Encyclopedia of race and ethnic studies

Encyclopedia of race and ethnic studies

Ellis Cashmore

Routledge
Taylor & Francis Group

LONDON AND NEW YORK

First published 2004
Paperback published 2008
by Routledge
2 Park Square, Milton Park, Abingdon, Oxon OX14 4RN

Simultaneously published in the USA and Canada
by Routledge
270 Madison Ave, New York, NY 10016

Routledge is an imprint of the Taylor & Francis Group, an informa business

© 2004, 2008 Routledge Ltd

Typeset in Sabon and Frutiger by Taylor & Francis Books Ltd
Printed and bound in Great Britain by
The Cromwell Press, Trowbridge, Wiltshire

British Library Cataloguing in Publication Data
A catalogue record for this book is available from the British Library

Library of Congress Cataloging in Publication Data
Cashmore, Ernest.
Encyclopedia of race and ethnic studies / Ellis Cashmore.
Includes bibliographical references and index.
1. Ethnicity–Encyclopedias. 2. Race relations–Encyclopedias.
3. Racism–Encyclopedias. I. Title.
GN495.6.C37 2003
305.8'003–dc21   2003046697

ISBN10 0–415–44714–3
ISBN13 978–0–415–44714–0

IN MEMORY OF
COLIN BELL
1942–2003
*Inspirational friend and
trailblazing scholar*

Contents

Editorial team
ix

List of contributors
x

Introduction
xiii

Entries A–Z
1

Internet resources
461

Index
474

Editorial team

Editor

Ellis Cashmore
Staffordshire University, UK

Consultant editors

Michael Banton
University of Bristol, UK

James Jennings
Tufts University, Massachusetts, USA

Online resources consultant

Stuart D. Stein
University of the West of England, UK

Contributors

Heribert Adam
Simon Fraser University, Canada

Anthony C. Alessandrini
Kent State University, USA

Suki Ali
Goldsmiths College, University of London, UK

Erna Appelt
University of Innsbruck, Austria

Molefi Kete Asante
Temple University, USA

Stephanie Athey
Lasell College, USA

Michael Banton
University of Bristol, UK

Pierre L. van den Berghe
University of Washington, Seattle, USA

Claudia Bernard
Goldsmiths College, University of London, UK

Dinesh Bhugra
Institute of Psychiatry, King's College London, UK

Frederick W. Boal
Queen's University Belfast, UK

Kingsley Bolton
University of Hong Kong

Alastair Bonnett
University of Newcastle upon Tyne, UK

Gillian Bridge
London School of Economics, UK

Roy L. Brooks
University of San Diego, USA

Richard Broome
La Trobe University, Australia

Bonnie Campodonico
Santa Clara University, California, USA

Lionel Caplan
University of London, UK

Bob Carter
University of Warwick, UK

Ellis Cashmore
Staffordshire University, UK

Emma L. Clarence
University of Aberdeen, UK

Robin Cohen
University of Warwick, UK

Naaz Coker
The King's Fund, UK

Simon Cottle
University of Melbourne, Australia

Guy Cumberbatch
The Communications Research Group, UK

Teun A. van Dijk
Universitat Pompeu Fabra, Spain

Joe R. Feagin
University of Florida, USA

James V. Fenelon
California State University, USA

Steven Fenton
University of Bristol, UK

John Gabriel
London Metropolitan University, UK

John A. Garcia
University of Arizona, USA

Mattias Gardell
*Stockholm University,
Sweden*

Jagdish Gundara
University of London, UK

Ian Hancock
University of Texas at Austin, USA

Leslie A. Houts
University of Florida, USA

Christopher Hutton
University of Hong Kong

James Jennings
Tufts University, Massachusetts, USA

Julia S. Jordan-Zachery
Wheaton College, USA

Evelyn Kallen
York University, Canada

Virinder Kalra
University of Manchester, UK

Robert J. Kerstein
University of Tampa, USA

Joseph Kling
St. Lawrence University, USA

Amy I. Kornblau
Florida Atlantic University, USA

Maxine Leeds Craig
University of Papua New Guineau

MichÒle Lamont
Harvard University, USA

Zeus Leonardo
California State University, USA

Sven Lindqvist
Stockholm, Sweden

Timothy J. Lukes
Santa Clara University, USA

Stanford M. Lyman
Florida Atlantic University, USA

Zine Magubane
University of Illinois, USA

Sarita Malik
Independent, UK

Stephen May
University of Waikato, New Zealand

Peter McLaren
University of California, Los Angeles, USA

Eugene McLaughlin
Open University, UK

Robert Miles
University of North Carolina at Chapel Hill, USA

VirÃg MolnÃr
Princeton University, USA

Kogila Moodley
University of British Columbia, Canada

Marshall Murphree
University of Zimbabwe

Ali Nasreen

Anoop Nayak
University of Newcastle upon Tyne, UK

Jan Nederveen Pieterse
University of Illinois, Urbana-Champaign, USA

Imari Abubakari Obadele
*House of Songhay Commission for Positive
Education, Louisiana, USA*

George Paton
Aston University, UK

Thomas C. Patterson
University of California, Riverside, USA

Laura Penketh
University of Central Lancaster, UK

Michael Pickering
Loughborough University, UK

Elizabeth Poole
Staffordshire University, UK

Peter Ratcliffe
University of Warwick, UK

Chris Rojek
Nottingham Trent University, UK

Bobby Sayyid
University of Salford, UK

John Solomos
City University, UK

Tony Spybey
Staffordshire University, UK

Stuart Stein
University of the West of England, UK

Betty Lee Sung
*City College of City University of New York,
USA*

Roy Todd
University of Leeds, UK

†Barry Troyna

Carol Tulloch
Victoria and Albert Museum, UK

Debra Van Ausdale
Syracuse University, USA

Steven Vertovec
University of Oxford, UK

†Robin Ward

Julia Wardhaugh
University of Wales Bangor, UK

Stephen M. Whitehead
Keele University, UK

Raymond A. Winbush
Morgan State University, USA

Loretta Zimmerman

Introduction

A multicultural dilemma

In time, ideas that once abounded with promise grow tired, exhausted by constant use and unable to cope with a changing world. Take MULTICULTURALISM: for over three decades it was a sound political ideal, a policy aspiration and an instrument with which to challenge RACISM. It gave purpose and direction to societies grappling with the often-conflicting demands of diverse populations. Then, the initial good impressions of multiculturalism started to change: what once appeared to be a treasure chest began to resemble Pandora's box. (Terms in SMALL CAPITALS have an entry of their own in the text.)

Global events prompted us to understand multiculturalism differently. And so it is with all the terms we habitually use. Their meanings change as the world turns. Multiculturalism had long occupied the status of an unquestionable good: social wellbeing depended on a degree of diversity and societies that tried to stifle or subdue this did so at their own peril. But the life of the concept of multiculturalism has been painful and ironic.

Since the 1980s, when it emerged in the vocabulary of students and practitioners of RACE and ethnic relations, multiculturalism was intended to be more than a grandiose gesture: it was meant to inform a process of directed change. As a student in Toronto in the 1970s, I recall the beginning of such a process. In contrast to the USA's melting pot, Canada promoted the image of a mosaic, a nationwide arrangement of different types, forms and colors that were all integral parts of an overall design. Canada was the first country to adopt multiculturalism as an official policy.

The USA pursued a rather different process by insisting on an adherence to core American values, while Britain followed the Canadian example and opted for INTEGRATION before, in practice, discarding this around the time of the STEPHEN LAWRENCE CASE. Other nations, including Australia and France, in their different ways, clung to ASSIMILATION as a goal. Still others like Germany and much of Europe did little to ameliorate stark inequalities among ethnic groups. But a dilemma now urgently confronts all of these countries and perhaps the world.

This is a dilemma quite unlike MYRDAL's *An American Dilemma* (Transaction Books, 1995), which was actually more of a paradox – a self-contradictory statement, such as "America is the land of opportunity for all; but AFRICAN AMERICANS are denied some of the opportunities afforded whites." A dilemma is a choice between two equally unattractive possibilities. In the current climate, it takes the form of (1) encouraging cultural divergence and – perhaps inadvertently – promoting the SEGREGATION it implies; or (2) reinstating a nucleus of standards, ethics and ideals and risk suffocating cultural differences while restoring a version of assimilation.

"What multiculturalism did was to confuse the fight against racism (which undoubtedly existed and exists today) with the business of nation-building," reflected BBC journalist George Alagiah, himself born in Sri Lanka, in his memoir *A Home from Home* (Little Brown, 2006). "Multiculturalism was the perfect excuse for those who wanted to ringfence their communities."

Alagiah argues that the uncritical acceptance of cultural differences has led to fragmentation and separation. On his account, one of the casualties of multiculturalism has been unity – the nation. Another, according to many writers, is basic HUMAN RIGHTS. The Somali-born feminist and Dutch politician Ayaan Hris Ali, condemns the denial of EQUAL OPPORTUNITY to Muslim women and rails at the DRESS, particularly the burka, a long, enveloping garment worn by Muslim women in public, which issues a reminder of "the stifling morality that makes Muslim men the owners of women," as she writes in her *The Caged Virgin* (The Free Press, 2006). Several other feminist writers also reject the PATRIARCHY of Islam.

No scholar seriously repudiates the significance of cultural differences and the need to protect and perhaps assist their nurturance, especially in resistant environments. But no CULTURE is inviolable or static and, for this reason, some writers have urged less reverence in the way we approach these differences.

Robert Young, for instance, in his *Colonial Desire* (Routledge, 1995) has insisted that, in the effort to confront racism, we have paid lip service to cultural features and experiences – what he calls "culturalism." In the process we have replaced one problem with another. Cultural diversity and the plurality of ethnic identity it encourages are tantamount to a new form of ESSENTIALISM in which culture is seen as fixed and immovable. History teaches us that the opposite is true. "Cultures are not impermeable," Edward Said memorably advised in his *Culture and Imperialism* (Vintage, 1993).

The problem is: many people want their cultures to be precisely that – resistant to change and impervious to the influences of the cultures of others. GLOBALIZATION has resulted in a denser coexistence of cultures than at any time in history. But it is often an uneasy coexistence. Attempts to maintain impermeable cultures have tested multiculturalism to its limits.

For example, Hina Saleem was a young Pakistani woman who was murdered by her Muslim father in August 2006. She was reported missing by her partner, an Italian-born carpenter with whom she shared a home in Brescia, northern Italy. Her father had insisted she return with her mother and sisters to Pakistan to get married in a traditional Islamic arrangement. When she refused, there was fierce argument. Her body was found under a meter of soil in the garden of her family's house.

The Vatican, in its official journal *L'Osservatore Romana,* denounced the crime as "the fruit of years of hostility and fighting which caused the father to lose every trace of reason and sentiment."

It was an interesting and somewhat ironic denunciation considering Italy's law offering the possibility of clemency in cases of "honor crimes" was repealed only in 1981. Even today, such crimes are not unknown in the south of the country.

Brescia has an immigrant population of 120,000, the largest group being Pakistanis. Hina Saleem's father, Mohammed, had lived in Italy for ten years. Historically a country of emigrants, Italy from the 1980s underwent considerable change, turning into a polyglot nation accommodating many different cultural groups. Unlike many other European nations, Italy had been slow to change, though, only weeks before the murder, the Interior Minister had announced a planned liberalization of rules for obtaining Italian citizenship. The murder gave him pause to think. "It is not enough to require adhesion to the values of the Italian Constitution," he commented. "Adhesion to fundamental rights is also necessary, such as the fact that women are to be respected according to rules which I consider universal."

Whether he meant it or not, he was alluding to what some saw as an incompatibility of priorities and perhaps even a *conflitto di civiltà* a clash of civilizations. Discourses on "fundamental rights" and universal rules are by no means new. For long, human rights were seen as compatible with multiculturalism. Some would argue they complemented each other. Perhaps they still do. Why then have critics raised doubts? The simple, if inaccurate answer is that they have grown impatient. The longer and more complex answer involves both an examination of recent history and of world events.

Global links

To study race and ETHNICITY without attention to history leaves the scholar stranded in the here-and-now with no depth of perspective or appreciation of how the past bears on the present. Historical processes have caused, facilitated or contributed to today's configurations of inequality. So race and ethnic studies have to be exercised in the historical context of the COLONIALISM that characterized Europe's relations with the rest of the world, including the Arab world and the USA's post-World War II switch from anti-colonial archetype to POSTCOLONIAL super-power.

What we are now forced to recognize is more confusing: that comprehensible cause and effect have been decoupled. Events that appear to be independent of one another in both time and space and have no logical connections might actually be related – though not in a way that necessarily lends itself to empirical analysis. Increasingly, one of the principal tasks of students of race and ethnic relations is to trace the links and explain why they are strengthened and sometimes weakened by changing circumstances.

Some contemporary events have echoes of larger conflicts. In 2006, a crowd demanding the expulsion of Chechens and other ethnic MINORITIES from Russia's North Caucasus region precipitated a riot in Kondopoga, 600 miles north of Moscow. Russian forces had been involved with groups demanding independence for the region of Chechnya for several years and the siege of a school in Beslan in 2004 was fresh in people's minds. A total of 344 people including 186 CHILDREN were killed in the siege, the leaders being Muslims with rumored ties to al-Qaeda. Chechen independence had been an historical source of conflict in Russia for decades.

Similarly the RIOTS in and around Paris in 2005 were less isolated incidents and more expressions of a momentum that had been gathering in France for years. When, in 2003, the government announced its intention to ban religious clothing in public schools, Muslims interpreted this as an instance of ISLAMOPHOBIA. While the ban also included Sikh turbans and Jewish yarmulkes, France's five million Muslims (constituting about eight percent of the total population) felt disproportionately affected as many females wear headscarves, the hijab being the most common. France has the largest population of Muslims of any European country. (Islam is the largest religion in the world, having nearly 20 million believers. Roman Catholicism is the next biggest with 17.34 million followers.) The ban took affect in 2004 amid stringent protests from both Muslims and human rights campaigners. President Jacques Chirac stood firm, pointing out that France was a secular republic and that secularism was "a crucial element of peace and social cohesion."

Neither peace nor cohesion was in evidence when the Paris riots broke out. Many of the rioters were young blacks of North African origin or descent and probably Muslims. Perhaps France's public indifference to minority ethics and preferences offered a matrix for understanding their experiences in the city. In these two cases, the tissues connecting specific episodes to wider events are apparent, though even these events have to be understood in terms of one cataclysmic conflagration.

If one event shaped the emerging uncertainties of the third millennium, it was the attack of SEPTEMBER 11, 2001, which brought about a dramatic shift in the relationship between the world's most powerful nation and many of its poorest, particularly Islamic states. It sounds trite to assert that this event changed everything, but it is difficult to think of an area of society, anywhere in the world that remained unaffected. The attacks "changed the terms of public discourse about race," as Stephen Small and John Solomos state in their 2006 essay "Race, immigration and politics in Britain" (*International Journal of Comparative Sociology*, 47(3–4): 235–57). They impacted the manner in which we address practically every aspect of race and ethnic affairs. They sparked debates about the larger themes about the supposed incompatibility of cultures.

Around the same time as the murder in Italy, eight young men appeared in an English court, accused of trying to blow up transatlantic planes. Alongside them, three others, including a seventeen-year old man and a mother, were accused of crimes relating to the alleged plot. They were all British-born Muslims, their families from the Asian subcontinent. Their arrest came amid talks about RACIAL PROFILING at British airports and debates about the influence of training camps known as *madrasahs* (religious schools), and the so-called "radicalization" of Muslim youth. The specter of Islamophobia re-appeared: stories of Muslims – or those who appeared to be Muslims – being marched off planes to appease the paranoia of other passengers, Asian youths being carefully avoided on public transport combined with all manner of conspiracy theories.

At the start of the century, the idea that young British-born and -educated Asians would prepare for the jihad in special training schools in leafy parts of England would have been preposterous. So would a figure like Abu Hamza, the Muslim cleric who was imprisoned for soliciting murder during his sermons at a London mosque. In the late 1990s, he might have been dismissed as a detestable but harmless crank.

Yet counter-terrorist police squads appeared to raid the most unlikely places – like Chinese restaurants – and uncover new evidence of young Britons' involvement with plots practically every month after the July 7, 2005 bombings in London.

BRITISH ASIANS were thrust into the center of arguably one of the most challenging questions to face scholars of race and ethnicity in the new century: why would young men and women, born and educated in Britain, some studying at university, others in professional careers, many with young wives and families, decide they wanted to kill innocent people, including other Asians, or, in one notable case, travel to Gaza on a suicide mission?

Even allowing for a degree of over-reaction from the forces of law and order, assisted by some hysterical sections of the MEDIA, there was enough evidence, direct and inferential, to suggest that many young British-born Asians considered themselves in a form of captivity. Their escape, as they saw it, was not achievable by departing the country, or with political protest: but by practicing the kind of incendiary VIOLENCE witnessed in many other parts of the world. It is not possible to understand this transformation of British Asian youth through the examination of the Asian experience in Britain since the war.

The cast of British Asians has frequently been distorted into a false inclusiveness. For those migrating to Britain from Asia and their offspring, experiences have been diverse. Those of Indian descent vied with the much smaller Chinese population as the country's educational elite. Others, in particular Pakistanis and Bangladeshis (90 percent of whom are Muslims), struggled in both EDUCATION and in the desirable professions. There was little to prepare anyone for the development of the early-century when youths decided to pursue tactics typically associated with Hezbollah, though not necessarily in the war-torn Middle East, but in urban England.

Young Muslims began to reflect on their own positions and that of their parents and elders who had been abused in the 1960s and 1970s by "paki-bashing" young whites, ridiculed by comedians and often forced to make a living out of the corner shops with which they became ineffaceably identified. Once the most vulnerable of Britain's ethnic minorities, Asians had their businesses frequently torched or vandalized and their places of worship regularly desecrated. For some, the experience of this generation was a microcosm of the Muslim experience. This was precisely the recognition that prompted the submission of some to a form of Islam that lay outside the normal scope of their parents' understanding. It was made more attractive because of precisely this.

Developments in race and ethnic relations frequently surprise us. British Asians' adaptation – and it seems appropriate to call it that – was startling. How is it possible to explain the involvement in mass violence of British-born and -educated young men whose Muslim parents communicated only a desire to follow their faith, go about their business and integrate as seamlessly as possible into British society?

At a different time in history, their behavior might be symptomatic of their estrangement from a society in which their access to education, political positions or high-ranking jobs was restricted by INSTITUTIONAL RACISM. Perhaps as a response to the persistent SOCIAL EXCLUSION of their parents from the mainstream, "highlighting how the children refused to accept many of the obstacles imposed upon, or hostility addressed against their parents," as Small and Solomos put it. These would have been citable reasons in the 1980s, but not in the twenty-first century when equal opportunity policies combined with social inclusion have taken some effect.

Research by, among others, Anthony Heath and Sin Yi Cheung Sin (*Unequal Chances: Ethnic Minorities in Western Labour Markets*, Oxford University Press, 2006), indicated that all ethnic groups, including whites, were converging in the job market and that a degree of parity was being approached. Amid the convergence was the sharpest divergence in the postwar period.

Many young British Asians have catalogs of complaints about their society. Given flashpoint events, such as the presence of far right political organizations, they might even resort to violence, as indeed they did in the riots of 2001. Yet typically, events such as these do not motivate people to GENOCIDE, suicide bombings or attempts to bring down aircraft. Young people from various ethnic backgrounds gripe about specific instances of DISCRIMINATION or more generic or institutional patterns. These have now been reconstituted in a grammar that includes other instances of perceived injustice elsewhere in the world. Bewildering at it may seem to some, a refusal at a bar or a brush with a discourteous police officer can be joined as if by a chemical chain to struggles in the Middle East or South Asia. The formula produces an apprehension of living in a culture without belonging to it, working with friends who are also enemies and being part of an alliance that may exist only in the imagination.

Some believe that this kind of mindset is shared by only a minority of a minority, an enclave of homicidal, obscurantist fundamentalists who want to create mayhem. Others suspect that it is rather more pervasive, offering a way of understanding the overall narrative in which the West and Islam have featured since Christian expeditions tried to recover Jerusalem from Muslims in the eleventh century. But historical accuracy is often a casualty of IDEOLOGY, as are policy driven directives. At a time when the western world has begun to see the maturation of numberless strategies all designed in some way to enhance integration, cohesion, EQUALITY of opportunity and the acceptance of cultural diversity as beneficial and racism as malevolent, an age-old discord has returned, albeit in a new guise.

It is no longer possible to view any of the cases covered so far as instances of what were once called RACE RELATIONS: as discrete expressions of psychological phenomena or as part of patterns of indigenous RACIAL DISCRIMINATION and structured DISADVANTAGE. Our scope needs to be much, much larger. We need to stay aware of the dangers of giving a spurious equivalence to dissimilar events, of course. But neither the Italian murder, the plot to demolish aircrafts or any of the other events make sense unless assessed in the context of Islam's frequently overwrought relationship with Western powers, especially over the past half-century, but with ancestry much deeper in history.

The wider conflict

While it seems astonishing from the vantage point of the twenty-first century, the USA was once a subjugated nation that fought for and gained its independence. Throughout the twentieth century, it rose to prominence, creating alternatives to its former master's hereditary hierarchy based on privilege, class distinction and cultural superiority. America advertised itself as the land of opportunity, but it was also a land of MIGRATION, the famous melting pot in which groups of all languages, faiths and customs could be blended. Some groups mixed and melted, either adjusting their differences in a way that made an accommodation possible, or simply assimilating to the American way of life.

African Americans' sense of betrayal after the war became clear in the 1950s, when the CIVIL RIGHTS MOVEMENT began its epic campaign to destroy the legal segregation that had been a feature of the American cultural landscape since the abolition of SLAVERY. Arabs felt similarly betrayed but for different reasons: the US government had supported ZIONISM after the war, buttressing the establishment of the Jewish state of Israel in 1948. An alliance of Arab armies led by Egypt was defeated. Israel was to remain a source of torment to the present day and, in a sense, it became a symbolic as well as political foundation for much of the conflict that ensued.

Egypt's change of status from monarchy to republic under the leadership of Gamal Abdul Nasser in 1953 was regarded portentously by the Muslim world. Egypt, having been subjugated serially since the seventh century BCE, might have developed into a theocratic Muslim state of 18 million people. Instead Nasser pursued his vision of a secular pan-Arab socialist state. In 1958 Egypt joined Syria to form the United Arab Republic. Among those disaffected by this was Sayyid Qutb, a member of the anti-British Muslim Brotherhood, who urged the unquestioning adoption of sharia, a legal code taken from the Koran, to regulate all aspects of social and personal life. Qutb was imprisoned by Nasser, but his written work circulated and became key texts for what later became known as Islamic fundamentalism.

For Qutb, the world was divided into Islam and *jahiliyya*, the latter describing not only the ignorant condition of the Western world, with its laxity and permissiveness, but also of much modernized Islamic culture which had been affected by commerce with the West. He encouraged the total rejection of Western rationalism and values. His vision was of a world split into two distinct and irreconcilably different halves that could not, or should not co-exist.

Qutb's influence grew, at first steadily, over the next several decades, enhanced by events in both the Middle East and the USA. In Iran the election of Mohammed Mossadegh in 1951 might have heralded an Islamic reformation, though the constitutional monarchy of the Shah offered more co-operation with the West. Mossadegh's removal after two years was largely attributable to British and American powers. The Shah of Iran was eventually overthrown in 1979 leading to a populist theocratic republic under the rule of Ayatollah Khomeini. It precipitated what became known as the Islamic Revolution. Relations with the USA deteriorated thereafter. The USA, often in tandem with Britain, armed and funded autocratic rulers across Muslim territories in exchange for access to oil and co-operation in the Cold War. In the absence of any type of meaningful democracy, Qutb's call for an Islamic regeneration became a credible alternative to western rule-by-proxy.

The deterioration spread, bringing the USA and its allies into conflicts with other Muslim nations. In 1986, the USA used British bases to launch bombing raids on Libya in retaliation for the bombing of a Berlin nightclub in which an American solider was killed. The bombing of the World Trade Center in 1993 and of the US Embassies in Dar es Salaam, Tanzania, Nairobi and Kenya drew retaliation with cruise missile strikes on Afghanistan and Sudan in 1998. The latter was followed by a dire warning from the World Islamic Front for Jihad against Jews and Crusaders, a movement fronted by Osama bin Laden, who acknowledged Qutb, who died in 1966, as an inspiration: "Strikes will continue from everywhere [against the USA]."

This was followed by the September 11 attacks in 2001, the stated aim of which was to avenge the desecration of Saudi Arabian soil by foreign troops in the first Gulf War. The retaliatory US attack on Afghanistan in 2002 added further impetus to a conflict that foreshadowed the invasion of Iraq in 2005. Attacks in Bali, Spain and London were interpreted as the manifestations of a mounting global calamity.

It is absolutely necessary to understand this context: every event that involves ethnic differences, whether concerning Islam or not, has to be set against this wider discord. It is as if the world has been offered new software that makes every type of cultural and political conflict intelligible in terms of, on the one hand, al-Qaeda (Islam), and on the other, the Global War on Terror (the West).

This might appear to be an odd way to explain the changes in meanings of, attitudes towards and emotions provoked by a single word – multiculturalism. It is intended, first, to remind readers that the terms of reference have changed significantly over the past few years and will probably go on changing, making the field of study perplexingly changeable. Second, to establish how no single word, term or expression in the lexicon of race and ethnic relations should be free from interrogation. We should reflect on every word we use in our discourses. Every one is loaded with meaning that can be explicated only through historical and social analysis.

Few of our terms of reference are eternally reliable: we need to revisit and revise them in the light of new developments. And it hardly needs stating that the developments witnessed in the first decade of the twenty-first century have shaken scholars of race and ethnicity into re-thinking their approaches.

Even before September 11, critics were rounding on multiculturalism. An ideal that implicates a society in a policy of inclusion is destined for trouble in the context of a world bent on exclusion. Yet the idea of groups with different, perhaps conflicting interests, predispositions and purposes being urged to become part of a collectivity and enjoy all of its benefits but without compromising, is arguably worth re-considering.

Cultural difference is surely something to be respected and valued rather than despised or feared. But is it reasonable to embrace without approval? We can include and value cultural standards, beliefs and practices that are radically different from our own. We can also fight others' rights to pursue a way of life that is singularly their own, though one that might be at odds with our own. We can even respect and honor cultural arrangements that seem slightly unusual compared with those with which we are accustomed. But how about those we actively discourage or of which we strongly disapprove?

Divergence among convergence

Imagine this: a Muslim woman, who now lives in Manchester (or it could be Baltimore, Sydney, Toronto, or practically any other city in the developed world), migrated from Nigeria several years ago and lives by the sharia code. She admits that she has had an adulterous relationship and is so ashamed of herself that she submits herself to an Islamic court. The judges, all of them men, sentence her to death by stoning, which is, of course, illegal in the West, but legal in her native northern Nigeria. She has an eight-month-old daughter and, in deference to her, the judges decide that she should nurture the child for two years, after which she should voluntarily return to Nigeria to face her death. She agrees, stating that her faith is unshakable and that her fate is in God's hands. The case prompts international outrage, especially when the Nigerian government confirms that it is prepared, however reluctantly, to allow the execution. But, the appeals for clemency are not effective and the woman confirms she is willing to surrender herself to God's will.

Actually, this is not dissimilar to the real case of Amina Lawal Kurami, the big difference being that she lived in Katsina in Nigeria, rather than in the West. Even then, the ruling created commotion around the world. The punishment seemed incomprehensibly out of proportion to the "crime," which would not be a crime in many other cultures, anyway. While most West-based Muslims insist that there is no contradiction between religious and national faiths and CULTURAL IDENTITY, there is no simple resolution between western notions of human rights, especially those of women, and Islamic codes. Women are habitually subordinated in many types of Islamic culture. Denied education and hospital treatment, women, in many Islamic cultures, are simply not valued as highly as men. In some Muslim cultures, female circumcision is permitted. While it might once have been possible to fret over such matters with the comforting assurance that they happened only in faraway places, the sobering reality is that they are not: they are happening everywhere.

Defenders of cultural diversity have, for years, rhapsodized over PLURALISM, difference, variety and the HYBRIDITY they nurture. Blissful inclusion is easy to come by if the diversity is all about cuisine, dress or music. These are what we might call aesthetic elements: parts of other cultures that have been appropriated and, for many, cherished. They form part of the "soft" side of culture. Execution by stoning and cliteridectomy are altogether different propositions. They tax even the most persistent devotee of cultural diversity because they pose a question: where do you draw the line?

There are cultures that have customs that openly deprecate women, such as footbinding or the other kinds of practices mentioned earlier. There are cultures that condemn homosexuality. These are clearly at odds with values the West has nurtured – and not always easily – over the past forty years. Most models of multiculturalism incorporate the demand for total equality without any dilution or compromising of cultural beliefs or values. Yet it raises logical and empirical questions, most urgently: how can a society abide by an imperative to destroy just because it is germane to a group's cultural credo?

The answer is, of course, that it cannot. So, why should it observe or respect other tenets of a culture that are inconsistent with and perhaps inimical to human rights? This is the dilemma to which I referred earlier. All of us, by dint of our birth, are members of a cultural group or collectivity and are raised to accept and respect its ethos. There is no choice in this, though, as we mature we may decide, after reflection and deliberation, to maintain or to drop our membership. In this respect, we are exercising freedom in a social context that acknowledges and respects our right to do so. If, for example, a young woman, like Hina Saleem, who was from a conservative migrant family, wanted to live with a young Italian man then her choice could not be opposed on the grounds of basic human freedom. Her father's attempt to prevent her from doing this, presumably justified on a traditional Islamic prerogative, might have drawn sympathy were he to have expressed his preference and allowed his daughter to make the final choice about her future.

In the particular case, he drew little sympathy because his prohibition involved killing her (though in fact one of the sayings of the Prophet Mohammed indicates that marriage must involve the consent of the marrying parties rather than just the parents). In many other contexts, the preservation of traditions specific to cultural groups, including the *rishda*, which describes the coordinated relationship, would be applauded as an instance of what used to be called integration – a process in which group boundaries and uniqueness are maintained amid an atmosphere of equality or equality of opportunity.

There is little comfort in this. It is probable that even approaching a solution would implicate every culture in throwing open the windows on itself and permitting others to make their critical evaluations openly and without fear. Some have argued that POLITICAL CORRECTNESS has prevented this, though, as the reader will discover, this should not have been the case. No conception of freedom or equality involves the suspension or suppression of criticism. Those who find what they regard as the laxity of the West odious have a right to say so. Others are at liberty to state that they think the values suggested by practices dating from early Islam are repulsive. If there is BIGOTRY implied in either view, only exposure and criticism can remove it.

No one seriously believes racism, in its every manifestation, has been vanquished. Equally, only a fool would deny that many of its toxic effects have been limited by a combination of policies and the inevitable mixing and melding that come of living in a culturally diverse society. Of course, these have not functioned like the river Alpheus, which Hercules diverted through the putrid stables of Augeas. Racism has not been flushed away in a purifying torrent. In particular, AFRICAN CARIBBEANS IN BRITAIN, like African Americans, are more likely to be unemployed or in prison than in universities. Some Asian groups, such as Pakistani and Bangladeshi males, are still disproportionately underrepresented in higher education and overrepresented in unskilled, manual occupations.

Over the past several decades, racism has been the crucial problem that has challenged scholars and practitioners. Now, in an ironic twist, the proffered solution to racism has become a problem. The transition of multiculturalism from an indisputable benefit to the source of a taxing dilemma illustrates the manner in which the words we use can affect our thinking on race and ethnicity. There has never been a more pressing need for clarity and precision.

The lexicon of race and ethnic studies has always been in flux, of course. Rightly so. Concepts, ideas, terms and expressions, like the world they describe, are in constant change. A book such as this can reflect their meanings at a particular time. What it can't do is anticipate accurately how continuing globalization will affect their reception and interpretation in years to come. The fate of multiculturalism is but one example of how our terms of reference can be affected by factors that have, in a way, forced us to re-examine the entire endeavor of race and ethnic studies.

Scope of the book

The vigilant student of race and ethnic relations needs to be both supple and acute, changing as situations change, staying sharp as subterfuge obscures. This book is intended to assist both those ends. It is designed to equip the reader, not only with a working lexicon, but an understanding of the meanings, importance and, where appropriate, implications of key terms, legal milestones, historically significant events, influential figures, illuminating theories and concepts that have inspired debates, discussion and sometimes polemics.

It is, of course, a sourcebook, though not one intended to sit in abeyance on library shelves. The paperback edition is a working book and is meant to earn its keep: it has been designed as a reference for virtually everything related to studies of race and ethnicity. It has been appended with a substantial index: so that, even if a term has not been afforded an entry of its own, it will almost certainly appear at one or more places in the text. The effort has been directed toward including not just the main terms of reference (though, of course, these are here), but more marginal words, concepts and people. Anything or anyone that has, in some way, shaped or continues to shape the way we approach, examine, understand or think about issues of race and ethnicity should appear in the text.

Race and ethnic studies, like any other branch of knowledge, does not stand still. As it moves, its terms of reference change. This is complicated by the fact that there were no ready-made terms of reference in the first place. In 1950, when ROBERT EZRA PARK published his *Race and Culture* (The Free Press), there was not a recognizable field of study dedicated to race and ethnic relations. Park regarded race relations as being present since the times of the ancient Greeks, though his own work established it as a newly demarcated field of academic study. Some of the terms and phrases used by Park and his peers are still in use, of course. Many, many more have been added over the years. And still more will be added in years to come.

While all the entries address aspects of race, racism and ethnicity, I have resisted appending headings with " ... and race" or " ... and racism" and so on. Essays headed, for example, HOMELESSNESS, SEXUAL ABUSE or SOCIAL WORK all engage with issues of race, racism and ethnicity as they affect and are affected by the topic suggested in the title. The entries raise issues that are both germane to the subject of the heading and specific to the themes of this volume. In this way, I have sought to introduce the reader to areas that are not always regarded as central to the study of race and ethnic relations, but which are nonetheless crucial to a comprehensive understanding of the ways in which race and racism impact on every aspect of global life.

There are several entries of a historical nature. This is a deliberate attempt to allow the reader to grasp the often-serpentine ways in which contemporary issues have arrived. Racism did not spring fully-formed from our consciousness; nor is it a natural impulse, as some claim. No exhaustive examination is complete without attention to frequently obscured historical factors that have cumulatively built toward the state of affairs we now face. The reader will find entries on a variety of figures (such as ERNST HAECKEL or BARTOLOMÕ DE LAS CASAS), whose importance have perhaps been forgotten, and issues (like ANTISLAVERY and the DOOMED RACES DOCTRINE) that are sometimes overlooked. Knowledge of these broadens our awareness of the scope and depth of race and ethnic studies. And to keep matters completely updated, there is, toward the end of the book, a section dedicated to INTERNET RESOURCES.

EC

A

ABOLITIONIST MOVEMENT *see* antislavery

ABORIGINAL AUSTRALIANS

Claude Lívi-Strauss termed indigenous Australians the "intellectual aristocrats" of early peoples because of the rich cultural heritage these
hunter-gatherers evolved in Australia since at
least 50,000 BCE. They were among the first
mariners, artists, and religious thinkers. The
name Aboriginal derives from the Latin phrase
ab origine, from the beginning.

1770–1930: Destruction, protection and assimilation

In 1770, the sovereignty of the 250 distinct
Aboriginal cultural-linguistic groups was contested by Lieutenant James Cook, when he
claimed the eastern half of the Australian continent for the British. Cook took possession
without negotiation or treaty since he judged the
indigenous people as not being owners, since
they were not numerous and had not blended
their labor with the land in an agricultural
manner. Colonialism in Australia was born with
his unilateral and incorrect declaration that the
land was *terra nullius* or waste – a perception not
legally reversed until 1992.

About a million Aboriginal peoples occupied
Australia before white contact, but smallpox
epidemics in the eastern portion of the continent
obscure a more accurate tally. These peoples
were pressured by a pastoral and mining frontier
that spread sporadically from southeast and
coastal areas across Australia in the century after
1788. A frontier guerrilla war was waged over
the land in most areas causing about 2,000

settler and possibly 20,000 Aboriginal deaths.
There was no policy of genocide, but at times
government forces supported settlers in local
killing actions. However, the clash between a
hunter-gatherer economy and the pastoral arm of
British industrial capitalism created unintended
relations of genocide. Within a generation many
Aboriginal groups had been reduced by over 80
percent while others disappeared totally through
the action of introduced diseases, economic disruption, white and *inter se* killings, and a
reduced birth rate through infertility and some
cultural fatalism.

Many Aborigines took a vital attitude to
culture contact and were not passive victims of
colonial expansion despite the violence. They
defended their land and resources, tried to control settlers through reciprocity and kinship, and
sought out Europeans by way of curiosity or to
extend their cultural opportunities and traditional power. Some material items such as glass
and steel were valued but only as adjuncts to
their own cultural imperatives. Many Aborigines,
particularly in the north, worked in the pastoral
industry, which supplanted their own traditional
economy. They provided cheap, servile, and
essential labor, but their nearness to traditional
lands and the indifference of their employers to
their culture, enabled the maintenance of the old
ways.

The gaining of responsible government by the
Australian colonies after the 1850s put the
settlers, not the British Colonial Office, in charge
of Aboriginal policy. This led to a century of
restrictive and racist controls under the name of
"protection," supported by social developmentalist and social Darwinist rationalizations. In
southeastern Australia, where two or three

generations of contact and miscegenation had left an Aboriginal population of mixed descent, policy after 1886 sought to end the "Aboriginal problem" through assimilation and absorption. People of mixed descent were forced from reserves formed earlier, and children were removed from their families for so-called "neglect," into orphanages, training homes, apprenticeships, and white foster care. Phillip Noyce's 2002 film *Rabbit-Proof Fence* relates the story of three such children's attempt in 1931 to escape an orphanage and walk the 1,500 miles back to their homeland using the eponymous fence (used to protect Western Australian farmlands from rabbits) as their guide.

The real reason for most removals that took an estimated 8,000 children from this region alone in sixty years and affected most Aboriginal extended families, was the children's Aboriginality. Such removals lasted into the 1970s. Their occurrence today is as welfare placements made after consultation with the Aboriginal community.

In the north and southwest, where people remained mainly of full descent, the policy was to protect and confine them on reserves under petty and strict controls though in practice half were moved to reserves. Thereafter they could be consigned to white employers as domestics or as pastoral laborers. The Aboriginal Acts removed their civil rights including freedom of movement, rights over property, freedom of marriage especially across racial lines, power over one's family, and the right to practice cultural activities. A dozen Christian missions carried out a similar but more benignly paternal role.

From the 1930s: struggles for self-sufficiency

Aboriginal activism from the 1930s, belated white Australian receptiveness by the 1950s to Aboriginal demands, and federal government leadership, led to a dismantling of the remaining state protective and discriminatory legislation in the 1960s. A landmark referendum in 1967 voted overwhelmingly to include Aborigines in the census with other Australians and to allow the federal government to legislate on Aboriginal affairs. Policy moved from "assimilation" to "integration." The reformist federal Labor government in 1972 introduced a policy of "self-determination" transformed to "self-management" by the succeeding Liberal-Nationalist government. Aboriginal community organizations mushroomed with federal finance, empowering people. The Northern Territory Lands Rights Act (1976) and South Australian legislation led to the handing back of a quarter of those states' lands – mostly arid – to Aboriginal people. The Aborigines were then pressured by an aggressive mining industry. A plethora of welfare officers and social scientists "found" the Aborigines, adding to the outside pressures. Self-managed reserves often fell to a new welfare colonialism – as white and black federal bureaucrats set overall funding and community development priorities.

Aboriginal people – less than 2 percent of the Australian population – continue to suffer social marginalization and political disadvantage despite antidiscrimination laws. Some of this social closure is due to the desire for cultural solidarity by Aboriginal people, but white prejudice, although dissipating, still plays a large part. Despite political advances, their socioeconomic indications languish. Aboriginal life expectancy is twenty years below that of other Australians, due to diabetes, kidney and heart disease, and drug abuse. Compared to other Australians their unemployment is five times higher and imprisonment rates fifteen times higher. Social welfare and work for unemployment benefit schemes raise their standard of living somewhat.

Almost 100 Aboriginal deaths in custody over seven years led to a Royal Commission (1987–91). While it found little official criminality in the deaths, it condemned the indifferent and racist treatment of Aborigines by authorities. This has led to new regimes of prison treatment and $4 billion spending on Aboriginal drug rehabilitation, education and job programs. The Commission, which received enormous daily publicity, also alerted the public to the extent of the removal of Aboriginal children since 1900. It led to a controversial national inquiry (*Bringing Them Home*, 1997) and an official Reconciliation Movement. The latter presented a compact of understanding in 2000 after a decade of work, but no treaty, which still remains a distant dream. However, Reconciliation has become a people's movement, changing the minds of many Australians.

A High Court ruling in the Mabo case (1992) over land claims at Murray Island in the Torres Strait dramatically overturned the notion of *terra nullius*. After a year of fierce controversy, the

Keating Labor government passed the landmark Native Title Act in late 1993; this gave Aboriginal people with traditional links to vacant crown land an opportunity to seek communal native title. The subsequent *Wik* decision in 1996 determined that pastoral leaseholders and native titleholders had potentially coterminous rights over leased areas, which formed two thirds of the continent. The incoming conservative federal government curbed native title rights in new legislation to counter the *Wik* decision. Native title claims, which clogged the courts, are now being settled outside court. Some groups have gained land, but Aboriginal factionalism over claims has caused much heartache.

However, six years of conservative federal Liberal-Nationalist rule since 1996 has placed Aboriginal people under siege. A resurgent Right succored by the federal government has attacked the truth of the stolen children, arguing they were "rescued", the violence of the frontier has been denied, the authenticity of Aboriginal tradition has been challenged in the six-year Hindmarsh Island Bridge saga, and Prime Minister Howard consistently has refused to say "sorry," even banning Cabinet ministers from joining Reconciliation marches. There have been renewed calls for assimilationism, using Aboriginal social problems as "proof" of their need to become like white Australians.

Traditional Aboriginal culture, which was forced underground in the century of paternalist control, is now flourishing in rural areas and many urban Aborigines are reclaiming their Aboriginal heritage. People now prefer to identify themselves as Aboriginal rather than "pass." An Aboriginal artistic renaissance attracts international interest and fosters new pride in Aboriginality. However, the old questions of cultural interface remain: how can Aboriginality thrive within the framework of Western culture?

SEE ALSO: American Indians; anthropology; assimilation; culturecide; Darwinism; Doomed Races Doctrine; ethnocide; ethnonational; eugenics; genocide; Hanson, Pauline; human rights; indigenous peoples; integration; miscegenation; One Nation; paternalism; reparations; social Darwinism

Reading

Aboriginal Australians, 3rd edn., by Richard Broome

(Allen & Unwin, 2001), is an overview of cultural contact from 1788–2001.
Annual Bibliography (1975/76–), Australian Institute of Aboriginal and Torres Strait Islander Studies, is a guide to sources.
Australians for 1788, edited by J. Mulvaney and P. White (Fairfax, Syme & Weldon, 1987), is an account of the diversity of the traditional hunter-gatherer in Australia.
Koori. A will to win by J. Miller (Angus & Robertson, 1985), is the first Aboriginal writer's view of black–white history since 1788.

RICHARD BROOME

ADOPTION *see* transracial adoption

AFFIRMATIVE ACTION

The policy of affirmative action is directed towards reversing historical trends that have consigned minority groups and women to positions of disadvantage, particularly in education and employment. It involves going beyond trying to ensure equality of individual opportunity by making discrimination illegal, by targeting for preferential benefits members of groups that have faced discrimination .

Employment

In the USA, the Civil Rights Act of 1964 was the initial important legislative effort that has served as a basis for later affirmative action efforts regarding employment. Title VII of this Act forbade employment discrimination on the basis of race, sex, religion, and national origin. This legislation also established the Equal Employment Opportunity Commission (EEOC) to investigate complaints of employment discrimination. Although initially the EEOC had to refer cases to the Civil Rights Division of Department of Justice for litigation, in 1972 Congress amended Title VII by passing the Equal Employment Opportunity Act. This legislation authorized the EEOC to file lawsuits in federal district courts against private employers if attempts at voluntary conciliation failed. It also authorized the Justice Department to bring local and state governments to court to challenge their hiring practices. Although many saw Title VII as merely a protection against discrimination, it has been interpreted in several court decisions as justifying affirmative action programs.

A significant early decision in the area of employment was *United Steelworkers of America*

v. *Weber*, 1979. This was the first Title VII case to come before the Supreme Court in which the plaintiff charged "reverse discrimination." The Court ruled that an affirmative action plan that was agreed upon by both the company and the union, and which included preferential promotions for blacks working for the company, was an acceptable policy designed to enhance the job opportunities for minorities, and did not constitute "reverse discrimination." The Court accepted this plan even though the company had not been found guilty of past discrimination. The Supreme Court ruled that, at least in this voluntary plan, Title VII does not forbid race-conscious affirmation action plans.

In *Johnson* v. *Transportation Agency, Santa Clara County*, 1987, the Supreme Court again approved a voluntary affirmative action plan as legitimate under Title VII. The Court noted that the plan could be acceptable even when the racial or sexual hiring imbalance is due to societal forces beyond the employer's control, rather than to discrimination by the employer.

The Supreme Court also has upheld court-ordered affirmative action challenges under Title VII (e.g., *Sheet Metal Workers Local 28* v. *EEOC, 1986, United States* v. *Paradise*, 1987), although it has made clear that it will accept court-ordered plans under more limited circumstances than voluntary plans. For example, in *Sheet Metal Workers*, the Court ruled that affirmative action must be a remedy for past discrimination, although the majority agreed that affirmative relief was not confined to actual victims of discrimination.

Although the 1964 Civil Rights Act did not originally apply to federal employees, Presidents Kennedy, Johnson, and Nixon all supported affirmative action efforts during their administrations. In 1961, Kennedy said it was the policy of the executive branch to encourage "positive measures of equal opportunity for all qualified persons within the government." This was reaffirmed by Johnson in 1965 in Executive Order 11246. Nixon issued an executive order in 1969 that required each federal agency to develop an affirmative action program to overcome past discrimination. Then, the 1972 Amendments to Title VII extended to federal employees the same protections as private employees and gave the EEOC jurisdiction over enforcement efforts regarding the federal service.

Disparate impact and consent decrees

An important issue facing the Supreme Court has been what constitutes the bases for proving discrimination, which then can serve as a basis for affirmative action agreements. In *Griggs* v. *Duke Power Company*, 1971, the Court held that Title VII forbids ostensibly neutral employment practices that are unrelated to job performance. The Court accepted the doctrine of *disparate impact* as a basis for affirmative action remedies. Instead of a plaintiff having to show a discriminatory intent on the part of an employer, the Court ruled that the plaintiff had to present information showing that women or members of a minority group were disproportionately under-represented in a firm or job category within that firm. In this case, a group of African American employees had charged job discrimination against the company under Title VII, arguing that the requirement that applicants have a high school diploma made it less likely that blacks would be hired. The Court ruled that the burden of proof rested on the employer to prove that the criteria that formed the bases for hiring were a legitimate business necessity and were clearly related to successful performance on the job. Even if the employer was successful in showing this, the plaintiff could still prevail by presenting other valid practices available to the employer that had less disparate impact. However, in *Wards Cove Packing Company* v. *Atonio*, 1989, the Supreme Court, which by then included several appointees of President Ronald Reagan, placed a greater share of the burden of proof on the plaintiff to demonstrate that particular job performance criteria specifically discriminate against minorities or women. Further, when the plaintiffs contended that several employment practices created a disparate impact, they had to show the disparity created by each separate practice. The Court also lessened the employers' burden in justifying the hiring practice. Congressional liberals quickly initiated legislative action to overturn *Wards Cove* and return to the *Griggs* criteria. This was accomplished with the Civil Rights Act of 1991.

During the same session in which the Supreme Court ruled on *Wards Cove*, it decided several other cases that had implications for affirmative action programs. One of the most significant was *Martin* v. *Wilks*. It had generally been assumed that "consent decrees" that resulted in affirmative action programs were not subject to court challenges based upon claims of reverse discrimination by those who had not been a party to the case. In *Martin*, the Supreme Court accepted the legitimacy of a suit filed by several white firefighters in Birmingham, Alabama, against a consent decree that had been accepted by the city, the black firefighters, and the federal government. It held that those who claimed reverse discrimination could challenge consent decrees as long as they were not participants in the original proceedings where the decrees were accepted. This decision was also overturned by the Civil Rights Act of 1991.

Government contracts

The federal government has focused affirmative action efforts on recipients of federal contracts. President Lyndon B. Johnson issued executive order 11246 in 1965 which prohibited federal contractors from discriminating on the basis of race, religion, or national origin. The Office of Federal Contract Compliance (OFCC) in the Department of Labor (reorganized in 1978 to become the Office of Federal Contract Compliance Programs) was established in 1966 to monitor these contractors. In 1968, OFCC mandated that all contractors above fifty employees and with contracts over $50,000 write affirmative action plans, and in 1969 it required some contractors in the construction industry to set goals and timetables for minority hiring. The policy became known as contract compliance.

The Public Works Employment Act of 1977, which amended the Local Public Works Capital Development and Investment Act of 1976, was an important legislative step regarding affirmative action in minority contracting. It required that at least 10 percent of the federal funds that are grants for local public works projects must be used by the local or state government to purchase supplies or services from minority business enterprises. The Supreme Court in *Fullilove v. Klutznick*, 1980, rejected a challenge to this Congressional action.

The Court, however, in *Richmond v. J. A. Croson* ,1989, narrowed the grounds upon which local and state governments could establish set-aside programs for minorities in the absence of a federal legislative mandate. In this case, the Court invalidated a set-aside program of the city of Richmond for minority contractors. Richmond had reserved 30 percent of its public works money for minority-owned construction firms after a study had shown that only a small percentage of its construction contracts had been awarded to minority-owned businesses. The Court ruled that Richmond would have to show previous discrimination against minority contractors in order to implement its program. As a result, several cities that had adopted Minority Business Enterprise programs to ensure that disadvantaged groups benefited from governmental contracts for construction and for the procurement of goods and services have had to undertake extensive studies to show discrimination against particular groups and must carefully tailor their programs around the findings of the studies.

The Supreme Court made a similar ruling in a 5–4 opinion in *Adarand Constructors Inc. v. Pe±a* in 1995. This case involved a policy of the federal Department of Transportation that gave contractors a bonus if they hired "disadvantaged business enterprises" as subcontractors, and the policy presumed that minority contractors fitted into that category. The majority opinion ruled that federal affirmative action programs would be subject to "strict scrutiny by the courts," meaning that they must be "narrowly tailored" measures to advance a *compelling governmental interest*. The Supreme Court emphasized that affirmative action programs must be examined to ensure that they do not infringe upon the personal right to equal protection under law.

Education

In addition to employment, affirmative action efforts in education have also come before the Supreme Court. The most discussed decision in education has been *Regent of the University of California v. Bakke*, 1978. Paul Allen Bakke was successful in challenging the University of California Medical School's affirmative action program, which included the set-aside of several slots exclusively for minorities. Bakke had applied for admission but was refused, despite holding better qualifications than some of the other candidates who were admitted as part of the school's quota. Although a deeply divided Supreme Court ruled in favor of Bakke, a majority of the Justices also concluded that minority candidates could receive some degree of extra consideration in a university's admissions policy.

Circuit Courts of Appeals have issued conflicting rulings on affirmative action in education. In *Hopwood, et al. v. State of Texas*, the Fifth Circuit Court of Appeals in 1996 ruled that the affirmative action program at the University of Texas law school was unconstitutional. The Eleventh Circuit (*Johnson v. Board of Regents*, 2001) has also ruled against affirmative action. The Ninth Circuit, however, in 1996 supported affirmative action (*Smith v. Washington State University*). In part due to these diverse rulings, the Supreme Court in its 2003 session issued a ruling on both *Grutter* and the *Gratz v. Bollinger* case, in which a lower court upheld an affirmative action program at the University of Michigan undergraduate school. In 2003 the Supreme Court declared that the University of Michigan's undergraduate affirmative action program had to be revised, but it allowed the law school's program to stand. The Court ruled that race could be a factor in admissions decisions to educational institutions, because racial diversity is a "compelling interest." However, universities could not use quotas for members of ethnic racial groups.

Affirmative action programs in education, as well as in public employment and contracting programs, were effectively terminated in California due to the passage of Proposition 209 in 1996. A federal district court issued an injunction in December of that year, delaying the implementation of 209, but the Ninth Circuit Court of Appeals upheld the legality of Proposition 209 in April 1997. Later that year the US Supreme Court refused to consider the case and, therefore, let Proposition 209 stand. Voters in Washington adopted a similar measure in 1998. California, Texas, and Florida have all adopted programs, which differ from traditional affirmative action plans, to try to achieve diversity in undergraduate programs at public universities.

The issue of affirmative action has been one of the most fiercely debated public policy issues for the past two decades. The conservative Reagan administration used the issue to try to strengthen its political support within the white working-class population and appointed members to the EEOC and the Civil Rights Commission who were unsympathetic to affirmative action programs that provided group benefits. The Clinton administration emphasized that affirmative action programs were appropriate under some circumstances. Clinton argued that they should be mended, when necessary, but not ended and the Civil Rights Division of the Justice Department during his administration supported affirmative action efforts. President Bush has argued for "affirmative access," as opposed to affirmative action, but it is still unclear what specific steps his administration will support.

SEE ALSO: African Americans; civil rights movement; disadvantage; equal opportunity; equality; ethnic monitoring; human rights; institutional racism; laws: civil rights, USA; merit; Thomas, Clarence; white backlash culture

Reading

Affirmative Action: An encyclopedia, vols. 1 & 2, edited by James Beckman (Oryx Press/ Greenwood, 2003), includes cross-disciplinary articles on a myriad of topics related to affirmative action issues in the USA and in several other countries.

Affirmative Action: The pros and cons of policy practice by Richard E. Tomasson, Faye J. Crosby and Sharon D. Herzberger (Rowman & Littlefield, 2001), offers a history of affirmative action and, as its title suggests, a balanced debate on the value of the policy.

Combating Racial Discrimination, edited by Erna Appel and Monika Jarosch (Berg, 2000), is a collection of essays focused on various measures designed to redress the effects of racism in the USA, Canada and Europe; among the questions raised are whether US-style affirmative action is applicable in Europe and whether the policy's preferential basis is at odds with the democratic ideal of individual equality.

Impacts of Affirmative Action: Policies and consequences in California, edited by Paul Org (Rowman & Littlefield, 1999), is a collection of essays all centering on California, which set precedents in establishing its first antidiscrimination policy in 1934.

CHECK: internet resources section

ROBERT J. KERSTEIN

AFRICA

The history of race and ethnic relations in Africa antedates the European colonial conquest by several millennia. The continent has been swept by numerous waves of migration and countless indigenous states conquered multiethnic empires. Indeed, the first European colonialism in Africa is over 2,000 years old: it began on a large scale with the defeat of Carthage by Rome in 146 BCE. Christianity entered Ethiopia in the fourth century; the Arabs conquered North Africa in the seventh, and Islam crossed the Sahara in the early years of the second millennium. The entire coast of East Africa has been in trade contact with

Arabia, India, Indonesia, and China for at least 3,000 years. In the interior, a succession of large multiethnic empires rose and fell in the Sudan belt from Senegal to Ethiopia.

The states of central, eastern, and southern Africa were on the whole smaller, somewhat more recent and more ethnically homogeneous, yet a number of them were also ethnically stratified as a result of conquest. Some of them developed indigenous forms of racism, for example the kingdoms of Rwanda and Burundi where a Tutsi minority of some 15 percent of the population dominated Hutu peasants and Twa serfs. The Tutsi claim to superiority was based in good part on their towering stature.

The second half of the fifteenth century marks the Portuguese expansion along the coasts of Africa. The Portuguese were followed in the sixteenth and seventeenth centuries by every other maritime power of Western Europe, principally the English, French, Spaniards, Dutch, and Danes. The Dutch settlement at the Cape of Good Hope in 1652 marks the first sizable European colony in sub-Saharan Africa and was the embryo of contemporary South Africa.

During the 1500 to 1850 period, Europe's relationship to Africa was dominated by the slave trade, which supplied with labor the European colonies of the New World. Contrary to common belief, such trade generally pitted Africans against Africans, and Europeans against Europeans, rather than Africans against Europeans. It was mostly Africans who waged war against their neighbors in order to enslave them, or to avoid being themselves enslaved, and then traded peacefully with European slavers on the coast. The Europeans, for their part, fiercely competed with each other for access to profitable markets and for control of the seas. In all, perhaps some fifteen million Africans crossed the Atlantic in chains, coming principally from West Africa, but also from the Zaire–Angola area, and, in the nineteenth century, increasingly from East Africa. The East African slave trade was centered in Zanzibar, and was largely the product of Arab entrepreneurship. The most massive trading took place during the last century of the traffic (1750–1850), with annual totals often exceeding 50,000 bodies.

After the abolition of slavery, the relationship between Africa and Europe entered a new phase. "Legitimate" trade continued, while the interior was gradually penetrated by "explorers," missionaries, and military expeditions. France con-

quered Algeria in 1830; the Boers and the British greatly extended their territorial encroachments in South Africa in the 1830s and 1840s. By the 1870s, the scramble was on; it consisted of a preemptive set of moves by competing colonizers (mostly the French, British, Belgians, and Portuguese, and belatedly the Germans and Italians), to claim vast stretches of African real estate as theirs. The Berlin Conference of 1884–85 divided the spoils and established the ground rules for fighting over the African carcass. It was not until World War I, however, that European colonial rule was well entrenched over most of Africa (except for Ethiopia, Liberia, and Egypt). When one considers that World War II marked the beginning of the end of European colonialism, the ephemeral nature of European political domination over Africa is evident: it achieved only a measure of solidity for one generation.

Much has been written of the differences between the colonial policies of the various powers. The British and the Belgians were probably more racist and less assimilationist than the French and Portuguese. The French, Portuguese, and Belgians had more centralized colonial administrations based on more direct rule, while the British favored indirect rule at least where they encountered large indigenous states as in Northern Nigeria and Uganda. However, the similarities between the European colonizers overshadow the differences. The basic ideology of colonialism was paternalism, and the reality was domination and exploitation.

A distinction was often made between colonies of settlement and colonies of exploitation. The former (such as Algeria, South Africa, Zimbabwe, the Kenya highlands, and the Angolan plateau) were opened for European rural settlement and were anticipated to have a substantial contingent of permanent European settlers. (The less tropical areas of the continent were preferred for that purpose.) Today, only South Africa retains a substantial population of European settlers. Colonies of exploitation, on the other hand, were meant to be administered by a rotating cadre of European administrators and managers exploiting native labor for the production of minerals and tropical crops (such as cotton, coffee, and cocoa). The economic exchange between metropole and colony was based on unequal terms of trade: costly European finished products against cheap African raw materials (mostly in mining, agriculture, and forestry).

The winds of change brought about by World War II affected the colonial relationship in Asia first (principally in India, Indochina, and Indonesia), but by the 1950s, the rumblings of independence were beginning to be heard in Algeria, Ghana, Kenya, Guinea, and elsewhere. The Mau Mau movement in Kenya and the Algerian war of independence were the violent exceptions to a largely peaceful process of political evolution of power leading to the great wave of independence of 1960.

By the mid 1960s, only the southern third of Africa remained under colonial or white-settler rule. The independence struggle in the south took a violent turn as it became clear that independence was not going to be granted through peaceful negotiations. Angola and Mozambique had to fight the Portuguese for fifteen years before achieving their independence in 1975. In Zimbabwe, too, the struggle was violent, and freedom had to wait until 1981. Finally, Namibia became independent in 1990 and South Africa came under majority rule after the elections of 1994.

Since independence, African states have developed different relationships to Europe. Some ruling elites of African states have maintained close economic, political, cultural, and educational ties with Europe in general, and their former colonial power in particular, a relationship often characterized as neo-colonialism. Countries such as the Ivory Coast, Senegal, and Kenya are examples. Others have taken a more militant course, and have sought to break their colonial ties, or, at least, to multilateralize their dependency. Tanzania, Guinea, Congo-Brazzaville, Ghana, and Nigeria might be put in that category. Some have sought alliance with communist states to achieve independence, only to fall into another form of dependency: Angola, Ethiopia, and Mozambique are cases in point.

Another interesting shift with independence has been one from race to ethnic relations. The accident of pigmentation differences between colonizer and colonized made the independence struggle to some extent a white–black conflict, even though many of the liberation movements stressed their nonracial and antiracist character. After independence, however, the racial issue receded into irrelevance, except for the expression of hostility against certain "middle-man minorities" such as Asians in East Africa (Uganda, under Idi Amin, forcibly expelled its Asians, for instance).

On the other hand, conflicts between indigenous groups for the spoils of independence quickly surfaced in many parts of Africa. Stigmatized as tribalistic, these movements were often, in fact, genuinely nationalist or irredentist. In some cases, ethnic conflicts led to open wars and massacres, as in the Sudan, Ethiopia, Rwanda, Burundi, and Nigeria. In other countries, the game of ethnic politics, while a constant reality, has remained relatively peaceful.

Terminological confusion reigns supreme in the analysis of ethnic relations in Africa. What is called nationalism in Africa is nothing like what the term conventionally has meant elsewhere. How can the concept of nationalism be applied to such multinational states as Senegal, Nigeria, or Zaire? Conversely, what is called tribalism in Africa is often genuine nationalism. The real nations of Africa are the Ibo, the Kikuyu, and the Ewe, not Nigeria, Kenya, and Togo. Only a few of these nations, like the Somali and the Swazi, have their state; the overwhelming majority are part of multinational states, or, even worse, are split between several states. It serves, of course, the interests of the ruling elites of these multinational states to stigmatize demands for national self-determination as tribalist, thereby also conforming to the old colonialist view of Africa as congeries of tribes.

Few African states show concrete signs of moving toward the creation of new nations coinciding with their geographical boundaries. Indigenous traditions and languages remain vigorous, and the official languages (French, English, Portuguese) remain tools of convenience of the ruling class, not the basis for the emergence of new national languages. Only Tanzania, with the effective spread of Swahili as a true national language, shows clear progress toward welding a multiplicity of ethnic groups into what may in time become a genuine new nation.

SEE ALSO: antislavery; apartheid; colonialism; Ethiopianism; exploitation; globalization; indigenous peoples; nationalism; *nigritude*; paternalism; pluralism; racism; Senghor, Líopold Sídar; slavery

Reading

Africa, the Politics of Independence by Immanuel Wallerstein (Vintage, 1961) is a brief treatment of the transition from colonialism to independence by a sympathetic American scholar.

The African Slave Trade by Basil Davidson (Little Brown, 1961) is a fascinating account of the African–European partnership in slaving, by a radical British scholar.

A History of Africa, 4th edn., by John Fage and William Tordoff (Routledge, 2001), is a comprehensive narrative with this edition taking into account contemporary issues, such as developments in Islamic North Africa and South Africa after apartheid.

Race and Ethnicity in Africa, edited by Pierre L. van den Berghe (East African Publishing House, 1975), is a collection of articles on North, West, East, and Southern Africa, with several general analytical pieces.

PIERRE L. VAN DEN BERGHE

AFRICAN AMERICANS

The term African American refers to the 36.4 million persons living in the USA in 2000 who described themselves as black, or African American, in the federal population count published by the US Bureau of the Census. This number represents 12.9 percent of the total American population of approximately 281 million persons. The term African American was revitalized in the late 1980s. During the 1960s, a similar self-description was popular in the black community: "Afro-American." While African American is a popular term utilized by many Americans, the term "black" is the most preferred self-description according to one survey published by the Joint Center for Political and Economic Studies, a black research think tank based in Washington, DC.

While both terms are considered interchangeable, it has been pointed out by some observers that black is more appropriate because it reflects the broader African diaspora and longer history than that associated with African American. Others have also expressed a preference for black because it includes many African-descent groups living in the US that do not use African American as a racial or ethnic self-description. One example of such a case are Haitians, who may identify themselves as black, but not necessarily as African American. In fact, in the 1990 federal population count by the US Bureau of the Census, black is defined as including persons who indicated their "race" as "black or Negro" or reported entries such as African American, black Puerto Rican, Jamaican, Nigerian, West Indian, or Haitian.

In the late 1980s two major national studies focusing on the status of African Americans were published. One study was commissioned by the National Academy of Science, and is titled *A Common Destiny: Black in America* (National Academy Press, 1988). This study represents a reexamination of the status of blacks in America within the framework of the classic study by the Swedish economist, Gunnar Myrdal, *An American Dilemma* (Harper & Row, 1944). The other major study was sponsored by a research think tank based at the University of Massachusetts, the William Monroe Trotter Institute. This study is titled *Assessment of African Americans in the United States* (1990).

While there are important differences in how these two studies approached issues related to black life in the USA, there is at least one important similarity. Both studies concluded that, while blacks have realized important progress in many arenas such as education, politics, military, government, housing, and the economy, many blacks have yet to enjoy social equality with whites. In other words, while there has been some progress and improvement in matters related to race, there still exists an entrenched racial divide and hierarchy in the United States. While some, such as Gunnar Myrdal in the 1940s, have referred to this racial paradox as an American "dilemma," others such as Malcolm X and Martin Luther King, Jr. in the 1960s, have described it as America's "hypocrisy." In 2001, one major study was published by the National Academy of Sciences, *America Becoming: Racial trends and consequences*. This two-volume study examined developments in the area of demography, health, education, racial attitudes, immigration and other areas. It utilized some of the most current census and survey data related to race and ethnicity in the USA. The conclusions of many of its contributing writers are similar to those of the two earlier studies.

Race relations

It cannot be denied that the USA has made enormous strides in improving relations between blacks and whites since the civil rights movement. Racial segregation as the official policy of many states was abolished in the United States as a result of important civil rights legislation. It is also reported in numerous surveys that more whites than ever before are tolerant of interaction with blacks in the areas of housing, schools, and jobs. Individual blacks continue advancing as trailblazers in places once completely barred to blacks. For example, Colin Powell serves as the top military official in the US government. Black sports figures such as the basketball superstar Michael Jordan, and TV and media personalities such as Bill Cosby and Oprah Winfrey, are embraced enthusiastically by white Americans.

Paradoxically, at the same time that this kind of progress is evident, there has been an increase in the number of incidents of racial harassment and violence across the nation. The Southern Poverty Law Center reported in 1989 that hate violence in the US has reached a crisis stage. Between 1980 and 1986 approximately 2,900 racial incidents were reported, including 121 murders, 138 bombings, and 302 assaults. This problem has continued since this period based on reports from this same organization. The number of organized and recognized hate groups, for example, grew to 676 in the year 2001. *Journal of Blacks in Higher Education* reported that during that same year the nation's newspapers and magazines used the term "hate crime" 12,971 times.

Several major studies suggest that in many ways the USA can still be characterized accurately as two societies, one black, the other white, as described in the Kerner Report, a national study which examined the causes of disturbances in the nation during the mid 1960s. While it is inaccurate to overlook the nation's racial and ethnic diversity that goes much beyond simply black and white, the implication that race remains a fundamental issue is valid. This is the conclusion of not only the two national studies cited earlier, but many other recent and scholarly studies as well: examples include *Quiet Riots* (1988) by Roger Wilkins, Jr. and Fred Harris, and Andrew Hacker's *Two Nations* (1992).

Families and health

Historically, the family structure of African Americans in the USA has been different to that of whites. Many factors have been proffered as explanation for the differences in black and white family structure including slavery and its lingering effects, economic conditions, African American culture, the impact of social welfare policies such as public assistance, and conditions

that dampen the availability of marriageable black men such as prisons, wars, drugs, and persistent high levels of unemployment.

Currently, there are many different kinds of families among African Americans as there are in other racial and ethnic communities in the US. There are several trends in the structure of families that are common to all families regardless of race and ethnicity. For example, there is an overall decline in the number of married-couple families, and an increase in the number of single female-headed families, as well as increasing rates of teenage pregnancies throughout society. Still, about one half of all black families were a married-couple family in 1990, compared to about 83 percent of all white families. Another difference between black and white families is the larger size of black family households (2.6 persons) in the USA in 1990; black household size is still smaller than the average family household size of Latinos (3.5 persons).

In the area of health a continuing crisis and racial gap in services has been documented by several researchers and organizations. For example, there is a racial gap in the infant mortality rates. The National Center of Health Statistics has reported that the rate for whites in 1995 was 6.3 percent per 1000 births reported (0–11 months), but 15.1 percent for black babies. Meanwhile, according to the Centers for Disease Control and Prevention the proportion of black pregnant women who did not receive any prenatal care in the first three months of pregnancies totaled 26.7 percent, compared to a figure of 12.0 percent for white women. And the Harvard University School of Public Health has reported that only 64 percent of the black patients in managed health care suffering from heart attacks were prescribed for beta blocker drugs, compared to a rate of 74 percent for white patients in a similar condition.

Education

America's racial paradox is reflected in the nation's educational systems. The gap in school enrollment between African American and white children is disappearing rapidly. By 1980, less than one half year separated the median schooling levels of African Americans (12.6 years) and whites (13.0 years). The difference between the high school completion rates of these two groups is also much smaller than in previous periods.

The scores on national, standardized tests such as the Scholastic Aptitude Test (SAT) and the National Assessment of Education Progress in the areas of reading, mathematics, and science continues to improve for black youth. And the number of blacks earning medical and law degrees has increased significantly in recent years.

Despite much progress in the arena of education many of the nation's public schools remain segregated as predominantly white, black, or Latino schools. Seldom can one find a public school in a major American city where black and white students have opportunities to interact as classmates in the same programs. Continuing disparities in educational experiences of black children and youth are taking place in a national context, where the proportion of black children composing the entire public school population is about 16 percent, and increasing rapidly.

In higher education, blacks now attend colleges and universities that have been hostile to their presence in earlier periods. But still, in 1986, the National Institute of Prejudice and Violence, based in Baltimore, Maryland, reported that "an increasing number of colleges and universities are reporting incidents of cross burnings and other acts of blatant bigotry or racial violence." Calls for multicultural curricula and a greater presence of students and faculty of color as a reflection of growing racial and ethnic diversity in society is still resisted widely. Many leaders and citizens see these calls and accompanying actions under affirmative action as "reverse discrimination" and therefore illegal. There are numerous court battles involving this issue. Additional factors dampening the presence of blacks in American higher education include federal cuts in financial assistance at the same time that the costs for attending college and graduate schools have risen dramatically.

Poverty and employment

Poverty continues to be a major feature of black life in the USA. While there has been a decline in the proportion of African Americans classed as below the poverty line from a rate of 55 percent in 1959 to 32 percent in 1989, this latter figure is still three times the poverty rate found among whites in the United States. This kind of poverty gap between blacks and whites remains despite the particular family structure of blacks, according to figures reported by the US Bureau of the Census. In other words, while black married-couple families had a much lower poverty rate than black female-headed families, blacks living in the former kinds of families were still more than twice as likely to be impoverished in 1990 than comparable whites in married-couple families. A large proportion of black youth and children, in particular, are mired in persistent poverty. In 1990 in the USA, approximately half of all black children under six years of age were poverty-stricken. In an article by Albert M. Camarillo and Frank Bonilla, "Hispanics in a multicultural society: a new American dilemma?" (in *America Becoming*), in 1995 approximately 6 percent of all white families were poverty-stricken. But the figure was much higher for black families; in this case 26 percent of all families were impoverished (the figure for Latino parents was 27 percent). While some may attribute this difference to the greater proportion of female-headed households among blacks, in fact the racial gap remains even controlling for this variable. For example, 22 percent of all white female-headed families were impoverished in 1995, but the rate for blacks stood at more than twice this rate, or 45 percent. The figure for similar Latino families was even slightly higher at 46 percent.

Unemployment rates in black communities continue to be between two and three times greater than white unemployment regardless of the health of the economy. In 1992 the official unemployment rate as reported by the US government's Bureau of Labor Statistics was 6.3 percent for white workers, while for black workers it was reported at 13.9 percent. The unemployment rate for white teenagers was 19 percent, but for black teenagers it was 39.9 percent. In some parts of the nation the unemployment levels for young blacks are in crisis proportions. For instance, in 1988 the Joint Center for Political and Economic Studies conducted a survey and reported that a majority of working-age blacks were not in the labor force in many US metropolitan areas where at least 100,000 blacks resided. In 1996 the unemployment rate for white males stood at 4.0 percent, but 14 percent for black males; white females registered an unemployment rate of 5 percent, but the rate for black females was 9 percent in the same year. When comparisons on the basis of wealth are made between blacks and whites, wide disparities are also found between these two groups. The US Bureau of the Census reported in 1988 that more than half (51.9 percent) of all black households had a net worth of $5,000 or less; but among white households only slightly more than one-fifth (22.6 percent) could be placed in this category. Only 15.5 percent of all black households had a net worth of $50,000 or more in 1988, compared to almost half (46.9 percent) of all white households.

Legal institutions and criminal justice

There is a general sense that some of the legal progress realized by blacks in the area of civil rights has been eroded under a conservative US Supreme Court. Several cases decided by the Supreme Court in 1989 have included legal opinions and interpretations that represent a narrow and circumscribed view of pursuing social and racial equality in the United States.

Such cases include the 1989 *Wards Cove* v. *Atonio* (109 S. Ct. 2115) which shifted the burden of proof of racial discrimination onto the alleged victim. The *Martin* v. *Wilks* (109 S. Ct. 2180) decision gave white male employees of the Birmingham, Alabama, Fire Department the right to challenge a 1974 consent decree to hire black firefighters, although these white firefighters were not employed at the time of the decree. The 1989 *Richmond* v. *Croson* (109 S. Ct. 706) outlawed a requirement for 30 percent construction contract minority set-asides in the city of Richmond, Virginia. The program had been established because over a period of time blacks, who comprised more than one third of this city's population, had received less than 1 percent of all construction contracts from the city. And in 1993, the Supreme Court declared unconstitutional congressional district boundaries drawn to facilitate black congressional representation.

Such state efforts have been based on the Voting Rights Act of 1965. *Shaw* v. *Reno* (113 S. Ct. 2816) suggested that such efforts represented segregation even though aimed at situations where black voters have never been able to elect black representatives due to racial discrimination.

These decisions have been made by a US Supreme Court dominated by the court appointments of Presidents Ronald Reagan (1980–88), and George Bush (1989–92). Together, these two appointed close to two thirds of all the federal judges in the USA. What has been perceived by some as the taking over of the Supreme Court by conservative forces continued with the retirement of legal giant Thurgood Marshall in 1991. His retirement capped a distinguished career devoted to social and racial justice and equality. Bush's replacement for Marshall, Clarence Thomas – himself African American – was criticized by many in the legal community as a conservative ideologue, and lacking in a distinguished legal career.

In the area of criminal justice there has been a significant increase in the number of blacks appointed to various positions, including judges, prosecutors, police officials, and police commissioners. Since 1960, however, the proportion of blacks in the nation's prisons has increased to a point where approximately half of all prisoners in the USA are black. In 1995, the Sentencing Project in Washington, DC reported that one third of all black males in their twenties are incarcerated or involved with the criminal justice system.

Some observers in the USA believe that such high rates reflect racial discrimination against black youth. This was one conclusion of a national report published by the National Association for the Advancement of Colored People, *Hearings on Police Conduct and the Community in Six American Cities* (1992). This report was based on hearing public testimony from a broad range of community representatives in several major cities.

Politics

The 1980s witnessed a black political explosion in the USA as blacks were elected mayors of Chicago and New York City for the first time; even in Boston, for the first time in its history, a black candidate won the mayoral preliminary election and qualified to run in the general election. The first black governor in this century was elected in the state of Virginia. And Jesse Jackson rocked the national political establishment by running for the Democratic Party's presidential nomination in 1984 and 1988; in the latter year he amassed approximately one quarter of the Democratic Party delegates needed to clinch the nomination. The traditional gap between the proportion of blacks and whites registered as voters was closed considerably. The increased electoral muscle of the black community was critical in the election, or reelection of several US senators, especially some representing the Southern states. It was due to this new muscle that several senators abided by the will of black voters and defeated President Ronald Reagan's nomination of conservative jurist Robert Bork as a justice to the Supreme Court.

As is the case with the other arenas of black life in the United States, however, many problems related to race persist, despite important progress. African Americans were unable to elect another black mayoral candidate in the city of Chicago after the death of the city's first black mayor, Harold Washington. David Dinkins, the first black mayor of New York City, was defeated in his bid for a second term.

Important political victories for blacks have not yet been translated into major improvements for a large sector that remain unemployed and in poverty. And at the national level, presidents have been hostile to the political growth and development of the black community since 1980. There have been only two instances in the last 120 years of the nation's history when the President has vetoed civil rights legislation passed by the US Congress, and both of these took place in the relatively recent past. The first instance was when Reagan vetoed the Civil Rights Restoration Act of 1988; the second veto was cast by President Bush when the Civil Rights Act of 1991 was presented to him for his signature. Despite these kinds of political ups and downs for black America, the possibility of major impact on the nation's electoral institutions at all levels remain hopeful. In 1992 blacks were elected to the US House of Representatives for the first time since the 1860s and 1870s in the Southern states of Florida, Alabama, North Carolina, South Carolina, and Virginia. The later 1990s witnessed the election of the first black female US Senator, Carol Moseley Braun. But while she won a seat as senator in 1992, Moseley was defeated after one term in 1998. In 1990 there were 313 blacks serving as mayors, but 451 by the year 2000. In spite of successes and failures of black electoral attempts, however, the unfolding demography of the USA will continue to ensure that blacks remain a powerful, albeit potential, factor to consider in the nation's politics.

SEE ALSO: affirmative action; Ali, Muhammad; Barry case, the Marion; black bourgeoisie in the USA; Black Panther Party; Black Power; blues; civil rights movement; Cleaver, Eldridge; Diageo case; Diallo case, the Amadou; disadvantage; double consciousness; drugs; Ebonics; empowerment; *Invisible Man*; Jackson, Jesse; Jackson, Michael; Jim Crow; Jordan, Michael; Kerner Report; Million Man March; King, Martin Luther; King case, the Rodney; Ku Klux Klan; law: civil rights, USA; Malcolm X; minstrelsy; Motown; Myrdal, Gunnar; *nigritude*; negrophilia; Park, Robert Ezra; reparations; riots: USA, 1921 (Tulsa); riots: USA, 1965–67; riots: USA, 1980 (Miami); slavery; Thomas, Clarence; tokenism; Tyson, Mike

Reading

America Becoming: Racial trends and their consequences, vols. I and II, edited by Neil J. Smelser, William Julius Wilson and Faith Mitchell (National Academy Press: Washington DC, 2001), is a comprehensive overview of racial data and characteristics in many areas. The data is among the most current available on topics like poverty, health, education, income, immigration, and other areas.

Assessment of the Status of African-Americans, vol. iv, edited by Winnie L. Reed, (William M. Trotter Institute, University of Massachusetts at Boston, 1990), is a comprehensive review of the status of African Americans in the areas of social relations, economy, politics, education, and criminal justice.

Journal of Blacks in Higher Education publishes an overview of "vital statistics" in each of its issues that is useful for providing snapshots of black life experiences in the USA. The information and data provided by this journal is particularly useful in understanding the dimensions of racial inequality in this country.

Quiet Riots by Roger Wilkins, Jr. and Fred Harris (Pantheon, 1988) is a series of essays that focus on changes in race and poverty in the US since the Kerner Report of 1968.

Two Nations by Andrew Hacker (Scribner, 1992) offers a bleakly analytical picture of a society "separate, hostile, unequal." "Race has made America its prisoner," concludes Hacker.

JAMES JENNINGS

AFRICAN CARIBBEANS IN BRITAIN

The post-World War II movement of African Caribbeans from their countries of origin to Britain, their routine experience of racism and discrimination in the metropolitan center, and their eventual location at the subordinate levels of Britain's class-stratified society are phenomena of colonialism. That is, the system geared toward the raw exploitation of human labor and natural resources. This system was secured and justified by the belief in racial inferiority and inequality, a belief which has remained firmly embedded in the collective consciousness of the indigenous white British population. What is more, it had enormous and far-reaching implications for the economies of the metropolis and periphery and, crucially, for the economic and social relations between them. A. Sivanandan has emphasized this point in his argument that:

> colonialism perverts the economy of the colonies to its own ends, drains their wealth into the coffers of the metropolitan country and leaves them at independence with a large labor force and no capital with which to make that labor productive. (*A Different Hunger*, Pluto Press, 1982)

Migration

At the end of World War II, the British and other Western capitalist nations embarked on a process of rapid economic growth which necessitated the import of migrant labor. This demand was only partially satisfied by the influx of workers from Poland and other parts of Europe, and it was at this juncture that Britain, almost in desperation, turned to its colonies and ex-colonies in Africa, India and the Caribbean.

Migration from the Caribbean, especially Jamaica and Barbados, had been a fairly routine experience – a conventional means of escape from the twin problems of overpopulation and under-unemployment, phenomena that had been determined by colonial exploitation. Until 1952, the migrants, for a variety of economic and social reasons, had generally headed for the United States; however, the enactment of restrictive immigration legislation by the US government in that year effectively blocked this route. Despite the reluctance of both Labor and Conservative parties to encourage black migrants to come to Britain, the economic situation demanded that this vast reservoir of cheap and alternative labor in the Caribbean could not be ignored. Especially as it could be attracted easily to the metropolitan center. The migrants, along with those who later arrived from India (and after 1947, Pakistan), collectively came to be known as "a reserve army of labor" for the British economy.

The nature of the work such migrants were put to in the metropolitan center was also predetermined by the colonial legacy. In a period of full employment, white indigenous workers inevitably moved into the higher echelons of the labor market. The vacancies which remained at the "cellar level" were filled by those such as African Caribbeans: these were the low status, often unskilled positions in the textile and clothing industries, engineering and foundry works, hotels, hospital and transport services. Prevailing perceptions of blacks as inferior, fit only for menial tasks, had originated in the colonial era; but experiences of black migrants in the metropolitan center reinforced these stereotypes. In short, because blacks were compelled to accept undesirable, menial work in Britain and were seen to demonstrate the veracity of colonial stereotypes about them, they were inevitably caught in the most vicious of vicious circles.

Class profile

In profile, the migrants formed a fraction of the working class: they occupied similar positions in relation to the means of production and supplied labor not capital. Nevertheless, though their objective interests were basically those of the working class generally, the migrants were often viewed as unwelcome competition. This was consolidated as the post-World War II economic boom began to recede in the late 1950s. As a corollary, hostility toward them increased. The outbreak of violence between blacks and whites in 1958 in the Notting Hill district of London and in Nottingham exemplified this growing trend. The increasing demands for selective immigration control, primarily to curtail the entry of nonwhite colonial and ex-colonial migrants, can also be understood from this perspective.

It is difficult to establish with any precision the collective response of the African Caribbean migrants to these circumstances, though research does indicate that there was widespread disillusionment with life in the "Mother Country." After all, they had not expected to compete with native workers for jobs, nor had they anticipated the individual and institutionalized discrimination and harassment that they habitually experienced in their day-to-day lives. Nor were they completely unmoved by these experiences: the manifestation of racist violence in 1958 highlighted the need for greater organization and militancy within the communities. It strengthened their fortitude and resistance and helped to set the scene for the publication of journals such as the *West Indian Gazette* and the establishment of the Standing Conference of West Indian Organizations in Britain. Despite these sporadic and important gestures of defiance however, it is difficult to disagree with the view that the energies of the African Caribbean migrants were geared primarily to a process of social involution: the cultivation of separateness from the hostile society and the emergence of group solidarity and community togetherness. The enormous growth of Pentecostalism in Britain testified to the extent of this withdrawal process. In 1970, it was estimated, for instance, that one branch of this sectarian movement alone had a following of nearly 11,000 congregations.

This tendency to eschew more militant postures against the daily inequalities of British hostility derived from a variety of factors. Some African Caribbeans adhered to what has been termed "the migrant ideology"; in other words, because their presence in Britain was based purely and simply on economic grounds, they saw themselves as transient workers who would return to their countries of origin once they had accumulated sufficient money. As such, they were prepared to tolerate conditions in Britain, because they regarded their stay as temporary. Others put up with what Nancy Foner, in *Jamaica Farewell* (Routledge, 1979), called "the pain of being black in Britain," largely because they believed that their children, born and brought up in Britain and therefore unencumbered by an immigrant culture, would not experience the debilitating effects of racial discrimination. They would, in effect, compete on an equal footing with their white counterparts in Britain's meritocratic education system.

The persistence of the colonial legacy ensured that this was false optimism however. The disadvantages experienced by the African Caribbean migrants in Britain were only tenuously related to their newness in the society; they were unlikely to diminish with the passage of time. It is precisely the fact that their disadvantaged positions are likely to be reproduced in the life patterns of their children that distinguishes the experiences of colonial migrants from those of other migrant workers. The result: citizens of African Caribbean origin continue to occupy subordinate positions in the labor market; tend to earn less than white indigenous workers; and

are more vulnerable to the risk of unemployment, especially in times of economic recession. Nor is this trend attributable in any significant measure to their alleged "underachievement" in school examinations. The proposition that, even in the midst of a severe recession, school leavers of equal merit stand an equal chance of getting a job simply cannot be sustained. Young unemployed blacks tend to be better qualified than their white unemployed peers.

Youth

After the rioting in Britain in 1981 and 1985, equal opportunities programs were addressed with more urgency and government assistance to entrepreneurship among ethnic minorities was stepped up. Several politicians of African Caribbean background grew to prominence. While these developments facilitated the improvement in material conditions of African Caribbeans, relations with the police remained tense, especially among the young. The murder of Stephen Lawrence in 1993 and the subsequent *cause cílØbre* did much to shift the often conflictual relations between African Caribbeans and the police into the public eye.

The stereotypes of disaffected, alienated black youth that were popular in the 1980s and 1990s have been replaced by another stereotype: that of the young black male raised in the ghetto with few aspirations beyond owning a gun and becoming a successful career criminal. As racially motivated crime has increased, young African Caribbeans are presumed to be both victims and perpetrators of violence.

SEE ALSO: black bourgeoisie in Britain; British Asians; colonialism; diaspora; education; equal opportunity; ghetto; Hall, Stuart; homelessness; institutional racism; Lawrence case, the Stephen; media; migration; Pentecostalism; policing; racial coding; riots: Britain, 1981; riots: Britain, 1985; Scarman Report; segregation; sexual abuse; social work; underachievement; welfare

Reading

Blacks and Britannity, edited by DaniØle Joly (Ashgate, 2001), is a collection of original essays, some based on empirical research. The volume covers the issue of violence and group identification.

Changing Britannia: Life experience with Britain, edited by Roxy Harris and Sarah White (New Beacon Books, 2001), is based on seven talks given by prominent members of the African Caribbean population and, as such, provides valuable perspectives.

Representing Black Britain: Black and Asian images on television by Sarita Malik (Sage, 2001) focuses on how ethnic minority people are depicted in the media and argues that these depictions affect their material lives.

Staying Power: The history of black people in Britain by Peter Fryer (Pluto, 1984) remains a classic text. It is a massive historical account of black presence in Britain, dating back to the sixteenth century; *The Making of the Black British Working Class* by Ron Ramdin (Gower, 1987) is another valuable history.

BARRY TROYNA

AFROCENTRICITY

Afrocentricity is a theoretical and philosophical perspective, as distinct from a particular system, based on the idea that interpretation and explanation derived from the role of the Africans as subjects is most consistent with reality. It became a growing intellectual idea in the 1980s as scores of African American, African Brazilian, Caribbean, and African scholars adopted an Afrocentric orientation to data. Afrocentricity is generally opposed to theories that "dislocate" Africans in the periphery of human thought and experience.

Afrocentrists argue that the Western dogma, which contends that Greeks gave the world rationalism, in effect marginalizes those who are not European. The Afrocentrists contend that the dogma is historically inaccurate and that the construction of Western notions of knowledge based on the Greek model is a relatively recent occurrence, beginning with the European Renaissance. In the standard Western view neither Africans nor Asians had rational thinking. Only Europeans had the ability to construct rational thought. In this view whatever occurred in ancient Egypt, Nubia, India, or China was never as important as what took place among Europeans. Thus, the Afrocentrists contend that the Eurocentric view has become an ethnocentric view elevating the European experience and downgrading all others.

Afrocentricity is not the counterpoint to Eurocentricity, but a particular perspective for analysis that does not seek to occupy all space and time as Eurocentrism has often done. For example, to say classical music, theater, or dance is usually a reference to European music, theater, or dance. However, this means that Europeans occupy all of the intellectual and artistic seats and leave no room for others. The Afrocentrists argue for pluralism in philosophical views, without hierarchy. All human cultures must be centered, that is subject to their own realities.

In the Afrocentric view the problem of location takes precedence over the topic or the data under consideration. The argument is that Africans have been moved away from the locus of social, political, philosophical, and economic terms for half a millennium. Consequently it becomes necessary to examine all data from the standpoint of Africans as subjects, human agents, rather than as objects in a European frame of reference. Afrocentricity has implications for fields as different as dance, architecture, social work, literature, politics, and psychology. Scholars in those fields have written extensively about the motifs of location and the constituents of decenteredness in various areas.

Two methodological devices have emerged to assist in the construction of a new body of knowledge: *reasonable plausibility* and *intelligent conclusion*. Both are common terms used in a definite and precise sense to deal with the issue of historical, social, and cultural lacunae in many discourses on African people. Although seen as speculative supports, these devices are central to understanding how Africans responded in situations where little information exists. Reasonable plausibility is based on Martin Bernal's *Black Athena* thesis of explaining lacunae in historical information (Rutgers University Press, 1987). One can assume that the ancient Greeks who lived and traveled in ancient Egypt were exposed to certain Egyptian values, ideas, and behaviors. Even if there were no documents saying that Plato or Lycurgus were actually in the great city of Waset reasonable plausibility would allow the researcher to make a highly probably statement of fact. Intelligent conclusion is derived from the work of Molefi Asante and is based on analysis of prejudicial and racist reportage in texts. When one knows by circumstances, effects, and policies that Africans were involved in an event or phenomenon, despite the lack of direct information, one can make an intelligent conclusion. The records of the Great Storm of 1928 in Florida reveal little about the role Africans played in the Florida economy prior to the storm. One could even get the impression that Africans were marginal to the society and the economy by reading the biased accounts of history. However, more than two thirds of the nearly 3,000 killed by the storm were Africans, indicating an enormous agricultural laboring sector that can be missed if one does not make intelligent conclusion.

Afrocentrists contend that human beings cannot divest themselves of culture, whether participating in their own historical culture or in that of some other group. A contradiction between history and perspective produces a kind of incongruity, which is called decenteredness. Thus, when an African American writes from the viewpoint of Europeans who came to the Americas on the *Mayflower*, or when literary critics write of Africans as 'Other,' Afrocentrists claim that Africans are being peripheralized within their own story.

Metaphors of location and dislocation are the principal tools of analysis as events, situations, texts, buildings, dreams, and literary authors are seen as displaying various forms of centeredness. To be centered is to be located as an agent instead of as Other. Such a critical shift in thinking means that the Afrocentric perspective provides new insights and dimensions to the understanding of phenomena.

Contemporary issues in Afrocentric thinking have involved the explanation of psychological misorientation and disorientation, attitudes which affect Africans who consider themselves to be Europeans, or who believe that it is impossible to be African and human. Severe forms of this attitude have been labeled extreme misorientation by some Afrocentrists. Additional issues have been the influence of a centered approach to education, particularly as it relates to the revision of the American educational curriculum. Hundreds of articles and books have been published examining social welfare, political institutions, crime and punishment, pan-Africanism, international politics and policies, and religion. Indeed, the contemporary Afrocentrist is interested in a variety of themes and topics.

SEE ALSO: Africa; African Americans; bigotry; colonial discourse; cultural identity; Ebonics; ethnocentrism; Fanon, Frantz; Garvey, Marcus; hybridity; Nation of Islam; *nigritude*; Other; postcolonial; racist discourse; Senghor, Líopold Sídar; subaltern

Reading

The Afrocentric Idea (Temple University Press, 1998),

Afrocentricity (Africa World Press, 2002), and *Kemet, Afrocentricity and Knowledge* (Africa World Press, 1990) by Molefi Kete Asante form a trilogy of works examining the origins of Africans, constituent parts and analytical methods of discovery in an Afrocentric sense.

The Afrocentric Paradigm by Ama Mazama (Africa World Press, 2003), is the definitive collection of theoretical and methodological articles by Afrocentrists.

Behind the Eurocentric Veils by Clinton Jean (University of Massachusetts Press, 1990), is an examination of how social and political institutions have been rationalized on a Eurocentric model and dislocated African institutions to the margins.

Journal of Black Studies (published by Sage), is a multidisciplinary forum related to issues concerning persons of African descent.

Social Work and Africa Centred Worldviews by Mekada Graham (Venture Press, 2002), is the first truly Afrocentric work written in the UK. It is a theoretical examination of the problem of social work in a multiracial environment where people of African descent are marginalized in the conception and execution of social work.

MOLEFI KETE ASANTE

AIDS *see* sexuality

ALI, MUHAMMAD (1942–)

The ethic of protest

Muhammad Ali was an emblem of black protest, a cipher for the anti-Vietnam movement, a martyr (or traitor, depending on one's perspective), a self-regarding braggart and many more things besides. While there have been several sporting icons, none have approached Ali in terms of complexity, endowment and sheer potency. Jeffrey Sammons suggests: "Perhaps no single person embodied the ethic of protest and intersected with so many lives, ordinary and extraordinary" (in "Rebel with a cause: Muhammad Ali as sixties protest symbol" in Gorn, below).

By the end of the twentieth century Ali, by then suffering from Parkinson's Syndrome, was an esteemed figure, acknowledged throughout the world as one of the finest athletes ever and as a global benefactor. It was easy to forget that, in the 1960s, he was despised and regarded by a great many as a malevolent presence.

Born in Louisville, Kentucky, in the segregated south, Cassius Clay, as he was christened, was made forcibly aware of America's "two nations," one black, one white. In his autobiography, he related how, after the euphoria of winning a gold medal at the Rome Olympics of 1960, he returned home to be refused service at a restaurant. This kind of incident was to influence his later commitments. Clay's amateur triumphs convinced a syndicate of white entrepreneurs to finance his early professional career.

Basing his approach on that of Gorgeous George a flamboyant and boastful wrestler, Clay both infuriated and fascinated audiences with his outrageous claims to be the greatest boxer of all times, his belittling of opponents, his poetry and his habit of predicting (often accurately) the round in which his fights would end. "It's hard to be modest when you're as great as I am," he once remarked.

In 1964, Cassius Clay forced the world heavyweight champion Sonny Liston into retirement and easily dismissed him in the rematch. Between the two fights, he had proclaimed his change of name to Muhammad Ali, reflecting his conversion to Islam. In fact, he had made public his membership of the Nation of Islam, sometimes known as the Black Muslims, prior to the first Liston fight, but the full ramifications of this move came later.

The Nation of Islam was led by Elijah Muhammad and had among its most famous followers Malcolm X, who kept company with Ali and who was to be assassinated in February 1965. Among the Nation's principles were (and are) that whites were "blue-eyed devils" who were intent on keeping black people in a state of subjugation and that integration was not only impossible, but undesirable. Blacks and whites should live separately; preferably by living in different states. This view was in stark distinction to North America's melting pot ideal.

Ali's camp comprised only one white man – Angelo Dundee, the trainer. Cassius Clay, Sr. was violently opposed to Ali's affiliation, not on religious grounds but because he believed the entourage of Black Muslims Ali attracted were taking his money. But Ali's commitment deepened and the media, which had earlier warmed to his extravagance, turned against him. A rift occurred between Ali and Joe Louis, the former heavyweight champion who was once described as "a credit to his race." This presaged several other conflicts with other black boxers whom Ali believed had allowed themselves to become assimilated into white America and had failed to face themselves as true black people.

Ali saved his most ardent criticism for Floyd Patterson whom he called an "Uncle Tom" and "the rabbit," after Patterson had refused to use his Islamic name. He seemed to delight in punishing Patterson in their fight in 1965. The almost malicious performance brought censure from sections of America, both black and white.

The events that followed Ali's call up by the military in February 1966 were dramatized by a background of growing resistance to US involvement in the Vietnam war. Ali failed to meet the qualifying criteria in the mental aptitude at first, but, by 1966, with the war intensifying, the US Army lowered the required percentile, making him eligible for the draft. A legal request for a deferment from military service was denied. Ali's oft-quoted remark, "I ain't got no quarrel with them Vietcong," made headlines around the world and positioned him in the eyes of many as the most famous-ever draft dodger. But he insisted that his conscience not cowardice guided his decision not to serve in the military and so, to many others, he became an emblem of pacifism.

Ali continued to defend his title, often traveling overseas in response to attempted boycotts of his fights. At the nadir of his popularity, he fought Ernie Terrell, who, like Patterson, persisted in calling him "Clay." The fight in Houston had a grim subtext with Ali constantly taunting Terrell. "What's my name, Uncle Tom?" Ali asked Terrell as he administered a callous beating. Ali prolonged the torment until the fourteenth round. The phrase "What's my name?" became a slogan of defiance. Media reaction to the fight was wholly negative. Thomas Hauser quotes Jimmy Cannon, a boxing writer of the day: "It was a bad fight, nasty with the evil of religious fanaticism. This wasn't an athletic contest. It was a kind of lynching ... [Ali] is a vicious propagandist for a spiteful mob that works the religious underworld."

In April 1967, Ali refused to be inducted into the armed forces. Despite claims that he deserved the same status as conscientious objectors from the Mennonite Church or other Christian groups, Ali was denied and found guilty of draft evasion. After a five-year legal struggle, during which time Ali was stripped of his title, a compromise was reached and Ali was set free. During his exile, Ali had angered the Nation of Islam by announcing his wish to return to boxing if this were ever possible. Elijah Muhammad, the supreme minister, denounced Ali for playing "the white man's games of civilization." Elijah had objected to sports for some time, believing them to be detrimental to the progress of black people.

Other critical evaluations of sport were gathering force. The Black Power-inspired protests of John Carlos and Tommie Smith at the 1968 Olympics, combined with the anti-apartheid movement in South Africa, where people such as Sam Ramsamy were rallying against racism, had made clear that sport could be used to amplify the experiences of black people the world over. While Ali was a *be?te noir* for many whites and indeed blacks, several civil rights leaders, sports performers and entertainers came out publicly in his defense.

"Still others in American society viewed Ali as a genuine hero," writes David Wiggins in his *Glory Bound: Black athletes in a white America* (Syracuse University Press, 1997). "Many people in the black community viewed Ali in this manner, considering him a champion of the black Civil Rights movement who bravely defied the norms and conventions of the dominant culture." As Michael Oriard, in his essay "Muhammad Ali: hero in the age of mass media" concludes: "There was not a single Ali but many Alis in the public consciousness" (in Gorn, below).

Ali's moves were monitored by government intelligence organizations: given the growing respect he was afforded, he was seen as an influential figure. Many of his conversations were wiretapped. He spent three-and-a-half years without his title, unable to earn a living. By the end of it, cultural conditions had shifted so much that he was widely regarded as a martyr by the by-then formidable antiwar movement and practically anyone who felt affinity with civil rights.

Return from exile

Ali's first fight after exile was in October 1970. He beat Jerry Quarry at an Atlanta where the majority of fans were African Americans. Any prospect of a smooth transition back to the title was dashed March 1971 by Joe Frazier, who had taken the title in Ali's absence and defended it with unexpected tenacity in a contest that started one of the most celebrated rivalries in sport. Ali had called Frazier a "white man's champion" and declared: "Any black man who's for Joe Frazier is a traitor." Ali beat Frazier twice over the following years, every fight being viciously fought and punishing for both men.

Ali had to wait until 1974 before getting another chance at the world title. By this time, Frazier had been dethroned by George Foreman and Ali, now thirty-two, was not favored; in fact, many feared for his well-being, especially as he had been given two tough fights by the unheralded Ken Norton (one win each; Ali won a third later, in 1976). The fight in Zaire was promoted by Don King, at that stage building his way toward becoming one of the world's most powerful sports entrepreneurs. The circumstances surrounding what was known as "The Rumble in the Jungle" are the subject of Leon Gast's documentary film *When We Were Kings*. Ali's remarkable Phoenix-like victory re-established him as the world heavyweight champion.

The death of Elijah Muhammad in 1975 led to a split in the Nation of Islam, Louis Farrakhan taking the movement in a fundamentalist direction, while Elijah's son Wallace D. Muhammad founded the World Community of Al-Islam in the West, which dwelt less on past atrocities of blue-eyed devils and more on the future. Ali sided with Wallace.

In June 1979, having lost and regained the title against Leon Spinks and beaten Frazier once more, Ali announced his retirement from boxing. There were clear signs of decline in both Spinks fights and, at 37, Ali appeared to have made a graceful exit when he moved to Los Angeles with his third wife Veronica whom he had married two years before. His first marriage had lasted less than a year, ending in 1966; Ali married again in 1967.

After joining the Nation, Ali split with the business syndicate that handled his early affairs. His manager now became Herbert Muhammad. Hauser estimates Ali's career earnings to 1979 to be "tens of millions of dollars." The three Frazier fights alone brought Ali $11m; the 1976 Norton fight grossed him $6m; his purse for the Foreman fight was $5.45m; he earned $6.75m for the two Spinks fights. His lesser-paid fights were typically worth $2m each to Ali. Yet, on his retirement, Ali was not wealthy. His wife had an extravagant lifestyle and his business investments were poorly judged. He also gave generously to the Nation of Islam and to various causes.

Within fifteen months of his announced retirement, Ali returned to the ring, his principal motivation apparently being money, though Ali himself reckoned it was the prospect of winning the world title for a record fourth time that drove him. While public sentiment seemed against a comeback at age thirty-eight against a peak-form Larry Holmes, who was employed as Ali's sparring partner between 1973 and 1975, box-office interest was strong enough to justify paying Ali $8m. Holmes, as champion, received less than $3m. It was the first fight in which Ali failed to last the full distance and seemed an inglorious, if lucrative, end to a grand career.

Ali's ill-fated business ventures took another bad turn when he became involved with Muhammad Ali Professional Sports, an organization headed by Harold Williams, and one which proved to be a fraudulent operation. A return to the ring appeared impossible after medical tests revealed all manner of complication and Ali relinquished his boxing license to the Nevada State Athletic Commission. But this still left him free to box elsewhere in the world and, in December 1981, he fought once more in Nassau, the Bahamas. It ended in another resounding defeat, this time by Trevor Berbick. James Cornelius, who was a member of the Nation of Islam, promoted the fight. As in the Holmes fight, there was plain evidence of Ali's acute deterioration and, although he lasted the ten-round distance, he spent much of the fight against the ropes soaking up punishment. He was now thirty-nine, and had fought 61 times, with a 56–5 record.

Further questionable business deals and an expensive divorce in 1986 followed. In 1984 he disappointed his supporters when he nominally supported Ronald Reagan's reelection bid. He also endorsed George Bush in 1988. The Republican Party's policies, particularly in regard to affirmative action programs, were widely seen as detrimental to the interests of African Americans and Ali's actions were, for many, tantamount to a betrayal.

Ali's public appearances gave substance to stories of his ill health. By 1987, he was the subject of much medical interest. Slurred speech and uncoordinated bodily movements gave rise to several theories about his condition, which was ultimately revealed as Parkinson's Syndrome. His public appearances became rarer and he became Hauser's "benign venerated figure."

Over a period of four decades, Ali excited a variety of responses: admiration and respect, of course, but also cynicism, anger and condemnation. At different points in his life, he drew the adulation of young people committed to civil rights, Black Power and peace. Yet, as Wiggins points out: "Members of the establishment were, moreover, infuriated by Ali because he exposed, for all the world to see, an America that was unwilling to honor its own precepts."

Ali engaged with the central issues that preoccupied America: race and war. But, it would be remiss to understand him as a symbol of social healing; much of his mission was to expose and, perhaps, to deepen divisions. He preached peace, yet aligned himself with a movement that sanctioned racial separation and the subordination of women. He accepted a role with the liberal Democratic administration of Jimmy Carter, yet later sided with reactionaries, Reagan and Bush. He preached black pride, yet disparaged and dehumanized fellow blacks. He preached the importance of self-determination, yet allowed himself to be sucked into so many doubtful business deals that he was forced to prolong his career to the point where his dignity was effaced. Like any towering symbol, he had very human contradictions.

SEE ALSO: African Americans; Barry case, the Marion; civil rights movement; Cleaver, Eldridge; Jackson, Michael; Jordan, Michael; King, Martin Luther; King case, the Rodney; Malcolm X; Nation of Islam; Tyson, Mike

Reading

Muhammad Ali: Celebrity trickster in an age of irony by Charles Lemert (Polity Press, 2004) is one of a number of high-quality scholarly accounts of Ali's life and his importance. Others include: Gerald Early's edited collection *I'm a Little Special: A Muhammad Ali reader* (Yellow Jersey Press, 1998) and Elliott Gorn's edited collection *Muhammad Ali: The People's Champ* (University of Illinois Press, 1995).

Muhammad Ali: His life and times by Thomas Hauser (Pan Books, 1997) remains the best biography, though Ali's own book, *The Greatest: My own story* (Random House, 1975), is, in its own way, an interesting document.

AMALGAMATION

This describes the merging of two or more different groups to produce a new and distinct group. It can be simply expressed as A+B+C=Z, where A, B, and C are individual groups and Z is the outcome of their mixing. Originally, the term referred to biologically different groups. Brazil had an official policy encouraging the intermarriage of its many distinct groups. More recently, the term is reserved for the fusion of cultural groups, whose mixing produces a new and unique culture. Contemporary Mexico combines elements of Spanish with Native American culture and the result is distinct from either. Amalgamation can be contrasted with assimilation, in which one culture tends to dominate and absorb all others into a single culture, i.e., A+B+C=A, in which A is the most powerful group.

This synethetical model avoids the essentialism implied in many other approaches: it views ethnic identity as in a continuous process of construction, the Zs always in interaction with others to produce new synetheses. It also permits the possibility that individuals simultaneously belong, move between and constantly engage in changing the groups to which they belong and which they constitute.

SEE ALSO: assimilation; Brazil; Myrdal, Gunnar; integration; multiculturalism; pluralism; welfare

Reading

Cultural Diversity in the United States, edited by Ida Susser and Thomas C. Patterson (Blackwell, 2001), is full of essays on ethnic amalgamations; in particular, parts III and IV contain valuable contributions from anthropologists studying historical and ever-shifting contemporary forms of cultural diversity and, as such, deliver an interesting corrective to static models of ethnicity.

"Race and ethnicity," by Richard Schaefer and Robert Lamm in their textbook *Sociology*, 4th edn., (McGraw-Hill, 1992), has a clear section on amalgamation with examples.

AMERICAN DILEMMA, AN see Myrdal, Gunnar

AMERICAN INDIANS

Nations and treaties

American Indians describes a generally accepted "race" of indigenous peoples in the Western hemisphere, especially North America, most likely derived from the mistaken Colombian usage of *Los Indios* for Caribbean peoples (actually *Taino-Arawak*) on *Hispaniola* in 1492, and is applied generically to the diverse nations that Europeans contacted and conquered, becoming a central feature of the social construction of

"races" of people by geophysical identifiers. The word took on different meanings in North, Central and South America, almost always derogatory, and changed politically, socially, and economically from one century to the next.

American Indians are the constructed category of indigenous peoples in the Americas that have survived 500 years of European and then American cultural domination, internal colonialism, holocaust-like demographic decline, and lately a limited resurgence. Often referred to as natives, their original societies ranged from vast empires such as those of the Aztecs, Mayans and Incas, to much smaller societies sometimes called "tribes" and more appropriately as nations or communities. Because of this incredible diversity spanning two major continents across five centuries in very different cycles of development, it is necessary to identify specific Indian nations and histories when describing their contemporary realities.

There are no countries or nation-states in the Western hemisphere still governed by Indian people, although there are millions of "Indians" throughout the Americas, especially in Central and South America. Some Indian tribes/nations have reestablished claims to sovereignty in homelands, while others struggle for recognition of autonomous relationships, or even as "minority" groups. There are generally sharp distinctions concerning recognition by the ruling nation-state between Indians in South and Central America (including Mexico), and North America (the USA and Canada). Even so, nearly all indigenous peoples in these areas have experienced some form of genocide, though there was very little state-sponsored mass-killing in the USA and Canada during the twentieth century.

Indigenous peoples have been referred to as "First Nations" in Canada for the last thirty or forty years, and are called "Indian Tribes" or, more recently, "Nations" in the United States, when so recognized, especially when developed from "Indian Reservations" still used in legal and social discourse. Federal recognition in the United States of Indian peoples, usually involves some complicated means of identifying a "blood quantum" or "descent-by-blood" rule that modern sciences have consistently stated is physically impossible to establish. Nonetheless, such distinction can be very important for Natives in these two countries, since otherwise they have few protections. Peoples that have moved or been forced to leave their homelands and live in cities are often referred to as "urban Indians," and at times lack meaningful connection to their home cultures. However, modern social activities such as generic "pow-wows" and intertribal or international gatherings that might include some ceremonial life are found among all Indian peoples.

Many nations struck treaties or other formal agreements with the USA and Canada which have been the basis for making the continued claims for lands and reparations for injustice which mark their continuous relationships with the dominant society. When such legal documents were upheld in courts, "tribal sovereignty" was reinserted back into the federal relationships, allowing political and economic activity to grow, including Indian Gaming. Lands have been restored in a few situations, as in the state of Maine or the province of British Columbia, but contested and limited monetary payments are the more common instrument.

Spectacular conflicts over these treaties stand out in definition of how incoming dominant governments have tried to avoid their mandated responsibilities in many of these treaties. The Lakota "Sioux Nation" is still in court over the 1868 Fort Laramie Treaty that included sacred territory known as the Black Hills for which the modern-day Lakota refuse to accept payment. Wars leading to treaties still affect many Native Nations, including the Apache, the Navajo, Ojibwa, Wampanoag, and Haudenosaunee (Iroquois), to name just a few. Peoples that were forcibly removed to reservations also contest the justice of their treatment, including many California Indians who have recently fought for and won state referendums on Indian Gaming, wherein a 150 years ago their population base was eliminated upwards of 90 percent. These and a host of related conflicts demonstrate the viability and survival of Indians.

Historical conflicts illustrate the complicated reality of most contemporary Native Americans. The Five Civilized Tribes were put under the genocidal policy "Indian Removal" from their Southeastern homelands to Indian Territory (Oklahoma), splitting up societies such as the Cherokee with recognized lands in North Carolina and Oklahoma. Similar policies were applied throughout the Northeast, Central Plains, and Northwest regions of the country. Many reservations contain people from different "tribes" or cultures, greatly complicating current social rea-

lities and nomenclature. The Seminole from Florida have added problems with race since they merged with runaway black slaves hundreds of years ago.

The intersection of race and culture with class is typical throughout Central and South America. Brazil, while not employing strict racial categories for blacks or Indians, nonetheless ends up with much greater poverty for both groups, and particularly oppressive policies towards indigenous peoples such as Yanomami in the Amazon rainforest under the guise of national "development." The Miskito in Honduras and during an uprising against Nicaraguan Sandinistas experienced the combined effects of being targeted by powerful elites in their own countries. Nearly all Central and South American nation-states oppress indigenous peoples through refusing to recognize historical, sovereign claims, or by typifying them as "minority" groups without any special rights. In a few instances, Indians have built coalitions to protest various injustices, as did those of Mayan descent in Chiapas, Mexico, with Zapatistas.

Earlier social movements often attempted coalitions in North America, leading to cultural revitalization movements that were historically put down with using military force, for example, the 1890 Ghost Dance. The 1960s and 1970s in the USA saw a resurgence that included the American Indian Movement (AIM) and the Trail of Broken Treaties, advocating resistance, such as at Wounded Knee. While ultimately unsuccessful, these movements supported, some would say spawned, current resistance groups, including the UN Indigenous People's Working Group and well established sovereignty claims in the USA and Canada, with Indian peoples demanding identification as nations within nation-states, rebuilding languages and cultures after 200 years of suppression.

Contemporary issues

The contemporary situations of "Native" American Indians as the indigenous peoples of the Americas must consider themes of cultural reproduction, commodification, education as oppression and liberation, environmental issues, globalization and resistance, identity issues in political constructs, media and representation, especially in respect of various stereotypes and ideological icons, sex and gender roles, traditionalism and modernity, social policy with inequality, and potential futures of indigenous peoples. Although much of the focus is on Indians north of Mexico, many of the most relevant issues apply to sociopolitical situations in Central and South America, furthering discussion of broad social movements shared across societies.

Cultural reproduction for nearly all American Indians is more a question of resisting cultural suppression and *culturecide*, through retaining social and cultural practices that more often than not were attacked and made illegal by governmental edicts. Within the political realm, these include systems of governance, law enforcement, and a maintenance of militias for defense. Modern Tribal Councils and Indian Police imperfectly now mediate these relations with the dominant society. Economically, land tenure systems were transformed via huge transfers and outright "takings" that left tiny, less desirable reservation areas. Property rights and trade are still restricted to those acceptable by the dominant nation-state. Cultural systems – language, family, learning, and religion – have become the primary conflict points for indigenous peoples' struggles to keep traditional knowledge alive while negotiating modern life.

Attempted commodification of "American Indians" has been centrally unique to profitable development of the American psyche, first by Euro-Americans and later by some Indian peoples. Besides continental land transfers noted above, and neo-colonial exploitation of natural resources still under Indian control, such as Crow coal, Navajo uranium, Inuit water/dam power, and timber/wildlife everywhere, imagery and culture are constantly commodified. Noble Savages in history and literature are a core of American ideologies, with many cities and states actually named after Native peoples. Even the instruments of war and domination, such as the Apache and Black Hawk helicopters, commodify American Indian culture. Lately, a few astute Native Nations have participated in these processes, as with Indian Gaming.

Education is the social sector that best represents American Indian oppression and now liberation, with coercive assimilation as the primary vehicle for destroying the cultural integrity of Natives attending public schooling. Historically, the Boarding Schools that forcefully extracted Indian children from their families for at least two years with many never returning, were clear attempts by the US and Canadian governments at ethnocide while building an oppressed racial minority. However, the twentieth century brought multicultural/bilingual education movements with positive influences over Indian Education, resulting in curriculum integration of indigenous perspectives on history, culture and social institutions.

Environmental issues have always commanded the attention of the conflict and competition between Indian peoples and their highly developed and industrialized dominant governments. Land tenure usage has been a critical factor, with Natives acknowledging natural cycles or a circle of life, while the USA and Canada have attempted maximum utilization of land for agricultural purposes and mineral extraction, recently trying to locate waste storage sites on Indian reservations. Conflicts over land and hydroelectric plants along with deforestation have arisen from Canada to Guatemala, Columbia, Brazil, and Chile. However, ideological concerns have caused divisions between indigenous peoples and environmental groups over such issues as whaling by the Makah in the Pacific Northwest.

These conflicts have exacerbated increasing globalization and resistance by indigenous peoples, best viewed through the lens of world systems perspectives. Collective or "tribal" rights and land use are central to Indian nations, even as capitalist accumulation on global levels through international trade and economies that rely on nation-states has become ever more hegemonic. Expansion into previously undeveloped areas, such as the Amazon region or circumpolar territories, combine with ongoing internal colonialism to fuel differences. New coalitions, sometimes between revolutionary groups with Natives, erupt in conflict spots, such as in Chiapas, Mexico, the Miskito in Nicaragua, and conflicts in Colombia, Peru and Venezuela. Similarly, armed conflict has often appeared within previously "settled" areas, such as on Pine Ridge, South Dakota, near Oka inside Canada, or around treaty lands in upstate New York. Ironically, constitutional fights at times accompanied by violent struggle began over Indian Gaming, illustrating differences between sovereign group rights/tribal distributions and corporate rights/individual profits. These conflicts and related issues connect to larger globalization processes.

Identity politics, often as offshoots to the question of "Who is an Indian?" contribute to internal conflicts as well. Federal recognition in the United States and Canada, with attendant bloodlines, causes some people of indigenous descent to be enrolled even as others cannot get on the rolls. Scientific racism once endemic in the late nineteenth and early twentieth century, still pervades identity and recognition issues for most Native Americans. Indians in Central and South America have few if any options in this respect, and usually suffer when it is noted that they are "Indios" from a certain community or a tribal group. Amazing connectivity transcends identity issues across nation-state borders for indigenous peoples, apparent when homelands straddle international borders, as the Mohawk (Canada /US), Yaqui (US/Mexico) Miskito (Honduras /Nicaragua) Yanomami (Venezuela /Brazil) and others show.

Media representations of Indians, especially in respect to various stereotypes or icons, plague American Indians to this day. In fact, indigenous peoples are the only racially identified groups whose identifiers serve as team names (Cleveland "Indians" or Washington "Redskins") and ominously are used as mascots ("Chief Wahoo" or "Dancing Chief Illiniwek"). Moreover, only recently have many movies, magazines and literature attempted to paint realistic pictures of Native peoples. Even linguistically accurate but historically erroneous movies such as *Dances With Wolves* perpetuate the Good Indian/Bad Indian stereotypes with origins in the Hostile and Savage icons. Lately, Native artists have picked up cultural production, resulting in accurate representations, as in movies (*Smoke Signals*) and books (*The Toughest Indian in the World*, by Sherman Alexie, Atlantic Monthly, 2000). Furthermore, American Indian scholars are producing analyses that take into account indigenous perspectives and knowledge, that are sensitive to imagery. Understanding gender roles as formulations of traditionalism has improved dramatically in recent years, demonstrating considerable sociopolitical activity by Native women in traditional societies.

Social policies, once exclusively the cause of inequality and stratification, can now be helpful to Indians. Although courts continue to side with dominant interpretations of law, and continue to try and reward injustice claims with monetary instruments, there are more support institutions and more Indian lawyers arguing for the benefit of their Native nations and the potential futures of many indigenous peoples. Canada has apologized to its First Nations, the USA has deliberated over the same, and states such as Mexico are allowing Indian leaders to address their governments directly. Indian Gaming and other economic developments have allowed some tribes to support those tribes without casinos, and politically to represent broad-based efforts assisting Native Nations and American Indians for an unsure but hopeful future for generations to come.

SEE ALSO: Australian Aboriginals; Brazil; culturecide; Doomed Races Doctrine; equality; ethnocide; *encomienda*; indigenous peoples; internal colonialism; miscegenation; representations; science; segregation; stereotype

Reading

500 Nations by Alvin Josephy (Gramercy, 2002) historically describes the complex and diverse Native nations in a context of conflict, conquest and dominance by European and American powers

American Indian Ethnic Renewal: Red power and the resurgence of identity and culture by Joane Nagel (Oxford University Press, 1996) is a good overall sociological description of Indian issues in the USA, including political struggles and census/identity issues.

Native America, Portrait of the Peoples, edited by Duane Champagne (Visible Ink Press, 1994), has both comprehensive sociological descriptions and is a cultural resource almanac that includes all peoples discussed in this essay.

Tribes, Treaties, and Constitutional Tribulations by Vine Deloria, Jr. and David E. Wilkins (University of Texas Press, 1999) considers many of the legal and sociopolitical issues of Indians in the USA, as well as colonial and constitutional justifications.

JAMES V. FENELON

ANGLO-INDIANS

Anglo-Indians are defined by the Indian Constitution, echoing the (British) Government of India Act of 1935, as persons of European descent in the male line, who are or were habitually resident in India. In practice, the term signifies people of mixed European and Indian ancestry, and excludes those of "pure" European extraction. Prior to the decennial Indian census of 1911, at which point they acquired the designation "Anglo-Indian," members of this hybrid group were referred to as Eurasians or Indo-Britons. Before this date, too, and occasionally after it, "Anglo-Indian" denoted a person of British or, not infrequently, other European birth who resided for an extended period in India. Those long-settled in the country, sometimes for generations, were labeled "domiciled Europeans." The distinctions among these three categories were by no means always clear. Anglo-Indians thus invite serious scholarly attention because, among other things, they blurred the divide between colonizer and colonized, questioning the very efficacy of these designations.

Economy and hybridity

Numerous British officers, soldiers and civilians in the service of the East India Company and later the government of India, as well as men of diverse European nationalities who, in the course of the colonial period, came to trade or seek employment in various sectors of the economy, established domestic unions with Indian women. These relationships, whether formal or informal, consensual or exploitative, resulted in the birth of children, and in the emergence of a hybrid population. Anglo-Indians are thus the inheritors of a diversity of national, ethnic and caste backgrounds. Moreover, during the colonial period, the ranks of Anglo-India fluctuated considerably, a result of attempts on the part of many Anglo-Indians to "pass" as Europeans, and of some members of the native population to become Anglo-Indians, in both cases to benefit from the special privileges enjoyed by the target groups.

Despite their disparate origins, Anglo-Indians professed Christianity from the start, while English soon became their principal tongue, the language in which they worshiped, studied and communicated with one another. By and large they settled and still reside in India's major urban centers – such as Calcutta, Bangalore or Madras (now Chennai) – and while estimates of their numbers varied considerably during the colonial period – one indication of the porosity of community boundaries – there were probably around a quarter of a million at the time of Independence in 1947. Large-scale emigration to the West (mainly Britain and Australia) in the years following the end of colonial rule has left about half that number resident in India today.

Like similar hybrid populations in the colonized world, Anglo-Indians were seen by their European rulers at times as potential enemies and at others as allies in their imperial adventure, alternately preferred and promoted, or discriminated against and victimized. In the early colonial period they were relatively free to follow a range of economic activities, but from the end of the eighteenth century – which saw a transformation in the relationship between British rulers and those over whom they exercised dominion – a series of measures restricted and diminished Anglo-Indian employment opportunities. They were excluded from higher civil and military services under government. Contemporaneously, the growth of "scientific racism" in Europe saw the hybrid become a trope for moral failure and degeneration. This led to an increasingly negative evaluation and status abasement of the Anglo-Indians. Branded with any number of degrading epithets, they became figures of contempt and ridicule. In both life and fiction they were frequently portrayed in disparaging stereotypes, many of which focused on women, regarded as the principal mimics of European mores and seducers of their men. Examples of such literature include " 'Representing' Anglo-Indians: a genealogical study" by Glenn D'Cruz (Ph.D., University of Melbourne, 1999) and "Piebald Trisanku: the Eurasian in Anglo-Indian fiction" by M. K. Naik, in *Postcolonial Perspectives on the Raj and its Literature* edited by V. Nabar and M. E. Bharucha (University of Bombay, 1994). Both deal with the formulaic ways in which Anglo-Indians were portrayed in the literature written mainly by Europeans in India.

The Sepoy uprising of 1857 contributed to the transformation of Anglo-Indian fortunes once again. Intermediate positions of moderate responsibility (below Europeans but above Indians) or those requiring technical competence in a variety of employment areas were reserved for Anglo-Indians, who were deemed more trustworthy than other Indians. Such positions were concentrated heavily in the railway industry: early in the twentieth century it was estimated that approximately half the community was either employed by or dependent on the railways (see "Miscegenations of modernity: constructing European respectability and race in the Indian railway colony, 1857–1931" by Laura Bear, in *Women's History Review*, vol. 3, 1994).

Identities

Notwithstanding Euro-colonial discriminatory social practices and disdainful attitudes directed at Anglo-Indians, a number of institutions and policies put in place by the colonial government during the nineteenth century in the spheres of education, religion, defense and security encouraged them to identify themselves with the colonial power. Moreover, from the second half of the century, developments in the employment field which favored Anglo-Indians further distanced them from other Indians and increased the tendency for members of the community to see themselves as British.

Only in the course of the twentieth century were more qualified and fragmented modes of belonging posited. As the end of British rule approached, increasing voices were heard within the community urging association with the nationalist project, and seeking an alternative identification as one among many Indian groups. Postcolonial Anglo-India reveals a disparate set of discourses about affiliation, influenced largely by class position. Anglo-Indian elites, who have benefited most from the removal of previous limitations on the advancement of colonized subjects, insist on a strong connection with India. Though encompassed within the multiethnic, multireligious, cosmopolitan and increasingly globalized ambience of the affluent, they nonetheless proclaim a local association. At the other end of the spectrum, among the most disadvantaged, enveloped in the surroundings of the poor, there is little in their quotidian demeanor or practices to distinguish them as belonging to a community claiming European antecedents.

It is principally within the middle ranks of the community that claims to a British affinity continue to be declared. It is within this segment of Anglo-India that economic uncertainties and downward mobility have been felt most acutely. They were deeply affected by Indianization programs during the latter years of the Raj, and subsequently by policies put in place by the government of independent India favoring disadvantaged groups ("scheduled castes" and "backward classes"), both of which developments eroded Anglo-Indian employment privileges and led to economic hardship. It is within these sections of the community that the hopes and fantasies of emigration to the West are most prevalent, and for which a European identity is thought to qualify them.

Alongside colonial discourses associating them with their British rulers, in specific circumstances or periods Anglo-Indians paradoxically exhibited a certain degree of self-awareness and group consciousness. In spite of their disparate origins they came to recognize themselves as possessing a separate if somewhat fluid identity, and to claim to be, if not always to act together, as a distinct people. Towards the end of the nineteenth century a number of formal organizations were established to represent them (the first was created in 1876), although there were smaller local bodies in existence for many years before then, as well as any number of ad hoc cooperative activities. While relations among the main associations (one based in north India, the other in the south) have seldom been harmonious, and can still be rancorous today, this bespeaks a vigorous politics of community.

Culture and hybridity

The colonial encounter, which brought together two quite distinct traditions, fashioned in the resultant Anglo-Indian community a distinctive, though creolized and complex, cultural regime. There has been a persistent rhetoric within Anglo-India, albeit less so today than in the past, of a clear distinction between their own cultural regime and that associated with other Indians. However, examination of a range of customary usage – related, for example, to their kinship, religious, language, dress, culinary and marriage protocols – reveals practices which obviously situate members of this hybrid community very firmly in their local surroundings. What we find now, as in the past, is a mílange fed by distinctive "cultural streams" – European and Indian – yet producing a set of routines which often defy ready apportionment to one source or another, though influenced in different measure by each. Throughout the extent of the Anglo-Indian fold, cultural elements whose provenance might be regarded as distinct are brought together in a creative synthesis.

Moreover, Anglo-Indian cultural usage, even that deemed by members as "emblematic" of the community, is differentially clustered within the population. Gender and age – not to mention personal predilection – are bound to affect individual behavior. Even more crucially, class location is an important influence on the practice of culture: people in the middle ranks clothe and feed themselves and celebrate their marriages in somewhat different ways from those at both ends of the socioeconomic spectrum. Anglo-Indian lifeways may be placed along a continuum, from cosmopolitan (or British, when referring specifically to colonial times) at one end, to "local poor" at the other.

While such a creolist image characterizes the contemporary no less than the colonial cultural world inhabited by the Anglo-Indians, it is important not to assume that even the most cherished and "traditional" of practices are unchanging. Of late, Anglo-Indian lifeways, though perceived by many as timeless and distinctive, have been profoundly touched by the dual magnets of globalization and Westernization.

In the face of claims that characteristic beliefs and observances circumscribe and set off the Anglo-Indian population (the "one people, one culture" view), we therefore have to acknowledge that cultural boundaries are no less porous than social ones, now as in the past. Not only do we find a heterogeneity of cultural behaviors within the community, as within all the constituent groups which comprise the urban social order, but also significant overlaps with non-Anglo-Indian groups in the urban milieu.

We see that Anglo-Indians evolved cultural routines which defied ready assignment to clearly bounded spheres and classes, underlining the fragility of the categorical edifice on which British colonial rule was predicated. Thus, perhaps more so than any other single colonial population, Anglo-Indians serve as both a factor in and a potent reminder of the fluidity of the urban social environment during the British no less than the contemporary periods. Their ambiguous positioning focuses attention on the theoretical importance of this or any other hybrid group, however demographically insignificant they might be.

SEE ALSO: Asian Americans; British Asians; colonial discourse; creole; cultural identity; diaspora; education; globalization; hybridity; migration; miscegenation; postcolonial; subaltern

Reading

The Anglo-Indian Community: Survival in India by Evelyn Abel (Chanakya, 1988) offers an account of recent political history based on a wide range of documentary sources; this may profitably be read in conjunction with *Britain's Betrayal in India: The story of the Anglo-Indian community* by Frank Anthony (Allied, 1969), which is a personal narrative of the community's struggle for recognition in the period leading up to and following Indian independence by the person who played a leading part in the events he describes.

The Anglo-Indians: A study in the problems and processes involved in emotional and cultural integration by V. R. Gaikwad (Asia, 1967) is the first substantial sociological study of this community; while now somewhat dated, it is still an ethnographic landmark.

Children of Colonialism: Anglo-Indians in a postcolonial world by Lionel Caplan (Berg, 2001) presents a historicized account of contemporary Anglo-India as it has experienced the transition from British Raj to Indian independence. It engages with recent theoretical debates surrounding colonialism, postcolonialism and hybridity.

Marginality and Identity: Anglo-Indians as a racially mixed minority in India by N. P. Gist and R. D. Wright (Brill, 1973) considers the concepts of "marginality," "marginal man," and "marginal situations" using Anglo-Indians as a case study.

Poor Relations: The Making of a Eurasian Community in British India 1773–1833 by Christopher Hawes (Curzon, 1996) proposes a detailed reassessment of the early years of the community, arguing that these five decades constituted a seminal period in its history.

LIONEL CAPLAN

ANTHROPOLOGY

The changing significance of race

Anthropologists have an historically complex relationship with the idea of race. On one hand, Daniel Brinton, in his *Races and Peoples*, published in 1890, asserted the existence of a hierarchy of races in which higher and lower races were distinguished from one another by combinations of morphological and mental traits. In this scheme, the white race of Northern Europe was separated from the colored races by a series of "not-quite-white" buffer races from Eastern Europe and the Mediterranean, many of whose members had recently emigrated to the USA (see Patterson and Spencer, below). Views such as Brinton's underpinned eugenics programs and served to legitimate a number of racist statutes that were enacted in the United States from the 1880s through the 1920s. During this period, Franz Boas criticized the anatomical and statistical foundations of racial classifications, and he and his students challenged the hegemony of eugenicist views in the wider society when they exposed the weaknesses of racial intelligence testing. By 1930, Boas had succeeded in pushing craniometry away from racial classification to the study of growth and development. Furthermore, his assertion that race, language, and culture constituted autonomous domains was ascendant.

During the 1930s, US anthropologists turned their attention increasingly to race relations and racism. For example, in *Deep South*, Allison Davis and the Gardiners, in 1941, examined the interconnections of social class and racial castes from both sides of the color line. In the 1940s *The Children of Bondage*, Davis and social psychologist John Dollard considered the impact that class and race had on educational achievement. St. Clair Drake and Horace Cayton's 1945 *Black Metropolis* offered an historically informed analysis of the articulation of class and African American culture in Chicago. In the early 1940s, Ashley Montagu's *Man's Most Dangerous Myth* and Ruth Benedict's *Race* explored the fallacy of race and the politics of racism in the USA. A number of anthropologists provided advice for Gunnar Myrdal's *An American Dilemma*, which focused on the contradiction posed by democratic ideals and pervasive racial discrimination and was published in 1944. A decade later, Chief Justice Earl Warren cited Myrdal's work in the US Supreme Court's landmark *Brown v. Board of Education* decision (Lee Baker's *From Savage to Negro* covers these developments).

Controversies over the nature of race and the significance of race differences flared again after World War II. In the 1950 UNESCO Statement on Race, Montagu and other committee members asserted that race was primarily a sociological category. Conservatives, critical of the initial statement, succeeded in weakening the revised version prepared in 1951. The resurgence of various eugenics arguments about the behavioral significance of race differences in the late 1950s sparked a lengthy dialogue in the pages of *Current Anthropology* during the early 1960s (Comas, below) and provoked biological anthropologist Frank Livingstone's statement on the nonexistence of human races. Carleton Coon's claim in *The Origin of Race*, that the modern races had distinctive characteristics and had evolved independently for the last 500,000 years, led biological anthropologist Sherwood Washburn to assert in his presidential address to the American Anthropological Association that "race isn't very important biologically" and "racism is based on a profound misunderstanding of culture, of learning, and of the biology of the human species." Washburn's concluding remarks echoed the sentiments of the UNESCO Statements: "Human biology finds its realization in a culturally determined way of life, and the infinite variety of genetic combinations can only express themselves efficiently in a free and open society."

By the mid 1980s, however, there was still no consensus among anthropologists regarding the existence of biological races. A 1985 survey showed that roughly half of the biological anthropologists in the USA believed that races were meaningful biological categories; this was particularly true of those who studied human evolution or who were involved in forensic investigations. Nearly two thirds of the sociocultural anthropologists either disagreed or were neutral; moreover, women rejected the idea at a higher rate than did their male colleagues, according to an analysis by Lieberman and Reynolds in 1996.

The effect was that many sociocultural anthropologists began to examine how social ordering principles – notably race, class, gender, ethnicity, and sexuality – intersect and articulate; how these principles are constituted socially; how they are manifest in liberalism and other forms of social thought; and how they have been manipulated historically by colonial regimes as well as by capitalist and socialist states. They recognize that these ordering principles are intimately related to the historical development of capitalism, which included both the enslavement of Africans and episodes of mass migration on a global scale. This has not resulted in a wholesale rejection of race as a concept, but rather in the recognition and textured appreciation of the fact that race has a number of distinct meanings that depend on social context.

In 1986, Michael Omi and Howard Winant used the term "racial formation" to describe "the process by which social, economic and political forces determine the content and importance of racial categories, and by which they are in turn shaped by racial meanings." In this view, race and the other ordering principles are also sites of political struggle. As a result, many anthropologists were clear that race had to be taken seriously, especially in a society that was purportedly color-blind; they realized that interpretations of biological variation were neither neutral nor immune from the influence of wider social and political-economic currents (e.g. Harrison, below). It also meant, of course, renewed attention to the matters of racism, its subtle and overt manifestations in contemporary practices and policies, and its interconnections with class exploitation and gender discrimination.

This led anthropologists to distinguish race from ethnicity rather than elide their differences. Both, of course, involve the creation of identities in the context of class and state formation. Ethnicity expresses a collective sense of shared experiences and inclusiveness that underlies group solidarity and identity. As Audrey Smedley notes "the physical markers of race are always open to interpretation by others," and the classifications based on these features are mutually exclusive categorizations. While ethnic identities are adopted by the members of groups, racial identities are assigned by the beholders, which are frequently state institutions with diverse, often contradictory agendas. Sally Engle Merry has explored the legal foundations of racialized identities in her essay "Racialized identities and the law" and Ann Stoler has examined the racisms of the state in her *Race and the Education of Desire: Foucault's history of sexuality and the colonial order of things* (Duke University Press, 1995).

Invisible normality

For the last decade, anthropologists have concerned themselves with the construction of whiteness, which was heretofore typically assumed to be an unmarked or neutral, dominant category whose peculiarities required no explanation. In 1997, John Hartigan examined race formation and identity at the local level in three neighborhoods in Detroit, a city that experienced "white flight" to more affluent suburbs, and where the whites who remained constitute a minority of its residents. Whites as racial subjects in the three sites experienced racial matters in quite different ways. The racial practices were complex. Whiteness was a heterogeneous, negotiated, relational category that was frequently conflated with class differences and history in these interracial settings.

In the 1990s, anthropologists also began to examine the processes by which the "buffer race" immigrants from Eastern and Southern Europe became white in the USA. In *How Jews Became White Folks*, Karen Brodkin (Rutgers University Press, 1998) pointed out that war preparations in the late 1930s, the disappearance in the 1940 US Census of the distinction between native-born whites with native-born parents and those whose parents were immigrants, and the GI Bill of Rights, formed the backdrop to the assimilation and whitening of immigrant ethnics to the status of American during World War II. After the war, 2.1 million veterans received educational benefits and many millions received low-interest loans to purchase homes. The vast majority of the beneficiaries were white; for the rest of the century, their rewards were passed to their children and grandchildren.

Anthropologists have begun to consider the myriad dimensions of what Helûn Page and Brooke Thomas, in 1994, called "white public space." This ranges from the upscale shopping mall to the classroom. Jane Hill describes white public space as "a morally significant set of contexts that are the most important sites of the practices of a racializing hegemony, in which Whites are invisibly normal, and in which racialized populations are visibly marginal and the [intense] objects of monitoring from individual judgment to Official English legislation." The linguistic practices involved in the construction of white public space was Hill's concern. She pointed out that, while the speech of Latinos and African Americans was often viewed by whites as a sign of disorder, the semiotics of the Mock Spanish used in white speech was complex and, in some circumstances, reproduced negative racialized stereotypes. Hill raised the question of whether and under what circumstances might the use of mock forms of speech subvert the order of racial practices.

Anthropologists are finally coming to terms with the import of "double consciousness" which W. E. B. Du Bois, in 1903, elaborated in *The Souls of Black Folk*. Double consciousness refers to the "complex and constant play between the exclusionary conditions of social structure marked by race and the psychological and cultural strategies employed by the racially excluded and marginalized to accommodate themselves to everyday indignities as well as to resist them," according to Essed and Goldberg. Their acknowledgment of double consciousness focuses attention on racism rather than race. It also

directs attention to everyday practices – such as
the insistence of many Puerto Ricans on a Puerto
Rican rather than a racialized identity – that
simultaneously affirm membership in a group,
subvert the racist practices and policies of at least
one agency of the state (the Census Bureau), and
provide a basis for other forms of accommodation and resistance.

SEE ALSO: Aboriginal Australians; Boas, Franz;
Brown v. Board of Education; caucasian; cultural
identity; culture; culturecide; Doomed Races
Doctrine; diaspora; Dollard, John; double
consciousness; ethnicity; ethnocide;
ethnonational; eugenics; Myrdal, Gunnar; Other;
Park, Robert Ezra; race: as classification;
racialization; science; UNESCO; white flight;
whiteness

Reading

"Establishing the fact of whiteness" by John Hartigan
(in *American Anthropologist*, vol. 99, no. 3, 1997)
discusses the construction of whiteness, while "Language, race, and white public space" by Jane Hill (in
American Anthropologist, vol. 100, no. 3, 1998)
examines language and the construction of white
public space; "White public space and the construction of white privilege in U.S. health care: concepts
and a new model of analysis" by Helûn Page and
Brooke Thomas (in *Medical Anthropology Quarterly*, vol. 8, no. 1, 1994) provides the initial
discussion of white public space.
*From Savage to Negro: Anthropology and the con-
struction of race, 1896–1954* by Lee Baker (University of California Press, 1998) discusses the dialectic
between anthropology and civil rights activists, while
" 'Race' and the construction of human identity" by
Audrey Smedley (in *American Anthropologist*, vol.
100, no. 3, 1998) examines the construction of race
from a more recent vantage point.
"Introduction: expanding the discourse on 'race' " by
Faye Harrison (in *American Anthropologist*, vol.
100, no. 3, 1998) outlines new directions in anthropology. Examples of this are "Racialized identities
and the law" by Sally Engle Merry in *Cultural
Diversity in the United States*, edited by Ida Susser
and Thomas Patterson (Blackwell, 2001), which
discusses how identities are codified by legal systems,
and *Racial Formation in the United States from the
1960s to the 1980s* by Michael Omi and Howard
Winant (Routledge, 1986) which analyzes the processes of racial formation.
"On the non-existence of human races" by Frank
Livingstone (in *Current Anthropology*, vol. 3, no. 3,
1962) argues the importance of clinal variation (i.e.
differences within the species); this may be read in
association with "The study of race" by Sherwood
Washburn (in *American Anthropologist*, vol. 65, no.
3, 1963), which argues that race is not a useful
biological category.

"The politics of the science of race: Ashley Montagu
and UNESCO's 'anti-racist declarations' " by Elazar
Barkan, in *Race and Other Misadventures: Essays in
honor of Ashley Montagu in his ninetieth year*, edited
by Larry Reynolds and Leonard Lieberman (General
Hall Publishers, 1996), describes the debates surrounding the UNESCO statements; this may profitably be read in conjunction with " 'Scientific' racism
again?" by Juan Comas (in *Current Anthropology*,
vol. 2, no. 4, 1961) which depicts the range of
opinions in the late 1950s; "Race: deconstruction of
a scientific concept," by Lieberman and Reynolds in
Race and Other Misadventures, analyzes what
anthropologists think about race; and the collection
Race Critical Theories edited by Philomena Essed
and David Goldberg (Blackwell, 2002).
"Racial hierarchies and buffer races" by Thomas
Patterson and Frank Spencer (in *Transforming
Anthropology*, vol. 5, nos. 1–2, 1994) discusses the
linkage between immigration and the construction of
buffer races and racial hierarchies.

THOMAS C. PATTERSON

ANTI-SEMITISM

The adherence to views, attitudes or actions
directed against the interests, legal rights, religious practices, or lives of Jews has been known,
at least since 1870, as anti-Semitism (Ernest
Renan was apparently the first to use the term).
But the mythology supporting its justification
derives from the image of Jews as demons,
"Christ killers" and the "devil incarnate" who
used Christian blood for rituals. According to A.
N. Wilson, in his biography *Jesus: A life* (Norton, 1992), early Christians, who were fearful of
Roman persecution, blamed Jews for Jesus'
death: they invented the idea that Jews had
turned on Jesus for blasphemy. "Such a distortion
of history would not have been so serious had it
not been used as an excuse for 2,000 years of
Christian antisemitism," writes Wilson. "Were
Jesus to contemplate the fate of his own people
at the hands of the Christians, throughout the
history of Catholic Europe," adds Wilson, "it is
unlikely that he would have viewed the missionary activities of St. Paul with such equanimity."
Paul, unlike Jesus, advocated the abandonment
of the Jewish Torah.

In eleventh-century Europe, the vast majority
of Jews were economically impoverished and
traditional in their beliefs. Their distinctive dress
and lifestyle made them readily recognizable
scapegoats in times of hardship. Voluntary migrations and forced expulsions in the thirteenth
and fourteenth centuries gave rise to a Jewish

diaspora. In 1492, over 150,000 Jews were expelled from Spain by Catholic monarchs; they were given two months to leave. Five centuries later, their ancestors still campaigned for their right to return to the homeland they called Sefarad, many still speaking Ladino, a form of medieval Spanish.

In *The Origins of Totalitarianism* (Harcourt Brace, 1951), Hannah Arendt argues that anti-Semitism began in the 1870s, in the aftermath of the Franco-Prussian war, and was an outgrowth of the French mindset of the late nineteenth century. "Race thinking," as Jacques Barzun described it in 1937 (in his *Race: A study in superstition*, Harcourt, Brace), manifested as "that remarkable urge to lump together the attributes of large masses." Clear political and social thought was replaced by crude, ahistorical reasoning and the introduction of categories imported from biology, anthropology and psychology, among other disciplines. Arendt makes the point that anti-Jewish feeling should not be automatically equated with anti-Semitism, which involves the creation of an Other, a fully developed, intellectual idea premised on the concept of race. Once this was established, a distinct entity that could penetrate the popular consciousness replaced more analytical thinking and supplied simplistic, yet plausible answers to questions about inherited inequality, natural nobility and the political state.

Anti-Semitism, on this account, was not just an extension of the pattern of persecution and driven rootlessness that had occurred throughout the Middle Ages, but a distinctly modern phenomenon. Indeed, for Arendt and several other scholars, such as Theophile Simar and George Mosse, the rise of anti-Semitism coincided with the emergence of the concept of race until the romanticism of the late eighteenth century (an artistic and literary movement that favored grandeur and passion, form rather than matter) combined with Darwinist thought. This style of thinking opposed classical thought, with its emphasis on tradition, continuity and the value of established forms (of art, culture, politics, etc.). This view contrasts with that of, for example, Norman Cohn (in his *Warrant for Genocide*, Penguin, 1970), who regards anti-Semitism as a variant on early types of anti-Jewish feelings and a collective psychopathology.

Anti-Semitism has been viewed in terms of both religion and race. The most virulent expression of the latter is clearly the Holocaust of World War II, which was intended to eliminate the European Jewry. While anti-Semitism has declined sharply in the years since the war, it remains a potent force in Europe, in Arab states and in the USA, among other places.

Many racist organizations still cling to *The Protocols of the Learned Elders of Zion*, a notorious text, first published in Russia in 1903, which purports to be the minutes of a secret meeting of Jews held in the early years of the twentieth century in which plans for world domination are outlined. This added to the image of Jews: they were cast as organizers of an intricate conspiracy geared to take over society's major financial institutions. It was originally used by the Russian tsars as a rationale for the oppressive policies against Jews, but also, in the 1920s, by the industrialist Henry Ford, who owned a newspaper which issued constant attacks on Jews. Ford later apologized.

Anti-Semitism has a long and well-documented historical pedigree. The suppositions, inclinations and actions of anti-Semitism suggest a mode of thought and behavior that is distinct from the disposition to exclude, repel and confront persons thought to be Jewish. In other words, anti-Semitism refers to a specific perception of alterity, or state of being different, that is based on a particular type of conjecture. It does not refer to a more generic hating, loathing or fearing of those who fall into the perceptual brackets of "outsiders" or the collective Other. Racist organizations, including neo-nazis, are often described as anti-Semitic; but their antipathy is not reserved for persons regarded as Jewish but for a miscellany of groups defined, for various reasons, as deserving of contempt and rejection, if not extermination. Similar conceptual problems confront those wishing to delineate manifestations of Islamophobia: is the expression reserved for those regarded as Muslims, or is it a less specific abhorrence of "outsiders"?

Like several other terms in the lexicon of race and ethnic studies, anti-Semitism has had its meanings and uses changed by circumstances. During the conflict in Palestine in the late twentieth and early twenty-first centuries, anti-Semitism was often employed as a smear on any group or individual opposing Israeli policies. It became inflated into an all-purpose slander against those who took issue with Israel. While this may have been a corruption of the meaning of anti-Semitism, its use became widespread.

SEE ALSO: bigotry; culturecide; diaspora; ethnicity; ethnocentrism; fascism; genocide; Holocaust; Islamophobia; Jackson, Jesse; neo-nazism; Oklahoma bombing; Other; pogrom; *Protocols of the Learned Elders of Zion*; racism; scapegoat; segregation; white backlash culture; White Power; Zionism

Reading

Anti-Semitism: The longest hatred by Robert Wistrich (Pantheon, 1992) traces the phenomenon from its early beginnings, especially from the third century BCE, to medieval and contemporary manifestations in Europe and the Middle East.

Guilty Victim: Austria from the Holocaust to Haider by Hella Pick (I. B. Taurus, 2000) argues that Austria, a nation which collaborated with Nazi Germany, is haunted by the ghosts of its past, as evidenced by the electoral success of the far right leader J?rg Haider.

In Search of Anti-Semitism by William F. Buckley, Jr. (Continuum, 1992) examines anti-Semitism in the US conservative movement today and may gainfully be read in conjunction with *Jewish Identity and Civilizing Processes* by Steven Russell (Macmillan, 1996), which traces the Jewish experience in Western Europe from the Middle Ages to the present, using a theoretical framework derived from Norbert Elias.

The Third Reich: Politics and propaganda, 2nd edn., by David Welch (Routledge, 2002), analyzes and appraises the most horrendous expression of organized anti-Semitism in modern times, paying particular attention to how populations were converted by propaganda.

CHECK: internet resources section

ANTIRACISM

Refers to forms of thought and/or practice that seek to confront, eradicate and/or ameliorate racism. Thus antiracism implies the ability to identify a process – racism – and to do something about it. The term antiracism is a twentieth-century creation. Indeed, it did not come into regular usage until the 1960s (and even then it was largely confined to English- and French-speaking countries). However, though the term is recent, much of its power relies on its ability to draw on ideas, such as human equality and cultural relativism, of considerable age. More-over, antiracism is not the product of a single culture or political imagination. To understand antiracism only through its European intellectual heritage is to marginalize its diversity and inter-national character. The challenge that presents

itself is to develop a global vision of antiracism that can see the connections that link different traditions yet neither homogenizes them nor avoids the existence of tensions between them.

Such a perspective also implies an unsentimental attitude towards a subject that is often the victim of panegyric and populism. Antiracism is a necessary yet politically fraught and often contradictory endeavor. Moreover, its relationship to the modern nation-state and globalization can rarely be adequately summarized simply in terms of resistance or struggle. The following portrait traces some of the principal intellectual roots of antiracism before turning to the often-complex relationship between antiracism and contemporary forms of national and international governance.

Roots of antiracism: a global heritage

Opposition to racism may be found from China to South America, from the Middle East to the Arctic Circle. Within this diverse landscape a number of intellectual traditions may be discerned. The five identified below have been chosen because, although they overlap, each has a central role in contemporary antiracist debate. I have exemplified each by reference to a key theorist or group of theorists whose work represents an *early and seminal* statement of an emerging tradition.

The "cosmic race": In the early twentieth century, in direct opposition to European notions of racial purism and European supremacy, Latin American theorists drew on established traditions of race mixing (*mestizaje*) in Latin America to propose that racial hybridization was the only way forward for humankind. The most prominent member of this group was Josí Vasconcelos whose critique of European racial hierarchies was influential throughout the continent in the decades following its publication as *La raza c?smica* in 1925. Vasconcelos identified European racism not simply as an imperialist ideology but as one that was subversive of the attempt to develop a new and better form of civilization in Latin America. The celebration of *mestizaje*, translated into its postmodern correlate of hybridity, remains a potent theme within contemporary antiracism. However, Vasconcelos's reputation in Mexico has suffered considerably in recent years. To understand why we need to appreciate that the notion of hybridization he employed relied upon a belief that there existed discrete primordial races with fixed attributes. Indeed, there exists a telling slippage in Vasconcelos's work between the notions of racial mixture and "absorption by the superior type."

Tradition versus race: If we accept that race is a modern European idea, elaborated in eighteenth- and nineteenth-century Europe as part and parcel of European science and global hegemony, it follows that a good place to look for opposition to the *racialization* process is within traditional practices and ideas. For example, scholars and other writers in nineteenth-century China, schooled in traditional Chinese forms of social representation, rejected racial thinking as a secular, alien and unwanted intrusion into their society (a view expressed in the *Scholar's Convenant*, written in 1898). In this instance, racial thinking was opposed, not because it was anti-egalitarian, but because it threatened established ways of understanding human difference. More precisely, the idea of race was considered part of a Western scientific, universalist worldview that downgraded the importance of the Chinese. For these conservative critics, racial science seemed to be suggesting that the Chinese, far from being at the center of creation (the established, Sinocentric, view), were just another people, to be placed alongside the rest of humanity. This example of conservative 'antiracial' thinking in China finds many parallels around the world where traditional social and religious dogma and Western racism have come into collision. The interaction of Islam and Western racism is, at the present time, perhaps the most well-known example. The claim that active resistance to Western scientific racism characterized an "Islamic response" to Western colonialism has been substantiated in historical research. However, this fact should not be confused with the idea that Islamic societies – or for that matter other societies dominated by religious traditions – are necessarily or inevitably socially egalitarian or, indeed, shun ethnic and color discrimination.

Racial solidarity and pride: Refers to the act of identifying a racially oppressed group's racial identity as a site of political organization and opposition to racism. Du Bois's *The Souls of Black Folk*, published in 1903, remains one of the most subtle articulations of this tradition. Du

Bois saw the affirmation of African identity not simply as the celebration of a fixed, unchanging African essence, but also as part of a process of social transformation. Thus Du Bois reflected on the construction of an American black identity that is within but rejected by US society, a situation that provided what he called *double consciousness*. Such a standpoint, suggested Du Bois, offered black people a self-awareness and critical insights unavailable to the insular, yet self-confidently universalist, perspective of white modernity.

Relativism: Refers to the belief that truths are situationally dependent. In the context of antiracism it refers, more specifically, to the idea that cultural and/or physical differences between races should be recognized and respected; that different does not mean unequal. The modern tradition of relativism is often traced back to the European Renaissance, more specifically to the writings of Michel de Montaigne. However, its political origins are more accurately located in the eighteenth century. One of the most influential ways European relativists articulated their position at this time was by writing fictional accounts of non-European travelers' perceptions of Europe. The most famous example of this type of literature is Montesquieu's *Persian Letters* (1721). Montesquieu's work consists of a series of letters, seemingly composed by two Persian travelers. The letters discuss national differences within Europe, constantly expressing surprise and interest in the *exotic* and *peculiar* nature of European customs. The antiracist implications and heritage of relativism suggest the importance of understanding the socially located limits of one's own knowledge and the refusal of suprematicism. "I do not find it surprising that the negroes paint the devil sparkling white, and their gods black as coal," notes one traveler to his friend, "It has been well said that if triangles had a god, they would give him three sides."

Universalism: The assertion of the validity, across all cultures and historical periods, of certain values, truths and processes. Within anti-racist discourse, universalism is often associated with the conviction that, whatever our race, we are all equally part of humanity and should all be accorded the same rights and opportunities. As this implies, the notion of prejudice is as central in universalist discourse as it is in relativism. However, the emphasis within universalism is on the task of overcoming prejudice in order to see, or enable, the true equality, the essential similarities, of people, rather than on conquering prejudice so as to enable a recognition of and respect for difference. Science is often understood as the archetypal universalist discourse. Despite racial science being one of the origins of the doctrine of biological racism, both the nineteenth and twentieth century saw the authority and testament of science being drawn on to oppose the idea of race. The development and dissemination of knowledge of human genetics in the 1920s and 1930s laid the ground for the relegation of race and racism to the realm of pre-scientific, popular myth. Indeed, the increasing association, from the end of the nineteenth century, but more especially after World War II, of racial thinking with irrationality and prejudice, led many who wished to align themselves with the authentic spirit of science to position "real science" as *inherently* antiracist.

The spread of antiracism

The rise of antiracism has, in part, been caused by the ability of previously marginalized and silenced groups to assert a critical and semi-autonomous political agenda and identity. Thus a relationship has developed between antiracism, postcolonialism and the activism of racialized minorities in the West. The development of research in human genetics and the defeat of Nazism in 1945 acted to provide further intellectual and moral authority to opposition to racism. Indeed, antiracism is, in some respects, a victim of its own success: the explicit advocacy of racial discrimination has come to seem so controversial and unacceptable that, today, a deracialized lexicon of ethnic and cultural hierarchy carries the burden of human hatreds and hierarchies (a lexicon that includes terms such as *ethnic cleansing* as well as more subtle and pervasive notions, such as the tautological use of the phrases Western civilization and Western modernity).

Moreover, opposition to racism has become a familiar element within the rhetorical repertoires of governments and international agencies. Antiracism is both laid claim to and a site of, sometimes, intense rivalry. Indeed, during the Cold War one of the most sensitive areas in US politics was the comparison of American racism and Soviet, and by extension, communist racial tolerance. The second half of the twentieth century saw the negative associations of racism become increasingly cemented into discourses of national, cultural and international political legitimacy. Thus President Pompidou's assertion, in 1973, that "France is profoundly antiracist," may be seen as part of a developing tendency to align modern government with government that does not – or, rather, claims not to – racially discriminate. At an international level, the UN has asserted the opposition to racial hierarchy as a key principle of international relations since its foundation in 1945. This concern is reflected in the UN Charter as well as within the UN Universal Declaration of Human Rights (1948). Alongside the rise of a 'corporate equity agenda' in the USA, these initiatives may be taken to indicate the assimilation of antiracism into what is often termed mainstream or status quo politics.

However, as has been shown many times, rhetorical claims on antiracism do not necessarily correspond to practical action. Moreover, since antiracism comprises not one but many traditions, any narrative of its "spread" or "rise" needs to be cognizant of how certain forms have been given legitimacy and other forms made marginal. The tendency for the blacks v. whites model of antiracist identities and struggle familiar from the US to be applied within other countries is one indication of this process. Another, even more recent yet potentially important, indication of the changing nature of antiracist debate concerns the way the globalization of neoliberal economics has acted to promote antiracism in certain countries in particular ways. In a number of non-Western nations, the process of being opened up to the free market and anti-protectionism has facilitated the identification of racism as an economic hindrance and as an anachronism that creates conflict and acts as a barrier to geographical and social mobility. The promotion of antiracism during Peru's move toward the free market in the 1990s may be taken as an example. Speaking to me in 1997, Patricia Oliart, a Peruvian activist-intellectual, noted that most antiracist work in the country is supported by USAID (the aid agency of the government of the USA).

This is just one voice from one country, but it tells us something significant; namely, that it is now difficult to isolate national traditions of antiracism or assume that antiracism represents only voices of resistance and the oppressed margins of society. Much antiracism consists of precisely this kind of experience and this kind of politics but much does not. The complex contemporary sociology and geography of antiracism is increasingly difficult to ignore, especially for those seeking to make their opposition to racism effective and far-reaching.

SEE ALSO: assimilation; beauty; double consciousness; ethnic cleansing; globalization; hybridity; international organizations; neonazism; Other; racialization; racism; science; United Nations; whiteness

Reading

Anti-racism by Alastair Bonnett (Routledge, 2000) provides a critical introduction to the international and national development of antiracism and includes a chapter on "anti-antiracism."

The Black Atlantic: Modernity and double consciousness by Paul Gilroy (Verso, 1993) is a work that successfully develops Du Bois's account of the distinctive nature of black experience and political consciousness.

The Force of Prejudice: On racism and its doubles by Pierre-Andrí Taguieff (University of Minnesota Press, 2001) is an important work exploring the close relationships between racism and antiracism, drawing on French and US material.

Racism and Anti-racism in World Perspective, edited by Benjamin Bowser (Sage, 1995), provides a decent overview of contemporary antiracism in the USA, Brazil and Britain.

The Silent War: Imperialism and the changing perception of race by Frank F?redi (Pluto Press, 1998) is a fascinating study of how and why the British colonial authorities began to critique racial allegiances from the 1930s once they had identified race as a subversive site of alliance and solidarity amongst nonwhites.

ALASTAIR BONNETT

ANTISLAVERY

Antislavery describes the associations, campaigns and organizations which expressed opposition to slavery between the seventeenth and nineteenth centuries. It embraced the Christian-inspired abolitionist movement and the various secular coalitions that sought to bring about an end to slavery rather than just the slave trade. Some factions of the movement also campaigned against imperialism. While the association between the term and this period is conventional, the sentiments and beliefs behind antislavery predate the seventeenth century and are probably

as old as slavery itself, which has its origins in antiquity.

From the middle of the eighteenth century, opposition to slavery coalesced into a collective effort to dispute the moral rightness as well as the practical value of slavery and the slave trade. Popular opinion against slavery became a catalyst in the intellectual transformations of the late eighteenth and nineteenth centuries: the discourse of ideas about the freedom of and differences between humans unsettled defenders of slavery and prompted further movements to oppose slavery. The antislavery movement enjoyed periods of success and of failure until emancipation was proclaimed in 1863 and slavery abolished two years later. The actual process of annulment was uneven and came about in stages, typically in accordance with the requirements of national economies and capitalist imperatives. While there is little doubt that the antislavery movement did play some part in removing slavery, it was perhaps not as important as the role played by economic considerations.

Religious dissent and Enlightenment thought

The earliest organized dissenting group was formed by George Fox in the 1650s. A member of the Christian movement without creed, the Society of Friends, Fox argued strongly that slavery was morally repugnant and contradicted Christian principles. Yet many Quakers were themselves involved in the slave trade, so it was not until 1776 that the movement finally prohibited slave ownership. The Quakers were one of several organized religious groups to oppose slavery. An alliance of evangelical Anglicans, English social reformers and politicians known as the Clapham Sect operated between the 1790s and about 1830 and worked toward not only the abolition of slavery, but also the improvement of prison conditions and other humane causes. Among its prominent members were William Wilberforce and Thomas Babington.

Wilberforce (1759–1833), in particular, was an influential figure, helping establish the Abolition Society in England in 1787 and, in his capacity as a politician, initiating a proposal legally to abolish the slave trade in 1792 (though the bill was defeated). At this stage, most of the efforts were directed at trying to end the trade in slaves in the Atlantic rather than the abolition of the institution of slavery itself. Many of those involved in antislavery activities owned slaves themselves and saw no necessary contradiction. Wilberforce actually supported slavery, fearing that the dissolution of both the trade and the institution together would leave ex-slaves untutored and unable to fend for themselves. Only after the abolition of the slave trade did Wilberforce turn his attentions to slavery, involving himself in the formation of the Anti-Slavery Society in 1823.

Eighteenth-century Enlightenment thinking was a great driving force behind antislavery. The concept that all men were by nature equal offered both an opportunity and a challenge to those committed to ending slavery. Science's response was to analyze human bodies in the minutest of detail, deploying new methods to measure and assess difference. The liberal ideologies emanating from the Enlightenment inclined most thinkers to align themselves with antislavery, though their opposition was not necessarily predicated on a belief in the natural equality of all. One of the most powerful doctrines influencing theories of race in the eighteenth century was the great chain of being: species were immutable entities arrayed along a fixed and vertical hierarchy stretching from God downward. This doctrine was regularly invoked to oppose the growing antislavery movement of the late 1700s. Many antislavery crusaders remained unconvinced that a dissolution of slavery and the trade that abetted it would result in a new era of human equality; rather another type of hierarchy would emerge, this time comprising free agents.

The church, while not unequivocal in its objection to slavery, maintained a persistent challenge. The French priest Henri Grígoire was one of the most effective radicals of his day, writing, lecturing and campaigning not only against slavery and the doctrines of racial inequality, but against clerical and noble privilege and the law of primogeniture. His text, *On the Cultural Achievements of Negroes*, first published in 1808, is still in print (University of Massachusetts Press, 1996). The book is an outstanding example of antislavery literature in that it attacks the assumption of black inferiority and amplifies the often-concealed accomplishments of black people. The first American study to echo this was conducted by another cleric, Reverend Samuel Stanhope Smith, who, in 1787, wrote a treatise expounding his ideas on the

equality of all races. The nub of these arguments concerned human variability: were humans simply created separately and destined to remain so, or were they, at least in part, products of different environments, their physical and mental forms reflecting these. If the former were the case, then there was no possibility of change.

In 1849 Thomas Carlyle wrote his notorious "Occasional discourse on the nigger question" in which he maintained that all men must work, if not voluntarily, then by compulsion. He aired grave doubts about the wisdom of emancipation and believed that the West Indies would be condemned to famine and dissipation. Shortly before writing, he had visited Ireland and witnessed at first hand the starvation which afflicted that country. While Carlyle's opinions, especially his attribution of natural characteristics, were opposed by many, they were influential.

Abolition in the British West Indies was phased in gradually, with owners compensated and slaves inculcated in alternative forms of servitude, such as apprenticeships. Ex-slaves were paid wages but their labor, when unburdened, was less productive – a fact that emboldened the pro-slavery Cassandras to gloat. The antecedents of abolition in British colonies include the moral pressure of antislavery, but also more influential economic factors, the most notable being the decline in demand for labor with the advent of automation.

America: ebb and flow of antislavery

America's first secular antislavery society was formed in 1775, its remit being "the relief of free negroes unlawfully held in bondage," and during the following ten years, three northern states passed laws that facilitated the abolition of slavery. A historic 1783 decision of the Massachusetts Supreme Court held that slavery violated the state constitution, which stated that "all men are born free and equal." While developments were uneven, the overall tendency was toward the end rather than the continuance of slavery in North America and the slave trade further afield, though in states such as Georgia and Maryland antislavery sentiment was not broached.

Even antislavery campaigners harbored beliefs about black inferiority. Thomas Jefferson, a slaveowner himself, opposed slavery and in many respects embraced the Enlightenment spirit, yet stated his belief in innate inferiority, most conspicuously in his *Notes on the State of Virginia*, first published in 1784.

Demand for slaves in the Americas declined in the late eighteenth century and this as much as antislavery lobbying was behind the eradication of trading. In 1807 both Britain and the USA annulled slave trading on the high seas (oceans not within the jurisdiction of any country) and, while this may have been greeted as a modest success, it was in fact the beginning of an ineffectual period for antislavery. In addition to the 1807 ruling, northern states of America provided for the eventual abolition of slavery, while, in the South, antislavery sentiment moved tentatively in the direction of total abolition until the late nineteenth century. By 1807, however, the energy of antislavery faded.

The reasons for this failure are varied. Winthrop Jordan believes that antislavery derived much of its early dynamism from the revolutionary struggles in Europe and America. Antislavery, on this account, was part of the ideology of revolution. Yet after the triumphs in Paris and Yorktown, natural rights, which was once the bedrock of revolution, lost relevance: more practical problems of government tended to take precedence. In America, the concept of private property was a basic natural right, anyway. Ownership of slaves was no different from ownership of other kinds of possessions. Compulsory manumission would be an effective violation of the rights of masters to their property. The absence of a distinction between human and property rights became a huge obstacle to abolitionists. There was also a question of exhaustion: the campaigns against the slave trade had absorbed much reformist energy, leaving the movement depleted after 1807. Jordan adds perhaps the most significant reason when he writes that the prohibition of the slave trade "salved the nation's conscience that *something* was being done about slavery."

But, there were other factors. The British economy had undergone a transition as steam power replaced human labor and industries needed raw materials rather than slaves from overseas. There was never slavery in Britain, of course. Cotton goods were staples of the English industrial revolution (beginning in the mid 1700s) and the market for cotton goods continued to expand. An important piece of machinery known as the cotton gin, which was used to separate cotton from its seeds, was invented in 1793. This permitted the production of cotton on a large scale and without the large numbers of slaves previously required to carry out the separating manually. But increasing production in America meant that slave labor was needed to plant and hoe. In other words, the flow of new slaves was less crucial, but the servitude of those already enslaved was.

Another factor that changed attitudes to slavery was the cluster of slave rebellions, starting in 1791 in Haiti (San Domingo), then in 1800, 1822 and 1831 in North America. The Nat Turner uprising was the largest slave rebellion in the history of North America (James T. Baker's *Nat Turner: Cry Freedom in America*, Harcourt College, 1998, conveys its importance). These uprisings suggested a different image of slaves to the ones suggested in popular literature of the day. "Responsive to kindness, loyal, affectionate, and co-operative" is how the typical slave was depicted in the novels of, among others, George Tucker, William Gillmore Simms, and James Kirke Paulding. It was what George M. Frederickson calls a "romantic racialist image," and while it continued to circulate through literature, its credibility was tested by the violent uprisings. Slaves, it seemed, were not at all happy about their servitude and were prepared to fight and, if need be, die in trying to escape it.

This goes some way to understanding the astonishing popularity of Harriet Beecher Stowe's celebrated text *Uncle Tom's Cabin*, which was originally published in an antislavery newspaper and published in book form in March 1852. It sold 300,000 copies in the USA alone in its first year of publication and two million copies by 1860. In one light, the book was a piercing diatribe against slavery, while, in another, it was a cavalcade of stereotypes, presenting slaves in terms of two basic images: submissive, or brutal. In Stowe's imagination, the likes of Turner or Denmark Vesey, both artful organizers, inspirational leaders and combative fighters, did not exist. "They are not naturally daring and enterprising," Stowe wrote of blacks; and in another passage, she described them as "simple, docile, childlike and affectionate." Within two years, pro-slavery writing replied to Stowe with at least fifteen novels, most arguing that slaves in the south were better off than free black workers in the north.

The success of *Uncle Tom's Cabin* delighted abolitionist campaigners who had been trying to halt the ebbing of antislavery sentiment. William Lloyd Garrison had been instrumental in setting up an influential journal called *Liberator* in 1831. This was an organ of an abolitionist society and encouraged contributions from both black and white writers. Garrison was also involved in setting up the American Anti-Slavery Society in 1833, the year in which slavery was abolished in the British Empire (800,000 slaves in British territories were freed). One of the movement's co-founders, Dwight Weld had written an antislavery polemic *American Slavery As It Is* in 1839.

For Garrison and his colleagues, doctrines of racial inequality were perversions of the Gospel and the American Declaration of Independence, both of which suggested that egalitarian society was possible. Apparent deficiencies of African Americans were not the result of the inherent inferiority advanced by scientific racism, but by repressive environments that were uncongenial to improvement. As idealistic Christians, abolitionists believed that the abundant prejudice and antipathy of whites toward blacks could be overcome just like other sinful human dispositions. This kind of view gained Garrison and his followers the epithet "perfectionist radicals" and, from 1840, he introduced more militant inclinations to the Anti-Slavery Society. Evil, in Garrison's view was an unwanted presence that would have to be conquered piecemeal; but human sin should be extirpated as soon as possible and, as such, needed more urgent attention. Even though most northern states had done away with slavery, Garrison demanded its complete eradication.

More pragmatic abolitionists were prepared to make tactical concessions to racism and, at times, even revealed their own residual prejudices. Yet the view that a fraternal Christian community which transcended racial differences was shared by all, and the doctrine of immediate emancipation (to which it was closely related), formed part of a general reform program – an evangelicalism that was intolerant of gradual change and temporary faults. Slavery denied black people the chance of moral, intellectual and religious self-development and so drove them to the depths of depravity. As the abolitionist writer Lydia Maria Child famously wrote in 1833: "The white man's influence directly cherishes ignorance, fraud, licentiousness, revenge, hatred and murder."

Slavery struck at perhaps the most fundamental of the abolitionists' beliefs: that all humans were free agents and, as such, were morally responsible for their own actions. Abolitionists argued that the evident degradation of slaves was not the result of racial attributes, but of the restrictions placed on them by the institution of slavery. The enactment of other laws banning slavery around the world spurred Garrison and his followers to make more strident demands.

Racial difference and Emancipation

An emerging scientific discourse about fundamental human differences, natural inequality, cultural diversity and inherent freedoms began from the late eighteenth century: arguments moved away from theological and philosophical realms and into the domain of science. The "geometry of race," as Stephen Jay Gould calls it, was effected by writers throughout the second half of the eighteenth century, Blumenbach's influential taxonomy creating the conception of a hierarchy in which caucasians were supreme. Nineteenth-century advances in science provided for what was to be known as "scientific racism," a set of theories, postulates or just conjectures that proposed essential inequalities between races. Much of the theorizing was informed by the theme of interbreeding and its possible consequence, degeneration. Often neglected amid the discussion of Gobineau, Haeckel, Nott, Gliddon and the many other champions of racial hierarchies, are the theorists whose work defined a counterpoint. Friedrich Tiedeman, for example, was an anatomist at the University of Heidelberg who examined the brains of cadavers and concluded "that no innate difference in the faculties can be admitted to exist between the negro and European races." French theorists, in particular, upheld the egalitarian ideals of the Enlightenment and challenged the racial doctrines; among these were Leonce Manouvrier, Alfred Fouillee, Celestin Bougle, and Jean Finot.

Audrey Smedley's argument is basically that the rise of racial science was a reaction to the success of antislavery movements. It finds favor with Jan Nederveen Pieterse who, in his *White on Black: Images of Africa and blacks in Western popular culture* (Yale University Press, 1992) writes that "the science of race developed *after* the first battle had been won in the struggle against slavery, with the British prohibition of the slave trade in 1807."

Slaveowners and all those with a personal stake in slavery had no need to justify their deeds. In the absence of sanctions, moral or material, they simply pursued their own best interests using whatever means were necessary. The success of antislavery prompted the search for a scientific justification for slavery. This view contrasts with the more orthodox explanation of racism as an ideology that was a convenient justification for slavery; if this were so, racism developed in spite of antislavery. In the account offered by Smedley, Pieterse and others, it developed because of its success. As Smedley detects: "Without the pressure of antislavery, especially by the abolitionists, there might have been less need or propulsion to construct the elaborate edifice of race ideology that has been our legacy."

The question of racial differences was aired in the *Dred Scott* v. *Sanford* decision of 1857 which concerned a fugitive slave who was taken by his owner to a free state where he lived for several years until he was taken back to a slave state. This, remember, came only eight years after the publication of Carlyle's cautionary article. Dred Scott, backed by moderate abolitionists, filed suit, claiming that, because he had lived in a state where slavery was prohibited, he had lost his status as a slave. The US Supreme Court ruled that he was still a slave and that the Constitution did not protect blacks, neither those free nor those held as slaves. "Negroes," it was concluded were not intended by the framers of the Constitution to be included in the category of citizen: "On the contrary, they were at that time considered as a subordinate and inferior class of beings." The text of the decision included phrases such as "scale of created beings," suggesting to Smedley that the arguments of biological science were invoked to justify the view that "the Negro was not fully human, but a separate and distinct class of being, isolated from whites by an 'impassable barrier'."

The case became a touchstone for antislavery movements vehemently refuting the decision and several northern legislatures passed resolutions denying its legitimacy. It also advanced America closer to a civil war. Three years before the decision, Robert Knox had famously declared "race is everything: literature, science, art – in a word, civilization depends on it." The decision offered a kind of confirmation of this.

In 1860 Abraham Lincoln was elected president. Seven slave states seceded and formed the Confederate States of America. Confederate troops attacked the federal Fort Sumter, South Carolina, on April 12, 1861, initiating a civil war. Opinion is divided on whether slavery was a central cause of the war, or just one of a number of issues. Regardless of the causes, the victory of the North brought Emancipation, the proclamation being delivered in January 1863. Within three years, the Thirteenth Amendment abolished slavery everywhere in the USA. Brazil was the last New World country to outlaw slavery when it did so in 1888.

SEE ALSO: caucasian; culturecide; Doomed Races Doctrine; emancipation; ethnocide; Finot, Jean; geometry of race; Grígoire, Henri; Hottentot Venus; human rights; Jim Crow; Las Casas, Bartolomí de; reparations; science; slavery; white race; whiteness

Reading

Race in North America: Origin and evolution of a worldview by Audrey Smedley (Westview Press, 1993) is an authoritative account of antislavery and its ironic relationship with racial ideologies.

Slavery, Abolition and Emancipation: Black slaves and the British Empire by Michael Craton, James Walvin, and David Wright (Longman, 1976) examines the changing historical conditions that affected the resistance to slavery.

The White Man's Burden: Historical origins of racism in the United States by Winthrop D. Jordan (Oxford University Press, 1974), *Race: The history of an idea in America* by Thomas F. Gossett (Schocken, 1965) and *The Black Image in the White Mind: The debate on Afro-American character and destiny, 1817–1914* by George M. Frederickson (Wesleyan University Press, 1987) are all excellent treatments of the way in which the antislavery movement strove to combat not only the institution but the ideas that underpinned it.

CHECK: internet resources section

APARTHEID

An Afrikaans word, meaning "apartness" or total separation. In the context of South Africa, where it defined official policy, it referred to the segregation of whites and those defined as "nonwhites." It was based on *baasscap*, a philosophy that asserted white supremacy.

Apartheid has its roots in the white master–black slave relationships of seventeenth-century colonialism. The Dutch developed a small slave colony in Cape Town (on the Atlantic coast) in the 1650s and began to supply fresh produce to ships sailing from Europe to Asia. In the eighteenth and nineteenth centuries, Dutch settlers known as Boers (farmers) moved into the inner regions of Southern Africa. The Boers' incursions brought them into severe conflict with native peoples, such as the Khoikhoi (Hottentots, as they were called by the Boers) from the Cape and Bantu tribes from the southeast. The black native peoples were suppressed by the 1870s and the Boers constructed a series of all-white republics in the Orange Free State and the Transvaal.

British interest in the area grew after the discovery of gold in Johannesburg and confrontation erupted into the Anglo-Boer War, 1899–1902. Britain emerged victorious and established the area as a colony, the Union of South Africa. This was declared a self-governing state, or white dominion, in 1910, with blacks excluded from all areas of political influence.

The division between blacks and whites was continued by the United Party under the leadership of Jan Smuts (1870–1950), who took office as Premier in 1919. He lost the support of the white working class and was defeated in a 1924 election. Returning to power in 1945, Smuts, who had once declared himself against segregation, asserted: "It is fixed policy to maintain white supremacy in South Africa." Between 1946 and 1948, Smuts pushed through a series of moves designed to remove blacks' already limited franchise and property rights. Apartheid was fully institutionalized in 1948 when the Afrikaner Nationalist Party won election.

Hendrik Verwoerd (1901–66) who, in 1948, became South Africa's Minister for Native Affairs and, from 1958, national leader, is acknowledged as the most important architect of apartheid. He was a Nazi sympathizer and reigned for eight years, his commitment to apartheid strengthened by his belief that he was an instrument of God's will. Verwoerd's recognition of the need to maintain South Africa's social division influenced his decision to withdraw his country's application for continued membership of the Commonwealth. In 1961, South Africa became a republic.

The first plots of land for native peoples, called Bantu reserves, were officially set up in the Transkei in 1962. South African state policy was that separate self-governing black states should be created with a view to their eventually becoming independent (a native reserve system had been started in the 1840s designed to restrict the natives' rural land to 13 percent of the total

area of the country). Blacks constituted about 72 percent of the total population of nearly thirty million; they were allocated 12 percent of the land. Whites constitute about 17 percent of the population (the remainder being composed of "coloreds" and Asians).

In order to sustain the economy, the system had to allow blacks to migrate temporarily to white urban areas, or zones. Blacks were issued with passbooks and required to carry them at all times; they were made to produce them on demand by the police; failure to carry or produce was made a punishable offense. Blacks, it was determined, were allowed to enter white areas only for the specific purpose of working; basically, they were needed to do menial jobs that whites refused to do, with whites sometimes earning up to twelve times as much as nonwhites.

After working, blacks were legally required to return to their reserves. This arrangement had actually started in the nineteenth century, when a solution had to be found to the problem of maintaining a supply of cheap labor (at the time for the mines) without disrupting the essential white–black division. Black workers were made to stay in austere barracks for the length of their contract of labor, then forced to return to their reserves. Overstaying was made punishable by long prison sentences.

Verwoerd pursued his policies with Bantu Laws Amendment Acts in 1963 and 1964; these eliminated any semblance of blacks' employment security and effectively reduced them to the status of chattel.

Certain other elements of apartheid, such as the illegalization of sexual relations between whites and nonwhites, were in effect before 1948, but the implementation of the system served to cement the segregation legally and totally. To complement the whole system, blacks were denied any effective political rights. So the whole thrust of the apartheid system was to: (1) ensure legally strict geographical and social segregation in all spheres of life; and (2) maintain a rigid pattern of inequality in which blacks were effectively kept powerless and without wealth.

Needless to say, such a harsh system experienced periodic challenges, two of the most important coming from black organizations: in 1960 (at Sharpeville) and 1976 (at Soweto). Both attempted coups were suppressed after horrific bloodshed. The South African army and police have, over the years, equipped themselves thoroughly to deal with uprisings, one of the common tactics being to torture and even kill suspected seditionaries. The death of Steven Biko in 1977 demonstrates this. Biko (1947–77) was, at the time, one of the most charismatic and influential leaders of the Black People's Movement, itself modeled on the American Black Power organizations of the 1960s. The 1976 atrocity at Soweto has marked a kind of watershed in South Africa's political history, and Biko's death was part of a ruthless crackdown by the Police Security Force. Section 6 of the South African Terrorism Act was regularly invoked to detain suspected black leaders. Biko was, in fact, the forty-sixth black person to die in police custody. "A struggle without casualties is no struggle," Biko himself tragically anticipated.

In a technical sense, apartheid's dissolution began in 1990 when South Africa's Premier, F. W. de Klerk, authorized the release of Nelson Mandela and announced the attempted transition from a fragmented and fractious society to a liberal, multiethnic, democratic nation. Agonizing resolutions between the ruling National Party and Mandela's Africa National Party yielded little obvious progress – only a decline in black living standards and a sharp rise in crime. The legacy of apartheid and the separation, isolation and poverty it created, made nation-building a forbidding task.

In 1996, a critical court case ruled against the continuation of apartheid in education. Despite the technical elimination of apartheid, the Potgietersrus primary school, 160 miles north of Johannesburg, refused to admit black children on the grounds that it was safeguarding Afrikaans language, religion and culture. When three black children enrolled, white parents blockaded the school, in a manner reminiscent of the incident at Little Rock, Arkansas, where in 1957 US troops had to escort black pupils to a high school. South Africa's Supreme Court ordered the Potgietersrus school to admit black children and thus remove one of the last vestiges of apartheid.

SEE ALSO: Mandela, Nelson; South Africa

Reading

Atlas of Changing South Africa by A. J. Christopher (Routledge, 2000) visually analyzes the spatial impact of apartheid using a series of maps.
Deconstructing Apartheid Discourse by Aletta J. Nor-

val (Verso, 1996) analyzes apartheid during the transformative period of the 1970s and 1980s and its disarticulation from the mid 1980s onwards. The author accentuates the specificity of the mode of social division instituted by apartheid which Norval calls "a failed hegemonic project." Complemented by *After Apartheid: Essays revisioning culture in the new South Africa*, edited by Abebe Zegeye and Robert Kriger (Ashgate, 2002), which focuses on the role of culture in the post-apartheid era.
A History of Africa, 4th edn., by John Fage and William Tordoff (Routledge, 2001), updates the comprehensive narrative history of the continent, paying particular attention to South Africa following the dissolution of apartheid.
Segregation and Apartheid in Twentieth Century South Africa, edited by William Beinhart and Saul Dubow (Routledge, 1995), is a collection of key texts that explore the historical and political origins of apartheid as well as its intellectual underpinnings.
South Africa's Racial Past: The history and historiography of racism, segregation, and apartheid by Paul Maylam (Ashgate, 2001) divides South Africa's history into phases and examines each, laying bare the political ideologies that informed each.
CHECK: internet resources section

ARYAN

Derived from *Åryas*, a Sanskrit word meaning noble (but apparently in earlier use as a national name), which was used in English primarily to denote the family of Indo-European languages related to Sanskrit. The word acquired greater currency when it was used in the 1850s and 1860s by Gobineau and Max M?ller to identify a group of people who produced a particular, and higher, civilization. Gobineau maintained that there was a hierarchy of languages in strict correspondence with the hierarchy of races. He wrote: "Human history is like an immense tapestry ... The two most inferior varieties of the human species, the black and yellow races, are the crude foundation, the cotton and wool, which the secondary families of the white race make supple by adding their silk; while the Aryan group, circling its finer threads through the noble generations, designs on its surface a dazzling masterpiece of arabesques in silver and gold." Most of the authors, who in the late nineteenth century mused upon the history of the Aryans, wrote less elegantly than this but often in almost equally general terms. Max M?ller came to regret the extension in the use of the word and complained: "To me an ethnologist who speaks of an Aryan race, Aryan blood, Aryan eyes and hair, is as great a sinner as a linguist who speaks of a dolichocephalic dictionary or a brachycephalic grammar. ... We have made our own terminology for the classification of languages; let ethnologists make their own for the classification of skulls, and hair, and blood."

SEE ALSO: anthropology; beauty; caste; caucasian; Chamberlain, Houston Stewart; fascism; geometry of race; Gobineau, Joseph Arthur de; science; *Volk*; Wagner, Richard; White Power; whiteness

Reading

The Aryan Myth by Leon Poliakov (Chatto, 1974) is a comprehensive account of the concept.
Race: The history of an idea in America by Thomas F. Gossett (Schocken, 1965) is a briefer treatment, which examines the manner in which the concept manifested in North America.
Race: The history of an idea in the West by Ivan Hannaford (Johns Hopkins University Press, 1996) traces the search for the origins of modern race-states through the genealogy of language.
CHECK: internet resources section

MICHAEL BANTON

ASIAN AMERICANS

Asians are considered to be one of the six major ethnic groups within the USA (White, Black, Hispanic, Asian, Pacific Islander and Native American). In 2000, the census counted 12 million Asians in the United States, including those of mixed ancestry. Of these, 24 percent are Chinese, 18 percent are Filipinos, 8 percent are Japanese, 16 percent Indian, 11 percent Korean, 11 percent Vietnamese and 12 percent Other. Asians comprise 4.2 percent of the US population, but in San Francisco are 33 percent of the city's population. In New York City, they already comprise 11 percent.

The term Asian American may be misleading in that it implies a commonality of experience which does not exist. There are an enormous variety of races, religions, and languages within this group. The nations from which they come are widely diverse in their cultures, customs, and traditions. Although the use of the term is often expedient for political categorization, it does not account for the diverse experiences of the individuals and communities which it attempts to encompass.

Migration

Asian Americans were among America's earliest settlers and have long been part of its history. Large-scale Chinese immigration began with the Gold Rush in 1849. For more than three decades, their labor contributed to the rapid economic development of the new nation. Between 1849 and 1880, over 200,000 Chinese entered America. The gold they mined filled the coffers of the Treasury, and without their muscle the transcontinental railroad that tied the country together and created a national economy would have been delayed for years. They tilled the soil and fed the settlers streaming West.

However, when the economy faltered, the Chinese, despite being pioneer settlers, became victims of prejudice and persecution. They became the focus of an "anti-coolie movement." Exclusion laws enacted in 1882 prevented all Chinese from entering the country.

The continuing need for labor led to recruitment of the Japanese in 1884. Like the Chinese before them, they soon met with racial prejudice and demands for their exclusion. In 1908, male laborers from Japan were restricted entry, but Japanese women continued to travel to the USA, laying the ground for a native-born Japanese American generation.

As each Asian group came *in seriatim*, they all were faced with similar conditions. After Japanese immigration was restricted, alternative labor sources from Korea and India were tapped during the early 1900s. The Indians were excluded by law in 1917, and by 1924 all Asian immigrants were classified as "ineligible to [*sic*] citizenship," and therefore not permitted to enter the country. With immigration blocked, the Asian presence in the USA declined. Most Japanese by this time were native-born Americans. Nevertheless, when the United States entered World War II, these Americans of Japanese descent were herded into relocation camps and detained for the duration of the war.

While legislation almost completely halted the immigration of Asians after 1924, Filipinos, being US subjects, were afforded a special status. Filipinos filled the labor gap created by the exclusion of all other Asians. However, their eventual fate was to follow that of other Asian groups. In 1934 the federal government promised independence to the Philippine Islands in exchange for the curtailment of immigration. Thus, the attitude toward Asians in the United States was characterized by a pattern of tolerance when their labor was needed followed by racism and eventual exclusion.

Postwar experiences

After World War II some Asians were permitted to enter the country, but quotas governing their admission hovered in the area of about 100 per country per year. This was tantamount to exclusion. Whereas earlier immigrants were able-bodied males, many women from Japan, the Philippines, and Korea arrived as war brides of American soldiers, since they were not subject to the quota limitations. This added a new dimension to the Asian population: inter-ethnic families and mixed-blood offspring.

The tide turned in 1965 with enactment of a new immigration law. The national origins quotas were abolished and countries were allowed up to 20,000 immigrants each. Change in the law, coupled with political unrest and the communist threat in many of the Asian countries, caused Asian immigration to balloon. Asians presently make up one third of legally admitted immigrants to the USA.

The aftermath of the Vietnam War in 1975 brought a new category of Asians to the United States: refugees from Vietnam, Cambodia, Laos, Thailand, and even Burma. The USA felt a moral obligation to help these refugees seek asylum from danger and persecution and to help them get resettled in this country. By 1990, more than a million refugees from Southeast Asia had entered the country through special refugee relief legislation. These numbers were in addition to the immigration quotas.

The decade 1981 to 1990 saw more than 2 million Asians admitted. In the period 1991–99, an additional 1.8 million Asians were admitted, with a breakdown for the major countries of origin as: China/Taiwan/Hong Kong, 657,000; Philippine Islands, 464,000; India, 304,000; Vietnam, 261,000; and Japan, 60,000. As economic and political conditions have improved in their homelands, Asian immigration has declined in recent years.

Profiles

Even within ethnic groups, Asians are not homogeneous. For example, Chinese immigrants may come from mainland China, Taiwan, Hong Kong, Singapore, or Vietnam, each with distinctive histories and backgrounds. Native-born Asian Americans have roots in America that might go back to the middle of the 1800s. However, a majority of Asians are foreign-born, The earlier immigrants were of the laboring class. Recent immigrants are well educated and better off than their compatriots of the past. However, Chinese from the Mainland and refugees from Southeast Asia come from war-torn or politically disrupted backgrounds. These groups experience greater problems trying to rebuild their lives.

Asian populations are concentrated along the East and West Coasts, the Hawaiian Islands and in urban centers. Approximately three out of five Asians live in the three states of California, New York, and Hawaii. They have introduced their cuisine to the American palate, so that Chinese restaurants, Japanese sushi bars, and Indian food stores dot the urban landscape. Asians tend to value education, so parents push their children to achieve academically. The educational profile of Asians is high: 44 percent of those over age 25 have a college degree or better. However, the language barrier and the relative recency of their immigration preclude them from getting jobs commensurate with their education. So they go enter the world of small business, for example, restaurants, green groceries, newspaper stands, motels, and garment factories.

Becoming Americans

Within the short time that Asians have been coming to the USA, they have made enormous contributions in technology, in the medical field, and in scientific discoveries: seven Asian Americans have been awarded the Nobel Prize, while Silicon Valley is dominated by Asian talent and entrepreneurs. Medical advances are often linked to someone with an Asian name. Slowly but surely, they are breaking into government. Gary Locke is governor of the state of Washington; Norman Mineta and Elaine Chow are cabinet members in the George W. Bush administration.

Although the doors of America have been opened to Asians since 1965, and many Asians have put down roots in their adopted country, they are perpetually considered foreigners and tied to US relations with their mother countries. An unfavorable trade balance with Japan will wreak hostility not only against Japanese Americans, but also against all Asians. In a 2001 survey conducted by an organization called the Committee of 100, two thirds of Americans see China as a future threat to US security and 24 percent think that Chinese Americans are taking jobs away from "Americans." In the survey, a great deal of admiration was expressed for Asian Americans for their family values, their hard work and commitment to education, but this was coupled with resentful reactions to their perceived success.

One phenomenon that may change the "foreigner" perception is the increasing incidence of intermarriage. The 2000 census delineated 1.7 millions persons of mixed Asian heritage. This is 14 percent of the combined Asian American population. In time, by blending in, Asians, too, will become part of the melting pot that is the United States of America.

SEE ALSO: Anglo-Indians; British Asians; cultural identity; diaspora; ethnicity; Islamophobia; law: immigration, USA; middleman minority; migration; Park, Robert Ezra; segregation; xenophobia

Reading

Amerasia Journal, edited by Russell Leong (UCLA: Asian American Studies Center Press, 1971–present) is a biannual publication of the Asian American Studies Association. The most valuable feature of the journal is a comprehensive bibliography of all publications and media output on Asian Americans for the year.

American Attitudes Toward Chinese Americans and Asian Americans (New York Committee of 100 Survey, 2001) shows the extent of negative perception by American public toward Chinese Americans; the survey was conducted by Yankelovich.

Asian American Almanac, edited by Susan Gail and Irene Natividad (Gale Research, Inc., 1995), is an encyclopedic reference work on Asians in the USA with lengthy articles on lesser-known Asian Americans such as Thais, Indonesians, Laotians, Pakistanis, etc.

Chinese American Intermarriage by Betty Lee Sung (Center for Migration Studies, 1990) deals with extent of, societal reaction to, and personal experiences of, marriage across ethnic boundaries by Chinese Americans in New York City.

Contemporary Asian America, edited by Min Zhou and James V. Gatewood (New York University Press, 2000), is a compilation of articles by Asian American scholars on issues such as identity, family, community, employment, culture, and discrimination.

Economic Diversity, Issues and Policies, edited by Paul Ong (LEAP and UCLA Asian American Studies Center, 1994), is a report on how public policy impacts on the economic situation, workforce, professions, and health care of Asian Americans and Pacific Islanders.

BETTY LEE SUNG

ASSIMILATION

Assimilation has two main meanings in popular English-language usage. The first is "making similar." The second is "the condition of absorption or incorporation." To assimilate is the process that is either to make like, or to absorb/incorporate. In the discussion of race and ethnic relations the primary sense of the word assimilation has been overlaid by the second meaning, that which denotes the absorption of nutriment by a living organism – as the body is said to assimilate food. The popularity of the organic analogy in early twentieth-century social science increased the tendency to give assimilation this secondary meaning. So did the concern in the USA at that time about the influx of immigrants from Eastern Europe and the Mediterranean countries: these were suspected of being of inferior stock and less easily *assimilable* (i.e. "absorbable") than immigrants from northwestern Europe. Thus under the pressures of the age, assimilation came to be equated with Americanization, just as in Britain in the 1960s it was identified with Anglicization.

The confusions in this oversimplification were exposed by Milton M. Gordon when he distinguished several different models then current in the US. One he called Anglo-conformity; this was the process by which immigrants were brought – or should be brought – to conform to the practices of the dominant Anglo-Saxon group. The second was the "melting pot," in which all groups pooled their characteristics and produced a new amalgam. The third model comprised two versions of pluralism: cultural and structural, according to whether the minority, while resembling the majority in many respects, retained elements of distinctive culture or could be distinguished by the way its members continued to associate with one another.

In sociology assimilation is one among a family of concepts that seek to grasp different kinds of relations between groups, like integration, insertion, inclusion and pluralism. By persons seeking to advance political arguments, assimilation has often been used as a foil to show off the superiority of the conception which is being advanced. For example, in 1965 the then British Home Secretary, Mr. Roy Jenkins, speaking in favor of a concept of integration, declared that he did not regard it

> as meaning the loss, by immigrants of their own national characteristics and culture … I do not think that we need in this country a "melting pot" … I define integration, therefore, not as a flattening process of assimilation but as equal opportunity, accompanied by cultural diversity, in an atmosphere of mutual tolerance.

If assimilation is "making similar," it is not a "flattening process," though if it is a synonym for incorporation it might appear one. Other writers have disparaged the idea of assimilation as incorporation because they have wanted minority groups to retain some at least of their distinctive character. Thus some have spoken of groups that "refuse assimilation."

From the mid 1960s until the end of the twentieth century social policy in the English-speaking countries and in Western Europe was sympathetic towards the maintenance of distinctive minority cultures. In France, there was much talk of a right to be different and of a *differentialist* outlook. Multiculturalism was in vogue. Towards the end of the century the pendulum swung back and the so-called "war on terrorism" generated new pressures on minority members to minimize any outward signs of difference. As a concept in social science the great weakness in the concepts of assimilation, integration, and the like, is their reliance on methodological collectivism. They treat the majority group as homogeneous, as if all its members are equally assimilated or integrated, and overlook the significance of social stratification within that group.

Using the first meaning of the word assimilation it is easier to allow for these considerations and to see it as one form of ethnic change in which people become more similar. It is contrasted with differentiation in which groups stress their distinctiveness, for example by observing food taboos or displaying distinctive signs and symbols. Members of a group who differentiate themselves in one respect (as, say, Sikhs wear turbans) may assimilate in another (e.g. language use). So in discussing ethnic change it is necessary to specify particular items of culture and to examine the direction in which change occurs and the speed with which it takes place. Moreover, ethnic change at the local level may in the short term run in a direction opposite to that at the national level. A group which is a numerical minority in the country may be in a majority locally, so that people belonging to the national majority may be under pressure to change toward the group which is the local majority. For example, immigrants from South Asia who have settled in Yorkshire speak English with a Yorkshire accent. In parts of British cities where there are substantial numbers of black children, some white and Asian children have interested themselves in black music and adopted black speech patterns. In the 1960s, there were neighborhoods in which most black families came from Jamaica. Black children whose parents came from other countries tended to adopt forms of the Jamaican dialect and that dialect contributed more than others to the new black speech patterns. In the USA black immigrants from the Caribbean have sometimes assimilated to African American cultural patterns.

Some minorities consciously adopt practices designed to resist the pressures toward assimilation that are generated within the national society, such as the advertising of consumer goods. Religious groups establish their own schools, while gypsies and travelers keep their children away from state schools if they fear that these threaten their family ties. In other circumstances, members of the majority may impede assimilation by withholding social acceptance, as white Americans have discriminated against black Americans although the latter were culturally much more Americanized than recent white immigrants. Students of race and ethnic relations should therefore be on their guard against the simple view of assimilation as a unitary or "straight-line" process on the group level which assumes that the minority will conform to majority ways and that the majority, in absorbing them, will not itself change. The processes of assimilation are much more complex. They need to be studied on both the individual and the group levels, with the focus on specific forms of behavior seen in their full political and social context.

SEE ALSO: Aboriginal Australians; amalgamation; American Indians; Boas, Franz; cultural identity; culturecide; ethnicity;

ethnocide; integration; *Invisible Man*; Irish; Las Casas, Bartolomí de; Myrdal, Gunnar; Park, Robert Ezra; pluralism

Reading

Assimilation in American Life by Milton M. Gordon (Oxford, 1964) remains the leading US discussion of assimilation; "The return of assimilation? Changing perspectives on immigration and its sequels in France, Germany and the United States" by Rogers Brubaker (in *Ethnic and Racial Studies*, vol. 24, no. 2, 2001) is a more contemporary review which argues that a new "transformed" version of assimilation has "returned" to policy debate.

Ethnic Change, edited by Charles F. Keyes (University of Washington Press, Seattle, 1981), is a useful collection of comparative essays, many focusing on this subject.

Racial and Ethnic Competition by Michael Banton (Cambridge University Press, 1983) devotes a chapter (chapter 7) to the discussion of the interrelation of processes at the individual and group levels.

MICHAEL BANTON

ASYLUM SEEKER

In terms of international refugee law, an asylum seeker is a person who is attempting to obtain official status as a refugee in some country by meeting the requirements of the asylum laws obtaining there. The substantive content of asylum law varies by country, but as nearly all countries are signatories to the 1951 United Nations Convention Relating to the Status of Refugees, and many have signed up to its 1967 Protocol, these provide the minimally accepted international standards for such laws.

Since the latter years of the 1980s the numbers of persons seeking asylum in the industrialized nations has increased substantially, for which there are a number of reasons. Economic migration posturing as political necessity has intensified. Civil wars in the former Yugoslavia prompted both short and long-term migration of millions of people from non-EU to EU countries and beyond. Famine, economic dislocation, civil wars, and state repression in Africa, the Middle East, and Asia accounted for very substantial increases in applications for asylum from countries in these regions. In the UK, the number of asylum applications rose from 5,444 in 1985 to 80,000 in 2000. Other EU member-states, Canada and Australia, and the USA have experienced similar surges. Among EU countries, Germany saw the largest number of asylum applications over the period 1990–2000 – 1,958,350 – followed by the UK with substantially less at 454,445, whilst Portugal had the least, with just fewer than 6,000 (*Asylum by Numbers*, Refugee Council Briefing, January 2002: available at *http://www.refugeecouncil. org.uk/infocentre/stats/stats001.htm*).

It should be noted, however, that the numbers of refugees that have been harbored by non-industrialized countries are substantially greater than those given either refuge or asylum by the more prosperous industrialized countries. Iran, Albania, and Pakistan, for example, have been the destinations of millions of refugees. The economic burden on the poorer countries is, of course, substantially more onerous in terms of GDP than it is on industrialized countries, but it is the latter, for the most part, that are most concerned to use political and legislative means to stem their inflows.

The overall picture is complex, as many industrialized countries have experienced very significant drops in the annual number of asylum applications between 1992 and 2002, whereas others have seen increases. Overall, as the UNHCR noted, the number of asylum seekers arriving in the EU in 2001 was only slightly over half the number that arrived in 1992. However, the political impetus for crisis management of asylum issues operates with substantial time lags. In the UK, for instance, concerns over asylum seekers, particularly their potential impact on social services such as education and housing, their receipt of state benefits, and the implied involvement of some of their numbers in criminal activities, have been fanned by substantial segments of the mass media. In the autumn of 2002 this culminated in the closure of the Sangatte Red Cross Center at Calais, which was a stepping off point for attempts by some refugees to obtain access to the UK, and the passage of the Nationality, Immigration and Asylum Act, 2002, which will substantially tighten up procedures, establish centers for housing of asylum seekers away from the general population, and limit the countries of residence from which persons will be entitled to claim political asylum. Other European countries have adopted similarly restrictive measures. Australia has also introduced extreme measures designed to make the seeking of asylum there less attractive, including the housing of refugees in centers in remote parts of the country.

There, as in some European countries, notably the Netherlands and France, concern over asylum issues has had significant electoral political impact. Heightened concerns over international terrorism is likely to further exacerbate these issues, particularly in connection with those seeking asylum from countries that are predominantly Muslim.

SEE ALSO: education; housing; human rights; international convention; law: immigration, Britain; law: immigration, USA; refugee status; UNESCO; United Nations

Reading

Arguing about Asylum: The complexity of the refugee debates in Europe by Niklaus Steiner (St. Martin's Press, 2000) is an examination of the handling of asylum and refugee issues in Germany, Britain and Switzerland from the 1970s to the mid 1990s, which explores the complex interplay of national interest, international norms and other factors in shaping policies on these questions.
Asylum Practice and Procedure: Country-by-country handbook, edited by Adele Brown (Trenton, 1999), is a valuable source.
Current Issues of UK Asylum Law and Practice, edited by Francis Nicholson and Patrick Twomey (Ashgate, 1998), has entries covering policy and procedures, as well as practical matters effecting refugees, such as health and benefits.
Saving Strangers: Humanitarian intervention in international society by Nicholas J. Wheeler (Oxford University Press, 2002) links a series of case studies with an argument in favor of an emergent norm of humanitarian intervention.
CHECK: internet resources section

STUART STEIN

AZTLŌN

A potent symbol of nationalist Mexican-American movements, *Aztlûn* refers to an ancestral homeland, utopian promised land, and a political emblem. *Aztlûn* first appeared in sixteenth-century records of Spanish missionaries. Aztec informants told of their ancestors' migration from a northern homeland to Tenochtitlan (now Mexico City). Missionary documents locate *Aztlûn* in present-day northeastern Mexico and southwestern Texas or immediately north of Mexico City. In the contemporary period, it is thought to be the land that Mexico ceded with the Treaty of Guadalupe Hidalgo in 1848.

In 1969, "El Plan Espiritual de *Aztlûn*" was collectively authored at the Chicano National Liberation Youth Conference and endorsed by Rodolfo "Corky" Gonzales, and this served to revive interest in the territory. The document outlined a plan for the cultural self-determination and unity of Chicanos. Prior to the 1960s, the word Chicano was widely regarded pejoratively. But, as the term "black" – once used to disparage African Americans – was recoded, Chicano was elevated to a new status, intended to accentuate the restoration of Mexican-American uniqueness amid US imperialism. The unifying force of the movement became known as Chicanismo.

As the nationalist agenda of Chicanismo gained impetus, the pragmatic efforts of Císar Chûvez and the United Farm Workers' Federation to unionize Mexican and Mexican-American agricultural labor seemed too limited in scope, and *Aztlûn* became something of a rallying cry for reappropriating the cultural unity and solidarity that had been dissipated in the USA. Followers laid claim to full rights of citizenship by ancestral birthright in the southwest.

Klor de Alva has called *Aztlûn* "the single most distinguishing metaphor of Chicano activism" (in *Aztec Confessions: On the invention of colonialism, anthropology and modernity*, Routledge, forthcoming). Its potency in mobilizing Mexican-Americans points up the power of Promised Lands for diasporic peoples. As Africa and Zion have been transformed from actual or mythical homelands into signifiers of resistance and, in some cases political defiance, so *Aztlûn* captured the hearts and minds of Mexican-Americans in uniting in a common cause. In fact, the very unity it fostered led to its downfall: as minority groups organized on the basis of gender, class and sexual orientation, the *Aztlûn* movement was considered too artificial in its homogeneous ethic and the concept of one people lost credibility.

SEE ALSO: Chûvez, Císar; cultural identity; diaspora; Ethiopianism; ethnonational; Latinos; Puerto Ricans in the USA; Zionism

Reading

Aztlûn: Essays on the Chicano homeland, edited by R. Anaya and F. LomelÖ (University of New Mexico, 1991), is the first collection of essays and political documents by scholars and artists on *Aztlûn* from the 1960s through to 1989.
"The Aztec palimpsest: toward a new understanding of *Aztlûn* cultural identity and history" (in *Aztlûn*, vol. 19, no. 2, 1992) by Daniel Cooper Alarc?n is an

excellent survey of the Mesoamerican history and contemporary political uses of the term as well as the current critiques concerning the changing nature of Chicano identity.

Youth, Identity, Power: The Chicano Movement by Carlos Mu±oz, Jr. (Verso, 1989) is the authoritative history of the Chicano movement by one of the key participants.

STEPHANIE ATHEY

B

BARRY CASE, THE MARION

In 1990, Marion Barry, the Democrat Mayor of Washington, DC, where about 80 percent of the population is black, was convicted and imprisoned for possession of cocaine. For over two decades, Barry had been part of a civil rights offensive on the notoriously conservative capital city. During his third consecutive term, a female friend lured him into a police drugs sting. At their assignation in a hotel room, hidden cameras captured them smoking crack cocaine. At the end of a six-week trial that seemed to have disgraced and possibly destroyed him politically, Barry went to jail for 180 days. The videotape was shown on a courtroom monitor.

Barry did not take the stand himself, but accounts of his drug binges and sexual propensities, backed by evidence from a collection of pimps and pushers, were relayed to homes across the USA via television. To many whites, Barry was a venal demagogue who betrayed the trust of the most needy of his own people and whose character deficiencies should have disqualified him from ever holding public office again. But to many African Americans (especially among DC's electorate), Barry was a heroic and defiant, if flawed, figure who was punished for confronting a white power structure. Three years after his release, he was reelected Mayor.

The suspicions harbored by many blacks about the criminal justice system were in evidence once more in 1991 when Mike Tyson was indicted by a Marion County, Indiana, grand jury of raping Desiree Washington, a contestant at a Miss Black America pageant; she claimed Tyson had forcibly had sex with her in an Indianapolis hotel room.

Washington later alleged that Tyson had given her a venereal disease. Tyson was released from prison in March 1995, and resumed his professional boxing career five months later under the guidance of Don King. Unlike the reaction to Barry, there was a less forgiving response to Tyson and a celebratory function following his release was stymied by protests from women's groups. There were similarities with the O. J. Simpson case: a conspicuously successful black sports performer-turned-movie star accused of a heinous crime.

All three cases elicited cynicism, mistrust, and a feeling that perhaps historical patterns were repeating themselves: black men were being punished for being successful.

SEE ALSO: African Americans; black bourgeoisie in the USA; Central Park jogger; consumption; cultural racism; drugs; Jordan, Michael; King case, the Rodney; race card; scapegoat; Simpson case, the O. J.; Thomas, Clarence; Tyson, Mike

Reading

Contemporary Controversies and the American Divide: The O. J. Simpson case and other controversies by Robert Smith and Richard Seltzer (Rowman & Littlefield, 2000) employs over forty surveys to analyze the racially divisive Barry case and other high-profile *causes cílØbres* that threw into relief America's ethnic cleavages.

"Racially based jury nullification: black power in the criminal justice system" by Paul R. Butler (in *Yale Law Journal*, vol. 105, no. 3, 1995) proposes "jury nullification" whereby African American jurors can consider race when acquitting black defendants; the authors argues that as most black crime has its origins in poverty and oppression, jurors are morally justified in releasing nonviolent black criminals under some conditions.

BEAUTY

Race and beauty

Beauty is an historically specific evaluation of physical attractiveness that expresses prevailing racialized social hierarchies. In most cases this has meant that the facial features, body type, and coloring of a society's culturally dominant group set the standard against which others were judged. Women of color were either categorically excluded from the possibility of being considered beautiful by dominant standards, or were beautiful only to the extent that they shared the features of the dominant racial or ethnic group, or were considered beautiful in particularly *eroticized* and *exoticized* terms. Standards of beauty have most often been used to rank women. Yet consideration of race complicates the generalization. Occupying an ambiguous location as objects of desire and as symbols of physical perfection and danger, idealized images of the black male body have become a focal point for cultural anxieties about sexuality and race. Even so, it generally holds that women are judged by and valued for their beauty as men are for their accomplishments.

Some of the most widely read popular and scholarly studies of the history or social consequences of beauty standards have been studies of the experiences of white, predominantly middle-class women. The race neutral titles of Lois Banner's 1983 *American Beauty*, Naomi Wolf's 1991 *The Beauty Myth*, and Debra Gimlin's 2002 *Body Work: Beauty and self-image in American culture* obscured the place of race in definitions of beauty as well as the function of beauty in racist ideologies, negated the alternative beauty standards that circulated within nonwhite communities, and ignored the distinctive experiences of women of color.

Claims of beauty or ugliness have been central to racism and to antiracist resistance. Ugliness – beauty's opposite – has historically been one of the ways in which racists disparaged the targets of their hatred. For example, in his *Notes on the State of Virginia*, Thomas Jefferson pointed to what he considered the self-evident superior beauty of whites as part of his justification for continued white supremacy. In Hitler's Germany, claims of superior Aryan beauty provided an ideological underpinning for Nazism.

Though public figures and mass media may promote narrow definitions of beauty, a variety of standards of beauty compete for dominance within every day life. Standards of beauty circulating within nonwhite communities have been neither monolithic nor identical with dominant standards. They have taken shape in dialogue with dominant standards, challenging some aspects of dominant ideals and incorporating others. The majority of research on the racialization of beauty has focused on black women. This focus was a response to the extent of black women's exclusion from dominant beauty standards. Asian, Latina, and Jewish women more frequently encountered exoticization than exclusion from dominant beauty standards.

Exoticization

Historically, exoticization has taken different forms. When exoticization meant that racialized women were seen as grotesquely sexual, it was a form of exclusion from beauty ideals. In the early twentieth century white showmen organized touring displays of South African Sarah Baartmann in Paris and London. Her protruding buttocks were the focus of the exhibitions. Called the "Hottentot Venus," she was displayed not as a beauty but as an oddity, and simultaneously as an example of the Otherness and hypersexuality of Africans.

At other moments exoticization meant representing particular groups of women as sexually inviting and seductively mysterious. Nineteenth-century white illustrators frequently depicted Asian women as grotesque and akin to animals and thus excluded them categorically from beauty. By the 1920s however, Hollywood movies began to portray Asian women as mysteriously alluring and dangerous. After World War II dominant representations of Asian women shifted again. Asian women were depicted as highly sexual but pleasingly submissive. No longer a threat, they became objects of desire. Latinas were represented as beautiful but "hot-blooded," "spitfires," an image established in Hollywood films of the 1930s. White beauties were represented through a wider range of images. Some white beauties were sassy, others dangerous, but many were the chaste but appealing girl next door.

Even as Asian, Latina, and Jewish women were valued in the dominant culture as exotic beauties, particular ethnically specific features were seen as deviant. As a result, Jewish women turned to rhinoplasty to have their "flawed" noses reshaped and Asian women submitted to blepharoplasty to create upper eyelid creases.

Beauty mattered to people of color because it was equated with goodness and absence of stigma in the larger culture. Men and women of color have used attestations of beauty as a way to make claims about the value of the racial or ethnic group. This strategy was particularly important for African Americans who were so categorically excluded from dominant images of beauty. Depending on the prevailing racial order and the range of available political responses, communities of color advanced claims to racial beauty through separatist or integrationist efforts.

Exclusion and the challenge to white norms

Through the first half of twentieth century, nonwhite women were officially barred from the Miss America pageant. As early as 1898, African American newspapers, social clubs, and civic organizations sponsored beauty contests as a form of entertainment that they promoted as evidence of the glory of the race. The contests that were documented by the black press were those sponsored by the black middle class. In these contests the winners were usually light skinned women of mixed African and European ancestry. Yet the beauty standards that reigned in these contests were regularly criticized within black communities. In the 1920s Marcus Garvey emerged as one of the most effective critics of the African American preference for light skin. Garvey himself favored the label "black" and praised the beauty of Africans.

In the early twentieth century, and with increasing intensity after World War II, civil rights groups challenged legal segregation. As part of this effort, African American organizations worked to win positions for black women in all-white beauty contests, and in the glamorous occupations of modeling and airline hostess from which they had been excluded. As a result of these organized efforts, concentrated between the 1940s and the late 1960s, black women won in increasing numbers regional, campus, and other small contests. However, that ultimate symbol of American beauty, the Miss America crown, remained out of reach.

By the late 1960s, when the ideological goals of black political organizers shifted from "integration" to "black power," black interest in integrating white beauty contests faded. Black women continued to enter beauty contests but they did so as individuals rather than as representatives of a collective effort. When Vanessa Williams became the first black Miss America in 1983, she entered the contest without social movement backing and was a reluctant symbol of racial pride. When the press asked her about the significance of being the first black Miss America, Williams responded by describing her crowning as a race-neutral individual achievement.

During the late 1960s black beauty was expressly politicized in the phrase "black is beautiful." The phrase neatly captured a broad effort to overturn white beauty standards and to celebrate African physical features and culture. Black activists encouraged African Americans to recognize dark skin and African facial features as beautiful. Of all the features that might have been the focus of the new aesthetic, hair became the emblematic way to embody racial pride. Hair straightening had been the normative practice for women within black communities. Proponents of the "black is beautiful" aesthetic stigmatized the practice of hair straightening and celebrated the unstraightened texture of African hair. Black male and female hairstyles converged as women cut their hair and men grew their hair longer to wear it in a round, unstraightened style called the "natural" or "afro." A waning of the social movement activism that had promoted the new aesthetic combined with commercialization of practices that had been invested with political meaning led to a decline in the articulation and practice of the black is beautiful aesthetic. Nonetheless, it can be argued that the broad challenge to white beauty standards that emerged during the late 1960s permanently expanded the range of skin tones and hair textures considered beautiful within black communities.

In the late 1960s the publishers and producers of mainstream magazines, films, television programs, and beauty contests began to include nonwhite women in their productions. Initially a response to organized pressure by antiracist social movement organizations, the inclusion of nonwhite women in venues that define beauty grew as corporations discovered the profitability of marketing difference. Feminist literary critic

Ann duCille argues that the inclusion of black women in beauty venues should be seen as the strategic inclusion of specific "signifiers of blackness" such as brown skin rather than the recognition that black women are beautiful. Difference, signified as dark skin or strikingly non-European features, has been included as an attention-getting novelty. Advertisers have also increased their use of nonwhite women in order to appeal to nonwhite consumers in national and international markets. Very often this has meant the inclusion of women who are identifiable as nonwhite but whose hair, facial features, and body types resemble contemporary Euro-American beauty ideals. There is evidence that global marketing strategies favoring models who are racially ambiguous but who conform to white norms, and the national prestige gained by winning international beauty pageants, have begun to influence international urban beauty standards to move toward a norm established in the USA.

The uses of beauty as a vehicle for making claims of racial pride as well as a niche market for minority entrepreneurs complicates the position of women of color with respect to critiques of the role of beauty in women's lives. Beauty culture, including hair straightening, coloring, cutting and styling, skin and nail treatments, and the sale of beauty products, has provided important opportunities for nonwhite female entrepreneurship. Madam C. J. Walker was notable among black female beauty entrepreneurs for establishing a beauty franchise that provided her sizable personal wealth, enabled large numbers of black women to open small businesses, and became an economic base for Walker's philanthropic endeavors for the race. Beauty culture continues to be a niche market open to women with little capital or formal education. Long after legal segregation ended, beauty shops remained segregated worlds. These racial boundaries have eroded as Asian immigrant women established businesses providing beauty products and services for white, black, and Asian women. The emergence of beauty shops as multiracial and multiethnic spaces may have consequences in terms of the social meaning of the beauty shop and continued redefinition of beauty standards.

White women and nonwhite women have stood in different positions in relation to dominant beauty ideals. The difference has been between categorical and individual exclusion, between objectification by inclusion and derision by exclusion. Nonwhite women are increasingly included in films, television, beauty contests, and fashion magazines but have been included in ways that fail to displace white norms of beauty.

SEE ALSO: Afrocentricity; Aryan; Black Power; consumption; dress; Garvey, Marcus; geometry of race; Hottentot Venus; masculinity; media; middleman minority; neo-nazism; *nigritude*; negrophilia; Other; patriarchy; racialization; racist discourse; representations; sexuality; whiteness

Reading

Ain't I A Beauty Queen: Black women, beauty and the politics of race by Maxine Leeds Craig (Oxford University Press, 2002) traces the uses of beauty as a political symbol and the transformation of black definitions of beauty in relation to black political movements.

Asian American Women and Men by Yen Le Espiritu (Sage, 1997) describes Hollywood's portrayal of Asian women as erotic or exotic Others; it may profitably be read alongside " 'Loveliest daughter of our ancient Cathay!' Representations of ethnic and gender identity in the Miss Chinatown U.S.A. beauty pageant" by Judy Tzu-Chun Wu (in *Journal of Social History*, Fall 1997), which explores the way pageant organizers used beauty contests to define and promote Chinese American identity.

"Black bodies, white bodies: toward an iconography of female sexuality in late nineteenth century art, medicine and literature" by Sander L. Gilman, in *"Race," Writing, and Difference* edited by Henry Louis Gates, Jr. (University of Chicago Press, 1986), uses the nineteenth-century exhibition of Baartmann's body as an example of racist representations of black women's bodies.

Hair Matters: Beauty, power, and black consciousness by Ingrid Banks (New York University Press, 2000) is an ethnographic study of black women's ideals and practices relating to hair; this may fruitfully be read in conjunction with *Hair Raising: Beauty, culture, and African American women* by Noliwe Rooks (Rutgers University Press, 1996) which discusses the meaning of beauty culture in black women's lives through a study of the career of Madam C. J. Walker; as well as *Hope in a Jar: The making of American beauty culture* by Kathy Peiss (Metropolitan Books, 1998), which traces the distinct histories of black and white American commercial beauty culture.

Nationalism and Sexuality: Middle class morality and sexual norms in modern Europe by George L. Mosse (University of Wisconsin Press, 1985) discusses the role of beauty in Nazi ideology.

Race Men by Hazel V. Carby (Harvard University Press, 1998) analyzes the use of Paul Robeson's body as modernist symbol of ideal black masculinity.

Skin Trade (Harvard University Press, 1996) by Ann

duCille analyzes the ways in which Mattel incorporated race and ethnicity into the Barbie line of dolls. duCille argues that Mattel's development of "other" Barbies did nothing to unseat the supreme position of white Barbies as the real Barbies.
"Young African-American women and the language of beauty" by Maxine Leeds, in *Ideals of Feminine Beauty: Philosophical, social, and cultural dimensions*, edited by Karen Callaghan (Greenwood, 1994), studies the daughters of the generation who shouted "black is beautiful" and finds that young black women hold and negotiate a contradictory mix of beauty ideals.

MAXINE LEEDS CRAIG

BELL CURVE, THE see intelligence

BIGOTRY

While conventionally defined in a narrow sense as a strong or extreme form of intolerance, bigotry may be usefully understood as a form of defense based on unexamined generalizations about others and built from resilient preconceptions or stereotypes of groups which have, for some reason, been defined as "outsiders." In this sense, bigotry occurs in greater or lesser degree both across time and social context. It is far from being only and invariably the inflexible, unchanging mindset associated with a particular repressed kind of individual. As such, it has reference to mainstream ideas and views about a diverse range of groups who are defined and labeled as "Other."

Bigotry is an unfashionable concept. Once a common term used to refer to an entrenched and only partially rationalized point of view, it has now fallen out of favor and only rarely appears in the index citations and glossaries of academic work. The concept has not come under sustained attack. It is currently overlooked for other reasons. While it has certain limitations, it remains a useful term in the critical lexicon and, with some conceptual refurbishment, it can be reclaimed as a valuable way of explaining forms of social antagonism, injustice and exclusion.

Unlike sexism and racism, bigotry is nonspecific. This is not in itself a problem. Its broad scope is shared with other commonly used terms such as prejudice and intolerance, yet the attention given to the conceptual elaboration of these other terms has not been given to that of bigotry. Commonly enough, lack of attention to a term is taken as meaning that it has become outmoded or redundant. This may or may not be so, but in the case of bigotry this assumption is reinforced by the suspicion that its sense and meaning are out of kilter with contemporary thought. Here lies the main reason for bigotry's conceptual neglect.

Bigotry as pathology

The basis for this neglect has been an understanding of bigotry that is narrow and restricted. Such an understanding associates it only or primarily with extreme forms of intolerance, with obdurate and fixed attitudes that often lead directly to hatred of particular groups, such as those of a different sexuality, gender or ethnic category to that of the bigot. Exclusive confinement of the term to strong forms of intolerance relates also to its close association with religious doctrine. Bigotry was often used in the past as a way of denoting the values and attitudes underlying religious forms of hostility and persecution, and this use remains among the most common applications of the term, whether with reference to the different branches of Christianity, or to the opposition between different religious creeds and traditions, for example Christianity and Islam. Dictionaries continue to apply the term in this way, as if fanatical or, at best, inflexible religious ideas and values are the main preserve of bigotry, but the assumption extends beyond such formal definitions, and has become even more prevalent as Western societies have become more secular and thus less in touch with sources of spiritual feeling and value, which are too easily associated only with "traditional" or non-Western societies.

Another assumption which the term trails in its wake is that bigotry is entirely a psychological problem, a pathological characteristic of a certain type of mind or mentality. This may have reference to religious doctrine, but is just as commonly used in connection with other forms of intense hostility. Understandably, this way of thinking about the forms of prejudice and intolerance with which bigotry has been aligned was common in the mid-twentieth century, following the ascendancy of nazism and fascism. It seemed then that the attraction of such movements, and the anti-Semitism they fueled, was felt primarily by those whose personality structure inclined toward a rigid sense of order and discipline, whose disposition was toward an absolute definition of things and an unbending view of what is right, and whose values resulted in a deep distrust, if not hatred, of foreigners, outsiders and dissidents. Such "authoritarian personalities" were those in whom bigotry, particularly racial bigotry, manifested itself. This reinforced the sense of the term's association with extreme forms of intolerance.

This is a convenient view in contemporary public culture where the tolerant co-existence of different groups and cultures has become a pervasive ethical value. Despite this change, forms of intolerance persist, and it is facile to see them simply as the reactionary attitudes of a few misguided zealots. While violence bred of intolerance is obviously a serious social problem, today as in the past, and may well be continuous with certain bigoted attitudes, bigotry and intolerance are not synonymous. Bigotry and intolerance seem to go hand-in-hand as pejorative terms whose common link is the assurance that they will somehow explain each other. They never do, and should for this reason be distinguished carefully. Conflating them provides a convenient way of dissociating oneself from any form of bigotry, of placing it well away from one's own ideas and practice. Even though his intention was partly humorous, it is this self-serving convenience that Ambrose Bierce punctured, in his *Devil's Dictionary*, when he defined a bigot as someone "who is obstinately and zealously attached to an opinion that you do not entertain." Bigots are always other people, and few would offer the term bigotry as a plain description of their own philosophy or beliefs, particularly as there is now almost a proscription on seeing certain common prejudices as bigoted because of the value which has become increasingly placed on a tolerant acceptance of social and cultural diversity. Bigotry has become the polarized opposite of this value in late modern culture, and this makes it that much easier to ignore in its less extreme and more everyday manifestations.

The construction of "we"

The term's rhetorical function as a way of distancing one's own beliefs and values from those with which there is strong disagreement or hostility remains common, in everyday parlance as much as in political discourse and the language of journalism. While the term is often used in this way, it further underwrites the narrow sense of bigotry as a strong or extreme form of intolerance, as for example with racial hatred based on biological features and genetic inheritance. As a way of offsetting the charge of bigotry, racists today are said to justify their beliefs on the grounds of cultural or national differences. Over the past twenty years or so, there has certainly been a decline in verbal and visual racist stereotypes based on crude biologistic notions of inferior racial types. Justifications of racism are now more likely to rest on assertions of cultural incompatibility, sometimes associated with an exclusive sense of national stock. While such justifications are commonly observable, they are not in themselves particularly new. Cultural racism may actually mask less warranted, longer established grounds for thinking of different ethnic groups or cultures as incommensurable. Racist bigots easily hide behind national pride, and in the West "culture" can become a camouflaged way of defending exclusion, exonerating marginality or equating social inclusion with cultural assimilation.

This is to talk of nationalist and culturalist forms of rhetoric, and even though "we" don't refer to ourselves as bigots, it shows how bigotry needs to be reconceived in the light of these ways of using national and cultural difference. Bigotry, then, acts as a defense of what it is "we" stand for, in a sort of essentialist character reference, while heritage operates as a euphemism for heredity. Behind the more positively valued language of particularism may lie unexamined generalizations about others, just as resilient preconceptions may endure beneath a superficial equalizing way of speaking. Preconceptions formed on the basis of exclusionary generalizations about groups different to one's own have always been key elements of bigotry, and they persist in bigoted views of stereotypical Others, whether these are gays and lesbians, black and Asian people, or any general national or religious category. These and other examples make clear that bigotry occurs in greater or lesser degree both across time and in any one temporal context. It is far from being only and invariably the inflexible, unchanging mindset associated with a particular repressed kind of individual. As such it has reference to mainstream ideas and views about a diverse range of "Othered" groupings that are defined and labeled as "outsiders."

Reconceived in this way, the concept of bigotry remains valuable as an aspect of stereotyping and associated distancing strategies such as subjugation, abjection and constructions of deviant or deficient alterity. It always has an important psychological dimension, but the analytical scope of the term extends beyond this into areas more usually treated by social and cultural studies. It is not reducible to psychology alone. Further, while we need to understand the career of the term – deriving, probably in the sixteenth century, from a similar word in French, but since then falling into a wide array of applications in Britain and other Anglophone countries – we also need to understand bigotry itself historically, as for instance with racial bigotry in its developing contexts of slavery, colonialism and imperialism. Along with racial forms of stereotyping to which it is clearly related, such bigotry is revealed as far from invariant, both within the long period of European imperialism as well as in its aftermath. It is seen instead as constantly mutating, able to shift in its terms of representation, vary in its scope and significance, and adapt to changing social contexts. Other forms of bigotry, relating for example to social class, gender, or sexual "difference," provide further examples of its differentiated character. While perhaps not as protean as sexism and racism – two major forms in which it is often manifest – it is hardly monolithic or without historical specificity and distinction.

Bigotry always implies a lack of perspective, for what is, in greater and lesser degree, characteristic of the term is its fixation on certain, usually stereotypical features of Others, and its insistence of definition of these Others only in terms of those features. The highly skewed nature of bigoted views turns around this fixation, sometimes to the extent that it is exaggerated out of all proportion, with other balancing or conflicting evidence cast out of sight. Bigoted forms of stereotyping attempt to install the Other into ideological place once and for all, even where changing circumstances or the accumulation of alternative data prove such attempts fallacious. Indeed, in its strongest manifestations, bigotry is impervious to that which negates it, and is then notoriously difficult to shift. This is not the same as saying that it is immutable, for one of the advantages of a historical perspective is that it shows how bigotry is usually generationally specific in character. Bigotry is rarely passed down wholesale or intact within families, from father to son or mother to daughter, in simple acquiescence of a parental worldview, yet it is clear that bigoted views do persist and recur

even as they adapt and change. This is difficult to explain, and is part of the broader problem of our limited understanding of the dynamics of continuity and change in the symbolic exchange of everyday culture.

Stabilizing normality

It follows from its characteristic element of fixation that bigotry is associated with a strong, sometimes unyielding, sense of normality and order. This is generally encouraged by the extent to which the boundaries of legitimate social conduct, roles and identities are built up and patrolled by those who are in a position of relative authority, with the power to censure in some way. Here normality and order are implicated in each other, since what is proper is also in place. Bigotry denotes an inability to deal with ambivalence and uncertainty, with things not being in their designated place in the order of things. Again, this should not be seen exclusively as a psychological condition, for the extent to which normality and order are prescribed and laid down, and infractions from them curtailed and punished, obviously varies within the modern epoch from one historical period to another, and even from one decade to another, as a new generation challenges the normative boundaries maintained by their elders, or a particular socially marginal group becomes symbolically central in cultural representation and practice. Bigotry is nothing without its less visible support within a broader collectivity, and so is likely to bulk larger in a social order with a rigid sense of normality than in a more libertarian social climate.

Bigotry may in some ways be seen as the product of rapid change within modernity, for as the conditions associated with the development of a generation's view are swiftly transformed, people need to modify their positions and adapt their frameworks of interpretation in order to keep apace with changes in the social world and in new ways of understanding it. Some find this difficult, and in sticking with increasing obduracy to their earlier outlook, may find in bigoted values some form of compensation for a sense of loss and disruption, whether of the world they once knew or the structures of meaning for making sense of it. Inability or refusal to adapt and change finds its positive manifestation in an increasingly conservative viewpoint as people grow older, and bigotry is then a likely if not necessary offshoot of this development so long as it is in some ways socially shared with others of the same group or generation. So, for instance, the "moral entrepreneurs" of campaigns for censorship or the increased control of cultural products such as popular music have been largely based in social groups who, because of age or social status, believe they have been marginalized and their views devalued. They "feel disadvantaged by the accelerating changes of modernity," according to David Chaney.

The consequences of feeling bypassed by social change and at a loss with one's acquired views may have broader ramifications in a denial of the values of pluralism, diversity and reflexivity in modern culture. When this is made in the interests of an idealized version of social normality and cultural identity, it is a product of historical disorientation. The flawed understanding of bigotry is then evidence of attempts to respond to this, to offset the difficulties of coming to terms with difference and change through opposition to social scapegoats and stereotypical projections of negative Others. Jews, gypsies, the Irish and Chinese are examples of groups who have found themselves the targets of such moral transposition in different historical contexts and conjunctures. While the bigotry associated with such examples is historically variable, it is clear that there are also elements of considerable longevity in the stereotypes that are central to its closure of intellectual view. Attempts to explain their resilience over time, their ability as it were to remain dormant for a considerable span of time and then, with apparent suddenness, seem to leap up with new invigoration when appropriate conditions and circumstances present themselves, remain theoretically impoverished. Without a better understanding of the interactive dynamics of symbolic continuity and change in cultural life there remains a strong temptation to fall back on the psychologistic model of bigotry that was developed in the early twentieth century.

For this reason, bigotry needs to be reconceptualized within a social and historical framework of understanding. Its forms of expression and representation need also to be studied for their discursive forms and features – how bigoted views are variously articulated, justified and made to appear rational and reasonable, in particular configurations of talk and text. This is important because of its political significance in the construction of normality and moral order, in the maintenance of exclusionary strategies and in such scapegoating practices as "blaming the victim."

It is also an urgent task because a crucial aspect of social antagonism and discrimination has been overlooked for too long. The current disuse of a term does not mean that the phenomena to which it refers have disappeared. This misconception follows from the idea of bigotry as confined to an extreme form of prejudice, particular examples of which are always likely to be the most notorious. If bigotry is seen as more prevalent and various than this, and as in practice less rigid and obstinate than is commonly assumed, it becomes less marginal to contemporary critical discourse. This suggests also that earlier intellectual traditions in which the concept has received more concerted attention should now be reexamined for their possible contemporary relevance, as well as their historical significance, rather than simply being dismissed as passí or worn-out. For all these reasons, bigotry needs to be put back on the analytical map if we are to improve our understanding of the social territory to which it applies, and of the distinctively historical forms it takes in particular social contexts and particular periods of time.

SEE ALSO: anti-Semitism; cultural identity; cultural racism; double consciousness; ethnocentrism; fascism; Islamophobia; nationalism; One Nation; Other; prejudice; racial coding; racialization; racism; racist discourse; scapegoat; stereotype; white backlash culture; White Power; whiteness; xenophobia

Reading

The Cultural Turn: Scene-setting essays on contemporary cultural history by David Chaney (Routledge, 1994) has a chapter which considers the relations between tolerance and intolerance in modern culture that is valuable for understanding forms of contemporary bigotry.

Stereotyping: The politics of representation by Michael Pickering (Palgrave, 2001) rehabilitates the concept of stereotyping through which bigotry usually achieves its expression. It also develops a historical understanding of stereotyping processes and shows their relevance within a number of academic disciplines.

Why Do People Hate America? by Ziauddin Sardar and Merryl Wyn Davies (Icon Books, 2002) shows how bigotry characterizes views of America both within and outside the USA, and how this is implicit in the commonplace attitudes of well-meaning, sensible people, rather than just the attitudes and actions of an extreme fringe.

MICHAEL PICKERING

BILINGUALISM *see* language

BIRACIAL *see* multiracial/biracial

BLACK BOURGEOISIE IN BRITAIN

Britain's black bourgeoisie emerged in the late 1980s/early 1990s and comprised South Asian and African Caribbean entrepreneurs who had turned to self-help as a guiding principle of "development," used here in the same sense as Shelby Steele: "the sum product of *individual* effort" (*The Content of Our Character*, St. Martin's Press, 1990).

The period marked a break with more traditional remedial social policies implemented by government and government agencies. Discouraged by over three decades of relative impoverishment, many ethnic minorities reassessed their position and opted for self-employment, leading to business ownership. The South Asian tradition of entrepreneurship has been a well-documented global phenomenon for many years, but the nature and scope of their enterprise changed and widened in the late 1980s. Margaret Thatcher's "enterprise culture" was intended to create a fertile environment for the growth of small businesses. During Thatcher's tenure as Britain's Prime Minister (1979–90) there was a series of policy reforms aimed at minimizing the role of the state and maximizing the responsibility of individuals. Ironically, few of the companies that started up in this period and went on to grow to at least medium-sized concerns were assisted by the various loans and incentive schemes offered during this time. By 1993, an estimated 7 percent of combined South Asian and African Caribbean population (accounting for 4.5 percent of Britain's total) were involved in some kind of entrepreneurial activity. The service sector was most favored, but a small minority of both South Asians and African Caribbeans were engaged in manufacturing.

Apart from the obvious difficulties facing ethnic minorities in a predominantly white society, Britain's black bourgeoisie faced three additional problems. The first was demonstrable:

generating capital through bank loans. Banks have shown a reluctance to venture loans to ethnic groups. The second concerned expansion. Many companies traded in a niche market, specializing in products and services for particular ethnic minorities. Expanding into other sectors proved troublesome, especially in the recession of the early 1990s.

The third problem was less visible and operated in such a way as to prevent black-owned companies being genuinely equal opportunity employers. "Racism by proxy" was the term given to the practice whereby black owners were compelled to employ white people at senior and middle management levels. Agencies and organizations with which the black bourgeoisie maintained business relationships were found to communicate to the owners their preference for dealing directly with white personnel. The dilemma facing the owners was whether to rebuff the request and jeopardize what might be a lucrative business relationship, or cooperate and covertly practice racism by proxy. Many opted for the second alternative and, effectively, kicked away the ladder they had themselves climbed.

SEE ALSO: African Caribbeans in Britain; black bourgeoisie in the USA; British Asians; middleman minority

Reading

The Asian Petty Bourgeoisie in Britain by Shaila Srinivasan (Avebury, 1995) is based on a study in Oxford, England and addresses key questions: Why do so many Asians enter into business? With what consequences? What are their class positions? Is business a vehicle for social mobility?

Middle-class Blacks in Britain by Sharon Daye (Macmillan, 1994) carries its central question in its subtitle: "A racial fraction of a class group or a class fraction of a racial group?"

"The new black bourgeoisie" by Ellis Cashmore (in *Human Relations*, vol. 45, no. 10, 1992) plots the growth of the ethnic business class and contains details of the various manifestations of racism by proxy.

BLACK BOURGEOISIE IN THE USA

This term generally refers to black individuals or families who are middle class in terms of social and economic status. The term was popularized in the USA by sociologist E. Franklin Frazier in his class work *Black Bourgeoisie*, published in 1957 (first published in 1955 under the French title, *Bourgeoisie noire*). A major theme of this work is that the behavior and actions of the black middle class as well as those who aspire to this social status are not responsive to the needs of poor or working-class sectors in the black community. Furthermore, the black middle-class sector described by this author concentrates on maintaining an image of status, even if illusory, rather than devoting time, energy, and collective resources toward the building of an independent black social and economic base in the USA.

In the 1960s, at the height of the Black Power movement, many in the black community used the term "black bourgeoisie" pejoratively. It was used to describe those blacks with overly integrationist and accommodationist tendencies, as illustrated by lifestyle, attitudes toward the black poor and working class, and economic status. The term was also used to describe those black professionals not connected to the political and economic struggles of the black community.

Despite an increase in the number of scholarly and popular works focusing on the US black middle class in the last twenty years, as pointed out by Bart Landry in *The New Black Middle Class*, there is no consensus in the literature on the definition of this term. While he refers to a broad range of characteristics in order to define and pinpoint the US black middle class, other observers have relied on income data. In 2000 the US Bureau of the Census reported that it did not use a particular income range to describe the middle class, but instead relied on the distribution of income and the degree of income inequality. This information was reported by quintiles in the general population, where the "lowest income quintile" is compared to the other and "highest income quintile" to determine the size of the "middle class."

Sociologist William J. Wilson revived discussions regarding the nature and obligations of the black middle class in his work, *The Declining Significance of Race* (University of Chicago Press, 1978); Wilson argued that, in the 1960s, the black middle class started to become similar to the white middle class in terms of education and upward mobility. At the same time, however, a highly impoverished sector is growing in size in American cities and becoming increasingly separated in terms of social and even geographical distance from the black middle class. Wilson's contention that the black middle class is becoming more geographically distant from the black

poor has been questioned by several social scientists studying this topic.

In *Introduction to Afro-American Studies* (Twenty-First Century Books, 1986), Abdul Alkalimat has pointed out that the black middle class has had a dual character in the history of black people in the USA. Due to the fundamental importance of race in American history, the black middle class has been a force for social change at the same time that it has been an instrument to maintain order among the poor and the working-class sectors in this community. The black middle class has struggled to weaken racial barriers in society in ways that would benefit the entire population, but as these same barriers are destroyed, it has not guaranteed that the interests of the poor and working class in the black community are being satisfied. Some observers, for example, have pointed to cities such as Atlanta or Los Angeles, where the black middle class have spearheaded successful political strategies that tend to tear down racial barriers. Such victories have been important for the growth and development of black professionals in many arenas, but in many of these same cities, poverty and economic dislocation have increased significantly for many blacks.

SEE ALSO: African Americans; black bourgeoisie in Britain; Black Power; empowerment; middleman minority

Reading

Behind the Mule: Race and class in African-American politics by Michael C. Dawson (Princeton University Press, 1994) is a general appraisal of the conditions of black Americans.

The Black Bourgeoisie: The rise of the new middle class by E. Franklin Frazier (The Free Press, 1957) is the original exposition.

The New Black Middle Class by Bart Landry (University of California Press, 1987) takes a more empirical approach and distinguishes between Frazier's subject and the "new" version comprising professionals as well as entrepreneurs.

JAMES JENNINGS

BLACK FEMINISM

This term is often used to designate an intellectual and political movement, referring specifically to the work of black female scholars and activists who are rethinking black experiences from a feminist perspective and revising white feminist politics from an Afrocentric perspective. This work draws on a long history of black women's political consciousness and resistance, a history which demonstrates: (1) the simultaneous operation and interlocking nature of gender, race and other oppressions; and (2) the centrality of black women's experience and knowledge to political struggle.

In defining the term, Patricia Hill Collins traces a tendency to equate "biology with ideology." Some texts adopt biologically deterministic criteria for the term black and conflate woman with feminism, regardless of her ideology. Other scholarship narrows the scope of feminist inquiry to research and activism focused exclusively on women. Ironically, adherence to race and gender classifications may give further credence to the very categories black feminism seeks to dismantle and redefine. Ann duCille, in "The occult of true black womanhood" (in *Signs*, vol. 19, no. 3, 1994), suggests any definition which grants "black women privileged access" to knowledge "rooted in common experience" actually "delimits and demeans" black feminist discourse as it "restricts this work to a narrow orbit in which it can be readily validated only by those black and female for whom it reproduces what they already know."

However, definitions which promote a race or gender "blindness" to the background of black feminist practitioners may further obscure the importance of black women's experience and analysis. It is the insidious and pervasive suppression of black women's knowledge and circumstance which necessitates black feminist work in the first place.

When calls for a specifically black feminist theory, criticism and activism emerged in the context of contemporary struggles, they stressed the suppression of black women's experience in other liberationist discourses. As the title of the groundbreaking collection by Gloria Hull *et al.* expressed it, *All the Women are White, All the Blacks are Men, But Some of Us are Brave* (Feminist Press, 1982).

Both black liberation and white feminist organizations marginalized black women's issues and analysis despite two facts: (1) black women's labor was deemed indispensable to the black liberation movement; and (2) black women had organized and promoted many feminist causes together with and often prior to the white women's segregated organizations. Thus the historic Black Feminist Statement of 1977 by the Combahee River Collective called for struggle against "manifold and simultaneous oppressions": "we are actively committed to struggling against racial, sexual, heterosexual, and class oppression, and see as our particular task the development of an integrated analysis and practice based upon the fact that major systems of oppression are interlocking."

Because of the history of racism within white feminist organizations and the eclipse of women of color within much white feminist theory, there is occasional hesitation about defining black women's politics as "feminist" in any sense. In her *In Search of Our Mother's Gardens* (Harcourt, Brace, 1983), Alice Walker advocated the term womanist – not feminist – to capture the unique perspective and strongly humanist vision she believed distinguished the activism of black women.

For those who adopt the term, womanist thought deepens the hue and broadens the issues associated with white-oriented feminism. Womanist philosophy is alert to racial hierarchy and combines a strong affirmation of manhood with an equally strong ideological critique of gender oppression. Walker emphasizes the need for solidarity with black men in the fight against racism as well as "patriarchy." In a similar vein Sherley Anne Williams in *Reading Black, Reading Feminist* (edited by H. L. Gates, Meridian, 1985), expands the province of black feminism beyond the study of black women's experience; she urges black feminists to turn gender analysis to a study of black men's self-representation as well.

Collins argues that black feminist epistemology has been shaped by the traditional role of black women as mothers, "othermothers" (adoptive-, foster-, community mothers), teachers and sisters. Black women were central to the retention and transformation of an Afrocentric worldview which survived within the all-black rural and urban locations created by segregation. In the USA, for instance, black women drew upon their grounding in traditional African American culture and thereby fostered the development of a distinctive Afrocentric women's culture. As black women's labor was increasingly ghettoized in domestic work, this gender-inflected and racialized political economy ensured black women a unique "outsider-within" perspective which demystified ideologies of white power through an "alien" insider's close observation of white households.

Through these contradictory locations black women have produced a unique "standpoint" on self, community and society, yet at the same time that black women's politicized thought protests these subordinate locations, the economic, political and ideological strategies of subordination work to suppress that thought. Because of this historic suppression, Collins and others maintain that black women's experience – as interpreted and theorized by black women – must form the core, but not the entirety, of black feminist work.

Black feminist scholarship accordingly exhibits some persistent themes, including black women's labor and role in the political economy, controlling images of black women in racist ideology and empowerment through self-definition, black women's health, the black family, motherhood as community leadership, and sexual politics in both the context of dominant society and the context of black women's relationships.

SEE ALSO: African Americans; Afrocentricity; equality; masculinity; patriarchy; rap; social exclusion; subaltern

Reading

Black Feminist Thought: Knowledge, consciousness and the politics of empowerment by Patricia Hill Collins (HarperCollins, 1990) is a solid introduction to black feminism and may usefully be read in conjunction with *Theorizing Black Feminisms: The visionary pragmatism of black women* edited by Stanlie James and Abena P. A. Busia (Routledge, 1993).

" 'Mama's baby, papa's maybe': an American grammar book" by Hortense Spillers (in *Diacritics*, vol. 17, 1987) suggests that the "ungendering" of African captives through the course of the Middle Passage constituted entirely new social subjects, with which feminism has yet to reckon. The black female stands outside of the bounds of "gender" and gender itself is a form of racial supremacy.

"Multiple jeopardy, multiple consciousness: the context of a black feminist ideology" by Deborah King (in *Signs*, vol. 14, no. 1, 1988) argues that black feminism is a multiple-level engagement stressing black women's self-determination and the "simultaneity of oppression" as a concept essential to this endeavor.

Notes of a White Black Woman: Race, color, community by Judy Scales-Trent (Penn State University Press, 2001) starts from the premise that "race" is best understood as an experience lived through interactions between individuals, within families and within communities.

STEPHANIE ATHEY

BLACK MUSLIMS *see* Nation of Islam

BLACK PANTHER PARTY

The Black Panther Party For Self Defense (BPP), founded in 1966 by Huey P. Newton and Bobby Seale, in Oakland, CA, represents a structure that organized the black community for revolutionary change in America. Its tenets included a commitment to armed self-defense, a tradition of community service, and support of self-determination for all people. In 1968, the BPP dropped "for self defense" from their name. Many focus on the armed self-defense aspect of the Party; however, there were many different aspects to the Party that included various programs that fed, clothed and provided medical assistance to community residents.

The Party emerged within the crucible of the Black Power movement. As a controversial radical organization, BPP played a prominent role in black liberation activism. Panthers represented a response to the nonviolent integrationist-directed civil rights movement. Additionally, the organization was born in response to the rebellions against the manifestations of institutional racism. The National Advisory Commission on Civil Disorders reported – in the 1968 Kerner Report – that forty-three racial riots occurred in the USA during 1966. This surge in racial uprisings, simultaneously occurring with the perceived stalemate of the traditional Southern-based nonviolent campaign for racial equality, gave birth to the Black Panther Party.

With an emphasis on racial solidarity and self-determination, the BPP issued a ten-point platform, "What We Want. What We Believe." This platform included two demands concerning the US criminal justice system and its treatment of African Americans. Additionally, the Party called for full employment of all people, the end of capitalism, decent housing, adequate and equal education, exemption of black men from military service, and fair and equal trials for African Americans. The final point called for "land, bread, housing, education, clothing, justice and peace. And as our major political objective, a United Nations-supervised plebiscite to be held throughout the black colony in which only black colonial subjects will be allowed to participate, for the purpose of determining the will of black people as to their national destiny" (The Black

Panther Party Platform and Program, 1966). However, Black Panthers, unlike other black nationalists, did not explicitly call for a black nation.

Panthers viewed black urban communities as colonies occupied by a white police state and thus organized African Americans to challenge and resist this power structure. As such, there was a military aspect to the BPP, somewhat reminiscent of the Nation of Islam and Marcus Garvey. BPP members were usually dressed in a uniform of a black beret, black pants, powder blue shirt, black shoes, and black leather jacket.

A core element of the Party's platform focused on self-help and advancement. The ideology of the Panthers was influenced by Mao Tse-tung's axiom of "picking up the gun," Malcolm X's nationalism, and Frantz Fanon's and Che Guevara's theories of revolutionary violence. BPP emerged as a black nationalist organization, but by its end had undergone a series of ideological changes. While maintaining nationalist tendencies they expanded their political ideology by embracing a revolutionary-socialist aspect. Leaders of the BPP believed that this would allow them to address and change not only racism, but also capitalism. The political ideology of the BPP expanded in terms of an international perspective. This growth was the result of viewing urban America as a colonized area, thus creating a similar context for African Americans as that in colonized areas in for example Africa and South America. The ideology of the BPP was captured in their propaganda newspaper *The Black Panther*, which became a weekly publication in January 1968.

The early development of the Party was hindered by male chauvinism. In the many reconceptualizations of the Party, the leaders would eventually present the organization as being better suited to deal with the "gender question" in comparison to other black organizations. However, gender played a role in influencing the Party's revolutionary nationalist ideology and its stances on various issues. Issues of gender also impacted on the BPP in a number of other areas, such as its ability to defend itself from state-sponsored repression, and its relationships with other black political organizations and communities. Some prominent women in the BPP included Akua Njeri, Elaine Brown, Ericka Huggins, Phyllis Jackson, and Assata Shakur. Many of these women served in central leadership positions and often brought many of the issues confronted by black women to the forefront. Like many other civil rights organizations, the BPP suffered from ongoing power struggles over gender identity and sexuality.

Pervasive political repression, internal conflicts, the resignation of key leaders, and a disillusioned membership, eventually culminated in the downfall of the BPP in the early 1980s. The Party suffered a number of incarcerations, assassination and exile of key male leaders. In 1969, for example, a rival black group killed the Black Panthers Bunchy Carter and John Huggins. They were succeeded by Elmer "Geronimo" Pratt, who immediately became a prime target for what the FBI called "neutralization." To this end, the Bureau recruited Julius Butler (among others) as an informant in its Counterintelligence program (COINTELPRO) against the BPP. In a May 15, 1970 memorandum, FBI Director J. Edgar Hoover declared that hindering the BPP's newspaper would be a great asset in crippling the organization. The Committee on Internal security of the United States House of Representatives thus investigated the newspaper in September 1970.

Part of COINTELPRO involved linking the BPP to the Communist Party and planting disinformation about the organization. This is explored in Mario Van Peeble's 1995 film *Panther*, which charts the rise and fall of the movement, the director suggesting that the FBI collaborated with the Mob to flood the ghettos with drugs and thus undermine the growing radicalism of African Americans.

Pratt, a Vietnam veteran and confidante of Eldridge Cleaver, was jailed for murder in 1972, though his defenders, including lawyer Johnnie Cochran, maintained that he was framed by the FBI. By systematically removing leaders and instigating rivalries, the Bureau eventually managed to wear down the Panthers. Internal wrangling also beset them. Cleaver wanted to build bridges with other radical movements, including those with white membership. Some, such as Stokely Carmichael, opposed this; he left the Panthers in 1969 (he later migrated to Guinea). The movement dissolved, though its main signifiers, the black beret and the gloved fist, remain in the public consciousness: they were worn by black athletes Tommie Smith and John Carlos, whose image on the victory rostrum of the 1968 summer Olympics remains one of the enduring icons of the twentieth century. The BPP's legacy of revolutionary politics can be found not only in the USA, but also globally.

SEE ALSO: African Americans; Black Power; Cleaver, Eldridge; double consciousness; Kerner Report; riots: USA, 1965–67

Reading

Elaine Brown: A taste of power. A black woman's story (Anchor Books/Doubleday, 1994), tells the story of Elaine Brown's personal development and later rise to power within the party. The memoir also portrays the role of women in the organization.

Revolutionary Suicide by Huey P. Newton (Writers and Readers, 1995) may be read in conjunction with *To Die for the People: The writings of Huey P. Newton*, a collection of the founder member's speeches and essays anthologized and edited by Toni Morrison, and a similar collection by Philip S. Foner entitled *The Black Panthers Speak* (Da Capo, 1995).

Seize the Time: The story of the Black Panther Party and Huey P. Newton by Bobby Seale (Black Classic Press, 1997) is an insider's account of the origins of the movement. The contrasting history is that of Hugh Pearson, who used interviews with members and ex-members of the Panthers to compile his *The Shadow of the Panther: Huey Newton and the price of black power in America* (Perseus, 1995).

This Side of Glory: The autobiography of David Hilliard and the story of the Black Panther Party (Little Brown, 1993) offers an account of Hilliard's life, inside and outside, as a Black Panther Party Chief of Staff.

JULIA S. JORDAN-ZACHERY

BLACK POWER

The Black Power movement of the 1960s represented another period of cultural renaissance in black America, one similar in some ways to the Harlem Renaissance of the 1920s. Many independent black cultural and educational institutions were founded during the movement, which lasted from the mid 1960s to the early 1970s. The Black Power movement in the United States – also referred to in some writings as the Black Consciousness or Black Arts movement – was significant for the debates it generated regarding the appropriate political strategies that should be pursued by blacks.

The call for Black Power first caught the focused attention of the US national media in the summer of 1966 when the chairman of the Student Nonviolent Coordinating Committee, Stokely Carmichael, used it several times in a speech at a civil rights rally in Mississippi. The term had previously been used by Congressman Adam Clayton Powell of Harlem. Since 1966, it was enunciated and endorsed in speeches by other civil rights activists during this period.

This term has not been defined precisely; it has remained vague in its meaning and use. As a concept, Black Power has been utilized differently by activists and organizations representing a broad ideological spectrum. During the late 1960s and 1970s many books and articles were written on this topic.

One of the first attempts to define this concept was a book co-authored by Stokely Carmichael and Charles V. Hamilton, *Black Power: The politics of liberation in America*. These authors implied that Black Power was quite an American concept in that it basically called for black people to act on the basis of organized group power. While for some in the civil rights movement the term was to be derided and avoided as racially divisive, eventually it was accepted by many black organizations and activists; as a matter of fact, even President Richard M. Nixon implicitly endorsed this term in the early 1970s, when he called for black capitalism as an appropriate response to the needs of blacks in the USA.

The Black Power movement helped to propel the first black mayors of major cities into office. Several congressional representatives were elected to the US Congress as a result of the Black Power movement. Additionally, this period gave rise to ideological debates within the black community that were muffled during the earlier civil rights movement as a result of the focus on racial desegregation.

SEE ALSO: African Americans; Afrocentricity; beauty; Black Panther Party; civil rights movement; Cleaver, Eldridge; cultural identity; culturecide; double consciousness; empowerment; equality; ethnocide; Fanon, Frantz; Garvey, Marcus; ghetto; *Invisible Man*; Kerner Report; King, Martin Luther; law: civil rights, USA; power; slavery; White Power; whiteness

Reading

Black Power: The politics of liberation in America by Stokely Carmichael and Charles V. Hamilton (Vintage, 1967), introduced the concept and fused it with social, economic, and political relevance.

The Black Revolt: A collection of essays, edited by

Floyd Barbour (Extending Horizons, 1968), brings together several different perspectives.

"Race, class and conflict: intellectual debates on race relations research in the United States since 1960" by Manning Marable (Sage, *Race Relations Abstracts*, 1981) discusses and critiques some of the major writings on the subject.

JAMES JENNINGS

BLUES

Blues was the first genre or musical expression that was universally acknowledged as being an integer of black culture. William Barlow, in his *"Looking Up at Down": The emergence of blues culture*, argues that: "The blues ... were an amalgam of African and European musical practices – a mix of African cross-rhythms, blue notes, and focal techniques with European harmony and ballad forms. There are many alternative histories of the music's formation and development (see, for example, James Cone's *The Spirituals and the Blues*, Orbis, 1991 and Stanley Booth's *Rythm Oil* [sic], Pantheon, 1992).

While interpretations differ, all agree that the music grew out of the collective work of the first generation of African Americans after emancipation. They had not directly experienced slavery, but their lives remained oppressively harsh and unpromising. The music they played embodied hopelessness and depression; the topics they sang about were sickness, imprisonment, alcohol, drugs, work, and the segregation forced by Jim Crow.

Blues was a secular music: it avoided the church's spiritual music which gloried in God's salvation and ecstatically encouraged the journey to the promised land in terms that generally avoided the more unpleasant aspects of life on earth. "Negro spirituals," which in the 1930s were displaced by gospel as the dominant religious music, conveyed the kind of hope offered by the church, particularly the Baptist church. Blues offered no such thing – only realism. Lawrence Levine provides a nice distinction by quoting the singer Mahalia Jackson, who refused to give up gospel music even though blues music would have given her a better living: "Blues are the songs of despair, but gospel songs are the songs of hope. When you sing them you are delivered of your burden" (in *Black Culture and Black Consciousness: Afro-American thought from slavery to freedom*, Oxford University Press, 1978)

Musically, the blue notes were the neutral or flattened pitch occurring at the major and minor points of the third and seventh degrees of the scale. But the connotations of depression and despair were much more resonant. As such, it had specific relevance to blacks: it documented a distinctly African American secular experience.

Blues was also highly individualized. Unlike early African American musical forms, blues was usually performed solo and without antiphony (i.e. a choral response). This suggests to Levine "new forms of self-conception." These features distinguished blues as what Levine describes as "the most typically American music Afro-Americans had yet created." As such, it "represented a major degree of acculturation to the individualized ethos of the larger society." West African influences may be there for some to detect, but there can be no denying that blues was very much part of an American consciousness, an adjustment of individuals to the here-and-now.

Muddy Waters and Howlin' Wolf are often credited with being the great modernizers of blues. Waters migrated from the Mississippi Delta to Chicago and replaced the acoustic folk blues with a sharper electric sound. By contrast, John Lee Hooker, who has continued to tour as a septuagenarian in the 1990s, maintained a more traditional approach.

SEE ALSO: creole; Jackson, Michael; Jim Crow; Motown; negrophilia; Pentecostalism; rap; reggae; Rock Against Racism

Reading

"The age of jazz and mass culture" by Edward L. Ayers, Lewis L. Gould, David M. Oshinsky and Jean R. Soderlund in their *American Passages: A history of the American people* (Harcourt, 2000) provides a social context in which to understand the rise of jazz.

Blues People by LeRoi Jones (Payback Press, 1995; originally published 1963) argues that both blues and jazz have a "valid separation from, and anarchic disregard of Western popular forms." "Blues," he adds, is "the most important basic form in Afro-American music."

"Looking up at Down": The emergence of blues culture by William Barlow (Temple University Press, 1989) begins its analysis from the premise that blues has deep roots in West African musical traditions.

Stomping the Blues by Albert Murray (Da Capo, 1989) is a colorful account of the development of the blues.

BLUMENBACH, JOHANN FRIEDRICH *see* caucasian; geometry of race

BOAS, FRANZ (1858–1942)

Boas was an anthropologist who was born and educated (in physics and geography) in Germany and worked professionally in the USA. His research on racial variation illustrates the transition from the pre-Darwinian concern with morphology to the statistically based approach later established in population genetics.

Boas's study of "Changes in the bodily form of descendants of immigrants" (first published in 1912), carried out on behalf of the immigration authorities, attracted particular attention. In it the stature, weight and head-shape of 18,000 individuals were measured, comparing US-born children with their European-born parents and with children born to such parents prior to immigration. He found that the round-headed ("brachycephalic") East European Jewish children were more long-headed ("dolichocephalic") when born in the USA, whereas the US-born long-headed South Italians were more round-headed. Both were approaching a uniform type. Moreover the apparent influence of the American environment made itself felt with increasing intensity the longer the time elapsed between the immigration of the mother and the birth of her child. Boas was puzzled by his findings. They were measures of phenotypical variation and anthropologists at this time were ignorant of the causes of the variation which had to be sought in the genotype.

The physical changes that Boas documented were not of great magnitude but they brought into question the assumption to which most anthropologists were then committed – that the cephalic index (the ratio of the breadth to the length of the skull when seen from above) was a stable measure of genetic history. Boas was an influential teacher, respected for his industry and devotion to objective analysis, someone who was willing publicly to challenge the racial doctrines propagated by the anti-immigration campaigners. Thomas F. Gossett, a historian of racial thought, was so impressed by Boas's record that he concluded "what chiefly happened in the 1920s to stem the tide of racism was that one man, Franz Boas, who was an authority in several fields which had been the strongest sources of racism, quietly asked for proof that race determines mentality and temperament."

SEE ALSO: anthropology; assimilation; culture; Darwinism; Doomed Races Doctrine; genotype; indigenous peoples; kinship; language; phenotype; race: as classification

Reading

"Diversity in anthropological theory" by Karen Brodkin, in *Cultural Diversity in the United States*, edited by Ida Susser and Thomas C. Patterson (Blackwell, 2001), sets Boas's contribution in context, showing how his "adamant anti-evolutionism" was a response to the way prevailing theories of his day "naturalized" the racism of American society.

Race: The history of an idea in America by Thomas F. Gossett (Shocken Books, 1963) has sections on Boas's analyses and his overall contribution to the field of research.

Race, Language and Culture by Franz Boas (Macmillan, 1912) is the classic text. Boas's work is appraised in *The Anthropology of Franz Boas* edited by Walter R. Goldschmidt (American Anthropological Association Memoir 89, 1959).

MICHAEL BANTON

BRAZIL

The arrival of the Portuguese in 1500 marks the historical beginning of Brazilian race relations. The most salient characteristic of that history is the gradual elimination of Brazil's indigenous populations, both physically and culturally, and their replacement by populations of African and European origin.

The Portuguese encountered "Indian" groups of thinly settled, small-scale, semi-nomadic, stateless, classless, tropical horticulturists. These native societies, numbering, in most cases, only a few hundred to a few thousand individuals each, were not only organizationally and technologically unable to resist the encroachments of the colonizers, but their lack of immunity to diseases imported from Europe (especially measles, smallpox, and influenza) made them vulnerable to disastrous pandemics.

Attempts to enslave the Indians proved mostly abortive, as they either withdrew into the less accessible parts of the interior, died of disease, or escaped. This secular process of retreat into the Amazonian jungle continues to this day, as the Brazilian frontier gradually encroaches over the last pockets of Indian populations. The latter now number well under 1 percent of Brazil's 160 million people, although perhaps 5 to 10 percent of Brazilians have some Indian ancestry, especially those of the interior states. (People of mixed Indian-European descent are often referred to as *caboclos*.)

This process of displacement of Amerindians in Brazil has sometimes been called genocidal. There has, of course, been sporadic frontier warfare between Indians and colonists, resulting sometimes in small-scale massacres, and there have been numerous allegations of deliberate spreading of epidemics through sale or distribution of contaminated blankets. It is untrue, or at least unproven, that the Brazilian government in this century has deliberately sought to exterminate Indians, although the effects of policies of frontier development and Indian resettlement have often been disastrous for the Indians, and continue to be so. As autonomous cultures, Amazonian Indians are fast disappearing, though surviving individuals become assimilated and interbreed with the encroaching settlers. The clash is more an ecological one between incompatible modes of subsistence than a "racial" one, and the process is better described as one of gradual "ethnocide" rather than as genocide.

The other main feature of Brazilian race relations is, of course, the relationship between people of European and African descent. Extensive interbreeding between them, particularly during the period of slavery, has created a continuum of phenotypes, described by an elaborate nomenclature of racial terms. Conspicuously absent from Brazilian society, however, are distinct, self-conscious racial groups. Nobody can say where "white" ends and "black" begins, and indeed, social descriptions of individuals vary regionally, situationally, and according to socioeconomic criteria, as well as phenotype. In Brazil as a whole, perhaps 40 percent of the population is of partly African descent and might be classified as "black" in, say, the USA. In northeastern Brazil, the heart of the sugar plantation economy, and hence of slavery, perhaps as many as 70 to 80 percent of the population is distinctly of African descent.

Much discussion has centered on how racially tolerant Brazil is. Brazilian slavery has been described as more humane than in the United States or the British Caribbean, and the Catholic Church has been seen as mitigating the harshness of the owners. It is probably true that the Portuguese were less racist and more relaxed and easygoing in their relations with blacks, and thus created a less rigid, caste-bound society than did the British and North Americans in their slave colonies. Thus, emancipation was more frequent and easier, and freedmen were probably freer than their counterparts in the American South, for example. On the other hand, the physical treatment of Brazilian slaves was undoubtedly inferior to that meted out to slaves in the USA. Mortality rates were extremely high, especially in the mines, which, next to the sugar plantations, were the main destination of Brazilian slaves.

A century after their emancipation, Afro-Brazilians continue to be overrepresented at the bottom of the class pyramid, but substantial numbers are found in the middle class, and conversely, many white Brazilians, especially first- and second-generation European immigrants, are also quite poor. Afro-Brazilians have never been subjected to the institutionalized racism, segregation, and discrimination characteristic of, say, South Africa, or the USA. They do not constitute a self-conscious group because Brazilians do not classify themselves into racial groups. This is not to say that they are not race conscious. Indeed, they are often very conscious of racial phenotypes, so much so that they commonly use a score or more of racial labels to describe all the combinations and permutations of skin color, hair texture, and facial features. Indeed, racial taxonomies are so refined that members of the same family may well be referred to by different racial terms.

Paradoxical as it sounds, it was probably this high degree of racial consciousness at the level of the individual phenotype which, combined with a high level of marital and extra-marital interbreeding, prevented the formation of self-conscious, rigidly bounded racial groups in Brazil. To be sure, blackness has pejorative connotations, but more in an aesthetic than in a social or intellectual sense. Courtesy calls for ignoring an individual's darkness, using mitigating euphemisms (such as *moreno*, "brown"), and "promoting" a person racially if his or her class status warrants it: "Money bleaches" goes a Brazilian aphorism. Thus, it is certainly not true that Brazil is free of racial prejudice, but it is relatively free of *categorical discrimination* based on racial group membership.

To be sure, class and race overlap to some extent, but there are no *institutional* racial barriers against upward mobility for blacks. Intermarriage between the extremes of the color spectrum is infrequent, but not between adjacent phenotypes. Race, or better, phenotype, is definitely a component of a person's status and attractiveness, but often not the most salient one. In many situations, class is more important. Indeed, race relations at the working-class level are relatively free and uninhibited, compared to for example the USA, and residential and school segregation is based almost entirely on class rather than race.

In short, Brazil may be described as a society where class distinctions are marked and profound, where class and color overlap but do not coincide, where class often takes precedence over color, and where "race" is a matter of individual description and personal attractiveness rather than of group membership. Brazil is definitely a race conscious society, but it is not a racial caste one. It is not a racial paradise, but neither is it a racially obsessed society such as South Africa or the USA.

SEE ALSO: caste; color line; ethnocide; Freire, Paulo; Freyre, Gilberto; phenotype; whiteness

Reading

Brazil by Ronald M. Schneider (Westview Press, 1995) examines the historical development of Brazil from 1500 to independence in 1822, the middle-class revolution of 1930, the military takeover in 1964, and the return to democracy after 1984.

The Masters and the Slaves by Gilberto Freyre (Knopf, 1964) is the classic account of Brazilian slavery by a distinguished Brazilian scholar of psychoanalytic orientation.

Race and Racism, by Pierre L. van den Berghe (Wiley, 1978), especially chapter 3, is a summary of Brazilian relations.

"Residential segregation by skin color" by Edward Telles (in *American Sociological Review*, vol. 57, no. 2, April 1992) analyzes patterns of geographical division.

PIERRE L. VAN DEN BERGHE

BRITISH ASIANS

The term British Asians refers to people from South Asia (principally from Bangladesh, India and Pakistan), as well as people of South Asian descent holding British passports domiciled in East Africa, who traveled and settled in Britain in the postcolonial period. The former traveled to Britain as migrants, mostly in the 1950s and, especially, the 1960s. The latter were political refugees who fled to Britain following the expulsions of the 1970s. More recent populations

derive from asylum seekers and refugees from Sri Lanka. While the population of South Asians in Britain is estimated to be only 5 percent of the total population (58.8 million), its presence marks a significant impact on urban areas where the population is concentrated.

The main areas of South Asian settlement are Britain's conurbations. The main regional concentrations are in London and the South-East, the West Midlands, the East Midlands, West Yorkshire and the North-West. These areas are post-industrial landscapes with highly concentrated housing and institutionally complete villages within the urban sprawl. According to most of the indicators of quality of life, Asians in Britain are seriously disadvantaged. They show the usual patterns of racialized deprivation: they tend to be overrepresented in prisons, among the unemployed and the poor, and underrepresented in positions of power, privilege or comfort. Beneath this rather overgeneralized statement, there are clear observable differences between the various constituent elements of South Asians: Indian groups do better in many indicators of social and economic well-being, while Pakistani and Bangladeshi groups tend to be clustered towards the more underprivileged end of society.

Migration, settlement and identification

The migration and settlement in Britain of a large contingent of South Asians cannot be accounted for outside the context of the relationships established between Europe and South Asia in general and post-Mughal India and the British Isles in particular. Indeed, Asian settlement of Britain is a postcolonial suffix to the colonial relationship between Britain and its Indian empire. The presence in Europe of South Asia was initially one reduced to goods, legends and a few hardy travelers. The modern entry of South Asia into the European imagination was not an event like the appropriation of the Western hemisphere, where an unknown landmass and its inhabitants were consumed by Europe. Many of those traits considered to be specifically South Asian were constituted by networks of trade, pioneered by the Portuguese – early modern India can be seen in terms of the way in which control of the Indian ocean passed from Islamicate and Chinese ships to Portuguese, Dutch and British fleets. The spices that were brought by the Portuguese from the Americas helped to define a global cuisine, which is now known perhaps too unproblematically as Indian. The voyages of Vasco de Gama can be seen as the beginning of the process by which South Asia becomes a looming presence on European horizons. Thus Portuguese voyages to *Al-Hind* coincide with the major transformation of European identity, in particular the way in which racialized discourses became central to the idea of *Europeanness*.

There is continued debate regarding the most appropriate way of classifying South Asian settlers; the debate also illustrates the changing contours of racialized politics that have dogged Britain's ethnically designated populations from the times of mass migration. The problem of identifying and classifying these settlers has not only academic relevance but also social and political implications for conceptualizing British society and Britishness. With the establishment of settled South Asian populations, the term black and its cognates were used to refer to all of Britain's ethically marked populations of non-European background.

By the early 1980s there were increasing demands that a separate "Asian" identity be recognized. In response to this "new" development, "Asians" became a homogenous category and the language of race relations changed from using race as basis of categorization to using ethnicity. This ethnic categorization and accommodation of ethnic identity did not prevent "Asian" being treated as a crude sociological group, Most research on "Asians" failed to recognize differences within the groups, and adopted an approach whereby complex identities were reduced to anthropological generalizations. Thus, whenever there was any acknowledgment of difference, the definitions of immigrants tended to revolve around oversimplified explanations of customs and beliefs inherited from localized family groups confined to small areas of South Asia. These tended to exoticize and ethnicize issues around religious, linguistic differences. Much of the research on "Asians" emerged from within this framework.

This neat split between black to denote Afro-Caribbean, African as well as all of Britain's non-European population, and Asian to refer to Britain's population of South Asian heritage, has been problematized by the emergence of a distinct Muslim identity. The general assertion of an Islamicate political identity and other religious identities has destabilized both the

categories of black and Asian. By end of 1980s and early 1990s, it was clear that many issues confronting Muslims could not be easily described in terms of black or Asian. The introduction of the term Islamophobia recognized this.

The appearance of distinct religious subjectivities as being more relevant for provision of local services and often of self-identification by British-born, educated people of South Asian heritage has also left the term Asian as a secular residue. It is worth noting, however, that more complex and subtle hyphenated identities such as Asian Muslim or British Hindu are beginning to emerge within the landscape of Britain's ethnically marked communities. This entails recognition that differential social, cultural and economic logics mark the various ethnicized minorities with increasing complex gradation. There is thus a growing discrepancy between official modes of classifying the South Asian population resident in Britain and the increasingly complex, fragmented and multiple ways in which members of these population groups seek to describe themselves.

Official records have increasingly sought to encapsulate the South Asian minority in Britain in ethnonational categories, such as Indian, Pakistani and Bangladeshi. With the inclusion of an ethnonational question in the 1991 census, ethnonational labels have become enshrined within public discourse, and thus the labels Pakistani, Indian, Bangladeshi in this sense are the most widely used in local and national state publications and media broadcasts. Subsequent to the 1991 census, surveys and monitoring forms have followed the same format in order to make longitudinal comparisons. This process has taken place despite the fundamental problem that these terms ascribe people born in Britain in terms of nation-states, which many may never have visited.

In contrast, many ethically marked groups seeking official recognition have sought to have their self-descriptions included in the data sets produced by governmental agencies, including the census. In particular the Kashmiris have been successful in gaining official recognition by being included as a distinct ethnic category by some local authorities. Partly in recognition of the salience of religious identity, the 2001 census also asked this question. It is not yet clear, however, how this will impact on the local construction of groups in terms of service provision and state response.

The term Asian has always served as short-hand for more complex identities, and is increasingly becoming displaced both nominally and in terms of certain socioeconomic, cultural and political experiences. However, it does still carry salience in both the world of popular culture and certain local state-sector contexts. There is for instance an increasingly visible presence in the mainstream and an ever-expansive set of outlets for music, film and art, though even here it is worth being careful about an overly romantic view of a unitary Asian popular culture.

Chain migration

"We are here, because you were there" is a slogan that came to epitomize the struggles that many of the new Asian settlers came to face in the factories and footpaths of the mother country. The impetus behind South Asian migration has generally been seen in terms of economic factors (push and pull). This is despite the accounts of the migrants, in particular the East African Asians and the Kashmiris, many of whom describe their displacement and relocation to Britain as being the result of political factors.

Marxist interpretations of this migration flow articulate the simple but powerful formulae that demand in the factories of the old industrial heartlands of England led to a very specific flow of workers from the periphery colonies to the center of empire. The seductive nature of this argument nonetheless erases the process by which this migration took place. A more nuanced account and one that assigns some degree of agency to the migrants is found in network migration theory, which articulates the process by which kith and kin played a significant role in the migration process. More controversially, migrant network theory maintains that the network takes on a life of its own, divorced from the initial structural causes of migration. This thesis has found much mileage in studies of Britain's South Asian populations, resulting in the idea of "chain migration." Migrants are linked like a chain, which also maintains links with the homeland. Perhaps the most important and significant contribution that studies of South Asian settlers have made to the theory of migration is a dismantling of the notion that migration is a one-way, one-off process. South Asian settlers have been remarkably adept at creating a transnational space in which the circulation of people, commodities and capital between various diasporic sites is the norm.

The end of primary migration in Britain is generally associated with the increasing racialization of the immigration issue from the late 1960s onwards. During this time successive Labour and Conservative governments passed restrictive immigration legislation. At the same time there was a declining demand for labor, a growing discontent, and some racial violence in inner-city areas marked most notably by the Notting Hill riots in 1958. All these have the effect of increasing the visibility of Britain's "black" population and focusing attention away from immigration to the difficulties of settlement.

Britain's early official response to the presence of large numbers of immigrants, who were distinguished by their skin color, language, religion and culture, was simply to declare that they must be assimilated to a unitary British culture. This implied the notion of the superiority of white dominant culture. Multiculturalism was a move towards acknowledging cultural diversity, the end goal of which is seen to be pluralism or living with difference. In other words, multiculturalism seemed to promise an abandonment of the idea that cultures were in some hierarchy in which ethically marked cultures were inferior to European culture.

Representations

The recognition of chicken tikka masala as one of Britain's favorite dishes is an useful metaphor for the emergence of cultural forms which are distinctly neither South Asian nor British but rather hybrid: since chicken tikka masala does not exist in South Asia it is a sign of South Asian cuisine invented in Britain. South Asian cultural forms have gone in and out of fashion in British society from Indian spiritualism in the 1960s to Bhangra in the late 1990s and Bollywood in the 2000s. These fads can be seen in light of the fetishization which has often been part and parcel of racist discourses. What is different is the appearance of a distinct British Asian culture constructed by and mainly consumed by Britain's South Asian population. The ubiquitous 'Indian' takeouts, halal butchers, mosques and temples, boutiques and jewelry stores all mark the transformation of Britain urban landscapes. This physical transformation of the various cityscapes is matched by the way in which networks based around newspapers, magazines and radio stations as well other patterns of communication stitch together a more or less coherent British Asian civil society that is parallel to the more extensive official British society.

Representations of South Asians in Britain have for the most part continued to rely on a conceptual vocabulary borrowed from the legacy of nineteenth-century anthropology of the South Asian subcontinent, such as the a priori use of concepts like caste (hierarchical divisions of Hindu society) and *biraderi* (kinship networks) to describe South Asian experiences. As a result, even though South Asians have been in Britain in large numbers for nearly fifty years, most of British society, including its elite, remain largely ignorant of South Asians, except as ethnographic exhibits. There is a strong tendency to see South Asians in Britain but not as part of Britain. The representation of Asians in Britain continues to be refracted through a prism, which is unable to come to terms with the postcolonial nature of the South Asian presence. South Asian culture continues to be regarded as static, traditional or antimodern, patriarchal and authoritarian. This is in contrast to British/Western culture. Implicit in these representations is the idea of Western culture and values as being the norm and criterion in relation to which other cultures have to be positioned. These representations and understandings of the South Asian presence are unable to deal with the decolonized and decolonizing aspect of this presence and thus remain increasingly unable to cope with the complexity of the postcolonial condition that continues to confront Britain.

It is also apparent that in the north of England and in particular with Asian Muslim young people a new resilience is appearing in relation to patterns of social exclusion and a sense of alienation with these modes of representation. The violent unrest of 2001 in England's northern towns following a decade punctuated by sporadic violence in Bradford indicates that the position of Asians in Britain is following a bipolar path. On the one hand it is an acceptable face represented by chicken tikka masala and Bollywood, a neat entry into the model of consumer multiculturalism and "new" Britain? Here consumption and economic high performance is the route to an integrated society. On the other hand are those who are excluded from the benefits of economic expansion and who occupy the lower rungs of postindustrial society's occupational ladder. These are the producers of the chicken tikka, the waiters in the restaurants and the cab drivers taking home the diners. It is clear that Britain has opened to some extent its metropolitan arms to the first group of Asians. It is not clear what is to become of the second.

SEE ALSO: Anglo-Indians; Asian Americans; asylum seeker; colonial discourse; colonialism; consumption; diaspora; disadvantage; education; essentialism; ethnonational; Islamophobia; kinship; law: immigration, Britain; media; migration; multiculturalism; postcolonial; racial coding; racist discourse; representations; riots: Britain, 2001; social work; stereotype; welfare

Reading

Asians in Britain: 400 years of history by Rozina Visram (Pluto Press, 2002) is a valuable chronicle. "Political blackness and British Asians" by Tariq Modood (in *Sociology*, vol. 28, no. 4, 1996) rejects attempts to class Asians as black for the purposes of color solidarity and political identity.

A Post Colonial People: South Asians in Britain by Ali Nasreen, Virinda Kalra and S. Sayyid (Hurst Publications, 2003) provides an elaboration of many of the themes suggested above.

ALI NASREEN, VIRINDER KALRA
AND BOBBY SAYYID

BRITISH NATIONAL PARTY

The British National Party or BNP was a neo-fascist organization that recruited many from disaffected white working-class youth in the late twentieth and early twenty-first centuries. It staged its rallies mainly in dense multicultural areas and was involved in a series of violent disturbances, particularly in 2001. BNP policy was a commitment to what it called "a homogeneous community."

The roots of the movement go back to 1957, when a fascist group called the White Defence League was set up and became a contributory factor in ethnic violence. In 1960, the League amalgamated with another group to become the British National Party, with Colin Jordan as its head. Jordan left to form the National Socialist Party, which he later relaunched as the British Movement. No more than a marginal organization with a commitment to anti-Semitism and other forms of racism, the BNP only started to acquire significance with the skinhead renascence of the 1970s.

The BNP recruited at soccer stadia, rock concerts, and openly on the streets, appealing to white British youth who were persuaded of the "threat" posed by ethnic minorities. By the early 1990s, the British Movement had receded from prominence, leaving the BNP as the main youth-oriented organization of the far right.

In the early twenty-first century, the BNP's rhetoric of racism was replaced, or perhaps just disguised, as a concern only with incoming refugees and, in 2001, a series of disturbances followed BNP marches in northern towns. Following September 11, 2001, the BNP attempted to link immigration with terrorism. Serendipitously perhaps, the involvement of two British Asians in a suicide bombing in Tel Aviv only days before local elections in English regions in 2003 helped boost the BNP. Fielding 221 candidates, it more than trebled its number of seats to 16, including five extra seats in Burnley, scene of the 2001 disturbances, making it the second largest party on that town's local council.

SEE ALSO: anti-Semitism; asylum seeker; British Asians; fascism; Islamophobia; Ku Klux Klan; Let's Kick Racism Out of Football; National Front; nationalism; neo-nazism; politics; prejudice; riots: Britain, 2001; Rock Against Racism; scapegoat; skinheads; September 11, 2001; White Power; white backlash culture; youth subcultures

Reading

The Extreme Right in Europe and the U.S.A., edited by Paul Hainsworth (Pinter, 1992), is a country-by-country analysis of neo-nazi groups.
"New-age nazism" by Matthew Kalman and John Murray (*New Statesman & Society*, June 23, 1995) looks at the way neo-nazi groups have aligned themselves with green and new age movements.
"Racist violence and political extremism" is the theme of a special issue of *New Community* (vol. 21, no. 4, 1995). It includes essays on this theme in relation to Britain and mainland Europe.

BARRY TROYNA

BROWN v. BOARD OF EDUCATION

Brown v. Board of Education of Topeka, Kansas was a legal case decided on May 17, 1954. It declared the fundamental principle that racial discrimination in public education was a viola-

tion of the 14th Amendment. All provisions of federal, state or local law that either permitted or required such discrimination were made to cease.

The eponymous Brown was Oliver Brown, whose daughter had been forced to travel by bus to an all-black school even though she lived close to an all-white institution. The National Association for the Advancement of Colored People (NAACP) threw its weight behind Brown and eventually secured the agreement of the presiding Chief Justice Warren who concluded: "In the field of public education, the doctrine of 'separate but equal' has no place." In ruling segregation unconstitutional, the *Brown* decision overturned the conclusions of *Plessy* v. *Ferguson*, 1896, which gave rise to the Jim Crow era.

States were instructed to proceed with "all deliberate speed" to abolish segregation in public schools. While five of the southern states, encouraged by governors, senators, representatives and white Citizens Councils, resisted the decision, twelve states and the District of Columbia (DC) immediately began to desegregate. The Supreme Court continued to hand down decisions that portended the further segregation that followed.

SEE ALSO: African Americans; busing; civil rights movement; education; equality; Jim Crow; King, Martin Luther; King case, the Rodney; law: civil rights, USA; Malcolm X; Million Man March; miscegenation; Myrdal, Gunnar; prejudice; Pruitt-Igoe; segregation; white backlash culture; xenophobia

Reading

The Negro in the United States: A brief history by Rayford W. Logan (Van Nostrand, 1957) includes transcripts from the case. Chief Justice Warren's summary can be found in *Annual Editions: Race and ethnic relations*, 12th edn., edited by John A. Kromkowski (McGraw Hill/Dushkin, 2002/03).

BUSING

In 1954, in the *Brown* v. *Board of Education, Topeka, Kansas* case, the US Supreme Court ruled that segregated education was unconstitutional and in violation of the 14th Amendment. By this ruling, schools had to be desegregated and special buses were to transport black and Latino students to schools in the suburbs. There, they would receive the same educational provision as white students. It was contended that the process of desegregation, or busing, would ensure that students would be treated first and foremost as individuals and not as members of a caste. Desegregation was based on a number of seductive, if not empirically tested, assumptions. First, it was anticipated that busing would equalize educational opportunities. Subsequent research showed unfortunately that this was little more than wishful thinking. The effect of desegregation on educational performance was erratic. Under optimal conditions it was likely to be effective. But as James Coleman pointed out, most school changes under optimal conditions have this effect.

Second, it was assumed that busing would help counteract the historically divisive nature of perceived racial difference and facilitate the emergence of a more tolerant society. This proposition was based on what is known as the contact hypothesis. This holds that enhancing interracial contact (in schools, residential areas, the workplace) is bound to improve relations between members of different groups. Once again, however, this is a romanticized view – a fiction that only under highly contrived conditions translated into an empirically verifiable scenario. Despite these profound reservations, in the USA busing was conceived as a liberal practice and its opponents, and their arguments, were generally characterized as racist.

Nine years after the *Brown* decision, a similar attempt was made in Britain to ensure a greater ethnic mix in schools. This provoked the opposite reaction however. Busing was seen as racist, a denial of equality of opportunity to colonial migrants and their children. Black and white liberals up and down the country vehemently opposed both its principle and practice. How do we account for these contrasting reactions?

In the United States, legally sanctioned school segregation embodied "a persisting badge of slavery," as David Kirp has put it. Schools in black neighborhoods were generally old and rundown and tended to be the last repaired, worst funded, and understaffed. Because education is conventionally viewed from the liberal democratic perspective as the gateway to social and occupational advancement, the provision of inferior education to black students was seen as a legally sanctioned instrument that endorsed and perpetuated black subordination. Not surprisingly then, the initiative for desegregation derived from the black American communities.

In Britain, on the other hand, there was no clear educational justification for the introduction of busing. The initiative came from a group of white parents in the Southall district of London who had complained to the Minister of Education, Edward Boyle, that the educational progress of their children was being inhibited in those schools containing large numbers of nonwhite, mainly South Asian pupils. Boyle subsequently recommended to government that the proportion of immigrant children should not exceed 30 percent in any one school. In 1965, "Boyle's Law," as it came to be called, received official backing from the Department of Education and Science. As a result, a few local education authorities followed the steps already taken in Southall and West Bromwich and formally implemented busing procedures.

The main imperative for this action was clear: to assuage the anxieties of white parents. The fact that skin color was used as the sole criterion for deciding which students were to be bused vividly demonstrated this point. But, as opponents of busing pointed out, these fears were largely unfounded in any case. Research carried out in primary schools in London has shown that the ethnic mix of a school has a minimal influence on the level of reading ability attained by pupils. Opponents also insisted that busing was premised on the racist assumption that schools with a large proportion of nonwhite students are inherently inferior to those in which white students are the majority.

By the late 1970s most of those local education authorities that had introduced busing had been persuaded by the efficacy of these arguments (if not by the threat of intervention by the Commission for Racial Equality) and abandoned the procedure. In the USA, the slow process of desegregation continues, despite the contention that it has encouraged "white flight" and has only slightly, if at all, led to educational or interpersonal benefits. Nevertheless, the different reactions to busing of the black and other nonwhite communities in the USA and Britain highlight its symbolic importance. On one side of the Atlantic it is seen as a catalyst for equality of opportunity; on the other, it is an instrument designed to undermine that ideal.

SEE ALSO: bigotry; *Brown v. Board of Education*; children; Ebonics; education; equal opportunity; law: civil rights, USA; multicultural education; racist discourse; transracial adoption; white backlash culture; white flight; whiteness

Reading

Contact and Conflict in Intergroup Encounters (Blackwell, 1986) comprises a series of critical essays on the contact hypothesis. The introduction by editors Hewstone and Brown and the essay by Steven Reicher are especially incisive.

Equality and Achievement in Education (Westview Press, 1990) by James Coleman, who in the 1960s advocated busing as a means of social engineering to enhance equality of opportunity. In this book he revisits some of his earlier assumptions and lays bare their weaknesses.

Just Schools by David Kirp (University of California Press, 1982) begins with a brief but critical discussion of the relationship between the Brown decree and equality of opportunity, then considers the experiences of five Bay Area communities in the twenty-five years since the introduction of desegregation.

CHECK: internet resources section

BARRY TROYNA

C

CAPITALISM

This refers to a particular type of socioeconomic structure bounded by a particular historical period. However, there are substantial disagreements between Marxists and non-Marxists, and between various strands of Marxism, over the defining features of the socioeconomic structure and historical period.

Non-Marxists tend to define capitalism in one of the following ways. First, it is conceived as any society characterized by the presence of exchange or market relations. Thus, the defining characteristic is individuals bartering or exchanging products for money. Second, as any society in which production occurs for the purpose of profit. Thus, the defining characteristic is the intention on the part of a group of people to organize the production and distribution of goods in order to realize more money at the end of the process than the sum with which they started. Third, as any society in which production is carried out by means of industry. In this instance, it is the specific use of power-driven machinery that is identified as the defining characteristic of capitalism.

The first two definitions imply that capitalism has existed over very large areas of the world since the earliest times of human activity. Proponents of these positions often also argue that this demonstrates that capitalism is a natural and inevitable form of socioeconomic organization. This conclusion is less likely to be accepted by some advocates of the market as the defining characteristic if they then wish to draw a distinction between market and nonmarket forms of socioeconomic organization (the latter being defined as some form of state socialist society).

The third is more historically specific, locating the development of capitalism in the later eighteenth century in Europe from where it has spread to characterize large areas of the world in the twentieth century.

Of these various positions, the most influential within sociology in the past two decades has been the identification of capitalism with the existence of market relations, as in the work of Max Weber. It is upon this tradition of theorizing that much of the sociology of "race relations" has drawn in its attempts to analyze race relations in some form of historical and structural context.

Similarly, within Marxism, there is a long-established debate over the origin and nature of capitalism. There are two main positions, although both are premised on the acceptance of Marx's method and labor theory of value. Thus, both accept that all previously existing societies are characterized by class exploitation which takes the form of one class living off the surplus product produced by another class. Despite other similarities with non-Marxist analyses, the acceptance of this claim makes the following two positions quite distinct.

The first position identifies capitalism with a system of production for the market which is motivated by profit. Thus, for advocates of this position, the appearance of markets and the development of trade, particularly international trade, marks the origin of capitalism in Europe in the fourteenth and fifteenth centuries. This position has been developed to the point that capitalism is seen to be synonymous with the development of a world market of exchange relations, in which Europe stands at the center of a series of dominant/subordinate relations with South America, the Caribbean, India, Africa and Southeast Asia. These analysts typically employ the following dualisms: center/periphery, metropolis/satellite, development/underdevelopment. It is argued that the development of the center metropolis is both product and cause of the underdevelopment of the periphery/satellite. In its most extreme form, it is claimed that capitalism refers to this system of international relations rather than to any national unit or units which participate in those relations.

The second position identifies capitalism as a mode of production sharing the following characteristics: (1) generalized commodity production, whereby most production occurs for the purpose of exchange rather than for direct use; (2) labor power has itself become a commodity which is bought and sold for a wage. On the basis of these characteristics, the origin of capitalism is located in England in the seventeenth century, from where it has spread out beyond Europe as nation-states have formed themselves around generalized commodity production utilizing wage labor. Advocates of this position place primary emphasis upon the character of the production process, to which the process of exchange is viewed as secondary. It accepts that the origin of capitalism lies partly in the accumulation of capital by means of colonial exploitation, but adds that this only led to capitalist production once a class of free wage laborers had been formed.

Both Marxist positions maintain that capitalism developed out of feudalism and that the development marked the beginning of a world division of labor and a world process of uneven development. They therefore suggest a determinant relationship between capitalism and colonialism, and this forms the backdrop to various Marxist accounts of historical and contemporary "race relations."

SEE ALSO: colonialism; conservatism; equality; exploitation; Freire, Paulo; globalization; hegemony; human rights; Marxism; migration; New International Division of Labor; slavery; social exclusion; underclass

Reading

Capital, vol. 1, by Karl Marx (Penguin 1976), especially Parts 2, 3, 5, 7 and 8, is Marx's analysis of the nature and origins of capitalism.

General Economic History by Max Weber (Transaction Books, 1981) is a general account of Weber's analysis of the nature and origins of capitalism.

Karl Marx's Theory of History: A defence by G. A. Cohen (Oxford University Press, 2001) is an attempt to "rehabilitate" Marx's theory of history, paying particular attention to the dissolution of the Soviet Union.

Sociological Theory by Bert N. Adams (Pine Forge, 2001) examines Marx and Engels's "radical anti-capitalism" in a direct and accessible way.

ROBERT MILES

CASTE

The concept of "caste" has been applied to a wide variety of social institutions, both human and nonhuman. Entomologists have used it to describe the functionally and anatomically discrete morphs (workers, soldiers, etc.) of many species of eusocial insects, especially ants, bees, and termites. Social scientists have spoken of castes in societies as different as those of Spanish American colonies until the nineteenth century, the Indian subcontinent, twentieth-century South Africa and the USA, and precolonial West Africa.

In the social sciences, there have been two main traditions in the use of the term caste. There have been those, mainly Indianists, who have reserved the term to describe the stratification systems of the societies influenced by Hinduism on the Indian subcontinent. The other tradition has extended the term to many other societies that lacked some of the features of the Hindu caste system, but nevertheless had groups possessing the following three characteristics:

- endogamy, i.e. compulsory marriage within the group;
- ascriptive membership by birth and for life, and, hence, hereditary status;
- ranking in a hierarchy in relation to other such groups.

These three characteristics have been called the minimal definition of caste, and such a definition has been extensively applied by W. Lloyd Warner, Gunnar Myrdal, and many others to white–black relations in the USA and in other societies, such as South Africa, with a rigid racial hierarchy.

There is a double irony in the position of those who want to reserve the term for India and related societies. First, caste is not a term indigenous to India at all; it is a Spanish and Portuguese word (*casta*), first applied to racial groupings, mostly in the Spanish American colonies. The *casta* system of the Spanish colonies, however, was not a caste system in either the Indian or the extended sense. There was little group endogamy, and extensive racial mixtures gave rise to a proliferation of "half-caste" categories such as *mestizos*, *mulatos*, and *zambos*. As a result, *casta* membership became rather flexible, negotiable and subject to situational redefinitions based on wealth and prestige.

Second, the term "caste," far from helping us understand the Indian situation, actually confuses it. It has been applied, often indiscriminately, to refer to two very different groupings: *varna* and *jati*. The four *varnas* (brahmins, kshatriyas, vaishyas, and sudras) are broad groupings subdivided into a multiplicity of *jati*. The effective social group in most situations is the *jati* rather than the *varna*. Yet most Hindu scriptural references are to *varnas*. Little seems gained by using a single exotic term such as "caste" to refer to two such different types of groups.

Beyond use of the term caste in Indian society and in racially stratified countries such as South Africa and the USA, the word has also been applied to certain specialized occupational groups, especially low-status endogamous pariah or outcaste groups in a range of other societies. For example the Eta or Burakumin of Japan, and the blacksmiths and praise-singers of many African societies, have been called castes.

There is little question that the Hindu caste system has a number of unique characteristics, but that is no reason to restrict to India the use of a concept to designate rigid ascriptive, stratified and endogamous groups. A useful distinction should be made, however, between genuine caste societies where the whole population is divided into such groups, and societies with some caste groups, where only a minority of the people belong to pariah groups. Perhaps only India, and South Africa until 1994, each in its own special way, could be described as caste societies, while many more societies, both past and present, have endogamous groups of pariahs and outcastes.

SEE ALSO: Cox, Oliver C.; cultural racism; ethnocentrism; miscegenation; Myrdal, Gunnar; race: as signifier; race: as synonym; racialization; segregation; underclass

Reading

Caste and Race, edited by Anthony de Reuck (Little Brown, 1967), is a collection of essays by leading authorities, covering many societies.

The Ethnic Phenomenon by Pierre L. van den Berghe (Elsevier, 1981), especially chapter 8, gives a more extensive discussion of the issues outlined above.
Growing Up Untouchable in India: A Dalit autobiography by Vasant Moon (Rowman & Littlefield, 2000) is a pathbreaking first person account of an untouchable born into the inescapable hierarchy of the Indian caste system.
Homo Hierarchies by Louis Dumont (Weidenfeld & Nicholson, 1970) is probably the best account of the Hindu caste system.
CHECK: internet resources section

PIERRE L. VAN DEN BERGHE

CAUCASIAN

A name introduced by Johann Friedrich Blumenbach (1752–1840) in 1795 to designate one of the "five principal varieties of mankind." Europeans were classified as Caucasians. The name was chosen because Blumenbach believed the neighborhood of Mount Caucasus, and especially its southern slope, produced the most beautiful race of men, and was probably the home of the first men. He thought they were probably white in complexion since it was easier for white to degenerate into brown than for a dark color to become white. The other four "principal varieties" were the Mongolian, Ethiopian, American, and Malay races.

Caucasian has continued to be used as a designation for white people into the twentieth century, although there is no longer any scientific justification for the practice. The distinctive characteristics of white populations need nowadays to be expressed statistically in terms of the frequency of particular genes, blood groupings, etc. Apparent similarities in appearance may be the basis for social classifications but are of little use for biological purposes.

SEE ALSO: anthropology; Aryan; Doomed Races Doctrine; genotype; geometry of race; Haeckel, Ernst; phenotype; race: as classification; race: as synonym; science; white race; whiteness

Reading

The Anthropological Treatises of Johann Friedrich Blumenbach, edited by Thomas Bendyshe (Longman, Green, 1865), is the original source.
Racial Theories, 2nd edn., by Michael Banton (Cambridge University Press, 1998), traces the development of ideas that have influenced thinking about race and racism.

MICHAEL BANTON

CENTRAL PARK JOGGER

In April 1989, a young white female who worked on Wall Street, was raped and beaten by at least nine young working-class African American and Latino men, aged 15–17, while jogging in New York's Central Park. She was beaten and left alone. The young men, from Harlem, were found guilty of raping and assaulting the woman and each was given a sentence of five to ten years, the maximum term for juveniles in New York State.

Within hours of the attack, the police had six suspects, accused of what was later described as "wilding." The internationally reported case provoked an almost hysterical reaction, which, critics argued, contributed to an unfair trial. While all but one of the accused made videotaped confessions of their involvement in the attack, DNA testing did not link any of the five to the rape. Physical evidence connected two to the beating.

Amsterdam News, the community newspaper, insisted that a "legal lynching" had taken place. It argued that the police were under severe pressure to "find a target" for the nation's anger and that the men were virtually coerced into making confessions. It also pointed out that the woman's name was withheld, though in comparable cases involving black victims, names had been released. The case both disclosed the intersecting fault lines of sex and race and prompted the specter of an attack motivated by racism.

In 2002, thirteen years after the attack, in an extraordinary development, Justice Charles Tejada of the State Supreme Court of Manhattan granted motions made by defense lawyers to vacate all convictions against five of the young men who had earlier admitted to attacking the jogger. The ruling was based on evidence that had come from a confession by Matias Reyes, a convicted murderer and rapist, who was the probable lone attacker. His confession cast doubt on the reliability of the confessions. By the time of their release, the men, who were teenagers at the time of the attack, were between 28 and 30 years old.

SEE ALSO: Barry case, the Marion; media; racist discourse; representations; Simpson case, the O. J.; Thomas, Clarence; Tyson, Mike; violence

Reading

Unequal Verdicts: The Central Park Jogger trial by Timothy Sullivan (Simon & Schuster, 1992) lacks analytical bite, but provides a good description of the case.

CHAMBERLAIN, HOUSTON STEWART (1855–1927)

"The Nazi Prophet," as he came to be called, was the son of a British naval admiral, who studied zoology under Carl Vogt in Geneva. He later moved to Dresden where he developed a theory that would influence world history. Published in 1899, Chamberlain's work was a gigantic exploration of what he called *The Foundations of the Nineteenth Century*. He traced these back to the ancient Israelites, locating the critical year as 1200, the beginning of the Middle Ages, when the *Germanen* emerged "as the founders of an entirely new civilization and an entirely new culture."

A large section of the work was intended to downplay the parts played by Jews, Romans and Greeks in the development of European culture. Yet Chamberlain was careful to note the increasing influence of Jews in the spheres of government, literature and art.

Inspired by the older theories of Gobineau and the newer work of Darwin, Chamberlain speculated that the indiscriminate hybridization, or mixing of races, was undesirable, though he remained convinced that the strongest and fittest race could, at any moment, be able to assume its dominance and impose its superiority and thus curb the degeneration process caused by racial mixing.

For Chamberlain, that race derived from the original peoples of Germany, created "physiologically by characteristic mixture of blood, followed by interbreeding; psychically by the influence that long-continued historical-geographical circumstances produce on that particular, specific physiological disposition." Interestingly, however, he was rather imprecise on the exact definition of race. The term *Germanen* referred to a mixture of northern and western European populations which were said to form a "family," the essence of which is the *Germane*.

Chamberlain's importance was not so much in his adding new knowledge to the concept of race itself, as in his general synthetical argument about the inherent superiority of one group over all others. There was a clear complementarity between Chamberlain's version of history and, indeed, the future and what was to become National Socialist philosophy.

Although he played no active part in the rise of nazism (he died in 1927 before the Nazis came to power in Germany), his work was used selectively to support theoretically many of the atrocities that accompanied the Nazi development.

SEE ALSO: anti-Semitism; Aryan; caucasian; culturecide; Doomed Races Doctrine; essentialism; ethnocide; fascism; genocide; geometry of race; Gobineau, Joseph Arthur de; Haeckel, Ernst; race: as classification; race: as signifier; racism; science; *Volk*; Wagner, Richard

Reading

The Foundations of the Nineteenth Century, 2 vols., by Houston Stewart Chamberlain (Fertig, 1968; first published 1899), is the infamous work translated by John Lee from the 1910 edition, but with a new introduction by George Mosse.

Man's Most Dangerous Myth: The fallacy of race, 6th edn., by Ashley Montagu (AltaMira, 1998), was first published in 1942 when Chamberlain's ideas were gaining currency through nazism and race was considered a determinant of thought and conduct. Montagu argued forcefully against both. This more recent edition includes revisions and updates from the author.

Race: The history of an idea in the West by Ivan Hannaford (Johns Hopkins University Press, 1996) contains a subsection entitled "The final synthesis" in which Chamberlain's work is assessed. "Chamberlain played upon all the diverse anxieties then afflicting Europe's industrial powers – militarism, anticlericalism, 'pan-isms,' extraparliamentary action, the degeneration of political life, the rise of technological and managerial society – in an effort to create an integrated theory of race," argues Hannaford.

CHŌVEZ, CÒSAR (1927–93)

As King had adopted Gandhi's nonviolent civil disobedience as a means of furthering the struggle of blacks, so Cìsar Chûvez did with Mexican-Americans. Chûvez became synonymous with the Chicano movement: his principal achievement was the creation of the United Farm Workers' Union (UFW) which attracted a considerable proportion of California's agricultural labor force and led to improvements in wages and working conditions for Chicanos.

UFW tactics were modeled on King's boycotts, strikes, mass demonstrations and pushing for new legislation. When violence did threaten to upset his tactics, Chûvez, like Gandhi, went on an extended fast in protest.

Before going further, a profile of Mexican-Americans might be useful. About 85 percent are born in the USA (approximately half of these being born to American parents). The vast majority are under thirty. Most speak Spanish as well as English and belong to the Roman Catholic Church. Since the 1950s, there has been a fairly rapid movement from rural areas into the cities, though this geographical mobility has not been accompanied by any upward social mobility.

Educationally, there have been improvements from one generation to the next, but the average Mexican-American child has less education than his or her white American counterpart and tends to achieve less. Thus, the children demonstrate little evidence for predicting an improvement in status and material conditions and remain a predominantly poor people with limited education.

During the 1950s Mexican-American war veterans founded the GI Forum, which became quite an important force in fighting discrimination against them, but out of the social upheavals of the 1960s grew the Chicano movement, which was committed to changing the impoverished circumstances of Mexican-Americans. The idea was to promote economic changes through uniting people. And the unity was achieved through the restoration of Mexican culture by making people of Mexican origins recognize the commonness of their background and current conditions; it was hoped to mobilize them for political action, and thus produce constructive change.

Chûvez had many obstacles to overcome, including the apathy of many Mexican-Americans, the resistance of agricultural businesses and their influential supporters, and also the opposition of the formidable Teamsters Union which, until 1976, challenged the UFW's right to represent Californian farm workers. Though his main success came in California, Chûvez spread his efforts to unionize agricultural workers elsewhere and became the single most important figure in the Chicano movement.

Beside Chûvez, other Chicano leaders emerged in the period. Some, such as Jerry Apodaca and Raul Castro, opted for party politics. Josí Anger Gutiírrez in 1970 founded the Partido de la Raza Unida organization in south Texas and successfully fought school board, city council, and county elections.

In addition to the visible successes of Chûvez in employment, Chicano groups have striven with some success for important educational objectives such as the reduction of school drop-out rates, the improvement of educational attainment, the integration of Spanish language and Mexican culture classes into curricula, the training of more Chicano teachers and administrators, and the prevention of the busing of Chicano schoolchildren.

After the impetus of the 1960s, Chicanos became more fiercely ethnic, establishing their own colleges and universities, churches, youth movements. More recently, the movement has spawned Chicano feminist organizations. A further development came in 1967 with the Brown Berets, a militant group fashioned after the Black Panthers. As the Panthers reacted to the nonviolent "working-the-system" approach of King *et al.*, so the Berets reacted to the Chicano resistance as led by Chûvez. This wing of the Chicano movement was perhaps inspired by the incident in New Mexico in 1967 when, led by Reies Lopez Tijerina, Chicanos occupied Forest Service land and took hostage several Forest Service Rangers. Tijerina and others were arrested, but escaped after an armed raid on a New Mexico courthouse. Several hundred state troopers and national guardsmen were needed to round them up.

Although the Chicano movement does not reflect the general experience of Mexican-Americans, it demonstrates the effectiveness of militant ethnicity in the attempt to secure advancement. Chûvez, in particular, created a broad base of support from a consciousness of belonging to a distinct ethnic group that was consistently disadvantaged, and thus pointed up the importance of ethnicity as a factor in forcing social change.

SEE ALSO: *Aztlûn*; Black Panther Party; civil rights movement; cultural racism; Gandhi, Mohandas Karamchand; King, Martin Luther; Latinos; Puerto Ricans in the USA; white backlash culture

Reading

Císar Chûvez: A triumph of spirit by Richard Griswold del Castillo and Richard A. Garcia (University of Oklahoma Press, 1995) is a biography of the farm worker-cum-labor organizer who was launched by events into a maelstrom of *campesino* strikes.

Latinos Unidos: From cultural diversity to the politics of solidarity by Enrique (Henry) T. Trueda (Rowman & Littlefield, 1998) shows how the adaptive strategies of Latinos in the USA embrace the establishment of bilingual and bicultural networks.

The Mexican-American People by Leo Grebler, Joan W. Moore and Ralph C. Guzman (The Free Press, 1970) is the most comprehensive historical source on the whole subject while *The Chicanos: A history of Mexican Americans* by Matt S. Meier and Feliciano Rivera (Hill & Wang, 1972) traces Chicano history and developments through the 1960s.

Mi Raza Primero: My people, first nationalism, identity and insurgency in the Chicano movement in Los Angeles, 1966–1978 by Ernesto Chavez (University of California Press, 2002) recounts the struggle.

CHILDREN

Learning racism

Children reared in societies with racial distinctions undergo a complex learning process in which they actually *learn* racism. Skin color and other racial markers provide overt indications of individuals' social worth and inform observers and institutions about individuals' potential in virtually all social realms, from friendships to education to employment and family formation.

Much recent work either assumes or suggests that children are more or less na?ve and innocent about racial and ethnic matters. Most adults refuse to accept that children, especially very young children, either can or would knowingly make use of racist epithets, emotions, or behaviors. When children do employ racial or ethnic terminology, they are typically assumed to be merely imitating adult behavior, with little or no awareness of the meanings and consequences of such conduct. In short, adults, from parents to researchers, deny that racism can exist in children. However, some research in cognitive psychology, sociology, and other social sciences, reveals that racial and ethnic ideas hold considerable salience for children, even those as young as three- or four-years-old. Some evidence demonstrates that by the age of three, children can use fairly sophisticated racially and ethnically informed ideas to organize their play, form friendships, define themselves and others, and establish dominance in social interaction (see Van Ausdale and Feagin, below). This finding indicates that children have had extensive experience with the ideologies of race and racism throughout their toddler years and that they grasp the significance of race on many levels. Yet such work remains rare, and much research on children's social learning remains dominated by traditional child development theories. We will now move to a review of the major theories of child development.

Cognitive/developmental

Perhaps the most influential theorist of child development in the twentieth century is Jean Piaget, whose paradigm asserts that children develop along fairly predictable and linear age-based stages of cognition. Piaget's work is a dominant force in developmental psychology and it is this field that has maintained hegemony in studies of children's cognitive capabilities. Piaget's primary notion is that children's systems of thought are fundamentally different from those of adults. This difference means that children are generally incapable of understanding information in the same way as adults.

As a result, information that is not developmentally appropriate for the individual child's stage of development will not be understood by that child, no matter how carefully and thoughtfully this information is delivered. The child's system of thinking is qualitatively different from that of adults. Central to this theory is the notion of egocentricity, which Piaget defined as a child's inability to perceive the perspectives of other people. Simply put, children cannot take the role of the Other, at least not until they are fairly well developed, and hence cannot be considered to be intellectually mature and responsible for their behavior, until they can approximate adult levels of thought. Social constructs such as race, ethnicity, gender and class are thought to require the development of higher-order ideas and are either absent from or indicative of imitative behavior in youngsters until about the age of seven.

Under developmental paradigms, children are assumed to be fairly isolated, their social experience limited primarily to contact with family. This is especially true for preschool age children. Thus, children's earliest experiences, which influence their basic development, are considered to reflect those of the immediate surroundings. Since they have little or no experience with the outside world, other than occasional forays to the market or church, they are limited in the scope and number of tools available to them for forming social ideas. These social tools are circumscribed by the family's social context, and

few children invent or discover alternative methods for understanding until they begin to have significant contact with society in contexts outside the home. For learning racism, then, children who are raised in a racism-free environment can safely be assumed to be free of racism. As they age and become more connected to the world they also begin to experiment with new ideas and forms of interaction.

Critics of cognitive and developmental models of child development point out that much of the research supporting these paradigms relies on experimental designs and individual orientations. Further, the theories themselves are deficit models, focusing on what children do not know rather than on what or how they do understand the world. Children are held in constant comparison to adult-centered standards, rather than being viewed as capable of creating and maintaining their own standards and understandings. Such research does not account for children's daily, lived experiences or for their own criteria on how racial and ethnic matters are used in social interaction. Typically, cognitive studies depend on psychological testing or experiments conducted under adult supervision. Children are shown pictures or read stories that represent stereotypical situations and are then questioned on their understanding of these pictures or stories. The goal is to determine whether children can successfully respond to the questions in a manner reflecting adult-level knowledge. These studies are useful for assessing children's level of development under the assumptions of age/stage progression, but they are not capable of gauging children's activities in the natural world.

A final note on cognitive developmental theories must draw attention to a contradiction apparent in much of this work. Generally, early experiences are considered to be critical for the development of later abilities. When learning to read, for example, experts insist that parents who read to their young children will encourage and develop in the children an orientation toward reading and learning that will last a lifetime, and there is some evidence to support this contention. Children have been seen as capable of developing complex, working hypotheses on social status, friendship, and religiosity, all highly social abstractions, at early ages. However, learning racism is not accorded the same significance. That is, early experience with racism is not considered consequential for the child's overall development.

When it comes to learning racism, also a highly abstract social construction, children remain na?ve and incapable.

Interpretive reproduction

Scholars using an interpretive reproduction perspective provide an alternative and significant influence in developing theories of racial and ethnic learning. That is, children rely on the meaning of social concepts to order their use of and responses to these concepts. This is a sociocentric orientation. Pioneering developmentalist William Corsaro and social psychologists Barry Troyna and Richard Hatcher propose that development is a process involving more than the solo individual. These researchers investigate the ways in which children of all ages construct their own cultures, incorporating many aspects of adult understandings of race and racism. In making sense of the collective contexts of children's learning and use of racial concepts, interpretive theories stress the social world as primary for human development. George Herbert Mead's idea of the "social mind" figures highly in this work, and posits that the ways in which we learn and develop are shaped by the social memory of past experiences and interpretations, both one's own and those of significant others. Interpretive approaches to studying racism center attention on the relationship between cultural, individual and generational levels of understanding. These relationships provide tools that both children and adults use to organize and conduct their lives. Those tools include racial and ethnic concepts.

Child development researchers have increasingly used the work of Lev Vygotsky. There are several components to Vygotskian theory that contribute to its usefulness in the sociological analysis of children's racial and ethnic relationships. Most importantly, Vygotsky proposed that social interaction precedes the development of the self. Most parts of a child's mental and conceptual development originates in actual social relations between individuals and relevant others or ideas. He also suggested that children's development does not proceed in a linear or straightforward manner, but rather that it progresses in "fits and starts," moving along rapidly at some times, regressing and stalling at others. The importance of social connections, context and development of mind cannot be exaggerated.

How children understand the world begins with their connections to the others in their lives.

This idea is stressed in the work of Maurice Halbwachs, who wrote on the formation and importance of the collective memory. According to Halbwachs, for almost all human beings, there is no possibility of being disconnected from the social world, as traditional developmentalists propose children must be. Human beings are constantly connected to others, and human experiences are perceived through the many lenses provided by these others. Nor are these connections limited to only those others with which we have immediate or personal contact. We rely on a wide variety of resources to inform our understandings, including mass media, language, family, play, and peers. We gather, interpret and adopt concepts that provide us with useful ways for negotiating the social world throughout our life span. These concepts include racism and ethnocentrism.

Race and ethnicity in early learning

The white majority in several developed nations is today less overtly racist than it was a few decades back, but many whites sill accept non-European Americans only on their own terms and in places and circumstances that whites determine. Racialized ideas and pressures remain a foundational aspect of American and other Western societies and affect people of all backgrounds in their interactive behavior and interpretations of racial-ethnic concepts. In the USA in particular, we remain a *de facto* deeply segregated society. Some significant change has occurred, but only in the past few decades, with deep-seated discriminatory attitudes and practices still in place. In surveys, many white Americans express racist beliefs and admit to racist behaviors. In-depth interviewing reveals that many hold prejudicial views in a deep and emotional way. American society remains separated in nearly all social realms, from housing and education to spirituality. An old saying suggests that the most segregated hour in America is at 11:00 am on Sunday mornings, when church congregations that are almost universally segregated by race meet to worship.

Recent research shows clearly that early learning includes race and ethnicity as crucial interactive and interpretive tools for children. These concepts inform much of children's social activity, from how children perceive themselves to how they select friends, explain social life and develop knowledge of racial hierarchies and power. From an early age, children are immersed in these societies where separation and mistrust dominate. In the course of their daily interactions they not only encounter a pervasive and informal system of racism, they also acquire the techniques of dealing with and understanding members of other racial and ethnic groups. Particularly important for the future is a way to understand the meanings of racial group membership and ethnicity in children's lives, and how they put these critical concepts to use. Racism and discrimination based on ethnicity are not fading societal realities but urgent, active and thriving ways of social life. Children's immersion in a social milieu that places such great emphasis on race must necessarily learn to both understand racism and to perpetuate it. The nature of everyday discourse and practice are laden with racial and ethnic meanings and children will make practical use of that discourse to create their social lives. Adult behaviors and attitudes, and our historical connections to centuries of discrimination, are a primary source of continuing racism. Efforts to eradicate racism, hence, must begin with a close examination of adult behavior and an attempt to cultivate a deeper insight into how our practices influence and perpetuate racism.

SEE ALSO: anthropology; Ebonics; education; epithet (racial/slang); ethnocentrism; language; media; prejudice; racialization; racist discourse; reading race; representations; segregation

Reading

The First R: How children learn race and racism, by Debra Van Ausdale and Joe R. Feagin (Rowman & Littlefield, 2001), uses a naturalistic observation technique to demonstrate the nature of race relations among American preschool children.
Gender Play: Girls and boys in school by Barrie Thorne (Rutgers University Press, 1993), while not specifically addressing racism, explores gendered practices among American elementary school children and is an excellent research model.
Interpretive Approaches to Children's Socialization by William A. Corsaro and Peggy J. Miller (Jossey-Bass Publishers, 1992) outlines the theoretical bases and methodological perspectives of interpretive reproduction in children's social relationships.
Racism in Children's Lives: A study of mainly-white primary schools by Barry Troyna and Richard Hatcher (Routledge, 1992) investigates the meaning

and construction of racist harassment in British primary schools.
"Racist thinking and thinking about race: What children know about but don't say," by D. Hughes (in *Ethos: Journal of the Society for Psychological Anthropology*, vol. 25: 117–25, 1997), examines the hidden nature of children's racist ideas and their efforts to keep their knowledge away from adult inquiry.

DEBRA VAN AUSDALE

CIVIL RIGHTS MOVEMENT

On December 1, 1955, Rosa Parks, a black seamstress, refused to give up her seat to a white man on a bus in Montgomery, Alabama. Her action was to prompt changes of monumental proportions in the condition of blacks in the USA. It provided the impetus for the most influential social movement in the history of North American race and ethnic relations.

Six months before the incident, the US Supreme Court had, in the *Brown* v. *Board of Education* case, reversed the 58-year-old doctrine of "separate but equal" after a campaign of sustained pressure from the National Association for the Advancement of Colored People (NAACP), which believed the issue of social equality rested on desegregating schooling.

Parks's refusal to surrender her seat resulted in her arrest, and this brought protest from black organizations in the South. The immediate reaction to the arrest was a black boycott of buses in Montgomery. So impressive was this action that it led to the formation of the Southern Christian Leadership Conference in 1957. This loosely federated alliance of ministers was the central vehicle for what became known collectively as the civil rights movement, or sometimes just "the movement." It was led by the Reverend Dr. Martin Luther King (1929–68), a graduate of Boston University who became drawn to the nonviolent civil disobedience philosophies of Gandhi. King was able to mobilize grassroots black protest by organizing a series of bus boycotts similar to the one in Montgomery which had eventually resulted in a Supreme Court ban on segregated public transportation.

Securing desegregation in education and obtaining black franchises were however more difficult, and King was made to mount a sustained campaign of black protest. Two laws in 1957 and 1960 aimed at ensuring the right of blacks to vote in federal elections were largely negated by the opposition of Southern states which actually made moves to reduce the number of black registered voters. Legal actions to desegregate schools were also foundering at state level as federal executive power was not widely available to enforce the law. By 1964 (ten years after the *Brown*case), less than 2 percent of the South's black students attended integrated schools.

At this point, King's movement was in full swing: boycotts were augmented with sit-ins (in streets and jails) and mass street rallies. As the campaign gained momentum, so did the Southern white backlash and civil rights leaders and their followers were attacked and many killed. By now John F. Kennedy was president, elected in 1960 with substantial black support. The first two years of his administration brought circumspect changes, but in 1963 Kennedy threw his support behind the civil rights movement, calling for comprehensive legislation to: (1) end segregation in public educational institutions; (2) protect the rights of blacks to vote; (3) stop discrimination in all public facilities. A show of support for the proposed legislation came on August 28, 1963, with a demonstration staged by some 200,000 blacks and whites. It was at this demonstration that King delivered his famous "I have a dream" speech.

The movement's campaign saw its efforts translated into results in the two years that followed. Following Kennedy's assassination, President Lyndon B. Johnson's administration passed acts in 1964 that extended the powers of the attorney general to enforce the prohibition of discrimination in public facilities and in 1965 to guarantee the right to vote (regardless of literacy or any other potentially discriminatory criteria). The latter piece of legislation significantly enlarged the black vote in the South and, in the process, altered the whole structure of political power, especially in Southern states.

But it was the former, the 1964 Civil Rights Act, that marked a dividing point in US race relations. Among its conditions were:

1   the enlargement of federal powers to stop discrimination in places of public accommodations;
2   the desegregation of all facilities maintained by public organizations (again with executive power to enforce this);
3   the desegregation of public education;
4   the extension of the powers of the Civil Rights Commission;
5   the prohibition of discrimination in any federally assisted program;
6   the total illegalization of discrimination in employment on the grounds of race, color, sex, or national origin;
7   the establishment of an Equal Employment Opportunities Commission to investigate and monitor complaints.

The Act was a comprehensive legal reformulation of race and ethnic relations and was due, in large part, to the sustained, nonviolent campaigns of the civil rights movement and the ability of King to negotiate at the highest political levels. The leader's assassination in Memphis on April 4, 1968 symbolized the end of the era of the civil rights movement, though, in fact, there had been a different mood of protest emerging in the years immediately after the 1964 Act. Whereas King and his movement brought, through peaceful means, tangible gains and a heightening of self-respect for blacks, the new movement was based on the view that no significant long-term improvements could be produced through working peacefully within the political system – as King had done. The alternative was to react violently to the system. For many, Black Power replaced civil rights as the goal for which to aim at.

SEE ALSO: African Americans; Ali, Muhammad; Black Power; *Brown v. Board of Education*; Cleaver, Eldridge; Gandhi, Mohandas Karamchand; Jim Crow; King, Martin Luther; law: civil rights, USA; Malcolm X; Nation of Islam; segregation

Reading

Black Civil Rights in America by Kevern Verney (Routledge, 2000) is perhaps the clearest, most accessible account of the origins and development of the civil rights movement, from the 1860s to the present; it may be read beneficially with other histories, *Freedom Bound: A history of America's civil rights movement* by Robert Lccisbrot (Plume, 1993) and *Debating the Civil Rights Movement, 1945–68* by Steven F. Lawson and James T. Patterson (Rowman & Littlefield, 1998), which focuses on influential figures in the struggle.

Eyes on the Prize: America's civil rights years, 1954–1965 by Juan Williams (Viking, 1987) is a companion volume to the brilliant Public Broadcasting System's television series of the same name; this may be read in conjunction with *Freedom: A photographic history of the African-American movement* (Phaidon, 2003) which tells the story of the struggle for civil rights through 550 images, edited by Sophie Spencer-Wood, with a concise text by Manning Marable and Leith Mullings.

The Making of Martin Luther King and the Civil Rights Movement by Brian Ward and Tony Badger (Macmillan, 1995) is an original reassessment of the movement, digging into the 1930s for its ancestry, evaluating its contemporary effects and making comparisons with the South African and British experiences.

CHECK: internet resources section

CLEAVER, ELDRIDGE (1935–98)

Author of *Soul on Ice*, one the most eloquent and provocative statements of black radicalism of the 1960s, Cleaver was, for a while, Minister of Information for the Black Panthers, the Oakland-based movement that advocated a revolutionary form of Black Power. Cleaver converted from Christianity to Islam, then to Marxism, before turning back to Christianity. He spent a total of nine years in prison for offenses ranging from drug dealing to rape. His career, in many respects, bears similarity to that of his peer and fellow radical Malcolm X.

Born in Wabbaseka, in rural Arkansas, Cleaver spent much of his early years on the streets of Los Angeles. His father was a waiter and night-club pianist, his mother a teacher. Both he and his mother received regular beatings from his father. Convicted on drugs and rape charges in 1953 and 1958, Cleaver was imprisoned. Whilst incarcerated, he underwent a tutelage of sorts and, in 1968, published what became a best-selling text. Paroled in 1966, Cleaver worked for the radical *Ramparts* publication and came into contact with Huey P. Newton and Bobby Seale, the founders of the Black Panther Party For Self-Defense. His involvement further shaped his political views, which were fused with Marxism and Freudian analysis.

While *Soul on Ice* is a passionately written diatribe against white society and one supported by a theoretical framework, its most provocative argument concerns the symbolic importance of rape. Cleaver had been convicted of rape and actually boasted of his deeds. For Cleaver, underlying white racism is sexual conflict. He believed that raping white women was a symbolic act of defiance, a kind of psychological emancipation.

Later, he recanted this position; though it was a huge factor in his notoriety.

Cleaver's notoriety was boosted further by his hatred of the police and his call to black people to kill them: "A dead pig is the best pig of all," he said. "We encourage people to kill them." Martin Luther King was killed the year of *Soul on Ice* was published and, in the following two years, the Black Panthers lost nineteen members at the hands of the police. Cleaver himself survived a shoot-out at his LA home. When charged for his part in a shooting, he fled the country, fearing that he would be killed if sent to prison. He left the USA in disguise, moving to Canada, then Cuba. Here he was accepted for his anti-American stance, though he soon tired of what he regarded as a different type of incarceration. Moving to Algiers, he was able to live on the royalties from his book, which became a best seller.

By 1972, he had become something of a political celebrity and was fe?ted when he moved to Paris. His illustrious guests included the playwright Jean Genet and the politician Roland Dumas. Complaining of restlessness, Cleaver left Paris for the C?te d'Azur, where he experienced a vision of Jesus in the process of a religious conversion.

Still wanted for his part in the 1968 shooting incident and for jumping bail, in 1976 Cleaver surrendered himself and spent eight months in prison before receiving a five-year probationary term and 2,000 hours of community service. He was later convicted of a cocaine violation. By this time, the radicalism of the 1960s had disappeared and Cleaver's fame – indeed infamy – had disappeared. During the 1980s, amid the revival of interest in 1960s black power, a resurgence of curiosity in Cleaver might have been expected. But, instead, new-found followers turned the legacy of Malcolm X into a virtual industry. In many ways, Cleaver's life parallels that of Malcolm X, moving from street crime to Islam and political radicalism.

In a rare interview in 1998, for PBS's *Frontline*, Cleaver reflected that, while the civil rights movement had gained access for black people to areas from which they previously had been excluded, "the burning issue right now is economic freedom and economic justice and economic democracy." Recanting his previous Marxist stance, he urged: "We [African Americans] have to be involved in owning and have an influence over the productive capacity of this country or else we are going to be perpetually dependent upon the largesse of those who rule." Black people who have acquired a degree of economic influence have "followed an assimilationist ethic," according to Cleaver (www.pbs.org/wgbh/pages/frontline/shows/race/interviews).

SEE ALSO: Ali, Muhammad; Black Panther Party; culturecide; ethnocide; Kerner Report; *Invisible Man*; King, Martin Luther; Malcolm X; Marxism; Nation of Islam; politics; power; riots: 1965–67, USA

Reading

The Shadow of the Panther: Huey Newton and the price of Black Power in America by Hugh Pearson (Perseus, 1995) is a history of the radical black movement in the 1960s, with an assessment of its impact.

Soul on Ice by Eldridge Cleaver (Delta, 1999) was first published in 1968 but remains a powerful read.

COLONIAL DISCOURSE

A concept employed as an alternative to forms of humanistic study, colonial discourse accentuates the role of domination, exploitation and disenfranchisement that is involved in the construction of any cultural artifact, including knowledge, language, morality, or attitude. Its sense derives from Foucault's analysis of power as exercised through discursive practices (speech, writing, knowledge – texts) as opposed to coercive force. So, the discourse is constituted by communicative and representational practices which are a form of power in themselves.

Interrogating the discourse reveals history as a palimpsest – as something on which original impressions are effaced to make room for further engravings, rather than a single narrative that describes reality. Discourse analysts are wont to examine or "read" the arts of description, in particular, literature. There is more involved than reading a text as a "reflection" of the discourse: in a sense, the text is made possible by the existence of the discourse. As Said writes: "References to Australia in *David Copperfield* or India in *Jane Eyre* are made because they can be, because British power (and not just the novelist's fancy) made passing references to these massive appropriations possible."

Colonial discourse redefines boundaries so as to "problematize" the ownership of the discourse. Fanon sought to treat metropolitan and colonial societies together, as discrepant but interconnected entities. And, following him, Bhaba asserts the unity of the "colonial subject," which includes both colonized and colonizer. This alerts us to the conflictual conqueror/native relationship, a Manichean struggle, in Fanon's phrase, and invites an investigation of how the discourse is held together using rules and codes that are observed by all.

JanMohamed distinguishes between "dominant" and "hegemonic" phrases of colonialism, the former characterized by the imposition of European military and bureaucratic control over native populations and the passive consent of natives. By contrast, the hegemonic phase involves the native population's internalization of the colonizers' entire complex of values, attitudes, and institutions. While the Europeans' covert aim was to exploit the natural resources of their colonies, the overt aim is to "civilize" the Other via subjugation. This is articulated in literature, which is a representation of a world at the boundaries of civilization.

Given its theoretical thrust, the role of individual properties, such as consciousness, motive or purpose, is superfluous. "Such is the power of colonial discourse that individual colonizing subjects are not often consciously aware of the duplicity of their position," write Bill Ashcroft *et al.*, stressing that "colonial discourse constructs the colonizing subject as much as the colonized." In other words, the discourse itself is the unit of analysis, not the human being. Humans are, on this account, creations more than creators of the colonial discourse.

A central idea informing colonial discourse analysis is that how we formulate or represent the past shapes our understanding of the present. By elevating the importance of the role of discourse in extending the imperial reach and solidifying colonial domination, we are better able to clarify the role played by culture (including aesthetics, ideas, values, and other items that have relative autonomy from the spheres of politics and economics) in perpetuating different kinds of domination in the postcolonial era.

SEE ALSO: diaspora; Fanon, Frantz; globalization; Hall, Stuart; hegemony; hybridity; Islamophobia; Other; postcolonial; race: as signifier; racist discourse; representations; subaltern; whiteness

Reading

"Colonial discourse" by Bill Ashcroft, Gareth Griffiths and Helen Tifflin, in their own introductory guide, *Postcolonial Studies: The key concepts* (Routledge, 2000), is a short essay and is the source of the quotation used in the main text above.

"The economy of the Manichean allegory" by Abdul R. JanMohamed, in *Race, Writing and Difference* edited by Henry L. Gates (University of Chicago Press, 1986), is one of several discussions on colonial discourses in the same book and may profitably be read in conjunction with another reader, *Colonial Discourse and Post-colonial Theory* edited by Patrick Williams and Laura Chrisman (Harvester Wheatsheaf, 1993).

Orientalism (Pantheon, 1978) and *Culture and Imperialism* (Vintage, 1994), both by Edward W. Said, luminously show how colonialism is not just an act of accumulation and acquisition: it is supported and perhaps impelled by ideological formations that include notions that certain territories and people *require* domination.

Power/Knowledge by Michel Foucault, edited by Colin Gordon (Harvester Press, 1980), is a selection of interviews organized around the theme suggested by the title; it is a useful primer for the Foucauldian approach.

COLONIALISM

From the Latin *colonia* for cultivate (especially new land), this refers to the practices, theories and attitudes involved in establishing and maintaining an empire – this being a relationship in which one state controls the effective political sovereignty of another polity, typically of a distant territory. This specific form has emerged over the past four centuries. While imperialism, from the Latin *imperium* for command or dominion, existed prior to this and was inspired by the belief in the desirability of acquiring colonies and dependencies, the particular practice of colonialism involved implanting of settlements on distant territories. This is the serviceable distinction between colonialism and imperialism offered by Edward Said in his *Culture and Imperialism* (Vintage, 1994), though Bill Ashcroft *et al.* argue that "European colonialism in the post-Renaissance [16th century onwards] world became a sufficiently specialized and historically specific form of imperial expansion to justify its current general usage as a distinctive kind of political ideology."

It is not possible to understand the complexities of race and ethnic relations without considering the historical aspects of colonialism, for many contemporary race relations situations are the eventual results of the conquest and exploitation of poor and relatively weak countries by metropolitan nations.

Following conquest, new forms of production were introduced, new systems of power and authority relations were imposed and new patterns of inequality, involving people of different backgrounds, languages, beliefs, and, often, skin color, were established. These patterns of inequality persisted for generation after generation.

In the colonial system, the more powerful, conquering groups operating from the metropolitan center, were able to extract wealth from the colonized territories at the periphery of the system by appropriating lands and securing the labor of peoples living in those territories. In extreme instances, this took the form of slavery, though there were what John Rex calls "degrees of unfreedom" less severe than slavery.

It was characteristic of colonialism that the conquering powers regarded the colonized peoples as totally unrelated to themselves. Their assumption was that the colonized were so different in physical appearance and culture that they shared nothing; they were Other. Racist beliefs were invoked to justify the open exploitation, the reasoning being that natives were part of a subhuman species and could not expect to be treated in any way similar to their masters. Even the less racist colonizers, such as Spain and France, held that, although the natives were human, they were so far down the ladder of civilization that it would take them generations to catch up. Racism, therefore, was highly complementary to colonialism (though it should be stressed that there are instances of racism existing independently of colonialism and vice versa, so there is no causal relationship between the two).

Colonization, the process of taking lands and resources for exploitation, has a long history. The great imperial powers (those countries acquiring colonies) were, from the sixteenth century, Spain, Portugal, Britain, France, and, to a much lesser extent, Holland and Denmark. These were quite advanced in navigation, agricultural techniques, the use of wind and water power, and the development of technology, so they possessed the resources necessary for conquest.

By 1750, all of South and Central America and half of North America were divided among these powers, with Britain the paramount force in North America. Britain's military might enabled it to conquer vast portions of India also, making its empire supreme; its conquests were successfully completed by white men with supposedly Christian ideals.

The interior of Africa remained for several hundred years untouched by the European empires because of the control of its northern coast, including Egypt, by dependencies of the Turkish empire and because of the prevalence of tropical diseases such as malaria in the center and south of the continent. The more accessible west coast of Africa, however, was comprehensively exploited, with Western Europeans establishing forts for slave trading right from Dakar to the Cape (Arabs had done similarly on the eastern coast). There was a triangular trade route involving Europe, West Africa, and the Americas (including Caribbean islands), so that a slave population was introduced to the Americas to supplement or even replace native Indian labor. An estimated fifteen million Africans were exported to the Americas, mostly from West Africa, but some from the east, in the late nineteenth century when the continent was divided up among France (which controlled 3.87 million square miles), Britain (2 million square miles), Belgium, Germany (both 900,000 square miles), Italy (200,000 square miles), Spain (80,000 square miles), and Holland (whose republic of Transvaal was subsumed in 1902 by British South Africa), leaving a mere 400,000 square miles of uncolonized territory.

European domination extended also to Australasia. The French, Portuguese, Spanish, and, especially, the Dutch made incursions in the sixteenth and seventeenth centuries and the voyages of Captain Cook in the 1770s led to the British occupation of Australia, New Zealand and Tasmania. Later, the Pacific islands of Fiji, Tonga, and Gilbert were absorbed in the British empire; other islands were taken by France and Germany, with some of Samoa, Guam, and Hawaii later being taken by the United States.

By about 1910, the "Europeanization" of much of the world was complete, with colonial rule extending over most of the globe – Russia held territories in Central and East Asia. Outside the zones of direct European control, the Turkish and Chinese empires were inhabited by paternalist European officials and merchants. Only Japan, Nepal, Thailand, Ethiopia, Liberia, and the rebel Caribbean island of Haiti were without European political direction.

The colonial structures of empire were maintained as they had been established: by military might. Despite this, it would be wise to recognize the pivotal parts played by missionaries in disseminating Christian ideas that were highly conducive to domination; for example, the basic concept of salvation encouraged colonized peoples to accept and withstand their domination and deprivation in the hope of deliverance in the afterlife, thus cultivating a passive rather than rebellious posture. This is not to suggest that the missionaries or their commissioning churches were deliberately engaging in some vast conspiracy. They were guided by the idea of a civilizing mission to uplift backward, heathen peoples and "save" them through Christianity. This was, indeed, as Kipling called it, the "white man's burden." Colonialism operated at many levels, crucially at the level of consciousness.

World War I did little to break the European colonial grip: Germany lost its African and other colonies, but to other European powers. After World War II, however, the empires began to break up with an increasing number of colonies being granted independence, either total or partial. Britain's empire evolved into a Commonwealth comprising a network of self-governing nations formerly of the empire; social and economic links were maintained, sometimes with indirect rule by Britain via "puppet" governments.

Colonialism worked to the severe cost of the populations colonized. For all the benefits they might have received in terms of new crops, technologies, medicine, commerce, and education, they inevitably suffered: human loss in the process of conquest was inestimable; self-sufficient economies were obliterated and new relationships of dependence were introduced; ancient traditions, customs, political systems, and religions were destroyed. In particular, Islam suffered inordinately: the military conquests of Africa simultaneously undermined the efficacy of the Islamic faith.

(The great imperial power of modern times was Russia: the Soviet area of control, whether through direct or indirect means, spread under communism to encompass countries in Eastern Europe, Cuba, and Afghanistan. Soviet systems did not, of course, operate slavery, but evidence suggests that their regimes were extremely repressive. The manipulation of consciousness, or "thought control," so integral to earlier colonial domination, was equally accentuated in Soviet systems.)

The basic assumption of human inequality that underlay the whole colonial enterprise has survived in the popular imagination and manifests itself in what has been called the "colonial mentality" (see *Introduction to Race Relations*, Barry Troyna and Ellis Cashmore, Routledge & Kegan Paul, 1983, chapter 1). The belief in the inferiority of some groups designated "races" has been passed down from one generation to the next and continues to underlie modern race relations situations. The colonial mentality which structures people's perceptions of others is a remnant of colonialism, but is constantly being given fresh relevance by changing social conditions.

SEE ALSO: Aboriginal Australians; Afrocentricity; antislavery; capitalism; colonial discourse; conquest; culturecide; emancipation; exploitation; Fanon, Frantz; Freyre, Gilberto; globalization; hegemony; ideology; internal colonialism; Irish; Las Casas, Bartolomí de; migration; Other; slavery; Third World; whiteness

Reading

"Colonialism" by Bill Ashcroft, Gareth Griffiths and Helen Tifflin, in their own guide, *Postcolonial Studies: The key concepts* (Routledge, 2000) is the source of the quotation in the main text above and contains the reminder: "No society ever attained full freedom from the colonial system by the involuntary, active disengagement of the colonial power until it was provoked by a considerable internal struggle for self-determination or, most usually, by extended and active violent opposition by the colonized."

Colonialism: An international social, cultural and political encyclopedia edited by Melvin E. Page (ABC-Clio, 2002) is a three-volume examination of all facets of colonialism.

Colonization: A global history by Marc Ferro (Routledge, 1997) is a thorough examination of the conditions under which colonies were built and may be read in association with Raymond Bett's *Decolonization* (Routledge, 1998) which looks at how the colonies achieved independence.

Globalization and the Postcolonial World: The new political economy of development, 2nd edn., by Ankie Hoogvelt (Palgrave, 2001), spends its first section, "Historical structures," discussing the colonial expansion and its structure of dependency.

COLOR LINE

The color line is that symbolic division between "racial" groups in societies where skin pigmentation is a criterion of social status. It is, of course, most clearly and rigidly defined in those societies which are most racist, that is, in societies that ascribe different rights and privileges to members of different racial groups. If access to social resources (such as schooling, housing, employment, and the like) is contingent on race, racial classification must be maintained and racial membership must be kept as unambiguous as possible. This is true even when racial discrimination is supposedly benign, as with affirmative action in the USA, for instance.

The simplest systems of racial stratification are the dichotomous ones, in which one is classified as either white or black, white or nonwhite, white or colored. An example is the USA, where any African ancestry places one in the social category of "Negro," "Black," "Colored," or "Afro-American" (to use different labels applied at different times to the same people). More complex systems have three groups, as do some Caribbean societies, with distinctions drawn between whites, mulattos, and blacks. South Africa under apartheid officially recognized four racial groups (Whites, Coloreds, Indians, and Blacks), but often lumped the three subordinate groups into the blanket category of nonwhite.

The color line may be more or less rigid. In some countries, for example some US states until 1967, interracial marriage was forbidden by law. In South Africa, both intermarriage and sexual relations between whites and nonwhites were criminal offenses subject to stiff penalties (up to seven years of imprisonment). To prevent "passing" (i.e. the surreptitious crossing of the color line), the South African government passed the Population Registration Act, providing for the issuance of racial identity cards and the permanent racial classification of the entire population.

Especially in societies that are virulently racist and attempt to maintain a rigid color line, the incentives for "passing" are great enough to encourage those whose phenotype is sufficiently like that of the dominant group to cross the color line. Even extensive "passing" does not necessarily undermine the color line. Indeed, "passing," far from defying the racial hierarchy, is a self-serving act of individual *evasion* of the color line. The very evasion implies acceptance of the system, a reason why "passing" is often resented more by members of the subordinate group for whom the option is not available than by members of the dominant group who are being infiltrated by racial "upstarts."

At the other end of the spectrum are societies where racial boundaries are so ambiguous and flexible that, even though they exhibit a good deal of racial consciousness, one may not properly speak of a color line. Brazil is an example of a country lacking any sharp breaking points in the continuum of color. Nobody is quite sure where whiteness ends and blackness begins.

SEE ALSO: affirmative action; apartheid; Brazil; caste; environmental racism; ethnic monitoring; Jim Crow; phenotype; reparations; South Africa; segregation; slavery; white race

Reading

Race Relations by Michael Banton (Tavistock, 1967) is a classic text on the subject, from a comparative sociological perspective.

Remembering Generations: Race and family in contemporary African American fiction by Ashraf H. A. Rushdy (University of North Carolina Press, 2001) suggests that the significance of the color line is reflected in particular types of literature that themselves impact on changing social circumstances.

Race Relations by Philip Mason (Oxford University Press, 1970) is a shorter account from a more historical point of view.

South Africa: A study in conflict by Pierre L. van den Berghe (University of California Press, 1967) is a detailed account of apartheid in South Africa.

PIERRE L. VAN DEN BERGHE

CONQUEST

Derived from the Roman *conquerere* (to seek or get), this refers to the acquisition and/or subjugation of a territory by force. Military conquest is the commonest origin of plural societies (societies composed of distinct ethnic or racial groups). It is also the most frequent origin of inequality between ethnic and racial groups. The other principal origin of plural societies is peaceful immigration, whether voluntary, semi-voluntary (e.g. indenture), or involuntary (e.g. slavery and penal colonies). Conquest, of course, is also a form of immigration, one in which it is the dominant group that enters and disperses to establish control over the natives. What is commonly meant by immigration, however, is a situation in which the dominant group is indigenous, and in which immigrants move in peacefully and disperse to assume a subordinate

position. Conquest and peaceful immigration lead to very different situations of race and ethnic relations.

Plural societies originating in conquest are frequently dominated by racial or ethnic minorities who exert their control through superior military technology and organization rather than numbers. Often ruled by minorities, such societies are typically highly despotic and characterized by sharp ethnic or racial cleavages and a large degree of legally entrenched inequality between ethnic groups.

Unlike in countries that owe their pluralism to peaceful immigration, conquest leads to relatively stable or slowly changing ethnic boundaries, largely because the conquered groups typically retain a territorial basis and remain concentrated in their traditional homeland. In contrast to immigrant groups who often disperse on arrival in their host countries, conquered groups, by staying territorialized, find it easier to retain their language, religion, and culture. Further, the dominant group often does not even seek to assimilate the conquered. So long as the conquered remain submissive and pay taxes, they are commonly left relatively undisturbed in running their daily affairs at the local level. They may even retain their native elite, under a system of indirect rule.

Two principal types of conquest can be distinguished, depending on the level of technology of the conquered. Where the natives belong to small-scale, stateless, thinly settled, nomadic groups of hunters and gatherers or simple horticulturists, the outcome is often their displacement by the invaders. Sometimes there is a definite policy of genocide, but often epidemic diseases, frontier warfare, and loss of a territorial basis for subsistence combine to bring about the destruction of native cultures as functioning groups, and the relegation of the remnants of their population to native reserves. In these "frontier" situations, which characterized countries such as Canada, the USA and Australia, the conquerors essentially replaced the indigenes, both territorially and demographically. The aboriginal societies were not only fragile and defenseless; their small numbers and their resistance to subjection made them virtually useless to the conquerors as a labor force.

Whenever the conquerors encounter a settled peasant population belonging to a stratified, state-level, indigenous society, however, the situation is very different. Initial resistance may be stronger, but, once control is achieved, the conquerors find an easily exploitable labor force (which often continues to be under the direct supervision of the collaborators from the former ruling class of the conquered groups). The result is exploitation rather than displacement. Examples are most traditional empires of Europe, Asia, Africa, and precolonial America, as well as most Asian and African colonies of Europe.

SEE ALSO: Aboriginal Australians; Africa; American Indians; bigotry; colonialism; culturecide; ethnocide; genocide; indigenous peoples; Other; race: as synonym; racist discourse; reparations; sexuality; slavery; South Africa

Reading

Ethnic Groups in Conflict by Donald Horowitz (University of California Press, 1985) is a study incorporating many case studies of ethnic conflict all over the world.

Imperialism After Imperialism by Bob Sutcliffe (I. B. Taurus, 2000) critically examines the concept of imperialism as a conceptual tool for understanding inequalities and conflicts.

Interethnic Relations by E. K. Francis (Elsevier, 1976) is a broad sociological treatment of ethnic and race relations, especially strong on Europe and North America.

Patterns of Dominance by Philip Mason (Oxford University Press, 1970) is much like the above, but more historical, and strongest on Asia and Africa.

PIERRE L. VAN DEN BERGHE

CONSERVATISM

As a political doctrine conservatism begins from a skepticism about the ability of human beings, acting within the constraints of consciousness, to understand the complexities of society. It follows that the only guide to governing society is *caution* in interfering with what is already established. This does not imply a hostility to change: conservatism accepts that societies must continually respond to circumstances; but the response should be anchored in custom, tradition, and established norms and values.

While this avoidance of change of a radical kind might be regarded as a timeless part of human disposition, conservatism acquired coherence as an intellectual doctrine in 1790 with

Edmund Burke's critique of the French Revolution and the rationalism (particularly the authority of individuals over privileged bodies such as church or government) that it extolled. Burke's *Reflections on the Revolution in France* countered the rationalist insistence on rebuilding entire societies in the spirit of innovation, as a break with the past: the present is never free from the past, Burke argued. Fundamental constituents of society, such as the state's legitimacy, are the product of traditions that stretch back for several generations.

This reverence for persistent structures, habits, and prejudices that have passed through generations has been a constant theme in conservative thought to the present day. (For Burke, "prejudice" refers positively to the wisdom and commonsense understandings that lie in tradition and which should not willingly be given up.)

Burke admired Adam Smith's *Wealth of Nations*, especially its arguments about the most effective means of preserving individual and communal liberties. The opposition to central governments' intercession and the respect for the free market as a "natural" mechanism continue to dominate conservative thought. Clearly, the free market generates inequalities and conservatives believe this is an inevitable consequence of protecting liberty. The inherent objective of equality is in a redistribution of unequally shared resources. According to conservative thought, this is not possible without violating individual (or familial) liberty, epitomized in the ability to own and protect property. Conservatives over the years have prioritized liberty over equality and have spurned any attempt to make such values seem compatible.

The state's role, as seen by conservatives, is to facilitate an environment that permits and even encourages freedom of competition, while protecting individual choice and freedom. One immediate consequence of this is a suspicion of state-initiated rules designed to regulate or control human behavior. In race and ethnic relations, this has prompted troublesome dilemmas. Civil rights, or race relations, legislation introduces norms intended to govern action. Affirmative action extends such government. But, while few doubt the necessity of the former in creating and protecting liberties, many remain mindful of Burke's remark, "Those who attempt to level, never equalize," when resisting affirmative action. Individual inequality and social hierarchy are vital to autonomy and, ultimately, a prosperous society. Removing such barriers to movement as segregation facilitates the freedom of opportunity so dear to conservatives. Yet, to reward on the basis of anything but merit is anathema.

Modern scholars, particularly Charles Murray and Thomas Sowell, have pointed out the baleful consequences of state policies to alleviate the condition of the poor – a group in which African Americans and Latinos are overrepresented. "We tried to provide more for the poor and produced more poor instead," Murray reflects on welfare programs, which, he argues, have destructive long-term effects in the shape of a chronically dependent underclass. In a similar vein, Sowell discounts all antidiscrimination laws and policies, instead blaming an alleged deficiency in African Americans for their continued impoverishment.

Support for moderate black political leaders (such as Douglas Wilder) and a disaffection with activists such as Jesse Jackson have led to a suspicion that ethnic minorities may be shifting towards conservatism. A study by the Center for Media and Public Affairs in 1986 reported a gap between blacks and organization-based leaders on several policy issues. Whether such a disillusionment will convert into conservatism is uncertain.

Modern black conservatives believe this is the case. Gary Franks, the first black Republican since 1937 to be elected to the House of Representatives, invoked Booker T. Washington to support the claim that "black economic nationalism" (as Washington called it) translates in practical terms to individual initiative, or self-help. Franks belonged to a faction of the black caucus that endorsed home ownership and entrepreneurial endeavor. The faction stresses the important distinction between desegregation, which was a matter to be tackled by social policy, and integration, which is a personal matter to be pursued by individuals.

The British Conservative politician Andrew Popat, who is of South Asian background, expressed his party's central values as: "Work, ambition, thrift, determination and the opportunity to get as far as your ability will take you."

SEE ALSO: affirmative action; capitalism; equality; Jackson, Jesse; merit; nationalism; politics; race: as synonym; Thomas, Clarence; tokenism

Reading

Black Politics in Conservative America by Marcus Pohlmann (Longman, 1990) looks in part at African Americans' allegiance to conservative politics; this might usefully be read in combination with Peter Eisenstadt's *Black Conservatism* (Garland, 1999).

A Critical Analysis of the Contributions of Notable Black Economists by Kojo A. Quartey (Ashgate, 2001) includes interesting essays on conservative and neo-conservative theorists, such as Thomas Sowell, Walter Williams, and Glenn Lowry.

Ideologies of Conservatism: Conservative political ideas of the twentieth century by E. H. H. Green (Oxford University Press, 2002) examines changes in conservative political thought.

Losing Ground by Charles Murray (Basic Books, 1984) and *Ethnic America* (Basic Books, 1981) by Thomas Sowell exemplify the intellectual conservatism in North American race relations, a trend roundly criticized by Thomas Boston in his *Race, Class and Conservatism* (Unwin Hyman, 1988).

CONSUMPTION

Consumption is the way we purchase and use goods that are available on the marketplace. Paradoxically, the *Oxford English Dictionary* offers two meanings of consumption that point to the utilization of products and five explications that point to destruction, evaporation, decay, and waste. This dual nature of consumption is reflected in the literature on the topic. On the one hand, authors such as Naomi Klein (in her *No Logo*, Flamingo, 1999) have written on the cultural alienation that results from industrial consumption, building on the earlier work of Frankfurt School scholars such as Theodor Adorno. On the other hand, students of culture have focused on how individuals use consumption to signal their identity, resist domination, and gain status. Both approaches are reflected in the research on the relevance of consumption for the study of race and ethnicity. Moreover, this research also focuses on consumption as a site for discrimination. This discussion centers on the three themes of *alienation*, *resistance* and *discrimination*, focusing on dominated racial and ethnic groups and on African Americans in particular. To conclude we will describe a more recent perspective that understands consumption as a site for the definition of collective identity of racial and ethnic groups.

Alienation

A large literature describes how dominated groups consume to compensate for oppression, exploitation, discrimination and humiliation: consumption offers immediate gratification and inclusion in mainstream society for affluent and not so affluent people. However, consumption also has negative consequences in that it erodes racial and ethnic solidarity and subordinates "uplifting the race" (or group) to private wealth accumulation. In his book *On the Edge: A history of poor black children and their American dreams* (Basic Books, 1993), Carl H. Nightingale offers a dreary account of how in the USA, inner-city black children define social integration by inclusion in the mainstream America mass market and hence compensate for the economic and racial exclusion they face in other parts of their lives. Marketing specialists devise advertising strategies to capitalize on this illusive and ultimately inefficient search for a compensatory identity. They produce images that equate personal worth with conspicuous consumption, which indirectly have devastating effects on the life of the inner city (e.g. the increasing number of clothing-related armed robberies, "sneaker murders," and the rise of violence between girls over jewelry). For Cornel West, market forces are threatening the very existence of black civil society as they produce a form of nihilism and meaninglessness (*Race Matters*, Beacon Press, 1993).

The affluent black middle class are similarly alienated and prone to engage in a desperate quest for status by means of consumption. In his *Black Bourgeoisie* (Free Press, 1957, 229–230), E. Franklin Frazier portrayed the black middle class of the 1940s and 1950s as "making a fetish of material things or physical possessions" to satisfy their longing for recognition and to "seek an escape in delusions involving wealth." However, "behind the masks," the black bourgeois struggled with insecurities and frustrations stemming from the futility of efforts to acquire membership in mainstream America, and with self-hatred and guilt for "elevating himself above his fellows." Today's "buppies" (upwardly mobile black professionals) are similarly described in the popular press as obsessed by consumption. They strive for career advancement and material wealth (designer wardrobes, elegant houses, furnishings, and fancy cars) to gain an ever-elusive

social acceptance, as their white counterparts often remain reluctant to acknowledge their status. As argued by Nelson George in his *Buppies, B-boys, BAPs and Bohos: Notes on post-soul black culture* (HarperCollins, 1992), consumption leads middle-class blacks to be doubly alienated, i.e. to be alienated from their own race as well as from mainstream society, in their pursuit of an ever-elusive integration. And indeed, poor and working-class blacks view the blossoming black bourgeoisie as preoccupied with conspicuous consumption, absorbed in egotistical pursuits, and drifting away from "uplifting the race." (see Michèle Lamont's *The Dignity of Working Men*, Harvard University Press, 2000).

The Frankfurt School's views on the perils of the "culture industry" and mass consumption have been applied to other racial and ethnic groups. Commodity fetishism is posited to generate "false consciousness" as people embrace the illusion that consumption will bring them fulfillment, just as they remain unaware of the inherent limitations of capitalism. At the same time, consumption and money are seen as intrinsically repressive forces, which precludes the possibility that individuals use them to transform their collective identity and improve their position in the hierarchy of status.

Resistance

Other writers understand consumption as a site where individuals express resistance and defiance to mainstream society and create and transform the meaning of commodity to suit their own purposes, against the dominant meanings provided for them by the advertising industry. This approach underplays the alienating forces of modern consumer culture and refocuses attention on the *polysemous* nature of commodities (in other words, they have many meanings). As described by Paul Willis (in *Common Culture*, Open University Press, 1990), consumer goods are "raw materials" for everyday creativity and consumption is an open-ended activity involving a great deal of interpretive freedom and negotiation rather than passive acquisition.

This perspective frames black consumption as "an active, celebratory process" whereby transfiguration of meaning is achieved by "blackening" mass-produced goods so as to subvert domination and contest their dominant, "mainstream" meaning (see Paul Gilroy's *There Ain't no Black in the Union Jack*, Hutchison, 1987). Black men and women who bleach their hair shades of blonde nowhere found in nature provide a handy example to this practice. Hip-hop culture, B-Boys and B-Girls (with their elaborately designed sneakers, gold chains, inverted baseball caps, and rap music) also poignantly illustrate the expressive use of consumption in contemporary black culture.

In *The Black Atlantic* (Harvard University Press, 1993), Gilroy also focuses on the use of consumption as a means of collective action within the black diaspora. For him, hip-hop culture in particular symbolizes a site of oppositional meaning and collective strength. It is a cultural practice that brings atomized individual consumers together and fosters collective action by generating an alternative public sphere. Thus Gilroy points to the potential link between the black empowerment movement and the mobilizing force of expressive black cultures through consumption. Similarly, in *A Consumer's Republic* (Knopf, 2003), Lizabeth Cohen offers an historical account of the significance of consumption in the civil rights movement. She underlines that blacks have associated their sense of citizenship with unrestrained access to consumer goods and services from the 1950s onwards. She also shows how the personal experience of indignity (or being "dissed") in everyday interactions and the political effectiveness of organized boycotts of stores, restaurants and buses in the struggle for desegregation, rendered the sphere of consumption a central scene of a social movement.

Discrimination

A third perspective on black consumption focuses on consumer discrimination and on the racialization of consumption. It describes how blacks encounter stereotypes (blacks are dangerous, without buying power, etc.) in shopping and how these stereotypes are enacted in the retail sector, often under the guise of security measures. An example is provided by Patricia Williams (in *The Alchemy of Race and Rights*, Harvard University Press, 1991), a distinguished black legal scholar and lawyer, who recalls how she was "buzzed out" of a Benetton store in New York City after the salesperson determined that she was an unpromising client, based on her racial characteristics only. Joe R. Feagin's (1992) large-scale study reporting on in-depth interviews with middle-class blacks suggests Williams's experience is not an isolated event, but is shared by an overwhelming majority of middle-class blacks. In fact, the incidence of discrimination is highest in commercial settings such as restaurants, retail stores, hotels, and banks, and it takes the form of poor service (or no service), excessive surveillance, or redlining. Consumption is a central site of discrimination and one that is particularly hurtful to blacks, because this discrimination sends the message that they are excluded from the American dream.

In this discrimination literature, a number of legal scholars also examine how blacks are taken advantage of in commercial transactions. In particular, Regina Austin explores how blacks' labeling as deviant legitimizes de facto limitations on their right to shop and sell freely. "It is assumed that blacks do not earn their money honestly, work for it diligently, or spend it wisely," writes Austin. "When blacks have money, they squander it and cannot save it. If blacks are cheated in the course of commercial transactions, it is because they cheat themselves either by being unsophisticated or incompetent consumers or by making it difficult for a decent ethical person to make profit from doing business with them. As a result, individual entrepreneurs feel perfectly justified in taking advantage of blacks as a means of privately policing or controlling blacks' spending malefactions."

Social identity

The social identity approach focuses on how ethnic and racial groups use consumption to define and signal their identity. In defining their identity, individuals must be able to differentiate themselves from others by drawing on criteria of commonality and a sense of shared belonging within their subgroup. This internal identification process must be recognized by outsiders for an objectified collective identity to emerge. Consumption plays a crucial role in internal and external definitions of collective identity. Virûg Molnûr and MichØle Lamont show that:

- cultural producers (here specifically, marketing specialists) identify and define categories of consumers, such as "the black consumer," which categories become objectified and shape the cultural tools available for the formation of collective identities;

- such cultural producers offer cues and cultural models to people about ways to achieve full social membership;
- individuals use consumption to signal aspiration to membership in symbolic communities (as citizens, middle class people, etc.); and
- consumers perform, affirm, and transform the social meaning attributed to specific collective categories (here, what is common to blacks, but also, eventually, to other racial and ethnic groups.)

The first two points address the social categorization process in the making, that is, the production of external definitions, while the latter two points address the role of consumption in the group identification process, – the production of internal definitions of collective identity.

Consumption is a particularly felicitous point of departure for examining the symbolic aspects of collective identity beyond the concern for the dynamic between internal and external processes. Indeed, its symbolic efficacy in "identity work" does not require that individuals be connected through networks and engage in face-to-face contact: It can operate either at the level of bounded subcultures, or at the level of widely shared cultural structures that exist beyond the enactment of specific interpersonal typification or ties. Consumption thus constitutes a useful lens for understanding how membership is acquired in symbolic communities (see Michèle Lamont's *The Dignity of Working Men*, Harvard University Press, 2000).

SEE ALSO: African Americans; beauty; black bourgeoisie in Britain; black bourgeoisie in the USA; cultural identity; dress; humor; inferential racism; institutional racism; racial coding; racialization; rap; segregation; stereotype; systemic racism

Reading

Common Culture: Symbolic work at play in the everyday cultures of the young by Paul Willis (Open University Press, 1990). Willis views consumer goods as instruments that can be employed to express resistance and defiance to mainstream society. Through use people can transform the meaning of commodities thereby counteracting the alienating force of modern mass consumer culture.

Consumer Culture and Modernity by Don Slater (Polity Press, 1997) surveys theories of consumer culture in relation to the rise of modernity. It investigates among other things the emergence of commercial

society, the relation between needs and social structures, the reproduction of social order, prosperity and progress, and changing identities in the post-traditional world.

"The continuing significance of race: anti-black discrimination in public places" by Joe R. Feagin (in *American Sociological Review*, vol. 56, 101–16, 1992) contests the widely held view that contemporary black middle-class life is substantially free of discrimination and shows that blacks remain vulnerable targets in public accommodations (large stores, restaurants) and other public places.

" 'A nation of thieves': securing black people's right to shop and to sell in white America" by Regina Austin (in *Utah Law Review*, vol. 1, 147–77, 1993) shows how blacks continue to be discriminated against when buying and selling goods and services.

"Social categorization and group identification: how African Americans shape their collective identity through consumption" by Virág Molnár and Michèle Lamont, in *Interdisciplinary Approaches to Demand and Its Role in Innovation* edited by Kenneth Green, Andrew McMeekin, Mark Tomlinson and Viven Walsh (Manchester University Press, 2002), presents the social identity perspective and contrasts it with the alienation, resistance, and discrimination perspectives.

VIRÁG MOLNÁR AND MICHÁLE LAMONT

COX, OLIVER C. (1901–74)

Cox was born in Trinidad and died in the USA. He studied law at Northwestern University and then continued these studies for a higher degree in law at the University of Chicago. While there, he contracted polio and the subsequent physical disabilities persuaded him that he would not be able to practice law. He chose to take a Master's degree in economics and then completed a Ph.D. in Sociology in 1938. Thereafter he became Professor of Sociology at Lincoln University, Missouri and, later, at Wayne State University.

Quantitatively, his main area of interest and writing was on the nature of capitalism as a system. This is evident in his following major publications: *The Foundations of Capitalism* (New York, Philosophical Library, 1959) and *Capitalism as a System* (New York, Monthly Review Press, 1964). The nature of capitalism and its evolution from the feudal system of Europe was the subject matter of one of his later articles, "The problem of social transition" (in *American Journal of Sociology*, vol. 79, 1120–33, 1973). However, his name is known primarily through renewed interest in the 1960s and 1970s in his earlier book *Caste, Class, and Race* (Doubleday, 1948; reprinted in 1959 and 1970 by Monthly Review Press). This became both the object of attack by radical "black" sociologists in the United States and of admiration by Marxist and leftist writers in Britain. The former regarded Cox as an assimilationist on the strength of some of the claims made in this text. The latter interpreted the text as the "classic" Marxist analysis of the origin of racism and of the relationship between class and "race." Both groups were referring to a text which was a product of an earlier time and set of concerns. Moreover, Cox's claims and predictions from that earlier time were contradicted by the events of the 1960s, leaving him, so others have observed, a lonely and disillusioned man.

Much of Cox's work was influenced by the writings of Marx, and this is clearly evident in *Caste, Class, and Race.* In this text, he defends two main contentions. First, he argued that "race relations" cannot be reduced to caste relations and so the text develops an extensive critique of W. Lloyd Warner and John Dollard. Second, he argued that what he preferred to define as "race prejudice" (he rejected the term racism) was not a natural phenomenon but was a direct consequence of the development of capitalism, from which he concluded that a solution to the "race problem" could be found only in the transition from capitalism to a democratic and classless society. It was in developing this second argument that Cox attempted to set out a detailed theoretical and historical account of the relationship between class and "race."

When viewed historically, Cox's text, published in 1948, was significant because it attempted to reassert the significance of Marxist categories of analysis in a context which was, to say the least, unfavorable to Marxism. This should be recognized, even when one goes on to argue that Cox's use of some of the Marxist categories was grounded in what would now be regarded as a very limited selection of Marx's work. Indeed, the way in which the concept of class is defined and employed has led others to argue that the work cannot easily be regarded as being within the Marxist tradition. Cox's tenuous relationship with Marxism is confirmed by the aforementioned article in the *American Journal of Sociology* of 1973, which is concerned with the transition from feudalism to capitalism and which makes no reference to the new classic Marxist contributions of M. Dodd and P. Sweezy, let alone vol. 1 of Marx's *Capital.*

SEE ALSO: capitalism; caste; Cleaver, Eldridge; colonialism; Dollard, John; empowerment; Fanon, Frantz; Hall, Stuart; Marxism; Myrdal, Gunnar

Reading

Caste, Class, and Race by Oliver C. Cox (Monthly Review Press, 1970), despite later criticisms, remains a challenging contribution when viewed historically.

"Class, race, and ethnicity" by Robert Miles in *Ethnic and Racial Studies* (vol. 3, no. 2, 169–87, 1980) is a critical analysis of Cox's attempt to theorize a relationship between class and "race."

The Idea of Race by Michael Banton (Tavistock, 1977) locates Cox's later work and criticizes it in the context of an analysis of the tradition of "race relations" analysis.

ROBERT MILES

CREOLE

A distinct culture produced as the result of the merging of two or more other cultures. It was originally taken from the Portuguese *crioulo*, meaning a slave brought up in the owner's household; the word became *criolli* in Spanish and *creole* in French, and came to take on a particular meaning in the state of Louisiana in the early 1800s. After the Louisiana Purchase of 1803, those of French and Spanish descent called themselves creoles as if to distinguish themselves culturally from Anglo-Americans who began to move into Louisiana at that time. The creoles evolved their own distinctive styles of cuisine, music and language. The term later came to refer to the group of "coloreds," that is, the products of miscegenation (black and white mixture). They were a self-conscious ethnic group who regarded themselves as different and separate. Based in New Orleans, they spoke French and developed their own educational institutions, such as Xavier University.

In a Caribbean context, creole referred originally to the descendants of Europeans who were both born and lived in the Caribbean; it was also used to distinguish a West Indian-born slave from an African one. Those born in the islands developed their own dialects, music and culture, and the word creole came to mean anything created anew in the Caribbean (it probably stemmed from the Latin *creara* for "created originally"). Thus particular dishes, dialects, art forms, etc. were known as creole, and this denoted something very positive and original.

Nowadays, the term creole describes homegrown qualities exclusive to ethnic groups, particularly in language and dialect.

SEE ALSO: amalgamation; hybridity; indigenous peoples; kinship; miscegenation; multiracial/biracial; phenotype

Reading

Ten Generations by Frances J. Woods (Louisiana State University Press, 1972) is the life story of an extended family of American creoles, who were something of an elite.

West Indian Societies by David Lowenthal (Oxford University Press, 1972) defines creole culture as based on a past history of slavery and a present legacy of color, and covers the whole development of creole culture. Less impressive, but still useful in this context, is Eric Williams's *From Columbus to Castro: The history of the Caribbean, 1492–1969* (Deutsch, 1970).

Jamaica Talk by Frederic G. Cassidy (Macmillan, 1969) is an interesting study of possibly the most important element of creole cultures: language.

CROSS-CULTURAL CONFLICT *see* ethnic conflict

CULTURAL DIVERSITY *see* multiculturalism

CULTURAL IDENTITY

The stable conception that a subject has of him- or herself as an individual is an identity. Cultural identity defines a junction between how a culture defines subjects and how they imagine themselves. Beyond this basic definition, there are two main versions of cultural identity. According to Hall, whose 1990 essay "Cultural identity and diaspora" did much to prompt interest in the term, the more conventional rendering of cultural identity is framed in terms of a collective "one true self" which people with a shared history and ancestry have in common and which is preserved through changes of fortune and the vicissitudes of history.

Cultural identity, in his sense, is a stable, consistent feature that unifies people, particularly during periods of struggle. Its relevance to colonized and oppressed populations is clear: it has been a powerful instrument in solidifying marginalized groups, especially in their resistance to colonial regimes and the values those regimes sought to impose. In the postcolonial era, cultural identity has brought to the fore continuities, a hidden history obscured by the colonial experience.

Representation has played an active part in constituting and perpetuating this unifying sense of self and collectivity. Hall specifies the importance of *nígritude* which offered images and visions of an Africa that lay at the center of all black people's cultural identity and provided meaning by restoring an imaginary fullness or "plenitude to set against the broken rubric of our past." Poetry, paintings and other representational forms sustained this.

The second, related conception of the term recognizes that, as well as the multiple similarities that unite groups, there are also deep and significant differences that shape not only what people have been, but what they have become. The ruptures and discontinuities that fragment populations are as important as the common experiences that unite them. "Cultural identity, in this second sense, is a matter of 'becoming' as well as of 'being'," writes Hall, highlighting how this conception avoids the assumption of an *essence* that remains inviolate. Cultural identity is not an unchanging spirit on which history has made no mark, but a set of unstable points of identification, constructed through a combination of memory, fantasy and myth. In other words, cultural identity is, in Hall's words, a "positioning" – a fluid arrangement, or configuration that is always in motion.

This is especially important when considering diasporic populations that are dispersed, yet feel as if they belong to a unified whole, or what Benedict Anderson calls "an imagined community," which may or may not be genuine – their reality is in the imagination. "Diaspora identities," is Hall's phrase to capture the manner in which, for example, Caribbean identities are framed along two axes, those axes being similarity/continuity and difference/rupture. His point is that slavery, transportation and colonization cut off disparate and diverse people from their pasts and, paradoxically, unified them. Difference persisted in and alongside continuity. The boundaries of difference are continually being repositioned in relation to different points of reference. For instance, Caribbeans in the developed West may remain similar to each other, sharing commonness of experiences; at the same time, Jamaicans and Martiniquans differ profoundly culturally and historically and those differences are as much part of their cultural identities as their similarities.

Every diasporic group has negotiated its particular relationship to "Otherness" and this too is inscribed in its cultural identity. Some groups remain at the economic and political margins, while others have made inroads. Yet this difference is never permanent: it is contingent on circumstances and, as such, is endlessly changing. Hall uses Derrida's concept of *diffirance* in this context. The term is suspended between the two French verbs to differ and to defer. "Diaspora identities are those which are constantly producing and reproducing themselves anew, through transformation and difference," says Hall.

How we think about ourselves is always "enunciated." This is an unusual use of the word enunciate, which means to express in definite terms (*nuntiare* is Latin for announce), and refers to the point that "We all write and speak from a particular place and time, from a history and a culture which is specific." Hall encourages, "instead of thinking of identity as an already accomplished fact ... we should think, instead, of identity as a 'production' which is never complete, always in process.

In contrast to psychological interpretations of identity, many of which begin from the premise of a stable "core" that provides a fixed concept of self, cultural identity is fashioned by history, by circumstance, and by the mode of thinking that prevails in any collectivity.

SEE ALSO: Anglo-Indians; culturecide; diaspora; double consciousness; essentialism; ethnic conflict; ethnocide; ethnonational; Fanon, Frantz; Hall, Stuart; hybridity; *Invisible Man*; *nígritude*; Other; post-race; whiteness

Reading

"Cultural identity and diaspora" by Stuart Hall, in *Identity: Community, culture, difference* edited by J. Rutherford (Lawrence & Wishart, 1990), is now accepted as classic statement on cultural identity

Diaspora and Visual Culture: Representing Africans and Jews, edited by Nicholas Mirzoeff (Routledge, 2000), takes an interesting approach to cultural identity and one which is consistent with Hall's second conception, exploring the manner in which diaspora have been visualized in art and how this both reflects and affects the experience of being part of a diaspora.

Imagined Communities: Reflections on the origin and rise of nationalism by Benedict Anderson (Verso, 1983) is the much-quoted treatise that outlines the ways in which communities, far from being territorial, encompass the globe.

The Making of the English Identity by Krishan Kumar (Cambridge University Press, 2003) is a detailed historical account of how the notion of Englishness evolved; as such it presents an illuminating case study of cultural identity in process, changing shape and content in response to changing circumstances. While the author challenges essentialist notions of cultural identity, he spurns purely theoretical models of identity, rooting his own analysis in evidence.

CULTURAL RACISM

On the surface, this term is an oxymoron in that it couples two seemingly contradictory expressions: "cultural" suggests the possibility of variation, transformation and exchange, while "racism" is predicated on the idea of permanence, separation and the improbability, if not impossibility, of change. In many senses, racism proposes that culture is actually determined or strongly influenced by "race." Despite these apparent contradictions, the term refers to a conceit: a way of disguising racist thought and behavior by phrasing it in a way that precludes reference to biological or psychological differences or indeed any of the indicators associated with what might be called, in the absence of a more appropriate term, orthodox racism. Racism, it should be remembered, does not necessarily involve the concept of race: it may have functional equivalents, culture being one of them.

The recent origins of cultural racism may lie in what Martin Barker called in the title of his 1981 book *The New Racism* (Junction Books). Barker advanced the view that the political rhetoric and action of the Conservative government of Britain (and, presumably, the USA) of the period were geared to the concept of a "way of life" that was threatened by "outsiders." As Barker summarized: "Human nature is such that it is natural to form a bonded community, a nation, aware of its differences from other nations ... feelings of antagonism will be aroused if outsiders are admitted." Barker argued that the roots of the new racism lay in the resentment stirred by Enoch Powell's speech of 1968, but flourished with Margaret Thatcher, who, as Prime Minister, famously declared: "The British character has done so much for democracy, for law and order and so much throughout the world that, if there was any fear that it might be swamped, people are going to react and be hostile to those coming in."

On this account, the form of racism that proliferated from the late 1960s was not based on the view that genetic or biological differences exert decisive effects on a person's aptitudes, capabilities, competencies and other attributes. It involved the acceptance that *there are* differences, but that these interact with other factors to influence individual or group propensities. Those other factors might typically include class, family, education, geographical and social environment, work experiences and so on – in other words, cultural context. This is the supposition on which a cultural version of racism is based.

Instead of maintaining that race *causes* differences that manifest in social behavior, this form of racism proposes that those very behavioral differences are themselves causes. Far from being susceptible to change, the cultural differences are as unbridgeable as racial differences. At the simplest level, a mother may object to her daughter's marriage to an Asian, not ostensibly on racial grounds, but because she insists that his upbringing makes him incompatible with her. He may have been socialized in a Sikh tradition and, as such, upholds particular kinds of values and beliefs that her daughter will not share. Ignoring the countless commonalties of background, experience, interests as well as values that the couple *will* share, the mother opts only to see what she regards as differences. This kind of selective focus implicates her in a prejudicial reading or interpretation of the situation that is tantamount to racism.

This type of reasoning and reaction seemed to appear in early twenty-first century Europe when attacks on those seeking asylum from, among other places, Afghanistan, Kosovo and Albania, were commonplace. Often, those opposing the presence of asylum seekers would emphatically deny racist motivations or intent, pointing out what they regarded as the unfairness of a system that allowed the inflow of those escaping persecution to claim refuge, as well as accommodation and living allowances, while taxpaying nationals, were not entitled to such provisions. Such reasoning invoked the language of migration discourse with its attendant denotations of parasitism, fraud and dishonesty. But there was no evidence of racial thinking, nor, for that matter, of any coherent theory or even conjecture: just a disposition to confront others suspected of being part of an unwanted population.

Even ostensibly non- or antiracist postures can secrete this form of repugnance. Those who uphold, defend and advocate cultural diversity

may encourage, for example, an acceptance of diverse institutions, such as arranged marriages or female circumcision. They may also harbor understandings of the cultural practices as obdurate and grounded in some unyielding "way of life" that remains permanent despite changing circumstances. In other words, the tendency to essentialize differences (envisage them as changeless structural features of a group, or class of people) actually undermines the attempt to steer clear of more overt forms of racism. The irony of these two examples is that, in the first, there is no evidence that the hostile party was prepared to reason through its actions to the point where there was speculation about the permanence (or impermanence) of cultural differences; in the second, there are grounds to suspect that the advocate of cultural diversity may well have reflected on cultural variation. Yet the consequences of the first have all the hallmarks of racist violence and exclusion, while those of the second are intended to further inclusiveness.

Often, racist motivations are imputed to hostile groups which only *appear* to harbor racist beliefs and sentiments, but who, on closer examination, are aroused by vague feelings of enmity against vaguely defined Others. Islamophobia, for example, was a term invoked to capture the antagonism toward Muslims, particularly after September 11, 2001. Yet, the rancor that followed the attack on the World Trade Center was not directed at Muslims: it was a more diffuse reaction against anyone or anything that was assumed to have some connection, no matter how spurious, to Islam (Hindu temples were attacked, as were many people of various faiths).

Do anti-Muslim sentiments, no matter how indefinite, qualify as cultural racism? Certainly, their effects are indistinguishable from those motivated by racism. In the absence of racist thinking by Islamophobes, it could be argued that their actions were functional equivalents of racism.

Racism does not lie dormant in every kind of culture at every stage in history, as if waiting to be activated by the right constellation of circumstances. Racist thinking and its behavioral consequences involve perhaps covert assumptions and conjectures about how the world's human population divides naturally into distinct groups, and how some of those groups are either destined to remain part of the lower orders, or should be pushed into those stations. One argument of those who defend the analytical value of the concept of cultural racism would be that any instance of assault on or exclusion of others designated as different is founded on racism. This may not be clear or overt, but deep down the assailants must entertain ideas that qualify as racist in the cultural sense.

Feelings of revulsion and tendencies to exclude, repel and oppose, qualify as cultural racism because they are given shape and coherence by beliefs, however imprecise, about the nature of the target. The fact that those beliefs will almost certainly change over time does not affect their qualification as culturally racist.

Understanding cultural racism in this extremely fluid and inclusive manner gives it analytical value in anatomizing episodes of conflict in which neither side subscribes to racist beliefs. Yet there are problems of extension. One obvious implication is that a loathing of, for example Scousers (people from Liverpool) or Okies (from Oklahoma), seems to approach qualification. And the antipathy of gangs of British soccer fans, who regularly engage in collective violence, certainly has a case. In all instances, the adversaries see their targets as irredeemably different, and this may, in itself, justify conflict and expulsion.

Defenders of a more exclusive conception of racism argue that the interpretation of these types of conflict in racist terms not only trivializes racism, but removes the element of white power, a power that has its historical sources in European imperialism. Logically, various forms of conflict, including conflict between ethnic minorities, are episodes of cultural racism: they are often based on the presumption that one group is culturally inferior to another, or perhaps just on perception of alterity (or "Otherness"). Ideologies of whiteness have no place in this type of conflict, even though they may carry the supposition that there is a natural correspondence of culture and superiority/inferiority.

The lexicon of racism has already been stretched by institutional racism and inferential racism (some terms, such as "camouflaged racism," as coined by Douglas Glasgow in his analysis of *The Black Underclass*, Jossey-Bass, 1980, have withered). The incorporation of cultural racism may serve the interests of analytical precision, but may also push the application of racism into much more general arenas of disunity.

SEE ALSO: bigotry; colonial discourse; culture; environmental racism; ethnocentrism; ethnonational; inferential racism; institutional racism; Islamophobia; One Nation; Other; Powell, J. Enoch; racist discourse; whiteness

Reading

The Clash of Civilizations: Remaking of world order by Samuel P. Huntington (Touchstone, 1999) provides a different perspective on the role of culture in superseding other sources of conflict; "civilizations," are cultural entities, the main antagonists of the future being Islam and the West, predicts Huntington.

Mistaken Identity: Multiculturalism and the demise of nationalism in Australia, 2nd edn., by Stephen Castles (Pluto, 1990), uses the term "covert racism" which seems to approximate cultural racism, and which is "based on the proposed incompatibility of certain cultures."

The New Racism by Martin Barker (Junction Books, 1981) is the book that described what the writer believed were new forms of racism that appeared beginning in the 1960s.

The Recovery of Race in America by Aaron David Gresson (University of Minneapolis Press, 1995) suggests that " 'racism' is a nearly defunct *topos*" but shows how that the meaning of "behavior called racist ... has become negotiable;" people can publicly disavow racism, yet still effect strategies that effectively maintain white supremacy.

CHECK: internet resources section under racism

CULTURE

Defined by Sir Edward Tylor in 1871 as, when "taken in its wide ethnographic sense," being "that complex whole which includes knowledge, belief, art, morals, law, custom and any other capabilities and habits acquired by man as a member of society." Since then, definitions have proliferated with little if any increase in precision. Sir Raymond Firth has written that "If ... society is taken to be an organized set of individuals with a given way of life, culture is that way of life. If society is taken to be an aggregate of social relations, then culture is the content of those relations. Society emphasizes the human component, the aggregate of people and the relations between them. Culture emphasizes the component of accumulated resources, immaterial as well as material."

In the USA in particular, culture is regarded as possibly the most central concept of anthropology as a discipline, but it has not been built into the sort of theoretical structure that can cause it to be defined more sharply for use in the formulation of testable hypotheses. Whereas it may be convenient to refer to say "Japanese culture" and its characteristics, and to recognize subcultures within such a unit, it is usually impossible to conceive of cultures as having clear boundaries. It is therefore impracticable to treat them as distinct and finite units that can be counted. Cultures tend to be systems of meaning and custom that are blurred at the edges. Nor are they usually stable. As individuals come to terms with changing circumstances (such as new technology), so they change their ways and shared meanings change with them.

It is important to bear in mind these limitations to the explanatory value of the culture concept when considering its use in the educational field. It is argued that the curricula for all subjects should be reviewed to ensure that schools make the maximum possible contribution to the preparation of children for life in a multiracial world, and in a society that includes groups distinguished by race, ethnicity and culture. At present there is a tendency to use the name "multicultural education" as an official designation for programs directed to this end, though the names multiracial and multi- or polyethnic education are favored by some people.

All these names are open to the objection that there is no finite number of stable constituent units. The use of "culture" in this connection is questionable since advanced technology is so readily identified with culture of the First World, the West. The culture of people living in India and Trinidad has many features in common with the culture of England – cars, radios, books, and so on – but the things taken to represent the cultures of Indians and Trinidadians tend to be festivals, songs, and recipes. This trivializes the culture of the people who live in those societies as much as it would were English children told that their culture was exemplified by Guy Fawkes Night, Morris dancing, and custard. It might be better to talk of education for cultural diversity were it not so difficult to know how much is desired in comparison with the traditional educational aims of literacy and numeracy.

SEE ALSO: amalgamation; anthropology; Boas, Franz; bigotry; consumption; cultural identity; cultural racism; culturecide; ethnicity; ethnocentrism; ethnonational; indigenous peoples; kinship; pluralism

Reading

Culture: A critical review of concepts and definitions by A. L. Kroeber and Clyde Kluckhohn (Peabody Museum Papers, 1952) has a systematic review of definitions; while *Culture and Society: A sociology of culture* by Rosamund Billington, Sheelagh Strawbridge, Lenore Greensides and Annette Fitzsimons (Macmillan, 1991) is a clear introduction.
Elements of Social Organization by Raymond Firth (Watts, 1952) is the source of the two definitions of culture quoted in the main text above.
Theories of Culture in Postmodern Times by Marvin Harris (AltaMira, 1998) reviews theories and opinions on the nature of culture and its relevance.

MICHAEL BANTON

CULTURECIDE

Culturecide, referred to also as *cultural genocide* or *deculturation*, signifies processes that have usually been purposely introduced and that result in the decline or demise of a culture, without necessarily resulting in the physical destruction of its bearers. These same processes have also been termed *ethnocide*, though some authorities insist that that concept should be applied only when there is also a deliberate attempt at the physical liquidation of the cultural bearers, as well as cultural eradication.

There is also a close affinity with the concept of *genocide*, which under the terms of the Genocide Convention 1948 refers to specified acts that are undertaken with the objective of destroying, in whole or in part, members of a national, ethnic, racial, or religious group, as such. During the drafting of that convention by the Division of Human Rights of the United Nations there was some debate as to whether or not "cultural genocide" should be incorporated. Raphþel Lemkin, the originator of the concept *genocide*, was one of the three experts consulted regarding the draft. He argued that a group could not continue to exist "unless it preserves its spirit and moral unity," and that the destruction of cultures was "as disastrous for civilization as was the physical destruction of nations." The general consensus appears to have been, however, that the inclusion of cultural destruction in the convention would divert attention away from its main purpose, namely, the prevention of the physical destruction of groups, and would also make securing agreement more difficult, if not impossible.

This, however, has not prevented various authorities from continuing with this line of argument, noting that the same objective – the eradication of a group of people differentiated by some distinct traits, such as ethnicity, race, religion, language, nationality, or culture – can be achieved just as effectively in the mid- to long-term, by gradual processes, as it might be by immediate physical liquidation. Consequently, the boundaries between culturecide, ethnocide, and genocide remain conceptually porous. This is frequently manifested in the experiences of the same group being described by different authorities using the terms culturecide, ethnocide, or genocide.

Culturecide is most often used to describe the experiences of many indigenous peoples. As Arens notes, deculturation "can involve some or all of the following: political and social institutions, culture, language, national feelings, religion, economic stability, personal security, liberty, health and dignity." Diverse authorities have noted the impact of policies implemented by colonizing powers on native populations. Churchill, commenting on the long history of policies pursued in the USA and Canada, noted that it was

> readily observable that both nations consistently engaged in what has been openly termed as "assimilationist policies" directed at indigenous populations within their borders. Aspects of these policies have and in many instances still include the legal suppression of indigenous religions and languages, the unilateral supplanting of indigenous governmental forms, the compulsory "education" of indigenous youth (often entailing their forced transfer

to "boarding schools") in accordance with the cultural and religious mores antithetical to their own ... Such policies make perfect sense when it is understood that the stated objective of forced assimilation is to bring about the complete dissolution of the targeted groups as such, causing their disappearance ("death") as individual members are absorbed into "mainstream society," they are but clinical descriptions of the process of cultural genocide.

The same argument has been laid in relation to the experiences of many other indigenous peoples.

SEE ALSO: Aboriginal Australians; assimilation; culture; Doomed Races Doctrine; ethnic cleansing; ethnic conflict; ethnocide; genocide; Holocaust; human rights; indigenous peoples; International Convention; Irish; language; UNESCO; United Nations

Reading

"East Timor: a case of cultural genocide," by J. Dunn, in *Genocide: Conceptual and historical dimensions*, edited by G. J. Andreopoulos (University of Pennsylvania Press, 1994) is a case study; as is *Tears of Blood: A cry for Tibet* by Mary Craig (HarperCollins, 1992).

"Genocide: toward a functional definition," by Ward Churchill, in *State Crime, Volume I: Defining, delineating and explaining state crime* edited by D. O. Friedrichs (Ashgate, 1998), discusses conceptual issues.

Genocide in Paraguay, edited by R. Arens (Temple University Press, 1976), is the source of the quotation in the main text above on "deculturation."

STUART STEIN

D

DARWINISM

Charles Darwin's influence upon the history of racial thought was profound. His demonstration of the mutability of species destroyed the doctrines of the racial typologists who assumed the permanence of types. He showed the debate between the monogenists and polygenists to be scientifically unproductive. He introduced a new conception of "geographical races, or subspecies" as "local forms completely fixed and isolated." Because they were isolated they did not interbreed and so "there is no possible test but individual opinion to determine which of them shall be considered as species and which as varieties." Darwin (1809–82) made no attempt to classify human races, observing that the naturalist has no right to give names to objects that he cannot define. As is to be expected, there are weaknesses in Darwin's work: he thought that acquired characteristics might be inherited; he believed that inheritance was an equal blending of parental characters, etc. Such problems were resolved when the scientific study of genetics became possible. As Jacob Bronowski once wrote, "The single most important thing that Charles Darwin did was to force biologists to find a unit of inheritance." Not until the statistical reasoning of population genetics had taken the place of the typologists' dream of pure races were the implications of Darwin's revolution for the understanding of race fully apparent.

Darwin's thought can be better understood if it is seen as combining several strands. Ernst Mayr distinguished five. In the first place, by assembling and ordering so much evidence of continuous change in the natural world, Darwin advanced a more convincing case for evolution than his predecessors had done. Secondly, he was the first author to postulate that all organisms have descended from common ancestors by a continuous process of branching; this constituted a theory of common descent. Thirdly, he insisted that evolution was a gradual process producing many forms intermediate between geographical varieties and species. Fourthly, he maintained that evolution is the result of natural selection, supplemented in some species by the process of sexual selection.

The theory of evolution proper does not depend upon acceptance of Darwin's argument about selection as its cause, or upon any assumption that evolution is gradual, or that selection is sufficient to explain speciation. It is a general theory that is used to generate falsifiable hypotheses.

Darwin's theory was at first the less convincing because it did not account for the origin of life and for the genetic code. Since then many gaps have been filled, particularly by new knowledge about the workings of viruses. Under the influence of population genetics, the Darwinian argument was developed into a mathematical theory of differential reproduction. Natural selection came to mean that some individuals were fitter because they left more offspring than others, without explaining which individual would leave more. The idea that it was those individuals best adapted to their environment that left more offspring was assumed, but it had no explicit place in the theory. So, in the words of C. H. Waddington, a geneticist writing in the late 1950s, "The whole guts of evolution – which is, how do you come to have horses and tigers and things – is outside the mathematical theory." That gap also is now much smaller.

The evolution of the transition from reptiles into mammals, with the loss of some bones and the acquisition of others, is now so well documented that it is virtually impossible to draw a dividing line between reptile and mammal. The evolution of flight, showing the contribution of gliding and soaring to the development of flapping flight has been exemplified through studies of gliding lizards and flying foxes. The evolution of horses is the better understood because there is now an almost unbroken fossil record over 60 million years of a succession of genera and species. It shows that there have been both gradual changes and sudden jumps, the latter supporting the theories of "punctuated equilibria" in evolution.

"Darwinism" is not an expression much used by specialists, but "neo-Darwinism" is sometimes employed to designate Darwin's original theory as modified by the genetical laws of inheritance first stated by Mendel. For readers interested in racial and ethnic relations in the late twentieth century, it is important to appreciate that the use of "race" as a social construct in ordinary English-language speech derives from pre-Darwinian science, and fails to allow for what has since been learned about the sources of variation in human as in other species.

SEE ALSO: anthropology; environmentalism; eugenics; heritability; social Darwinism; sociobiology

Reading

Darwin by Adrian Desmond and James Moore (Penguin, 1991) is a much-praised account of his life and work.

Evolution by C. Patterson (1978) and *Mammal Evolution* by R. J. G. Savage and M. R. Long (1986, both British Museum – Natural History) are more general texts.

The Evolution of Human Sociality: A Darwinian conflict perspective by Stephen K. Sanderson (Rowman & Littlefield, 2001) is an ambitious attempt to use a Darwinist framework to understand the development of human societies; this may be read in conjunction with the similarly motivated *Crisis in Sociology: The need for Darwin* by Joseph Lopraeto and Timothy Crippen (Transaction, 2001).

The Growth of Biological Thought by Ernst Mayr (Harvard University Press, 1982) locates Darwin's work in the history of biology.

CHECK: internet resources section

MICHAEL BANTON

DEVELOPMENT

The elevation of the concept of development to its current status as a loosely defined but ubiquitously accepted definition of means and goals for socioeconomic advancement has been a comparatively recent phenomenon, although it has roots in such earlier concepts as social Darwinian notions of evolutionary societal progress and Marxist notions of phased sequences in history. The phenomenon is closely associated with the growth of bureaucratic and technocratic modes in government, and the assignment to state structures of a central role in the planning and implementation of programs of social betterment. Thus discussions on development characteristically take as their focus contexts where state bureaucratic vanguardism typifies government, either in the formerly planned economies of Eastern Europe or in the "developing" societies of the Third World. Here "five year development plans" and "development ministries" abound, to a degree not found in the industrialized societies of the West.

Theories

Socioeconomic conditions in the postcolonial states of the Third World have provided a particular locus for development thinking. First, Third World nationalism, 'has played a major role in placing development at the center of the state's agenda. In its anticolonial phase, nationalism was primarily concerned with political and cultural liberation. This phase having been successfully concluded, nationalism has turned its attention to concomitant goals of material well-being, social equity and national integration all subsumed under the rubric of development. Secondly, the notion of development has an important comparative dimension. With their colonial histories, Third World states have suffered from an exploitative location in a global economic system, which has inhibited the growth of structures of self-sufficiency. On a number of economic performance indicators they compare unfavorably with the industrialized world of the West. "Development" for these countries thus has often carried the inference of improved performance as measured by these indices. This inference informs both of the two major perspectives in development thinking, which emerged after World War II.

Modernization theory. The first movement, dominant during the 1950s and 1960s, saw development as a linear path in economic growth marked by stages through which all countries had to pass. Strongly influenced by neo-classical economics, this perspective placed emphasis on capital formation and employment generation through the creation of economic/technological enclaves, which would act as "engines of progress" for entire economies. Such progress was to be measured primarily by economic indices, the assumption being that economic growth would "trickle down" to create diffused societal benefits. In following this path Third World countries would be emulating the stages of growth of Western industrial societies; in this mode the perspective is often termed "modernization theory."

Underdevelopment theory. The second perspective, which came to prominence during the 1970s, also starts from the premise that economic growth constitutes the main criterion for development but differs radically in its analysis of the obstacles to its achievement. This perspective holds that the development of the industrialized former colonial powers was historically and reciprocally linked to the underdevelopment of the colonial periphery in a system of global economic exploitation. Little change has been effected in this system by political decolonization. Through transnational investment, trade and technology, abetted by the complicity of local elites, the system remains largely in place. Capital and resource flows continue to the benefit of the developed societies at the expense of the underdeveloped, which cannot develop until the system is either destroyed or radically modified. Generally termed "underdevelopment theory," in some of its forms this perspective sees the global economy as presenting a zero-sum situation in which the development of the Third World inevitably implies redistributive costs to the other participants in the system.

Theoretical debates between the proponents of these two perspectives during the 1980s tended to modify the sharp contrasts suggested, the attempt being to identify and synthesize valid points made by each. More important, however, is their continuing influence as rationalizations for the policies of major actors on the international politico-economic scene. Many of the activities of international aid and technical assistance agencies continue to draw on assumptions rooted in modernization theory; the international political stances of many Third World countries continue to be informed by perceptions embedded in the underdevelopment theory.

Basic needs theory. A third perspective on development has evolved since the early 1970s, which challenges the centrality assigned to economic growth indicators as a measure of development. From this perspective these indicators, with their implication that Western patterns of production and consumption constitute a standardized objective, are an incomplete definition of human and social good. Furthermore they can be dangerously misleading in that they set goals which, given resource/demand ratios in the Third World, are unattainable. In some of its forms referred to as the "basic needs" approach to development, this perspective accepts an economic dimension to development objectives in the production of the food, shelter, and commodities required for the necessities of life. Development also concerns access to basic educational, health and welfare services; equity issues therefore form an important aspect of this approach. Finally, an emphasis is placed on progress toward the growth of cultural and moral values, participatory involvement by all members of society and the evolution of a sense of national identity within the framework of viable, representative, and integrative political structures.

The intersection of ethnic and development issues

Within the Third World this perspective has gained considerable currency, not as a substitute for the first two approaches but rather as a component in a spectrum of development definitions, which is selectively evoked in given contexts. Its emphasis on equity, cultural identity, and national integration provide a useful link for the analysis of the ethnic factors in development. Given the multiethnic composition of most Third World states, ethnicity is clearly an important variable when issues of national integration are addressed and is often seen as obstructive to integrative objectives. On the other hand, the emphasis placed on cultural identities introduces a different value perspective, and some analysts have argued that "ethnodevelopment" must be an important component in larger developmental schemes. Popular national slogans such as "Unity in Diversity" reveal an awareness of the contradictions raised by the ethnic issue and also frequently disguise the lack of coherent programs for dealing with them. The debate over assimilationist or pluralist policies is only infrequently made explicit in Third World politics, not because the issue is considered unimportant but because its sensitivity is regarded as requiring covert, *ad hoc* policy shifts. That this is a critical gap in development planning is demonstrated by the recent and largely unanticipated eruptions of ethnic conflict in "developing" countries such as Fiji and Sri Lanka.

The intersection of ethnic and development issues in the economic arena has also been largely neglected both by analysts and by policy makers. More consideration is required of the notion of ethnic identity as social capital. Some recent analyses of peasant modes of agricultural production in the Third World, based on affective principles of economic reciprocity, have shown how these can create rational and functionally beneficial structures for the peasant populations involved but which also frustrate the macroeconomic objectives of state development. The affective affinities involved include ethnicity, and the "economy of affection" hypothesis is a useful corrective to approaches which can only see ethnicity through the prism of political action, opening up a search for its salience in a broad spectrum of affectively informed behavioral loci within the structures of economic development.

SEE ALSO: Africa; assimilation; capitalism; colonialism; conquest; cultural identity; culturecide; ethnonational; exploitation; globalization; human rights; international organizations; Marxism; minority language rights; social Darwinism; South Africa; Third World; UNESCO; United Nations

Reading

Culture and Development by K. C. Alexander and K. P. Kumaran (Sage, 1992) investigates the uneven developments in regions of India after forty years of planning.

Development Perspectives by P. Streeten (Macmillan, 1981) is an essay collection by one of the subject's foremost analysts.

"Ethnicity and third world development" by Marshall W. Murphree in *Theories of Race and Ethnic*

Relations, edited by J. Rex and D. Mason (Cambridge University Press, 1986), is a more extended discussion of the ethnic factor in development.

Human Development Report was published by the UNDP in 2000 and may be read in conjunction with *The Least Developed Countries 2000 Report*, published by the UNCTAD also in 2000.

The Sociology of Developing Societies, 2nd edn., by Ankie M. M. Hoogvelt (Macmillan, 1978), has a broad survey of issues and perspectives.

The Sociology of Development edited by Bryan Roberts, Robert Cushing, and Charles Wood (Edward Elgar, 1995) is a colossal (1,232 pages) two-volume collection of essays on such themes as dependency, modernization, and the global economy; its focuses include Africa, Latin America, China, and Mexico.

MARSHALL MURPHREE

DIAGEO CASE

In 2001, Diageo, the giant food and drinks corporation, settled a potentially damaging racial discrimination case after its Burger King operation had been sued by the proprietor of twenty-six of its US franchises. La-Van Hawkins, an African American businessman who owned UrbanCity Foods, accused Burger King – the USA's second biggest fast food chain – of racism and trying to force him out of business, claiming the fast food chain reneged on a deal to let him open 225 outlets.

Hawkins operated twenty-three restaurants in Detroit, Atlanta, Chicago and the Washington/Maryland area. He maintained that the group blocked his expansion plans; he also insisted that it demanded repayment of loans. Backed by the Reverend Al Sharpton, the black activist leader, Hawkins publicly accused Burger King of racism and launched a legal action, demanding $1.8 billion (à1.1 billion) in punitive damages. Burger King retaliated, including among its supporters Jesse Jackson and Thomas Dortchy, who headed a prominent black business group. It counter-sued Hawkins to try to retrieve more than $6.5m it claimed Hawkins owed on a 1998 loan. Burger King won two key rulings in 2000, but, in early 2001, brokered a deal that ended the dispute.

The settlement not only allowed Burger King to release a $55m provision it had set aside to cover possible losses, but also removed a potential obstacle to its planned demerger of the business from Diageo. The affair became something of a *cause célèbre* with Hawkins claiming that there was a conspiracy against successful black business people.

Hawkins agreed to sell back his twenty-three restaurants to Burger King, though planned expansions in other parts of his operation were not affected.

Diageo sold Burger King to a consortium of US venture capitalists led by Texas Pacific in mid 2002, in a deal worth $2.2 billion (à1.4 billion)

SEE ALSO: African Americans; black bourgeoisie in the USA; capitalism; equal opportunity; globalization; inferential racism; institutional racism; Million Man March; minorities; race card; reparations

Reading

"Burger King, Hawkins settle" by R. J. King is one of a series of articles written by the same writer for the *Detroit News* (Business section, October 1, 2001).

Fast Foot, Fast Track? Immigrants, big business and the American dream by Jennifer Parker Talwar (Westview Press, 2002), while not about the Diageo case, provides another perspective on the fast food industry's relationship with ethnic minority workers: the author spent four years working behind the counter in New York City, talking to ethnic minority workers about their attempts align poor wages and equally poor prospects with their bigger ambitions.

DIALLO CASE, THE AMADOU

The most notorious case of race-charged police brutality since the Rodney King beating in 1991 involved the killing of Amadou Diallo by New York police officers in 1999. The four officers involved were all acquitted, prompting protest throughout the USA. The incident was compared to Britain's Stephen Lawrence case, though without the sense of disgrace that accompanied that. New York Police Chief and Mayor Rudolph Giuliani emphasized the probity of the subsequent investigation and rebuked protesters.

Twenty-one-year-old Diallo was from Guinea, West Africa and worked in New York as a street vendor, selling hats and clothing. In the early morning of February 4, he returned from work to his apartment in the Bronx. Four white police officers investigating a cab shooting approached him. They later said that they believed Diallo motioned his hand toward his pocket, reaching for a gun. He was subsequently found to be unarmed. The officers, who were members of the NYPD's Street Crime Unit and carried nine-millimeter semiautomatic weapons, opened fire, discharging forty-one shots and killing Diallo

instantly. The Reverend Al Sharpton was later to declare: "Even an execution squad would not have fired so many shots. Are we talking about policing or are we talking about a firing squad?"

The sheer quantity of gunfire turned what would have been a controversial case into a *cause cílØbre*, with inchoate protests escalating to a fully-fledged campaign after the acquittal of the officers. Over a thousand arrests were made in the aftermath of the killing.

The trial of the officers was moved from the Bronx to Albany, where the jury was mainly white. The prosecution did not raise the possibility of racism during the trial. Unlike the initial absolution of the four Los Angeles police officers who were acquitted after the Rodney King trial, this did not touch off riots (the King riots left fifty people dead). There were street marches involving thousands, mostly in New York. Banners bearing "Jim Crow Justice" and "KKK Cops" were carried.

Perhaps the most significant event in helping raise awareness of the killing was the performance of a song by Bruce Springsteen, who wrote "American skin (41 shots)" specifically about the Diallo case and sang it at a number of concerts. Although the song was not recorded, it was downloadable from the internet. It included the line: "You can get killed just for living in your American skin." By the time of Springsteen's appearance for a concert in New York, in June 2000, the police officers had been acquitted. Diallo's parents praised Springsteen for keeping the memory of their son alive, but the police condemned him.

The Diallo killing came within two years of another globally publicized case involving an ethnic minority suspect and the police. In 1997, Haitian migrant Abner Louima was arrested, taken into custody and sexually assaulted by police officers in Brooklyn.

New York's Street Crime Unit was known to use racial profiling in its stop-and-search policy. According to the NYPD's own estimates, sixteen black stops are made for every arrest.

SEE ALSO: African Americans; Central Park jogger; institutional racism; King case, the Rodney; Lawrencc case, the Stephen; media; Million Man March; policing; racial profiling; racist discourse; scapegoat; violence

Reading

"The Amadou Diallo case: the social and political roots of police violence" by the editorial board of *World Socialist Web Site*, February 28, 2000: available at *www.wsws.org/articles/2000/feb2000/dia2-f28.shtml*). A punchy article written just after the acquittal of the NYPD officers, it reflects on the reforms promised in the wake of the King riots: "The impact of these initiatives has been nil."

DIASPORA

Drawn from ancient Greek terms *dia* (through) and *speir?* ("dispersal, to sow or scatter,"), diaspora and its adjective diasporic have been utilized in recent years in a variety of ways. Among these uses – some rather new, all inherently related – three approaches to the notion of diaspora emerge and a fourth unrelated approach reacts to them.

As a social category

"The Diaspora" was at one time a concept referring almost exclusively to the experiences of Jews, invoking their traumatic exile from an historical homeland and dispersal throughout many lands. With these experiences as reference, connotations of a "diaspora" situation were negative as they were associated with forced displacement, victimization, alienation, and loss. Along with this archetype went a dream of return. These traits eventually led to the term's application comparatively to populations such as Armenians and Africans.

Now, however, "diaspora" is often used to describe practically any community which is transnational, that is, whose social economic and political networks cross the borders of nation-states. Such current overuse and under-theorization – which sees the conflation of categories such as immigrants, guestworkers, ethnic minorities, refugees, expatriates, and travelers – threatens the term's usefulness. More rigorous theoretical work germane to the category, however, is being developed contiguously (as witnessed in academic journals such as *Public Culture, Cultural Anthropology* and *Diaspora*).

As a form of consciousness

Here, with a direct allusion to W. E. B. Du Bois's notion of "double consciousness," diaspora refers to individuals' awareness of a range of decen-tered, multi-location attachments, of being simultaneously "home away from home" or "here and there." It is in this sense that Paul Gilroy (in *The Black Atlantic*, Verso, 1993) both presents stimulating ideas surrounding the exposition of a people's historical "roots and routes" and passes on the proposition (originally made by rap artist Rakim) that "It don't matter where you're from, it's where you're at."

As a mode of cultural production

In this approach, the fluidity of constructed styles and identities among diasporic people is emphasized These are evident in the production and reproduction of forms which are sometimes called "cut'n'mix," hybrid, or "alternate." A key dynamic to bear in mind, according to Stuart Hall, is that cultural identities "come from somewhere, have histories" and are subject to continuous transformation through the "play of history, culture and power" ("Cultural identity and diaspora" in *Identity: Community, Culture and Difference* edited by J. Rutherford, Lawrence & Wishart, 1990). For Hall, diaspora comprises ever-changing representations which provide an "imaginary coherence" for a set of malleable identities.

As a new kind of problem

According to this line of thinking – typically associated with right-wing groups – transnational communities are seen as threats to state security and potential sources of international terrorism. In this view too, people's links with homelands and with other parts of a globally dispersed community raise doubts about their loyalty to the "host" nation-state. Hybrid cultural forms and multiple identities expressed by self-proclaimed diasporic youths, too, are viewed by "host-society" conservatives as assaults on traditional (hegemonic and assimilative) norms. Such appraisals are countered by persons who see strong transnational networks as unsurprising features of globalization (particularly involving the enhancement of telecommunications and the ease of travel) and who welcome the construction of new compound identities and hybrid cultural forms as a way of valuing cosmopolitan diversity.

SEE ALSO: African Americans; African Caribbeans in Britain; Anglo-Indians; Asian Americans; British Asians; cultural identity;

culturecide; double consciousness; essentialism; ethnocide; ethnonational; globalization; Hall, Stuart; Holocaust; hybridity; Irish; migration; postcolonial; Roma; Zionism

Reading

"The concept of diaspora as an analytical tool in the study of refugee communities" by ½sten Wahlbeck (in *Journal of Ethnic and Migration Studies*, vol. 28, no. 2, 2002) applies the concept to a study of how refugees in exile maintain transnational links between countries of origin and settlement.

"Diasporas" by James Clifford (in *Cultural Anthropology*, vol. 9, no. 3, 1994) provides a superb overview of theoretical issues surrounding diasporas and related social and cultural topics.

Global Diasporas: An introduction by Robin Cohen (UCL Press, 1997) includes an historical overview of the concept in addition to a wide-ranging typology.

"Introduction" by Steven Vertovec and Robin Cohen, in *Migration, Diasporas and Transnationalism*, edited by Steven Vertovec and Robin Cohen (Edward Elgar Publishing, 1999), examines distinctions and inherent relationships between social patterns concerning migrant communities, diasporas and transnational practices.

STEVEN VERTOVEC

DISADVANTAGE

In the context of social policy, "disadvantage" generally refers to individuals or groups suffering a handicap in competition with others, by virtue of membership of a social category such as class, ethnicity or race. While ostensibly neutral and silent about the causes of disadvantage, the term is often used as a euphemism to hide the discrimination and exploitation at the root of "disadvantage." Indeed, the term often puts the burden of explanation for inferior status on supposed disabilities of the victims. *Underprivilege* is an equally convenient obfuscation of the sources of inequality.

The concept of "disadvantage" has been central to a set of ameliorative strategies devised in the USA, supposedly to redress ethnic and racial differences, mostly in income, education, and access to employment and schools. Certain minorities are defined as disadvantaged or underprivileged, and, therefore, qualify for affirmative action. Existing differences are principally ascribed to racial or ethnic factors, to the nearly complete exclusion of class. Minorities are alleged to be in a "disadvantaged" position partly because of ethnic or racial discrimination against

them, and partly because of unfortunate failings of their own which they must be helped to overcome (e.g. lack of education, lack of a work ethic, hedonism, "externality," or the latest psychologistic fad).

Social remedies for disadvantage consist mostly of making supposedly benign exceptions for minorities rather than in changing the class structures which perpetuate inequalities. Affirmative action, or positive discrimination, takes the form of racial and ethnic quotas in university admissions and in hiring, remedial courses for minorities, racial busing for school "integration," and the like. The common denominator of some fifteen years of these policies has been their lack of success, or even their boomerang effect (in the form of white backlash, increasing salience of racial consciousness, and devaluation of credentials of all minority group members).

Long before the United States, the government of India, both under British rule and since independence, adopted similar policies to relieve the disadvantage of the "backward" castes. The results were quite similar: far from reducing the significance of caste status, a political incentive was created for people to organize along caste lines, and to claim "backward" status for economic or political advantage. In Israel, too, the government has initiated policies of benign discrimination in favor of Oriental Jews, though not toward Arabs, whose position is far worse and who suffer from much more blatant discrimination.

SEE ALSO: affirmative action; caste; drugs; education; equal opportunity; equality; ghetto; homelessness; minorities; Park, Robert Ezra; racial discrimination; racism; social work; underachievement; welfare

Reading

Affirmative Discrimination by Nathan Glazer (Basic Books, 1975) is a critique of the policy and of its impact in the USA, by an American sociologist.

Minority Education and Caste by John Ogbu (Academic Press, 1978) is a lucid analysis of the source of educational "disadvantage" for minority groups in the USA, Britain, India, Nigeria, and elsewhere, by a Nigerian anthropologist.

PIERRE L. VAN DEN BERGHE

DISCRIMINATION *see* racial discrimination

DOLLARD, JOHN (1900–80)

Dollard was a US psychologist who, having undergone psychoanalysis in Berlin, became the first writer to apply Freudian interpretations to black–white relations in North America. According to Freudian doctrine, social living and human culture require a degree of orderliness and discipline that conflict with the desires of the young human. Socialization entails frustration. The basic reaction to frustration is the aggressive response, designed to reassert mastery, but a child finds it unprofitable to attack a parental figure who provides nurture. The child must either turn the aggression in on itself or store it up, waiting for a convenient opportunity to discharge it onto a suitable scapegoat. The first key concept is therefore that of generalized or "free-floating" aggression held in store; the second, that of social permission to release this aggression onto a particular target group; the third, that scapegoats must be readily identifiable (as the Negro's skin color served as a sign telling the prejudiced person whom to hate). According to this view racial prejudice was always irrational.

In a later article, Dollard distinguished between direct and displaced aggression according to whether it was discharged against the agent of the frustration (direct) or a scapegoat (displaced); he stressed that in a situation of direct aggression some displaced aggression would also be released, adding an emotional element which might be responsible for the irrational behavior often observable in situations of rational conflict. Dollard's main contribution was his book *Caste and Class in a Southern Town* (first published in 1937), which brought together the Freudian interpretation and a description of black–white relations in the Mississippi town of Indianola. In it, blacks and whites were presented as separate castes after the manner of W. Lloyd Warner, though without carrying through the sort of analysis three of Warner's students (Allison Davies, B. B. Gardner, and M. Gardner) achieved in their book about another Mississippi town. This was published a little later under the title *Deep South*.

SEE ALSO: anthropology; caste; Cox, Oliver C.; Myrdal, Gunnar; Park, Robert Ezra; prejudice; racial discrimination; scapegoat; segregation; transracial adoption

Reading

"Hostility and fear in social life" by John Dollard (in *Social Forces*, vol. 17, 1938), is a short but comprehensive statement of the author's views about the sources and nature of racial prejudice.

MICHAEL BANTON

DOOMED RACES DOCTRINE

The discourse on extinction

The doctrine that certain "lower races" were condemned to extinction was held by many white scholars during the greater part of the nineteenth and the early twentieth centuries. According to the doctrine, the indigenous inhabitants of the continents into which Europe was expanding – Siberia, North America, South America, North Africa, South Africa, Australia and the islands of the Pacific – were the first to be consigned to their fate. In the wishful thinking of many whites, blacks in America, the "savages" of Africa and the Chinese "barbarians" were also doomed. Extinction was regarded as their inescapable destiny, decreed by God or by nature.

The idea of *extinction* is fairly recent. The concept originated in 1796, when a young French anatomist, Georges Cuvier (1769–1832), proved that whole species of animals, even animals as large as the mammoth and the mastodon, could die out, and had in fact died out. Cuvier, a child of the French Revolution, believed that the animal species had become annihilated through some vast catastrophes, which he called "revolutions of the earth." Charles Lyell (1797–1875), the father of British geology, did not experience the siege of the Bastille, but he witnessed the Industrial Revolution in England during the late eighteenth and early nineteenth centuries. He saw society becoming fundamentally reshaped through small, gradual changes, and thought the same thing happened in nature – an animal species dies out just as a firm goes under when it cannot adapt to changing markets.

Charles Darwin (1809–82) read Lyell's *Principles of Geology* (1832) on his voyage on the *Beagle*, and took Lyell's idea one step further. If old species could slowly and naturally die out, why then should not new species be able to appear in the same way, for the same natural reasons that had eradicated their predecessors? If dying out did not require a catastrophe, why then should coming into being require creation? Darwin continued to work on this question after his return to England. 1838 was a year of severe depression – 400,000 unemployed emigrated from Great Britain. That solved some of Britain's economic problems, but where the immigrants arrived, they were regarded as angels of death by the native peoples. Darwin noted that when two human races meet, they behave like two animal species: they fight, they eat each other, and they infect each other. "The strong are always extirpating the weaker," and in his opinion "the British were beating the lot."

A Parliamentary Select Committee on Aboriginal Tribes, reporting in 1837, surveyed the fate of native peoples from Newfoundland, where British settlers shot the last native in 1823, to South Africa and Australia where whole peoples were on the verge of extinction. As a conclusion, the Report quoted one witness who held peaceful trade to be the only way to approach the natives without destroying them: "The alternative is extermination, for you can stop nowhere; you must go on; you may have a short respite when you have driven panic into the people, but you must come back to the same thing until you have shot the last man." "From all the bulky evidence before us," the Report continued, "we come to no other conclusion; and considering the power, and the mighty resources of the British nation, we must believe that the choice rests with ourselves."

The Doomed Races Doctrine offered a way for the "superior" race to evade this choice. Whatever whites did, the peoples of color would perish. According to Samuel Morton in *Crania Americana* (1839), the "Indian" and the "Negro" had insufficient cranial capacity: their small skulls condemned them to be exterminated or else enslaved. The Scottish doctor, Robert Verity, in his *Changes Produced in the Nervous System by Civilisation* (1839) held that the extinction of the peoples of color is caused by a deficiency of the nervous system. He predicted that "the present numerous Negro population will in all likelihood decline like the Indian races and in the course of time become extinct." Further, there was a law-like certainty about the outcomes of contact between "the stronger and more intellectual races" and "the inferior and weaker": the latter will succumb. "Those which cannot assimilate will end by disappearing," Verity concluded,

referring to high mortality rates of free African American males in Philadelphia and New York as evidence.

Racial extinction was seen as a way to improve mankind. The great liberal philosopher Herbert Spencer in his *Social Statics* (1851) praised imperialism for clearing the "inferior races" from the earth. "The forces which are working out the great scheme of perfect happiness, taking no account of incidental suffering, exterminate such sections of mankind as stand in their way ... Be he human or be he brute – the hindrance must be got rid of."

Darwin's *On the Origin of Species* (1859) did not mention human beings, but readers were quick to draw their own conclusions. And in his *The Descent of Man* (1871), Darwin explicitly made the extermination of native peoples a natural element of evolution. Animal species had always exterminated each other, so had savages; and now when there are civilized people, the savages will be completely exterminated: "When civilised peoples come into contact with barbarians the struggle is short, except where a deadly climate gives its aid to the native race."

And the climate will not alter the inevitable outcome: "At some future period, not very distant as measured by centuries, the civilised races of man will almost certainly exterminate and replace throughout the world the savage races."

Darwin had seen it happen, in Argentina, Tasmania and Australia, and had reacted very sharply to what he saw. But incorporated into his evolutionary theory, the extermination of native peoples no longer stood out as a crime, but as the inescapable result of natural processes.

Culture shock and depopulation

The scientific study of these "natural processes" began with the German anthropologist Georg Gerland's *èber das Aussterben der Naturv?lker* (*On the Extinction of Primitive Peoples*, 1868). Gerland evaluated every conceivable reason for depopulation mentioned in the literature on doomed races: primitive peoples' lack of care for their own bodies and for their children, personality traits such as indolence and melancholy, sexual depravity and addiction to intoxicants, cannibalism and human sacrifice and, finally, influence from higher cultures. He concluded that the diseases of the whites have often been decisive exterminating factors. Even more important was the hostile behavior of whites. Physical force was the clearest and most tangible factor in extermination. But what might be called "cultural violence" is sometimes just as harmful.

The way of life of primitive peoples is so wholly adapted to climate and nature that sudden changes, however innocent and even useful they may seem, have devastating effects. Radical changes such as the privatization of land that was previously held in common, disturb the basis of a whole way of life. Europeans destroyed out of rapacity or lack of understanding the basis of everything the natives thought, felt and believed. When life lost its meaning for them, they died out. But that did not mean that their dying out was a law of nature. Nowhere had any physical or mental inability to develop been found among them, concluded Gerland. If the natural rights of the natives are respected, they will survive.

Another landmark in the study of doomed races was anthropologist W. H. R. Rivers's *Essays on the Depopulation of Melanesia* (1922). An important factor in depopulation, he found, was the forced export of labor to Australia. "It would be difficult to exaggerate the evil influence of the process by which the natives of Melanesia were taken to Australia and elsewhere to labour for the white man. It forms one of the blackest of civilisation's crimes."

Like Gerland before him, Rivers held "loss of interest in life" to be the most important cause of low birth rates. After having had their society and way of life destroyed by white invaders, the inhabitants asked: "Why should we bring children into the world only to work for the white man." Rivers had been studying the psychological effects of trench warfare on soldiers in the Great War. In Melanesia he found that the victims of "culture shock" showed many of the symptoms of "shell shock."

Ludwik Krzywicki, professor of social history in Warsaw, came to much the same conclusion in his 600-page study *Primitive Society and its Vital Statistics* (1934). Krzywicki studied cases of depopulation all over the globe and found the main cause to be the destruction of native society following white invasion. "The victorious advance of our civilisation swept and sweeps away primitive peoples mercilessly, partly by force of arms, partly by epidemics, but mostly by a far-reaching social break-down."

Science, progress and genocide

After World War II research interest switched from the causes of depopulation to the problem of why some peoples were thought to be dying out while their numbers actually were increasing. George M. Fredrickson, in his *The Black Image in the White Mind*, showed how white thinking about blacks for nearly a century was dominated by the vain hope that they were heading for extinction. Reginald Horsman, in *Race and Manifest Destiny*, told the story of how American expansion westwards was destined to cross both the Rio Grande and the Pacific Ocean, rapidly replacing such doomed races as the Mexicans and the Chinese, both of whom showed no sign of disappearing. Russell McGregor, in *Imagined Destinies*, showed how the Doomed Races Doctrine had, for the better part of the previous 200 years, been dominating Australian thinking about the indigenous inhabitants of the continent.

The most surprising thing about the Doomed Races Doctrine is how easily whites accepted the thought of vast numbers of "inferior" human beings just vanishing out of existence. After Darwin, extermination elicited a response of indifference: only the poorly educated would respond emotionally to the inevitable demise of inferior groups. "Nothing can be more unscientific," wrote George Chatterton Hill in his *Heredity and Selection* (1907), "nothing shows a deeper ignorance of the elementary laws of social evolution, than the absurd agitations, peculiar to the British race, against the elimination of inferior races." The truth is that the British race "by reason of its genius for expansion, must necessarily eliminate the inferior races which stand in its way. Every superior race in history has done the same, and was obliged to do it."

If the workforce of a colony cannot be disciplined into producing the profits rightly expected by the mother country, wrote Henry C. Morris in his *History of Colonization* (1900), "the natives must then be exterminated or reduced to such numbers as to be readily controlled."

Professor Karl Pearson, founder of mathematical statistics, wrote in his *National Life from the Standpoint of Science* (1901): " The path of progress is strewn with the wreck of nations; traces are everywhere to be seen of the hecatombs of inferior races, and of victims who found not the narrow way to the greater perfection. Yet these dead peoples are, in very truth, the stepping-stones on which mankind has arisen to the higher intellectual and deeper emotional life of to-day."

In France, Jules Harmand wrote in his *Domination et colonisation* (1910): "When these miserable populations have become unusable by, or dangerous to, the superior race they are destined to be sooner or later annihilated."

An authoritative French handbook of colonial law published in many editions between 1892 and 1923 was called *Principes de colonisation et de lígislation colonial*. The question of the right of colonization, it stated, alluding to cannibalism, "is whether Europeans should have to resign themselves to the miseries of overpopulation for a few thousand natives to be able to continue to eat each other … The gradual eradication of the lower races, or if another choice of words is preferred, the annihilation by the strong of the weak, is the actual prerequisite for progress."

Consequently, there was no reason for the members of a "superior" race to regret the extinction of "inferior" races. The survival of the natives will only cause trouble, wrote anthropologist George H. L.-F. Pitt-Rivers in his *The Clash of Cultures* (1927): "In fact, the Native Problem might well be defined 'the problem' created by the survival of those native races or their hybrid descendants that have not been exterminated by the 'blessings of civilisation'. That is to say there is no native problem in Tasmania and only one of very little importance to the European population in Australia, for the very good reason that the Tasmanians are no longer alive to create a problem, while the aboriginals of Australia are rapidly following them along the road to extinction."

In statements such as these the Doomed Races Doctrine was used to defend, or even to recommend, what has since 1949 been condemned in international law as genocide. "A special kind of genocidal practice is directed against overseas populations," writes genocide historian Irving L. Horowitz in *Taking Lives* (1980).

One of the fundamental characteristics of 19th century European imperialism was its systematic destruction of communities outside the "mother country". Decimation of Zulu tribesmen by British troops, the Dutch-run slave trade, and the virtual depopulation of the Congo by Belgians, typify this form of colonial genocide.

[…]

The conduct of classic colonialism was invariably linked with genocide. It is the hypocritical heritage of European nations that they proclaimed concepts of democracy and liberty for their own populations while systematically destroying others. This was the bequeathal of 19th-century "civilised" existence. This bequest of the past became the norm of the 20th century.

The Doomed Races Doctrine tended to become a self-fulfilling prophecy, used to legitimize acts of violence and dispossession for which the survivors today claim compensation. The Herero people of Namibia require the Germans to pay for genocide which wiped out 80 percent of their ancestors in 1904. Native Americans, Australian Aborigines and Scandinavian Laplanders call for the return of lands that were taken from them when their extinction was considered inevitable. These are but a few examples of a landslide of demands for apology, reparations and restitution from those who survived the "doomed races" epoch.

SEE ALSO: Aboriginal Australians; American Indians; Chamberlain, Houston Stewart; culturecide; Darwinism; ethnocide; genocide; Gobineau, Joseph Arthur de; indigenous peoples; reparations; science; self-fulfilling prophecy; slavery; White Power

Reading

The Black Image in the White Mind: The debate on Afro-American character and destiny 1817–1914 by George M. Fredrickson (Wesleyan University Press, 1971) analyses the Doomed Races Doctrine in white perceptions of African Americans.

Exterminate All the Brutes by Sven Lindqvist (The New Press, 1996) analyses the Doomed Races Doctrine in Joseph Conrad's *Heart of Darkness*; and Lindqvist's *The Skull Measurer's Mistake* (The New Press. 1997) portrays some of the early critics of the doctrine.

The Guilt of Nations by Elazar Barkan (Norton, 2000) shows how restitution for historical injustices have in some cases been successfully negotiated.

King Leopold's Ghost: A story of greed, terror and heroism in colonial Africa by Adam Hochschild (Macmillan, 1999) tells the story of the depopulation of the Congo; while in Irving L. Horowitz, *Taking Lives: Genocide and state power* (Transaction, 1980), colonial terror is compared with other forms of mass murder.

Race and Manifest Destiny: The origins of American racial Anglo-Saxonism by Reginald Horsman

(Harvard University Press, 1981) shows the doctrine applied to Mexicans and Chinese, while Russell McGregor has documented it for Australia in his *Imagined Destinies: Aboriginal Australians and the doomed race theory 1880–1939* (Melbourne University Press, 1997).

SVEN LINDQVIST

DOUBLE CONSCIOUSNESS

W. E. B. Du Bois defined double consciousness as "this sense of always looking at one's self through the eyes of others, of measuring one's soul by the tape of a world that looks on in amused contempt and pity. One ever feels the twoness – an American, a Negro; two souls, two thoughts, two unreconciled strivings; two warring ideals in one dark body." He introduced this idea in *Atlantic Monthly* in August 1897 and later elaborated on it in his *The Souls of Black Folk*, published in 1903. The first chapter of this contains the following insight:

> The American Negro is the history of this strife – this longing to ... merge his double self into a better and truer self. In this merging he wishes neither of the older selves to be lost. He would not Africanize America ... He would not bleach his Negro soul in a flood of white Americanism ... He simply wishes to make it possible for a man to be both a Negro and an American.

Du Bois referred to white people's refusal, generally, to acknowledge the way their society has transformed the physiological characteristic of skin color into the political category of race. Given the consciousness of race as a hierarchical construct, a consciousness members of both groups share, albeit from polar modes of apperception, most whites, however open, find it difficult to relate to persons of color as individuals. There is a tendency among whites to experience persons of color not as persons of color experience themselves, as conscious human agents with the same inner stream of subjectivity that defines all conscious human agents, but as racialized Others. As, that is, members of the category white society has itself created; subjects who exist on the outside of a socially invented barrier of exclusion. It is a barrier of no one's personal or particular or individual making, but an immanent cultural presence nevertheless, and the persons whom it structures as Other recog-

nize that they are being perceived and responded to not as ordinary human beings, but as problematic ones. Whites tend to be uncomfortable in informal relations with persons of color, then, a discomfort that, in the desire not to appear to want to avoid the subject, manifests itself as a seemingly friendly reference to race when, in fact, there is no reason to refer to race at all.

It is this distancing, the feeling that one's humanity is being cordoned off, that gives rise to the next component of the over-all construct of double consciousness, the Du Boisian notion of *duality*, "this sense of always looking at one's self through the eyes of others." Our own, immediate subjectivity is experienced as alien to the way in which other people – no, not other people, white people – reflect that subjectivity back at us. The white Other communicates only a diminished recognition of the stream of perceptions that flow together to create what we experience as the culturally embedded self. In interactions and social exchanges with white people, this self is estranged, and seems not to be as one knows it *is*.

It is important to recognize that double consciousness, as an existential element of African American life, is not universally accepted in black political thought. Cornel West tells us, for example, that, for Malcolm X, "double-consciousness [was] less a description of a necessary black mode of being in America" than it was "a particular kind of colorized mind set [that] seems to lock black people into the quest for white approval ...." And Adolph Reed, who prefers to read Du Bois, not through the lens of the philosophical idealism of his early years, but through that of his identity with the progressive and socialist movements of his time, is skeptical of the general applicability of the concept. "As a proposition alleging a generic racial condition – that millions of individuals experience a peculiar form of bifurcated identity, simply by virtue of a common racial status – the notion seems preposterous on its face."

Yet there are problems with the suspicion of duality that both nationalists and Marxists express. For it is not, as the nationalists would have it, a dubious moral category to be banished through a personalistic and transformative act that wills into being an authentic black identity and consciousness. It is, rather, an attempt to describe in realistic terms the psychological impact of finding oneself embedded in a contradictory and marginalized social position. Indeed, nationalism itself can be read as one particular response to that condition, a response seeking to negate one's connections to white society, with its deformed definitions of blackness, all together. And if, as Reed would have it, the overall construct of double consciousness has resonance only in terms of the academic conventions of late nineteenth-century essentialist thought, one needs to explain why, as those conventions dropped away, duality remained central to efforts to comprehend African-American life. Thus, Reed is correct in pointing out that, after *Souls*, Du Bois does not again use the phrase "double consciousness." Still, duality continues to run as a metaphor not only through all of his work up through *Dusk of Dawn*, but appears and reappears in many of the defining texts of African American thought generally. As Bernard Bell writes, "Johnson's *Autobiography of an Ex-Colored Man*, Tooter's *Cane*, Wright's *Native Son*, Ellison's *Invisible Man*, Baldwin's *Go Tell It on the Mountain*, and Morrison's *Beloved* readily come to mind as improvisational variations on Du Boisian themes and tropes of double-consciousness." And this is to name only a few.

"Duality" leads immediately to the tangle that emerges from the third component of double consciousness, the struggle "to make it possible for a man to be both a Negro and an American." This seems a legitimate enough aspiration, no more than the just demand, in fact, that American society finally extend to its people of African descent the freedom and dignity and inalienable rights that, according to the founding documents, are self-evidently the property of all men (though, alas, not so self-evidently the property of women or slaves). There is a paradox however. For such an aspiration cannot be realized as long as the cultural assumptions that fuse "American" with "whiteness" remain in place. But it is just the hegemonic position of such assumptions that creates the dilemma of dual-consciousness in the first place, that habituates black Americans to internalize the collective images and historical narratives that devalue their worth, and justify the premises of their material subordination.

What Du Bois is demanding in his condemnation of the double consciousness that informs the social context of most people of color in the USA is that the historical and ideational link between "American" and "whiteness" be broken apart, shattered, and replaced by a radically new conception of American identity. This is not readily achieved by a society that, from its beginnings, defined blacks as a separate, distinct, and lower species of humanity. For it was only by characterizing black people as being of lesser worth than whites, as having no role in the nation's self-image as a place of freedom for all, that it could allow slavery as an institution in the South, and discrimination and denial of equality in the North. The notion of black folk as outside the frame of American identity is an integral part of American heritage, and a nation, whatever constitutional changes it accepts, whatever laws it passes, whatever principles it routinely affirms in its schoolbooks, does not so easily walk away from its heritage.

Bernard Bell writes that "for most contemporary African Americans double-consciousness is the striving to reconcile one's ancestral African and diasporic slave past – however remote, mythic or spiritual – with one's American present; one's sense of being a subject with that of being an object, of being an outsider with that of being an insider ..." What, in different ways, both Du Bois and Baldwin recognized, however, was that the issue is not merely one of blacks in America finding an identity that joins their cultural past to the values and aspirations of their present nation. Embedded in all their writings is the insistence that there cannot be an African American identity unless there is a profound and revolutionary transformation of the hegemonic identity that America has inherited, a transformation the nation consistently has resisted.

Du Bois and African American identity

In *Dusk of Dawn*, the autobiography he published in 1940, aged seventy-two, Du Bois wrote:

> Not only do white men but also colored men forget the facts of the Negro's double environment ... The American Negro, therefore, is surrounded and conditioned by the concept which he has of white people and he is treated in accordance with the concept they have of him. On the other hand, so far as his own people are concerned, he is in direct contact with individuals and facts. He fits into his environment more or less willingly. It gives him a social world and mental peace. On the

other hand and especially if in education and ambition and income he is above the average culture of his group, he is often resentful of its environing power; partly because he does not recognize its power and partly because he is determined to consider himself part of the white group from which, in fact, he is excluded.

Du Bois decided to deal with the bonds of double consciousness by extending his vision beyond its American and integrationist context. Without repudiating his connection to white America, he committed himself to pan-Africanism on the one hand, and to the strategy of black economic, political, and cultural autonomy on the other. Both stances got him into trouble, not only with the US Government and many of his white colleagues, but with the black professional leadership of the country generally, including that of the NAACP, which he had helped found in 1910, and whose journal, *Crisis*, he edited. But Du Bois's own relation to his American identity changed as he engaged in these conflicts, and I want to take a brief look at those changes in this section.

The Great War had a tremendous impact on Du Bois's theory and politics. It began the process whereby he abandoned the aspiration implicit in *Souls*, that white people, if educated about the spiritual and material conditions of black life, would join with their black compatriots in the effort to tear down the veil between them and end racial injustice. His basic theory, he wrote later, had been that racial prejudice was primarily a matter of ignorance, and that when the truth was properly presented, the monstrous wrong of race hate would quickly melt before it: "All human action to me in those days was conscious and rational."

But the response of America to the black soldiers who had risked their lives for their country no differently than had white soldiers enraged him, and started him on the path that led to his eventual break with the integrationist sentiment of the progressive politics of his time. Sent in 1919 to France by the NAACP to investigate the status of black soldiers, he documented the cruel and discriminatory treatment they suffered at the hands of their white officers, most of whom were Southerners. When he attempted to publish these documents in the NAACP journal, the Post Office delayed the

mailing for a day, considering whether to suppress the issue. The government relented, and the issue sold 106,000 copies, but Du Bois was attacked in the House of Representatives for allegedly inciting race riots, and, along with other black journalists, was investigated by the Department of Justice.

The aftermath at home of the Great War also hardened Du Bois in his attitude toward American society and culture. The response to returning black veterans was a horror, as these men began to leave the South and compete with whites for jobs in the cities of the North. Perhaps it had to be made clear that their service to America should not lead them to believe that their subordinate position was about to change. Seventy-seven black citizens were lynched in 1919, Du Bois writes, one of them a woman. Fourteen of these people were publicly burned, eleven of them alive. There were race riots in twenty-six American cities that year, including Washington, where six people were killed. In Chicago, the toll was thirty-eight.

The war had a double impact on Du Bois's philosophical and political outlook. For not only did it demonstrate that the governing forces in the USA were not about to legitimize any movement toward racial equality, it established in his mind the primacy of pan-Africanism as a pressing issue for black political consciousness and identity. Du Bois had long understood that the question of the relation between white and nonwhite was global in nature. It was in an address to an early pan-African conference, in London in 1900, that he made his prophetic statement that "the problem of the twentieth century is the problem of the color line." But as the war drew to a close Du Bois and a group of his colleagues recognized that, at the coming Peace Conference, while the future direction of the African nations would be decided, no provisions were in place for any black representatives to be heard. The group delegated Du Bois to be their spokesman, and once in Paris, working through Blaise Daigne, Senegalese member of the French Parliament, he received permission to convene a pan-African Congress. There were fifty-seven delegates at the meeting, and "the results were small," but the importance of this gathering was not in its immediate effects, but in the way it oriented Du Bois to a concept of African American identity that went beyond the domestic arena. He organized four more such meetings over the course of the following decade, though the final meeting, scheduled to be held in Tunis in 1929, was canceled by the French Government. What mattered, however, was that Du Bois had begun to challenge the hold of double consciousness by stepping beyond the boundaries of American life, and providing a much broader canvas against which the notion of African American identity could develop.

There is no space in what is a brief survey article to trace the fullness of the way in which Du Bois's thought shaped black American politics and identity. It is important to point out, however, that in the years between his return from Paris and the publication of *Dusk of Dawn*, he broke with the NAACP over the issue of what we would today call self-determination, or black political autonomy. "I proposed," he wrote in describing his conflict with the NAACP, "that in economic lines, just as in lines of literature and religion, segregation should be planned and organized and carefully thought through. ... This plan did not establish a new segregation; it did not advocate segregation as a final solution of the race problem; exactly the contrary; but it did face the facts and faced them with thoughtfully mapped effort ...." Whether self-segregation for his protection, for inner development and growth in intelligence and social efficiency, will increase his acceptability to white Americans or not, that growth must go on.

Du Bois never abandoned his notion that double consciousness outlined the parameters of the African American experience. What he did, however, was to insist, in his life and practice, on an orientation to African American identity that never compromised the independence of black people as he saw and understood their situation. But this orientation came at a price, for, in the years of the Cold War, Du Bois drifted towards a Marxist worldview, and aligned himself more and more with the Stalinist politics of the time. And as he did so, he became isolated from the mainstream of African American life. For most American blacks were not prepared, as was Du Bois, to step outside the traditional American aspiration towards equal treatment within the frame of liberal democratic values.

In 1963 Du Bois renounced his American citizenship and became a citizen of Ghana, where he died, and remains buried.

James Baldwin

James Baldwin came on the scene holding to the liberal values that Du Bois rejected, though he struggled mightily with them as the violence of the civil rights movement escalated, Malcolm X and Martin Luther King were assassinated, and police departments across the country, orchestrated as it later turned out by the FBI's COINTELPRO operation, began systematically to harass and brutalize the Black Panthers. However, while Baldwin, too, died in self-imposed exile, in France, there is a sense in which he never left home.

Baldwin's understanding of "race" in America is infused with paradox. His sense of estrangement from American society – and Western culture – was acute, but his sense of belonging to that society and culture was equally passionate. His entire corpus flowed from the premise that peoples of color in the West had to construct their own social identities in order to become free. But he insisted, just as vehemently, that neither could whites realize their humanity until they also reordered their relation to the world. He wanted a society that was race-blind, but which recognized that it could not escape the politics of identity. He was profoundly political, but, at the same time, suspicious of political solutions. He rejected assimilation, doubted integration, and refused nationalism. If he fell out of favor for a time during the late 1970s and 1980s, Lawrie Balfour writes, it was "because of his appreciation for the complexity of American racial dilemmas."

Baldwin never used the term double consciousness. But, in 1955, in his first essay in his first published collection, *Notes of A Native Son*, he identified the precise nature of its meaning.

In any case ... the most crucial time in my own development came when I was forced to recognize that I was a kind of bastard of the West; when I followed the line of my past I did not find myself in Europe but in Africa. And this meant that in some subtle way, in a really profound way, I brought to Shakespeare, Bach, Rembrandt, to the stones of Paris, to the Cathedral at Chartres, and to the Empire State Building, a special attitude. These were not really my creations; they did not contain my history; ... I was an interloper; this was not my heritage. At the same time I had no other heritage which I could possibly hope to use.

Baldwin begins with the affirmation that he is both outside the Western heritage, and within it. It is not his, but it is all that he has in front of him to work with. He can come to self-recognition only by forging a new identity, one which both reflects the shaping of his character by that heritage, and brings to bear not only his exclusions from it, but the unique history that is his own. A difficult task, since much of that history has been deliberately hidden from him.

Nowhere in his work does Baldwin ever specify what that new identity will look like. There are a number of reasons for his silences here, I suggest. First, Baldwin was not in the business of defining anyone else's identity for them. In that sense, he was the supreme individualist. Not because he rejected the notion that human beings were social in nature, or dismissed the role of the state in meeting human needs, and certainly not because he had any love for capitalism – although it must be said he wasn't much impressed by socialism, either. Rather, it was because he believed that, within the construction of race, which he saw as both illusory and real, each individual had to find and name her or his own particular identity and sense of who s/he was.

Baldwin's individualism, at bottom, followed from his conviction that race itself was an externalized imposition on human agency. It had no rightful claim to be part of anyone's consciousness. Given, however, its uses as an instrument of power in the history and contemporary politics of the West, one had no choice but to affirm one's dignity within its confines, even as one struggled to break loose from its hold.

When the black man's mind is no longer controlled by the white man's fantasies, a new balance or what may be described as an unprecedented inequality begins to make itself felt: for the white man no longer knows who he is, whereas the black man knows them both. For if it is difficult to be released from the stigma of blackness, it is clearly at least equally difficult to surmount the delusion of whiteness ...

"Black" and "white" are invented categories, one, a false stigma, the other a delusion. Since they mask the uniqueness of each individual human being, black or white, it is a fruitless effort to attempt to define a general and collective identity for the fabricated groups to which these beings belong. And since "race" is invented, there is no reason to assume that, within the groups themselves, there will be any agreement as to how such identity should be named and affirmed in any event. In fact, there is much reason to doubt that such agreement will, or can, emerge. It remains the responsibility of the particular members of these groups to figure out, in ways that violate the dignity of no one, who they are and who they wish to be.

There is at least a third reason Baldwin offers no fixed definitions for black identity. For, to the extent that the identity of any one "race" is grounded in the denial of the humanity of another, the attempt to affirm a general cultural identity for either the oppressed or the oppressor is a meaningless act. Baldwin rejected not only the legitimacy of the white social order on this basis, but that of the black Muslim as well, though he always felt the former was responsible for making the choices of the latter seem plausible to American blacks, whether they agreed with those choices or not. In the face of such a distorted set of cultural relationships, individual determination of one's identity, and the dignity and sense of self that go along with that determination, is the only workable alternative. Baldwin could only articulate and name the condition existentially. He could not make the determination.

In the end, Baldwin's most profound conviction is that, in a shared society, the choices and identity of one group, whatever its position in relation to power, will be inextricably connected to the choices and identity of all other groups. Thus, his conclusion was that, no matter what black people did, America could realize its promise only to the extent that whites ultimately saw the reflection of themselves in the black people whom they had constructed as racial objects but who were, it turned out, their intimates.

Baldwin incorporates double consciousness into his apprehension of the world, understanding it as the consequence of a white society's commitment to the construction of a dehumanized black object. But white people are not irrelevant to the effort to transcend it. In Baldwin's eyes, and it is perhaps what made him anathema to the militant nationalists with whom he disagreed, but deeply respected, there is no solution to the racialized catastrophe of American life without black and white recognizing the dialectic that, like it or not, binds them together. The question of the identity of one is inseparable from the question of the identity of the other.

SEE ALSO: African Americans; bigotry; Black Panther Party; color line; Cox, Oliver C.; cultural identity; essentialism; *Invisible Man*; Marxism; Myrdal, Gunnar; Nation of Islam; *négritude*; Other; racialization; whiteness

Reading

Collected Essays by James Baldwin (Library of America, 1998) is full of insights.
Race Matters by Cornel West (Vintage, 1994) is the source of the argument outlined in the main text.
The Souls of Black Folk by W. E. B. Du Bois (Bantam, 1989) is the classic 1903 text; it may profitably be read with the same author's *Writings* (Library of America, 1986).
W. E. B. Du Bois and American Political Thought: Fabianism and the color line by Adolph Reed Jr by Adolph L. Reed. Jr. (Oxford University Press, 1997) is worth reading alongside Bernard W. Bell's "Genealogical shifts in Du Bois' discourse on double-consciousness as the sign of African-American difference", in *W.E.B. Du Bois on Race and Culture* edited by Bernard Bell, Emily Grosholz, and James B. Stewart (Routledge, 1996).

JOSEPH KLING

DRESS

Identity and dress

To discuss dress, whether its production, consumption or use, is to engage with objects that touch a body, an individual, a group, a society and a culture – physically, visually and psychologically. The components of dress are:

- clothing
- accessories
- styling
- fashion
- hairstyles
- body art

These have been used in a variety of combinations by individuals and groups to define their identity within their society. To make such a cultural statement through the adornment of the body, and as an expression of the self, affords dress a crucial place in cultural and critical practice. Where, how and why people wear clothes are determined by external sociocultural issues and events. Within the context of ethnicity and race, the interrelated issues of skin color and social class, group and individual identity, colonialism and imperialism, are signifiers of how societies can be subdivided. Therefore the dress of different groups or individuals can reference different values and unlock a multiplicity of meanings associated with dress and how it is worn and used by its wearer, turning their dressed body into a prism of social-cultural commentary and critique.

The transformation of the body into an aesthetic form can express a whole gamut of emotions, from the seemingly simple act of dressing up to the expression of full-blown political ideologies. This style of dressing the body can lessen the anxiety of *who* one is and *how* one is. The constitutive principle of dress is to be the conductor of abreaction between the self and the non-self: it provides an opportunity for the wearer to release and express some repressed emotions. Dress is also a compelling reminder of the human dependency on, or acknowledgment of, boundaries – to reject or confront them – for the purpose of self-construction, and thereby constitutes the mechanics of cultural identity and the crystallization of one's ethnicity.

The historiography of dress is predominantly Eurocentric, with notable concentration on Britain and Paris. Published works have mainly concentrated on the heroes of dress culture – again European-based and white. Due to the advent of postcolonial studies, the mechanics of that discipline have enabled a growing field of study on the dress worn by the colonizer and the colonized and their descendants. When considering dress within a colonial context, race informs the historiography, the rhetoric and the material effect of imperial discourse and at once renders the host body visibly invisible. Notably, the construct of ethnicity, whilst inextricably linked with race, allows investigation across races. For example, studies of the dress practices amongst the larger groups of the British colony of Jamaica during the late nineteenth and early twentieth century – African Jamaicans, White Jamaicans and Indian Jamaicans – were carried out under the intrusive tenets of British imperialism and colonialism. Researching the resources on that island, as elsewhere, provides an alternative history, an alternative "truth" to the established representation of black, white and Indian people in Jamaica that had been disseminated through imperialist discourse, and thereby helps to overturn misconceptions.

Counter-discourse

In relation to the dress practice of colonized people, the use of traditional or Western-inspired dress was a means of "voice-consciousness," to apply Gayatri Chakravorty Spivak's term, providing the Other with an alternative form of communication on their place and identity. When artfully worn dress becomes the most resonant sign language; it can be a disturbingly powerful resource as a counter-hegemonic discourse based on commonalities such as race and ethnicity.

Frantz Fanon's work *A Dying Colonialism* (Penguin, 1965) presents an aphoristic treatise on the cultural and colonial significance of the veil to the colonized Algerian woman during the country's fight for independence during the 1950s. Fanon refers to the veil as the visible identification and signification of the Arab world. It was targeted by the French colonial administration as the dismantling mechanism of the colony's strength. It objectified, and was imbued with, the culture of that world as a symbol of strength, an anchor and a shield: "If we want to destroy the structure of Algerian society, its capacity for resistance, we must first of all conquer the women: we must go and find them behind the veil where they hide themselves." Kadiatu Kanneh's *Feminism and the Colonial Body in Post Colonial Studies Reader* (Routledge, 1995) offers a feminist reading of Fanon's essay that surmises that "ethnic dress becomes interchangeable with tradition and essentialism, and the female body enters an unstable arena of scrutiny and meaning." In this context, then, an authority of dress is the empowerment of the dressed body to undermine the tenets of authority.

The dress worn by the colonizer in the captured land generally conveys the meaning of power and superiority. For example, the practice of English men and women to wear full evening dress in the African bush, despite the impracticalities of women wearing layers of garments and restrictive underwear and men in thick suiting materials, was confirmation in alien surroundings and practices of their origins and the retention of the standards that came with those origins, and

simultaneously a means of retaining self-respect. It was a visual marker of race, gender and social rank of the different groups – the colonizing representative and the subaltern – who exist in a colonial place. Those associated with the rank of colonizer who chose to engage in the "ethnic" dress of the subaltern were branded as *going native*, thereby losing a sense of morality and damaging the dignity of their country of origin in the eyes of loyal colonial representatives. To engage in this change of clothing practice was seen as a desertion of the former self and the creation of a new self, thereby crafting one's identity on one's own terms and life experience.

The dressed body is also a "projection surface" for personal goals or beliefs which are fed into the self-imaging of an individual. To dress and style the body in a particular way, most notably in the use of Western dress, to meet certain personal criteria, places the components of dress as a metaphor of progressive action. The African-American Muslim and civil rights activist Malcolm X, for example, used dress throughout his life as one method to define his self. It was a process he refers to continuously in *The Autobiography of Malcolm X* (Hutchinson & Collins, 1966) as part of his explanation as to why his life was what he called a "chronology of changes." In 1961 the white photographer Eve Arnold took what has become one of the most iconic images of Malcolm X. Arnold has stated that the photograph was a collaboration with the man himself, who knew how to use the power of photography as an affective tool for positive representation. The portrait is dominated by his accessories: a trilby hat, horn-rimmed glasses, a Nation of Islam ring and a watch.

The trilby, the most overbearing item in the portrait, has, in the climate of the persistent Jim Crow etiquette in which this photograph was taken, the most foreboding and subversive communication. During the "racist etiquette" that plagued America during the 1950s and on through the 1960s nonwhite men were warned in 1959 that to wear a hat in the presence of whites could constitute an arrest, and in some extreme cases if they were to wear it when addressing a white woman, to mob violence, the action constituting "alleged rape of white women by non-white men." For a black man to have himself photographed by a white woman whilst wearing his hat, and more conspicuously, for that hat to be worn in such a cocksure manner –

tipped forward and perched nonchalantly on the subject's head – was an act of repudiation of the Jim Crow laws, and everything those laws meant in the separation of the races; it was a very public flouting of his "uppitiness."

The above examples of how men and women have used dress to situate their self centrally in the debate about race and ethnicity, place and identity, typify the possibilities of what a study of dress can do in the history and critique of different groups within this context.

SEE ALSO: beauty; bigotry; colonial discourse; colonialism; consumption; cultural identity; essentialism; ethnicity; ethnocentrism; Fanon, Frantz; hegemony; Jim Crow; Malcolm X; Orientalism; Other; postcolonial; representations; subaltern

Reading

Clothing and Difference: Embodied identities in colonial and post-colonial Africa, edited by Hildi Hendrickson (Duke University Press, 1996), demonstrates that the systems of studying dress in Europe and America can be applied to a study of colonial and postcolonial Africa.
Clothing Matters: Dress and identity in India by Emma Tarlo (Hurst, 1999) is an anthropological treatise on dress and identity to redress the lack of work in anthropology about clothing practice in India.
Dress and Ethnicity, edited by Joanne B. Eicher (Berg, 1995), acknowledges the essential need for such a study whilst outlining the complexities that must be addressed in such an undertaking.
Fashioned from Penury: Dress as cultural practice in colonial Australia by Margaret Maynard (Cambridge University Press, 1994) uses dress to unlock other aspects of Australia's history and the relationships between the dominant culture and the periphery.
"My man, let me pull your coat to something: Malcolm X" by Carol Tulloch, in Fashion Cultures, edited by Stella Bruzzi and Pamela Church-Gibson (Routledge, 2000), focuses on the dressed body of Malcolm X and his political activities as outlined by him in The Autobiography of Malcolm X.
"Out of many, one people? The relativity of dress, race and ethnicity to Jamaica, 1880–1907" by Carol Tulloch (in Fashion Theory, vol. 2, 1998) presents the methodology applied to research the dress practice of black, white and Asian women in Jamaica.
"The veil: postcolonialism and the politics of dress" is a special topic of Interventions: International Journal of Postcolonial Studies edited by Alison Donnell (vol. 1, 1999) which brings together a number of academics on the areas that need to be uncovered with regard to dress, ethnicity and identity.

CAROL TULLOCH

DRUGS

It is important at the outset to draw a distinction between drug usage and drug dealing. One who uses illicit drugs recreationally may not trade in illicit drugs professionally, and vice versa. It is unclear how sharply the distinction should be drawn. For, even though drug use and drug dealing are not coextensive, it cannot be gainsaid that a small percentage of drug users trade in drugs as a means of supporting their own drug habit.

Some would argue that the cry of racism is given as a convenient excuse for those who wish to engage in illicit drug use or dealing or both. They see no other connection between drugs and racism and, in fact, would argue that drug users or dealers would pursue their private crusades even in the absence of racism. Along these lines, others would argue that it is a kind of reverse racism even to attempt to place the blame of drug use or drug dealing on racism.

On the other hand, it is argued also that there is a definite relationship between drugs and racism. For example, in the USA racism contributes both to drug use and drug dealing in at least two ways. First, past racism – two centuries of slavery and nearly a century more of government-sanctioned racism under the Jim Crow system that ended only in the late 1960s – left black communities with tremendous social and economic disadvantage: less well-paying jobs, inadequate housing, and lower quality education than in white communities. Second, present-day racism that motivates racial discrimination in employment, housing, and education exacerbates the dismal living conditions today's black Americans have inherited from past racism. Both forces – past racism and present-day racism – have converged on generations of black families living in racially isolated communities.

Caught in an intergenerational cycle of poverty and despair, it is not surprising that black Americans use or deal in drugs at disproportionately high rates. The recreational use of drugs offers temporary relief (if not the only relief) from the pain and frustration of trying to succeed against insurmountable social and economic odds. While some might be able to fathom this connection, they have a more difficult time comprehending the nexus between these conditions or racism and drug dealing.

They, like society as a whole, tend to view drug dealing strictly as a form of criminal activity. In contrast, black Americans who live in poverty and deal in drugs view drug dealing as "an important career choice and major economic activity." Beepers hanging from the belt and briefcase swinging from the hand; drug dealing is what they do for a living. It is not simply their job (they view themselves as "capitalists," not as laborers), it is their business. Indeed, studies have shown that, not unlike those formally educated in Harvard Business School principles of finance, these drug dealers consciously seek to establish the optimum level of risk and return. Another study has concluded that: "The structure of drug-dealing organizations is complex and contains many roles with approximate equivalents in the legal economy." In racially isolated communities, drug dealing is sometimes the only business in town.

Critical race theorists (legal scholars who believe racism in the USA is permanent) add a more nuanced view to our understanding of racism. They argue that most racism today is unconscious; that is to say, it consists of negative attitudes or stereotypes about racial groups that are part of a person's cognitive makeup. Unconscious racism arises from an individual's cultural experiences, often transmitted by tacit understandings. Even if a child is never explicitly told that black Americans are inferior, the child learns that lesson by observing social arrangements and the behavior of others. When whites see disproportionately more blacks living in ghettoes, working at minimum-wage jobs, or failing to succeed in school, these negative images become mental referents for their understanding of what it means to be a black American. Jim Crow images beget Jim Crow cognitive categories.

SEE ALSO: African Americans; Barry case, the Marion; bigotry; black bourgeoisie in the USA; disadvantage; ethnocide; ghetto; homelessness; Jim Crow; racial profiling; representations; stereotype; underclass; violence

Reading

Bad Kids: Race and the transformation of the juvenile by Barry C. Feld (Oxford University Press, 1999) is an excellent discussion of black kids and their prosecution in the juvenile justice system for drugs and other criminal offenses.

"Drug abuse in the inner city: impact on hard-drug users and the community" by Bruce D. Johnson, Terry Williams, Kojo A. Dei, and Harry Sanabria, in *Drugs and Crime*, edited by Michael Tonry and James Q. Wilson (University of Chicago Press, 1990: 1–67), is a sophisticated discussion of drug use and drug dealing in the inner city.

Life with Heroin: Voices from the inner city by Bill Hanson, George Beschner, James M. Walters, and Elliot Bovelle (Lexington Press, 1985) gives the inner-city drug user's perspective.

Malign Neglect by Michael Tonry (Oxford University Press, 1995) argues that racial bias is built into the mandatory sentencing laws.

Petit Apartheid in the U.S. Criminal Justice System: The dark figure of racism by Dragan Milovanovic and Katheryn K. Russell (Carolina Academic Press, 2001) offers a conceptual scheme for understanding racial profiling and similar forms of racism in drug enforcement and, more generally, in the administration of justice.

Pipe Dream Blues by Clarence Lusane (South End Press, 1993) proposes that racism motivates government policy on drugs; not to be confused with *The American Pipe Dream: Crack cocaine and inner city* by Dale Chitwood, James Rivers, and James Inciardi (Harcourt Brace, 1996) which examines the impact of crack on city populations.

ROY L. BROOKS

DU BOIS, W. E. B. *see* double consciousness

E

EBONICS

A compound of ebony and phonics (of sound), Ebonics has been defined by Molefe Kete Asante as the "language spoken in the United States by African-Americans which uses many English words but is based on African syntactic elements and sense modalities" (in his *Afrocentricity: The theory of social change*, Amulefi, 1980). In December 1996, it became known internationally after the Board of Education of Oakland, California, passed a resolution to respect the legitimacy of Ebonics in order to facilitate African American pupils' acquisition and mastery of English language skills.

Ebonics combines West African grammar and pronunciation with the language of European colonial plantation owners and has about fifty distinct characteristics. Mostly an oral language, it typically involves dropping consonants at the end of words, which is, of course, common among many dialects. While it was presented by the Oakland board as a separate language, rather than a dialect or patois, it shares a basic vocabulary with standard English, the major differences being the conjugation of verbs, particularly "to be," with only the infinitive used in the present tense (e.g. "she be going") and only the past participle used in the past tense ("she been gone a while").

Much of the considerable criticism directed at the Oakland resolution was based on the misconception that African Americans would be taught Ebonics. In fact, the resolution provided for pupils who were fluent in Ebonics to become proficient in standard English in the same way as Asian American, Latino, Native American and other minority groups whose primary language was other than English. African Americans were considered equally entitled to educational programs designed to address their specific needs. The idea of treating black American children as effectively bilingual was, for many, insulting; though, for others, Ebonics was an authentic language and deserved to be regarded as such. Still others accused the Board of Education of seeming to pander to political correctness while applying for additional federal funds for remedial English.

Persistently low scores by black pupils in English and reading tests had been a problem in US schools for decades. At Oakland, 53 percent of pupils were black, 71 per cent of them in special classes and 64 per cent held back by at least one year because of underachievement. Two years before the Oakland resolution the infamous book *The Bell Curve: Intelligence and class structure in American life* by Richard Herrnstein and Charles Murray had raised the specter of differential intelligence based on genetics, or "the race-IQ" argument. While the Ebonics resolution did not directly address this, it alluded to essentialism in maintaining that Ebonics was one of a number of African language systems that were not dialects of English. It asserted that West and Niger–Congo languages were "genetically-based" and elements of them had been transmitted through several generations.

SEE ALSO: African Americans; Afrocentricity; beauty; children; education; essentialism; intelligence; language; racist discourse; whiteness

Reading

"The Ebonics controversy in my backyard: a socio-linguist's experiences and reflection" by John R.

Rickford (in *Journal of Sociolinguistics*, vol. 3, 1999) may be read in conjunction with the earlier *Ebonics: The true language of black folks*, edited by Robert L. Williams (St. Louis Institute of Black Studies, 1975). "Mock Ebonics: linguistic racism in the parodies of Ebonics on the Internet" by Maggie Ronkin and Helen E. Karn (in *Journal of Sociolinguistics*, vol. 3, 1999) is an empirical study of the caricatures of Ebonics that appeared on the internet in the wake of the Oakland decision.

EDUCATION

In its widest sense, education refers to the development of character or mental faculties in an intellectual and moral framework. Given this, education takes radically different forms, its content and methods of instruction reflecting and, sometimes, refracting the social context in which it takes place. When the context is one of cultural variation and increasing heterogeneity, systems of education are responsive to change.

Studies of the educational response to cultural diversity have explored a number of substantive themes against a bewildering backcloth of contradictory understandings of key conceptual and theoretical themes. If researchers tend to be out on a definitional limb when they grapple with the protean concept, multicultural education (and cognate terms such as multiracial education, multiethnic education, intercultural education, polytechnic education, antiracist education, and education for prejudice reduction), this is not surprising. After all, they derive from concepts which, burdened with the weight of ideological baggage in the disciples of sociology, anthropology, philosophy, psychology, and politics, fail to travel well either within or between these disciplines. The result: they remain diffuse, complex and, above all, contested terms.

Some educational researchers have admonished their peers for failing to explicate the denotative and connotative meanings of multicultural education (and its variants) when used as explanatory or analytical tools. It is easy to see why. On some occasions, terms such as multicultural, multiethnic and multiracial education are used synonymously and interchangeably. On others, particular concepts are assigned privileged status in the design, execution, and dissemination of research, but remain ill defined.

In Britain, this debate has tended to be structured around an intensive exploration of the distinction, if any, between multicultural and antiracist education. For some writers, the distinction is more apparent than real. They argue that despite protestations to the contrary, antiracists have tended to mobilize concepts, pedagogical strategies and policy imperatives which bear more than a passing resemblance to those associated with the (discredited) multicultural education paradigm. Antiracists maintain that their conception of racism and their strategies to combat its reproduction in education differ in profound ways from those which are operationalized by advocates of multicultural education.

There are other researchers, however, in Britain and elsewhere who show their impatience with efforts to consolidate conceptual clarity. For them, such enterprises are self-indulgent; displacement activities which distract attention away from the formulation and implementation of concrete policies to mitigate racial inequality in education.

There is a further complication, especially for those researchers and practitioners involved in comparative studies. This relates to the limited exportability of terms across national and cultural boundaries. In Britain, for instance, the discourse is heavily racialized, with terms such as "black," "racism," and "antiracism" naturalized in the literature and associated practices. This contrasts sharply with, say, the discourse in other Western European contexts. Similarly, terms such as "immigration" and "integration" have assumed a specific denotative and connotative status in Britain which is not necessarily shared in other national contexts.

This conceptual muddle is paralleled in the debate surrounding multilingualism. There, phrases such as mother tongues, community languages, and home languages are often used interchangeably without explanation or precision.

In spite of this terminological and conceptual confusion, there is some common ground. Above all, multicultural education assumes a view of an ethnically and culturally diverse society to which the education system should respond in a positive manner. In this sense, it may be distinguished from monocultural education and its attendant ideology of assimilation. It is also generally accepted that multicultural education embraces two distinct but complementary objectives. First, meeting the particular educational needs of ethnic minority children. Second, preparing all children for life in a multicultural society.

Of particular interest is the level of articulation between these particularistic and universalistic idioms of multicultural education and their relative contribution to the realization of equality of opportunity in education. If the "multicultural society" is interpreted as social description then it could be argued that *de facto* structural assimilation offers the most fruitful route to equality of opportunity. It assumes the pre-eminence of a transmissionist education primarily concerned with endorsing cultural hegemony and conserving the organization of the school, pedagogy, assessment, and curriculum accordingly.

Alternatively, the perception of the "multicultural society" in prescriptive terms demands the legitimation of cultural pluralism through transformative education. In this scenario, educational structures and experiences are reconstituted to ensure that cultural pluralist and antiracist ideals are normalized in administrative, pedagogical, curricular, and appraisal procedures. The dilemma facing educational systems in culturally diverse societies is both real and demanding. Too little allowance for diversity can lead to alienation, unrest and loss of control; too much, to fragmentation and loss of control.

SEE ALSO: antiracism; children; cultural identity; equality; ethnicity; intelligence; merit; multicultural education; multiculturalism; transracial adoption; underachievement; white flight

Reading

Critical Ethnicity: Countering the waves of identity politics, edited by Robert H. Tai and Mary L. Kenyatta (Rowman & Littlefield, 1999), examines the interactions of education, ethnicity and race through the work of mainly North American academic writers.

Diversity and Multicultural Education: A reference handbook by Peter Appelbaum (ABC-Clio, 2002) focuses on both the practicalities and the philosophical underpinnings of diversity and multicultural education; for a different perspective, and one which confirms the educational system's role in perpetuating inequalities, *Teach Me! Kids will learn when oppression is the lesson* by Murray Levin (Rowman & Littlefield, 2000) is recommended.

Interculturalism, Education and Inclusion by Jagdish S. Gundara (Sage, 2000) provides a British perspective.

"Race" Identity and Representation in Education, edited by Warren Crichlow and Cameron McCarthy (Routledge, 1993), is a comprehensive series of essays, drawing on contributions from the USA, UK, Canada, and Australia, where centrality is given to the issue of racial inequality contexts.

Rethinking Multicultural Education: Case studies in cultural transition, edited by Carol Korn and Alberto Bursztyn (Bergin & Garvey, 2002), investigates how pupils and educators negotiate the transition between home and school.

BARRY TROYNA

ELIJAH MUHAMMAD *see* Nation of Islam

EMANCIPATION

In Roman Law, *emancipare* meant literally "to transfer ownership," specifically the release of a child from paternal authority. By extension, emancipation came to mean the freeing of slaves, and, in an even broader sense, the lifting of legal restrictions on certain groups, as when we speak of the emancipation of Jews in eighteenth- and nineteenth-century Europe, of serfs in nineteenth-century Russia, or of women in twentieth-century Europe.

In the context of race relations, "emancipation" usually refers to the collective manumission of slaves in specific countries or colonial territories, especially in the Western hemisphere. France was the first to issue an emancipation proclamation of its slaves, in 1794, but the edict was rescinded by Napoleon in 1802, and actual emancipation only took place in 1848. Britain legally abolished slavery in its empire in 1833, with a five- to seven-year transition period of "apprenticeship." Most Spanish-American colonies emancipated their slaves within a few years of achieving independence from Spain in the 1820s. In the USA, the first Emancipation Proclamation was issued in 1862, but it only became effective in 1865. Brazil was the last major country of the Americas to abolish slavery, waiting until 1888, only a couple of years after the remaining Spanish colonies of Cuba and Puerto Rico.

The late eighteenth century saw the rise of an abolitionist movement in Europe and America, especially in Britain, France, the United States, and Brazil. The movement achieved its first major success when Britain and the United States outlawed the transatlantic slave trade in 1807. However, it was not until the early 1860s that the trade was effectively abolished. Rates of manumission of individual slaves during the slavery period differed widely from territory to territory. Some countries that were late in abolishing slavery, such as Brazil and Cuba, had much higher rates of manumission than countries where final abolition came earlier (e.g. the British colonies and the United States).

Whether slavery is considered extinct in the world at present is largely a matter of definition. A number of traditional forms of serfdom and clientage subsist in parts of Africa, Asia, and even Latin America which are difficult to distinguish from domestic slavery. As for large-scale chattel slavery, the Soviet and Nazi concentration camps would seem to qualify as modern revivals.

SEE ALSO: antislavery; Brazil; colonialism; diaspora; *encomienda*; Las Casas, Bartolomí de; miscegenation; race: as synonym; racism; science; slavery

Reading

Race and Class in Latin America, edited by Magnus M?rner (Columbia University Press, 1970) devotes Part 1 to "The abolition of slavery and its aftermath."

Slave and Citizen by Frank Tannenbaum (Random House, 1946) is a classic account of differences between the slave regimes in various parts of the Western hemisphere.

Slavery and Social Death by Orlando Patterson (Harvard University Press, 1982) is an impressively detailed sociological study; this may be read in conjunction with Kevin Bales's *Disposable People* (University of California Press, 2002), which suggests that, for twenty-seven million people in the world today, emancipation has still not arrived.

PIERRE L. VAN DEN BERGHE

EMINEM *see* rap

EMPOWERMENT

The term "empowerment" has been used in different, even contradictory ways. In some discussions it refers to a sort of psychological liberation; that is, someone has been "empowered" to act on his or her own behalf. In others, it refers to the capacity of individuals or a group to pursue an economic agenda free of interference from excessive government. As a descriptive term empowerment has become increasingly used and popularized in discussions focusing on race and poverty. Empowerment is utilized with increasing frequency especially in policy and political circles.

The US Federal Government and a range of public agencies at the local and state levels have used this term without clearly defining it. During the administration of President George Bush, Snr., an "Empowerment Task Force" was established by the White House staff. The US Secretary of Housing and Urban Development (HUD) at that time, Jack Kemp, utilized the term many times to describe the general strategy of the national administration in the area of urban public housing. The administration of President Bill Clinton pushed successfully legislation for the creation of "empowerment zones" throughout parts of poor urban and rural America and aimed at local economic revitalization.

Mack H. Jones used the word empowerment to describe the electoral victories and accomplishments of blacks in Atlanta, Georgia from the late 1960s to the mid 1970s. As used in this particular article, therefore, empowerment is a description of blacks gaining electoral office. Jones does add, furthermore, that the empowerment of the black community will not be adequate for improving living conditions due to the fact that the agenda for public policy is determined by the hierarchical relationship between white power and influence, and black political life. The major quality of this relationship is "the subordination of blacks by whites and the concomitant institutionalized belief that white domination is a function of the inherent superiority of white."

Lawrence J. Hanks uses the term empowerment, as does Jones. He suggests that black political empowerment reflects three components: proportional distribution of electoral positions based on the number of blacks in the total population, development and enactment of public policies benefiting blacks, and improvement in the social and economic status of the black community. For both Jones, and Hanks, empowerment refers primarily to the electoral victories of blacks in various settings. Thus, the black community becomes empowered as it gains electoral office.

But Jones and Hanks critique this process by pointing out that the gaining of political office by blacks does not necessarily mean the pursuit of public policies more favorable to black social and economic needs. Both authors see other political and economic limitations on the potential for empowerment – as they use the term – to improve drastically the living conditions of blacks.

Roberto Villareal *et al.* attempt a slightly different, and concrete, definition of political empowerment by writing that this term refers to "an increasing capacity to win value satisfaction through the organization of aggregation of individual resources and through the skill of organizational leadership in striking mutually beneficial bargains with other participants in the coalition-building process." Like Jones and Hanks, however, Villareal *et al.* state that electoral progress must be an integral part of a group's empowerment.

I have used the term empowerment here to mean specifically political mobilization aimed at challenging relationships of wealth and power in American society. The winning of electoral office by blacks or Latinos, therefore, is not enough to justify a descriptive term suggesting that a group has "empowered" itself. Though winning electoral office is one critical component of an empowering process, by itself such victories do not guarantee that a group is capable of challenging the relationships of economic and social hierarchy that Jones described in Atlanta, Georgia.

SEE ALSO: African Americans; Black Panther Party; Black Power; conservatism; Jackson, Jesse; Kerner Report; Latinos; Million Man March; Motown; politics; power; racist discourse; reparations; riots: USA, 1965–67; riots: USA, 1980 (Miami); whiteness

Reading

"Black political empowerment in Atlanta: myth and reality" by Mack H. Jones (in *Annals*, no. 439, September 1978) discusses black empowerment in terms of the first wave of city-level electoral victories in urban America. He uses Atlanta, Georgia, as a case study to argue that electoral victories will not be enough to significantly improve the living conditions of masses of blacks.

Latino Empowerment by Roberto E. Villareal, N. G. Hernandez, and H. O. Neighbor (Greenwood Press, 1988) describes empowerment as the ability to bargain successfully for group demands. Such bargaining is not confined to the electoral arena. Two critical elements for the empowerment of Latinos, according to these authors, are aggregation of individual and community resources, and the quality of leadership.

The Politics of Black Empowerment by James Jennings (Wayne State University Press, 1992) examines the complex political processes that need to be negotiated en route to black political and economic power in the urban USA.

The Struggle for Black Political Empowerment in Three Georgia Counties by Lawrence J. Hanks (University of Tennessee Press, 1987) focuses on how blacks

have attempted to mobilize themselves politically in three locations in the southern region of the USA. His study seeks to answer how political empowerment of blacks does or does not translate into public policy benefit for blacks.

JAMES JENNINGS

ENCOMIENDA

A practice used by Spanish conquerors and colonizers of Latin America to secure the labor of indigenous peoples in the sixteenth century. Derived from the Spanish *encomendar*, to entrust, the *encomienda* gave the Spanish rights to tribute in acknowledgment of submission, or as the price of peace or protection.

The system was used earlier in Spain after the 1492 treaty, which formally ended the Moors' occupation of the Iberian peninsular. Under an oath of capitulation, Moors were granted property rights and civil and religious liberty until 1499, when forcible conversion held sway; in 1502 Moors were expelled completely from the territory. Earlier, over 150,000 Sephardic Jews were driven out of Spain (Sefarad is the name they used to refer to their Spanish homeland).

The colonization of areas of Central and South America brought problems of labor. Indians subsisted primarily as farmers, while the Spanish, inspired by visions of *El Dorado*, sought to exploit the abundant land. Within the first hundred years of conquest, the Spanish had mined gold and silver, produced cacao, sugar cane and wheat and bred cattle, sheep and pigs. All enterprises demanded labor and, from 1511, the Spanish Crown began sending African slaves, especially to Hispaniola, for sugar production, and Puerto Rico, for gold mining. Black slaves proved more robust than indigenous workers, sharing with Europeans an acquired resistance to certain diseases, such as measles and smallpox.

While Africans were held as slaves, Indians were initially required to pay tribute to the Spanish from their lands; in return they were made subjects of the Spanish Crown and, as such, entitled to its protection. They were also provided with instruction in Christianity and allowed to subsist on their land. The idea of the *encomienda* was to exact loyalty by permitting modest reward.

The costs of the system were punishing and, combined with European-borne diseases and famine, the native population was decimated.

Also, pressure from campaigners against slavery, most notably Las Casas, persuaded Spain to introduce its New Laws in 1542. While these humanitarian regulations were designed to suppress the *encomienda*, the practice continued informally until perhaps the middle of the seventeenth century.

SEE ALSO: anti-Semitism; antislavery; capitalism; colonialism; culturecide; emancipation; Las Casas, Bartolomí de; Latinos; slavery

Reading

The Encomienda in New Spain: The beginning of Spanish Mexico, 3rd edn., by Lesley B. Simpson (University of California Press, 1981), is an authoritative guide.

ENCULTURATION *see* assimilation

ENTERTAINMENT *see* Jackson, Michael; Lee, Spike; minstrelsy; Motown; negrophilia; rap; reggae

ENTREPRENEURSHIP *see* middleman minority

ENVIRONMENTAL RACISM

This term has its origins in a 1987 report by the US Commission on Racial Justice, which found a pattern of "environmental racism" in the siting of toxic waste dumps and incinerators, and concluded that most of the largest and most dangerous landfills were in communities with majority black or Latino populations. Now it refers more generally to the various ways in which minorities fare badly in relation to the quality of the built environment; poor housing quality (and the failure to secure renovation grants), poor location, high noise and chemical pollution levels, and so on.

A key issue is residential settlement patterns: ethnic segregation is a common feature of many, perhaps most, contemporary societies; differing only in degree. This is not a problem *per se*: those sharing a common heritage may clearly wish to share residential space. But, majority and minority communities differ in the extent to which this desire can be actualized in the context of what those involved would regard as a "desirable" environment. In other words, for a variety of reasons such as those outlined at the end of the previous paragraph, minorities tend disproportionately to live in environmentally

poor neighborhoods; poor, in this context, meaning neglected and decaying urban infrastructure, high pollution levels and lacking inward investment and therefore employment opportunities.

Compounding the effects of this widespread material disadvantage is another key dimension of environmental racism. This is where minorities are deemed to be the root cause of their own predicament (rather than, say, individual or institutional racism). "Victim blaming" can take a number of forms. They are often wrongly blamed for the state of the properties in which they live, through lack of investment or lifestyle. Blacks, and young male blacks in particular, are disproportionately targeted by environmental health officers as a source of noise pollution, for example through loud music and parties. Minorities may also be seen as creating a wider problem through their cultural and religious practices. Hence, in the UK at least, halal butchers face an increased likelihood of inspection on the grounds that they (allegedly) pose a potential threat to public health.

Urban policy, certainly in Britain and the USA, has tended over the past few decades (officially at least) to take a "color-blind" approach in dealing with problems of urban decay. For example, a 1994 report by the US Environmental Protection Agency concluded that, though ethnic minorities were likely to be more exposed to hazardous chemicals, the pattern was determined less by race than by poverty. The policy implication was that poverty in the general sense should be targeted. An exception to this was the set of guidelines prepared by the Clinton administration in 1994: this required federal agencies to make sure that their programs did not inflict an unfair degree of environmental damage on poor white or ethnic minorities.

One of the key problems in the inner urban areas relates to the levels of unfitness and disrepair in the older housing stock. In Britain in the 1960s the central policy was one of clearance, i.e. the poorest housing was razed to the ground to make way for new developments. John Rex and Robert Moore, in their seminal research on Birmingham, Alabama showed how policy decisions led to the exclusion from clearance plans of areas with large numbers of black residents; local policy makers used the pretext that the statutory obligation to rehouse those displaced would provoke anger from white residents who did not benefit in this way. The effect was not only that such individuals were destined to remain in poor, substandard housing, they also suffered from urban blight (as a direct result of the clearance of contiguous areas). When policy moved away from clearance to renewal (in the mid 1970s), the question for researchers shifted to one of assessing the impact on minority populations of more localized investment within designated Housing Action Areas or General Improvement Areas. The investment was more likely to benefit white residents. All of these matters have significant implications for health, given the established links between poor housing and certain sources of high morbidity (and mortality) levels.

SEE ALSO: ghetto; homelessness; institutional racism; medicine; Park, Robert E.; Pruitt-Igoe; race relations: as activity; race relations: as construction; racial profiling; rational choice theory; segregation; social exclusion; welfare

Reading

Environmental Health and Racial Equality (Commission for Racial Equality, London, 1994) presents a review of attempts to undermine discriminatory practices, but concludes that local authorities in Britain have in general done little to control "environmental racism."

Race, Community and Conflict by John Rex and Robert Moore (Oxford University Press, 1967) spells out very clearly both how and why minority populations in Birmingham in the 1960s were located in areas which suffered from environmental decay.

"Renewal, regeneration and 'race': issues in urban policy" by Peter Ratcliffe (in *New Community*, vol. 18, no. 3, 1992) shows how urban policy has consistently failed to improve the position of minority residents.

CHECK: internet resources section under racism

PETER RATCLIFFE

ENVIRONMENTALISM

Environmentalist explanations of racial diversity were first developed in the eighteenth century at a time when many scholars looked to the Bible for their understanding of the world. The Bible presented all mankind as descended from Adam and Eve. How then could differences of physical appearance have arisen? The French naturalist Georges-Louis Buffon maintained that originally there was one species of man which, after being dispersed, changed "from the influence of climate, from the difference of food, and of the mode of living, from epidemical distempers, as also from the intermixture of individuals." The attainment of civilization depended on a society's ability to develop a social organization appropriate to its environment. The environment of tropical West Africa was seen as a particularly adverse one so that one strand in the defense of the slave trade was the belief that it provided an opportunity for Africans to attain human fulfillment in a more favorable setting. The natural humanity of West Africans was denied neither by the slave traders nor by the contemporary books of geography. Some eighteenth-century writers assumed that the prevailing adaptation to environment had been achieved over a long period and that it was dangerous for people to migrate to a region with a different kind of environment. The implication of Voltaire's *Candide* was that it was best for people to remain and cultivate the gardens of their own country. Europeans who settled in North America were expected to degenerate, and biblical support was found for the view that God had determined the bounds of each nation's habitation (*Acts* 17: 26).

The high point of eighteenth-century environmentalism in its application to race relations was the 1787 *Essay on the Causes of the Variety of Complexion and Figure in the Human Species* by Samuel Stanhope Smith (later president of Princeton College). Smith insisted that the Bible showed all men to be of one species. There was a general association between skin color and the degree of latitude marking out a people's habitat once allowance had been made for the "elevation of the land, its vicinity to the sun, the nature of the soil, the state of cultivation, the course of winds, and many other circumstances." Color, he wrote, might well "be considered as a universal freckle." Races could not be clearly distinguished from each other and it was therefore impossible to enumerate them with any certainty. All that stood in the way of the advancement of Negroes and other peoples of non-European origin was their removal to a better environment. If Negroes "were perfectly free, enjoyed property, and were admitted to a liberal participation of the society, rank and privileges of their masters, they would change their African peculiarities much faster."

Environmentalist explanations of racial diversity were under sharp attack during the first half of the nineteenth century from writers who stressed hereditarian causes of difference. Both kinds of explanation were brought together in

Darwin's theory of natural selection. With the establishment of genetics as a field of scientific research, it became possible to examine the relative importance of environmental and hereditarian explanations of particular observations. It is quite reasonable, however, to describe as environmentalists those writers who stress the relative importance of social, cultural, economic, nutritional, and similar factors in the differential performance of individuals of different socioeconomic status or different ethnic group membership when, for example, taking intelligence tests.

SEE ALSO: Africa; antislavery; Darwinism; equality; hereditarianism; heritability; science; self-fulfilling prophecy; slavery; social Darwinism; sociobiology

Reading

Mirage in the West by Durand Echevaria (Princeton University Press, 1957) describes European conceptions of America and the degeneration of those who settled there.

White Over Black by Winthrop D. Jordan (University of North Carolina Press, 1968) is a masterly study of the environmentalist strand in the development of racial thought in North America; this may profitably be read in association with *The Image of Africa* by Philip D. Curtin (Macmillan, 1964).

MICHAEL BANTON

EPITHET (RACIAL/SLANG)

Epithet is a term often used pejoratively to describe a person or group in disparaging terms. In its original use, epithet merely meant a short phrase or word to describe a person or object. For many years, it has almost exclusively been associated with a negative reference or name-calling of a racial and/or ethnic group, particularly persons of color. Thus, the term *racial epithet* has been employed in most instances when racist language is used to describe ethnic groups.

Racial epithets are centuries old and have often been used by a majority group in a society to denigrate minority groups that its members may hold in contempt.

A casual glance in dictionaries of slang lists defines over 1,500 racial epithets for nearly every ethnic and racial group in the world.

Epithets seem to be used more when an ethnic group is deemed to be dangerous to the majority of society or is viewed by the majority population as threatening its economic base. For example, during the latter part of the nineteenth century, American workers were alarmed with the increasing presence of Asian workers and businesses in the US and described them, as well as "it," as the "Yellow Peril." Similarly, after the World Trade Center attacks on September 11, 2001, "Towel Heads" and "Camel Jockey" re-emerged as slurs for Arabs or even people who "resembled" them.

Epithets have been ruled as "fighting words' by the US Supreme Court as far back as 1919 in *Abrams* v. *United States* in which the court ruled that words could be of such a nature and said in such a manner as to incite violence and would not necessarily be covered under the First Amendment of the US Constitution which guarantees freedom of speech. Entire books such as Randall Kennedy's *nigger* have been written on epithets, and the efforts to keep them out of dictionaries have been mounted by groups such as the NAACP (National Association for the Advancement of Colored People).

One irony of an epithet is that its use can evolve from being a term of pride to one of derision. "Colored" for example was the most common designation that Africans in America used to refer to themselves until the early part of the nineteenth century. This replaced the term "African" which the newly captured Africans called themselves for nearly two hundred years. The African Methodist Episcopal Church founded by Richard Allen in 1787 took pride in its name. So did most Africans in America until the Colored Conventions which began around the first quarter of the nineteenth century, encouraged the use of that term – "colored" – to describe Africans in America since it was thought that "African" made them seem more "African" than "American." It was reasoned that they would be more quickly be absorbed into the social fabric of the United States if they dropped "African" as an appellation and used "colored." The NAACP was founded with this in mind, but W. E. B. Du Bois, one of its original founders, thought that "Negro" was a more assertive term and used it in much of his writings for many years. "Black" replaced "Negro" as a symbol of racial pride and "colored" not only fell into disrepute but also became a term of derision and "fighting words" for most blacks along with its close etymological cousin, "Negro."

In one sense, the evolution of epithets reflects the dilemmas that ethnic and racial groups face in societies that are often responsible for the racism directed toward them. Furthermore, "co-opting" epithets has also become a strategy for removing the sting from racial slurs. "Nigger," or "nigga" is a term used by many rap artists in music as a way of lessening its impact on the hearer. Such use, however, is *only* for the in-group; use of such terms by out-group members is viewed with hostility. The denunciation of Jennifer Lopez, a Latina singer, for her use of the term "nigga" in one of her sounds is illustrative of the "exclusivity" of epithets to the targeted group.

Comedians also engage in the use of epithets in what some refer to as "gallows humor." Jewish comedians will make fun of being Jewish. So will Asian, black and other entertainers who encourage laughter from their ethnic group as well as others by using epithets. This "dangerous" comedy is epitomized in the humor of Chris Rock, Dave Chappelle and in the recent past by the early Richard Pryor.

At its core, however, is the persistence of epithet as a way of marginalizing groups that the society views as questionable. Often such terms are used incorrectly to include *anyone* resembling in speech, custom or dress the group in question. In Europe, "Turks" are sometimes viewed as *any* person working in Europe and having their ethnic roots in the Middle East. "Nigger" is widely used as a term that includes any person of African descent regardless of their country of origin. Efforts to eliminate epithets from dictionaries and other word lexicons, though heroic, fail at eliminating them from the language of most people.

SEE ALSO: bigotry; double consciousness; humor; *Invisible Man*; Islamophobia; Jim Crow; language; media; Other; racial coding; representations; September 11, 2001

Reading

A Dictionary of Epithets and Terms of Address by Leslie Dunkling (Routledge, 1990) and *The Dictionary of American Slang*, 3rd edn., edited by Barbara Kipfer, Harold Wentworth and Robert L. Chapman (HarperCollins, 1998), are both serviceable sourcebooks.

nigger: The strange career of a troublesome word by Randall Kennedy (Pantheon, 2002) is the Harvard law professor's essay on what he calls the "paradig-

matic" racial slur in the English language; a neutral noun in the seventeenth century, *nigger* had, by 1830, become an "influential" insult; the book examines the word's history in literature, song, film and other forms of popular entertainment.

RAYMOND A. WINBUSH

EQUAL OPPORTUNITY

Originally advocated by the US civil rights movement, this principle was appropriated by conservatives in the late 1970s and used as an alternative to policies that emphasized equality of results, as opposed to opportunities. As such, it was a perfect complement to the conservative egalitarianism that was pre-eminent in the USA and Britain through the 1980s and 1990s. The components of equal opportunity comprised:

- The adequacy of the marketplace in the fair distribution of rewards appropriate to ability, innovation and endeavor.
- The need to encourage the elimination of discrimination at the point of entry into the job market.
- The absence of state responsibility for racism in history.
- The standardization of merit-oriented criteria in employment; as embodied, for example, in typical equal opportunities employers' job advertisements " ... encourage applications for all suitably qualified candidates irrespective of ethnic origin, race, sex, ... etc."
- The undesirability of government interference in protecting groups that, for historical reasons, have been disadvantaged or rendered vulnerable.
- The need only for fine tuning in the matters of professional expertise and job proficiency to give presently disadvantaged groups the skills and values necessary to be competitive in the job market; and correspondingly the essential soundness of present structural arrangements.
- The dire consequences of policies designed to improve the conditions of specific groups by favor, preferment or protection. Dependence on the state, it was thought, was the most likely result.

Equal opportunity was perfectly consonant with the ideological frameworks erected by Ronald Reagan in the United States and

Margaret Thatcher in Britain in the 1980s. The appeal to market forces, absence of government in the expansion of opportunities, and the opposition to the granting of special privileges or rights made it a successful weapon with which to challenge some forms of modern liberalism. In contrast to policies that urged an active role for government in the advancement of disadvantaged groups, conservative egalitarianism emphasized *laissez-faire* and "supply-side" economic theory as the way to correct glaring inequities in the distribution of resources.

While the moral legitimacy of the concept has been established on both sides of the Atlantic, equal opportunity has been limited in practical results, primarily because it ensures no discrimination in appointments. Managing its implementation in promotion or transfer has proved more difficult and has lessened its potency.

SEE ALSO: affirmative action; disadvantage; equality; ethnic monitoring; human rights; institutional racism; law: civil rights, USA; law: race relations, Britain; medicine; merit

Reading

Against Equality of Opportunity by Matt Cavanagh (Oxford University Press, 2002) is a full-blown critique of the concept, which the author believes is too vague to be useful in determining how jobs should be allocated.

Chain Reaction by Thomas and Mary Edsall (Norton, 1991) contains a chapter on "Race, rights, and party choice," which examines the symmetry between equal opportunity and Republican ideologies of the 1980s in the USA. For comparison, *Racism and Equal Opportunities Policies in the 1980s*, edited by Richard Jenkins and John Solomos (Cambridge University Press, 1987), addresses the problem of equal opportunity and methods of ensuring its maintenance in Britain.

Equal Opportunity Theory by Dennis E. Mithaug (Sage, 1996) addresses the discrepancy between the concept of a human right and the experience of self-determination.

Ethnicity, Equality of Opportunity and the British National Health Service by Paul Iganski and David Mason (Ashgate, 2002) is a study of equal opportunity in action, in this case in the form of the provisions and initiatives operative in the health service; it may profitably be read with *Equal Opportunities and Social Policy: Issues of gender, race and disability* by Barbara Bagihole (Longman, 1997), which also has a British focus.

EQUALITY

Greek, Roman and Christian conceptions

Equality is a key term in contemporary theories about justice and about democracy. It has been a keyword of the revolutionary movements fighting against hierarchies and privileges in the last centuries and a crucial term of the affirmative action debate in the last decades. Besides this, equality is an important idea in the discourses about modernity and tradition. However, the term equality causes considerable confusion in academic as well as in everyday discussions. Thus, in the affirmative or positive action debate both supporters and opponents attempt to justify their respective positions. These controversial perspectives could suggest either that the participants in this debate are victims of semantic confusion, or they are using, in bad faith, the notion of equality in a purely ideological manner (according to Julio Faundez).

However, one of the main sources of the problem lies in the unclear notion of equality. This fuzziness had already started with Aristotle, who saw the key element of justice in treating like cases alike – an idea that has set later thinkers the task of working out which similarities (need, desert, talent) should be considered as relevant. Aristotle's conception of justice provided a framework that had to be filled in before it could be put to use and, in fact, over centuries it was used to legitimize hierarchies between the sexes or between free people and slaves.

Looking at its history, we have to distinguish between the history of the normative concept of (Western style) equality and the never-ending fight over hierarchy, privileges and justice in the name of equality. However, preceding the normative concept of equality is the ubiquitous idea of reciprocity in so-called primitive societies. From ethnological accounts we know that systems of reciprocity have been rather complex and far-reaching. It seems that both reciprocity and hospitality have been considered as highly esteemed values; and in fact both were necessary conditions for the survival of individuals and societies in endangered situations. However, alongside this, the most widespread understanding of humankind in those societies (including the Greek *polis*) has been the identification of their own group as the true representatives of human beings, and that of all the other people not only as aliens but as inferior.

The Stoics are reportedly the first to elaborate the conception of general equality, based on their conviction that all human beings share the capacity to reason. This led them to a fundamental sense of equality, which went beyond the limited Greek conception of equal citizenship. From the belief in human reasoning capacities the Stoics drew the implication that there is a universal moral law, which all people are capable of appreciating. Based on the doctrine of a universal moral law the Stoics rejected ethical relativism.

However, the derivation of the conception of equality from the capacity to reason is a rather dubious one, because it cannot clarify what should be considered as reasonable and what should not. The history of humankind provides us with plenty of examples that the more powerful also claimed to be the (more) reasonable. And those who were excluded from resources as well as from participation in the normative discourse, such as women, men and women of color or simply the "have-nots," have been denied both the capacity to argue reasonably as well as access to equal rights or benefits.

In contrast to both the Greek and Roman understandings, the Christian ethical standards developed a new sense of the equal moral status of all human beings. For Christians, humans are equal because they are all potentially immortal and equally precious in the sight of God. This allowed them to treat slaves as human beings. In contrast to the earlier conception of equality, the Christian understanding of equal value has been more inclusive and – taken seriously – would not provide the powerful with arguments to deprive the powerless from equal value. However, over centuries the Christian conception of equal value of all human beings as well as the creed in the virtue of poverty coexisted with a highly hierarchical understanding of church and society. Whereas the protest against hierarchy and privileges never could be silenced, most of the time it was left to heretics, rebels or mendicant orders within the church.

Goods, claims and burdens

In response to a question raised by the Academy of Dijon, Jean-Jacques Rousseau, in 1754, developed his understanding of the origin of inequality among men. Quite pathetically Rousseau claimed that the first man who enclosured a piece of land and named it his property did both: he founded civil society and at the same time brought crime, wars, killing, suffering and terror to the world. In his treatise Rousseau went on to regret that nobody had stopped him, saying that all would be lost if one forgot that the fruits of the earth belong to everybody whereas no human being can be the owner of the earth. Like Thomas Hobbes, John Locke, and Emmanuel Kant, Rousseau realized that within property-based societies only a *social contract* could provide rules creating equality among citizens. The fictional idea of *social contract* has been the fundament of modern constitutions. However, the concept of *social contract* also has been both an instrument of inclusion, endowing the included with equal rights, and an instrument of exclusion to the rest, i.e. again to women, men and women of color, and aliens (see, for instance, Pateman, below).

Today, it is a matter of fact that modern democracies are based upon the principle of equality of all human beings. The Constitution of the United States, the Declaration on Human Rights of the French Revolution, the UN's Universal Declaration of Human Rights (1948), many other international documents, and the great majority of the national constitutions all over the world declare themselves committed to the principle of equality. However, the modern conception of equality does not provide us with any specific interpretation of the term. For instance, Ronald Dworkin maintains that the equal protection clause of the US Constitution anchors the concept of equality without providing any particular conceptions of it. Thus, the term equality does not give us any information about the question of which goods and claims are the entitlement of human beings or which burdens are incumbent on them.

Besides this unclearness, it has to be stressed that all political and moral debates and all modern legal documents deal with a prescriptive and not with a descriptive equality. In his *Equal under Law*, Jacobus tenBroek rightly pointed out that the sentence of the American Constitution "All men are created equal" is a demand, a prescription, not a description. However, no conclusions can be drawn from this prescription, i.e. from this political consensus in which respect equality should be realized.

To give a picture of the possible confusion when it comes to the question of equal distribution, consider Bruce Ackerman's story, in *Social Justice in the Liberal State*, about the discussion in a fictional assembly about fair and just rules to distribute manna. Agreeing that a just distribution should be based on the concept of equality, very different rules could be formulated: Some rules distribute manna on the basis of merit, others on the basis of need; some classify people by their contribution to overall happiness; others consider their contribution to the worst-off class; some say that manna should be distributed in a formally equal way.

Equal treatment/equal rights

In order to clarify the possible meaning of equality we should differentiate between *formal* equality of opportunity and *fair* equality of opportunity. Formal equality of opportunity requires that laws and quasi-legal devices are not used to deprive subjects of means already in their possession or within their present capacity to obtain in the future (see Rosenfeld, below). Fair equality of opportunity, on the other hand, requires, for John Rawls, that those with similar abilities and skills should have similar life chances irrespective of the income class into which they are born. Individuals from all economic and social backgrounds should be able to develop those skills for which they are naturally suited. Thus, fair equality of opportunity demands correction for socially relative disadvantages.

Next to this differentiation we have to distinguish two different kinds of equality rights: (1) the right to equal treatment and (2) the right to be treated as an equal. Ronald Dworkin explains the difference between the two legitimate moral and legal claims as follows:

The first is the right to equal treatment, that means, the right to equal distribution of a chance, a resource, or a burden. For instance, every citizen in a democracy has the right to an equal vote; it is the nerve of the decision of the Supreme Court that a person has to have a vote, even if other and more complex arrangements would better secure the collective well being. The second one is the right to be treated as an equal, this does not mean the right to receive the same share in a burden or in a utility, but the right to be treated with attention and consideration in the same way as all the others. If I have two children and one is in danger of dying from a disease which causes an indisposition to the other, I do not consider both in the same way, if I throw a coin to decide who of the two is to receive the remaining dose of a medicine. This example shows that the right to be treated as an equal is the fundamental one and that the right for equal treatment has been derived from it. The right to be treated as an equal will implement a right for equal treatment into some circumstances; this will, however, by no means be the case in all situations. (in *Taking Rights Seriously*)

Consequently the right to be treated as an equal may legitimize the right to certain preferential treatment without violating the principle of equality.

Besides the theoretical discussions we need to consider under which condition even a modest form of equal distribution and equal opportunities can be realized. In today's capitalist societies the liberal idea of equality seems to be the most effective legitimization of an endless increasing unequal distribution. In the last decades this statement seems to be true more than ever. Thus, a worldwide household survey that covered 84 percent of the world population and 93 percent of the world GDP (gross domestic product) gave evidence that the richest 1 percent of people in the world (i.e. less than 50 million people) receive as much as the bottom 57 percent (i.e. 2.7 billion poor people). The ratio between average income of the world top 5 percent and the world bottom 5 percent increased from 78:1 to 114:1 between 1988 and 1993 (figures from Milanovic, below).

With respect to this development we can conclude that the liberal concept of equality serves as an effective instrument of removing unfair disadvantages for those who have at least some access to resources and only within those states which have developed effective redistribution institutions. For those who have no access to any resources and who live within states without effective redistribution instruments, the liberal concept of equality seems to be no more than a useless phrase. As long as there exist no institutions for substantial redistribution both within states and also between states on a global level, the ideal of equality will be misused to legitimate an unjust status.

SEE ALSO: affirmative action; disadvantage; equal opportunity; ethnocentrism; human rights; ideology; merit; patriarchy; rational choice theory; underclass

Reading

Affirmative Action: International perspectives by Julio Faundez (International Labor Office, 1984) reviews affirmative action policies from an international perspective.

Affirmative Action and Justice – A Philosophical and Constitutional Enquiry by Michel Rosenfeld (Yale University Press, 1991) provides a systematic analysis of the philosophical background of affirmative action; while *Equal under Law* by Jacobus tenBroek (Collier, 1969) defends affirmative action policies as a legitimate instrument in liberal societies.

The Sexual Contract by Carol Pateman (Oxford University Press, 1988) analyzes the concept of social contract from a feminist point of view.

Social Justice in the Liberal State by Bruce Ackerman (Yale University Press, 1980) analyzes the compatibility of liberty and equality from a theoretical standpoint.

Taking Rights Seriously by Ronald Dworkin (Duckworth 1987) defends the concept of substantial equality as one of the basic fundaments in liberal societies; this should be read in conjunction with *A Theory of Justice* by John Rawls (Harvard University Press, 1971), which presents the most influential theory of justice in the twentieth century.

"True world income distribution 1988 and 1993: first calculation based on household surveys alone" by Branco Milanovic (in *The Economic Journal*, vol. 112, 2002) scrutinizes worldwide unequal distribution on an empirical basis.

ERNA APPELT

EROTICIZATION *see* beauty; sexuality

ESSENTIALISM

Deriving from the Platonic conception of essences, or intrinsic features, qualities or elements, essentialism is an approach based on the assumption that groups, or classes of people and objects, have one or more fundamental features exclusive to members of that group or class. This essential set of characteristics not only work to distinguish one group from others, but remain largely unchanged over time and exert decisive influences over other facets of the group.

Essentialism as a modern mode of thought is a product of the eighteenth-century Enlighten-ment's search for ways of ordering and understanding. The effort to discover distillations of difference was a response not to the question "how are things different?" but "what makes them different?" Scientific research geared toward the discovery of natural qualities that were in some way linked to capabilities promoted a doctrine that held that all living phenomena possess essences that may bind them together as well as separate them from others. The search was promoted by Rení Descartes's proclamation that human reason could potentially disclose all the so-called mysteries of the universe.

Jacques Barzun, in his 1937 classic *Race: A study in superstition* (Harcourt, Brace & Co), wrote that: "In recent times, the first systematic division of mankind into races is that by [FranÆois] Bernier in 1684." Bernier proposed four or five *espØs ou races*, based on geography, color and physical traits. Bernier followed Descartes's injunction to use reason by applying a scientific method in his effort to uncover basic qualities that separated human populations. His theory was the first of several grander attempts to ascertain properties that defined human groups, though his work was overshadowed by a larger and more ambitious project.

The recent ancestry of essentialism can be traced to Carolus Linnaeus (1707–78), the Swedish botanist who devised a comprehensive system for naming, ranking and classifying organisms according to "natural" differences. The class of a plant, for example, was determined by its stamens, and its order in the arrangement by its pistils. These are the plant's reproductive organs. For Linnaeus, species of organisms were entities that were grouped into higher categories called *genera*, the singular of which is *genus*. The idea informing this taxonomy was that groups of living entities have common structural characteristics distinct from those of all other groups. The concept of race, of course, distills this very idea. In other areas of human culture, tribes, nations and classes are among the many ways in which humans align themselves with similar concepts. It follows that members of such alignments share cultural identities and that those identities will either echo, reflect or incorporate characteristics that define an essence.

Race, racism and other modes of what Barzun called "race thinking" exemplify essentialism. The signification of an Other involves essentializing what are perhaps diverse, disparate and variegated populations by the selection of one or more features. In this instance, political and economic purposes inform the designation. But even measures designed to challenge those purposes and their consequences may venture into essentialism. The idea of ethnicity, for example, has been construed as a constructive response to racism: ethnic groups, which have been racialized, articulate positive and inclusive tendencies as if to repudiate the stereotyping that typically accompanies racism. Yet, as some writers, including Floya Anthias, have pointed out, "a common experience of racism may act to 'ethnicize' diverse cultures, as in the case of the 'Black' category in Britain" (in "Connecting 'race' and ethnic phenomena," *Sociology*, vol. 26, 1992). "Ethnicizing" heterogeneous populations becomes tantamount to creating essential categories; attempting to escape one trap leads to another.

Afrocentrism, or Afrocentricity, provides a comparable example. Conceived initially as a way of reminding African-descended populations throughout the world of their common heritage, it emphasized the dignity of Africa and celebrated its history, culture and achievements in counterpoint to those of Europe. In other words, it was an alternative to worldviews that presented European motifs as central – Eurocentrism. Subsequent varieties of Afrocentrism became more robust, advancing a conception that, doctrinally, resembled the very phenomenon it opposed. From this followed "Extreme intellectual and cultural separatism, involving belief in fundamentally distinct and internally homogeneous 'African' ways of knowing and feeling about the world, ways which only members of the group can possibly understand" (see Howe, below).

The conception of a natural, spiritual and perhaps even psychic unity of all people of African descent is essentialist, and, as such, faces the same kind of criticism leveled at other such movements, i.e. that they insulate themselves from the possibility of falsification, render meaningful differences insignificant details and imagine unity where there is often division. The dangers of simply inverting or transposing the categories of oppressor and oppressed without revealing the genesis of such binary classifications are ever-present for all movements challenging racism and, indeed, other forms of essentialism.

The women's movement faced comparable problems. It made good strategic sense to accept established sexual divisions and radicalize their contents: women were not biologically ill-equipped to perform the kind of intellectually demanding work associated with men, nor especially well-equipped to nurture and care. But women nevertheless possessed characteristics that equipped them for a range of activities, many of which required a combination of attributes, some of which were traditionally associated with men, others of which were uniquely women's.

Yet, closer historical investigation reveals that the essentialism of sexual differences is relatively recent. Thomas Laqueur's studies of medical texts indicate that the concept of a sharp division between male and female is a product of the past 300 years and, for 2,000 years before that bodies were not visualized in terms of differences. In other words, there were people, some of whom could have children, others of whom could not; sexual difference was not a concept, so it was impossible to conceive a distinct bifurcation of types based on sexual identity. Even those physical differences we now regard as obvious were not so obvious without a conceptual understanding of sexual differences. In some periods a woman's clitoris was thought to be a minuscule protuberance, an underdeveloped version of the equivalent structure in men, the penis.

For most of human history the stress was on similarities, the female body being just a "gradation," or nuance, of one basic male type. This vision complemented and bolstered a male-centered worldview in which, as Laqueur puts it, "man is the measure of all things, and women does not exist as an ontologically distinct category." Nelly Oudshoorn's work extends that of Laqueur by identifying how the female body became conceptualized in terms of its unique *sexual essence* only in the 1920s and 1930s when hormones were discovered.

While opposition to essentialist ways of thinking has escalated with the rise of postcolonial challenges, the tendency to slide back toward or retain a residual essentialism remains. *Négritude* and subaltern, for example, both oppose yet step in the footprints of essentialism. And while the concept of diaspora is explicitly used to undermine, indeed atomize, essentialist notions, its own status must remain open to ontological review. In other words, residual essentialism may be detectable in many of the efforts to deconstruct it.

SEE ALSO: Afrocentricity; cultural identity; diaspora; ethnocentrism; Hall, Stuart; hybridity; *nigritude*; race: as signifier; race relations: as construction; racial coding; racist discourse; subaltern; transracial adoption; white race; whiteness

Reading

Afrocentrism: Mythical pasts and imagined homes by Stephen Howe (Verso, 1998) is a full-frontal assault on the doctrine in which the author exposes its limitations and its dangers.

Making Sex: Body and gender from the Greeks to Freud by Thomas Laqueur (Harvard University Press, 1990) is the text quoted above and should be read in association with two pieces of research that extend the author's analysis: Nelly Oudshoorn's *Beyond the Natural Body: An archeology of sex hormones* (Routledge, 1994) and Londa Schiebinger's medical history *The Mind Has No Sex: Women in the origins of modern science* (Harvard University Press, 1989), as well as Laqueur's edited collection with Catherine Gallagher, *The Making of the Modern Body: Sexuality and society in the nineteenth century* (University of California Press, 1987).

ETHIOPIANISM

The expression of black nationalistic-messianic movements organized around the vision of an Africa redeemed and liberated from colonial rule. Its sources derive from nineteenth-century chiliastic Christianity, missionaries, and black nationalism, whilst its origins lie in the sixteenth century. As Jenkins points out in his *Black Zion*: "From the first day on which an African was captured then blessed by some swaggering Portuguese cleric and consigned to a terrible Atlantic crossing, there have been two distinct Africas. There is the geographical entity with its millions of social realities, and there is the Africa of the exiled Negro's mind, an Africa compounded of centuries of waning memories and vanquished hopes translated into myth."

Jenkins notes how slaves being transported to the Americas threw themselves overboard still locked in irons in vain attempts to swim home. In the early 1830s, Samuel Sharpe, a Jamaican slave, organized a rebellion based on the belief in a messianic deliverance to Africa. Sharpe used a combination of Christian concepts, particularly the idea of the "second coming," and African beliefs to generate enthusiasm for his uprising. Before him, slave preachers from America had traveled to the West Indies to establish what was called Native Baptism, again a fusion of Christianity and African beliefs.

At the turn of the nineteenth century, Paul Cuffee, a black sea captain living in Massachusetts, attempted a migration program, but succeeded in returning only thirty-eight people to Sierra Leone. After Cuffee, the vision of a mass migration of blacks to Africa was sustained, albeit with some modifications, by various leaders, one of whom, Bishop Henry M. Turner, succeeded in settling an estimated 500 people in Liberia.

One of the most vivid expressions of Ethiopianism came in the 1920s with the Universal Negro Improvement Association (UNIA) under the leadership of Marcus Garvey, whose slogan "Africa for the Africans" captured the philosophy of the movement. Blacks in the USA and the West Indies were implored to abandon hopes of integration into white society and turn their sights toward Africa.

Garvey adopted the national colors of Ethiopia for the UNIA and constantly referred to the Ethiopian empire as a source of inheritance and ancestry in counterposition to the imperial dominance of Western powers. "We negroes believe in the God of Ethiopia," insisted Garvey. "He shall speak with the voice of thunder that shall shake the pillars of a corrupt and unjust world and once more restore Ethiopia to her former glory." Like other similar movements, the UNIA identified the whole African continent as "Ethiopia," the idea being that, in ancient times, there was just one vast nation called Ethiopia; the conquering Europeans found it expedient to split up the continent into separate countries because it facilitated domination – the "divide and rule" principle.

Elements of Ethiopianism can be found in many twentieth-century messianic movements, such as those led by Daddy Grace, Father Divine, J. Arnold Ford, and W. D. Fard, who started the movement which became today's Nation of Islam.

Perhaps the most universal manifestation of Ethiopianism is Rastafari. This movement emerged in the 1930s, taking the basic ideas of the UNIA but grafting them on to an apocalyptic vision of the future in which the whites' political control of the West would be loosened and all black peoples would be returned.

In Europe the movement called *nigritude* became a cultural counterpart to the more obviously political movements. This gave artistic expression to what were taken to be distinct African modes of thought. One of its leading proponents, Líopold Senghor, told his followers to attempt to rid their minds of "white" thoughts, reject white values and immerse themselves in Ethiopia, which he also used synonymously with Africa.

SEE ALSO: Afrocentricity; diaspora; double consciousness; essentialism; Fanon, Frantz; Garvey, Marcus; Malcolm X; Nation of Islam; nationalism; *nígritude*; Rastafari; Senghor, Líopold Sídar; whiteness

Reading

Black Messiahs and Uncle Toms: Social and literary manipulations of a religious myth, rev. edn., by Wilson J. Moses (Penn State University Press, 1993) chronicles the extraordinary continuity in Ethiopianist themes among African American social and religious movements.

Black Nationalism by E. U. Essien-Udom (University of Chicago Press, 1962) is essentially a study of the Nation of Islam, but with interesting sections on its forerunners, such as the Moorish Science Temple of America and Father Divine's Peace Mission.

Black Zion by David Jenkins (Wildwood Press, 1975) is a clear exposition of the various manifestations of Ethiopianism since the early slave days, showing how they are sometimes purely religious. This may be read in conjunction with *Black Exodus* by Edwin S. Redkey (Yale University Press, 1969) which covers much the same ground, but gives more emphasis to the American movements, particularly Southern slave rebellions, such as that of Nat Turner.

Civil Rights, Blacks Arts and the Black Power Movement in America: A reflexive analysis of social movements in the United States, edited by James L. Conyers Jr. (Ashgate, 2001), is full of essays on movements and organizations that in some way embody Ethiopianist values and ideas.

ETHNIC CLEANSING

Conceptual and historical background

Broadly, ethnic cleansing refers to a policy of forced population movement to render a geopolitical locality homogeneous in relation to ethnicity. As with many concepts employed in the field of race and ethnic relations, the terminology is of more recent derivation than the practices it designates. The term first began to be extensively deployed during the wars that accompanied the disintegration of the former Yugoslavia, particularly in connection with the warfare and attendant ethnic/religious violence in Bosnia-Herzegovina and Croatia, 1991–95, and later in connection with the conflict in Kosovo in 1999. A Commission of Experts established by the Secretary-General of the UN to inquire into "grave breaches of the Geneva Conventions and other violations of international humanitarian law committed in the territory of the former Yugoslavia," referred in its report of April 1994 to ethnic cleansing as "a purposeful policy designed by one ethnic or religious group to remove by violent and terror-inspiring means the civilian population of another ethnic or religious group from certain geographic areas. To a large extent, it is carried out in the name of misguided nationalism, historic grievances and a powerful driving sense of revenge. This purpose appears to be the occupation of territory to the exclusion of the purged group or groups" (*http://www.ess.we.ac.uk/comexpert/III-IV_D.htm#III.B*, accessed September 16, 2002).

Ethnic cleansing is a subtype of population cleansing, one that involves the forcible removal of members of an *ethnic* group from a particular locality. In terms of the orientation and motivations of its perpetrators, and their interactions with victims, it is conceptually difficult at times to demarcate entirely satisfactorily ethnicity, religion, nationality, and culture in connection with forced population movements. Many of the underlying factors associated with ethnic cleansings are common to the motivational, aetiological and interactive contexts of other types of cleansings, as in those where the demarcation lines are drawn on the basis of religion, culture or nationality. Similarly, ethnic cleansings can be associated with other policies designed to disempower and discriminate against targeted populations, in some instances being associated with mass killings, rape and torture. In extreme instances these policies shade into genocides.

Bell-Fialkoff suggests that it is fruitful to view such population transfers in the context of a continuum. At one end of this is emigration, which may or may not be *encouraged* by state polices involving the creation of a negative climate conducive to the attainment of such an objective. Nazi Germany, between 1933 and 1939, created a climate that encouraged many of its Jewish inhabitants to leave, and established bureaucratic procedures to expedite this. The violence that accompanied the partition of India and Pakistan encouraged mass migrations in both directions. The next node on the continuum is the exchange of populations, such as those that occurred between Greece and Turkey in the years 1920–23. Toward the middle point of the continuum are situated transfers of populations under pressure – deportations or expulsions – such as those directed at Ugandan Asians in the 1960s, and Kosovar Albanians in the late 1990s. At the other end of the continuum Bell-Fialkoff situates genocide. It is, however, necessary to view such a continuum as a useful classificatory mnemonic rather than as an accurate representation of contiguous underlying realities. Although emigration, population exchanges, deportations, expulsions and genocide may all achieve the *cleansing* of a particular locality from an undesired population group differentiated by some trait, it is, nonetheless, not unreasonable to contend that there may be qualitative differences between achieving this objective by way of their physical relocation, and policies designed to secure the destruction of the group in whole or in part.

Many examples of population cleansings from all eras can be cited. In antiquity the Assyrians allegedly resettled millions of subjects in conquered territories, during 883–859 BC and 669–627 BCE. In 146 BCE the Romans, having laid siege to the city of Carthage for three years, razed it to the ground and prohibited any of its former inhabitants who survived from returning. It is presumed that they were exiled and enslaved. Similarly, the wars between the Romans and the Jews, in AD 66–70, the Great Jewish War, and during AD 132–35, the Bar Kochba revolt, were accompanied by the displacement of nearly the entire Jewish population from its settled lands.

In medieval and early modern Europe, the cleansing of religious groups from various lands was not unusual. Bell-Fialkoff suggests that the modern notion of cleansing can be derived from the medieval dichotomy of religious purity/impurity: "The impure, by the very logic of such a Manichean dichotomy, have to be banished. It was therefore natural that nationalism, with its strong religious and messianic components ... would display the same tendency toward (self-) cleansing and (self-) purification."

Twentieth-century expulsions

Many large-scale twentieth-century cleansings have been associated with wars and their aftermath. The Balkan wars of 1912–13 were characterized by massacres and expulsions on both sides, designed in part to legitimize claims for territory based on the ethnic homogeneity of their inhabitants. At their conclusion, the terms of the Turkish–Bulgarian Convention, 1913, allowed for population exchanges of 48,570 Turks and 46,764 Bulgarians from the frontier zones. As Martin notes, "the populations concerned had already been expelled and the treaty served only to formalize the expulsions and regulate property claims." Population exchanges were also one of the consequences of the successful resistance of the Turks to the Greek invasion of 1919. The Treaty of Lausanne, 1923, formalized the expulsion from the Aegean area of Turkey of a million Greeks, the forcible expulsion of Turkey's remaining Greek population, as well as that of Greece's Turkish population.

During World War II Germany engaged in an abortive demographic experiment, transferring *Volksdeutsche* from recently conquered areas to that part of Poland annexed to the Reich, the *Warthegau*, and banishing Poles, both Christians and Jews, to that part of Poland known as the *General Gouvernement*, in the quest for an ingathering of all racially pure Germans to the Reich. Although the policies were never fully implemented due to the containment of German advances on the eastern front, by October 1941 some 1.3 million Christian and Jewish Poles had been relocated eastwards, whereas some 1.25 million Germans from Eastern Europe and the Reich had been resettled in their place.

The defeat of the Reich was accompanied by a demographic tidying operation, in which between 10 and 14 million Germans were removed from countries of Eastern Europe. These expulsions had been authorized under the terms of Article XIII of the Protocol of the Potsdam Conference, which allowed for the transfer of the eastern Germans to what remained of the Reich. Some 2.5 million were expelled from Czechoslovakia, 3 million from Poland, 500,000 from Yugoslavia, and smaller numbers from Hungary, Romania and elsewhere. Other millions fled to the western part of Germany to escape the clutches of the advancing Soviet armies. Although Article XIII of the Potsdam Protocol had stipulated that the removals were to be conducted in an orderly and humane fashion, this was far from being the case, particularly in the early phases. Germans were often given only moments' notice to move to the railway stations, without any opportunity for collecting belongings, including warm clothing. Trains arrived in Berlin with cattle cars full of dead adults and children.

Population relocations have characterized more recent wars as well, both international and internal. In the course of the wars in the former Yugoslavia, during the 1990s, both Serbs and Croats implemented policies designed to achieve ethnic homogeneity in particular localities. The Croats banished Serbs from the Krajina salient, and the Serbs forced the flight of millions of Muslims through calculated policies of terror, rape and massacre, as well as by forcibly deporting them from recently conquered territories. The Israeli authorities, on a much smaller scale, have deported Palestinians from the Occupied West Bank to the Gaza Strip, and to Lebanon. During the course of the Israeli–Lebanon conflict in the 1980s the Israeli authorities were also instrumental in securing the deportation of large numbers of Palestinians to Tunisia and the flight of undesired Arab populations from Lebanese border regions.

Population relocations on a large scale were undertaken in the USSR during the 1930s and in the course of World War II, and have also occurred in some of the successor states. Armenians have been expelled from Azerbaijan, and Azeris, in turn, from Armenia. Ethnic Russians have felt pressured to relocate to Russia. The formation of many other states during the twentieth century, or the galvanization of their populations around notions of ethnic interest or purity, have been accompanied by forced cleansings of targeted *out-groups*. The partition of India was accompanied by the flight of millions on both sides, encouraged by widespread massacres, burnings, and property confiscation and looting. The partition of Cyprus also resulted in the *unmixing* of ethnic groups. In Rwanda, in 1994, the desire for ethnic homogeneity led to the mass killings of some 800,000 Tutsi and noncompliant Hutu. Although generally characterized as genocide, it was at the same time an ethic cleansing, this constituting a pre-eminent underlying motive.

Ethnic cleansing, as the above indicates, is not a rare historical occurrence. There are many etiologically related considerations that prompt it: security, population subjugation, ethnic and religious hatreds, economic and political conflicts and advantages, modern ideological imperatives, and a desire for political and cultural autonomy. Pressures toward population cleansings are exacerbated by wars, state creation, state and empire disintegration, political maneuverings, variable economic circumstances of constituent groups in a political entity, and ideological proclivities. Generally, cleansings are drawn across certain social fault lines: race, ethnicity, nationality, religion, and language, though there are others, including gender and class. Ethnic and other population cleansings are likely to persist for as long as such social fissures constitute significant sources of personal and group identity.

SEE ALSO: anti-Semitism; culturecide; Doomed Races Doctrine; ethnic conflict; ethnocide; fascism; genocide; Holocaust; human rights; International Convention; language; nationalism; pogrom; UNESCO; United Nations

Reading

Ethnic Cleansing by Andrew Bell-Fialkoff (St. Martin's Press, 1996) provides a broad historical overview.
Fires of Hatred: Ethnic cleansing in twentieth-century Europe by Norman M. Naimark (Harvard University Press, 2001) includes discussion of the Armenian genocide, the Holocaust, the Soviet expulsions of the Chechen-Ingush and the Crimean Tartars, expulsions following World War II, and the ethnic cleansings accompanying the wars in the former Yugoslavia.
Nemesis at Potsdam: The expulsion of the Germans from the East, 3rd edn., by Alfred M. De Zayas (University of Nebraska Press, 1989), and "The origins of Soviet ethnic cleansing" by T. Martin (in *Journal of Modern History*, vol. 70, no. 4, 1998) focus on European experiences.
"Schindler's fate: genocide, ethnic cleansing and population transfers" by R. M. Hayden (in *Slavic Review*, vol. 55, no. 4, 1996) focuses on conceptual issues in the context of the expulsions of Germans following World War II and the wars of succession in the former Yugoslavia.

STUART STEIN

ETHNIC CONFLICT

Conflict and competition

Conflict is to be distinguished from competition. Football teams compete with one another according to agreed rules. A team that breaks them may be suspended from the competition. The players in a team may speak different languages, practice different religions, and have little in common with one another except a commitment to play football. If so, the aggregation of individuals constitutes a group on one social dimension only. Conflicts, by contrast, are struggles that observe few rules between groups that are distinguished on several social dimensions. There are laws of war, but most war crimes are those arising from the abuse of noncombatants. The groups that engage in protracted conflicts are aggregations of individuals who share distinctive characteristics that may be based on territory, economic interest, language, religion, and culture. Conflicts are by definition political, being struggles over interests, either material or immaterial. Conflicts in which ethnic differences between the parties are prominent may be identified in popular speech as ethnic conflicts, but for the purposes of social science it is not possible to distinguish them sharply and clearly from conflicts between groups that are not regarded as ethnic. In English-language usage, particularly in North America, racial groups are often thought to differ from ethnic groups, but when intergroup conflicts in various parts of the world are compared, it is not possible to separate ethnic conflicts either from racial conflicts or from national conflicts.

Many examples point to such a conclusion. When the Indonesian economy was damaged by the Asian currency crisis of 1998, mobs attacked the Chinese minority that had been established there for several generations. Members of the minority were of distinctive appearance; among themselves they had their own language and few shared the religion of the majority population. Chinese-Indonesians dominated the economy. Neither their ethnic origin, nor any presumption of racial distinctiveness, explains why they were attacked. Official policies excluding them from government service, the tensions associated with economic relations, the instigation of the military, and the search for scapegoats, were more important. In the Rwanda genocide of 1994 the Hutu intent on slaughtering Tutsi could not necessarily identify their victims by their appearance. They had to be pointed out as Tutsi or recognized as such by their official identity documents. The Hutu majority had been brought to believe that the only way they could overcome an imagined threat from the previously dominant political group was by massacring them. The break-up of the former Yugoslavia after 1991 exacerbated conflicts between Serbs, Croats, Bosniacs and Kosovo Albanians; these were groups distinguished by ethnic origin, and often by national aspiration, language and religion, but not necessarily by appearance. In early 2002 the pogroms in India, in which Hindu mobs slaughtered Muslims in retaliation for an attack on some Hindus, showed that the atrocities associated with what was regarded as a religious conflict could be as grave as any associated with ethnic difference. The granting of independence to Sri Lanka in 1948 and the establishment of the state of Israel in the same year both gave rise to protracted conflicts between political groups with different ethnic origins. Tamils and Sinhalese spoke different languages and practiced different religions, as did Arabs and Jews. In each instance the military repression of the minority's national aspirations has led some of its members to engage in suicide bombing. In Northern Ireland there has been a protracted conflict identified with the two main political groups, Unionist and Republican, which are often simultaneously identified as Protestant and Catholic, and sometimes seen as of different ethnic origin.

These cases illustrate the way that the significance attributed to shared ethnic origin can be one dimension of a more complex conflict. Anyone who wished to maintain that ethnic conflicts are distinctive would have difficulty specifying some criterion that differentiated them from the larger number, while it should be noted that the parties to such conflicts use proper names (such as Serb and Croat) when they refer to each other, not to abstract notions of ethnic origin. From a social science standpoint the common characteristics shared by all group conflicts are more important than their particular dimensions. For example, the processes by which national, linguistic, religious and other kinds of group are mobilized differ little from those by which ethnic groups are mobilized. So too the processes by which they are maintained and sometimes dissolved. Another common characteristic, of both conflict and intergroup competition, is that group interests can take priority over individual interests. A football team is more successful if its players subordinate any search for individual glory to a desire that their team wins. In a conflict between Tamils and Sinhalese, or Arab and Jew, the parties believe they must put their collective interests before their private interests.

Ethnic mobilization and collective action

Many people prefer to associate with others of the same ethnic origin as themselves. This is a relative preference, and there is much variation in its potential as a basis for collective action. The most remarkable mobilization in the twentieth century occurred during World War I when men from many countries marched into battle knowing that they had little chance of survival. Some eight million servicemen were killed and another twenty-two million permanently disabled or seriously wounded. In few countries today could servicemen and their families be persuaded to make comparable sacrifices. With greater popular knowledge of other countries, their peoples, and their points of view, they are less easily persuaded than their predecessors to pursue what political leaders tell them are their long-term collective interests. In a consumer society people's priority interests tend to lie in repaying the mortgages on the houses they have purchased, the loans on the cars they are using, saving for their holidays, arranging their children's schooling, and so on. The scope of shared class or national interest has declined.

Just as relative preferences change over time, so they vary between situations. In Malaysia the preferences of middle-class urbanites for association with co-ethnics have been measured against their preferences for financial advantage, status advantage, and personal obligation to co-workers or neighbors. The studies showed that in certain situations these other factors were more influential than ethnic preferences. Very different results would have been expected had similar studies been conducted in rural areas where Malay–Chinese tensions can be strong. At elections times also, other preferences are likely to be subordinated to ethnic alignment.

These principles can help explain why after the fall of the Berlin Wall there were more serious outbreaks of ethnic conflict in Eastern Europe than in Western Europe. During the Cold War the superpowers suppressed internal tensions in order to maintain the solidarity of their alliances. Soviet theorists and politicians had regarded ethnic groups and nations as natural units that formed stages in historical development. Moscow's policy was to protect the right of Soviet peoples to self-determination, not to promote assimilation; educational standards in the ethnic republics were lifted dramatically, but there was

continuous lobbying for recognition as the boundaries of nations and national groups were drawn and then reduced in number. Even in 1999, as some of these units were fragmenting, one politician (V. Zorin) could assert that "any nation, any people, is a manifestation of nature, which must be respected, with which we must come to terms in the same way as we do with the sun, with the water, with the air."

Valery Tishkov, a former Minister of Nationalities in the government of President Boris Yeltsin, has poured scorn on this view of group difference, insisting that "the crucial factor" in the recognition of ethnic groups and nationalities in the USSR was not "the existence of a shared name held in common by a group of people and thereby signifying a primordial entity," but "the political will of 'outsiders' or group elites, and intellectual/academic exercises." He has described how first the organization and then the dissolution of the USSR offered political entrepreneurs the opportunity to exploit popular sentiment in building careers for themselves. The construction of ethnic units was driven by private interest.

The destruction of the Berlin Wall at the end of 1989 and the collapse of Soviet power weakened the forces that had held together the communist bloc. Croatia's precipitate declaration of independence in 1991 was followed by waves of "ethnic cleansing" in the former Yugoslavia. The dissolution of the multinational USSR caused ethnic tensions to escalate into conflicts in Georgia, Armenia-Azerbaijan, Tadjikistan, Kazakhstan, Chechnya and the Baltic republics of Estonia, Latvia and Lithuania, which, like some of the former Soviet republics, contained substantial Russian minorities. Republics that had been part of the Soviet Union declared themselves independent. The creation of new states was to be the solution to any ethnic problem. The new governments then had to enact constitutions, adopt national languages, declare national holidays, select national anthems and take other steps to cultivate national unity. Inevitably they drew upon the cultural heritage of their ethnic majorities, to the alarm of their ethnic minorities. Now that these could no longer be protected by Soviet power, they attempted to break away. When Armenia and Azerbaijan went to war with each other there was no Soviet power to suppress the conflict, though Chechenya's break with the new Russian Federation was repressed with startling ferocity.

There were also tensions with an ethnic dimension in Western Europe, for example, the mistrust between Greece and Turkey, the independence movement of the Basques and the linguistic struggle between Fleming and Walloon in Belgium, but these were not significantly affected by the decline in East–West tension. Greece and Turkey had to cooperate within NATO (North Atlantic Treaty Organization). In other countries minorities that wished to protect or promote their distinctiveness had to work through political parties, most of which wanted to make only relatively small changes to their political systems. There was less pressure for radical action and less incentive to exploit ethnic consciousness in the service of political campaigns.

At the level of the state, ethnic tensions are generally held in balance by contrary forces. On the one hand, ever-smaller groups want to become national states. On the other, states are bound into the international treaty system that underpins powerful bodies such as the World Trade Organization and regional organizations such as the European Union and the Organization of American States. On the one hand, the consumer society elevates the satisfaction of individual desires. On the other, individuals have a greater need for state bodies to secure their defense, provide them with passports, and regulate their relations with persons and institutions in foreign states. Within states there can be a deadlock in the opposition between two groups, as between Unionist and Republican in Northern Ireland, Francophone and Anglophone in Quebec, and Fleming and Walloon in Belgium, but most such struggles cannot be static. As the international environment changes, so do the priorities that individuals attach to their preferences and negotiation becomes possible, often more easily with respect to ethnic differences than religious ones.

Aims of conflict

The preceding paragraphs illustrate the need to develop better concepts in this field. Competition can occur between individuals, and be unconscious, but conflict has to be between groups and to be a conscious mode of social interaction. In sociology, conflict is conventionally defined as a struggle in which the parties seek to neutralize, injure or eliminate their opponents. The distinction is preserved in references to "class struggle" rather than "class conflict." Many tensions in industrial societies that are referred to as conflicts in popular speech, such as those between young males and the police, do not meet the sociological criterion; the parties do not seek to eliminate one another and, generally speaking, observe many rules even while disliking one another. However, the conventional definition of conflict is not always observed. For example, the analysis of modes of conflict resolution can cover relations of competition and struggles in which the parties seek to eliminate opposition without physically eliminating their opponents. The very difficulty of drawing distinctions between struggles in which the parties observe agreed rules, or few rules, or none at all, suggests that other concepts, informed by sociological or psychological theories, are needed in the examination of the nature and effects of intergroup tension. The principles that explain ethnic conflict need to be extended and made more general.

SEE ALSO: empowerment; ethnic cleansing; ethnicity; ethnonational; human rights; minorities; minority language rights; racial coding; rational choice theory; violence

Reading

"Ethnic conflict" by Michael Banton (in *Sociology*, vol. 34, no. 2, 2000) summarizes the general issues and applies them to conflict in Malaysia.

Ethnicity: Racism, class and culture by Steve Fenton (Macmillan, 1999) explores the ethnic dimension to inter-group relations in Britain, the USA, Hawaii and Malaysia.

Ethnicity, Nationalism and Conflict in and after the Soviet Union. The mind aflame by Valery Tishkov (Sage, 1997) provides a review of recent developments in Eastern Europe.

World Directory of Minorities (Minority Rights Group International, 1997) surveys data on ethnic conflicts; while a record of the number of armed conflicts in progress is maintained by the Department of Peace and Conflict Research, Uppsala University (*www.peace.uu.se*).

CHECK: internet resources section

MICHAEL BANTON

ETHNIC HUMOR *see* humor

ETHNIC MONITORING

A method of assessing the effectiveness – or lack of effectiveness – of affirmative action, or analogous programs, by recording the ethnic background or origin of the recruits or existing personnel of an organization. Applicants or members would be asked to describe themselves according to specified criteria, a typical case being the British National Union of Journalists' application form which lists: "A – Black (Afro-Caribbean, including Black British whose forebears originate in or recently came from Guyana or an island in the West Indies). B – Black (African including Black British whose forebears originate in or recently came from Africa). C – Black (Asian, including Black British whose forebears originate in or recently came from the Indian subcontinent). D – White (UK); or E – Irish."

Proponents of such procedures (such as the Commission for Racial Equality) argue that this is the only means of either measuring the progress of organizations in creating equal opportunities in recruitment, selection and promotion, or of exposing discrimination over periods of time. Opponents (who include personnel managers of employers and many ethnic minority groups) contend that the questions asked are, at best, impertinent and, at worst, racist in that they encourage the perpetuation of differences in areas where ethnic differences are irrelevant. There is an additional fear over the uses to which such data can be put.

Frank Reeves has called the procedure a "benign form of discursive racialization," meaning that "racial characteristics" are identified in policy, albeit for benign purposes – the elimination of racism being the primary one. This is in contrast to malevolent forms, for example, when fascists delineate populations in terms of their alleged race.

SEE ALSO: affirmative action; equal opportunity; homelessness; law: civil rights, USA; law: race relations, UK; social work; welfare

Reading

British Racial Discourse by Frank Reeves (Cambridge University Press, 1983) explores the use of racial evaluations in political discourse, suggesting that this may be overt or covert, or geared to either benign or racist ends.
Race Relations in Britain since 1945 by Harry Goulbourne (Macmillan, 1998) maps out the field and includes sections on producing and maintaining what the author calls "good race relations."
Racism and Equal Opportunities Policies in the 1980s, edited by Richard Jenkins and John Solomos (Cambridge University Press, 1987), addresses the problem of equal opportunity and methods of ensuring its maintenance.

BARRY TROYNA

ETHNIC NATIONALISM *see* ethnonational

ETHNICITY

Identification and inclusion

The actual term derives from the Greek *ethnikos*, the adjective of *ethnos*. This refers to a people or nation. In its contemporary form, *ethnic* still retains this basic meaning in the sense that it describes a group possessing some degree of coherence and solidarity composed of people who are, at least latently, aware of having common origins and interests. So, an ethnic group is not a mere aggregate of people or a sector of a population, but a self-conscious collection of people united, or closely related, by shared experiences.

Those experiences are usually, but not always, ones of deprivation; for example, those characterizing immigrants and their descendants. The original migrants might have left their homelands to seek improvements elsewhere or maybe they were forcibly taken from their lands, as were African slaves. Conversely, the deprived peoples might have been the natural inhabitants of lands that were invaded and from which they were then alienated. North American Indians and Australian Aborigines would be apposite examples of this. Whatever the circumstances, those people coming under the total or partial domination of either a hostile indigenous population or a conquering group of intruders go through experiences of deprivation. They may be materially deprived, culturally denuded, politically neutered; or quite often all of these.

After they become aware of their common plight, their response may be to generate stability, support and comfort among others who undergo similar experiences. By emphasizing the features of life, past and present, they share, they define boundaries inside which they can develop their own particular customs, beliefs, and institutions – in short, their own cultures. The ethnic group, then, is a cultural phenomenon, even though it is based originally on a common perception and experience of unfavorable material circumstances.

Some have argued for the replacement of the word "race" with "ethnic group," although this argument seems to stem from a fundamental confusion. Ethnic groups do flourish in times of adversity and quite frequently there is a relationship between a group that is considered a distinct "race" by the dominant population and the group that considers itself a unified people sharing a common experience. But whereas "race" stands for the attributions of one group, "ethnic group" stands for the creative response of a people who feel somehow marginal to the mainstream of society. There is no necessary relationship between the two concepts, though, in actuality, there is often a strong overlap in the sense that a group labeled a race is often pushed out of the main spheres of society and made to endure deprivations; and these are precisely the conditions conducive to the growth of an ethnic group. These are the very people likely to band together to stress their unity or common identity as a way of surviving. Michael Banton has summed up the essential difference between an ethnic group and a "race": "the former reflects the positive tendencies of identification and inclusion where the latter reflects the negative tendencies of dissociation and exclusion."

Floya Anthias writes that: "A common experience of racism may act to 'ethnicize' diverse cultures, as in the case of the 'Black' category in Britain" (in "Connecting 'race' and ethnic phenomena," *Sociology*, vol. 26, 1992). Anthias goes on to point out that ethnicity can militate against, as well as promote the advancement of, political goals, in particular goals related to class and gender. "Ethnicity can be a vehicle for diverse political projects," she argues, adding that often ethnicity is antithetical to "the notion of emancipation," and supportive of gender inequalities. Her bracing argument cautions against championing ethnic pluralism as a tool in the fight against racism (the argument is extended in *Racialized Boundaries* by Floya Anthias and Nira Yurval Davies, Routledge, 1992).

Ethnicity, then, defines the salient feature of a group that regards itself as in some sense (usually, many senses) distinct. Once the consciousness of being part of an ethnic group is created, it takes on a self-perpetuating quality and is passed from one generation to the next. Distinct languages, religious beliefs and political institutions become part of the ethnic baggage and children are reared to accept these.

The ethnicity may, of course, weaken as successive generations question the validity of the ethnic group. An example of this would be the responses of many children of South Asian migrants in the UK; the "second generation" found the cultural demands (ranging from arranged marriages to dress restrictions, etc.) excessive and in sharp contrast to the culture they were associated with when away from their families. Whereas the original migrants found the maintenance of their culture highly necessary, their sons and daughters found it irrelevant. Yet the ethnic affiliation cannot be freely dropped as if a cultural option; frequently, it is deeply embedded in the consciousness through years of socialization within the ethnic group. The ethnic boundary is difficult to break out of.

"The convenient fiction of ethnicity" is how Beryl Langer describes the management strategy devised to contain Salvadorean migrants within Australia in the 1990s. In her essay "Globalisation and the myth of ethnic community: Salvadorean refugees in multicultural states" (in David Bennett's edited collection below), Langer disputes ideas of ethnicity as an organic unity and argues that, for Salvadoreans, migration meant stepping out of civil war "into the cast of an 'ethnic group' in which divisions of class and politics are glossed by the unities of culture and language." In other words, ethnicity was a ready-made construct and one which had to be exchanged: refugees were obliged to leave behind historical differences in exchange for a new ethnic identity which minimized conflict. Ethnicity was not only imposed, however: it was embraced. There were advantages for those who were prepared to trade older discord for new harmony, however artificial and imposed in the first instance.

This is another way in which ethnic awareness can be actively promoted to serve immediate purposes. The development of the Chicano movement attests to this. Disparate groups of Mexicans and people of Mexican descent were made aware of their own common plight, principally through the efforts of people such as César Chûvez (1927–93) who galvanized agricultural workers into a strong ethnic-based labor union. In this case, ethnicity was used quite openly as a resource to promote the feeling of "we" and "them" (the white business-owners who exploited them) in the achievement of both short-term and long-term tangible goals. The generation of this "we-ness" prompted confrontation in the form of strikes, sit-ins, boycotts, and demonstrations. The Chicano ethnicity was not a mere spontaneous rearing of a new awareness, but a deliberate manipulation of people's perceptions of their own situations. In this sense, ethnicity can be used as an instrument in the effort to achieve clearly defined ends. The Italian-American Congressman Vito Marcantonio (1902–54) successfully drew on strong ethnic support to keep him in power in the 1934–40 period, and his attempted reforms included ethnic progressive programs.

In Nigeria, the dynamics of ethnicity were intertwined with nation-building, as the work of Obi Igwara shows (*Ethnicity and Nation-building in Nigeria*, Macmillan, 2000). Across the Commonwealth states of Australia, Canada and New Zealand, dispossessed groups have enclosed themselves ethnically, yet have gradually opened out to become prime movers in cultural change.

Imagination of tradition

In other situations, ethnicity may be an utter irrelevance or even a liability. Emphasizing or exaggerating cultural differences may not only distinguish a group from the rest of a population, but also incur the wrath of the wider society. Witness, for example, the experiences of Yosif Begun (1932–), one of countless Russians sentenced to Siberian exile for the "crime" of sustaining Jewish ethnicity through the teaching of Jewish language, history and culture. Western anti-Semitism still prevails, possibly sustained by the view that "Jews keep themselves to themselves … they like to think of themselves as superior." Despite the social mobility of Jews, their progress is still, to a degree, inhibited by such postures.

Situations such as these mean that the ethnic group is widely recognized by other nonethnics. The group has a significance quite apart from the members of the group. This does not make the group any more or less "real" in an objective sense. The whole point about ethnicity is that it is as real as people want it to be. The group may have no significance at all outside the perceptions of the group members themselves; yet it is real to them and their subjective apprehension of the group motivates them to organize their lives

around it. Ranger, Samad, and Stuart favor the term "imagination of tradition" to explain how ethnicities can become "concretized" (in *Culture, Identity and Politics*, Avebury, 1996).

For instance, it might be possible to expose many of the beliefs on which the Rastafari movement is based as ill-founded. Rastas themselves feel united by a common ancestry as well as current material circumstances. The bonds that hold the "brotherhood" together have their origins in a conception of an ancient Africa, united and glorious in a "golden age." The fact that many of the ideas held by Rastas may be erroneous does nothing to weaken the ethnic bonds, for Rastas themselves find them meaningful and structure their day-to-day lives around them. The strength of ethnicity lies at source in the subjective relevance it has for the group members.

There is a clear parallel between the Rastas' ethnic response and that of black Americans in the 1960s. Previous generations of blacks had attempted to imitate the lifestyles of middle-class whites, attempted – perhaps vainly – to move physically and intellectually away from the ghetto life and all its associations with the past. Pale skin and straight hair symbolized the attempt to remove the "taint" of blackness and aspire to white standards. Young blacks in the 1960s reversed this. They plunged back into history in a search for their roots, and, to signify this, grew their hair into "Afros" and changed their names to African equivalents, at the same time declaring "black is beautiful." For the blacks themselves, they were "discovering" their past and, therefore, themselves. For others, they were creating ethnicity anew. True, they were basing that ethnicity on the conception of a common ancestry, but the way in which they reformulated it was a product of their imaginations. Thus the ethnicity was a subjective phenomenon that was lent credibility by the many thousands of members it attracted.

Ethnic growth, then, can emerge from a number of sources. It can be a defensive mechanism, as with, say, Italians, who moved to America, faced antagonism and hardship, and so turned in on themselves to recreate their own Italian culture in the new context. The basic characteristics of the culture were carried over and given fresh relevance. On the other hand, the Afro-ethnicity of young blacks was a new construction.

Reactions to constraint

Underlying these and other responses is the theme that ethnicity is basically reactive: it is elicited and shaped by the constraints and limits on opportunities imposed on the people who seek to be ethnic. Those people perceive that they are up against something and organize themselves (survive) or advance themselves (achieve). But the ethnic group is always a reaction to conditions rather than a spontaneous stirring of people who suddenly feel the urge to express themselves through the medium of a group. As stressed before, ethnicity appears as a cultural phenomenon, but it is a response to material conditions.

Over time, those conditions may disappear, leaving an ethnic group united or at least self-aware enough to recognize its own interests and feelings. The term "ethnic Chinese" is used throughout Southeast Asia: it both describes and reinforces solidarity among groups who may be dissimilar in a great many other respects, but who perceive a common lineage. Similar "ethnic Muslims" in Bosnia observe commonality of purpose as well as descent. This use of ethnic as an adjective preceding either a geographical or religious designation has become current since the 1980s when Bulgarian citizens of Turkish origin were referred to as ethnic Turks.

The more general "ethnic revival," however, predates this and has prompted some writers to theorize that ethnicity has displaced social class as the major form of cleavage in modern society. Ethnicity, they conclude, is "a more fundamental source of stratification." While it seems untenable to dismiss class as the critical factor in all forms of social conflict, there is certainly sufficient material to predict that ethnicity and ethnic conflict will be, in the future, at least as significant as class conflict. Having stated this, it would be unwise to separate the two forms, except for analytical purposes, for there is often a very intimate connection between class position and ethnic response.

Ethnic groups are more often than not fractions of the working class, an underclass that is especially vulnerable to the kinds of exploitation upon which capitalism is based. This is not to suggest that ethnic groups must stay anchored in this position. The actual fact of organizing ethnically is often instrumental in furthering the interests of the members and some groups, for example Irish Catholics and Jews in the USA, overcome material deprivations and aspire to elites. Quite often the ethnic impulse spills over into political realms and strong political organizations are built up to represent the ethnic groups' interests. But nearly always the group begins life from a low-class position of marginality.

To sum up: (1) ethnicity is the term used to encapsulate the various types of responses of different groups; (2) the ethnic group is based on a commonness of subjective apprehensions, whether about origins, interests or future (or a combination of these); (3) material deprivation is the most fertile condition for the growth of ethnicity; (4) the ethnic group does not have to be a "race" in the sense that it is seen by others as somehow inferior, though there is a very strong overlap, and many groups that organize themselves ethnically are often regarded by others as a "race;" (5) ethnicity may be used for any number of purposes, sometimes as an overt political instrument, at other times as a simple defensive strategy in the face of adversity; and (6) ethnicity may become an increasingly important line of cleavage in society, though it is never entirely unconnected with class factors.

SEE ALSO: African Americans; African Caribbeans in Britain; American Indians; Anglo-Indians; anthropology; Asian Americans; assimilation; *Aztlân*; British Asians; culture; culturecide; Ebonics; Ethiopianism; ethnic conflict; ethnocide; ethnonational; integration; kinship; Latinos; multiculturalism; *nígritude*; Park, Robert Ezra; Pentecostalism; pluralism; Puerto Ricans in the USA; Rastafari; Roma; transracial adoption

Reading

Ethnic Identity: Creation, conflict and accommodation, 3rd edn., edited by Lola Romanucci-Ross and George de Vos (Sage, 1995), is a wide-ranging examination of ethnicity in areas such as the former Yugoslavia, the Baltic States and Sri Lanka, with the themes of language and nationalism linking the analyses.

Ethnicity: Racism, class and culture by Steve Fenton (Macmillan, 1999) contextualizes ethnicity, situating its expression in specific historical circumstances and making comparisons between the USA, Europe and Malaysia.

The Politics of Ethnicity in Settler Societies: States of unease by David Pearson (Macmillan, 2001) examines the historical foundations of ethnic politics in Australia, Canada, New Zealand and compares these with the experience in Britain and the USA.

Multicultural States: Rethinking difference and identity,

edited by David Bennett (Routledge, 1998), is the collection cited in the main text above and contains several challenging essays.

Racial Disadvantage and Ethnic Diversity in Britain by Andrew Pilkington (Macmillan, 2001) examines the relationship between deprivation caused or compounded by racism and the proliferation of ethnicity in Britain since World War II.

Rethinking Ethnicity: Arguments and explorations by Richard Jenkins (Sage, 1997) argues that ethnicity is imagined, though its effects are palpable; this theoretical approach can be compared with those in *Theories of Ethnicity: A classical reader*, edited by Werner Sollors, and Henry and Anne Cabot (Macmillan, 1996), which draws together a wide range of essays written on conceptual and practical facets of ethnicity.

ETHNOCENTRISM

From the Greek *ethnos*, for people or nation, and *kentrikos*, relating to the center, ethnocentrism describes the tendency to understand the world only from the viewpoint of one's own unit of affiliation, and evaluating all others strictly in one's own group's terms. This disposition is based on the assumption that one's own unit of affiliation is inherently superior to all others and defines the standard by which all others should be measured There is a corresponding reluctance or inability to empathize with the manner in which those outside one's own unit of affiliation perceive, understand and approach the world. The unit of affiliation may be an ethnic group, "race," nation, society, or whatever putative institution persons attach themselves to, identify with and invest with meaning. Derivative terms include *phallocentrism* (the inclination to see the development of females as a reaction to males) and *eurocentrism* (though this term rests on the disputable premise that there exists a uniform perspective that encompasses what is, in reality, a variegated assembly of cultures, languages and religions accommodated in the European continent). More recent related additions to the vocabulary are *ecocentrism* (centering on the value of nature) and its converse *anthropocentrism* (regarding humans as central).

There is no absolute condition of ethnocentrism: rather a spectrum across which runs a range of shades and hues. Some groups exhibit a preparedness to consider and appreciate others' faiths and forms of worship, while refusing to countenance, for example, their customs about marriage. Others may be not be prepared to

accept, less still approve of any cultural practice that deviates from their own. Still others may, on occasion, receive and perhaps embrace the institutions and customs and practices of others, but maintain an immovable conviction that they are inferior to their own. Nor can ethnocentrism be seen as stable over time: the onset of migration may initially prompt ethnocentric responses from the host society; but, after a while, some sort of accommodation is typically made and a modification of attitudes and precepts follows.

Some writers, for example David Levinson, believe that "Ethnocentrism is a cultural universal in that it is displayed to some degree by members of all cultures." Levinson points out that one culture may be ethnocentric in regard to some groups and less ethnocentric in regard to others.

If, as Levinson supposes, ethnocentrism is a "cultural universal," meaning it is present in all known human societies throughout history, then it would need a particular type of explanation. A *universal* describes a property of, or belonging to, all persons in the world, making the prefix "cultural" redundant – the property is invariantly present everywhere, regardless of differences of culture. If ethnocentrism is such a property, then it may have its sources in biological realms, perhaps in the effort to maximize reproductive fitness within a particular group. Nepotism, or favoring one's nearest kin, may have the corollary of disfavoring out-groups and ethnocentrism can facilitate this. In this explanation, ethnocentrism is rooted in human nature. The property may also be linked with xenophobia, which was once explained as a psychological condition in which members of "out-groups" are detested or even feared and typically considered inferior in some permanent sense. Ethnocentrism, according to this conjecture, is based on the recognition of others who are perceived as threatening or offensive and is a kind of psychological reflex. Again, it is understood as a feature of the human condition rather than a cultural variable.

Ethnocentrism is certainly widespread and persistent, but it may not be universal. "The history of all cultures is the history of cultural borrowings," wrote Edward Said in his *Culture and Imperialism* (Vintage, 1993). "Cultures are not impermeable." We can cite Western science, which borrowed from Arabs, who had, in turn borrowed from India and Greece. Martin Bernal's *Black Athena: The Afroasiatic roots of classical civilization*, vol. 1 (Rutgers University Press, 1987), shows how Egyptian and Semitic influences bore on Greek civilizations, though these influences were either obscured or left unacknowledged. Evidence that ethnocentrism dissolves and ossifies is abundant: it is in every culture, every one based on some sort of appropriation, common experience and interdependency. In the 1970s, for example, American whites seemed close-mindedly ethnocentric about African Americans. In the twenty-first century, white youths admire and enthuse over music such as rap that was once seen as an exclusively black art form. White British were once repulsed by South Asian cuisine, though the proliferation of Indian and Pakistani restaurants attests to their current devotion to such food. Were ethnocentrism to be a changeless universal, cultures would petrify. The fact that they do not suggests that ethnocentrism should be visualized as temporary aversion, incapacity or unwillingness rather than a permanent human condition.

SEE ALSO: anti-Semitism; bigotry; cultural racism; neo-nazism; power; prejudice; race card; racism; stereotype; subaltern; whiteness; xenophobia

Reading

"Ethnocentrism" by David Levinson, in his *Ethnic Relations: A cross-cultural encyclopedia* (ABC-Clio, 1994), is a clear, succinct statement on ethnocentrism, though the author tends to understate the perceptual components and overstate the cultural invariability of the condition.

"Jewish and Arab ethnocentrism in Israel" by Sammy Smooha (in *Ethnic and Racial Studies*, vol. 10, 1987) is a case study in which the politically powerful and more numerous Jews and the Arab minority live in a situation of mutual mistrust and demonstrate an utter unwillingness to entertain the viewpoint of each other.

ETHNOCIDE

The term *ethnocide* is generally taken to refer to the destruction of members of a group, in whole or in part, identified in terms of their ethnicity. Its use is conceptually and theoretically closely linked with the term *genocide*.

The term *genocide* was introduced by Raphþel Lemkin in his *Axis Rule in Occupied Europe* (1944), as follows: "By 'genocide' we mean the destruction of a nation or of an ethnic group. This new word ... is made from the Greek word

genos (race, tribe) and the Latin *cide* (killing)." In a footnote to this section he notes that: "Another term could be used for the same idea, namely, ethnocide, consisting of the Greek word 'ethnos' – nation – and the Latin word 'cide'."

Although the term has been employed by a number of authorities, its close affinity with the concept genocide, and the somewhat varied and confused amplification of its meaning without adequate reference to the derivative attributions of the Genocide Convention of 1948, or Lemkin's work, tends to render it superfluous for both analytic and descriptive purposes. The Genocide Convention stipulates quite clearly that the acts associated with it apply to ethnic groups, as well as those demarcated by race, nationality or religion. Accordingly, inasmuch as ethnocide is used to refer to the destruction of members of a group, in whole or in part, on the basis of their ethnicity, this practice would simultaneously constitute genocide.

A contextual examination of some of its referents indicates that the term is often being used to refer to a subtype of genocide, or to indicate processes that were excluded from inclusion in the 1948 convention. It is most frequently used in connection with the plight of indigenous peoples. Israel Charny prefers to employ "a specific category of *ethnocide* for major processes that prohibit or interfere with the natural cycles of reproduction and continuity of a culture or nation, but not to include this type of murderous oppression directly under the generic concept of genocide," which he prefers to reserve for "actual mass murders that end the lives of people." In other words, Charny's use of *ethnocide* is homologous with the use of the word *culturecide* by other authorities, namely, processes that contribute to the disappearance of a culture without necessarily entailing the immediate physical destruction of its bearers.

The close relationship between *ethnocide* and *culturecide* is evident in Beardsley's specification that it refers to the "commission of acts of specified sorts with the intention to extinguish utterly or in substantial part, a culture. Among such ethnocidal acts are the deprivation of the opportunity to use a language, practice a religion, create art in customary ways, maintain basic social institutions, preserve memories and traditions, work in cooperation toward social goals." The connection with *genocide* is explicitly developed in his contention that the extermination or dispersion of the sole bearers of a culture "is to commit *both* genocide and ethnocide" (italics added). Other authorities have also commented on the fact that writers have conflated the two terms. Leo Kuper, one of the early writers on genocide, noted that although culturecide was excluded as a crime from inclusion in the 1948 convention, "it is commonly treated as such in much contemporary writing where it is described as ethnocide."

Given that each authority, or agency, tends to have a somewhat unique notion of what the concept subsumes, and as embellishment is an ongoing characteristic of social scientific work, it is unlikely that the term will prove systematically useful for analytical purposes in the future.

SEE ALSO: Aboriginal Australians; culturecide; Doomed Races Doctrine; ethnic cleansing; ethnic conflict; genocide; Holocaust; human rights; indigenous peoples; International Convention; Irish; language; slavery; UNESCO; United Nations

Reading

Axis Rule in Occupied Europe by RaphÞel Lemkin (Carnegie Endowment for International Peace, 1944) is the text in which the term originally appeared.
Genocide by Leo Kuper (Penguin Books, 1981), though published over two decades ago, contains timeless insights.
"Reflections on genocide and ethnocide" by M. C. Beardsley, in *Genocide in Paraguay*, edited by R. Arends (Temple University Press, 1976), is a worthy, albeit dated, contribution.
"Toward a generic definition of genocide" by Israel W. Charny, in *Genocide: Conceptual and historical dimensions* by G. J. Andreopoulos (University of Pennsylvania Press, 1994) takes a conceptual approach.

STUART STEIN

ETHNONATIONAL

An ethnonational group usually refers to populations which express an ethnic identity *and* make a claim to being recognized as nation. The ethnic identity is often grounded in region, common culture, religion or language, or a combination of some of these. The claim to "national" status is by groups within a larger (nation)-state or lying across several states; the latter would include for example the Basques and Kurdish peoples. The

ethnonational claim (or ethnonationalist ideology) may represent a threat to the larger state(s).

Origin and uses

The term "ethnonational," used with considerable frequency in social science publications at least since the early 1980s, is deployed to capture something of the meaning of both "ethnic" and "national." It is used to denote groups and movements that lie between the meaning of the two terms, or has connotations of both. Its etymological origins would annoy language purists since (like "television" and "genocide") it combines a Greek beginning with a Latin ending. Curiously the Greek *ethnos* and the Latin *natio* are approximately the same in meaning; both could be translated as meaning "people" or "nation." The fact that they have come to be combined in a single word could only be explained by tracing the separate histories of *ethnos* and *natio* as they have come to be used as "ethnic" and "nation" in English.

The word ethnic entered English usage in the fourteenth and fifteenth century when it was largely used with a meaning of foreign and pagan, as neither Christian nor Jew. It was used substantively and adjectivally but is now usually adjectival. It has retained this sense of "foreignness" and later of a *minority*. In the USA and other contexts "ethnic groups" came to mean groups of foreign origin or ancestry, especially insofar as they retained distinctions of language, religion and culture. By contrast *nation* has not usually anything of this minority sense and has come to mean the people of a society or state, (sometimes) mythically conceived as having common ethnic origins. Thus nation has tended to become strongly linked to the idea of *state*, therefore producing the combined term nation-state.

A civic or universalistic idea of the nation is said to emphasize a non-ethnic conception of the nation as a body of citizens, which can incorporate multi-ethnicity. For this reason the idea of a nation which is infused with a strong notion of common ethnic origins (i.e. the idea of ethnicity as comprising the ideas of *common ancestry* and *common culture*) could be described as *ethnonational*. On this construction, ethnonationalism would have a meaning similar to that of *ethnic nationalism*, often contrasted with civic nationalism. In most contexts it means something rather different: the claim to be a nation by groups whose nationhood is not recognized in a fully fledged state form.

Autonomy and distinctness

There are many nations (or ethnonational groups) which live within the boundaries of a larger nation-state. Examples would be Catalonia, Scotland, and Quebec, entities that are often described as "ethnonational" in the literature. But this terminology can be problematic. To take only the case of Scotland, Scottish nationalism has focused primarily on the autonomy, devolved power, or independence of the territory called Scotland rather than on the (putatively shared) ethnic origins of the "Scottish people." It is possible therefore to envisage nationalism of regional groups within a larger state which is not primarily ethnic in ideology. Such is the strength of the twentieth-century idea of the self-determination of peoples (nations) that a claim to be a nation virtually implies a claim to an existence separate from or autonomous within a larger community.

Nonetheless *multi*-national states (such as Spain or Great Britain) persist although others (such as the former Soviet Union or Yugoslavia) have recently broken into smaller "national" units. This is not an indication of the power of ethnonationalism as some, such as Walker Connor, have argued. The reasons for collapse of these multinational states include many more factors than the strength of ethnonational sentiments in their former component parts. The break-up of the Soviet Union however has been an important prompt for the use of the term ethnonational, referring to groups with some language and/or religious distinctiveness who may have been recognized as autonomous regions, nationalities or ethnoses (see Banks, Tishkov, below) in the Soviet period.

English-language journal literature from 1980 reveals the usage of ethnonational(ism) in many contexts including Yugoslavia, the former Soviet Union, Spain, Papua New Guinea, South Africa, Turkey (and the Kurds), the Middle East, India (and Sikhs) and many other contexts where the connotation is a subnational group with a claim to recognition. That recognition may vary from "equal treatment" to "separation" or secession. Eriksen quite specifically used the term ethnonational groups to mean proto-*nations* or would-be

nations, which were incorporated in a larger entity, and this meaning is reflected in many of the examples above. Sometimes it is used more loosely so that it is almost equivalent to the concepts of ethnic mobilization or "communalism." But the mobilization of ethnic groups as minorities in urban centers usually falls short of the "national" claims or would-be national claims of ethnonational groups. By contrast Guiberneau and Conversi have both written about sub- or proto-nationalisms in Spain (Basque, Catalan) without using the word ethnonational.

Connor is one writer who has used the word ethnonationalism quite prominently and wrote a 1994 volume with that title. He differs significantly from many other commentators in two important respects. The first is that he wishes to reserve the term nation for those communities who are truly united by an ethnonational bond. For him therefore the word "nation" cannot have its civic sense, except in the limiting case where the people of a state are a single ethnonation. The sentiment of attachment to country or state should not be confused with the attachment to nation; the former is patriotism, the latter nationalism. Thus he is able to argue that an individual's Basque nationalism may be in conflict with their Spanish patriotism. In this way national/ism and ethnonational/ism are the same things. The second distinctive feature of Connor's arguments is that he insists on the nonrational and emotional nature of the ethnonational bond. This is in contrast to those who have seen national myths as "constructed" and nationalism as instrumental or politically opportunistic. Connor's are minority views.

The persistent meaning of ethnonational remains a fusion of ideas associated with ethnicity and with nation, and in particular with respect to claims for recognition which are somehow less than and contained within a larger state framework. The theorization of ethnonationalism (i.e. as nonrational, instrumental, constructed), i.e. explanations for the apparent rise and fall of ethnonational sentiment, remains, of course, contested.

SEE ALSO: American Indians; cultural identity; cultural racism; culture; culturecide; diaspora; ethnic cleansing; ethnic conflict; ethnicity; ethnocide; globalization; human rights; hybridity;

indigenous peoples; language; minorities; multiculturalism; nationalism; pluralism

Reading

The Basques, the Catalans, and Spain by Daniele Conversi (Hurst, 2000) examines the separatist movement in Spain; *Ethnicity, Nationalism and Conflict in and after the Soviet Union* is by Valery Tishkov (Sage, 1997).

Ethnicity: Anthropological constructions by Marcus Banks (Routledge, 1996) is an overview of the creation of ethnicities; this may profitably be read in conjunction with *Ethnonational Identities*, edited by Steve Fenton and Steve May (Palgrave 2002), Thomas H. Eriksen's *Ethnicity and Nationalism: An anthropological perspective* (Pluto 1993) and *Contemporary Nationalism: Civic, ethnocultural and multicultural politics* by David Brown (Routledge 2000).

Ethnonationalism: The quest for understanding by Walker Connor (Princeton University Press, 1994) argues for the emotional nature of ethnonational bonds.

Nations without States: Political communities in a global age by Montserrat Guiberneau (Polity, 1999) analyzes the mobilization of ethnic forces and sentiments without using the term ethnonationalism.

STEVEN FENTON

EUGENICS

A social movement originated by Francis Galton (1822–1911), author of *Hereditary Genius* (1869). It is currently defined as an applied science directed toward the improvement of the genetic potentialities of the human species. Its history, particularly with respect to questions of racial relations, has been punctuated by controversy.

Galton argued that mental ability was inherited differentially by individuals, groups, and races. He showed that this ability, like the physical trait of height, followed a normal curve of distribution within the population and that the relatives of outstandingly able individuals tended to be very able themselves. Galton drew on his own money to create a research fellowship, and a eugenics laboratory at University College, London which was directed by his friend Karl Pearson. Later he bequeathed funds to endow a chair of eugenics for Pearson. The American Eugenics Society was founded in 1905 and similar societies followed in many other countries. There is currently a Galton Institute in London.

Following Darwin's theory, a race is a line of individuals of common descent. A race which transmits more of its characteristics to future generations is fitter than other races and therefore is likely to predominate in the future. This gives rise to the same sort of controversy as other theories (such as those of Marx) that claim to predict the course of future development. Those who adopt a "naturalistic" stance contend that ethical decisions should be based on the knowledge of what is going to happen anyway. Antinaturalists insist that "what is good" and "what the future will bring" are questions requiring different kinds of answer. Their objections are expressed with humor in C. S. Lewis's "Evolutional hymn" (reprinted in *The Oxford Book of Light Verse*). Another position is that humans differ from other forms of life in having the ability to direct the course of their future evolution. A government can enact legislation to prevent unfit persons (mental defectives, persons suffering from hereditary diseases, etc.) from having children; this is called negative eugenics. Equally, it can take action (through tax incentives, special allowances, etc.) to encourage persons considered to be of the best stock to have more children; this is called positive eugenics.

The eugenics movement's campaign for the institutional segregation of the mentally backward led to the (British) Mental Deficiency Act of 1913, while its ideas influenced the 1924 National Origins Quota Law regulating immigration into the USA. By 1931 sterilization laws had been enacted by twenty-seven US states; four years later nearly 10,000 persons had been sterilized in California alone. By 1935 similar laws had been passed in Denmark, Switzerland, Germany, Norway and Sweden. The laws provided for the voluntary or compulsory sterilization of those thought to be insane, feebleminded, epileptic and (sometimes) to be habitual criminals. With the advance of scientific knowledge the justification for such legislation increasingly came into doubt, but many people of politically progressive views continued to favor quality controls upon population growth. In 1939, under the Nazis, Germany moved from the sterilization of individuals to the killing of whole categories of persons; but note that the eugenics movement cannot be held responsible for Nazi conceptions of inheritance.

Many of the aims of the eugenics movement have been achieved by other means. In many countries pregnancies can be terminated when tests reveal genetic defects in an embryo, though where there is a cultural preference for male children the prenatal identification of an embryo's sex may result in the differential abortion of female embryos. Advances in assisted reproduction have given rise to concerns about "designer babies" with particularly desired genetic attributes, but such matters are now considered in connection with medical genetics and medical ethics, not eugenics.

SEE ALSO: Darwinism; environmentalism; fascism; Haeckel, Ernst; genocide; hereditarianism; heritability; social Darwinism

Reading

Eugenics and Politics in Britain, 1900–1914 by G. R. Searle (Woordhoff, Leyden, 1976) describes the establishment of eugenics in its social context.
"Galton's conception of race in historical perspective" by Michael Banton, in *Sir Francis Galton FRS: The legacy of his ideas*, edited by Milo Keynes (Macmillan, 1993), examines Galton's ideas about racial difference.
CHECK: internet resources section

MICHAEL BANTON

EUROCENTRISM *see* ethnocentrism

EXOTICISM *see* beauty; Hottentot Venus; negrophilia; Orientalism; Other; sexuality

EXPLOITATION

This has both a narrow and a more broad usage. The narrow usage is found within Marxist writing to refer to the process by which a class of nonproducers are able to live without working by extracting a surplus from a class of direct producers. This process of exploitation takes a number of different historical and structural forms. Within a feudal society, the serfs produced crops and other items both for themselves and for the various levels of the aristocracy, either by directly working the lord's land (and handing over to him all the product), or by handing over a proportion of the product from their activity on their customary land. Despite variations in the specific form that the transfer of surplus took, what characterized the process was a legal/customary constraint upon the serfs to produce directly for the dominant class.

By way of contrast, for Marxists the process of exploitation in a capitalist society is obscured by the very form that it takes. Within capitalism, the worker sells labor power for a wage to a capitalist. The capitalist uses the labor power, in combination with raw materials and machinery, etc., to produce commodities which are then sold. By virtue of the fact that the worker receives a given sum of money for every hour worked or item produced, it appears that he or she is fully rewarded for the time spent laboring for the capitalist. In fact, the value received by the worker in the form of wages is less than the value of the commodities that are produced as a result of the employment of his or her labor power. Profit originates in the difference between these two values (in the sphere of production) and not in the difference between the combined price of all the "factors of production" and the price of the product as paid by the purchaser (in the sphere of exchange).

In both these instances, exploitation is being used to refer to the extraction of surplus value at the point of production. The process is, however, not simply an "economic" one. Rather, it occurs within supporting political and ideological relations. Hence, in feudal societies, there were customary/legal definitions of the amount of time that the serf should spend laboring for the lord. And, in a capitalist society, the relationship between worker and capitalist is surrounded and linked by a wide range of legal provisions and ideological notions concerning a "just wage" and "acceptable" working conditions, etc. This integral political/ideological dimension to exploitation within Marxist analysis provides the bridge to broader and, ultimately, non-Marxist uses of the concept of exploitation.

To illustrate this point, we can take two examples: slave labor, and contract, migrant labor. In the case of slave labor, the slave is owned as a thing by a master who receives the total product of the slave's labor, but in return for which the slave has to be provided with food, clothing, and shelter. However, the ownership of a human being as a thing requires that the human being be divested partially, or completely, of humanity. Thus, one can identify an historical, *ideological* process by which those human beings who were enslaved were defined as less than human by virtue of their condition of "heathenness" and, later, by their supposed "race." In the case of a contract, migrant worker, entry into the society in which capital employs his or her labor power in return for a wage is legally and ideologically structured in such a way that the conditions under which this exchange occurs are inferior to those applying to indigenous labor. Hence, the contract worker may have no permanent residence or voting rights.

These political and ideological processes are, in both cases, integral to the process by which a surplus product is obtained from the utilization of labor power. In other words, in Marxist analysis, they are integral to the process of exploitation. However, it is common for the notion of exploitation to be used to refer directly to the ideological and political processes in themselves, and without reference to the appropriation of surplus value. This broader usage tends to arise from theoretical perspectives that regard wage labor as a natural or acceptable form of appropriation of labor power, against which other forms are then evaluated and analyzed. Thus, in the case of slave labor, exploitation is used to refer to both the harshness of the treatment of the slave and the way in which the slave is dehumanized, as assessed relative to the "freedom" of the wage labor. And in the case of contract, migrant labor, exploitation is located in the comparative legal/political disadvantages of the worker when compared with "indigenous, free" labor.

We find parallels in the way in which writers analyze the position of New Commonwealth migrants and their children in Britain. This is judged to be the sole or primary product of racism and discrimination and therein, it is argued, lies their exploitation. In other words, racism and discrimination are forms of exploitation in and by themselves, as measured by the fact that "white" people are not the object of such experiences and processes. In this usage, exploitation loses any direct connection with production relations and comes to refer to any process by which one group is treated less equally than another. Thus, the many ways in which men treat women, whites treat blacks, and parents treat children, can all fall within the rubric of exploitation. This move towards extreme generality, and the analytical problems that it causes, is evident in the way in which the notion of exploitation is increasingly qualified by a descriptive adjective as in racial exploitation, sexual exploitation, and parental exploitation.

SEE ALSO: capitalism; consumption; disadvantage; empowerment; human rights; ideology; Marxism; postcolonial; race relations: as activity; racist discourse; segregation; slavery

Reading

Capital, vol. 1, by Karl Marx (Penguin, 1976), where, in Parts 3, 4, and 5, he details his analysis of the nature of exploitation in a capitalist society through the concepts of absolute and relative surplus value.

Ethnic Minorities and Industrial Change in Europe and North America, edited by Malcolm Cross (Cambridge University Press, 1992), provides comparative data on the scale of persisting exploitation of minority workers.

Racial Oppression in America by Robert Blauner (Harper & Row, 1972) is an example of an analysis which tends towards a broad utilization of the notion of exploitation.

ROBERT MILES

F

FANON, FRANTZ (1925–61)

Diagnosis of racism

Fanon was one of the most important theorists of the political, psychic, and existential effects of racism and colonialism in the twentieth century. Fanon's life and work has influenced both political movements and academic disciplines over more than a half-century and his writing has formed one of the foundations of postcolonial studies.

Born in Martinique, Fanon grew up in Fort-de-France, the island's capital. Since he belonged to a middle-class family (his father worked as a government official, his mother kept a shop), the Fanon children were among the very small percentage of blacks in Martinique who were able to be educated at the *lycée*. Fanon was to later write about the lasting effects of receiving a French colonial education, which encouraged black schoolboys in the Antilles to identify with "our ancestors, the Gauls," as he put it. Certainly his writing shows the influence of French literature and philosophy, alongside that of Francophone writers belonging to the *négritude* movement such as Aimé Césaire and Léopold Sédar Senghor, on his intellectual development. This youthful identification with France led Fanon to join the Free French Army in 1944, and he returned to Martinique two years later, having been wounded at the front and having received the Croix de Guerre for bravery. But his first traumatic experience of French racism, which he would go on to chronicle so eloquently in his first book, *Peau noire, masques blancs* (*Black Skin, White Masks*), had changed him irrevocably.

Fanon wrote the essays that make up *Black Skin, White Masks*, first published in 1952, while studying medicine at the University of Lyons (he had returned to France in 1947, with the original intention of studying dentistry on a scholarship for veterans). The book is a groundbreaking study of the multiple effects of racism in both colonized territories, such as the Antilles and North Africa, as well as in metropolitan centers in Europe. Combining political and economic analysis, psychological case studies, existentialist philosophy, linguistic data, and literary criticism, and written in a prose that moves from scientific to poetic to polemical, often on the same page, *Black Skin, White Masks* has become a key text for those who want to understand the dynamic and complex process that comes to be regarded as racism. Fanon's approach, he tells us, is "sociodiagnostic": "This book is a clinical study," he declares in the introduction. But what many find so striking is the way Fanon constantly moves from the position of analyst to that of subject of analysis. For example, in the book's most famous chapter, "L'expérience vécue du Noir" (translated as "The fact of Blackness"), Fanon narrates his various attempts to analyze and understand a particular moment in which he is made violently aware of his racial identity (by being confronted with a racial epithet) soon after his arrival in France. He makes the startling suggestion that such an epithet is identical to a seemingly neutral sounding phrase, "Look, a black man!" is tantamount to violence: it freezes or "fixes" his racial identity, forcing him to perform the role of absolute Otherness for the white man.

Fanon goes on to investigate, but ultimately challenge, the understandings of race offered by liberalism, *négritude*, and Marxism, striving instead for a new way of thinking and living. This is best spelled out in the book's conclusion, where Fanon declares, "The black man is not. Any more than the white man," and ends with a "final prayer": "O my body, make of me always a man who questions!"

Psychiatry in a colonial situation

Meanwhile, Fanon continued his medical studies. He defended his medical thesis in 1951, and was admitted to a residence program in psychiatry at the Hôpital de Saint-Alban. His hope was to work in Senegal, but when he failed to obtain a post there, he accepted the opportunity to work in Algeria, and in 1953 he became the chef de service of the Blida-Joinville Hospital, the largest psychiatric hospital in the country. Fanon introduced a number of innovative techniques at Blida-Joinville, many of which bore the influence of François Tosquelles, his mentor. He also wrote and co-wrote many articles on the practice and theory of psychiatry, and while these articles are not as widely read today as much of his other writing, he was undoubtedly responsible for initiating radical changes in the practice of colonial psychiatry in Algeria.

But it was precisely the problem of practicing psychiatry in a colonial situation that began to take its toll upon Fanon's work. As the struggle for national liberation in Algeria became more conspicuous, and French repression became more brutal, Fanon found himself treating both Algerian freedom fighters and French police officers, the tortured and the torturers. The case studies documenting these years of treatment form the astonishing penultimate chapter of Fanon's last book, *Les Damnés de la terre* (*The Wretched of the Earth*). Fanon finally concluded that the practice of psychiatry was impossible under colonial conditions: "The social structure in Algeria," he later wrote, "was hostile to any attempt to put the individual back where he belonged." In the summer of 1956 Fanon resigned his post at Blida-Joinville, writing in his "Letter to the Resident Minister" (later published in *Pour la Révolution Africaine*, or *Toward the African Revolution*, a collection of his journalistic and political essays): "If psychiatry is the medical technique that aims to enable man no longer to be a stranger to his environment, I owe it to myself to affirm that the Arab, permanently

an alien in his own country, lives in a state of absolute depersonalization."

From this point on, Fanon dedicated himself more and more to political activities for the Front de Libération Nationale (FLN), although he continued to practice medicine and his background in psychiatry and psychoanalytic theory continued to be central to his writing. In January 1957, Fanon was expelled from Algeria, and for the rest of his life was one of the most wanted persons of the French secret police. He was also targeted by French settlers in Algeria and survived several assassination attempts. After leaving Algeria, Fanon arrived at the FLN headquarters in Tunis and served in a number of capacities, including editing the movement's newspaper, *El Moudjahid*, working as a doctor in FLN health centers, and acting as an ambassador to several African nations. During his time in Tunis, Fanon also wrote *A Dying Colonialism*, a sociological study of the Algerian liberation struggle. Written with a manifesto-like intensity, the book received enough attention in France for the government to ban it six months after its publication. The book's best-known chapter, "Algeria unveiled," continues to be at the center of debates, since Fanon offers the provocative argument that the veil worn by Algerian women (the *hëik*), which would seem to be the symbol of an unchanging patriarchal culture, is in fact used for strategic purposes by women active in the revolution, and that the revolution in turn would transform gender relations in the society. Some have argued that Fanon's analysis in *A Dying Colonialism* is hampered, in spite of his commitment to the revolution, by his lack of detailed knowledge of Algerian society, for example, Fanon never mastered Arabic, something for which he has been criticized. What is certainly the case is that Fanon was working towards an analysis that saw Algerian culture as shifting and mutable rather than static and unchanging.

In 1960, while traveling in Mali as an FLN representative, Fanon became ill, and shortly afterwards he was diagnosed with leukemia. He was taken to Moscow for treatment, and Soviet doctors suggested that he seek treatment in the USA. Instead, Fanon returned to Tunis, and writing from what he realized was his deathbed, he produced in a period of ten weeks his final and most famous book, *The Wretched of the Earth*. Finally, despite his disgust at the idea of dying in "that nation of lynchers," he agreed to travel to Washington, DC for treatment, but it was too late to stop the progress of the disease. Frantz Fanon died on December 6, 1961, aged thirty-six. His body was taken to Tunisia, then smuggled across the border to Algeria, where he was buried in an FLN cemetery with full military honors.

New skin, new concepts

While *Black Skin, White Masks* has been highly influential in recent years, *The Wretched of the Earth* remains central to Fanon's legacy. As polemical as *A Dying Colonialism* and as wide-ranging in its critical concerns and tone as *Black Skin, White Masks*, Fanon's final work is a direct statement of what an anticolonial revolution in Africa needed to look like. The opening chapter, "Concerning violence," became famous (or perhaps infamous) on its own, and led critics such as Hannah Arendt to label Fanon a prophet of violence for statements such as: "To work means to work for the death of settler." But far from suggesting that violence would, in and of itself, bring an end to colonialism and its legacy of racism in Africa, Fanon's argument is that colonialism is itself violence in a pure state, and thus leaves the colonized with no arena in which to fight, no political public sphere, no mediation between ruler and ruled, except for that of pure violence. But Fanon goes on to question the very spontaneity that seemed to be the strength of the anticolonial movement, and in the remarkably prescient chapter entitled "The pitfalls of national consciousness," predicts precisely what would go wrong after the national bourgeoisie took over in newly independent African states. Fanon's response to this sense that things will almost certainly go wrong is not despair, however, but a call to create a new form of national culture, inspired by a national consciousness that distinguishes itself from nationalism by its universal dimension: "National consciousness, which is not nationalism," he declares, "is the only thing that will give us an international dimension." This same call is to be found in the book's justly famous conclusion, in which Fanon simultaneously offers his most withering critique of the form of "humanism" that has underwritten European imperialism and racism – "Leave this Europe where they are never done talking of Man, yet murder men everywhere they find them," – as part of a larger call to bring about a new postcolonial form of humanism. The book's final sentence, written on his deathbed, makes this call to the wretched of the earth clear: "For Europe, for ourselves, comrades, and for humanity, we must grow a new skin, we must work out new concepts, and try to set afoot a new man." This is Fanon's challenge, and it remains as urgent today as it was when he wrote these words over forty years ago.

SEE ALSO: colonial discourse; colonialism; cultural identity; dress; Hall, Stuart; hybridity; Islamophobia; *négritude*; Other; postcolonial; racist discourse; Senghor, Léopold Sédar; sexuality; subaltern

Reading

For translations of Fanon's writings into English, see *Black Skin, White Masks* (Grove, 1991); *A Dying Colonialism* (Grove, 1988); *The Wretched of the Earth* (Grove, 1986); and *Toward the African Revolution* (Grove, 1988).

Frantz Fanon by David Macey (Picador, 2001) is the authoritative biography of Fanon.

Frantz Fanon: Critical perspectives, edited by Anthony C. Alessandrini (Routledge, 1999), provides examples of contemporary critical writing inspired by Fanon's work.

Rethinking Fanon's Legacy, edited by Nigel Gibson (Humanity Books, 1999), provides a survey of critical responses to Fanon's writings.

ANTHONY C. ALESSANDRINI

FARRAKHAN, LOUIS *see* Nation of Islam

FASCISM

Refers to a political movement which aspires to a particular form of authoritarian class rule within a capitalist society. It emerged in Western Europe in the period after World War I, although its ideology has much deeper roots in European political action and political thought. As a form of class rule, it is characterized by an acceptance of a form of capitalism as an economic structure and process, by the elimination of all independent working-class and other political organizations, and by authoritarian forms of political rule and administration. The latter is evident in the rejection of bourgeois liberal conceptions of party organization and representation in favor of the establishment of a permanent political elite, and in the establishment of a corporate state. As an ideology, it is characterized by an extreme nationalism (which commonly but not characteristically becomes racism) and an "irrationalism," which asserts that the interests of "the nation" must always predominate over all other interests. Although fascist movements have existed in all European countries since the 1920s, only in Germany, Italy, and Spain have they attained political power.

Fascist movements of the early twentieth century represented a revolt against bourgeois society and the liberal state as well as against the growing working-class political and trade union organizations. The early support for these movements came from sectors of the population excluded from both financial and political bourgeois privilege, and working-class organizations, notably the petit-bourgeois, clerical and professional strata, and the peasantry. Such strata were facing extreme political pressure from "above" and "below" in a context of the major social and economic dislocation in Europe after 1918, and so any explanation must take full account of both the nature of the strata that gave support to fascism and the structural conditions that permitted fascism to become a solution. Fascism represented a solution insofar as it constituted a new route to political power and promised through national reorganization a new and radically different political and economic future. This revived support from sections of both the petit-bourgeoisie and the working class, but the political and financial support of monopoly capital became the decisive factor in ensuring the attainment of political power. The route to political power was based upon only tactical support for electoral activity, combined with paramilitary organization and activity, not only for "self-defense" but also for a coup d'état. Its vision for the future was a national state purged of all forms of internationalism (from finance capital to communism) and bourgeois privilege in which the ordinary man (and sometimes woman) would have his (and her) rightful place as a member of a national community. The explicit political subordination of women to the task of biological reproduction of the nation, with all its implications, has received particular attention in more recent analyses of fascism. It also aimed at dispensing with bourgeois parliamentarianism as a form of government, to be replaced by the rule of the Fascist Party which would embody all national interests.

The routes to power in Italy, Germany, and Spain differ in important ways. However, in all three cases, the support of important sections of the ruling capitalist class became crucial, both in terms of political credibility and financial support. The emphasis on national regeneration and suppression of working-class political organization promised greater economic and political rewards to sections of the dominant class, faced with economic crisis and a strong and politically conscious working class, than did bourgeois parliamentarianism. It is in this sense that fascism, once in power, is to be understood as a form of class rule.

The relationship between fascism and racism is a particularly controversial issue. It was only in Germany that racism came to play a predominant part in political ideology and strategy, and this has led some commentators to conclude that a firm distinction can be drawn between fascism and nazism. It is certainly the case that the fascist movement in Germany explicitly reproduced a notion of German nationalism which was biologically based and excluded the Jews as an allegedly distinct and inferior "race" which threatened biological extinction if allowed to remain. An explicit biological nationalism was not as important in Italy or Spain but it does not follow that the resulting treatment of the Jews makes German fascism a special case. Not only, in all three cases, was fascism an alternative form of class rule which guaranteed a modified capitalism, but, moreover, the historical coincidence of the generation of the ideas of "nation" and "race" as means of political mobilization in the nineteenth century means that nationalism contains within it the potential of becoming expressed by means of an explicit racism. This is not simply a matter of historical coincidence but also of the nature of nationalism per se, characterized as it is by the belief in the historical/natural existence of populations sharing a common heritage and culture which must receive expression and organization in a territorial state. The notion of natural, cultural distinctiveness can, in particular historical circumstances (given the predominance of the common-sense idea of "race"), easily come to be expressed in terms of "race."

The defeat of the fascist powers in World War II has not led to the elimination of fascist movements in Western Europe. Although the political ideology and strategy of fascism was discredited in defeat and in the discovery of the activities of nazism against the Jews and other sections of the German and other European populations, small fascist parties have been allowed to continue to exist and have, since the mid-1970s, shown signs of increasing support and activity throughout Europe. In some cases, particularly in Britain, this has been on the basis of the articulation of an explicit racism in reaction to the presence and settlement of migrant labor. But this should not be allowed to obscure the more general, common features of fascist movements, in particular their tactical support for bourgeois democracy combined with paramilitary, repressive activity of various kinds.

SEE ALSO: Aryan; caucasian; Chamberlain, Houston Stewart; Doomed Races Doctrine; eugenics; genocide; Gobineau, Joseph Arthur de; Holocaust; nationalism; neo-nazism; pogrom; science; Wagner, Richard; White Power

Reading

Fascism by Mark Neocleous (Open University Press, 1997) is a short introduction to the topic, representing it as an expression of the destructive potential of modernity and a form of reactionary modernism designed to remove movements of emancipation.

Fascism: A history by Roger Eatwell (Chatto, 1995) is a wide-ranging survey that provides a general history of fascism; it is complemented by *Fascism*, edited by Roger Griffin (Oxford University Press, 1995), which offers more than 200 extracts on fascism written by its precursors, practitioners, and critics, including one by the nineteenth-century composer Richard Wagner. Both books argue that fascism constituted a serious intellectual alternative to socialist or liberal progress.

Fascism Reader by Aristotle Kallis (Routledge, 2002) explores the various manifestations of fascism, including the lesser known ones in Hungary and Portugal as well as Britain (through the British Union of Fascists); this may profitably be read in conjunction with Stanley G. Payne's *A History of Fascism, 1914–1945* (UCL Press, 1996) and Philip Morgan's *Fascism in Europe, 1919–1945* (Routledge, 2002).

ROBERT MILES

FINOT, JEAN (1859–1922)

Author of *Le Préjé des races* (first published in 1905), Finot was part of a diverse group of writers who attacked the racial science that emerged in the nineteenth and early twentieth centuries. Finot, who was French, confronted the theories of Gobineau, Chamberlain, Ammon and others who advanced ideas of natural hierarchies

based on racial classifications, for the purpose of showing their scientific limitations and moral dangers. "Based on craniological differences, the largeness or smallness of the limbs, the color of the skin or hair etc., they endeavor to appeal to a sort of pseudo-science, with its problematic laws, unexamined facts and unjustifiable generalizations," wrote Finot about racial theorists.

He criticized what became known as scientific racism for trying to sell itself as "dogmas of salvation and infallible guides for humanity." The concept of race, for Finot, existed "only as a fiction in our brains." Much of his work focused on dismantling the scientific foundations of racial theories and, as such, he was part of a collectivity. Like many other writers associated with Enlightenment thinking, Finot saw the contradiction between the egalitarian ideas that issued from the era and the implications of the scientific thought that grew out of the period of discovery. The science, or pseudo-science as Finot called it, suggested an objective basis for human inequality. According to Jennifer Michael Hecht, Finot, together with fellow left-wing theorists, Alfred Fouillee and Celestin Bougle, decided that, given the choice between Enlightenment ideals and Enlightenment methods, they should preserve the ideals. "In so doing," writes Hecht, Finot "proposed a sort of metaphysical leap of faith that would hold certain basic human values beyond the reach of scientific theories, however persuasive they might seem."

Finot became a key figure in what Thomas F. Gossett called "The scientific revolt against racism." Often obscured by the more dramatic and menacing racial theories, the *ur*-antiracism of Finot and others, opposed, though not always unequivocally, racist theories. The English philosopher John Stuart Mill, for example, in 1848, wrote that, of all the malign influences on the rational mind, "the most vulgar is that of attributing the diversities of conduct and character to inherent natural differences." This was, of course, a deduction from prevailing theories, rather than an attempt to undermine racism through empirical means.

More systematic analyses came with the German Theodor Waitz, the Englishman William Dalton Babington, and the American William Z. Ripley, all of whom subjected racist theories to critical scrutiny and exposed their shallow, overly simplified character. The most formidable antagonist of racial theorists in the early twentieth century was Franz Boas.

SEE ALSO: anthropology; antislavery; Boas, Franz; Chamberlain, Houston Stewart; Gobineau, Joseph Arthur de; Grégoire, Henri; Hottentot Venus; human rights; Las Casas, Bartolomé de; science; sexuality; slavery

Reading

Race: The history of an idea in America by Thomas F. Gossett (Schocken, 1965) has a chapter "The scientific revolt against racism" in which he uncovers the diverse theorists who, in one way or another, opposed the racial theories of the nineteenth and twentieth centuries.

"The solvency of metaphysics: the debate over racial science and moral philosophy in France, 1890–1919" by Jennifer Michael Hecht (in Isis, vol. 90, 1999) examines the political and natural scientists who fought for Enlightenment ideals in the face of scientific racism.

FREIRE, PAULO (1921–97)

A Brazilian educator and philosopher, Freire is best known for his work on critical literacy, first articulated in his landmark volume, Pedagogy of the Oppressed (first published in English in 1970). In this book, Freire developed a revolutionary pedagogy for liberation, arguing that the act of reading is a politically transformative event. In the ensuing years and up to the present, Freirean literacy programs designed for both developing and postindustrial countries around the world have attempted to free the oppressed from the powerlessness resulting from illiteracy and pre-critical literateness under the system of "banking education" where subjects are regarded as passive "receptacles" of information.

For Freire, the act of reading is simultaneously an act of reading the world. In other words, subjects exist with the world rather than merely living in it. Thus, one of his central ideas is that humans come to know the world as beings-for-themselves-and-others and have the capacity to transform concrete everyday lives and the lives of others. Through critical literacy, people read both the word and the world, and consequently become critically empowered to make their own history.

An important concept in Freire's writings is that of reflection. By critically interrogating the objective reality in which individuals and groups find themselves, people become reflectively aware of the relations that oppress and dehumanize them. Reflection is a necessary but not sufficient act of liberation: pure introspection results in what Freire calls "verbalism," while acting, when unaccompanied by critical reflection, degrades into mere "activism." Together, critical reflection and action create what Freire refers to as praxis (theory linked with practice).

Praxis is accomplished in part by acting with others in order to collectively transform the material conditions of existence. As such, Freire's pedagogy is dialogical and establishes the conditions of learning an act of knowing between subjects. The goal of this act of knowing (dialogical communication) is freedom from oppressive material and social conditions. Becoming literate is not just a cognitive process of decoding signs, but requires living one's life in relation to others. Freire's (essentially phenomenological) literacy method invites learners to examine the concrete lived conditions of their existence. Such conditions come to be understood as social, political, and economic "codifications" through which everyday reality for the oppressed has become naturalized and made into an inevitable and presumably inescapable part of their situation.

Further, these codifications are made into a "knowable object" by the oppressed through a process of "decodification" in which the codified totality is broken down and "retotalized' through a form of ideology critique. Freire's goal is to create epistemic shifts in the consciousness of the oppressed through a focus on "action-object wholes" and "forms of orientation in the world" that eventually leads to concrete goals, strategies, and programs. In other words, such epistemic shifts lead to the creation among the disenfranchised of political subject positions and forms of collective subjectivity. In this way, Freire's literacy method enables the disenfranchised to alter their structural condition in Brazilian society through challenging the coercive power relationships of the dominant social order that support the privileging hierarchies of race, class, and gender.

In this conception, reading is already social. In order to liberate oneself and others from the kind of dehumanization experienced by subordinated groups under colonialism, subjects must criticize their lived context, or "limit situations." True dialogue among subjects is realized when they speak to one another as authentic human beings, as subjects free from oppression.

SEE ALSO: children; colonial discourse; education; human rights; Freyre, Gilberto; Hall, Stuart; multicultural education; racial coding

Reading

The Paulo Freire Reader, edited by A. Freire and D. Macedo (Continuum), 1998, is a valuable collection.

Pedagogy of Freedom: Ethics, democracy and civic courage by Paolo Freire (Rowman & Littlefield, 2001) is a visionary text that reminds readers of the "incompleteness" of any project designed to approach freedom.

Pedagogy of the Oppressed (Continuum Press, 1970, rev. edn., 2000) is Freire's influential text and may fruitfully be read in conjunction with *Pedagogy of Hope* (Continuum Press, 1994).

PETER MCLAREN AND ZEUS LEONARDO

FREYRE, GILBERTO (1900–87)

Brazilian social anthropologist and member of the Brazilian parliament (1946–50), Freyre is best known for his work, *The Masters and the Slaves* (first published in 1933), a detailed analysis of plantation society which re-established the positive contribution of Africans in shaping Brazilian character and culture. The book punctured the myth of a cordial Brazilian democracy, or melting-pot culture, where ethnic groups and classes had dissolved racism and prejudices.

Sexual contact between white masters and black slaves was the key to Freyre's concepts of racial informality and flexibility: the mulatto offspring was considered the symbol of racial democracy, transcending class barriers and integrating cultures and ethnic identities – an idea expressed as *mesticismo*. But, Freyre argued, such democracy always assured the supremacy of white European culture as the goal toward which the process of integration was to advance. The vision of a "meta-race" of brown Brazilians only camouflaged the location of class power and domination.

Mass migration and the proletarianization of Brazil in the twentieth century brought a sharpening of class conflict and an end to traditional sexual intimacy, which was a legacy of the oppressive patriarchal relations of plantation economies. Freyre was jailed in the reign of Getúlio Vargas before World War II.

SEE ALSO: Brazil; conquest; creole; Freire, Paulo; miscegenation; slavery; whiteness

Reading

The Masters and the Slaves by Freyre (Knopf, 1964) is the influential text.

G

GANDHI, MOHANDAS KARAMCHAND (1869–1948)

Leader of the Indian nationalist movement which successfully repelled British colonial rule, Gandhi was born in Porbandar on the western coast of India and had an arranged marriage in the customary Hindu way at the age of thirteen. His wife Kasturbai was his lifelong supporter. At nineteen, he went to England to study law and graduated as a barrister before returning to India in 1891. There his lack of self-confidence led him to accept a post in South Africa, where he felt professional demands were less stringent.

It was in South Africa that he first encountered racialism, a pivotal experience being when he was ejected from a Pretoria-bound train despite holding a first-class ticket – Indians were allowed only in third-class compartments. His ejection was based solely on his color. After this, he committed himself to campaigning for the rights of Indians in South Africa through the vehicle of the Natal Indian Congress, formed in 1894.

To attain his objectives, Gandhi came to formulate his central method of nonviolent civil disobedience, or passive resistance, which later became known as *Satyagraha*, meaning "truth force"; for example, whenever he or his followers were beaten or imprisoned, there would be no retaliation, only a refusal to comply with others' demands. In the years that followed, the method was adopted by movements the world over, particularly by Martin Luther King's Southern Christian Leadership Conference.

During his twenty-one-year stay in South Africa, he edited an influential publication, *Indian Opinion*, which was distributed throughout the country. He became internationally renowned for his campaigns. His intermittent imprisonments served only to elevate his status. During the Anglo–Boer War, 1899–1902, Gandhi organized an ambulance corps in support of the British government. At this stage, he believed in the virtues of British colonial rule. The reversal of this opinion was to feature centrally in his subsequent operations in South Asia. After the war, the civil disobedience continued, culminating in a massive protest march in 1913 which resulted in the granting of many of Gandhi's demands for Indians.

His growing reputation in South Africa was constantly relayed to India, thus producing an invitation by the Indian National Congress (INC) for him to return to India to help his own country win *swaraj*, or self-rule. He took up the invitation in 1915, taking over the unofficial leadership by 1921. The INC was formed in 1885 mainly as a liberal middle-class movement dedicated to reviving interest in traditional Indian culture; it later developed a political edge when it campaigned for greater freedom from British political control. Gandhi was responsible for transforming the INC from a more or less elitist organization into a mass movement with the support of the Muslim League and other smaller movements. Instead of constitutional lobbying, the INC opted for mass direct action in the form of nonviolent civil disobedience.

Gandhi was able to unify and mobilize the movement to such measures because his leadership was premised on charisma; in Gandhi, Indians saw not only a leader, but a person endowed with supernatural powers. This he acknowledged: "Men say I am a saint losing myself in politics. The fact is I am a politician trying my hardest to be a saint." He came as a messiah, bringing images of sainthood with his severe dietary restrictions, his vows of celibacy, his insistence on wearing only homespun *khaddar* and his Utopian vision of an independent, agrarian India freed of the modern science and technology, which, he argued, were instruments of Western domination.

At the outbreak of World War I, at Gandhi's insistence, India offered support to Britain in anticipation of a stronger elected element in government led by the INC and the Muslim League. This was provided in the Montagu–Chelmsford Reforms of 1919, but was insufficient to stem the tide of postwar dissatisfaction. The British government, in its concern for the maintenance of order, passed the Rowlatt Acts, which gave the government greater powers to punish Indian dissidents.

Gandhi implemented a massive campaign of civil disobedience and urged his followers to withdraw from all schools and government positions. Whenever violence erupted, Gandhi embarked on extended fasts as if to blackmail his followers into ceasing their violence. This invariably succeeded. One such incident was when nearly 2,000 villagers burned alive 21 Indian policemen in their station in Chaura Chaura in the United Provinces in February 1922.

One of the nonviolent protests against the reforms of 1919 turned into an atrocity when General Dyer ordered British troops to fire on a crowd of unarmed Indians at Amritsar, the result being 379 people killed and 1,137 injured. General Dyer himself said, after the massacre: "It was no longer a question of merely dispersing the crowd, but one of producing a sufficient moral effect. My intention was to inflict a lesson that would have an impact throughout all India."

During the events leading to the Amritsar incident, Gandhi's attitude toward the British colonialists changed completely: he became convinced that "the British government today represents satanism." This change led him into alignment with some factions of the INC who were strongly anti-British, and served to win him leadership of the organization.

There were three decades of turmoil in India before the country won its independence from the British in 1947. Although Gandhi's influence was in decline in the years immediately preceding independence, it was his charismatic leadership which gave the Nationalist movement its impetus on a mass basis, for which he became known as

the *Mahatma*, "the great soul." In 1948 he was assassinated by a Hindu extremist.

Martin Luther King acknowledged Gandhi as his inspiration and used the INC as the model for his own movement. King, like Gandhi, demanded great, almost inhuman self-discipline of his followers in restraining themselves when subjected to violence. As Gandhi strove to acquire independence and equality for Indians, King strove for freedom and equality for black Americans.

SEE ALSO: Anglo-Indians; apartheid; Chávez, César; civil rights movement; colonialism; human rights; King, Martin Luther; Mandela, Nelson; postcolonial; power; South Africa

Reading

Gandhi: Prisoner of hope by Judith Brown (Yale University Press, 1989) sets Gandhi in an historical, colonial context.
Gandhi's Political Philosophy by Bhiku Parekh (University of Notre Dame Press, 1989) is a scholarly attempt to systematize the leader's thoughts.
M. K. Gandhi: An autobiography (Penguin, 1982) is the Mahatma's own account of his experiences and philosophy translated from the original Gujerati.

GARVEY, MARCUS (1887–1940)

One of the enduringly influential black leaders of this century. His actual achievements do not compare with those of King, Washington, or even Du Bois, but his general thrust to elevate black people by forcing them to recognize their African ancestry was to have a lasting impact.

Born in Jamaica, Garvey traveled throughout the Caribbean and Central America before starting his organization in the USA. His Universal Negro Improvement Association (UNIA) went strongly against the grain of other black American movements. As his biographer E. David Cronon puts it: "Garvey sought to raise high the walls of racial nationalism at a time when most thoughtful men were seeking to tear down these barriers." Whereas leaders such as W. E. B. Du Bois and his National Association for the Advancement of Colored People (NAACP) were campaigning for the greater integration of blacks and whites (principally through legislation), Garvey declared integration impossible and implored his followers to make a sharp break with whites. His simple aim was to restore all blacks to what he considered their rightful "fatherland," Africa. "If you cannot live alongside the white man, even though you are his fellow citizen; if he claims that you are not entitled to this chance or opportunity because the country is his by force of numbers, then find a country of your own and rise to the highest position within that country" was Garvey's message, and he summed it up in his slogan, "Africa for the Africans."

To show that this was no empty slogan, Garvey made efforts to realize his ambition by buying a steamship line, called "Black Star," and even entered into what were ultimately abortive negotiations with the Liberian government to make possible a mass migration. Garvey, at the peak of his popularity, claimed four million followers all willing to forsake America and migrate to Africa to start a new life as what Garvey called "The New Negro."

This concept of the New Negro was pivotal in Garvey's movement. Blacks were told to rid themselves of any notions of inferiority and cultivate a new sense of identity; they were urged to take pride and dignity in the fact that they were truly Africans. Their subordination was the result of whites' attempts to control them not only physically, but mentally too. One method used by whites was religious instruction: blacks were taught to believe in conventional Christianity and worship whites' images. But Garvey augmented his UNIA with a new, alternative religious movement called the African Orthodox Church. Its leader, George Alexander McGuire, instructed UNIA members to tear up pictures of white Christs and Madonnas and replace them with black versions. Garvey explained: "Our God has no colour, yet it is human to see everything through one's own spectacles, and since white people have seen their God through white spectacles we have only now started to see our own God through our own spectacles."

Often, Garvey would fuse his practical policies with biblical imagery, sometimes hinting at the inevitability of the exodus to Africa: "We have gradually won our way back into the confidence of the God of Africa, and he shall speak with the voice of thunder that shall shake the pillars of a corrupt and unjust world and once more restore Ethiopia to her ancient glory." Messages like this and continual reference to Ethiopian royalty helped generate the kind of interest that eventually turned into the Rastafarian movement, members of which even today regard Garvey as a prophet.

At a time when black organizations, particularly in the United States, were assiduously trying to implement gradual integrationist policies, Garvey's program was an outrage. He was vigorously condemned by Du Bois *et al.* and there were assassination attempts. Further notoriety came when Garvey entered into negotiations with the Ku Klux Klan; in a bizarre way, both harbored the same ideal: the removal of blacks.

Throughout the 1920s, Garvey's influence spread in the USA and in the Caribbean and he cultivated a mass following. The steamship line failed and negotiations for a migration to Africa broke down, so his following eventually faded. A spell in Jamaican politics ended after a series of clashes with the law and Garvey left for England where in 1940 he died.

Yet his influence amongst blacks continued; as his wife was to express it, "Garvey instilled in them *new concepts* of their rightful place on earth as God's creation." Garvey had instigated what he called "a second emancipation – an emancipation of the minds and thoughts." He identified the evil not so much in whites who controlled blacks, but in the minds of blacks themselves: they accepted their own inferiority and so failed to recognize their own potential. Garvey provided a blueprint for banishing the sense of inferiority with his conception of the New Negro. Even in the 1990s, Garvey is revered by a great many blacks as one of the most important leaders, not in terms of practical achievements, but in terms of transforming consciousness.

SEE ALSO: Africa; African Caribbeans in Britain; beauty; Black Power; diaspora; essentialism; Ethiopianism; Fanon, Frantz; Malcolm X; Nation of Islam; nationalism; *négritude*; Rastafari; Senghor, Léopold Sédar; whiteness

Reading

Black Moses by E. David Cronon (University of Wisconsin Press, 1974) is a well-researched biography of the man and his movement with attention given to the social contexts of the times.

Marcus Garvey: Anti-colonial champion by Rupert Lewis (Africa World Press, 1988) is an appreciation of Garvey's contribution, as is the concise *Marcus Garvey, 1887–1940* by Adolph Edwards (New Beacon Books, 2001).

Philosophy and Opinions, 3 vols., by Marcus Garvey (Cass, 1967), is a collection of speeches and essays edited by Garvey's wife Amy Jacques Garvey; the best account of the complex, sometimes contradictory, patterns of Garvey's thought.

GENOCIDE

There are many definitions of genocide (formed from the Greek *genos*, meaning a species or class, and *cida*, Latin for kill). The most commonly referred to, and the one of most immediate practical significance, is that incorporated originally in the Convention on the Prevention of the Crime of Genocide, 1948. Therein it is defined, in Article II, as a series of specified acts committed with intent to destroy, in whole or in part, a national, ethnical, racial, or religious group, as such. The acts specified were: (a) Killing members of the group; (b) Causing serious bodily or mental harm to members of the group; (c) Deliberately inflicting on the group conditions of life calculated to bring about its physical destruction in whole or in part; (d) Imposing measures intended to prevent births within the group; (e) Forcibly transferring children of the group to another group.

The concept of genocide was originally introduced by a Polish lawyer, Raphäel Lemkin, in a book that was published in 1944, *Axis Rule in Occupied Europe*. His analysis of the phenomenon and his formulation of the concept have been critical to the development of the field of genocide studies as these were to some degree incorporated in the 1948 Genocide Convention, the drafting of which he participated in as one of the expert advisers to the Division of Human Rights of the United Nations. The definition of the 1948 Convention has been carried over, unchanged, to the Rome Statute of the International Criminal Court.

Another factor of critical importance bearing on the formulation of the Convention, its subsequent interpretation, and the deployment of the concept by scholars, has been that the destruction of European Jewry was the paradigm case of group destruction that informed its drafting. It is difficult to think of the concept of genocide without associating it with the killing policies of the Third Reich, particularly as they were applied in concentration and death camps to Jews, although they were by no means the sole victims of such policies.

Even a cursory glance at the content of Article II indicates that its clauses raise substantial issues of interpretation. Moreover, many authorities have argued that its construction restricts the application of the concept to too few instances of hypothesized deliberate group destruction, militating against the development of an adequate theoretical framework for considering such behaviors. Accordingly, a major focus of genocide studies has been conceptual clarification and classification, which has generally advanced from noting flaws in the Article II definition relative to the requirements assumed by the author. This is invariably followed by an explication of necessary additions or modifications, and, at times, assimilation of a case study under consideration by the author to the category *genocide*, or some other category that is assumed to be not too dissimilar from it in essence.

To a degree, the preoccupation with issues of classification has been dictated by the specifications of Article II, and the fact that the destruction of European Jews has been the paradigm case that informed its construction. The problems that this has been perceived as creating have been fivefold:

1 Few other clusters of mass killings originally appeared to meet the requirements of Article II. This was both because the Holocaust was perceived as being the "archetype of twentieth-century evil," and because of the complexity and comprehensiveness of this destructive process. As Bedau has argued, "accusations of genocide in our time are coloured by the paradigm case ... there is a strong disinclination to describe as genocide any crime that fails to measure up to the fury of the Nazi's 'final solution'." There was also an element of what Harff referred to as "parochial and sectarian divisions," a tendency of many scholars to "reserve the right to consider their particular genocide unique." This gave rise to the somewhat sterile *uniqueness* debate, a main premise of which has been that the destruction of European Jewry was a unique event, in the sense that it differed from every other instance of large-scale mass killing in significant ways. Although various distinguishing criteria have been referenced, including ideology, bureaucracy, modernity, and intention of finality, these have never been systematically contrasted across a sizeable number of case studies.

2 Many scholars assumed that the *essence* of the notion *genocide* was the intention to

destroy the collectivity/group, but those included under Article II, namely national, ethnical, racial, or religious, did not exhaust those targeted. During the deliberations that accompanied the passage of the convention through the numerous UN committees that scrutinized it, the question of *political* groups was raised repeatedly. In the end, reference to political groups was omitted.

Drost, one of the earliest legal scholars to question this omission, noted that the inclusion of political groups under the umbrella of the convention, as with the exclusion of economic, social and cultural groups, would not entail any greater problems than those that already existed in relation to groups that were included. Excluding such groups, he contended, "left a wide and dangerous loop-hole for any Government to escape the human duties under the Convention by putting genocide into practice under the cover of executive measures against political or other groups for reasons of security, public order or any other reasons of state."

Many other authorities have since concurred. The destruction of individuals on the basis of membership in political groups – *politicide* – is now often included alongside genocide as a largely homologous category. Other categories have been added on the grounds that the groups which they designate have, similarly, been unjustifiably excluded from the umbrella genocide definition, Article II. These include gendercide and ethnocide.

3   Some authorities considered that the category genocide was insufficiently comprehensive to cover the clusters of mass killings that they wished to analyze. Others considered that there were other categories of mass killings that were similar in many respects to those that accompanied clusters of killings and policies referred to as genocides, but which were either not directed at the *complete* destruction of the group, or were much smaller in scale, and, thus, on a slightly lower point on a scale of severity. Rummel noted that whilst the concept genocide "provided yeoman service in denoting government murder," it "hardly covers the variety and extent of ruthless murder carried out by governments." It excludes, for instance, "starving civilians to death by a blockade; assassinating

supposed sympathizers of antigovernment guerrillas; purposely creating a famine; executing prisoners of war; shooting political opponents; or murdering by quota (as carried out by the Soviets, Chinese communists and North Vietnamese)." Rummel introduced the concept *democide*, defining it as "the intentional killing of people by government." In this framework, genocide becomes a variant of democide.

4   The practices designated by the term *culturecide*, although considered and rejected when the Genocide Convention was under consideration, are employed by authors to refer to processes that are considered to be genocidal in import although not covered under the terms of Article II. It is generally used in connection with the erosion or extinction of indigenous cultures and in connection with certain types of cultural assimilation programs. Kuper elaborates it as "the commission of specified acts with intent to extinguish, utterly or in substantial part, a culture." These include, "the deprivations of opportunity to use a language, practise a religion, create art in customary ways, maintain basic social institutions, preserve memories and traditions, and work in cooperation toward social goals." As noted earlier, some authorities employ the term *ethnocide* in illustration of similar processes. Charny uses this term to designate "major processes that prohibit or interfere with the natural cycles of reproduction and continuity of a culture or nation," whilst Katherine Bischoping and Natalie Fingerhut define it as processes "in which ways of life rather than individuals are destroyed ("Border lines: Indigenous peoples in genocide studies," *Canadian Review of Sociology and Anthropology* vol. 33, 1996: 482)."

5   The Genocide Convention, like other humanitarian law legal instruments, was a product of drafting compromises that reflected differences in approach, interests, and legal cultures of the participants. No surprise, therefore, that sections of Article II are ambiguous and difficult of incontestable interpretation. This has been another important factor in stimulating the advancing of alternative definitions designed to designate the same or allied phenomena. As elaborated in some detail in the report of the Special

Rapporteur of the Human Rights Commission in 1978, these relate to the groups included, issues concerning the extent of the destruction of the group that must take place to justify the imputation of genocide, and problems associated with the subjective component, that is, the phrases with intent to destroy and as such.

No surprise, therefore, that there is no overall consensus among scholars as to which clusters of policies should be designated as genocides. The three on which there is general agreement are the massacres of the Armenians during World War I in Turkey, with virtually the only dissent coming from the Turkish authorities; the destruction of European Jews during World War II; and the killings of Tutsi and noncompliant Hutu by Hutus during three months of 1994. Others that are frequently mentioned are various indigenous peoples who have been the victims of colonizing policies, especially the Herero in Namibia, Native American Indians, and Australian Aborigines.

SEE ALSO: Aboriginal Australians; culturecide; Doomed Races Doctrine; ethnic cleansing; ethnic conflict; ethnocide; Holocaust; human rights; indigenous peoples; International Convention; Irish; slavery; UNESCO; United Nations

Reading

Century of Genocide: Eyewitness accounts and critical views, edited by Samuel Totten, Williams S. Parsons and Israel W. Charny (Garland, 1997), is a collection of papers employing common headings on a wide range of twentieth-century genocidal type events.
"Democracy, power, genocide, and mass murder" by R. J. Rummel, in *State Crime, vol. I: Defining, delineating and explaining state crime*, edited by David O. Friedrichs (Ashgate, 1999), takes a conceptual approach.
"The Drafting of the 1948 Convention on the Prevention and Punishment of the Crime of Genocide" by Matthew Lippman (in *Boston University International Law Journal*, vol. 3, no. 1, 1985) and *The Crime of State: Book II, Genocide*, by Pieter N. Drost (A. W. Sythoff, 1959) examine legal issues.
Genocide by Leo Kuper (Penguin, 1981) and *Axis Rule in Occupied Europe* by Raphäel Lemkin, (Carnegie Endowment for International Peace, 1944) remain valuable.
"Genocide as state terrorism," by Barbara Harff, in *Government Violence and Repression*, edited by M. Stohl and G. A. Lopez (Greenwood, 1986), may be read in conjunction with *Genocide in International Law* by William A. Schabas (Cambridge University Press, 2000).
Rwanda: Death, despair and defiance by African Rights (rev. edn., August 1995) is a lengthy and detailed account of the Rwanda genocide of 1994, while the question of whether the Vietnam atrocities constituted genocide is raised by H. A. Bedau in "Genocide in Vietnam?" (in *Worldview*, vol. 17, 1974).
CHECK: internet resources section

STUART STEIN

GENOTYPE

The genotype is the underlying genetic constitution of an organism in respect of a particular trait or traits, as opposed to the *phenotype*, or appearance, of that organism. All people with brown eyes have the same phenotype in respect of eye color, yet some of them may carry a recessive gene for blue eyes and therefore have a different genotype. For predicting inheritance, it is the genotype that is important.

Genes control enzymes and in that way control the nature of physical characteristics. They are located on chromosomes and since all chromosomes exist in pairs, so do genes. The two members of a gene pair may be either identical or different. A person who carries blue-eye genes on both chromosomes is said to be homozygous for that characteristic; someone with a blue-eye gene on one chromosome and a brown-eye gene on the other is heterozygous in that respect. If a man who is homozygous for brown eyes and a woman who is homozygous for brown eyes have children they will all be brown-eyed. If a man who is homozygous for blue eyes has children with a woman who is homozygous for brown eyes the outcome is more complicated. Every egg cell the mother produces will contain one brown-eye gene; every sperm cell the father produces will contain one blue-eye gene. No matter which sperm fertilizes which egg, the fertilized ovum will be heterozygous, containing one blue-eye and one brown-eye gene. Each child will be brown-eyed since the brown-eye gene forms more of the chemical (tyrosinase) that colors the eye; it is therefore said to be dominant, whereas the blue-eye gene is recessive; although it is part of the genotype and cannot be seen in the phenotype.

If the father and mother are both heterozygous with respect to blue and brown-eye genes, they will form sperm and egg cells with one blue and one brown-eye gene. When these cells interact, three combinations are possible for the ovum:

two brown-eye genes; one gene of each; two blue-eye genes. Since the one of each combination is twice as likely as either of the others, and since the brown-eye gene is dominant, the probability is that of four children three will have brown eyes and one will have blue.

This example oversimplifies the inheritance of eye color because, as everyone can see, there are eyes of other colors than blue and brown. Possibly other genes at other places in the chromosomes or other kinds of eye-color genes are involved in the production of the relevant chemicals, but the example serves to clarify the differences between phenotype and genotype. It also illustrates Mendel's laws: first, that inheritance is particulate, resulting from the interrelation of distinctive genes rather than from the blending of hereditary elements to produce a mixed character; and, second, that characters are independently inherited, so that a child's inheritance of his or her father's eye color does not indicate the likelihood of the inheritance of his or her father's hair or skin color.

SEE ALSO: anthropology; eugenics; heritability; kinship; phenotype; science

Reading

The Race Concept by Jonathan Harwood and Michael Banton (David & Charles, 1975) examines the often confused theorizing over "race."

MICHAEL BANTON

GEOMETRY OF RACE

This is a term used by the late Harvard zoologist Stephen Jay Gould when explaining how the modification of taxonomies of human diversity in the eighteenth century resulted in a shift from the geographical arrangement favored by the Swedish botanist Carolus Linnaeus (1707–78) to the hierarchical ordering of humanity advanced by Johann Friedrich Blumenbach (1752–1840). According to Gould, the shift "must stand as one of the most fateful transitions in the history of Western science – for what, short of railroads and nuclear bombs, has had more practical impact, in this case almost entirely negative, upon our collective lives?"

Linnaeus, whose *Systema Naturae*, first published in 1758, is regarded as the first systematic attempt to classify *Homo sapiens* by race, intro-

duced a taxonomy (the word is from the Greek *tasso*, meaning arrange and *nomina* for distribution) based fundamentally on geographic criteria, without any explicit hierarchy. His divisions were *Americanus rubescus*, *Europaeus albus*, *Asiaticus luridus* and *Afer niger*. He also included *Homo ferus*, feral men. Each division was attributed with features, such as their disposition, color and posture, but with no evaluation, less still prescription. It was part of a much wider project to classify all living phenomena, including plants and animals, which were arranged according to their *genus* and *species*.

Blumenbach, the German anatomist and naturalist, studied at the University of Göttingen. He submitted his doctoral thesis in 1775 and, twenty years later, published a revised edition *De Generis Humani Varietate Nativa* (*On the Natural Variety of Mankind*). In the intervening years, Blumenbach, who had originally subscribed to Linnaeus's scheme, added a new category.

Blumenbach's taxonomy catalogued humans into five files, defined by geography and appearance. The Caucasian file contained populations of Europe and contiguous parts of Africa and Asia, with pale skins. Mongolians were, for the most part, from Asia and had slightly darker complexions. Darker still were those in the Ethiopian category, which, in this schema, covered most of Africa. The American division comprised native populations of the New World. These four were all presented in Blumenbach's original thesis. The Malay, including Pacific Islanders and Aboriginal Australians, was added only in the 1795 edition; these groups were originally included in the Mongolian group. Ivan Hannaford notes that only in the 1781 edition of the book did Blumenbach use the word Caucasian (which is, of course, still used, quite inaccurately, by all manner of official organizations) to describe Europeans.

The introduction of the Malay class was pivotal: it changed the entire geometric structure of the model and set up a scheme that has, as Gould puts it, "served racism ever since." While Blumenbach may not have intended to encourage scientific racism, he lived during the Enlightenment, the period when reason, rationality and individuality were emphasized as determinants of human thought and behavior. As such, he would have absorbed ideas of human progress and of the cultural and technological superiority of Europeans. Conceptions of racial hierarchies, with Europeans at the apex of development, were not out of place in scientific discourse. Blumenbach's reformulation offered a tiered five-race model, which he described as "consonant with nature."

In his model, Blumenbach saw races as groups sharing characteristics, but not entirely separate, bounded units. In fact, he subscribed to a monogenetic conception of human origins: diversity was the result of climate, topography and cultural adaptation (*monogenesis* is the theory that all humans share common ancestors; its alternative is *polygenesis*, that human diversity is the result of separate origins). In this respect he anticipated Darwin, whose magnum opus was published eighty years after Blumenbach's. He identified the European variety as the finest representatives of humanity, physical beauty being his central criterion when making this evaluation. In particular, he chose the people around Mount Caucasus as the most beautiful. Caucasus was the most likely place of human origin and subsequent departures from the original ideal were the result of degeneration. The term is taken from the Latin *de*, meaning away or from, and *generare*, propagate; it would not have carried the same connotations as it does today, though there remained the implication that a deviation from a former state of excellence had taken place among those who were not Caucasians.

Blumenbach believed that the most extreme deviations from the Caucasian ideal were Asian and Ethiopian races, and that, to maintain symmetry and stay true to his monogenetic beliefs, he needed intermediate races, which were neither immutable nor static, but which overlapped. The Native American race served this purpose, connecting Caucasians with Asians. The introduction of Malays – which did not appear in the original doctoral thesis – was intended as a device to link Ethiopians with Caucasians. So the final arrangement resembled a triangle.

It was a simple expedient that allowed Blumenbach to complete his model, but one with far-reaching consequences, as Gould points out: "With this one stroke, he produced the geometric transformation from Linnaeus's unranked geographic model to the conventional hierarchy of implied worth that has fostered so much social grief ever since."

SEE ALSO: beauty; caucasian; Chamberlain, Houston Stewart; Doomed Races Doctrine; Finot, Jean; genotype; Gobineau, Joseph Arthur de; Grégoire, Henri; Haeckel, Ernst; intelligence; phenotype; science; White Power; white race

Reading

"The geometer of race" by Stephen Jay Gould (in *Discover*, November 1994, reprinted in *Race and Ethnic Relations*, 11th edn., edited by John A. Kromkowski, MacGraw-Hill/Dushkin, 2001) is the illuminating article that compares Linnaeus and Blumenbach.

Race: The history of an idea in the West by Ivan Hannaford (The Johns Hopkins University Press, 1996) locates the thought of both Linnaeus and Blumenbach in "the first stage in the development of an idea of race, 1684–1815," which occupies chapter 7 of his text. His other stages are: 1815–70, when the theories of Gobineau became influential, and 1870–1914, which Hannaford describes as "the high point of the idea of race" and when Haeckel and Chamberlain came to prominence.

GHETTO

Meanings

The origins of the term ghetto can be traced back to Europe in the Middle Ages when it described how Jews voluntarily established corporate areas within the city, largely for protective purposes. The word may be derived from the Italian *geto vecchio*, or old foundry. It is thought that, in 1516, the site of a foundry was converted into a Jewish-only enclave. More latterly, the word came to mean the congregation of particular groups who share common and ethnic cultural characteristics in specific sectors of the city. This often takes the form of a segregated area, described as a ghetto.

The concept, ghetto, however, is notoriously imprecise and, in popular usage, it has assumed pejorative connotations. Areas such as Bel-Air in Los Angeles, Hampstead in London, and Solihull in the English city of Birmingham, are rarely considered as urban ghettos despite their homogeneous nature: after all, their residents are overwhelmingly white and upper-middle-class. In contrast, areas in those cities such as Watts (LA), Brixton (London), and Sparkbrook (Birmingham) – which contain relatively large black populations – are frequently characterized as ghettos. Clearly then, the term, ghetto, is not simply a descriptive term which refers to areas of ethnic and cultural homogeneity. It has highly potent connotations, symbolizing all that is negative about city life: high crime rates, pollution, noise, poor quality housing, bad sanitation, and so on.

On the whole, most commentators agree that, technically, a ghetto should comprise a high degree of homogeneity, all residents sharing similar backgrounds, beliefs, and so on. They should also be living amid poverty, in relation to the rest of the city's population. By these two criteria, then, New York's Harlem and the Watts district in Los Angeles can be defined legitimately as ghettos. In Britain, however, the term ghetto is wholly inappropriate even to areas such as Brixton and Sparkbrook. Despite the concentration of colonial migrants and their descendants in these and other districts within the major urban centers of Britain, they are nowhere approaching all-black areas. On the contrary, whites continue to constitute the majority of residents in these areas, with the presence of blacks and South Asians largely confined to a few streets. But, despite its technical inappropriateness, the term ghetto continues to be popularly applied to these areas. In short, "ghetto" is emotive and racist in its connotation.

Ghettoization

The voluntaristic nature or otherwise of the "ghettoization" process, however, is a contentious issue. Some writers adopt a "choice" model of interpretation in which they focus on the attitudes and behaviors of ghetto residents themselves. Those who put forward the "constraint" theory tend, in contrast, to adopt a broader perspective, which engages more directly with social and political processes. In other words, theirs is a more deterministic account of ghetto formation. Not surprisingly, these different interpretations of the process lead to contrasting appraisals of their function. Louis Wirth, for instance, presented a romantic version of ghetto life in Chicago in the 1920s, in which he stressed its voluntaristic nature, and hence, its positive community features. On the other hand, Robert Blauner (*Racial Oppression in America*, Harper & Row, 1992) saw ghettos as an "expression of colonized status" and a means by which the white majority is

able to prevent blacks from dispersing and spreading discontent. He argued that black ghettos in America are controlled by white administrators, educators, and police who live outside the ghetto but in effect administer its day-to-day affairs. In other words, they exert "direct rule" over the black communities, a relationship which Blauner termed "internal colonialism." Under this system, blacks in the ghetto are subject people, controlled from outside: the "burn, baby, burn" episodes of the 1960s, therefore, represented an attempt by the ghetto dwellers "to stake out a sphere of control by moving against (US) society and destroying the symbols of its oppression."

In Britain, a similar debate surrounds the pattern of ethnic segregation in the cities: some writers stress the discriminatory practices of the housing market as the determinant of migrant residence; others insist that clustering is actively sought by the migrants and occurs independently of such discriminatory practices.

All in all, then, the term ghetto tends to lack conceptual clarity and provides limited analytical precision. While its connotative powers continue to remain intact, its value as a social scientific concept is limited.

SEE ALSO: environmental racism; homelessness; inferential racism; internal colonialism; institutional racism; Jim Crow; Kerner Report; Park, Robert Ezra; prejudice; race: as signifier; race: as synonym; racial coding; segregation; social exclusion; white flight; xenophobia

Reading

Code of the Street by Elijah Anderson (W. W. Norton, 1999) is a convincing case study in Philadelphia which exposes the self-perpetuating dynamics of ghetto life.

The Ghetto by Louis Wirth (Chicago University Press, 1928) is a classic account of ghetto life in Chicago in the 1920s by a student and colleague of Robert Park, co-developer of the "urban ecology" theory.

Racism, the City and the State edited by Malcolm Cross and Michael Keith (Routledge, 1993) explores the relationship between racism, the city and the state by addressing urban social theory, contemporary cultural change, and racial subordination.

The South Side: The racial transformation of an American neighborhood by Louis Rosen (Ivan R. Dee, 1999) reveals how a ghetto was converted.

BARRY TROYNA

GLOBALIZATION

Consumption, communications and production

Globalization may be understood as a tendency for routine day-to-day social interaction to be imbued with patterns that are, to an increasing extent, shared across the planet, which has in turn been brought about by the increasing interdependency of societies across the world and complemented by the expansion of international media of communications that has made people all over the world more conscious of other places and the world as a whole.

Beyond this broad definition, there is little agreement on globalization's precise meaning or its consequences. For this reason, its relevance to race and ethnic studies is open to dispute. Some scholars emphasize the importance of global migration in the formation of transnational identities, others accentuate its role in promoting new forms of ethnic conflict, while still others point to the changing patterns of exploitation precipitated by global production and consumption processes. Despite these differences of emphasis, globalization, since the 1990s, has become a central part of the lexicon of race and ethnic relations.

Perhaps the reason for its popularity and the speed of its growth in use is undoubtedly because it captured a moment. That moment was when the ramifications of the take up of personal computers in general and the internet and email in particular became more apparent. Communication has always been about the exchange of knowledge and instant global communication therefore represents global exchange at speeds hitherto unthought of. The ability to exploit such possibilities came in the wake of the continued broadening of mass consumption, which had made broadened mass production feasible. The connection between these two has been potentiated by intensive mass communication and instant electronic exchanges have in turn enhanced the process.

The twentieth century's "holy trinity" of mass *consumption*, mass *communication* and mass *production* had, long before the word globalization came into use, brought about a trend toward the homogenization of culture in all sorts of ways. Mass production in its full sense can reasonably be attributed to Henry Ford's development of assembly line production. His dream was to produce the fruits of advanced engineering at a price that everyone, including his own workers, could afford. (He paid them $5 for an eight-hour day when the going rate was $2 for nine hours.) And, despite his subsequent lurch from philanthropy to ruthless autocratic control, it should not be forgotten that he championed the role of African Americans in ways that were unfashionable at the time. In drawing labor to his vast Dearborn plant he substantially increased the black population of Detroit, in the north of the USA, with all that this implies. He grasped that one could not have mass production without mass consumption and with that came, whether he liked it or not, mass communication. With Ford and his emulators in other industries the twentieth century became the age of the consumer and what became known as "the American dream" was aspired to by the rest of the world. Possibly, the spread of consumerism is as important and emancipatory, if not democratic, process as any of the others, social and political.

If the twentieth century, up to its last few decades, is seen as the century of mass society based upon production – communication – consumption, these last few decades have been labeled those of the communications revolution and the knowledge industry. These latter developments have resulted in a situation in which it is difficult for anyone to consider anything other than against a background of global developments. The process of globalization has penetrated the local, implicitly by definition, and what goes on in the locale therefore becomes part of the continuing globalization process. As Roland Robertson put it in his text *Globalization*, one of the first substantial approaches to the subject, the process is actually one of *interpenetration* between the global and the local.

As such, globalization is at its core a process of increasing awareness and is of immense importance to any understanding of race and ethnicity. Whilst the cutting edge of technology has limited application due to price, computers and their ancillary equipment have been subject to very dramatic price reductions enabling unanticipated levels of take up. The phenomenal growth of the Microsoft Corporation alone is evidence of this. Bill Gates is the Henry Ford of the information age. To illustrate another dimension, the humblest desktop computer has on occasion been used successfully to hack into the Pentagon.

Ethnic awareness

It is no coincidence therefore that the decades referred to here have seen not only a revolution in communication but also an intensification of ethnic awareness. The global has revolutionized the local and one outcome of this is renewal of identification. The modern world has been a world of nation-states. The establishment of the UN in 1945 may be seen as a confirmation of this. At first there were some fifty members, but now there are around two hundred as successful independence movements have been followed by membership. Yet the nation-state is an engineered entity, one designed to administer the population of a designated parcel of land by giving them a convenient identity to which to subscribe. In so many cases, however, this does not align itself to the underlying identity to which people, in their hearts, feel they belong.

Consider a map of Africa based upon tribal lands. Then superimpose upon it the colonial map as defined by Europeans, largely at a conference in Berlin in 1884–85. The latter survived the various independence movements and continues to project on Africans identities formed under colonialism. For instance, Ibo, Hausa, Yoruba and others became Nigerians, a process replicated in various ways elsewhere about the continent. How much blood has been shed disputing these assertions ever since? The process is not restricted to Africa of course. Taking a random sweep across the accustomed map of the world we can find seemingly endless examples of ethnic resurgence stimulated to varying degrees by instant communication and the exchange of knowledge. Native Americans; Zapatistas in Mexico; Northern Irish Catholics; Basques in Spain; Bosnians, Croatians and Kosovans in the former Yugoslavia; Chechnyans on Russia's border; Kurds in several Middle Eastern states; Tibetans in China; Timorese in Indonesia, will not nearly exhaust the list. Even the simple split of Czechoslovakia into Slovakia and the Czech Republic is a case in point.

Globalization has affected our assumptions about ethnicity, nation and state by reproducing and extending knowledge about these issues on a day-to-day basis with an intensity that could not be achieved previously by the printed news media or earlier means of broadcasting. Observers and commentators describe globalization penetrating our lived communities and ourselves as individuals not only at the level of communication through the internet and cable/satellite television, but also at the level of the territorial state and global politics, the expanding reach of organized violence, global trade and markets, shifting patterns of global finance, corporate power and global production networks, and people on the move, according to David Held *et al*.

Migration, citizenship and racism

To this latter should be added, especially, multi-cultural citizenship, new (and old) forms of racism, the racisms of globalization, citizenship and the Other in the age of migration analyzed by Stephen Castles in his *Ethnicity and Globalization*. The nation-state has, in a sense, been transcended by revived ethnicities within, and, at the same time, by the entry of people on the move carrying their ethnicities with them. An English politician once asked which cricket team some migrants living in England supported? The England team, or that of their country of origin in the Commonwealth (or former British Empire). Their response appears to be obvious from watching the networked broadcasts of international test matches and is reinforced in some cases by (illegal) ethnic national identifications on the newer European-style number plates displayed by some groups. Fans' allegiance tends to be with the countries of their forebears, countries that they may never even have visited.

Globalization has enhanced not only communication but also travel. Air travel can take one to an airport anywhere in the world in about 24 hours. Tunnels and bridges enable motor vehicles to make continuous journeys over great distances across the borders of many nation-states. Whether traveling by air or in the secret compartment of a juggernaut lorry the movement of people is now much faster than it has ever been. Refugees from the many conflicts involving ethnicity (and/or religion) and the nation-state, and the relatively new category of asylum seeker (as opposed to economic migrant) are part of the process of globalization. Their identities and their common predicament are a foremost item on the global agenda as communicated continuously. They are the stuff of the media news and they have their own web sites. New diasporas are in a continuous process of construction and the wretched outcomes are an illustration of apparent powerlessness.

The other side of the coin to the movement of people is the movement of economic activity to people hitherto untouched by it. What has often been referred to as de-industrialization is more specifically the de-industrialization of the West and the transfer of production to formerly non-industrialized areas. The prime reason for this has of course been access to lower, often dramatically lower, labor costs. The globalization of knowledge has however made known the grimmer side to this when it has been revealed that, for instance, the phenomenally successful sports goods manufacturer Nike has had the advantage, directly or indirectly, of child labor, while the owners of the global icon McDonalds have accessed some of their vast demand for beef from areas which exploit both people and the environment. Almost universally this exploitation is of black or Asian populations. Inasmuch as globalization has created such malpractice it has also been instrumental in uncovering it, but alas not, so far, in putting an end to it.

SEE ALSO: asylum seeker; colonialism; colonial discourse; diaspora; ethnonational; exploitation; human rights; International Convention; international organizations; migration; minority language rights; postcolonial; UNESCO; United Nations

Reading

Ethnicity and Globalization by Stephen Castles (Sage, 2000) usefully links globalization, through migration, to the difficulties of ethnicity in a globalized world.

Global Transformations by David Held, Anthony McGrew, David Goldblatt, and Jonathan Perraton (Polity Press, 1999) has established itself as the key work on the globalization process.

Globalization by Roland Robertson (Sage, 1992) remains the best theoretical approach to the social culture of globalization; it may be read in conjunction with *Globalization and World Society* by Tony Spybey (Polity Press, 1996).

TONY SPYBEY

GOBINEAU, JOSEPH ARTHUR DE
(1816–82)

A Frenchman born into a bourgeois family with aristocratic pretensions, and who claimed the title "Count," Gobineau was educated in German as well as in French. He earned a living from journalism until 1849, after which he obtained a succession of diplomatic appointments up to 1877. It would seem that in the Paris salons Gobineau obtained an acquaintance with contemporary anthropological speculations, notably with those of Victor Courtet de l'Isle, author of *La Science politique fondée sur la science de l'homme*. These were important to his four-volume *Essai sur l'inégalité des races humaines* (*Essay on the Inequality of Human Races*), the first two volumes of which appeared in 1853 and the last two in 1855. The question of racial inequality receives little attention in Gobineau's remaining writings (which included twenty-six other books).

Some sections of the *Essay* are unequivocal in asserting a philosophy of racial determinism, but there are ambiguities and inconsistencies, so that different commentators emphasize different themes of his work. If anything can be seen as the book's central problem, it is probably the assertion that "the great human civilizations are but ten in number and all of them have been produced upon the initiative of the white race" (including, apparently, those of the Aztecs and the Incas, though their civilizations are never examined). What explains the rise and fall of civilizations? Alongside this problem, and at times overshadowing it, is the author's desire to lament the breakdown of the old social order and to insist that the process of *degeneration* has advanced so far as to be irreversible. To answer the historical question Gobineau contends that races differ in their relative worth; and that "the question on which the argument here turns is that of the permanence of type." Whereas the whites are superior in intellect they are inferior in the intensity of their sensations so that "a light admixture from the black species develops intelligence in the white race, in that it turns it towards imagination." Mixtures of blood seem to be necessary to the birth of civilizations but mixtures, once started, get out of control and the "historical chemistry" is upset. Thus there is a subsidiary theme in the book that stresses the complementarity of races as well as their hierarchical ordering. Logically there is no reason why the inability of racial types to lose their fundamental physical and moral characteristics, plus the idea that "ethnic workshops" can be built to diffuse a civilization, should not lead to the birth of an eleventh civilization. The prophecy of decline ("what is truly sad is not death itself but the certainty of our meeting it as degraded beings") therefore has its origin not in Gobineau's borrowed anthropology but in his personal pessimism.

One message that the book conveyed is the impotence of politics: nothing that men do can now affect the inevitable outcome. Nor does it lend support to nationalism, since Gobineau's "German" and "Aryan" are not to be equated with *die Deutsche* but include the Frankish element among the French population. The country that has best preserved Germanic usages and is "the last centre of Germanic influence" is England, though in some degree the leadership of Aryan-Germanism has passed to Scandinavia. Gobineau emphasizes status differences as well as racial ones ("I have no doubt that negro chiefs are superior," he writes, "to the level usually reached by our peasants, or even by average specimens of our half-educated bourgeoisie"). If it had been taken seriously, therefore, the *Essay* would not have been ideologically valuable as a basis for German nationalism, or for claiming European racial superiority. But because of its ambiguities and its pretensions as a comprehensive philosophy of history, its political potential was greater than that of other works in the typological school. The first volume was quickly translated into English because it appealed to white supremacists in the South of the United States. The Wagnerian movement in Germany cultivated Gobineau's ideas and in 1894 a Gobineau Society was formed to give them publicity. In Hitler's Third Reich, the *Essay*, suitably adjusted, became a popular school reader. Michael Biddiss states that in the political literature of nazism there are many phrases and conceptions echoing Gobineau's work: "above all, there is in the *mode* of thinking every similarity."

SEE ALSO: Aryan; caucasian; Chamberlain, Houston Stewart; fascism; geometry of race; Haeckel, Ernst; hereditarianism; Holocaust; language; *Volk*; Wagner, Richard

Reading

Father of Racist Ideology: The social and political thought of Count Gobineau by Michael D. Biddiss (Weidenfeld & Nicolson, 1970) is a biographical treatment.

Gobineau: Selected political writings by Michael D. Biddiss (Cape, 1970) is a particularly useful anthology.

MICHAEL BANTON

GRÉGOIRE, HENRI (1750–1831)

Grégoire was a French prelate and radical thinker who challenged, among many other things, the institution of slavery. His scholarly writing and ecclesiastical position made him one of the most masterful European antislavery campaigners of the eighteenth and early nineteenth centuries.

He became a member of the Estates General and Constituent Assembly in 1789 and was bishop of Loir-et-Cher the following year. Over the next several years, he became a member of the National Convention, the Council of Five Hundred and the French Senate. As a senator, he opposed the Concordat of 1801, an agreement between church and state, and resigned to become a simple priest. Throughout his life, he opposed French imperialism, though, ironically, Napoleon I made him a count. Elected to the chamber of deputies in 1819, he refused his seat and eventually died in poverty.

Among his publications were two exemplars of antislavery literature: *An Enquiry Concerning the Intellectual and Moral Faculties and Literature of Negroes*, which was originally published in 1810 and remains in print (translated by David Warden and Graham Hodges, published by M. E. Sharp, 1996) and *On the Cultural Achievements of Negroes*, first published in 1808 (translated by Thomas Cassirer and Jean-Marie Briere, published by University of Massachusetts Press, 1996). In both these works, Grégoire argued against the racial theories that had been emerging since the seventeenth century. French theorists, in particular, had contributed to a debate concerning the fixity of types of humanity.

In 1684, François Bernier (1625–88) published his "Nouvelle division de la terre par les differents espèces ou races qui l'habitent," in which he argued that humanity could be broken into *espèces ou races* and analyzed accordingly. This was a significant departure from the more conventional ways of understanding humanity in terms of Christian–heathen or human–animal, and paved the way for later racial classifications in which the influence of environment was considered. Georges Cuvier (1769–1832) argued that, while there must be some environmental influence, changes occur only in periods of catastrophic physical change that brought one form of life to an end and replaced it with another. For the most part, types were fixed. Georges-Louis de Buffon (1707–88) proposed an environmentalist case, suggesting interaction between milieux and human development. Amid this theoretical debate, slavery and the slave trade were in full swing. It is in this context that Grégoire's work should be understood to appreciate the discord it must have created.

SEE ALSO: antiracism; antislavery; environmentalism; Finot, Jean; hereditarianism; Hottentot Venus; Las Casas, Bartolomé de; science

Reading

"Henri Grégoire, 'The friend of men of all colors' " by J. F Briere (in *Journal of Blacks in Higher Education*, issue 17, Fall 1997) is an appreciation of Grégoire's work and may be read profitably in association with the two works quoted in the main text above.

GYPSIES *see* Roma

H

HAECKEL, ERNST (1834–1919)

A famous German zoologist, academic entrepreneur, and popularizer of science, who constructed a vacuous philosophy of life called "Monism" on a Darwinian foundation. He coined a variety of new terms, some of which have survived; among them was the "biogenetic law" that ontogeny recapitulates phylogeny. This doctrine had been discussed in biology since the 1820s and appears in Robert Chambers's anonymously published *Vestiges of Creation*. The doctrine stated that before birth all embryos were supposed to pass through the earlier stages of evolution, thus European babies passed through Ethiopian and Mongolian stages in the womb.

Haeckel's significance for the study of racial thought lies firstly in his decisive influence upon the development of the Volkish movement, a special kind of romantic German nationalism. Haeckel and the Monists were an important source and a major inspiration for many of the diverse streams of thought that later came together under the banner of National Socialism. Secondly, he publicized a distorted version of Darwinism in which racial differences were fundamental. Haeckel wrote of "woolly haired" Negroes, "incapable of a higher mental development," and of Papuans and Hottentots as "fast approaching their complete extinction." One of his major theses was that "in the struggle for life, the more highly developed, the more favored and larger groups and forms, possess the positive inclination of the certain tendency to spread more at the expense of the lower, more backward, and smallest groups." In this way, Haeckel and the Monists became the first to formulate a program of racial imperialism and *lebensraum*

for Germany. Haeckel himself supported the Pan-German League, one of that country's most militant, imperialistic, nationalistic, and anti-Semitic organizations.

Haeckel had a direct and powerful influence upon many individuals important to the rise of racial anthropology and National Socialism. One of them was Ludwig Woltmann, a member of the Social Democratic Party who attempted to fuse the ideas of Haeckel and Marx, transforming the latter's concept of class struggle into a theory of worldwide racial conflict. Another was Adolf Hitler. According to Daniel Gasman, Hitler's views on history, politics, religion, Christianity, nature, eugenics, science, art, and evolution, however eclectic, coincided with those of Haeckel and were at times expressed in very much the same language. At least two significant ideological contacts can be established between Hitler and the Monist League that propagated Haeckel's doctrines. Among many Nazi scientists and intellectuals there was a general acclaim for Haeckel as an intellectual ancestor and forerunner, but he was never lauded as a major prophet of the movement (as was Houston Stewart Chamberlain). Chamberlain's conception of race derived from the pre-Darwinian theory of racial typology which permitted enthusiasts to regard the Aryans as being of distinctive origin and permanently superior. Darwinism was included in the German curriculum in biology but the Nazis were suspicious of a doctrine that attributed an inferior anthropoid ancestry to all men and was incompatible with their belief that Aryans had been racially superior from the very beginning.

SEE ALSO: Aryan; caucasian; Chamberlain,

Houston Stewart; Darwinism; Doomed Races Doctrine; environmentalism; fascism; Finot, Jean; genotype; Gobineau, Joseph Arthur de; Grégoire, Henri; Haeckel, Ernst; hereditarianism; Hottentot Venus; phenotype; science; social Darwinism; *Volk*; white race

Reading

The Scientific Origins of National Socialism by Daniel Gasman (Macdonald, Elsevier, 1971) demonstrates the historical importance of Haeckel's teaching.

MICHAEL BANTON

HALL, STUART (1932–)

An "organic intellectual" in the mold of Antonio Gramsci, Hall contrasted himself with "traditional intellectuals" by emphasizing the political payload of intellectual labor. He attempted to synthesize continental traditions of Marxism, discourse analysis and poststructuralism with the native tradition of culturalism, the study of culture as, in the words of Raymond Williams, "a whole way of life." In the 1980s his work influenced a generation of researchers by situating the study of racism within the wider context of culture and politics.

Background

Born in Kingston, Jamaica, Hall was the son of lower-class, upwardly mobile black parents. His father rose through the ranks of the United Fruit Company, the leading private employer on the island, eventually becoming Chief Accountant. The decisive formative influence on Hall's politics of race was his experience and observation of colonialism in Jamaica. The Brown Man movement and its campaign to achieve dominion status within the British Commonwealth dominated his school years. The movement did not envisage the end of Eurocentrism or, still less, the positive promotion of Africa and African culture. As such, Hall quickly recognized that it was fatally flawed because it could not generate a realistic politics of difference.

In 1951 Hall migrated to England, where he enrolled as a Rhodes scholar at Merton College, Oxford. His Ph.D. was on the relationship between Europe and America in the novels of Henry James. Given the passionate interest that Hall evinced later in his career in questions of position, difference, power, the nuance of discrimination, diaspora and hybridity, the choice is revealing. Politically speaking, Hall's mature outlook was formed in 1956 by what he called "the double conjuncture" of the Anglo-French invasion of the Suez Canal and the Soviet invasion of Hungary. He regarded the first to symbolize the last gasp of Empire and the second to expose the despotic character of the Soviet *imperium*.

Hall abandoned his Ph.D. and worked as a supply teacher in London, while continuing his part-time career as a left-wing writer and activist. Between 1961 and 1962 he was editor of the *New Left Review*. In 1962, he became lecturer in media, film and popular culture at Chelsea College, University of London. Two years later he was appointed Research Fellow at the newly established Centre for Contemporary Cultural Studies (CCCS) at the University of Birmingham.

The Birmingham Centre for Contemporary Cultural Studies

Hall's work in Birmingham is generally acknowledged to be a seminal influence in the development of cultural studies. It harnessed a rich fund of continental theory to combat the empiricism and humanism of the native tradition exemplified in the work of Raymond Williams, Edward Thompson and Richard Hoggart. The primary intellectual influences were the writings of Gramsci and Althusser. The groundbreaking work in the Centre on youth culture, education, the media, the state and policing, published in the 1970s, can be interpreted as an attempt to fuse the best elements in Gramsci with Althusser. The most important work produced in this period was the powerful analysis of state formation and hegemonic rule in Britain, *Policing the Crisis*, published in 1978.

In 1979 Hall became Professor of Sociology at the Open University. In these years, through his analysis of Thatcherism, a political formation that he described as "authoritarian populism," he established himself as Britain's leading black intellectual and a role model for many other intellectuals. While he continued to work in the tradition of neo-Marxism, he now embraced new continental influences of poststructuralism and postmodernism, notably in the work of Derrida, Laclau and Mouffe. These influences existed in some tension with the central tenets of classical Marxism, in particular by questioning identity and class politics. By the 1980s Hall claimed to be practicing a "Marxism without guarantees." His "New Times" thesis called upon the Left to overhaul the traditional emphasis on class politics by recognizing the transformative influence of globalization, multiculturalism and "the politics of difference."

The latter emerged as a fundamental concept in Hall's later writings, although its meaning remains elusive. In fact, there are at least three meanings of the concept in Hall's writings: (1) the recognition of multiethnic difference in Britain; (2) the acceptance that Black British ethnicity is divided along generational lines between the values and aspirations of the first wave of postwar migrants and their British-born children; (3) the recognition that identity is always split, mobile and divided. The third meaning shows how far Hall had moved from mainstream Marxism and the conventional critique of the race relations school of, for example, Gunnar Myrdal, Michael Banton and John Rex. He approached race as "a floating signifier." His work on "multicultural drift" in Britain continuously returns to the failure of both right and left-wing traditions to adequately understand racism and ethnicity.

New ethnicity: diaspora and identity

For the mature Hall, the focus of research is no longer between antiracism and multiculturalism. Instead it has moved to the notion of identity itself. This entails de-anchoring the notion of ethnicity from its moorings in discourses of race and nation and developing a new positive concept of ethnicity. "New ethnicity" demarginalizes the position of ethnicities in Britain and validates ethnic forms of experience from which it draws its strength. Hall breaks with the conventional notion of diaspora, as a scattered population. Instead he redefines it to refer to a realm of ideas, discourses and practices that connect dispersed groups.

These contributions shows how much he has been influenced by Lacan, Derrida, Laclau, Mouffe and Foucault in redefining the crisis in contemporary society as primarily a crisis of the West, rather than a mere question of redistributive justice.

Hall was an influential member of the Parekh Report of 2000 on the future of multiethnic Britain. It proposes a variety of policy initiatives

in education, employment, policing, immigration and asylum, welfare, the arts, sport and media to expunge racism and discrimination. It reinforces the idea of "unity through difference" constructed around three unbreakable principles of cohesion, equality and difference. The main characteristic of Hall's thought is anti-essentialism. It is evident in his refusal to be confined by the limitations of traditional Marxism, particularly in his rebuttal of the base/superstructure distinction that underpinned vulgar Marxism. It is also apparent in his resistance to English "culturalism" as expressed in the work of Raymond Williams, Edward Thompson and Richard Hoggart, his audacious advocacy of *New Times* and his espousal of "new ethnicities" and the "politics of difference." This necessarily produces a strong streak of eclecticism in Hall's work. Some critics accuse him of confusing being *au fait* with being *au courant*; in other words, of being a theoretical faddist.

In mitigation Hall's self-image as an intellectual is shaped profoundly by Gramsci's concept of the organic intellectual. This concept foregrounds the relationship between intellectual work and political responsibility, and dismisses the objectivity and impartiality of traditional intellectuals. It follows that topicality and change are bound to figure prominently in the work of the organic intellectual, just as they do in the course of human history and development. The emphasis on the centrality of politics is welcome, but it does not absolve organic intellectuals from outlining the kind of politics and the kind of society they positively support. Hall has been richly sarcastic about "third way" politics and New Labour. However, his own concepts of the politics of difference and unity through difference remain unclear.

SEE ALSO: colonial discourse; cultural identity; diaspora; essentialism; Fanon, Frantz; globalization; hegemony; hybridity; Marxism; media; multiculturalism; postcolonial; post-race; race: as signifier; racial coding; racist discourse; representations

Reading

The Future of Multi-ethnic Britain: The Parekh Report by The Runnymede Trust (Lanham Books, 2002) analyzes the contemporary situation of Britain and makes recommendations for the future.

Policing The Crisis by Stuart Hall, Charles Critcher, Tony Jefferson, and John Clarke (Macmillan, 1978) is the most significant harvest of Hall's collaborative work in Birmingham, which demonstrates most cogently the attempt to marry Althusserian and Gramscian traditions in the context of a social and historical analysis of hegemony in Britain.

Stuart Hall by Chris Rojek (Polity Press, 2003) is the first full-length attempt to critically engage with Hall's writings.

Stuart Hall: Critical dialogues in cultural studies, edited by David Morley and K.-H. Chen (Routledge, 1996) is a curate's egg which mixes key selections from Hall's *oeuvre* with original papers of critical assessment and appreciation.

CHRIS ROJEK

HANSON, PAULINE (1954–)

Pauline Hanson was elected to the Australian House of Representatives as an independent candidate in the 1996 federal election. In the 1998 federal election, Hanson failed to win the newly redistributed seat of Blair. However, during that two-year period Hanson and the political party founded and organized around her, One Nation, dramatically altered the Australian political landscape. Hanson's economically populist views, her attacks on multiculturalism, immigration, and programs directed at indigenous Australians, all garnered her not insignificant popular support.

Initially preselected as the Liberal Party candidate for the Queensland-based seat of Oxley, she was deselected after widespread reports of controversial comments regarding indigenous Australians. Hanson's deselection came too late for the federal election and she appeared on the ballot as the Liberal candidate. The importance of this was difficult to judge, however: the significant swing towards Hanson (nearly 23 percent – more than the national average towards the Liberal Party) suggested that Hanson had wide-ranging support for her outspoken views.

What Hanson stood for following her election was broadly an attack on much of the political and economic agenda that had dominated the 1980s and 1990s. Hanson rejected economic liberalism, central to the ideas of the dominant political parties, in favor of economic nationalism; she demanded increased government intervention, tariffs and subsidies. Accompanying such ideas was a rejection of multiculturalism and associated government-sponsored programs, as well as demands for zero immigration during periods of unemployment in Australia. In essence, Hanson envisaged a return to a (nonexistent) "golden era" of economic prosperity and social stability. The lack of factual accuracy which marked many of Hanson's claims, and which was epitomized by her parliamentary maiden speech, did not stop her from developing support from across a wide demographic spectrum.

It can be argued that much of Hanson's early success sprang not only from the nebulous policies she espoused but also from the image she created of herself. To the electorate Hanson was a struggling single mother who ran a fish and chip shop in a provincial town in rural Queensland. Whilst the reality of her situation may have been somewhat different (she was reportedly a millionaire), her plain speaking appealed to many Australians who felt alienated from the mainstream political parties. The perception that both the Australian Labor Party and the Liberal Party had become distanced from the "little Aussie battler" enabled Hanson's plain speaking, "battler" persona to gain widespread appeal. Hanson was willing "to tell it like it was" and was thus perceived to be a radically different politician from those professional politicians who had come to dominate the mainstream parties. Her tours of Australian towns and cities drew in support and furthered her image as a "battler" and a patriot – at one meeting she famously draped herself in the Australian flag. Indeed, attacks on mainstream politicians, the press and educational institutions gained her even more support. In an infamous television interview, Hanson, when asked if she was xenophobic, said "please explain"; her apparent ignorance, rather than losing her support, actually appeared to increase it.

It is difficult to judge to what extent the Hanson phenomenon in its early days was a media construction. The shockwaves that her election had sent through the mainstream political elite and the liberal press ensured Hanson wide press coverage. The newly elected Liberal Prime Minister, John Howard, sought to characterize Hanson as a "meteorite" which would pass quickly across the sky, and he refused to condemn her outright racist sentiments. As a result, his reluctance and inability to tackle the perceived threat Hanson posed to mainstream Australian politics ensured that Hanson remained the focus of media attention for many months after her election.

Hanson's rise to prominence was quick, however her success was ultimately to be short lived. The establishment of One Nation in 1997, with Hanson as party leader, was clearly a high point. However, the 1998 federal election saw her seat of Oxley redistributed and she failed to win the seat of Blair (also in Queensland) which she contested. Internal, but very public, wrangling within One Nation quickly followed its establishment and highlighted Hanson's lack of political experience or understanding, although it did not appear to significantly diminish her support.

After a number of difficult years, the 2001 federal election appeared to offer Hanson an opportunity to re-enter federal politics, particularly following the electoral success of One Nation in state elections in both Queensland and Western Australia. Choosing to stand for election for the Senate (which is elected proportionately), Hanson failed to win the necessary support and abruptly resigned from politics to raise cattle. However, controversy continued when, in 2002, Hanson was committed to stand trial for fraud. Hanson and the co-founder of One Nation, David Ettridge, were alleged to have obtained $500,000 of electoral funding dishonestly and of fraudulently registering One Nation in Queensland and New South Wales.

Despite her retirement and the pending trial, Hanson suggested in 2002 that she wished to re-enter politics, probably in Western Australia. However, the party which had evolved around her, made it clear that Hanson was no longer welcome. Although now largely absent from Australian politics, Hanson had a profound impact within the field. The mainstream political parties found themselves responding to the policy and political agenda set by Hanson, and in some policy areas drifting toward Hanson's ideas in order to win back some support. Arguably, not all of Hanson's impact was negative. The legitimacy Hanson gave to a resurgent racism was countered by the emergence of groups which sought to reject her ideas and promote social and cultural diversity. Notably, indigenous Australians and ethnic minority groups became increasingly aware of, and sensitive to, each other's needs and concerns. In April 2003, the leader of One Nation's political career received what appeared to be a fatal blow when Hanson tried but failed to win a seat in the Upper House of the New South Wales parliament.

Hanson may no longer be involved in politics, her legacy continues both in the mainstream political parties which have taken up some of her concerns and in the revival of overt support for diversity which before Hanson had appeared only a marginal interest.

SEE ALSO: Aboriginal Australians; bigotry; indigenous peoples; multiculturalism; nationalism; neo-nazism; One Nation; politics; racist discourse; white backlash culture; xenophobia

Reading

One Nation and Australian Politics, edited by Bligh Grant (University of New England Press, 1997), is an early collection that provides an initial analysis of the emergence and popularity of Pauline Hanson and One Nation.

The Resurgence of Racism: Howard, Hanson and the race debate, edited by Geoffrey Gray and Christine Winter (Monash Publications in History, Melbourne, 1997), examines the resurgence of racism within Australia following the election of Pauline Hanson and the Howard-led Liberal government in 1996.

Two Nations: The causes and effects of the rise of the One Nation Party in Australia (Bookman Press, Melbourne, 1998) is a valuable anthology of essays by politicians, journalists and academics which seeks to explain the success of Pauline Hanson and One Nation.

EMMA L. CLARENCE

HATE GROUPS *see* neo-nazism

HEALTH *see* medicine

HEGEMONY

From the Greek *hegemon*, meaning leader or ruler, this term has become associated with a particular brand of twentieth-century Marxism, especially that espoused by the Italian Antonio Gramsci (1891–1937). Hegemony describes the total domination of the middle class (bourgeoisie), not only in political and economic spheres, but also in the sphere of consciousness. Marx theorized that the dominant ideas of any age are the ideas of the ruling class, and this is taken as a central point in Gramscian interpretations of capitalist societies. What is accepted as common sense, the obviously correct way things are, is not a neutral perception of the world, but a particular way of grasping reality which fits in neatly with the existing social order. In other words, the bourgeoisie's leadership extends from the material world into people's minds. In other words, domination effectively becomes domination-by-consent.

For Marx, consciousness was not separable from material existence. This means that what goes on in our heads can never be divorced from how we live the rest of our lives; so practices such as how we feed and clothe ourselves, our place in the social order, and how we work, are all influences on our consciousness. People have a certain view of reality and, for the most part, they believe in the legitimacy or "rightness" of that reality. Under capitalism, the working class (the proletariat) live in a social order which works against their true interests: they are systematically exploited. However, and this is crucial, they do not oppose that order because they believe in its legitimacy; so they accept their own subordination. They believe it is part of common sense.

The actual mechanisms through which common sense is disseminated and transmitted from one generation to the next (thus ensuring the perpetuation of capitalism) are complex, but the Algerian philosopher Louis Althusser (1918–90) has offered an influential version using the concept of an ideological state apparatus (ISA). An ideology is a way of viewing reality; for Althusser (and other Marxian theorists), ideologies distort or mask true reality and serve ruling-class interests (i.e. enable them to keep control). Through schooling, going to church, attending to the media, people piece together a picture of reality. By accepting this common-sense picture of reality, people make themselves available for exploitation by those who dominate (and therefore control agencies such as education, the media, etc.). One of the critical features of this is that the people accepting the common sense remain unaware of their exploitation. Hence there is a hegemonic control and the bourgeoisie maintains its leadership without having it seriously questioned.

According to Gramsci, hegemonic control and the consent it yields is never totally secure and must continually be sought; there is always room for resistance through subversive – or counter-hegemonic – cultural work.

The relevance of all this to race and ethnic relations became apparent in the early 1980s, particularly through the theoretical work of the University of Birmingham's Centre for Contemporary Cultural Studies (England). Racist ideologies are seen as components of common sense: ideas about the inferiority of blacks and Asians have deep roots in history, but they are "reworked" over and over again and serve to divide working-class people. "Problems" connected with so-called racial groups are interpreted as "pathological" because these groups are seen as somehow different. This kind of common-sense thinking operates at local levels (for example, in riots and with regard to unemployment) and at international levels, as Errol Lawrence points out: "The relative 'under-development' and poverty of many 'Third world' countries is of course not viewed as the outcome of centuries of imperialism and colonial domination, but rather is thought to be expressive of a *natural state of affairs*, in which blacks are seen as genetically and/or culturally inferior."

Images of primitiveness, backwardness and stupidity are associated with blacks and Asians and these are unquestioningly accepted as part of common sense. They are integrated elements of a wider ideology, however, and the ideology's strength rests on people's failure to unmask it and examine alternative ways of viewing reality. So racism, in this Gramscian interpretation, is not a peculiarity of extreme right-wing forms of society, but part of everyday common-sense knowledge in modern society. The continued subordination of blacks and Asians is as much the result of ideology as it is to do with the more easily identifiable form of inequalities in work, housing and education.

SEE ALSO: empowerment; Hall, Stuart; ideology; Marxism; media; power; racial coding; racism; racist discourse; representations

Reading

Ethnic Minorities and the Media, edited by Simon Cottle (Open University Press, 2000) and *Representing Black Britain: Black and Asian images on television* by Sarita Malik (London, 2002) both draw on hegemony to disclose how the media sustains racism.

Hegemony by R. Bocock (Tavistock, 1987) is a short, accessible introduction to the concept, while "Just plain common sense: the 'roots' of racism" by Errol Lawrence in *The Empire Strikes Back*, edited by the Centre for Contemporary Cultural Studies (Hutchinson, 1982), is a strongly argued case for understanding racist ideologies within a Gramscian framework; this article uses interesting historical material to show how imperialist regimes created racist images that have been transmitted from one generation to the next and have gained purchase in the context of the "organic crisis" of capitalist societies.

Policing The Crisis by Stuart Hall, Charles Critcher, Tony Jefferson, and John Clarke (Macmillan, 1978) is an old but influential analysis which traces the processes through which race came to be recognized as a social problem. Hall developed the approach in a paper, "Race articulation and societies structured in "dominance," in *Sociological Theories* (UNESCO, 1980).

HEREDITARIANISM

The argument that racial differences are hereditary arose in opposition to the belief that, since all mankind is descended from Adam and Eve, diversity must be a product of adaptation to environment. In 1520 Paracelsus maintained that peoples "found in out-of-the-way islands" were not descended from the sons of Adam; early hereditary theories followed this thesis by claiming that racial differences had existed from the beginning of humanity. At the start of the nineteenth century, the influential French anatomist Georges Cuvier classified *Homo sapiens* as divided into three subspecies, Caucasian, Mongolian, and Ethiopian, each of which was further subdivided on geographical, linguistic and physical grounds. He represented the races as constituting a hierarchy and contended that differences in culture and mental quality were produced by differences in physique. This line of reasoning was developed into an international school of racial typology, as expressed in Britain by Charles Hamilton Smith (1848) and Robert Knox (1850), in France by Arthur de Gobineau (1853), in the USA by Josiah Clark Nott and George Robbins Gliddon (1854), and in Germany by Karl Vogt (1863). This school has more often been referred to as that of "scientific racism." Its adherents maintained that racial types were permanent forms, at least for the period for which evidence was available, and might have been separately created.

The stricter typologists, such as Knox and Nott, believed that the various human types were adapted to particular zoological provinces. Just as marsupials were peculiar to Australia, so Australian Aborigines exemplified the kind of men who belonged in that province. Other animals would not long survive there. It was the height of foolishness for Europeans to attempt to colonize North America, Australia, or tropical regions because they were not suited to these environments; if they attempted it their descendants would degenerate and die out. The typological theory of racial differences appeared some three decades before the main phase of European imperial expansion, and its doctrines provided little, if any, support for imperialist campaigns.

Whereas environmentalist theories offered explanations for the diversity of racial forms and hereditarian theories for the stability of these forms within particular environments, both kinds of explanation were brought together in Darwin's theory of natural selection. With the establishment of genetics as a field of scientific research, it became possible to examine the relative importance of hereditarian and environmental explanations of particular observations. It is quite reasonable, however, to describe as hereditarians those writers who stress the importance of genetic inheritance relative to environmental influences in the differential performance of individuals of different socioeconomic status or different ethnic group membership when, for example, taking intelligence tests.

SEE ALSO: antislavery; Darwinism; environmentalism; geometry of race; Gobineau, Joseph Arthur de; Haeckel, Ernst; heritability; science; social Darwinism

Reading

The Black Image in the White Mind: The debate on Afro-American character and destiny, 1817–1914, 2nd edn., by George M. Fredrickson (Wesleyan University Press, 1987), is another historical account.

The Leopard's Spots by William Stanton (University of Chicago Press, 1960) is a historical study of hereditarian thought.

Racial Theories, 2nd edn., by Michael Banton (Cambridge University Press, 1987) explains the origins and some of the consequences of early theories of race.

MICHAEL BANTON

HERITABILITY

A measure of genetic inheritance. More technically, a heritability estimate for a particular trait expresses the proportion of trait variation in a population which can be attributed to genetic variation. Suppose, for example, that in a certain population individuals vary in stature. If all the variation can be traced to genetic differences the heritability estimate for stature will be 1; if it can all be traced to differences in the environments of individuals the estimate will be 0.

Every organism is the product of both inheritance and environmental influence. A hereditary trait (e.g. skin color) may be modified by environment (e.g. sun tanning). Equally, a trait sensitive to environmental modifications (e.g. weight in humans) may be genetically conditioned. Geneticists speak of genes being "switched on and off" by environmental stimuli. The difficulties involved in studying the interactions between heredity and environment can be illustrated by the inheritance of genes for yellow or colorless legs among certain kinds of chicken. If they are fed on white corn they all have colorless legs. If they are fed on yellow corn, or on green feed, some have yellow legs. If those belonging genetically to the yellow-leg variety are fed, some on white and others on yellow corn, the former have colorless and the latter yellow legs, so that the difference can be attributed to an interaction between environmental factors (i.e. nutrition) and genetic ones. This is why heritability has to be estimated for particular populations and the estimates for different traits in the same population vary substantially.

There was an angry debate in the early 1970s about the heritability of intelligence as measured by IQ tests. Studies in the USA had consistently recorded an average of about a 15 percentage-point difference in the scores of black and white samples, while Asian Americans regularly scored better than whites. It was not in question that environmental factors could account for individual IQ differences of 20–30 points, or that US blacks and whites differed in several IQ-relevant environmental respects. The dispute centered upon whether environmental differences could account for all the differences between groups. Hereditarians such as Arthur R. Jensen maintained that since heritability estimates for IQ can be as high as 0.8, the intergroup difference is likely to be in part genetic. However the available heritability estimates only expressed the relative importance of environmental factors for IQ differences within the white population, and no reliable estimates were available for blacks. The hereditarian argument was blocked by the lack of evidence that environmental differences operated between the groups in the same way as within the white population. Moreover, if discrimination against blacks in the USA was itself an intellectual handicap, this made intergroup comparison impossible because like was not being compared with like.

SEE ALSO: environmentalism; hereditarianism; intelligence; science

Reading

The Bell Curve: Intelligence and class structure in American life by Richard Herrnstein and Charles Murray (The Free Press/Simon & Schuster, 1994) is a recent statement of hereditarian views.

The Race Concept by Michael Banton and Jonathan Harwood (David & Charles, 1975) is an elementary exposition.

The Science and Politics of I.Q. by Leon J. Kamin (Penguin, 1977) gives a critique of the evidence about intelligence; the opposition of views is analyzed in "The race-intelligence controversy" by Jonathan Harwood (in *Social Studies in Science*, vol. 6, 1976 and vol. 7, 1977).

MICHAEL BANTON

HISPANICS *see* Latinos

HOLOCAUST

Usually referred to as *The Holocaust*, this broadly refers to the experiences of European Jews in territories occupied or controlled by the Third Reich and its allies during the years 1933–45, with particular emphasis on the varied discriminatory laws and regulations to which they were subjected, confiscation of property, brutality and violence, concentration in ghettos, and starvation and killings, especially in the death and concentration camps. (The word derives from the Greek *holos*, for whole, and *kauston*, burnt.) Although it is not possible to estimate accurately the number of European Jews who died as a direct result of Nazi policies, the figure that is widely accepted is that of six million.

The Holocaust is viewed by many as the pre-eminent genocide of the twentieth century, the series of events that most directly gave rise to the formulation and adoption of the 1948 Convention on the Punishment and Prevention of the Crime of Genocide. In the view of some prominent scholars the Holocaust constituted a major rupture of, and a critical turning point in, the development of Western civilization. The philosopher Theodor Adorno speculated on this by postulating that there could be no poetry after Auschwitz.

The Holocaust is one of the most intensely studied events of twentieth-century history, and has given rise to an enormous literature. Although tens of thousands of publications have dealt with matters relating to its origins, its implementation, and with issues focusing on why various categories of participant assisted in the persecution, plundering, concentration, deportation, starvation, and the killing of Jews, whilst others, the great majority, failed to take significant steps to protect them, the field is still characterized by a lack of consensus relating to some fundamental issues. Thus, whilst it is generally acknowledged that the wellspring from which the policy was fed was the long tradition of anti-Semitism of many European countries, there is no consensus that the decision to embark on the final phase of the campaign against the Jews – their physical liquidation – can be explained largely in terms of a decision to draw out the ideological implications to their operational conclusion. There has been a long-standing debate between scholars who take the view that the decision to liquidate the Jews was already foreshadowed in Hitler's speeches of the 1920s, and those who argue that the liquidation program was only implemented because of certain contingencies that arose out of the military campaign being waged on the Eastern front, and the demographic experiments being conducted in Nazi-controlled Poland. Although it is acknowledged by the latter grouping that the racist anti-Semitic ideology was a necessary precondition for targeting a particular segment of the population for liquidation, it is their contention that in the absence of certain unforeseen contingencies that arose during the Russian campaign, an extermination program would not have been undertaken. That is, a decision to liquidate European Jewry was not conceived of or undertaken prior to the first half of 1941.

Similarly, there has been no overall systematic analysis relating to matters focusing on the motivations of perpetrators. Explanations range from psychoanalytically oriented perspectives that emphasize sadism, to sociologically focused analyses that emphasize the banality, or normality, of even those participants who were most directly implicated in the planning, bureaucratic implementation, and day-to-day execution of such policies. Thus, quite a few scholars have argued that the extermination of European Jewry was executed, not by racial fanatics who were incensed and vitriolic anti-Semites, but by mild-mannered bureaucrats who were, essentially, carrying out routinized jobs under the direction of persons in authority, who, in turn, were in the majority of cases not particularly ill-disposed toward their victims. Even those who were participants in the special action units and police battalions that were responsible for rounding up Jews and executing them with firearms have been represented as "ordinary men." Such an approach is not discordant with analyses that suggest that the Holocaust is in some way a direct by-product, or even manifestation, of modernity, its most importantly relevant attributes being scientism and bureaucratization.

SEE ALSO: anti-Semitism; culturecide; ethnocide; fascism; genocide; nationalism; pogrom; UNESCO; xenophobia

Reading

Eichmann in Jerusalem: A report on the banality of evil, by Hannah Arendt (Penguin, 1977). Adolf Eichmann, a Lieutenant-Colonel in the SS, was head of *Referat* IV B4 of the Reich Main Security Office (Gestapo), its expert on *Jewish Affairs*, between 1939 and 1945; he was responsible for the bureaucratic coordination of the *final solution to the Jewish question*. Arendt, a prominent political philosopher, who attended the trial for the *New Yorker*, addresses, among many issues, the question of what type of persons were implicated in the implementation of what is considered by many the greatest crime in history.

Hitler's Willing Executioners: Ordinary Germans and the Holocaust by Daniel J. Goldhagen (Little, Brown & Company, 1996) is a controversial discussion of German anti-Semitism, which he characterizes as *eliminationist*, and of the implementation of various policies relating to the destruction of European Jewry. This book is best contrasted with Christopher Browning's approach in *Ordinary Men* (see below) which, to a degree, it is in conversation with. Its publication gave rise to extensive academic exchanges, and the publication of numerous articles and books, most of which sought to refute his thesis. Although the cauldron has cooled somewhat, the issues have by no means been resolved.

The Holocaust: The Jewish Tragedy by Martin Gilbert (Collins, 1986) is a detailed and well-organized descriptive account of the varied phases and programs of the Holocaust, from anti-Semitism to extermination camps, and the aftermath.

Modernity and the Holocaust by Zygmunt Bauman (Cornell University Press, 1989) discusses the relationship between attributes of modernity and the occurrence of the Holocaust.

Ordinary Men: Reserve Battalion 101 and the Final Solution in Poland, by Christopher R. Browning (HarperCollins, 1992) is a pathbreaking analysis by one of the foremost Holocaust scholars; it explores the complex of factors that allowed a unit of largely middle-aged men who were not fervent Nazis to round up and then execute Jews in occupied Poland. *The War Against the Jews 1933–1945* by Lucy Davidowicz (Penguin, 1987) may be read in conjunction with *Why Did the Heavens Not Darken? The Final Solution in history* by Arno Mayer (Pantheon, 1988), which puts forward probably the most radical formulation of the argument that the extermination phases of the Holocaust occurred because of contingencies that arose in the course of the Eastern Campaign.

CHECK: internet resources section

STUART STEIN

HOMELESSNESS

Homelessness is notoriously difficult to define, and establishing its parameters has political and policy implications. In this context, a broad definition is adopted, to include statutory homelessness (those accepted as such by housing authorities), street homelessness (those without any form of shelter, also known as the roofless and as rough sleepers), and hidden or invisible homelessness (those living in inadequate and/or vulnerable circumstances, such as bed and breakfast accommodation). In general, it is true to say that minority ethnic people are over-represented in all forms of homelessness, due to a combination of institutional racism, concealed housing needs, and higher levels of economic disadvantage and social exclusion. Minority ethnic people are represented among all types of homeless groups, including runaways from home, young people leaving care, single people and families, women escaping domestic violence, people with mental health needs, and ex-offenders.

Patterns of homelessness

Black and minority ethnic homeless people are likely to be significantly under-recorded by homelessness statistics. There are three main reasons for this: first, a reluctance to use statutory or voluntary services perceived to be oriented towards the ethnic majority and potentially racist institutionally; second, the racism that may pervade the street homeless culture; and third, a community pride that may lead people to adopt informal solutions to homelessness (e.g. sleeping on a friend's floor) in preference to a public acknowledgment of their status. This contributes to high levels of hidden homelessness, and so the extent of housing need is not officially recognized. This situation may become self-perpetuating, whereby agencies concerned with homelessness may believe that black and minority ethnic people always prefer to "look after their own."

There is very little documentation of homelessness culture in relation to issues of racism; most studies focus on policy issues concerned with the provision of accommodation and other services. The qualitative studies that do exist suggest a level of racism within street homeless culture and in venues such as hostels and day centers. In the 2000 study *Sub City: Young people, homelessness and crime*, Wesley, a young man of twenty-four who described himself as of mixed race, gave the following account:

> You do get a bit of trouble … you get abuse 'cause you're homeless. At first it was a bit upsetting, but you just get used to it after a while … It's not normally racist abuse, it's normally about being homeless, getting called scruffy and a tramp … [But] it can make it harder [being black], it can get a bit depressing, makes it seem worse.

Despite the under-recording of their levels of homelessness, minority ethnic groups still tend to be over-represented in most measures of homelessness. In 2002, a Downing Street briefing revealed that among the statutory homeless, 22 percent consist of black and minority ethnic households, though they constitute 8 percent of the general population of England. The British government expressed its concern over this level of social exclusion, and announced measures to investigate and tackle the causes of this homelessness.

In London, minority ethnic people are around three times more likely than white people to be staying in direct access hostels or winter shelters. Among young people, housing need is at a very high level. One study showed that over two-fifths of young people applying for help to homeless agencies are from minority groups, while in London this rose to 54 percent, according to Centrepoint in 1996.

The Rough Sleepers' Initiative (RSI) has collected information on ethnic origin of the roofless population. Findings confirm other reports which suggest that white people are much more likely to sleep rough, with other ethnic groups being more likely to make informal and temporary arrangements with friends and family. One evaluation of the work of the RSI found that about 80 percent of white homeless people had slept rough, compared to only 30 percent of black homeless people (HMSO, 1993). At present it is only possible to speculate about the reasons for this difference, but possible explanations include the greater vulnerability of minority groups while sleeping rough.

In response to significant housing need, social exclusion and institutional racism, many specialist agencies have developed services for homeless minority ethnic groups, while many other general agencies have responded by developing specific resources. For example, there now are black housing associations and shelters for women of South Asian, Chinese and African descent.

The specific needs and experiences of different ethnic groups are considered below.

South Asians: The stigma of homelessness is often felt particularly acutely within the South Asian community. For many, to be homeless is to lose *izzat* or personal and family honor. Those who do become officially homeless may in some cases be faced with the loss of family and community links. Overcrowded households may be maintained in preference to someone becoming officially designated as homeless. Such households may also be defined as being homeless (see voluntary organizations such as Shelter), but unless their need is registered with the relevant housing authorities, then they will remain the hidden homeless.

On becoming homeless, a number of issues may face the South Asian individual. In addition to institutional and peer group racism faced by all minority ethnic people, there may also be a range of cultural concerns. First-generation settlers, in particular women, may need hostels and other agencies to provide services in one of the community languages, such as Urdu, Hindi, Bengali or Gujarati. Knowledge of cultural backgrounds on the part of workers is also important. A small number of hostels cater for specific groups, such as South Asian women escaping violence within the home. Often these are located far from the woman's hometown, and therefore alternative support networks may be needed.

Homeless South Asian women may find themselves excluded from both their own communities and from wider society. In the *Sub City* study Ruksana, a young Muslim woman, gives this account of her experiences since leaving home:

> I don't consider myself as an Asian, even though I am ... I've left my community ... Once you're married, if you don't like your husband you're bloody stuck with him. If you leave your husband and you go back to your parents' house, they'll still force you to go back to him. It's your only place ... if you get a divorce society is going to spit on you.

Finding herself alone in a hostel in the English Midlands, Ruksana, like women of all ethnic groups in similar circumstances, was attempting to rebuild her life and gain access to permanent housing and employment. Although the need for shelter is universal, ethnicity, gender and other social identities mediate the specific experience of homelessness.

Irish people: One of the earliest migrant groups to mainland Britain, the Irish have long been over-represented among the homeless population, the result of historic economic and social conditions. Throughout much of the nineteenth and early twentieth centuries, famine and poverty in Ireland led to high levels of emigration, with many people settling in Britain. Significant anti-Irish discrimination, coupled with employment and economic difficulties, contributed to high levels of homelessness among this group.

In the late twentieth and early twenty-first centuries, a buoyant Irish economy has altered traditional patterns of out-migration, and those young Irish who do migrate often do so in order to take up employment in mainland Europe. However, homelessness is still a problem for first and second-generation Irish settlers in Britain. Evidence is scattered, but some studies have found significant over-representation of the Irish among the homeless in cities such as London.

Travelers: Traditional Traveler-Gypsies, or Roma, are unlikely to define themselves as homeless. For them, the itinerant lifestyle is a chosen one, and part of their culture. They do however face both discrimination and a lack of sufficient sites on which to settle. Although not homeless in any official sense, they do experience problems in relation to accommodation, problems that some would argue are exacerbated by both official and local community prejudice against this ethnic group.

Relevant legislation includes the Criminal Justice and Public Order Act 1994, which served to render more difficult the lifestyle of Travelers.

Unlike Traveler-Gypsies, New Age travelers have not been designated as an ethnic group under the Race Relations Act, though some are actively seeking this definition. They may or may not perceive themselves to be homeless, but like the Traveler-Gypsies they find that negative stereotypes and discrimination serve to make more difficult their chosen Traveling lifestyle.

Refugees and asylum seekers: Virtually all ethnic groups are represented among the refugees currently in Britain. National groups such as Somalis, Afghans and Bosnians form a significant proportion of refugees, reflecting recent wars and political conflicts across the world. After an initial period of time which may be spent in prisons or reception centers, if refugees are granted asylum they then face the process of permanent resettlement. Currently a contentious political issue, refugees are often blamed by the media for a range of social ill; they face discrimination in housing, education and employment; and they often encounter resistance from many rural and urban communities during the settlement process. Already facing poverty, unemployment, language and cultural adaptations and an uncertain future in their adopted country, refugees also encounter a range of housing problems. The most common circumstances are those of insecure, overcrowded and inadequate accommodation. Groups such as Shelter include such circumstances in their definition of homelessness. Their access to public housing provision and to welfare benefits has been restricted in recent years by the Immigration and Asylum Act 1999.

A global perspective

While this entry concentrates on homelessness in Britain, a global perspective reminds us that in many parts of the world, ethnicity is closely connected with homelessness. In recent years many thousands, and in some cases millions, of people have become homeless refugees because of their ethnic identity. This has been true for the Tutsi and Hutu peoples of Rwanda and for Bosnian Muslims in the former Yugoslavia, following the process euphemistically described as "ethnic cleansing." The beginning of the twenty-first century has seen communal violence

between Hindus and Muslims in North India, leading to the displacement of thousands of Muslim households in towns throughout Gujarat. People displaced by ethnic conflicts of this nature often remain homeless for many years, either in their own country or in other nations.

SEE ALSO: asylum seeker; British Asians; ethnic cleansing; globalization; housing; human rights; institutional racism; Irish; law: immigration, Britain; Roma; social exclusion; social work

Reading

"Black women and housing" by Perminder Dhillon-Kashyap, in *Housing Women*, edited by Rose Gilroy and Roberta Woods (Routledge, 1994). This includes an overview of the housing conditions and homelessness experienced by black women.

Discounted Voices: Homelessness among young black and minority ethnic people in England by J. Davies, S. Lyle, A. Deacon, I. Law, L. Julienne and J. Kay. (University of Leeds, 1996) reports on homelessness among various minority ethnic groups, including statistics and policy recommendations; this may profitably be read in conjunction with *Hidden Crisis* by Sheron Carter (Frontline, 1998), a study of black and ethnic minority homelessness in London.

Homelessness in Global Perspective by Irene Glasser (Macmillan, 1994) provides an international perspective on homelessness, with some reference to ethnic identity in various nations.

Planning for Action: The Children Act and homeless young people, a black perspective (CHAR, 1995) provides a report on the implications of the Children Act 1989 for young black homeless people.

Sub City: Young people, homelessness and crime by Julia Wardhaugh (Ashgate, 2000) is a study of youth homelessness and crime and includes some case studies of the experiences of homeless minority ethnic people.

"Theorising homelessness and 'race' " by Malcolm Harrison, in *Homelessness: Exploring the new terrain* (Policy Press, 1999), provides a theoretical perspective in a policy-dominated field of inquiry.

JULIA WARDHAUGH

HOTTENTOT VENUS

This was the name given to Saartjie Baartmann (1789–1816), a member of the Griqua tribe of South Africa, who was taken to Europe as a slave, exhibited like a circus freak and, after her death, dissected by the French anatomist, Georges Cuvier (1769–1832), who used her body as evidence to support his theory of fixed racial types. Baartmann became a symbol of the humiliation and subjugation experienced by both the indigenous Khoikhoi and blacks under colonialism and then apartheid. The term "Hottentot" is an Afrikaans word used by the Dutch to describe indigenous South Africans.

In 1810, Baartmann was transported from the British colony on the Cape of Good Hope to London. She was in the custody of a ship surgeon, Alexander Dunlop, who persuaded her that she could make a fortune by exhibiting herself in European capitals. Spectators were charged to view and, if inclined, feel her prominent buttocks. Antislavery forces started court proceedings to stop the exhibition on the grounds that Baartmann had been traded as a slave. The slave trade had been abolished in 1807. Baartmann's keepers countered that she had entered into an agreement of her own volition and was actually a paid servant. The case was dismissed. While in England, she was baptized and given the name "Sarah."

Moving to Paris, she appeared in an animal show but attracted scientific interest, particularly from Cuvier who was developing his theory of permanent racial types. His view was that there were a finite number of material species that were not susceptible to change, but could be eliminated by periodic catastrophes and replaced with others. At the time of Baartmann's arrival in France, the country was in the midst of a bitter scientific and theological dispute. Monogenists basically contended that a single species had been created in one act of creation and that the diversity of life was the result of environmental influences. Polygenists disputed this account of creation and the universe, arguing that humankind had been created out of several different sets of ancestors, giving rise to a multiplicity of types, all with separate origins.

Baartmann died penniless age twenty-six and her body was used for further examination. Cuvier was especially interested in her genitalia, the labium of which he considered a "special attribute of her race." After dissecting her body, Cuvier presented this aspect of her anatomy to the French Academy. *Le règne animal destribué d'après son organization* was published in 1817 and included Cuvier's conclusions on the specimen he called *Vènus Hottentotte*. He compared the structure and functions of her body to those of the great apes. The comparison extended to the way he discharged her dismembered cadaver: preserved in formaldehyde-filled bell jars and either sold, loaned or donated to natural history

museums. Cuvier made a cast of her body and allowed it to be displayed at the *Musèe de l'homme* in Paris until 1974 when it was stashed in a backroom with some of her remains.

The post-apartheid South African government pressed France to release her skeleton and bottled organs and, in August 2002, they were returned to Hankey, 470 miles east of Cape Town, where there was a solemn burial ceremony attended by thousands. At the ceremony, President Thabo Mbeki reflected on Baartmann's life: "It is the story of the loss of our ancient freedom ... it is the story of our reduction to the state of objects who could be owned, used and discarded by others."

SEE ALSO: antislavery; beauty; bigotry; geometry of race; Grégoire, Henri; negrophilia; race: as classification; science; sexuality; South Africa; subaltern

Reading

"The Hottentot Venus" by Percival Kirby (in *African Notes and News*, vol. 6, 1949) is an early account, the same author later contributing "More about the Hottentot Venus" to the same journal (vol. 10, 1953); the case is also recorded in Stephen Jay Gould's *The Flamingo's Smile: Reflections in natural history* (Norton, 1985) and chapter 5 of Londa Schiebinger's *Nature's Body: Gender in the making of modern science* (Beacon, 1993).

The Idea of Race (Tavistock, 1977) and *Racial Theories*, both by Michael Banton (Cambridge University Press, 1987), set Cuvier's theories in context.

"Which bodies matter? Feminism, poststructuralism, race and the curious theoretical odyssey of the 'Hottentot Venus' " by Zine Magubane (in *Gender and Society*, vol. 15, no. 6, 2001) is a critique of an earlier argument by Sander Gilman ("Black bodies, white bodies: toward an iconography of female sexuality in late nineteenth century art, medicine and literature," in *"Race," Writing and Difference*, edited by H. L. Gates, University of Chicago Press, 1985).

HOUSING

Housing is the provision of accommodation, including shelter, lodging, rented and owned dwellings; it can also refer to residential patterns, or zones. A salient characteristic of many ethnic groups is that their housing shows significant differences from that of the wider society within which they find themselves. They tend to be relatively highly segregated and their housing tends to be of lower quality. A number of questions then arise: (1) what processes create and maintain these patterns; (2) to what extent are they external impositions on ethnic groups; and (3) to what extent can they be attributed to the actions and attitudes of the groups themselves? In addition, since housing is profoundly interwoven with quality-of-life issues, the housing of ethnic groups is a matter of major concern in public policy formulation.

The dwelling and its context

The dwelling must be central to any discussion of housing. The dwelling is the built structure occupied by one or more people defined as a *household*. The dwelling may be a house, an apartment, or flat, or some other people container. The dwelling, however, must not be viewed in isolation. It exists in the context of other dwellings, which, together, comprise the street, the block, the apartment building, the neighborhood and so on. These spatial units in turn are not just characterized by their built form but by the characteristics of those who inhabit them ("the neighbors"). Thus, when we examine housing and ethnicity we will focus not only on the dwelling but also on the surrounding area in which it is located. Dwelling and neighborhood are fundamentally linked.

Members of ethnic groups are distributed in distinctive ways within the housing system of their country or countries of residence. They will be found in a range of tenure types (such as owner-occupation, rental from private landlords, or rental from social housing landlords). Their distribution could be a mirror image of the wider societal distribution or it could be deviant from that distribution – for instance, unduly concentrated in a particular tenure, overconcentrated in dwellings of a particular quality, or spatially concentrated in certain limited areas of cities.

Explanations for the distribution of ethnic groups in housing systems have been offered on the basis of two approaches: *constraint* models and *choice* models. With constraint the particular position of members of a given ethnic group is attributed to the limits within which they seek housing. These limits may be household income, the operation of institutions such as mortgage lenders or social housing allocators, or the discriminatory attitudes and behaviors of other households.

On the other hand, a range of researchers has emphasized the choice dimension. The early work of Robert Park and his associates in Chicago tended to stress the choices made by European immigrants as they sought residential niches for themselves in American cities. In the 1960s and 1970s, work in Britain on the circumstances of Asian immigrants has also stressed choice – where the culturally based preferences of the various groups or the ways in which they organize self-help are considered to be key contributors to the observed housing patterns.

At times there has been a tendency to polarize the constraint–choice debate. More realistically, however, it is now widely accepted that choices *and* constraints jointly shape ethnic housing outcomes. Choices are made within constraints. In some cases the constraints are quite loose, in others very tight indeed. One might view the constraints as a box within which choices are to be made. Some ethnic groups find themselves confined in very small boxes (they have very limited choice) while others operate in much larger ones (they have much greater freedom).

Perhaps the most balanced statement of the constraint–choice perspective is that provided by Roger and Catherine Ballard. They were describing the general position of ethnic and racial minorities in British society, but their words can be read as applying specifically to the housing system:

It is clear that any understanding of racial and ethnic minorities must rest on a consideration of both the internal preferences and the external constraints that act simultaneously upon them. But at the same time, it should also be recognized that the external constraints, such as the migrant's position on the labour and housing markets or the discrimination he [she] faces, are ultimately prior to the internal preferences of the group.... It is the external constraints of discrimination, which set the limits within which South Asians, and West Indians in Britain may operate. But the particular behaviour of different groups can only be finally explained in terms of the culturally determined choices made within these limits. ("The Sikhs: the development of South Asian settlements in Britain," in *Between Two Cultures: migrants and minorities in Britain*, edited by James L. Watson, Blackwell, 1977).

In examining the relationship between housing and ethnicity, it is tempting to try and come up with universal theories and models. However, we must also recognize that universal processes are likely to be profoundly shaped by the particular circumstances of whatever ethnic group is being studied. What are the distinctive cultural attributes of group members, and how variant are these (in fact or in perception) from the wider society? How long have group members been present – are they recent immigrants, or are they second or third generation, or has their group formed a distinct ethnic presence for many generations?

The enormous variety of circumstances that impinge on housing and ethnicity means that each case needs to be examined in its own right, though general processes will be acknowledged. To provide some indication of the processes at work, a number of brief case studies are now offered, focusing, in turn, on tenure, on quality and on location.

Ethnic groups in housing markets

Here we refer to Asian-origin immigrants in Britain. The data are drawn from a survey carried out in 1974, a time when most of the immigrants were recent arrivals (see David J. Smith's *Racial Disadvantage in Britain: The PEP Report*, Penguin Books, 1977). Strikingly, we note that Asian immigrants were disproportionately found in owner-occupied housing. Moreover, while owner occupation amongst the general population was at its highest for wealthier households, precisely the opposite was the case for the Asians. Providing a further contrast with the host society was the fact that Asian occupancy of public (social) housing was at a very low level indeed. Again, this seems surprising, given that social housing was aimed at low-income households and Asians, at the time of the survey, were generally low-income. Finally, the survey recorded that the Asian owner-occupied dwellings were of lower quality than those of the general population, this being particularly true for those immigrants of Pakistani and Bangladeshi origins.

What factors contributed to these patterns? Firstly, most Asians in the 1970s were excluded from social housing because they had not at that time been in the country long enough to qualify under the regulations used to allocate such housing. In addition many Asian households inadvertently excluded themselves because the public housing stock did not provide large enough dwellings to meet their needs.

Most Asian immigrant households started out in housing rented from private landlords. Much of this housing was located in neighborhoods of growing Asian concentration, as many immigrants sought the support of their fellow ethnics in their struggle to gain a toehold in a strange world. However the rental housing itself was very unsatisfactory, and so they began to enter the only segment of the housing stock that was open to them and that could provide dwellings appropriate to their needs. These owner-occupied dwellings were old, were located in inner-city neighborhoods and were of relatively poor quality.

West Indians, or African Caribbeans, in Britain provide a further illustration of the dynamic interplay of housing and ethnicity. In this example we can look at the position of West Indians with respect to public (social) housing. In the early days of large-scale immigration from the Caribbean, West Indians were underrepresented in this housing tenure (bearing in mind their low socioeconomic position). Explanations for this situation focus on the qualifying criteria for gaining entry to social housing. In particular, residence qualifications tended to exclude those who had moved to the country only recently. However, as time passed, West Indian households found themselves increasingly in social housing. In this case, the evidence available shows that the dwellings so occupied were on average of lower quality than those that had been allocated to whites. The dwellings, on average, were older, tended to be located in less popular, inner-city neighborhoods and a disproportionate number were located in high-rise buildings. There have been many investigations of this situation. Reasons for the observed patterns include discrimination by institutions and individual "gatekeepers" engaged in managing the social housing sector, exclusionary attitudes and actions by elements in the wider population, and the wish, at least for a portion of West Indians, to live in neighborhoods where a significant number of their "own people" were present. Here clustering may have been for reasons of cultural support and may also have been a defensive response to fear of harassment in predominantly white neighborhoods.

One of the characteristics of the relationship between housing and ethnicity is the tendency for some degree of locational concentration. Here the constraint–choice debate again intervenes when interpretations are offered for this segregation.

To illustrate this we can look at the USA. In the nineteenth and early twentieth centuries those immigrants from a range of European countries who ended up in urban centers initially settled in older neighborhoods downtown. Being predominantly of low income they had to seek low-cost accommodation close to the main sources of employment. They also tended to cluster according to ethnic origin, seeking dwellings in close proximity to their fellow-countrymen or co-religionists. In this way they attached themselves to socially supportive networks. Thus the immigrant ethnics were constrained by income and by employment accessibility needs, while they chose to locate in those segments of the housing market that met their requirements and which were densely occupied by co-ethnics.

The classic American immigrant settlement model then has the groups begin to disperse away from the inner-city concentrations as their income improved and as they lessened their dependence on the cosiness of the ethnic cluster. For African Americans (though mainly internal migrants), the inner-city also served as the reception area. In their case, however, inner urban segregation did not decline with time. Instead, powerful external pressures (prejudice, violence and discriminatory behavior by key players in the housing market) maintained the *ghetto* concentration as a trap. Here constraints were dominant, while choice was extremely limited or virtually nonexistent.

Overview and policy

The three basic dimensions of housing and ethnicity (tenure, quality and location) have briefly been illustrated above. These three dimensions of course are intimately interwoven and are found in an environment characterized by constraint and choice. A very useful way of pulling all this together was offered back in 1970 by R. F. Haddon, in his "A minority in a welfare state society: the location of West Indians in the London housing market" (in *The New Atlantis*, vol. 1, 1970). Haddon offered six dimensions for consideration:

- A stock of housing differentiated as between tenure types, location, age and condition.
- A number of means of access to these different types of housing and the rules of eligibility that govern these means of access.
- A particular group of the population with its characteristic needs and preferences that result from their cultural background and from the current social situation they find themselves in.
- The interaction between the means of access and the rules of eligibility, on the one hand, and the needs and attributes of the ethnic group being examined, on the other.
- The additional factor of discrimination (by other population groups; by institutions) on the basis of ethnicity, leading to exclusion or to the steering of ethnically defined households into narrowly defined niches in the housing market. This discrimination may be directly intentional or it may be unintentional.
- A group of people who have been referred to as "gatekeepers" who operate the rules of eligibility and who are in a position to discriminate.

Governments are inextricably involved in the dynamics of ethnicity and housing. They may have operated apartheid policies (separate and unequal), they may have been content to let market processes operate unhindered, they may have intervened to impose specific levels of ethnic mixing (for instance in Singapore) or they may have decided to operate a pluralistic housing policy, where choice is as unconstrained as possible and where unacceptable imbalances (for instance in housing quality or in excessive degrees of segregation) are confronted. In all this, ethnic record keeping will be essential. Otherwise decision-makers will be ill informed both about the circumstances with which they have to deal, and the consequences of the policies they initiate and attempt to carry out.

Segregation, poor housing and distorted tenure choices are factors limiting social, educational, political and economic advancement for many members of ethnic groups. Consequently such matters are of considerable public policy concern.

SEE ALSO: African Americans; apartheid; British Asians; environmental racism; ghetto; homelessness; institutional racism; integration; internal colonialism; Jim Crow; Park, Robert

Ezra; pluralism; Pruitt-Igoe; segregation; social exclusion; social work; violence; welfare; white flight

Reading

Ethnicity and Housing: Accommodating differences, edited by Frederick W. Boal (Avebury, 2000), offers a wide range of case studies of attempts to house members of ethnic groups in a "pluralistic" manner.

"Housing and urban space", chapter 7 in *Race and Ethnicity in Modern Britain* by David Mason (Oxford University Press, 1995), provides a succinct summary of housing and ethnicity in Britain.

"The housing careers of Polish and Somali newcomers in Toronto's rental market" by Robert A. Murdie (in *Housing Studies*, vol. 17, no. 3, 2002) provides a useful picture of the varied housing experiences of two immigrant ethnic groups.

"Immigration and settlement, 'race' and housing," chapter 1 in *Ethnic Minority Housing: Explanations and policies* by Philip Sarre, Deborah Phillips, and Richard Skellington (Avebury, 1989), is a good overview of explanations offered for ethnic group disadvantage in housing.

"Towards the comparative exploration of public housing segregation in England and the United States" by John M. Goering (in *Housing Studies* , vol. 8, no. 4, 1993) concentrates on commonalities and contrasts in the social housing field.

FREDERICK W. BOAL

HUMAN RIGHTS

International human rights are rights that belong to every human being solely by virtue of his or her membership as part of humankind. Universally endorsed human rights are expressed in the pivotal principles of social equality, social justice enshrined in the provisions of the UN Charter, the International Bill of Human Rights (United Nations, 1978, 1988) and related covenants.

This conception of universal human rights is a twentieth-century phenomenon: it should not be equated with the historical concept of natural rights because to do so would be to overlook the crucial fact that so-called natural rights were not rights held solely by virtue of one's humanity. Indeed, race, gender and nationality were also relevant criteria. Natural rights, in reality, were the rights of dominant Westerners: white European men. Some 80 percent of all human beings were excluded.

Today, the primary source and authority for international action against racial, ethnic and gender discrimination is the UN Charter, which declares in article 55 that the UN shall promote "universal respect for, and observance of, human rights and fundamental freedoms for all without discrimination as to race, sex, language, or religion."

International human rights principles set down in the provisions of the various international human rights treaties and covenants are prior to law: essentially, they serve to challenge states to revise laws in ways which offer guaranteed protections for the rights of citizens, especially members of minority groups, against abuses of state power. Principles are advocated by UN authoritative bodies as moral guidelines, the universal human rights standards to which all systems of justice should conform.

While UN international human rights principles are put forward as global moral standards, this is not to say that these principles are absolute or that they leave nothing further to be desired. Indeed, these principles are continuously evolving ascensions and concerned citizens within nations reconsider them and develop ever-newer covenants to protect more explicitly the human rights of persons and groups throughout the globe.

The development of international human rights covenants

The various human rights covenants in which international principles of human rights are put forward were developed soon after World War II, in response to the world's outrage when the full account of Nazi atrocities – enslavement, torture, genocide – became public knowledge. These resolutions represent the attempt by nations to prevent such crimes against humanity from ever happening again.

On December 9, 1948, the UN General Assembly approved the Convention on the Prevention and Punishment of the Crime of Genocide. On the very next day, December 10, 1948, the General Assembly adopted and proclaimed the Universal Declaration of Human Rights (UDHR), a declaration which represents a statement of principles or moral guidelines for the recognition and protection of fundamental human rights throughout the globe. Articles 1 and 2 of the UDHR set out the three cardinal principles of human rights: freedom, equality and dignity as rights and freedoms to which everyone is entitled, without distinction of any kind. The twenty-eight articles which follow identify particular rights and freedoms exemplifying the three central principles. Since its proclamation, the Universal Declaration has had international impact, influencing national constitutions and laws, as well as later, more specific international declarations.

The bulk of the declarations advanced in current international human rights instruments build upon the three guiding principles of the Universal Declaration and address a common, threefold theme: the right of every human being to participate in the shaping of decisions affecting one's own life and that of one's society (freedom to decide/political rights); reasonable access to the economic resources that make that participation possible (equality/equivalence of opportunity/economic rights); and affirmation of the essential human worth and dignity of every person, regardless of individual qualities and/or group membership (dignity of person/social rights).

The right to equality principle is probably one of the most misunderstood (and variously interpreted) of all tenets of fundamental human rights. The right to equality essentially represents equality/equity of opportunity and results. Equality does not necessarily mean sameness. In some instances, equal (standard or same) treatment (e.g. equal access to jobs and promotions for members of all racial and ethnic groups) is appropriate, but in other instances, equivalent (special) compensatory treatment may be required (e.g. architectural adaptation of public buildings; provision of ramps and handrails as well as stairs to enable access to the facility by wheelchair-bound and mobility-impaired as well as ambulatory persons).

Justifiable restrictions on human rights

Under current UN human rights covenants, the three pivotal human rights principles – freedom to decide, equality/equivalence of opportunity and dignity of person – are held to be inalienable. What this means is that these fundamental human rights can be claimed equally by all human beings, regardless of demonstrated or assumed differences among individual persons in their talents, abilities, skills and resources and regardless of their membership in different human groups. While fundamental human rights are held to be inalienable, they are not absolute: in the exercise of his or her fundamental rights,

each human being must not violate; indeed must respect, the fundamental human rights of others. Human rights, then, are not unconditional: they are conditional on the exercise of social responsibilities or duties to others.

The fundamental principles of the interdependence of the individual and community and of the reciprocity of rights and duties provide the underpinnings for the moral justification of necessary restrictions on individual human rights. For, from a human rights view, any restriction or denial of the exercise of the fundamental human rights to freedom, equality and dignity of any human being can be justified only in instances where violations of the human rights of others can be fully substantiated. In such cases, restrictions justifiably may be imposed on the violator's exercise of human rights, but only to the extent necessary to prevent further violations of the rights of others.

Everyday life provides us with endless examples of rights in conflict. For instance: does the freedom of the individual include the freedom to kill, maim, rape, and assault? The assailant and the victim cannot both have absolute freedom of choice. Thus, we must face the fundamental paradox. The existence of freedom demands the imposition of restrictions. In order to accomplish this task, democratic societies have developed systems of justice: laws, law enforcement agencies, courts and so forth.

The enduring critical question concerns the kind and the extent of restrictions or laws are appropriate in a society, which seeks to promote the greatest possible freedom of the individual and, at the same time, to promote the greatest good of the society as a whole?

Twin principles of human rights: human unity and cultural diversity

Fundamental individual human rights are rooted in the distinctive biological attributes shared by all members of humankind as a single species, *Homo sapiens*. Recognition of the essential biological oneness of humankind provides the scientific basis for the universal principle of fundamental individual human rights. A primary assumption, then, behind international human rights covenants is that of the fundamental unity and kinship among all members of humankind.

Yet every human being is born not only into the human species, but also into a particular human population and ethnocultural community. Collective cultural rights represent the principle of cultural diversity, the *differentness* of unique ethnocultures or blueprints for living developed by the various ethnic populations of humankind. Taken together, individual and collective human rights represent the twin global principles of human unity and cultural diversity.

The concept of cultural diversity and collective rights of culture as ethnoculture underscores protections for collective cultural rights endorsed in the provisions of article 27 of the International Covenant on Civil and Political Rights (UN, 1978, 1988) and reinforced in the provisions of the Declaration on the Rights of Persons Belonging to National, Ethnic, Religious and Linguistic Minorities (UN, 1992).

The principle of collective human rights recognizes the collective right of every ethnic community to practice and to perpetuate the distinctive culture or way of life developed and shared by its members. Just as all human beings, as members of humankind, must respect the fundamental individual rights of all other human beings, so, also, all human beings as members of particular human cultures must respect all of the different ethnocultures shared by other human beings.

Conflict of rights: individual v. collective (cultural) rights.

While the universality of human rights in a global context of cultural diversity has, since the inception of the UDHR in 1948, continued to spark debate in the realms of international politics and law in recent years, only a few non-Western countries, especially those from Asia, have questioned the universal character and international force of the Declaration. However, given the increasingly multicultural nature of modern societies, the same conflict between individual and collective cultural rights is posed within nations. Freedom of cultural expression, like freedom of speech, is not absolute. All human rights, both individual and collective are conditional on the cardinal principle of nonviolation of the rights of others. The critical question here concerns the nature of restrictions or laws, which are appropriate in a society which seeks to promote individual rights and freedoms as well as harmonious relations between the different ethnocultural communities in the society.

International human rights instruments: key provisions of the special covenants

Since its proclamation, the Universal Declaration has had international impact, influencing national constitutions and laws, as well as international declarations such as the UN Declaration on the Elimination of All Forms of Racial Discrimination (1963) and the International Convention on the Elimination of All Forms of Racial Discrimination (1965). This impact notwithstanding, the UDHR represents only a general statement of ideals: It is morally but not legally binding on member-states of the UN. Some countries sought a more forceful declaration, which would establish binding obligations on the part of member states. As a result, two additional Covenants were drawn up and came into force in 1976: The International Covenant on Economic, Social and Cultural Rights (ICESCR) and the International Covenant on Civil and Political Rights (ICCPR). In 1978, the UDHR and the two later covenants (ICCPR) and (ICESCR) were incorporated into the International Bill of Human Rights (IBHR).

Protection for the collective right of self-determination of peoples is provided under the provisions of article 1 of both the ICCPR and ICSCER. Until quite recently, legal interpretation of this article has been based on a very narrow concept of "people" which applied only to peoples as nations whose cultural/territorial boundaries coincide with or have the potential to coincide with the boundaries of a state unit. This restrictive interpretation afforded no support for the nationhood claims of peoples/nations living inside the territorial boundaries of recognized, sovereign states. Over the last two decades, however, largely in response to resolute lobbying by organizations and coalitions representing the world's "internally colonized" aboriginal (indigenous) peoples, there has been increasing support for a broader interpretation of article 1 among international legal scholars. A draft proposal for an International Covenant on the Rights of Indigenous Peoples was adopted in principle by the Third General Assembly of the World Council of Indigenous Peoples in May 1981.

A preliminary document, the Universal Declaration on Indigenous Rights, was introduced in August 1988. While this draft, and later drafts, including the present 1994 declaration, recognizes the collective cultural and aboriginal rights of indigenous peoples as well as their collective right to autonomy in matters relating to their own internal and local affairs within the institutional structures of recognized states, it falls short of an explicit recognition of aboriginal peoples as nations with an inherent right to self-government. In response, aboriginal representatives have continued to press for unambiguous recognition of the right of self-government of aboriginal nations in the declaration.

Human rights as legal rights

At this point, it is important to distinguish clearly between international human rights principles and public policies or laws enacted by governments. Laws and government policies may violate human rights. While some laws are modeled on human rights guidelines (e.g. human rights statutes prohibiting discrimination on specified grounds, such as race or ethnic origin), others violate human rights principles (e.g. laws which discriminate against particular populations on specified grounds, such as race or religion). When human rights principles do become incorporated into law, they become legal rights which can be invoked by persons or groups who perceive that their human rights have been violated in order to seek redress for the alleged violation.

Human rights legislation and human rights claims

A legal framework of human rights protection allows those whose rights have been violated to bring forward claims for legal redress and recompense. Any member of a particular social group who perceives that s/he has experienced violations of his/her fundamental, individual right/s to freedom, equal opportunity or dignity on the arbitrary basis (assumed) of an identified group can make individual rights claims (e.g. black, Sikh or Greek immigrants denied jobs on the grounds of race, religion and ethnicity, respectively, can make complaints for employment redress). By way of contrast, collective cultural rights claims can only, justifiably, be put forward by representatives of ethnic communities with distinctive ethnocultures. As indicated earlier, the basic principle behind collective cultural rights is the right of ethnic communities legitimately and freely to express their cultural dis-

tinctiveness. When this right is violated, then a collective cultural rights claim can legitimately be put forward (e.g., aboriginal, Jewish or Muslim minorities whose distinctive language, religion, customs or lifestyles have been denigrated, suppressed or destroyed can make claims for recognition and protection of their distinctive cultural practices.)

The one component of ethnicity which differentiates the kinds of collective rights claims that may be put forward by particular ethnic groups is that of territoriality. As indicated earlier, there is growing support among legal scholars for the view that all ethnic communities which can demonstrate a continuing, integral association between the people, their ancestral territory and their distinctive ethnoculture within the boundaries of a given state unit (such as the Kurds in Iraq, the Palestinians in Israel, the Basques in Spain and the Franco-Quebecois in Canada) can claim collective nationhood rights. When such communities have been denied their collective right to self-determination as internal nations within their own territorial bounds, they can put forward nationhood claims.

Territoriality has a unique dimension in connection with the collective claims of aboriginal ethnic groups. Aboriginal (land) rights are seen as derived from a collective form of land occupancy and use; they are collective rights of aboriginal communities, not rights of individuals.

Those aboriginal peoples whose ancestors never signed land cession treaties with state authorities whereby their aboriginal right and title were deemed, by the state, to be "extinguished," can make land claims based on aboriginal rights (e.g. Australian Aborigines, Sami in Lapland, and Maxi Indians in Brazil). Aboriginal nationhood rights, on the other hand, derive from the historical fact that, prior to the destructive impact of colonialism, aboriginal peoples were self-governing nations with distinctive cultures and recognized territorial boundaries. It is on this premise that some aboriginal peoples are putting forward nationhood claims (American Indian Movement (AIM), Canada's First Nations peoples).

SEE ALSO: Aboriginal Australians; American Indians; ethnonational; exploitation; indigenous peoples; International Convention; international organizations; minority language rights; UNESCO; United Nations

Reading

"Cross-cultural dimensions of human rights in the twenty-first century" by S. K. Murumba, in *Legal Visions of the 21st Century: Essays in honour of Judge Christopher Weeramantry*, edited by A. Anghie and G. Sturgess (Kluwer Law International, 1998), presents a comprehensive overview of the ongoing debate concerning the universality of human rights.

Discrimination and Human Rights, edited by Sandra Fredman and Philip Alston (Oxford University Press, 2001), offers a series of essays about human rights legislation and how it addresses racial discrimination.

Ethnicity and Human Rights in Canada: A human rights perspective on ethnicity, racism and systemic inequality by Evelyn Kallen (Oxford University Press, 2003) offers a social scientific analysis which provides: first, an understanding of the way in which human rights violations lead to the social construction of group-level racial/ethnic inequalities; second, the analysis shows how members of Canadian racial/ethnic minorities can use international human rights principles, incorporated into Canada's system of legal protections for human rights, to gain redress for past human rights violations; third, the analysis provides an outline of strategies for change designed to facilitate a goal of equity and justice for all racial and ethnic groups in society.

CHECK: internet resources section

EVELYN KALLEN

HUMOR

Humor is the faculty of sensing and enjoying the amusing, comic or ludicrous. *Ethnic humor*, as defined by M. L. Apte (in *American Behavioral Scientist*, vol. 30, no. 3, 1987), is "a type of humor in which fun is made of perceived behavior, customs, personality, or other traits of a group or its members by virtue of their specific, socio-cultural identity."

Joking-down and joking-up

Ethnic humor reflects the lack of symmetry in social relations between different ethnic groups. It articulates ambiguities, ambivalence and incongruities in perception. Historically, ethnic groups, which have been marginalized, materially deprived and rendered politically powerless have invariably been unable to avoid the attribution of ethnic humor used to justify their sufferance of discriminatory treatment.

Such humor can be traced back at least to the Ancient Greek Empire where the butts of jokes about their alleged stupidity made by urbanized Athenians at the core of Greek civilization were the non-Greek and designated barbarian inhabitants of peripheral Greek colonies and cities, for example, the Milesians and Boeotians. The prominent and influential Ancient Roman satirist Juvenal, ridiculed as comic butts ethnic Syrians, Greeks, Egyptians and Jews, who could variously be found on the streets of Imperial Rome. In the latter case their out-group marginality was reinforced by widespread perceptions and hostile misunderstandings of their unfamiliar religion of Judaism, their use of magic and their begging, as well as other aspects of moral and social behavior regarded as incompatible with and reprehensible in Imperial Roman culture.

Hostile humor and ethnic jokes directed at groups defined as outsiders in society, or Other, reflect *social* attitudes, in this case anti-Semitism, and deployment of serviceable pejorative stereotypes and myths leading in the case of migrating Jews since ancient times to their becoming the universal butt of ethnic humor, a status reinforced by the concept of the Wandering Jew in their Western Diaspora. This illustrates what Anton Zijderveld (in *Social Research*, vol. 35, 1968) calls "joking-down" and "joking-up": making fun of (and with) members of ethnic groups either above or below one's own status group or class as a way of corroborating social distance, ethnic boundaries and hierarchical power relations. Thus, in traditionally dehumanizing and belittling Jews to the level of crude stereotypes and caricatures by joking-down, the joke is a form of social *control* and corrective employed to reduce the credibility and humanity of Others. Joking not only conveys the racism of the joke-teller, but also sustains it.

Joking-up, by contrast, has created a distinctive in-group Jewish humor and wit, including black and gallows humors, originating in self-deprecation – joking about one's own marginality and perceived cultural characteristics. In this sense, humor serves as a form of resistance and a powerful weapon in the assimilation and emancipation of Jews in Western societies. The wit of retaliation and the comedy of revenge function similarly as symbolic victories over majority groups. Such humor further acts as a source of social cohesion and distinctive ethnic identity for members of the minority group, especially among first-generation immigrants. Once established, the self-mocking humor is frequently appropriated by the majority group and given wider social approval. The humor works to remind the majority what they are *not* (not miserly or mean, in this instance). Thus in twentieth-century America, large numbers of gentiles have been drawn into the magic world of Jewish humor (see P. Berger's *Redeeming Laughter: The comic dimension of human experience*, De Gruyter, 1997). Indeed, the greatest contributions to the American world of comedy, especially in the media in recent years, have come not from the socially dominant group (WASPs) but from those at the margins of society – Jews and African Americans.

"Race" through the prism of humor

Given the history of modern slavery and the large number of black African slaves transported to Southern states of America between the seventeenth and nineteenth centuries, it is hardly surprising that slaves and their descendants have been the objects of disparaging humor. Such humor has been based on crude and often vicious racial stereotypes.

In his pioneering study (in *American Sociological Review*, vol. 2, 1946), J. H. Burma differentiated between "anti-Negro" humor as expressed by whites to reflect their alleged supremacy and control and "anti-white" humor, in which Southern whites were depicted as being outsmarted by cunning blacks. In the former, the derogatory Jim Crow stereotype of the nineteenth century was employed and this was later transmitted as the urbanized Sambo character, dull-witted and always trying unsuccessfully to imitate white culture with humorous consequences. In the latter, blacks made use of an inverted corruption of the trickster figure Sambo as a weapon to confront and accommodate adversity and racial competition and conflict in the late nineteenth and early twentieth centuries; the central character of black humor was a city slicker and con-man who mocked the features ascribed to him by rebelliously exposing the bigoted prejudices of redneck whites. Thus Jesse B. Simple and Slim Greer are symbols of the ridiculing of whites' values and lifestyles by means of role reversal, cultural code-switching and code-mixing. They are profound parodies of the dominant white society. This joking-up emancipatory tradition, which humorously plays on the realities of street life and self-mockery, has been continued and augmented by such late twentieth-century comedians as Godfrey Cambridge, Dick Gregory, Red Foxx, and Richard Pryor, who whilst offering running commentaries on white American culture at the same time importantly drew attention to their own exclusive counterculture and history. (Note: Eddie Murphy's rise has been seen less as an extension of this tradition and more a modification of "anti-Negro" humor merely substituting homosexuals, women, and other minority groups in place of blacks.)

Christie Davies argues that in the West orally communicated jokes about ethnic groups, for example as the Irish and "Pakis" (South Asians), are the most popular. The attribution to such Others of ignorance and stupidity, especially with respect to machinery and artifacts, as well as the organized marketplace, serves the cause of efficiency and rationality by denigrating their opposites in terms of the "comic spirit of capitalism." It defuses the anxieties of those living in the "joyless economy" of modern capitalism. By joking-down about the failure of stereotyped groups to fit into the modern world, ethnic disparagement humor and hostile wit act as a social control mechanism in interethnic relations, inculcating in both the jokers and their ethnic butts a sense of "what is right": deficient minorities should be more like the adequate and rational majorities.

Hugh Dalziel Duncan, in *Communication and Social Order* (Oxford University Press, 1962), has further confirmed that laughter derived from joking-down at a succession of ethnic immigrants (German, Irish, Scottish, Scandinavian, Italian, Polish and Yiddish in turn) acts as a form of social discipline, corrective or control of initially marginalized out-groups which has served to keep them in place until they have learned how to behave like established Americans. This suggests that such ethnic humor functions as a complex and subtle form of social probing in interethnic relations to discover what attitudes, motives, and values members of a particular ethnic group share and whether they are socially acceptable, particularly to dominant groups, in assimilating to a multicultural society such as America.

A growing area of interest is the way in which the mass media have confirmed or modified stereotypes in expressions of the humor of ethnic marginality. Obvious examples are British sitcoms of the 1960s and 1970s – *Love Thy*

Neighbour, Till Death Do Us Part and its American offshoot All in the Family. The most outrageous display of racism and ethnocentrism in a TV show came in the British-produced Mind Your Language about a polyglot language class, every member of which was a grotesque caricature of ethnic characteristics. Despite this, the militant humor of African American comedians on late night satire programs such as Saturday Night Live in the 1970s not only resisted and mocked white racially stereotyped attitudes and ambivalence but comically exposed and played with the gamut of residual bigotry, racial slurs and black images expressed in traditional mass media. While confirming the norm enforcement function of the media in reinforcing cultural conformity or reflecting society's ambivalence about ethnic minorities, the alternative and subversive humorous depiction of suppressed minorities can also provide the social analyst with a barometer registering changing ethnic situations and statuses of groups vis-à-vis the wider society. From the 1960s, the social exposure of America's race relations was furthered when black humor (in the generic sense) made significant inroads into mainstream popular comedy, especially stand-up, releasing previously suppressed satirical aspects of African American comedy and thus gaining currency in the dominant white society (see Mel Watkins, below).

One seeming breakthrough in status conferral which challenges the stereotype of African Americans is the ratings success of The Cosby Show, the most popular American sitcom between 1984 and 1992. Bill Cosby, by pioneering shows about African Americans as multidimensional black characters, also exemplified the recent acquisition by African Americans of power positions as US TV executive producers and directors, enabling non-clichéd portrayals. Despite this, Cosby's depiction of a well-meaning, middle-aged, professional black father with three children, an expert on child-rearing with pious views, does little more than reaffirm the more benign ways that the white middle class perceives black participation in American society: "The black male should be individualistic, racially invisible, professionally competent, successful, and upwardly mobile expressions of racial conflict and black collectivity are absent," writes D. Crane in The Production of Culture: Media and the urban arts (Sage, 1992).

Racial ventriloquists

A further dimension of humor and ethnicity accompanying the burgeoning study of women's humor is the case of African American women who are traditionally attributed with employing verbal wit and wordplay denied their white sisters until comparatively recently. This is evidenced by the man-and-wife stage acts developing out of the older minstrelsy from the early 1890s. Thus Jackie "Moms" Mabley played the lewd widow in stand-up comedy routines for much of the century, working within the joking frames of folk humor recognized by her predominantly black audiences.

Classic female blues singers, such as Lucille Bogan and Clare Smith in the 1920s and 1930s, challenged male sexual potency with the raunchy epithets and double entendres of their songs. In all these comic formats, the black woman played the antagonist to the man. Zora Neale Hurston (1903–60), one of the first widely acclaimed African American women novelists, assimilated folk tradition in modern literature. She dramatized verbal duels of mock courtship and post-courtship routines in the South. Munroe observes that she "played out in the liminal land of the porch." The singularity of her comic achievement is seen as advancing, however indirectly, a pioneering feminist agenda. Male African American literature, both poetry and novels, from the mid nineteenth century onwards was at best tinged with irony, its authors sparing in their use of humor and satire. Following the example of early twentieth-century satirical cartoons and editorials in black newspapers emphasizing the irreconcilability of America's racial policy and its humanitarian pretensions, significant satirists and folk humorists of the Harlem Renaissance of the 1920s and 1930s characterized the urban wise fool and trickster. George Schuyler, in his 1931 novel Black No More, lampooned racial bigotry and false racial pride, as well as race leaders, both black and white. Incorporating the rhythms and tones of authentic black street humor, Rudolph Fisher earned the title of the "first Negro to write social comedy." Langston Hughes, whose finest works of humor emerged in the form of his most popular folk hero and "Socratic clown" Jesse B. Simple, first appeared in 1943 in the Chicago Defender column which continued until 1965 as a humorous mouthpiece unmasking the pretensions and follies of both white and black opponents.

It was not until 1952 however that an African American comic novelist – Ralph Ellison, with his *Invisible Man* – gained recognition from literary critics for having written one of *the* best American novels. His employment of the full range of genres that define the comic spirit helped revise stubbornly wrong-headed (white and black) notions of the double-edged nature of African American humor aptly labeled by Watkins as "racial ventriloquy." Charles Wright's novel *The Wig*, set in the 1960s, with its connection to mainstream anti-establishment humor, further unmasked through a series of absurd situations and use of dark humor the continuing confusion between black identity and American identity. During the late sixties and early seventies humor, not least its satirical aspect, suddenly emerged as one of the staple elements in contemporary African American literature, affirming its distinctly comic resonance as reflective of the worldview of many ordinary African Americans.

Another post-1980s contributory factor in the demise of public hostile racial and ethnic humor has been the onset and rapid growth of political correctness. This forced humorists, especially joke-tellers such as alternative comedians in popular cultural contexts, to become more circumspect in their humorous utterances, primarily before interethnic audiences. Apte has pertinently suggested that such contemporary sensitivity to ethnic diversity and the rise of cultural pluralism in America has created a new sociocultural reality of "situational ethnicity" whereby minority ethnic groups " increasingly have the option of affirming, negating, obfuscating, or underplaying their ethnic identity in small group social interactions, commensurate with their motives and their perceptions of the significance of the social situation" (in *Humor*, vol. 10, 1997). Ethnic humor has thus become "obscure humor," as Joseph Boskin calls it, or a form of whispered humor disseminated as joke-lore in the private domain.

The more malign and hostile humor in the cause of white racism has been driven underground or at best into cyberspace and virtual reality via the internet with its explosive growth in the early nineties. This has been highlighted in a critical study by Michael Billig (in *Discourse & Society*, vol. 12, 2001) of recent humor on joke sites linked to the American Ku Klux Klan. When such jokes and parodied dictionary entries are examined in the context of the extremist politics of racism, hatred and bigotry which the KKK has long espoused, allowing for the fact that the language of the extreme right with its coded messages is not straightforward, their presentation of racist humor indicates a complex and dissembling rhetoric which in extreme forms presents lynching of blacks as a joke to "murderers in their imagination." Similarly, privatized racial humor on World Wide Web pages followed the 1996 resolution of the Oakland (California) Unified School District to respect the legitimacy and richness of Ebonics in order to facilitate African American students' acquisition and mastery of English language skills (Maggie R. Ronkin and Helen E. Kern in *Journal of Sociolinguistics*, vol. 3, 1999). Such web sites reveal the employment of "mock Ebonics" as a form of linguistic racism parodying African American vernacular English stereotypes to articulate an anti-Ebonics language ideology and deflect the blame for the poor scholastic performance of African Americans from a racist society to learners and the community from which they come.

SEE ALSO: bigotry; Ebonics; epithet (racial/ slang); *Invisible Man*; Jim Crow; Ku Klux Klan; language; media; minstrelsy; Other; political correctness; racial coding; representations; scapegoat; stereotype

Reading

"Courtship, comedy, and African American expressive culture in Zora Neale Hurston" by B. Munroe, in *Look Who's Laughing: Gender and comedy*, edited by G. Finney (Gordon & Breach, 1994), examines some key twentieth-century female comics and genres in African American comic expression.

The Humor Prism in 20th Century America, edited by Joseph Boskin (Wayne State University Press, 1997), contains a wide range of articles on the significance of ethnic and racial humor in multicultural American society in recent years.

The Mirth of Nations by Christie Davies (Transaction, 2002) examines the origins and persistence of ethnic jokes both historically and comparatively in a worldwide context in terms of stereotyped characteristics of stupidity or canniness attributed to ethnic groups.

On the Real Side: A history of African American comedy from slavery to Chris Rock by Mel Watkins (Transaction, 1999) is the definitive work on African American humor, humorists and comic genres from minstrelsy to stand-up comedy.

CHECK: internet resources section

GEORGE PATON

HYBRIDITY

The term hybrid has developed from biological and botanical origins to become a key term in contemporary cultural criticism. "Wherever it emerges it suggests the impossibility of essentialism," writes Young. In Latin *hybrida* originally meant the offspring of a tame sow and a wild boar, though in the nineteenth century it became a physiological phenomenon, referring to a "half-breed" (as the *Oxford English Dictionary* expresses it) or a "mongrel or mule" (according to *Websters*). Theories of racial typologies warned of the dangers of hybridization and degeneration that would result from the mixing of distinct races which occupied different hierarchical positions. Anxiety about hybridity served to keep "races" separate.

More recently, hybridity has been appropriated by cultural critics and deployed against the very culture that invented it to justify its divisive practices of slavery and postcolonial exploitation. William Rowe and Vivian Schelling refer to hybridization as "the ways in which forms become separated from existing practices and recombine with new forms in new practices" (in *Memory and Modernity*, Verso, 1991). So, while hybridity originally denoted an amalgamation or mixture, it now describes a dialectical articulation. For example, in Hall's work on the black experience in Britain, he recalls a moment of homogenization in which "blackness" contests dominant representations of black people. Out of this awareness of commonality (of being black) comes an awareness of heterogenity, of diffuseness, of being part of a dispersed population – what Hall calls "diaspora-ization."

In this sense, hybridity describes a *culture* composed of people retaining links with the territories of their forebears but coming to terms with a culture they inhabit. They have no wish to return to their "homeland" or to recover any ethnically "pure" or absolute identity; yet they retain *traces* of other cultures, traditions and histories, and resist assimilation.

Bakhtin uses hybridity in another way, to describe a language's ability to be simultaneously the same and different: "An utterance that belongs ... to a single speaker, but actually contains mixed within it two utterances, two speech manners, two styles ... the division of voices and languages takes place within the limits of a single syntactic whole, often within the limits of a single sentence." The application of this to colonial settings, through the work of Bhaba, reveals hybridity to be a moment of challenge and resistance against a dominant cultural power: "Hybridity ... is the name for the strategic reversal of the process of domination through disavowal (that is, the production of discriminatory identities that secure the 'pure' and original identity of authority)."

In this perspective, colonialism has actually produced hybridization: in establishing a single voice of authority or dominion over *others*, it *in*cludes the *ex*cluded Others in its discourse (i.e. by representing them) and simultaneously estranges the basis of its authority. Hybridity is the antidote to essentialist notions of identity and essentialism: the colonial authority and Other are locked into the same historical narrative, their cultures and identities contingent on each other.

SEE ALSO: Anglo-Indians; colonial discourse; colonialism; creole; diaspora; essentialism; Hall, Stuart; Other; postcolonial; post-race; race: as signifier; racial coding; racist discourse; subaltern; youth subcultures

Reading

Colonial Desire: Hybridity in theory, culture and race by Robert J. C. Young (Routledge, 1995) connects old racial theories with present cultural criticism by showing how we retrospectively construct old notions of race as more essentialized than they actually were: "Culture and race developed together, imbricated within each other."

Global Diasporas: An introduction by Robin Cohen (Routledge, 2001) makes the point that hybridity may not be the most appropriate term to denote the evolution of new, dynamic, mixed cultures, for, "as plant breeders know, hybrids have marked tendencies towards sterility and uniformity." Cohen prefers "syncretism" and his book contains an interesting section on this.

Hybridity and its Discontents: Politics, science and culture, edited by Annie Coombs and Avtar Brah (Routledge, 2000), applies the concept to a range of cultures.

The Location of Culture by Homi Bhaba (Routledge, 1994) is a dense and sometimes perplexing text on what the author calls "beyond theory." "Hybridity is the sign of the productivity of colonial power, its shifting forces and fixities ... [it] represents that ambivalent 'turn' of the discriminated subject into the terrifying, exorbitant object of paranoid classification – a disturbing questioning of the images and presences of authority."

"New hybridities, old concepts: the limits of 'culture' " by Floya Anthias (in *Ethnic and Racial Studies*, vol. 24, no. 4, 2001) describes hybridity as "inadequate in addressing the issue of the multifarious nature of identifications, since it constructs identity in a singular, albeit synthetic form"; in other words, and, according to the author, the concept does not move far away from more conventional notions, such as culture and ethnicity.

Post-colonial Studies: The key concepts, edited by Bill Ashcroft, Gareth Griffiths, and Helen Tiffin (Routledge, 2000) pulls together a wide range of writings by, among others, Fanon, Spivak, and Said, all united by postcolonial theory and criticism.

I

IDENTITY *see* cultural identity

IDEOLOGY

This concept is the object of continuing debate and argument, though all uses of it suggest that it refers to a complex of ideas. This reflects the origin of the term in the late eighteenth century when it was used to refer, in a technical sense, to the science of ideas. It took on another meaning around the same time, one which is still predominant in common-sense discourse and in conservative political thought. This is the uses of the term in a pejorative sense to refer to impractical or fanatical theory, to ideas which are abstract and which ignore "the facts." Neither of these two uses are of any direct relevance to the way in which the concept is employed analytically now.

Contemporary analytical usage reflects the different ways in which the concept was employed by Marx. In Marx's own writings, one finds two distinct usages. The first is his use of the concept to refer to false and illusory descriptions of reality, a meaning that is synonymous with the notion of false consciousness. This usage is found clearly expressed in *The German Ideology*, written by Marx and Engels in 1846. This notion of ideology is used by both Marxists and critics of Marxism in combination with a mechanical interpretation of the base/superstructure metaphor. This is evident in arguments which claim that ideology is the reflection and product of ruling-class interests and has the function of obscuring from the working class the "real" nature of its domination and exploitation by capital.

The second use of ideology in Marx's writings is to refer to the complex of ideas that correspond to particular sets of material interests and experiences. This usage is found in Marx's later work, notably in the *Grundrisse* and *Capital*. However, this usage itself fragments into two different emphases. On the one hand, ideology is used to refer in a general sense to the content of the forms of consciousness which come into being and are reproduced in the course of the reproduction of material life. On the other, it is used to refer to the structural fact of consciousness: in this sense, ideology is used to refer to a particular level or dimension of a social formation. However, both usages are usually associated with a further distinction between ideology and science, which implicitly (if not explicitly) returns us to an elaboration on the theme of illusion. The introduction of the concept of science as a polarity is necessary in order to permit a critical evaluation of the nature and content of ideology in these two latter senses.

The work of Althusser and Poulantzas has been the site of much of this recent debate, from which have emerged some important clarifications and developments. One of these is pertinent to an analysis of racism and nationalism as ideologies. It has been argued recently that although ideologies refer to accounts of the world that are, in totality, false, they must be analyzed and understood in such a way as to allow for the fact that people who articulate them can nevertheless make sense of the world through them. This means that ideological generation and reproduction cannot be understood simply and solely via some notion of false perception or ruling-class domination. The latter may empirically be the same in particular instances but this is not the complete substance of ideology. Rather, it is more important to explain why and how ideologies "work" in relation to the essential relations of the mode of production, thus allowing a certain autonomy to the formation and reproduction of ideology. Thus, ideologies are mistaken, not so much because of false perception or indoctrination, but because of the determinate forms in which production relations can be experienced and expressed phenomenally.

The other important clarification to emerge from recent debates is consequent upon renewed interest in the work of Gramsci, from which has emerged the concept of common sense. This refers to the complex of ideas and perceptions, organized without coherence, which are a consequence of both historical tradition and direct experience and by which people negotiate their daily life. The term ideology can refer to this common sense which is characterized not only by its "matter-of-factness" but also by its internal disorganization. Ideology can therefore refer not only to a complex of ideas that are the product of "systematic" thought, but also to the internally contradictory and incoherent set of ideas through which daily lives are lived.

These general debates are refracted in the ways in which racism is analyzed as ideology. One classic, Marxist tradition has been to argue that racism is an ideology created by the ruling class in a capitalist society to justify the exploitation of colonial populations and to divide the working class. This clearly reproduces the notion of ideology as an illusory creation of the bourgeoisie. More recently, drawing upon the second general notion of ideology found in Marx, racism has begun to be analyzed as an ideology (complex of "facts" and explanations) which refracts a particular experience and material position in the world capitalist economy. It has independent conditions of existence, although those conditions are not themselves fully independent of the material parameters of the social formation. From this perspective, what is significant is that the ideology of racism allows sections of all classes to intellectually interpret and understand the world in a way that is consistent with their experience. Although the illusory nature of the ideas is openly acknowledged (on the basis of analytical historical analysis of the idea of "race," i.e. science), it has been argued that they nevertheless provide at one level a relatively coherent explanation of the world as perceived and experienced. In its extreme form, in this argument, racism becomes one further dimension of the ideological level of the social formation. Within this level of the social formation one can therefore identify an ideological struggle and conflict, between racists and antiracists, which is not assumed to be between purely proletarian and bourgeois forces.

SEE ALSO: capitalism; Hall, Stuart; hegemony; inferential racism; language; Marxism; nationalism; political correctness; racism

Reading

Karl Marx: Selected readings, 2nd edn., by David McLellan (Oxford University Press, 2000), brings together valuable extracts from Marx's formidable oeuvre.

Marxism and Historical Writing by P. Q. Hirst (Routledge & Kegan Paul, 1986) is a critical discussion of contemporary Marxist theorists, with a view to assessing the materialist science of history; this may be read in conjunction with the old, but useful On Ideology by the Centre for Contemporary Cultural Studies (Hutchinson, 1978).

Political Ideologies: An introduction, 2nd edn., by Andrew Heywood (Macmillan, 1998), is a clear, accessible account; this may be read alongside the more demanding Ideologies and Political Theory: A conceptual approach by Michael Freeden (Oxford University Press, 1998).

ROBERT MILES

INDIGENOUS PEOPLES

Prior to the expansion of Europe, many regions of the earth were occupied by peoples who lacked the art of writing and pursued technologically simple ways of life. Such peoples are now more usually referred to as indigenous peoples. Indigenous means belonging naturally to a territory and derives from the Latin indigena (indi, meaning in, gen, for be born).

Columbus thought he had discovered a new route to the Indies, thus the Europeans described the peoples of the Americas as Indians. The native people of Australia were called Aborigines (from the Latin ab origine, from the beginning, probably because they were seen as primitive). In Africa and Oceania the expression "native" was commonly used. The Europeans described themselves as civilized but, ironically, the weaker the native peoples, the greater was the brutality shown toward them. In the USA and Australia, the native peoples were at times hunted by armed whites who regarded this as a form of sport. In Brazil and Australia diseases were deliberately spread among the native peoples and poisoned food left out for them.

In New Zealand, prior to the European invasions, there were about 200,000 Maoris. Before the end of the nineteenth century they seemed to be dying out, so many of them having succumbed to European diseases or having been shot by other Maoris using imported muskets. Then Maori cultural pride and the Maori birth rate began to revive. A similar three-stage sequence of defeat, despair, and regeneration can be discerned among the Native Americans of the United States, whose lands were appropriated more savagely than in the European colonies to the north and south. In North America, European occupation was legitimated by international treaties, the "Indian tribes" being regarded in law as nations on an equal status to that of the invaders. Different European powers were eager to make such treaties because they were in competition with one another. The political claims of Native Americans today are that the whites should observe the promises they made in these treaties.

No issue is more important than that of "Native Title" to land. In Canada, where indigenous peoples are called the "First Nations," aboriginal (or "native") title to land has been recognized under the common law as existing alongside the treaty-making process, but ownership of minerals rests with the Crown. In Australia there were no treaties between the invading and indigenous peoples following British settlement from 1788. In law, the land was regarded as *terra nullius* (land belonging to no one) until January 1992 when, in an historic judgment in the case of *Mabo* v. *Queensland*, the High Court held that native title had survived the Crown's annexation, and that, under closely specified conditions, persons of indigenous origin could enjoy rights deriving from it.

In New Zealand, the 1840 Treaty of Waitangi was given new life in 1975 with the establishment of the Waitangi Tribunal; this is authorized to assess Maori land claims. Under US law, the British Crown, by "discovery," acquired title to all the land, but this was subject to an indigenous right of occupancy. That occupancy has to be protected by the government against third parties but can be extinguished by Congress.

In Sweden, the indigenous people are called Sami (formerly Lapps). Though most persons of Sami origin are now urban dwellers, Sami culture is identified with reindeer breeding. The law protects the rights of persons belonging to recognized Sami communities to their traditional use of reindeer pasture, and associated hunting and fishing rights, but it does not accept Sami ownership of land itself.

At the UN, representatives of the world's indigenous peoples have been pressing for better recognition of their distinctive rights as the original inhabitants of their countries and owners of the land. Draft paragraphs of a Declaration on the Rights of Indigenous Peoples have been under discussion for many years; it is hoped that it will be adopted before the end, in 2004, of the International Decade of the World's Indigenous Peoples. Since international law recognizes that "All peoples have the right of self-determination," many governments are reluctant to regard indigenous groups as "peoples" and prefer to speak of "indigenous people."

The International Labor Organization's (ILO's) Convention 169 "Concerning Indigenous and Tribal Peoples in Independent Countries" applies to distinctive tribal peoples and to peoples "who are regarded as indigenous on account of their descent from the populations who inhabited the country, or a geographical region to which the country belongs, at the time of conquest or colonization or the establishment of present state boundaries and who, irrespective of the legal status, retain some or all of their own social, economic, cultural and political institutions." Governments are supposed to accept self-identification with such a group as the criterion of being indigenous, but the criteria for deciding which groups are indigenous vary from one world region to another. The ILO believes that there are some 5,000 different indigenous and tribal peoples living in around 70 countries, the greatest number being in Asia.

In the Latin American region forest peoples are threatened by colonists who occupy and clear their land and by the operations of companies prospecting for oil. In a landmark judgment of September 2001, the Inter-American Court of Human Rights affirmed the existence of indigenous peoples' collective rights to their land, resources, and environment by declaring that the Mayagna Community of Awas Tingni's rights to property and judicial protection were violated by the government of Nicaragua when it granted concessions to a foreign company to fell trees on that community's traditional land without consulting them or securing their consent. The government was found to have violated its obligations under international law to give effect to its duties under the Inter-American Convention on Human Rights. The Court ordered the government to demarcate and recognize the title of the Mayagna and other communities to their traditional lands, to submit biannual reports on measures taken to comply with the Court's decision, and to pay compensation and legal costs. In some African countries indigenous peoples are threatened by the actions of governments that commandeer their land for the creation of national parks intended to serve their tourist industries.

Ruling elites in many less developed countries believe that the interests of indigenous groups must be subordinated to those of national development. This is sometimes described as development racism, and the damage to their habitats as environmental racism.

SEE ALSO: Aboriginal Australians; American Indians; anthropology; culture; environmental racism; ethnonational; human rights; minority language rights; United Nations

Reading

The Indigenous World, Yearbook of the International Workgroup for Indigenous Affairs (Copenhagen), is valuable for annual surveys of current developments, as is the report *Land Rights and Minorities* by Roger Plant (Minority Rights International, 1994).

International Law and the Rights of Minorities by Patrick Thornberry (Clarendon Press, 1991) describes and assesses the legal situation.

"Should we have a universal concept of 'indigenous peoples' rights'?" by John R. Bowen (in *Anthropology Today*, vol. 16, 2000), together with Marcus Colchester's "Indigenous rights and the collective conscious" in the same journal (vol. 18, no. 1, 2002) and "Defining oneself, and being defined as, indigenous" by Ian McIntosh, Marcus Colchester, John Bowen and Dan Rosengren, also in *Anthropology Today* (vol. 18, no. 3, 2002), provide reviews of the anthropological approach to the subject.

White Settlers and Native Peoples by A. Grenfell Price (Cambridge University Press, 1950) remains a useful historical review.

CHECK: internet resources section

MICHAEL BANTON

INFERENTIAL RACISM

This describes language, images and other textual materials from which racism can be inferred, i.e. deduced, concluded, conjectured or presumed. Its source implies hints or allusions to racism rather than spells it out explicitly. The term was used by Stuart Hall in a series of essays in the 1980s in which he considered the shift in racist discourses from overt forms of racism to more implicit forms that remained embedded in dialog.

Explicit or overt racism, on this account, is clearly in evidence when unambiguously racist arguments and opinions are advanced and publicized. The advent of legislation curbing the public dissemination of such forms and the rise of political correctness resulted in a decline, though not disappearance, of such racist forms. Inferential racism, while not new, has become more prevalent in recent years, though it often remains "invisible even to those who formulate the world in its terms."

Inferential racism represents reality in a "naturalized" way, embodying a set of unquestioned *assumptions* about the status of groups designated "races" and their relationship with whites. As Hall wrote: "These enable statements to be formulated without ever bringing into awareness the racist predicates on which the statements are grounded."

Neglecting to examine the assumptions confers the statements that flow from these with authenticity. Even statements that are made with the best of intentions can have racist inferences. One of the most historically notable examples of this is the 1992 reference of US presidential candidate Ross Perot when addressing an audience of African Americans as "you people." Less naïve and certainly not well intentioned was British politician Enoch Powell's warnings of the effects of Caribbean and South Asian immigration in the 1960s. The unstated assumption was, as Hall put it, "that *blacks* are the *source of the problem*."

While inferential racism has become more apparent recently, it has co-existed with more open racism. For example, popular literature during the period of European colonialism was "saturated" with representations of colonized people as being inferior to Europeans and possessing negative attributes. "We find them in the diaries, observations and accounts, the notebooks, ethnographic records and commentaries of visitors, explorers, missionaries and administrators in Africa, India, the Far East and the Americas," wrote Hall in his essay "The whites of their eyes."

Analysis of inferential racism is consistent with Hall's advocacy of research that investigates not racism per se, but the ways in which racist ideas and ideologies are "constructed and made operative under different historical conditions."

While he does not actually use Hall's term, John Hoberman reveals inferential racism in the glorification and honoring of African American athletes (see his book *Darwin's Athletes: How sport has damaged black America and preserved the myth of race*). The failure to address the question of why so many African Americans succeed only in the two main areas of sport and entertainment induces the media to celebrate black sports success uncritically. This leaves assumptions about the natural athletic superiority of blacks and their concomitant intellectual inferiority intact. It also contrives to ignore the fact that African American success is limited to specific areas. In Hall's language, the media's treatment naturalizes inequalities and normalizes failure.

While Hall would not exculpate all journalists, he would not necessarily blame them: there is a sense in which they are reflecting popular sentiments and articulating widely held beliefs. Inferential racism, as its name suggests, is communicated via inference. Its sources may not willfully convey racism, though they may imply it. The power of inferential racism lies in the manner in which it is received.

SEE ALSO: colonial discourse; Hall, Stuart; hegemony; institutional racism; language; media; National Front; neo-nazism; Powell, J. Enoch; racial coding; racist discourse; representations; scapegoat; systemic racism; Tyson, Mike; welfare; white backlash culture

Reading

Darwin's Athletes: How sport has damaged black America and preserved the myth of race by John Hoberman (Houghton Mifflin, 1997) is the study referred in the main text above.

"The whites of their eyes" by Stuart Hall, in *Silver Linings* edited by G. Bridges and R. Brunt (Lawrence & Wishart, 1981), is perhaps the author's clearest account of inferential racism.

"Race, articulation and societies structured in dominance" by Stuart Hall in the 1980 UNESCO publication *Sociological Trends: Race and colonialism*, is a much-anthologized essay that influenced a generation of researchers.

CHECK: internet resources section under racism

INSTITUTIONAL RACISM

Institutional racism refers to the anonymous operation of racist discrimination in associations, organizations, unions, professions, or even whole societies. It is anonymous in that individuals can deny the charge of racism and absolve themselves from responsibility. Yet, if a pattern of exclusion persists, then the causes are to be sought in the institutions of which they are part, the unspoken assumptions on which those organizations base their practices, and the unquestioned principles they may use. The term was popularized in 1999 after the Macpherson Report on the case of the murdered black student Stephen Lawrence used institutional racism to describe the methods and practices of London's Metropolitan Police. Its origins are deeper however.

The term itself was introduced in 1967 by black activists Stokely Carmichael and Charles V. Hamilton in *Black Power: The politics of liberation in America* (Penguin). Racism is "pervasive" and "permeates society on both the individual and institutional level, covertly and overtly," they wrote. Later writers, such as Douglas Glasgow, sought to restrict the use of the concept to express the fact that, in the 1960s and 1970s "[t]he 'for colored' and 'whites only' signs of the thirties and forties had been removed, but the institutions of the country [United States] were more completely saturated with covert expressions of racism than ever" (in *The Black Underclass*, Jossey Bass, 1980). Glasgow wrote further: "Institutional racism (which involves ghetto residents, inner-city educational institutions, police arrests, limited success models, undernourished aspirations, and limited opportunity) does not only produce lowered investment and increased self-protective maneuvers, it destroys motivation and, in fact, produces occupationally obsolete young men ready for underclass encapsulation."

On these accounts, institutional racism is to be camouflaged to the point where its specific causes are virtually undetectable, but its effects are visible in its results. The racism itself is concealed in the procedures of industries, political parties, schools, etc. Defining it as inclusively as this makes institutional racism a resonant term and one which has gained currency of late. But its generic status has invited criticism about its lack of specificity and, therefore, its limited usefulness as a tool of analysis.

While the concept was either alluded to or explicitly recognized in academic literature, its use was often imprecise. Beyond academic discourse it was known only vaguely, at least until Macpherson's application. Widely quoted by the British media, Macpherson offered a new definition in section 6.24 (page 28) of his report:

A collective failure of an organisation to provide an appropriate and professional service to people because of their colour, culture or ethnic origin. It [institutional racism] can be seen or detected in processes, attitudes and behaviour which amount to discrimination through unwitting prejudice, ignorance, thoughtlessness and racist stereotyping which disadvantage minority ethnic people. It persists because of the failure of the organisation openly and adequately to recognise and address its existence and causes by policy, example and leadership.

In this construction, the vital element was that racism and all its cognitive and behavioral constituents were "unwitting," unintentional, or inadvertent. This induced a plethora of large-scale British organizations to own up to the fact that they, like the police, may be "institutionally racist," in the sense of not knowing that racism operated. Macpherson offered a definition that exculpated organizations that may have discriminated habitually but without any individual or group of individuals realizing this was the case. Even "enlightened" organizations such as religious and educational institutions could own up to racism with relative impunity.

Because institutional racism highlights the consequences rather than causes of racism, it tends to absolve individuals from responsibility and lay blame on the entire organization. From some perspectives, this is a strength: for example, by capturing the manner in which whole societies, or sections of society, are affected by racism, or perhaps racist legacies, long after racist individuals have disappeared. The racism that remains may be unrecognized and unintentional, but, if never disclosed, it continues uninterrupted. But its strength is, from a different viewpoint, also its source of weakness: an accusation of institutional racism may allow everyone to escape; only the abstract institution is blameworthy. Critics insist that institutions are, when all is said and done, the product of human

endeavors and it is a category mistake to suppose that *institutional* racism is a *cause* (i.e. terms from uncombinable categories are put together). Some, like Gurchand Singh, argue that its uncritical use means "that social researchers do not even begin to identify causal relationships that structure 'black' inequality."

Conceptual criticism apart, institutional racism has demonstrated practical value in highlighting the need for positive, continuous action in expunging racial discrimination rather than assuming it will fade. Even organizations committed to "worthy" causes, which would seem to complement the efforts of civil rights and equal opportunities, are bound to inspect their own procedures for ensuring equality of opportunities and outcomes, as a case in 1990 in Washington, DC indicates. Eight major national environmental organizations, including the Natural Resources Defense Council, the Wilderness Society, and the Sierra Club, were charged by civil rights group with racism in their hiring practices. None of the leaders of any of the organizations were African American or Latino and few of the middle managers were from minority groups; of 315 staff members of the Audubon Society, three were black. Friends of the Earth's staff of forty included five minority workers. The Natural Resources Defense Council had five ethnic minority staff out of 140. The Sierra Club had one Latino among 250 staff.

The accused organizations' reaction was typical; the claim that there was a scarcity of black or Hispanic people among the pool of trained environmental specialists. The organizations added that they were not aware of the "whiteness of the green movement" and would implement a "concerted effort" to remedy the imbalance (*New York Times*, February 1, 1990).

In none of the attacks on the organizations were individuals singled out, nor were any motives imputed. No one was actually accused of refusing to appoint or promote anyone on racist grounds. Criticisms were based on clinical analysis of figures, with the result that institutional racism was found, in this case, in unlikely settings. This was an example of how accusations of institutional racism can crystallize awareness and promote more aggressive attempts to discourage it. Other examples of institutional racism that have come to light in recent years include:

- The credit policies of banks and lending institutions that prevent the granting of mortgages to people living in neighborhoods densely populated by ethnic minorities.
- Seniority rules when applied to jobs historically occupied by whites, that make more recently appointed ethnic minorities (and females) more subject to dismissal ("last in, first out" policies) and least eligible for advancement (the "glass ceiling").
- Restrictive employment leave policies, coupled with prohibition on part-time work or denials of fringe benefits to part-timers that make it difficult for the heads of single-parent families, most of whom are women, and a disproportionately high amount of them of African descent, to get and keep jobs and maintain a family.
- Implementing height requirements that are unnecessarily and unintentionally geared to the physical proportions of white males and so exclude certain ethnic minorities from jobs.
- Using standardized academic tests or criteria that are geared to the cultural and educational norms of middle-class white males and are not relevant indicators of the ability to perform a job successfully.

Institutional racism has become central in the contemporary race and ethnic relations vocabulary and, despite its conceptual elasticity, has shown utility in analyzing how institutions can operate along racist lines without acknowledging or even recognizing this and how such operations can persist in the face of official policies geared to removal of discrimination.

SEE ALSO: Diallo case, the Amadou; inferential racism; Lawrence case, the Stephen; policing; representations; social work; systemic racism; violence; white backlash culture

Reading

"Black power" by Stokely Carmichael and Charles Hamilton, in *Racism: Essential readings*, edited by Ellis Cashmore and James Jennings (Sage, 2001), is an extract from the source text and is set in context by the other readings in this volume, all of which conceptualize racism.
"The concept and context of institutional racism" by Gurchand Singh, in *After Macpherson: Policing after the Stephen Lawrence inquiry*, edited by Alan Marlow and Barry Loveday (Russell House, 2000), is a thorough examination of the concept's various uses and criticisms which concludes that, while flawed,

"It is useful in directing our attention to how racist discourses can become embodied within the structures and organisations of society."
Institutional Racism and the Police: Fact or fiction, edited by David G. Green (2000) and *Racist Murder and Pressure Group Politics: The Macpherson Report and the police* by Norman Dennis, George Edos, and Ahmed Al-Shahi (2000) are both published by the Institute for the Study of Civil Society, in London, and present critical evaluations of the concept, particularly in the context of the Lawrence Case.
"The life and times of institutional racism" by Jenny Bourne (in *Race and Class*, vol. 43, no. 2, 2001) offers a way of understanding the concept in the interplay with the larger culture of state racism.
CHECK: internet resources section under racism

INTEGRATION

This describes a condition in which different ethnic groups are able to maintain group boundaries and uniqueness while participating equally in the essential processes of production, distribution and government. Cultural diversity is sustained without the implication that some groups will have greater access to scarce resources than others. For a society to be fully integrated, it must remove ethnic hierarchies, which permit differential access, and it must encourage all groups' contributions to the social whole.

In Britain, integration has been a policy ideal since 1966, when the then Home Secretary Roy Jenkins defined it as "not a flattening process of assimilation, but as equal opportunity accompanied by cultural diversity in an atmosphere of mutual tolerance." The contrast with assimilation is important: far from facilitating an absorption of one culture by another, integration entails the retention or even strengthening of differences of ethnic groups. The popular metaphor for assimilation has been the melting pot; for integration, it is the salad bowl, with each ingredient, separable and distinguishable, but no less valuable than the others. (Canada has favored the concept of an ethnic mosaic, with the different pieces of society joined together in one arrangement.)

In the USA, integration is used synonymously with pluralism, specifically "equalitarian pluralism" as Martin Marger once called it, in which balance and cohesion are maintained among the various groups and there are no ethnic minorities because there are no ethnic hierarchies. In a sense, ethnic groups become political interest groups that compete for society's rewards. But these competitive differences do not lead necessarily to conflict: they are dealt with by "reasonable give and take within the context of the consensual mores of society," according to Marger (in *Race and Ethnic Relations*, 2nd edn., Wadsworth, 1991). Group differences are never threatened because mutual respect for such differences is an essential part of the social order and there need only be an agreement about the governing framework in which the production and distribution of scarce resources is fairly handled and in which the law is operated.

In some societies, such as Belgium, Canada, and Switzerland, institutional provisions are made to ensure an ethnically proportionate distribution of resources, thus protecting cultural differences while keeping groups integrated into the whole. Integration means more than coexistence: it implies an active participation of all groups and an agreement on the appropriate methods of organizing the allocation of power, privileges, rights, goods, and services without compromising cultural differences.

In both Britain and the USA, integration remains more of an ideal than a reality. Despite a plethora of culturally distinct groups, there has been slow progress toward involving them in mainstream politics, commerce, professions and other key areas. While persistent racism has retarded the progress of integration in both contexts, groups have mobilized around their ethnic identity to force some measure of integration.

Essentially, the two main strategies employed to achieve integration have involved equalization at the point of entry into public and private domains, such as the job markets, education and training sectors and health care systems and equalization of outcome in competition for appointments and positions. The first is underpinned by the philosophy of equal opportunity, all entrants being granted equivalent chances regardless of status, success or failure being determined solely on merit. The second actively promotes inequality of opportunity, advantaging groups that have, historically, been underrepresented in particular domains as a way of balancing out the skewed effects of the past – which are invariably reflected in a preponderance of whites in positions of prestige and authority. Affirmative action, or positive discrimination as it is known outside the USA, embodies this

approach. Neither has been conspicuously successful.

SEE ALSO: affirmative action; amalgamation; assimilation; education; equal opportunity; equality; indigenous peoples; merit; multiculturalism; pluralism; segregation

Reading

The Enigma of Ethnicity: Another American dilemma by Wilbur Zelinsky (University of Iowa Press, 2001) confronts the puzzle of how to integrate in a culture of perplexing diversity.

The Ordeal of Integration: Progress and resentment in America's "racial" crisis by Orlando Patterson (Basic Civitas, 1998) understands the USA's struggle with integration as full of paradoxes arising from fundamental inequalities, and may gainfully be read with *Citizenship in Diverse Societies*, edited by Will Kymlicka and Wayne Norman (Oxford University Press, 2000), the latter providing European perspectives on the points of conflict and convergence between concerns for citizenship and cultural diversity.

Philosophies of Integration: Immigration and the idea of citizenship in France and Britain, 2nd edn. (Palgrave, 2001), compares the British ideal of the integration of diverse cultures with the French philosophy of republican integration; another case study, this time of migrant settlement and integration, is *Immigrant Integration: The Dutch case*, edited by Hans Vermeulen and Rinus Penninx (Transaction, 2001); it is also a critique of the view that assimilation is the most effective strategy to achieve upward mobility.

Race and Ethnicity in the United States: Issues and debates, edited by Stephen Steinberg (Blackwell, 2000), is a collection of essays, many of which center on the problems of achieving integration.

INTELLIGENCE

Intelligence may be described as the capacity to comprehend, understand and reason in a way that enables successful adaptation to changing environments. The issue of racial differences in intelligence has raged for well over a century, especially in relation to people of African descent. Blacks have long been regarded in the West as intellectually inferior to whites and Asians, and, starting in the nineteenth century, the racist doctrines of Joseph Arthur de Gobineau, Houston Stewart Chamberlain and others, have sought to give the stamp of scientific approval to theories of mental differences classified according to race. With World War I, when IQ tests began to be widely applied to army recruits, school pupils, and other groups in the USA, interest in

racial differences in intelligence was given another boost. Test results were used to "prove" the
inferiority not only of blacks, but also of Eastern
and Southern European immigrants.

In more recent times, the work of Arthur
Jensen and other psychometricians has kept the
controversy alive, especially Jensen's 1969 article
in the *Harvard Educational Review*, and his text,
Bias in Mental Testing (Methuen, 1980). For the
last thirty years, however, the great weight of
scientific opinion has been cast on the environmentalist side of the interpretation of group
differences in IQ test performance. Jensen has
repeatedly been attacked for asserting that black
Americans were innately inferior in certain intellectual abilities, and that some 80 percent of
the variance in IQ performance is due to heredity.

Jensen's "hereditarian" position has two principal components, which are, theoretically, separable. One consists of stating that the heritability
of *individual* intelligence is high; and the other is
to ascribe *group* differences in intelligence to
genetic factors. The second statement in no way
follows from the first. It is the consensus of most
geneticists that human intelligence is determined
by many genes, and that any assessment of such
a complex set of abilities by an IQ test is suspect.
Even if one accepts the validity of the test, to
make statements of heritability concerning such a
polygenic trait goes well beyond the scope of
modern genetics. Finally, to transpose a guess on
heritability of the individual phenotype to the
level of group differences represents another
giant leap beyond the data.

Indeed, any assessment of heritability is always
time- and situation-specific: it only holds under a
precise set of environmental conditions. The
heritability of a given trait differs widely from
group to group if environmental conditions vary
(as they clearly do for white and black Americans). In short, Jensen's conclusions are not only
based on unwarranted assumptions; they have
absolutely no standing in human genetics.

There is much evidence that Jensen is wrong in
attributing "racial" differences in IQ scores to
differences in native intelligence. Similarly disadvantaged groups, quite unrelated to Afro-
Americans, have also shown an IQ score gap of
about 10–15 points (the average white–black gap
in the USA). This includes such disparate groups
as European immigrant groups in the United
States in the earlier decades of the twentieth

century, and Oriental Jews in contemporary
Israel. Conversely, some subgroups of Afro-
Americans in the USA, notably people of recent
West Indian extraction, do considerably better
than old-stock continental Afro-Americans (who,
like West Indians, come principally from West
African populations).

Scarcely anyone denies that there is an important genetic component in phenotypic intelligence, but our rudimentary knowledge of human
genetics does not permit even an informed guess
as to degree of heritability. Perhaps the safest
conclusion is that intelligence, like other behavioral phenotypes, is 100 percent heredity and
100 percent environment. Even if heritability of
intelligence in one group could be ascertained, it
would not be the same in another group, and
within-group heritability would not be a valid
base for explaining between-group differences.

It is, of course, possible that significant differences in frequencies of genes affecting intelligence
exist between human groups, but no such differences have yet been found, nor is it plausible to
infer any from existing data. The weight of
evidence points to an environmental explanation
of intergroup differences in IQ scores. In any
case, mean differences between groups are much
smaller than individual differences within groups.
Individual differences in IQ performance are
probably attributable to a mixture of genetic
and environmental factors, in unknown proportions. Most problematic of all is the extent to
which IQ tests are a meaningful measure of
intelligence.

SEE ALSO: Chamberlain, Houston Stewart;
Darwinism; education; environmentalism;
eugenics; genotype; Gobineau, Joseph Arthur de;
hereditarianism; heritability; phenotype; race: as
synonym; science; underachievement

Reading

*The Bell Curve: Intelligence and class structure in
American life* by Richard Herrnstein and Charles
Murray (The Free Press/Simon & Schuster, 1994) is a
controversial statement on the relationship between
intelligence, race, class, and various other social
characteristics such as crime, occupation, and education.

*The Bell Curve Wars: Race, intelligence and the future
of America,* edited by Steven Fraser (Basic Books,
1995) focuses on the debates triggered by the best-
selling book and evaluates its impact on race
relations in the USA.

"How much can we boost I.Q. and scholastic achieve-

ment" by Arthur Jensen, in *Harvard Educational Review* (vol. 39, pp.1–123, 1969), is the most scholarly treatment of the hereditarian position.
CHECK: internet resources section

PIERRE L. VAN DEN BERGHE

INTERCULTURAL EDUCATION *see* multicultural education

INTERNAL COLONIALISM

A term first used by Robert Blauner to describe the situation of minorities in contemporary America. In classic colonialism, a country's native population is subjugated by a conquering colonizing group. In internal colonialism, by contrast, the colonized groups are minorities under white bureaucratic control; they have been conquered and forcibly taken to the United States, in the process having their culture depreciated or even destroyed. North American Indians and Mexicans were forced into subordinate status in much the same way as Asians, Africans, and Latin Americans were conquered by Europeans. White Americans treated native populations (Indians and Mexicans) as colonizers treated the groups they colonized.

According to Blauner, blacks, although they were not conquered and enslaved on their own land, were nevertheless conquered and forced into subordinate status in America. This experience of lack of voluntary entry into the country marks blacks, Native Americans and Mexicans off from all other migrant groups: Europeans who enter the USA voluntarily (whatever their motives) form an immigrant minority.

The groups conquered and colonized undergo unique experiences in the process of becoming a colonized minority: (1) they are forcibly made to exist in a society that is not their own; (2) they are subjugated to the extent that their social mobility is limited and their political involvement restricted; and (3) their own culture is depreciated or even extinguished. As a result, the colonized group becomes trapped in a caste-like situation. This, in turn, affects that group's self-conception: it accepts the "superior" ways of life of the colonizing group and tends to view itself as inferior.

Specific areas, likened to internal colonies, were the basis of segregation in all areas of urban life: politics, education, occupations, and virtually every other area of social interaction. This spatial segmentation ensured that certain groups were herded together and were therefore easier for white bureaucracy to control.

By examining how the various minority groups first came into contact with white American society, Blauner contends, we can understand their differential treatment in the generations that followed. So: colonized minorities' positions are structurally quite different from those of immigrants. Whereas Irish, Italians, Poles, and others have advanced socially (albeit in a restricted way), blacks, Native Americans, and Mexicans have not. The latter groups remain disadvantaged. Similarly, the institutions and beliefs of immigrants were never brutalized in the same way as were colonized groups. Underlying this is the fact that white racism is much more virulent when directed against colonized minorities than against immigrant groups.

Taxonomically, Blauner's thesis has many problems, not the least of which is: where do groups such as Puerto Ricans, Chinese, and Filipinos fit? The experience of these groups leads to a more fundamental conceptual problem of defining forced and voluntary migration. As Blauner's argument rests on this distinction, it may be asked whether so-called voluntary movement to America might not be precipitated by a complex of circumstances that severely limit the emigrants' alternatives. It may well be the case that the migrants' conditions are so intolerable that a migration is imperative – if only in the interests of survival. Even more extreme would be cases in which political situations actually motivate the migration. Such instances weaken the notion of involuntary movement.

Nevertheless, Blauner's model of internal colonialism has made an influential contribution to theories of race relations and has at least directed attention away from current circumstances and toward history as a starting point for investigation.

SEE ALSO: black bourgeoisie in the USA; colonialism; cultural racism; environmental racism; ghetto; Kerner Report; King case, the Rodney; migration; pluralism; policing; power; segregation; slavery

Reading

Internal Colonialism by Michael Hechter (University of California Press, 1975) accounts for the causes of nationalism in Britain between the years 1536 and

1966 by using the internal colonialism model; the author's more general explanation is given in *Containing Nationalism* (Oxford University Press, 2001). *Racial Oppression in America* by Robert Blauner (Harper & Row, 1972) is the original text in which the author sets out his important thesis; though dated, it still repays reading.

INTERNATIONAL CONVENTION

The International Convention on the Elimination of All Forms of Racial Discrimination (ICERD) is a treaty prepared under the auspices of the UN and adopted by the General Assembly in 1965. By August 2001, 158 states (including all the major powers) had acceded to it. By accession, states undertake to fulfill the obligations of the Convention and to report every two years on what they have done in fulfillment to a committee of eighteen individuals whom they themselves elect. This body, the Committee in the Elimination of Racial Discrimination (CERD), reports to the General Assembly on the outcome of its examination of state reports and there is an annual debate towards the end of the calendar year. CERD started its work in 1970.

By August 2001, thirty-four states had made declarations under article 14 of ICERD permitting persons within their territories to petition CERD if they consider that the state has failed to provide them with the protections promised under the Convention; CERD issues opinions on such petitions. This is of importance to European states because ICERD, unlike the European Convention on Human Rights, offers protections against racial discrimination in the exercise of economic rights.

SEE ALSO: human rights; international organizations; law: civil rights, USA; law: racial discrimination, international; law relations, Britain

Reading

International Action Against Racial Discrimination by Michael Banton (Clarendon Press, 1996) sets out the history of the Convention and of CERD's activities; it is updated in *Combating Racial Discrimination: the UN and its Member States* (London: Minority Rights Group International, 2000), a report that summarizes states' records of reporting under the Convention and CERD's observations on their fulfillment of their obligations.

MICHAEL BANTON

INTERNATIONAL ORGANIZATIONS

As the international organizations with responsibilities for regulating ethnic and racial relations on a global scale are described in the entry on the UN, this entry will be restricted to international organizations on the regional scale.

The governments of West European countries founded the Council of Europe (COE) in 1949 "to achieve a greater unity ... for the purpose of safeguarding and realising the ideals and principles which are their common heritage." Its statute required every member-state to "accept the principles of the rule of law and of the enjoyment by all persons within its jurisdiction of human rights and fundamental freedoms." In the following year the Council adopted the European Convention on Human Rights and Fundamental Freedoms that included, as article 14, a prohibition of racial discrimination. Persons who claim that their governments have failed to protect their rights under this Convention can appeal to the European Court of Human Rights in Strasbourg. In 1952 some of the same countries joined in the creation of common institutions for the regulation of the coal, steel and atomic energy industries, and then later for establishing a common market. In 1993, following upon the Maastricht Treaty, these countries formed the EU. The Conference on Security and Cooperation in Europe, convened on a proposal from the USSR in Helsinki in 1972–75, adopted a Final Act that included declarations about cooperation in humanitarian fields. In 1994 it became the Organization for Security and Co-operation in Europe (OSCE). There are therefore three chief regional organizations in Europe. The OSCE is the largest, including among its fifty-three member-states, the USA, Canada, the Russian Federation, and states of the former USSR stretching to Uzbekistan and Tajikistan; it has a special orientation to security. The COE, with forty-two member-states, is much concerned with human rights and has established a European Commission against Racism and Intolerance (ECRI) that reviews state compliance with COE conventions. The EU, with fifteen members, is starting to construct a constitution of its own with a common citizenship in order to supplement its orientation towards economic relations. It has adopted directives on the equal treatment of persons irrespective of racial or ethnic origin that can be enforced by the Court of Justice in Luxembourg.

International organizations in other regions are following a similar course, notably those established by the Organization of American States, like the Inter-American Indian Institute. An American Declaration on the Rights of Indigenous Peoples is under active consideration. The Inter-American Commission on Human Rights issues country reports and receives complaints alleging violations of the Inter-American Convention on Human Rights. The Inter-American Court of Human Rights issues opinions on whether such complaints disclose any failure on the part of a government to give effect to its obligations under the Convention. The Court in 2000 ruled upon the mass deportations of Haitians from the Dominican Republic, which involved what many regard as elements of racial discrimination. In a landmark judgment of September 2001 the Court affirmed the existence of indigenous peoples' collective rights to their land, resources, and environment by declaring that the rights to property and judicial protection of the Mayagna Community of Awas Tingni had been violated by the government of Nicaragua when it granted concessions to a foreign company to fell trees on that community's traditional land without consulting them or securing their consent. The Court ordered the government to demarcate and recognize the title of the Mayagna and other communities to their traditional lands, to submit biannual reports on measures taken to comply with the Court's decision, and to pay compensation and legal costs.

The Organization of African Unity (OAU) in 1981 adopted the African Charter of Human and Peoples' Rights that provided for the establishment of a Commission and a Court of Human and Peoples' Rights. In 2002 the OAU was reconstituted as the African Union. African states are beginning to submit periodic reports to the Commission, to send high-powered delegations to speak for them when necessary and to take heed of its conclusions. As the states of the Asia-Pacific region constitute the largest and most diverse of the UN's regional groups, it is little wonder if they have greater difficulty in agreeing upon common action. Nevertheless, they are moving in the same direction, helped by the UN's strategy for strengthening national capacities for the promotion and protection of human rights.

SEE ALSO: globalization; human rights; International Convention; law: civil rights, USA; law: racial discrimination, international; law relations, Britain; UNESCO; United Nations

Reading

www.ecri.coe.fr
www.oas.org
www.oau.org.

MICHAEL BANTON

INTOLERANCE *see* bigotry; prejudice

INVISIBLE MAN

Ralph Ellison's novel, *Invisible Man*, was published in 1952. This novel is full of symbolism that captures the socioeconomic and racial hierarchal structure of the USA. The invisibility of the narrator symbolizes what it means to be a black man in a society that is both capitalist and race conscious. He details his invisibility not only to the white power structure, but also to those of his own race. The protagonist battles, through allegory and symbolism, with issues of the slavery and emancipation of African Americans and the betrayal of the US democratic system to these now free individuals. He tackles issues such as integration and nonviolence (when he gives an impromptu speech against rioting) and black nationalism. There are two consistent themes running throughout the book: one is a sense of betrayal, individually and collectively, and second is the quest for enlightenment – that is, for freedom. These two themes can actually summarize the life of African Americans. In essence this is a book of social protest – a man in search of equality in order to gain his visibility.

The opening of the novel tells the story of a man living underground in a place that is filled with 1,369 light bulbs, which are fueled by stolen power. This symbolizes a man in search of enlightenment, in search of the methods and techniques to deal with the invisibility that has been cast on him by a sociopolitical structure that fails to recognize and value his contributions. From there the invisible man begins to tell the tale of the circumstances and situations that led him to this state of hibernation. The story is told in the first person, by an unnamed protagonist. The nameless narrator details his lessons in disillusionment as he encounters life as a black boy in the South and as a black man in the North.

Invisible Man opens with a tale that captures the essence of race relations in the USA. The narrator tells the story of a young black boy who has been awarded a scholarship by some whites in a Southern town. A group of young men, including the Invisible Man, is forced to watch a nude white woman, with a tattoo of the American flag on her belly, perform a seductive dance. The nude white woman symbolically serves to psychologically castrate black men. She also captures much of the legacy of lynching in the South in the post-emancipation period, where black men would be hanged for the mere appearance of looking at a white woman. After watching the dancer, the young men are forced to engage in a battle royal, where they fight among themselves, blindfolded. These young boys are then "rewarded" with fake gold pieces scattered on an electrified rug. Ellison uses this tale to tell the story of how black men are pitted against each other and are apparently rewarded with fake societal benefits. Upon the completion of the battle royal, the valedictorian, who is Invisible Man, is then forced to give a speech with a mouth full of blood on "social responsibility" as he is laughed at by a roomful of whites. Eventually he is given a briefcase and awarded a scholarship to a black college in the South.

Invisible Man's experience at the black educational institution further highlights how the social structure pits blacks against each other and perpetuates white superiority. Over time this becomes institutionalized and taught. The nameless narrator is expelled from school by a black president, a race leader who advocates the strategy of saying "yes sir" to whites and confirming their false sense of reality. Mr. Bledsoe, the black president of a black college, adopted the plantation/slave master mentality, in his "training" of young black men and instructed them to lie to please the white man. After being expelled, and given a letter that recommends that he not be employed, Invisible Man ends up in Harlem, New York.

In Harlem, he is exploited by the capitalist system, as are so many African Americans who were pushed out of the South and pulled into the North by racism. The symbolism of Invisible Man's employment at Liberty Paints captures much of the racial, and economic tensions in the US. Liberty Paints represents a patriotic devotion to the free market system and the maintenance of white supremacy. The physical plant is adorned in flags, and a screaming eagle is the company's trademark. Liberty Paints prides itself on providing America with the whitest white paint, which by the way is manufactured by a black man. While in Harlem, Invisible Man also encounters the Communist Party, which Ralph Ellison refers to as the "Brotherhood." As a member of the Party, Invisible Man is used as a tool for the achievement of the Party's goals at the expense of the black community. Not only does he encounter this white group, but Invisible Man must also deal with black nationalists as captured by Ras, the Exhorter. The clash of these distinct ideological groups, the communists focused on class issues and the nationalists focused on race, results in the uprising in Harlem. Interestingly, the uprising occurs on the Fourth of July and results in the demolition of a thriving black community, a community known as the mecca of black intellectuals and artists. This race riot results in Invisible Man retreating from society, withdrawing from relationships with both blacks and whites, and withdrawing from the society that refuses to recognize him.

Invisible Man is a book about the emotional and intellectual perils faced by educated African Americans, specifically African American males. It is a book that challenges the status quo; that challenges democracy, capitalism, and the social construction of race. Ralph Ellison explores, on many different levels, social norms of the United States, especially racialized social norms. Ellison informs the reader that the search for visibility among African Americans is not simply limited to them, but that it permeates the fabric of American society. He suggests that the search for visibility is synonymous with the search for humanity.

SEE ALSO: African Americans; Black Panther Party; Black Power; consumption; double consciousness; Jackson, Michael; Jordan, Michael; Malcolm X; Million Man March; minstrelsy; Motown; Nation of Islam; riots: USA, 1965–67; Thomas, Clarence; tokenism; Tyson, Mike; whiteness

Reading

The Critical Response to Ralph Ellison, edited by Robert J. Butler (Greenwood, 2000), offers early and current reviews and provides an analysis of Ellison's short fiction and nonfiction work.

JULIA S. JORDAN-ZACHERY

IRISH

The Irish emigrant experience can only be understood by recognizing the dramatic impact that centuries of British colonialism has had on the Irish people. As a result of its geographical position and internal political feuds Ireland became the first English colony.

Colonization

Although the Normans established settlements in the twelfth century, it was not until the sixteenth century that systematic colonization took place under the Tudors and their successors. While the Normans had been eventually assimilated into traditional Gaelic society, the sixteenth-century invaders were not. As a result of England's break with Catholicism, the common link between the two countries was finally broken. Consequently, religion became the mechanism whereby colonizer was distinguishable from colonized. This was exacerbated by the fact that significant numbers of Scottish and English Protestant settlers were subsequently given the lands of native Catholics by the English Crown, most notably in the province of Ulster. The native Irish were depicted as savage heathens who were "more uncivill, more uncleanly, more barbarous and more brutish in their customs and demeanours, than in any other part of the world that is known."

Consequently, it was justified through military conquest and legislation such as the 1697 Penal Laws to deprive the native population of their religious, civil and land rights. By the beginning of the eighteenth century, almost 90 percent of the land was in the hands of non-Catholics of foreign origin. Virtually the only legal way that Catholics could retain ownership of their land was through renouncing their religion.

For the majority of the Irish population – the peasantry – colonialism brought destitution. An English agricultural reformer, Arthur Young, compared the position of the Irish peasantry in the late eighteenth century to that of slavery. They subsisted on one crop, the potato, while the rest of the crops they produced were exported. When the crop failed between 1845 and 1849 it is estimated that 1.5 million died of starvation and disease. There is a school of thought that insists that Ireland did not suffer from famine but from genocide caused by the *laissez-faire* principles of the British government. The prime minister of the period, Lord Russell, stated, "it must be thoroughly understood that we cannot feed the people." There can be little doubt that the famine resulted from the nature of the economic system fostered under colonialism. Of all the countries in northwestern Europe, only in Ireland did such a large percentage of the population depend on one crop for their daily survival.

The famine had drastic consequences for Irish society. Military force and repressive legislation had never resulted in acceptance of colonization by the Irish. However, the sheer magnitude of the disaster undermined the infrastructure of a distinctive Gaelic culture and generated collective trauma. For example, the Gaelic language, the medium of that culture, was virtually wiped out because the famine impacted so severely in the geographical areas where it had been extensively used.

Mass emigration also became part of the Irish experience. Although migration to Britain had existed for centuries it had been seasonal. And of course many Irish found their way to Australia, mainly as convicts. However, between 1841 and 1861, half a million Irish settled in Britain. Of even more significance was the fact that between 1846 and 1861 approximately 900,000 migrated to North America and by 1860 the Irish population had leapt to 1.5 million. Many Irish did not survive the desperate journey across the Atlantic in "coffin ships." In 1848, for example, of the 100,000 who left for Canada, 17,000 died on the journey and 20,000 died soon after their arrival. On Grosse Island, an immigrant landing station in Quebec, an inscription reads: "In this secluded spot lies the mortal remains of 5,294 persons, who flying from pestilence and famine in Ireland in the year 1847, found in America but a grave." On the other side of the border, on Deer Island (Boston Bay) where Irish immigrants were quarantined, 1,000 are buried in paupers' graves. This tragic Irish diaspora lasted until 1921.

In both Britain and North America the Irish endured anti-Catholic hostility and were accused of taking jobs, undercutting wages, creating slums, and being political troublemakers. Anti-Irish cartoons in magazines such as *Punch*, supported by respectable writers such as Charles Kingsley, Thomas Carlyle and Elizabeth Gaskell, depicted them as being a less evolutionarily developed race. Kingsley stated that, "to see white chimpanzees is dreadful; if they were black, one would not feel it so much, but their skins, except where tanned by exposure, are as white as ours." The American historian, Edward A. Freeman, commented that "This would be a grand country if only every Irishman would kill a Negro and be hanged for it." It is in this context of Irishophobia that the racist caricature of the unpredictable, drunken, violent, ignorant "Paddy" was established. Their supposed wildness meant that writers questioned whether the Irish could ever be assimilated into civilized society. Anti-Irish riots occurred in many towns in Britain and the USA during the nineteenth century.

However, the Irish in America did adapt and did find mechanisms for resistance and assimilation, something that they did not manage to do in Britain. Because of their urban concentration, their domination of municipal services such as the police and the fire service, their transformation into an urban proletariat, and their mastery of the Anglo-Saxon democratic process, the Irish in America were able to build powerful Democratic political machines in many cities that enabled them to gain respectability in society, challenge their WASP opponents and establish their socioeconomic superiority in relation to other racial and ethnic groups. It is argued that the election of John F. Kennedy represented the final assimilation of the Irish into respectable American society and signed the seal on the notion of the fully white Irish American. Kennedy's election removed any lingering sense of social inferiority and insecurity. But many believe that President Kennedy, and his brother, were assassinated precisely because they were Irish Americans.

The construction of Irishness

Throughout this complex process of generational transition, adaptation and assimilation many Irish never forgot their homeland. These reluctant exiles carried with them a lasting sense of banishment, a hatred of the English, and a romanticization of the Emerald Isle. It is hardly surprising that the Irish communities in America provided recruits, money and support for successive revolts against the English presence in Ireland. In many respects, notions of Irishness as a

clear ethnic identity in America were constructed in opposition to Englishness.

Ireland was dramatically affected by its colonial experience. In 1922, as a result of the war of independence, the country was partitioned. This seriously damaged the national psyche, and hindered the process of decolonization and the construction of a postcolonial national identity. In the six counties of Ulster the descendants of the seventeenth-century settlers consciously created "a protestant state for a protestant people." Catholic minorities were deprived of their basic civil rights and suffered systematic discrimination. In the late 1960s, using methods borrowed from the American civil rights movement, Catholics challenged the status quo and triggered a violent sectarian struggle over the existence of Northern Ireland that lasted until the signing of the Good Friday Agreement in 1998.

Partition also had considerable consequences for the rest of Ireland. The Ulster Crisis threatened the stability of the Irish Republic because of the possibility of the violence spilling over the border. Economically, Partition deprived the Republic of its most industrialized region and successive governments had to deal with the consequences of colonial underdevelopment of the rest of the country. As a result the only product that the country exported was successive generations of its young people. During the 1980s and early 1990s for example, because of the state of the Irish economy tens of thousands emigrated for mainland Europe, America and Australia. Fortunately, the threatened demographic decimation of Irish towns and villages was blocked by the emergence of the fully Europeanized and globalized and highly successful Celtic Tiger economy. For the first time population movement of the Irish would be much more fluid, moving back and forth rather than immigration for good.

This new diaspora demographically revitalized existing Irish communities and contributed to a simultaneous resurrecting and re-imagining of Irish cultural identity Ironically, this has triggered yet another culture war over the nature of Irishness. On one side are those who yearn for a clearly defined, authentic Irish identity and condemn what they see as crass "shamrockery" and global "Paddywhackery." On the other are those who condemn essentialization and wish to celebrate all aspects of *being Irish*, including St. Patrick's Day Parades, the Boston Celtics, the

Fighting Irish of Notre Dame, the Irish theme pub, Ned Kelly, *The Quiet Man*, *Angela's Ashes* etc., in the hope that this will facilitate diverse, postcolonial, postnational, postmodern constructions and cultural markers of Irishness appropriate to twenty-first-century realities.

SEE ALSO: assimilation; bigotry; colonialism; cultural identity; culturecide; diaspora; empowerment; essentialism; ethnocide; genocide; globalization; migration; Other; postcolonial; race: as synonym; racialization; slavery; social Darwinism; stereotype; systemic racism; white race

Reading

Irish America: Coming into clover, by M. Dezell (Doubleday Books 2001), provides a systematic overview of the Irish American experience.
The Irish Diaspora by A. Bielenberg (Cork University Press, 2000) is a comprehensive theorization of the diasporic experience.
The Irish Worldwide: History, heritage, identity, edited by P. O'Sullivan (St. Martin's Press, 1992), remains an important interdisciplinary reference point for the Irish abroad. The key volumes are as follows:

Volume 1: Patterns of Immigration
Volume 2: The Irish in New Communities
Volume 3: The Creative Immigrant
Volume 4: Irish Women and Irish Migration
Volume 5: Religion and Identity
Volume 6: The Meaning of the Famine

New Perspectives on the Irish Diaspora, edited by C. Fanning (Southern Illinois Press, 2000), is an overview of key research by North American scholars.

EUGENE MCLAUGHLIN

ISLAMOPHOBIA

Islamophobia has been defined by the Runnymede Trust as "an outlook or world-view involving an unfounded dread and dislike of Muslims, which results in practices of exclusion and discrimination." The Trust's 1997 report *Islamophobia: A challenge for us all* gave the term its currency although, as the authors argued, it already had a presence in the British Muslim community due to Muslim experiences of discrimination. Its first documented use in the USA was in 1991, when *Insight* (February 4, 1991) used it in relation to Russia's activities in Afghanistan.

The Runnymede Trust argued that a new term was necessary both for: (1) describing the experience of groups who fall outside the categories (of race) used to monitor discrimination and inequality resulting in structural disadvantage; and (2) for the existence of Islamophobia to be recognized and challenged. The report argued that Islamophobia consists of "closed views" of Islam, which do not constitute legitimate criticism, and characterize Islam as separatist, monolithic, inferior, and a manipulative enemy that rejects any criticisms made by the West. In this conception, Western hostility is justified and Islamophobia is "normal." Islamophobia is evident in the discrimination experienced by Muslims in employment, health, education and their exclusion from politics.

History and political context

Islamophobia is often seen to have its origins in Orientalism, an ideological process by which, according to Edward Said, eastern cultures have been constructed as Other by the West allowing for their domination (see Said's *Orientalism*, Penguin, 1978). The institutional reproduction of this discourse has resulted in its naturalization. However, we should not see Islamophobia as part of an unbroken history of incompatibility: aspects of Orientalism have been reworked and reinvested with new significance at different historical moments and for different functional reasons. While there are continuities with historical anti-Muslim feelings, Islamophobia is not just an extension of previous forms.

It is as a result of contemporary political, economic and social processes that Islam has become a globally salient issue. This is attributed to shifts in the global power equation with the collapse of communism, which has led to anxieties and attempts by the West to maintain its hegemony. Political Islam, which has emerged out of different experiences of colonialism and oppression – its initial signifier being the Iranian Revolution, 1979 – has allowed "the West" to construct Islam as the new enemy (a global force which represents an ideological and physical threat) based on a "clash of civilizations" thesis. This has been necessary for "the West" to both reassert its power over an economically rich area and in so doing to defend its supreme Western identity.

Several events in Britain, beginning in the early 1980s, pushed Islam into the national arena. These included the Salman Rushdie Affair, of 1989, which was precipitated by the *fatwa* that followed the publication of the author's *The Satanic Verses*, a text that was interpreted by some Muslims as heretical and which prompted the author to go into hiding for fear of his life. Earlier, in 1984, Raymond Honeyford, then head teacher of Drummond Middle School in Bradford, Yorkshire, sparked controversy by writing an article in the right-wing magazine *The Salisbury Review* in which he asserted a that a gulf in values between white pupils and their South Asian counterparts was threatening British schooling. South Asian pupils constituted about 90 percent of his school's population. The article started a *cause célèbre*.

These events raised questions amongst dominant groups about the ability of Muslims to integrate. Attempts by Muslims to preserve their culture and exercise their liberal rights have been interpreted as separatism and perceived as a threat to what are seen as traditional British values. The responses have increased the desire for cultural autonomy by Muslims and resulted in their politicization. The result has been a strengthening of *cultural racism* whereby religion and culture (rather than color or origins) constitute the dominant signifiers of the Other, forcing Muslims into a central target position for these forms of discrimination. Extreme right-wing, including neo-nazi, groups have responded to these circumstances by adopting a form of racism which argues that separation has already occurred and is driven by cultural rather than racial disparities. In other words, difference is based on religion: Islam.

Successive attempts by Muslim groups to secure laws against religious discrimination have been rejected in favor of freedom of speech. Because Muslims do not constitute a race and Islam is a religion of many nationalities and races, they are not protected under the Race Relations Act in the UK.

Additionally, the increasing visibility of Muslims to non-Muslims in a global mediated world, within which Muslims are homogenized, has resulted in their construction as a threat to non-Muslims. This ideology allows Muslims to be suppressed, the practical consequences of which are experiences of discrimination.

Evidence of discrimination

Current statistics show that Muslims in Britain are severely disadvantaged in relation to other groups. It is important to note, however, that many of these statistics have been compiled through the 1991 British census which, having no question on religious affiliation, have been calculated through the conflation of ethnic groups and countries of origin (and results in an estimation of the Muslim population in Britain varying between 1.5 and 2.5 million). This usually includes mainly Bangladeshis and Pakistanis (approximately 95 percent of whom are Muslim) along with a percentage of people of Middle Eastern, North African and Indian origin (obscuring white Muslims). Also, as The Runnymede Trust suggest, other statistics, such as those provided by the Prison Chaplaincy Service, which show an increase in Muslim prisoners in England and Wales of 40 percent between 1991–95, may be distorted by changes in self-definition.

Nevertheless, those statistics show the extent of Muslim disadvantage. At the time of the Gulf war, there was evidence for an increase in racially motivated crime towards South Asians in Britain. For example, statistics from the British Crime Survey of 1996 show that nearly a third of Pakistani respondents who have been victims of crime recorded their attacks as racially motivated, compared to just under a fifth of Indians and 14 percent of Afro Caribbeans. For Pakistanis this rose to 70 percent in relation to threats. A *Guardian*/ICM (June 17, 2002) poll of 500 British Muslims found 1 in 3 have experienced personal abuse because of their faith, a situation which 61 percent said has deteriorated since the attacks on New York and Washington on September 11, 2001.

This has also been the case across Europe according to the EU's watchdog, the European Monitoring Centre on Racism and Xenophobia (EUMC), which has found increasing evidence of Islamophobia in the form of physical and verbal abuse and attacks on property across its fifteen member-states. One of the problems of this approach is that it is difficult to differentiate or distinguish racism from Islamophobia. In fact, it is highly probable that the perpetrators of racial violence are not aware of the religious affiliation of their victims, and vice versa. It is likely, however, that in the current climate there has been a convergence of these hostilities, and evidence bears witness to this. One example, provided by The Runnymede Trust, is the nine Muslim names present in the list of thirteen racist and religious murders which took place between 1992 and 1993. Another, the attacks that took place on Sikh men following September 11 as reported by the EUMC.

In education, both Bangladeshi and Pakistani children are underachieving as a recent OFSTED (Office for Standards in Education) survey shows. In 1998 an average of 31 percent achieved grade A–C in their GCSEs compared to 47 percent of white pupils and 54 percent of Indian. Bangladeshi and Pakistani groups combined accounted for only 2.8 percent of entrants into higher education in 1998, compared to 89.8 percent of whites and 4 percent of Indians.

Various studies by the Cabinet Office (2002), TUC (Trade Union Congress, 2002), Home Office (2001) and the Policy Studies Institute (1997) have examined the complex factors which result in employment disadvantage for Muslims. The 2001 Labour Force Survey reported that 24.6 percent of Bangladeshis and 16 percent of Pakistanis were out of work compared to 5.4 percent of white people. These studies show that those Muslims who are in work tend to occupy low income, low status positions but are underrepresented at every level of employment.

Muslims continue to be discriminated against in the allocation of facilities such as housing. The Guardian/IMC poll found that 43 percent of Bangladeshis live in council housing and 54 percent of Bangladeshi and Pakistani homes receive income support, both higher than the national average. Their overall standards of living and health are therefore lower than other groups. These statistics provide evidence for the severe social exclusion of Muslims in Britain.

Media representation as a case study

The media has received particular scrutiny as a perpetrator of Islamophobia. Its role in the production of institutional and dominant discourses has resulted in the demonization of Islam, portraying it as a threat to Western interests, and sustaining the ideology necessary to subjugate Muslims both internationally and domestically. There is now significant evidence which demonstrates the negativization of Muslims in the media across Europe and in the USA. However, it should be noted that the form that

this takes varies according to differing political circumstances and motivations. For example, a study of the representations of British Muslims in the British press, which examined articles quantitatively from 1994–2000 and prominent stories from 1997 qualitatively, found Muslims are generally underrepresented. Coverage of Islam amounts to about 2,000 articles a year, in total, in the newspapers The Times and the Guardian, only 10 percent of which are about British Muslims. The reporting of Islam globally, therefore, accounts for 0.7 percent of The Times' total coverage and 1.7 percent of the Guardian's, whilst coverage of British Muslims accounts for just 0.16 percent of The Times' total annual copy compared to 0.28 percent of that of the Guardian.

The research uncovered the negative and reductive framing of events that illustrate Muslim attempts to gain legal redress for their socioeconomic disadvantage. This included attention to the funding of Muslim schools and the teaching of religious education within them; attempts to bring about legislation on religious discrimination (often interpreted as extending the blasphemy laws which allowed the Rushdie Affair to be invoked); attacks on Muslim attempts to enter politics (with the vilification of the first Muslim Member of Parliament, Mohammed Sarwar); a disproportionate focus on the relationships of mainly Muslim (often non-British) men with British non-Muslim women who then convert and are subject to abuse; and finally the activities of extremists in the UK involved in, for example, raising funds for Islamist groups abroad. Together, these stories express broadly similar themes:

- Muslims are a threat to security in the UK and, indeed, the USA due to their involvement in deviant activities.
- Muslims are a threat to "mainstream" values and thus provoke integrative concerns.
- There are inherent cultural differences between Muslims and the non-Islamic traditions which create tensions in interpersonal relations.

However, there was also evidence of the increasing strides made by Muslims to achieve recognition in public life, in education and politics for example, with the image of the "loyal citizen." Unfortunately, since September 11, it appears that coverage of the "enemy within" has dominated. The image of the "loyal citizen" thus functions to position Muslims as one or the other, and forces conformity if they do not wish to be seen as extremist.

Whilst this would appear to justify accusations of Islamophobia in the media, such a stance is problematic if we understand it to be based on the intentional bias of journalists. Simplification occurs as a result of a combination of a liberal secular media which fails to understand religious identity, cultural ignorance and institutional constraints in producing copy.

Current context

Media coverage which questions the loyalty of British Muslims, which has intensified since September 11, has contributed to a climate where repressive policies can be enacted without public dissent. Security measures, for example the British Anti-Terrorism, Crime and Security Act, which was passed through Parliament in December 2001, has particular implications for minority groups in relation to increased police powers to detain suspects for indefinite periods without charge. The only part of this legislation which potentially favored minority groups – the religious discrimination laws – was again withdrawn in order to ensure consent to the rest of the Bill.

The increase in the activity of far right, neo-nazi groups in Britain, who have been explicit in targeting Muslims for scapegoating (equally evident across Europe and for which September 11 supplied further ammunition to manipulate fears), combined with experiences of violence, poverty and dislocation, gave rise to a series of disturbances involving South Asian (mainly Muslim) communities in impoverished northern towns in Britain in the summer of 2001. Again, rather than provoke more liberal policies, the government has responded by resurrecting an assimilationist model of multiculturalism, demonstrated by the Home Secretary's proposals that immigrants should swear their allegiance to Britain and take citizenship classes.

However, there have also been several initiatives that draw on the sixty recommendations the Runnymede report made. For example, following the report's release an umbrella body, the Muslims Council of Britain, was set up in order to represent Muslims in the public sphere, to lobby government and other institutions. More recently FAIR (the Forum against Islamophobia and Racism) was established to monitor media coverage and has been active in challenging examples of Islamophobia through dialog with media organizations. Following September 11, a number of cultural events have been launched to promote good relations including Islam Awareness Week in November 2001 and the Best of British Islam Festival which ran from March to August 2002. However, these activities have been initiated mainly by the victims of Islamophobia. There is still a long way to go in offering Muslims political legitimization (this has not occurred when seen to inconvenience the majority).

Xenophobia and "anti-Muslimism"

The Runnymede Trust has been successful in that the term Islamophobia is now widely recognized and used, though many right-wing commentators either reject its existence or argue that it is justified. However, now becoming a catch-all label to describe any kind of harassment involving Muslims, it should not be considered unproblematic.

The *Guardian*, for example, claims that its poll is evidence of "high levels of Islamophobia" in Britain. Yet we have already questioned how far the anti-Islamic and xenophobia overlap. For example, a spokesmen for the Cabinet Office, quoted in the *Guardian*, June 18, 2002, suggested that their evidence of disadvantage points to a "country of origin effect" rather than religion, citing, for example, the success of Middle Eastern Muslims. Equally, the loose methodologies of these studies raise questions as to their validity. One way of clarifying the term conceptually would be utilize the distinctions defined by the University of Derby in its analysis of religious discrimination for the British Home Office, 2001. This consists of five different dimensions of religious discrimination, including *religious prejudice*, *religious hatred* and *religious disadvantage*, and differentiates between *direct* and *indirect* discrimination. Another is to recognize the intersection of Islamophobia and xenophobia which results, according to the EUMC report, in forms of ethnic xenophobia.

Fred Halliday takes a more radical approach, questioning the worth of the term on several levels including the possibility that it reinforces ideas of Islam as a unitary entity and closes down legitimate criticism of the activity of Muslims. More centrally, he argues that Islam itself and its central tenets are no longer the enemy but its people and therefore a more appropriate name for the kind of discrimination experienced by Muslims is *anti-Muslimism*. This is a legitimate point although there are plenty of examples of discourse which is aimed at what are perceived to be Islamic beliefs and practices. Clearly, the term is proving useful for describing a multitude of practices that are not primarily or solely racial. However, if the term is to maintain any meaning, in using it we should recognize the complexity and diversity of the situations we are defining as Islamophobic and the different degrees of religious, political and racial motivations behind them.

SEE ALSO: Asian Americans; bigotry; British Asians; cultural racism; human rights; hybridity; media; Nation of Islam; Orientalism; Other; racialization; racist discourse; representations; September 11, 2001; whiteness

Reading

Islamophobia: A challenge for us all by The Runny-mede Trust (1997) is the source of the basic defini-tion, while *Summary Report on Islamophobia in the EU after 11 September 2001* by Christopher Allen and Jorgen S. Nielsen (European Monitoring Centre on Racism and Xenophobia, May 2002) is a more up-to-date treatment of the concept in the wake of September 11.

Islamophobia and Muslim Recognition in Britain by Steven Vertovec (*www.oup-usa.org*) examines the relationship between Islamophobia and increased Muslim prominence in public life. Vertovec argues that the two can be seen as interlinked in a circular process whereby Muslims achieving greater accom-modation in institutional arenas leads to intensified Islamophobia, further increasing Muslim activity.

"Islamophobia" Reconsidered by Fred Halliday (in *Ethnic and Racial Studies*, vol. 22, no. 5, 1999) reviews recently published books that examine rela-tions between "Islam" and the West, criticizing a monolithic approach; this may be read in conjunc-tion with Edward Said's classic text, *Orientalism* (Vintage, 1978).

Reporting Islam: Media representations of British Muslims by Elizabeth Poole (I. B. Tauris, 2002) explores how particular kinds of representations of Muslims have contributed to the demonization of Islam.

ELIZABETH POOLE

J

JACKSON, JESSE (1941–)

An active member of the Southern Christian Leadership Conference in the crucial 1966–71 period, South Carolina-born Jackson developed into an extraordinarily energetic and flamboyant leader and spokesman for black Americans. He claimed to have been a close confidante of Martin Luther King and reflected on how the leader had died in his arms – a claim disputed by many present at the leader's death. In 1969 he led the Active Black Coalition for United Community Action, but, more significantly, in 1971 he created People United to Save Humanity (PUSH), based in Chicago. This pressure group had an ingenious repertoire of strategies, one based on the threat of mass black boycotts of company products should the companies in question fail to implement a set of PUSH demands, such as hiring or promoting to senior positions more black employees.

Reverend Jackson was unsuccessful in his bid to become the presidential nominee of the Democratic party in 1984, but his sometimes controversial campaign drew much attention. He ran against Michael Dukakis in 1988. He continually stressed the "multicultural" nature of US society with his concept of the "Rainbow Coalition," which called for the political unity of all groups traditionally marginalized in electoral politics, including ethnic minorities, women, the poor, and environmentalists. Jackson tried to move beyond an ethnic interests-based agenda, eschewing the questionable title of the "black candidate" and appealing to a wider spread of groups – an attempt which was not wholly successful, as indicated by the antagonism he aroused among the Jewish community.

After 1988, Jackson eschewed attempts at securing political office, even when strenuously urged to do so (as in the mayoral race for Washington, DC in 1990). Despite having no official government position, Jackson retained prominence and several polls in the early 1990s confirmed that he was among the most widely recognized figures in North American public life. In 1989, he visited the then Soviet Union and Africa in a series of high-profile international travels. Such was his prominence that he was able to meet and negotiate with heads of state. In 1990, he hosted a television panel discussion series. The PUSH strategy, which had brought success in the 1980s, suffered a reverse in 1991, when the sports goods manufacturer Nike, which contracts many blacks to endorse its products, refused to negotiate. Jackson's boycott faltered and Nike was unscathed.

In the midst of the Gulf War of 1991, Jackson flew to Iraq to try to persuade Saddam Hussein to release hostages. Despite strong speculation in 1992, Jackson refused to run for the presidency, claiming "the basis of my strength and credibility is not in any office or position, but my relationship with people." He added that those who assumed government office "ended up conservative and cautious."

Jackson's previously high profile fell during Bill Clinton's Democratic administration and he became more of a celebrity, giving occasional lectures and appearing on television shows, though without seeking public office. The Rainbow Coalition's early promise to become an instrument of antiracism faded.

SEE ALSO: affirmative action; Ali, Muhammad; Barry case, the Marion; black bourgeoisie in the

USA; Black Panther Party; Black Power; civil rights movement; Cleaver, Eldridge; Diageo case; Diallo case, the Amadou; double consciousness; drugs; Ebonics; empowerment; *Invisible Man*; Jackson, Michael; Jim Crow; Jordan, Michael; Kerner Report; King, Martin Luther; King case, the Rodney; Ku Klux Klan; law: civil rights, USA; Malcolm X; Million Man March; Motown; politics; reparations; riots: USA, 1965–67; riots: USA, 1980; Thomas, Clarence; tokenism; Tyson, Mike

Reading

Black Civil Rights in America by Kevern Verney (Routledge, 2000) contextualizes Jackson in the civil rights struggle.

The Jesse Jackson Phenomenon by A. L. Reed (Yale University Press, 1986) argues controversially that Jackson's campaigns have hurt rather than helped the American black political movement; another, perhaps more damaging interpretation of Jackson came through Kenneth R. Timmerman's *Shakedown: Exposing the real Jesse Jackson* (Regnery, 2002), which alleged that Jackson was – and is – a self-serving hypocrite who has exploited his own status among the African American population.

"Profiles: Jesse Jackson" by Marshall Frady is an 89-page, 3-part article in *The New Yorker* (February 3, 10 and 17, 1992), while "Jesse Jackson and the new black political power" by William Strickland (in *Black Enterprise*, vol. 21, no. 1, August, 1990) is another profile.

JACKSON, MICHAEL (1958–)

During the last two decades of the twentieth century, Michael Jackson was one of the supreme icons of popular culture. Few performers and certainly no African American performer has ever commanded a following like that of Jackson: in one remarkable decade, Jackson sold 110 million records (over 75 million as a solo artist). *Bad*, his follow up to *Thriller*, was considered a virtual failure, selling 20 million copies. The tour to promote it in 1987 was watched by a total of 4.5 million people. The video of his single "Black or White" was simultaneously shown to an estimated 500 million television viewers in 27 countries in 1991. A six-album deal with Sony was worth up to one billion dollars. Jackson's rare public appearances, though fleeting and uneventful, were accorded a status akin to a royal visit. The word enigmatic is overused when describing taciturn pop and movie stars, but, in Jackson's case, it fits. He was truly an enigma,

and this played no small part in deepening the public's interest in him. Of all the questions asked of Jackson, the most perplexing concerns his physical transformation: was he a black man trying determinedly to become white?

Creating the enigma

Seven years separated the ages of the Jackson 5, Michael being the youngest. By the time he was ten, he had featured on two singles released on a small independent label, Steeltown Records. The band was, of course, five brothers, managed, often dictatorially, by father Joe. In 1969, Berry Gordy, the head of Motown Records, spotted the potential of the band. Influenced by the success of the assembled-for-TV band The Monkees, Gordy initially wanted to create a black version, complete with cartoon series and a range of merchandise. He launched the Jackson 5, using established stars such as Diana Ross and Sammy Davis Jr. as endorsers. In fact, the band's first Motown album was *Diana Ross Presents the Jackson 5*.

A white version of the band, the Osmonds, flickered briefly, but the Jackson brothers went from strength to strength with Motown in the early 1970s, Gordy cleverly issuing single releases by Michael independently of the band, while keeping the unit together. Like all artists in the Motown fold, the Jackson 5 were given the full grooming treatment: no detail was ignored. As such Michael was a seasoned showbusiness professional by the time he was a teenager. His father, however, was dissatisfied with Gordy's handling of his son's career and, in 1976, negotiated a deal with CBS's subsidiary label, Epic. For contractual reasons, the band became known as The Jacksons, the first album being released in 1977. While both the band and Michael continued to sell records, progress was unspectacular until 1979 when a collaboration with producer Quincy Jones yielded Michael's *Off the Wall* album, which sold six million copies – and continues to sell. The album spawned four hit singles. Around this time, the facial changes that were to become the stuff of myth began: two rhinoplasty operations followed an accident in which Jackson broke his nose.

Despite his commercial success, MTV was impervious to Jackson for a long while. In 1983, the 24-hour all-music cable TV channel rejected Jackson's "Billie Jean," giving rise to the suspicion that the station wanted only "safe" acts that appealed to white youth. CBS threatened MTV with a boycott by all its artists, forcing a change of heart. In a way, MTV's decision may have been a historic one, providing a black artist with a genuine mainstream showcase. The track was taken from Jackson's album *Thriller*, which turned him into the bestselling recording artist of his time. It became the top-selling album in history. The title track's video was made into an extravagant TV event, receiving a première in December 1983 and going on to sell 48 million copies independently of the album.

As the world's leading artist, Jackson had to contend with the attendant publicity. This was intensified by the fact that consumers' fascination with celebrities, the gossip about them, the stories surrounding them, and the minutiae of their personal lives, had begun in earnest. Jackson's response was to become a virtual recluse, giving interviews sparingly and making infrequent public appearances. Perversely, this promoted even greater interest in him; and the hearsay multiplied.

Throughout his career, the questions that contributed so fulsomely to his enigma were rarely answered. Did he really sleep in an oxygen tent? Why did he want to buy the bones of the Elephant Man? Was he so obsessed with Diana Ross that he actually tried to look like her? Did he seriously believe, as suggested in an *Ebony* interview, that he was a messenger from God? And, how come he always seemed to be in the company of young boys? This last question was asked time and again and eventually turned into one scandal too many.

In 1993, Jackson was accused of child molestation by a thirteen-year-old boy. Jackson agreed to talk about the charges on a "live" satellite hookup from his Neverland ranch in California. He complained that the police had subjected him to a humiliating inspection and taken photographs of his genitalia. In 1994, Jackson agreed to pay Jordy Chandler, then fourteen, an undisclosed sum, thought to be more than $25m, to stop a sexual abuse suit ever reaching court. Jackson was never put under oath for a civil deposition which could be used in a criminal trial. The deal was negotiated on Jackson's behalf by his lawyer, Johnnie Cochrane, Jr., later to represent O. J. Simpson, and Larry Feldman, who was retained by Chandler's parents. Part of the agreement reached was that the payment did not constitute an admission of guilt by Jackson. After the charges, Jackson was forced out into the open and made to defend himself, whether he liked it or not. In the process, the qualities that were once integral to his appeal became implements of immolation. Was he "weird-unusual," or "weird-sicko?"

His fans, indeed, consumers around the world, drew their own conclusions. Jackson's career slid from that point, though the decline was not as sharp as might have been expected; after all, scandals have crushed many a star's career almost immediately.

Paradox

Jackson epitomized a perfect confluence of personality and history. A black male, precociously talented as an entertainer, he emerged as a child star in the 1970s, a time when America's dilemma had become a glaring paradox. The land of opportunity had finally granted civil rights to all citizens, yet continued to deny whole portions of the population access to the kinds of jobs, goods and other resources germane to an egalitarian society. As the rioting of the 1960s subsided and African Americans poured their fury into more cultural expressions, Jackson came to the fore, sporting an Afro hairdo and a clenched fist salute. He was a young man who looked like he had all the trappings of Black Power.

In reality, he was an innocent, a child who could be admired paternistically, living proof that black people had gifts that were uniquely their own. For some, he was testimony to the continued self-hatred that tormented African Americans. For all his success, Jackson seemed ill at ease with his blackness, and his transformation might be seen as proof of this. In a 1991 interview with Oprah Winfrey, Jackson said that he suffered from a skin disorder called vitiligo, which causes discoloration, but few accepted that Jackson had not undergone some sort of treatment. His face seemed to be a state of perpetual alteration, giving rise to the suggestion that he was actually trying to rid himself of his blackness. Certainly, his blanched complexion, small pointed nose and thin lips lent substance to this theory, though Jackson himself remained silent on the subject and was famously prickly about unflattering descriptions. Speculation about his motives fueled the abundant mysteries surrounding Jackson.

It is not necessary to impute motives: no one will ever know whether Jackson actually wanted to rid himself of his blackness. But he certainly gave many precisely that impression. He was a black man so successful that he could have had almost anything in the world. In one stroke he convinced America that it was truly the land of opportunity, while emphasizing that whiteness was still the most valued commodity in that land. Don King, who promoted a world tour for Jackson and his brothers, once said of Michael: "He's one of the megastars in the world, but he's still going to be a nigger megastar" (quoted in Taraborelli's book, below).

SEE ALSO: Black Power; blues; double consciousness; Jackson, Jesse; Jordan, Michael; Lee, Spike; masculinity; Million Man March; minstrelsy; Motown; race: as signifier; rap; Simpson case, the O. J.; Thomas, Clarence; Tyson, Mike; whiteness

Reading

The Black Culture Industry by Ellis Cashmore (Routledge, 1997) has a chapter on Jackson, "Infant icon," in which many of the themes in this entry are expanded and set in the context of black music's development over the past 120 years.

Michael Jackson: The magic and the madness by Randy Taraborelli (Birch Lane, 1991) is a detailed biography; it might gainfully be read in association with *Michael Jackson: Unauthorized* by Christopher Andersen (Simon & Schuster, 1994).

JIM CROW

"Jim Crow" was a common slave name used as a song title by the nineteenth-century entertainer Thomas Dartmouth "Daddy" Rice (1808–60). Rice ridiculed blacks as amusing fools, as congenitally lazy but with an aura of childlike happiness. The name was applied to legislation that provided for the practice of segregating whites and African Americans.

The conclusion of the Civil War brought about the 1863 Thirteenth Amendment to the US Constitution, the Emancipation Proclamation that provided for the freedom of all slaves. It also prompted the question of whether white responsibilities toward blacks should end with the prohibition of physical bondage: should the federal government provide protection and eco-nomic resources for freed ex-slaves? In formulating answers to this, the federal government attempted to reconstruct the South on a new basis of equality.

So, when eight Southern states tried via legal means – designated the "Black Codes" – to deny blacks access to desirable, well-paying work, the federal government introduced two additional amendments to provide: (1) equality of protection for all under the law; and (2) equality of voting rights for all men (not women).

Reconstruction had barely begun when the military occupation of the South ended in 1875. The belief was fostered that blacks would prosper through their own initiative and application and without federal intervention. The Civil Rights Bill of 1875 was designed to grant equal access for all citizens to all public facilities. But only limited government aid was provided; economic security and political equality were matters of individual enterprise. Hostility toward blacks was rife, especially in the South, and resentment surfaced whenever blacks did show enterprise. The Thirteenth Amendment ended slavery, but did nothing to erode the racist beliefs that underpinned slavery.

In 1883, the US Supreme Court ruled that the 1875 Bill did not apply to "personal acts of social discrimination." Effectively, this meant that state laws requiring segregated facilities for blacks and whites were constitutional. The feeling was that the federal government had done too much to help blacks in their transition to free men. So the US Supreme Court deprived the previous legislation of its cutting edge and restored the determination of civil rights to state rather than federal levels. What followed became known as the "Jim Crow" era: Southern states enacted a series of statutes that provided for the segregation of blacks and whites in such spheres as education, transport, marriage, and leisure.

The *Plessy v. Ferguson* case of 1896 was a legal milestone: the Supreme Court upheld the state of Louisiana's requirement that seating on trains be segregated. The doctrine emerging from this decision was that blacks and whites were "separate but equal." Mr. Plessy was, he claimed, seven-eighths "white," yet he was, for all intents and purposes, a "Negro" and therefore not allowed to travel in "whites only" railroad cars. The doctrine of "separate but equal" spread throughout the South and, by 1910 there was a virtual caste system in practice. It served to maintain blacks in their subordinate positions by denying them access to reasonable education and jobs; sharecropping was their principal means of survival.

"Jim Crow" was a type of *de jure* segregation; a separation required by law. When the law was not available to support segregation, the forces of the Ku Klux Klan were invoked. Hence, lynchings were widespread and largely overlooked by legal authorities. Blacks were thus inhibited from challenging the segregation and were more or less forced into accepting their inferiority. In other words, blacks were provided with no facilities for improving their education, for showing skillful application, nor for protesting aggressively their conditions (at least, not without fear of violent reprisals); so they were virtually made to conform to the white popular "Jim Crow" image of them.

The court decision that brought an end to the Jim Crow era came in 1954 with the *Brown* v. *Board of Education* case. Segregated schools were declared unconstitutional; the principle was then extended to buses, restaurants, parks, etc. Over the next decade the Jim Crow laws were gradually overturned, their total dissolution coming with the 1964 Civil Rights Act.

SEE ALSO: blues; *Brown* v. *Board of Education*; civil rights movement; double consciousness; humor; *Invisible Man*; Ku Klux Klan; law: civil rights, USA; minstrelsy; Myrdal, Gunnar; segregation; slavery

Reading

Black Civil Rights in America by Kevern Verney (Routledge, 2000) and *The Shaping of Black America* by Lerone Bennett, Jr. (Penguin, 1993) are both authoritative general histories of the black experience with ample discussions of the Jim Crow era.
The Color Line: Legacy for the twenty-first century by John H. Franklin (University of Missouri Press, 1994) argues that the "color line" instituted by Jim Crow still holds in education, housing, health, and the legal system.
Fighting in the Jim Crow Army: Black men and women remember World War II by Maggi M. Morehouse (Rowman & Littlefield, 2000) is a collection of personal reminiscences of officers who served in a segregated army.
Race, Ethnicity, and Class in American Social Thought 1865–1919 by Glenn C. Altschuler (Harlan Davidson, 1982) is a historical monograph detailing developments in this crucial period in American race relations.
CHECK: internet resources section

JORDAN, MICHAEL (1963–)

Status

While Jordan's athletic prowess and his global popularity are beyond doubt, his position in the panoply of African American achievements and overall cultural significance are less clear. His attainments in basketball were unprecedented and may never be eclipsed. He was also formidably rich, commanding a yearly income of over $35m in the 1990s. In terms of appeal, there were no rivals to his uncommon popularity, even in parts of the world where basketball is not played. Jordan essayed films, television shows, made videos and lent his name to a miscellany of commercial products; in short, he submitted to remaking himself into a commodity that could be consumed by anyone, anywhere. In the 1990s it seemed that Jordan enjoyed a godlike status. Yet, a question remains: to whose advantage or to what purpose did he turn that status?

Unlike, say, Muhammad Ali, Paul Robeson, even Bill Cosby – all influential figures by virtue of their renown – Jordan rarely, if ever, committed himself on issues of the day. He was either silent or judicious on the Million Man March, the Rodney King case or the killing of Tupac Shakur, all occasions when a prominent African American may have been expected to have opinions or issue statements that may have had some productive effect. On the other hand, and in his defense, Jordan played sports: his reputation was that of a basketball player *par excellence*, not of a public figure or self-appointed spokesman in the mold of Jesse Jackson or Al Sharpton. At a time when some outstanding black athletes were better known for their trespasses than their athletic accomplishments, Jordan remained aloof, his only very minor indiscretion being a gambling debt, which, to a man of his substance, was an oversight rather than an avoidance.

In a career free of controversy and scandal, Jordan was, for some, too anodyne to be an effective leader. For others, he was right for his times: an all-purpose African American icon, a faultless symbol of achievement, a wholesome family man (though he eventually divorced) and an inspiration to a generation. But what did he inspire? Certainly, he inspired millions, perhaps billions, of consumers to spend a great deal of money on, and in some cases fight each other for,

Nike sportswear. He also persuaded people to buy Gatorade, Wheaties, or any number of the many other products he endorsed. And the National Basketball Association (NBA), which was ailing when Jordan first appeared for the Chicago Bulls in 1984, profited enormously from Jordan's presence in its league. Jordan even pulled moviegoers to his film *Space Jam*, in which he co-starred with Bugs Bunny and other Warner Bros. cartoons. Jordan was a marketing phenomenon that could be used to sell virtually anything.

Triumph of capital over culture

Jordan was the youngest of three sons, his father an affluent corporate executive. Between 1981 and 1984, he studied at North Carolina University and won an Olympic gold medal with the USA basketball team in the Los Angles games of 1984. He was a third draft pick, going to Chicago Bulls. Represented by the sports marketing agency ProServ and, in particular, by David Falk, he entered into a complex series of commercial arrangements with the Bulls and Phil Knight, the founder and owner of Nike.

Jordan went to Chicago at the same time that the NBA was desperately trying to rid itself of its reputation of being "too black" for the major TV networks (most of the players were African Americans). The game was also known for its inordinate number of drug-using players. A new commissioner, David Stern, imposed harsh sanctions on drug violators and convinced TV companies that he could deliver a product that white viewing audiences would embrace. Jordan was part of his plans. Clean, wholesome, with none of the uncertainty or menace typically attributed to black males, Jordan was perfect. By 1991, when the Bulls began their domination of the NBA championships, the final games were transmitted not only across the USA but also to over seventy other countries. By 1996 the play-offs were televised to 175 countries, the commentaries in 24 languages. In this period, Jordan earned about $25m a year, just 15 per cent of which was his salary, the rest coming through endorsements. He remained the top-earning endorser up to 1999, when Tiger Woods signed a $90m deal with Nike.

The relationship with the sportswear company Nike was mutually rewarding. As Jordan's name and image helped sell Nike products, so Nike's

ingenious advertising elevated Jordan to national, then international prominence. The "mythmaking," as Naomi Klein calls it (in *No Logo*, Flamingo, 2000) was engineered by Nike's advertising: "You'll believe a man can fly," advertisers told consumers, creating transcendent images of Jordan that were nearer to those of a comic book superhero. Children were encouraged to "Be like Mike." While the source of his early appeal lay in his preeminent sports skill, his clean-cut, near-colorless appearance and his too-good-to-be-true devotion to American family values, this later transmuted into something more otherworldly. Appellations included "His Royal Airness" and "The light." Unlike any other sports figure in history, Jordan was able to fuse himself with an artifice, a cunning contrivance constructed by advertisers and marketers whose principal interest lay in selling products.

By 1998 Jordan products were estimated to have grossed about $2.6 billion for Nike alone (figures from *Fortune* magazine writers Roy S. Johnson and Ann Harrington, "The Jordan effect," vol. 37, no. 12, June 12, 1998). Changes in the marketplace enabled this. Ten, perhaps five, years before Jordan's ascent, it would have been unimaginable for a black male to have become, as the *Chicago Tribune* once called him, "the world's most popular marketing commodity." Falk had earlier noted that: "The problem from a corporate point of view was that he [Jordan] was black."

Jerry Reinsdorf, the owner of the Bulls, remarked that: "Michael has no color." Later, another ostensibly black, yet color-free sports star, Tiger Woods, was to prove that the market had become yielding enough to accept African Americans as endorsers in a way that was not possible before Jordan. Black celebrities, many from sports, had helped market products. Joe Louis, Hank Aaron and, of course, O. J. Simpson, were among the many African American sports stars to have endorsed commercial products. None, however, approached Jordan's redoubtable capacity for moving goods off shelves.

Were he to have, for example, turned on Nike when Jesse Jackson and his PUSH organization tried to prompt a boycott of its products (because of the corporation's equal opportunity record), his status would have been placed in doubt. He might have become involved in any number of issues that affected African Americans in the 1990s. Advertisers may not have thrilled to the idea of a newly politicized Jordan. In the event, he remained neutral, sustaining interest in himself by segueing into baseball, with limited success, returning with the Bulls, retiring, then mounting an astonishing comeback with the Washington Senators (which he co-owned).

Some writers, such as John Hoberman, would argue that Jordan's impact was only in bolstering the decades-old stereotype about physically gifted but intellectually limited black athletes. The very last thing African Americans needed in the late twentieth century was a new superstar who personified the achievement ethic, but not in politics, business, the professions or other areas that demanded intellectual rather than physical attributes.

Other writers, his biographer Walter LaFeber included, argued that Jordan was "a triumph of capital over culture." For LaFeber, Jordan was both a catalyst for and product of America's "soft power" – its cultural influence around the world. The USA has written the "grammar" of international television by creating its formats and concepts. Sport is one such format; Jordan was one such concept.

Television moguls such as Rupert Murdoch and Ted Turner created the conditions under which Jordan the icon was possible when they launched satellites and laid cables that enabled virtually the whole world to access American TV at the push of a remote control button. US television spread like "an out-of-control bacteria," according to LaFeber. Needing product to fill their channels, TV execs sent out as much sport as they could. This was a low-risk, high-entertainment strategy. Who better than the ultra-safe and hugely engaging Jordan to take American culture to the world?

"American media, advertising, and marketing entered an unexplored, unimagined era" when it started sending out global communications. "Michael Jordan personified that new era," argues LaFeber. Constructed by Falk, packaged by Knight, "synergized" by Stern and distributed by Murdoch et al., Jordan was living confirmation that culture can be assimilated into a commercial program, then sold to the world. Michael became as integral to late twentieth-century culture as his alliterative cousins Microsoft, Madonna and Mickey Mouse.

One possible way to make sense of Jordan is in terms of a more widespread enthusiasm among predominantly white consumers for black culture, or at least the version of black culture that was offered by the entertainment industry. From the 1970s, white consumers progressively embraced the output of black culture, its music, its art, its movies and so on. The mainstreaming of rap in the late twentieth and early twenty-first centuries epitomizes this enthusiasm. While African Americans made headway in many other spheres, the basic racial inequalities of American society stayed intact. It is at least possible that the ardor over black culture and its appropriation by whites was a resolution of sorts to the age-old American dilemma: black symbols and cultural expressions were a way of reminding whites of how tenderly they had clasped black culture; it also helped them overlook, or, perhaps more accurately, disremember how the material position of black people remained in large part unchanged since the 1970s. By welcoming, appreciating and even adoring Jordan, consumers could absolve themselves of any responsibility for the obstinacy of racism – and point to their idolatry of a black athlete, not to mention enthusiasm for black music and movie stars as evidence.

Approached in this way, the contribution and significance of Jordan is in providing a wide constituency of mainly white consumers with comfort and reassurance and a smaller but still appreciable body of black fans with evidence that African Americans could defy the odds and become conspicuously successful. In many ways, Jordan, as David L. Andrews puts it, "erased" race, replacing it with "a universal circumspect human nature that knows its place in the order of things." Jordan supplied more comfort than challenge, delighting his audience and making his skill available for their delectation. But when he finally retired he left behind a society essentially untouched by his presence.

SEE ALSO: African Americans; Ali, Muhammad; assimilation; Central Park jogger; consumption; Jackson, Jesse; Jackson, Michael; Lee, Spike; Let's Kick Racism Out of Football; Simpson case, the O. J.; Thomas, Clarence; tokenism; Tyson, Mike; whiteness

Reading

Darwin's Athletes: How sport has damaged black America and preserved the myth of race by John Hoberman (Houghton Mifflin, 1997) is a powerful argument that helps create a framework in which

Jordan's significance might be assessed; it includes the insight that both blacks and whites have bought into the "myth" and how identifying with black athletic success has made black professional achievement "a seldom-noticed sideshow to more dramatic media coverage of celebrities and deviants"; it may be read fruitfully with Mark Kohn's "Can white men jump," which is chapter four of his *The Race Gallery* (Vintage, 1996).

"Decontructing Michael Jordan: reconstructing postindustrial America," edited by David L. Andrews, is a special issue of *Sociology of Sport Journal* (vol. 13, 1996) containing several interesting essays; Andrews has also co-edited (with Steven J. Jackson) the similar *Sport Stars: The cultural politics of sporting celebrity* (Routledge, 2001).

Michael Jordan and the New Global Capitalism by Walter LaFeber, (Norton, 1999) is a short and pithy essay on Jordan that situates him in a globalization process for which American wrote the "grammar."

Playing for Keeps: Michael Jordan and the world he made by David Halberstam (Random House, 1999) credits Falk with helping to "revolutionize the process of representing a basketball player, going into a team sport and creating the idea of the individual player as a commercial superstar, an iconographic act that was considered breathtaking at the time."

K

KERNER REPORT

The shorthand name for the report of the National Advisory Commission on Civil Disorders chaired by Otto Kerner. The commission was set up by President Lyndon Johnson in 1967 with the aim of investigating the causes and consequences of a series of uprisings that had occurred in many US cities over the previous two years. One of its conclusions was that the USA was "moving toward two societies, one black, one white – separate and unequal."

The first of the riots started on August 11, 1965. A confrontation between white police and young blacks in Watts, Los Angeles's largest black ghetto, marked the end of the period of nonviolent protest at black oppression in the United States and presaged the start of a series of "race riots." By the end of 1968, the catchword, "burn, baby, burn" had been heard in virtually every major US city, coast to coast, north to south. In 1967 alone, over 150 "race riots" were recorded during the "long hot summer," the most serious taking place in Newark and Detroit. By the end of 1968, police had reported 50,000 arrests and more than 8,000 casualties.

Black and white left-wing radicals characterized the "riots" as revolutionary insurrection, comparable to the colonial rebellions in Africa and Asia. White reactionaries, while agreeing with this description, maintained that the episodes had been inspired by foreign agitators and black communists and urged the authorities to meet fire with fire. President Johnson, on the other hand, tended to agree with moderate black leaders that the relatively small caucus of young troublemakers had acted against the will of the vast majority of black Americans.

In his address to the nation on July 27, 1967, Johnson announced his intention to set up an investigation to determine the causes of the riots, to examine the characteristics of the areas affected and of those who participated, to appraise the media's presentation and treatment of the riots and its effects, and, most importantly, to pinpoint strategies which would avert the possibility of further disorders.

The more speculative accounts of the "burn, baby, burn" disorders were largely repudiated by the wealth of statistical and documentary material presented by Kerner and his colleagues in their 1968 report. Not surprisingly perhaps, in view of the significance and authority with which the Commission was endowed, some of the Commissioners' results and research methodology have since been subject to careful scrutiny by social researchers and, in some instances, found to be flawed. Even so, the profile of "the typical rioter" sketched out by the Commissioners has generally been accepted: a young, single black male who had been born and brought up in the state and who shared a comparable economic position to blacks who had not participated in the disorders. He tended to be slightly better educated than other ghetto residents, though he was positioned in the lower echelons of the labor market, rarely worked full-time and was frequently unemployed. Although he was slightly more likely than nonparticipants to have been brought up at home in the absence of an adult male, the statistical difference was insignificant and its impact marginal. The evidence adduced by the Commission, and subsequently verified by other research, suggested that the motives of the "rioters" were primarily political: they were not responding to their own particular disadvantage, nor indeed that of their local communities, but to the more general disadvantaged and oppressed position of the entire black community in the USA.

The most fundamental of the "underlying forces" which had precipitated the disorders was, in the words of the Commission: "the accelerating segregation of low-income, disadvantaged Negroes within the largest American cities." As they put in their conclusion to the report: "Our nation is moving toward two societies, one black, one white – separate and unequal." They identified three paths along which government policies could proceed: the first was the "present policies choice" which, the Commissioners warned, carried the "highest ultimate price" of an even greater likelihood of further civil disorders, perhaps surpassing even the scale of the "burn, baby, burn" incidents. An "enrichment" policy, or "gilding the ghetto," constituted the second strategy. This recognized some of the positive aspects of ghetto life and was premised on the notion of separate but equal communities. Although a similar strategy had been advocated by many Black Power leaders, the Commission pointed out that "gilding the ghetto" to enhance its status would require a considerable deployment of national funds.

The preferred course of ameliorative action combined "gilding the ghetto" policies with "programs designed to encourage integration of substantial numbers of Negroes into the society outside the ghetto." In other words, the enrichment policy would be an interim measure: the goal was dispersal. This, they contended, would not only improve the educational and social standards of American blacks, but would also facilitate social integration and help secure social stability. Put simply, dispersal constituted the most effective means of crisis management.

Despite its many limitations, the Kerner Commission made a deliberate attempt to present the disorders in a sociological perspective rather than one which dealt exclusively in a "law and order" framework. Although the report tended to overlook the more insidious and ultimately more wide-reaching forms of institutional racism as an instrument of oppression in the United States, it highlighted the central role that white racism (and the modes of action that this impels) played in the outbreak of the disorders. In this sense

alone it presented a far more sophisticated appraisal than its UK counterpart, the Scarman Report, though, like that document, it evoked a sporadic and highly selective response from central government.

SEE ALSO: African Americans; Black Panther Party; Black Power; civil rights movement; Cleaver, Eldridge; ethnic conflict; ghetto; King, Martin Luther; King case, the Rodney; Malcolm X; Motown; riots: Britain, 1981; riots: USA, 1921 (Tulsa); riots: USA, 1965–67; riots: USA, 1980 (Miami); Scarman Report; segregation

Reading

Let Nobody Turn Us Around: Voices of resistance, reform and renewal – an African-American anthology, edited by Manning Marable and Leith Mullings (Rowman & Littlefield, 1999), contains, as its title suggests, excerpts from writers on the black struggle in the USA.

Locked in the Poorhouse: Cities, race and poverty in the United States, edited by Fred R. Harris and Lynn A. Curtis (Rowman & Littlefield, 1999), is interesting because Harris served on the Kerner Commission and, thirty years on, was able to reflect on the long-term impact of the report.

"Parameters of British and North American racism" by Louis Kushnick (in *Race and Class*, vol. 23, nos 2/3, 1982) argues that despite its liberal pretensions, the Kerner Commission advocated coercion and co-option. Its recommendations for more effective police control, for instance, were most enthusiastically and expeditiously implemented.

Report of the National Advisory Commission on Civil Disorders (*Kerner Report*) is the original document, with an introduction by Tom Wicker (Bantam Books, 1968), while *Prevention and Control of Urban Disorders* by the US Department of Justice (US Government Printing Office, 1980) is a more up-to-date assessment of the riots.

BARRY TROYNA

KING, MARTIN LUTHER (1929–68)

Born of a middle-class Atlanta family, King was educated at Morehouse College (Atlanta), Crozer Theological Seminary (Pennsylvania), where he was ordained into the National Baptist Church, and Boston University, where he received his doctorate in theology in 1955.

Almost a year after receiving his doctorate, King was serving as a Baptist pastor in Montgomery, Alabama, when he heard of Rosa Parks's refusal to give up her seat in the "whites only" section of a municipal bus. This historic action was to provide King with the opportunity to initiate a series of boycotts that eventually gelled into a movement of national importance, designed to secure civil rights for blacks, at that time still suffering from the vestiges of the "Jim Crow" era, despite the technical ending of racial segregation brought about by the *Brown* decision of 1954.

King worked with black civil leaders Ralph Abernathy, E. D. Dixon, and Bayard Rustin to promote a boycott of Montgomery's buses. Throughout 1956, about 95 percent of the city's blacks refused to use public buses. In November 1956, a Supreme Court ruling declared the bus segregation laws of Montgomery unconstitutional. During the eleven months preceding the decision, King had emerged as a leader of substance, but the tangible success of the campaign transformed him. As Manning Marable observes in his book, *Race, Rebellion and Reform* (Macmillan, 1984): "Overnight, King became the charismatic symbol of the political aspirations of millions of coloured people across the world."

The effect of the Montgomery success was to spark a series of isolated boycotts, though no coherent mass campaign materialized until the 1960s. King had, in 1957, formed the Southern Christian Leadership Conference (SCLC), of which he was president and which was to become his vehicle for civil rights reform. Influenced by the teachings of Thoreau, and especially Gandhi, King employed the tactic of nonviolent disobedience, staging street demonstrations, marches, sit-ins and even jail-ins. After 1960, the sit-ins became more frequent and were used to particularly good effect by black students to protest against lunch-counter segregation at educational institutions.

King and his followers had to endure violent attacks from whites and even from some blacks who were fearful of reprisals. King himself was sentenced to four months imprisonment after leading a protest in Atlanta. Charges were dropped, but King was imprisoned for violating his probation on a traffic offense conviction. John F. Kennedy used influence to obtain King's release, a strategic move which undoubtedly played a part in Kennedy's election to President in that same year (in most cities and states, three-quarters of all votes cast by blacks were for Democratic nominees).

King enjoyed fruitful associations with both John and Robert Kennedy, negotiating civil rights reforms, the most important of which were the two laws passed in 1964 and 1965. The latter, which was signed by Kennedy's successor, Lyndon B. Johnson (whose presidential candidacy was endorsed by King), ensured voting rights for blacks and was preceded by a 4,000-strong march from Selma to Montgomery. In December 1964, King received the Nobel Peace Prize.

In his book, *Martin Luther King, Jr.*, W. R. Miller describes his subject's most remarkable achievement as his success in making middle-class blacks the "backbone" of his crusade. When King began to mobilize his organization in the Southern states, one-fifth of the population in that region was black and, of these, at least one in three was above the poverty line. The import of this is that there was a sizable proportion of blacks who were beyond worrying about sheer physical survival and were ambitious enough to become the "backbone" of a mass movement for reform. King's association with, and support from, the emergent black middle class was one of the keys to his success in leading a movement of great scale and force. But, it was also the reason why, even as early as 1960, when he was 31, "he seemed rather remote from the mind and mood that simmered across black college campuses," as Marable puts it.

By 1963 the "mood" had spread. For example, in that year, he delivered his famous "I have a dream" speech to an audience of 250,000 and several million television viewers. In content, it was a relatively mild speech, incorporating passages from many other, older deliveries and lacking any reference to the violent white backlash his sympathizers were having to endure. Also in 1963, he gave another speech in Harlem, before an audience of 3,000, many of whom jeered and chanted "We want Malcolm [X]!" to signal their discontent with King's gradual and moderate programs.

The same sentiment was articulated more aggressively from 1965 when Black Power spurred rioting in many major US cities. King remained steadfast in his condemnation of violence, but was clearly troubled by both dissension within his own movement and external pressures from militants. From this point, King seems to have been drawn toward a more extreme position. In 1966 he admitted that his policy of "a little change here, a little change there" was an idea he had, as he put it, "labored with." His departure from this was heralded by his criticism of the Vietnam War; in particular, the disproportionate number of blacks involved in military action. Many blacks disapproved of King's position and turned sharply against him. Thus the final years of his life were spent struggling not only against the reactionary forces of white America, but against the radical demands of militant blacks who advocated violent solutions to the problems King addressed.

In April 1968, King traveled to Memphis to support a strike by black sanitation workers. Here he was assassinated. Following this, 70,000 troops were needed to quell violence that broke out in 125 American cities.

SEE ALSO: African Americans; Ali, Muhammad; Barry case, the Marion; black bourgeoisie in the USA; Black Panther Party; Black Power; blues; civil rights movement; Cleaver, Eldridge; disadvantage; double consciousness; empowerment; Gandhi, Mohandas Karamchand; Garvey, Marcus; *Invisible Man*; Jackson, Jesse; Jim Crow; Kerner Report; Ku Klux Klan; law: civil rights, USA; Malcolm X; minstrelsy; Motown; *négritude*; riots: USA, 1921; riots: USA, 1965–67; Thomas, Clarence; tokenism; Tyson, Mike

Reading

And the Walls Came Tumbling Down by Ralph Abernathy (Harper & Row, 1989) is a biography by the slain leader's confidante and adviser, which discloses hitherto neglected facets of King's personal life. Other life histories include: *King: A biography* by D. C. Lewis (University of Illinois Press, 1978), *Martin Luther King* by K. Slack (SCM Press, 1970) and *Martin Luther King Jr* by W. R. Miller (Avon Books, 1968).
The Last Crusade: Martin Luther King Jr., the FBI and the Poor People's Campaign by Gerald D. McKnight (Westview Press, 1997) focuses on J. Edgar Hoover's orchestrated attempt to undermine King in the more general effort to construct a "black menace" within America; this should be read alongside *Orders to Kill* by William Pepper (Carroll & Graf, 1995) which alleges that King was killed by the US intelligence agencies; written by a London-based attorney, it dismisses the theory of the lone assassin (James Earl Ray, who was sentenced to ninety-nine years) and argues that King was killed because it was thought that his crusade for blacks was turning into a campaign against involvement in Vietnam.
Martin Luther King Jr by Peter Ling (Routledge, 2002) asks the provocative question: was King the inspirational prime mover he is usually thought to be, or was he carried along by forces which were to a great degree beyond his control?

KING CASE, THE RODNEY

In March 1991, Rodney King, an African American male, was stopped for speeding by Los Angeles police officers. The four white officers administered a brutal beating, which was videotaped by a member of the public and later broadcast worldwide. In 1992 the four police officers were acquitted, a verdict that sparked off three days of violent unrest in LA and elsewhere in the USA, resulting in fifty deaths, with 4,000 more injured, 1,100 arrested and $1 billion in property damage. King eventually received compensation of $3m.

While ostensibly the uprising was in protest at the acquittal, there were other contributory factors. Cornel West wrote that the "riot" was "the consequence of a lethal linkage of economic decline, cultural decay, and political lethargy.... Race was the visible catalyst, not the underlying cause" (in Gooding-Williams, below).

The King verdict was extraordinary in the sense that it seemed to contradict the available evidence – an amateur videotape showing him receive fifty-six baton blows, punches and kicks. But its power to provoke a full-scale riot may have lain in the fact that it dramatized what is a quotidian feature of blacks' relationships with the police in Los Angeles.

The four officers were brought to trial and acquitted by a jury comprising six males and six females, one of whom was Hispanic, another Filipino, the rest white. The acquittal prompted protests outside the LAPD headquarters and these later spiraled out of control.

Anticipating the reaction to such a verdict, the LAPD had allocated $1m in overtime wages. Yet the police response to the initial outbreaks was sluggish and the LAPD hesitated to restore order. Police Chief Daryl Gates – who was forced to resign because of the King incident, but still held office at the time of the uprising – answered critics by saying he feared a police presence would worsen matters.

The LAPD deployed only two officers per 1,000 residents, the lowest ratio in the USA (New York City deploys 3.7) and fifteen per square mile (compared with 89 for New York). Neighborhood involvement was sought through community policing, but, with so few officers, the approach was largely ineffectual. When the LAPD failed to quell the initial violence, 1,000 federal law enforcement officers and 4,000 Army and Marine troops were sent to Los Angeles, ready to move in at the express command of the President; 1,400 Californian National Guard members were placed on stand-by. A state of emergency was declared by California Governor Pete Wilson.

In the ten years leading to the violence, Los Angeles county had experienced demographic changes in its ethnic minority population. While the African American population had dropped from 13 to 11 percent, both the Latino and Asian populations had grown. Collectively, the unemployment level among the three groups was nearly 50 percent. As whites moved out of the area to places such as Simi Valley (where the trial was held) and Ventura County, interethnic conflict surfaced – in much the same way as it had done in Miami twelve years before. The predominantly Asian district known as Koreatown was particularly badly damaged.

The rioting forced the "race" issue to the fore, after a period of relative "tranquillity" in which "universal programs" of reform were advocated over group-targeted policies. The view was inspired by the groundswell of scholarly opinion predicated on the idea that racial inequality had nonracial origins; that the impersonal forces of the market economy explained more about the impoverishment of inner-city blacks than notions of racial discrimination. The King case seemed vividly to remind the nation – indeed, the world – that assumptions that racial discrimination had faded were ill-founded.

Ten years after the rioting, memories of King's beating were evoked when Donovan Jackson, an African American, was pulled over for a routine driving violation and pummeled by LAPD officers. As with the King case, the initial incident was captured on tape. A police officer was suspended immediately after the presentation of the videotape, which showed him slamming Jackson on the trunk of a car and punching him in the face while his arms were held by other officers.

SEE ALSO: Barry case, the Marion; Central Park jogger; Diallo case, the Amadou; policing; race card; racial profiling; rap; riots: USA, 1965–67; riots: USA, 1980; Thomas, Clarence; Tyson, Mike

Reading

Contemporary Controversies and the American Divide:

The O. J. Simpson case and other controversies by Robert Smith and Richard Seltzer (Rowman & Littlefield, 2000) uses survey data to highlight how public opinion on several *causes célèbres* of the 1990s divided black and white populations.

"How the rioters won" by Midge Decter is part of a series of articles in a special issue of *Commentary* (vol. 94, no. 1, July 1992) on the LA disturbances while "Causes, root causes, and cures" by Charles Murray appears in a special collection of papers in an issue of *National Review* (vol. 44, no. 11, June 1992) devoted to analyses of the uprisings.

The Los Angeles Riots: Lessons for the urban future, edited by Mark Baldassare (Westview Press, 1994), address three questions: what were the causes of the riots, what actually took place, and what were the consequences?

Official Negligence: How Rodney King and the riots changed Los Angeles and the LAPD by Lou Cannon (Westview Press, 1999) examines both the circumstances leading up to the riots and the fallout. Written by a *Washington Post* journalist, the text is based on extensive interviews with witnesses and participants

Reading Rodney King, Reading Urban Uprisings, edited by Robert Gooding-Williams (Routledge, 1993), is devoted to an analysis of the case and its effects; it contains the West chapter cited in the main text above.

KINSHIP

Kinship should be distinguished from *affinity* (a relationship traced through marriage) and *descent*. It is also important to differentiate kinship as a personal network, as a means of recruiting corporate groups, and as a sentiment of identification. Sir Raymond Firth wrote in 1958: "The way in which a person acquires membership of a kinship group is termed descent. The way in which he acquires rank and privileges is termed succession, and the way in which he acquires material property after the death of its former owner is termed inheritance."

Descent may be traced in the following ways: (1) from a male ancestor through males (patrilineal); (2) from a female ancestor through females (matrilineal); (3) through both simultaneously but for different purposes (double unilineal); or (4) through a mixture of lines (variously called omnilineal, cognatic, or bilateral). Two persons are kin when one is descended from the other (lineal kin, as with grandparent and grandchild) or when they are both descended from a common ancestor (collateral kin, as with a man and his brother or uncle). Any table of kinship requires a reference point, that of ego, from whom relationships are reckoned. When kinship is a basis for claiming rights it is also necessary to establish a boundary to the range of degrees of relationship (as the medieval German kinship group included kin only up to the sixth cousins). It will be apparent that only some of ego's kin will be of the same unilineal kinship group as ego, so that kinship reckoning comprehends more persons in the present generation than unilineal descent reckoning, whereas descent lines can list large numbers of ancestors who would be outside the range of recognized kin. The rights of kinship can be created, as by adoption, and they depend upon the social recognition of relationships, not upon genetic relationships (or consanguinity).

Most men and women grow up in families and therefore experience relationships of kinship as principles organizing the social world. They are therefore apt to organize their perceptions of the natural world according to similar principles, seeing family resemblance and relationships in animals, plants, etc. They also utilize the sentiments of identification generated within the kinship network as norms for judging social relations. For example, fraternity is considered an important value on the assumption that brothers support and care for one another, ignoring the frequency with which, in some social systems, brothers struggle with one another for primacy. Sentiments of kinship are extended in many ethnic movements to comprehend a much wider network (for example, the use of "brother" and "sister" in the African American revitalization movement). Relationships of descent are also replicated in the organization of ethnicity. Just as someone can be a MacDonald over a Campbell, a Highlander in opposition to a Lowlander, a Scot and not an Englishman, but a Briton or a European when overseas, so an immigrant may be able to utilize a series of ethnic identities of different magnitudes according to the social situation in which s/he finds himself. One identity nests inside another in an order of segmentation.

SEE ALSO: anthropology; Boas, Franz; culture; culturecide; Dollard, John; ethnicity; ethnocide; patriarchy

Reading

Human Types by Raymond Firth (New English Library, 1958) is the source of the quotation in the main text above.

Introduction to Social Anthropology, 2nd edn., by Lucy Mair (Clarendon Press, 1972), is a textbook on the subject of anthropology, the writing in which is clear; the literature on kinship is extensive but, in some cases, very technical.

MICHAEL BANTON

KU KLUX KLAN

A racist organization, originating at the end of the American Civil War in 1865, taking its name from *Kuklos* (Greek for circle or band), and Klan (from the Scottish clan), denoting common ancestry. At first intended as a secret society, the Klan opposed the new social and legal rights granted to four million blacks after the abolition of slavery. At various stages in its development, the KKK terrorized blacks, Jews, Catholics, Mormons, and communists, while retaining one constant imperative: to uphold white supremacy. The Klan remains one of the most vigorous white racist organizations in the USA and, to a much lesser extent, in Europe. In 1998 one of the Klan's chapters was ordered by a South Carolina jury to pay $37.8m (£24m) in damages to the congregation of a black church torched by KKK members in 1995. It was the largest ever award for a hate crime (in 1987, a different chapter of the organization was ordered to pay $7m for its role in the lynching of a black teenager in Mobile, Alabama.)

Throughout its history, the Klan has fought to maintain the supposed purity of the white Anglo-Saxon Protestant – the WASP. As with neo-nazi organizations, the KKK philosophy was based on a vision in which the white race (its term) reigned supreme. For two hundred years of its history, America had housed a majority of Protestants of English descent, Anglo-Saxons. According to Klan philosophy, it was obvious that God constantly looked over, protected and designated whites as the supreme, ruling group. It was demonstrated by their material well-being compared to the other two main groups: (1) American Indians were subhuman savages fit only for mass extermination; (2) blacks were also less than human and were to be used as a form of property to relieve whites of the harder forms of labor.

The Klan believed that there was a divine plan in which the WASP was to dominate; this plan had been violated by the freeing of slaves and the growing presence of Catholics. William Randel quotes from a KKK manifesto: "Our main and fundamental objective is the MAINTENANCE OF THE SUPREMACY OF THE WHITE RACE in this republic. History and Physiology teach us that we belong to a race which nature has endowed with an evident superiority over all other races, and that the Maker, in thus elevating us above the common standard of human creation, has to give us over inferior races a dominion from which no law can permanently derogate."

The Klan chose an assortment of methods to achieve its aim. At the respectable extreme it ventured into national politics, both independently and through the mainstream parties. At the other extreme, it simply annihilated whole groups of people. Just after its formation, the Klansmen used to clothe themselves in white robes and hoods and terrorize blacks: there were regular lynchings, castrations, and destruction of blacks' properties. But, even as recently as 1978, in Greensboro, the Klan ambushed a meeting and killed five people; though perhaps the Klan's most famous atrocity of recent times was in 1963 when a church in Birmingham, Alabama, was bombed, killing four black girls.

The KKK has gained momentum since the 1920s when it acquired an organizational structure, principally through the influence of William Mason. Ostensibly, it took the form of a secret society, much like Freemasonry, with a hierarchy of lodges and a network of communications. The head of this "invisible empire," as the Klan called itself, was the Imperial Wizard, and under his command were Grand Dragons, Grand Titans, Lictors, and so on.

In the 1920s, racism was rife in the USA, and there was growing hostility to the new immigrants from Europe. Charles Alexander wrote of the southern branches in this period: "The Klan was only doing what the regional majority wanted – preserving the American way of life as White Southerners defined it." Randel estimates that, at this time, about five million people were in some way affiliated to the Klan. In some respects it was regarded as a positive moral

force, and this image was fostered by philanthropic enterprises and church-like rituals. Support was gained through charity appeals.

Its membership today is impossible even to estimate if only because the Klan carefully preserves its status as a secret organization. It has international links with other fascist groups and has branches in Britain, where it established a base in the mid-1960s. Its presence in England was signaled by a spate of burning crosses either nailed to or laid at the foot of doors of selected persons, usually black or Asian.

Bill Wilkinson, an Imperial Wizard, illegally entered Britain in 1978 with the expressed intention of generating support, but it seems his impact was nugatory. The British scene at that stage was full of neo-fascist groups ranging from the "respectable" National Front, through the virulent League of St. George to the paramilitary Combat 18. But the Klan has maintained its principal strength in the United States and remains one of the most potent racist underground organizations.

SEE ALSO: Aryan; bigotry; Doomed Races Doctrine; fascism; Jim Crow; National Front; neo-nazism; Other; prejudice; reparations; skinheads; White Power; white race; whiteness

Reading

Encyclopedia of White Power: A sourcebook on the radical racist right, edited by Jeffrey Kaplan (Alta-Mira, 2000), as its title suggests, provides valuable reference material on the Klan as well as other white supremacist groups.

The Ku Klux Klan by William P. Randel (Hamish Hamilton, 1965) remains one of the most authoritative accounts of the growth of the organization in America and is complemented by *The Fiery Cross* by W. Craig (Simon & Schuster, 1987), in which the KKK is called "an American institution."

The Ku Klux Klan in the Southwest by Charles C. Alexander (University of Kentucky Press, 1965) is an historical case study of one segment of the KKK in the United States and may be read alongside the more contemporary *White Man Falling: Race, gender and white supremacy* (Rowman & Littlefield, 1998), which includes excerpts from Klan publications.

CHECK: internet resources section

L

LANGUAGE

The term language is capable of a range of meanings: it can refer to the individual's "mother tongue," the descriptions of languages found in dictionaries and grammatical descriptions, the property of a community (as in the "standard" language of a particular nation), or the language that people actually speak or write. Language, like "race," thus derives many of its broader meanings from the symbolism that attaches itself to the mental concept, however blurred that image might be. There are parallels between the issues encountered when subjecting language to scrutiny and the way in which the term "race" is now regarded as problematic.

Language, "race" and ethnicity

The concepts of "race" and "ethnicity" have a long and complex history within the fields of language and linguistics. According to a number of accounts, the English term "race" appears to date from the sixteenth century, when we also have *razza* in Italian, *raza* in Spanish, *raça* in Portuguese, and *race* in French. Until the eighteenth century, the term was typically associated with membership of a noble house or lineage. In the late nineteenth century, the term was increasingly employed in the anthropological and biological categorization of human beings, and thus became associated with the range of modern meanings that persist to the present.

As the anthropological classification of race based on physical (or phenotypical differences) developed during the nineteenth century, evidence in support of such theories was sought from the study of language. Scholars sought to reconstruct language "families" based on linguistic evidence, in order to measure the "congruence" of racial groups to such groupings of languages throughout the world. The languages of India and the European languages were classified together in the Indo-European group of languages. At the same time, the myth was established of a long-lost Indo-European or "Aryan" race that had spoken a proto-language from which Indo-European descended and who were the ancestors of the Slavs, Romans, Germans, and other European races.

Although nineteenth-century race theory is ineluctably linked to the Nazi Holocaust of the 1930s and 1940s, many linguists in Nazi Germany were aware that the congruence between language and race was inexact at best. Indeed, what was most disturbing to many in the Third Reich was that so many Jews spoke German so flawlessly and assimilated linguistically so well in many key areas of German society, including the professions and academia. Since World War II, discussions of the links between language and race have been muted in many fields of European linguistics, a consequence of an association with neo-Darwinian theories of scientific racism. Nevertheless, the notion of race, it might be argued, has survived in discussions of language and *ethnicity* (with its earliest attestation in its modern sense in the *Oxford English Dictionary* dating from 1953).

Multilingualism and multiculture

Within sociolinguistics (the study of language and society), it is axiomatic that the term "language" cannot be explained adequately by reference to linguistic criteria alone. There are many examples in the world – for example, in

Scandinavia or the Dutch–German border – where political or cultural forces leading to the creation of separate "languages" have segmented dialect continua almost arbitrarily. The vast majority of societies in the world are *multilingual* rather than monolingual. It is estimated that the approximately 190 nation-states of the world share around 5,000 languages. Even in Britain, which was traditionally considered a monolingual society, a report from *The Times* (January 22, 2000) claimed that "London is the most linguistically diverse city on earth," and that 307 languages were spoken by schoolchildren attending the city's schools. Overall, this survey showed that only two-thirds of London schoolchildren spoke English at home, and that thirty-nine languages other than English were used extensively at home.

One major reason for multilingualism of this kind in Europe today has been the migrations of large numbers of former colonial subjects from erstwhile colonies to metropolitan European societies. In the colonial era, European languages such as English, French, Spanish, and Portuguese became established throughout the Americas, the Caribbean, South Africa, Africa and Asia. As the British Empire retreated after 1945, the spread of English was sustained by the increasing economic and technological power of the USA. Traditional European colonialism may now have almost totally vanished, but English has been retained in many former colonial territories. The English language is currently spoken by over 300 million "native-speakers" in the USA and Britain, but it also has a wide currency among another billion or so speakers in such "outer circle" or "second language" societies as Nigeria, Kenya, India, Singapore, Hong Kong, and the Philippines. In societies such as these, the language has typically been retained as a language of government, law and education, as well as a medium of international communications of various kinds.

Following this, one of the foremost problems in language planning worldwide has been the choice of official or national languages for newly emergent independent states in the developing world. For various reasons, this choice has often involved a compromise between an international language, such as English, and indigenous languages, as can be seen in many ex-colonial nations in Africa, India, Singapore, and the Philippines. As a result, there are now large numbers of people of African and Asian origin who speak what were originally European languages, and, in the case of English, many such second-language varieties have become at least partly "nativized" so that it is possible to speak of Nigerian English, Indian English, Singaporean English and so on. In the case of Singapore, the promotion of English as an official language has been motivated in part by the need to adopt a neutral *lingua franca* in a culturally diverse multiethnic nation. In other postcolonial societies, however, rather different considerations of race and ethnicity have played a role in the promotion of national vernacular languages, such as Hindi in India, and Bahasa in Indonesia and Malaysia. In Malaysia, for example, this policy was partly designed to privilege the native-born sons of the soil (or *bumiputera*) over those who belonged to the Chinese and Indian populations.

While it is misleading to assume that speakers of the same language are necessarily members of the same race, or that speakers of apparently related languages are racially related to one another, language often plays a role in symbolizing or signifying membership of a particular ethnic group. Central to the relationship between language and ethnicity are issues of self-identity and identification with others, as noted by the British sociolinguist Robert Le Page. Language issues related to ethnicity may be seen in the conflicts experienced by minority language groups in multilingual societies, as with the case of the French in Canada, or Hispanics in the USA. The importance of ethnicity may also been seen, however, in the way in which the distinct identity of ethnic groups is expressed not only by different languages but also by different varieties of the same language.

Black English

The case of "Black English" both in the USA and Britain provides a good example of the latter point. The study of the Black English Vernacular (or African American Vernacular English, AAVE) was pioneered by the American sociolinguist William Labov. His and subsequent studies have emphasized the distinctive patterns of AAVE in terms of both its pronunciation and its grammar. In 1979 an historic trial, the so-called Black English Trial, took place in Ann Arbor, Michigan, during which the judge found that the failure of the school authorities to recognize Black English as a separate language had handicapped the educational progress of black children in the area. Similar issues arose in 1996–97, when the Oakland School Board made the decision to recognize AAVE, or Ebonics as it is better known, as a variety of language used by many African American children. The proposal immediately drew flak from a range of conservative quarters in educational and political circles and a somewhat muddled debate ensued. The leading US professional organization for linguists, the Linguistic Society of America (LSA) was then moved to pass a resolution on the issue, which avowed that Ebonics was "systematic and rule-governed like all natural speech varieties," and that the Oakland School Board's recognition of the Ebonics variety was "linguistically and pedagogically sound."

In Britain, a number of linguists have set out to describe "British Black English," a term typically used to refer to a type of modified Jamaican Creole spoken by second-generation British of Caribbean descent. Whether Black English is a fully developed language "variety" is a matter of interpretation, as most British speakers of Black English will invariably have a command of other varieties of the language as well. However, it seems clear that the adoption of creole speech forms by youths of Caribbean parentage in Britain is closely linked to the assertion of an ethnic identity closely related to black interests and activities (such as Rastafari and reggae music). In addition, the use of creole or patois is also linked to values of solidarity, and ethnic blacks perceive it as expressing resistance to a repressive and racist society.

Many linguists today believe that one of the most important contributions of linguistics as a profession is in advocating the "language rights" of minority groups (immigrant and other) in Europe and North America, as well as in supporting the survival of many of the world's endangered languages. It is currently estimated that a majority of the world's approximately 5,000 languages face "language death" in the next thirty years. Local varieties of speech are being displaced by national and international languages, often in tandem, with economic and social developments within the modernizing Third World and with the effects of cultural and economic globalization. Those working on the issue of language rights are concerned not only by the projected demise of many language varieties, but also by the unequal treatment accorded to speakers of minority languages, particularly in education, by governments and state institutions. Internationally, the claims of minority groups have received formal recognition in agreements such as the UN Declaration on Indigenous Rights and the European Charter for Regional and Minority Languages.

The current idealism shown by linguists on such issues is not without its ironies, however, since research by Christopher Hutton has shown that much of the rhetoric on the sanctity of the "mother tongue" can be traced back to debates among Nazi linguists in the 1930s (including Heinz Kloss, who later played a leading role in founding "sociolinguistics" in North America). Many scholars today nevertheless argue that linguists should play an active role in defending the ethnolinguistic rights of minority groups, and that scientific linguistics is an important weapon against racism. At another extreme, however, there are also other linguists still committed to the notion of an Indo-European and proto-Indo-Ayran language now seeking help from archaeology and genetics to scientifically unravel the linguistic and racial mysteries of the past. Historical tensions concerning both language and race persist in many societies and at times explode violently, as in the demise in the former Yugoslavia of Serbo-Croatian, which was replaced by two varieties of ethnically purer "Serbian" and "Croatian." Despite the widely held assumption that many of the more banal ghosts of our intellectual past have been laid firmly to rest, the at times unholy alliance between race theory and linguistics seems certain to persist and to find new expressions in the academic as well as the general community.

SEE ALSO: Afrocentricity; Anglo-Indians; anthropology; Aryan; colonial discourse; colonialism; creole; Ebonics; epithet (racial/slang); ethnic cleansing; ethnocide; ethnonational; globalization; Holocaust; human rights; media; migration; minority language rights; multicultural education; multiculturalism; phenotype; race: as classification; race: as synonym; racial coding; racist discourse; Rastafari; reggae; science; subaltern; transracial adoption; youth subcultures

Reading

"Language and race: some implications for linguistic science" by John Baugh, in *Linguistics: The*

Cambridge Survey IV: Language: The socio-cultural context, edited Frederick J. Newmeyer (Cambridge University Press, 1994) presents the contemporary view that "scientific linguistics" can be a useful weapon against racism, particularly within debates about African-American Vernacular English (AAVE) in the US context.

"The language myth and the race myth: evil twins of modern identity politics?" by Christopher Hutton, in *The Language Myth in Western Culture*, edited by Roy Harris (Curzon Press, 2002), presents a scholarly and revealing account of the notions of "race" and "language" in the intellectual history of linguistics.

Linguistics and the Third Reich: Mother-tongue fascism, race and the science of language by Christopher Hutton, (Routledge, 1999) provides a fascinating account of the beliefs and practices of linguists in the Third Reich and reveals the intellectual links between the German linguistics of the era and the role of "mother-tongue" ideologies that have now found a place in contemporary sociolinguistics.

Linguistic Human Rights: Overcoming linguistic discrimination, edited by Tove Skutnabb-Kangas and Robert Phillipson (Walter de Gruyter, 1994), provides an overview of the growing debate on linguistic human rights, with discussions of language rights in many societies throughout the world, including the USA, New Zealand, Latin America, and postcolonial Africa.

London Jamaican: Language systems in interaction by Mark Sebba (Longman, 1993) is a study of the forms of Jamaican creole spoken by black youth in Britain.

KINGSLEY BOLTON

LAS CASAS, BARTOLOMÉ DE (1474–1566)

Bartolomé de Las Casas was a Spanish conquistador who went to Hispaniola in the Caribbean (now Haiti and the Dominican Republic) in 1502, ten years after Christopher Columbus's first voyage, and entered the priesthood eight years later, age nine. He later turned into one of the first and fiercest critics of Spanish colonialism in the New World. As a Dominican priest, he became one of the most effective antislavery writers and campaigners of the sixteenth century, arguing that Indians, far from being akin to beasts or belonging to some indeterminate category of being, were sentient human beings and entitled to the protection of God, along with all the rights of human subjects. On his return to Europe in 1547, he was drawn into a renowned public debate with the theologian Gines de Sepúlveda on the nature of Indians. Three years later, he published his *The Devastation of the Indies: A brief account*, a passionate denuncia-

tion, which did much to sway public opinion against the *encomienda*, the Spanish system of slavery.

A slaveowner himself, Las Casas is said to have experienced an epiphany in 1514 while preparing a sermon on a verse in Ecclesiastes: "He that sacrificeth of a thing wrongfully gotten, his offering is ridiculous and the gifts of unjust men are not accepted."

Las Casas interpreted this against the background of the Spanish conquests and concluded that "everything done to the Indians thus far has been unjust and tyrannical." He immediately freed his slaves and began to preach against slavery. In fact, he dedicated the remainder of his life (and he lived until the age of 92) to the cause of Indians and against slavery. He was a forceful writer, chronicling the atrocities initiated by Spaniards against native Americans. His text contained horrific details of how Spaniards wagered whether they could split Indians in two with a single stroke of their swords and trained dogs to hunt them for sport. Regularly, the Spanish disemboweled men, women and children, "as if dealing with sheep in a slaughterhouse."

Despite witnessing such deeds, Las Casas never doubted the virtue of the Christian mission and garnered the support of both Pope Paul III and the King of Spain, Ferdinand V. In 1530 he helped secure the prohibition of slavery in Peru and, in 1537, the Pope bowed to Las Casas's solicitation by proclaiming that Indians were "truly men" and should not be treated as "dumb brutes" or deprived of freedom and property; *they had souls worth saving*. Although, in 1517, he had requested African slaves from the king, he later regretted this. He once refused to administer the last rites to a colonial landowner until the dying man agreed to free his indigenous slaves.

Several Papal edicts had been issued from the eleventh century onwards, all attesting to the Spanish right to rule over infidel lands, but Las Casas countered that Indians, having the power of reason, possessed the potential to become not only Christians, but also citizens of *res publica*. The abolition of slavery in Spanish colonies was uneven, with some territories abolishing outright and others maintaining the institution.

Las Casas spent most of his life campaigning in the New World though he made a number of visits to Spain where he engaged in discussions on the subject of Spanish policy in regard to

Indians. Many of the debates would invoke the subject of natural inequality. In one debate, Las Casas was made to answer the question: if Indians were, as he insisted, human, were they of the same order as their masters? Or were they the functional equivalents of children, without the sophistication of civilized beings? Among those who argued that Indians were naturally idle and thick skulled was Sepúlveda, who maintained that Indian inferiority was natural rather than a product of the circumstances imposed by their masters (the sociologist Oliver C. Cox was later to describe Sepúlveda one of "the first great racists"). A debate between Las Casas and Sepúlveda took place at Valladolid on July 8, 1550, and, while no minutes of the meeting were taken, Las Casas is thought to have emerged with credit. He maintained his position that Indians did indeed have souls. The decision of the Council was that Aristotle's work was not sufficient justification for the natural superiority of one people over another. Las Casas's written and spoken work was widely circulated and used to limit the savagery of the exploitation in Spanish colonies.

"Las Casas' accomplishment was formidable," wrote Thomas Gossett in the 1960s. "Indians had been admitted to equality with Spaniards under the law. By the pronouncement of the Pope, the Indians had the status of rational beings, and henceforth it was heretical to maintain the contrary."

In 2000, Seville's Dominican community requested canonization for Las Casas, arguing that his central ideas on human rights were timeless.

SEE ALSO: antislavery; culturecide; *encomienda*; ethnocide; exploitation; human rights; indigenous peoples; slavery

Reading

Bartolomé de Las Casas (1474–1566) in the Pages of Father Antonio de Remesal by Antonio de Remesal, translated by Felix Jay (Edward Mellen, 2002), is a translation of a document written by a fellow Dominican sixty years after Las Casas's death.
Bartolomé de Las Casas: An interpretation of his life and writings by Lewis Hanke (Nijhoff, 1951) is complemented by the same author's *Aristotle and the American Indians: A study in race prejudice in the modern world* (Hollis & Carter, 1959), which focuses on the Council at Valladolid in 1550–51 when the Spanish court was asked to pronounce on the status of the peoples of America.
The Devastation of the Indies: A brief account,

translated by Herma Briffault, is Las Casas's texts, originally published in 1552, but still in print (Johns Hopkins University Press, 1992).

LATINOS

Latinos, or Hispanics, refers to persons of Spanish origin, usually with ancestry in either Spanish-speaking Latin America or the Iberian peninsula. There are 35 million Latinos in the USA, which slightly exceeds the population of the African American community. This represents almost a 60 percent increase over the decade up to 2000, compared to an overall population increase of 13.7 percent, making Latinos the fastest growing minority group.

Composition and growth

The Mexican origin community continues to be the largest national origin group at almost 60 percent of the Latino community. It is noteworthy however to highlight the faster growing segments of the Latino community as well. The Dominican community, especially in the New York metropolitan area, exceeds over 750,000 persons; while the number of El Salvadorans (largest Latino segment in the Washington, DC metro area) and Colombians on the East coast also represent marked gains. For the general grouping of Latinos, those of Central and South Americans origin constitute the fast growing segment of the Latino community. The results of the 2000 US Census shows that the second largest Hispanic subgroup is that of "other Hispanic." The ten million persons who indicated that they were of Hispanic, Latino, Spanish origin could specify being Mexican, Puerto Rican, Cuban, and Central/South American or other Hispanic. Currently, over ten million Latinos responded as "other Hispanic or Latino," rather than from a designated origin, for example Mexican, Puerto Rican, and Central/South American. There is little evidence to suggest who these individuals are and how much of this response is a function of the format of the Hispanic origin question in the Census. At the same time, the presence of a broader notion of associating with a large array of Latino national origin groups does add to the force of a growing political community.

The other interesting element to note about the composition of the Latino community is the governmental information on specific Latino subgroups. That is, more information has been available for the Mexican origin, Puerto Rican and Cuban populations than for the other Latino subgroups. Recently, Dominican and Colombian organizations requested that more complete and accurate data be disseminated regarding all of the Latino subgroups. The bases for the concerns were affected by their need for an accurate count. It is contended that the absence of subgroup affiliation or identification hinders the provision of subgroup specific information (i.e. family structure, income, educational attainment, etc.). While the status of Latinos is portrayed usually as all subgroups, there are subgroup differences and regional concentration for some groups (i.e. over 90 percent of Dominicans are found in the New York metro area, etc.) such that there is a need to establish the specific group's policy needs and issues. One difference between the 2000 Census and the previous one was that examples were provided under the "other Hispanic" designation.

The percentage growth among Hispanics for the decade up to 2001 was seven times greater than for non-Hispanics in the USA in the same period. The Mexican origin population increased by 52.9 percent over the decade, while the other Hispanic category increased by 97 percent. Levels of population increases were highest among Central and South American subgroups. Over seventeen million Latinos reside in California and Texas, which represents half of the total Latino population. At the same time, significant numbers of Latinos are found in the eastern states of New York, Florida, and New Jersey. One the other noteworthy results of Census 2000 information is the wider distribution of Latinos in the South and the Midwest. States such as Arkansas, North Carolina, Georgia, and South Carolina experienced triple-digit percentage gains. Interestingly, the states in which Latinos are located are in the most populous states with the highest number of electoral votes for the presidential elections.

The themes of significant growth, new areas of growth, and greater concentration in the more established Latino areas are reinforced with the observation that the ten states with the largest Latino population represent over four-fifths of all Latinos and their regional presence is extensive. In 1999, California became a majority–minority state in which the combined populations of Latinos, African Americans, and Asian Americans exceeded 50 percent of the state's total population. One-half of all Latinos live in the two states of California and Texas. In addition, their concentration in the Sunbelt region and the more industrialized northeast positions Latinos in key electoral states for both national and state elections.

Correspondingly, the major political parties have targeted greater efforts toward getting the Latino communities to support their candidates and policies. The 2002 mid-term elections illustrate this increased political capital for Latinos. With control of Congress a primary concern, significant partisan funding and national leaders, including President George W. Bush, have traveled to many of the states on behalf of congressional and gubernatorial candidates and incumbents. To some extent, both parties have courted Latinos voters and, in addition, the number of Latino candidates is increasing over previous elections. On the latter point, Latinos are vying for the governorship of New Mexico and Texas. Characteristic of this "demographic imperative" are: a more noticeable Latino middle-class, saliency of organizations and increased levels of participation, all of which have warranted greater attention by the conventional institutions of the US political system. That said, increased population growth and size is not totally sufficient to insure significant and effective political influence and power for Latinos.

Overall, two out of every five Latinos are born outside of the USA. In addition, the naturalization rates for Latinos tend to be lower than for foreign-born persons, with Mexican immigrants among the lowest. However, English language acquisition and length of time in the US are important to social mobility. Since the mid 1990s, federal immigration policies (dealing with legal permanent residents' access to social service programs, deportation, and anti-terrorist monitoring) as well as statewide initiatives – such as those in California limiting access of undocumented immigrants to education, health and social welfare services – have become part of the decision-making process. Thus, in addition to becoming citizens as part of a sociopolitical attachment to the USA, some immigrants do pursue naturalization as a means to protect their status, improve immigration priorities for fellow family members and access social services for which they meet the means testing.

There has been an increase of naturalized Latinos in the past five years for the range of reasons suggested above. In addition, Latino organizations such as the National Association of Latino Elected and Appointed Officials have actively promoted naturalization to Latino immigrants and have lobbied the Immigration and Naturalization Service to streamline its processing and allocate more staff to facilitate a quicker turnaround time for final citizenship completion. While the number of Latino naturalized citizens has been increasing, there still remains a major untapped reservoir of political participants (especially electorally) to activate. At the same time, with potentially greater numbers of naturalized Latinos, the educational process of political familiarity and motivation is still required to convert an expanded Latino electorate.

Public opinion and policy preferences

Latinos exhibit modest levels of trust toward the "government in Washington," with 44 percent trusting the national government most or all of the time. Comparatively, these response patterns are similar to those for non-Hispanic whites but not as low as for African Americans. On the other hand, Latinos have a greater expectation that government should provide more services than other groups, and are willing to pay higher taxes in exchange for such services.

The issue of immigration has been a consistent focus for the past three decades. Latinos and many of its organizations have advocated immigrants' rights and protections, higher legal immigration ceilings, and amnesty for the current undocumented resident population. Latinos believe that there are too many immigrants living in the USA On the other hand, Latinos are more likely to favor a higher immigration ceiling for those from Latin America. Similarly, Latinos exhibited a more positive view about the contributions of undocumented or illegal immigrants to the American economy, as well as more support for legalization of the status of undocumented residents.

Yet there are other relevant policy concerns for Latinos. Research indicates that, overwhelmingly, education is the most important issue. The economy is also a pressing issue, followed by health care and social security. There is support for bilingual education programs, expansion of programs for proficient students who have limited English, school financial equalization measures, overall educational quality improvements. The area of the economy would include: wages and unemployment insurance coverage; unionization protection; job training; workplace safety; and more vigorous economic growth. Health care access, medical benefits, HIV/AIDS treatment as well as for other health conditions (i.e. higher incidences of tuberculosis, cervical cancer, high blood pressure, etc.) are part of the Latino policy agenda in the health care area. A growing national Latino political agenda revolves around opportunity, access and participation in the main areas of American life. The significant proportion of the Latino community that is foreign-born helps to maintain immigration policies as a key element of the agenda. Latino organizations such as the Mexican American Legal Defense and Education Fund, and the National Association of Latino Elected and Appointed Officials have served as advocates for both native and foreign-born Latinos.

Finally, primary attention to issues and political activities focusing on Latinos has been directed at the national level; yet much of Latino politics centers on local issues and arenas. Increased representation, access to decision making, quality and range of services available to Latinos, and local issues around education, health care, and the local economy are mirrored at the state and local arenas. Local organizations have been formed and operate on a sustained basis on local issues and enhanced political empowerment. In addition, many of the Latino organizations have incorporated immigrants into their association and issues. In some cases, the unions such as the janitorial/custodian have relied heavily on their immigrant members (both documented and undocumented) for their membership base and for union activists. The old cliché that politics is local has quite a bit of relevance in the characterization and understanding of Latino politics.

Political behavior and empowerment

While attitudes and orientations about the political system provide some indication about political involvement, information about actual political participation enlarges the portrait of Latino politics in the USA. For the most part, Latino political participation has been characterized as exhibiting low levels in most modes of participation (i.e. voting, campaigning, organizational, contacting, etc.). The major sets of explanations have centered on lower socioeconomic status (i.e. education, income levels and occupational status), youthfulness of the population, cultural factors (including language, familiarity with American organizational society, isolation) and high levels of cynicism and alienation. Yet there are clear signals that greater political involvement exists.

An examination of the political participation of Latinos presents a mixed picture, with Latinos involved in voting, campaign-related activities, communal or organizational activities, particularized contact with officials, and the holding of office. While more attention is directed toward the electoral arena, organizational involvement and activities have served as a means of direct interaction with specific policy-makers and public policies, with females participating less than males. Overall, the level of Latino participation is lower than that for Anglos and African Americans, yet there are noteworthy variations in which, depending on the participatory mode, the political "engagement" gap is very slight.

The number of Latinos who voted over the last eight presidential elections portrays similar patterns to the registration data; that is, consistently lower levels of turnout than other groups. Again the voting age population base or the denominator, which includes all adults, affects the lower percentage. In any event, 2000 proved to be a marker in which the turnout rate increased substantially from the previous election years. The increase has been affected by the continued population growth among Hispanics; a higher percentage of 18+ voters, more concentrated voter registration, and education drives over the latter part of the 1990s; as well as targeted mobilization efforts.

Two factors have enhanced the political capital of Latinos: (1) a more defined policy and political agenda; (2) targeted efforts by Latino organizations and leaders to encourage more positive political orientations. In the case of the former, the policy areas of education, immigration, economic well being and the corresponding labor market and social service programs, and health care access and status are the primary issue clusters for Latinos. Within each of these policy areas more targeted concerns would include: education (i.e. support and expansion of bilingual education, equalization of school finances, educational quality and resources); immigration (i.e. rights and protections for undocumented and permanent resident persons, potential guestworker programs, legalization or amnesty, protection of workers' right to organize); economic well-being (i.e. access and expansion of social service programs, increased wages and benefits, protection from employment discrimination); and health care (i.e. access to health care services, research and treatment of health conditions and diseases prevalent among Latinos, language and health services).

The role of Latino organizations and leaders become critical to educating, mobilizing, and targeting Latino communities to political institutions and leadership. At the same time, external factors such as statewide initiatives and public policies (e.g. anti-immigrant and anti-Latino propositions, and political officials raising the issue of political loyalty to the USA) have served to activate politically a greater portion of the Latino community.

The electoral arena is one in which Latinos have lagged over the past decades (in part due to the youthfulness of the population, high percentage of noncitizens and high levels of participatory orientations). Yet voter participation among Latinos increased in the 2000 national election. The combination of active Latino organizations, increased numbers of Latino candidates and office-holders, greater partisan appeal, increased voter registration levels, and salient issues and propositions, contributed to gains in the electoral process. Similar patterns were evident in the 2002 elections, where Latinos picked up four more congressional seats (in Florida, California and Arizona) and a governor in New Mexico, though they were unsuccessful in capturing the Texas gubernatorialship and a Senate seat in New Mexico. Nevertheless, increased numbers of Latino candidates are retaining and challenging current office-holders at all levels of the American political system, especially at the local levels. At the same time, statewide offices (governors, attorney generals, etc.) and the US Senate remain challenges for the near future.

Any discussion of Latino politics and its future lies with the inclusion of internal political developments and external pressures and factors. The former centers on the continual political capital accumulation within each of the Latino subcommunities and the "coalitional efforts" to enjoin more regularized and effective activities over common concerns and issues.

The experiences of the late 1990s have indicated that when they feel "under siege," there is a wider range of Latinos who become more politically aware and involved. Thus, in addition to the punitive and negative responses within the American system, there have been more proactive efforts by political parties to encourage and solicit Latino political involvement.

SEE ALSO: affirmative action; African Americans; Chávez, César; education; *encomienda*; ethnonational; Las Casas, Bartolomé de; multicultural education; Park, Robert Ezra; politics; Puerto Ricans in the USA

Reading

Changing Race: Latinos, the census and the history of ethnicity in the U.S. by Clara Rodriguez (New York University Press, 2000) situates Latinos in a wider context.

Immigration and Race: New challenge for American democracy, edited by Gerald Jaynes (Yale University Press, 2000), is a collection with several essays on Latinos.

Latino Politics in America: Community, culture, and interests by John A. Garcia (Rowman & Littlefield, 2003) is a comprehensive analysis of the development of political engagement among Latinos.

Voice and Equality: Civic voluntarism in American politics by Sidney Verba, Kay Scholzman, and Henry Brady (Harvard University Press, 1995) is a valuable study; it may profitably be read in conjunction with Louis DeSipio's Counting the Latino Vote: Latinos as a new electorate (University of Virginia Press, 1996).

JOHN A. GARCIA

LAW: CIVIL RIGHTS, USA

Apart from the brief period immediately after the Civil War, American legislation up to 1938 had the effect of maintaining discrimination against blacks and other minority groups. Reconstruction was an exception to the general pattern, which denied blacks civil rights such as voting, access to education, and so on. The 1866 Civil Rights Act signaled the end of *de jure* discrimination (that is, legal racialism), but various federal actions had worked to diminish racialism in various sectors before that time.

In 1938, for example, the Supreme Court ruled that the University of Missouri should admit a black applicant to law school because the state had no comparable institution open to blacks

(*Missouri ex. rel. v. Canada*). Four years later, governmental agencies were instructed to end discrimination in employment; and, in 1946, segregated interstate travel was made illegal. Segregated transport was generally more widespread in Southern states than in the North, though *de facto* segregation was rife throughout America, with public facilities having all-white and all-black areas.

In housing, blacks were prevented from buying certain properties by restrictive housing covenants (a provision attached to a deed in which the buyer must agree not to sell or rent to a member of a particular group, such as blacks, Jews, or Latinos). In 1948, the Supreme Court, in the *Shelly v. Kraemer* case, ruled that the restrictive covenants were not enforceable by the states any longer. This did not eliminate the covenants however: it simply meant that they were no longer enforceable. The 1968 Act eventually banned them.

Perhaps the single most important piece of legislation in regard to race relations came in 1954 with the famous case of *Brown v. Board of Education of Topeka, Kansas*. The Supreme Court overturned the "separate but equal" principle established in 1896 by the *Plessy v. Ferguson* case in which it was established that different facilities should be made available to blacks. In the area of education, black institutions were truly separate but rarely equal to their white equivalents. The 1954 decision ended this and made segregation in schools illegal. The importance of the decision was magnified by the fact that many believed that the whole issue of equality hinged on integrated schooling. The National Association for the Advancement of Colored People (NAACP) precipitated the 1954 ruling by arguing the case of Oliver Brown, whose daughter had been forced to travel by bus to an all-black school even though she lived close to an all-white institution. The NAACP insisted that school segregation was unconstitutional and the Supreme Court agreed, the presiding Chief Justice Warren concluding: "In the field of public education, the doctrine of 'separate but equal' has no place."

Between 1957 and 1960, civil rights legislation introduced enforcement powers through a Civil Rights Division of the US Department of Justice. But the critical period in antidiscrimination legislation came over the following four years. Pressure from Martin Luther King's movement resulted in the strengthening of voting rights for blacks (in 1960) and the banning of discrimination (including sex discrimination) in employment and trade union membership as well as in access to privately owned accommodations, such as hotels, restaurants, and theaters. Enforcement of provisions against discrimination in education was also given more weight.

Constitutionally, the Civil Rights Act of 1964 was something of a watershed in US race relations, extending federal powers to eliminate discrimination in places of public accommodation and enable the desegregation of all public facilities maintained by public organizations. In addition, public education was desegregated and the Civil Rights Commission granted new powers. Discrimination in employment on the grounds of "race, color, sex, or national origin" was made illegal. The Equal Employment Opportunity Commission was established to investigate and monitor complaints pertaining to this.

The most widespread requirement limiting minority voting was the literacy test that existed in various forms in numerous states in the South, West, and Northeast of the US. This tended to reduce voting opportunities for black, Hispanic, and Native American groups because these groups suffered extensive educational discrimination and, therefore, did not always match up to the literacy test requirements (in some cases, this was compounded by the fact that more stringent demands were made of minorities than whites). The Voting Rights Act of 1965 largely ended the tests. Discrimination of sorts continued, with some states operating policies that governed voter registration and made voting easier for whites; but the 1965 Act made discrimination in access to the ballot box considerably more difficult.

Five key court decisions in 1989 paved the way for new legislation. The most important was *Wards Cove* v. *Atonio*, which involved the concept of "disparate impact," meaning a practice which is not intentionally discriminatory but which results in a statistically disproportionate effect on minority group members or women. It was decided that the plaintiff had to prove that a minority was underrepresented in a particular type of job and demonstrate that there were qualified applicants in the labor market. *Price Waterhouse* v. *Hopkins* deliberated whether a "mixed motive" could lie behind discrimination:

for an employee to win a case against an employer, he or she would need "clear and convincing proof" that the motives behind an action were completely discriminatory and not just that discrimination was present.

The 1991 Civil Rights Act, signed by President George Bush (Sr.), was effectively a response to the Supreme Court decisions that had narrowed the scope of existing antidiscrimination legislation. It upheld the *Wards Cove* principle that the plaintiff needed statistical proof but it overturned *Price Waterhouse*. It became necessary to prove that discrimination was only part of the mixed motive. But the major change brought about in 1991 was the fact that parties taking action against intentional discrimination under the terms of the 1964 Civil Rights Act (specifically Title VII) would be entitled to a hearing by jury, who could decide the extent of compensatory damages, both monetary and emotional.

SEE ALSO: affirmative action; *Brown* v. *Board of Education*; civil rights movement; empowerment; equal opportunity; Jim Crow; Ku Klux Klan; law: race relations, Britain; law: racial discrimination, international; segregation

Reading

Black Civil Rights in America by Kevern Verney (Routledge, 2000) is a political and social history of the evolution of civil rights legislation.

Eye on the Prize by Juan Williams (Viking, 1987) is a tie-in with the celebrated television series documenting the civil rights years, 1954–65, showing how each piece of legislation was hard won.

"Race and ethnicity in the American legal tradition" is Unit 1 of *Annual Editions: Race and ethnic relations*, 12th edn., edited by John A. Kromkowski (McGraw-Hill/Dushkin, 2002), and comprises six extracts focusing on key legal decisions and their effects.

The Routledge Atlas of American History, 4th edn., by Martin Gilbert (Routledge, 2002), describes the struggle for voting rights through maps that are thoroughly augmented with captions, facts and text.

Unlikely Heroes by Jack Bass (University of Alabama Press, 1992) is an account of the implementation of the *Brown* decision.

LAW: IMMIGRATION, UK

The seventeenth and eighteenth centuries saw Britain and other Western European powers occupy vast portions of Africa, Asia, and the Caribbean. This colonial expansion laid the economic basis for the development of Western capitalism: the colonies provided a source of cheap labor, raw materials and, in some cases, markets. In the years immediately following the end of World War II, Britain exploited this source of cheap labor to the full. The introduction of the 1948 British Nationality Act by the Labour government facilitated access to this source, and while some members of what is commonly referred to as "the lunatic fringe" of the House of Commons protested publicly at the unregulated influx of black (and later South Asian) migrants, their demands tended to fall on deaf ears; quite simply, while many of their colleagues on both sides of the House shared this concern with the increased settlement of black migrants in Britain, priority ultimately was given to the country's economic priorities. Britain was experiencing rapid economic growth and the import of cheap labor to fill the subordinate levels of the labor market was essential. Nor did central government intervene in the settlement of the migrants in Britain. They were seen and treated simply as factory fodder and no attempt was made to facilitate settlement by the provision of educational, housing and welfare advice and facilities.

It was not until the economy began to take a turn for the worse in the mid 1950s and the demand for labor in major industries began to recede did the efficacy in Britain's approach to immigration come to under serious question. On the one hand, local authorities which had borne the brunt of migrant settlement complained that their limited resources were stretched to the full. On the other, the outbreak of violence between blacks and whites in Notting Hill and Nottingham in 1958 highlighted the resentment felt by some sectors of the white population toward the black migrants. Against this background of imminent social and economic stress, the racialization of Britain's immigration policies emerged as an important fulcrum on which political debate was balanced. At the risk of oversimplification, two courses of action were available to the government: first, the implementation of policies designed to ameliorate the social problems highlighted by the settlement of colonial migrants in certain parts of Britain. Alternatively, central government could abandon its "open door," or noninterventionist, immigration policy and impose entry controls. On the face of it, this second approach was entirely unnecessary; as the leader of the opposition Labour party explained in the House of Commons in the early 1960s, migration was self-regulating: as the economy

had entered a downward phase and the number of job vacancies gradually diminished, the number of migrants from the Caribbean had fallen accordingly. Nor was there much prospect of long-term unemployment. In this light, claims that the migrants would spend long periods drawing security benefits were completely untenable.

In the event, the Conservative government eschewed the more constructive and logical step of attacking social problems through policies to improve the living and working conditions of black and white residents. Instead, it embarked on a policy of surrender. The reasons behind this course of action are both complex and, in part, a matter of speculation. Nonetheless, recent research into cabinet and ministerial debates of this period indicate that immigration controls had always been favored. What seems to have inhibited, or at least delayed, their introduction was the embarrassment which might have accompanied their initiation, given Britain's status as head of the Commonwealth and Colonies.

The Commonwealth Immigrants Act 1962 formally marked the end of Britain's allegedly (if not committed) *laissez-faire* approach to immigration. It established a precedent for the introduction of progressively more restrictive and, *de facto*, racially discriminatory immigration legislation, and presaged the start of what some parliamentary members and others had identified as the defining characteristic of the race relations debate: numbers.

Briefly, the Act qualified the right of free entry into Britain for migrants from the New Commonwealth; that is, for black and brown migrants. Although skin color was not openly declared as the criterion for entry, the exclusion of citizens of the Irish Republic from the constraints of the Act signified its racially discriminatory nature.

By 1965, selective immigration control had become bipartisan policy. Despite its relatively strong opposition to the 1962 legislation the Labour party had, by 1965, completed a *volte face* on this issue and, for the sake of political expediency, introduced an extension of the earlier Act. In short, 1965 marked the point of public consensus in Westminster based on an identification of black and brown people as "the problem" and "turning off the tap" as the solution to that problem. "Keeping numbers down is good for race relations" became the organizing principle of this bipartisan policy. As Labour MP Roy Hattersley put it: "Without integration, limitation is inexcusable; without limitation, integration is impossible."

This principle has subsequently been put into practice by both major political parties in 1968, 1971, 1981, and 1988. Although blacks in Britain retain formal citizenship, the effect of these laws has been successively to undermine their welfare and security. In all, these selective controls have institutionalized the notion of differential rights and status between white and nonwhite populations in relation to Britain. The 1971 Immigration Act, for example, effectively ended all primary immigration (that is, heads of households) from the New Commonwealth and placed colonial migrant workers in Britain on an equal footing with, say, "guestworkers," or *Gastarbeiter*, in Germany. The 1981 British Nationality Act went even further by curtailing, among other things, the citizenship rights of black and brown people brought up in Britain. The 1988 Immigration Act goes further down the line of restrictive and racist legislation by introducing "means-tested" conditions on entry. It is quite clear that inequalities in the global distribution of wealth means that potential migrants from Bangladesh who wish to join their families in Britain will be more likely to be hit by this regulation than many of their white counterparts.

In 1978, Ann Dummett pointed out that although immigration laws formally constitute part of the country's external policies, they cannot be divorced entirely from its general policy on race relations; this is because they express "by means of their definition of wanted and unwanted newcomers, what kind of society each Government is aiming for" (*Citizenship and Nationality*, Runnymede Trust, 1976). The pertinence and veracity of this observation in the case of Britain is clear. The external immigration controls in Britain have become more restrictive, so the government's reliance on internal controls, such as passport checking and police surveillance of "suspected" illegal immigrants has become correspondingly greater. The 1981 British Nationality Act and 1988 Immigration Act ensured that this pattern of internal harassment was sustained. The Asylum and Immigration (Appeals) Act received Royal assent in 1993 and, over the next two years, refusals of asylum applications increased from 16 percent to 76 percent. Further restrictions on asylum seekers were debated in 1996 when the Asylum and Immigration Bill came under consideration. Included among its provisions were: (1) excluding asylum seekers from a "white list" of countries; (2) removing asylum seekers to a "safe" third country if they passed through such a designated country before arriving in Britain; (3) reducing the right of in-country appeal for many asylum seekers; (4) introducing a legal category of "immigrant" which included many long-term residents of Britain who would not automatically have the same rights as other citizens; (5) increasing the powers of police and immigration officials; (6) making employers criminally liable for the status of their employees.

The reintegration of former British colony Hong Kong into the People's Republic of China in June 1997 introduced the question of whether the 3.3 million Hong Kong-born residents had the right to live and work in Britain. Special British Nation Overseas passports were issued and these entitled holders to visit but not to work in Britain. Exceptions to this were those passport holders who were prepared to invest £1m ($1.6m) in government treasury bonds.

In 2002, the British government's Nationality, Immigration and Asylum Bill prompted controversy after it was pointed out that key parts of the draft proposed law were in conflict with the Human Rights Act, 1998 (which made rights from the European Convention on Human Rights into a form of higher law in the UK). The bill was designed to address the issue of so-called "asylum shopping," whereby asylum seekers, many from Eastern Europe, looked for the most convenient way to enter Western Europe. It also confronted illegal immigration and its associated problems of people-trafficking and illegal working.

While there was consensus over many of the proposed measures, others were criticized. These included excluding children of asylum seekers from mainstream schools, powers of entry and search without warrant, and a proposal to confiscate an individual's citizenship if he or she committed an offense that compromised national security. The bill also included a measure giving the government's Home Secretary or immigration officer the power to remove an asylum seeker's right of appeal if there were no legitimate grounds for the application.

SEE ALSO: asylum seeker; colonialism; environmental racism; law: immigration, USA;

migration; National Front; nationalism; Powell, J. Enoch; refugee status; scapegoat

Reading

British Immigration Policy Since 1939: The making of multi-racial Britain by Ian R. G. Spencer (Routledge, 1997) chronicles the developments and their impact on Britain's changing demography.

British Immigration Policy Under the Conservative Government by Asifa Maaria Hussain (Ashgate, 2001) examines the development of immigration legislation and rules since 1945 and balances this with empirical case studies.

Citizenship and Immigration in Postwar Britain by Randall Hansen (Oxford University Press, 2000) interprets archival material in a provocative way, suggesting that the transformation of Britain to a multicultural society through immigration policy was not fueled by racist fears, but by rational, liberal intentions.

CHECK: internet resources section under law: immigration

BARRY TROYNA

LAW: IMMIGRATION, USA

The history of USA immigration policy falls into five distinct periods: 1609–1775 (colonial period); 1776–1881 (open door phase); 1882–1916 (regulation phase); 1917–64 (restriction phase); 1965–present (liberalization phase).

In the seventeenth century, colonial immigration policy was shaped by the need for labor to work the virgin lands of the New World. Schemes were designed to attract people to the colonies from Europe and the British Isles. Transportation was laid on and subsidies for the purchase of land and tools for new settlers provided. Bounties were paid to those who could secure the services of indentured laborers and take them to America.

The availability of work and property was the major incentive for migrating, though the religious policy of most of the colonies was also a magnet. Apart from New England, all areas tolerated most varieties of Christianity. Some places became religious enclaves, such as Maryland for English Catholics, and Pennsylvania for Quakers. There were three important components established in this phase:

- local government exercised jurisdiction over immigration and settlement;
- local government and private entrepreneurs were responsible for recruiting immigrants from overseas;
- economic developments stimulated an active search for new sources of labor, so that policy was directed toward encouraging the flow of immigrants.

The British government's refusal to recognize general naturalization acts bred conflict as it restricted settlement in areas where labor was required. In fact, this was one of the grievances that led colonists to take up arms against the British in 1775. The War of Independence brought with it a new concept of national identity and the new Americans began to see themselves as a unique "frontier people." This influenced the Constitution drafted in 1787 and made foreign people ineligible for high political positions until they fulfilled residential qualifications.

Congress passed federal laws in 1790 allowing for the granting of citizenship to any whites who resided and abided by the law for two years. This was a very relaxed policy and laid the basis for the massive population growth of the nineteenth century. From 1820 to 1860, there was some regulation of migrant traffic at major entry ports, particularly New York, and ships' masters were made to give details of their passengers, making it possible to identify and possibly deport the infirm and destitute who could make no meaningful contribution to the labor force. Criteria for entry were such things as medical health, trade or craft, and religion, so there was little control over immigration. Federal officials kept no records of immigrants until 1820. The emphasis was very much on getting as much labor as possible; so much so that there was intense competition between states.

By the 1870s, over 280,000 immigrants a year were disembarking at American ports. Overwhelmed by the growing volume, Congress declared existing state laws regulating immigration unconstitutional and enacted a series of statutes to bring immigration under federal control.

In the late nineteenth century, the federal government erected the bureaucratic structure to operate the new immigration control. Restrictions gradually got tighter as speculation about the links between immigrants and social problems mounted. One notable flashpoint arose over the issue of Chinese workers: labor organizations felt threatened by the non-unionized, unskilled laborers who were willing to work for low wages. Pressure resulted in new legislation preventing Chinese workers from acquiring citizenship (thus making them more amenable to control).

The Chinese Exclusion Act of 1882 was a significant move in identifying a group thought unable to assimilate as well as threatening. Again, in the 1890s, a group was perceived as undesirable: this time it was "new immigrants" from southern and eastern Europe who were filing into urban centers. More stringent rules were added in regard to health and competence, with the result that by the end of the century about 15 per cent of migrants were being rejected.

However, the "alien wedge" continued to be driven in, particularly by the Japanese in California. In 1910, the Dillingham Report on the harmful effects of immigration argued, albeit implicitly, that the "new immigrants" were racially inferior to those from Northern and Western Europe. So people like Slavs and Sicilians became the source of panic as they were thought incapable of becoming "Americanized."

The 1917 Immigration Act was the first of a sequence of severely restrictive statutes based on the report. Restricted zones were located, literacy tests introduced and a ranked order of eligible immigrants drawn up. No limits on the Western Hemisphere were imposed and the lack of restrictions on neighbors ensured a steady, cheap supply of Central American labor. Southern and Eastern European immigration was sharply curtailed and no labor was allowed from the so-called Asiatic Barred Zone (which included India, Indo-China, and other smaller Asian countries). This effectively signaled the beginning of the era of restriction. Quota systems were later introduced, allowing for annual quotas of immigrants from specific countries. The thrust of later acts was to select those groups considered best suited to American society.

Unfortunately there existed inadequate methods of classifying national origins which undermined the quota system and the effort to thwart "unassimilable" groups was not effective. However, by the 1930s, the system was fully operative and immigration began to drop, especially with the onset of the Great Depression; large portions of the quotas went unfilled. In fact, for the first time in its history, the number of people leaving the USA exceeded the number entering. World War II prompted the US government to make special provisions for groups suffering hardship as the result of war experiences.

Perhaps the most significant piece of immigration legislation in modern times is the McCarran–Walter Act of 1952. This tightened restrictions on migrants from the colonies of quota-receiving countries, so that black immigrants from the West Indies who had previously entered under the British quota were sharply reduced in number (this, in turn, stimulated many migrants to turn to Britain as an alternative and so precipitated a massive rise in Caribbean migration to Britain). There were, however, liberalizing elements in the Act, such as the allowance of no less than 85 percent of the total annual quota to Northern and Western European countries and the extension of quotas to Asian countries.

The Kennedy administration attacked the national origins quota system as having no "basis in logic or reason" and its reform eventually resulted in the 1965 Hart–Celler Act (the provisions of which took effect in 1968). The quota system was abolished and the ceiling on annual immigration raised to 290,000, at the same time removing any preferential treatment for Western countries (this was later revised in 1976 to give priority to Western immigrants with training, skills or family ties).

Reforms since the mid twentieth century have served to dismantle some of the exclusionary measures installed when the federal government assumed control over immigration without removing the crucial link between immigration flow and labor requirements which has become a feature of all industrial societies. The importance of this link is reinforced by the concern over illegal immigration, particularly from Mexico (over half a million arrests and deportations take place annually and between one and eight million Mexicans are thought to reside illegally in the USA).

The Immigration Reform and Control Act of 1986 was designed specifically to combat such illegal immigration: it established sanctions against employers who hired unauthorized workers who could show they had worked at least ninety days in agriculture in the United States in the year ending May 1, 1986. But inadvertently, the law also gave rise to a market in counterfeit documents that undermined the objectives of the legislation. Unless a document was obviously bogus, it was usually evidence enough to protect an employer from penalties, ranging from a $100 fine to six months' imprisonment. A 1992 report on the law by the Commission on Agricultural Workers found that the law had made virtually no difference to the flow of illegal immigration, and it proposed changes to toughen enforcement. The report was submitted to Congress in 1993.

The years 1995–96 witnessed a spate of activity to curb immigration. California's Proposition 187, as it came to be known, triggered a national debate: it was an "initiative that bars undocumented aliens from receiving public education and most government-funded social and health services," and, as such, had an adverse effect on illegal migrants from Mexico and their children. In a similar vein, the Clinton administration and the Republican leadership in Congress advocated stronger efforts against illegal migrants and sponsored separate bills that would reduce legal immigration by about one third.

While much of the debate centered on whether immigrants would take jobs from Americans, the subtext concerned population growth and ethnic diversity. In 1996, a report by the Census Bureau in Washington, DC, predicted a significant demographic shift fueled by immigration and high birth rates among Latino women. The proportion of whites would shrink from 74 percent to 53 percent in 2050, with the number of Latinos increasing from 10.2 to 24.5 percent and Asians from 3.3 to 8.2 percent. The African American population, the report forecast, would rise just 1.6 percent.

SEE ALSO: Asian Americans; assimilation; Latinos; law: immigration, Britain; migration; September 11, 2001

Reading

The Distant Magnet: European emigration to the USA by Philip Taylor (Eyre & Spottiswood, 1971) analyzes the movements from Europe and the "pull" factors drawing people to America; it may be read in conjunction with *Immigration as a Factor in American History* by Oscar Handlin (Prentice-Hall, 1959) which is a classic text on early migration.

Encyclopedia of American Immigration by James Ciment (Eurospan, 2001) is a comprehensive four-volume, 2,000-page reference work.

Immigration and the Nation-State: The United States, Germany and Great Britain by Christian Joppke (Oxford University Press, 1999) is an ambitious and valuable attempt to compare policies of the three nations.

Immigration in America's Future by David Heer (Westview Press, 1996) focuses on migration trends in the USA and raises questions about the nature of immigration policy. Covering the dispute over Proposition 187, the influx of Cuban refugees into Florida, and the illegal border crossings into California and Texas, Heer links the reaction to these episodes with basic concerns over standards of living, the preservation of "American culture," ethnic and class conflict, and the nation's role in foreign affairs. This may usefully be read alongside Louis DeSipio and L. M. García Y. Griego's *Making Americans, Remaking America* (Westview Press, 1998).

Making Americans: Immigration, race and the origins of the diverse democracy by Desmond King (Harvard University Press, 2000) documents how America moved from an "open door" policy in the nineteenth century to a "finely filtered regime of selection" from the 1920s. King argues that, far from being a welcoming society for everyone, America has used eugenics and intelligence testing to exclude various groups from either entering or becoming citizens.

CHECK: internet resources section under law: immigration

LAW: RACE RELATIONS, UK

The development of antidiscrimination laws in the UK has to be considered, first and foremost, against a background of increasingly draconian measures designed initially to reduce the number of black and brown migrants entering the country, and subsequently to eliminate this process entirely. By invoking the principle, "keeping numbers down is good for race relations," both major political parties consistently have presented antidiscrimination laws as a complementary aspect of their policy initiatives on this issue. The imperative for these laws has been to secure equality of opportunity for all people in Britain, irrespective of ascribed features such as skin color. The reality of the situation, however, suggests that such laws are seen as little more than a token gesture by the nonwhite populations of Britain whose confidence in the state's commitment to "harmonious race relations" has been irrevocably undermined by the obsession with the numbers question, the development of external and internal immigration controls, the division of family units, and so on. These constitute the thrust of state policy and formally legitimate the second-class status of the nonwhite communities in Britain. In short, the avowed intention to create a society in which "every citizen shares an equal right to the same freedoms, the same responsibilities, the same opportunities (and) the same benefits" is no nearer its realization in the 1990s than when it was first declared in 1968 by the Labour government's Home Secretary, James Callaghan.

Framework

Moves to ensure equal opportunities for the nonwhite communities in Britain has most often been associated with the Labour Party, but it was not until 1965 that the development of an exclusionist immigration policy was accompanied by any action to improve the position of these communities. In that year, the Labour government introduced its White Paper, *Immigration from the Commonwealth*, which tried to sweeten the pill of further immigration restrictions by introducing protective laws to combat racial discrimination. Compared to similar initiatives in Canada and the USA, the 1965 Race Relations Bill was very limited in scope. It outlawed racial discrimination in "places of public resort" such as restaurants, hotels, places of entertainment, and on public transportation, and set up the Race Relations Board which was charged with the responsibility to deal with complaints of discrimination and resolve them through conciliation.

But, quite apart from its practical limitations – it failed to protect nonwhites from discriminatory practices in housing and work spheres, for instance – the 1965 Bill was also logically incoherent. On the one hand, it insisted that the black and brown migrants were not depriving whites of jobs, did not have lower health and sanitation standards, and were not sponging off the welfare state. Having denounced racialism and dissociated itself from racialist practices, however, the Labour government then proceeded to orchestrate and support racist views by implementing immigration policies which deliberately excluded nonwhites.

The limited practical use of the antidiscrimination laws included in the 1965 Bill was highlighted by the findings of the PEP investigation two years later. This revealed the extent of discrimination along color lines in employment and housing. The need for an extension to the 1965 measures was further underlined by the eruption of violence in the Watts district of Los Angeles, and elsewhere in the USA around this time. It was precisely the systematic denial of equal opportunity that had precipitated the volatile reaction of blacks in the United States. Fearful of a similar occurrence in the UK, the Labour government initiated new legislation in 1968, the Race Relations Act. This enlarged the scope of the law to the important spheres of employment and housing but, crucially, the powers of the Race Relations Board were not extended. It remained a reactive body, permitted to respond to complaints rather than to initiate investigations into racialist practices. Quite obviously, a law that required proof of deliberate acts of racial discrimination could have only a limited effect on the more widespread patterns of inequality between whites and nonwhites; after all, it could do nothing to cope with the more subtle, less visible and conspicuous expressions of racial discrimination.

The veracity of this argument was demonstrated in the next PEP investigation which reported its findings in the mid 1970s. The report showed that the proscription by law of racialism in housing and employment had led to a substantial decrease in its incidence; at the same time however, the apparent success of the 1968 Race Relations Act may have been mitigated by the replacement of overt racialist practices by less conspicuous and detectable forms of its operation. What is more, the PEP study showed that discrimination along color lines remained common and that many nonwhites who had been discriminated against had failed to inform the Race Relations Board.

Commission for Racial Equality

Along with the development of innovative and antidiscrimination laws in the USA and the introduction of Britain's Sex Discrimination Act (1975), the PEP survey provided the catalyst for further legislation in this field. In 1976, the Labour government introduced a new Race Relations Act. This totally restructured the machinery dealing with antidiscrimination and integrated the functions of the Race Relations Board and the Community Relations Commission (which had been established in 1968 to promote "harmonious community relations") into a new body, the Commission for Racial Equality (CRE). Unlike its predecessor, the CRE had been empowered to initiate investigations where it suspected discrimination has taken place and, where its investigations proved positive, to issue nondiscrimination notices.

Since its inception, the CRE has been assailed on all sides; in 1981, for instance, a team from the Home Affairs Sub-Committee on Race Relations and Immigrations was severely critical of the CRE's lack of direction, its lack of cohesiveness and consequently, its ineffectual attempts at eliminating racial discrimination.

It is difficult to deny the legitimacy of these and other criticisms of the CRE. Put bluntly, the CRE suffers from the tension created by its two principal – some might say irresolvable – functions: the promotion of "harmonious community relations" and the investigation of alleged discrimination. Which of these should assume priority remains a dilemma which continues to tantalize. At the same time, it needs to be recognized that the CRE functions in a political climate that is not only indifferent to a coordinated policy on race relations but is in fact wholly antagonistic to such a policy. Regardless of the internal faults of the CRE, any organization integrated into the state machinery is unlikely to be effective either in combating racial discrimination or in assuaging the anxieties of the nonwhite communities in Britain. How can the CRE or the range of antidiscrimination measures be effective when they are linked to governments which are resolutely determined to prevent black and brown settlement in Britain and to sanction the low status of these communities? In this context, policies to combat racial discrimination, however determined and well organized, can never be sufficient to ensure equality between white and nonwhite citizens in Britain.

The Race Relations (Amendment) Act, 2000, strengthened the scope of the 1976 Act in two ways: (1) it extended protection against racial discrimination by public authorities; and (2) it placed an enforceable duty on public authorities. Like the Human Rights Act of 1998, the legislation defined public authority widely: for instance, the police, government, health service or any private or voluntary agency carrying out public functions (running prisons, schools, detention centers, parking controls etc.) were included.

Introduced while debate over the Stephen Lawrence case was continuing, the Act made Chiefs of Police liable for acts of discrimination by officers under their direction or control. Individual officers were also to be liable. Racial profiling in any sphere of police activity was rendered unlawful; this included the controversial stop and search approach as well as arrests, detentions and the control of demonstrations.

The Act also placed responsibilities on the immigration service. Immigration officers carrying out policing functions, such as searches or arrests in relation to immigration offenses, were responsible for carrying out their duties without discrimination on the grounds of "race or colour." Discrimination on the grounds of nationality or ethnic or national origin was also made unlawful, except where authorized by a government minister (or under immigration legislation or rules).

SEE ALSO: affirmative action; antiracism; equal opportunity; equality; ethnic monitoring; human rights; law: civil rights, USA; law: racial discrimination, international; Lawrence case, the Stephen; merit; migration; multiculturalism

Reading

Equal Opportunity or More Opportunity? The good thing about discrimination by Richard A. Epstein (Civitas, 2002) argues that Britain's antidiscrimination legislation creates more injustice than it solves; the author calls for the abolition of the Commission for Racial Equality and other agencies charged with the responsibility of reducing discrimination.

Race and Racism in Contemporary Britain, 3rd edn., by John Solomos (Macmillan/Palgrave, 2001), provides a readable account of the origins and impact of antiracial discrimination legalization in Britain and might be read with a reflective essay "From legislation to integration: twenty years of the Race Relations Act" by Anthony Lester, in *Race Relations in Britain: A developing agenda*, edited by Tessa Blackstone, Bhikhu Parekh and Peter Sanders (Routledge, 1998).

Racial Disadvantage and Ethnic Diversity in Britain by Andrew Pilkington (Macmillan/Palgrave, 2001) looks specifically at changes since the 1990s; while Mark Bell's *Anti-Discrimination Law and the European Union* (Oxford University Press, 2002) provides an overview of legal developments in the EU.

BARRY TROYNA

LAW: RACIAL DISCRIMINATION, INTERNATIONAL

The accepted definition of racial discrimination is that found in the International Convention on the Elimination of All Forms of Racial Discrimination, article 1: "any distinction, exclusion, restriction or preference based on race, color, descent, or national or ethnic origin which has the purpose or effect of nullifying or impairing the recognition, enjoyment or exercise, on an equal footing, of human rights and fundamental freedoms in the political, economic, social, cultural or any other field of public life." This definition specifies: [i] a prohibited ground of action (one "based on race" etc.); [ii] four protected classes of persons (those differentiated by race, etc.); and [iii] a sphere in which the protections must operate (in public life).

A similar definition is the basis for the Discrimination (Employment and Occupation) Convention (No. 111) of the International Labor Organization. According to article 26 of the International Covenant on Civil and Political Rights, states are bound to "guarantee to all persons equal and effective protection against discrimination on any ground such as race, color, sex, language, religion, political or other opinion, national or social origin, property, birth or other status." Discrimination is also prohibited under various regional instruments, such as the African Charter on Human and Peoples' Rights, the American Convention on Human Rights, and the European Convention for the Protection of Human Rights and Fundamental Freedoms.

The international definition is inspired by a concept of human rights as the rights of all peoples, which are above the state and which the state must respect. States give effect to this obligation in different ways. Some embody it in their constitutions, thus the USA treats racial discrimination as a breach of the rights of citizens as set forth in the Constitution of 1789. Others, such as the UK and Australia, prohibit discrimination by statutes enacted by the legislature.

SEE ALSO: human rights; International Convention; law: civil rights, USA; law: race relations, Britain; racial discrimination

Reading

The Lawful Rights of Mankind by Paul Sieghart (Oxford University Press, 1986) and *Equality and Discrimination under International Law* by Warwick McKean (Clarendon Press, 1983) both take a global perspective on the subject.

MICHAEL BANTON

LAWRENCE CASE, THE STEPHEN

The Lawrence Case was widely regarded as one of the, if not *the*, most important episode in British race relations. It prompted saturation media coverage, searching critical evaluations and an immediate response from the government. Seen by some as a watershed, it introduced the term institutional racism into the popular vocabulary, officially confirmed the reality of racism in the police force and set in motion initiatives designed to reform said force. The government-commissioned Macpherson Report on the case condemned the police's handling of the case and made far-reaching recommendations. The report triggered a national debate and moved the issue of racism into public focus in the most dramatic way since the urban disorder of the early 1980s.

The facts of the case were: on April 22, 1993, in Eltham, London, Stephen Lawrence, an 18-year-old student, was murdered after an unprovoked knife attack by a group of white youths. Later, the British Home Secretary, Jack Straw, reflected: "There was only one reason for his [Lawrence's] murder. He was black." In July 1993, two white teenagers, Neil Acourt, and Luke Knight were released from custody after the Crown Prosecution Service dropped murder charges against them, stating that there was insufficient evidence to proceed. Lawrence's parents launched a private prosecution against five white youths, including Acourt and Knight, though charges against two were dropped and the other three were cleared after identification evidence against them was ruled inadmissible. In February 1997, an inquest jury returned a verdict that Lawrence was unlawfully killed in an attack by five youths, prompting the Home Secretary to announce a public inquiry, headed by Sir William Macpherson of Cluny, a retired High Court judge. The day after the verdict's announcement, a British national newspaper, the *Daily Mail*, named the five suspects as Stephen Lawrence's "murderers." The paper later challenged them to sue for libel.

The inquiry opened in 1998 with a description of the police's investigations as "seriously flawed." Neville Lawrence, Stephen's father, disclosed to a visitor at his home that the suspects had been seen washing blood off themselves on the night of the murder. Detective Superintendent Ian Crampton, who led the initial investigation, admitted that he should have made arrests within 48 hours of the murder. The report was later to conclude that: "Considerable time elapsed before they (the suspects) were taken into custody and before the unsatisfactory searches of their premises did eventually take place." It added that: "There was no wall of silence. A vital and fundamental mistake was made in failing to arrest the suspects."

The strategic decision not to arrest the suspects was crucial, according to the report. The police failed to recognize the murder as motivated purely by racism and this, in itself, was evidence of some sort of racism, according to the report. Dennis *et al.* later pointed out: "Yet, Macpherson, six years after it occurred, did not at first see it as a *purely* racist murder. On their own argument, therefore, had the Macpherson people concerned with preparing and presenting early statements about the problem inadvertently proved themselves to be racists?"

One of the most dramatic pieces of evidence to emerge was a secret video used to film the suspects without their knowledge when waiting in a room. The suspects were seen fantasizing about killing ethnic minorities and gesticulating as if stabbing.

The full conclusions, which were published in February 1999, were that the police investigations were full of "fundamental errors" and "professional incompetence." In fact, London's Metropolitan Police had earlier carried out its own investigation under the leadership of Detective Chief Superintendent John Barker. This was singled out by Macpherson as "pulling its punches" and reflecting "a continuing lack of open and meaningful communication with the Lawrence family and their representatives." While the review was "condemned" by Macpherson, it was not considered tainted by collusion or corruption; only by a lack of rigor, direction and control.

The report accused the Met of institutional racism, which it defined as "the collective failure of an organisation to provide an appropriate and professional service to people because of their colour, culture or ethnic origin." This was a somewhat limited conception of the concept and one that was criticized from many quarters. A report by the De Montfort University, Leicester, argued that Macpherson's "emphasis on unwitting and collective failure allows institutional racism to become almost accidental." Gurchand Singh (in the Marlow and Loveday collection, below) maintained that the concept of institutional racism actually hindered "the formulation of effective anti-racist strategies."

The report made several recommendations, the seven main ones being as follows:

- Attempts to recruit more ethnic minority officers should be stepped up (at the time, the Met had about 860 black and Asian officers, or 2.3 percent of the total force; while the ethnic population of London was about 20 per cent. The total ethnic minority population of Britain was estimated as 5.6 percent). The Home Secretary later set target numbers of ethnic minority recruits.
- The Home Secretary should declare improving relations a major priority.
- An immediate review of racism awareness training throughout the police should be undertaken.
- A "forthwith" inspection of the Metropolitan Police should be carried out to restore public confidence.
- A shake-up of the structure of the Metropolitan (London) Police should make it as accountable as other forces in Britain.
- The school national curriculum should be changed so that it "values cultural diversity" and reflects contemporary society.
- Investigations into complaints against the police should be conducted independently.

The Race Relations (Amendment) Act, 2000, extended the legislation's protection against racial discrimination by public authority and made Chief of Police officers liable for acts of discrimination by officers under their direction or control. It became unlawful for police officers to discriminate on racial grounds in exercising any policing function, including stops and searches, arrests, detentions and control of demonstrations. Police chiefs were made responsible for demonstrating that they had taken all reasonable steps to prevent discrimination and officers found guilty of discriminating were also liable. Effectively, some of the recommendations of the report were given the force of law.

While much of the focus of the Lawrence Case fell on the police, public attention in its aftermath turned toward the persistent number of incidents involving black victims. The Lawrence case threw into relief the extent to which black people were attacked by perpetrators with racist motives. For example, in 1997 Michael Menson, the son of a Ghanaian, was doused with gasoline and set fire for "a joke" by men who believed he might have upset one of their girlfriends. Menson died later in hospital. An Asian youth, Lakhvinder "Ricky" Reel, was found dead after being attacked in 1997. Roger Sylvester died in hospital eight days after an alleged disturbance, which culminated in his being restrained by eight police officers. These were among 157 incidents identified by the National Civil Rights movement: in all cases, black people had died as a result of racism of one kind or another. In several cases, the families of the victims claimed that the police had been at fault either in the way they carried out investigations or in their unwillingness to bring prosecutions to court.

When accepting the recommendations of the Macpherson Report, the then Home Secretary Jack Straw had urged: "In terms of race equality, let us make Britain a beacon to the world." But, in the six months following, the reported number of racially motivated attacks rose sharply. This may have been a reflection of more aggression against ethnic minorities, or perhaps a greater preparedness to report such incidents to the police. For example, the Home Office recorded 11,000 racist incidents in Greater London alone in 1999, a rise of 89 percent. Attacks more than doubled in Cheshire, Durham, Gloucestershire, Lincolnshire, Suffolk, Surrey and the whole of Wales. The situation was compounded by a debate on the question of asylum seekers in Britain.

While the Lawrence case was undeniably a momentous symbolic event and one that stimulated long, probing investigations and soul searching, the palpable improvements in ethnic relations that many suspected would follow were not in evidence. Indeed, the rise in attacks on ethnic minorities that followed might be interpreted as a backlash against the case itself.

SEE ALSO: Diallo case, the Amadou; institutional racism; law: race relations, Britain; media; policing; racist discourse; representations; riots: Britain, 2001; Scarman Report; violence; white backlash culture; whiteness

Reading

After Macpherson: Policing after the Stephen Lawrence inquiry, edited by Alan Marlow and Barry Loveday (Russell House Publishing, 2000), and *Racist Murder and Pressure Group Politics: The Macpherson Report and the police* by Norman Dennis, George Erdos and Ahmed Al-Shahi (Institute for the Study of Civil Society, 2000), are both sharp, critical evaluations of the case and its fallout.

The Case of Stephen Lawrence by Brian Cathcart (Viking Press, 1999) provides a thorough description of the murder and its investigation; this should be read in conjunction with *A Culture of Denial*, which is the "alternative" to the official Lawrence report offered by the trade union Unison (De Montfort University/1990 Trust), and Simon Cottle's *Media Performance and Public Transformation: The case of Stephen Lawrence* (Praeger, 2003), which highlights the media's transformative role in the case.

The Stephen Lawrence Inquiry by Sir William Macpherson (London TSO Cmnd 4262–1, 1999) is the official document. The British government's response can be found at "Stephen Lawrence Inquiry: Home Secretary's Action Plan, " available at *http://www.homeoffice.gov.uk/hmic.htm*.

CHECK: internet resources section

LEARNING RACISM *see* children

LEE, SPIKE (1957–)

Perhaps the most original and, in many ways, iconoclastic black filmmaker of his generation, Lee was born in Atlanta, Georgia, the oldest of five children. His father was Bill Lee, an acclaimed jazz bassist, and his mother Jacquelyne (Shelton) Lee, a teacher. Shelton Jackson Lee, as "Spike" was christened, moved with his family to Chicago and, in 1959, to Brooklyn, New York – where his early films were set. He took an interest in film during his studies at Morehouse College and, after graduating, gained an internship at Columbia Pictures in California, before returning to New York where he obtained a master's degree at the Institute of Film and Television, New York University. His master's thesis film, *Joe's Bed-Study Barbershop: We Cut Heads* received a student Academy Award and was screened internationally at film festivals.

His first two commercial films, *She's Gotta Have It* (1986) and *School Daze* (1988) were both popular successes, but his third eclipsed both, in terms of its commercial success and critical acclaim. *Do the Right Thing* (1989) was dropped by Paramount Pictures after Lee refused to change its ending – a violent conflict in which African Americans torch an Italian-owned pizzeria and a white police officer kills a black youth. The film essayed ethnic tensions in New York's Bedford-Stuyvesant district and showed blacks as flawed and fallible. It was eventually released by Universal Pictures. Subsequent films, such as *Mo' Better Blues* (1990), avoided the homeboy/drugs/violence stereotype favored by many of Lee's peers. *Jungle Fever* (1991), in particular, portrayed blacks and other ethnic minorities as complex, multifaceted and prone to the kinds of prejudices conventionally reserved for whites. The film told of an ethnic *mésalliance* between a black male and an Italian woman.

Lee's career-defining movie was a film biography of *Malcolm X* (1992), the directorship of which was originally awarded to Norman Jewison, a white male. Lee won the job after arguing forcefully and typically that white directors are unable to convey the richness of black culture on film. He had previously singled out Steven Spielberg for his film version of Alice Walker's *The Color Purple* (1986). Lee has contended that "we (blacks) can't just sit back and let other people define our existence, especially when they're putting lies out there on the screen" *(Washington Post*, October 22, 1986).

Lee made a prodigious sixteen films in the ten years following *Malcolm X*, yet without ever matching the acclaim of his early period. High-quality products, such as *Clockers* (1995), *Summer of Sam* (1999) and the overlooked *Bamboozled* (2000), were mixed with modest contributions like *Girl 6* (1996), *He Got Game* (1998) and *25th Hour* (2002). His *Get on the Bus* (1996) commemorated the Million Man March, focusing on a variegated group of African Americans traveling from LA to Washington, DC for the occasion. The interest in biopics which started with Malcolm X continued with the television film *A Huey P. Newton Story* and *Jim Brown, All American*, the first about the Black Panther leader, the second about the football star.

SEE ALSO: African Americans; Afrocentricity; black bourgeoisie in the USA; humor; Jackson, Jesse; Jackson, Michael; Jordan, Michael; King case, the Rodney; Malcolm X; media; Million Man March; minstrelsy; tokenism; Tyson, Mike

Reading

Reel Racism: Confronting Hollywood's construction of Afro-American Culture by Vincent Rocchio (Westview Press, 2000) investigates cinema's contribution to racism; while Norman K. Denzin's *Reading Race: Hollywood and the cinema of racial violence* (Sage, 2001) probes the depiction of African American violence in contemporary film, taking particular note of Lee's efforts.
Spike Lee by Alex Patterson (Avon Books, 1992) is an unauthorized biography, which revealingly quotes Lee: "Black people have been dogged in the media since Day One [but] we overreact when we think that every image of us has to be 100 percent angelic."
"Spike Lee hates your cracker ass" by Barbara G. Harrison (in *Esquire*, October 1992) features an interview with Lee on the subject of Malcolm X, whose philosophies, Lee urges, should be mixed with those of Martin Luther King: "the synthesis is not going to include total nonviolence."
Toms, Coons, Mulattoes, Mammies and Bucks: An interpretive history of blacks in American films, 3rd edn., by Donald Bogle (Continuum, 1998), argues that Lee's films "revealed the presence of a large black audience eager for movies with specific African American cultural references, subjects, issues, and stars."

LET'S KICK RACISM OUT OF FOOTBALL

An initiative designed to address the presence of racism in British soccer. Abusive behavior from fans directed at ethnic minority players had followed the appearance of significant numbers of black players in British leagues in the late 1970s. Barracking and chanting had been commonplace for many years before, but they took on racist overtones and were augmented with the pelting of fruit and coins when directed at black athletes. Let's Kick Racism Out of Football was a campaign designed to extirpate this.

While the mistreatment of black players by fans had been evident for at least fifteen years, in 1993 the British Commission for Racial Equality (CRE) joined forces with the Professional Footballers' Association (PFA, which represents players) to mount an organized campaign against it. The PFA had for long had concerns over the habitual assailing of its ethnic minority members and sought a liaison with the CRE, a government agency charged with the responsibility of investigating, monitoring and minimizing racial discrimination. The campaign was launched with the instigation "Let's kick racism out of football." It became the slogan for the campaign, which was largely based on publicity materials admonishing racists and encouraging fans to rid the sport of racism. By the mid 1990s, African Caribbeans made up about 20 percent of all professional soccer players in England.

Over the next two years, a steering group known as the Advisory Group Against Racism and Intimidation developed and all of soccer's governing federations and representative bodies became involved in the CRE/PFA campaign. The scope of the campaign was broadened, largely at the behest of soccer's governing federation, so that all forms of intimidation, not simply racist abuse, were confronted. Its two themes were "Let's kick racism out" and "Respect all fans."

Despite this, the abuse continued and took on a more organized form. This became dramatically evident in February 1995, when a game between the Republic of Ireland and England in Dublin was abandoned after serious violence in the crowd. The involvement of C18, a neo-nazi organization, was strongly suspected. C18 was a loosely coordinated group composed of cells of various other organizations, including the British National Party, which was to feature in the 2001 riots in England.

English soccer's central governing Football Association (FA) became involved in the campaign, though its agenda was, as Les Back *et al.* observe, "driven by an interpretation of racism as a product of fan cultures and, more particularly, 'hooligan' or unruly neo-Nazi fans." This, for Back and his co-writers (all of whom were involved in some way with the campaign) restricted the definition of racism. "To accept that the notion that racism plays a part within the administrative structures of the game would be to draw parallels with the behaviour of the racist-hooligan fan pariahs."

In other words, the strategy identified racism as a phenomenon carried by and expressed through the behavior of fans, not as a pervasive force that affects all institutions. An alternative emerged in the mid 1990s, known simply as "Kick it out," and this involved liaising with local groups around England, establishing and running educational and equality of access workshops and seminars, and generally trying to operate as a rubric under which any initiative to counter racism in sport could organize. Its partnership with Football Unites, Racism Divides (FURD) produced exhibitions, a magazine *The United Colours of Football 2*, and the support of high-profile sports celebrities.

While the aims of such campaigns are laudable, the presence of racism in British soccer has remained and, in the early twenty-first century, seems resurgent as sports fans have identified a new pariah group in asylum seekers.

SEE ALSO: British National Party; Lawrence case, the Stephen; National Front; neo-nazism; reggae; riots: Britain, 2001; Rock Against Racism; skinheads; whiteness; xenophobia

Reading

The Changing Face of Football: Racism, identity and multiculture in the English game by Les Back, Tim Crabbe, and John Solomos (Berg, 2001) is based on an empirical study of racism in English soccer and is full of quotations from fans and those who govern the sport.

"Racism in football: a victim's perspective" by Richie Moran, in *The Future of Football: Challenges for the twenty-first century*, edited by Jon Garland, Dominic Malcolm, and Michael Rowe (Frank Cass, 2000) reveals the limits of the initiative.

LINNAEUS, CAROLUS *see* geometry of race

M

MACPHERSON REPORT *see* Lawrence case, the Stephen

MALCOLM X (1925–65)

A prominent spokesman for black nationalism in the USA in the 1950s and 1960s, Malcolm Little (as he was christened) has become arguably more influential intellectually since his assassination in 1965 at the age of forty. His radical arguments for black separatism and endorsement of violence make him, in many ways, Martin Luther King's alter ego. At a time when King's Southern Christian Leadership Conference was using non-violent disobedience as its main strategy in securing civil rights reform, with integration its ultimate goal, Malcolm X urged blacks to disavow themselves of Christianity, reject the very concept of integration, and abandon any thoughts that the material conditions of blacks would be improved through white patronage.

Malcolm was born on May 19, 1925 in Omaha, Nebraska. His father, Earl Little, used his itinerant Baptist ministry to preach the black nationalist ideas of Marcus Garvey; he was a member of Garvey's Universal Negro Improvement Association. This was a factor in his murder by whites when Malcolm was six years old. The murderers were never found. Malcolm moved to Boston when he was fifteen to live with his half-sister, Ella. A few years later, he moved to Harlem, New York, and earned a living pimping and pushing drugs, activities that brought him into conflict with the law.

Malcolm became attracted to the Nation of Islam (Black Muslims) while serving a jail sentence which began in 1946. He studied the writings of Elijah Muhammad and, on his release in 1952, went to Chicago to meet Elijah. He took the name of Malcolm X (which he later changed to El-Hajj Malik El-Shabazz). Two years later, he left to lead a mosque in Harlem.

His rift with the Nation of Islam came about in 1963 when he was suspended for regarding the death of John F. Kennedy as a case of "the chickens coming home to roost." (He later explained that, as a farm boy from Omaha, he regarded the return of chickens to roost as a joyous event.) He parted with the movement, though privately he had had misgivings for some time before, as he revealed in his autobiography: "I was convinced that our Nation of Islam could be an even greater force in the American Black Man's overall struggle – if we engaged in more *action.*"

In 1964 Malcolm, having left the Nation of Islam, began to espouse his own distinct ideas of a black international struggle. The organization he founded to express these views was the Organization of Afro-American Unity (OAAU). He retained his Islamic beliefs, making a pilgrimage to Mecca. He also traveled to West Africa, where he met personally several national leaders. His reputation was growing at a time when King was pushing steadily and successfully for civil rights legislation, but also when many blacks, dissatisfied with the slow-paced reforms, were looking for alternative, more direct approaches. Although he actually met with King in 1964, the year before he had strongly denounced him and his movement in a speech (reprinted in *The End of White Supremacy*, edited by I. B. Karim, Arcade Publishing, 1971). "I think any black man who goes among so-called Negroes today who are being brutalized, spit upon in the worst fashion imaginable and teaches those Negroes to turn the other cheek, to suffer peacefully, or love their enemy is a traitor to the Negro," said Malcolm. "If it is all right for black people to be drafted and sent to Korea or South Vietnam or Laos or Berlin or some place else to fight and die for the white man, then there is nothing wrong with the same black man doing the same thing when he is under the brutality in this country at the hands of the white man."

During his last three months of life, he linked national progress in Africa to the emancipation of women. He dropped his earlier proposal for an independent black state in the United States and relaxed his strictures on ethnically mixed marriages. He also endorsed voter registration and political involvement, though he warned that civil rights legislation did not defuse the "social dynamite" in the ghetto. It was a prescient warning, as 1965 saw the beginning of a two-year period of black uprising. While he was not alive to witness this, he would have endorsed it, as he taught that "a person who is fighting racism is well within his rights to fight against it by any means necessary" – a phrase for which he is remembered.

His assassination at an OAAU rally in Harlem on February 21, 1965, is still surrounded by mystery. Rumors of plots had circulated when he visited Paris shortly before his death. He was known to be under FBI surveillance. Three members of the Nation of Islam were convicted of shooting him, but speculation remains about the guilt of two of the convicted men and about the complicity of the New York City Police, the FBI and, possibly, the CIA.

Twenty years after his death, Malcolm underwent a cultural resurrection courtesy of rap music, and a canonization on the authority of film director Spike Lee. The title of Michael Dyson's book, *Making Malcolm*, suggests the process by which legacy was commodified and sold to a new generation of blacks. By the early 1990s, "X" had become a logo and political pronouncements ("by any means necessary"; "I don't even call it violence when it's self-defense, I call it intelligence") mere bromides.

SEE ALSO: African Americans; Black Panther Party; Black Power; Cleaver, Eldridge; *Invisible Man*; Kerner Report; King, Martin Luther; Marxism; Nation of Islam; riots: USA, 1965–67

Reading

The Autobiography of Malcolm X, written with Alex Haley (Hutchinson & Collins, 1966), and *Victims of Democracy* by Victor Wolfenstein (Guildford, 1993) are two of several life histories.

From Civil Rights to Black Liberation: Malcolm X and the organization of Afro-American unity by William W. Sales (South End Press, 1994) focuses on Malcolm's influence on black politics in the 1960s, with particular reference to the OAAU.

Let Nobody Turn Us Around: Voices of resistance, reform and renewal – an African American anthology, edited by Manning Marable and Leith Mullings (Rowman & Littlefield, 1999), contextualizes Malcolm's thoughts alongside those of many other African American activists and thinkers, including Claude MacKay, James Baldwin, Martin Luther King, and Maria W. Stewart.

Making Malcolm: The myth and meaning of Malcolm X by Michael E. Dyson (Oxford University Press, 1995) analyzes the emergence of Malcolm as an icon of militant black nationalism.

MANDELA, NELSON (1918–)

Nelson Mandela was born into the royal family of the Tembu in Transkei in 1918. Groomed to become a chief, he attended Head-town School in the Eastern Cape and later Fort Hare University College, from where he was expelled in 1940 for his activities in student politics. Many African leaders, including Robert Mugabe, later President of Zimbabwe, studied at that time at Fort Hare which became the center of early anticolonial sentiments and liberation strategies. After moving to Johannesburg, Mandela studied law and, together with Oliver Tambo, set up the first African attorneys' practice in 1952.

Together with Walter Sisulu, Mandela was active in the African National Congress (ANC) Youth League, of which he became national president in 1950. He helped to organize the passive resistance campaign to defy apartheid laws which led to his first arrest and suspended sentence under the Suppression of Communism Act. Banned from political activity, he nevertheless reorganized the ANC branches into small cells for their expected functioning underground. In 1956 Mandela was among the 156 political leaders charged with high treason, followed by the anti-pass campaign and demonstrations against the declaration of the Republic. In 1961, after the ANC and PAC (Pan-African Congress) were outlawed, Mandela went underground and traveled to Addis Ababa, Algeria and London where he addressed conferences and conferred with political leaders.

A few weeks after his return to South Africa in July 1962, Mandela was arrested and charged with incitement and leaving the country illegally. Together with his fellow conspirators on the Rivonia farm outside Johannesburg, he was sentenced to life imprisonment on June 12, 1964.

On February 11, 1990, Mandela was finally released unconditionally after he had rejected earlier offers to be freed on condition that he undertook not to engage in violent resistance.

After twenty-six year of imprisonment, Mandela quickly filled a gaping vacuum in the heterogeneous ANC camp. His leadership unified the oldest and most popular liberation movement as he straddled the divide between a militant youth and older traditionalists, revolutionaries and pragmatists, Africanist nationalists and liberal universalists, orthodox socialists and social-democratic capitalists. Without Mandela's mythos, the ANC would not have been able to rally its skeptical constituency behind the new politics of negotiations, suspend the armed struggle, and soften promises of nationalization and redistribution. Likewise, Mandela's remarkable lack of bitterness and his moderation were crucial in convincing the white segment to share political power and agree to universal franchise without being defeated militarily.

At the same time, the gloss of liberation wore off as Mandela entered the fray of political wheeling and dealing as the first democratically elected South African president between 1994–99. Mandela's support for Arafat's PLO, Libya's Gadhaffi, and Cuba's Castro have raised questions about his political judgment. Many critics charge that the erstwhile global prisoner was in danger of becoming a mere figurehead, a symbol more powerful behind prison bars than in the harsher world of "realpolitik."

After handing over to his anointed successor Thabo Mbeki, Mandela did not retire politically. Invigorated by his new marriage to Graca Machel, he traveled the world fundraising and was honored with the most prestigious awards in every country. As a global conscience and universally revered icon, he actively championed many causes, from peacemaking in Burundi to opposing US unilateralism. He admonished the Zimbabwe government for human rights violations when other African leaders kept an expedient silence. He did not shy away from criticizing his own party on various issues, especially its inexplicable AIDS policy. Some former comrades denounced Mandela as an undisciplined dissident and the government sidelined him for a while. Together with fellow Nobel laureate Desmond Tutu, Mandela almost assumed the role of informal opposition leader, but simultaneously remained a loyal member of the ANC.

The unprecedented moral authority of Nelson Mandela resembles the influence of Mahatma Gandhi half a century earlier. Like the failed leader of a united India, Mandela, too, may eventually fail with his noble advocacy of non-racialism, inclusiveness and reconciliation. However, like Gandhi, a principled Mandela remains faithful to the ANC ideals which still may save his beloved South Africa from the fate of many failed states to the north of his beloved home.

SEE ALSO: Africa; apartheid; colonialism; culturecide; ethnocide; human rights; King, Martin Luther; minorities; segregation; South Africa; white backlash culture

Reading

Long Walk to Freedom (Little, Brown, 1994) is Mandela's own autobiography.
Mandela: The authorized biography (2000) by Anthony Sampson is so far the most comprehensive and astute assessment by a veteran analyst of the South African situation.

HERIBERT ADAM

MARXISM

Marxist discussion of the interrelationship of class relations and forms of social differentiation based on racial and ethnic categories has become intense over the last two decades. The explosion of Marxist debate on this issue certainly contradicts the oft-cited argument that the preferred response of Marxism to nonclass forms of social division is either silence or an attempt to force a complex reality into narrow and determinist models.

A number of key questions have dominated recent debates. Firstly, there is the issue of Marx's and Engels's views on the subject, or rather their supposed failure to analyze it systematically. Secondly, there is the problem of how Marxist concepts of class can help us understand the dynamics of societies that are structured by racial and ethnic categorization. Thirdly, there is the question of how recent Marxist debates on ideology, hegemony, and overdetermination can help us understand the development of racism as an important ideological force in contemporary societies. Fourthly, there is the question of how the important debates about class position of women and about sexism interlink with the analysis of race. Finally, a lively discussion has taken place on the alleged Eurocentric bias of Marxist theory.

Class and nationalism

The starting point of the majority of recent Marxist studies of the dynamics of race and class is that classical Marxism contains no systematic treatment of this question. It has been pointed out, for example, that although the words of Marx and Engels contain a number of scattered references to the pertinence of racial and ethnic relations in certain social formations, e.g. the reference to race as an economic factor in the slavery in the USA, they contain little historical or theoretical reflection on the role of such processes in the capitalist model of production as a whole. Perhaps even more damagingly, a number of critics have argued that several statements on race by Marx and Engels reveal traces of the dominant racial stereotypes of their time and an uncritical usage of common-sense racist imagery. Additionally, a number of critics of Marxism have argued that the reliance by Marxists on the concept of class has precluded them from analyzing racial and ethnic phenomena in their own right, short of subsuming them under wider social relations or treating them as a kind of superstructural phenomenon.

In the writings of Marx and Engels, references to racial and ethnic divisions, along with related issues of religious differences, regional identity, and nationality, are organized around two central themes. The first is the question of internal divisions within the working class. A good example of this strand is the question of the Irish workers who migrated to England and Scotland in search of employment. Both Marx and Engels commented at various points in their work on the impact of this division on the consciousness of the English working class and the manner in which it was perpetrated.

The second theme to be found in the works of Marx and Engels is the issue of the nation and the national question. They frequently drew attention to the significance of national identities and their interrelationship with class relations. For example, they initially highlighted the effect that the development of Irish nationalism had on the consciousness of the English proletariat. Later, they came to perceive the development of a nationalist movement in Ireland as essential to the emergence of a strong labor movement in England. Their historical works are suffused with references to the emergence, development, or demise of nationalities. The analysis provided is by no means as detailed as it could have been, but (1) it does allow us to question the notion that Marx and Engels were silent on forms of extra-class differentiation, and (2) it provides a basis for later attempts by Marxists to analyze the impact of nationalism and racism within the working class.

Early Marxist work on racial and ethnic divisions concentrated particularly on race and class as modes of exploitation. Oliver Cox's *Caste, Class and Race* (Monthly Review Press, 1948) is an early example of this focus. Cox was primarily interested in the economic interests that produce racist exploitation and ideologies historically, and explained racial inequality as an outcome of the interests of the capitalist class in super-exploiting sections of the working class. Since he saw class divisions as the fundamental source of exploitation in society, the main thrust of his work was to conceptualize racial exploitation as a special form of class exploitation. This model subsequently was to exercise a deep influence on the work of Marxist writers on race in the USA, and to a more limited extent in European and other societies.

Reductionism

New life was breathed into this question during the 1960s, particularly as a result of the regeneration of Marxist debates on class and historical materialism which sought to transcend economic reductionism and through increasing political awareness that contemporary racial inequalities were being reproduced in a complex manner which could not be reduced to economistic notions of class. This rethinking of class theory and the historical context of race–class relations is evident in new research on slavery in the USA, studies of racisms and labor market segmentation, the analysis of state racism in South Africa and the large body of work on the economics of migrant labor. Out of this large body of research and historical writing, a number of main themes have emerged. These have centered on:

- the question of the autonomy (relative or otherwise) of racism from class relations;
- the role of the state and political institutions in relation to racial and ethnic issues;
- the impact of racism on the structure of the working class and dynamics of class struggle and political organization;
- the processes through which racist ideologies are produced and reproduced.

The question of autonomy in relation to race and class introduced into this field theoretical problems which had been posed through the analysis of class formation and the capitalist stage. This influence is particularly clear in the work of Stuart Hall and other Marxist writers in Britain, the writings of a number of American scholars and the work of several writers on European migration. The starting point of Hall's work is the assertion that it is incorrect to juxtapose race to class in a simple manner, since it is the articulation between the two in historically specific situations that is the core issue. For example, in a study of Jamaica, he stresses the manner in which class is overdetermined by race, color, and culture. Thus while one cannot reduce racism to class or other social relations, he also maintains that it cannot be adequately understood in abstraction from wider economic, political, and ideological forces.

Studies by Omi and Winant (*Racial Formation in the United States*, Routledge & Kegan Paul, 1986) and by the CCCS Race and Politics Group (*The Empire Strikes Back*, Hutchinson, 1982) have focused more specifically on the role of the state as a site for the reproduction of racially structured situations. Drawing partly on recent Marxist debates on the nature of the capitalist state, a number of studies have analyzed the interplay between politics and racism in specific historical settings. Studies on the role of state institutions in maintaining racialized structures in a number of societies, particularly the USA and South Africa, have highlighted the importance of the political context of racism. This has raised important questions and problems: what is the precise role of the state in the reproduction of racially structured social relations? How far can

the state be transformed into an instrument of antiracist political action? These, and other questions, are currently being explored and debated.

As mentioned earlier, the claim that racism is a source of division within the working class was central to the work of early Marxist writers such as Cox. This theme has once again become central to contemporary debates about racism and class formation, partly as a result of the growth of working-class support for racist political groups and the emergence of black politics. In their study, *Immigrant Workers in the Class Structure in Western Europe* (2nd edn., Oxford University Press, 1973), Castles and Kosack deal with the way in which the state has intervened to create two distinct strata within the working class through the system of contract labor, which denies political rights to the essentially foreign lower stratum. This lower stratum is said to perform the function of a reserve army of labor. In Britain, the work of Robert Miles and Annie Phizacklea on working-class racism represents another strand of the debate (see *Racism and Political Action in Britain*, Routledge & Kegan Paul, 1979). Their writings reflect a deep concern with overcoming the potentially divisive impact of racism on class organization and radical political action. In the United States similar questions have been raised and, given the political climate in many advanced capitalist societies, this is bound to be a source of concern for some time to come.

Ideology

The final theme to emerge from Marxist debates on race and class is that of ideology. The development of racist ideologies, and the various forms such ideologies have taken at different stages of capitalist development, has traditionally not been an issue which has received much attention among Marxists. But renewed interest in the analysis of ideology has helped to overcome this neglect, and questions have begun to be asked about the historical, cultural, literary, and philosophical roots of ideologies of race. Specifically, questions are being asked about the role that ideological relations can play in providing a basis for the articulation of racist ideologies and practices.

An important aspect of recent debates about the pertinence of Marxism to the analysis of race and racism is the question of whether there is an intrinsic Eurocentric bias in the core of Marxist theory. This is a theme that has been taken up in recent years by a number of critics of Marxism and by others who profess to be sympathetic to the Marxist tradition. Perhaps the most important statement of this position is Cedric Robinson's *Black Marxism* (Zed Press, 1983), which argues forcefully that Marxism is inextricably tied to Western European philosophical traditions that cannot easily incorporate the experience of racism and ethnic divisions. This and other studies seem certain to raise questions which will play a part in Marxist discussions for some time to come.

At the present time, however, the broader crisis in Marxist theory has resulted in the development of new perspectives which clearly go beyond Marxism. Above all, recent advances have been made in our understanding of the role of racial ideologies and the racialization of social and political discourses. Originating largely from the USA, such studies have looked at a number of areas, including literature, motion pictures, and other popular cultural forms. They have sought to show that within contemporary societies our understandings of race, and the articulation of racist ideologies, cannot be reduced to economic, political, or class relations. The work of literary and cultural theorists in the United States and Britain has in recent years begun to explore seriously the question of race and racism, and has led to a flowering of studies which use the debates around post-structuralism and postmodernism as a way of approaching the complex forms of racialized identities in colonial and postcolonial societies.

Perhaps as a result of broader transformations in social theory, this is an area of research which has developed rapidly in recent years. Apart from studies of contemporary trends, there has also been a growth of interest in historical research on the origins of ideas about race and in the dynamics of race, class, and gender during the colonial period. This has been reflected in important and valuable accounts of the changing usage of racial symbols during the past few centuries and in accounts of the experience of colonialism and its impact on our understandings of race and culture.

These recent accounts are clearly a long way from the work of Oliver Cox and contemporary Marxist writers such as Robert Miles. But they highlight the ways in which many writers who were once influenced by Marxism have begun to question the relevance of the Marxist paradigm to the analysis of race and racism in contemporary societies.

SEE ALSO: capitalism; Cox, Oliver C.; exploitation; Hall, Stuart; hegemony; ideology

Reading

Marxism and Leninism: Different ideologies by John H. Kautsky (Transaction Books, 2002) provides a clear exposition of the conceptual apparatus of Marxism, paying particular attention to ideology: "No one advocates a policy, becomes or supports a politician, joins an organization, votes, rebels – without some thought motivating his or her behavior, and that thought is ideological."

"Race," Writing and Difference, edited by H. L. Gates, Jr. (University of Chicago Press, 1986) and *Anatomy of Racism*, edited by D. T. Goldberg (University of Minnesota Press, 1990), are two collections that examine strengths and limitations of models of action, including post-Marxist models.

Racism by Robert Miles (Routledge, 1991) provides a critical analysis of racism from a Marxist perspective, while *There Ain't No Black in the Union Jack* by Paul Gilroy (Hutchinson, 1986) provides a critique of contemporary Marxist accounts of racism.

"Varieties of Marxist conceptions of 'race', class and the state" by John Solomos, in *Theories of Race and Ethnic Relations*, edited by J. Rex and D. Mason (Cambridge University Press, 1986), is a critical review of the main strands of Marxist writing on racism.

JOHN SOLOMOS

MASCULINITY

Masculinities are those behaviors, languages and practices, existing in specific cultural and organizational locations, which are associated with males and thus culturally defined as not feminine. There is not just one masculinity but countless *masculinities* manifest in diverse cultural sites. Although there will be massive variations between them, all masculinities have one common feature: each signals a culturally acceptable way of acting like a boy or man, thereby symbolizing male behavior. Most social scientists now accept that masculinities are not something with which males are born but ways of thinking and acting that are learnt over time.

So, it is the environment, not DNA or hormones, that plays the major role in influencing how males think about themselves as gendered beings and how they respond to other males and to females. In other words, masculinity is *culturally* specific, not biologically grounded. The other important point is that males do not generally assume one type of masculinity throughout their lives. Just as a man's life, and the environment within which he lives it, will change over time, so too does his sense of himself as a male. This alerts us to the fact that masculinity is highly contingent, never fully secure and always in process rather than finally accomplished.

So masculinity is a complex concept, and it becomes more so when the variable of race is added. Over recent years notions of race, nationhood and ethnicity have come to be recognized as important avenues of research and understanding within the critical study of men and masculinities.

Respect and cool pose

Richard Majors coined the term "cool pose" to describe the expressive behaviors of many African American males, situated as they are in a society where "institutional racism and constricted structure of opportunity ... restrict their access to education, jobs and institutional power." Majors argued that the adoption of a cool pose by black males is a strategy of resistance to white power structures and as such is an "attempt to carve out an alternative path to achieve the goal of dominant masculinity."

One of Major's questions concerned the relationship between black males and sporting achievement, in particular how a sense of power and purpose was enhanced and sustained through the dynamics of masculine identity processes in sport. This relationship has been interrogated by a number of writers. Several writers have challenged the myth that sporting achievement by black men undermines or removes institutionalized racism, suggesting that black athletes' dominance of certain sports was a sign of racism rather than progress. Michael Messner's research reveals that black men, especially those from lower status backgrounds, seek to achieve a sense of "respect" as masculine men through their successful participation in sports, thus further locking them into activities which have, for most, a limited potential to change their material and social status (see his *The Politics of Masculinities: Men in movements*, Sage, 1997). It

is apparent that this phenomenon is not exclusive to the USA, but can be seen in most white dominated societies.

While research into men, masculinities and race was gathering pace in the US, similar studies were being initiated and undertaken in the UK. One of the most influential of these was that undertaken by Mac an Ghaill in which he explored local student cultures of masculinity and sexuality. In his *The Making of Men* (Open University Press, 1994), Mac an Ghaill argued that "school microcultures of management, teachers and students are key infrastructural mechanisms through which masculinities and femininities are mediated and lived out." Mac an Ghaill's study is particularly important because it exposes the contrasting yet self-sustaining masculine behavior patterns being enlisted and adopted by both white and black young males of different cultural and social backgrounds. Prominent black male icons have also been subject to scrutiny in terms of the types of masculinity they exhibit. An example here is Mike Tyson. Jefferson has provided an illuminating study of Tyson, highlighting how different discourses of masculine identification compete within Tyson for subjective dominance, thereby providing him with some of the impetus for his more visible competition with the world around him.

In line with similar movements within sociology more widely, the sociology of masculinity has undergone some important shifts in more recent years. Such shifts have led to a different set of questions being asked about masculinity and race. For example, in the 1980s and early 1990s some of the key questions being raised by critical gender theorists were: how is male power sustained, what are its origins, and how might such power be challenged? These questions reflected the dominant influence on feminism of structural concepts such as *patriarchy*, *gender order* and *hegemonic masculinity*, where power was seen as top-down rather than a fundamental product or condition of the social network (see Whitehead, below, for discussion). However, the increasing influence of postmodern and poststructuralist theories has led to a reappraisal of the centrality of power as a determinant of male behavior, and toward a recognition that masculinities are discursive in origin, multiple and contingent: neither biologically nor psychologically static and grounded. In short, masculinities are more about identity work than about the conscious pursuit of power by men. Following Michel Foucault and Judith Butler, the questions increasingly being asked of masculinity and race concern the relationship of identity process to the reification of male attitudes and behaviors.

Drawing attention, then, to the provisional character of racial masculine identities, several writers have made significant contributions to our understanding of how cultural dynamics, gender, sexual and racial performativities, and micro-subjectivities and transactions, come to inform and define black males' sense of themselves as males. Recognizing that no identity constructs exist in cultural or social isolation, H. Stecopoulos and M. Uebel make the point that "definitions of black masculine identity crucially hinge on investments in white male identity," with neither identity existing in social isolation of the other.

There is clearly a "crossing and uncrossing" taking place of white and black identity processes within the countless, complex discourses which serve to constitute male behavior in a globalized world. A similar argument is put forward by D. Marriott (in "Reading black masculinities" in *Understanding Masculinities*, edited by M. Mac an Ghaill, Open University Press, 1996), who discusses the ambivalence of, for example, inter-racial desire and sexuality, and the inherent contradictions and problematics contained in the notion of an "authentic" black masculinity.

The idea of a singular *black masculinity* may have some popular appeal to those unwilling to acknowledge the complexities of gender identity, but it has little place in the sociology of masculinity, not least because it rests largely on a white phallocentric view of the black male and on a racist-inclined determinism whereby black skin equals black subjectivity. However, because black males exist in a complex structure/agency dynamic, cleaved with positive/negative dualism and associated discourses of "problem," "power" and "resistance," official pronouncements concerning black male issues often exhibit all the language of a moral panic, thereby serving to reinforce the idea of a black masculinity, albeit one perceived to be at the margins of mainstream society. Marriott has challenged such reductionist thinking, arguing that there is a dynamic diversity within black male experience which undermines any idea that cultural identity can be reduced to an easily assimilated and identifiable

structure or dualism, or that race is somehow functionally added on to gender, thereby producing predictable effects and responses in certain racial and social groups.

Politics of race/politics of masculinities

As the study of race and masculinity has developed, so has it broadened out to include ethnic groups previously less visible within gender studies. Examples here include the study by K. Woods and R. Jewkes (2001) which looks at violence, rape and sexual coercion in a South African township ("Violence, rape and sexual coercion: every love in a South African township," in Whitehead and Barrett, below). Sampath's 2001 study of the "reforming" of male identities in Trinidad, which Sampath sees as a response to new gender discourses in that society (" 'Crabs in a bucket': reforming male identities in Trinidad," in the same collection); and the 1997 research by A. Mirande into Latino culture, masculinity and machismo (*Hombres y Machos: Masculinity and Latino culture*, Westview Press, 1997).

Whatever their cultural location, much of the research into masculinity and race shows that while gender politics may have come to exhibit a highly visible presence, such politics remain unpredictable, riven as they are by contrasting pressures, all of which conspire to make their understanding somewhat elusive. For example, Messner's research into black men's responses to feminism and sexual identity politics reveals the "growing sense of urgency among African American males" over their need to "respond collectively to the institutional decimation of Black Males." As Messner discusses, one obvious example of such a response was the Million Man March by African American males in Washington, DC in 1995. In my own research, I show that the responses of black males to the demands for feminist-inspired equal rights have been neither uniform nor predictable.

On one hand there has been something of a cultural backlash by some black men against (black) women's rights, most obviously apparent in the attitudes and language of rap artists such as 2 Live Crew and Ice Cube. Similarly, in her study of African American intellectuals and artists, *Race Men* (Harvard University Press, 1998), Hazel Carby argues that dominant black and white cultural discourses and representations, arising from male-centered assumptions, continue to locate black women as a "decorative function" outside of the main political spheres. In contrast to these positions, prominent black feminist writers such as bell hooks take a more accommodating view of the diverse responses of black men to issues of gender equality, arguing that " 'the ties that bind' black women and men are unique and thereby beyond the everyday politics of gender discourse" (in her "Men: comrades in struggle," in *Men's Lives*, edited by M. S. Kimmel and M. A. Messner, Allyn & Bacon, 1995)

It is clear that the politics of race are inextricably intertwined with the politics of masculinities. Like men of all social and ethnic groups, men of color exist in a discursive landscape not entirely of their own making or choosing. At the level of their individual subjectivity, black, Latino and Asian men exist beyond the understanding or interpretation of any single, overarching theory of identity or power. Yet at a macro level, being black, Latino, or Asian places those who occupy such identities in a discursive power regime whose contingency rests on the cultural and geographical spaces inhabited by the individual.

In other words, to be black, Latino or Asian is to occupy a political category which, in white dominated regimes, constitutes that person as Other and therefore marginal and peripheral. It is within this political and cultural embodied reality that dominant and subordinate discourses of masculinity flourish or wither, though in recognizing this one should never assume that such a political category automatically constitutes either a singular masculinity or femininity. As I have written in *Men and Masculinities*: "The black male body may appear singular, as might its expression of masculinity, but the authoritative gaze on black men's bodies takes multiple forms." It is in this management, coping, enhancement and negotiation of the self as Other that much of black, Latino and Asian men's sense of themselves as men draws meaning and takes shape.

SEE ALSO: bigotry; black feminism; cultural identity; Jordan, Michael; media; Million Man March; Other; patriarchy; power; racial coding; racist discourse; rap; representations; sexuality; stereotype; Tyson, Mike

Reading

Black Masculinities and Schooling by T. Stewell (Trentham Books, 1997) is an ethnographic study of African Caribbean students in a British comprehensive school.

"Cool pose: black masculinity and sports" by Richard Majors, in *The Masculinities Reader*, edited by S. M. Whitehead and F. J. Barrett (Polity Press, 2001), is the study cited in the main text above; this may be read in conjunction with Tony Jefferson's "Muscle, 'hard men' and 'Iron' Mike Tyson: reflections on desire, anxiety and the embodiment of masculinity" (in *Body and Society*, vol. 4, no. 1, 1998).

Men and Masculinities: Key themes and new directions by Stephen Whitehead (Polity Press, 2002) is a comprehensive and detailed introduction to the sociology of masculinity.

Men's Lives, edited by M. S. Kimmel and M. A. Messner (Allyn & Bacon, 1995) is an anthology of fifty-seven articles, many of which address contemporary debates in race and masculinities.

Race and the Subject of Masculinities, edited by H. Stecopoulos and M. Uebel (Duke University Press, 1997), is an examination of the social construction of masculinities and race and their dynamic relationship with sexuality.

STEPHEN M. WHITEHEAD

MEDIA

The media describes the channels, systems or methods of communication, encompassing television, radio, newspapers, magazines, journals, advertising and other public platforms, including the internet. As sources of information, the media carries great weight in influencing our knowledge of the world. Its impact on race and ethnic relations is considerable. Two of the main issues concerning the media's impact revolve around the under-representation of minority groups in the media; and the manner in which images of minority groups are portrayed.

Under-representation

In 1827 the first newspaper for African Americans was launched: *Freedom's Journal*. In its first issue it proclaimed: "From the press and the pulpit we have suffered much by being incorrectly represented" and "too long have the publick been deceived." Similar concerns have been voiced over the years about each new mass medium – notably motion pictures, the radio and television. Centrally the complaints have been that ethnic minorities are both under-represented and negatively stereotyped.

The importance of such concerns lies in the cultural significance of the mass media. For example, television predominates as a human activity throughout the Western world – the average is around thirty hours per week per person in the USA and the UK. In many countries, it is the third most time-absorbing activity after sleep and work. Not surprisingly, public opinion surveys regularly show that television is cited as by far the most important source of information about what is going on in the world, well above newspapers and radio.

The history of media representation of ethnic minorities is important. While there has been considerable progress in the last two decades, numerous persistent problems remain. Concerns about the media's portrayal of ethnic minorities became mainstreamed following the explosion in the 1960s of racially linked riots in the USA. In 1967, the President (Lyndon B. Johnson) created the National Advisory Commission on Civil Disorders directed by Otto Kerner. The Commission's report concluded that "the overall treatment by the media of the Negro ghettos, community relations, racial attitudes, urban and rural poverty" left much to be desired, and that much was reported "from the standpoint of a white man's world" and reflected "the biases, the paternalism, the indifference of white America."

One explanation of this bias was seen to be the relatively low employment rate of black people in journalism – Kerner estimated this to be around 5 percent (compared with a population then estimated at around 11 percent). Ten years later, the first census by the American Society of Newspaper Editors (ASNE, 1978) found that a mere 4 percent of newsroom employees were from *any* ethnic minority. In the 2001 ASNE survey this had risen to only 12 percent, which it compared with a population estimate of 30 percent. Surveys of the television industry have been more sporadic but point to similar patterns among news reporters and editors, with African American representation at around 8–10 percent but Hispanic only 1–3 percent and Asian/Pacific even lower (compared with census data indicating 13 percent; 12 percent and 4 percent respectively).

It is important to note here that the overall population of most ethnic minorities is rising unevenly but much faster than that of white people. Current US Census Bureau projections are that around one half of the population will be from an ethnic minority group by 2050 (roughly 24 percent Latino, 15 percent African American and 9 percent Asian and Pacific Islanders). Thus, the modest increase in numbers of ethnic minority journalists employed cannot disguise their continuing and serious under-representation. This is particularly acute with Hispanic and Asian/Pacific groups.

Studies of the organizational culture of newsrooms suggest that ethnic minority recruits have made little impact – news values are predominantly socialized ones and are those of white middle-class males. Following the civil unrest in 1992 which stemmed from the police brutality to Rodney King in Los Angeles, the National Association of Black Journalists issued a task force report noting the "simmering frustration" about how its members were used and regarded and "about the slow pace of racial change in newsrooms." Indeed, around the same time, a survey of job satisfaction among press journalists (*The Newsroom Barometer*, 1991) found that more than seven out of ten minority respondents said their papers covered minority issues and concerns "marginally" and "poorly" while 50 percent of white journalists agreed.

Content analyses of television news over the years have tended to support the critical views of ethnic minority journalists. A persistent complaint has been that African American people in particular are problematized by a focus on black poverty, drugs or crime out of all proportion to the reality. Indeed Entman and Rojecki (2001) found that in local TV news reports, the mug shot of the accused was four times more likely to be used when the defendant was black rather than white. They observe that, while there has been an increase over the years in the representation of black people, in network television news this is mainly in crime, sports and entertainment stories. Only rarely do blacks contribute to the serious business of the nation in stories about foreign affairs, economics or electoral politics.

Portrayals

Despite the growth of multiethnic portrayals in children's programming debuted in 1969 with *Sesame Street*, the world of prime-time television remained dominated by able-bodied, single, heterosexual white male adults under forty – until quite recently. By the mid 1990s it was possible to claim that African Americans had achieved equivalence in terms of the number of roles enjoyed. Nevertheless, the quality and variety of roles may be disputed, with a pronounced clustering (ghettoization) in situation comedy such as *The Cosby Show* and in those of entertainer and athlete. In the most recent analyses, the demographics of prime time were: 73 percent white; 16 percent African American; 4 percent Hispanic; 3 percent Asian/Pacific Islanders, 0.2 percent Native American and 3.8 percent Others, emphasizing the growing need for greater inclusion of all ethnic groupings.

This need is not simply one driven by political correctness in order to reinforce notions of equal opportunity. It has become quite clear that ethnic groups do not necessarily share the same tastes in media consumption. For example, the main US audience data generated by Nielsen Media Research (2002) reveals that only one TV program in the top ten list for white people appears in the top ten list for African American homes. Similarly, only one television program in the top ten for African Americans appears in the top ten for white people. Moreover, ethnic minority groups record far greater use of television than their white counterparts. Thus, with the shifting demographics where white people decline as a proportion of the population, it is just as much a matter of pragmatics: television companies need to address issues of representation and inclusion in order to hold on to their market shares of audiences.

The growth of "narrowcasting" (i.e. the specialized channels of satellite and cable) has helped minority groups to achieve better representation. For example, the dedicated channels Telemundo and Univision reach almost nine out of ten Hispanic households in the USA. In recent years, new, cheaper and more sophisticated technologies of production are increasingly accessible, allowing minority groups more independence from the traditional power base of wealthy broadcasters. Thus, the proliferation of such channels would seem inevitable.

Since the Kerner Report of 1968, the cultural, economic and social gap between white people and others may well have reduced somewhat, but it could well be aggravated by such "narrowcasting," which might be seen as essentially divisive and perhaps too by the growth in migration and new religious conflicts in the world. As Entman and Rojecki argue: "all of us are shaped by popular culture" but television images have rarely shown a commitment to what they call "racial comity" or community building. The need for this remains as strong today as at the time of the Kerner Report and with it the need to mainstream and indeed celebrate ethnic diversity may become an increasingly important imperative.

SEE ALSO: African Americans; globalization; Hall, Stuart; Kerner Report; King case, the Rodney; language; political correctness; racial coding; racist discourse; representations; stereotype

Reading

The Black Image in the White Mind: Media and race in America by Robert M. Entman and Andrew Rojecki (University of Chicago Press, 2001) is a well-researched, sophisticated account of how television presents "complicated and conflicted racial sentiments."

Images of Savages: Ancient roots of modern prejudice in Western culture by Gustav Jahoda (Routledge, 1998) is a well-documented reminder of how history continues to shape cultures and provides a foundation for racism.

"Minorities and the mass media: television into the 21st century" by Bradley S. Greenberg, Diana Mastro, and Jeffrey E. Brand, in *Media Effects: Advances in theory and research*, edited by Jennings Bryant and Dolf Zillman (Lawrence Erlbaum, 2002), provides a useful summary of research evidence and pressure group initiatives in the USA.

GUY CUMBERBATCH

MEDICINE

The profession charged with the responsibility for maintaining and restoring health is, of course, highly valued by society. The medical profession's ethical codes emphasize the importance of care for the individual, always putting their best interests first. "The duty of the clinician is to care and comfort as well as to treat," writes Chantler. "When faced with disease and disability the question *'what should be done?'* requires a deep understanding of the human condition and the particular circumstances of the patient." As such: "Medical education must include the opportunity to learn about and understand the needs of people, their families and society." These are high aspirations indeed and yet racism, in various forms, keeps the medical profession and its institutions from achieving their avowed aims and objectives.

Racism at all levels

Racial discrimination in the medical profession has been found at all levels, from entry into medical schools to career development, promotion, in the allocation of discretionary awards (which have a financial value) and in the complaint procedures. A study into 12,000 applications to British medical schools in 1997 found that applicants from minority ethnic communities had significantly less chance of obtaining a place than white applicants. Research conducted by Chris McManus found that eighteen of the UK's twenty-seven medical schools had "disadvantaged applicants from ethnic minority backgrounds. In some cases black and Asian students were three times less likely than white students to gain a place."

However, it is not just medical schools who were found to discriminate. Studies carried out by Aneez Esmail and Sam Everington in 1993 found racist attitudes in the medical profession generally ("Racial discrimination against doctors from ethnic minorities," in *British Medical Journal*, vol. 306, 1993). Their research showed that if applicants had an Asian-sounding name, they were half as likely to get an interview for a National Heath Service (NHS) post. Research published by the King's Fund in 2001 highlighted the experiences of doctors who had encountered racism within the medical profession. Even after obtaining work, black and Asian doctors, particularly those who qualified overseas, tend to get the least attractive jobs in the NHS. The medical specialties with the largest proportions of black and minority ethnic doctors are geriatrics, accident and emergency, and psychiatry; these are specialties that were considered less attractive within the profession. Ethnic minorities are poorly represented in general surgery, cardiology and oncology, which tend to be the most highly regarded specialties. Black and Asian doctors are also far more likely than their white colleagues to be in the more junior staff grade and associate specialist posts that do not lead to a consultant position.

Even professional bodies such as the Royal Colleges and the General Medical Council (GMC) have not escaped allegations of racism; for example, doctors from minority ethnic communities were six times more likely than white doctors to have complaints upheld against them by the Professional Conduct Committee of the GMC. Although the GMC brought in an ex-ternal body, the Policy Studies Institute, to investigate the allegation of racial bias in its handling of complaints, it seems the findings were somewhat ambiguous and the GMC still has to demonstrate that any bias has been removed from its handling procedures.

The term Black and Minority Ethnic (BME) groups together all nonwhite people from minority ethnic communities, British born and those born overseas. The term *overseas doctors* includes all doctors who gained their primary qualifications outside the countries of the EU. The largest group of overseas doctors comes from the Indian subcontinent (often referred to as South Asian). Currently there are many European doctors in Britain mainly from the EU; most of them are white and do not encounter the same level of prejudice and discrimination faced by overseas doctors.

Overseas-trained doctors say that they encounter the greatest amount of discrimination; they get "selected out" of the process from the outset because of their names and country of qualification. However, there is a dearth of research in the experiences of doctors from black and minority ethnic communities who were trained in the UK. Anecdotal evidence suggests that many continue to experience discrimination.

Overseas doctors have been employed in the NHS for over a century; however they were actively recruited during the 1950s to compensate for the underestimation of the medical manpower requirements which led to a significant shortfall in numbers of doctors graduating from British medical schools. Many doctors came from India, Pakistan, Bangladesh and Sri Lanka, a group referred to as South Asian. Further expansion of the NHS in the 1960s resulted in greater recruitment of overseas doctors, especially from India. These were qualified doctors with several years' experience. The GMC, which recognized the qualifications obtained from foreign medical schools, made this migration possible.

At this time, such doctors were welcomed. The mood soon changed. In 1975, a Government inquiry into regulations in the medical profession, the Merrison Report (Department of Health, 1975), called into question the clinical competence and language skills of overseas doctors. Doctors of Asian origin came under particular scrutiny. There was a specific anti-Asian sentiment in British society that was reflected among hospital doctors, according to K. Decker

("Overseas doctors: past and present," in Coker, below)

A 1980 survey conducted by the Policy Studies Institute and published as *Overseas Doctors in the National Health Service*, summarized the views of 60 percent of white British doctors: "Their view is that the general level of competence is lower among Asians, that there is among Asians a relatively high proportion of doctors who are below a minimum acceptable standard, that there is greater variation of competence among Asians, but there is not, among Asians, a relatively high proportion who are outstandingly good doctors."

This rather unforgiving criticism of Asian doctors has affected their careers. These views were widely expressed in the medical press. The belief of the poor standard and language skills of overseas doctors persists and is still being expressed in the twenty-first century.

Impact of discrimination

The main impact of the prejudice and discrimination faced by minority, overseas doctors over the years has been:

- high levels of demoralization, bitterness and anger;
- they have been clustered in the lower ranks of associate and staff-grade specialist posts, (these are subconsultant secondary careers);
- many trained under the worst, rather than the best, training practices and usually had to construct their own vocational training schemes;
- many left the hospital service frustrated after ten to fourteen years to become overqualified and not genuinely motivated general practitioners, or primary carers;
- many have ended up in single-handed practices in the inner cities with a heavy workload;
- poor job satisfaction among a significant number;
- racial harassment, bullying and isolation are commonplace;
- many claim that they do not have equal access to merit awards;
- a waste of talent among people denied opportunities in a profession with serious shortages in key specialties.

Racial harassment covers a wide range of unacceptable, and often unlawful, behavior, including verbal abuse and violence. There are the more obvious and overt forms of harassment such as racist language and physical intimidation. However, racial harassment is frequently more covert. These more subtle forms of racial harassment, such as deprecating the way people dress or speak, are equally distressing and can create an intimidating and unpleasant atmosphere at work. There is still reluctance on the part of the medical establishment and the NHS to acknowledge that racism exists within their organizations.

Doctors from minority ethnic groups believe that they cannot achieve their full potential because of the limitation in other people's minds. If the contribution of black doctors is defined in white norm terms, then their contribution will never be given equal merit. The result is a workforce that is not being enabled to meet its full potential. The medical profession is falling below the threshold of being a meritocracy and will continue to do so until it embraces positive action to promote genuine equality. The color-blind approach that the profession's leaders have, in good faith, pursued until now will have to be replaced by a very different way of tackling racism within its ranks. That action will need to be matched by a similarly determined strategy for promoting equality by medical organizations.

History could repeat itself as medical organizations recruit abroad in efforts to meet the planned increase in medical manpower. The medical system must learn from its past mistakes. What is needed now is some real leadership in the fight against racism in medicine. Senior doctors, managers, politicians and others have a duty to promote equality within the health system, both for patients and workers.

SEE ALSO: British Asians; equal opportunities; inferential racism; institutional racism; mental illness; racial discrimination; transracial adoption; violence; welfare

Reading

Equalising Opportunities, Minimising Oppression: A critical review of anti-discriminatory policies in health and social welfare, edited by Dylan R. Tomlinson and Winston Trew (Taylor & Francis, 2002), examines attempts to reduce inequalities in health.

"Factors affecting likelihood of applicants being offered a place in medical schools in the United Kingdom in 1996 and 1997: retrospective study" by I. C.

McManus (in *British Medical Journal*, vol. 317, no. 7166, 1998) is a valuable study.

Medicine and Humanity by C. Chantler (King's Fund London, 2001) is the source of the quote in the main text above.

Racism in Medicine – an agenda for change, edited by Naaz Coker (King's Fund London, 2001), contains detailed research and first-hand experiences of doctors who have encountered racism and discrimination within the medical profession.

Report of the Committee of Inquiry into the Regulation of the Medical Profession, known as the Merrison Report (British Department of Health: HMSO, 1975), gave an early indication of patterns of discrimination that were emerging in the medical profession; this may profitably be read in conjunction with *Health, Race and Ethnicity: Making sense of the evidence* by C. Smaje (King's Fund London, 1995) and the more general *Genes, Peoples and Languages* by Luigi L. Cavalli-Sforza (Penguin, 2000).

NAAZ COKER

MELTING POT *see* assimilation; Myrdal, Gunnar

MENTAL ILLNESS

Mental health is often described as absence of mental illness. As a concept, it does apply evenly across cultures: different cultures include spiritual well-being as part of their well-being, whereas Western-trained psychiatrists often ignore the spiritual aspect. There is considerable research and clinical evidence to suggest that individuals from black and ethnic minorities have higher rates of certain conditions defined as mental illness, or disorders of the mind. Yet, they also have more difficulty in accessing psychiatric services. There is some evidence to suggest that the pathways they choose in seeking help are not straightforward and the quality of services they receive is often not up to mark and does not necessarily meet their needs. Furthermore, such groups are more likely to be treated by physical means and less likely to receive psychotherapeutic interventions. The reasons for this differential in access and acceptance of services are many and include culturally inappropriate services, their past experiences of seeking help from statutory psychiatric services and culturally defined lay referral systems.

Conditions

Schizophrenia is broadly defined as a psychiatric condition where the individual has lost touch with reality, is experiencing hallucinations in any sensory form, and is also experiencing delusions (the unshakable belief held by the individual contrary to the evidence available) which cannot be understood by others taking into account the individual's cultural and educational standing.

Schizophrenia is probably the most researched psychiatric condition among ethnic minorities. It is a heterogeneous condition and its diagnosis cannot be made after one examination. Different studies use different methods to identify cases, e.g. some use case notes, others use research diagnoses. The heterogeneity of ethnic minorities has often been ignored. In spite of advances in research methods and studies spanning several decades, some key generalizations can be made.

African Caribbean populations in the UK have diagnosis rates of schizophrenia that are between twice to fourteen times higher than for the white population. Whereas some studies have indicated an increase varying from twice to four times, others have argued that there is no increase and rates are broadly similar when compared to the native white population. Data for the Irish are more limited. In the only study of its kind, it was found that rates of admission to psychiatric hospitals were elevated among the Irish when compared with the native whites in Britain.

Ethnic minorities are likely to be economically disadvantaged and as a result will have poor housing and social support may be limited. The contribution of discrimination to the stress of being in a minority and therefore feeling alienated, plus the inherent sense of disappointment and disillusionment, are all significant factors for mental illness.

Although some authors have indicated that the rates of common mental disorders were higher among the ethnic minorities, this finding has not been upheld subsequently.

In one study it was reported that 30 percent of the Asian females attending a general practice in West London had a common mental disorder. The authors found that the general practitioners' diagnosis of common mental disorder had a sensitivity of 17 percent (i.e. they picked up only 17 percent of cases) and a specificity of 91 percent (i.e. their diagnostic accuracy). Individuals who suffered from a common mental disorder also had a higher rate of consultation and were less likely to see depression as a medical condition. Asian females who had common mental disorder were more likely to withhold information from their primary carer. The individual's admission of emotional distress in response to a direct question during the interview correlated well with the diagnosis of common mental disorder. The rates of common mental disorder among the younger generation and among those who speak English show a relative increase in rates for this disorder. Other studies had indicated that the rates among Asians were lower than predicted.

There is considerable evidence in Britain that rates of deliberate self-harm have increased among South Asian females when compared with native whites, whereas there has been no increase among African Caribbean females. Interestingly, this increase among the South Asian females is also reflected among other South Asian diaspora in Fiji, Malaysia and Trinidad. The variation in the rates are more pronounced in Asian females aged 18 to 20 (where the rates are 2.5 times higher) compared to Asian adolescents who show no such increase. The rates are higher among females compared to males and among Asians compared to whites. The rates of completed suicide among Asian females are also elevated compared to white females or Asian males. The method of attempted suicide was not related to ethnicity. Interestingly, Asian females were also more likely to repeat their attempts compared to Asian controls. One of the hypotheses put forward has been that culture conflict contributes to higher rates. Refugees and asylum seekers may well be more vulnerable to stress compared to those who migrate in a planned way and may have had plenty of time and opportunity to prepare themselves for the stress.

From these three conditions, it is clear that differential rates exist in different ethnic minorities. The following can be put forward as possible explanations. For both depression and schizophrenia, misdiagnosis must be ruled out. Several languages do not have words which refer to depression, and there are no clear ways of identifying it. Furthermore, some communities see depression as part of life's ups and downs for which doctors have little to offer. Combined with the notions of stigma, these conditions can be seen as nonmedical responses, and by medicalizing them there is a danger that these become even more of a stigma.

Reasons

Misdiagnosis of schizophrenia in cultural and ethnic groups, whose cultural mores may not be easily understood, is often offered as an explanation for high rates of schizophrenia. Misdiagnosis by itself is unable to explain fourteen-fold differential in rates however. Furthermore, patients in research studies are recruited according to symptoms (which would have been identified as abnormal or odd by their carers) and not by diagnosis.

However, little consideration has been given to differences in symptom patterns of schizophrenia across different cultural groups. For example, some groups report higher levels of auditory hallucinations when compared to others.

For schizophrenia, one suggestion to explain high rates in African Caribbeans is that the countries from which patients had originated had high rates and thus that there was a genetic vulnerability to schizophrenia. However, three well-designated studies from three islands in the Caribbean (Trinidad, Jamaica and Barbados) have demonstrated that the rates of schizophrenia are not higher among the sending countries. Similarly, rates from north India have indicated the same. The other interesting finding has been that the rates are even higher among the second generation – differential rising to about sixteen-fold. Thus the question arises, why should the second generation have even higher rates? Another observation has been that the siblings of second-generation cases of schizophrenia have higher than expected (four times) rates of psychosis compared to controls. This points toward a theory of social causation or contribution, which may be related to socioeconomic discrimination and alienation.

Among whites, rates of schizophrenia have been shown to be related to increased rates of pregnancy and birth complications, suggesting physical assault as a cause, but this finding has not been upheld among the African Caribbeans in the UK or in Trinidad.

There had been previous suggestions that the stress of living in an alien society may produce increased rates. However, bearing in mind that stress produces elevated rates of other psychological morbidity as well, it is difficult to explain high rates of schizophrenia using this.

Two additional factors in the social causation model are worth mentioning. Firstly, discrimination may lead to social and economic disadvantage and may further alienate the vulnerable individual. Secondly, it is possible that if an individual had been led to believe high levels of expectation and their achievement is lower than expected, this discrepancy may contribute to a further sense of alienation. It has been reported that among African Caribbean male patients, the rates of unemployment were twice those of whites and Asians. These patients were also more likely to be living alone in poor housing. Although no causation can be attributed, a clear association suggests that social factors may contribute to the increase. Asians in this sample were more likely to be married and living with their families and their one-year outcome was better compared to white and African Caribbean patients with schizophrenia. It has been indicated that in north India, expressed emotion among relatives of patients with schizophrenia was low, contributing to better outcome.

Racism has played an important role in the way ethnic minorities have been treated at both individual and group levels. It has to be linked with social, political, historical and economic contexts in which ethnic minorities have survived. Psychiatry and psychiatrists have both been seen as tools of the state in controlling deviance.

Racism can be linked with both misdiagnosis and under-diagnosis. There was a collective conviction among British psychiatrists that natives (in the Far East and in Africa) were happy and psychologically underdeveloped and therefore did not suffer from depression. Having believed that this was a rare phenomenon they did not bother to look any further for evidence. The possibility that this perceived or missing difference may be real and significant did not appear to occur to them. A clear reflection of lack of rapport and understanding between the two participants in (this or any other) therapeutic encounter did not appear to occur to them.

Studies in the US and UK have suggested that some psychiatric conditions may be linked with ethnic density of the individual, in that if members of one group are living isolated lives they are more likely to develop schizophrenia, whereas if they are living with others from the same group around them, they are likely to experience culture conflict and may respond by deliberate self-harm, using the act as time out. Another possibility is that if individuals from

sociocentric societies live in egocentric settings; their stress levels are likely to be significantly ill managed. The role of social networks and ethnic density have been studied separately, but not together. Similarly, the impact of a move from one kind of society to another (i.e. egocentric to sociocentric and vice versa) may produce problems.

Linked with socio- or egocentrism is the individual's cultural identity. Studies have shown this to be related to culture conflict, which has been clearly linked with increased rates of depression, anxiety and deliberate self-harm. Thus, understanding aspects of an individual's cultural identity in the context of their own culture as well as in the context of other cultures is useful in understanding emotional and psychological distress.

Cultural identity is bound to play an important role in the genesis of schizophrenia also, because the splitting of the self may well contribute to a sense of loss of reality and delusional perceptions.

Loss of self-esteem related to poor achievement, socioeconomic disadvantage, alienation and disrupted cultural identity, could all contribute to the genesis of depression. Other factors such as loss or separation from parents at a young age can add further to the stress. It has been demonstrated that African Caribbean males with schizophrenia are more likely to have been separated from their fathers for more than four years compared to community controls. Again, this observation cannot be taken as possible causation, only as an association, and needs to be explored further. Similarly, the role of vulnerability factors in the genesis of depression among ethnic minorities needs to be studied and explained.

Medication and psychotherapies

There is a likelihood that patients from ethnic minorities will be given higher dosages of medication without clear indications and for longer periods. Research shows that ethnic minorities often have higher rates of side effects, yet clinicians ignore these observations. In addition, there is evidence that some ethnic groups have different metabolic rates, and pharmacokinetics and pharmacodynamics of drugs vary. The pluralistic approaches followed by some groups may also lead to drug interactions, as may dietary and religious factors.

Psychoanalytic theories developed by Freud and post-Freudian thinkers cannot be applied blindly to all cultures and ethnic minorities. Unless and until the social milieu in which the patient lives and works is understood, no amount of psychotherapy will work. Counseling and other psychotherapies are not often available to ethnic minorities, either because of a genuine lack of resources or more often on the misunderstanding that they are not psychologically sophisticated, or minded, to accept such treatment. Psychological concepts are culture bound and indigenous therapies are often ignored. Group therapy and behavior therapy may work if the clinician takes into account all the relevant factors. For example, in cognitive behavior therapy, the cognitive triad of depression may not be universally applicable because cognitive schema may vary.

Any clinical management of ethnic minorities' health care needs must be in the context of social, economic, political and health care systems, and the trends in application of standard psychiatric criteria for diagnosis and intervention. The concepts of underlying personality also vary across cultures and need to be assessed accordingly.

SEE ALSO: African Caribbeans in Britain; asylum seeker; British Asians; cultural identity; diaspora; language; medicine; Other; racism; refugee status; underachievement; welfare

Reading

Handbook of Cultural Psychiatry by W. S. Tseng (Academic Press, 2001) provides theoretical background as well as practical advice aimed largely at an American audience, though European readers may find some chapters useful.

Mental Health of Ethnic Minorities: An annotated bibliography by Dinesh Bhugra (Gaskell, 1999) provides and annotated bibliography of nearly 100 significant papers which deal with mental health issues in ethnic minorities.

Psychiatry in Multicultural Britain by Dinesh Bhugra and R. Cochrane (Gaskell, 2001) is an edited collection of essays written largely by black and ethnic minority researchers which provides an overview of current clinical practice in different psychiatric subspecialties; it contains all the research cited in the main text above.

DINESH BHUGRA

MERIT

Merit is a term often used in the debate over affirmative action. The debate is complicated by the fact that both sides lay claim to the concept. Both opponents and supporters of affirmative action insist it is their position that protects merit and rewards individuals for meritorious behavior.

Opponents claim that the beneficiaries of affirmative action programs do not "merit" the advantages they receive because advantages are allocated on the basis of gender and skin color instead of individual talent. Talent, supposedly, relates to more legitimate distinctions among individuals, such as intelligence, aptitude, and ability. Opponents of affirmative action would prefer that these traits be recognized as meritorious and that individuals who possess them should receive rewards like college admission or job placements because they "earn" them. The success of talented people ought not be obstructed by government programs that recognize and reward individuals merely on the basis of group membership. Instead, critics of affirmative action advocate an environment of equal opportunity, wherein legitimately meritorious individuals compete fairly for society's perquisites.

For supporters of affirmative action, however, merit is obstructed in an environment without affirmative action. Supporters of affirmative action complicate the concept of equal opportunity by asking: what if society's reward system is so skewed that it becomes easier for people of one color or gender to develop and exhibit their talents? In such cases, the emergence of talent would have less to do with individual traits such as energy and creativity, and more to do with genetic privilege. Thus, it is possible, in a discriminatory society, that merit is associated with sex or skin color even though it is ostensibly assigned on the basis of talent.

In response to this problem, supporters of affirmative action argue that *talent alone* does not necessarily define merit, since recognized talent in some societies can be acquired from privilege rather than industry. Instead, supporters of affirmative action argue that considerations of merit ought to include the role of effort, industriousness, and persistence in the formation of an individual's talent. It may be that an African American inner-city child has a harder time preparing for college than does an affluent white child living in the suburbs. Supporters of affirmative action argue that this discrepancy in difficulty should be recognized in calculations of merit. Affirmative action policies, whether in academia or the business community, address this discrepancy and provide greater access to what is considered true potential because they acknowledge those individuals with unrecognized or unhoned talents.

The debate over merit, then, comes down to a difference in emphasis. Opponents of affirmative action prefer to consider proficiency alone as worthy of merit; they emphasize personal qualities independently of the origin of those qualities. Affirmative action supporters, on the other hand, recognize the sacrifices and efforts expended in the achievement of proficiency. The measure of merit, then, is the distance traveled by the individual instead of just the final destination. And if it is determined that groups such as African Americans and women usually have more distance to travel in the acquisition of recognized talent, then it is quite legitimate for society and government to grant them preferential concessions. In any case, if there is to be a consensus regarding the issue of affirmative action, it is clear that differences in concepts of merit must be recognized and resolved.

SEE ALSO: affirmative action; education; equal opportunity; equality; institutional racism; Marxism; multicultural education; underachievement; welfare

Reading

"Deserving jobs" by David Miller (in *The Philosophical Quarterly*, vol. 42, no. 167, April 1992) examines the underpinnings of social policies designed to ameliorate inequalities in the job market.

"The end of equality: the ugly truth about America's future" by Mickey Kaus (in *The New Republic*, vol. 206, no. 25, June 1992) and "The concept of desert in distributive justice" by Julian Lamont (*The Philosophical Quarterly*, vol. 44, no. 174, January 1994) are both useful articles.

Sex, Race, and Merit: Debating affirmative action in education and employment, edited by Faye J. Crosby and Cheryl Van De Veer (University of Michigan Press, 2000) is a collection that examines the pros and cons of affirmative action.

When Race Counts: The morality of racial preference in Britain and America by John Edwards (Routledge, 1994) critically examines the principle of merit and looks at conditions under which it can be overridden without damage to justice.

TIMOTHY J. LUKES AND BONNIE CAMPODONICO

MIDDLEMAN MINORITY

The term has been used to describe the wide range of minorities concentrated in intermediate economic niches in which they engage in trade and broking but encounter hostility in so doing. The term occurs in analyses of the history of the Jewish Diaspora but it has also been used widely in descriptions of many other ethnic groups, principally those from the Indian subcontinent, China, Lebanon, Armenia, and Greece.

While there is full agreement on the widespread occurrence of this phenomenon, attempts to explain the mechanisms whereby ethnic status, economic specialization in trading and host society hostility are associated have taken various and conflicting forms. Key elements in the debate focus on:

- why particular minorities feature as middlemen;
- how they come to be concentrated in these economic niches; and
- the origins of the hostility to middlemen minorities.

On the first point, those groups who are most regularly found as middlemen can usefully be compared in terms of economic background, family system, and cultural attributes. It is also notable that there are no well-documented examples of minorities of African as opposed to Asian origin acting as middlemen. The social processes whereby blacks come to be concentrated in public sector employment rather than in middlemen roles provide a related focus of inquiry.

Second, explanations of how middleman minorities come to enter trading and broking niches vary between those stressing features of the structure of economic opportunities ("status gap") approaches (Zenner, below) and those which emphasize the possession of relevant qualifications and cultural values that facilitate trading.

Finally, some explanations of the origins of hostility to middleman minorities stress the interests and actions of the dominant elite who may find such groups useful as sources of economic growth and as scapegoats in times of hardship. Other approaches locate the origins of hostility to middlemen in relations with competitors, clients, or employees. Bonacich argues that middleman minorities are characteristically "sojourners" and that their primary allegiance to another homeland to which they expect to return reinforces the effects of cultural separateness in encouraging negative attitudes within the host society. While this formulation has not stood up well to critical analysis (Zenner, below), it has stimulated further testable hypotheses which have done much to illuminate the relationship between ethnicity and economic specialization.

SEE ALSO: beauty; black bourgeoisie in Britain; black bourgeoisie in the USA; capitalism; diaspora; globalization; migration; Motown; Nation of Islam; scapegoat

Reading

Immigrant Businesses: The economic, political and social environment, edited by Jan Rath (Macmillan, 2000), is a European study, while *Immigrant Entrepreneurs: Venturing abroad in the age of globalization*, edited by Robert Kloosterman and Jan Rath (Berg, 2003), is a wide-ranging comparative analysis.
"Middleman minority theories: a critical review" by Walter Zenner, in *Sourcebook of the New Immigration*, edited by Roy Bryce-Laporte (Transaction Books, 1980), summarizes the main contributions in this field. Zenner concludes that while a satisfactory theory of middleman minorities has not yet been put forward, the debate has given rise to many useful and testable hypotheses which can be applied in a wide variety of contexts.
Race and Culture: A world view by Thomas Sowell (Basic Books, 1994) has a provocative argument viz: "Middleman minorities have ... tended to exhibit similarities in certain social traits, despite their great differences from each other in specific cultural features such as religion, food, dress, and language."
"A theory of middleman minorities" by Edna Bonacich (in *American Sociological Review*, vol. 38, 1973) is a sophisticated version of a theory of middleman minorities.

ROBIN WARD

MIGRATION

Population shifts are present at the dawn of human history – the phenomena of hunting and gathering, transhumance (seeking seasonal pasture) and nomadism are as old as human social organization itself. Flight from natural disasters, adverse climatic changes, famine and territorial aggression by other communities or other species is also a common occurrence. The biblical story of the epic flight of the Jews from ancient Egypt is well known, but other great empires – notably those of the Aztecs, Incas, Mesopotamians, Indus, and Zhou – also constructed immense monuments using subordinated peoples dragooned into work, often brought from long distances.

The mercantile period

The "modern world system" was marked by the flourishing of long-distance trade and the opening up of global lines of communication. Along these arterial links flowed not only commodities such as spices, precious metals, and ivory, but also seamen, settlers, merchants, and slaves. European mercantilism also initiated the hitherto largest process of forced migration – the shipment of ten million slaves from Western Africa to the New World. The Caribbean, Mexico, Brazil, and the Southern states of the United States all have large populations descended from these Africans.

At the end of slavery, indentured labor from China, India, and Japan worked the sugar plantations of the European powers in the Caribbean, Indian, and Pacific Ocean areas. Indentured labor was deployed mainly from 1834 to 1920, when the program ceased in British India under the impact of Indian nationalist demands. But the Coolie Ordinance permitting the use of indentured labor in the Dutch East Indies was only finally revoked in 1941.

In addition to compelled and indentured migrants, European global expansion was associated with involuntary and voluntary settlement from Europe itself – particularly to the colonies of settlement and the Americas. Involuntary and state-induced migration from the European mercantile powers included "redemptioners," convicts, demobilized soldiers, and servants. In the English case, a State Paper delivered to King James I by Bacon in 1606 provided justification of the principle: England would gain, Bacon claimed, "a double commodity in the avoidance of people here and in the making use of them there." The poor rates would be relieved and idlers, vagrants, and criminals would be put to good use in the colonies. Political dissenters such as the Levellers, troublesome Irish peasants, and dispossessed Scottish crofters were shipped out in considerable numbers. Even children were not immune from this ruthless logic. Under the various child migration schemes, commencing in 1618 and concluding only in 1967, a total of

150,000 orphaned and indigent children were sent to the British colonies (descendants of these children make up 11 percent of the current Canadian population.)

As largely voluntary migrants, British settlers went to the Dominion societies of Canada, New Zealand, and Australia where they monopolized the political and economic life of these countries at the expense of the local inhabitants. British settlers also migrated to the USA, Rhodesia, and South Africa, where their exclusive political hegemony was slowly eroded by other settlers or by the autochtonous peoples themselves. The Portuguese settled in Angola, Brazil, Mozambique, and a few smaller places. Large parts of North Africa and Indochina were populated by the French. Such was the level of identification with their new homes that the Dutch in South Africa called themselves Afrikaners (Africans) while many French settlers in Algeria called themselves *pied noirs* (black feet), to signify their attachment to the African soil. But, despite the localization of the Afrikaners and the Dominion-British, European settlements did not always endure. The French and Portuguese, in particular, had to absorb large repatriate populations at the end of their colonial empires.

The colonial and industrial era

Mercantilism propelled the commercialization of agriculture, the export of manufactured goods and the growth of the European empire. This was to lead both to massive internal population shifts to staff the colonial enterprises and to the internationalization of the labor market.

The colonial powers needed large gangs of laborers to service the mines, cut the timber, establish the rubber plantations, and to build the docks, railways, roads and canals needed to cement their commercial supremacy and promote their imperial visions. Often the colonial powers adapted local systems of unfree labor recruitment for their own purposes. The Spanish commandeered *repartimiento* workers to dig the silver mines at Potosi in Bolivia and used the *mita* system in Peru. The gold mines in South Africa recruited, through a system of circulating migration, millions of African quasi-free workers from the surrounding countries. Free labor migrants were recruited for work on the various Panama canal schemes, but the death toll was so enormous it threatened the completion of the project.

The free labor market was internationalized notably by growth of the new mass industries in the USA. The collapse of feudalism and the second serfdom in Europe was followed by the Great Atlantic Migration when, over the period 1870–1914, thirty-five million Europeans were transshipped to the United States. Similar international movements of Poles to Germany and the Irish to Britain accompanied industrial development, although the French, Italian, and Japanese were able to staff their factories largely by internal supplies from their floundering rural areas.

Rural–urban migration

Few small countries and only the most remote parts of large countries have been able to resist the seemingly inexorable drift from agriculture to industry, from rural to urban life. This process is often depicted as a natural, if regrettable, fact of life flowing from "population pressures." In trying to develop a more satisfactory explanation of rural–urban migration, it is however worth recalling Marx's remark that "population does not press on capital, capital presses on population."

This aphorism is a useful reminder that a wide range of phenomena – such as land enclosures, the occupation of land by settlers, fights between ranchers and farmers, the move to cash-cropping, the growth of prairie farming and agribusiness, and the introduction of high-yield seeds needing irrigation, fertilizers and large tracts of land – are all examples of commercial pressures on agricultural areas. They all result too in the migration of landless or small peasants, farmers, and rural craftsmen, who find it more and more difficult to subsist in the countryside.

Projections of the demographic consequences of this process have yielded the following figures: globally, the percentage of population expected to be living in the urban areas in the year 2025 is 65.2 percent. This will comprise 86.7 percent in the most developed regions and as many as 60.9 percent in the least developed regions. The destabilizing effects of such large-scale movements on the capacity to provide housing, food, stable government, and a sustainable livelihood for the majority of the population is self-evident.

Current migratory flows

Four forms of migration predominated in the post-1945 period. Firstly, state formation arising from nationalist pressures resulted in mass displacement. Examples include the swap of Muslims from India with Hindus from Pakistan and the expulsion of Palestinians from Israel. This phenomenon is also currently seen in the former state socialist bloc, notably in former Yugoslavia. Mass displacements have arisen from the two World Wars, localized interstate wars, civil wars, famine, economic crises and political instability. By the mid 1990s some seventeen million "refugees" (the word being used in a general, not a legal sense) had been compelled to leave their homes.

Secondly, the unskilled labor migration characteristic of the postwar period has continued despite the immigration restrictions imposed by European countries and North America in the 1970s. Sometimes the flows have gone to new destinations, like such as the oil-rich countries of the Gulf or Venezuela. In other cases, illegal, undocumented, and contracted laborers have continued to migrate to rich countries in an often desperate search for work.

Thirdly, skilled migrants have used the globalization of the economy to secure their comparative advantage in employment. International civil servants, independent entrepreneurs, scientists, doctors and dentists, business executives, skilled engineers, and architects are examples of highly mobile, skilled workers who cross international frontiers with little difficulty.

Fourthly, asylum seekers, i.e. those hoping for *legal* recognition as refugees under the international Conventions have arrived in Europe and North America in significant numbers. Constitutional provisions in Germany and France and the perception that the USA is willing to accept the world's "huddled masses" act as factors in encouraging movement, but the growth in the numbers of asylum seekers has triggered a xenophobic, hostile, and often violent reaction to the newcomers. Increasingly restrictive measures to slow the flow of asylum seekers have been imposed or announced in all destination countries.

SEE ALSO: asylum seeker; colonialism; cultural identity; diaspora; ethnic conflict; globalization; human rights; hybridity; Irish; law: immigration, Britain; law: immigration, USA; middleman minority; refugee status; slavery; xenophobia

Reading

The Cambridge Survey of World Migration, edited by Robin Cohen (Cambridge University Press, 1995), provides the most wide-ranging coverage of migration in a single volume. In 95 contributions from scholars in 27 countries, the authors cover regional migration patterns, labor migration, the flights of refugees, and illegal migration. The book contains both historical and contemporary contributions

Citizenship and Migration: Globalization and the politics of belonging by Stephen Castles (Routledge, 2000) may be read in conjunction with *The Age of Migration* by Stephen Castles and Mark J. Miller (Palgrave, 1998); both deal with global migrations and their impact in the past several decades.

Guests and Aliens by Saskia Sassen (The New Press, 2000) explains the economic and political migrations of Italians and Eastern European Jews during the nineteenth and early twentieth centuries as part of a much wider history of global border crossing.

Migration Theory: Talking across disciplines by C. B. Brettell and J. F. Hollifield (Routledge, 2000) takes an eclectic approach.

The New Untouchables: Immigration and the New World worker by Nigel Harris (I. B. Taurus, 1995) describes the conflict between increasing state restriction on the one hand and the increasing mobility of workers on the other. Harris suggests that the pressures of globalization will ultimately challenge the capacities of the nation-state to control its borders.

The State of the World's Refugees 1995: In search of solutions is a report written by the United Nations High Commission for Refugees (UNHCR) and published by Oxford University Press in 1995. While arguing that the right of asylum should be scrupulously respected, the authors of the report argue that greater efforts need to be made to tackle the problem of refugees and displaced people at source. The report is trenchantly written and beautifully produced, with excellent graphics.

CHECK: internet resources section

ROBIN COHEN

MILLION MAN MARCH

The Million Man March was the name given to an assembly of African Americans who, on October 16, 1995, converged on Washington, DC at the behest of Louis Farrakhan, leader of the Nation of Islam. The rally was intended to solidify an African American population that Farrakhan believed was heading toward self-destruction: "Unity, atonement and brotherhood" were the watchwords.

Drugs, black-on-black violence, persistent criminality and female-led single parent families were among the issues Farrakhan believed were causing divisions among America's black population. He implored those attending the rally to take a pledge not to " ... raise my hand with a knife or a gun to beat, cut, or shoot any member of my family or any human being except in self-defense ... never abuse my wife ... never engage in the abuse of children ... for sexual gratification ... never again use the 'B' word to describe any female ... not poison my body with drugs."

African Americans from across the country gathered at DC's National Mall, many from Christian churches, as well as schools and all types of social organizations. While the number of delegates did not reach the million target, it far surpassed the 250,000 who gathered for Martin Luther King's historic "I have a dream" speech in 1963.

Joining Farrakhan on the steps of the US Capitol were civil rights leaders, Benjamin Chavis, Jesse Jackson, Rosa Parks and Dick Gregory. Stevie Wonder sang and Maya Angelou recited poetry.

The march, which became the subject of Spike Lee's 1996 movie, *Get on the Bus*, was not without dissent. The Baptist church pointed out that the separatist Nation of Islam was at odds with the aims of many African American churches, which pursued greater integration. Farrakhan's chosen title for the march reflected his movement's stance on women. Myrlie Evers-Williams, chair of the National Association for the Advancement of Colored People (NAACP), objected to the explicit sexism of the event. The Jewish Anti-Defamation League's leader Abraham Foxman pointed out Farrakhan's record of anti-Semitic remarks: "We have a problem with the fact that the man who calls us together continues to be a racist, sexist, homophobic, anti-Christian."

Farrakhan claimed that evidence of the rally's effects was seen in the following year's presidential election when 1.7 million more African American men voted than did in 1992. There were, of course, many other contributory factors.

SEE ALSO: African Americans; Afrocentricity; civil rights movement; culturecide; human rights; Lee, Spike; Nation of Islam; racist discourse; reparations; white backlash culture

Reading

"Million Man Messenger, Not Message, Causing Divi-

sion," *CNN US News*: available at *http://www.cnn.com/US/9510/megamarch/10–15*.
Race and Ethnic Relations in Today's America by Greg Oswald (Ashgate, 2001) has a chapter "Politics" in which the author contends that the march mobilized African Americans and "Farrakhan definitely did make a contribution" to the increase in the black vote in 1996; after the big event, however, "the militant leader has reverted to his earlier racist message and attendance at his rallies has fallen off."

MINORITIES

In the field of race and ethnic relations, the term minority has been confusing because of the double component of its meaning: the *numerical* and the *political*. In the USA, where the term has become entrenched in official terminology, a minority group is defined primarily in terms of disadvantage, underprivilege, or some such euphemism for a combination of political oppression, economic exploitation and social discrimination. In recent American usage, the noun "minority" can refer both to a racial or ethnic group, or to an individual member thereof. Since the groups that are so defined (principally Afro-Americans, Amerindians, Hispanics, and groups of Asian origin) are all numerical minorities of the total US population, this usage is relatively unproblematic in North America, although it may reflect class interests. (The only possible confusion is with the political usage of minority to refer to party representation in government, as in "the minority leader of Senate.")

As a term to be used in the comparative study of race and ethnic relations, minority is a liability, since many numerical minorities have been politically dominant and economically privileged. Nearly all tropical colonies of European powers, for example, have been ruled by minorities, often very small ones of under 10 percent, or even 1 percent of the total population. Obviously, to speak of the indigenous populations of India, Algeria, Nigeria, or South Africa as minorities in relation to their colonial masters does not make much sense.

Even in a political context such as that of the United States, where the ethnically and racially disadvantaged are numerical minorities, the term minority is an analytical liability. Its popularity, however, may well be due to the fact that it serves political interests precisely *because* it obfuscates reality.

First, in a representative system, where small numbers are disadvantageous in themselves, it is not clear where the status of minority begins and ends. In the USA, for example, many voices have argued for the inclusion of groups such as Jews and Japanese Americans on grounds of past discrimination as well as small numbers, while others have sought to exclude the same groups on the basis of above-average success on educational or economic indices. If minority status confers preferential access to resources (as under affirmative action policies in the US) then, of course, the terminological confusion of minority can be manipulated for political and economic gain.

Second, the definition of minority in racial and ethnic terms, and the association of that term with political and economic exclusion from the majority mainstream, represents an obfuscation of class realities. Specifically, it ascribes the status of dominant group (WASP, White Anglo-Saxon Protestant) to a group much larger and much more diffuse than the actual ruling class of American society. It also, of course, divides the working class along ethnic and racial lines, and militates against class-based organization by rewarding ethnic and racial affiliation. Perhaps most insidiously, it disguises the fact that the USA is, like all societies, ruled by a small elite, not by a large amorphous group such as WASPs; that is, the term minority salvages the majoritarian myth of bourgeois democracy.

SEE ALSO: affirmative action; Asian Americans; British Asians; disadvantage; empowerment; equality; ethnic monitoring; indigenous peoples; Park, Robert Ezra; power; racial discrimination; rational choice theory; reverse racism; tokenism

Reading

Debating Diversity: Clashing perspectives on race and ethnicity in America, 3rd edn., edited by Ronald Takaki (Oxford University Press, 2002), examines the similarities and differences between the experiences of minorities in the USA; the essays are structured around a series of debates.

Minorities in an Open Society by Geoff Dench (Transaction Books, 2002) challenges many widespread assumptions about the manner in which minority groups adapt and are adapted to.

Protection of Ethnic Minorities, edited by Robert G. Wirsing (Pergamon Press, 1981), is a good summary of the treatment of ethnic minorities in capitalist, socialist, and Third World countries.

PIERRE L. VAN DEN BERGHE

MINORITY LANGUAGE RIGHTS

Minority language rights are the linguistic and wider social and political rights attributable to speakers of minority languages, usually, but not exclusively within the context of nation-states. Given their close association with the wider discourse of human rights, they are also regularly described by some commentators as *linguistic human rights*.

Advocacy of minority language rights arises out of three principal concerns: (1) the decline of languages; (2) language hierarchies; and (3) legal rights.

Decline of languages

The current exponential decline and loss of many of the world's estimated 6,000 languages stands at 50 percent predicted to "die" or no longer be spoken by a community of speakers by the end of the twenty-first century. A further 40 percent of languages are also said to be threatened or endangered. This suggests that as few as 600 languages may survive over the longer term. These predictions are reinforced by a 1999 US Summer Institute of Linguistics survey that found that as many as 5,000 languages currently have fewer than 100,000 speakers and that 96 percent of the world's languages were spoken by only 4 percent of its people.

Language decline and loss always occur in bilingual or multilingual contexts, in which a majority language (a language spoken by groups with political power, privilege and social prestige) comes to replace the range and functions of a minority language. The inevitable result is that speakers of the minority language shift over time to speaking the majority language. In this sense, language loss is not a new phenomenon: languages have risen and fallen, become obsolete, died, or adapted to changing circumstances in order to survive, throughout history. In response, proponents of minority language rights often adopt a linguistic ecology perspective, arguing that the current parlous state of many of the world's languages is analogous to processes of biological/ecological endangerment and extinction; indeed, is far greater than the threat of extinction facing animal and plant species. Unless this process of languages loss is seriously and urgently addressed, they argue, the world's linguistic "gene pool," along with the cultural knowledge associated with these languages, will be irremediably diminished.

Hierarchies

The second principal concern has to do with the reasons why certain languages and their speakers come to be minoritized in the first place. Advocates of minority language rights argue that the establishment of majority/minority language hierarchies is neither a natural process, nor primarily even a linguistic one. Rather, it is a historically, socially and politically constructed process and one that is deeply imbued in wider (unequal) power relations.

There are two specific points at issue. One concerns what actually distinguishes a majority language from a minority language or a dialect. This distinction is not a straightforwardly linguistic one. For example, we cannot always distinguish easily between a language and a *dialect* on linguistic grounds, since some languages are mutually intelligible, such as Danish, Swedish and Norwegian, while some dialects of the same language are not. Similarly, the majority/minority status ascribed to particular language varieties may well change over time, depending on wider social and political events. Thus, Norwegian was regarded as a dialect of Danish prior to independence and only attained the status of a "language" in 1905. A contemporary example can be seen in the former Yugoslavia, where separate Serbian and Croatian language varieties (re)emerged in the 1990s to replace Serbo-Croat, itself the artificial fifty-year product of the Yugoslav Communist Federation under Tito. Place also plays a significant part here: for example, Spanish is regarded as a majority language in Spain and many Latin American states, but as a minority language in the USA.

What this demonstrates is that languages are "created" out of the politics of state making, not the other way around. This highlights, in turn, the second key point at issue: the central and ongoing influence of nation-state organizations in the establishment and maintenance of majority/minority language hierarchies. Modern nation-states, with their origins in the nationalism of the last few centuries, are organized on the principle of cultural and linguistic homogeneity, itself a consequence of the nationalist idea of nation-state congruence (that a nation, or national group, should be represented by a state). Following from this, nation-states have been concerned primarily with the replacement over time of the wide variety of language varieties spoken with a nation-state's borders with one "common national language (sometimes, albeit rarely, a number of national languages). This process usually involves the legitimization and institutionalization of the chosen national language.

Legitimization is understood to mean the formal recognition accorded to a particular language by the nation-state. Institutionalization refers to the process by which this language comes to be accepted or taken for granted in a wide range of social, cultural and linguistic domains or contexts, both formal and informal. Both elements achieve a central requirement of the modern nation-state: that all its citizens adopt a common language and culture for use in the civil or public realm. At the same time, the chosen "national" language comes to be associated with modernity and progress, while the remaining minority languages become associated with tradition and obsolescence,

Proponents of minority language rights argue that the emphasis on culture and linguistic homogeneity with nation-states, and the attendant hierarchizing of languages, is neither inevitable nor inviolate: particularly given the historical recency of nation-states and the related, often arbitrary and contrived processes by which particular languages have been accorded "national" or "minority" status respectively. These arguments about the historical and geopolitical situatedness of national languages also apply at the supranational level, particularly in relation to the burgeoning reach and influence of English as the current *lingua mundi* or world language.

Minority language rights proponents argue that the hegemonic influence of English, though clearly aided by the processes of globalization, has longer and geopolitical antecedents. Firstly there was the initial preeminence of Britain and the British Empire in establishing English as a key language of trade across the globe. Secondly, there has been the subsequent social-political dominance of the USA, along with its current preeminent position in the areas of science, technology, media and academia. Recent geopolitical events, such as the collapse of the former Soviet Union and much of communist central and Eastern Europe along with it, have further bolstered the reach and influence of English.

As with the construction of national languages, the current ascendancy of English is also invariably associated with modernity and modernization and the associated benefits which accrue to those who speak it. The result, minority language rights proponents argue, is to *position* other languages as having less "value" and "use" and, by extension – and more problematically – to delimit and delegitimize the social, cultural and linguistic capital ascribed to non-English speakers: the phrase itself reflects the normative ascendancy of English. And this brings us to the third principal concern underlying advocacy of minority language rights: the often-deleterious consequences facing the speakers of minority languages.

Minority language rights point out that the promotion of national languages and/or English is, because of the social and political processes outlined above, almost always couched in terms of "language replacement": that one should/must learn these languages at the expense of one's own first language. Consequently, the promotion of cultural and linguistic homogeneity at the collective/public level has come to be associated with, and expressed by, individual monolingualism. This amounts to a form of linguistic social Darwinism and also helps to explain why language shift, loss or decline has become so prominent. In response, minority language rights proponents argue that the clear importance of learning or acquiring majority languages does not – indeed *should* not – preclude individuals from continuing to speak other languages, particularly their first language should they so choose.

Legal rights

Following from this, proponents of minority language rights have increasingly drawn upon the discourses of minority rights within international law to argue that minority language speakers should be accorded at least some of the protections and institutional support that majority language speakers already enjoy. These arguments include the enforcement of basic human rights such as the ability to speak one's first language when and where one likes. Surprisingly, this right is still regularly usurped in the contemporary world: Kurds in Turkey, for example, continue to have their language proscribed in all

public domains. More contentiously, arguments for minority language rights have also increasingly been framed in terms of wider emergent concerns about the inherent individualism and Western ethnocentrism of human rights law. This is particularly evident in the way human rights have come to be conceptualized and employed in the post-World War II era and is in contradistinction to earlier formulations of international law which did recognize and attribute specific cultural and linguistic rights to minority groups, notably in minority treaties overseen by the League of Nations.

As a result of these wider debates, a more accommodating approach to the rights of minorities has emerged, particularly in the post-Cold War period, including more direct recognition of and protection for minority language rights. At the supranational level, two key examples of recent legislation demonstrate this. One is the UN Draft Universal Declaration of Linguistic Rights, of 1996, which argues that explicitly legal guarantees be provided for the linguistic rights of individuals, language communities (in effect, national minorities and indigenous peoples) and language groups (other ethnic minority groups). This includes the right of the individual "to the use of one's language both in private and in public" (article 3.1).

Another key example is the 1993 UN Draft Declaration on the Rights of Indigenous Peoples, which in article 14 states: "Indigenous peoples have the right to revitalize, use, develop and transmit to future generations their histories, languages, oral traditions, philosophies, writing systems and literatures." States shall take *effective* measures, whenever any right of indigenous peoples may be threatened, to ensure this right is protected."

These more accommodating developments with respect to minority language rights have also been reflected within some nation-states. Thus, in Brazil, the adoption in 1988 of a new constitution recognized for the first time the indigenous Indians' social organization, customs, languages, beliefs and traditions. Norway also moved in 1988 to revise its constitution in order to grant greater autonomy for the indigenous Sami, including the specific directive that governmental authority take the necessary steps to enable the Sami population to safeguard and develop their language, their culture and their social life. The effects of this are most apparent in the regional area of Finnmark, in the north-ernmost part of Norway, where the largest percentage of Sami live. The formal recognition accorded to Sami has led to the subsequent establishment of a Sami Parliament in Finnmark in 1989, while the Sami Language Act, passed in 1992, recognized Northern Sami as its official regional language and resulted in the formal promotion of the language within the Sami Parliament, the courts of law and at all levels of education.

These recent developments within both inter-national and national law are clearly significant, but they also face two key and ongoing chal-lenges. One is the degree to which these general claims to rights are actually enforceable, since they are still dependent on the commitment of individual nation-states to provide the effective measures necessary for implementing such claims. The second concerns the contentious and ongoing debates within academic, political and policy arenas about group-differentiated rights per se, of which minority language rights clearly forms a part. The latter challenge has been debated within the social and political theory, as well as within anthropology, with respect to what actually constitutes a "group" and, given the complexities involved in defining groups, whether any rights – linguistic or otherwise – can actually be attributed to them. In this respect, early discussions of minority language rights were found to be problematic because they tended simply to assume that the linguistic community in question was easily definable in the first place – or, rather, that all members of this group were (or would want to be) principally identified and identifiable by their language. This led in turn to the further potential problem of essentialism – of essentializing the language–identity link – something which runs counter to the many conceptions of cultural identity. More recent work has specifically acknowledged the contingency of language and identity, while still providing sociohistorical and sociopolitical argu-ments along the lines outlined above for the greater recognition and promotion of minority language rights.

But there still remains continuing opposition to minority language rights and group-differentiated rights more broadly, within the political and policy domains, and particularly at national levels. Again, this has much to do with the allied notions of nation-state congruence and

cultural and linguistic homogeneity, which con-tinue to underlie the public organization of nation-states. Opponents of minority language rights argue that recognition of minority language rights will inevitably undermine the cohesiveness of nation-states, resulting in their ethnic, cultural and/or linguistic Balkanization, as well as con-tributing directly to wider ethnic, social and political conflict. These arguments are broadly employed against the public promotion of multi-culturalism as well. An example of both can be seen in the rise of the English Only movement in the USA, which aims specifically to undermine and dismantle bilingual education, particularly for Spanish speakers, while Pauline Hanson's One Nation party in Australia employed a wider agenda against group-differentiated rights, parti-cularly for Aboriginal Australians, as a case of "special privilege" and/or "special pleading."

This opposition to minority language rights is likely to continue because of the ongoing public purchase of the arguments employed, although proponents of minority language rights point out that it is the *suppression* of minority language rights that has most often led to wider conflict and destabilization, not their recognition. This is demonstrated by numerous historical and con-temporary examples throughout the world, in-cluding in the Baltic, Belgium, Canada, Spain, Sri Lanka, Turkey and the former Yugoslavia.

SEE ALSO: Aboriginal Australians; American Indians; anthropology; cultural identity; culturecide; education; essentialism; ethnocentrism; ethnocide; ethnonational; globalization; Hanson, Pauline; human rights; indigenous peoples; language; minorities; multicultural education; multiculturalism; nationalism; One Nation; social Darwinism; United Nations

Reading

Language: Ideological debates, edited by Jan Blom-maert (Mouton de Gruyter, 1999), is a collection that explores, via a range of widely different national contexts, the historical interconnections between language, political ideology, nationalism and the subsequent influence on the implementation (and contestation) of language policy and planning.

Language and Minority Rights: Ethnicity, nationalism and the politics of language by Stephen May (Long-man, 2001) is an interdisciplinary and critical analy-sis that draws together sociological discussions of ethnicity and nationalism and social and political theory discussions of minority rights in order to explore their specific implication for minority language rights; it develops a nonessentialist defense of minority language rights and includes in-depth discussion of key case studies from around the world. *Linguistic Genocide in Education or Worldwide Diversity and Human Rights?* by Tove Skutnabb-Kangas (Lawrence Erlbaum, 2000) is a highly polemical and voluminous but accessible and informative overview of current processes of minority language shift and loss, or what the author terms "linguistic genocide" and its obverse, minority language rights or linguistic human rights; the text is enhanced by a large number of vignettes and exercises.

STEPHEN MAY

MINSTRELSY

Troupes of public entertainers with blackened faces performing songs and dances ostensibly of African or African American origin in the nineteenth and early twentieth centuries were called minstrels and their entirety was known as minstrelsy. In this context, the word is faithful to its origins: it derives from the Old French *menestral*, which means both entertainer and servant. Minstrels entertained predominantly white audiences by portraying buffoons and supposedly depicting authentic scenes from African American life. Robert Toll, in his history of the minstrelsy, sees enormous significance in this "because it was the first indication of the powerful influence Afro-American culture would have on the performing arts." But, as Toll points out: "It does not mean that early minstrels accurately portrayed Negro life or even the cultural elements that they used. They did neither."

The minstrel troupes deliberately stretched and distorted the aspects of black culture they deemed useful in such a way to endorse popular stereotypes held by whites about blacks. Popular entertainers had amused American audiences by ridiculing blacks from the start of the nineteenth century. The name "Jim Crow" came from a ludicrous character created by Thomas Rice (1808–60) who amused audiences with his characterization of the fictional, indolent and enchantingly childlike fool. Joseph Boskin notes that: "By the early 1820s, songs and dances by white actors along the eastern seaboard expanded the character of the black." White performers wore "black" clothes, imitated "black" accents and acted in an absurdly cheerful style.

Boskin's research centers on *Sambo: The rise and demise of an American jester*. The dependable Sambo character was the stuff of lore. According to Boskin, the type was instrumental in persuading whites that the popular fictions about African Americans had some substance. Like Jim Crow, the mild-mannered and light-hearted dimwit comforted whites in the knowledge that black people, far from being resentful and threatening, were content, if not happy in their enslavement.

This became an important motif as the 1863 Emancipation Proclamation approached and many feared the consequences. The Ethiopian Opera, burlesque shows featuring artists in blackface (as the makeup was called), was the most popular form of entertainment at the turn of the century, eventually ceding place to vaudeville, theater, then film. It comprised white singers and dancers playing banjos, wisecracking and, generally, imitating crude caricatures of inoffensive "plantation niggers" or "coons," the popular name for Southern blacks – memorably defined by Donald Bogle as "unreliable, crazy, lazy, subhuman creatures good for nothing more than eating watermelons, stealing chickens, shooting crap, or butchering the English language." The Rastus character was added to the gallery of stereotypes depicted in the minstrelsy.

After slavery was outlawed, fearful imagery circulated among whites. It was suspected that African Americans, once released from bondage, would invade job markets and perhaps even seek to exact vengeance for past injustices. The minstrelsy did much to allay the fears of whites.

Occasionally, whites would claim to have researched their characters by observing Southern blacks. One in particular, Edwin P. Christy, studied the "queer words and simple expressive melodies" of New Orleans blacks in the 1830s. He eventually created the Christy Minstrels, acknowledged as one of the leading troupes of the day.

Minstrel troupes featuring black performers began to appear in the mid 1800s, but few of them rivaled the white-owned companies until Charles Callender, a white tavern owner, started up minstrel shows with a black cast. By 1875 Callender had two black troupes, one of which toured the East Coast, the other the Mid-West. In 1878 he sold out to J. H. Haverly, who, with more marketing know-how, took the company from strength to strength. His ploy was to present his minstrels not as entertainers, but as true representatives of plantation "Negroes"; "like animals in a zoo," Toll remarks. The success of the enterprise indicates the perverse amusement whites took in having popular images of uneducated, pitiful and brutish blacks presented, albeit in theatrical form. It also served to legitimize plantation caricatures.

African Americans also ran their own minstrel businesses. Lew Johnson, for example, began his operation in the 1860s and kept it afloat for twenty-five years. A small-time outfit comprising between six and eight players, Johnson's "Black Baby Boy Minstrels" (one of several names) was effectively shut out of the big cities but worked the frontier territories with modest success. In the same period, another black company owner, Charles Hicks, found getting into the lucrative city markets a problem and so opted for Europe and Australia. Hicks continually challenged white owners, sometimes luring their performers away, sometimes losing out to owners who could offer better money. He died in 1902 on the Pacific island of Java, where his troupe was performing. Not for sixty years after his death was a black entrepreneur able to wrest control of a sector of the black entertainment industry large enough to rival white-owned corporations; and that man was Berry Gordy, the owner of Motown.

Despite the difficulties of black impresarios, African American entertainers were welcomed. Billy Kersands, for example, was the highest paid minstrel of the late nineteenth century. His stardom was founded on his ability to perform with his mouth full of billiard balls, cups and other objects. His cartoonish contortions and cod-poll manner made him a perfect enactment of the Sambo type. Less of living stereotypes were Wallace King, a noted tenor balladeer, Horace Weston, a banjo virtuoso, and James Bland, a noted singer-songwriter who gained fame in Europe and reputedly earned, at his peak in the 1880s, $10,000 per year.

By the end of the nineteenth century, there was a bizarre coexistence of African American entertainers and white performers mimicking them, or more specifically, parodying them. And, if Toll is to be accepted, black performers copying white performers copying them. The shows presented by both white and black minstrels were aesthetically fraudulent in that both misrepresented black culture.

Lawrence Levine contends that the black performers of the early twentieth century were influenced by, and in turn influenced, many white Southern country singers. This "black–white musical admixture," as he calls it was not limited to song, but to vaudeville, phonograph records, radio and movies, all of which succeeded minstrelsy. We should also add ragtime.

White audiences eventually grew tired of the minstrels, black and white. Public curiosity, concern and interest declined in almost direct relation to the abatement of any threat that the post-emancipation period seemed to hold. Yet the minstrels' impact lasted beyond their own lives. Black people established a presence in popular entertainment and whites had accepted, perhaps even encouraged, this. LeRoi Jones, in his book *Blues People*, lauds the minstrelsy: "For the first time Negro music was heard on a wider scale throughout the country, and began to exert a tremendous influence on the mainstream of the American entertainment world." Of course, the influence continued through the twentieth century to the present day.

"Live" minstrel shows dwindled as vaudeville's star rose. This offered new opportunities for black musicians, especially those who were prepared to mix drops of mirth into the serious business. Louis Armstrong not only recorded inferior material for the sake of appealing to a white audience, but also introduced comic routines into his act. In this sense, he did not stray too far away from the minstrels' maneuvers. During the first two decades of the twentieth century, the popularity of minstrelsy waned, though *The Jazz Singer*, released in 1927, featured the Jewish singer Al Jolson blacked up in evocation of minstrelsy days.

While the genre declined, Boskin argues that the self-mocking fashion of many black actors, singers and other kinds of theatrical performers continued, albeit in slightly revised ways. Boskin's observation is that black entertainers were able to draw short of total compliance with old stereotypes, subtly undermining them in a way that was probably more recognizable to blacks than whites. While he does not mention it, a nice example of this was the "cakewalk" often enacted by minstrels: this was a ridiculous caricature of whites' dancing originally used slyly by black minstrels. It was made ironic by white minstrels who intended to mock blacks without understanding they were compounding their own indignity.

Toll writes that: "Minstrelsy was the first example of the way American popular culture would exploit and manipulate Afro-Americans and their culture to please and benefit white Americans."

SEE ALSO: blues; humor; Jackson, Michael; Jim Crow; Ku Klux Klan; Lee, Spike; Motown; negrophilia; race: as signifier; racist discourse; rap; representations; self-fulfilling prophecy; tokenism; Tyson, Mike; white race; whiteness

Reading

Black Culture and Black Consciousness by Lawrence Levine (Oxford University Press, 1978) may profitably be read in conjunction with Alan Locke's classic *The Negro and his Music* (Arno Press, 1969) and LeRoi Jones's *Blues People* (Payback Press, 1995).
Blacking Up: The minstrel show in nineteenth century America by Robert Toll (Oxford University Press, 1974) remains the most valuable historical account of minstrelsy.
Sambo: The rise and demise of an American jester by Joseph Boskin (Oxford University Press, 1986) is the source of the quotations in the main text above; it examines what the author calls the "defusing process" – the way black performers would subtly live up (or down) to white expectations, while secretly mocking whites.
Toms, Coons, Mulattoes, Mammies and Bucks: An interpretive history of blacks in American films, 3rd edn., by Donald Bogle (Continuum, 1998), shows how many of the stock-in-trade types of the minstrelsy were exported to other media, particularly film; those types are summarized in the book's title.

MISCEGENATION

This term derives from the Latin *miscere*, for mix, and *genus*, for stock, kind, species, or race, and refers to the interbreeding of subjects deemed to belong to different racial stocks, especially whites and African-descended peoples. It was coined in connection with the 1854 presidential election in the USA. Campaigners for the Democratic Party published a book contending that mating between persons of different racial stocks produced superior stock in an attempt to insinuate that it was the policy of the Republican Party to encourage such unions. Use of the word reinforces the pre-Darwinian idea that there are pure races and, for this reason (among others), is out of place in contemporary discourse.

SEE ALSO: anthropology; caste; caucasian; cultural racism; Darwinism; Doomed Races

Doctrine; eugenics; hybridity; Jim Crow; multiracial/biracial; race: as classification; race: as synonym; slavery; transracial adoption; white race; whiteness

Reading

Victorian Anthropology by George W. Stocking, Jr. (The Free Press, 1987) examines the debates over race and evolution in the nineteenth century.

MICHAEL BANTON

MOTOWN

The music corporation started by Berry Gordy in 1959 and named Motown (an abbreviation of Motor Town) after its original base, Detroit, both represented and helped shape black culture in succeeding decades. Yet, its commercial success was founded on the appeal of its music to white consumers. While previous African American-owned record labels had tried to broaden their markets, none succeeded in crossing over to the mainstream in the way that Motown did, particularly in the 1960s. The Motown label still exists, though it was sold by Gordy in 1988 and has long since lost its status as a symbol of black cultural and economic independence; yet the name Motown still resonates.

Gordy came from an entrepreneurial family, in which all members were encouraged by their father, who was born in Georgia but moved to Detroit where he ran his own grocery store; all eight children worked there at some stage. The Gordy family had a cooperative association in which all members could pool their resources and draw from when business needs arose. After several ventures in the music industry, Berry met William "Smokey" Robinson, then a member of a band called the Matadors. The two began collaborating, Gordy co-writing and producing the band, which was later renamed the Miracles. Gordy rented a studio and set up a production business.

In 1960, Gordy took on the major challenge of writing, producing, advertising, marketing and distributing a record nationally. "Way Over There" by the Miracles was a modest success, selling 60,000 copies. His earlier experiences with a record he co-wrote, "Money (That's What I Want)" alerted him to the fact that, in the music business, the writer is often, as he put it in his biography, "furthest away from the money." His aim was to control all facets of the operation whereby a record was turned into a commercial success. One of Gordy's philosophies was based on his experiences working on the Lincoln-Mercury assembly line, where he had watched cars start out as a frame pulled along on a conveyor belt until they emerged at the end of the line as complete cars ready for the road. He believed that, given the right internal organization, he could produce hit recording artists by comparable processes.

Another Gordy philosophy was that his products should appeal to the widest possible market, meaning white as well as black Americans. To this end, he hired Barney Ales as his head of sales. "Gordy knew that Ales, one of the company's first white executives, could give Motown crucial access to the broader national record market, which traditionally excluded independent black record producers," writes Suzanne E. Smith. Previously labeled "race music" and, later, "rhythm and blues," music produced by black artists was regarded, as were other institutions and cultural expressions, as distinct from and, for the most part, inferior to that of whites. Gordy's ambition was to effect a crossover: to produce material that was valued artistically and was accessible to white consumers. In this, he succeeded: Motown's back catalog is still revered.

Critics of Motown argued that Gordy consciously designed his acts for the delectation of whites. Spurning the more spontaneous expression of earlier forms of black music, such as blues and soul, Gordy encouraged precision and polish both in Motown music and its presentation. Motown artists carefully rehearsed everything. So much so, that Charles Shaar Murray referred to "Gordy's Motown plantation" in his book *Crosstown Traffic: Jimi Hendrix and the rock'n'roll revolution* (St. Martin's Press, 1989). Certainly, Gordy oversaw every dance step, every hand movement, and every note in trying to calibrate his products to the needs of the mainstream market. Marvin Gaye told his biographer: "Sometimes I felt like the shuffle-and-jive niggers of old, steppin' and fetchin' for the white folk."

Another criticism of Gordy's handling of Motown artists was summarized by producer Clarence Paul, who worked closely with Gordy: "Just about everybody got ripped off at Motown" (quoted in Ritz, below). Many artists and writers made similar complaints, several leaving the company after disputes over money; some even filed suit to recover what they believed they were owed. More grumbling concerned the inordinate attention Gordy paid to Diana Ross when he launched her solo career. Troubled by changing tastes and sniping among his employees, Gordy attempted to restore stability by financing a film biography of Billie Holiday, featuring Ross in the lead. *Lady Sings the Blues* (1972) received five Academy Award nominations and encouraged Gordy to venture further into film, though without comparable success.

The emergence of Motown not only coincided with but was encouraged and perhaps affirmed by the passing of the 1964 Civil Rights Act, which outlawed all forms of racial discrimination in public facilities, the development of technologies, particularly domestic television and transistor radio, and the widespread recognition of black cultural expression as both authentic and valuable. As well having a cultural impact, Motown also held political potential, as Smith writes: "The role of black cultural expression, in conjunction with its production, in the cause of civil rights and black empowerment was gaining currency by late 1964 and early 1965."

While Gordy aligned himself with a variety of causes, including civil rights, he never claimed to be using his music either to reflect or provoke social change. This did not stop commentators inferring messages in numbers such as Martha and the Vandellas' "Nowhere to run" and "Dancing in the street," which, as Smith puts it, "expressed the emotions of the moment." Stevie Wonder's output was often quite explicitly political, much of his material embodying the conflictual spirit of the times. "Living in the city," which was released in 1973, remains one of the most enduringly poignant commentaries on the condition of black America.

Gordy never satisfactorily reconciled his entrepreneurial mission with his commitment to black causes. This was highlighted in 1970, when he shifted Motown from Detroit to Los Angeles, a move that upset many of his artists and supporters (Gordy had been moving Motown piecemeal for a few years). Predictable cries of "sell-out" greeted the move. Among the artists who moved west with the company was Michael Jackson, then a member of the Jackson 5. The band was to become one of the most commercially successful Motown acts ever, despite leaving the fold amid legal dispute in 1975. With their Afro hairdos and funky sound, the band members appeared to refract the black power ethic, but without ever endorsing it.

In the 1980s tastes changed and Motown's fortunes declined to the point where Gordy decided to sell his company to the MCA corporation for $61m; it was sold to Polydor in 1993 for $301m. The label kept its identity, though by then it was largely of historical importance. Gordy retained the lucrative publishing portion of his business until 1997 when he sold 50 percent of Jobete Music and Stone Diamond, which he owned with his sister, Esther Edwards, for $132m (with an option to buy the remaining shares for about $250m).

Criticism of Gordy gradually ceded place to more considered appraisals of his achievements. At one stage the chief of the USA's largest black-owned company, he created an exemplar of black capitalism. His ruthlessness, especially with his own artists, and his autocratic approach to running Motown have been understood as failings. But, if they are failings, they might also be the reasons for his success where others failed. If there is a fault in Gordy, it may not lie in his endorsing a success ethic, but in demonstrating that its pursuit requires a degree of assimilation many may find abhorrent.

SEE ALSO: African Americans; Ali, Muhammad; black bourgeoisie in the USA; Black Power; Jackson, Michael; Kerner Report; Malcolm X; minstrelsy; rap; reggae; riots: USA, 1965–67

Reading

The Black Culture Industry by Ellis Cashmore (Routledge, 1997) explores Motown in the wider context of commercialized African American culture. Gordy's trailblazing enterprise was the most conspicuously successful venture to sell black cultural product to a white market. It investigates the many criticisms of Motown's originator before concluding: "If there is a fault in Gordy, it is not in endorsing a success ethic, but in showing that its pursuit requires a degree of assimilation many find abhorrent."

Dancing in the Street: Motown and the cultural politics of Detroit by Suzanne E. Smith (Harvard University Press, 1999) is a scholarly dissection of the role of Motown in Detroit's corporate economy. Smith analyzes Motown as "a product of and an agent within" the "unique, and distinctly urban, cultural formation" of Detroit, an industrial city with a strong black middle class and a long history of racism."

To Be Loved: The music, the magic, the memories of Motown by Berry Gordy (Headline, 1994) is Gordy's own account of the rise of Motown and, because so many of the accusations against him are either ignored or glossed over, should be read alongside David Ritz's *Divided Soul: The life of Marvin Gaye*, which presents a somewhat different perspective of Gordy and his project, and *Supreme Faith: Some day we'll be together* (HarperCollins, 1990) by ex-Supreme Mary Wilson and Patricia Romanowski, which is effectively a critique of Motown.

MULTICULTURAL EDUCATION

Multicultural education, or *intercultural* education, as it is sometimes known, refers to the provision of intellectual and moral training within a framework of instruction that accurately and appropriately reflects the diversity and plurality of the surrounding culture. *Multi* means many; *inter* between. It follows that any discussion of this term must begin with a consideration of the notion of culture.

Meanings and difference

A culture is a system of signs and meanings; it constitutes a collective framework for giving order and coherence to ways of thinking and understanding. The concept of culture cannot be equated to definitions of cultural groups; nor is it a substitute for the term ethnic or minority. Although dominant cultural groups are normally not defined as ethnic, every society consists of diverse cultural groups, and in that sense every society is made up of different cultures and, indeed, different languages.

Cultures are also linked to identities and identities inevitably mean differences. We define ourselves in contradistinction to each other. If there is a continual process of marking out between different cultural groups and attitudes, then all relations, within all societies, are undoubtedly multicultural and intercultural. Initially, there is a need to develop the culture of multicultural relations, so that issues about multicultural education can be clearer.

If culture is a system of signs and meanings, then it is essential that we understand the meaning of difference and work to construct a culture that relates between cultural groups in a non-threatening and positive way. Democratic processes are deficient but necessary and issues within culturally diverse polities are about the educated and educative, and participatory democracy. They are not about *majoritarian* democracy, which continually constructs for itself, and against itself, minority groups of all kinds, including cultural, linguistic and racial minorities. The fact that terms and concepts are ambivalent or that one can disagree with some of their meanings should not lead to surrendering them. There is a continuing power struggle over meanings within and between languages.

Diversity, rights and shared values

An important issue is how to define culturally diverse or multicultural societies. A taxonomic framework of states – which includes linguistic, religious, social class, nationality and ethnic groups – means that most societies have been historically as well as contemporaneously diverse. Hence these states need inclusive modalities to ensure that in legal and legislative terms all groups who reside in a polity have citizenship rights. Much is made of the Renaissance, the Scientific Revolution and the Enlightenment, but if these are to have a reality, then the rational principles on which states educate citizens inclusively have to be reflected in educational policies and practices of the state.

In societies where educational provision is developed as a result of historical analysis of society, immigrants can be seen as merely highlighting the underlying features of diversities based on the taxonomy referred to above. If educators and policy-makers use an historical and contemporaneous framework for analyzing society and develop policies to address issues of cultural diversity, it is less likely that such issues can be marginalized.

A complex set of issues revolve around the issue of the Janus-headed nature of the nation, which may have "ethnic" features as well as constructions based on modern constitutions which ensure equality, liberty and fraternity in legal terms. The development of inclusive multicultural educational policies for socially diverse societies is important, so that citizens do not only possess the rights but also adhere to their obligations or responsibilities. This may also obviate the development of patriarchies, fundamentalism and siege mentalities amongst the disadvantaged and excluded groups in society.

The development of a core of shared value systems based on a democratic basis amongst all children would enhance the development of a common civic culture in the context of an inclusive civil society. The limited notions of a capitalist market system require further discussion in terms of a social market democracy to minimize inequalities and the development of excluded groups or a large underclass in society.

The development of multicultural and intercultural public and social policies ought to ensure that all groups have the opportunity of getting a job given the rapid technological changes in society and rising levels of de-skilling and unemployment. The clear and present danger of certain groups of immigrants, refugees, travelers and Roma being made increasingly vulnerable is exceedingly high. Hence, the role of educating whole populations and providing the possibility of an appropriate noncentric and ethnocentric curriculum is critical. To enable access to knowledge of all pupils the development of noncentric curricula should remain a priority for educators in the twenty-first century. The substitution, for example, of Afrocentric or Sinocentric for Eurocentric knowledge is not sufficient. Such an education ought to have a lifelong span and include a training provision which can take on the issue of providing relevant provision of skills which lead to gainful employment in complex plural and urban environments. In the absence of such provision there has been the growth of a large underclass of unemployed people, including women and migrants, who have become impoverished. This has in turn feminized poverty. These groups have little access to relevant skills and educational provision and remain excluded from society in socioeconomic terms.

The challenge therefore is of constructing prophylactic and inclusive public and social policy, and of developing common curricula, which are able to realize the vast potential of multiculturalism for all citizens in contemporary societies.

Development of intercultural education has to start from negating the racism, xenophobia and narrow nationalism and ethnicisms. Such multicultural/intercultural education can only be meaningful if they can dissolve theories and practice of exclusionary power and powers of exclusionary institutions. Hence, the task is one of developing a critical multiculturalism, which is based on constructions based on modern democratically derived constitutions, which ensure equality in educational terms.

Exclusions from education and other social provision in socially and culturally diverse societies can in turn breed exclusivity. This has led to ethnic Armageddon in many parts of the world.

States therefore ought to safeguard educational access and rights of all groups to ensure greater levels of equity, which strengthen democratic engagements. Such national policies can help to bridge ethnic, religious, linguistic and racial differences in culturally diverse polities and negate the rise of narrow nationalism and xenophobia.

Citizenship

A key term that requires reflection is *citizenship*. Is there not a need to construct a notion of citizenship that does not involve identification with one city, one space or place? Or a citizenship that is not the same as nationality and certainly not synonymous with nationalism? A citizenship that carries rights and sustains obligations and is rooted in a basis of equality, both economic and cultural?

Democratic processes that may deliver such a citizenship cannot be the traditional nation-state structures as developed in Western Europe, and unsuccessfully exported elsewhere. Can the failed guarantee of equal cultural citizenship, promised, but never delivered by the nation-state model, be provided by a combination of international, regional and personal, cultural autonomy?

This also necessitates clearer understanding of the meanings of terms such as "multicultural education or learning" and "multicultural society." It leads to a whole range of options and ways of exploring discussions which allow us to develop some common meanings which emanate from such multicultural learning. The task is one of developing a critical multiculturalism, which is based on sounder intellectual foundations.

The notion of analyzing multicultural societies also requires critical engagement. If societies are considered to have become multicultural or culturally diverse because of the presence of immigrants then educators confront a totally different set of questions and issues than if societies are seen as historically diverse or multicultural. In many states, territorially based nationalities are a further feature and a representation of this important issue. Hence, terms such as "ethnic," "national minorities" or "ethnic majorities" raise complex, analytical issues. The historical and contemporaneous analysis of societies makes such issues less likely to be marginalized.

If issues of intercultural relations and an equitable intercultural education are to become a reality, they have to be treated as being central rather than marginal to most societies.

SEE ALSO: Afrocentricity; children; cultural identity; Ebonics; education; equality; ethnocentrism; ethnonational; language; multiculturalism; Other; patriarchy; racist discourse; Roma; transracial adoption

Reading

Intercultural Education, World Yearbook of Education, edited by D. Coulby, J. S. Gundara and C. Jones (Kogan Page/Sterling, 1997) examines the variety of educational responses to differing forms of diversity within states. It considers the ways in which these diversities proclaim themselves and are categorized; the growth of nationalism and regionalism in many parts of the world is considered alongside the emergence of international structures.

International Perspectives on Methods of Improving Education Focusing on the Quality of Diversity, edited by Rose M. Duhon-Sells, Halloway Sells, Alice Marie Duhon-Ross, and Gwendolyn Duhon (Edward Mellen, 2003), is a collection of thirteen essays on a variety of subjects related to multicultural education.

Interculturalism, Education and Inclusion, by J. S. Gundara (Paul Chapman Publishing, 2000) raises a range of critical issues for educators as a consequence of historical and contemporary aspects of social diversity using a historical and social science framework; it examines issues concerning national minority and immigrant communities.

Theorizing Multiculturalism: A guide to current debate, edited by C. Wilett (Blackwell, 1998), contains a range of chapters including many from North America; they provide a useful background, debates and theoretical readings about multiculturalism.

JAGDISH GUNDARA

MULTICULTURALISM

There is cultural diversity in most, if not all, societies. As a result of conquest, colonization, or migration, almost all societies contain groups whose culture, language, religion, or identity does not conform to that of the majority. In these circumstances of diversity, multiculturalism has been a focus of critical analysis and political debate, as well as a source of legislation and cultural and social policies.

The concept of multiculturalism is broad and contested, although the ideal of the harmonious coexistence of differing cultural, ethnic, national, or indigenous groups within a complex society remains at its core however it is specifically defined. For Parekh, in his *Rethinking Multiculturalism: Cultural diversity and political theory*: "Multiculturalism ... is about cultural diversity or culturally embedded differences." In their *Unequal Relations: An introduction to race and ethnic dynamics in Canada*, Augie Fleras and Jean Leonard Elliott explicitly incorporate additional dimensions in their definition of multiculturalism as "a principle and a practice for engaging diversity as different yet equal." Images used to clarify the diverse nature of multicultural societies, and to contrast them with the "melting-pot" notion of a society based upon assimilation, include "mosaic" and "kaleidoscope."

Canada can be taken as a unique example of state promotion of policy on multiculturalism. Official multiculturalism in Canada is dated as beginning in 1971, within the context of a policy of bilingualism reflecting colonization by the British and the French. Since then multiculturalism has been built into the Constitution Act (1982), the Charter of Rights and Freedoms, and the Multiculturalism Act (1988). The Multiculturalism Act's coverage includes recognition of cultural and racial diversity, promotion of understanding and respect for diversity, and a commitment to equality. Canada's pattern of social and cultural diversity includes indigenous peoples, two official languages, a large and complex immigrant population, and global cities such as Toronto and Vancouver. In this context, policies and practices relating to policing, education, health, and social and child welfare are all subject to scrutiny on grounds of their cultural sensitivity, and equality of treatment for different groups. At the same time the principles of societal integration, social inclusion, individual and group rights, and the tensions between equality and difference are a rich source of debate in the country.

Britain's transformation as a nation during the twentieth century by the influx of refugees and immigrants from Eastern and Western Europe, Ireland, the West Indies, India and Pakistan (amongst others) has led to discussion about the nature of British society and its governance. Through the latter part of the twentieth century piecemeal policies and practices have been implemented in response to cultural diversity and to racism, in, for example, areas of education, policing and health services. An overview of this is provided by the Parekh Report of 2000 (revised in 2002), which gives a critical analysis of progress towards a just and tolerant multiethnic society in Britain and makes recommendations for new legislation and new policies. The report drew upon the considerable experience of a large panel, incorporated evidence from individuals and organizations in many regions of the country, used interview data, and assimilated the results of seminars.

The report argues that Britain should move from "multicultural drift" to deliberate change based upon recognition of the multiethnic, multifaith, multicultural, multicommunity of British society. Starting from principles of justice based upon concepts of equality and diversity, the report calls for a new Equality Act (offering a model based upon the Canadian Multiculturalism Act) and for organizational and policy change in criminal justice, policing, education, health and welfare, and employment. Its discussion of key cases, statistics on inequality and discrimination, and existing practice in each of these areas is grounded in a clear view of the ways in which principles and practice may lead to positive change toward equality and justice.

The differing demographic realities of plural societies, coexistence of and conflict between different groups, drafting of legislation and implementation of policies, continue to promote political and philosophical debates about multiculturalism. These debates, while highlighting some of the tensions and conflicts between cohesion and division, and some of the cultural conflicts between groups, are also a source of new frameworks for understanding and implementing policies that promote equality and justice.

SEE ALSO: assimilation; British Asians; colonialism; cultural racism; culturecide; ethnicity; ethnocide; globalization; Hall, Stuart; human rights; multiracial/biracial; pluralism; representations; social exclusion; white backlash culture

Reading

Citizenship in Diverse Societies, edited by Will Kymlicka and Wayne Norman (Oxford University Press, 2000), covers debates about conflict and convergence between citizenship and diversity in pluralist societies.

Global Multiculturalism: Comparative perspectives on ethnicity, race and nation by Grant H. Cornwell and Eve Walsh Stoddard (Rowman & Littlefield, 2001)

provides case studies of ethnic, racial and cultural diversity in thirteen countries.

Multiculturalism by C. W. Watson (Open University Press, 2000) gives a concise overview of the concept and discusses themes such as minority rights and education while drawing upon examples from several countries.

Rethinking Multiculturalism: Cultural diversity and political theory by Bhikhu Parekh (Macmillan/Palgrave, 2000) develops a theory of multicultural society and discusses a wide range of examples; this should be read in conjunction with *The Future of Multi-ethnic Britain: The Parekh report* by The Runnymede Trust (Lanham Books, 2002) which analyzes the contemporary situation of Britain and makes recommendations for the future.

Unequal Relations: An introduction to race and ethnic dynamics in Canada by Augie Fleras and Jean Leonard Elliott (Prentice-Hall, 2003) gives an analysis of multiculturalism in Canada; it may be read in conjunction with *Debating Diversity: Clashing perspectives on race and ethnicity in America*, 3rd edn., edited by Ronald Takaki (Oxford University Press, 2002) and *Un/Settled Multiculturalisms: Diasporas, entanglements, transruptions* by B. Hesse (Zed Books, 2001).

ROY TODD

MULTIRACIAL/BIRACIAL

These terms typically describe persons who have parents of different "racial" heritage. Biracialism refers to those with two heritages, usually one black parent, one white; while multiracialism is a more inclusive term, suggesting a plurality of heritages through several generations.

From the sixteenth to the twentieth century, *mulatto* (the Portuguese term for a young mule) was used in the West Indies and the USA when referring to children of mixed heritage. Other dehumanizing terms included the US and Britain's use of "half-breed" and "mixed breed." In the twentieth century "half-caste" was the predominant term. Though still in use today, this offensive term became less pervasive in Britain after 1945, except in Liverpool where its common usage continued longer. It was only in countries such as Brazil where persons of mixed heritage became the majority of the population that multiracialism ceased to be an issue of social reproach.

Other terms more recently used in the United States and Britain, which are not considered to be derogatory, are "multiracial" and "mixed heritage." During the late 1980s it has also become more common to see references to the adjective, "ethnic." For instance, "ethnic Muslim" in Bosnia

and "ethnic Chinese" of South-East Asia. In 1994, the Council of the Royal Anthropological Institute of Great Britain and Ireland adopted a motion in favor of the expression "mixed origin." Though not ideal, the Council believes the term to be preferable to the expression, "mixed race." "Mixed parentage" has also been widely used in Britain during recent years.

Traditionally, social attitudes in the United States have been based on the "one drop of black blood" rule (adopted by some states following the abolition of slavery) which classified individuals with the aforementioned "drop" as black. While most individuals of black and white parentage presumably internalized this rule and identified themselves as black, others "passed" for white. The children from these unions have often experienced rejection from both whites and blacks, and indeed from society.

It was not until 1967 that a US Supreme Court ruling repealed the remaining antimiscegenist laws. *Loving* v. *Virginia* came as the result of action by Richard and Mildred Loving, a couple who were arrested in their home town in Virginia in 1958 for being married; he was white, she was black. They fled to Washington, DC, rather than face prosecution, but fought and eventually won their case.

In addition to the repealed antimiscegenist laws, other significant changes during the 1960s in both the USA and Britain may have contributed to the development of more positive identities of multiracial individuals. Such changes include the scientific discrediting of white superiority and the rise of multiculturalism. Ironically, the "one drop of black blood" rule experienced a resurgence as black leaders argued for people of mixed heritage to regard themselves, and be perceived by others, as black. Although this view was more widely accepted in the United States, the extent of this view's acceptance in Britain remains uncertain.

During the past decade, however, the denial of part of one's heritage has come under question. Individuals identifying themselves as multiracial have argued that it is psychologically damaging to deny the white part of their heritage and that to do so would in essence support the discredited theory of distinct biological "races."

Some of the particular problems faced by biracial adolescents were uncovered in a study by Gibbs and Hines (in Root, 1992, below) which found that conflicts regarding ethnic identity could be attributed to the failure to integrate the ethnic and "racial" heritages of both parents into a cohesive identity. While several subjects identified with only the white aspects of their identity, others "overidentified" with the minority parent and rejected whiteness, sometimes taking on stereotyped characteristics. Others experienced pressure to identify with one group or the other and felt ambivalent over the "racial" heritages of both parents. Other biracial adolescents switched between one heritage and the other, reflecting "divided loyalties."

During the late 1990s, both the United States' and Britain's monoracial census categories were re-examined. Dissatisfied with what they understood to be the inadequacy of existing statuses, advocates of a separate status designated as multiracial rather than "Other" believed this category would provide official recognition and a more accurate representation of American and British demographics.

Although the 2001 UK Census multiracial statistics were not released in time for inclusion in this publication, the 2000 US Census revealed that nearly seven million individuals (more than 2 percent of the nation's 281.4 million people) stated they belonged to more than one race. Compared to five racial categories of a decade ago, the 2000 Census provided sixty-three possible racial designations. Interracial categories most commonly chosen were white and black, white and Asian, white and American Indian/Alaska native, and white and "some other race." Census officials admit that in hindsight the "some other race" category might have been eliminated from the form as people could already select more than one race.

Those who opposed a multiracial category on census forms cautioned that as more blacks choose this "racial" category and reduced their numbers under the category of black "race," blacks may lose political strength behind governmental policies designed to promote "racial" equality. The mere admission of new "racial" categories into an already contested discourse may serve to perpetuate divisions that other policies have tried to break down.

Finally, there is the issue of multiracial organizations to consider. While there are over six dozen formal multiracial organizations across the USA, some of the organizations maintain political agendas challenging racial perceptions that guide social policy, while others primarily serve as social groups. Yet, Dalmage argues, "without an antiracism agenda, multiracial organizations seem to be distancing themselves socially and politically from blacks, creating one more layer in the racial hierarchy in which whites remain privileged, blacks disadvantaged, and multiracials somewhere in the middle."

SEE ALSO: antiracism; antislavery; Brazil; children; creole; cultural identity; ethnicity; hybridity; miscegenation; multiculturalism; race: as synonym; racial coding; transracial adoption

Reading

Beyond Black Biracial Identity in America by Kerry Ann Rockquemore and David L. Brunsma (Sage, 2002); Jill Olumide's *Raiding the Gene Pool: The social construction of mixed race* (Pluto, 2002); and G. Reginald Daniel's *More Than Black? Multiracial identity and the new racial order* (Temple University Press, 2002) are parts of a growing body of literature on the subject.

Black, White Or Mixed Race? Race and racism in the lives of young people of mixed parentage by Barbara Tizard and Ann Phoenix (Routledge, 2001) is a revised edition which examines multiracialism from an historical context and explores the "racial" identities of adolescents of black and white parentage in Britain.

Mixed Feelings: The complex lives of mixed race Britons by Yasmin Alibhai-Brown (Women's Press, 2001) explores racially mixed people and race relations in the UK.

Multiracial Couples: Black and white voices by Paul Rosenblatt, Terri Karis, and Richard Powell (Sage, 1995) and *Black, White, Other: Biracial Americans talk about race and identity* by Lisa Funderburg (William Morrow, 1994) are both based on qualitative interview studies.

The Multiracial Experience: Racial borders as the new frontier, edited by Maria P. P. Root (Sage, 1996), is a collection of articles which explore the dynamics of multiculturalism; it is complemented by the same editor's earlier work *Racially Mixed People in America* (Sage, 1992), which looks at multiracial identity and concludes with a section on challenging the US Census's "racial" categories.

Multiracial Identity: An international perspective by Mark Christian (Palgrave, 2000) examines multiracial identity from an historical and sociological perspective.

"Social science and the citizen: multi-racial census report" (in *Society*, vol. 38, no. 5, July–August, 2001) provides multiracial statistics regarding the 2000 US Census.

"Race: questions and classifications" by Claudette Bennett, in *Encyclopedia of the U.S. Census*, edited by Margo J. Anderson (CQ Press, 2000), provides 2000 US Census information including coverage of the new "racial" classifications; this may be read in conjunction with C. Alexander's "Beyond black: rethinking the colour/culture divide" (in *Ethnic and Racial Studies*, vol. 21, no. 2, 2002).

Tripping on the Color Line: Black–White multiracial families in a racially divided world by Heather M. Dalmage (Rutgers University Press, 2000) provides unique insight into the dynamics of multiracialism and the powerful issues and challenges facing black–white multiracial families.

AMY I. KORNBLAU

MYRDAL, GUNNAR (1898–1987)

Swedish economist and sociologist, and Nobel laureate (Economics, 1974). Among his prolific works are *Asian Drama, Beyond the Welfare State, Challenge to Affluence,* and *Rich Lands and Poor.* His main contribution to the field of race relations was his monumental study on black Americans, commissioned by the Carnegie Corporation of New York, conducted through a large staff of collaborators between 1937 and 1942, and published in 1944 as a 1,300-page, two-volume, forty-five-chapter book, *An American Dilemma.* This massive research effort has left its imprint on at least a quarter-century of scholarship on Afro-Americans, and the list of Myrdal's collaborators was virtually a *Who's Who* in the field: Charles S. Johnson, Guy B. Johnson, Melville Herskovits, Otto Klineberg, E. Franklin Frazier, St. Clair Drake, Arnold Rose, Allison Davis, to name but a few.

An influential feature of *An American Dilemma* was *Appendix 2, A Methodological Note on Facts and Valuations in Social Science.* This classic statement of the role of the social scientist's values was widely acclaimed and emulated.

The central thesis of the book is that the USA has long lived with a painful dilemma caused by the discrepancy between its democratic and libertarian ideals of freedom and equality for all, and its shabby treatment of Afro-Americans, first as disfranchised chattel slaves, then as segregated outcastes. Myrdal predicted that this dilemma would, however slowly and painstakingly, be resolved by bringing the treatment of blacks in line with the lofty ideals of the American Republic.

An American Dilemma was also influential in its analysis of white–black relations in terms of caste and class. The first statement in print of the caste and class school was authored by the American sociologist and anthropologist W. Lloyd Warner in his introduction to a 1941 book by some of Myrdal's collaborators, but the concept was widely adopted thereafter. Warner, Myrdal, and others saw whites and blacks as representing two almost impermeable castes, characterized by ascriptive, lifelong membership, hierarchy, and endogamy. Each racial caste was internally divided into permeable classes, but class status was not directly transferable from one caste to another because the castes themselves were in a hierarchy.

Myrdal was not without his critics. In 1948, Oliver C. Cox published his massive attack on Myrdal and his associates, *Caste, Class and Race.* From a Marxist perspective, Cox regards American racism as a capitalist device to divide the working class, and to produce false consciousness. He attacks Myrdal's idealist formulation of a dilemma, and analyzes the situation in terms of the class interests of the ruling capitalists. He also rejects the description of Afro-Americans as a caste, stressing the nonconsensual nature of the American system, compared to what he saw as the consensual nature of the classical Hindu caste system.

SEE ALSO: *Brown* v. *Board of Education*; caste; civil rights movement; Cox, Oliver C.; equality; Jim Crow; Ku Klux Klan; Marxism; Park, Robert E.; prejudice; segregation

Reading

An American Dilemma: The negro problem and modern democracy by Gunnar Myrdal (Transaction Books, 1995; originally Harper & Row, 1944) is the towering study of black Americans in the early 1940s; the edition cited here has an introduction by Sissela Bok, Myrdal's daughter. The tome is condensed by Arnold Rose in *The Negro in America* (Harper, 1948).

The Essential Myrdal by Gunnar Myrdal, edited by Örjan Appelqvist and Stellan Anderson (The New Press, 2000) shows the full range of Myrdal's expertise on such topics as economics, the population problem, and ethics in the social sciences; the book also contains excerpts from Myrdal's study of development in Asia.

PIERRE L. VAN DEN BERGHE

N

NATION OF ISLAM (OR "BLACK MUSLIMS")

The largest and most important African American sectarian movement, the Nation of Islam, has 15,000 registered members and countless sympathizers, all convinced that whites have been at the center of a centuries-long conspiracy to deny black people their ancestry and conceal their historical achievements. The movement can be described through the activities of its imamate.

Noble Drew Ali

The first twenty years of this twentieth century saw many black sects and cults emerge in Chicago and New York City. One such sect was the Moorish Science Temple of America founded in 1913 by Timothy Drew (1886–1929), who later changed his name to Drew Ali. The sect was based loosely on Islamic principles and adapted a version of the Koran. Drew bade his followers to look for their origins in the ancient Moors, and explained that whites had stripped blacks of their religion, their power, their land and their culture. In 1929 Drew was murdered, but his followers believed him to be a prophet ordained by Allah and searched for a reincarnation.

Wallace D. Fard

Fard sold silk products door-to-door in Detroit's ghettos. In the late 1920s, he began to claim he was "Arabian," a prophet sent to help blacks discover their dual African and Islamic heritages. According to Fard, African Americans were descended from the first humans, the "original race" whose descendants could be found in their purest form among Muslims in the Middle East, Africa, and Asia. Fard taught that the world was once ruled by blacks who established a highly advanced civilization: twenty-four scientists populated the earth with animals, created trees, mountains and oceans, and even the moon. According to Fard, they had communication with life on Mars. After 8,400 years, a scientist named Yacub discovered that within blacks there were two "germs," a strong black germ and a weak brown germ. Yacub separated the two and, through some form of genetic engineering, was able to reproduce the lighter and weaker people, who eventually migrated to the cold wastelands of Europe. But the pale race were adept at robbing, scheming, and cheating and used these skills to gain mastery of the world. Once in power, no evil was beyond them, and they enslaved blacks physically and mentally by convincing them they were inferior beings and that the true prophets were white. Only when blacks realized this would their oppression end.

Elijah Muhammad

In 1934, Fard disappeared in mysterious circumstances and one of his converts, Elijah Muhammad (formerly Elijah Poole) – whom he had first met in 1931 – dedicated himself to promulgating Fard's revelation. Elijah proselytized vigorously and built a coherent organization for the movement, which attracted a variety of well-known figures, including Malcolm X in the 1950s and Muhammad Ali in the 1960s, all of whom converted to the Nation of Islam.

In 1963, Elijah became embroiled in a scandal concerning rumors that he was sleeping with his secretaries in breach of his own moral code.

Malcolm X believed that this discredited Elijah and this became a factor in his eventual departure from the movement. In the December 4, 1964 issue of the Nation's magazine *Muhammad Speaks*, one of Elijah's loyal supporters, Louis Farrakhan, wrote: "The die is set and Malcolm shall not escape. ... Such a man is worthy of death." Two months later, Malcolm was assassinated.

Louis Farrakhan

When Elijah died in 1975, his son Wallace Deen Muhammad took over the leadership of the movement, which by then had over 50,000 members. Farrakhan, born Louis Walcott, was born in 1933 in the Bronx, New York, but grew up in Boston. A one-time calypso artist under the name of Louis X (he made a record, "White Man's Heaven is a Black Man's Hell"), Farrakhan was a strict follower of Elijah and objected to reforms initiated by Deen to relax the restriction of whites' membership and seek a closer integration with Muslims around the world. The movement divided, Deen changing his organization's name to the World Community of Islam, while Farrakhan retained the original. Farrakhan also revived the militant wing called The Fruit of Islam. His teaching was essentially that of Elijah and Fard, though he did take the unprecedented step of aligning himself with a party political candidate, Jesse Jackson. In 1984, during Jackson's Democratic nomination campaign, Jackson was overheard to have referred to New York City as "Hymietown" when in conversation with Farrakhan. It started a series of remarks over subsequent years that was to alienate Jews. This was to elevate Farrakhan into the most infamous imam in the Nation of Islam's history. In a speech in New Orleans in 1989, he professed to have traced the origin of AIDS to the attempts of the US government to destroy the population of Central Africa. He similarly explained the influx of crack cocaine and other hard drugs into black neighborhoods. He proposed reparations for the centuries of slavery; part of which included freeing blacks from prisons and setting aside a separate territory exclusively for blacks. The concept of having a voluntarily separated territory with self-sufficiency has been central to Nation of Islam philosophy since Elijah.

In 1995, after years of relative obscurity, Farrakhan leapt back to prominence when he organized a march on Washington, DC, where he gave an address to an estimated 600,000 African Americans. And while he made no claim to such a status, Farrakhan may have been the single-most influential black leader in a period that had witnessed the fall from grace (and later restoration) of Marion Barry, the dismissal of Benjamin Chavis as executive director of the NAACP, and the political disappearance of one-time presidential nominee Jesse Jackson.

SEE ALSO: Afrocentricity; Ali, Muhammad; anti-Semitism; Barry case, the Marion; Ethiopianism; Garvey, Marcus; Jackson, Jesse; Malcolm X; Million Man March; *négritude*; race card; Rastafari; reparations; Tyson, Mike

Reading

Black Nationalism by E. V. Essien-Udom (University of Chicago Press, 1962) is based on a two-year study in Chicago and New York City, while *The Black Muslims in America* 3rd edn by C. Eric Lincoln (Africa World Press, 1994) is an in-depth analysis of the movement in its historical context. Both are solid works, albeit dated.

Elijah Muhammad: Religious leader by Malu Halasa (Chelsea House, 1990) is a short biography of the influential leader in the "Black Americans of Achievement" series. *Malcolm X* (1989) by Jack Rummel is also in this accessible, but rather superficial, series.

"False prophet – the rise of Louis Farrakhan" is a critical two-part article by Adolph Reed in the journal *Nation* (vol. 252, issues 1 and 2, January 21 and 28, 1991); Reed traces Farrakhan's development and argues that Farrakhan appeals to whites because he legitimizes the idea that blacks should help themselves. Another critic of Farrakhan, Nat Hentoff, laments that there are not more credible or inspiring black leaders than the Nation's imam (see "I am to black people as the Pope is to white people," in *Village Voice*, vol. 36, no. 21, May 21, 1991).

"The Nation of Islam: A historiography of Pan Africanist thought and intellectualism" by James L. Conyers, Jr., in his own edited collection *Civil Rights, Blacks Arts and the Black Power Movement in America: A reflexive analysis of social movements in the United States* (Ashgate, 2001), is one among several essays that explore facets of the Nation, including Emerson Mungin's "Drew Ali and the Moorish Science temple" and Malachi D. Crawford's "Understanding the Honorable Elijah Muhammad."

Prophet of Rage: A life of Louis Farrakhan and his Nation by Arthur J. Magida (Basic Books, 1997), is a study of demoguery; as its subtitle suggests, it chronicles the Nation's fortunes under Farrakhan's controversial leadership.

NATIONAL FRONT

A British fringe political party which ran in political races with some measure of success during the 1970s. The National Front's premise was that those Britons of African Caribbean and Asian descent threatened the job prospects of indigenous whites. In a context of high unemployment, the message gained some credibility among factions of the British working class. The party was launched in 1967 after an amalgamation of other neo-nazi groups. Its avowed aim was to contest by-elections (i.e. local political elections). It is also the name of the French far right party which split into rival movements in 1999; this National Front was once led by Jean-Marie Le Pen.

The other main thrust of its political activities was its decision to hold demonstrations and meetings organized either around explicitly racist themes or within areas containing relatively large black, brown, or Jewish communities. Quite rightly, these consistently provoked opposition both from the local communities and from antiracist organizations such as the Anti-Nazi League and often degenerated into volatile occasions. In 1974, for instance, an anti-NF protestor, Kevin Gately, was killed at the NF's demonstration in Red Lion Square. A little less than five years later, in April 1979, a London teacher, Blair Peach, was killed as antifascists tried to prevent the NF's pre-general election meeting in the Southall district of London.

Despite its claim to be Britain's "fastest growing party," its successes were minor and it suffered an embarrassing reverse at the 1979 polls. After this time, its membership dropped and it lost its initiative to the more aggressive and youth-oriented British Movement and, later, the British National Party (BNP). Opportunistically, the National Front attempted to capitalize on the reaction to the hand-wringing period that followed the publication in 1999 of the Macpherson Report on the Stephen Lawrence murder investigation. Two years later, violence erupted in several northern towns and both the BNP and National Front were present. While the BNP garnered most publicity, the National Front claimed it was articulating the fears and grievances of white people who felt victimized.

SEE ALSO: British National Party; Hanson, Pauline; Ku Klux Klan; Lawrence case, the Stephen; nationalism; neo-nazism; One Nation; Powell, J. Enoch; racial coding; riots: Britain, 2001

Reading

Fascists: A social psychological view of the National Front by Michael Billig (Academic Press, 1978) scrutinizes the consistencies between the NF and earlier fascist organizations and personalities. It also includes interviews with members of an NF branch in the West Midlands.

"In a foreign land: the new popular racism" by Arun Kundnani (in *Race and Class*, vol. 43, no. 2, 2001) argues that the state and the media combine to foment a consensus of hostility that manifests in the kind of "popular racism" that the National Front can harness to its own ends.

The National Front in English Politics by Stan Taylor (Macmillan, 1982) looks critically at various aspects of the party, including its ideological background, its apparent electoral advances in the 1970s and the effectiveness of anti-NF groups such as the anti-Nazi League.

BARRY TROYNA

NATIONALISM

A term that refers to an ideology which was formulated after the French Revolution. It became a major determinant of political action in the course of the nineteenth century throughout Western Europe and, in the twentieth century, throughout the world. Many writers want to draw a firm distinction between this conception of nationalism as an ideology, and the notion of national sentiment which refers to a sense of collective solidarity within identified geographical and cultural boundaries. Thus, this distinction can account for the fact that a particular population may express some notion of national identity in the absence of a coherent and organized political movement to bring into being or reproduce territorial boundaries within which a state formation has political power.

As an ideology, nationalism contains three main ideas. First, it argues that an identified population should be able to formulate institutions and laws with which to determine its own future. Second, it maintains that each such population has a unique set of characteristics, which identify it as a "nation." Third, and consequently, it claims that the world is divided naturally into a number of such distinct "nations." This combination of ideas and claims constitute the basis for political strategies and movements which, since the nineteenth century, have had a major influence on the way in which the world is organized politically. The formation and reproduction of national boundaries is, therefore, not a natural or inevitable process, but one which is the consequence of human action in particular historical circumstances. Indeed, that process need not be directly prompted by the ideology of nationalism, as the examples of England, France, Spain, and Holland illustrate.

The origin of the ideology is the object of continuing debate, although there is considerable agreement with the claim that it is connected with what some writers call industrialization and what others define as capitalist development. What unites these different theoretical traditions is the employment of the notion of uneven development. What is claimed is that from the late eighteenth century, the process of industrialization/capitalist development occurred in particular geographical areas, with the result that certain groups in adjoining areas desired to emulate the advances made elsewhere in order to share in the consequential material and political advantages. The ideology of nationalism was a means of politically mobilizing populations to construct a particular political framework for economic/capitalist development, i.e. to "catch up" with the development of those who had developed first.

This process can be observed to have continued in the twentieth century particularly in connection with the consequences of decolonization. A rather different process occurred in connection with the redrawing of political boundaries after the two "World Wars" in Europe, although, again, nationalism was a prominent factor. Such a wide diversity of instances where nationalism has been a political force, particularly in the twentieth century, supports the contention that nationalism can be combined with political movements of the "left" and "right," a fact that can cause particular difficulties for Marxist writers. One can illustrate this point by referring to the way in which nationalism has been a component elsewhere in the rise of fascism in Europe and in liberation movements in Africa and Southeast Asia. Moreover, the latter examples constituted political inspiration for black people in the USA in the 1960s, where political resistance to institutionalized racism came to be expressed in terms of nationalism. For Marxists, these examples have posed a problem insofar as they claim that classes constitute the major force for revolutionary change. The relative failure of Marxists to be able to account for the political significance of nationalism in the twentieth century has been paralleled by the increasingly common claims by sociologists and political scientists that nationalism constitutes the major political force of the twentieth century.

The fact that nationalism emerged as a coherent and explicit ideology at the same time that racism was formulated as a "scientific" doctrine is of significance. Both ideologies assert that the world's population is naturally divided into distinct groups, although the nature of the group and the foundation for supposed natural division differs. Nevertheless, the fact that racism asserts some form of deterministic relation between attributed or real biological features and cultural characteristics means that nationalism, although ostensibly focusing on cultural/historical differences, can nevertheless merge into or develop out of the former. This is particularly evident in British politics since the 1960s, when expressions of British nationalism increasingly came to contain a form of racism, although without explicit use of the idea of "race" in the case of the main political parties. However, in the case of the neo-fascist parties, nationalism is expressed explicitly through a notion of "race," in line with central strands of fascist ideology.

SEE ALSO: colonialism; ethnonational; fascism; ideology; neo-nazism; politics; Powell, J. Enoch; race: as signifier; race: as synonym; racism; science

Reading

The Break-up of Britain by Tom Nairn (Verso, 1981) is an influential Marxist analysis of nationalism which breaks with both previous Marxist analyses and sociological explanations.

Myths and Memories of Nation by Anthony D. Smith (Oxford University Press, 1999) takes what the author calls an "ethno-symbolic" approach, revealing the power of symbols and myths to mobilize, shape and define people, their ethnic attachments and their national identities.

Nation and Identity in Contemporary Europe, edited by Brian Jenkins and Spyros Sofos (Routledge, 1996), asserts that "nation" is an ideological construct and that nationalism, far from being a natural response, is a political program; this can be read alongside *Modern Roots: Studies of national identity*, edited by Alain Dieckhoff and Natividad Gutiérrez (Ashgate, 2001).

Nationalism: A critical introduction by Philip Spencer and Howard Wollman (Sage, 2002) introduces the reader to the main theories and central debates about nationalism; the authors favor a fluid account of nationalism, ethnic identity, and culture.

ROBERT MILES

NATIVE AMERICANS *see* American Indians

NATIVE NATIONS *see* American Indians; ethnonational

NÉGRITUDE

A movement begun in the 1930s by the Martinique-born poet Aimé Césaire and other French-speaking black artists who wanted to rediscover ancient African values and modes of thought so that blacks could feel pride and dignity in their heritage. In its broadest sense, *négritude* was "the awareness and development of African values," according to Léopold Senghor, who helped develop the original ideas into a coherent political movement.

Though principally an artistic and literary critique of Western society and its systematic suppression of blacks' potentiality by dissociating them from what were regarded as their true roots, *négritude* took on a more programmatic dimension with Senghor, who later became president of Senegal. The impulse was, according to L. V. Thomas, "the rediscovery of one's past, one's culture, one's ancestors and one's language." Inspired by the African ethnographer and historian Leo Frobenius, Senghor delved into African culture to which he attributed the characteristic of being "Ethiopian" as a way of coming to grips with the different conception of reality he presumed existed in ancient African societies.

Leo Kuper writes, "Initially, *négritude* developed as a reaction to white racism, as dialectical opposition to cultural values imposed by whites," but the Africa oriented to was not, as G. R. Coulthard (below) puts it, "of African civilizations or African cultural values, but of Africa itself as a vague geographical region, and the imaginary and emotional fatherland of all the Negroes in the world."

Négritude never advocated a return to Africa in a physical sense, as did Marcus Garvey. Nor did it spurn the otherworldly elements of black religions, as did W. E. B. Du Bois. It sought to make Africa's presence felt by the millions of "exiled," scattered blacks who had been "brainwashed" into Western ways of thinking. It was an attempt to create an African consciousness for blacks wherever they were; a return to Africa through realizing its presence in the *mind* of blacks. As the Haitian poet Jean Price-Mars put it: "We belong to Africa by our blood."

Like other Ethiopianist movements, *négritude* condemned conventional Christianity as a tool of colonialism designed to keep blacks in a state of subjection and perpetuate their physical and mental enslavement; it was seen, as Coulthard points out, in "hypocritical connivance with colonialism and imperialism." Colonialism had culturally denuded blacks to the bone, but as the *négritude* poet Léon Damas wrote:

We have stripped off our European clothes ...
Our pride in being Negroes
The glory of being black

This sums up the *négritude* effort: to upgrade black people not so much through overt political means, but through instilling in them a sense of history and culture compounded of the distinctive qualities deriving from Africa; a new pride and dignity in being black and being African.

SEE ALSO: Afrocentricity; colonialism; double consciousness; essentialism; Ethiopianism; Fanon, Frantz; Garvey, Marcus; Nation of Islam; negrophilia; Rastafari; Senghor, Léopold Sédar

Reading

Race and Colour in Caribbean Literature by G. R. Coulthard (Oxford University Press, 1962) is an assessment and appreciation of *négritude* set in its historical context.

"Senghor and *négritude*" by L. V. Thomas (in *Présence Africaine*, vol. 26, no. 54, 1965) details the poet-president of Senegal's appreciable contribution to the movement and his attempts to convert it into practical policies.

Voices of Négritude by J. Finn (Quartet, 1988) charts the origins and development of the movement and its relationship with the "Negrista" in Latin America, cults in the Caribbean, and the Harlem Renaissance.

NEGROPHILIA

Negrophilia, from the French *négrophilie*, means an affection, liking or love for black culture. It is evidenced in all manner of art and popular culture which has absorbed black influences, and in the attitudes of those who, in the nineteenth century, opposed slavery. There is a historical ambiguity about the term: at times, to be called a negrophile was abusive, while at other times it was almost honorific. While negrophilia is used primarily to characterize a particular period in history, its contemporary expression is to be found, for example, in the appropriation of rap music by white musicians, most infamously, Eminem.

The term has been used in the wider sense of "popular representations of Africa and black people in the West," consisting of visual material (for example, prints, illustrated magazines, advertising, toys, etc.). An exhibition entitled the "Negrophilia Collection" began in Amsterdam in 1989 and subsequently toured Europe. Many of the exhibition's contents are pictured in Jan Nederveen Pieterse's book *White on Black: Images of Africa and blacks in Western popular culture*. Nederveen Pierterse's illuminating text suggests that the connotation of blackness with negative traits began appearing in European iconography in the twelfth century. The visual representations of blacks both reflected and assisted the racial classifications and modes of thought that developed, particularly from the end of the eighteenth century.

Nederveen Pieterse charts how stereotypes migrated into the popular imagination via illustrations and other visual forms; the imagery of advertising was especially potent in the late nineteenth and twentieth centuries, depicting grotesque typifications and caricatures that, in many ways, comforted whites in the knowledge that black people were, for instance, threatening, comical, bestial and never part of the same order of humanity as whites.

While such depictions went largely unchallenged in the West up until the late twentieth century, there were exceptions. As Nederveen Pieterse points out: "French popular representations of Africa and of blacks are less racist, but it certainly is a *different* racism." France was the first European country to entertain the concept of *l'art nègre* and was home of the journal *Présence Africaine*. France's colonial ideology, in stark contrast to those of most other European powers (Portugal excepted), was informed by the view that colonized groups, given sustained contact with the French, could be acculturated, or assimilated. In some circles, however, the cultural power of Europe had corrupted African values and needed to be resisted.

Petrine Archer-Straw's study of negrophilia focuses on Paris during the 1920s, a period when black culture was embraced by avant-garde writers and artists such as Guillaume Apollinaire and Marcel Duchamp, who wished to emphasize their extremism through *l'art nègre*, and surrealists like Georges Bataille and Michel Leiris, who advocated an interest in, for instance, cannibalism, ritualism and fetishism. Black culture, or at least a conception of black culture, was juxtaposed with or contrasted to other art forms to exaggerate their conflict with "traditional" values. "Blackness" was interpreted as a sign of modernity, reflected in styles of music, dancing, sculpture and texts.

The avant-garde's appetite for what it regarded as exotic, primitive and "real" involved the assimilation of black aesthetic forms into Parisian culture. In fact, the appropriation involved what Archer-Straw calls a "primitivizing" of black culture: it was thought to stand for a world set apart from Western society, one in many ways untouched by European science and rationality. The "Othering" of black subjects included excavating a spurious symbolism that connected blackness with death, ignorance, sensuality and virility; in other words, the very features that validated whiteness as pure, chastened and enlightened. By enthusiastically clasping what they regarded as authentic black culture, the avant-garde reinforced the outsider status of black subjects. Unwittingly, perhaps, the negrophile aesthetes provided Europeans with a conception of what they were not. "Debates about blackness were really about whiteness," writes Archer-Straw of discourse in the 1920s.

Jazz is one such example. Seized upon so eagerly that it warranted the epithet "craze" (with all its connotations of pathology), jazz became popular in the 1920s, many black American musicians appearing in Parisian clubs. The music promoted the spread of negrophilia, attracting a young, bohemian following that associated jazz with vitality, potency and the opportunity for expression, all of which were lacking in European musical forms. Jazz complemented the burgeoning awareness of black performers, Josephine Baker being one of the most celebrated.

Celebrating black culture and black artists had the effect of reinforcing stereotypes of black people as having emerged from a continent unaffected by many of the constraints and problems of the West, yet lacking the basic civilized values of Europe. The uninhibited exhibitions of Baker, whilst lauded, fueled fantasies of exotic sexuality. Her performances at *Revue Nègre* were outrageous for the time.

Negrophilia is perhaps best understood as a creation of "Otherness". As Nederveen Pieterse concludes of negrophiliac representations, they "reflect, not changes in the characteristics of the labelled group but rather in the circumstances of the labelling group."

SEE ALSO: Afrocentricity; beauty; essentialism; Hottentot Venus; Jackson, Michael; masculinity; minstrelsy; Other; rap; representations; sexuality

Reading

Hogarth's Blacks: Images of blacks in 18th century art by David Dabydeen (I. B. Taurus, 2000) discloses previously neglected features of William Hogarth's images of London and, in the process, offers new perspectives on what Dabydeen calls "the invisible man" of English art and social history – the black subject. This may gainfully be read alongside Anne Mangum's study, *Reflections of Africa in Elizabethan and Jacobean Drama and Poetry* (Edward Mellen, 2002) which examines the depiction of Africans in the work of, amongst others, Shakespeare, Donne and Johnson, amid the colonization and slavery of the sixteenth and early seventeenth centuries.

Negrophilia: Avant-garde Paris and black culture in the 1920s by Petrine Archer-Straw (Thames & Hudson, 2000) focuses on Paris in the grip of *le virus noir* in the early twentieth century. The ambiguous fascination with black culture is visible in much of the art of the period, as well as in advertising, furniture design, fashion, journalism, and literature.

White on Black: Images of Africa and blacks in Western popular culture by Jan Nederveen Pieterse (Yale University Press, 1992) presents inarguably the most exhaustive and revealing study of imperial European iconography and how it both refracted and contributed to the changing patterns of racism.

NEO-NAZISM

From the Greek *neos*, meaning new or revived, and the German phonetic spelling of the first two syllables of *Nationalsozialist*, the fascist party that seized political control of Germany in 1933 under Adolf Hitler. The term refers to contemporary groups, parties and organizations that exhibit features associated with the original Nazi party: authoritarian, hierarchical, right-wing government; opposition to democracy, liberalism, pluralism, and an assembly of minority groups, especially Jews and blacks.

The term has been applied to white supremacist groups, including the Ku Klux Klan, the Order, and the Aryan Nation Church affiliates, including the Michigan Militia and the Aryan Republican Army that is thought to have been involved in the Oklahoma bombing of 1995. That episode revealed the preparedness of such US-based groups to turn to terrorist activities in pursuit of their goals. In Britain, neo-nazi groups such as the British National Party and the National Front have developed along conventional political party lines, putting up candidates for election, occasionally with modest success.

Studies by, among others, James Aho (*This Thing of Darkness: A sociology of the enemy*, University of Washington Press, 1994) in the USA and Nicholas Goodrick-Clark in Europe (see below) suggest that the worldview of members is often shaped by economic insecurity, a deep suspicion of government, and, in many cases, a religious fervor that anticipates an apocalyptic battle in the unspecified future. Goodrick-Clark describes neo-nazism as Manichean, that is, understanding the universe as divided between forces that are essentially good and evil. This absolves individuals from meaningful moral responsibility and extends the promise of an ultimate triumph when "good" overcomes "evil," in this reading the Jewish World Government.

Many groups, including the Order, harbor conspiracy theories, particularly about the operations of Jews in government and commerce. Christian patriotism is typically invoked to justify such views: historically there has been a close connection between neo-nazi groups and church organizations. Yet there are other wings that veer away from Christianity and toward Paganism. At the more esoteric fringes, members hold that the origins of Aryans lie in the star of Aldebaran some 68 million light years away.

SEE ALSO: Aryan; bigotry; British National Party; ethnic cleansing; ethnocentrism; fascism; intelligence; Ku Klux Klan; National Front; Oklahoma bombing; One Nation; Other; riots: Britain, 2001; science; skinheads; White Power; white race; whiteness; youth subcultures

Reading

Black Sun: Aryan cults, esoteric nazism and the politics of identity by Nicholas Goodrick-Clark (New York University Press, 2002) interprets the Aryan cults and neo-nazi movements as symptoms of major divisive changes in Western democracy: a deskilled white working class destabilized by migration and the supposed favoritism extended to migrants, turn to political movements that offer unduly simplified accounts and uncomplicated remedies.

Encyclopedia of White Power: A sourcebook on the radical racist right, edited by Jeffrey Kaplan (Alta-Mira, 2000), is an exhaustive 600+ page tome that is unquestionably the best of its kind. It might effectively be augmented with *Extremism in America* (New York University Press, 1995), an uncredited collection of racist texts including the infamous *Turner Diaries*, which is revered by many neo-nazis.

Religion and the Racist Right by Michael Barkun (University of North Carolina Press, 1994) explores the Christian Identity movement, which believes that white people are the literal descendants of the tribes of Israel; that Jews are the product of a sexual union between Eve and Satan; and that these are the last days before a cosmic apocalypse. It may be read in conjunction with *The Politics of Righteousness: Idaho Christian patriotism* by James A. Aho (University of Washington Press, 1994).

White Man Falling: Race, gender and white supremacy by Abby L. Ferber (Rowman & Littlefield, 1998) tries to construct an image of the world through the eyes of neo-nazis.

CHECK: internet resources section under hate groups

NEW INTERNATIONAL DIVISION OF LABOR (NIDL)

First published in English in 1980, the NIDL thesis, as promulgated by Fröbel *et al.* advances the argument that, since 1970, there has been a shift of capital from industrial centers to peripheral undeveloped nations, where cheap and unorganized labor is available. The movement away from industrial centers was hastened by difficulties in securing and realizing high profits, as industrial conflict, increased production costs, and the unionization of migrants and ethnic minorities prevented high levels of labor exploitation.

In Germany, where the thesis was developed, there were obvious economic advantages attached to importing large numbers of temporary migrant "guestworkers." But technical and managerial developments in the labor process later permitted use of peripheral labor power, with little training. Third World governments further facilitated the outward tendency by legislating against labor/trade union power.

The thesis is, in part, intended to account for the decline in the traditional industrial metropolis. When the policy of attracting cheap migrant labor began to show signs of weakness, a new policy of exporting capital was pursued, often to the cost of those in the job markets at the centers.

The NIDL thesis has been roundly criticized on a number of fronts. Cohen, in particular, notes a lack of originality in the observation that global labor markets have been located abroad; this strategy dates back to the mercantile period. He also objects to the "logic" implied in its sequence of phases, forms of labor changing in an inexorable movement. The conception of a single division of labor Cohen also doubts; there are a number of different forms of labor utilization that have implications for the patterning of migration flows.

SEE ALSO: capitalism; colonialism; development; exploitation; migration

Reading

"Migration and the New International Division of Labour" by Robin Cohen, in *Ethnic Minorities and Industrial Change in Europe and North America*, edited by Malcolm Cross (Cambridge University Press, 1992), is one of many critical discussions of the NIDL thesis in this volume.

The New International Division of Labour by F. Fröbel, J. Heinrichs, and O. Kreye (Cambridge University Press, 1980) and *The New International Division of Labour, Technology and Under Development*, edited by D. Ernst (Campus Verlag, 1980) are the two basic expositions.

O

OKLAHOMA BOMBING

The bomb attack on the Alfred P. Murrah federal building, Oklahoma City, in 1995, which resulted in 168 deaths, including those of 19 children, was committed by Timothy McVeigh, who claimed to have acted alone but was almost certainly in collaboration with members of the Aryan Republican Army (ARA), a white supremacist group affiliated to the Ku Klux Klan and the neo-nazi network spread across the USA and Europe.

While McVeigh admitted blame for the bombing and was subsequently executed (in 2001), the nature of his relationship with the ARA and other groups, the extent of the involvement of the far right, and McVeigh's precise motives remain unclear. Evidence, some conclusive, some inferential, suggests that the bombing, which took place on the morning of April 19, was the work of an organized group and its purpose appears consistent with the political ideology of Aryan Nation groups – to attack government buildings as a way of drawing attention to its own right-wing cause and create as much chaos as possible.

McVeigh was picked up within 48 hours of the bombing, after being stopped for a minor motoring violation (a missing license plate). He had not worked regularly for three years before the attack and lived an itinerant lifestyle, accumulating gambling debts. At his trial, it was said that he supported himself largely from the proceeds of a theft in 1994 which netted him $8,700 cash and $60,000 of silver bars. He also made visits to an armed religious compound in a remote part of Oklahoma called Elohim City. The compound had strong associations with a group of Aryan supremacists who had previously plotted to bomb the Murrah building in the 1980s. One of the original conspirators, Richard Wayne Snell, was executed in Arkansas on the day of the bombing for murdering a state trooper and a pawnbroker whose name sounded Jewish. His body was buried at Elohim City. This may or may not have been coincidence.

McVeigh was also known to associate with Richard Guthrie and Pete Langan, both bank robbers and founders of the ARA. Guthrie hanged himself in prison in 1996, having written a 300-page ideological tract in which he advocated attacking "utilities, railways, communications and even government installations" so that the ARA would become a force with which the government would have to reckon. He had previously collaborated with Langan to make an ARA recruitment video full of racist propaganda and denouncements of "government whores." Langan, who is serving life imprisonment without parole, denied any involvement with the Oklahoma bombing and actually cooperated with Mark Hamm, author of studies of both the ARA and the Oklahoma bombing.

The ideology of the ARA was shaped largely by Nazism, the Klan and other racist, anti-Semitic movements that vilified "outsiders" (defined effectively as non-WASPs) and those that were understood to protect them. It drew inspiration from the Order, a neo-nazi organization that subscribed to a Zionist conspiracy in which strategic government positions were occupied by either Jews or those with connections to Jews. The Order was responsible for the killing of Jewish radio talk show host Alan Berg, and stealing $3.8m from an armored truck in the 1980s (Berg's murder is the subject of Oliver

Stone's 1988 film, *Talk Radio*, based on Stephen Singular's book *Talked to Death: The life and murder of Alan Berg* and the investigation into it forms the basis of Costa-Gavras's 1988 movie *Betrayed* in which the FBI agent goes undercover to penetrate the Order). McVeigh was known to have read and liked the infamous *The Turner Diaries*, a novel written by a leading neo-nazi in which a group blows up the FBI headquarters in Washington, DC. The text is accorded almost biblical status by neo-nazis.

Hamm's research reveals that the "lone wolf" interpretation of McVeigh's actions is implausible, particularly when set against the number of eyewitness accounts of what appeared to be at least one accomplice. Hamm argues that the ARA must have been involved in the planning, financing and execution of the bomb attack. McVeigh lacked expertise in bomb handling, but Guthrie was a Navy Seal and had trained in explosives. Langan was a veteran of bank raids and was well versed in the subterfuge and strategy necessary in planning robberies.

Within months of McVeigh's execution, there were two violent sprees involving members of white supremacist organizations. In July 1999, Benjamin Smith, of the World Church of the Creator, went on an Independence Day weekend rampage, shooting Jews, African Americans and Asians in the Chicago area before taking his own life as police closed in. In August, Buford Oneal Furrow, who was a companion of Debbie Mathews, widow of the Order's former leader, Robert Mathews (who died in a shoot-out with the police), walked into an FBI office in Las Vegas and surrendered after shooting a group of children and their teachers at a Jewish community center in suburban Los Angeles. He said that his actions should be "a wake-up call to America to kill Jews." Police found that he had stocked his van with explosives, ammunition, bulletproof vests, freeze-dried food, a US army ranger handbook and neo-nazi literature. Police maintained that he had acted alone, though, as with the Oklahoma bombing, suspicions persist that neo-nazi organizations facilitate, support and perhaps even conspire in such events.

SEE ALSO: anti-Semitism; Aryan; culturecide; ethnic cleansing; ethnocide; nationalism; neo-nazism; *Protocols of the Learned Elders of Zion*; scapegoat; white backlash culture; White Power

Reading

Apocalypse in Oklahoma: Waco and Rugby Ridge revenged by Mark S. Hamm (Northeastern University Press, 1998) should be read in conjunction with Joel Dyer's *Harvest of Rage: Why Oklahoma City is only the beginning* (Westview Press, 1998); taken together, the reader is allowed to understand the culture from which people such as McVeigh emerged – powerless, disenfranchised agricultural workers in search of reasons, however spurious, for their plight.

The New White Nationalism in America: Its challenge to integration by Carol M. Swain (Cambridge University Press, 2002), while not specifically concerned with the bombing, is a study of racist white nationalist movements that gained strength in the USA from the early 1990s.

"The Oklahoma conspiracy" by Andrew Gumble (in *Independent*, "Friday Review," May 11, 2001) is an exceptional, detailed disclosure of McVeigh's involvement with the ARA and other neo-nazi groups that completely undermines McVeigh's own testimony that he acted alone and strongly suggests that the confusion over the case was deliberately engineered by the ARA.

ONE NATION

The voiceless Australians

One Nation was formed in Australia, March 26, 1997 as the political party that coalesced around the populist far right ideas propounded by Pauline Hanson. Socially, One Nation called for zero immigration, the ending of financial support for indigenous Australians, immigrants and ethnic minority groups, and the abolition of the policy of multiculturalism. Economically, the party sought greater support for the agricultural and manufacturing sectors, demanding increased subsidies and the imposition of tariffs on imports.

Through its focus on the mythical "little Aussie battler," One Nation sought to draw support from those people whom, it argued, had become voiceless and marginalized by "special interest groups." The alleged dominance of such groups – which included the inaccurately and broadly defined multicultural industry, ethnic minority groups and indigenous Australians – had led to social policies being directed at them which, it was claimed, were divisive and "unfair" to other Australians.

The surge of popular support for Pauline Hanson following her election as an independent in 1996 led to the formation of One Nation. As a result, the fortunes of the party, particularly in its early years, are difficult to disentangle from those of its figurehead and leader. The opposition which Hanson had engendered extended to One Nation and there was significant resistance to the registration of the organization as a political party. Protests against One Nation, Hanson and the growth of racism that their emergence had precipitated throughout 1996 and 1997 took a range of different forms. The Australian Electoral Commission received over eighty submissions which argued against the registration of the group. Regular demonstrations outside One Nation meetings were accompanied by attempts to deplete the resources of One Nation – a free telephone inquiry line had to be discontinued after opponents encouraged people to telephone One Nation, thereby increasing their telephone bill. State governments, notably Victoria and New South Wales, vocally rejected the ideas of Hanson and One Nation on multiculturalism, immigration and indigenous affairs. However, such resistance arguably proved ineffectual, with One Nation quickly receiving significant levels of polled support.

One Nation's support

The Australian Labor Party (ALP) and the Liberal-National coalition had long dominated the Australian political system and One Nation was able to gain support by drawing upon disaffection with them. Such disillusion emanated from the neo-liberal economic policies which the ALP had pursued in government, and which the Liberal Party had broadly supported, and the belief that special interest groups and "big business" had marginalized the concerns of the "average" Australian. The role of Hanson was important in garnering support for One Nation because her plain speaking appealed to those disillusioned by the professional politicians of the main political parties.

The success of One Nation became evident when, in the 1998 Queensland state election, it won 22.7 percent of the votes cast and took eleven seats. Following this win, it was presumed that the 1998 federal election would see One Nation securing significant support; particularly given that it was being fought in the shadow of the High Court of Australia's *Wik* decision that had further extended the native title land rights of indigenous Australians. Such optimism was misplaced: One Nation received only 8.4 percent of the vote for the House of Representatives and

Pauline Hanson failed to win the seat of Blair. A 9 percent share of the vote in the Senate earned it only one seat. The result was disappointing given the suggested (polling) support for One Nation, although it is a significant result given the short time One Nation had been in existence and the long dominance of the main political parties.

Acrimonious and melodramatic internal feuding followed electoral success. In Queensland, where One Nation had been successful in taking eleven seats in the 1998 state election, the party imploded. In 1999 six members left to form the City Country Alliance, one committed suicide and the remainder became independents. There had been internal turmoil within the wider party even before the 1998 elections which culminated in 1999 with the Supreme Court ruling that One Nation were alleged to have obtained $500,000 of electoral funding dishonestly and of fraudulently registering One Nation in Queensland and New South Wales.

Despite these problems, the 2001 state elections signaled a resurgence of support for One Nation after the political infighting and near collapse of the party. In the 2001 Queensland state election it won three seats and averaged 21 per cent in the seats in which it stood (around half of all constituencies). It was the conservative parties which suffered the most at the hands of One Nation, with the Liberal Party reduced from nine to twelve seats and the National Party from twenty-three to twelve. In the Western Australia state election One Nation took nearly 10 percent of the vote and three seats in the legislative council. Success in these state elections was not matched by success in the 2001 federal election where One Nation failed to win a seat in either the House of Representatives or the Senate.

The impact of One Nation

One Nation's impact went far beyond its size. Politically, the Liberal Party, and particularly the National Party (the rural-based coalition partner), found themselves electorally threatened as it won support in once traditional Liberal-National areas. One response on the part of the Coalition was to shift towards accepting aspects of One Nation's concerns. Whilst the Coalition federal government was unwilling to alter its neo-liberal economic approach, it was far more willing to address One Nation's calls for lower immigration and the reduction of financial support for key social policy areas in indigenous affairs and multiculturalism. Perhaps most crucially, the emergence of One Nation appeared to legitimize racist and divisive language that had previously been marginalized by mainstream politics.

SEE ALSO: Aboriginal Australians; bigotry; Hanson, Pauline; indigenous peoples; multiculturalism; neo-nazism; politics; racist discourse; white backlash culture; xenophobia

Reading

One Nation and Australian Politics, edited by Bligh Grant (University of New England Press, 1997), is an early collection that provides an initial analysis of the emergence and popularity of Pauline Hanson and One Nation.

Two Nations: The causes and effects of the rise of the One Nation Party in Australia by Robert Manne (Bookman Press, 1998) is a valuable anthology of essays by politicians, journalists and academics which seeks to explain the success of Pauline Hanson and One Nation.

EMMA L. CLARENCE

ORGANIZATION OF AFRICAN UNITY *see* international organizations

ORIENTALISM

While, for long, the term referred to characteristics of cultures east of the Mediterranean, its contemporary use typically derives from the work of Edward Said whose 1978 book *Orientalism* offered an influential interpretation. The concept's root is *orientalis* (Latin for rising or sunrise); it came to describe a place or position that faced east (one of the meanings of the verb "to orient" is to turn eastward). The Orient emerged as a way of collectively describing civilizations that lay to the east of, and stood in distinction to, Western civilization.

Orientalism, from the eighteenth century onward, referred to, for example, the pursuits of scholars, journalists and artists who specialized in work on North African, Middle Eastern and East Asian subjects. Active during the colonial period, these practitioners depicted a civilization that was at once exotic, remote, mysterious and beguiling. The products of their work gave rise to arcane images of "Orientals," mostly based on stereotypes. Unfathomable in their worship and other cultural practices, impenetrable in their wisdom, vexing in their erudition, the Chinese epitomized this and were bestowed with the enduring adjective *inscrutable*.

Through the 1960s, criticisms were raised against crude conceptions of Eastern cultures, though it was Said's much-lauded text that revealed Orientalism as a mode of thinking that was crucial to the maintenance of unequal power relations between the colonial powers and those cultures they sought to subordinate and exploit.

In Said's conception, Orientalism invited a way of conceiving Others, those groups who, as Fanon had earlier suggested, functioned to remind subjects of colonial nations of who they were *not*. Cultural identities are forged in contrariety. Western knowledge of those whom they dominated may have been based on ignorance and, in some cases, reverie, but they served a purpose. Said's approach was to read Orientalism *contrapuntally*: by understanding the entire nature of Orientalism, the art, literature and reportage that constituted it in a contrary way to those traditionally accepted, he was able to expose the manner in which representations legitimize and perpetuate colonial authority.

Cultures emanating from Western Europe were conceived not only as dramatically different from those of the East, but as self-evidently superior. Far from visualizing cultures as incommensurate or, as Said suggested, permeable, colonialists saw in Oriental cultures inferior and impervious entities. Qualities that were regarded as linked with the Orient were at once alluring and repulsive. Women, for example, were variously understood as either inherently erotic and lacking the self-control of Western women, or as restricted by Eastern men and unable fully to express themselves. Either way, the West was their savior.

Orientalism continued to flourish through the twentieth century, sustained by films and television series. Peter Sellers's last film *The Fiendish Plot of Dr Fu Manchu* – in which he played the iniquitous lead – was released in 1980, shortly after the finish of the TV series *Kung Fu*, in which American actor David Carradine played a nomadic martial artist from China. The Kung Fu genre that grew out of the 1970s continues to the present day, albeit modified in line with politically correct imperatives. However, for most of the century, clichéd Oriental archetypes, such as Charlie Chan and Mr. Moto (both fictional detectives, with "inscrutable" methods of inquiry), circulated in popular film and comic books.

In his essay "Orientalism," Ali Rattansi notes how Japanese advances in technology, when combined with popular representations of Japanese (while he does not mention them, one presumes he refers to *Manga* publications), have produced new images of Japanese as cold, impersonal and machine-like and their culture as authoritarian and lacking emotional connection to the rest of the world.

The value of the concept of Orientalism, certainly in the way depicted by Said, lies not so much in its ability to counterpoise Western conceptions with more "realistic" ones, but as an investigation into the manner in which cultural materials that ostensibly have no connection with the distribution of power or other elements of political economy are actually integral parts of processes that confirm the rightness of colonial and postcolonial arrangements. So Orientalism prescribes and maintains a discourse that upholds the essential distinction, if not opposition, between cultures and their products.

SEE ALSO: bigotry; colonial discourse; cultural identity; essentialism; exploitation; Fanon, Frantz; hybridity; Islamophobia; language; Other; political correctness; postcolonial; racial coding; racial profiling; reparations; representations; sexuality; stereotype

Reading

Orientalism by Edward Said (Routledge, 1978) is the seminal text, which may be read in conjunction with the same author's later work "Orientalism reconsidered," which was published in 1988 in *Europe and its Others*, vol. 1, a collection of essays edited by F. Barker, P. Hulme, and M. Iverson (University of Essex Press).

"Orientalism" by Ali Rattansi, in *Dictionary of Race, Ethnicity and Culture*, edited by Guida Bolaffi, Raffaele Bracalenti, Peter Braham, and Sandro Gino (Sage, 2002), provides a valuable guide, before concluding that Orientalism is a "blunt analytical tool for understanding the forms in which Western culture sustains its unitary identity as the most 'progressive' force on the globe."

OTHER

The theme of Otherness originates in philosophical queries about the nature of identity. Wherein lies the identity of a thing? Is the difference between Same and Other a matter of essence or existence? With Hegel identity and difference translates into the antinomy of being and nothing, spirit and matter that unfolds in history. What he calls the life and death struggle with the Other, for instance between master and slave, is a relationship that changes dialectically over time. Schopenhauer speaks of Will and Representation, Heidegger of Being and Time, Sartre of Being and Nothingness. These and other queries yield various notions of Otherness such as the Unthought, the Implicit (Husserl), the Virtual or Unfulfilled Possibilities (Marcuse). From psychoanalysis and the unconscious as the ego's Other arises the theme of oneself as An Other. In the words of Julia Kristeva, "Nous sommes étrangers à nous-mêmes." In *I and Thou* Martin Buber addresses the Other in social relations as a potential partner in dialog. In the work of the philosopher Emmanuel Levinas *alterity* becomes a relational concept.

Cultural difference is a major part of Otherness. From times immemorial peoples have considered themselves as "the people" and all the rest as "Others" – the Greeks and *barbaroi*, Jews and *goyim*, the Japanese and *gajjin*. In the West, the distinction between Christians and heathens long served as the main boundary between Self and Others. Heretics and believers in other faiths such as Muslims, Jews and Orthodox Christians occupied in-between niches. In the Renaissance the distinction between Ancients and Moderns overlaid these differences. The Enlightenment introduced a preoccupation with classification and scientific attempts to classify humans on the basis of "race" and language. In the wake of the French Revolution, nationhood became a defining element of identity. The notions of race, language and nationality mingled (nations were thought of as races and races were viewed as language groups). Romantic preoccupation with the unknown in its ambivalent character of attraction and repulsion was yet another face of the Enlightenment. The pathos of the unknown (wild, remote) was like a secular version of pantheism or else of the hidden God (*deus absconditus*). Others were the embodiments of ideals (the good or noble savage), fears (monsters, cannibals), objects of desire, windows of mystery. Others were targets of hatred – scapegoats, as in anti-Semitism and pogroms: "Nothing but otherness killed the Jews." Genocide of indigenous peoples – Native Americans, Tasmanians, Armenians – and dehumanizing treatment of slaves, Natives, Gypsies are part of the history of Otherness. In nineteenth-century Orientalism and exoticism all these attitudes are reflected in a general setting of Western expansion, imperialism and colonialism.

Decolonization destabilized these relations. Imperial identities were decentred. In this context, the question of the Other became a critical theme, first in structuralist anthropology and its understanding of culture as a system of systems on the model of language. Tzvetan Todorov is a classic representative of this approach that uses a binary schema of Self and Other. In Michel Foucault's work, relations of power and domination are analyzed through discourse analysis as knowledge regimes or epistemological orders. How others are represented is a key to understanding the structure of knowledge regimes and their truth claims. Foucault concentrated on others in French society, those classified as deviant, criminal, heretic, insane, diseased. In *Orientalism* Edward Said applied discourse analysis to the texts produced by European Orientalists about the Orient, the colonized world.

Cultural and postcolonial studies now examine how others are represented. The main axis of difference is the Big Three of race, class, and gender. Representations of racial (ethnic, national) others often overlap with those of women and lower-class people. Increasingly the Other is left behind as too narrow and static a notion. There are so many kinds of Others that there is little point in generalizing about them. Besides, the "Self" no longer represents a fixed identity; witness ideas of multiple identity and the decentering of the subject. The universalist Enlightenment subject (white, male, middle-aged, rational) is no longer being taken for granted.

Jacques Derrida rephrases the question of Otherness in terms of identity and difference, returning it to the wider terrain of philosophical questioning from whence it originated. In sociology, gender and cultural studies *difference* increasingly takes the place of Otherness. The terminology of identity/difference is more matter of fact than that of Self/Other. Difference, of course, also comes in many forms: as ontological difference, the difference of God, gender, cultural difference and diversity. Migration opens up new frontiers of difference centered on citizenship status (here Others include asylum seekers, refugees, undocumented aliens, illegal immigrants). The most recent Others are "terrorists" (as in war on terrorism).

Over time, then, Otherness has referred to questions of being and nonbeing, immanence and transcendence, and to cultural differences along lines of language, religion, civilizational or evolutionary status (savages, primitives), "race," ethnicity, nationality, gender, class, development, ideology, age, citizenship, and so forth. All along it has been basic to the construction of boundaries of community.

SEE ALSO: American Indians; anthropology; anti-Semitism; antislavery; asylum seeker; beauty; colonial discourse; cultural identity; culturecide; double consciousness; ethnocide; Fanon, Frantz; genocide; Hall, Stuart; hybridity; Irish; language; orientalism; postcolonial; race: as signifier; racial coding; racist discourse; representations; Roma; September 11, 2001; sexuality; slavery; subaltern

Reading

The Conquest of America: The question of the Other by Tzvetan Todorov (Harper and Row, 1984; original French edition, 1982) is a classic source in structuralist anthropology.

Madness and Civilization: A history of insanity in the Age of Reason by Michel Foucault (Random House, 1965) is also relevant, as is Jacques Derrida's *Writing and Difference* (Chicago University Press, 1978). These may profitably be read in conjunction with Edward Said's pathbreaking study *Orientalism* (Penguin, 1978), which discusses the construction of the Orient as fundamentally Other, different from the West.

White on Black: Images of Africa and blacks in Western popular culture by Jan Nederveen Pieterse (Yale University Press, 1992) focuses on representations of Africa, black people and on colonialism, and may be usefully read in association with Nicholas Thomas's *Colonialism's Culture: Anthropology, travel and government* (Polity Press, 1994), *Representing Others: White views of indigenous peoples*, edited by Mike Gidley (University of Exeter Press, 1992), and Iris Marion Young's *Justice and the Politics of Difference* (Princeton University Press, 1991).

JAN NEDERVEEN PIETERSE

P

PARK, ROBERT EZRA (1864–1944)

One of the foremost contributors to the development of a sociology of race and ethnic relations and of urban sociology, Robert Ezra Park was born on February 14, 1864 near the town of Shickshinny, Pennsylvania. His father, Hiram Asa Park, had been a soldier in the Union army and during his term of service with the First Regiment Iowa Cavalry he married Theodosia Warner. The couple settled down in Red Wing, Minnesota, the town in which Robert Park spent his formative years.

"Progress" and human waste

In 1887, Park graduated from the University of Michigan, having been awarded a Bachelor of Philosophy degree and membership in Phi Beta Kappa. For the next eleven years he worked as a journalist on newspapers in the Midwest and in New York City. Park's journalism concentrated on what later would be called "human interest" stories. He especially undertook assignments that covered proceedings in night court. There a rough and instantaneous mode of justice was meted out to prostitutes, derelicts, drunkards, petty thieves, and other members of that element which Park would later recall as the "human junk" of civilization. It was during this period of his life that Park began to formulate his conceptions of civilization and progress. Likening the forward movement of society to the passage of a speeding locomotive, Park took interest not only in the outcome of the "train" and its "road" to "progress," but, more significantly, in the human waste that was piled up along the side of those tracks. Thus, early in his career, Park showed an interest in both the positive and negative effects of rapid industrialization, urbanization and the "progress" these were supposed to bring.

Seeking to enlarge his outlook on life and society, Park left the field of journalism and entered Harvard University seeking a master's degree in philosophy. There he studied with William James who, like his undergraduate professor – the young John Dewey – would have an important influence on his subsequent development as a sociologist. James warned Park against seeking a career in philosophy and urged him to undertake a broader outlook than that which could be obtained from immersion in the classical scholars. Park accepted this advice and, like so many others of his generation, undertook doctoral studies in Berlin and Heidelberg. During his years in Germany, Park took his only sociology course from Georg Simmel, whose essays "The stranger" and "The metropolis and mental life" would figure in both Park's understanding of immigration and the emerging urban *mentalité*. Park completed a doctoral dissertation entitled *Masse und Publikum, Eine Methodologische und Sociologische Untersuchung* in 1904. This work was not translated into English until 1972.

Upon his return to the USA Park served for one year as a teaching assistant at Harvard and then founded an American branch of the Congo Reform Association, an organization established to expose the atrocities committed by the agents of Leopold II, king of Belgium, in the Congo. Park wrote and published a series of essays in a style that today would be called "investigative journalism" and in his day was called "muckraking." Although later biographers of Park would place little emphasis on his writings on the Congo conditions, in fact, as Stanford M. Lyman would show, there is implicit in these essays a sociological critique of both modernization and capitalism. However, Park's perspective belongs to a now-forgotten genre which Lyman calls "Gothic sociology." Employing the metaphor of the "vampire," Gothic sociology teaches its readers about the actual horrors that are produced and that prevail in modernity. Using preternatural imagery and occult phantasy, Park likened the Belgian king to a vampire who preys upon the abject native laborers of Belgium's African colony. In the event, he showed how capitalist imperialism fed itself on the exploitation of abject labor, the victims of a system's vampiric drive for hegemony.

With the death of King Leopold in 1908 Park turned to new areas of investigation. He was invited by Booker T. Washington, who had served as vice president of the Congo Reform Association, to go to Tuskegee Institute and serve as Washington's private secretary and ghost writer. Park would hold this position until 1913 when he was invited by Professor William I. Thomas to join the faculty of sociology at the University of Chicago. While in service to Washington, Park investigated aspects of Negro life and labor in the "new South." It is in this period that Park formulates his conception of a biracial community drawn from his analysis of the racial situation in Winston-Salem, North Carolina.

Race relations cycle

Park's most important contribution to the understanding of race and ethnic relations was presented as what he called a "race relations cycle." Combining Simmel's conception of forms with Windelband's conception of historical movements, Park proposed that race relations occur in four successive stages: contact; competition; accommodation; assimilation. As Park conceived of the matter, these stages are progressive and irreversible. A universal perspective on race and ethnic relations, Park's cycle would fit every instance in which two or more races encountered one another in areas that he called "racial frontiers." Park's race relations cycle provided a paradigm for studies of African, Asian, Hispanic and European interactions throughout the world, but especially in the USA. However, neither Park nor his disciples could demonstrate empirically that the stages occurred for each and every racial and ethnic group or that they occurred in the

order that he had proposed, or that the stages were irreversible. Nevertheless, the idea of an inevitable and progressive resolution of the race problem served to inspire both sociological investigations and public policy. Assimilation, the final stage of Park's cycle, was held out as a "promissory note" upon "payment" of which race conflicts would disappear. In 1937 Park reconsidered the ultimate stage of his cycle and suggested that race relations might end in one of three possibilities: a caste system, permanent minority status, or assimilation. However, Park was noticeably silent about how race relations would culminate in the United States. Moreover, in a later essay, he suggested that the end of the race relations cycle would merely clear the sociocultural space for a class struggle to begin.

Collaboration with Burgess

Park's other major contribution to sociology is found in his analysis of the city and urban life. Working together with Ernest W. Burgess, Park proposed a cycle of stages that would describe urban development geographically and socioculturally. Park believed that his race relations cycle could be envisioned as a part of urban development and reach finality in the ultimate establishment of a civic civilization. His outlook on urban development concentrated attention on what Burgess called "zone 2," in which were to be found the several unassimilated ethnic and racial communities as well as numerous forms of deviance and social disorganization. In this matter, Park's perspective differed from that of virtually all of his disciples. Where such sociologists and anthropologists as Louis Wirth and Robert Redfield spoke of the anomie of urban life and the joys of the small community and the primitive tribe, Park looked forward to the onset of a global civilization rooted in cosmopolitanism, commerce and capitalism. Although Park was nostalgic for the racial ghetto, the ethnic community and the *Gemeinschaft* (characterized by strong social bonds) that prevailed in zone 2, he would not allow his sentiments to obscure his judgment that all those would eventually disappear. Park understood fully what one of his critics called "the romance of culture in an urban civilization," but his ultimate belief was that civilization would triumph over all. His concept of the "marginal man" captured the sociopsychological status of those in transition from a folk culture to an urban society.

Park died in 1944. His final lectures were devoted to an analysis of America's failure to live up to the promise of its professed aims in World War II. Park called attention to the contradiction entailed in the failure of the USA to have established full freedom and equality for African Americans, Asian Americans and Native Americans, while the nation claimed that the defeat of fascist totalitarianism and Japanese militarism were justified by American's proclamation of the four freedoms. Although Park's race relations cycle is no longer regarded as the dominant perspective on the race question and although Burgess's urban theory has been discredited by later empirical studies, Park remains one of the most significant contributors to the development of sensitizing concepts on each of these issues.

SEE ALSO: African Americans; anthropology; Asian Americans; assimilation; disadvantage; ethnicity; ghetto; Latinos; minorities; racism; whiteness; youth subcultures

Reading

Militarism, Imperialism and Racial Accommodation: An analysis of the early writings of Robert E. Park in American sociology by Stanford M. Lyman (University of Arkansas Press, 1992), is, as its title suggests, an examination of Park's pioneering forays into the study of race and ethnicity; this may be read in conjunction with the same author's "The Gothic foundation of Robert E. Park's conception of race and culture," in *The Tradition of the Chicago School of Sociology* edited by Luigi Tomasi (Ashgate, 1998); and *Color, Culture, Civilization: Race and minority issues in American society* (University of Illinois Press, 1994), also by Lyman.

Quest for an American Sociology: Robert E. Park and the Chicago School by Fred H. Mathews (McGill-Queen's University Press, 1977) is one of a number of appraisals of Park's work; others include Winifred Raushenbush's *Robert E. Park: Biography of a sociologist* (Duke University Press, 1979); Barbara Ballis Lal's *The Romance of Culture in an Urban Civilization: Robert E. Park on race and ethnic relations in cities* (Routledge, 1990); and *Robert E. Park and the "Melting Pot" Theory* edited by Renzo Gubert and Luigi Tomasi (Reverdito Edizioni, 1994).

Race and Culture by Robert E. Park (The Free Press, 1964) is perhaps the best way to begin Park's impressive oeuvre, which includes *The Immigrant Press and its Control* (Scholarly Press, 2001); with Ernest W. Burgess, *Introduction to the Science of Sociology* (University of Chicago Press, 1985); and,

with Roderick D. McKenzie, *The City* (University of Chicago Press, 1984).

STANFORD M. LYMAN

PATERNALISM

From *pater*, Latin for father, this refers to what is essentially a legitimation of despotism, or tyranny. A model of familialistic relations, especially of father to child, is applied to relations of economic, social and political inequality. Thus, subjects' freedoms are limited by regulations that are ostensibly "well-meant."

There is, of course, an element of despotism in parent–child relations, but the despotism is both tempered and legitimated by "love." In the colder phrasing of sociobiology, kinship makes for a commonality of genetic interests between relatives. Parents can indeed be expected to exert authority for the benefit of their children, if not all the time, at least much of the time, since their children's interests overlap with their own.

In the absence of such a commonality of genetic interests, unequal relations of power are characterized by a highly asymmetrical distribution of costs and benefits, that is, by exploitation. It is, therefore, in the interest of the dominant party to seek to disguise the coercive and exploitative nature of the relationship by claiming that domination is in the best interests of the oppressed. This is done by asserting that the dominated are in a state analogous to childhood, that is, are dependent, immature, irresponsible, and unable to run their own affairs, and that the rulers "love" their subjects, and act *in loco parentis*, for the best interests of the oppressed.

Paternalism is probably the most widespread legitimating ideology of pre-industrial societies, and has been independently reinvented time and again in a wide range of social situations. It characterized, among others, patron–client relationships in many pre-industrial societies; godparent–godchild ties in class-stratified Latin American countries; the white man's burden and civilizing mission ideology of European colonialism in Africa; master–slave relations in the chattel slavery regimes of the Western hemisphere, and teacher–student relationships in universities.

The British attitude toward Aboriginal Australians, while initially one of indifference, from the middle of the nineteenth century changed to one of guardianship, with "protectors" appointed to assist assimilation and absorption. While the methods adopted were frequently appalling, the aims were ostensibly guided by paternalistic motives – to seek an end to the "Aboriginal problem." The solution was effectively the elimination of the Aboriginal population.

The acceptance of the legitimizing ideology by the subordinates is generally a function of the degree of perceived benevolence in the relationship, and of the age difference between the parties. Thus, the model is more acceptable between teacher and students than between masters and slaves. As a type of race and ethnic relations, paternalism has characterized many societies, although acceptance of that ideology by the oppressed has always been problematic. Perhaps the two situations in which paternalism was most explicitly formulated as a legitimation of despotism are European colonialism, particularly in Africa, and plantation slavery in the Americas.

There has been much debate on the extent to which colonial subjects and slaves accepted their masters' view of them and internalized a sense of their own inferiority (the so-called Sambo mentality). There is much evidence that servility and subservience were only opportunistic survival mechanisms, although one cannot entirely discount that some slaves and colonials did indeed develop a dependency complex. This was probably more the case under slavery than under colonialism, because the slave plantation did, in fact, represent a somewhat closer approximation to a large family (though far from a happy one) than the typical colony.

Indeed, extensive mating (often forced, and nearly always extramarital) between male owners or overseers and female slaves was characteristic of all slave regimes. For the dominant males, mating with slaves was a way of combining business and pleasure, hence the popularity of the practice, both in North and South America. (The Latins tended to be less hypocritical and more open in their acceptance of miscegenation than the Dutch and English, but there is no evidence that the actual incidence of the practice differed between slave regimes.) These liaisons across racial lines did, of course, create numerous ties of sexual intimacy and of kinship between masters and slaves, and did make many plantations big families of sorts, albeit of a perverse

type. The undeniable fact, however, is that sexual and kin ties across racial lines necessarily affected the master–slave relationship, and consolidated the paternalistic model of legitimation by giving it *some* factual basis.

SEE ALSO: Africa; antislavery; apartheid; Brazil; colonialism; Doomed Races Doctrine; Freyre, Gilberto; indigenous peoples; slavery; South Africa

Reading

The Masters and the Slaves by Gilberto Freyre (Knopf, 1964) is the classic account of Brazilian slavery by a psychoanalytically oriented Brazilian sociologist.
Race and Racism by Pierre L. van den Berghe (Wiley, 1978) is an analysis of race relations in Mexico, Brazil, South Africa, and the USA, stressing the contrast between "paternalistic" and "competitive" race relations.
Roll, Jordan, Roll by Eugene Genovese (Pantheon, 1974) is an account by a Marxist historian of the US plantation system from the point of view of the slaves.

PIERRE L. VAN DEN BERGHE

PATRIARCHY

Patriarchy is a social system that emerged during the age of antiquity and continues in various forms to the present. It has existed in various types of nation-states. Whether feudal, capitalist, or socialist, the essential underpinnings of such a system have not differed. In all patriarchal settings, dominance in power and authority have been male-centered, primarily expressed in female sex-gender control and economic discrimination.

Origins

The origins of patriarchy may be traced to primitive sexual divisions of labor, resulting from the transition from food-gathering and foraging/scavenging modes of survival to hunting, perhaps three million years ago. Women, unable during pregnancy and periods of early child rearing to engage in the more physically challenging feats of big game hunting and, later (10,000 years ago), subsistence agriculture, were relegated to different chores, that were labeled as lesser in worth. Male economic power was augmented with the domestication of animals and male proprietorship of herds and their associated wealth was interwoven into many patriarchy systems. The emergence of property as private rather than communal was a major factor in the establishment of subordinate female sex-gender relationships. The establishment of property as private altered more egalitarian sex-gender relationships for it changed the ways in which basic functions in the family operated. The labor of women was transformed from services of survival or for the betterment of society to an act that enhanced family wealth. In time, many patriarchal cultures denied women the right to acquire, hold, and dispose of property.

In many ancient city-kingdoms or states, the first components of patriarchy were evidenced in male control of two of a woman's biological capacities, namely her sexuality and procreativity. Female sexual subordination ultimately was written into codes of law which were not only enforced within the family, one of the first and primary institutions constructed on the basis of patriarchial values, but also by the state. Besides laws, males resorted to the use of force, assignment of class privileges, economic dependency, and confirmation of respectability or nonrespectability upon women in order to assert control. Within time, patriarchy entailed also the placement of women in a subjugated class, devoid of rights equal to those accorded males. The right of women to own, use, and sell property was denied in most ancient societies, and is still a feature of female subjugation in many nation-states today.

In the ancient world, as well as today, patriarchy was expressed in a number of ways. Within a patriarchal family, a male possessed the right to sustain life or inflict death upon females. In other patriarchal settings, female right to life was state-controlled. The primary subjugation devices utilized by males in such states were the allocation of awards for obedience or punishments, even physical in nature, for disobedience. In all situations, the male was designated head and power figure in the family.

The city-kingdoms of the Mesopotamian world were some of the earliest agencies of state to employ patriarchal ideology to justify sex-gender-class stratification. A patriarchy was established in the Fertile Valley: the ultimate sanction of patriarchy in Mesopotamia was evidenced in the codification of law, most notably Hammurapi's code, which included statutes that guaranteed, in many areas of life, abrogation of the rights of women. Women in the Mesopotamian system were disowned by their husbands

for sterility, infidelity, and other types of non-approved conduct; rewards and punishments were dictated by males. Married Mesopotamian women could be given to their husband's creditors in order to cancel a debt. Yet, on the other hand, women of Mesopotamia were permitted to own property and to engage in commercial enterprises free of male control.

A genuine expression of patriarchy did not become a major feature of life in every ancient kingdom that was transformed from an archaic organization into a centralized and structured nation-state with a flourishing culture. Many early horticultural societies, for example, were structured around women as dominant forces in society. If matriarchy is defined as the exact opposite of patriarchy in terms of power and control, a mirror image of a patriarchial system, history does not provide an example of a matriarchal culture.

The Mesopotamian model was in many ways duplicated in a large percentage of the societies of antiquity and extended, with some modifications, into the modern world. Greek and Roman civilizations were societies in which patriarchy prevailed. English society in the seventeenth century was patriarchal in nature and the same was true in the USA. Aspects of patriarchy remain features of both societies as the twentieth century draws to a close. In fact, the expressions of patriarchy that still exist in England and the USA are referred to as *de facto* patriarchy, for in both societies the state does not intervene when certain female rights, within a household or in the workplace, are abrogated by a male figure who assigns rewards for what is deemed accepted behavior and inflicts punishment for "unseemly" acts.

African American matrifocality

Scholars suggest that the African American family structure represents an exception to patriarchy, by arguing that African American family life demonstrates the existence of a matriarchal system marked by matrifocality and consanguine households. This view derives from the belief that African American females, out of necessity, assumed control of power and authority in families. The African American female, from the period of slavery into the modern era, was forced to assert dominance as a result of the need to preserve the family unit because of the absence or prolonged unemployment of the male head of household. Also, African American matriarchal culture is reinforced by the ways in which modern government assistance is allocated. Most notably, Aid to Families with Dependent Children (AFDC) stipends are allocated on the basis of the absence of an adult male from a household, what is called the "no-male in the household" restriction.

Opponents of this argument note that the African American familial experience is characterized by a system of kinship networks. With the destruction of nuclear and polygamous family units, lineage could no longer be reconstructed under slavery, so networks based on marriage, friendship, and relatedness developed. Such a system still exists today, and is made even more necessary, scholars suggest, by other forces that further erode the nuclear family. The boundaries of the African American family units are elastic and the inner workings of such groupings produce behaviors that allow for a great degree of adaptiveness to crises, such as unemployment, welfare payments restrictions, and lack of permanent dwelling forcing frequent movement of the family unit.

In the African American system of kin networking, according to many, adult females play a key role in acquiring resources to meet needs. But they do not hold absolute power and authority within the kinship structure. African American kin networks are cooperative units: all members – males, females, and children – are called upon to assist in order that the kinship survives. All members, to an extent not found in white families, expend effort to acquire critical resources to overcome multiple disadvantages. African American kinship systems are usually three-generational, co-residency households with boundaries that are flexible and exist within a larger kinship system that is extended and adaptive. The role of the woman within this double-tiered social system is *matrifocal*. Her role is both cultural and structural: adult females, primarily mothers, transmit cultural values and are participant in almost all interkinship decision making, the creation of family and kinship ties, and the acquisition of resources.

In the African American kinship network, young women are socialized to demonstrate strength and to become active members. Both males and females exemplify qualities of assertiveness, initiative, autonomy, and decisiveness. A significant aspect of the socialization process is the training of females to act independently of males. Also, in such a matrifocal, bilateral arrangement, a close affinity between mother, child, and sibling exist, more so than within conjugal relationships. Human bonding in the African American kinship system is decidedly mother–child oriented, as in many other cultures where matrifocality is present.

Among the Ibo of Nigeria, the Javanese, and two Indonesian ethnic groups, the Minangkabau and the Atjehnese, family systems have been constructed in which degrees of matrifocality also exist. Like the African American kinship system, that of the Javanese is also bilateral. Among the Javanese, as in many matrifocal cultures, bonding is mother–child arranged, rather than husband–wife.

Patriarchal families are sometimes consanguine: that is, organized in terms of blood relationships. Male power is vested in senior male members of the family. Examples of this type of patriarchy are found in many Chinese families. Other examples of consanguine patriarchal family structures are ancient Israel and ancient Rome. Both blood as well as extended relationships, such as friendship and culture, are the social blocks that create the contemporary African American family kinship system.

Religion

Another force that has given rise to patriarchy and sustained its existence into modern times is religion. Religions such as Judaism, Christianity, Hinduism, and Islam led to the development of tenets and practices that enhanced existing patriarchal ideologies. Employing a metaphysical rationale, males were able to legitimate extensively their own superiority and establish for women an inferior, even precarious position in society.

In the Judeo-Christian tradition, a God-ordained male-dominated hierarchy was constructed. Important was the idea that male creation was a primary act, while that of the female was secondary in nature: the female was created to serve the male and bear children. As the rites of Judeo-Christianity unfolded, women were not ordained as priests, were denied the position of sacramental celebrants, and were forced to veil their heads, especially in religious gatherings, to signify male authority.

Other ancient metaphysical covenants negated the role of the woman as priestess, divine healer, or seer. The dominant male god that surfaced in Hebrew monotheism in some cases destroyed and in others decreased the presence of influential and powerful goddesses in ancient societies.

Under Hinduism, women are deemed to be more erotic than males. If their eroticism is left unchecked, it is believed that the male's quest for spirituality and a high level of asceticism would be impeded. Hindu women have been cloistered, never seen by males who were not members of the family, and wear veils concealing garments. In traditional Hindu society, all property acquired by a wife was transferred to male ownership.

The same was true in ancient Greece, Rome, Israel, China, and Japan. Also in England and America the right to own property did not exist until the modern period. Currently in Islamic Iran and Saudi Arabia, female property rights are still denied.

Theories of patriarchy

Socialist-Marxist feminists contend that a capitalistic-materialistic organization of society invokes patriarchy. It gives rise to a functional arrangement of the workforce that is based on sexual division; neither equity in labor assignments, pay, nor worth are accorded to women. Patriarchy is sustained by the manner in which class relations occur. Class relations and the sexual division of labor are mutually supportive of one another under capitalism. Patriarchy in this perspective is a universal system that will not alter *unless* a radical restructuring of society takes place.

Other feminists turn to psychoanalysis to provide explanations for the emergence of patriarchy. They note that once male and female gender classifications were devised, a double standard evolved and women were accorded a lesser position in society. The authority of male as father was the main structural device that was employed for the inclusion of gender in the social order.

Another group of social theorists differ from the more radical feminists and advance the concept that patriarchy was, and still is, only one of a number of sex-gender systems. Their viewpoint rests on the position that patriarchy can and does function independently of political systems and is autonomous. There is general acceptance that not all past societies were universally patriarchal. Any assertion included in prior scholarship that such was the case was due in large measure to patriarchal assumptions introduced by ethnographers and anthropologists. While it is contended that a number of past societies were culturally more egalitarian than others, and the role of women was more than that of child bearers and child providers, they were not genuinely matriarchal systems. No society of the past was a matriarchy; women acquired positions of importance but did not gain and utilize a dominance in power and authority.

SEE ALSO: African Americans; anthropology; beauty; bigotry; black feminism; essentialism; ethnicity; Hottentot Venus; kinship; Marxism; Other; sexual abuse; sexuality; transracial adoption

Reading

The Creation of Patriarchy, vol. 1, by Grada Lerner (Oxford University Press, 1986), is a stylistic and informative investigation of the evolution of patriarchy in ancient cultures.

Myths, Dreams and Mysteries: The encounter between contemporary faiths and archaic realities by Mircea Eliade (translated from the French into English by Philip Mairet, Harper Torchbooks, 1967) has as its central theme the delineation of two types of thought: *traditional*, as archaic and Oriental in nature, and *modern*, as Western in type. Each affects a culture's attitudes towards women.

Women Culture & Society, edited by Michelle Zimbalist Rosaldo and Louise Lamphere (Stanford University Press, 1974), comprises sixteen articles that explore various theories that have been offered to explain the role of women in the development of various societies and cultures. This is complemented by *Women, Politics and the Third World*, edited by Haleh Ashfar (Routledge, 1996), which examines strategies of resistance adopted by women.

LORETTA ZIMMERMAN

PENTECOSTALISM

A term used to describe a collection of religious sects that proliferated particularly among African Caribbeans and African Americans. Doctrinally, the assemblies revolve around the Day of the Pentecost spoken of in the Bible's Acts, 2:1–2: "And the day of the Pentecost was now come, they were all together in one place. And suddenly there came from heaven a sound as of the rushing of a mighty wind, and it filled all the house where they were sitting."

Pentecostal members, or "saints," were to await this day of judgment when they would reach their salvation; in the meantime, they were to withdraw as far as possible from the "outside world" and restrict contact with outsiders. They believed themselves to be the "chosen people," the saved who would be rescued on the day of the Pentecost when all others would be damned.

The precise origins of Pentecostalism are obscure, but it seems there were antecedents in both North America and the Caribbean, where there flourished a movement called native baptism. This was based on Christianity but was fused with elements taken from African belief systems. Slavery played a significant part in shaping native baptism, as Malcolm Calley points out: "Possibly the most important role of slavery in the West Indies was to hinder the diffusion of a detailed knowledge of Christianity to the slaves thus stimulating them to invent their own interpretations and their own sects."

Lay native Baptist preachers were exposed to Christian teaching in America and their mixture of biblical concepts and African ritualism was enthusiastically met by American and, later (in the 1780s), Jamaican slaves. Native baptism survived the attempts of plantation owners to suppress it and sprouted a variety of different forms which later transmuted into Pentecostalism.

The sects maintained a presence in the Caribbean and the USA after emancipation and grew in Britain in the 1950s and 1960s – coinciding with the arrival of tens of thousands of Caribbean migrants. The response of the first wave of immigrants to white racialism was characterized by the writer Dilip Hiro as "evasion": they turned inward, developing postures designed to minimize their visibility. Black clubs, shops, and, of course, churches developed. Calley locates the beginnings of Pentecostalism in Britain in 1954 when services were held in private homes. By 1967, Clifford Hill revealed that a single branch of the movement – the New Testament Church of God – alone commanded a following of 10,861 congregations, employed fifteen full-time ministers, and owned its own buildings, including a theological college for the training of its own ministry.

The growth of Pentecostalism is even more surprising when we consider the strictures placed on its members: forbidden were the consumption of tobacco and alcohol, the wearing of jewelry or cosmetics, the use of bad language, and sexual laxity. Avoidance of contact with the "contaminated" outside world was recommended. Observance of these rules and adherence to Pentecostalist practices ensured the believer a special relationship with God, a relationship that was expressed through ecstatic experience in which the individuals became "filled" with the spirit of God and threw convulsions, twitching and being able to speak in tongues (glossolalia): "And they were all filled with the Holy Spirit, and began to speak with other tongues, as the spirit gave them utterance" (Acts, 2:4).

Pentecostalism indicates how many ethnic groups, particularly blacks in the USA and Britain, rather than articulate any outright protest against their treatment by society, develop alternative lifestyles, creating their own autonomous religions, passively withdrawing and seeking salvation not in this world but in an afterlife.

SEE ALSO: African Caribbeans in Britain; kinship; Nation of Islam; Rastafari; segregation

Reading

God's People by Malcolm Calley (Oxford University Press, 1965) is a piece of social history: a detailed study of Pentecostalism's growth in Britain in the 1950s, with useful chapters on the ancestry of the sects.

The Making of the Black Working Class in Britain by Rom Ramdin (Gower, 1987) has a section on "black churches" and the rest of the book supplies detailed contextual information.

"Pentecostalism" by Grant Wacker, in *Encyclopedia of American Religious Experience*, vol. II, edited by C. Lippy and P. Williams (Charles Scribner's Sons, 1988), is an excellent summary of the whole tradition and is complemented by the fuller treatment of John T. Nichol's *Pentecostalism* (Harper & Row, 1966).

PHENOTYPE

The visible or measurable appearance of an organism in respect of trait or traits. The phenotype is what one sees; the appearance or behavior of an organism, in contrast to the genotype or underlying genetic constitution. For example, all people with brown eyes have the same phenotype in respect of eye color; equally, the behavior of a particular strain of rats when confronted with a series of puzzles in a maze is a behavioral phenotype. The outward appearance of humans in respect of skin color, hair form, bone structure, etc. is best identified as phenoty-pical variation; this is a relatively culture-free way of designating differences as opposed to using the word "race," the meaning of which varies from one historical period and one culture to another.

SEE ALSO: genotype; intelligence; race: as classification; race: as synonym; science; transracial adoption

Reading

Personality and Heredity by Brian W. P. Wells (Long-man, 1980) is an introduction to the study of psychogenics.

The Race Concept by Michael Banton and Jonathan Harwood (David & Charles, 1975) discusses the concept of phenotypes.

MICHAEL BANTON

PLESSY V. FERGUSON, 1986 *see* Jim Crow; law: civil rights, USA

PLURALISM

This refers to a pattern of social relations in which groups that are distinct from each other in a great many respects share aspects of a common culture and set of institutions. Each group retains its own ethnic origins by perpetuating specific cultures (or "subcultures") in the form of churches, businesses, clubs and media. It also encloses itself with its own set of primary group relations such as friendship networks, families and intragroup marriages. Yet, all those groups participate collectively in some spheres and, collectively, make up a "plural society."

J. S. Furnivall used societies in Burma and Indonesia as illustrations of plural societies: there, people of very different ethnic back-grounds did not meet each other except in the marketplace, where they had to dispose of goods and services to other groups. The marketplace was the glue that held the different groups together like different pieces of stone in a mosaic. The mosaic is a useful metaphor for pluralism: one flat entity made up of many separate and distinct elements.

There are two basic types of pluralism: cul-tural and structural. Cultural occurs when groups have their own religions, beliefs, customs, atti-tudes and general lifestyles, but have others in common. Structural pluralism is when groups

have their own social structures and institutions, while sharing others. For example, several groups may support a single government, and recognize the same law and use the same money, yet they might go to their own churches, speak a second language among themselves, have their own specialist educations and occupations, and marry only within their own group.

Pluralism, as an analytical tool, purports to explain how many different groups with different backgrounds and, perhaps, different interests can live together without their diversity becoming a basis for conflict. This is especially so if power is distributed fairly evenly among the groups. Where one of the groups has control of power, conflict is likely to erupt. Historically, pluralism seems to apply to pre-industrial or industrializing countries such as East Africa or Caribbean societies where there are more or less equal segments rather than hierarchical classes as in industrial societies.

Plural society is based on cultural and social heterogeneity (i.e. it is composed of diverse elements), but a heterogeneity that does not necessarily create deep divisions and produce serious conflict. Groups maintain their own distinct features and corporate identities, thus adding to the richness of society, without being excluded or relegated to lowly positions.

Pluralism has been used as an ideal in some circumstances, something to aim at; a society in which all groups can express their differences and cultivate their uniqueness without engaging in wholesale or even petty conflicts. The ideal encourages self-awareness and development in some spheres and unification and cooperation in others. This has been particularly popular in North American countries which house a variety of ethnic groups, but can foster only a limited unity despite attempts to balance out interests. But, well intended as the goal may be, it is constantly interrupted by racism, which denies different groups access to certain types of re-sources (such as well-paying jobs and good housing).

The term pluralism is also used in political science in a slightly different sense: it describes a situation in which there are several different interest groups segmentalized horizontally with no single group exerting complete dominance. The similarities with ethnic pluralism are appar-ent: division on the basis of difference without severe inequality of power; horizontal not vertical differentiation.

SEE ALSO: anthropology; culture; ethnicity; ethnonational; integration; minority language rights; multiculturalism; indigenous peoples; power

Reading

Crises of Governance in Asia and Africa, edited by Sandra J. Maclean, Fahimul Quadir and Timothy M. Shaw (Ashgate, 2001), contains several essays that focus on the political management of plural societies.
Netherlands India by J. S. Furnivall (Cambridge University Press, 1967, first published in 1947) is a very early account of plural societies and provides the theoretical model for the later work by M. G. Smith, *The Plural Society in the British West Indies* (University of California Press, 1965).
"Pluralism: a political perspective" by Michael Walzer, in *Harvard Encyclopedia of American Ethnic Groups* (Harvard University Press, 1980), is an assessment of the pluralist development of the USA, while David Levinson's essay, "Pluralism" in his own *Ethnic Relations: A cross-cultural encyclopedia* (ABC-Clio, 1994) applies the concept to Mauritius, in the Indian ocean.
"Pluralism, race and ethnicity in selected African countries" by M. G. Smith, in *Theories of Race and Ethnic Relations*, edited by J. Rex and D. Mason (Cambridge University Press, 1986), is a more recent re-evaluation by one of the perspective's original proponents.

POGROM

The term is of Russian derivation (*gromit'*, destroy), meaning riot or outburst, referencing organized massacres directed at a particular body or class. The term has been applied particularly in connection with the massacres of Jews, especially, but not exclusively, to the periodic outbursts of violence against them that occurred in the latter decades of the nineteenth century, down to the conclusion of the civil war of the Bolshevik revolution. Although some scholars of Jewish history employ the term, it is in more widespread colloquial than academic use, and it is not unusual to encounter the word's application to situations that are also described as riots, communal violence and massacres.

SEE ALSO: anti-Semitism; bigotry; culturecide; ethnic cleansing; ethnocide; genocide; Holocaust

Reading

Pogromchik: The assassination of Simon Petlura, by Saul S Friedman (Hart, 1976) and *The Slaughter of the Jews in the Ukraine in 1919* by Elias Heifetz (Thomas Seltzer, 1921) concentrate on specific pogroms.
Pogroms: Anti-Jewish violence in modern history, edited by J. D. Klier and S. Lambroza (Cambridge University Press, 1992), is a valuable sourcebook.

STUART STEIN

POLICING

The majority of police forces worldwide claim as their mandate preventing crime, bringing law breakers to justice, maintaining the peace, and protecting the community. Many pledge to discharge their duties with integrity, respect human rights obligations, treat all sections of the community equally, and deploy only minimum force. However, evidence emanating from North America, Latin America, South Africa, Indonesia, and Australia and across the EU indicates that racial minorities are still at the forefront of discriminatory and abusive policing practices. There are a number of distinctive but interrelated allegations of racially biased police practices that divide into the overpolicing of racial minorities and underpolicing in relation to the specific law and order needs of these minorities.

Zero tolerance

Allegations of overpolicing relate to the discriminatory use of police powers when dealing with members of racial minorities, particularly in relation to powers of surveillance, traffic stops, street frisks, arrest, detention, investigation and resort to excessive use of force. As well as incidents of individual harassment, minority communities have complained about racial profiling of certain crime categories, saturation policing by specialist police squads, incursions on cultural and political events, as well as immigration raids. Well-publicized incidents emanating from the USA in the late 1990s and early years of the twenty-first century dramatize how the routine policing in minority neighborhoods can tip over into extremely coercive and violent forms of social control. New York, during the 1990s, acquired a global reputation for pioneering zero tolerance policing practices that targeted petty crime, low-level disorder and incivility on the grounds that they were indicators of potentially serious criminal behavior. The spectacular drop in the official crime rate resulted in zero tolerance policing being exported to Europe and Australia. However, while the crime rate plummeted, the intensive policing practices associated with zero tolerance strained the already frayed relationship between the NYPD and the city's racial minorities. Two incidents provoked a nationwide discussion on the desirability of letting the police off the leash in sensitive multiracial contexts. In August 1997 it become known that Abner Louima, a Haitian immigrant, was brutalized by white police officers after an altercation outside a nightclub. As this high-profile case was making its way through the courts, in February 1999 Amadou Diallo, an unarmed Guinean immigrant street vendor, was shot dead by four white undercover officers from the proactive Street Crime Unit. What was particularly controversial was the fact that the police officers had fired forty-one bullets, nineteen of which hit the young African immigrant. In Los Angeles, during 1999, it was established that a core group of officers of the Rampart Division of the LAPD were responsible for beating and shooting suspects, fabricating evidence, planting incriminating evidence and rigging crime scenes in order to entrap suspects. This turned into the biggest police scandal in the history of the LAPD. The sensational revelations were extremely damaging for the police force because they struck at the heart of the force's anti-gang crime fighting methods in some of the city's poorest and most ethnically dense streets. The Rampart scandal revealed a new level of criminality and coined a new criminal justice concept: "the gangster cop." In New York and Los Angeles the common complaint voiced was that certain communities were living in fear of the police as well as the criminals.

As a result of what they perceive to be constant harassment, discrimination and racial profiling, across a variety of jurisdictions, significant sections of these communities, particularly young people, have become alienated from the police. The ultimate manifestation of the near complete breakdown of the police–community relationship is the anti-police riot. Riots in the UK during the 1980s and in France during the 1990s were precipitated by what were perceived to be heavy-handed police actions in minority neighborhoods. The USA watched in shock as the most serious riot of the postwar period engulfed South Central Los Angeles, claiming fifty-four

lives and causing millions of dollars' worth of damage. Triggered by the acquittal of four white police officers for the brutal beating of Rodney King, the ferocity of the May 1992 riots indicated the depth of anger, frustration and despair that existed in minority communities. For many respectable community leaders the verdict represented a final loss of faith by African Americans in the fairness of the criminal justice system. It also suggested that white middle-class America was willing to condone systematic police brutalization and the mistreatment of minority populations.

Hands-off policy

The second facet of racially discriminatory policing relates to the alleged refusal of the police to provide an adequate response to minority community needs. Critics of the police claim that responding to the needs of residents in crime-ridden ghettos and inner cities is a lower police priority than responding to the needs of respectable neighborhoods. For the sake of maintaining public order the police have virtually abandoned certain neighborhoods. Such a hands-off policy effectively leaves these neighborhoods in the hands of local criminals. Critics also claim to have identified a consistent pattern in the response of the police to racist crimes: that is, a lack of effective response; a reluctance to prosecute; the definition of such crimes as nonracist; treating the victim as the criminal; and reacting harshly to community self-protection measures. With the recent upsurge of right-wing extremism across the EU and the increasing seriousness of attacks on guest workers, refugee camps, and immigrant communities, the apparent lack of police protection has become a major cause for concern. This lack of intervention stands in stark contrast to the overpolicing that racial minorities claim they are normally subjected to. In the UK, the murder of black teenager Stephen Lawrence by a gang of young white men in April 1993 propelled the issue of how the police respond to racist crime to the center of public debate. A public inquiry was established to examine why the Metropolitan Police had failed to bring the killers to justice and to make recommendations to ensure that such a miscarriage of justice did not happen in future. The report of the inquiry, chaired by Sir William Macpherson, was published in a blaze of publicity in February 1999.

To the consternation of the Metropolitan Police it concluded that the police investigation was characterized by a combination of professional incompetence, institutional racism and a failure of leadership by senior officers. As a result, UK police forces have been required to overhaul their approach to the recording, investigation and prosecution of racist crime and to ensuring that their work practices meet the requirements of specific communities. In the USA during the 1990s pressure groups began to demand an effective police response to "hate crime" violence and intimidation directed at minority communities. As a result of prolonged campaigning, federal, state and local authorities began to recognize the category of hate crime. New categories of criminal behavior and corresponding sentencing guidelines were established and police forces, in certain parts of the country, established specialized investigative units to concentrate on the perpetrators of hate crime. Similar campaigns for passing "hate crime" legislation have also been established in Australia and Europe.

Various explanations have been forwarded to account for problematic relations between the police and racial minorities in various jurisdictions. The orthodox police position has tended to deny the problem of racial harassment and discrimination. Police representatives continue to argue that the real source of the problem is the overrepresentation of certain racial groups in criminal activity. Thus it is argued that the criminality of certain communities results in proactive policing practices and that in the "war against crime" there will be casualties. They also point to the anti-police attitudes that are entrenched in these communities. Complaints about harassment and discrimination are interpreted by many police officers as attempts to undermine the efficiency of anti-police operations and lower morale. As far as rank and file police officers are concerned they are required by law to exercise their powers and they have the right in the fight against crime and criminals to use force where necessary. In the aftermath of the April 2001 riots in Cincinnati, police officers complained that the city was experiencing an epidemic rise in violent crime for the simple reason that, because they would be accused of racial profiling, officers were not willing to enforce the law. More enlightened senior officers would argue that the problem of racial prejudice lies with the attitudes of a minority of individual officers rather than the institution. They also acknowledge that the racist attitude of one officer can destroy the quality of service and any nondiscriminatory efforts by the rest of the police force. From this perspective, the screening of applicants should be tightened, psychological testing of potential recruits improved, training in community and race relations extended, recruiting practices overhauled to ensure that the forces are representative of the communities that they serve, supervision of front-line officers intensified; and community outreach programs established.

The reordering of criminal justice policy

However, research primarily from the USA and UK suggests that racially discriminatory policing is not just the prerogative of a few "rotten apples." In the aftermath of the Los Angeles riots there were numerous news reports indicating that in certain US police forces racist attitudes were widespread among officers. The alternative explanation argues that the source of this conflictual relationship lies with the police mandate and the structural position of racial minorities. From the late 1960s, it is argued, there has been a fundamental shift as tough law and order tendencies emerged both in the USA and the UK. Those who have suffered most from this reordering of criminal justice policies have been racial minorities. They have no longer any core role to play within the new economic order and are suffering in a disproportionate manner from structural unemployment, the effects of cutbacks in welfare, and urban disinvestment. They are to all intents and purposes politically and socially powerless, existing on the margins of the reconstituted edifice of citizenship. Within this context a potent ideological connection has been made between "race" and crime and this has provided the *raison d'être* for the introduction of aggressive policing tactics. Racial minorities have been criminalized and scapegoated and white support has been mobilized for "the thin blue line." Related to this perspective is the observation that police forces have utilized news media scares to foster an image of a crisis-ridden threatened society in which racial minorities are responsible for an inordinate amount of predatory criminal activity. As a result, police forces have been able to demand more autonomy and the resources necessary to meet the challenges of the purported crisis. The police, on this account, have actually contributed to the sense of racial crisis.

From this perspective, suggestions for improving police training and race relations courses, recruiting minority officers, and making racism a disciplinary offense will not work because the source of the problem is structural not individual. Racism is institutionalized in the police. The charge of *institutional racism* has been denied vehemently by police forces in the USA and UK and by various official inquiries into controversial police actions. However, in the UK, in the first years of the new century, the terms of the debate have changed as a result of the finding that institutional racism played a central role in the inability of the Metropolitan Police to bring the murderers of Stephen Lawrence to justice. Police forces in the UK are now required to consider how the Macpherson Report's definition of institutional racism affects their routine policies, procedures and practices:

> [institutional racism consists of the] collective failure of an organisation to provide an appropriate and professional service to people because of their colour, culture or ethnic origin. It can be seen or detected in processes, attitudes and behaviour which amount to discrimination through unwitting prejudice, ignorance, thoughtlessness and racist stereotyping which disadvantage minority ethnic people. (Macpherson, 1999: 321)

Police forces in the UK have formally acknowledged the problem of institutional racism and have formally committed themselves to implementing a reform program that will enable them to become antidiscriminatory public services and to ensure that officers do not engage in inappropriate language, behavior or perpetuate stereotypes. Critics remain skeptical about the ability and willingness of police forces to instigate the policies needed to root out racist and abusive officers and dismantle the "blue wall of silence." They argue that external pressure needs to be exercised to force change upon police forces and to monitor the functioning of reforms. In the USA, Human Rights Watch has recommended that federal aid should go only to those police departments that can demonstrate that they are taking tangible steps to respect human rights and curb police abuse. The organization also supports the creation and strengthening of civilian review agencies, establishing early warning systems to identify and track officers who are the subject of repeated complaints, and creating a special prosecutors office to pursue cases against police officers accused of criminal conduct.

SEE ALSO: bigotry; Diallo case, the Amadou; human rights; institutional racism; King case, the Rodney; Lawrence case, the Stephen; racial coding; racial profiling; racialization; riots: USA, 1965–67; riots: USA, 1980 (Miami); scapegoat; social work; violence; welfare; white backlash culture

Reading

Ecology of Fear by M. Davis (Metropolitan Books, 2000) is a striking account of the socioeconomic forces driving police–community conflict in Los Angeles.

Official Negligence: How Rodney King and the riots changed Los Angeles and the Los Angeles Police Department by L. Cannon (Westview Press, 1999) is a detailed account of the impact of the Rodney King case on the LAPD.

Shielded From Justice by Human Rights Watch (New York, 1998) is an overview of the abusive police practices that continue to undermine good police–community relations in US cities.

The Stephen Lawrence Inquiry by Sir William Macpherson (London TSO Cmnd 4262-1, 1999) is the most important policy document on police community relations in the UK; this may be read in conjunction with John Grieve's *Institutional Racism and the Police: Fact or fiction?* (Civitas Publications, 2000) and *Search and Destroy* (Cambridge University Press, 1997) by J. G. Miller.

EUGENE MCLAUGHLIN

POLITICAL CORRECTNESS

Much-derided as excessive conformity, political correctness (PC) describes the observance of guiding principles and directives of liberal or radical opinion in the public sphere. It involves the avoidance of language and behavior considered as discriminatory, offensive or patronizing, especially toward ethnic minorities and women.

PC became a virtual orthodoxy at many US universities in the early 1990s. While it was based on sound academic concepts, its enactment was quickly interpreted as a form of censorship. It aimed to redress the balance of North American academies, which were understood to be mired in the same racism and sexism that existed in and was promoted by much American culture. The pervasive character of racism and sexism ensured that the language of instruction and the content of curricula reflected these. Given that knowledge is disseminated through educational institutions, it was thought unlikely that such knowledge would serve emancipatory goals unless it consciously rejected racism and sexism and actively embraced alternatives based on multicultural, antiracist, and antisexist articles.

Inspirations behind PC were diverse. Rather strangely, a term appears in Vladimir Nabokov's 1947 novel *Bend Sinister*: "A person who has never belonged to a Masonic Lodge or to a fraternity club, union, or the like, is an abnormal and dangerous person. It is better for a man to have belonged to a politically incorrect organization than not have belonged to any organization at all."

While the Frankfurt School of philosophy taught the importance of subjecting even profound and heartfelt beliefs to critical scrutiny in the 1920s, the main source for PC seems to be French linguistic philosophy, in particular Michel Foucault. His analysis of the coterminous power/knowledge was important in pointing out that the production of intellect and imagination represent not so much the capacities of the authors producing them, but the relations of power and the ideologies that define the boundaries of discourse – this being, in very general terms, the context in which the knowledge is produced. There has also been a recognition that concepts are not formed in the human mind independently of the language we use to express them. The world is not experienced as a series of facts, but as a series of signs encoded in language. This makes it possible for us to experience the world as "natural" and "right." But, according to writers such as Roland Barthes, it is possible to uncover invisible codes and conventions through which the meanings of experience are accepted.

Jacques Derrida's method of deconstruction was a challenge to the language in which rational argument is expressed. Derrida argued that the Western tradition of thought is founded on assumptions about a final source, or guarantee, of meaning in language. Language is an instrument, but it is not a neutral one. PC followers believe language has been used to perpetuate racism and sexism, but in ways which almost defy conventional analysis.

Because of this, PC began its attempt to counter the Western, or Eurocentric, conceptions of knowledge by targeting language and the discourse it inscribes. Terms and text did not carry thought; they perpetuated it, often in an unreflective way. Apart from the more obvious cases where "black" or its corollaries were used in a derogatory way and in terms of implied abuse, PC carefully screened out all manner of words, such as "beauty," "burly," "dear," and "leader." Any word with a vaguely sexist or racist inference, or one that reflected poorly on disabled persons, the aged, or the young, was anathema.

PC also scrutinized curricula, often finding Eurocentric biases in traditional subjects such as English literature and philosophy, the domains of the DWMs, or "dead white males" (Shakespeare, Aristotle, *et al.*). It sought to make some courses on multiculturalism requisite for all students. This was pursued so zealously at US universities that it led to hostility from faculty members who sensed an encroachment of "academic freedom." In one notable case at Duke University, classroom behavior was monitored to root out racism. The process uncovered only "disrespectful facial expressions or body language aimed at black students." At Stanford University, a student chant went "Hey hey, ho ho, Western culture's got to go," to signify the complete rejection of the established literary canon. This kind of finding hastened the trivialization of PC, and so reduced its impact as an intellectual force.

Much of the contempt for PC was based on hearsay. For example, the *causes célèbres* created by the supposed banning of the nursery rhyme "Baa baa black sheep" on account that it conjured up negative images of blackness was actually advice dispensed by a Working Group against Racism in Children's Resources to the city council of Birmingham, England. The advice was never heeded.

Despite the derision typically afforded PC, its influence spread, albeit surreptitiously and sensibly. "Actresses" became actors, to avoid a gendered term. Flight attendants replaced "air hostesses" or "stewardesses" for the same reason. Comedians specializing in racist material faded away, as did drama that depicted minority groups in baseless negative ways.

SEE ALSO: Afrocentricity; antiracism; education; ethnocentrism; humor; language; media; multiculturalism; racial coding; reverse racism; subaltern; transracial adoption

Reading

After Political Correctness, edited by Christopher New-field and Ronald Strickland (Westview Press, 1995), centralizes the PC debate as a struggle over the very purposes of higher education.

Beyond Political Correctness: Social transformation in the United States by Michael S. Cummings (Lynne Rienner, 2001) argues that "progressives" have been too preoccupied with agreeable pursuits rather than the politically sensitive issues that demand attention; similarly critical of PC is Herman Vuijsje, who focuses on *The Politically Correct Netherlands: Since the 1960s* (Greenwood Press, 2000).

The Politics and Philosophy of Political Correctness by Jung Min Choi and John W. Murphy (Praeger, 1993) explores the assumptions that underpin the PC debates.

Unthinking Eurocentrism by Ellas Shohat and Robert Stam (Routledge, 1994) has a chapter "The Politics of Multiculturalism in the Postmodern Age" that offers a challenging view of PC by reversing Spivak's memorable question thus: "Can the non-subaltern speak?"

POLITICS

Politics refers to the civil government of organized society. The idea of "race" has been taken up and employed as an object of political action in a variety of ways in different countries. Put another way, one can trace different forms in which political processes have become racialized. In the vast majority of these instances, the idea of "race" has been employed in order to justify or legitimate discriminatory action of some sort. At the extreme, as in the instance of Germany in the 1930s and 1940s, the idea of "race" was employed by the Nazi Party to justify a solution to identified economic and political problems which involved the mass murder of Jews. In South Africa, from the early nineteenth century to the 1950s, the idea of "race" was employed to justify the physical segregation and extreme exploitation of African labor.

Both these examples represent twentieth-century instances of a relationship that characterizes European colonial domination and expansion in the late eighteenth and nineteenth centuries, and the exploitation of African labor in the USA in the same period. In these instances important sections of the dominant class justified their economic and political activity by labeling those whose labor they exploited in various ways as belonging to an inferior "race." The political application of the "race" label was explicitly accompanied by the employment of racist ideol-

ogy: Africans, both in Africa and the USA, were defined as belonging to the "Negro race," which was held to be inferior, biologically and culturally, when compared with the "race" to which their exploiters allegedly belonged.

The fact that this racism was used to justify mass murder in the heartland of a European continent which various national ruling classes defined as the epitome of "civilization" and "democracy" was one of the reasons why the manner in which politics were racialized changed in Europe after 1945. Another, equally important, factor was the process of decolonization that was well under way by the 1950s. Although direct political control over colonies was conceded, often after direct armed struggle, European and North American capital wished to retain economic control as far as was possible and this necessitated no longer defining the emerging ruling classes as members of an inferior "race." For this same reason, European and North American policy toward South Africa changed to the extent that political opposition toward the manner and content of the means of domination of its ruling class was expressed while trade and investment continued relatively unhindered. The necessary desire to maintain the international domination of capital was not the sole determinant of this changing ideological content of ruling-class ideology, but it provided the parameters for such a change. It also had major repercussions within European and, particularly, American societies. The contradiction between political legitimation of the American ruling class in terms of "freedom" and "equality," when combined with changing world political relationships in the 1950s and 1960s, was clearly contradicted by the position and experience of the African-descended population within the USA. The result was the rebellion and revolt of those who were the object of that contradiction, and, as a longer term consequence, a redefinition by the exploited of what "race" meant to them.

This general process was neither uniform nor universal. Moreover, it did not mean that the idea of "race" was removed from political discourse. Rather, although the language of biological racism was removed from bourgeois politics, the language of "race" remained and was accompanied by assertions of cultural inferiority. Only the neo-fascist right retained the "old" racism; parliamentary politicians articulated the "new" racism. The process is particularly clear within Western Europe (in Britain the process is evident in the extreme form) where, since 1945, the racialization of politics has become an internal issue.

Before the major labor migrations beginning in the 1940s, the racialization of politics occurred primarily in connection with colonial affairs. The political reaction to these migrations was at first out of step with the economic reaction: capitalists required labor power and so welcomed migrant labor as a solution to their problem. But there was a hostile political reaction from the start, and this gained in strength through the 1960s. The hostility was expressed by drawing attention to cultural differences and by linking these with the idea of "race" (in that the migrants were identified primarily by certain phenotypical features). On the basis of this new form of racialization, a wide range of racist legislation was passed in different European countries to confine the migrants to a marginal legal/ideological position. In some instances, the legislation preceded and directly structured the entry to migrants.

As a result of this process, "race" is widely defined as a political problem requiring attention and policy decisions in Europe. This is the case irrespective of the fact that not only has the language of nineteenth-century scientific racism been largely absent from official political discourse, but also that elected governments have consistently denied being motivated by, or having institutionalized in law, racism. The official explicitly defined object and problem is "immigrants," but the language and imagery used by all classes to discuss this "problem" draws directly, yet separately, upon that store of late eighteenth- and nineteenth-century racism.

SEE ALSO: colonialism; conservatism; cultural racism; empowerment; fascism; Hanson, Pauline; migration; National Front; neo-nazism; One Nation; Powell, J. Enoch; power; racialization; science; systemic racism; white backlash culture

Reading

Critical Ethnicity: Countering the waves of identity politics, edited by Robert H. Tai and Mary L. Kenyatta (Rowman & Littlefied, 1999), is a collection of essays from scholars, each examining a facet of identity politics.
The New Politics of Race: From Du Bois to the 21st century, edited by Marlese Durr (Praeger, 2002), is a collection of essays, ranging from white backlash culture to occupational mobility.
Race and Racism in Britain, 3rd edn., by John Solomos (Macmillan/Palgrave, 2001), is an introduction to the politics of racism and provides a framework in which to understand trends and developments.
Racism, edited by Martin Bulmer and John Solomos (Oxford University Press, 1999), contains a section "Racism and the state" which has five readings, taken from around the world.
Rethinking Multiculturalism by Bikhu Parekh (Macmillan/Palgrave, 2000) addresses theoretical questions about such matters as national identity, citizenship, and political discourse.

ROBERT MILES

POST-RACE

The prefix "post" has been attached to a range of phenomena, including various strands within social theory, as an indication of the move from the early modern through to the "late," "high" or "postmodern" era. Despite no real agreement as to how best define this term or its relationship to the linked term post-structuralism, it seems that we can at least acknowledge that it is intended to mark an end to the grand theories which characterized much of the modern era; to sign a move away from universalizing accounts of the social world and a shift in focus to issues of diversity, dispersal and contradiction. Much academic work that investigates identity now uses some kind of post-structural or postmodern theories of the self. A major part of this work shifts analyses from constructive approaches to *deconstructive* approaches to social categories that make up our sense of who we are, our identity; with one of the most important being race. Such theorizing is connected to debates about globalization, flows of information, technologies and people, and the loss of simple discrete categories for classifying groups or communities. Within these new world relations everything becomes multiplicitous, fluid, changeable and porous. Academic disciplines such as sociology and cultural studies and postcolonial studies have begun to theorize race and racism, colonialism and imperialism in ways that consider not only how to combat discrimination in its current form, but also how to bring about a post-race era in which current forms of racist discrimination will no longer be meaningful.

For purely analytic purposes we can identify two strands to post-race thinking. These are, in reality, neither discrete nor antagonistic, but do have different emphases in their approach to the problem of racism arising from ideas of race.

Social constructionism still holds to the idea of race as some kind of ontological category, a real foundation for what one "is," and thus provides the basis for questions about equality and difference – and how they may be tied to a "racial identity." It is on this basis that the 1980s saw the rise in what is commonly known as "identity politics," the political fight against discrimination based on one's identity as, for example, Asian or black. Such a position excluded groups such as Muslims and Jews and as such was inadequate to the task of challenging "racism" and "racialism" in all their forms.

From this position it follows that instead of uncritically focusing on race, which is an erroneous social construction, we need to incorporate ethnicity and culture as sites of struggle and discrimination, and as articulating factors in what race itself is.

This first way of thinking about postracial potential is to be found in a whole range of writing, which argues that race is in fact constituted "along the axis of ethnicity." Many authors challenge simple discussions of multiculturalism and a tolerance for difference, arguing that all kinds of racism are in fact better analyzed by drawing on theories of culture and ethnicity. Utilizing the concept of "new ethnicities" Stuart Hall argued against an essentialized black subject and pointed to the diversity within the category "Black," and its contingency. Writers such as Les Back have shown that antiracist work in multicultural locations has to be conducted with an appreciation of these new and complex ethnic identities that are not based on simple notions of, for example, "blackness" that is based on skin color or "pure" ethnic or national heritage, but are part of new hybridized forms of identification. By researching race in this way it becomes "ordinary"; one aspect of political action that must be seen to articulate with others such as cultural discrimination, class discrimination, and so on.

The second, rather more contentious, post-race position suggest that race is itself "performative," that it is a set of practices, citations, utterances and expressions that "materialize" the body through their repetition and reiteration. Judith Butler has argued that gender is performative, and that race too may be seen in the same way.

Deconstructive approaches look to move us into thinking about the possibilities for post-race thinking by dismantling the foundations to the meanings of race and "emptying it out" as a category. There can be no certainty that, for example, race is based upon meanings attached to skin color – because the very uncertainty of "skin color" is emphasized. The meanings attached to skin color may change, and the body and skin itself are also changeable, through tanning, skin whitening, aging and so on. Culture itself has also been reconfigured to find a new way of understanding that it is a dynamic and changing process of constant change and creolization – that there are no *originary* cultures – just many influenced by a huge range of things. Such methods of analysis are extremely useful to the complexity of invisible categories such as whiteness, or European ethnic identities such as that of Italian migrants.

There are, inevitably, critiques of post-race thinking, and those who hold to the idea of race as an ontological category of being especially are skeptical about both losing the "fact" of race, whether through emphasizing its embeddedness in ethnic and cultural processes or – more seriously – its abolition through deconstruction. In addition, whilst those who fall within the first category (see above) are clearly emphasizing that the social meanings of racism are as real as ever, on a theoretical level the second stance has been charged as apolitical – or rather with being an attack on the politics of race for which many have fought bitter battles to gain recognition for. However, there are increasing numbers of writers, such as Anne-Marie Fortier, who are using such approaches with empirical work in ways that draw upon the realities of racial economies in contemporary societies.

SEE ALSO: beauty; colonial discourse; creole; cultural identity; culture; dress; essentialism; globalization; Hall, Stuart; hybridity; postcolonial; race: as signifier; representations; whiteness

Reading

Between Camps: Nations, cultures and the allure of race by Paul Gilroy (Penguin, 1999) is the most clear call for post-race thinking; it should be read in conjunction with *Migrant Belongings: Memory, space identity* by Anne-Marie Fortier (Berg, 2000), which uses post-structuralism and cultural theory in an ethnography about Italian communities in England.

Bodies that Matter: On the discursive limits of sex by Judith Butler (Routledge, 1993) continues to develop the theories of performativity and introduces a racial analysis; the same author's *Gender Trouble: Feminism and the subversion of identity* (Routledge,1990) is influential.

New Ethnicities and Urban Culture: Racism and multiculture in young lives by Les Back (UCL Press, 1997) is a wonderful ethnographic study using young people in south London that shows the interplay of culture and ethnicity in urban environments.

"Reading racialised bodies: learning to see difference" by Suki Ali, in *Cultural Bodies: Theory and ethnography*, edited by H. Thomas and J. Ahmed (Blackwell, 2003), uses the author's ethnographic material to explore the potential for post-race identities; this may profitably be read in conjunction with a special edition of the journal *Ethnic and Racial Studies* (vol. 25, no. 4, July 2002) which looks at the "future of race" in Britain.

"The third space: interview with Homi Bhabha" in Jonathon Rutherford's edited collection *Identity: Community, culture difference* (Lawrence & Wishart, 1990) lays out Bhabha's thoughts on hybridity and cultural translation.

SUKI ALI

POSTCOLONIAL

A term used to describe theoretical and empirical work that centralizes the issues emerging from colonial relations and their aftermath, colonial here meaning the implanting of settlements by imperial powers on distant territories. The "post" aligns it with other intellectual movements, such as postfeminism, postmodernism and, most significantly, post-structuralism, in that it connotes a transition beyond more obsolete discourses; in this case, an age or historical epoch (colonialism) *and* a type of theorizing (nationalistic anticolonial critique). Its ascent in popularity coincided with the descent of the older "Third World" paradigm.

A product largely of European and US academies, postcolonial discourse concerns itself not only with the former colonies that gained independence following World War II, but with the experiences of people descended from inhabitants of those territories and their experiences in the metropolitan centers of the "First World" colonial powers – with the diaspora. It focuses on the institutional forces that shape and set limits on the representation of what have been/are considered subordinate humans and on the efforts of those subordinated groups to challenge the representations.

Postcolonial literary theory concerns itself with the analysis of texts produced by all societies in some way affected by colonial regimes, both colonizer and colonized. Edward Said's "contrapuntal reading" of Joseph Conrad's *Heart of Darkness*, for example, uncovers "a structure of attitude and reference" that animates and articulates the relationship between England and Africa in the nineteenth century.

Postcolonial theory encompasses the work of a wide variety of writers from diverse backgrounds, including Frantz Fanon, Jean-Paul Sartre, and Gayatri Spivak. Its critics include Carole Boyce Davies, who objects to it on a number of counts, including the fact that it is too premature a formulation, it is ahistorical and it "remales and recenters resistant discourses by women." The last point refers to the tendency of postcolonial theory to become a single narrative, what Davies calls "the center announcing its own political agenda without reference to indigenous self-articulations." In becoming integrated into "theory," postcolonial work has become the property of Western (male-dominated) academies, even if the writing is by scholars who have no heritage in the West.

SEE ALSO: colonial discourse; cultural racism; development; diaspora; essentialism; Fanon, Frantz; globalization; hybridity; inferential racism; Irish; migration; Other; post-race; subaltern; whiteness

Reading

Black Women, Writing and Identity by Carole Boyce Davies (Routledge, 1994) contains the critique outlined in the main text above.

Post-colonial Studies: The key concepts, edited by Bill Ashcroft, Gareth Griffiths and Helen Tiffin (Routledge, 2000), is an accessible, alphabetically organized introduction to the entire field of study.

The Post-colonial Studies Reader, edited by Bill Ashcroft, Gareth Griffiths and Helen Tiffin (Routledge, 1994), pulls together a wide range of writings by, among others, Fanon, Spivak and Said; it may be read in conjunction with a similar text, *Colonial Discourse and Post-colonial Theory*, edited by Patrick Williams and Laura Chrisman (Harvester Wheatsheaf, 1993).

Postcolonialism: Critical concepts in literary and cultural studies, edited by Diana Brydon (Routledge, 2000), is a comprehensive five-volume set, packed with essays.

The Turbulence of Migration: Globalization, deterritorialization and hybridity by Nikos Papastergiadis (Polity Press, 1999) engages with the work of Spivak,

Bhaba and Canclini to map the new forms of migration around the world.

The Wretched of the Earth (Grove Press, 1964) and *Black Skin, White Masks* (Grove Press, 1967) by Frantz Fanon are seminal texts about which post-colonial theorists rhapsodize; Fanon's influences include Hegel, Marx, Freud, and Nietzsche.

POWELL, J. ENOCH (1912–98)

Powell was a controversial member of the British Conservative Party, whose speech in his home-town Birmingham in 1968 sparked one of the most contentious and conflictual discourses on race relations of the twentieth century.

"Those whom the gods wish to destroy, they first make mad," warned Powell. "We must be mad, literally mad, as a nation, to be permitting the annual inflow of some 50,000 dependants, who are for the most part the material of the future growth of the immigrant-descended population." In a notable 1968 speech, Powell, in allusion to Virgil's prophecy of war, spoke of "the River Tiber flowing with much blood," predicting that "in this country in fifteen or twenty years' time, the black man will have the whip hand over the white man" (the text of the speech can be found in Seymour-Ure's book listed below).

The now-infamous speech had a mixed reception from newspapers, some decrying the sentiments, others applauding them. Whatever the tenor of the response, it was forceful. Front-page headlines included RACE BLOCKBUSTER (*Sunday Express*, April 21), EXPLOSIVE RACE SPEECH (*Sunday Times*, April 21) and RACE ROW (*Daily Mirror*, April 22). For ten solid days, there was coverage of Powell's speech and its possible repercussions, two immediate ones of which were his dismissal from the Shadow Cabinet and, following this, a one-day "we back Powell" strike augmented by a protest march by dockers. A Tory politician receiving such ful-some support of traditional Labour voters is a rare occurrence.

Powell's denials of racism belied some of the implications of his views, which were soon put to overtly racist use. Writing in the 1970s, John Thackara argued this was assisted. "The media reinforce Powell's racism by their failure either to recognize that he uses them as a stage or to ensure that his contentious 'proposals' are put in critical context" (in "The mass media and ra-cism" in *Media, Politics and Culture*, edited by C. Gardner, Macmillan, 1979).

While there were critical evaluations of Po-well's speech, these were largely eclipsed by the more sensationalistic stories. Apart from these, the sheer intensity of the coverage effectively changed the rules of discourse. As Peter Braham wrote of the intense coverage in his 1982 essay "How the media report race," it "signified that what could now be taken for granted in public debate over race and immigration had changed" (in *Culture, Society and the Media*, edited by M. Gurevitch, T. Bennett, J. Curran and J. Woolla-cott, Methuen).

Powell helped shape a new agenda for future discussions about race relations: from 1968, the media, politicians and public debate colluded with Powell's interpretation of the developing situation. Questions revolved around: how migrants should be allowed into Britain and how long before violence erupts? The episode presents an example of what Stuart Hall calls "inferential racism." In contrast to explicit, or overt, racism, inferential racism, as the name suggests, is deduced or interpreted by others. The source – in this case Powell – implied rather than laid bare the racism of his commentary.

Powell was first elected as a Conservative Member of Parliament for the West Midlands city of Wolverhampton (south-west) in 1950; he held the seat for twenty-four years. A strong believer in the value of the free market, Powell resigned as financial secretary to the Treasury in protest at the Conservative government's plans for increased public expenditure in 1958. This preparedness to sacrifice his own political career rather than compromise personally held princi-ples surfaced again ten years later when his "Rivers of Blood" speech virtually guaranteed the end of his career as a front-ranking politician. After his dismissal by Tory leader Edward Heath, Powell continued to attract considerable support, some from neo-nazi elements that were then emerging in the form of the White Defence League (launched in 1957, later in 1960, becom-ing the British National Party), an organization that, after several mutations, continues to main-tain a presence in the early twenty-first century.

Powell claimed he received over 100,000 letters of support in the wake of his speech, though a group of politicians who formed a "Powellite" movement to advance his views never attracted more than 600 members. Other evidence suggested that, while there was, as Elaine Thomas puts it, "extensive interest and community involvement in issues related to immigration and the social tensions it produced, it was mainly directed toward the reduction of discrimination and efforts to promote interracial harmony" ("Muting interethnic conflict in post-imperial Britain: the success and limits of a liberal political approach," in *The Myth of 'Ethnic Conflict'*, edited by B. Crawford and R. D. Lipshutz, University of California Press, 1988). Despite this, the legitimacy that he conferred on antimigrant views contributed to a diffuse racism that permeated Britain in the 1960s, a period when several academic studies confirmed a consistent pattern of exclusion. These studies included W. W. Daniel's *Racial Discrimination in England* (Penguin, 1968), R. B. Davison's *West Indian Migrants* (Institute of Race Relations, 1962), Sheila Patterson's *Immigrants in Industry*, Ceri Peach's *West Indian Migration to Britain* and Peter Wright's *The Coloured Worker in British Industry*, the last three all published in 1968 by Oxford University Press. The most exhaustive survey of the time was modeled on Gunnar Myrdal's huge American study and yielded comparable results: ethnic minorities were "less well-represented than the total population in those occupations usually considered most desirable and over-represented in those considered most undesirable," concluded the *Colour and Citizenship* survey published by the Institute of Race Relations/Oxford University Press and led by E. J. B. Rose, in 1969.

The context in which Powell's speech was received was one of widespread discrimination and uncertainty. Outbreaks of violence against ethnic minorities in 1958 had been interpreted as the result of instability and mounting unemployment. Scapegoating became commonplace. Powell's notoriety may have been attributable to his articulation of ideas and sentiments that were more widely held than suspected. He certainly gave shape and explicitness to what might have been previously formless, implicit ideas. When allied to the exhaustive media coverage he attracted, Powell's ideas all but mandated the kind of political expression of racism not seen in Britain since the anti-Semitism of Oswald Mosley's British Union of Fascists in the 1930s. (The various neo-nazi organizations started by Colin Jordan and Colin Tyndall in the 1950s and 1960s were only ever marginal to mainstream politics.)

Some speculated that Powell's speeches contained the potential of a self-fulfilling prophecy. His contemporary and fellow Tory Quintin Hogg alluded to this when he remarked: "If one is going to say ... that the streets of our country might one day run with blood ... one ought to consider whether in the more immediate future, one's words were more likely to make that happen" (quoted in Seymour-Ure, below).

In the event, the period immediately following Powell's address was relatively calm, systematic racial violence not appearing till the 1970s and the neo-nazi skinheads. By this time, Powell had slid from the public gaze. His attempts to re-enter the debate on race and immigration in the aftermath of the 1981 riots were largely ignored, his colorful language (" ... mistrust and resentment builds up like water filling a cistern ... it is collective instinctive, human, the imperative of territory, possession and identity") were, by then, seen as the ranting of a politician desperate to regain his former standing. He was no longer a Conservative party member, opting to join the Unionists of Northern Ireland and gaining election as the candidate for Down South. He lost his seat in 1992, largely because of boundary changes rather than a loss of popularity. He died in 1998, at the age of 85.

SEE ALSO: British National Party; Hanson, Pauline; inferential racism; law: immigration, Britain; law: race relations, Britain; media; migration; National Front; nationalism; One Nation; politics; race: as synonym; racist discourse; riots: Britain, 1981; scapegoat

Reading

Enoch Powell by Robert Sheperd (Pimlico, 1997) is a biography of Powell, published just a year before his death.

Immigration and Enoch Powell by Tom Stacy (T. Stacey, 1970) was written in the 1960s at the height of Powell's infamy and relates how Powell's indifference to ethnic minorities conflicted with his ostensibly Christian values; this may usefully be read in combination with Paul Foot's *The Rise of Enoch Powell: An examination of Enoch Powell's attitude on immigration and race* (Cornmarket Press, 1969).

"Muting interethnic conflict in post-imperial Britain: the success and limits of a liberal political approach" in *The Myth of "Ethnic Conflict": Politics, economics and "cultural violence"*, edited by Beverly Crawford and Ronnie D. Lipschutz (University of California International and Area Studies Research Series/no. 98, 1998) sets the wider context in which Powell emerged and subsequently declined; it may be read beneficially with Anthony Messina's *Race and Party Competition in Britain* (Oxford University Press, 1989).

The Political Impact of the Mass Media by Colin Seymour-Ure (Constable, 1974) is dated but contains an account of Powell at a time when his impact was still fresh in people's minds.

POWER

Power refers to the ability to exact a degree of compliance or obedience from others in accordance with one's own will. As such, it is a crucial concept in race and ethnic studies. Power may be vested in individuals, in groups, in whole societies, or even in blocs of societies; the distinguishing feature is the capacity to influence others into performing and, possibly, thinking in accordance with one's own requirements.

There has been great debate over the exact nature of power and there are many different forms. For example, slavery is an extreme example of what might be called "raw power" – an unmitigated coercion based on physical might. It entails one group exercising its will over another through almost total control of circumstances; conformity is enforced through the application of negative sanctions to undesirable behavior. But, as the French philosopher Jean-Jacques Rousseau noticed: "The strongest man is never strong enough to be always master unless he transforms his power into right and obedience into duty."

Sheer compulsion works effectively under some conditions, particularly where there is a large disparity in material resources, but race relations today usually have more complex power relationships entailing a recognition by the power*less* group of the powerholding group's right to exercise its will. For instance, in many situations a group will retain its power because other groups accept the *legitimacy* of its position and so never challenge the unequal relationship. It could plausibly be argued that blacks in the USA, for many years, did not seriously question the legitimacy of the power relationship of which they were part: they acknowledged the right of whites to rule and so accepted their own subordinate position. So the threat of force that lay behind the whites' power in slave days was not necessary to the maintenance of the power relationship.

Power is sometimes operationalized through a unified framework of rules, such as the laws existing in the USA until civil rights legislation.

These institutionalized whites' power and ensured blacks were kept powerless through legal means. The extreme example of this is the law relating to apartheid, which effectively denies nonwhites access to power. This type of arrangement was characterized by the sociologist Max Weber as "rational-legal," but there are alternatives. There may be a "traditional" mode of legitimation in which authority has been vested with one group for a long period of time. On occasions, there may emerge a "charismatic" leader who is attributed with power because his followers believe him or her to be endowed with some special gifts, perhaps from some supernatural agency. In these situations, the ultimate legitimating power may be the "will of God" and such leaders often engender forces for changes in power relationships rather than those securing existing arrangements. Gandhi's successful campaign against British power over India is an obvious example.

The Gandhi case is an illustration of the loss of plausibility of the legitimacy of one power relationship and the gain in plausibility of an alternative. Once legitimacy is lost, then forms of resistance to it are likely to proliferate. Basically, all ethnic struggles are about power relationships. Where there is a diversity of groups with divergent interests and no absolute attribution of legitimacy to a power relationship, a perpetual resistance is likely to take place.

SEE ALSO: Black Power; civil rights movement; colonialism; empowerment; ethnicity; ethnonational; Gandhi, Mohandas Karamchand; hegemony; King, Martin Luther; politics; rational choice theory; slavery; whiteness

Reading

Ethnicity: Racism, class and culture by Steve Fenton (Macmillan, 1999) offers an analysis in which power is central to the articulation of ethnicity and, indeed, racism.

Max Weber: The lawyer as social thinker by Stephen Turner and Regis Factor (Routledge, 1994) is an exposition of the influential theorist's thought; this may be read with the later *Theories of Power and Domination: The politics of empowerment in late modernity* by Angus Stewart (Sage, 2000) which critically assesses contemporary accounts.

Power, Racism and Privilege by William J. Wilson (The Free Press, 1973) is an old but enduringly useful analysis of race relations that uses a power framework and some good comparative material.

Race, Ethnicity and Power by Donald Baker (Routledge & Kegan Paul, 1983) remains a model study of the way in which power has factored into ethnic relations in Australia, North America, and southern Africa.

PREJUDICE

From the Latin *prae*, before, *judicium*, judgment, this may be defined as learned beliefs and values that lead an individual or group of individuals to be biased for or against members of particular groups prior to actual experience of those groups. Technically then, there is positive and negative prejudice, though, in race and ethnic relations, the term usually refers to the negative aspect when a group inherits or generates hostile views about a distinguishable group based on generalizations. These generalizations are invariably derived from inaccurate or incomplete information about the other group.

For example, we might say a person (or group) is prejudiced against Asians; we mean that they are oriented toward behaving with some hostility toward Asians (that behavior is called discrimination). The person believes that, with the odd exception, all Asians are pretty much the same. But the general characteristics they attribute to Asians are faulty. The generalization is called stereotyping, and means assigning properties to any person in a group regardless of the actual variation among members of the group. In a recent piece of research it was found that many white residents of British housing developments were prejudiced against Asians, believing them all to be, among other things, "unhygienic, crafty, and antiwhite." The views were not gleaned from valid experience, but from hearsay or secondhand images.

Such prejudices might not be restricted to ethnic groups, but can be used for virtually any group (including whole nations or continents) to which generalized characteristics can be applied. Thus, individual members of those groups are denied the right to be recognized and treated as individuals with individual characteristics.

Examples of this process are rife in history, although the anti-Semitism of World War II stands out: millions were identified as sharing alleged characteristics because of their Jewish background. Gross generalizations were made about Jews and these were used as the basis of all manner of atrocities.

In the aftermath of the war, a large-scale study of prejudice was made by Theodor Adorno and his colleagues. Published in 1950, *The Authoritarian Personality* concluded that certain people are prejudiced because their prejudices meet certain needs associated with their personality. Further, those who were highly prejudiced were likely to have authoritarian personalities; they tended to be submissive and obedient to authority and to reject "out-groups" in a punitive way. They also saw people in dichotomous terms – "either you're with us or against us."

The upshot of this was that, if prejudice was bound up with a fundamental type of personality, people with this type of personality would be prejudiced not just against one particular "out-group" but against all people and groups who were considered different in some way.

This general and complex form of prejudice the researchers called *ethnocentrism*, as contrasted to the more one-dimensional *anti-Semitism*. This ethnocentrism referred to a tendency to regard one's own group as the standard and all other, different groups as strange and, usually, inferior. One's own ways of thinking and behaving were seen as normal, the natural way of doing things. The main finding of the research was that there was a strong relationship between this consistently high degree of prejudice against all "out-groups" and a personality with the following features: possession of "conventional values;" intolerance of weakness; rigidity of beliefs and views; tendency to be punitive and suspicious; respectful of authority to an extreme degree. Hence the "authoritarian personality."

Adorno *et al.* traced the development of this personality complex and prejudice to early childhood experiences in families tending to be harshly disciplinarian. As a child, the possessor of an authoritarian personality was insecure, dependent on, fearful of, and unconsciously hostile toward parents. As an adult he or she has a high amount of pent-up anger which, because of basic insecurity, manifests itself in a displaced aggression against powerless groups. At the same time, the individual remains respectful of and obedient toward those in authority.

Though *The Authoritarian Personality* has become a classic study of the causes of prejudices, modern psychologists and sociologists have tended to take the emphasis away from unconscious childhood conflicts and to lay it instead on pressures and influences in the social context. In particular, many have pointed to prejudice as a matter of learning: people simply pick up prejudices against groups from others with whom they identify. Those others may be parents or they may be peers. Either way the individual feels a pressure to conform, and so adjusts their views accordingly. This helps explain why prejudices seem to pass from one generation to the next. Thomas Pettigrew has argued in *The Sociology of Race Relations: Reflections and reform* (Collier Macmillan, 1980) that although personality features may account for some prejudice, the greater proportion of it stems from a straightforward conformity to prevalent standards. So that if one grows up in an environment in which all those with Spanish-sounding names are regarded as imbeciles fit only for menial work, then one strongly feels a pressure to align one's own negative prejudices to conform with this generalization.

Other explanations also invoke social factors. For example, the phenomenon known as scapegoating implicates minority groups in situations that are not of their own making, yet produces high amounts of prejudice against them. A general social decline might lead to a sharp contraction of the job market and a general deterioration in material conditions. The underlying causes of decline may be complex, so people may look for something more immediate and locate it in the form of a minority group. So an immigrant or minority group might be made into a scapegoat and negative prejudices against that group can be created.

Prejudice, then, can be explained as a result of childhood experiences, the pressure to conform, or scapegoating. There are many other explanations; it can be approached as an individual or a social phenomenon. But, however it is explained, one must consider it an important factor in race and ethnic relations. For being aware of another group's presence and holding negative values and beliefs about that group bears a crucially strong influence on how behavior toward that group will be organized and, therefore, on the general pattern of race relations.

SEE ALSO: anti-Semitism; bigotry; children; Dollard, John; ethnocentrism; inferential racism; Other; racial coding; racial discrimination; rational choice theory; scapegoat; stereotype; xenophobia

Reading

The Authoritarian Personality by T. S. Adorno, E. Frenkel-Brunswick, D. J. Levinson, and R. N. Sanforo (Harper & Row, 1950) is the most influential study of prejudice since the war.

The First R: How children learn race and racism by Debra Van Ausdale and Joe R. Feagin (Rowman & Littlefield, 2000) is drawn from Van Ausdale's original research and shows how children as young as three exhibit racist attitudes; the research should be compared with the earlier *How Young Children Perceive Race* by Robyn M. Holmes (Sage, 1995), which was also based on empirical work.

The Nature of Prejudice by Gordon W. Allport (Perseus, 1979) is the "25th anniversary edition" of the 1954 text, which was, in its day, a major statement on the psychology of race relations; it remains an impressive, scholarly account of the causes of, and solutions to, prejudice.

Peer Prejudice and Discrimination: The origin of prejudice, 2nd edn., by Harold D. Fishbein (Lawrence Erlbaum, 2002), is very basic, but contains some useful reminders.

Race and Ethnic Conflict: Contending views on prejudice, discrimination and ethnoviolence, 2nd edn., edited by Fred L. Pinchus and Howard J. Ehrlich (Westview Press, 1998), reviews the psychological research on prejudice and tries to align this with perspectives derived from sociology, political science and other social sciences.

Understanding Prejudice, Racism and Social Conflict, edited by Martha Augoustinos and Katherine Jane Reynolds (Sage, 2001), investigates the several levels at which prejudice is expressed: individual, interpersonal, intergroup, and institutional.

PROTOCOLS OF THE LEARNED ELDERS OF ZION

The Protocols of the Learned Elders of Zion is an infamous and, in many ways, mythical text, first published in Russia in 1903, which purports to be the minutes of a secret meeting of Jews held in the early years of the twentieth century in which plans for world domination are outlined. It has been exposed as a hoax, but continues to inspire anti-Semitic, neo-nazi and other forms of hate groups. In the text, Jews were depicted as organizers of an intricate conspiracy geared to take over the world's major financial institutions. It was originally used by the Russian tsars as a rationale for the oppressive policies against Jews, but also, in the 1920s, by the industrialist Henry Ford, who owned a newspaper which issued constant attacks on Jews. Ford later apologized. Many US-based white supremacist groups affiliated to the Aryan Nations subscribe to the central tenet of the text, i.e. that of a world Zionist conspiracy.

SEE ALSO: anti-Semitism; Aryan; Doomed Races

Doctrine; Ku Klux Klan; Oklahoma bombing; pogrom; scapegoat; violence; white backlash culture; White Power; white race; whiteness; xenophobia

Reading

The Protocols of the Learned Elders of Zion by Sergyei A. Nilus, translated from the Russian by Victor E Marsden: available at *ftp://ftp.std.com/obi/Rants/ Protocols/The_Protocols_of_The_Learned_Elders_ of_Zion*
CHECK: internet resources section

PRUITT-IGOE

The name of two areas in St. Louis that were designated by city planners as the sites of a large-scale housing project. In the early 1950s, big, high-rise apartment blocks situated in grounds intentionally left open for the use of both the resident and surrounding community were erected in the two areas.

The project was developed in the spirit of good ethnic relations, the idea being that blacks would live more harmoniously together and away from whites. Originally, the plan was to house whites in one estate and blacks in the other, but the US Supreme Court considered this unconstitutional, and the two areas were eventually occupied by some 10,000 mostly black residents. The first families moved in during 1954; by 1959, the project had become a total scandal, not only because of the unusual architecture but because of the high incidence of crime, vandalism, and prostitution. Its unattractiveness was reflected in its vacancy rate, which exceeded that of any housing complex in the USA.

Lee Rainwater studied the area and noted: "The original tenants were drawn very heavily from several land clearance areas in the inner city.... Only those Negroes [*sic*] who are desperate for housing are willing to live in Pruitt-Igoe."

The place became a "dumping ground" for poor blacks. Street violence became an everyday occurrence, robbery was commonplace and buildings were allowed to deteriorate. Families left as quickly as possible: a vacancy rate of 65 percent attested to the ultimate failure of the project. Twelve years after its construction, Pruitt-Igoe was quite literally blown up.

The "public housing monstrosity," as Oscar Newman called it, served as a reminder of the negative effects of projects based on *de facto* segregation.

A similar policy almost materialized in Britain in 1978 when the Greater London Council announced its proposal for a "racially segregated" area for Bengalis in the Tower Hamlets borough. Its divisiveness was, however, noted and it came to nothing. Herding is a simple "response" to inner-city problems, but is in no sense a solution to them; it submits to people's prejudices and fears and can lead to the artificial creation of vast ghettos – as Pruitt-Igoe demonstrates.

SEE ALSO: disadvantage; environmental racism; ghetto; homelessness; housing; institutional racism; integration; racial profiling; segregation; social exclusion; systemic racism

Reading

Behind Ghetto Walls by Lee Rainwater (Penguin, 1973) is a study of life as lived by the residents of Pruitt-Igoe and includes an assessment of the effects.
Defensible Space by Oscar Newman (Architectural Press, 1972) is an analysis of how people's physical environments can affect their social behavior, with particular attention taken of Pruitt-Igoe.
Ethnicity and Housing: Accommodating differences, edited by Frederick W. Boal (Ashgate, 2000) is a sizable collection of essays gathered from scholars all over the world.

PSYCHOLOGY *see* Dollard, John; prejudice; scapegoat

PUERTO RICANS IN THE USA

About a third of the total Puerto Rican population lives in the USA, with over half of that migrant group domiciled in New York City. Between 800,000 and 900,000 Puerto Ricans live in New York, around twice as many as live in San Juan, the capital city of Puerto Rico.

Puerto Rico itself is a Caribbean island about 1,000 miles southeast of Florida. It was conquered by the Spanish and made into a slave colony with the introduction of African labor in the early sixteenth century. The dominant cultural influence remains Spanish. After the Spanish-American War, Puerto Rico was given to the United States under the terms of the Treaty of Paris, 1898, and was granted a measure of local government until 1917 when Puerto Ricans were declared citizens of the United States. This precipitated a migration to the mainland.

Improvements in health and sanitation on the island produced a decline in the death-rate, thus swelling Puerto Rico's population and putting pressure on the economy. This hastened migration in the pursuit of employment; access to the USA was simplified by the availability of citizenship and migration increased rapidly in the 1920s.

Natural disasters in 1928 and 1932 devastated coffee plantations (the major source of income for the island) and stimulated more migration. World War II curtailed the movement, but the development of inexpensive air travel after the war (e.g. to New York in six hours for about $50) resulted in a mass migration. By 1973, almost five million people were traveling to and from the USA in search of work they could not find in their homeland.

New York became the center of gravity for migrants, particularly the area of East Harlem called *El Barrio* (the neighborhood), which is still the prototype Puerto Rican ghetto. Like most other immigrants, Puerto Ricans faced problems of family fragmentation, inadequate living conditions, poor health, exploitation at work, the handicaps of language and education, and the underlying obstacles of racialism. These had the effect of binding them together and the perception of sharing common problems produced a vigorous ethnicity.

With little improvement, ethnicity was sustained and had the perhaps unwanted consequence of compounding the deprivation. Oscar Lewis, in his study of Puerto Ricans in New York, describes a "culture of poverty" in which Puerto Ricans grow up in a tightly bonded community and assimilate poverty as a way of life instead of trying to break away from it. Catholicism is all-pervasive and enhances the sense of group identity, and family solidarity has worked as a kind of fetter to social and geographical mobility. Often, educational and occupational advancement necessitates moving away from the community and therefore from the family unit (which is rather large – about four people – compared to the New York average). Adherence to this culture alone vitiates any prospect of betterment and locks the Puerto Rican into a world of fatalism and the kind of street violence portrayed in *West Side Story*.

The indications are that today's Puerto Ricans are trying to advance in both education and occupations, but at the expense of family solidarity and, ultimately, Puerto Rican ethnicity. Marrying outside the ethnic group will also work to weaken the sense of community and identity Puerto Ricans have displayed since the war.

SEE ALSO: ethnicity; Latinos; minorities; racial profiling; segregation

Reading

La Vida: A Puerto Rican family in the culture of poverty – San Juan and New York by Oscar Lewis (Secker & Warburg, 1967) is a classic study of Puerto Rican life, rich in illustrations and theoretically strung together by the author's "culture of poverty" thesis.

Puerto Ricans: Born in the USA by Clara E. Rodriguez (Westview Press, 1989) is a slightly dated but thoughtful portrait of the condition of Puerto Ricans.

The Semiotics of Exclusion: Puerto Rican experiences of language, race and class by Bonnie Urciuoli (Westview Press, 1996) is a study based on ethnography and interviews and maps the experiences of working-class Puerto Ricans in the USA.

R

RACE: AS CLASSIFICATION

A group or category of persons connected by common origin. The word entered the English language at the beginning of the sixteenth century; from then until early in the nineteenth century it was used primarily to refer to common features present because of shared descent. But it was also used more loosely, as when John Bunyan in 1678 wrote "of the Way and Race of Saints," or, a little over 100 years later, Robert Burns addressed the haggis as "the chieftain o' the pudding race." The literary usage to designate the descendants of an ancestral figure, or as a synonym for nation, continues to the present day, although it now appears archaic. Since the beginning of the nineteenth century the word has been used in several other distinct senses. It is important to notice these changes in the use of the word in order to avoid any assumption that there is one scientifically valid way of using it. Physical differences catch people's attention so readily that they are less quick to appreciate that the validity of race as a concept depends upon its use as an aid in explanation. From this standpoint the main issue is not what "race" is but the way it is used. People draw upon beliefs about race, as they draw upon beliefs about nationality, ethnicity, and class, as resources for cultivating group identities.

The changes in the way the word race has been used reflect changes in the popular understanding of the causes of physical and cultural differences. Up to the eighteenth century at least, the chief paradigm for explaining such differences was provided by the Old Testament. This furnished a series of genealogies by which it seemed possible to trace the peopling of the world and the relations that different groups bore to one another. Differences of outward appearances could then be interpreted in one of three ways: firstly, as part of God's design for the universe; secondly, as caused by environmental differences irrelevant to moral issues; thirdly, as arising from different original ancestors. In any event, the dominant meaning attaching to the word race was that of descent. In the early nineteenth century increased knowledge about the differences between the world's peoples suggested to many people that they were part of a more general pattern of natural differences encompassing the animal and vegetable kingdoms. Under the influence of Georges Cuvier, the French comparative anatomist, such differences were seen as expressing distinctive types. "Type" was defined as a primitive or original form independent of climatic or other physical differences. Types were thought to be permanent (for this was a pre-Darwinian view of nature). Race came to be used in the sense of type as designating species of men distinct both in physical constitution and mental capacities. This conception survives to the present and forms the core of the doctrines often designated "scientific racism."

Darwin showed that no forms in nature were permanent. His work led to a new interpretation according to which the physical differences between people stem from their inheriting different genes. Race (or geographical race in Darwin's vocabulary) became a synonym for subspecies, i.e. a subdivision of a species that is distinctive only because its members are isolated from other individuals belonging to the same species. If their isolation did not reduce opportunities for mating between these populations, the distinctiveness of their gene pools would be reduced. The theory of natural selection and the establishment of genetics as a field of experimental research had revolutionary implications for the study of racial differences, but it took some two generations for these implications to be properly appreciated. For half a century after the publication of Darwin's *Origin* in 1859, anthropologists continued to propose racial classifications of *Homo sapiens* in the belief that in this way the nature of the differences could be better understood. Subsequent research suggests, to the contrary, that classifications based upon phenotypical variation are of very limited value and that it is of more use to ascertain the frequency with which various genes occur in different populations.

In 1935, Sir Julian Huxley and A. C. Haddon maintained that the groups in Europe that were commonly called races would be better designated "ethnic groups." They wrote that "it is very desirable that the term race as applied to human groups should be dropped from the vocabulary of science. ... In what follows the word race will be deliberately avoided and the term *(ethnic) group* or *people* employed."

Too few have followed their advice. In the English-speaking countries "race" is widely used as a social construct. For example, in the USA, a person of, say, one-eighth African ancestry and seven-eighths European ancestry, may account himself or herself black and be so accounted by others. This assignment follows a social rule, not a zoological one. In most other countries such a person would not be accounted black. In France (and in some other non-English-speaking countries), the English-language expression "race relations" is regarded as misconceived if not racist. Yet it would be difficult to stop the use of race as a social construct and substitute references to ethnicity, because the idiom of race is important to measures for combating racial discrimination. In Britain, as in some other countries, the law prohibits discrimination "on racial grounds" and provides protection to "persons not of the same racial group." The use of the expression "race" in the law, in the census, and in official documents, may appear to give government sanction to a classification which is no longer of explanatory value in zoology, and to keep alive a pre-Darwinian belief that it is important to the understanding of differences which are now known to be of a social, cultural, and economic character.

SEE ALSO: Darwinism; Doomed Races Doctrine; geometry of race; race: as signifier; race: as synonym; science; social Darwinism; UNESCO; whiteness

Reading

The Concept of Race, edited by Ashley Montagu (The Free Press, 1964), is a useful collection of essays which might profitably be read in conjunction with the 6th edn. of the same author's *Man's Most Dangerous Myth: The fallacy of race* (AltaMira, 1998, originally published 1942).

Race: The history of an idea in the West by Ivan Hannaford (Johns Hopkins University Press, 1996) traces the "confused pedigree" of the concept.

The Race Concept by Michael Banton and Jonathan Harwood (David & Charles, 1975) is an elementary history combined with a simple scientific exposition of the concept.

We Europeans: A survey of racial problems by Julian S. Huxley and A. C. Haddon (Cape, 1935) is the early text that recognized the inappropriateness of race when applied to human populations.

MICHAEL BANTON

RACE: AS SIGNIFIER

In contrast to other approaches to race, discourse analysis treats "race" (the quotation marks are conventional) as a *signifier* – an utterance, sound or image whose meanings are made possible only by the application of rules or codes. So the meanings of race are encoded and may be decoded only within the parameters of the discourse. The indeterminacy of "race" (and, for that matter, all signifiers) provides for its *polysemy*, or openness of interpretation (the term polysemy is preferred to ambiguity, which suggests only a double meaning). "Race" is a shifting signifier that means different things to different parties at different points in history and defies definitive explication outside specific contexts. The manner in which the signifier "race" is decoded and read by subjects is known as *signified*, and this again is made possible only through appeal to discursive rules.

The approach moves beyond the critique of "race" as a biological misnomer or even as a synonym for cultural difference: it is interested in the popular usage of the term. "Race" is removed from its status as something with characteristics and stable features and conceived instead as diffuse; how it is used in a discourse is of paramount concern. Decentering the concept in this way necessarily changes the way it is analyzed.

"Race," it is contended by Gates, has become "a trope of ultimate, irreducible difference between cultures, linguistic groups, or adherents of specific belief systems . . . it is so very arbitrary in its application." The concept has sutured otherwise vague and possibly incoherent beliefs about white supremacy by synonymizing skin color and other phenotypical features with deviance and inferiority.

The admission of the word into our language and so into the discourse enables and encourages us to *will* the sense of natural difference into our formulations. For Gates: "To do so is to engage in a pernicious act of language, one which exacerbates the complex problem of cultural or ethnic difference rather than to assuage or redress it."

In other words, the mere mention of "race" commissions our understanding of a permanent difference and hence a conception of "Otherness." Criticism of the term "race" and disclosures of its redundancy as an analytical construct have destabilized and dismembered the understanding of "race" as a meaningful criterion in biological and social sciences, but as long as contemporary conversations continue to include the word, its potency remains. This is so because "race" purports to describe something, but simultaneously inscribes difference.

The focus then is on language not merely as a conveyor of the word and the assembly of beliefs and metaphors it embodies, but as a sign of difference, cultural as well as biological, and a way of maintaining space between superordinate and subordinate groups. Language is both a medium and an active constituent in the process of "racializing."

Cultures are never impermeable and the signifier "race" appears in various cultures of resistance to colonial and racist orders. W. E. B. Du Bois wrote of this in his *The Souls of Black Folk* (first published in 1903) when he argued that a creative solution to the divisiveness of "race" should be sought. Indiscriminate and wholesale attacks on white or Western culture were not productive. He warned against separatist nationalism which was a reaction rather than an imaginative response and, instead, urged an entry into the discourse of white America to make it acknowledge marginalized and suppressed histories. So, while he rejected "race" as

a unit of hierarchy, his effort actually needed it not so much to occlude or eliminate as to question and expose.

In contemporary conceptions, there is no race "out there" in the domain or biology or any other part of the world; "race" exists only as a way of understanding and interpreting difference through intelligible markers. "Problematizing" the concept in this way creates the possibility of unsettling the intellectual foundations on which it has for so long rested. Writing with this in mind, Rod Brookes uses the phrase "floating signifier" (originally coined by Stuart Hall) to suggest that the apparently unsinkable concept never stays still, but bobbles, changing position and shape at any moment. In his *Representing Sport* (Arnold, 2002), Brookes writes: "In analysing the representation of black athletes in media and sport, as there are no essential meanings but only historically specific ones, it is important to locate these within the specific historical political, economic and social context in which media representations are produced, circulated and consumed."

In other words, few people today may cling to the kind of stereotypes that characterized black athletes as "naturally gifted" or endowed with superhuman capacities. The appearance of black athletes as diverse as Tiger Woods, Mike Tyson, or, in England, Rio Ferdinand have rendered fixed notions of race redundant. What meanings are attributed to these and other figures are neither fixed nor distinct; yet there is still a sense in which their blackness is an apparent feature of the way in which they are popularly addressed, while whiteness is normalized.

SEE ALSO: colonial discourse; cultural racism; double consciousness; Hall, Stuart; hybridity; *Invisible Man*; One Nation; Other; postcolonial; race: as classification; race: as synonym; race card; racism; white backlash culture; white race

Reading

Imperial Leather: Race, gender and sexuality in the colonial conquest by Anne McClintock (Routledge, 1995) explores the historical instability of the concept of race, embracing, as it did, not only colonized peoples, but the Irish, Jews and, at times, prostitutes in what the author calls "the imperial narrative."
"Race," Writing and Difference, edited by Henry L. Gates (University of Chicago Press, 1986), contains several articles previously published in vol. 12 of

Critical Inquiry and addresses aspects of the importance of "race" in literature and its shaping influence as "a persistent yet implicit presence" in the twentieth century.

Racist Culture by David Theo Goldberg (Blackwell, 1995) and "Is there a 'neo-racism'?" by Etienne Balibar, in *Race, Nation, Class*, edited by Balibar and Immanuel Wallerstein (Verso, 1991), both deal with the near-universal norm of "race" and may profitably be read in conjunction with *The Meaning of Race: Race, history and culture in Western society* by Kenan Malik (Macmillan, 1996), a textbook that attempts to reconstruct the "evolution of the modern discourse of race."

The Recovery of Race in America by Aaron David Gresson (University of Minnesota Press, 1995) is about shifts in the "locus of meaning" or race and racism.

RACE: AS SYNONYM

As applied to groups of living organisms, the term "race" has been used in at least four different senses. The most common use of the term in biology has referred to a subspecies, that is, a variety of a species that has developed distinguishing characteristics through isolation, but has not yet lost the ability to interbreed and to produce fertile hybrids with other subspecies of the same species. Today, biologists prefer the term subspecies or breed (in the case of a domesticated species) to "race," and thus avoid the confusion associated with the latter term.

Physical anthropologists used to speak of human "races" in the sense of subspecies, the most common scheme being the great tripartite division of mankind into Negroid, Mongoloid, and Caucasoid. Over the last forty to fifty years, however, it became increasingly clear that no meaningful taxonomy of human races was possible. Not only were numerous groups not classifiable as belonging to any of the three main groups, but physical anthropologists could not agree with each other as to where the genetic boundaries between human groups were to be drawn, or even on how many such groups there were. The essential condition for subspeciation is breeding isolation, often maintained by ecological barriers. Humans, on the contrary, have migrated over large distances and interbred extensively for thousands of years. Especially with the maritime expansion of Europe starting five centuries ago, this process of interbreeding has greatly accelerated, thereby blurring "racial" boundaries, and contributing more than ever to the genetic homogenization of our species.

A second usage of "race" is as a synonym for species, as in the phrase "the human race." That usage is often deliberately antithetical to the first one, when the stress is put on the unity of humankind.

A third meaning of "race" is as a synonym for what we usually call a nation or an ethnic group, as, for example, "the French race" or "the German race." This third usage has become obsolete, but it was common in the nineteenth and early twentieth centuries.

Finally, a "race" can mean a group of people who are *socially* defined in a given society as belonging together because of *physical markers* such as skin pigmentation, hair texture, facial features, stature, and the like. To avoid the confusion, some people specify "social race" when they use "race" in this fourth meaning. Nearly all social scientists *only* use "race" in this fourth sense of a *social* group defined by somatic visibility. It is important to stress here that any resemblance with the first usage is little more than coincidental. For example, "blacks" in South Africa and in Australia, although they occupy somewhat similar *social* positions in their respective societies, are no more closely related genetically to each other than each of them is to the "whites." Even where there is some shared ancestry in broad parental stocks (as, for instance, between the Afro-American populations of Brazil and the USA, both of which came predominantly from West Africa and interbred with Europeans), the same social label may cover very different blends of ancestry. In Brazil, a "black" is a person of predominantly African ancestry, while, in the USA, the term often refers to persons of predominantly European stock who would be called "white" in Brazil.

The significance of racial labels is thus purely a function of the specific content attached to racial terms at a particular time and place. Social races are *not* genetically bounded subspecies. In fact, members of different social races are frequently close kin of each other in many multiracial societies, particularly those with a history of slavery.

It is also important to note that not all societies recognize social races. In fact, the great majority of human societies have not used physical phenotypes as the basis of group distinctions. Where social races exist, there is invariably an attribution of social and behavioral importance to physical markers. Societies that recognize social races are invariably *racist* societies, in the sense that people, especially members of the dominant racial group, believe that physical phenotype is linked with intellectual, moral, and behavioral characteristics. Race and racism thus go hand in hand.

SEE ALSO: apartheid; Darwinism; Doomed Races Doctrine; eugenics; geometry of race; phenotype; pluralism; race: as classification; race: as signifier; science; social Darwinism; race relations: as activity; racism; UNESCO; whiteness

Reading

Cultural Diversity in the United States, edited by Ida Susser and Thomas C. Patterson (Blackwell, 2001), devotes Part II to "The Biology of Difference?" and contains four essays.

The Idea of Race by Michael Banton (Tavistock, 1977) is a thorough investigation of the development of racism in the West.

Man's Most Dangerous Myth: The fallacy of race, 6th edn., by Ashley Monagu (AltaMira, 1998), expands and revises the original 1942 text, covering the *Bell Curve* controversy, ethnic cleansing and other contemporary topics.

Race: The history of an idea in the West by Ivan Hannaford (Johns Hopkins University Press, 1996) is a scholarly dissection of the concept in its historical and political contexts.

Race and Racism by Pierre L. van den Berghe (Wiley, 1978) is a comparison of four societies (Brazil, Mexico, South Africa, and the USA), attributing different degrees of importance to "race."

PIERRE L. VAN DEN BERGHE

RACE CARD

The term "race card" is full of symbolic value and captures much of the racial history in Great Britain, the USA, and other territories. The race card is employed to suggest that: (1) a specific group is being unfairly victimized; or (2) as a mechanism to highlight white interests in a particular political situation. The term is usually given its history starting with the O. J. Simpson trial for the murder of his ex-wife and her friend. Simpson's attorneys were accused of playing the "race card" because of their suggestion that a key detective's motives to pin the murder on O. J. Simpson was the result of racism. Simpson's defense team were accused of relying on racism (real or perceived) to change the tone of the trial away from one focusing on murder to one about racism; that is, black–white relations and issues of power.

According to some observers, various leaders in their quest to end affirmative action and other race-conscious public policies have used the race card. It has also been used in other policy areas such as welfare and crime as a means of swaying public sentiment. The race card was employed in the post-emancipation period in the USA to justify the lynching of blacks and their continued subjugation. Blacks have also used the race card in their quest to end police brutality and socio-economic and political inequalities. Both the left and the right in the debate over immigration employ the race card.

The race card relies on racial stereotypes that are often deeply embedded in society's culture. These stereotypes, which often elevate the dominant group at the expense of all other racial and ethnic groups, serve as political and sociological tools for presenting an ideology of what society should look like and how it should act. As such, it structures the meaning of society.

Use of the race card permeates society through different media, including politics and entertainment for example. It is often employed as a political tactic. George Bush's use of Willie Horton during his 1988 presidential campaign is often cited as a prominent use of the race card. Its use in this instance was relied upon as a tactic to invoke racial fears and resentment. After the 2000 presidential election in the US, some organizations, such as the National Association for the Advancement of Colored People, have employed the race card not only to challenge the election results, but also to rally minorities, specifically African Americans, to vote in future elections.

What the race card produces is a construction of categories of race, a racial hierarchy, and it further suggests how this racial hierarchy should be challenged and by whom. The race card has been used to challenge a system of racial domination and control, but also to maintain a system of domination and control.

SEE ALSO: Barry case, the Marion; inferential racism; race: as signifier; racialization; systemic racism; Simpson case, the O. J.; stereotype; Thomas, Clarence; tokenism; welfare; white backlash culture

Reading

Playing the Race Card: Melodramas of black and white from Uncle Tom to O.J. Simpson by Linda Williams (Princeton University Press, 2001) suggests that to engage in a honest discussion about race relations, in the US context, society must acknowledge the influence of the melodrama of race. Williams traces this melodrama throughout American culture and shows how images of race continue to influence attitudes of racial empathy and enmity.

The Race Card: Campaign strategy, implicit messages, and the norm of equality by Tali Mendelberg (Princeton University Press, 2001) looks at how politicians evoke racial stereotypes, fears, and resentments – that is, play the race card – many times without voters being aware of the fact. Mendelberg argues that politicians often resort to subtle uses of race to win elections. The author uses a number of data sources, including national surveys, and content analysis of campaign coverage to show how politicians manipulate white voters' sentiments without overtly violating egalitarian norms.

Welfare Racism: Playing the race card against America's poor by Kenneth Neubeck and Noel Cazenave (Routledge, 2001) examines the role of racism in shaping public assistance policies and practices. The authors trace the racialized political backlash against welfare from the 1960s to the 1990s.

JULIA S. JORDAN-ZACHERY

RACE RELATIONS: AS ACTIVITY

Race relations describes a specific form of social relations: it emphasizes the operation, activities, processes and what might be termed the mechanisms involved in creating, maintaining and changing relationships between groups that are in some way affected by the apprehension of race. This conceives of race relations less as condition, more as an activity or, perhaps, series of evolving activities.

This type of approach argues that the term race relations can and, indeed, must be applied to a specific form of social relationship. This approach fully recognizes and endorses the hollowness of the concept of race itself, but, at the same time, insists that, in many situations, people believe in the existence of race and so organize their relationships with others on the basis of that belief. In other words, people predicate their relationships with others on what they believe about those others. If they believe those others belong to a group that is genetically and permanently different (and possibly inferior in some respect) then we have a situation of race relations. And this is the object of inquiry.

The exact nature of race is not at issue, though the biological concept has been refuted many times over. The point is, however, that people, rightly or wrongly, accept it as a reality and so act in accordance with their belief. This makes race subjectively real: no matter how offensive we may find race and how unimpressed we are by the (largely spurious) scientific research on it, it remains a powerful motivating force behind people's thoughts and behavior. It is as real as people want it to be and cannot simply be wished away. Recognition of this is the starting point of the study of race relations in this perspective.

This allows for the acceptance of Michael Banton's advice that "the student who wishes to understand the nature of the field of race relations study ... should approach it from the standpoint of the growth of knowledge." Believing in race is tantamount to holding a form of knowledge (even if that knowledge is built on uncertain foundations). This in no way denies the huge influences on race relations which lie outside people's minds and are quite beyond their control. In fact, the approach stresses that study of race relations should proceed at levels: (1) to discover the reasons why people might believe others are so different, culturally or biologically; (2) to find out how this belief affects their actions towards others – this usually takes the form of maintaining social (and often geographical) distance in the attempt to keep unequal relationships; and (3) to analyze the ways the belief and the terminology that complements it are used in such a way as to perpetuate a context in which the concept of race continues to have relevance – a racialized discourse.

Such discourses have been encouraged by globalization. In fact, some authors have argued that an entirely new manifestation of race relations has emerged as a result of global reformations of economic, political and cultural relations. Shifts in global patterns have led to shifts in relations between racialized groups, i.e. those groups that have been seen in racial terms. It follows that race relations should not be seen in domestic, but in international, terms.

This sets the scope of the field very widely because the distinguishing feature of race relations is the consciousness of race, and it is possible to identify many situations and complexes of social relations where this consciousness is present. It will inevitably influence the conduct of social relations, but will almost certainly operate in combination with other influences. Processes of inclusion and exclusion can be heavily influenced by being conscious of race – or racism – yet it need not be assumed that this is the only, nor indeed the strongest, influential factor. Often we cannot decide the contribution that racism makes to the maintenance of a social activity except in evaluative terms. The precise contribution is the topic of empirical inquiry.

Race relations as a program of empirical study seeks to analyze the relations between sets of factors, one of which is racism. If, for example, the phenomenon to be explained – the *explanandum*, in formal terms – is the educational underachievement of black schoolchildren, we may compare samples of black children with their white peers and find something in the experience of black children that accounts for their poor performance. Suspending judgments about innate (genetic) characteristics, we might trace antecedent factors that either lead to or are associated with underachievement. Clearly, there may be a range of factors, many of which do not involve racism. Yet it may be possible to identify factors involving the awareness of race that will exert an influence on the child's ability to achieve at school. This would draw attention to the value of an emphasis on racism as an approach to some of the problems confronting ethnic minorities. Many ethnic minorities may have problems that are not unique to themselves, but which they share with whites. We can proceed to analyze the two with quite different explanatory factors – *explanans* – or precisely the same. The former may reveal racism as something that affects the position of ethnic minorities, while the latter should disclose broad similarities in conditions and experience.

The presence of racism is presumed from the outset. The analysis then takes the form of a search for its origins (in general or particular settings), tracing back in an aetiological manner an elaboration of racist thinking, a consideration of its effects, behavioral and cognitive, and an assessment of its functional importance in the wider culture.

A narrow conception of this program of study might locate the answer to these types of questions in the individual, suggesting for example why certain groups are prejudiced and examining how this has impact on their behavior and relationships over a period of time. The classic study in this vein is *The Authoritarian Personality* by Theodor Adorno and his colleagues (Harper & Row, 1950). The preferred approach would be much wider in scope, seeking to integrate historical analyses of the colonial conditions underlying most contemporary race relations situations with an examination of how culture mediates these situations.

In many instances, globalization has precipitated the social fragmentation that creates the conditions under which race relations come into being (through, for example, widening divisions between black and white workers). But it is proposed that this does not prove that race relations cannot exist independently of globalization; so there may be a close, but not direct, relationship between the two. The present forms that racism takes and the forms it has taken in recent history indicate that it is related to the development of modern capitalism and the widespread political and cultural transformations this has fostered. This does not assume a causal relationship between them, however. Nor even a logical relationship between racism and ethnicity.

Historical and empirical studies do, however, demonstrate a parallelism between the presence and development of racist practices and the cultural and political expression of ethnic bonds. Steve Fenton's work draws on material from, among other places, the USA, Europe and Malaysia to illustrate precisely this point.

Race relations situations are not a perfectly defined series of events, but rather an evolving complex. A mature race relations study should be able to incorporate the investigation of changing events and interpret these in the context of historical, political and social conditions. In this way, it is possible to acknowledge that race as a concept is analytically redundant, yet still identify race relations situations as the focus of study.

SEE ALSO: bigotry; colonialism; ethnicity; ethnocentrism; globalization; Other; post-race; prejudice; race: as signifier; race relations: as construction; racial profiling; racism; slavery; white race

Reading

Contemporary Racisms and Ethnicities: Social and cultural transformations by Mairtin Mac an Ghaill (Open University Press, 1999) offers an unusual perspective, focusing on the fragmentation of social relations due to globalization; in other words, changes in race and ethnic relations are linked to wider changes in culture and politics.

Ethnicity: Racism, class and culture by Steve Fenton (Macmillan, 1999) is the study cited in the main text above and might usefully be read alongside *Race and Power: Global racism in the twenty first century* by Gargi Bhattacharyya, John Gabriel, and Stephen Small (Routledge, 2001) which suggests that race relations have been transformed by globalization.

From Immigrants to Ethnic Minority: Making a black community in Britain by Lorna Chessum (Ashgate, 2000) is a thoughtful historical account of African Caribbeans in Leicester, England; it is a good example of race relations research, examining how racism affected people's identities and behavior and how these, in turn, led to the construction of an "ethnic minority."

Race and Racism in Britain, 3rd edn., by John Solomos (Macmillan Palgrave, 2003) is a textbook in which the first chapter considers various theoretical approaches to race relations.

BARRY TROYNA

RACE RELATIONS: AS CONSTRUCTION

A term used in academic writing and in the everyday world to refer to a particular category of social relations. There is an academic tradition that focuses upon these relations and this has come to be known as the sociology of "race relations," now a distinctive and institutionalized subdiscipline within sociological analysis. However, within and outside that subdiscipline, there is controversy about what characterizes this apparently distinct category of social relations, a controversy which arises from the recognition that *Homo sapiens* is one species. The biological sciences take account of genetic variation, but this does not correspond to what, in the everyday world, is regarded as a difference of "race," founded as it is on phenotypical variation. Hence, "race relations" cannot be naturally occurring relations between discrete, biological groups but have come to be seen as relations between groups which employ the idea of "race" in structuring their action and reaction to each other.

This latter notion of "race relations" links together the pioneering work of Robert Park, John Dollard, W. Lloyd Warner, Gunnar Myrdal, and Oliver C. Cox in the USA, all of whom were concerned in one way or another with "race relations." A large proportion of the work in the United States in the 1950s and 1960s refracted the new political definitions that arose out of the renewed struggle against racism and discrimina-tion but agreed that "race relations" were a real and distinct category of social relations. Hence, for them the idea of "race" was employed with a new positive content as a collective characteristic of the Afro-American population, one that set it apart from the majority American population of European origin. But they agreed that the rela-tions between these two defined groups were "race relations."

This American-derived conception influenced political, media and academic reactions to the labor migration from the New Commonwealth to Britain in the 1950s, although this reaction also drew upon that deep reservoir of imperialist thought about the inferior "races" of the empire. The consequence was that "race relations" "appeared" within Britain in the 1950s, displaced as it were from the colonies or, more particularly, from Africa (especially the ill-fated Central African Federation). Most writers and commentators took this definition, and its history, for granted. Some academics went further and attempted explicitly and analytically to classify "race rela-tions," not only as a discrete category of social relations, but also as having a specific place within sociological theory. The project was de-fined as setting out the defining features of a "race relations" situation and classifying different types of such a situation.

The sociology of "race relations" that has developed from these analytical concerns has been preoccupied with two main themes, first, with assessing the extent and effects of racism and discrimination upon those who have been its object; and second, with the political struggle against racism and discrimination. It is thereby a sociology of conflict which reflects everyday conceptions of what "race relations" are, though it offers a quite different explanation for that conflict from that employed in the everyday world.

More recently, a new line of inquiry has developed which is critical of this tradition of work and which moves toward a rejection of "race relations" as a legitimate form of study. This emerging position is firmly grounded in historical analysis of both the idea of "race" and the academic study of relations between groups who utilize the idea of "race" to organize their social relations. It is concluded from this analysis that because "race" is no more than a socially constructed phenomenon, then so are relations between the groups that are constituted through this social construction. Consequently, there is nothing distinctive about the resulting relations between the groups party to such a social construction. Put another way, what are called "race relations" are quantitatively no different from other forms of social relations.

There remains the problem of determining how such historically and socially constructed relations are, therefore, to be analyzed. To this problem, one can currently distinguish two solutions. The first sees "race and ethnic relations" as a subdivision of a sociology of intergroup relations. This is premised on the observation that a tradition of inquiry has been established and that any new development should be contained within the tradition established by earlier contributors. But, more significantly, it is argued that the circumstances under which individuals are ascribed, or ascribe themselves, to membership of a "race" (together with the varied and various consequences of such ascription) warrant explanation in terms of a theory of intergroup relations. The second position, developed using Marxist categories of analysis, claims that this process of social ascription should be analyzed as an ideological and political process and, for that reason, it cannot employ everyday conceptions of "race" and "race relations" as either descriptive or analytical categories. This leads to the conclusion that there can be no theory of race relations because this only serves to reify what is a historically specific political and ideological process.

SEE ALSO: anthropology; capitalism; Cox, Oliver C.; Dollard, John; equality; ideology; Marxism; Myrdal, Gunnar; nationalism; Park, Robert E.; race relations: as activity; racial profiling; racialization; racism; rational choice theory

Reading

"Progress in ethnic and racial studies" by Michael Banton (in *Ethnic and Racial Studies*, vol. 24, no. 2, 2001) reflects on the knowledge generated by the study of "ethnic and racial relations" and encourages a "wider recognition of the value of theoretical frameworks which can exploit the possibilities of comparison" and a "careful consideration of the applicability to other regions of concepts developed in Europe and North America."
Race Relations in Sociological Theory by John Rex (Weidenfeld & Nicolson. 1970) is an analysis which claims a theoretical status for the sociological analysis of race relations.
Racism and Migrant Labour by Robert Miles (Routledge & Kegan Paul, 1982) is an elaboration of the latter critique but within a Marxist frame of reference which concludes that the analytical task is not to develop a theory of "race relations" but to explain, historically, why certain forms of social relations are racialized; this can be read with the later critical review from the same author, *Racism After "Race Relations"* (Routledge, 1993).

ROBERT MILES

RACIAL CODING

First principles

Racial coding is a process through which people, objects and events are understood, communicated and given meaning. We associate certain codes and signs with certain concepts and ideas and, in turn, attribute certain qualities to certain races through the process of racial coding. Codes have two essential parts: one, the basic units of the code (or signs); and two, a set of rules around how these units are put together in order to be used in communication. Codes of communication can be verbal (these are representational codes such as speech, writing, music or art) or non-verbal (these are presentational codes such as sign language, facial expressions, movements, tone and gestures).

The use of codes, or the process of coding, is not always apparent, and in fact the more habitually and naturally we use certain codes in everyday communication, the more ordinary and neutral they may appear. Semiology is concerned with the breaking down and analysis of the grammar, vocabulary and rules of codes and coding which often pass themselves off as commonsense. There is nothing intrinsic in the people, objects or events which the code refers to; the code is simply a system through which people, objects or events are represented. Meaning is therefore constructed through the coding process, which is at the heart of the system of representation. The way in which the system of coding develops is called codification; all messages involve codification.

A signifying structure or text is made up of codes and signs. Structuralist semioticians focus on this internal structure of the text, and argue that meaning lies within the text. Ferdinand de Saussure (1857–1913), the Swiss linguist, argued that the meaning of language is to be found in its function as a system, and referred to "the role of signs as part of social life." As such, he argued that we need to look beyond the text to find meaning and in order to analyze culture, which is also a system of codes and signs.

Leading thinkers such as sociologist Stuart Hall have refuted textually deterministic approaches which presume that all meaning is contained within a text and focused on the process of decoding and encoding (or how a message is produced and received). Hall, in his 1980 essay, "Encoding/decoding," focuses on the field of mass communication, and argues that "decodings do not follow inevitably from encodings." This is central to understanding the processes used in decoding popular messages because it helps us to understand the importance of the "decoder" as well as the "encoder." That is, it considers other discourses and processes beyond the "original" text itself by insisting that the moment of decoding or reception (for example, by the viewer or reader of a media text) is as important as the moment of encoding or production (for example, by the television report or newspaper article). There is greater insistence therefore on a *circuit of communication* producing meaning rather than a linear or definitive pattern of meaning being produced.

A context is needed to help us understand what the text means. Coding itself is the correlation between our language system and our conceptual system, and this is shared and communicated by members of the same culture who are able to recognize the codes and contexts. Language and the language we use literally allow thinking. Signs are organized as codes (or signifying codes) which are formulated in agreement and used by members of a social or cultural group. They are therefore socially and culturally constructed and operate as a collectivist method of producing and sharing information.

These first principles of coding help us to understand that codes based around racial lines are not innate in the race of a person, but are concepts agreed and shared by human beings within a society. In any case, race itself is a social construction, not reliably or wholly rooted in biological difference. Racial codes are often dependent on the location, politics and moment in which the society that devises those racial codes is situated. For example, certain commonly agreed codes around the Jewish race in 1940s Nazi Germany (as cunning, grasping and clannish) are arguably quite different to the way in

which the Jewish race is looked upon in the current-day USA (as intelligent, entrepreneurial, and industrious). The racial codes formed around a particular set of people can alter over time and according to the context within which they arise. Racial codes are therefore rooted in context, although the essence of the codes can transcend this. For example, the dominant racial codes around Jewish people in Nazi Germany may still linger and be used to represent them in other contexts today.

Political ideologies

Although racial codes themselves can alter over time, they are devised, fixed and sustained by human communication in such a way that they present themselves and maintain their position as natural and inevitable. The real danger of (racial) codes is that they are not generally recognized as codes but are taken to be "the truth."

Lurking beneath the system of coding are ideologies. Ideologies can be understood as "sets of political ideas and values" that might belong to the specific interests of a particular group, hence the Marxist notion of a *dominant ideology* which is imposed through consciousness or structures. The term *discourse*, in relation to ideology, helps us to understand the textual process by which coded meanings are constructed. Discourse analysis considers the content and context of verbal and nonverbal codes and systems of representation. It stresses that there are no pre-given ideologies which are adopted and then simply represented, but that ideologies themselves are formed through discourse.

The work of Michel Foucault (1926–84), the post-structuralist philosopher and historian, is particularly useful here for its emphasis on discourse serving not the "will to truth," but the "will to power." Foucault was less interested in "the great model of language and signs" than in "that of war and battle"; more concerned with the relations of power, not relations of meaning. This discursive approach is fundamental, because it helps us to understand how racial coding itself is something that we are all involved in, in some way or another, and that it carries with it associations of power. For example, there are some racial codes and messages that mobilize themselves more vociferously and consistently than others and these are arguably those which "belong" to what are most commonly perceived as the "obvious" or marked races within that society.

Broadly speaking, it is minority people and cultures that are seen and depicted as Other and as diametrically opposed to ourselves. This binary configuration between Self and Other inevitably means then that codes and signs are used to represent not just Others, but also ourselves. So, for example, if Jews are greedy, then "we" are generous, if African Caribbeans are criminal then "we" are law-abiding, if Muslims are barbaric, then "we" are civilized. This opposition-based schema indicates how "our" racial Others are typically racially coded in correlation with the negative. These are codes which feed off, are supported by, and framed within dominant popular messages.

One of the key routes through which racial codes are strengthened and delivered is through popular media messages. In turn, the routine or popular usage of racial codes becomes part of everyday culture. Those of us to whom the codes are presented, or those of us who are expected to understand the codes, are involved in this circulation of popular culture. Public service broadcasting codes, for example, organize themselves around presenting a cohesive "we"; uniting the nation to whom the medium speaks. Television news, for example, constructs its own codes and conventions around representing different (racial) groups. Familiar racial codes and conventions are created through the news production process of selection and editing. News is a useful example, because news frameworks are a central knowledge system through which the (national) common sense about in-group cohesion and out-group difference is established, disseminated and authorized. The domestic rituals involved in watching news, and the fact that it is engaged with as a matter of course, makes the "truth" of the news text and those who tell it (the newsmakers or the enunciators) appear both natural and legitimate. The presence of racial codes is actively concealed in order to support the realism of the news text. In fact, in the making of a news story, certain groups are included or excluded; certain images, views, backgrounds, cultures and contexts are selected over others; and certain groups are more actively involved in the process of producing the news story.

If we think briefly about dominant Western news representations of black people (specifically African Caribbean), we can identify certain racialized codes through which that racial group is routinely represented. We know from their recurrent appearance in certain types of news themes – immigration, "race rows" and race riots – that black people have typically been positioned in relation to crisis and the problematic and coded as containing "the problem." The codes used within these racialized geographies – and they could include images, speech, facial expressions or language used in the news reports – create a kind of network, a shorthand system of translation that indicates that black people signify trouble. This representational process is often discussed in terms of "racial stereotyping," which is just one element of racial coding practice.

Or we might take the image of Islam, which is a religion with dominant racial associations (Arabs, Pakistanis, etc.). Many in the West instantly recognize this religious/racial image through messages (made up of codes and signs) which have most vigorously been used to represent Islam. The idea or symbol of Islam – vis-Á-vis popular messages based on key recent encounters such as Salman Rushdie's *Satanic Verses* (1988) book-burning and fatwa affair or the Gulf War in 1991 or post-September 11, 2001 discourse – is that Islam is menacing, barbaric and extreme. This works within broader contexts around "Orientals" and is just one example of the way non-Western cultures, religions and peoples are "Othered" in Western discourses and popular media messages through the process of coding.

Palestinian-American intellectual Edward Said (1935–) has been the leading thinker around the concept of Orientalism, the grand narrative that hooks up imperialistic thinking with Western knowledge. His ideas draw on the poststructuralist ideas of Michel Foucault, and have most prominently attempted the decoding of anti-imperialist ideas. According to Said, so deep are the racialized codes representing the Orient that the Orient cannot be imagined in non-Orientalist terms; the Eurocentric discourse is so deeply entrenched in Western ideologies and patterns of thinking.

One of the most dominant racially coded narratives of recent times has centered on Islam v. the USA. Such is the powerful force of this binary code that those who are critical of the US government are instantly labeled and coded as "anti-American." Of course, the US government does not represent all the views of all the American people and to criticize a country's political stance does not amount to or entail a criticism of all that country's citizens. As writer, Arundathi Roy argues: "To call someone anti-American, indeed, to be anti-American, is not just racist, it's a failure of the imagination. An inability to see the world in terms other than those that the establishment has set out for you: if you don't love us, you hate us. If you're not good, you're evil. If you're not with us, you're with the terrorists" (in *Guardian*, September 27, 2002).

Challenging popular racial codes

The process of racial coding within popular media messages is ongoing, and continues to be formed and re-formed in different historical moments and contexts. It is interesting therefore to observe how the popular media responds when it faces criticism from other parties about its role in processing these racial codes. On the whole, the media contains a lack of reflexivity or awareness about its role in mobilizing racially inflected messages. Let us take the example of the report by the Runnymede Trust, a UK-based independent think-tank on race and cultural diversity issues. In 2000 the Runnymede Trust published *The Future of Multi-Ethnic Britain: The Parekh Report* (Runnymede Trust, 2000). One of its key observations was that "Britishness has racial connotations" which are not inclusive of Britain's culturally diverse communities and which are still assumed essentially to belong to the White English. To this extent, the report proposed that the term "British" was racially coded.

The *Guardian* newspaper's response to the Parekh Report carried the misleading headline, "British tag is 'coded racism'." The popular media responses to the report were speedy (coming days before the report was even published) and defensive. Phrases such as *"racial* connotations" were misreported as *"racist* connotations" and thus the report was increasingly packaged in popular media messages and subsequently accepted by the general public as alarmist, unmerited and significantly "un-British." (See *www.runnymedetrust.org* for a range of responses to the report.)

These responses mobilized a discourse of denial that Britain could be racist, which in any case, was not the thrust of the report's argument.

Samir Shah, the chair of the Runnymede Trust, explained the important distinction: "Consider the difference between calling a group of, say, Chinese a 'racial' group as opposed to a 'racist' group. The word British – rather like Chinese – conjures up many images. And just as you or I would be unlikely to imagine a black or brown face when thinking of the word Chinese, so the images brought to mind with the word British are more likely to be of an Anglican church rather than a Sunni mosque, warm beer rather than a cold lassi, a white face rather than a black or brown one ... the meaning embedded in words often lags behind reality" (*Guardian*, October 20, 2000). Shah's example is useful here for it highlights the racial codes that are most likely to come to mind when we think of a "Chinese" person or "British" culture. It is no coincidence that the more obvious the association, the more habitually such associations are supported and coded within popular messages.

SEE ALSO: anti-Semitism; bigotry; colonial discourse; ethnocentrism; Fanon, Frantz; Hall, Stuart; ideology; Islamophobia; language; Marxism; media; multiculturalism; nationalism; neo-nazism; Other; policing; post-race; race: as signifier; race card; racist discourse; representations; September 11, 2001; stereotype

Reading

Encoding and Decoding in the Media Discourse in Stencilled paper 7, Centre for Contemporary Cultural Studies (University of Birmingham, 1973) by Stuart Hall is a rudimentary paper which focuses on coding and meaning as a circuit of communication. Hall provides a useful cross-reference with the theoretical framework laid out by Saussure, and pays particular attention to how messages operate in relation to popular media and mass communication.

Orientalism: Western conceptions of the Orient (Penguin, 1978) and *Culture and Imperialism* (Verso, 1993) by Edward W. Said are two books that map out and deconstruct the West's depiction of the East and draw on examples ranging from Jane Austen to the media coverage of the Gulf War.

"Reading racial fetishism: the photographs of Robert Mapplethorpe" by Kobena Mercer, in his *Welcome to the Jungle* (Routledge, 1994), provides an in-depth analysis of Mapplethorpe's approach to photographing black men and masculinity.

Representation: Cultural representations and signifying practices, edited by Stuart Hall (Open University, 1997), provides an excellent survey of questions of cultural representation using extensive examples and case studies to explain representational structures and techniques.

Representing Black Britain: Black and Asian images on television by Sarita Malik (Sage, 2002) traces the history of racially coded images of black people on British television and positions questions of representation (including coding) at the center of its analysis.

SARITA MALIK

RACIAL DISCRIMINATION

Also known as *racialism*, this is the active or behavioral expression of racism and is aimed at denying members of certain groups equal access to scarce and valued resources. It goes beyond thinking unfavorably about groups or holding negative beliefs about them: it involves putting them into action. Often, racialism and racism are mutually reinforcing in a self-fulfilling way because, by denying designated groups access to resources and services, one creates conditions under which those groups can often do no more than confirm the very stereotypes that inspired the original racist belief.

Racial discrimination, as distinct from many other forms of discrimination, operates on a group basis: it works on the perceived attributes and deficiencies of groups, not individualized characteristics. Members of groups are denied opportunities or rewards for reasons unrelated to their capabilities, industry, and general merit: they are judged solely on their membership of an identifiable group, which is erroneously thought to have a racial basis.

The racial discrimination may range from the use of derogatory labels, such as "kike" or "nigger," to the denial of access to such institutional spheres as housing, education, justice, political participation, and so on. The actions may be intentional, or unintentional. The use of the terms racialist and racial discrimination has diminished in recent years as racism and institutional racism have come into popular use as expressions of both thought and action. Institutional racism, in particular, is now used widely to describe the discriminatory nature and operations, however unwitting, of large-scale organizations or entire societies. A pedant would insist that the correct term should be institutional racial discrimination, or institutional racialism.

SEE ALSO: anti-Semitism; bigotry; cultural racism; environmental racism; ethnocentrism; homelessness; *Invisible Man*; institutional racism; law: civil rights, USA; law: race relations, Britain; law: racial discrimination, international; race relations: as activity; race relations: as construction; racialization; racist discourse; reverse racism/discrimination; social exclusion; social work; welfare; white backlash culture

Reading

African Americans, Labor, and Society: Organizing for a new agenda, edited by Patrick L. Mason (Wayne State University Press, 2000), is a collection of essays on how to combat racial discrimination in the workplace.

Clear and Convincing Evidence, edited by Michael Fix and Raymond Struyk (University Press of America, 1992), explores the "auditing" method of assessing discrimination in such areas as housing, hiring, mortgage lending, and credit extension: two individuals are matched on all relevant criteria except the one presumed to lead to discrimination: each member applies for the same job, housing, or service and the differential treatment they receive provides a measure of discrimination.

Combating Racial Discrimination, edited by Erna Appelt and Monika Jarosch (Berg, 2000), surveys the methods employed and their shortcomings.

Race, Gender and Discrimination at Work by Samuel Cohn (Westview Press, 1999) examines racial and gender discrimination and offers some explanations.

Understanding Prejudice, Racism and Social Conflict, edited by Martha Augoustinos and Katherine Jane Reynolds (Sage, 2001), investigates the several levels at which prejudice manifests: individual, interpersonal, intergroup and institutional.

RACIAL PROFILING

Meaning

Profiling is a process of representing a group, person or thing by selecting salient features and integrating these into a coherent image designed to guide inquiry (the origins of the term are obscure, but may lie in the Italian *profilare*, to draw in outline). When the various features are collapsed into just one salient characteristic, the purported race or ethnicity of a subject(s), racial profiling is said to occur. Particular groups or persons are identified because of their apparent race or ethnicity alone. While this is intended to direct inquiry, it typically results in the selection of visually distinguishable minority groups for particular types of treatment. Racial profiling is an instrument to identify, select and guide and, as such, should not be confused with the more generic racial *discrimination*.

The term racial profiling is North American in origin and, while it came into popular currency during the 1990s, the practice of selecting subjects by their suspected race or ethnicity is, of course, age-old. In the twentieth century, racial profiling was at the core of US internment camps, shattering the lives of Japanese Americans.

Kang argues, "Viewing these 'Orientals' as incurable foreign, speaking foreign languages, perpetuating foreign cultures, practicing foreign religions (Shinto, Buddhism), American society could not distinguish between the Empire of Japan and Americans of Japanese descent." By December of 1942, nearly all Japanese on the West Coast had been concentrated into ten camps with armed sentries and barbed wire ensuring their confinement. In 1982, a congressionally appointed blue ribbon commission concluded that "broad historical causes which shaped these decisions were race prejudice, war hysteria, and a failure of political leadership."

Decades after the internment camps, racial profiling began its significant presence in the sphere of policing. Earl Ofari Hutchinson argues that the escalation of police power following the 1960s launched the particular type of racial profiling we recognize today. In its contemporary use, it refers to a pattern of inquiry operated at institutional levels and, in this sense, differs from *stereotyping*, which has a cognitive component, and *bigotry*, which frequently involves a refusal to countenance alternative perspectives. Racial profiling accommodates elements of both and activates them in routine practices and procedures such as the police's stopping African American drivers for minor violations because they seem to be members of a group that fits a certain kind of profile. That profile may be a "drug courier," "gangbanger" and so on.

Racial profiling can take place in any sphere of activity, though it has come to the fore principally through policing. David A. Harris argues that the "emergence of crack in the spring of 1986 and a flood of lurid and often exaggerated press accounts of inner-city crack use ushered in a period of intense public concern about illegal drugs" and initiated the targeting of "poor, minority, urban neighborhoods where drug dealing tended to be open and easy to detect." After the Rodney King case of 1991/92, attention was paid to the manner in which the police habitually conduct their inquiries. From 1994, the US government has been legally obliged to collect data on police brutality.

Similarly, police activities were thrown into relief after the publication of the report on the Stephen Lawrence case in London in 1999. Apart from the incompetent investigation into the killing of the African Caribbean youth, the police's practice of stops and searches was revealed to involve a degree of racial profiling.

It is possible that the racial profiling is not deliberate, but may be the outcome of unexamined conventions: ways of working that have never been subject to critical reflection. It may also be based on conscious and deliberate targeting that has become routinized over years. In this case, *pretext stops* may become intentional maneuvers: the routine stops for minor (alleged) violations become a tactic to discover more serious offenses. Harris identifies the case of *Whren v. US*, which reached the US Supreme Court in 1996, as a key ruling. This concluded that that stops and searches of vehicles after minor infractions did not invite discriminatory enforcement and were not violations of the Fourth Amendment. In other words, Harris argues, this gave license for pretext stops.

One of the most notorious racial profiling incidents involving what may have been a pretext stop occurred in April 1998 when four young males – three African Americans, the other Latino – were pulled over by state troopers for speeding on the New Jersey turnpike. As the police officers approached the vehicle, it backed up, knocking one trooper down as it hit the patrol car. The troopers opened fire, wounding three of the four passengers, who later contended they were not speeding. Critics maintained that this was a case of racial profiling and that the only reason that the police stopped the vehicle was that they saw an ethnic minority driver and passengers. Others rebutted this, insisting that the shooting was justified by the way the driver reversed the vehicle toward the police car. Whether or not this was a case of racial profiling, the episode became an infamous illustration of the dangers of "driving while black," or DWB as it is often abbreviated.

In another highly charged incident Amadou Diallo, a West African resident of New York, was killed by members of the New York Police Department's Street Crime Unit in 1999. Diallo was found to be unarmed. His death prompted mass street protests. These were instances of what many regard as a widespread pattern of selective policing.

The term *disproportionality* was coined in Britain to characterize the lopsided numbers of stops and searches of ethnic minority groups compared to their numbers in the total population. While the police typically defend such disproportionate apprehensions as the result of an overrepresentation of certain groups in crime, others suggest the opposite logic. Ethnic minorities tend to appear in crime statistics *because* the police targets them in the first place. Joe Feagin gives an example of disproportionality in his *Racist America: Roots, current realities, and future reparations* (Routledge, 2001). While black and Latinos made up only 5 percent of drivers on a highway in Volusia County, Florida, for many years they were in the majority of those stopped.

Mikal Muharrar calls racial profiling "an instrument of modern, deniable racism." It enables authorities to deal with urgent social problems, such as crime, welfare fraud and drug dealing, without making explicit reference to race. "The trait of blackness associated with the problem is viewed as nothing more than an unfortunate reality," writes Muharrar, who argues that the media plays a part in "fostering stereotypes" that inform public perceptions.

Muharrar's argument is that the media acts as the "missing link": the public has become so accustomed to seeing, hearing or reading about ethnic minority persons suspected of crimes that, "even when the race was not specified, viewers tended to remember seeing a black suspect." On this account, the media engage in a form of racial profiling that complements that of the police and encourages public fears about the racial nature of crime. It may also affect victims' accounts of crimes and their identification of perpetrators. Harris's report (below) provides a catalog of such searches that occurred in the aftermath of the aforementioned *Whren* decision.

While policing has commanded the focus of attention, racial profiling has been discovered among the practices of US customs officials, who tend to body search a disproportionate number of black or Latino passengers. After September 11, 2001, travelers from Islamic countries were afforded particular attention. Racial profiling was again used as an instrument to guide inquiry.

"Driving While Black" allegations have made Washington uneasy about officially sanctioning profiling. However, racial profiling may find itself politically correct after all in the form of post-September 11 terrorism-risk profiling where race became only one of many characteristics making up a profile. Specialists in criminology and terrorism suggest a detailed terrorism-risk profile which might incorporate one's travel patterns, education background, ties to radical mosques and evidence of "visa shopping." Gorman argues advocates of terrorism-risk profiling maintain that this form of profiling is based on a multitude of factors, thereby deflecting sole emphasis from such politically sensitive issues as race and religion. Once political correctness is stripped away, however, terrorism-risk profiling is clearly racial profiling however "soft" it may be.

"Hard" and "soft" racial profiling

Writing in *City Journal*, Heather MacDonald introduces a distinction between "hard" racial profiling in which "race" is used as the *only* factor in assessing suspects, and "soft" racial profiling, when "using race as one factor among others in gauging criminal suspiciousnessness [*sic*]." She argues that many procedures identified as cases of "hard" racial profiling may not be so straightforward. To arrive at this conclusion the kind of data needed would include answers to: do ethnic minorities tend to drive more miles, have equipment violations, have more young drivers (young people tend to get stopped more than older drivers), drive more on weekend nights, get involved in more accidents than population figures would predict? All these factors affect stop patterns.

MacDonald believes that "soft" racial profiling is commonplace. This might involve "pulling someone over because driver *and* car *and* direction *and* number *and* type of occupants fit the components of a [drugs] courier profile." This, she argues, is just a case of statistical probability: experience corroborates intelligence reports that certain groups traveling in certain directions in particular types of vehicle etc. fits a pattern of typical offenders. "When an officer has many independent indices of suspicion, adding his knowledge of the race of major trafficking groups to the mix is both legitimate and not overly burdensome on law-abiding minorities," writes MacDonald. She contends that the apparent race of a suspect combines with an assortment of other factors which guide "assertive policing," and that this approach has led to a measure of success in the war on drugs. But, the repeated criticism of the police for apprehending ethnic minority suspects has given rise to what she calls the "myth of racial profiling." In other words, the police may be operating with several cues as to the most likely offenders, and ethnic identity is only one of them.

Reasons

Racial profiling is a form of discrimination that is habitually practiced in an environment where racism is ostensibly condemned and censured. It was at the root of the Japanese internment camps during World War II, an abhorrent event in US history, and continued its course in the twentieth century in the hands of the police. Never acknowledged nor made an explicit policy, it is a covert form of racism, though one that is widely recognized, particularly by critical commentators on the police. The police force has been harangued for several decades, critics decrying the institution as racist and its members as incorrigible bigots. With the events of September 11 and America's subsequent "War on Terrorism," a new dynamic to racial profiling proliferates into the twentieth century.

SEE ALSO: bigotry; cultural racism; Diallo case, the Amadou; Islamophobia; King case, the Rodney; Lawrence case, the Stephen; policing; political correctness; racialization; reparations; September 11, 2001; stereotype

Reading

Driving While Black: Racial profiling on our nation's highways by David A. Harris (American Civil Liberties Union, 1999) is a commissioned report; it is also available at *www.aclu.org/profiling/report/*.
"Media blackface: 'racial profiling' in news reporting" by Mikal Muharrar (in *Racism Watch*, September/October, 1998) accuses the media of racializing crime, i.e. defining a social problem in "blackface": available at *www.fair.org/extra/9809/media-blackface.html*.
"The myth of racial profiling" by Heather MacDonald (in *City Journal*, vol. 11, no. 2, 2001) argues that "too many enforcement interactions with minorities" has become equated with racism and that policing is in danger of being "emasculated."
"National Security: Profiling terror" by Siobhan Gorman (in *National Journal*, vol. 34, no. 15, 2002) examines profiling methods to prevent potential terrorists from obtaining visas to enter the USA.
"Racial profiling: another tragedy of the terror attacks"

by Earl Ofari Hutchinson (in *African-American Village*: available at: *www.imdiversity.com/villages/african/article_detail*, 2002) is a short argument about how racial profiling was intensified in the wake of the September 11th attack.
"Thinking through internment: 12/7 and 9/11" by Jerry Kang (in *Amerasia Journal*, vol. 27, no. 3, 2001) examines racial profiling in the context of internment camps and the events of 9/11.

AMY I. KORNBLAU

RACIALISM *see racial discrimination*

RACIALIZATION

A term that emerged in analysis in the 1970s to refer to a political and ideological process by which particular populations are identified by direct or indirect reference to their real or imagined phenotypical characteristics in such a way as to suggest that the population can be understood only as a supposedly biological unity. This process usually involved the direct utilization of the idea of "race" to describe or refer to the population in question.

The use and meaning of the term emerges from historical analysis. This work demonstrates that the idea of "race" is not a universal idea, but, rather, emerges at a particular point in western European history, and, over time, comes to be used to refer to supposedly fixed and discrete biological categories of the world's population. This shows that "race" is not a biological fact but a social construction. The first use of the notion of racialization arose in the course of establishing these claims and was used to refer specifically to the development of the idea of "race," first in historical writing and, later, in European "scientific" writing of the late eighteenth and nineteenth centuries.

The term's usage has been developed and widened in time with the fact that the process of identifying particular populations as "races" is not confined to level of "intellectual" activity. By a process not yet adequately understood and analyzed, this social construction of "race" was passed down to the level of everyday categorization and action. In recognition of this, the notion of racialization has been used in a broader sense to refer to any process or situation wherein the idea of "race" is introduced to define and give meaning to some particular population, its characteristics and actions. Hence, the fact that the public and political reaction to the Irish migration and presence in Britain in the nineteenth century employed the idea of "race" to refer to the Irish can be understood, analytically, as an instance of racialization. Similarly, when the political and ideological consequences of New Commonwealth migration to Britain in the 1950s began to be defined by politicians by reference to the idea of "race," one can refer to this process as the racialization of British politics.

In the narrower usage, the ideological content of the process of racialization will warrant description as racism, or more specifically, scientific racism. In the wider usage, referring in addition to the attribution of social significance and meaning to phenotypical/genetic variation in all dimensions of social life, the ideological content of the identified process is not necessarily racist. Before that can be determined, it is necessary to analyze the content of the attributed significance and those populations party to the attribution (both object and subject). In this way we can take account of the fact that those who have historically been the "victims" of racialization may employ the idea of "race" in turn to refer to these who so label them without necessarily concluding that their response is racist in content. This, therefore, requires that the concepts of racism and racialization be kept analytically distinct.

SEE ALSO: double consciousness; ideology; intelligence; Irish; Lawrence case, the Stephen; phenotype; policing; race: as signifier; race: as synonym; race relations: as activity; race relations: as construction; racial coding; racial profiling; racism; science

Reading

The Idea of Race by Michael Banton (Tavistock, 1967) contains one of the first uses of the term to refer to historical and scientific writing in the eighteenth and nineteenth centuries.

"Racialization: the genealogy and critique of a concept" by Rohit Barot and John Bird (in *Ethnic and Racial Studies*, vol. 24, no. 4, 2001) traces the origins and emergence of the concepts of racialization and deracialization in contemporary debate.

Racism and Migrant Labour by Robert Miles (Routledge & Kegan Paul, 1982) is an example of the utilization of the term in a wider sense.

Racism and Society 3rd edn by John Solomos and Les Back (Macmillan Palgrave, 2001) has a section on the racialization of political life; this is complemented by an application of racialization in the context of Asian youth in Britain: "The construction of

'Asian' criminality" by C. Webster (in *International Journal of the Sociology of Law*, vol. 25, 1997).

ROBERT MILES

RACISM

Racism was a relatively new word in 1940 when Ruth Benedict defined it as "the dogma that one ethnic group is condemned by nature to congenital inferiority and another group is destined to congenital superiority." She maintained that, like religion, it was a belief that could be studied only historically, and that "racism was first formulated in conflicts between classes." Up to the late 1960s most dictionaries and textbooks defined it as a doctrine, dogma, ideology, or set of beliefs. Its core element was the claim that "race" determined culture. At that time social scientists agreed that what were then called "race relations" had three main dimensions: that of ideology had racism as its basic concept; whereas the study of the psychological dimension was organized around the concept of prejudicial attitudes; and the analysis of the behavioral dimension used the concept of discrimination to examine social relations. These distinctions were dismissed by Stokeley Carmichael and Charles Hamilton, black leaders of the civil rights movement in the USA when, in 1967, they insisted that by "racism" they meant "the predication of decisions and policies on considerations of race for the purpose of subordinating a racial group and maintaining control over that group" (*Black Power: The politics of liberation in America*, Penguin, 1967). The influence of the movement was such that thereafter the word racism was increasingly used in political contexts to make negative judgments of a wide range of beliefs, attitudes and practices. This expanded use was to the forefront in the UN World Conference Against Racism in 2001. In the 1970s it stimulated in Britain a movement arguing for an "antiracist" program in education. A flexible conception of racism suited the purposes of the antiracist movement.

The word will continue to be used in English and other languages as part of the international campaign against racial discrimination. The question for social scientists is what part it may have as a concept for explaining intergroup attitudes and behavior. Is racism an *explanandum* (something to be explained) or an *explanans* (something that accounts for an observation)? For Ruth Benedict the concept of racism helped explain the persecution or subordination of one group by another. Some of those who followed her historical approach maintained that the expansion of capitalism in the New World required the exploitative use of African labor. As this could be achieved more effectively were black labor treated simply as a commodity, a whole complex was created to facilitate this exploitation. For these authors, beliefs about black inferiority could be adequately understood only as part of a new historical creation – racism; in subsequent centuries this has been modified in step with changes in the economic structure.

At the end of the 1960s sociologists detected a new tendency for the unequal treatment of groups to be defended on political and cultural instead of on biological grounds. In everyday relations, stereotypes, proverbs, symbols and folklore could serve as functional substitutes for the theories of the armchair philosophers. In social science writing, as well as in popular speech, more and more forms of ideology, attitude and behavior were described as racist, even when there was no explicit mention of "race." This resulted in what Robert Miles called "a process of conceptual inflation." Trying to call a halt, he proposed a more limited definition of racism as the attribution of social significance (meaning) to particular patterns of phenotypical and/or genetic difference which, along with the characteristic of additional deterministic ascription of real or supposed other characteristics to a group constituted by descent, was the defining feature of racism as an ideology. But, additionally, those characteristics had, in turn, to be negatively evaluated and/or designated as the reason to justify unequal treatment of the defined group.

Another response to conceptual inflation has been the identification of historically specific racisms, differentiating, for example, the racism of the US slave in the South from the industrial employment of blacks in the post-bellum North, or the racism of Caribbean slave societies from that of European societies. If this proposal is taken seriously it should eliminate any reference to "the phenomenon of racism" as if this were a sufficiently coherent unit to constitute a single *explanandum*. It breaks with the assumption that racism was a product of European imperialism and makes it possible for the ideology and

practices of the Japanese when they occupied part of the Chinese mainland to be examined in parallel with those of Europeans in Africa and India. It remains an approach that emphasizes top-down constraints and tends to collectivism in its generalizations about groups; nor has it inspired any program of empirical research. Its main weakness is the failure to find a satisfactory way of deciding what is to qualify as a racism. Some of the difficulties have been exemplified in the bitter debates about whether Zionism is a form of racism. In many situations of ethnic and national conflict, individuals think of members of opposed groups as essentially different from themselves and their reasoning is little different from that which underpinned older racial ideologies.

At the present juncture it seems best to concentrate on the closer specification of what is to be explained. Scholars who have sought uniformities in social and economic development have delineated the capitalist system and used the concept of racism to account for interrelations between some of its component parts. Others have used it when they have tried to distinguish a special quality in popular beliefs about alterity, the "Otherness" of rival or subordinate groups. Relations between ethnic groups following the break-up of Yugoslavia were not characterized by differences of physical appearance but they showed many of the features that elsewhere might have been called racist. So too did the attitudes of Hutu towards Tutsi in Rwanda, Turk and Cypriot in Cyprus, Hindus towards Muslims in Gujarat and Russians towards Caucasians. Some writers do not employ the word as either an *explanandum* or an *explanans*. They find it a convenient name for an area of study in the way that in a library a set of books may be classified as being about politics.

Racism has often been represented as a kind of social pathology, as when it has been likened to a cancer or a virus, and whole societies have been described as racist. It can equally well, or perhaps better, be represented as a crime, and, like other forms of crime, as a normal behavior to be expected from members of all social groups even if it is one that is to be prohibited and punished. Thus some of the significant advances since the 1960s in the understanding of the behavioral dimension to intergroup relations have been associated with developments in the law against racial discrimination. These are relevant to situations in which two groups are distinguished by both race and something else, for example, religion. If a member of one group treats another less favorably, is that because of the racial difference or the religious difference? The law now prohibits both less favorable treatment on purpose (sometimes called direct discrimination or disparate treatment) and treatment that is less favorable in effect (sometimes called indirect discrimination or disparate impact). This has a bearing upon any conception of racist behavior. The Carmichael and Hamilton definition, for example, was limited to purposive behavior.

When attempting to account for an observation about intergroup tensions it is inadvisable to accord a privileged status to any one kind of *explanans*. It is best to focus on a specific question and consider which concepts are most useful to an answer. Examination of the nineteenth-century doctrines that have been called scientific racism shows that they were not homogenous and can profitably be divided into two: the racial typology of the 1850s, and the later selectionist theories that have sometimes been called social Darwinism. The names "racial typology" and "selectionism" direct attention to the distinguishing features of these doctrines better than does the name "scientific racism." Its accusations of racism enabled the civil rights movement to drive great changes in US society but other kinds of concept are required to analyze how it did this and to account for contemporary patterns of segregation and racial discrimination in that country. It is advisable to look for the concepts that can best relate the beliefs, attitudes or behavior under study to social science theories. Racism will eventually be superseded as one of these, but whatever happens in social science, the word will surely continue to be important in political argument about current affairs.

SEE ALSO: bigotry; cultural racism; environmental racism; essentialism; ethnic conflict; ethnocentrism; inferential racism; institutional racism; Park, Robert Ezra; race: as classification; race: as signifier; race: as synonym; race card; racial coding; racialization; racist discourse; reverse racism; science; systemic racism; White Power; white race; whiteness

Reading

The Arena of Racism by Michael Wieviorka (Sage, 1995) exemplifies the conception of racism as a social pathology; it is the perspective of a French sociologist who argues that "the spread of racism takes place against a background of the breakdown, absence or inversion of social movements and, more generally, of a crisis of modernity." It has been criticized as leaving no place for the victims as acting subjects.

Race and Racialism, edited by Sami Zubaida (Tavistock, 1970) provides assessments of the concept of racism as it was seen at the end of the 1960s.

Race and Racism by Ruth Benedict (Routledge, 1943) is the early influential work mentioned in the text above.

Racism by Robert Miles (Routledge, 1989) is an influential critique of subsequent writing, while *The International Politics of Race* by Michael Banton (Polity Press, 2002) contains proposals for superseding the use of the concept.

CHECK: internet resources section

MICHAEL BANTON

RACIST DISCOURSE

Racist discourse is a form of discriminatory social practice that manifests itself in text, talk and communication. Together with other (non-verbal) discriminatory practices, racist discourse contributes to the reproduction of racism as a form of ethnic or "racial" domination. It does so typically by expressing, confirming or legitimating racist opinions, attitudes and ideologies of the dominant ethnic group. Although there are other racisms elsewhere in the world, the most prevalent and devastating form of racism has historically been European racism against non-European peoples, which will be the focus of this essay.

Two forms of racist discourse

There are two major forms of racist discourse:

1 racist discourse *directed at* ethnically different Others;
2 racist discourse *about* ethnically different Others.

The first form of racist discourse is one of the many discriminatory ways that dominant group members verbally interact with members of dominated groups: ethic minorities, immigrants, refugees, etc. They may do so blatantly by using derogatory slurs, insults, impolite forms of address, and other forms of discourse that explicitly express and enact superiority and lack of respect.

Since today such blatant forms of verbal discrimination are generally found to be "politically incorrect," much racist discourse directed at dominated ethnic group members tends to become more subtle and indirect. Thus, white speakers may refuse to yield the floor to minority speakers, interrupt them inappropriately, ignore the topics suggested by their interlocutors, focus on topics that imply negative properties of the ethnic minority group to which the recipient belongs, speak too loudly, show a bored face, avoid eye contact, use a haughty intonation, and many other manifestations of lack of respect. Some of these verbal inequities are more generally a problem of multicultural communication; others are genuine expressions of racial or ethnic dominance of white speakers.

In other words, these are the kinds of discourse and verbal interaction that are normally considered deviant or unacceptable during conversation with in-group members, and therefore are forms of domination that have has been called "everyday racism." Of course, they also occur in conversations with people of the "own" group, but are then sanctioned as being rude or impolite. The fundamental difference is that minority group members *daily* are confronted with such racist talk, and not because of what they do or say, but only because of what they are: different. They are thus subjected to an accumulating and aggravating form of racist harassment that is a direct threat to their well-being and quality of life.

The second form of racist discourse is usually addressed to other dominant group members and is *about* ethnic or "racial" Others. Such discourse may range from informal everyday conversations or organizational dialogues (such as parliamentary debates), to many written or multimedia types of text or communicative events, such as TV shows, movies, news reports, editorials, textbooks, scholarly publications, laws, contracts, and so on.

The overall characteristic of such racist discourse is the negative portrayal of *Them*, often combined with a positive representation of *Ourselves*. The corollary of this strategy is to avoid or mitigate a positive representation of Others, and a negative representation of our own group.

Typical for the latter case is the denial or mitigation of racism.

These overall strategies may appear at all levels of text and talk, that is, at the level of visuals, sounds (volume, intonation), syntax (word order), semantics (meaning and reference), style (variable uses of words and word order), rhetoric (persuasive uses of grammar or of "figures" of style), pragmatics (speech acts such as assertions or threats), interaction, and so on.

Topics

Thus, *topics* of conversation, news reports, political debates or scholarly articles about minorities or immigrants may be biased in the sense that they focus on or imply negative stereotypes. Thus, immigration may be dealt with in terms of an invasion, a deluge, a threat, or at least as a major problem, instead of as an important and necessary contribution to the economy, the demography or the cultural diversity of the country.

Research into conversation, media, textbooks and other discourse genres has shown that of a potentially infinite number of topics or themes, text and talk about minorities or immigrants, typically clusters around three main topic classes.

The first class features topics of discourse that emphasize the *difference* of the Others, and hence their distance from Us. Such emphasis may have a seemingly positive slant if the Others are described in exotic terms. More often than not, however, the difference is evaluated negatively: the Others are portrayed as less smart, beautiful, fast, hardworking, democratic, modern, etc. than We are. These topics are typical in everyday conversations, textbooks and especially the mass media. This first step of in-group–out-group polarization in discourse, which also characterizes the underlying attitudes and ideologies expressed in these discourses, usually also implies that They are all the same (and We are all individually different).

The second group of topics takes polarization between Us and Them one step further and emphasizes that the behavior of the Other is *deviant*, and hence breaks Our norms and rules: They do not (want to) speak our language, they walk around in funny dress, they have strange habits, they eat strange food, they mistreat their women, and so on. The presupposition or conclusion of such topics is generally that They do not, but should, adapt to Us. On the other hand, even when they totally adapt, the Others will still be seen as different.

Thirdly, the Other may be portrayed as a *threat* to Us. This happens from the moment they arrive, for instance when immigration is represented as an invasion, until the new citizens have settled in "our" country, in which case they may be seen as occupying our space, running down our neighborhood, taking our jobs or houses, harassing "our" women, and so on.

The most prominent threat theme however is crime. All statistics on the coverage of immigrants – or otherwise marginal or marginalized people – show that in everyday conversations, the media and political discourse, various kinds of crime invariably show up as a permanent association with minorities and immigrants: passport fraud, assault, robbery, and especially drugs. Indeed, the quite common expression "ethnic crime" suggests that such crime is seen as a special and different category: crime thus becomes racialized. Doing drugs in the USA and other countries is seen as a typically "black" crime. On the other hand, "normal" topics, such as those of politics, the economy, work, or ("high") culture are seldom associated with minorities. If they are reported positively in the news, blacks do so mostly as champions in sports or as musicians.

According to the overall strategy of positive Self-presentation and negative Other-presentation, neutral or positive topics about Us are preferred, whereas the negative ones are ignored or suppressed. Thus, a story may be about discrimination against minorities, but since such a story is inconsistent with positive Self-presentation, it tends to be relegated to a less prominent part of the page or newspaper.

The discursive logic of racist positive Self-presentation and negative Other-presentation not only controls the fundamental level of global content or topics, but extends to all other levels and dimensions of discourse. Thus, lexicalization, or the choice of words, tends to be biased in many ways, not only in explicit racial or ethnic slurs, but also in more subtle forms of discourse, beginning with the very problem of naming the Others. There has been opposition to changes in naming practices: for example, the movement from (among other terms) "colored," "Negro," "Afro American," "African American" to "people of color" was opposed at different stages in history and by different groups, including, we might add, some African Americans.

Another well-known way to emphasize *Their* bad things is to use sentence forms that make bad agency more salient, such as active sentences. On the other hand, if *Our* racism or police harassment needs to be spoken or written about, the grammar allows us to mitigate such acts that are inconsistent with a positive Self-image, for instance by using passive phrases ("They were harassed by the police," or "They were harassed") or nominalizations ("harassment") instead of the direct active phrase ("Police harassed black youths").

Similar forms of emphasis and mitigation are typically managed by rhetorical figures, such as hyperbole and euphemisms. Thus, few Western countries or institutions explicitly deal with (own!) racism, and both in political discourse and well as in the media, many forms of mitigation are currently being used, such as "discrimination," "bias," or even "popular discontent." On the other hand, the opposite takes place whenever the Others do something we do not like. Thus, for starters, and as we have seen, immigration is often described using the military metaphor of an invasion. Similarly, large groups of immigrants or asylum seekers are described not only and simply in large numbers, but typically in terms of threatening amounts of water or snow in which *We* may drown: waves, floods, avalanches, etc. The same is true for the so-called "number game," used broadly in politics and the media, a strategy that emphasizes the number of immigrants in society by constantly emphasizing how many new people have arrived.

Strategies of presentation

Discourse is more than just words or sentences. It is typically characterized also at more global levels of analysis, as we have seen for the study of topics. In the same way, discourse has more global forms, formats or schemas that may become conventionalized, such as the typical format of a story, a news report in the press, a scientific article or a mundane everyday conversation. Although these formats are quite general and hence do not normally change in different contexts, and hence are the same in (say) racist or antiracist discourse – indeed, a racist story or joke is just as much a story or joke as an antiracist one – there are some interesting ways in which such structures may be related to different intentions or opinions of language users.

Thus, we found that in negative everyday stories about foreign neighbors, people tended to emphasize the *Complication* category, contrasting it with the peaceful *Orientation* category ("I was just walking on the street, and then suddenly..."), but often leave out the *Resolution* category, as if to stress that the presence of foreigners is a problem which cannot be resolved. Typically, the less-biased speakers in such a case *do* mention some form of (positive) resolution, even if they were initially confronted with some "trouble."

Similarly, in parliamentary debates, editorials, scientific articles and any other discourse in which arguments are very important, we also may expect ways in which the argumentation tends to be biased against the Other. Authoritative sources, such as the police or (white) experts, are being mentioned in order to "prove" that the immigrants are illegal, cannot be trusted, or need to be problematized, marginalized, removed or expelled. This move is typical for the well-known fallacy of "authority." Immigration debates are replete with such fallacies, for example, the fallacy of exaggeration, in which the arrival of a small group of refugees may be extrapolated to a national catastrophe by a comment such as, "if we have lax immigration laws, all refugees will come to our country."

Finally, discourse is also more than words and global structures in the sense that it is semiotically associated with visual information, such as page layout, placement, pictures, tables, and so on, as is the case in the press, or for film on TV, or on the internet. These nonverbal messages are also powerful ways of implementing the general strategy of positive Self-presentation and negative Other-presentation. Thus, articles in the press that are about *Their* crime or violence (such as urban disturbances defined as "race riots") tend to appear on the front page, on top, in large articles, with big headlines, with prominent pictures in which *They* are represented as aggressive or *We* (or Our Police) as victims. On the other hand, our racism, or the harassment of blacks by "Our" police will seldom occupy such a prominent place, and will tend to be relegated to the inner pages, to less substantial articles, and not emphasized in headlines.

In sum, we see that in many genres, and at all levels and dimensions of text and talk, racism and prejudice may daily be expressed, enacted and reproduced by discourse as one of the practices of a racist society.

Such discourse, however, does not come alone, and takes its conditions, consequences and functions in communicative, interactional and societal contexts. Biased or stereotypical news is produced in media organizations, by journalists and other professionals. Parliamentary debates are conducted by politicians. Textbooks, lessons, and scholarly publications are produced by teachers and scholars. They do so in different roles and as members of many different professional and other social groups, and as part of daily routines and procedures. News is gathered under the control of editors, and typically under majority institutions and organizations, such as government agencies, the police, the universities or the courts. Minority groups and sources are systematically ignored or attributed less relevance or expertise. The newsrooms in North America, Europe and Australia are largely white. Minority journalists are underemployed and discriminated against, with the usual fake arguments. No wonder that the dominant discourse of society, especially also about ethnic affairs and minority communities, is badly informed and hence informs badly. In other words, racist societies and institutions produce racist discourses, and racist discourses reproduce the stereotypes, prejudices and ideologies that are used to defend and legitimize white dominance. It is in this way that the symbolic, discursive circle is closed and dominant elite talk and text contributes to the reproduction of racism.

Fortunately, the same is true for antiracist discourse. And once such discourse is engaged in by responsible leaders in the media, politics, education, research, the courts, corporate business and the state bureaucracies, we may hope that society will become diverse and hence truly democratic.

SEE ALSO: bigotry; colonial discourse; cultural racism; epithet (racial/slang); humor; inferential racism; language; media; Other; policing; postcolonial; race: as signifier; racial coding; racialization; representations; systemic racism; whiteness

Reading

Discourses of Domination: Racial bias in the Canadian English-language press by Frances Henry and Carol

Tator (University of Toronto Press, 2002) presents a critical discourse analysis of a number of case studies of the ways the Canadian media portray minorities and immigrants and of the difficulties minority journalists have to get a job within the white media; this may productively be read in conjunction with *Debating Diversity: Analysing the discourse of tolerance* by Jan Blommaert and Jef Verschueren (Routledge, 1999), which focuses on debates on immigration in Belgium; and *Die vierte Gewalt: Rassismus in den Medien* (*The Fourth Power: Racism in the media*), edited by Siegfried Jöger and Jrgen Link (Duisburg, Germany, DISS, 1993), which presents studies of the way in which the German media, and especially also the tabloids, deal with immigration. This is one of many studies on racism published by the Duisburg Institute for Language and Social Research.

Mapping the Language of Racism: Discourse and the legitimation of exploitation by Margaret Wetherell and Jonathan Potter (Harvester-Wheatsheaf, 1992) is a discursive sociopsychological study of racism and discourse in New Zealand; this may be read alongside Philomena Essed's *Understanding Everyday Racism* (Sage, 1991), a study of the daily experiences of African American women in California and Surinamese women in the Netherlands, which provides a detailed theoretical account of the notion of "everyday racism."

Prejudice in discourse by Teun van Dijk (Benjamins, 1984) is the first monograph in English of the author's long-term research program on racist discourse. This study focuses especially on racism in everyday conversation and storytelling, and presents his first theoretical framework for a multidisciplinary study of racist discourse. Other work by the same author includes: *Communicating Racism* (Sage, 1987), a social psychological study on how ethnic and racial prejudices are expressed and reproduced by discourse, based on data collected in the Netherlands and California; *Racism and the Press* (Routledge, 1991), a quantitative and discourse-analytical study of the portrayal of immigrants and minorities in the Dutch and English press; *Elite Discourse and Racism* (Sage, 1993), which summarizes the author's earlier research on racist discourse, emphasizing the prominent role of the elites in the reproduction of racism, and offers new data and analyses of parliamentary debates, textbooks, scholarly discourse, and discourse in business enterprises; and *Racism at the Top: Parliamentary discourses on ethnic issues in six European countries*, edited with Ruth Wodak (Drava Verlag, 2000), which features studies by the team of the international project "Racism at the Top," in which parliamentary debates on immigration and ethnic affairs in seven western European countries (Austria, Italy, Spain, France, the Netherlands, the UK and Germany) are being studied.

The Semiotics of Racism: Approaches in critical discourse analysis, edited by Martin Reisigl and Ruth Wodak (Vienna: Passagen, 2000), is one of a series of books on the critical discourse analysis of racism and anti-Semitism edited and written by the team directed by Ruth Wodak at the University of Vienna; the papers contributed to this volume deal with such topics as explaining right-wing violence, diversity, the discourse of social exclusion, parliamentary debates on immigration, linguistic discrimination, and visual racism; it may be read alongside *Discourse and Discrimination. Rhetorics of racism and antisemitism* by Reisigl and Wodak (Routledge, 2000), which is a discourse-historical study of racism and anti-Semitism in Austria, dealing with everyday anti-Semitic discourse, political and media about a petition by right-wing leader J—rg Haider, as well as bureaucratic discourse refusing residence permits.

TEUN A. VAN DIJK

RAP

The term is taken from the slang for talk and refers to the half-spoken, half-sung genre that became musical shorthand for the African American experience in the 1980s and 1990s. By the twenty-first century, rap had become mainstream music, though without losing the undercurrent of rage and sexuality that had been integral to its popularity.

It began in the 1970s in the predominantly black neighborhoods of New York and New Jersey. Carried mainly by DJs rather than musicians, it consisted of abstracting, or "sampling," pieces of previously recorded tracks, playing them repeatedly, sometimes backwards, often with another track playing simultaneously, and voicing over them.

DJs would "toast" across the music in the manner of Jamaican DJs: as the music played, the DJs would speak or dub over their own rhymes or doggerel. Many accounts credit a Jamaican-born DJ named Kool Herc with pioneering the approach in the late 1960s. Several US DJs adopted and refined the technique, which, by the 1970s, had become known as rapping. Radio DJs in the New York/New Jersey area, particularly Gary Byrd, had used conversation, or rap, over prerecorded music in his shows, though it was the traveling DJs who originated "scratching," which meant manipulating a stylus on a record to produce new sounds. Used together, the techniques made possible a unique and inexpensive approach to music.

"Rapper's delight," by the Sugar Hill Gang, released in 1979, was the first commercially successful rap record, logging up two million in sales. This was eclipsed in 1981 by Grandmaster Flash and the Furious Five's "The message," which was a long, spoken rather than sung statement on life in the ghetto as seen through the eyes of a black youth – "Rats in the front room/roaches in the back/Junkies in the alley/ with a baseball bat." The lyrics were very different from those of the earlier Sugar Hill hit and showed how music could radicalize the black experience, turning it into an invective against the police and an injunction to challenge its authority; criminal acts could be made political ones. This strain of rap became particularly popular on the West Coast.

The first commercially successful record from a Los Angeles rap band was NWA's *Straight Outta Compton*, which, in its credits, thanked "gangstas, dope dealers, killers, hustlers, thugs, hoodlums, winos, bums" and a variety of other bona fide members of the underclass. Two million copies of the album were sold. NWA's infamy, rather than just fame, gave one member, Ice Cube, the exposure he needed to launch a solo career, so that, when he left in 1989, he was already an established writer/producer. He went on to start his own label and management company. On his first album, *AmeriKKKa's Most Wanted*, Cube set out to personify the black criminalized population. He pushed the rap genre by integrating various perspectives from law enforcement officers, judges and so on. The album starts with the character described in the title being led to the electric chair.

In 1991, the NWA follow-up album, *Nigga-z4Life* entered the Billboard pop chart at number two unassisted by a trailer single or a video. The low-budget underground record productions that had been so prized in the 1980s became things of the past as big money began to roll into the ghettos.

Churches, mainstream African American organizations, women's groups, two US presidents and a battery of other right-minded people and groups condemned Ice-T's "Cop killer," which told of a young man intending to shoot a police officer. "Die, pig, die" he raps as he discharges his "twelve-inch sawed off." In common with other gangsta tracks, it mythologized its eponymous hero. In 1992, Warner Brothers Records recalled copies of the CD after death threats, protests from police associations and denunciations from the White House. Later, Warners dropped Ice-T after a disagreement over the artwork of his album *Home Invasion*. It was the beginning of an extremely vexed relationship between Time Warner and rap. The media conglomerate sold its interest in Interscope Records,

a company that had on its roster Snoop Doggy Dogg, who was arrested on murder charges. His album *Doggy Style* sold four million copies, generating $40m, despite being banned by, among others, Radio KACE in Los Angeles and New York's WBLS. The artist toured Britain while on a $1m bail bond. He was one of many best-selling rap artists who blurred the boundary between life and art.

Rap began as innocent rhapsodies about boys and girls, but changed to angry and often malevolent diatribes often against women. Early evidence of this came in Ice-T's "Six in the morning" – "As we walked over to her, hoe continued to speak/So we beat the bitch down in the goddam street" and Ice Cube's "Gangsta fairytale" "Jack and Jill went up the hill to take a nap/Young bitch gave him the clap."

The "considered" response to rap's abuse of women was to explain how black males were engaged in a search for the causes of their obvious disempowerment. State authority figures, as epitomized by the police, were located, as were black women. Houston Baker suggested that the defense for the crudely sexist 2 Live Crew might rest on the "But, officer, the cars in front of me were speeding too!" plea. Cornel West writes effusively about the rappers' role in "the repoliticizing of the black working poor and underclass" in his book *Keeping Faith* (Routledge, 1993) yet parenthesizes "(despite their virulent sexism)."

Many female rap artists recoiled against this. In her 1994 single "Unity," Queen Latifah asked: "Who *you* callin' a bitch?" Roxanne Shante proclaimed "Brothers ain't shit." Others used names in parody of their male counterparts: Hoes with Attitude was one example. Bytches with Problems was another, though their track "Two minute brother," in deriding a less than spectacular lover, affirmed rap's homeboy patriarchal values, the ones that celebrated the kind of man who could provide for his woman (or, more usually, women) both materially and sexually and ridiculed others as "fruity" or "punks." As Tricia Rose observed: "This sort of homophobia affirms oppressive standards of heterosexual masculinity."

The popularity of rap with mainstream audiences has ensured the profitability of several once-independent record companies specializing in rap. Over the years, a tier of young entrepreneurs has emerged, the most celebrated being

Russell Simmons, of Rush Communications. Others include Andre Harrell, Sean "Puffy" Combs aka P. Diddy and Antonio "LA" Reid, all of whom have made personal fortunes from what became in the mid 1990s a rap industry.

By the start of the twenty-first century, rap's incorporation into the mainstream was complete: albums by rappers DMX, Mystikal and Nelly regularly headed the best-selling lists and Eminem's *The Marshall Mathers LP* was the biggest selling album in the world in 2000.

Andy Gill explained the rise of rap in terms of a reaction against capitalism. He reasons that, since the 1950s, pop culture has become so pervasive that it is in effect *the* global common culture. "But the entertainment industry has become so much more skilled in moulding teenage desires, that it is all the harder for modern youth to carve themselves a little authentic personal space," wrote Gill, suggesting that disenfranchised youth of all class and ethnic backgrounds seek expression of their situation in the swearing, sexuality and criminal glamor of rap.

The seal of approval was given to rap by Tipper Gore (wife of presidential candidate, Al Gore) when she lobbied the American music industry to put parental advisory stickers on albums deemed obscene – which meant a great deal of rap's output. The sticker became a powerful signifier. In Britain, a consignment of NWA's *Efil4zaggin* was impounded, though later released after a court case.

But, it was Eminem, a white artist, who managed to horrify while, at the same time, dominating the mainstream. Likened to Elvis Presley, "he represents a threat to established values," wrote Gill in 2001. "The ostensible threat is different in substance, but ultimately of little consequence; what both men really represent is the championing of a black art form over their 'native' white European heritage."

SEE ALSO: African Americans; blues; consumption; cultural identity; humor; hybridity; Jackson, Michael; Jordan, Michael; Lee, Spike; minstrelsy; Million Man March; Motown; media; racial coding; reggae; representations; Rock Against Racism; Tyson, Mike; youth subcultures

Reading

Black Noise: Rap music and black culture in contemporary America by Tricia Rose (Wesleyan University Press, 1994) analyzes rap as an oppositional practice, a vehicle through which the voice from the margins can be heard. Houston S. Baker's *Black Studies, Rap and the Academy* (University of Chicago Press, 1993) takes a similar approach, while *The New Beats* by S. H. Fernando, Jr. (Payback Press, 1995) is in effect an oral history of rap music and the general hip-hop culture of which it is part. All provide generally appreciative interpretations.

"How rap conquered the world" by Andy Gill (in *Independent*, Friday Review, February 23, 2001) is the interesting account of the rise of rap cited in the man text above.

"The rap on rap" by David Samuels (in *The New Republic*, November 11, 1991, pp. 24–9) and "Jazz, rock'n'roll, rap and politics" by M. Bernard-Donals (in *Journal of Popular Culture*, vol. 28, no. 2, Fall 1994: 127–38) offer a cynical contrast from the above readings and understand the rap genre as a white-driven operation.

RASTAFARI

Arguably the fastest-growing black movement of the 1970s/80s, it first appeared in Jamaica in 1930 just after the decline in fortunes of Marcus Garvey, who organized his Universal Negro Improvement Association around the ambition to return to Africa. "Africa for the Africans" was Garvey's basic philosophy, and he worked at mass migration programs, buying steamship lines and negotiating with African governments.

Garvey had some success in the West Indies (he was born in Jamaica), but was more influential after his demise, for he was reputed to have prophesied: "Look to Africa when a black king shall be crowned, for the day of deliverance is near." Around this prediction a whole movement was mobilized. In 1930, Ras Tafari was crowned Emperor of Ethiopia and took his official title of Haile Selassie I. Garvey, at this stage, had slipped from prominence, but at least some black Jamaicans remembered his prophecy and made the connection between "the black king" Haile Selassie and "the day of deliverance," the return to Africa. The connection was reinforced by a new element added by new adherents of Garvey. They made the conclusion that Haile Selassie was not just a king but also their God and Messiah, who would miraculously organize a black exodus to Africa (used synonymously with Ethiopia) and simultaneously dissolve the imperial domination by Western powers – "Babylon" to the new Garveyites.

It is worth noting that in no way did Garvey endorse this new interpretation of his philosophy. Indeed, he assailed Haile Selassie as "a great coward" and "the leader of a country where blackmen are chained and flogged." Further, Garvey insisted on practical organization and de-emphasized the value of spiritual salvation; his new followers went in the other direction, making no provision for returning to Africa, simply awaiting the intervention of their Messiah, Ras Tafari.

However, what Garvey actually said was less important than what he was reputed to have said, and, quickly, the new movement gained followers among the socially deprived black Jamaicans, hopeful of any kind of change in their impoverished lives and willing to cling to the flimsiest of theories of how they might escape their condition. They adopted the Garvey movement's colors of red, black, and green (from the Ethiopian flag) and twisted their hair into long matted coils called dreadlocks as if to exaggerate their primitivity in contrast to Western appearances. Some made use of ganja, a type of cannabis found in Jamaica, and even endowed this "weed" with religious properties. They used it in ritual worship of *Jah* (the form of "Jehovah" used in bibles before the King James version). Many took to the hilly inner regions of the island and set up their own communes, a celebrated one being that led by Leonard Howell, who, with Joseph Hibbert and H. Archibald Dunkley, is popularly attributed as one of the original formulators of the new Garveyism.

Garvey remained a reluctant prophet, although a careful reading of his speeches and published comments reveals his great interest in Ethiopian royalty and his repeated use of biblical, often apocalyptic, imagery to strengthen his beliefs. "We Negroes believe in the God of Ethiopia, the everlasting God," wrote Garvey in volume one of his *Philosophy and Opinions*. His conception of a black god was also significant; he implored his followers to destroy pictures of white Christs and Madonnas and replace them with black versions. "No one knows when the hour of Africa's Redemption cometh," he once warned his followers. "It is in the wind. It is coming. One day, like a storm, it will be here."

Periodically, the Rastas, as they came to be called, gathered at ports to await the ships to take them to Africa and, at one stage, a faction of the movement resorted to guerrilla tactics in a vain effort to assist the destruction of Babylon. More recently, the movement in Jamaica has gained a more respectable status and, nowadays, has become a vital cultural force on the island.

In the middle of the 1970s, the Rastafarian movement manifested itself in such places as the USA, England, Holland, France, New Zealand and Australia. Its growth was stimulated by the rise in popularity of Rasta-inspired reggae music, which was given a personal focus by the almost prototype Rasta Bob Marley (1945–81). It seems that the vision of a united African continent and a black god was a potent one. It was used in sharp counter-position to the imperial dominance of the West. Blacks feeling disaffected with society and searching for alternatives found in the movement a new force which upgraded blackness and instilled in them a sense of identity, of belonging to a unity.

Despite an infinite variation in interpretation of Garvey's philosophy, two themes remained central to Rastafarian beliefs: the divinity of Haile Selassie (whose death in 1975 did little to dissuade Rastas of his potency in instigating the transformation) and the impulse to return to Africa – if not physically then in consciousness (as the Rasta reggae musician, Peter Tosh, sang; "Don't care where you come from, as long as you're a black man, you're an African").

In 1989, Trevor Dawkins, a Rasta born in Birmingham, England, won a case of racial discrimination against a British government agency and, in the process, threw the legal status of Rastas into confusion. Under the terms of the 1976 Race Relations Act, Rastas became officially recognized as an ethnic group and, as such, could not be lawfully discriminated against on the basis of their cultural characteristics. They were liable to the same kind of protection afforded to Sikhs (who cannot be refused work for wearing turbans, for example). The decision was subsequently reversed, leading to a legal debate on the subject.

SEE ALSO: Ethiopianism; Garvey, Marcus; kinship; Nation of Islam; *nÕgritude*; reggae; youth subcultures

Reading

Rastafari and Other Afro-Caribbean Worldviews, edited by Barry Chevannes (Macmillan, 1995), is a collection of conference papers, most of which discuss aspects of the movement.
Rastafari and Reggae by Rebekah Mulvaney (Greenwood Press, 1990) is a dictionary of Rasta terms.
The Rastafarians, 2nd edn., by Ellis Cashmore (Minor-

ity Rights Group, 1992), is an update of an earlier report, which documents legal changes in the status of Rastafarians in Britain. It focuses on the Dawkins case.

RATIONAL CHOICE THEORY

A theory that treats behavior as the selection of means to obtain given ends. The preferences, dispositions, or prejudices of those who control access to scarce resources are understood as comparable to consumer tastes for particular kinds of product.

Maximizing gains/minimizing costs

A successful theory explains many observations. Take, for example, the observation that, in the 1940s, black- and brown-skinned students at London University had to pay more than white-skinned students to obtain lodgings in private houses. They called the differential a "color tax" because it appeared that the darker the student's complexion the more he or she had to pay. The differential could be explained as the result of supply and demand. The supply of lodgings was at the discretion of property owners, who at that time were frequently middle-aged women; sometimes they were widows who had inherited relatively large houses and could continue living in them by renting out rooms. They provided breakfast and an evening meal; they often arranged for the washing of their lodgers' clothing, they might require them to be home by a particular hour, and did not permit guests of the opposite sex to visit lodgers in their rooms. It was a quasi-familial relationship. Taking in students did not demean their social status as much as taking in other kinds of lodger would have done because university students were then an elite among their age group. The landladies' reluctance to accommodate students from India and Africa was a compound of fears that relations with them might be more difficult and a concern for their own status. If they took in black- or brown-skinned students the neighbors might think that they did so only because they could not get white students, and that this must be because the standard of their rooms was not high enough. In such circumstances the color tax can be seen as compensation to the landlady for departing from her preferred course of action. The level of the tax was determined by student demand and the landladies' preferences.

This explanation treats the legal sanctions that can be imposed on those who discriminate unlawfully as costs that can discourage such persons from indulging their tastes. It is a theory of aggregate behavior in that it explains the behavior of landladies as a group, not that of any individual lady (some of whom did not prefer white students or ask a higher rent from Indians or Africans). The color tax measured the price that they placed upon their preferences. These could change. Some landladies may have had bad experiences with a particular kind of lodger and have concluded that it would be risky to accept any others of this kind. The theory assumes that the landladies were attempting to maximize their gains and minimize their costs (both material and in social status). It does not attempt to explain the origin of tastes (such as why many ladies preferred as lodgers students of the same color or ethnic origin as themselves), nor why so many Indian and African students studied in London rather than elsewhere.

The theory is one example of the many exercises in the latter part of the twentieth century that applied economic reasoning in the study of social life. It is one among a group of theories that have common characteristics but go under different names, such as theories of exchange, of games, of public choices, of transactions, of rational action and of *rational choice*. This last name has sometimes been misinterpreted as designating theorizing about rational choices only, as if irrational choices had to be explained by other kinds of theory. Those who favor the theory contend, to the contrary, that it is not limited to intentional and utilitarian behavior, but that it prescribes the examination of all kinds of choice against the standard of rationality. If someone chooses a course of action that does not maximize his or her benefits, he or she will learn from the experience and try to do better next time.

Applications of rational choice theory have been extended to explain why less racial discrimination is to be expected in more competitive markets. The search for profit should lead an employer to engage the best workers irrespective of their color, but when political pressure has been exerted to promote racial segregation (as in apartheid South Africa) white workers have been able to exploit their political advantage to secure a monopoly of the better paying jobs and to extract higher wages than they would have been able to obtain in competition with black workers. Mining employers at one time built a labor *monopsony* (one buyer, many sellers) to force black workers to take lower wages than they would have been able to obtain had the employers competed with one another for labor. A segregated labor market would reinforce employers' tastes for association with employees of their own color and ethnic origin. If the segregation were eliminated these tastes might persist, but the effects of competition would increase the cost of indulging them.

A prime stimulus to the application of economic theories to political life was the analysis of the problem of the "free-rider" in Mancur Olson's book *The Logic of Collective Action*. This explained how it could be in the interest of individuals to draw benefit from the collective action of others without paying their share. Thus students seeking accommodation can pursue their ends by individual action (beginning by scanning the appropriate columns in the local newspaper for addresses) or by collective action (joining with others to press their university to build special student accommodation). A student who secured a place in new university accommodation without having supported those who campaigned for it would have taken a free ride on the back of others' efforts. Much of the behavior constituting the substance of ethnic and racial relations is collective action by persons cooperating in the pursuit of shared ends. If it is to succeed some means must be found to minimize free-riding. The cultivation of a norm of solidarity with other members of the same racial or ethnic group can be one means to this end. Whereas in what is sometimes call "act utilitarianism" a person acts to maximize his or her net advantages, the cultivation of such a norm illustrates "rule utilitarianism," the process by which people adopt a rule that reduces their individual freedom (and is therefore a cost) but which maximizes their long-term benefits.

Ethnogenesis and group identity

Confronted by the apparently distinctive character of racial and ethnic relations, rational choice theory has to account for the formation, maintenance, and sometimes the dissolution, of racial and ethnic groups. Notable examples of group formation have been the ethnogenesis of African Americans and of Palestinians. Afro-Americans descend, in varying degree, from persons originating from a great variety of peoples in Africa, mostly near the West coast. They came to feel themselves a single people because of the circumstances in which they found themselves in North America. Whereas African Americans were brought to a new country, the Palestinian identity was forged in reaction to the immigration of another people. In 1881, just before the birth of the Zionist movement, there were 25,000 Jews in that part of the Ottoman Empire called Palestine. The first suggestion of a Palestinian ethnic identity appeared in 1911. The Arab population came to feel themselves a people, and to call themselves Palestinians, as a result of the tensions associated with the foundation of Israel. New ethnic groups were also sometimes created in Africa when the colonial powers grouped smaller peoples into larger units or when migrants from one region came together in the cities. In such settings ethnic identity is negotiated rather than pre-existent.

A group mobilizes to pursue its members' shared ends, changing an aggregation of individuals into what is, for the time being at least, a *solidary* group (i.e. one that it is held together by shared interests, feelings and action). The processes by which this is achieved are similar whether the group is a minority or a majority, and whether it is based on shared race, ethnicity, religion, language or class. With the formation of a group comes a sense of obligation to fellow-members, so that membership can be a useful resource providing access to help and cooperation when wanted. Sometimes ethnic groups dissolve. In England after the Norman Conquest the ethnic tension between Saxon and Norman had dissipated two centuries later. In the USA many persons of European origin, because of intermarriage and their way of life, now feel themselves only "white American." Groups persist only if they are maintained in daily life by the exchange of services and modes of identification (like images on television). When they persist, feelings of group solidarity can make it difficult for anyone to leave the group (increasing what is called the exit cost). In racially divided societies the pressure to show solidarity reinforces the boundaries between the groups. When individuals are free to compete with others of both their own and other groups, this tends to weaken group boundaries and give way to group formation based on other shared characteristics, such as those of social class, nationality and religion.

Group processes interact with individual preferences. A person choosing a holiday resort may like to go to a place where there will be many other persons of the same ethnic origin, may be indifferent as to whether there are, or may want to go somewhere where he or she will meet no co-ethnics. Such a person will have either a positive preference for association with co-ethnics, or a zero preference, or a negative one. In similar fashion, a set of persons might share a wish to constitute a political unit populated only by persons of their ethnicity, but give this goal a low priority because they think it impracticable. A mobilizer could appear to persuade them that the means are to hand to create an ethnically pure state and a new movement could start. Moving the preference for association with co-ethnics up the popular scale of priorities relative to other priorities increases ethnic tension. Elevating some other priority (such as lifting the standard of living or improving personal security) can decrease it.

Opposition between two major groups (as in apartheid South Africa or Northern Ireland in the last decades of the twentieth century) resembles a zero-sum game in which a gain for one side can be only a loss for the other. Those on one side may sacrifice short-term benefits in order to reduce the other side's benefits and threaten further sanctions. Resolution of the struggle in Northern Ireland may provide an example of a positive-sum situation in which in the longer term both sides benefit from the bargaining over rewards. The study of bargaining has been developed in connection with wage and tariff negotiation and applied to negotiation between the super powers over nuclear disarmament. It suggests that, applied to racial and ethnic relations, the key consideration is that of representation. If all the parties are represented by agents able to reach bargains on behalf of those they represent, much is possible. Often those who come forward as bargaining agents are not able to control elements within their own groups who insist on holding out for more favorable terms.

Methodological individualism

All the varieties of the theory of rational choice are examples of bottom-up as opposed to top-down theorizing. Their potential explanatory power is considerable, but many current critics within sociology are unimpressed by them. The critics do not advance alternative theories that can provide better explanations of observations like that about the color tax, but maintain that there are more interesting or politically important questions to pursue. Some of the critics look to top-down theories that seek historical interpretations of trends within national societies. They try to formulate more comprehensive explanations of such trends than rational choice theorists believe epistemologically possible. Rational choice theory relies on the principle of methodological individualism. Critics sometimes regard this as a weakness, but the alternative is methodological collectivism, which treats groups as units. Methodological collectivism ignores the problems of free-riding, of political differences about strategy inside groups (e.g. calculations of long-term as opposed to short-term benefits). It leads easily to essentialist conceptions of race and ethnicity, as if the character of a group was determined by some inner essence. Since much of the writing that is currently classified as "theory" fails to identify researchable questions, it is difficult to compare the explanatory power of the different theories.

Critics maintain that some expositions or applications of rational choice theory emphasize agency at the expense of structure. Weaknesses of such a kind are not inherent in the theory and can be remedied, but there are limitations of a more fundamental character. The main one is reliance on the axiom that individuals seek to maximize their net advantages with its associated concept of revealed preference, a preference that is revealed after the event (e.g., the landladies' preference for student lodgers of their own color or ethnic origin) for which there may be no independent evidence. This weakness can be remedied to some extent by empirical inquiry into what are called positive preferences (the landladies could be interviewed), but since stated preferences can change when a decision has to be taken it is difficult to test their influence upon actual decisions.

The techniques for analyzing collective action offer the best prospect for overcoming the opposition between bottom-up and top-down approaches in social science, because they take account of the particular character of the circumstances in which members of groups find themselves; they entail empirical inquiry into the extent to which group members share ends and can agree upon means to pursue them, and they lead on to the analysis of interaction between groups.

SEE ALSO: assimilation; ethnic conflict; Marxism; racial discrimination; social exclusion

Reading

The Logic of Collective Action: Public goods and the theory of groups by Mancur Olson (Harvard University Press, 1965) has inspired much of the theorizing in this field.

Principles of Group Solidarity by Michael Hechter (University of California Press, 1987) presents a sophisticated analysis of the conditions under which groups are more or less solidary.

Race and Economics by Thomas Sowell (McKay, 1975) is a stimulating application of the theory to the USA.

Racial Theories, 2nd edn., by Michael Banton (Cambridge: Cambridge University Press, 1998) discusses explanations of discrimination and of mobilization at pages 140–58 and 219–26 respectively; while a special issue of the journal *Ethnic and Racial Studies* (vol. 8, no. 4, 1985) is devoted to the examination of rational choice theory.

MICHAEL BANTON

READING RACE

To read is to interpret or make sense of. The use of the term reading is particularly relevant to the way in which race is visualized and how we read visual clues in order to understand how someone or some group is raced, or subject to the process of racialization.

We could also say the same for other signs – such as clothing and style, but also language, rituals and so on – all the markers of what is now called ethnicity and culture, but are often then mapped back onto particular *racial* groups.

For adults, reading race is something that is for the most part "second nature," what is perhaps more interesting is the work done with children which shows how reading race, ethnicity and culture as embodied signs or practices can, at an early age, form the basis for racism. In addition, the reading processes can offer unique insights to the actual processes of racialization as they may differ from those of adults.

It is only comparatively recently that children have been taken seriously as respondents in social research. Recent studies into race and racism in schools has shown that from a very early age children learn about racial difference

and that it is value-laden. Paul Connolly's 1997 work with children as young as five and six in multiethnic schools shows this in shocking clarity. However, even children in mainly white areas are learning to read race, sometimes at a distance, through their use of popular culture. For example, in recent research with children aged eight to eleven in a semi-rural location, many of them reported having heard about the Stephen Lawrence inquiry on the TV news and that was how they had learnt about racism.

Others thought that "most Black people on television are American" and drew on the stereotypes of sport and music to support their assertion. The most interesting finding was that when shown images of famous people from popular culture, the mostly white, middle-class children (and to a lesser extent their peers in multiethnic areas) would look for certain "visual clues" in order to assess a person's race and then, from that, their ethnic or national heritage. The American R'n'B star Coolio was identified as Jamaican on a number of occasions on the basis of his hair, which was in dreadlocks at the time. This seems a fairly logical process, but obviously is an impossible task for the most part as in reality skin color, hair styles and so on are much more ambiguous. In working through the same sorts of ideas with Scary Spice (Melanie Brown) who claims a mixed-race and black identity, children showed the potential pitfalls of attempting to read race. Using a range of discourses they tried to show a knowledge of her mixedness but also admitted that her skin color alone could *not* reveal her race beyond all doubt, and even less give information about her background or heritage.

There are two important points in much of this work that provide valuable resources for dismantling racial hierarchies and combating racism.

1   We can look at how it is that race comes to make sense to us at an early age. In particular, through studying the "errors" in racial readings we can challenge the naturalization of race, and find concrete points of intervention into the negative and positive values attached to different aspects of embodied racialization.

2   These same misreadings and creative readings not only remind us forcibly of the erroneous nature of racial categories, but

also show how they are simply inadequate to the task of dealing with the increasingly multiplicitous nature of racial heritages in modern urban lives.

The research with children showed how they are attempting to make sense of a range of clues in order to ascribe race in the first instance, but also how that is attached to a range of other identifications, the most significant of which was nationality. So, for example, in attempting to place a pop group containing "white" men and women, a selection of Western countries would be invoked that could range from Belgium to Australia. Reading race is just one way in which children make sense of, and begin to order, perceived difference, but is arguably still relevant to the way in which adults too position themselves in relation to others.

SEE ALSO: bigotry; children; dress; Lawrence case, the Stephen; Other; racialization; stereotype

Reading

"Black Bodies, White Bodies" in *"Race," Culture and Difference*, edited by J. Donald and A. Rattansi (Sage, 1992), may profitably be read in conjunction with *Anatomy of Race* by David T. Goldberg (University of Minnesota Press, 1990)

Racism, Gender Identities and Young Children: Social relations in a multi-ethnic, inner-city primary school by P. Connolly (Routledge, 1998) contains details of the interesting study cited in the main text above.

"Reading racialised bodies: learning to see difference" by Suki Ali, in *Cultural Bodies: Theory and ethnography*, edited by H. Thomas and J. Ahmed (Blackwell, 2003), explores in more detail several of the issues raised in the main text above.

SUKI ALI

REFUGEE STATUS

Colloquially, a refugee is a person who seeks refuge outside the country of his/her habitual or recent residence on grounds of persecution, which may be based on a variety of factors, including race, religion, color, culture, nationality, or political or sexual orientation. The term was apparently first applied to the French Huguenots who sought sanctuary in England after the revocation of the Edict of Nantes (*rõfugiõ* from *rõfugier*, to flee). In national and international law it refers to persons who are seeking official status as a refugee in a particular country,

under the terms of the domestic law of that country and/or international law.

Most countries are signatories to the 1951 UN Convention relating to the Status of Refugees, and many to the 1967 Protocol thereto. As of August 8, 2002, 141 states had ratified the Convention, 139 the 1967 Protocol, and 136 state parties had ratified both. The domestic laws of these signatories are expected, minimally, to comply with their provisions, although the asylum laws of some countries may be wider in scope. The Convention specifies that a refugee is a person who "owing to a well-founded fear of being persecuted for reasons of race, religion, nationality, membership of a particular social group, or political opinion, is outside the country of his nationality, and is unable or, owing to such fear, is unwilling to avail himself of the protection of that country."

The Convention specifies the protections that someone who is a refugee is entitled to, as well as the obligations of refugees to the laws of the host country. The rights include freedom of movement, freedom of religion, and access to travel documents. Their rights, in the view of the UN High Commissioner for Refugees, should approximate those of other foreigners in the country where they seek asylum who are legally resident there. One of its key provisions specifies that a person who has sought refugee status should not be forcibly returned, *refouled*, to a country where he or she fears persecution. It is the task of the host country to make a determination as to whether the applicant is entitled to the status of a refugee, and to put in place procedures that will enable such to be achieved expeditiously. The source of such controversy concerning refugees/asylum seekers in many countries at present, particularly in some western European countries and Australia, relates to issues of whether applicants face a *genuine* and *well-founded* fear of persecution in the countries from which they have fled. Economic migrants, those seeking to re-establish in other countries because of the perceived economic benefits for doing so, are not covered by the 1951 Convention or the 1967 Protocol.

The implementation of the Convention and Protocol, as well as the wider interests of refugees, and, in many but not all instances, those of internally displaced persons (IDPs), are overseen by the UN High Commissioner for Refugees UNHCR, which was established in

December 1950. In the course of its history it has assisted more than fifty million refugees in establishing lives in other countries, and has provided assistance to millions of refugees who have been caught up in international and internal wars.

The table below provides some overall UNHCR statistics, by UN major area, for asylum seekers, refugees and others of concern at the end of 2001.

In this table *Refugees* refers to persons recognized as refugees under the 1951 UN Convention/1967 Protocol, the 1969 OAU Convention, in accordance with the UNHCR Statute, persons granted a humanitarian status and those granted temporary protection, whereas *asylum seekers* designates persons whose application for asylum or refugee status is pending in the asylum procedure or who are otherwise registered as asylum seekers. In countries with various stages in the asylum procedure, a case (person, family) may have been counted more than once.

SEE ALSO: asylum seeker; bigotry; diaspora; human rights; International Convention; scapegoat; UNESCO; United Nations; xenophobia

Reading

The Law of Refugee Status by James Hathaway (Butterworths, 1991) is slightly dated and should be read in conjunction with *Guide to International Refugee Law Resources on the Web*: available at *http://www.llrx.com/features/refugee.htm*, compiled by Elisa Mason, who worked for six years with the UNHCR, published July 2000.

The Price of Indifference: Refugees and humanitarian action in the new century by Arthur C. Helton (Oxford University Press, 2002) focuses on forced displacement and the role of the United Nations.

Refugee Law, Status and Rights, available at *http:// www.refugeecaselaw.org/Refugee/Default.asp*, provided by the University of Michigan Law School: "The site currently collects, indexes, and publishes selected recent court decisions that interpret the legal definition of a 'refugee.' It presently contains cases from the highest national courts of Australia, Austria, Canada, Germany, New Zealand, Switzerland, the United Kingdom, and the United States." Also available are the British Home Office Country Assessments.

UNHCR, available at *http://www.refugeecaselaw.org/ Refugee/Default.asp*, provides access to extensive information relating to refugees/asylum seekers, as well as access to relevant international legal instruments and procedures.

CHECK: internet resources section

STUART STEIN

REGGAE

An amalgam of various musical forms, reggae – probably derived from "raggamuffin," a raggedly dressed person – became a near-universal cultural phenomenon. In the 1970s, it was the music of the Rastafari: its messages and motifs were diffused primarily through the music of Bob Marley (1945–81), whose albums continued to sell in the 1990s. Stylistic derivatives of reggae included ragga, moshing and jungle.

	Refugees	Asylum seekers	Returned refugees	Others of concern			Total population of concern
				Internally displaced	Returned IDPs	Various	
Africa	3,305,070	107,159	266,804	421,574	42,000	30,920	4,173,527
Asia	5,770,345	33,111	49,246	2,720,462	–	247,502	8,820,666
Europe	2,227,900	335,375	146,457	1,185,914	198,950	760,781	4,855,377
Latin America and the Caribbean	37,377	7,878	194	720,000	–	–	765,449
Northern America	645,077	441,681	–	–	–	–	1,086,758
Oceania	65,351	15,587	–	–	–	313	81,251
Various/unknown	–	–	22	–	–	–	22
Total	12,051,120	940,791	462,723	5,047,950	240,950	1,039,516	19,783,050

Essentially a music of protest, reggae fused several different elements of popular music in Jamaica where it originated. Indeed, its origins may be traced way back to the hybrid music that was born out of slave days. But it seems that the significant stage in the development of reggae was in the 1950s, when the sound of black American rhythm and blues and soul music filtered across to the Caribbean via radio stations and West Indians who migrated temporarily to the USA to look for work. Early attempts to imitate American music foundered, but inadvertently gave rise to a unique style that came to be called "blue beat" and, later, "ska." This was popularized in the West Indies, particularly in Jamaica, by peripatetic disc jockeys who operated a "sound system." The DJs stamped their own identity on the music by "dubbing" or toasting over the music, literally speaking into the microphone while the records were playing, in efforts to urge the dancers; this became known as "toasting" and many DJs established more prestigious reputations than the musicians they dubbed over.

In the 1960s, ska was introduced into Britain and was received enthusiastically by sections of white youth without ever growing into a popular music. Occasionally, ska records would become commercial successes, "Long shot kick the bucket" and "The return of Django" being examples.

Late in the 1960s, however, ska underwent mutations and the flavor of its lyrics became altogether more political. Musicians, either adhering to or being sympathetic with Rastafarian ideals, began expressing statements on the condition of black people through the music. Themes included exploitation, poverty, inequality, liberation, and the critical experience of "suffering." They were articulated through Rastafarian imagery, the system of control being Babylon, as contrasted with the liberty of Zion. Predictions of "war in a Babylon" and "Catch a fire, the wheel will turn, slavedriver you gonna get burn" were incorporated into the music.

In his book *The Black Atlantic*, Gilroy writes of reggae's contribution to the creation of a "self-consciously synthetic culture"; he writes: "Once its [reggae's] own hybrid origins in rhythm and blues were effectively concealed, it ceased, in Britain, to signify an exclusively ethnic Jamaican style and derived a different kind of cultural legitimacy both from a new global status and from its expression of what might be termed a pan-Caribbean culture." Reggae, in this view, articulates the consciousness of being part of a black diaspora.

SEE ALSO: Afrocentricity; blues; diaspora; Ethiopianism; Motown; rap; Rastafari; Rock Against Racism

Reading

Catch a Fire by Timothy White (Elm Tree Books, 1983) is the best and most comprehensive biography of Bob Marley based on interviews with Marley and members of an "inner circle" of friends during a seven-year period before the artist's death in 1981; the book chronicles Marley's childhood and early involvement with reggae and shows how he was promoted to the position of "superstar" in the 1970s; it also contains a full "discography" of Marley, the Wailers, and his backing singers, the I Threes.

Cut 'n' Mix by Dick Hebdige (Comedia, 1987) offers a concise definition of reggae, but also considers other Caribbean music idioms as expressions of the black experience in the New World.

Rastafari and Reggae by Rebekah Mulvaney (Greenwood Press, 1990) is a dictionary and sourcebook.

There Ain't No Black in the Union Jack by Paul Gilroy (Hutchinson, 1987) contains a sustained analysis of reggae and may be read as a precursor to the author's later work *The Black Atlantic* (Verso, 1993).

RELIGION *see* Islamophobia; Nation of Islam; Pentecostalism; Rastafari

REPARATIONS

Reparations are forms of compensation for damage inflicted on a nation, culture or ethnic group. They have been enshrined in US legislation since 1946, when Congress quietly passed an act that created an Indian Claims Commission, though their ancestry is much older. Since the late 1980s, proponents of reparations in the USA have organized and rallied through the National Coalition of Blacks for Reparations in America (N'COBRA). Their demand is that the US Government make amends for centuries of slavery and for discrimination after slavery. Interestingly, because employed persons of African descent in the USA, except for the poorest, pay income taxes, they will be helping to pay their own reparations.

Origins in slavery

While reparations have contemporary associations, they have a long history. The last of the great Roman emperors, Justinian, is held to be the author of the conclusion *Summa itaque divisa de jura haec personarem est, quod homines aut Libere aut Servi* ("The principal difference between the rights of men is this, that all men are either free or slave"). By AD 529, Justinian had outlawed slavery among Christians in Europe. His rule would be followed in the Thirteen English Colonies in that European whites were considered Christians, although this was not the case for baptized Africans. Whites could be indentured; blacks, baptized or not, could be enslaved.

To be sure, slavery in Africa after Justinian and Muhammad sometimes had a face as cruel as that in the American colonies, but sometimes its face was the same as that reported for ancient Egypt when Joseph was allowed to become a ruler. The King James version of the Protestant Bible bears a reparations story, "revealing" an interesting version of "slavery" and an account of reparations to which some black reparationists refer. God is said to have told the Jewish leader Moses that he would smite the first-born of the Egyptians, who were said to be holding Jewish people in slavery. Interestingly it appears that to distinguish Jewish homes from Egyptian homes it was necessary to mark the Jewish homes with blood: in short, there were no "slave quarters." The Lord is reported to have instructed Moses that unleavened bread was for the Jews but that "every man's servant that is bought for money, when thou hast circumscribed him, then shall he eat thereof."

When the Egyptian Pharaoh decided to command all the Jewish people to leave Egypt, the King James Bible reports that Moses directed his people to ask "of the Egyptians jewels of silver and jewels of gold and raiment." And the Egyptians "gave unto them such things as they required."

Slavery has played a major role in questions of reparations. At the end of World War I, in 1919, the victorious Allies used the term reparations in documents requiring the defeated Germans to pay for "damage caused to civilians by being forced by Germany or her allies to labor without just remuneration." Again, toward the end of World War II, in 1945 at Yalta and again in Paris after the war in 1946, the Allies wrote of the necessity of reparations from Germany for rehabilitation. Later, in 1999, persons used as slaves in German factories reached a settlement with the German government and some of those companies which had enslaved them: over $5.2 billion for several hundred thousand victims.

In the USA, the foundation of the modern reparations movement was established by Callie House, a woman who in the 1880s was so moved by the poverty and suffering of the people freed from slavery twenty-five years earlier without any compensation that she began an organization called The National Ex-Slave Mutual Relief Bounty and Pension Association. House successfully gained members in several southern and mid-South states, and the movement kept an agent in Washington, DC. But the US government attempted to destroy the organization and in 1917 engineered her imprisonment for a year and a day. She continued with her commitment.

Legal foundations

The previously mentioned 1946 law was designed to allow American Indian nations to come before Commission judges and argue for redress for arrangements made with them which lacked "fair dealings" without the structures normally required by federal civil procedures. By the time the Commission terminated in 1978 Commission judges had considered many cases. Indian representatives argue that the process provided only small benefits.

While this was a precedent, the piece of legislation that became an alarm for persons in the Americas, Africa and, indeed, Europe who claimed to suffer racial discrimination based on an African heritage, came in 1988 – a year after the USA celebrated the 200th anniversary of the approval of its Constitution. It was a reparations bill for persons of Japanese ancestry who were US citizens and/or resident aliens, living mainly in California, when the Empire of Japan began war against the United States at Pearl Harbor. The Japanese Americans, while having committed no acts of sabotage or other delinquency against the USA, were put under curfew and exclusion orders and most were transferred to inland concentration camps. They remained in these camps from 1942 to 1946. Congress' 1988 legislation, which included an apology and a payment of $20,000 to each of the constrained

Japanese and their non-Japanese spouses, was the Civil Liberties Act of 1988.

During the passage of the Act, attorney Adjoa Aiyetoro, a veteran of civil rights work in Mississippi, organized a panel on reparations for persons of African descent in the USA. Under the auspices of the National Conference of Black Lawyers, the panel examined how the Thirteenth Amendment to the US Constitution, which ended slavery, might be changed to provide reparations and justice.

These events were pivotal in the rebirth of the struggle for reparations in the United States. In 1988 the Provisional Government of the Republic of New Afrika (PG-RNA) – a movement building on the work of Malcolm X and seeking to establish an independent country in the south of what is now the USA – asked its vice president Kalonji Olusegun, living in Washington, DC, to undertake the work of building a coalition of people of African descent, basically in the US, which was broader than the nationalists who were fostering the reparations rebirth. He joined with Adjoa Aiyetoro and out of their work was born the National Coalition of Blacks for Reparations in America, or N'COBRA. By the beginning of the present century, N'COBRA was the leading grassroots reparations organization in the US. It was also playing a role in the development of the Pan-African reparations movement seriously underway from September 2001.

As N'COBRA held its first organizing meetings in Washington, DC, Congressman John Conyers of Detroit sent to the conferees a copy of a draft reparations study bill. It was patterned after a congressional study that had preceded passage of the Japanese bill. Re-introduced every two-year session since 1969, the bill had not been provided a committee hearing as the session ending in January 2003 came to a close – despite visits to Congressional offices by N'COBRA members.

In this same period, the state of Florida reviewed the murder and community devastation visited upon the black town of Rosewood in January 1923. Florida voted reparations to survivors and began paying in 1994. Oklahoma, by contrast, undertook a legislative investigation of murder and destruction visited upon an appendage of Tulsa, Oklahoma, known as "Black Wall Street" but declined to pay reparations for this well documented crime of 1921, involving aerial bombing of the town.

At the start of the twenty first century, lawsuits against Aetna and several insurance companies and businesses were filed under the leadership of a young black lawyer, Deadria Farmer-Paellmann. Also in 1999 a suit seeking reparations for people of African descent, based on the Civil Liberties Act of 1988, was filed in the US Court of Federal Claims by Atty. Maynard M. Henry, Sr., for Dr. Obadele, Mr. Olusegun, and General Kuratibisha X Ali Rashid, all of the RNA Provisional Government. Chief Judge Lawrence Baskir dismissed the suit after three years of contest, yet commented that "the plaintiffs have made a powerful case for redress." Attorney Henry promptly appealed.

The state of California in the year 2001 passed a law forcing all companies doing business with the state to reveal any dealings during the era of slavery which were designed to create profit from any aspect of slavery. Following this, in 2002, Chicago became the first city in America to require firms seeking official contracts to disclose past links with slavery. Companies bidding to do business with the country's third largest city, which had over one million African American residents, were told to search their archives and make known any profits made from owning, insuring or trading in people held as slaves. Firms attempting to conceal their historical links were threatened with having their contracts with the city canceled. Supporters of the initiative, known as the Slavery Era Disclosure Ordinance, hailed it as a step toward securing payment of reparations to descendants of enslaved persons almost 140 years after emancipation. Dorothy Tillman, of Chicago's city council, went so far as to suggest that companies which might have conducted slave-related business, often through predecessor companies, could be shut out of city contract even if they did acknowledge such histories.

International movement

The rebirth of the reparations movement in the United States in late 1988 can be said to have borne international fruit when, in 1990, the Nigerian Head of State General Ibrahim Babangida, serving as head of the Organization of African Unity (OAU), made a speech which led the OAU to create a Group of Eminent Persons. Its chairman was Dr. Dudley Randall of Jamaica.

The prolific writer Chinweisu and the millionaire Bashorun Mashood K. Abiola, who lost his fortune and his life when the military, led by General Sani Abacha, seized the Nigerian government, drove this auspicious new beginning, which was derailed.

The Pan-African reparations movement was pursued on the continent, particularly at the UN in Geneva but also at the capitals of Zimbabwe and other African countries, by the International Secretariat of a New York-based organization known as The December 12th Movement. Viola Plummer and Roger Wareham led this. Their work helped to lead the way to a UN-sponsored World Conference Against Racism held in Durban, South Africa, during two weeks at the end of August to the beginning of September 2001. In October 2002, a Pan-African Congress, building on the Durban conference – at which one of the resolutions had declared slavery and the slave-trade to have been a crime against humanity – was held in Barbados with 900 participants from Africa, Europe, Asia, Australia, South America, the islands of the Americas, the USA and Canada.

SEE ALSO: Afrocentricity; American Indians; antislavery; Asian Americans; culturecide; emancipation; ethnocide; genocide; Holocaust; Malcolm X; Million Man March; Nation of Islam; riots: USA, 1921 (Tulsa); slavery; United Nations

Reading

Criminalizing A Race by Charshee C. L. McIntyre (Kayode Publications, Ltd., 1992) offers an interesting interpretation of law and politics making slavery the peculiar institution it was in the Thirteen Colonies and the USA.

The Debt, What America Owes To Blacks by Randall Robinson (Penguin Putnam, 2000) is an important argument for the rightness and value of reparations.

In The Matter of Color, by A. Leon Higginbotham (Oxford University Press, 1978) studies slavery and law as they developed in the Thirteen English Colonies.

Race, Racism and American Law by Derrick Bell (Little, Brown & Co., 1973) provides, among other things, insights into aspects of English law respecting slavery.

"Reparations for freedmen" by Mary F. Berry (in *Journal of Negro History,* vol. LVII, no. 3, 1972) includes a relatively full account of Callie House, her movement during the 1890–1916 period and the reparations bills submitted in Congress.

"Symposium: The constitution and race" (in *New York Law School Journal of Human Rights,* vol. 5, Part Two, 1988) reproduces papers on reparations and other racial issues that helped create the rebirth of the reparations movement in the USA.

IMARI ABUBAKARI OBADELE

REPRESENTATIONS

Boundary construction and the media

Representations consist of the images, ideas, signs, symbols, discourses and debates that feature within and are circulated by the channels and genres of the mass media. They transmit meanings and, as such, affect and are affected by the life of society; this is because media representations do not simply *reflect* society, but can play an active part in *constituting* what the nature of that society is, of how its social relations are conducted, and in defining what its future can be.

Historically, representations reveal the dominant thinking about "race" at moments in time and how prevailing cultures legitimize racist practices and perpetuate inequalities. Two outstanding analyses of this phenomenon are Jan Nederveen Pieterse's *White on Black: Images of Africa and blacks in Western popular culture* (Yale University Press, 1995) and Anne McLintock's *Imperial Leather: Race, gender and sexuality in the colonial context* (Routledge, 1995), both of which recover the racist ideologies and meanings embedded within earlier cultural formations. They make explicit how representations in, for example, advertising illustrations and the packaging of literature and consumer goods, encoded the dominant Western hegemony of the time and its racisms, either implicit or openly expressed.

However, the meanings of media representations need not only serve to legitimize dominant ideas of race or make racial inequalities appear natural: they can also become the site of contestation and challenge. The meanings of media representations are neither fixed for all time nor necessarily always accepted; increasingly they are acknowledged to perform actively a more benevolent (if sometimes patronizing) role in the changing cultural politics of "race" and ethnic identity in multicultural societies. Today's media, it seems, are capable of polluting the cultural pool of images and ideas about minority groups, thereby reinforcing or *re-inscribing* prejudicial views and racist practices. But they can also challenge stereotypes and promote multicultural understanding and intercultural dialog. In other words, media representations can help construct boundaries of inclusion as well as exclusion.

Boundaries erected by today's media extend to the outer geopolitical frontiers of nation-states, designed to keep migrants and asylum seekers out, as well as inwards to the core of one's intimate sense of self and personal identity. Media representations actively contribute to processes of boundary construction and maintenance by affirming the sense of who "we" are in relation to who we are *not*, whether as Us and Them, "insider" and "outsider," colonizer and colonized, the West and the rest, citizen and foreigner, normal and deviant, or even friend and foe.

When positioned in exclusionary ways, minorities can become ontologically disenfranchised from humanity, misrecognized as Other, exploited and oppressed and rendered, *in extremis*, vulnerable to lethal and systematic violence. But so too can the media – both mainstream and minority-based – serve to promote increased recognition and understanding of ethnic differences, the histories and struggles that inform these, as well as the richness and gains that identities of difference can bring to culturally diverse societies. In such ways, then, media representations variously and often powerfully enter into the life of society.

Three problematics

A problematic describes conditions that both enable and restrict thought; it defines the limits of what is thinkable. The three problematics of *race relations, racism/racialization* and *new ethnicities* have tended to guide the questions asked by researchers as well as the conceptualization of differing objects of inquiry and modes of approach.

Race relations. Early research conducted under the race relations problematic had relatively little to say about how media representations entered into the conduct of race relations and the problems of adjustment and assimilation of newly arrived immigrant groups. In this problematic the concept of "race" was often unquestioned and, in common-sense terms, seemingly assumed to have a biological basis. It was also to be at the root of "racial conflict situations." Media representations were

implicitly treated as seemingly irrelevant or as straightforward accounts of reality.

Racism/racialization. In contrast, this questions common-sense thinking and draws attention to the systematic and powered nature of racism in society as well as the ways in which minority groups become racialized – a representational process by which a group becomes ascribed with racial characteristics and defined as Other. Clearly, this second problematic helps draw attention to the roles of media in circulating racist ideas and images in society, including cultural ideas of "new racism," and its specific involvement in processes of racialization.

New ethnicities. More recently, a third problematic, based on a theorization of the cultural complexities of ethnic identities, processes of identity formation and change, has sought to engage with the discursive complexities and "positionalities" involved in ethnic identity and diasporic communities. In an influential essay, "New ethnicities," Stuart Hall has argued that the strategic mobilization of "the essential black subject" deployed earlier in the struggle against stereotypical representations and underrepresentation within the media, has subsequently given way to an acknowledgment of important ethnic minority differences and the multiple "subject positions" that exist within and between these. This emergent problematic thus encourages us to take seriously issues of ethnic minority differences and the complexities of media use, appropriation and sense making within processes of identity formation, contestation and change.

How diasporic communities and those positioned at the margins of society creatively utilize media technologies and integrate mainstream media representations within their daily lives and local cultural practices are theoretically prefigured in this problematic. Interestingly, the focus on processes of identity formation and change at the margins is also thought by some cultural theorists to help illuminate processes of hegemonic "ethnicity" and the construction of whiteness at the center.

The influence of these three overarching problematics can be detected in the research approaches to media representations of race, racism and ethnicity reviewed below.

Baseline research findings

Considerable research now exists that has examined the media's representations of "race," racism and ethnic minorities over a considerable period of time. The collective findings of this research effort can be summarized as follows: the media have often perpetuated underrepresentation and stereotypical characterization within entertainment, drama and fact-based genres and exhibit a tendency to ignore structural inequalities. In Britain from the late 1950s through to the 1970s, for example, studies observed how immigrants were reported in relation to the so-called race riots of 1958, public health scares, problems of numbers (of migrants) and tensions of "race relations" and how this effectively concealed problems of British racism.

In the 1970s and 1980s, studies of news, and other fact-based genres, identified the ways in which a moral panic orchestrated around mugging, the portrayal of street violence, and inner-city disorders, served to criminalize Britain's black population and ignored continuing social inequalities and growing anger at policing practices and harassment. In the late 1980s and 1990s, studies charted virulent press attacks on antiracism campaigns, the vilification of black representatives and the support given to statements of "new racism" by prominent politicians, as well as xenophobic reportage of refugees and migrants – actively disparaging attempts to further multicultural and antiracist agendas. Across the years, numerous studies have also observed the media's use of stock stereotypes of black people as troublemakers, entertainers and dependents.

In *Black Looks: Race and representation* (South End Press, 1992), bell hooks has maintained that "there has been little change in the area of representation. Opening a magazine or book, turning on the television set, watching a film, or looking at photographs in public spaces, we are most likely to see images of black people that reinforce and reinscribe white supremacy."

These and many other studies provide evidence of the general patterns, impoverished representations and sometimes starkly racist portrayals found in mainstream media. As *general* findings, however, they can perhaps inadvertently create a sense of media representations as historically static and ideologically uniform and, in consequence, cover over important processes of historical change, media differentiation and representational complexity.

Dynamic and differentiated media representations

Studies are now beginning to recover historically how changing ideas and political agendas, whether those of assimilation, antiracism or multiculturalism, have informed the development of media representations including those of television, the press and cinema. The influence of liberal TV producers as well as "responsible" newspapers and journalists has also contributed to, respectively, the downplaying of white racist fears and the selective curbing of sensational press treatments of civil disorder in earlier periods of conflict reporting. Studies such as these demonstrate something of the less-than-uniform representational portrayal of past media output. There has also been a greater ethnic minority presence in television, including advertising. A commodification of black music, dance and fashion has also taken place. These too are important features of contemporary ethnic minority media representation.

Contemporary societies increasingly accommodate ideas of multiculturalism, a growing sensibility that can sometimes provoke forms of white backlash culture as well as more subtle forms of modern racism. Attempts to move beyond old-fashioned racism by portraying, for example, African Americans in more positive ways within news representations, can sometimes create an impression of black social advance and thus undermine black claims on white resources and sympathies. Similar criticisms have also been leveled by Sut Jhally and Justin Lewis in their study *Enlightened Racism* (Westview Press, 1992) which argues that a successful "black" TV program such as *The Cosby Show* "tells us nothing about the structures behind success or failure" and "leaves white viewers to assume that black people who do not measure up to their television counterparts have only themselves to blame."

These studies increasingly point to the dynamic nature and subtleties of media discourse and representation, features that cannot always be captured through simplistic and static applications of the concept of stereotype. Ideas concerning new ethnicities and the cultural politics of difference, with their fluid understanding of contested subject positions, are today prompting a more diversified stance towards the politics of representation – one that increasingly questions essentialist stereotypes whether negative or positive. Ella Shohat and Robert Stam, in *Unthinking Eurocentrism: Multiculturalism and the media* (Routledge, 1997), also document representational complexities in the historical developments of film and uncover the continuing tensions within multicultural representations, a finding that is updated and theorized by Norman Denzin in *Reading Race: Hollywood and the cinema of racial violence* (Sage, 2001).

Recovering the play of difference

In order to address such representational complexities, studies today increasingly deploy an array of sophisticated textual methods when analyzing the myths, narratives, discourses and language embedded within media representations of "race." The work of Stuart Hall and Kobena Mercer demonstrates how recent images of black bodies often embody ambivalent meanings that deliberately play on ideas of cultural difference, stereotypes and intertextuality, and thereby prompt readings or interpretations that go against the grain.

Other studies also detect at least some discursive contestation and/or challenge to dominant viewpoints across mainstream genres and within minority media outlets, whether, for example, in representations of urban disorders in the USA or the portrayal of inner-city disturbances in the UK. None of the studies suggest that dominant views of "race" no longer inform media representations or that these can often serve to *racialize* media events. But these outcomes are precisely that: *outcomes* that have to be secured and managed if definitions, interpretations and prescriptions are to be effectively imposed on represented events. In other words, media representations of "race" are a product of social and discursive processes mediated through cultural forms; they are not a foregone conclusion and they most certainly are not beyond challenge or change.

Sensitized to the textual forms and discursive nature of media representations, recent studies have tended to reflect the growing influence of cultural studies and the wider linguistic (and cultural) turn in contemporary social theory. Here empiricist ideas of representation and

"ideology" have become increasingly challenged by approaches that explore the ways in which "reality" is constituted (and/or known) within language, discourse and representations. Approached in such discursive terms, representations do not so much "distort" reality as productively provide the means by which "reality" is actively constructed and/or known.

While this culturalist turn has helped to sensitize many to the discursive forms in which "reality" is literally made to mean, or "signify," a strict adherence to structuralist (and poststructuralist) preoccupations with language, texts, signifying systems or "regimes of truth" must always, according to its critics, collapse into forms of textual determinism, cultural relativism and political idealism. For these commentators, the culturalist analysis of *texts* needs to be integrated into a deeper appreciation of the contexts of production and reception. It becomes fatally undermined if permanently severed from the sociological analysis of social relations, unequal life chances and the wider play of power. In other words, interrogation of the social world via media representation – the politics of recognition – needs to be augmented with a power-based analysis of the politics of redistribution.

An influential example of this approach arrived in 1978 in the form of *Policing the Crisis* (Macmillan) by Hall and his colleagues, a study that theorized popular culture as the terrain on which, and through which, hegemonic struggles for consent were ideologically conditioned and discursively played out. It sought to keep both the interactions (and "articulations") of the "cultural" and the "social" in view and proved to be extraordinarily influential in its ideas; they continue to inform analyses of media representations of "race" in the UK and the USA.

The study had sought to analyze how black youth had become criminalized and symbolized as folk devils by the media in the mugging scare of the early 1970s. This "moral panic," it was argued, helped pave the ideological way for a new form of state "authoritarian populism" (neoconservative politics) that itself was a response to processes of national economic decline and growing political dissensus. It was popularly known as Thatcherism in Britain, and Reaganomics in the USA. The analysis explained the exact mechanisms through which media institutions, professional practices and cultural representations were linked to political forces of change.

Media events and media performance

More recent studies in the US have also made connections between "media events" and deep cultural anxieties around issue of "race." These studies generally observe, however, that though racialized media events serve conservative political projects they can also sustain counter-hegemonic discourses. Major "media events," such as the O. J. Simpson trial in the US, are often, according to John Fiske in *Media Matters: Race and gender in US politics* (Minnesota Press, 1996), *hyperreal* in nature because of their massive and determining media exposure and are therefore indicative of our increasingly *mediatized* "postmodern times." He argues that they receive such phenomenal interest and media exposure because they tap into the deep conflictual cultural undercurrents of "race" within American society.

Massive media exposure is not always dependent upon high-profile celebrity involvement, whether that of O. J. Simpson or Mike Tyson. The media can also serve to propel issues of race and social injustice to the top of the political agenda. For example, in the reporting of the Stephen Lawrence case in Britain, the media adopted a championing role in support of Lawrence's parents and their calls for justice. *Media Performance and Public Transformation: The case of Stephen Lawrence* (below) demonstrates how the media enacted a "public crisis" and performed a potentially transformative role in shifting the contours of racist Britain.

Going against the grain of earlier baseline research expectations, prominent sections of the media, both press and TV, performed a complex of roles in which elite authorities and institutional power (notably, the Crown Prosecution Service, the Metropolitan Police and its Chief Constable, Sir Paul Condon, Sir William Macpherson, the Public Inquiry Chair, the then Home Secretary, Jack Straw, and the Home Office) all became embroiled in intense public criticism. Symbolic power here played a part in sustaining critique and challenge from below. Doreen and Neville Lawrence, the parents of the murdered youth, effectively took possession of the moral high ground via the media in their quest for justice for their son, and by extension all those subject to racist violence and discrimination. In such ways, the racist murder of their son turned into a public crisis and, as such, conditioned elite discourse and served to move public awareness from the indicative mode – of "what is" – to a subjunctive mode – of "what should be." Media performance, in this instance, served to unleash widespread processes of institutional and social reflexivity.

Studies such as these, then, remind us how media representations can both register and contribute to the shifting terrain of "race," racism and ethnicity, a contested landscape that by definition is constantly on the move. They also serve to underline the central nature of media representations that are best approached not as "reflections" of society but rather as active agents that exert influence and have consequences within the life of society.

SEE ALSO: cultural identity; diaspora; essentialism; Hall, Stuart; humor; language; Lawrence case, the Stephen; media; negrophilia; Other; racial coding; racialization; racist discourse; Simpson case, the O. J.; stereotype; Tyson, Mike

Reading

Ethnic Minorities and the Media: Changing cultural boundaries, edited by Simon Cottle (Open University Press, 2000), both introduces the field of media communication research into "race," racism and minority ethnicity and also brings together the latest thinking and findings from international researchers working in the field today.
"The spectacle of the 'Other'," by Stuart Hall, in his *Representation: Cultural representations and signifying practices* (Sage, 1997), outlines and develops cultural studies approaches to the analysis of racialized representations and meanings and is written by one of the world's most influential cultural studies theorists; Hall's "New ethnicities" is in *Black Film, British Cinema*, edited by Kobena Mercer (British Film Institute, 1988); Mercer's *Welcome to the Jungle* (Routledge, 1994) is also valuable.
Four up-to-date accounts of the complexities, continuities and changes now characterizing representations of "race," racism and multiculturalism in news, television genres and cinema respectively are: *Race in the News* by Ian Law (Palgrave 2002); *Representing Black Britain* by Sarita Malik (Sage, 2002); Simon Cottle's *Media Performance and Public Transformation: The case of Stephen Lawrence* (Praeger, 2003); and *Reading Race: Hollywood and the cinema of racial violence* by Normal K. Denzin (Sage, 2001).

SIMON COTTLE

REVERSE RACISM/ DISCRIMINATION

In recent years, expressions of hostility, prejudice, discrimination, or even indifference to whites by ethnic minorities, have been interpreted by some as reverse racism. In terms of actual content, some of the beliefs and theories held by ethnic minorities, particularly African Americans and African Caribbeans, resemble a photographic negative of white racism. The beliefs involve an acceptance of the basic categories imposed by whites to justify their historical domination and contemporary privilege, followed by a denial of the validity of the meanings attached to those categories by white doctrines.

Accepted is: that blacks and whites constitute distinct races. Rejected is: that the black race is inferior and degenerate. This is modified to include the view that blacks are superior. We find examples of this in the philosophies of the Nation of Islam. Robert Miles believes that the statements of its leader Louis Farrakhan "warrant description as racism." And, while he does not spell out his argument, Miles presumably refers to the sometimes acerbic anti-Semitism of Farrakhan, whose theories had a disarming symmetry with the purported Zionist world domination conspiracy of the *Protocols*, which has inspired white racist organizations for generations and in which Jews are depicted as spiders at the center of a vast political web they have spun about the world.

By contrast, Joe Feagin believes the term reverse discrimination is an "oxymoron." He acknowledges that "today many whites believe that they are likely to be the victims of governmental policies helping black Americans." But, such beliefs, he argues, succeed in pushing aside "the central issue of the systemic racism still routinely oppressing Americans of color."

In a similar vein, Aaron David Gresson argues that it is "folly to cry 'reverse racism' and claim that Blacks, Hispanics, poor white ethnics, and other disenfranchised groups have turned the tide of oppression and now oppress privileged white men in some wholesale fashion" (in his *The Recovery of Race in America*, University of Minnesota Press, 1995).

If it were a straightforward question of beliefs, then there would be little argument about the existence of reverse, or black, racism. But, content is but one component of racism. Black populations have been affected by the experience of forced migration and enduring oppression. The material element of blacks' relationship with whites has affected both groups' mentalities, or mindsets and approaches to each other. One big difference is that white racism is a legacy of imperialism, whereas the black version is a reaction to the experience of racism. This qualitative difference is disguised by the term "reverse racism," or "reverse discrimination," which implies too simple a comparison with its white counterparts.

Black reaction to white racism takes many forms; accepting racial categories and articulating them in a way that mimics those of white racists is but one of them. Analytical purposes would not seem to be served by calling this reverse racism. The term misguidedly suggests that racism today can be studied by examining beliefs and without careful consideration of the vastly different historical experiences of the groups involved.

SEE ALSO: bigotry; cultural racism; ethnic conflict; Malcolm X; Nation of Islam; *Protocols of the Learned Elders of Zion*; racial discrimination; systemic racism; White Power

Reading

Racism by Robert Miles (Routledge, 1989) is the short book cited in the main text above.
Racist America: Roots, current realities and future reparations by Joe R. Feagin (Routledge, 2001) is the book in which the writer refutes the suggestion that reverse discrimination is anything more than a term to deflect attention away from more potent forms of racism.

RIOTS: BRITAIN, 1981

The term "race riot" was used in both popular and political discourse to describe and define the wave of violent disturbances which erupted first in Brixton, London, in April 1981 and subsequently in a range of Britain's other major cities during the "long, hot summer" of that year. The typification of these incidents as "race riots" not only helped to shape ensuing political debate on the matter but also helped to determine the nature of subsequent policy interventions.

In fact, careful scrutiny of what took place at Brixton, Southall, Toxteth, Moss Side, and elsewhere in 1981 reveals that "race riot" is a wholly inappropriate mode of classification: not only is it a factually incorrect description, it also denudes the incidents of any political complexion and the participants of any political edge to their protest.

Of the various and often disparate violent episodes of 1981 only the confrontation in the Southall district of London could be labeled legitimately as "racial" insofar as the clashes were primarily between white youth, on the one hand, and the young local Asian residents, on the other. A concert in a local public house by the 4-Skins – a group which constantly made reference to Nazi slogans – had attracted a large following of skinhead youths into the district; a contingent of this group abused an Asian shopkeeper, smashed a few windows, and had set off down the main street of Southall intent on more malicious damage. Local Asian youths reacted strongly and despite (or because of) police intervention the scene outside the concert venue degenerated into a battle. Molotov cocktails were thrown and the public house was eventually gutted.

The violence which had erupted three months earlier in Brixton and which was soon to engulf Toxteth, Moss Side, and other districts was of an entirely different nature. Here, hostilities were directed, first and foremost, at the police and, like the Watts outbreak in Los Angeles in 1965, were precipitated largely by what the residents perceived as racial harassment and intimidation by police officers. What is more, though these disturbances took place in districts containing relatively large black populations, they were not simply black youth versus police confrontations; a substantial number of white youngsters participated. In fact of the 3,074 people arrested during the disturbances, over 2,400 were white, according to Home Office figures.

Historically, and in its current usage, the term "riot" popularly connotes an image of widespread mindless violence, perpetrated by people who are intent, purely and simply, on creating havoc and inflicting malicious damage on people and property. What came to be called the "burnin' and lootin' " episodes of 1981 were presented via media and political debate largely in these terms. Indeed, the media assumed a major role in this process of "depoliticizing" the incidents; first, by including under the riot heading a whole series of events which on other occasions might never have been reported or which would simply have been recorded as normal crime. The media were also accused of

producing a "copycat effect"; by showing graphic and dramatic scenes of the Brixton disturbances, the media were said to have encouraged youths in other parts of the country to imitate their Brixton counterparts. This interpretation of the "burnin' and lootin' " episodes was in part supported by Lord Scarman in his official report. But there is no evidence to sustain this view, nor does it explain why the youths in Toxteth, Moss Side, and elsewhere waited almost three months after the Brixton disturbances before deciding to imitate those scenes. Most importantly, however, the "copycat" interpretation plays a significant ideological role in undermining the notion that the disturbances were inspired by real and substantive political grievances. As one youth in Handsworth, Birmingham, explained: "We're fighting for our rights – against the police – it's not copycat."

If the disturbances were neither "race riots" nor "copycat riots" but forms of protest against specific conditions, one has to establish what these conditions actually were. Clearly, the dramatic rise in unemployment, especially among the young, both locally and nationally constituted one of the most significant of the underlying causes. Although as the studies of the "burn, baby, burn" incidents in the United States revealed, unemployment does not directly and inevitably provoke social unrest. What is more, unemployment levels in parts of Scotland and the northeast of England exceeded those in Brixton, Toxteth, and Moss Side, but were no scenes of disorder there.

When they took to the streets, the youths made it clear that their hostility was directed towards the police. In all the major districts affected in 1981, relations between the police and the local community had reached a low ebb; mutual distrust, suspicion, and resentment characterized this relationship. On the one hand, the communities insisted they were maltreated by the police, subjected to racial harassment and to an intensification of police control, e.g. the Swamp 81 exercise in Brixton in which the Metropolitan Police saturated the district with extra police, including the Special Patrol Group. The police, on the other hand, justified these modes of action by pointing to the disproportionately high crime rates in Brixton and other multiracial areas.

The characterization of the Brixton and July 1981 episodes as "riots" ensured that the thrust of political debate and policy prescriptions would be firmly with a "law and order" framework. The imperative for action, in other words, has been to ensure that there is no repetition. An intensification of policing in the affected areas and, more generally, a broadening of police powers have been the most significant of the subsequent initiatives. But, while the incidents of 1981 may have included some wanton acts of destruction and thieving, the participants in general were remarkably selective in their choice of targets. To have responded to these episodes purely and simply in terms of a law and order crisis degrades and disparages the communities' sense of grievance. Worse still, it is myopic because it leaves untouched the underlying causes of these incidents and increases the possibility of further, perhaps even more severe, rebellions.

SEE ALSO: African Caribbeans in Britain; ethnic violence; Kerner Report; media; policing; Rastafari; riots: USA, 1965–67; Rock Against Racism; Scarman Report

Reading

"Muting interethnic conflict in post-imperial Britain: the success and limits of a liberal political approach," in *The Myth of "Ethnic Conflict": Politics, economics and "cultural violence"*, edited by Beverly Crawford and Ronnie D. Lipschutz (University of California International and Area Studies Research Series/no. 98, 1998), provides a broad perspective on these earlier and subsequent disturbances.

Public Disorder by Simon Field and Peter Southgate (Home Office Research Study no. 72, 1981) comprises two reports: the first considers the "burn, baby, burn" episodes in the USA and the relevance of the studies to the 1981 incidents in Britain; the second is a survey of the views and experiences of male residents at Handsworth, Birmingham – scene of one of the 1981 disturbances.

Race and Class, special double issue, "Rebellion and repression" (vol. 23, nos. 2/3, 1982) presents an account of the disturbances with due regard to historical and contemporary factors.

Uprising by Martin Kettle and Lucy Hodges (Pan, 1982) is a detailed account of the 1981 disturbances which discusses the various explanations adduced and identifies policing as the main catalyst of what took place.

BARRY TROYNA

RIOTS: BRITAIN, 1985

The disturbances of 1985, like those of 1981, occurred in major urban centers, involved a great many (but not only) black youths and were precipitated by incidents involving the police. The first three episodes in Birmingham, Brixton (London), and Liverpool suggested that it was possible to assess the events in much the same terms as their precursors. While there were two deaths at Birmingham, these seemed largely accidental; no one apparently aware that two Asians were trapped in a burning post office. But, at Tottenham, in North London, the final outbreak of the sequence took a new turn when a police officer was attacked and killed in the midst of the riot. Rioters, armed with guns, fired at the police; the police deployed (although they did not use) CS gas and baton rounds for the first time ever in Great Britain.

In Birmingham, events had been spurred by a traffic offense on September 9. Ironically, the day before had been one of celebration, when residents of Handsworth congregated at their local park (about one mile from the incident) for the district's annual festival. A standard operation was handled indelicately, drawing an overreaction and a burst of violence which escalated through the night. Heavy-handed policing, culminating in the shooting of Mrs. Cheryl Groce, a black mother of six, triggered more violence at Brixton. A week later, another black mother, Mrs. Cynthia Jarrett, fatally collapsed during a police raid on her Broadwater Estate home in Tottenham. A day later, violence broke out, and during the violence of October 6, PC Keith Blakelock was killed.

Popular explanations for the riots were familiar: criminality, inner-city deprivation, institutional racism, mass unemployment, innate indiscipline, left-wing political agitation, and, most implausible of all, drug abuse. The prescriptions were unimaginative: order another Scarman-type inquiry, democratize the police force, crack down in the courts, and increase spending in the inner cities.

One of the interesting political figures to emerge in the aftermath of the riots at Tottenham was Bernie Grant, a local council leader who later became an elected Labour Member of Parliament. To many people, Grant was an extremist who talked coldly of the police getting a "good hiding" (223 police were injured and one died during the disturbance; 20 public were injured). Yet his unequivocal opposition to violence in his discussions with black youth, his attempts to persuade them to use the political process, and his refusal to condemn the subsequent trial of forty-five people charged with riot and affray ("You can't support the jury system when it suits you, but not when it results in a verdict you don't like") estranged him from many black youths. Despite being pilloried from all sides, Grant became a politician of note, active in the Labour Party's "black section" and strongly opinionated on all aspects of race relations.

SEE ALSO: media; policing; riots: Britain, 1981

Reading

"Forms of collective racial violence" by Terry Davis (in *Political Studies*, vol. 34, nos. 40–60, 1986) and "Metaphysics of paradigms" by Michael Haas (in *Review of Politics*, vol. 48, no. 4, 1986) both analyze theories of urban violence and the assumptions underpinning them.

The Racialisation of Disorder in Twentieth Century Britain by Michael Rowe (Ashgate, 1998) is a full-scale analysis of how disorders were turned into "race riots."

The Roots of Urban Unrest, edited by John Benyon and John Solomos (Pergamon Press, 1987), is a textbook comprising contributions from a variety of scholars and practitioners on the question "what has gone wrong in the 1980s?"

RIOTS: BRITAIN, 2001

Britain's most serious disturbances involving racial components in two decades occurred in Spring 2001, when several towns in northern England were scenes of violence, most of it precipitated by the appearance of far right political movements in deprived, predominantly Asian areas. Research into the causes of the riots concluded that the separate and distinct cultures into which ethnic minorities had crystallized contributed significantly to the outbreaks, though the provocation of neo-nazi movements was certainly a major factor.

With a national debate on asylum seekers gathering momentum and the Lawrence case still fresh in minds, the far right British National Party (BNP) made political capital by focusing on an attack on a 76-year-old white man, Walter Chamberlain, who was attacked when returning home from a rugby game. A national radio report suggested that some areas of Oldham, in Greater Manchester, had become "no-go" to whites. The BNP and the National Front (NF), another party of the far right, seized the opportunity to promote their causes, campaigning and

leafleting in one such "no-go" zone in Oldham. The NF was subsequently banned from marching in the town.

This contributed to a sense of unease in the town. So, when a dispute between an Asian and white youth outside a chip shop escalated, this became the catalyst for a widespread spate of violence involving several hundred Asians and which resulted in 50 arrests over three days. The disorder proved to be a flashpoint for further disturbances across the north of England. Barely a week after the Oldham incident, Asian, white and black youths clashed with police in Leeds after three Bangladeshi youths were arrested. Violent clashes between whites and Asians broke out in Burnley, Lancashire, and nearby Accrington.

In the lead-up to a General Election, the BNP announced it would put up candidates in the Oldham area. The organization's election results were seen as a "victory" of sorts: the party won more votes than expected (16 per cent of the total) and gained national publicity. The party was accused by many of creating a climate conducive to violence by its presence in multicultural areas; but, when violence occurred, it quickly distanced itself, often condemning ethnic minorities as perpetrators. In a well-publicized radio interview, the BNP leader, Nick Griffin, blamed the Burnley disorder on "Asian thugs."

Oldham erupted again after the election when Muslim graves were desecrated and an incendiary device was thrown at the home of the town's deputy mayor Riaz Ahmad. NF marchers clashed with members of the Anti Nazi League. This was followed by an outbreak in Bradford. Things started with a rumor that a group of white youth had been shouting racist remarks. Asians stabbed two whites, five people were arrested and about 300 congregating Asians were pushed away from the scene by 180 riot-shielded police. "Airbombs," as the fiery missiles were called, were thrown at the police. Buildings were torched. In all thirty-six arrests were made – twenty-three Asians and thirteen whites.

Subsequent analyses and reports disclosed little new information, though, interestingly, second and third generation Asians (the children and grandchildren of migrants to Britain in the 1950s and 1960s) had traveled from across the nation to support resistance to the far right presence. Oldham, in particular, was depicted as a starkly divided community, whites occupying a separate social sphere to ethnic minority populations. Many of the conditions underlying the riots were to be found elsewhere in England: poor education, youth unemployment – as high as 50 per cent among Asians – *de facto* segregation and accusations of insensitive policing. The British Commission for Racial Equality played down racism, insisting that the disorder was a response to shared social circumstances more than the goading of the far right. As is often the case in such situations, a combination of factors were at work.

Oldham's town council co-commissioned an inquiry which found that "poverty and social exclusion" aggravated by government funding had caused the violence, though the town's municipal leaders repudiated its conclusions, pointing to Oldham's regenerative efforts and arguing that segregation played no part in the outbreaks.

The timing of the riots was significant. The liberal response to the Macpherson Report of the Lawrence case involved much hand wringing, expressions of regret and a resolve to begin a new era in race relations. For two years following the publication of the report, in February 1999, the police inspected its own policies and procedures, while all major employers were mindful of accusations of institutional racism. There were also a number of opportunistic cases that tried to capitalize on the fallout from the Lawrence case by spuriously attributing racist motives to culprits, while, in reality, there was no evidence of racism at all. As these developments unfolded the BNP and NF recruited zealously among the ranks of disaffected whites, who were persuaded by the far right's argument that the pendulum had swung in favor of ethnic minority groups and that working-class whites were the new disenfranchised. The modest success of the far right in recruiting and in articulating a sense of injustice among some factions convinced it that it could pounce on *causes cõlÒbres*, such as that of Walter Chamberlain, and promote its own cause.

In the process, it sparked the most serious rioting in Britain since the 1980s.

SEE ALSO: British Asians; British National Party; consumption; education; Lawrence case, the Stephen; media; National Front; neo-nazism; riots: Britain, 1981; riots: Britain, 1985; social exclusion

Reading

"All quiet on the Northern Front?" by Paul Vallely (in the *Independent*, Review, July 3, 2002) revisits the scene of the riots twelve months on and found that, as an Asian resident put it, "We have gone from assuming that most of our neighbours were decent and friendly to sleepless nights, footsteps in back alleyways and strange cars on the street."

"From Oldham to Bradford: The violence of the violated" by Arun Kundnani (in *Race and Class*, vol. 43, no. 2, 2001) links the riots with multiple deprivations and policing, and presents a sympathetic interpretation of the disaffected youth involved in the disorder.

From Textile Mills to Taxi Ranks: Experiences of migration, labour and social change by Virinder S. Kalra (Ashgate, 2000), while not about the uprising, is a study of a Mirpuri/Pakistani population in Oldham and, as such, provides interesting background to the violence.

RIOTS: USA, 1921 (TULSA)

On June 1, 1921, Greenwood, also known as "Black Wall Street," was looted and burned to the ground over a twelve-hour period. Thirty-five blocks in the Greenwood district, a predominately African American community in Tulsa, Oklahoma, were razed during race riots. Black economic success, an unbearable insult to the social order of white supremacy, appeared to be at the heart of events. The National Guard, the local police – some of whom actively participated in the riot – deputized citizens, and the Ku Klux Klan converged in order to destroy violently Black Wall Street. This event is often viewed as one of the worse race riots on American soil.

Greenwood was a healthy and viable black community supporting black business including doctors, lawyers, hotel financiers, real estate, hairdressers, and grocery stores. It was the home of one of the most prestigious churches at the turn of the twentieth century, Mount Zion Baptist Church. Common to many towns during this era, Greenwood also had its share of gamblers, prostitutes, and other lawless individuals. Greenwood, like many of its surrounding towns, benefited from the booming oil industry. While there were no oil deposits in the city limits, the city was able to thrive by offering itself to the oil industry as a conduit for business.

As Tulsa evolved economically, racial tensions appeared. Tulsa was known to support some of the toughest Jim Crow laws in the nation. Additionally, the city prided itself on its vigilantism.

This was an area that often did not hesitate to use lynching as a means of keeping African Americans in their "rightful" place.

The catalyst of the riot was the arrest of "Diamond" Rowland, an arrest that represented racial and sexual insecurities among whites. Dick (Diamond) Rowland, a nineteen-year-old shoe shiner, was accused of assaulting a seventeen-year-old white female elevator operator, Sarah Page. *The Tulsa Tribune*, a local newspaper best known for its inflammatory journalistic style, published a story of the attempted assault. The paper featured an editorial entitled "To Lynch Negro Tonight" and informed readers that "mobs of Whites were forming in order to lynch the Negro." Such reporting incited both sides. Black World War I veterans and other concerned citizens of Greenwood approached the court building where Rowland was held to secure his safety and freedom. On the steps of the Court House they were met by a throng of whites. Eventually a shot was fired and "the riot was on."

Retreating for cover, African Americans made their way back to the Greenwood business district where they sought to protect themselves. However the residents of Greenwood could not escape the white mob that torched, looted, and flew airplanes overhead that allegedly dropped incendiary material. In the aftermath of the planned sunrise attack, some 35 city blocks were charred, 1,200 homes, 35 grocery stores, 8 doctors' offices, 5 hotels, 21 churches, 21 restaurants, theaters, a bank, post office, libraries, schools and law offices were burned. The National Guard demolished the pride of Greenwood, the Mount Zion Baptist Church. As initially reported, thirty African Americans were killed; however, it has been suggested that the number is actually closer to 300. The estimated cost of this devastation is over $16m (in 2001 dollars). African Americans who did not flee, or who were not killed, were rounded up and held prisoner in local jails and the Convention Hall. The once thriving Greenwood never recovered.

This race riot suffered a relatively quiet afterlife, until the issue of reparations arose. The formation of the Tulsa Race Riot Commission, in 1997, was an attempt to gather as much comprehensive information on the incident and to determine if reparations would be appropriate. After years of fact-finding, etc., the Oklahoma legislature voted against the bill designed to compensate the known living survivors and against reparations for the first-generation descendants of the riot victims. One explanation for the vote against reparations was that the bill's language painted white people as "thugs."

SEE ALSO: African Americans; bigotry; blues; ethnocide; human rights; *Invisible Man*; Jim Crow; Ku Klux Klan; minstrelsy; policing; reparations; riots: USA, 1980 (Miami); segregation

Reading

Death in a Promised Land: The Tulsa race riot of 1921 by Scott Ellsworth (Louisiana State University Press, 1982) is a social history, case study of American racial ideologies and race relations.

Reconstructing the Dreamland: The Tulsa race riot of 1921, race, reparations and reconciliation by Alfred L. Brophy (Oxford University Press, 2002) draws on extensive research including contemporary accounts and court documents to chronicle this devastating riot, showing how and why the rule of law quickly eroded. Brophy offers a portrait of mob violence and racism run amok, both on the night of the riot and the morning after. Equally important, he shows how the city government and police not only permitted the looting, shootings, and burning of Greenwood, but actively participated in it.

The Tulsa Race War and its Legacy: Riot and remembrance by James S. Hirsch (Houghton Mifflin, 2002) tells the story of the riots using court records, newspaper reports, and eyewitness accounts. He ponders the question of whether the event was a mass murder/war or necessary governmental action.

JULIA S. JORDAN-ZACHERY

RIOTS: USA, 1965–67

South Central Los Angeles contains the largest concentration of blacks in the city. It includes the district called Watts. On August 11, 1965, blacks took to the streets and for six days engaged in what became known as the "Watts riots." Some whites were attacked, but mostly the destruction was aimed at property: cars were overturned, stores were looted, and buildings set afire. The watchword of the riots summed up the imperative: "Burn, baby, burn." The burning continued for two years, ravaging ghetto areas in such places as Detroit and New York City.

The actual incident that precipitated the Watts riots involved a white police officer's attempted arrest of a black youth (a similar episode started the Brixton riot in 1981). More and more people became involved and police reinforcements were brought in. Five arrests were made before the police withdrew under a hail of stones from an angry mob. Instead of dispersing, the crowd grew and began assailing whites. Over the next few hours, there were periodic bursts when rocks and Molotov cocktails were thrown.

Then came a lull: police called in the National Guard and the situation seemed under control. This tactic, however, served to aggravate matters and the rioting escalated: buildings were burnt and looting was rife. "One of the most ravaging outbursts of Blacks in the history of this nation," is how Douglas Glasgow described the event. "Their rage was directed at white society's structure, its repressive institutions, and their symbols of exploitation in the ghetto: the chain stores, the oligopolies that control the distribution of goods; the lenders, those who hold the indebtedness of the ghetto bound; the absentee landlords; and the agents who control the underclass while safeguarding the rights of those who exploit it."

One estimate placed the total number of participants as over 30,000, or 15 percent of the adult black population of the area. Of the 3,927 people arrested, most were black, but only 556 were under eighteen, while 2,111 were over twenty-five; 602 were over forty. It was not a youth riot as such.

All manner of explanation was invoked to determine the causes of the Watts riots; these ranged from the excessively warm weather (the "long, hot summer theory") to the influence of outside agitators. Glasgow is probably the most plausible when he cites the conditions: "Poverty, racial discrimination, long-term isolation from the broader society." Added to this was the sense of frustration elicited by the failure of the civil rights movement to instigate any immediate, tangible changes after years of campaigning for social reform.

Clearly, there was a frustration that was not just confined to blacks in Los Angeles, but which existed throughout the USA; for over the next two years, similar outbursts occurred at other American cities. They reached a virtual climax in July 1967 when a Detroit vice squad conducted raids on gambling clubs frequented by blacks. There were several arrests (there is an uncanny parallel here with the incident in Bristol, England, in 1980 when police raided a cafe used by blacks; this sparked a mass disturbance, with police eventually withdrawing to leave a virtual

"no go area"). By the following morning, some 200 blacks had gathered on the streets; a bottle hurled from the crowd smashed through the window of a leaving police car. The crowd grew to about 3,000 by 8.00 a.m. and the police mobilized for action. As in Watts, rocks were thrown and buildings were burnt, prompting a police withdrawal. Reports of gunfire filtered back to the police, who, in midweek, when the initial outburst had died down, started a series of raids on residents' homes. Once more, the services of the National Guard were invoked. The efforts to restore order and re-establish control only exacerbated the situation and violence erupted again, so that by the end of the week, 7,200 people had been arrested. Forty-three people were killed, thirty or more by the police. Property damage exceeded $22m.

The mid 1960s were a period of severe black discontent. Rioting may not have been an effective method for overthrowing the social order, but it certainly enlisted the attention of the American population and forced problems unique to blacks into public visibility. In this sense, the riots were spectacularly successful. As one observer put it: "Reporters and cameramen rushed into the ghettoes; elected and appointed officials followed behind; sociologists and other scholars arrived shortly after. The President established a riot commission; so did the governors." That commission was to conclude that the cause of the riots lay in racism and the resulting poverty suffered by blacks, leading to their being undernourished, underpaid, badly clothed, and poorly housed. The civil rights movement had complained about precisely these features of blacks' lives, but it is arguable that the violent pressure of two years of rioting achieved more than had ten years of peaceful protest.

SEE ALSO: African Americans; bigotry; Black Power; civil rights movement; Cleaver, Eldridge; ghetto; internal colonialism; Kerner Report; media; riots: Britain, 1981; underclass

Reading

The Black Underclass by Douglas Glasgow (Jossey-Bass, 1980) is a reflective summary of the reasons behind and the aftermath of Watts and an appraisal of blacks in modern America.

Fire This Time: The Watts uprising and the 1960s by Gerald Home (University Press of Virginia, 1995) documents the impact of race on postwar Los Angeles.

Ghetto Revolts by Joe R. Feagin and H. Hahn (Macmillan, 1973) examines the reasons for and the effects of the riots in a book that embraces many perspectives. This may profitably be read in conjunction with *The Politics of Violence* by D. O. Sears and J. B. McConahay (Houghton Mifflin, 1973) which has as its central theme "new urban blacks and the Watts riot."

RIOTS: USA, 1980 (MIAMI)

The disorder that centered on the district of Liberty City signaled a slight variation on the pattern established by the urban disturbances of the 1960s. The earlier riots tended to be precipitated by blacks in response to what they perceived to be police provocation. Also, the violence was more frequently directed at property rather than persons. The grievances of blacks were about poverty and racialism, particularly that practiced by the police.

Liberty City was slightly different. The first incident started in court. Four police officers who had been accused of beating to death a black Miami businessman were acquitted. Many suspected a miscarriage of justice with underlying racist themes. In addition to this, there was a feeling among blacks that the needs of migrant Cubans in the area were being given priority over their own.

Like the 1960s riots, conflict with the police proved to be a catalyst for violence, but, unlike the 1960s version, the violence concentrated on white people. As one eye-witness described it: "the anger is so intense, the feelings are so rampant now, that the attacks have been aimed at white people with intent to do great bodily harm to people."

Whites were attacked as they walked the streets, they were dragged out of cars and chased through the city. Property was vandalized too, but the Liberty City riots were distinguished by the gross violence done to people. Eighteen people were killed and the cost of the destruction was put at hundreds of millions of dollars.

SEE ALSO: consumption; ethnic conflict; ethnicity; Kerner Report; Latinos; policing; riots: USA 1965–67; underclass

Reading

The Miami Riot of 1980 by B. D. Porter and M. Dunn (Lexington Books, 1984) is a comprehensive account of the riots with due emphasis given to the inter-

ethnic conflict between blacks and Cubans that exacerbated the riots.

Race, Reform and Rebellion by M. Marable (Macmillan, 1984), *The Underside of Black American History* by T. R. Frazier (Harcourt, Brace & Jovanovich, 1982), *Race, Ethnicity and Socioeconomic Status* by C. Willie (Prentice-Hall, 1983), and *The Black Community* by J. E. Blackwell (Harper & Row, 1985), all cover similar ground and include sections on urban disorders.

RIOTS: USA, 1992 *see* King case, the Rodney

ROCK AGAINST RACISM

Rock Against Racism was the name given to a loose coalition of musicians and rock fans who came together in Britain during the 1970s to organize concerts, marches, demonstrations, rallies and various other activities, all designed to galvanize and publicize opposition to the neo-nazi movement that grew amid social discord.

Records and magazines were produced under the rubric of Rock Against Racism. *Temporary Hoarding* sold 12,000 copies per issue in the 1970s. In 1980, Virgin Records released an album called *Rock Against Racism's Greatest Hits*, though, by this time, the impetus behind the campaign had slowed and the neo-nazi elements had receded.

The context of Rock Against Racism was one of severe unemployment, especially among the young and particularly among African Caribbeans. The far right political organization known as the National Front emerged from obscurity to canvass in areas of job scarcity. Focusing on cities such as Birmingham, Leeds and London, the NF, as it was often abbreviated, enjoyed modest political success and appeared to have recruited well among young whites. An affinity between the NF and the British skinheads developed.

Rock Against Racism challenged this tendency and publicly celebrated the multicultural aspects of popular music. Many of the bands which were associated, however tenuously, with Rock Against Racism had black, white and Asian members. The Birmingham band UB40 and Coventry's The Specials AKA were among these.

Whether the idea of using music to combat racism among the young was effective is open to question. Racist attacks continued unabated and, of course, unemployment remained unaffected; though support for the NF dwindled and all but disappeared in the early 1980s. This may be evidence of some measure of success. It could also be regarded as testimony to the rise of Margaret Thatcher's Conservative government, which appropriated some of the right-wing policies that had been advocated – albeit in more extreme ways – by the NF.

Rock Against Racism certainly highlighted the power of music in mobilizing people around social causes, and later efforts, such as Band Aid and Amnesty International, were able to capitalize on this.

SEE ALSO: consumption; Let's Kick Racism Out of Football; media; Motown; National Front; neo-nazism; representations; riots: Britain, 1981; Scarman Report

Reading

Beating Time: Riot'n'race'n'rock'n'roll by David Widgery (Chatto & Windus, 1986) is a journalist's account of the rise of Rock Against Racism and, indeed, the whole musical challenge to right-wing extremism.

Key Concepts in Popular Music by Roy Shuker (Routledge, 1998) has a short, but useful essay on Rock Against Racism, and another essay is "Rock against Racism and the Red Wedge" by S. Frith and J. Street (in *Rocking the Boat: Mass music and mass movements*, edited by R. Garofalo, South End Press, 1992); both might be read alongside Robin Denselow's more detailed and wide-ranging *When the Music's Over: The story of political pop* (Faber & Faber, 1990).

ROMA

Popularly though misleadingly known as Gypsies, Roma (singular: Rom) are diasporic people of Indian origin who arrived in Europe at the end of the thirteenth century before moving to other continents. They now number between ten and twelve million worldwide, with between six and seven million in Eastern Europe, two million in Western Europe, one million in North America and one million in South America.

The widely held view is that Roma were from Egypt (hence "Gypcian" or "Gypsy"), though others suggest that they originate with the 10,000 musicians who were gifted from the King of India to the Shah of Iran in the fifth century. It is now accepted that the source population was of composite non-Aryan origins (principally Dravidian and Pratihara, though with some African input from the Siddis or East Africans conscripted to fight for both the Muslim and Hindu armies). They were persons marshaled into battalions to resist the incursion of the Islamic Ghazi (a fighter against non-Muslims) into India in the eleventh century. They begin to appear in Europe from 1300.

The Romani word for a non-Rom is *gadzo* (from the Sanskrit *gajjha* for civilian). Romani language, in many ways, reflects migratory patterns: it has elements of Hindi (from northern India), traces of Iranic (from northern Africa) and Armenian, Georgian, and Ossetic words (from the Caucasian area of Eastern Europe). The presence of Greek suggests a long stay in the Byzantine empire in western Asia and southern Europe.

The move into Europe, like the move away from India, was the result of Islamic expansion. In the Balkans, Roma provided a much-need artisan population and were employed in the Wallachian and Moldavian principalities in southeastern Europe. The need for Romani labor precipitated a movement to other parts of Europe where their weapon-making skills made Roma sought-after workers – so sought-after that legislation permitting the enslavement of Roma was written into many constitutions. Emancipation came about in the second half of the nineteenth century.

By 1500, Romani groups had reached every country in northern and western Europe. The exodus that followed the abolition of slavery began in the 1860s and took hundreds of thousands of Vlax (Romanian and Bulgarian) Roma to Russia, Serbia, the Americas and elsewhere. Today, the Vlax Roma are the most numerous and widely dispersed Romani group, and their dialect of Romani is the most popular. Other political events, such as the fall of the Austro-Hungarian empire and two world wars, stimulated migrations. After the collapse of communism in 1989, a major migration out of Eastern Europe took more Roma to western Europe and North America.

Anti-Gypsy sentiment has been a feature of the Roma experience. As nonwhite, non-Christian, nonterritorial people entering Europe near the height of Ottoman imperialism, they were first identified with Muslims and seen not only as a threat to the Christian church, but to the European economy, which was supported by trade with the East. Their dark skin was associated, using biblical rhetoric, with evil; racism was Hitler's rationale for wanting to eradicate Roma. As a diasporic people, Roma were trespassers everywhere. Romani culture itself forbade – and still forbids – overly intimate contact with non-Roma, thereby reinforcing their marginal status to and nonparticipation in various host societies. Laws have been variously enacted to keep Roma at a distance. When western European countries entered the period of colonial expansion, their overseas territories became dumping grounds for unwanted Romani populations: Roma were shipped as slaves from Britain, France and Portugal to their colonies in the Caribbean and elsewhere in the 1660s.

The Balkanization of Europe into several ethnically distinct republics after 1989 led to another wave of enforced Romani migration and harassment. In Bosnia-Herzegovina, Poland, Slovakia, Bulgaria, and the Czech Republic, anti-Romani activity was especially severe. In 1995, twenty-four houses were set on fire in Bacu, Romania and five Roma were injured in a letter bomb attack in Bucharest, giving rise to the suspicion that, in certain parts, there was a genocidal intent in some of the attacks. In 1994, there was a Congressional Hearing on this very issue: the human rights abuses of Roma. The rise of skinheads in the USA brought fresh problems for Roma, who were regularly victimized by neo-nazi youth.

In June 1999, nearly 1,000 Roma fled in four separate areas of Naples, Italy, after an organized attack in which camps were burnt. The raid was the backlash of a hit-and-run accident involving a Serbian Rom who was living in one of Naple's rundown suburbs. The entire Roma community was punished for the actions of one of its members.

SEE ALSO: Aryan; bigotry; culturecide; diaspora; ethnocide; human rights; minorities; Other; prejudice; racial coding; racialization; racist discourse; scapegoat; skinheads; slavery; social exclusion; white backlash culture

Reading

The Gypsies by Angus Fraser (Blackwell, 1991) is an historical treatment of origins and migrations and may profitably be read in conjunction with a collection edited by David Crowe and Johri Kolsti, *The Gypsies of Eastern Europe* (Sharpe, 1986).

The Gypsy-American: An ethnogeographic study by David J. Nemeth (Edwin Mellen, 2002) presents a rare insight into Roma culture, or the "Gypsy-American inscape," as the author calls it, "a vital activity space that produces and reproduces a Gypsy-American ethos."

A History of the Gypsies of Eastern Europe and the U.S.S.R by David Crowe (St. Martin's Press, 1995) is a country-by-country account of the history and sociopolitical situation of Roma.

The Pariah Syndrome: An account of Gypsy slavery and persecution by Ian Hancock (Karoma, 1987) deals mainly with the five centuries of Romani slavery, with chapters on anti-Romany laws in Europe and the USA; this may profitably be read in conjunction with *We Are The Romani People*, also by Hancock (University of Hertfordshire Press, 2002).

The Time of Gypsies by Michael Stewart (Westview Press, 1998) provides an assessment of the Roma experience in the USA.

CHECK: internet resources section

IAN HANCOCK

S

SCAPEGOAT

The term originated in the Hebrew ritual described in the Book of Leviticus: "Aaron shall lay both hands upon the head of the live goat, and confess over him all the iniquities of the children of Israel, and all their transgressions, even all their sins; and he shall put them on the head of the goat" (16:20–2). In other words, the sins of the people were symbolically transferred to the goat which was then let go into the wilderness taking with it the guilt of the people.

At a different level, a schoolgirl may be humiliated by a teacher at school; she can't hit back at the teacher, so she gets frustrated. When she gets home, she might take it out on her younger brother or sister, who is a more accessible target.

In race and ethnic relations, similar processes often take place: people shift the responsibilities for their misfortunes and frustrations onto other groups and those groups are usually visibly identifiable minorities, such as blacks, Asians or Mexicans, who have little power. These groups can be singled out and attributed with blame for all manner of evil, whether unemployment, housing scarcity, or literally anything else.

Jews and blacks have been recent popular scapegoats; they have had to shoulder the blame for almost everything from the economic decline of whole societies to the escalation of crime rates. Political groups, such as communists, and religious denominations, such as Roman Catholics, have historically been used as convenient scapegoats. It is, of course, no accident that the scapegoated groups are invariably powerless; they can be blamed and picked on without the possibility that they might hit back and resist the attribution. Lynchings and pogroms were carried out against blacks and Jews, when it was reasonably certain that those groups didn't have the power to fight back with any effectiveness.

One important feature of the *scapegoating* process (the actual practice of apportioning blame) is the failure of the group doing the blaming to analyze fully the circumstances producing the apparent misfortunes. Economic decline, for example, may be caused by a complex of factors, some rather obscure and difficult to comprehend. Yet scapegoating removes the need to analyze: it provides ready-made explanations: "the blacks caused it" is simple and comprehensive – but wrong.

For the scapegoating to work best, there must be an available stereotype, so that the blame can be transferred with a minimum of ambiguity. If people have a fairly well-defined stereotyped conception of Asians as people who work too hard, make too much money, and engage in less-than-orthodox business dealings, then they have a convenient group to scapegoat. If there is widespread recognition that a great many Asians work in bad conditions for poor wages and are overcrowded in rundown homes, then this complicates the stereotype and makes the scapegoating more difficult – depending, of course, on what problems Asians are meant to be blamed for. The abiding rule seems to be not to analyze in any depth the group to be scapegoated.

A further point about the scapegoat should be borne in mind: the image of the group identified and blamed may be created anew for the purpose of scapegoating, but, more frequently, it exists as a stereotype in the popular imagination; the scapegoating adds new dimensions to the image.

Karim Murji argues that the objects of scape-goating may be "able to challenge the images and representations." Far from being an inexorable process, scapegoating can simply backfire: groups targeted for blame may resist the label of scapegoat and answer critics.

SEE ALSO: anti-Semitism; bigotry; Dollard, John; National Front; neo-nazism; policing; prejudice; race card; racial discrimination; racism; racist discourse; representations; skinheads; stereotype; Thomas, Clarence

Reading

American Minority Relations, 4th edn., by James Van der Zanden (Knopf, 1983), has a chapter on "Personality bulwarks of racism," which considers scape-goating as a "theory of prejudice."

The Nature of Prejudice by Gordon W. Allport (Perseus, 1979) is the "25th anniversary edition" of the 1954 text, which was, in its day, a major statement on the psychology of race relations; it contains a chapter on "The choice of scapegoats."

"Scapegoating" by Karim Murji, in *The Sage Dictionary of Criminology*, edited by Eugene McLaughlin and John Muncie (Sage, 2001), makes the point that: "The powerful can also be scapegoated, for instance when army commanders and politicians are held responsible for particular defeats, or more generally, for national decline."

"The ultimate attribution error" by Thomas F. Pettigrew, in *Readings About the Social Animal* (Freeman, 1981), is designed to test some of Allport's theories about prejudice.

SCARMAN REPORT

The findings of a commission headed by Britain's Right Honorable Lord Scarman to investigate the causes of urban disorders in Brixton, London, in 1981 and make recommendations in the wake of the events. During the course of the inquiry, violence erupted in the streets of Birmingham, Liverpool, and Manchester (in July 1981), and in his subsequent report to Parliament, Scarman made passing reference to these disorders, focusing particularly on the ways they shared with or differed from prevailing social and economic conditions in Brixton. Scarman also considered the claim that there had been an imitative, or "copycat" element, to the July outbreaks, stimulated by media portrayals of the Brixton disorders.

The Scarman inquiry differed in at least two significant ways from its US counterpart, the Kerner Commission's report on the "burn, baby, burn" disorders of the 1960s. Firstly, the gathering of evidence by the US Commission was completed by a team of researchers; in Britain, this role was undertaken solely by Lord Scarman. The result: Scarman collected a less detailed and comprehensive account of the extent of racial disadvantage and the grievances of the black communities than his US counterparts. Secondly, Scarman presided over a quasi-judicial inquiry, established under section 32 of the 1964 Police Act. The nature of the inquiry, then, enhanced already existing skepticism about its function and relevance and deterred a number of members of the black communities from submitting either oral or written evidence. This further underlined the contention that the report, published in November 1981, presented only a partial view of what actually happened.

Scarman's appraisal of the Brixton district highlighted the social and economic privations experienced by the local black and, albeit to a lesser extent, white communities. Poor-quality housing, the paucity of recreational and leisure facilities, and the almost obscene levels of un-employment especially among black youngsters constituted some of the most important of the underlying causes of the disorders, wrote Scarman. But the evidence received indicated unequivocally that oppressive – some might say repressive – policing procedures in the locality provided the spark which ignited the flames in April 1981. Scarman was extremely critical of the decision taken by the local police chief, Commander Fairbairn, to inaugurate Swamp 81 on April 6. The essence of the Operation was to "swamp" certain areas of the district with police officers who were empowered to stop and search suspected criminals. Despite the notoriously poor police–community relations in Brixton – especially in the Railton Road/Mayall Road area – the "Front Line" as it is often called – the decision was taken independently of discussions with local community leaders. As Scarman pointed out: "I am ... certain that 'Swamp 81' was a factor which contributed to the great increase in tension ... in the days immediately preceding the disorders" (para 4.43).

Among the various criticisms of the police received by the inquiry – harassment, unimaginative/inflexible policing, overreactions, etc. – Scarman was informed that certain police officers were racists. With some circumspection, Scarman conceded that this might have been a legitimate appraisal of a small caucus of police officers in Brixton and elsewhere. He was insistent, however, in his denunciation of accusations that the police force, and Britain in general, were characterized by institutional racism (see paras 2.21 and 9.1). His remarks on this issue have subsequently attracted considerable and widespread dissent and may have been based on an inchoate understanding of this concept.

Scarman's tendency to divide policing into "hard" and "soft" methods and to advocate the latter – in the form of community policing, and putting "bobbys back on the beat" – also attracted criticism, largely from within the police force. The argument here is that "soft" policing is not a cure-all for crime and is simply not appropriate for all circumstances. Others, from outside the police force, are also critical of community policing, though for distinctly different reasons: they argue that it is a more subtle, though no less invidious, form of ensuring repressive control over the communities.

The notion of "police accountability" figures prominently in the report: "Accountability" wrote Scarman, "is, I have no doubt, the key to successful consultation and socially responsive policing" (para. 5.57). His recommendation that accountability be statutory has met with little enthusiasm from most police forces, however, who maintain that it would undermine the operational independence of their forces. A contrasting view is that policing can only take place, effectively, with the consent of the public; therefore, legislative action was necessary to provide the statutory framework for consultation at the local level.

Scarman's emphasis on the role of the police, both in the context of the disorders and in general, was not surprising in view of the fact that the inquiry was set up under a section of the 1964 Police Act. He did, however, engage in wider questions of social policy both in the substantive sections of the report and in his subsequent recommendations. As he pointed out, issues such as housing, education, local community relations councils and the media, and their specific relation to the needs of ethnic minority communities, "must be kept constantly in view if the social context in which the police operate is not to continue to breed the conditions of future disorder" (para. 6.42).

The Scarman inquiry was designed to function within a liberal-reformist framework; the aim was to identify those factors which precipitated the disorders in Brixton in April 1981, and elsewhere in Britain three months later, and to recommend those policies and practices necessary to restabilize the foundations and structures of society. Consequently, those who perceived the disorders as exercises in mindless violence, as a further indication of the erosion of traditional values and mores, criticized the report for its liberal orientation. On the other hand, those who viewed the disorders in terms of an uprising or rebellion against regressive state institutions and who advocate the eradication of those institutions, rejected the report as conservative, myopic and largely irrelevant. Either way, Scarman was bound to disappoint and antagonize – and he did.

SEE ALSO: disadvantage; ethnic violence; institutional racism; Kerner Report; policing; politics; racial discrimination; riots: Britain, 1981; riots: Britain, 1985; scapegoat

Reading

The Brixton Disorders, 10–12 April 1981 by Lord Scarman (HMSO, Cmnd. 8427, 1981; also published by Penguin, 1982).
"From Scarman to Lawrence" by Stuart Hall (in *Connections*, Spring, 2000) reflects on changes in British race relations in the period between the two major reports.
The Racialisation of Disorder in Twentieth Century Britain by Michael Rowe (Ashgate, 1998) is a full-scale analysis of how disorders were turned into "race riots."
Scarman and After, edited by John Benyon (Pergamon, 1984), is a set of readings reflecting on the disturbances, the report, and the aftermath.

BARRY TROYNA

SCIENCE

Race science and scientific racism

A science of race (or "race science") involves the comparative study of human diversity with the aim of clearly distinguishing a set of distinct human races. *Scientific racism* is the label applied to racist ideologies supported by appeals to scientific method and observer objectivity. Whilst race science and scientific racism overlap to a considerable degree historically, they are logically distinct. It is possible to believe that human races exist as scientific facts without necessarily being committed to the belief that there is a natural hierarchy in terms of ability, morality, intelligence, etc. Likewise, not all followers of racist ideologies justify their theories by reference to modern science. Contemporary academic disciplines such as physical anthropology use methodologies of human biometrics (the comparative study of human physical variation), but practitioners explicitly oppose racist ideologies.

One can think of science having a number of contrasting roles in relation to ideas concerning human racial or ethnic diversity. Firstly, modern science played a key role in the rejection of the biblical framework for understanding the origins and history of humankind. Secondly, the discourse of science was extended in the course of the eighteenth and nineteenth centuries to include human physical diversity, giving rise to a new "science of race." Ideas about the origins and nature of human diversity formulated by scientists were given additional cultural and political power by their association with the prestige of the natural sciences. Thirdly, scientists have observed the importance of categorization by group and the prevalence of racism and other forms of stereotyping in human societies, and offered arguments grounded in evolutionary biology or psychology for the persistence of strong in-group loyalties and hostility toward outgroups in modern societies. Finally, scientists have argued that the category "race" is not well defined in any scientific sense, and they have drawn the boundary between science and non-science so as to exclude theories of race. Scientists have in many contexts led the attack on racist ideologies.

In the twenty-first century we face a highly complex situation as regards science. On the one hand, science as a so-called "objective" mode of knowledge is discredited in the eyes of many critics (feminists, environmentalists, postmodernists), who point to the role of science and scientists in the human, political and environmental catastrophes of the nineteenth and twentieth centuries. From this perspective, the development of a science of race with racist characteristics is a specific instance of a more general destructive tendency latent in science, held to be grounded in authoritarian social and political structures. As an example, one could take the science of eugenics developed by Francis Galton (1822–1911), which was self-consciously developed as an instrument of authoritarian

social engineering. Yet, science is now enjoying a period of resurgence in the public arena, as a mode of knowledge production said to offer potential solutions for problems in public health, alternative energy sources, and in the treatment of inherited disease.

Scientific questions are at the heart of contemporary debates about human identity, potential and the relation of human beings to "nature" (gender, race, sexuality, animal rights). Advances in technology, in relation to genetic manipulation, and reproductive technology, are raising new and complex ethical questions. But if these questions are primarily scientific questions, which are opaque to all but scientifically trained specialists, how can an informed debate be carried on in relation to their impact on social policy? For example, some scientists argue for a close link between genetic factors and behavior. What account should be taken of this scientific trend when formulating educational or other fundamental social policies?

In practice, scientists rarely reach a total consensus, but there are broad trends observable in the understanding of topics such as the nature of human diversity. Issues that confronted eighteenth-century intellectuals, such the monogenesis versus polygenesis debate, the age and development of the human species and its subdivisions, the influence of the environment and climate on human diversity, the philosophical nature of human unity and diversity, and the understanding of human cultural and ethical difference, underlie in modified form contemporary controversies. It is important to remember when considering the history of ideas about race that theories discredited by mainstream science can remain powerful, as any search of the World Wide Web for materials concerning race and race politics will show. Race science and scientific racism also retains a marginal place in the academy, as evidenced in the work of the psychologist J. Philippe Rushton.

The mastery of nature

Broadly speaking, one could talk of the development of a science of race in the modern sense in the eighteenth century, with the extension of zoological and botanical taxonomic methods to human diversity in the works of Carolus Linnaeus (1707–78), Johann Friedrich Blumenbach (1752–1840), Georges Cuvier (1769–1832) and Immanuel Kant (1724–1804). The notion that there could be a science of race arose in the context of aspirations to classify and order in hierarchies all the natural phenomena of the world, mankind included. Following the development of the taxonomic disciplines of zoology and botany, race theory located human beings decisively within nature, and thus marked a stage in separating questions about the origins and nature of human diversity from the biblical account. Advances in geology, paleontology and archeology increasingly put a strain on the biblical account of the time lapsed between the creation and the present, and the rapidly expanding knowledge of the world and the varieties of plants, animals and human groups made it increasingly difficult to map the diversity of the world's peoples directly onto the family tree of Noah and his sons Shem, Ham and Japheth. In one sense, human beings were demoted by science from their supreme and God-ordained position at the pinnacle of creation. In another, however, their ascendancy was affirmed by a growing belief that science could categorize, explain and give laws for the development of all phenomena, and that it gave humankind the key to the mastery of nature.

Whilst the Bible had been used to justify the institution of slavery (Genesis 9:xxv, "Cursed be Canaan! The lowest of slaves will he be to his brothers") and could be read as a description of a world of fixed types and natures in hierarchical order ordained by God, it also could be used to assert the fundamental unity and equality of human beings under God, with each human being possessing a unique soul. (Of course, there were potential ambiguities about defining the boundaries of the human race, with eighteenth and nineteenth century debates about whether the Negro was of the same species as the rest of humanity.) Once human beings were seen as part of nature, this notion of spiritual equality could not be defended on scientific grounds.

The nineteenth century – Darwin's century – saw the academic institutionalization of the study of race in the form of physical anthropology, as well as the diffusion of racial ideologies into the worldview of broad segments of European society. The almost unchallenged rise of science in the late nineteenth century, and its dominance over the developing social sciences, led to increasing conflicts between social philosophies self-consciously informed by "laws of nature"

(e.g. social Darwinism) and ideological trends towards mass education and health care, democracy and political equality, which to a degree had inherited or adapted the Christian notions of human equality, rights and dignity. Metaphors taken from a popularized theory of evolution of life as a ceaseless struggle involving the "survival of the fittest" (Spencer) were applied to relations between nation-states, classes and individuals. Thinking "scientifically" meant taking an objective or unsentimental view of social issues (e.g. poverty), and crime and antisocial behavior were seen as pathological features akin to disease of a population understood as a collective organism. These conflicts continued in the twentieth century in a politicized "nature" versus "nurture" debate.

The crimes against humanity committed by the National Socialist regime (1933–45) led to the widespread discrediting of political philosophies that denied a fundamental equality to all human beings (regardless of actual abilities, mental or physical handicap, race or ethnicity). Liberationist philosophies drove the social reforms of the 1960s in the West and experiments in socialism followed the end of the colonial era in the developing world. Social scientists took the lead in rejecting genetic determinism in favor of a belief in an open-ended human potential, self-fashioning, and human liberation. Feminism involved a rejection of a science-inspired physical or genetic determinism and argued for a total separation of biological identity from social role. Gender, like race, was deemed a "social construct," and equal civil and political rights were seen as the basis for marginalized or oppressed groups to achieve their full potential.

Since its high point in the 1970s, "social constructionism" and its associated belief in the determining power of the environment have been under concerted intellectual attack. With the rise of sociobiology and evolutionary psychology, the failure of experiments in state socialism, the triumph of metaphors of competition and struggle in political economy (e.g. Thatcherite conservatism in the UK), and most significantly the massive potential impact of new advances in genetics, it has again become intellectually fashionable to link genetic factors with behavior. Whilst the traditional notion of "race" is rejected by most geneticists, the contemporary intellectual climate once again favors the scientific study of human genetic diversity, either with regard to individual and population-specific medical-related features (e.g. susceptibility to particular diseases or drugs), or – in the style of the late nineteenth century – of relating intelligence or criminality to genetic, or even racial, factors.

The social and political contexts of science

It is possible to view the history of the scientific study of race as a textbook case of the "chauvinism of science" (to borrow a phrase from the philosopher of science Paul Feyerabend). Contemporary followers of Michel Foucault, for example, point to the nexus between race theory, the Enlightenment and European colonialism. The science of race in some contexts is used to stand for the "Enlightenment project," i.e. the oppressive and rationalistic regimes of modernity, especially the Nazi state. Race theory is held to represent the totalitarian tendencies of that modernity, such as the desire to gain mastery through acts of classification, the unequal power relations between the West and other cultures (summed up in the colonial projects of surveying, ethnographic measurement, census-taking, etc.). However appealing though this argument is in many respects, it leaves a number of serious questions unanswered. A rejection of (modern) (Western) science as a mode of knowledge is incompatible with the labeling of race theory as "pseudo-science." For the label "pseudo-science" to have any force requires a belief in "real" science. Similarly, we cannot attack race theory as exemplifying oppressive rationality if we wish to use rationality as a mode of argumentation against it.

The problem for the nonscientist is that genetics and related sciences are moving extremely rapidly, and for someone without specialized training there is no simple way to follow those developments critically. One tactic employed by nonscientist critics is to look at the social and political consequences of such theories, and to judge them on the level of the metaphors of the worldview which they seem to express. In this sense, evolutionary psychology can be seen as a backlash against feminism, and a reaffirmation of the traditional roles assigned to women in premodern societies. The debate over IQ and race, which is carried out partly in terms of complex statistical models, is evaluated in terms of the kinds of social policies that would

follow from accepting that race is correlated with IQ and therefore with class. Similarly, if behavioral traits are largely inherited, then issues such as housing, poverty, diet and access to education may be seen as irrelevant to important areas of social policy.

This approach to science has its attractions, not least because science clearly is itself a product of its sociopolitical environment, in the metaphorical language used by scientists, in the kinds of question they ask (and get funded), and also in the questions that they fail to ask. But it also has its dangers, which are intrinsic to the "two cultures" organization of contemporary knowledge, in which there is a lack of communication and understanding between the sciences and the humanities. Scientists can dismiss critics in the social sciences and humanities on the grounds that they do not understand the basic science which they are discussing. For example, the argument that race is a "construct," while it has its place in an explanation of why scientific racism is to be rejected, cannot do justice to the complexity of contemporary scientific debates about the nature of genetic diversity, including the origins and evolutionary development of human beings.

A generalized hostility to science is not necessarily going to serve the cause of progressive politics in relation to race, gender and other key issues; nor, on the other hand, is it necessary to accept blindly the scientific authority of every pronouncement about the relationship between a character trait and a particular gene. In this context, it is worth pointing out that many scientists have used their authority and training in genetics to attack the use of racist argumentation by scientists and nonscientists. Many geneticists caution that we have little or no real understanding of the relationships between genetics and human diversity, even in relation to a seemingly unproblematic and uni-dimensional human feature such as height. Further, in the history of race theory, race scientists were not necessarily exclusively reactionaries in relation to causes such as the emancipation of slaves or theoretical debates about the unity of the human species.

Just as theoretical concepts postulated by linguists and historians came to have a political life and real political consequences, so scientific understandings of human identity have the potential to transform popular self-understandings.

A good example of this is the contemporary use of DNA testing to locate an individual in a set of biological – and therefore cultural and ancestral relationships – which would otherwise have remained opaque or irrelevant. For this if no other reason, scholars in the humanities and social scientists need to take account of developments in science that relate to human identity. The humanities' perspective can also bring to the scientific debates a sense of history, i.e. the recognition that there is a cycle to the debate between genetic determinism in its various forms, environmental determinism, and various forms of humanism. The existence of fashions in debates as fundamental as these serves as a warning against acceptance of facile scientific reasoning in relation to complex multidimensional phenomena such as the causes of human behavior.

SEE ALSO: anthropology; caucasian; Darwinism; environmentalism; eugenics; fascism; genotype; geometry of race; hereditarianism; ideology; intelligence; phenotype; race: as classification

Reading

The Idea of Race in Science by Nancy Stepan (Macmillan, 1982) is a valuable work written by a specialist in the history of medicine and history of science.
Lifelines: Biology, freedom, determinism by Steven Rose (Penguin, 1997) offers an accessible guide to debates in science about genetics and determinism, as well as trenchant criticism of the naïve use of metaphors in scientific thinking.
The Mismeasure of Man by Stephen Jay Gould (Penguin, 1981) offers a critical and highly influential reading of the history of science in relation to human diversity.
"Race and ethnicity: a sociobiological perspective" by Pierre van den Berghe, in *Racism: Essential readings*, edited by Ellis Cashmore and James Jennings (Sage, 2001), argues that we should understand concepts of race and ethnicity within the framework of kinship relations, and seek to understand the biology of human racial and ethnic loyalty from an evolutionary standpoint.
Victorian Anthropology by George W. Stocking, Jr. (The Free Press, 1987) remains an excellent guide to the intellectual debates of the nineteenth century concerning race, evolution and science.

CHRISTOPHER HUTTON

SCIENTIFIC RACISM *see* science

SEGREGATION

There are two modes of segregation: *de jure* and *de facto*. *De jure* represents the situation whereby groups defined in terms of putative "racial" or ethnic difference are formally separated by law. In the latter (*de facto*) situation, such group separation exists in the absence of a formal legal framework.

Although there have been countless examples of legal separation historically, the most obvious would be the "Jim Crow" laws of the postbellum era in the Southern states of the USA and apartheid in South Africa. In the former case, levels of residential segregation between the black and white communities were effectively increased following the abolition of the slave regime. Most commentators saw this as the result of a fear of equal status contact between freed slaves and their former masters: it was certainly a way of maintaining a system of subordination rooted in the notion of an ethnic/"racial" hierarchy. In South Africa, from 1948 until the 1990s, apartheid extended and formalized the process of strict residential segregation, this being enshrined in the Group Areas Act and the "Bantustan" policy.

In both countries, legally enforced segregation went much further than the question of residential settlement. "Nonwhites" were prevented from sharing a whole range of facilities with whites; ranging from education, employment and health to places of public resort such as restaurants, cafes, cinemas, clubs, public transportation and swimming pools/beaches. Apartheid even went as far as providing for separate entrances to public buildings, separate park benches, drinking fountains, and so on.

De facto segregation sometimes follows the formal abolition of its *de jure* equivalent. Thus, in the USA residential segregation in the South remained high for a number of reasons. Poverty, high unemployment levels and institutionalized discriminatory practices within the housing market meant that the mobility of African Americans was severely constrained, and the threat of racially motivated violence deterred those for whom such a move was feasible. Beyond the arena of structural constraints, they would also have been isolated from those who shared their cultural heritage. African Americans who migrated from the rural South to the northern cities in search of work had little choice but to replicate their previous patterns, becoming concentrated in poor urban ghettos.

It is important to recognize, therefore, that *de facto* segregation cannot normally be interpreted as voluntary segregation. There are also certain "gray areas" in the policy sphere in that, even in the absence of a legal framework, "custom and practice" may conspire to produce localized segregation. Thus, in response to complaints of racial harassment from Bangladeshi in Tower Hamlets in London in the 1970s, the local authority elected to place complainants in (for them, totally unsuitable) flatted accommodation (apartments) in a small number of hard-to-let high rise blocks. Enforced segregation therefore resulted from the Greater London Council's unwillingness to tackle the root problem: it was easier to move an already marginalized community than to deal with the perpetrators of the harassment who were for the most part established white residents.

Segregation may also appear to be a conscious "choice" on the part of minority families when it is in reality more a reflection of fear: fear for the safety of kinfolk where they to move to a white, or mainly white, area. Although segregation levels in the UK are rarely comparable to the (high) norm in US cities (in respect of white and African Americans), there is increasing concern about their long-term effects. Segregation is seen as antithetical to the idea of an "inclusive society." The inequalities associated with segregation are compounded by communities effectively living separate, or parallel, lives: residential segregation leads to segregated schooling and segregation at work, prayer and leisure. Such was the key finding of a recent inquiry into rioting in the UK in 2001 (see the Ouseley Report, below).

Even more significant in the context of involuntary segregation without a formal legal framework is the process which has become known euphemistically as "ethnic cleansing." Based often on systematic ethnic genocide, as in Bosnia and other parts of the former Yugoslavia in the early 1990s, this is a consciously policy-driven process. In the Bosnian case, the Dayton Peace Accord, signed by all warring parties in December 1995, drew clear "ethnic boundaries" in spatial terms, thus "segregation as a policy" became formal *de jure* segregation.

Except in certain extreme cases, a few of which have been noted here, segregation is not a phenomenon that is either present or absent: it tends to be a matter of degree. The question for researchers then becomes one of measuring the level of segregation.

A number of measurement problems, mainly associated with the arbitrary nature of bureaucratically defined spatial units, complicate comparative analyses (see Massey and Denton, below). It is important to tackle these problems, however, as the detailed analysis of changing spatial patterns, particularly when looked at in conjunction with issues such as social class, can provide crucial insights into the dynamics of social change.

SEE ALSO: apartheid; ghetto; homelessness; Pruitt-Igoe; racial discrimination; racial profiling; racialization; riots: Britain, 2001; social exclusion; white flight

Reading

Community Pride Not Prejudice: Making diversity work in Bradford by Sir Herman (now Lord) Ouseley (Bradford Vision, 2001) is the report of an inquiry into serious "race riots" in Bradford in the summer of 2001. Written by a former head of the UK's Commission for Racial Equality this looks at the broader impact of self-segregation in an ethnically diverse city.

Ethnic Segregation in Cities, edited by Ceri Peach, Vaughan Robinson, and Susan Smith (Croom Helm, 1981), contains theoretical and substantive contributions from some of the key researchers in the field.

Social Geography and Ethnicity in Britain: Geographical spread, spatial concentration and internal migration, edited by Peter Ratcliffe (*Ethnicity in the 1991 Census*, vol. 3, OPCS, 1996), contains a detailed appraisal of current and past residential patterns in Britain and assesses the likely direction and significance of future changes.

"Trends in the residential segregation of blacks, Hispanics, and Asians: 1970–1980" by D. S. Massey and N. A. Denton (in *American Sociological Review*, vol. 52, 1987) discusses the problem of measuring levels of spatial segregation.

PETER RATCLIFFE

SELF-FULFILLING PROPHECY

This term, first used to effect by the sociologist Robert Merton in 1948 (*Antioch Review*, vol. 13), refers to the processes by which false beliefs are converted to practical realities. Merton's seminal argument begins with W. I. Thomas's proposition, "If men define situations as real, they are real in their consequences." Merton offered an example of northern American whites who had genuinely held beliefs about the typical migrating black from the non-industrial south: "Undisciplined in traditions of tragic unionism and the art of collective bargaining … a traitor to the working class." The whites saw these views not as prejudices, but as "cold, hard facts"; that is, they defined the reality. They then acted on the "facts," excluding blacks from unions so that the only way in which they could find work was as scab labor; this served to confirm the whites' original beliefs. (The John Sayles movie *Matewan*, 1987, brings this point to life.)

"The self-fulfilling prophecy is, in the beginning, a *false* definition of the situation evoking a new behavior which makes the originally false conception come true," wrote Merton. In the 1960s, a study by Rosenthal and Jacobson illustrated this: the researchers selected 20 percent of children on San Francisco school rolls completely at random and informed the relevant authorities, including teaching staff, that these children were intellectually promising; in their terms, "bloomers." Returning to the schools later, the researchers found that the children in the 20 percent were excelling, not, they concluded, because of their own capacities or efforts, but because of the schools' heightened expectations of them and the extra attention they were accorded. Teachers accepted the researchers' completely erroneous observations and adjusted their behavior toward the "bloomers" in such a way as to create conditions under which they could achieve good results. One might easily imagine the experiment in reverse, with specific groups of pupils falsely defined, perhaps through racist assumptions, as "slow learners," and a reality being created to fit the beliefs, or fulfill the prophecy.

Merton showed how this had consequences beyond the school experiment when he wrote, "If it appears to the white in-group that Negroes are *not* educated in the same measure as themselves, that they have an 'unduly' high proportion of unskilled workers and an 'unduly' low proportion of successful businesses and professional men, that they are thriftless and so on through the catalogue of middle class virtue and sin, it is not difficult to understand the charge that the Negro is 'inferior' to the white." One especially damaging effect of this is what Merton called "self-hypnosis," in which the group labeled inferior come to believe this of itself.

"Ethnic and racial out-groups," as Merton called them, have no simple task in breaking out of the self-fulfilling cycle, for, even when they display characteristics that are valued by whites,

their behavior can be evaluated differently. Merton described the "moral alchemy" by which key American values, such as industry, resolution, and perseverance, when shown by Jews or Japanese, can bear witness to "their sweatshop mentality, their ruthless undercutting of American standards, their unfair competitive practices." Whites transmute their own virtues into others' vices, so that ethnic "out-groups" are, in Merton's phrase, "damned-if-you-do and damned-if-you-don't." Whether they achieve or not, they are condemned.

Merton's old but absolutely crucial article points out some of the logical paths in the "intricate maze of self-contradictions" of white mentalities, showing how racism, far from being a matter of blind prejudices, is sustained and nourished by actions which at one level seem to defy racist beliefs, but, at another, can be interpreted as support for them.

SEE ALSO: children; disadvantage; education; ethnocentrism; prejudice; stereotype; tokenism; underachievement; xenophobia; whiteness

Reading

Pygmalion in the Classroom by R. Rosenthal and L. Jacobson (Holt, Rhinehart & Winston, 1968) includes details of the school study, while Jacobson's edited collection with P. Insel, *What Do You Expect?* (Cummings, 1975), is a set of studies exploring the general principle of self-fulfilling prophecy.

"The self-fulfilling prophecy" by R. K. Merton is reprinted in the author's book *Social Theory and Social Structure* (Macmillan, 1968) and in several texts, including *Social Problems*, 2nd edn., edited by E. McDonagh and J. Simpson (Holt, Rhinehart & Winston, 1969).

SENGHOR, LèOPOLD SèDAR (1906–2001)

Senegal-born politician, poet and writer and an advocate of *nÕgritude*. Senghor was educated in France and served in the French government before returning to Senegal, on the west coast of Africa, where he was president for over twenty years. Throughout his career, he pushed strongly for decolonization, which he defined in terms of the expurgation of the "superiority complex in the mind of the colonizer and the inferiority complex in the mind of the colonized."

Born in Joal, on the Senegalese coast, his father a trader who had converted to Christianity,

Senghor was sent to missionary school and, later, to the LycÕe Louis le Grand and the Sorbonne. He taught in France: during his classes he is said to have disarmed students who may have been intrigued by the unusual sight of a black teacher with: "Let's spend the next few minutes in silence so that you look at me and see how black I am."

During World War II, he served in the French army and was taken prisoner by Germans. In 1944 he was appointed to a chair at the University of Paris and made deputy from 1945 to 1958, then served as a minister in the governments of Edgar Faure and Charles de Gaulle. While he was often credited with being the originator of *nÕgritude*, he usually denied this, recognizing AimÕ CÕsaire, the poet from Martinique, as the prime mover of the movement. Still, he remained true to the ethos of *nÕgritude* and, more than any other, helped shape the values and beliefs into political programs. Leading the party Bloc DÕmocratique SÕnÕgelais, Senghor was elected the first president of an independent Senegal.

Senghor argued against a complete separation from France and that the decolonization of Africa should not lead to a division of small and possibly antagonistic states. De Gaulle accepted that the Fifth Republic should extend to a Franco-African community, though he was unconvinced by the union of Senegal and the former French Sudan which was to be known as the Mali Federation. In the event, the Federation lasted only two years as the decolonization process swept across Africa and each state demanded its independence.

Senghor was president between 1960 and 1981, during which time he pursued a form of democracy, though he refused to break completely with France in a cultural sense: he insisted that French be taught in schools, for example. His reign was beset by conflicts with the region of Casamance and with Muslim factions. He resigned in 1981 and died in France twenty years later.

SEE ALSO: Afrocentricity; Black Power; colonialism; Ethiopianism; Fanon, Frantz; Garvey, Marcus; *nÕgritude*; negrophilia; Rastafari

Reading

Black, French and African: A life of LÕopold SÕdar Senghor by Janet G. Vaillant (Harvard University Press, 1990) and *LÕopold SÕdar Senghor: An intellectual biography* by Jacques Louis Hymans (University of Edinburgh Press, 1971) provide two different slants on Senghor's life and achievements.

"Senghor and *nÕgritude*" by L. V. Thomas (in *PrÕsence Africaine*, vol. 26, no. 54, 1965) was written during the poet-president's presidency and evaluates his achievements.

SEPTEMBER 11, 2001

No date in recent history is weighted with as much symbolic importance as September 11, 2001. This was, of course, the date on which hijackers commandeered American aircraft and attacked strategic targets, including New York's World Trade Center. The loss of life, estimated as over 3,000 (the actual figure was never known), the unprecedented breach of US security, the absence of a discernible adversary, and the realization that America's enemies were as fanatical as they were resolute, ensured that the event would be momentous in its consequences. Of the consequences relevant to race and ethnic studies are the following: (1) a restriction of constitutional rights; (2) a sharp rise in Islamophobia; (3) a separation of opinion along ethnic lines.

Restriction of constitutional rights

In the immediate aftermath of the attacks, thousands of US residents and hundreds of foreign nationals were detained for questioning. Washington ordered law enforcement officers across the US to detain and arrest anyone with potential knowledge of the hijackers or involvement in any other suspected terrorist plots. As panic ensued, persons who might in some way have qualified as "enemies of America" were rounded up, though none of them were subsequently charged with terrorism-related offenses. Criticism of this immediate, perhaps excessive, reaction mounted only with time. Many detainees were held for months without criminal charges or legal representation. Most were young Muslim men, who were not US citizens and who had traveled to the US on visas.

The incident began the most severe restriction of constitutional rights in the US since the end of World War II, when 100,000 Americans of Japanese descent were released from internment camps where they had been held for the duration of the war. The post-September 11 detentions were distinguished both by the covertness with which they were executed and the way in which they reversed a recent trend. In the previous decades, an untold number of illegal immigrants had won amnesty, the rights of women and minority groups were legally assured, and criminal defendants secured remarkable legal protections. Ironically, in a mood of national contrition, regret had been expressed for the internment of American GIs by the Japanese.

Much of the secrecy and duration of the detentions was justified in terms of national security. In one notable instance, several men were arrested in the Detroit area in September 2001, but were not named in a terrorist indictment for eleven months. The manner in which the detentions were made raised suggestions that the majority of the suspects were Muslim. While the Justice Department insisted that Muslims were not targeted, the widespread suspicion was that a large number of Muslims and Arab Americans were taken into custody.

In the twelve months following the attack, the Immigration and Naturalization Service (INS) made zealous use of immigration law to arrest and detain more than 1,200 suspects in its terrorism investigation. Secret hearings outside the view of the public and media were held. No charges were made in connection with the attack. An unknown number of deportations were ordered. Immigration law became an instrument in holding persons suspected of having ties with terrorist organizations.

Critics argued that pretextual law enforcement, in which a version of racial profiling is used, was used to identify likely suspects. Legal challenges, however, were often met with deportations. Once a detainee leaves the USA, the legal challenge to his or her detention is nullified.

Sharp rise in Islamophobia

"Islamophobia" was invoked to describe the wave of attacks on anyone suspected of being a Muslim, or on mosques and businesses bearing Islamic-sounding names. While Islamophobia may be an inadequate term to describe abuse directed at persons and groups who may, in fact, have little or no connection with Islam (Hindus, for example, were attacked in the streets), the term came to characterize the vicious reaction in the several months following September 11. Islamophobia took hold in many European nations as well as the USA. Families were encour-

aged to order in food, to keep children out of school and to travel in groups if they needed to go out at all. Whether Islamophobia was a genuinely new form of prejudice-based hatred or a subterfuge for existing racism – a new name for old practices – is uncertain.

Muslim groups strenuously emphasized that the radical organization suspected to have been behind the attack was in no way representative of Islam; but the attacks continued and abated only during the military offense on Afghanistan – presumably because only then had a tangible enemy been identified and targeted. (Julia Jordan-Zachery reminds me that a spurious rationale invoked during the bombing of Afghanistan was that Muslim women would be "liberated" once the Taliban regime had been defeated, though a necessary condition of this deliverance was the incarceration or wasting of men. Another patriarchal device to inveigle Muslim women into Western modes of thought, some might suspect.)

Separation of opinion along ethnic lines

Much as the O. J. Simpson trial exposed a divide that separated black and white America in the mid 1990s, the accusations following September 11 brought sharply divergent views of the world into focus. For most Americans and their allies, there seemed to be little doubt of the guilt of Osama bin Laden, who was suspected of masterminding the attack and orchestrating it through the al-Quaeda network. Yet, for much of the Muslim world, the US campaign against him appeared vengeful, unsubstantiated and prejudicial. These differences reflected a gulf of suspicion between US and Muslim societies. The almost instant attribution of blame for the bombing in Bali thirteen months after the World Trade Center attack to Jamaah Islamiya, a radical Islamic group with ties to al-Quaeda, lent weight to Muslim suspicions.

Much-quoted immediately after the attack was the "I've never felt so American" proclamation of African Americans, while reports of the Stars and Stripes flying in the 'hood were commonplace. Coinciding with this was a change in the accent of racial profiling, with Muslims, or persons who appeared to be Muslim, now targeted. Blacks became more self-consciously American as that identity was progressively denied other groups in an action that evoked similarities with the late seventeenth-century transformation of English, Irish, Scottish and other Europeans into members of a *white race*, while that privilege was denied African American slaves (I am grateful for Zine Magubane for bringing this parallel to my attention). The situation changed gradually as African Americans began to realize that the profiling of Muslims in fact afforded no new status to black people: it was possible to be both Muslim and phenotypically black.

Often underestimated in the wake of September 11 was the scarcity of objectivity in media reports. Emerging from the crisis was Al-Jazeera, an Arabic television station which broadcast tapes of bin Laden. Founded in 1996 with the Emir of Qatar's $160m backing, the uncensored satellite station was later threatened by an advertising boycott created by political pressure in the Middle East. In the West, Muslims complained that too little criticism of the common accord brokered by George Bush and Tony Blair, the respective premiers of the USA and Britain, created a sense of consensus that was reflected in the media. An urban myth of the time captures this. A man in New York rescues a child who is being mauled by a ferocious dog. A journalist witnesses the heroic act and tells the man that tomorrow's headline in his paper will read NEW YORK MAN SAVES BOY. He is corrected by the man: "I'm not from New York." The journalist replies: "Then, it will read AMERICAN HERO SAVES BOY," only to be informed that the man is from Pakistan. "Oh!" Next day, the headline is: ISLAMIC FUNDAMENTALIST STRANGLES PUPPY.

SEE ALSO: ethnocentrism; globalization; human rights; inferential racism; Islamophobia; law: immigration, USA; media; racial coding; racial profiling; reparations; representations; white race; xenophobia

Reading

The Cell: Inside the 9/11 plot and why the FBI and CIA failed to stop it by John Miller and Michael Stone (Hyperion, 2002) is an investigative report that traces the errors in US security and claims knowledge of the "plot."

"National security: profiling terror" by Siobhan Gorman (in *National Journal*, vol. 34, no. 15, 2002) examines how the methods to prevent potential terrorists from obtaining visas to enter the USA were tantamount to racial profiling.

The War on Freedom: How and why America was attacked, September 11, 2001 by Nafeez Mosaddeq Ahmed (Tree of Life, 2002) was one of several publications purporting to analyze the cultural and political conditions that led to the attack.

SEXUAL ABUSE

The term sexual abuse refers to the involvement of children under the age of sixteen in sexual activities that they do not fully comprehend and to which they are unable to give informed consent. It is generally taken to refer to behaviors that range from sexual touching, indecent exposure, rape and incest, to exploiting children in child pornography. It is significant to note that most children are abused by someone they know and trust. Research shows an overwhelming predominance of men (fathers, stepfathers, grandfathers, male relatives and other trusted male adults known to the child) as the perpetrators of sexual abuse. However, in a minority of cases, women also sexually abuse children.

Race as a compounding factor in child sexual abuse

In formulating an exploration of sexual abuse and race, there are two main strands that deserve close attention: (1) the way that race impacts victims' subjective experiences of abuse, and (2) how race profoundly influences responses to sexual abuse. Despite the substantial body of research on child sexual abuse in Britain, questions of race and racism as they frame experiences of sexual abuse have not been issues of central concern. The actual extent of child sexual abuse in black and ethnic minority families is therefore difficult to establish and poses a major problem in understanding the scale of the problem in black communities. It is important to recognize that, as secrecy and denial typically characterize sexual abuse, it is possible to infer that a good deal of it is not reported and thus does not appear on official statistics. Therefore, generalizations about prevalence rates of sexual abuse in black and ethnic minority families could be misleading because of difficulties in obtaining reliable figures.

Whilst there is no doubt that sexual abuse affects children from all racial and social class backgrounds, it seems probable that the meaning that "race" has in the everyday lives of black children will be a compounding factor in how they make sense of sexual abuse. First-person narratives by black women recovering from childhood sexual abuse provide vivid accounts of the dilemmas and complexities for victimized black children. These accounts give voice to the devastating effects of sexual abuse on black children's physical, psychological and emotional lives and offer rich insights into the psychosocial processes of children in the aftermath of sexual abuse. A central theme throughout adult survivors' testimonies is the significant role race plays in shaping the specific dynamics of child sexual abuse for black children.

An essential consideration is racism as a key component in the social devaluation of black and ethnic minority children. From a very early age, overt and covert forms of racism contribute to a feeling of poor self-worth for black children, and sexual abuse further distorts and diminishes the sense of self. Predictably, the concurrent effects of sexual victimization interact with the cumulative effects of racism to undoubtedly compound feelings of worthlessness. In nonabusive families, parents work doubly hard to provide guidance and support to counteract the societal racism that diminishes their children's self-worth. In effect, in families where sexual abuse is occurring, the actions of abusive parents are actively reinforcing children's perceptions of poor self-worth. Of course, the cruel irony for black children is that their parents, who should be a primary source of safety from a hostile racist world, pose the main threat to their day-to-day safety. That is a major contradiction for children to grapple with as they find ways to come to terms with sexual abuse. Essentially, the myth of the protective family is exploded and this contributes to their trauma. Specifically, those black children who have internalized a poor self-worth as a result of racism may believe that they were abused just because they are black, or that abuse only happens in black families.

Moreover, the impact of intrafamilial abuse may be compounded by negative valuations of black families in the wider society, which may intensify the trauma. In all probability, depending on the age and cognitive understanding of children, they will be well aware of how racism informs the perception of their families as flawed, and fuels the prevailing view of the supposed deficit in parenting skills of their parents. The interconnectedness of these experiences for black children means that the trauma

that ensues from sexual abuse becomes inextricably linked with the effects of stigmatization that is rooted in a societal racism, which fosters a negative valuation of the self. In essence, black children may be doubly traumatized by the experience of coping with the effects of racism and being sexually abused by someone from their own racial or cultural background.

In short, black children may have difficulties unraveling whether their feelings of worthlessness (a common occurrence in victims of sexual abuse) may be due to the abuse they have experienced, or to the pervasive effects of racism. Black children, along with most victims of child sexual abuse, experience conflicting emotions of fear, anxiety, shame, guilt, denial and self-blame. Arguably, for black children these conflicted emotions interlock with the debilitating effects of racism powerfully to shape the way sexual abuse is experienced as something that is shameful and should be kept hidden. Thus, as a coping mechanism, some victimized children may feel they must keep silent about the abuse, which means denying or undervaluing their experiences.

It is also the case that race is a contributing factor in affecting black children's abilities to access help through child protection services. When black children are abused within their families, it is especially traumatic, which makes it difficult for them to disclose sexual abuse to outsiders. Moreover, black children are in a position of powerlessness, in that they are dependent for care on their families, and there are strong pressures on them not to discuss the family secrets outside the home. Notably, the emotive nature of sexual abuse means telling about the abuse may not be safe for children, and they may feel they are betraying their families. One of the risks for children is that disclosing sexual abuse could incur marginalization, isolation, or even exclusion from families and communities.

A major problem associated with the reporting of sexual abuse in black families is that there is a fear and mistrust of statutory and law enforcement agencies. One concern is that exposing sexual abuse in black communities will bring about a coercive intervention by statutory agencies. The perception of many in the black community is that there will be little justice in the criminal justice system and, consequently, some may feel their concerns will not be taken seriously when they are victims of crimes. In many regards, black people may feel alienated from the whole notion of law enforcement. Significantly, victimized children, as well as nonabusive parents, may not want to disclose abuse to outsiders, ultimately protecting themselves from public scrutiny.

Race, gender and power relations

Raising the issue of black men's involvement in the sexual abuse of their own children is probably the most contentious of issues. It opens up uncomfortable questions and fundamentally challenges core assumptions about family life. A primary factor that makes it difficult to address this issue frankly is that prevailing stereotypes conveyed through the media and other social institutions, discourses and practices, shape an image of black males as violent, dangerous, hypersexual and absent fathers. In particular, the complex relationships between ideologies of masculinity and discourses of race influence deeply the way they are responded to by social welfare agencies. Keep in mind, too, that in a climate of institutionalized racism, and where the state plays a significant role in demonizing black men, for black women to raise the issue of their violence and abusive behavior in public is to risk the accusation of disloyalty. To name the reality of child sexual abuse means confronting difficult questions that ultimately may evoke strong reactions within black communities, as well as risk the possibility of a racist interpretation. Given these sets of concerns, it is hardly surprising that there is ambivalence about lifting the veil of silence surrounding childhood sexual abuse in black communities. Consequently, the subject becomes shrouded in silence because of black women's complex relationships with black men and general feelings of responsibility to the black community.

The complex ways that the simultaneity of oppressions operate to mute the voices of victims, as well as nonabusive parents, about child sexual abuse in black families must also be considered. Black feminist analyses of gendered power relationships raise challenging questions about the silence surrounding child sexual abuse in black families and call attention to the contradictory position of black mothers, who are often the nonabusive parent. Such analyses highlight the intersecting effects of racial and gender oppression as they contribute to contradictory feelings of loyalty, and fuel a climate of silence around the subject of childhood sexual abuse in black families. More specifically, on discovery of the abuse, nonabusive mothers may be too distraught or sidetracked by their own emotional crises to be able to attune empathetically and be responsive to the emotional needs of their children. Typically, it becomes easier to protect oneself by adopting defensive reactions such as avoidance and denial to deal with an intolerable reality.

Specificities and complexities

In essence, by critically interrogating the interwoven nature of race and gender in the sexual abuse of black children we can better elucidate the specificities and complexities embodied in their experiences. Through such analyses we gain a deeper insight into the ways that societal racism compounds the trauma of sexual abuse for black children, precisely because it reinforces feelings of worthlessness. Where black children's lived experiences are deeply enmeshed in a racism that devalues their selfhood and diminishes their moral worth, their capacity to disclose sexual abuse will be affected. Unquestionably, living with the experience of racism means that black children may grow up with a perception of themselves as worthless, presenting them with obstacles in how they make sense of, and articulate, their perspective of sexual abuse. Sexual abuse has shattering effects on children's emotional and psychological development, and it can take a lifetime for their wounds to heal. Children are also left susceptible to mental health problems in later life. An analysis of the sexual abuse of black children that has at its center an understanding of how race and gender coalesce to trap black children and their families into a web of contradictions will provide a valuable framework for thinking through the traumatizing effects of abuse.

SEE ALSO: anti-Semitism; black feminism; children; human rights; mental illness; patriarchy; race: as signifier; race: as synonym; racial coding; racism; racist discourse; sexuality; social work; violence; whiteness

Reading

Child Sexual Abuse: Feminist perspectives, edited by Audrey Droisen and Emily Driver (Macmillan, 1989), is a key text for its exploration of racism and anti-Semitism in child sexual abuse from a feminist perspective.

Constructing Lived Experiences: Representations of black mothers in child sexual abuse discourses by Claudia Bernard (Ashgate, 2001) is written from a black feminist perspective and explores the links between race and gender as important markers of experience for shaping responses to child sexual abuse in black families.

Crossing the Boundaries: Black women and incest by Melba Wilson (Virago, 1993) is a groundbreaking text written from the perspective of a survivor of sexual abuse. This book is a landmark for its illuminating account of the effects of abuse on women and children. By interrogating issues of race, sex, gender and power relationships, the dynamics of sexual abuse are located in the broader context in which it takes place.

Racism and Child Protection: The black experience of child sexual abuse by Valerie Jackson (Cassell, 1996) examines the effects of racism on the protection and support of black children who have been sexually abused.

CLAUDIA BERNARD

SEXUALITY

Sexuality references the instincts, drives, and behaviors associated with reproduction as well as those connected with the pursuit and/or satisfaction of erotic desires. Sexuality, like race, is a socially constructed category of power, which operates politically by defining and regulating desire, determining whose body and what body parts are eroticized, and what erotic acts are acceptable. Historically speaking, issues of race, sexuality, class, and nation are interwoven. Whether we are speaking of slavery, colonialism, or Jim Crow, domination inevitably referenced and implicated sexuality in some way.

Racialized imagery

Slavery, for example, was a system predicated on the sexual commodification of the black body and the sexual abuse of black women. Slave masters had strong economic incentives to govern black women's reproduction as all children borne by a slave belonged to the slave owner from the moment of conception. The control of black procreation was thus the linchpin of the slave system and black women's sexuality and fertility were irreversibly connected with the global system of capitalist exploitation. The ideology that underpinned slavery, however, consistently denied the vested interest that white slaveholders had in exploiting the sexual vulnerability of

black women and, instead, produced images of black women as sexually licentious beasts intent on seducing white men and destroying white families. Thus the images of white female sexual purity and black female sexual depravity, rather than being opposed, actually were closely connected. The popularization of the image of the black man as a sexually aggressive beast, intent on violating white female purity, must also be seen as part of the harnessing of black reproduction to the reproduction of a system of capitalist exploitation. Motherhood and racism became symbolically intertwined as slave laws dictated that freedom was a condition bestowed on children by their mothers. Forbidding black men to have sexual relations with white women of any social class reduced the possibility that children of African descent would be born into freedom, thus curtailing the profits of slaveholders.

Colonialism was, likewise, predicated on the ideas of sexual objectification and domination. The iconography and imagery associated with colonialism equated conquered lands with female bodies and the unexplored continents – Africa, the Americas, and Asia – were usually libidinously eroticized. Africa was represented as a land of hyper-fecundity and sexual profligacy, peopled with men with enormous sexual organs and women with excessive sexual appetites. The idea that Africans were people who were unable to control their sexuality, and thus should be subject to control – political, social, and economic – by others was one of the core ideas underlying the ideological justification of conquest. The discovery of America, on the other hand, was depicted in a famous fourteenth-century drawing by Jan van der Straet as an eroticized encounter between Vespucci, the explorer, and a naked woman, who represents the as-yet-to-be conquered land. Within the USA westward expansion was also sexualized as the land itself was feminized in the metaphor of the virgin land and westward movement was imagined in terms of masculine penetration and conquest. Pocahontas, an early seventeenth-century Native American woman who saved Captain John Smith, a colonialist, from execution epitomized the self-sacrificing female heroine who legitimized white male domination of the American frontier. In a contrasting, yet related, move, Orientalist discourse produced Asia and the Middle East as the equivalent of erotically mysterious, veiled women that were simply waiting for European explorers and missionaries to emancipate, unveil, and ultimately rule, them.

Sexuality was also connected to the exercise of racialized state power in the sense that race, one of the primary categories through which states exercise governmentality, is generally presumed to be a heritable characteristic. Most white settler colonies established government departments responsible for overseeing the sorting of human bodies into manageable racial categories, and administering tests to determine people's degree of racial purity or admixture. It was thus that sexuality and human reproduction became profoundly implicated in the evolution of the colonial state, as a racially stratified colonial system would quickly have become inoperable without a systematic method of racial classification. An obsession with racial purity found its highest expression in white settler colonial societies such as Rhodesia, Kenya, and South Africa, which developed laws like South Africa's Prohibition on Mixed Marriages Act, aimed at eliminating interracial sexual contact.

The family played a particularly important symbolic role in the exercise of racialized state power as it is and was the primary metaphor of the nation. In the United States, for example, the family is presumptively white, symbolizing the status of America as a white nation. As Dorothy Roberts observes, in her *Killing the Black Body: Race, reproduction, and the meaning of liberty* (Pantheon, 1997), America was and is "obsessed with creating and preserving genetic ties between white parents and their children."

Threats to the white family and threats to the nation are thus often symbolically conflated. The lynching of African Americans, for example, escalated immediately in the wake of Reconstruction, when the possibility of racial and social equality became frightening reality for white Americans. Lynching emerged as the specific form of sexual violence visited on black men, with the myth of the black rapist and the image of the bestial black man as its ideological justification. Thus, it was through manipulating images of black sexuality that the state was able to legitimize its refusal to put an end to the waves of politically motivated violence and terror being directed against African Americans. Likewise, in the early twentieth century, the rape or attempted rape of white women by Asian men was actualized in the myth of the "Yellow Peril,"

which gained ascendancy during America's transition from a republic to a small empire with sovereignty over Hawaii, the Philippines, Guam, and Samoa.

Moral pollution

The Asian in America, who has been described as a "third sex – an alternative or imagined sexuality that was potentially subversive," accordingly *was* imagined as an erotic threat to American domestic tranquillity; this was for two reasons, argues Robert G. Lee, in his *Orientals: Asian-Americans in popular culture* (Temple University Press, 1999).

Firstly, during the latter decades of the nineteenth century 10,000 Chinese women were forcibly brought to the USA as prostitutes. Chinese prostitutes were popularly seen as posing a serious threat to the physical and moral development of young white men. Secondly, thousands of immigrant Chinese men became servants in American households, which not only opened up the possibility for cross-class and cross-racial intimacy but also threatened the nation, the working-class family popularly being seen as the source of national rejuvenation. The construction of Asian women as prostitutes was closely connected to the issue of the extension of citizenship as fears of moral and racial pollution by sexually deviant Chinese women were used as justification for the Page Act of 1870, which severely curtailed Chinese immigration into the US.

The family, the state, sexuality, and race became connected in nationalist discourse as racial science – particularly eugenics – became instrumental in fostering the view that birth control was a means of solving social and national problems. Although the father of eugenics was an English scientist, Francis Galton, his ideas were immensely popular in the United States where, at the turn of the century, white Americans were paralyzed by fears of "race suicide," believing that immigrants were reproducing faster than native Anglo-Saxons. The eugenics movement thus aimed to prevent socially undesirable races from procreating. Lothrop Stoddard, the founding father of the American eugenics movement, which argued that intelligence and other personality traits were genetically determined, believed that the principal threat to the white race came from Asia. He saw immigration, assimilation, and miscegenation between the "white" and "yellow" races as ultimately leading to the swamping of the Anglo-American by the Asiatic. Eugenicists were equally worried, however, that interracial sex between blacks and whites would dilute the white race, to its detriment. Nineteenth- and early twentieth-century eugenicists advocated compulsory sterilization to improve society by eliminating races that were "unfit" – a movement popularly known as "negative" eugenics. They also advocated so-called positive eugenics, which encouraged the breeding of superior citizens. During the Depression negative eugenics became even more popular as sterilization became the preferred method of preventing the birth of children, particularly if they were black and would need public assistance.

Eroticized bodies

Racialized imagery remains deeply inscribed in the psychic imagery of the West. Colonial discourses about racial Others have been projected from the past into the postcolonial present. This obsession is principally evident in contemporary fantasies about the deviant sexuality of black and brown people. The black male, in particular, remains a repository of white fear and desire. In his *Rituals of Blood: Consequences of slavery in two American centuries* (Basic/Civitas, 1998), Orlando Patterson observes that "the Afro-American man as demon represents the evil side of violence, the violence we dread, the violence that Euro-American males do not dare to admit is a core part of their psychic being." The obsession of white males with black male bodies has long been channeled through entertainment and popular culture. During the nineteenth century, for example, minstrelsy allowed the continued enactment and reenactment of white male homoerotic desire for African Americans. White males' subversive sexual enjoyment of black males continues in the form of obsessive interest in the athletic black body, which has become a key repository for contemporary fears and desires around blackness. Sports today, like minstrelsy in the nineteenth century, provide a safe context for the exercise of the racialized, homosocial gaze, which simultaneously hyper-masculinizes and feminizes black male bodies.

The bodies of black women are also eroticized in commodity culture, wherein they are represented not as integrated human beings, but rather as collections of erotic parts, with particular attention paid to their buttocks. The continuing fetishization of the buttocks of black and Latina women in contemporary culture recall the public exhibition of Sarah Baartmann, a Khoikhoi woman taken from South Africa and exhibited as a curiosity in London during the early nineteenth century due to the purportedly "over-developed" state of her buttocks.

Contemporary media culture is notable for the degree to which historical colonial fantasies about the racial excesses of the Other continue, as the eroticized black body has become a highly valued commodity within the sign economy. At the same time that black and brown bodies are becoming increasingly valuable commodities in the sign economy, however, actual black and brown people are becoming increasingly peripheral in the formal economy. Thus, the precipitous increase in the visibility of black bodies in commodity culture must be considered in tandem with the changing nature of politics, particularly the shift from coalition politics to what Paul Gilroy calls "bio-politics." In his essay "After the love has gone: bio-politics and ethno-poetics in the black public sphere," Gilroy argues that, whereas black liberation politics used to be focused on achieving social and economic rights in the public sphere, they now reflect the preoccupations of commodity culture and focus on iconic black bodies "engaged in characteristic activities – usually sexual or sporting – that ground and solicit identification if not solidarity" (essay in *The Black Public Sphere*, edited by the Black Public Sphere Collective, University of Chicago Press, 1994)

Discussions of race and sexuality have always encompassed a medical dimension. In the early twentieth century, for example, a debate ensued over what colonial officials in the Uganda protectorate felt was a "syphilis epidemic" among the indigenous population. Similar fears surfaced amongst officials in India and the so-called Orient. These panics over the spread of venereal disease were constructed as problems of morality and thus the solution was seen to lie in the control of the sexuality of the Other. In the contemporary era, the epidemic that has attracted the most attention is that of Acquired Immune Deficiency Syndrome, or AIDS, which is currently the leading cause of death among sexually active youth and adults in a number of developing countries. It is also becoming a leading cause of death amongst poor African Americans, particularly women. Since 1995 the USA has been conducting experiments on pregnant women infected with HIV in Africa, Thailand, and the Dominican Republic, in which some women are given drugs that can prevent the transmission of the deadly AIDS virus and others receive only placebos. Some critics have suggested that these studies are reminiscent of the Tuskegee experiment, in which the US Public Health Service withheld treatment from black males with syphilis so that it could observe the disease's progression.

Race and reproduction also continue to be deeply implicated in global discourses about "overpopulation" in the developed world as well as in contemporary discussions about race and the new reproductive technologies. Poor women in the developing world, as well as black and brown women in the developed world, have routinely been subject to forced sterilization. At the same time, though middle-class white women are routinely advised and encouraged to seek fertility treatments, poor women of color are routinely steered away from reproductive technologies. As Dorothy Roberts explains, "high tech means of procreation may magnify racial inequities ... by strengthening the ideology that white people deserve to procreate while black people do not, the new reproduction may worsen racial inequality." The new reproductive technologies have also provided an opening for the reemergence of nineteenth-century eugenics discourse. Spurred on by fears about Singapore's growing Indian and Malay populations, the Singapore government, for example, has recently invested heavily in the development of new reproductive technologies in order to increase the fertility of the educated elite, particularly those of Chinese ancestry.

SEE ALSO: African Americans; Asian Americans; beauty; colonialism; culturecide; Doomed Races Doctrine; essentialism; ethnocide; eugenics; Hottentot Venus; intelligence; Jim Crow; Jordan, Michael; masculinity; minstrelsy; miscegenation; negrophilia; Other; patriarchy; racist discourse; sexual abuse; slavery; South Africa; Tyson, Mike

Reading

Empire and Sexuality: The British experience by Ronald Hyam (Manchester University Press, 1990) looks at the sexual attitudes of British colonial elites and argues for the importance of understanding the role that sexuality played in the project of imperial expansion.

Imperial Leather: Race, gender and sexuality in the colonial contest by Anne McClintock (Routledge, 1995) examines how the categories of gender, race, and class became articulated through an historical examination of British imperialism.

Love and Theft: Blackface minstrelsy and the American working class by Eric Lott (Oxford University Press, 1995) discusses the way in which white working-class masculinity has, historically, been channeled through imaginary black interlocutors.

Race and the Education of Desire by Ann Laura Stoler (Duke University Press, 1995) is a critique of Foucault's genealogy of European sexuality; Stoler argues that Foucault overlooked the degree to which colonial bodies were sites for the articulation of nineteenth-century European sexuality.

Race and the Subject of Masculinities, edited by Harry Stecopoulous and Michael Uebel (Duke University Press, 1997), explores the ways in which masculinity intersects with other categories of identity, especially those of race and ethnicity.

ZINE MAGUBANE

SIMPSON CASE, THE O. J.

It has been argued that the trial of Orenthal James Simpson (b. 1947) for murder was America's defining cultural experience of the 1990s. It claimed the front-page of every newspaper in the USA, Britain and probably everywhere else in the world. Television companies afforded it gavel-to-gavel coverage and were rewarded with record-breaking viewer ratings.

Simpson, relatively unknown outside the USA, became perhaps the most talked-about person in the world. A rich and decorated former football player, Simpson had made the transition to comedy actor, featuring in the *Naked Gun* series, before he was charged, in June 1994, with the murder of his estranged wife Nicole Simpson and her friend Ronald Goodman. His defense, led at great cost (estimated $4–5m) by celebrity lawyer Johnnie Cochrane, Jr., revolved around the claim that the Los Angeles Police Department (LAPD) had planted evidence. In the wake of the Rodney King case, it was not unreasonable to suppose that racism was a motive in some LAPD actions and Cochrane skillfully played the "race card." Simpson was acquitted.

Born in San Francisco to a poor family, Simpson developed rickets soon after birth, a condition that left him bowlegged and pigeon-toed. His father, Jimmy Lee, abandoned the family. His mother Eunice encouraged O. J. to pursue sport mainly to ameliorate his physical problems; he soon showed enough promise to win an athletics scholarship at a parochial school, where he played baseball. After moving to a different school, Simpson became an outstanding football player. Despite his physical handicap, he was big for his age. Also on the team was Al Cowlings, who became his close friend and confidante in years to come.

Simpson enrolled in the City College of San Francisco and continued to impress on the football field. Teresa Carpenter tells of a superstition Simpson held for many years: his head was so large that the City College needed to order a new helmet. There was no time to paint the college's logo and Simpson played so well that he insisted on wearing a plain helmet from that stage. This aided his instant recognition by the local media.

With offers from 50 universities, Simpson opted for University of Southern California (USC) where he distinguished himself as the 1968 Heisman Trophy winner. USC was a predominantly white school and Simpson was not, it seems, eager to become involved in the racial politics of the late 1960s. He did not support the attempt to boycott the Mexico Olympic games in 1968 and was not conspicuously supportive of the Black Power revolt of the era. The Nation of Islam's best-known athlete member Muhammad Ali was embroiled in all manner of controversy and his acts of defiance inspired many black sports performers to pledge their allegiance. But Simpson was noncommittal. "A lot of my brothers in sports have joined the Black Muslims," he once said. "But ... they're not allowed to eat pork – and I love bacon too much" (quoted in Teresa Carpenter's article, "The man behind the mask," in *Esquire*, vol. 122, no. 5, 1994).

A semester before he was due to graduate in public administration, Simpson dropped out and signed a three-year deal with Chevrolet worth $250,000 – the first of several highly lucrative endorsements that would make Simpson one of the wealthiest athletes of his time. By 1985, it was estimated that he had earned $10m from sponsors such as Schick, Foster Grant and Tree Sweet orange juice. The money pales besides that earned by Michael Jordan in the 1990s, but in the 1980s sponsors were only learning the value of having products endorsed by sports performers. All the same, Simpson was an African

American and commercial companies were known to favor white product endorsers.

Drafted by the then unfashionable Buffalo Bills in 1969, Simpson failed to deliver for three years. But in 1972 a new head coach, Lou Saban, played him with protective blockers, who released him to exploit his speed (he was a useful track athlete in his early career). The records went tumbling: he topped 1,000 yards' rushing five consecutive times, had six 200-yard games and broke Jim Brown's season record for rushing yards with 2,003 in 1973. He traded to the San Franciso 49ers in 1978, but injuries dogged him and he was forced to retire the following year, age thirty-two. He was inducted into the Pro Football Players' Hall of Fame in 1985.

The expected glut of film offers did not materialize, but he picked up some minor parts and became well-known for his role in David Zucker's 1984 comedy *The Naked Gun*, which spawned a series. He had a brief but ill-starred commentator spot on ABC's Monday Night Football. Hertz rental cars featured Simpson in its advertising and, interestingly, did not void the contract during Simpson's trial.

Stories of Simpson's alleged abuse of his first wife, Marguerite Whitley Simpson, had circulated during their twelve-year marriage, during which they had three children. Simpson left her and sued for divorce in 1978. But Marguerite Whitley refused to be drawn and filed no official complaint. In fact, the first recorded account of O. J.'s violence was not until New Year's Eve, 1989, when Nicole Simpson called the police; when the police arrived, Nicole was hiding. O. J. received a $200 fine and two years' probation.

Simpson had met Nicole in 1977, when she was waiting tables. They had an affair and married shortly after she became pregnant in 1985. Over the next four years, it is understood that Nicole made up to thirty emergency calls to the police without pressing formal charges or filling out incident reports.

His dramatic arrest, flight, trial and subsequent civil suit have been exhaustively documented. Coming so soon after the *causes cõlòbres* involving Marion Barry, the black former mayor of Washington DC, and Mike Tyson, the Simpson trial became yet another prism through which to view America's racial condition. As well as the racist dimensions inherent in the case (including taped racist remarks of LAPD officers), there were other factors that went beyond the courtroom. Research conducted while the trial was in progress revealed that a majority of African Americans believed Simpson to be innocent, while a majority of whites thought him to be guilty.

Simpson was, of course, acquitted of the charges in 1995. The acquittal did not bring immediate rehabilitation as far as commercial America was concerned; there was not a glut of movie or endorsement offers. Simpson had been demonized. A successful athlete-turned-movie actor with millions in the bank, Simpson was widely regarded as fortunate: had he been just another African American without the kind of resources to hire formidable defense teams, it is at least statistically probable that the verdict would have been different.

SEE ALSO: Barry case, the Marion; Central Park jogger; Jordan, Michael; King case, the Rodney; Million Man March; Nation of Islam; race card; sexual abuse; Thomas, Clarence; Tyson, Mike

Reading

Contemporary Controversies and the American Divide: The O. J. Simpson case and other controversies by Robert Smith and Richard Seltzer (Rowman & Littlefield, 2000) interprets the Simpson case as one of a number of "racially divisive" issues that affected the USA in the 1990s; these include the Rodney King trial, the Marion Barry case, the Clarence Thomas affair and Louis Farrakhan's Million Man March (all covered elsewhere in this volume). What elevates this book over others is that it is based on public opinion survey analyses, which highlight the differences between ethnic groups and explains these differences of opinion in terms of distinct historical and social experiences, and the gap in economic conditions. A similar theme is explored in "The influence of racial similarity on the O. J. Simpson Trial" by L. Mixon, A. Foley, and K. Orme (in *Journal of Social Behavior and Personality*, vol. 10, no. 3, 1995).

Reasonable Doubts: The O. J. Simpson case and the criminal justice system by celebrity lawyer Alan Dershowitz (Simon & Schuster, 1996) is a level-headed assessment of the trial which concludes that the appropriate verdict was reached and that justice was served.

SKINHEADS

While many other white supremacist movements have declined in recent years, skinheads have continued to attract adherents from all over Europe and the USA. They have followed the examples of British counterparts in the 1970s, who formed alliances with neo-fascist organiza-tions such as the National Front (NF) and the British Movement (BM) and linked up with established political movements. Although they have no formal organizational structure themselves, skinheads have been welcome supplements to such groups as the Ku Klux Klan, the Liberty Lobby, White Aryan Resistance (WAR), and Germany's radical right-wing Nationalist Front and Deutsche Alternativ parties.

Originating in England in the late 1960s, skinheads defined a hostile working-class reaction to the cultural changes sought by youth of the day. Drawing support from young people in Britain's inner cities, skinheads preyed on groups perceived to be "outsiders," most particularly South Asian migrants – in their terms, "Pakis." Their uniform was shorn hair, braces (suspenders), denim jeans, and industrial boots. After a period of decline, skinheads reappeared in 1978 as part of a racist revival.

As skinheads faded slightly in Britain in the 1980s, US equivalents came to light. Many cases of brutality and vandalism involving skinhead attacks on ethnic minorities emerged in the 1980s and 1990s, the best-known involving Tom Metzger, a former Klan Grand Dragon and leader of WAR, which had a large skinhead membership. In 1990, Metzger and his son were found guilty by a court in Portland, Oregon, of inspiring a group of skinheads to beat to death Mulvgeta Seraw, an Ethiopian migrant. Metzger was ordered to pay $12.5m to Seraw's survivors and his assets were liquidated. Metzger was in court again in 1993 when charged with a felony count of conspiracy to violate the municipal fire rules of San Fernando Valley, California, by ritually burning a cross Klan-style. His lawyer invoked the First Amendment (free speech), arguing that Metzger was being persecuted for "his beliefs."

In 1992 the German government banned the sale, manufacture and distribution of the skinhead music known as "Oi!," the lyrics of which advocated racism and genocide. According to George Marshall (in *Spirit of '69: A Skinhead Bible*, ST Publishing, 1991), "Oi!" was started in 1980 by the English band The Cockney Rejects. The German bands affected by the ban included St—rkraft (Disruptive Force), Endstufe (Final Stage), and Kahlkopf (Bald Head). At the same time, skinheads were appearing in the Eastern European states of Poland, Hungary, Slovakia, and the Czech Republic. Their targets were, variously, Gypsies, Jews, and asylum seekers.

SEE ALSO: Ku Klux Klan; Let's Kick Racism Out of Football; neo-nazism; Rock Against Racism; scapegoat; stereotype; White Power; white race; youth subcultures

Reading

Black Sun: Aryan cults, esoteric nazism and the politics of identity by Nicholas Goodrick-Clark (New York University Press, 2002) interprets neo-nazi movements as symptoms of major divisive changes in Western democracy: a deskilled white working class destabilized by migration and the supposed favoritism extended to migrants, turn to political movements that offer unduly simplified accounts and uncomplicated remedies.

Blood in the Face by James Ridgeway (Thunder's Mouth Press, 1990) plots the rise of what the author calls a "new white culture," which includes skinheads and other white supremacist movements.

"Long day's journey into white" by Kathy Dobie (in *Village Voice*, vol. 37, no. 17, April 1992) discusses female skinheads and their involvement with neonazi organizations.

SLAVERY

Forms of unfreedom

"Slavery is the status or condition of a person over whom any or all of the powers attaching to the right of ownership are exercised," according to the United Nations Slavery Convention (I (1), Geneva, 1926). The condition invariably involves the forced, unremunerated labor of the person held as property and his or her exclusion from any kind of participation in politics or civil rights.

The process by which this condition comes about is the "slave trade," defined by the UN as: "all acts involved in the capture, acquisition of a slave with a view to selling or exchanging him; all acts of disposal by sale or exchange of a slave acquired with a view to being sold or exchanged and, in general, every act of trade or transport in slaves" (I (2), Geneva, 1926).

The origins of the term are interesting. They lie in the Latin *sclavus*, meaning captive, which eventually became Slav. "For it was from among the pagan Slavs that Western Europeans, reluctant to enslave fellow Christians, turned for slaves," writes Ronald Seagal in his book *The Black Diaspora* (Faber & Faber, 1995).

Pierre van den Berghe explains the reason for this: "Slavery is a form of unfreedom and disability that is largely restricted to ethnic strangers – to people who are defined as outside the solidarity group."

Types of unfreedom have been institutionalized in ancient Greece, imperial Rome, in China and Korea. The Domesday Book, which was a record of land in England in 1066, registered slaves in the counties of Cornwall and Gloucestershire. As in other situations, the availability of labor was the decisive factor: when free, waged labor became more available, it became more economical to hire, rather than own and keep manual workers.

From about CE 650, the Islamic world engaged slaves. In fact, Islamic slavery is the most enduring form of the institution: it was banned in Saudi Arabia in 1962 and in Oman as late as 1970. Historically, "ethnic strangers" were from the Balkans and Africa and were crucial to the Ottoman Empire (Ottoman Turks ended Christianity's Byzantine Empire in 1453). Slaves were responsible for physically laborious work and domestic service, including concubinage. In total, about eighteen million slaves were taken by Islamic nations in the period 650–1900. There was also slave trade between Africa, the Middle East and Southeast Asia. Unlike some other forms of slavery, the Islamic tradition allowed for manumission either by length of duty, purchase or birthright – children of concubines, for example, were not enslaved.

West African societies retained slaves to work for royalty, for example, as trained metalworkers, or porters. They exported some slaves to North Africa, though this commerce was eclipsed by the large-scale traffic from the sixteenth century onward. This was precipitated by European demands.

While Europeans had relied mainly on serfdom after the fall of Rome in AD 410, the economic revival of the Middle Ages (from about 1000) brought about a demand for labor. In conquering territories previously held by Muslims, Christian Crusaders also took slaves, mostly white, though some Africans too. Black slaves became more common only after about 1300. The occupation and exploitation of the New World from 1492 introduced both new possibilities and new demands for labor to cultivate sugar. It also brought new sea routes, southwards from Europe to the African coast, then west to the Indies in an Atlantic triangle.

Chattel slavery

The particular type of slavery operated by European powers when expanding and maintaining their colonies between the sixteenth and nineteenth centuries was chattel slavery, the term "chattel" deriving from the same root as cattle (the Old French *chatel*). The especially virulent form of racism that is the source of contemporary race relations issues was, in large part, born out of the desire and need to defend, justify and preserve this form of slavery. The main European nations responsible for chattel slavery were Britain, France, Holland, Portugal and Spain. It was based on the chattel slaves' having no legal rights at all and, in this sense, differed from some earlier forms of slavery. For example, under Roman law, slaves were allowed limited legal privileges and rights as people as well as property; and the Spanish practiced a system known as *encomienda*, in which settlers had the right to tribute and work from Indians. France, more than any other imperial power, tried to formalize the legal position of slaves with its *Code Noir* of 1685. As in Roman Law, slaves' rights as well as rights of ownership were established. Under French imperialism, slaves were baptized and subject to control only by Roman Catholics; they were allowed to rest on Sundays and holy days; they were also allowed to marry with the consent of owners. These and other entitlements were prescribed by law. Other European powers were more prohibitive. Yet, in all cases, the status of the slave as chattel was validated and owners were invested with extensive powers over them.

Essentially, slaves were needed for labor. They were denuded of their humanity as an economic expedient; in other words, they could be captured, bought, sold, traded and put to use if they were not considered human, at least not in the same sense as were Western Europeans. The conditions for this slavery were quite basic: the conquest of a territory, followed by the capture of its people and their sale to traders, then their transportation to a distant country where they were forced to work. Slaves from West Africa were captured mainly by Africans from other ethnic groups, who then traded them to Europeans. Most of the Europeans' attentions were concentrated on Africa, so the native peoples underwent what Stanley Elkins calls a series of "shocks" in the process of enslavement: "We may suppose that every African who became a slave underwent an experience whose crude psychic impact must have been staggering and whose consequences superseded anything that had ever happened to him."

Before the trade in slaves ended in the mid nineteenth century, between twelve and fifteen million Africans were transported to North, Central, and South American countries to work as slaves (about 60 percent of them were taken in the eighteenth century when the slave trade peaked). Most came from a narrow strip of the West African coast, with a significant majority coming from Central Africa. The areas now known as Angola and southern Nigeria were fertile grounds. The native peoples' robustness and acclimatization to tropical conditions were thought to make them suitable for cotton or sugar plantation work in such places as Brazil, the Caribbean, and the southern states of America. The physical environments were harsh and demanding, but the first slaves had come from lands rife with diseases and subject to droughts and famines. An unknown number of indigenous peoples were enslaved by the Spanish and Portuguese in South America.

Slaves were made to labor on plantations, in mines (especially in Brazil), or in houses (as domestic servants or artisans). The motivation for keeping them working in this way and depriving them of any sort of freedom was in most cases (but not all) profit-maximization. Productivity was paramount and slave owners and traders were unaffected by moral considerations. Racist ideologists served useful purposes in several contexts, for clearly it was morally wrong and unchristian to subject a fellow human being to all manner of atrocity in the pursuit of wealth. If all men were equal before God, then it was simply not right to hold another in bondage and deprive them of all basic human rights.

Racism provided a legitimization of sorts, however, for it proposed a theory of human types in which some races were superior to others. In this instance, whites were thought to be obviously superior: their military and technological advancement demonstrated that. Blacks were considered a race apart: inferior, and even subhuman. So, if they were not equal, there was no reason to treat them equally. There was not an agreement among scholars as to the exact relationship between slavery and the racist ideologies that appeared in Europe and North America in the nineteenth century. The abolition of the slave trade (as opposed to the institution of slavery itself) in 1807 was a victory for abolitionists and other antislavery movements. It also propelled the need "to construct the elaborate edifice of race ideology that has been our legacy," as Audrey Smedley puts it in her *Race in North America: Origin and evolution of a worldview* (Westview Press, 1993). The response to the flow of public and legal opinion was to garner scientific evidence to support the view that slaves were innately inferior and undeserving of treatment as equals.

The problem with racist ideologies is that, unlike chalk marks on a board, they cannot be rubbed away when no longer needed. After the abolition of slavery racism did not disappear, of course. Rather, it endured in the popular imagination and continued to affect relationships between whites and the descendants of slaves most substantially. Racism permanently stigmatized the succeeding generations of those who had previously been enslaved.

In 1772, a British judgment ruled that slaveowners claiming to hold 10,000 slaves could not do so. While the planters took their property (i.e. slaves) to Britain as servants, they could not be sent back to the West Indies against their will. In 1807, the legal slave trade ended after a period of antislavery pressure, much from religious abolitionist groups. The following fifty years saw some small improvements in slaves' conditions, such as housing, clothing, and diet, though the average life expectancy of slaves was at least 12 percent below that of whites by 1850. In 1833, some 800,000 slaves in British territories were freed and ten years later slavery was abolished in British colonial India; one year later it was abolished in Ceylon (now Sri Lanka). Full emancipation came in 1865, though a system of indentured labor in some areas ensured that ex-slaves in the Americas remained tied to plantations. By this time, other European powers, including Denmark (1848), Holland (1863) and Sweden (1847) had ended slavery. France abolished (1794), then restored (1802), before finally ending slavery in 1848. Mexico abrogated in 1829 and Brazil in 1888. Many Latin American countries phased out slavery by granting freedom to children of slaves.

Technically, emancipation meant that slaves were released from their bondage and relieved of their status as chattel (that is, someone's possession). Yet, various pieces of legislation and other developments made sure that, for the next hundred years, their progress towards some form of equality would be painfully slow.

Servitude today

The particular combination of slavery and racism was a potent one, and one which was to have far-reaching effects. There are, however, instances of slavery without racism and it seems that some system of unfreedom can be imposed wherever conditions facilitate slavery; the prime condition being where human labor can profitably be exploited. This is attested to by the endurance of various forms of chattel slavery. The ownership of one human by another persists in the contemporary world, particularly in India, where a system of *debt bondage* ensures that an estimated 6.5 million people are held in a slave-like state. The absence of bankruptcy laws in India means that a creditor can claim back money or goods owed by acquiring his debtor as his property. Kevin Bales provides details of what he calls the "new slavery" in which adults who are destitute sell themselves and their children to those who are not. In most cases, the transaction is bound by a contract and, once bonded, the initial debt grows. Debt bondage emerges in countries that provide little or no welfare, where unemployment is high and where expanding populations have been driven off the land. Another type of slavery in Asia is the kidnapping of women from Bangladeshi villages, followed by their transportation and sale as servants in the Gulf states. One feature of interest in the "new slavery" is that the slaves are not always "ethnic strangers" but are often from the same ethnic group, though inevitably further down a hierarchy that may be based on matrices not recognizable to (or long since disappeared in) the West.

In South America, there are various types of labor that come very near to slavery, such as in Peru where certain tribes are classed as "savages" and denied citizenship, or Brazil where the *yoke* keeps unpaid laborers working the plantations while in bondage.

There is evidence to suggest that slavery exists in such unlikely places as the People's Republic of China, the ex-Soviet Union, and even the USA. As recently as 1982 arrests were made involving the sale of illegal Indonesian immigrants to wealthy Los Angeles homes as domestic servants. The number of illegally held Haitians, Mexicans,

and Salvadorans in the United States is speculated to be in the tens of thousands.

In 1992, the London-based Anti-Slavery International submitted to a UN working group
reports on slavery in Brazil. These estimated
5,000 men, women and children were found in
slave conditions, mostly on Amazon cattle
ranches or sugarcane distilleries in Mato Grosso.
The usual practice was to recruit unemployed
people in one state, transport them hundreds of
miles to another, promising good pay and conditions. On arrival they would find their fares, and
the food and tools they were obliged to buy at
inflated prices, were deducted from their wages,
leaving them in debt to the rancher or distiller.
Escapees were hunted, tortured, or even murdered. The debt-bonded system, as it is called,
was not confined to remote regions. Paraibuna,
80 miles from SÐo Paulo, harbored seventy
slaves, some of whom were forced to live among
livestock.

The most visible state of slavery in recent
times is that practiced in the Islamic republic of
Mauritania in West Africa. Although technically
outlawed, a system of chattel slavery is an
integral part of the economy and continues to
thrive with about 100,000 held in bondage.
Having reviewed the relevant research, Russ
Vallance, the Development Secretary of the Anti-
Slavery Society (to whom I am grateful for the
information on slavery today), concludes that
there are "probably more slaves in the world
today than were freed by the great reformers of
the 19th century" (personal communication,
April 13, 1983). This view was later validated in
Bales's *Disposable People*, which estimates that
some twenty-seven million individuals are enslaved. This reinforces the idea that slavery
surfaces in virtually any social situation where
there are disparities in wealth and where human
labor can be forced and exploited.

SEE ALSO: Africa; antislavery; Brazil;
colonialism; *encomienda*; exploitation; Fanon,
Frantz; Freyre, Gilberto; ideology; indigenous
peoples; Las Casas, BartolomÕ de; racist
discourse; reparations; science; white race;
whiteness

Reading

*The Diligent: A voyage through the world of the slave
trade* by Robert Harms (Perseus, 2002) estimates
that there are over twenty million slaves around the
world today – more than were exported from Africa
during the entire Atlantic trade.
Disposable People: New slavery in the global economy
by Kevin Bales (University of California Press, 2001)
explains that the population explosion and poverty
in the underdeveloped world has created a surplus of
potential slaves who are cheap and, as the title
suggest, disposable.
Roll, Jordan, Roll by Eugene D. Genovese (Pantheon,
1974) is something of a classic text on slavery,
complemented by *Race and Slavery in the Western
Hemisphere*, edited by Genovese with Stanley L.
Engerman (Princeton University Press, 1975); *Slavery*
by Stanley Elkins (University of Chicago Press, 1968)
provides a contrast to these.
Slavery: A world history by Milton Meltzer (Da Capo,
1993) is one of the most comprehensive guides to
slavery available.
Slavery and Social Death by Orlando Patterson (Harvard University Press, 1983) is an original treatment
of slavery, tracing its many historical forms and
theorizing why this form of domination and exploitation occurs even when it is economically useless;
slavery is seen as a form of "social death" and slaves'
membership of society is totally negated; the author's
earlier work was *The Sociology of Slavery* (MacGib-
bon & Kee, 1961). Patterson also writes the fore-
word for Junius P. Rodriguez's sourcebook
Chronology of World Slavery (ABC-Clio, 1999).
*The White Man's Burden: Historical origins of racism
in the United States* by Winthrop Jordan (Oxford
University Press, 1974) is an historical analysis
which argues that English explorers in the eighteenth
and nineteenth centuries conceived of Africans as
heathen savage beasts which were in need of severe
discipline; in this way, the adventurers were able to
be consistent with the moral tone of the Protestant
reformation. Also on the British experience, see
Slavery and British Society, 1777–1846 by James
Walvin (Macmillan, 1982).
CHECK: internet resources section

SOCIAL DARWINISM

Social Darwinism is widely, but misguidedly,
regarded as a distinctive school of thought that
flourished at the end of the nineteenth and
beginning of the twentieth centuries. Authors
commonly said to be members of this school
include Herbert Spencer, Walter Bagehot, Ludwig
Gumplowicz, William Graham Sumner, Gustav
Ratzenhofer, Franklin H. Giddings, and Benjamin Kidd. Some textbooks identify a separate,
and contemporaneous, school of "anthroposo-
ciology" led by Otto Ammon and Georges
Vacher de Lapouge, writers who showed similarities of approach with some of the authors in the
first list.

The Origin of Species was published in 1859.
Within twenty years Bagehot and Gumplowicz

were consciously attempting to apply in the study of society principles they believed to have been established by Darwin, but the expression "social Darwinism" did not make an appearance for almost another thirty years, when it was employed by critics to designate a political philosophy that they considered pernicious. Social Darwinism came to be seen as a doctrine defending free-market economics and opposing state intervention. This was far removed from a literal interpretation of the name, which could with greater justification have been applied to the argument that social evolution results from the natural and sexual selection of favorable inherited variations.

Within the early twentieth-century debate about social evolution, several contending schools can be distinguished. As described by R. J. Halliday, the Oxford idealists explained it in terms of the dominance of rational mind over instinct. The Spencerian individualists represented human evolution as primarily a genetic or hereditarian process with a stress upon man's biological make-up rather than his rational mind. A third group, the civics movement, presented evolution as an adaptive process resulting from the interaction between man and his environment: man was unique because of his ability to plan and to influence his own evolution. A fourth group, identified with the Eugenics Society, was closer to Darwin's conception of natural selection as resting upon a theory of population. Spencer disagreed with almost all the components of the eugenic doctrine and retained in his biology a strong environmental emphasis, insisting in particular upon the inheritance of acquired characteristics. The eugenicists can be seen as the true Darwinians in that they interpreted the social problem of reproduction in terms of the biological problem of competition for resources. On such a view, the conventional definition of social Darwinism as a *laissez-faire* economic ideology is misleading: the economic theory presupposed an ability rationally to allocate scarce means to competing ends, whereas those who started from biological principles saw human rationality as relatively unimportant. It is also misleading to label particular authors as social Darwinists without allowing for changes in their positions. Gumplowicz and Sumner each at one stage of their careers advanced Darwinist arguments but then moved on to write in quite other ways. Spencer's arguments were so special to himself

that nothing is gained by classing him as a social Darwinist.

Arguments appealing to Darwinist principles had a significant influence upon racial relations in the early twentieth century. They introduced an element of ruthlessness and immorality into the justification of European expansion into overseas territories. They gave additional force to the anti-immigration campaign in the USA that resulted in the exclusion act of 1924 establishing quotas for different national groups. They produced a theory that represented racial prejudice as a positive element in human evolution (most elegantly expressed by Sir Arthur Keith). This theory reappeared in the 1970s in connection with the approach known as sociobiology; it has been applied, in an updated form, by Pierre van den Berghe to racial and ethnic relations. Whether sociobiology is properly described as a new version of social Darwinism is disputable. It has been maintained that for the study of racial relations the best resolution is to isolate what is called the selectionist theory. This holds that: (1) evolution may be assisted if interbreeding populations are kept separate so that they can develop their special capacities (as in animal breeding); (2) racial prejudice serves this function and in so doing reinforces racial categories in social life; (3) therefore racial categories are determined by evolutionary processes of inheritance and selection. Where the pre-Darwinian racial typologists inferred that pure races must have existed in the past, the selectionists see racial purity as something constantly advanced as humans adapt to new circumstances and cause their groups to evolve. Sociobiologists often advance some version of the selectionist theory; this enables their arguments to be classified without entering into the dispute as to whether or not they are social Darwinists.

SEE ALSO: anthropology; Darwinism; Doomed Races Doctrine; environmentalism; eugenics; hereditarianism; science; sociobiology; White Power

Reading

Racial and Ethnic Competition by Michael Banton (Cambridge University Press, 1983) provides further observations on the selectionist theory: see pp. 47–50.

"Social Darwinism: a definition" by R. J. Halliday (in *Victorian Studies*, vol. 4, 1971) reviews the definitional problem.

Social Darwinism in American Thought by Richard
  Hofstadter (Beacon Press, 1975) is a more conven-
  tional history.
CHECK: internet resources section

MICHAEL BANTON

SOCIAL EXCLUSION

Social exclusion describes either the condition
of, or the processes contributing to, either the
opting-out, or the expulsion or removal, of
certain groups from participation in mainstream
economic, political and cultural activities. The
processes may include racism, sexism, ageism,
geographical segregation, as well as unemployment and homelessness. The resulting condition
has been known as marginalization, dislocation,
disaffection or alienation, all of which have, at
some stage, been used popularly to describe the
general condition of groups that lie outside
central social institutions and processes.

While the term social exclusion has been used
for decades, it entered the popular vocabulary in
the 1990s. Derided by some as a neologism
coined to mask some of the harsher consequences
of mature capitalism's structured inequalities,
social exclusion was introduced into a public
discourse shaped by the liberalism that followed
the rightist regimes of the 1980s in Britain and
the USA. The stress on the sovereignty of the
market and the rights of individual citizens
chimed perfectly with the replacement of work
and production by lifestyle choice and consumption as the principle modes of identity creation.
In other words, inclusivity became more a matter
of choice than circumstance. A residual number
of groups may have been shut out or forced to
the margins of society; but others made conscious decisions to remain excluded.

Trevor Bradley argues that there have been
three trends of relevance to the appearance of
social exclusion. (1) The economic crisis of the
1970s and the erosion of the state, particularly in
respect of the provision of welfare payments. As
state intervention in public policy decreased so
the conception of individual freedom as meaning
the absence of state regulation grew. (2) The
departure of full employment as a legitimate
target and its replacement with structural unemployment and casual or part-time work. These
led to economic insecurity, uncertainty and un-
predictability as staple ingredients of life under
late capitalism, (3) The changes in ideas of

citizenship and identity. These are constructed
around consumption as opposed to production.
"The state now argues that the inclusion of
individuals is not its proper role and instead it is
the responsibility of the individual to gain inclusion via choices made in the market place,"
argues Bradley.

So, for example, racism, while still acknowledged to be at work in the twenty-first century,
was understood as surmountable. Ethnic minority groups which had been stymied by racism in
the past but which had progressed economically
were held up as exemplars of achievement who
had embraced democratic values. Other ethnic
minorities positioned in what was once called the
underclass were regarded as lying outside the
mainstream, their condition as much to do with
their own lack of motivation as with the persistence of racism. This means that the exclusion
that was once explained as the consequences of
racism has been rendered explicable as the result
of differential aspirations among ethnic minorities. Some work their way inside the system;
others prefer to stay on the outside.

While the term social exclusion has not replaced racism or, indeed, many of the other -isms,
it has provided a rubric under which disparate
forms of hindrance and ejection can be collected
and thus managed. Like "disadvantage," it also
contrives either to obscure the causes that lead to
some groups' removal, or create misleading impressions about those causes.

SEE ALSO: affirmative action; children;
consumption; disadvantage; equal opportunity;
equality; ghetto; homelessness; human rights;
merit; minorities; racialization; segregation;
social work; underclass; welfare; white backlash
culture; whiteness

Reading

Social Exclusion by David Byrne (Open University
  Press, 1999) is an introduction to this concept,
  reviewing theories of social exclusion and tracing
  the source of the condition to the creation of a postindustrial order founded on the exploitation of low-
  paid workers, while "Social exclusion" by Trevor
  Bradley, in *The Sage Dictionary of Criminology*,
  edited by Eugene McLaughlin and John Munice
  (Sage, 2001) is a short, but useful essay that
  encapsulates many arguments neatly.
*Tackling Social Exclusion in Europe: The contribution
  of the social economy*, edited by Roger Spear,
  Jacques Defourny, Louis Favreau, and Jean-Louis
  Laville (Ashgate, 2001) and *Social Inclusion: Possi-*

bilities and tensions, edited by Peter Askonas and Angus Stewart (Macmillan, 2000) are both collections on the antidotes to social exclusion.

Understanding Social Exclusion, edited by John Hills, Julian Le Grand, and David Piachaud (Oxford University Press, 2002) addresses several questions, including what influences social exclusion and how can it be reduced?

SOCIAL WORK

The racial dimension of social problems

Social work is a professional activity designed to promote social change, and to apply knowledge, skills and values to help people solve problems in their lives. How the profession has approached the subject of racism is troubled and contentious, provoking strong and often hostile responses from many sources. Even social work academics cannot reach agreement. For example, in his *Anti-Discriminatory Practice* (Macmillan, 1993), Neil Thompson argues that "traditional social work has seriously neglected the racial dimension of the social problems it seeks to tackle, and the impact of racism on ethnic minority communities." In contrast, R. A. Pinker describes the endorsement by Central Council for Education and Training in Social Work (CCETSW) of antiracism, and the obligation to teach social work students how to challenge all forms of structural oppression, as "disastrous policies, which have ripped the professional credibility out of British social work" (in "Playing the devil's advocate," *Community Care*, vol. 24, 1994).

Inevitably the divisive and passionate feelings provoked in this debate mean that it is almost impossible to conduct an objective discussion, and to avoid research bias. The conflicts apparent in the profession mirror the current, unresolved debates in society. For example, antidiscriminatory legislation sits uncomfortably with the increasingly restrictive legislation relating to asylum seekers. On the one hand, the state imposes stringent immigration controls, while on the other, sustains a raft of legislation aiming to challenge racism (see part II.8 of David Denney's *Social Work and Social Policy*, Oxford University Press, 1998, for an analysis of this).

Social workers, who are primarily concerned with a wide range of ethnic communities, cannot do their jobs effectively without an understanding of ethnic difference, and the impact on their clients of individual and institutional racism, whether unwitting, deliberate or structural. Additionally, social care legislation in the 1990s, notably the Children Act 1989 and the National Health and Community Care Act 1990, requires them to take into account "race, language and culture" in their practice. A way of overcoming some of these dilemmas, and bringing some objectivity to this stormy area, is to place the debates about racism in its historical context by tracing changing attitudes to racism throughout the last century. This may produce a sounder understanding of the conflicts and dilemmas, even if resolution seems unlikely.

Changing approaches

The origins of social work in the UK lie in nineteenth-century philanthropy, which was driven by intentions to mitigate the harsh impact on the poor of the Poor Law of 1834. In the literature before 1980, minimal references were made to the presence of people of different race and cultures apart from isolated studies, an example being Kathleen Fitzherbert's study *West Indian Children in London* expressing concern at the number of "colored" and mixed race children in the care of the London County Council's Children's Department in 1967. Despite the increasing numbers of Commonwealth immigrants beginning in 1958, social work appears to have gone along with the prevailing colorblind approach in society that immigrants should be assimilated. Underlying this was the usually unspoken imperialistic attitude that white people were inherently superior to these black immigrants, whose task was to integrate themselves into British society.

Nevertheless, the psychodynamic casework approach to client work, characteristic of the 1950s and 1960s, stressed respect for individuals and the unique nature of each person's situation. As this approach emphasized the personal resolution of problems, paying less attention to external, structural contributors to distress, practitioners rarely identified racism in their assessments.

Concern about racism dates from the 1980s in social work literature. This mirrors the growing recognition in society that race relations could not be ignored. In 1981, Juliet Cheetham, Walter James, Martin Loney, Barbara Mayor, and William Prescott, editors of *Social & Community*

Work in a Multi-racial Society, advocated a multiracial approach to social work, as did Vivienne Coombe and Alan Little in their 1986 training guide, *Race and Social Work*. In 1982, the British Association of Social Workers urged social workers to be "responsive to the changing environment," and included racism as a major social issue of the day. A year later, CCETSW published a report, *Teaching Social Work for a Multi-racial Society*, in recognition that the implications for social work of the development of a multicultural society had not been fully appreciated, and that there were "exciting and challenging consequences for professional training." Emphasis was placed on changing perceptions of multiculturalism, from being seen as "a problem," to providing opportunities for social workers to "become aware of the positive and creative opportunities offered by the rich cultural resources."

Meanwhile, the prevailing climate about racism in society was becoming turbulent. Legislation to curb racism was introduced in 1965, 1968 and 1976. The riots of 1981 and the ensuing Scarman Report, which argued that training police officers in race relations was an imperative, reflected growing fears that there were strong links between racism and crime. As society acknowledged the pervasive nature of racism, social work was shaken into action by outspoken, critical and hostile voices from within the profession. Radical social workers challenged psychodynamic intervention methods, promoting acknowledgment of structural explanations for human need. The earliest expressions of concern about racism emerged in the child care field. Those responsible for adoption expressed concern about the unacknowledged racist assumptions underlying transracial adoption practices, and advocated same race placements in recognition of the significance of racial identity for healthy emotional development (two studies published in 1986 cover this issue: J. Small's "Transracial placements – conflicts and contradictions" and J. MaximÕ's "Some psychological models of black self-concept," both in *Social Work with Black Children and their Families*, edited by S. Ahmed, J. Cheetham and J. Small, Batsford Books).

In addition, black writers drew attention to the lack of power that black people had over their own lives, emphasizing their lack of access to powerful white-dominated institutions (see D.

Naik's "An examination of social work education within an anti-racist framework," in *National Curriculum Development Project: Setting the context for change, anti-racist social work education*, CCETSW, 1991). Burgeoning social work literature of this period exudes hostility and political polemic. A selection of work from the late 1980s and early 1990s illustrates this: Lena Dominelli's 1988 *Anti-racist Social Work*, Macmillan Education; Bandana Ahmad's, 1990 *Black Perspectives in Social Work*, Venture Press; D. Divine's "The value of anti-racism in social work" and A. Sivanandan's "Black Struggles against Racism," the latter two in *Setting the Context for Change, Northern Curriculum Development Project*, CCETSW, 1991.

Explanations for the high proportion of black people in prisons, psychiatric hospitals and in the child care system, and the low numbers of black social work practitioners and managers were given in terms of these writers' Marxist analyses.

A return to roots?

In 1989, CCETSW required that students of the Diploma in Social Work should "recognise, understand and confront racism and other forms of discrimination and demonstrate their ability to work effectively in a multi-racial society" (Paper 30, 1989). Inevitably there has been a political and professional backlash. Social workers have been derided by the media and government for espousing "politically correct" attitudes, at the expense of providing high quality services, and in particular for failing to prevent child deaths. While some of these criticisms were blatantly unjust, social work did lose direction in some ways in the 1990s. Whilst explanations for this cannot be laid at the doors of the antiracism movement, the internal professional disputes undoubtedly weakened professional credibility. The lowering of training standards resulting from operating a positive discriminatory policy towards recruitment is indisputable, and a cause for concern. That the proliferation of antiracist literature within social work appears to have become "an academic industry benefiting trainers and consultants rather than the recipients of service" is possibly the most serious outcome, according to Denney.

The question remains as to the direction for social work in the twenty-first century. Perhaps the answers lie in returning to social work's roots, to universal respect toward all human kind in the tradition of Christian Socialism (see, for instance, Butrym, below). This means improving the lives of vulnerable people by the application of knowledge, skills and values. Foremost among values must be commitment to responding to inequalities and injustices in society, and in particular to combating racism. This must be achieved without sacrificing professional standards of knowledge, and skills in practice, some of which are not concerned with racism. Society has not resolved race relations questions. Nor is it the primary role of the social work profession to achieve this. Rather, antiracism should permeate their tasks, directed toward "promoting social change and problem solving in human relationships," as the International Federation of Social Workers (IFSW) expressed it in 2000.

SEE ALSO: homelessness; Marxism; policing; riots: Britain, 1981; Scarman Report; sexual abuse; transracial adoption; welfare

Reading

Anti-racist Social Work by Lena Dominelli (Macmillan 1988) provides serious criticism of the profession's neglect of racism. This theme is echoed in a collection of papers, *Setting the Context for Change* (CCETSW, 1991), and in *Black Perspectives in Social Work* by Bandana Ahmad (Venture Press, 1990).

" Minimising discrimination: a case for excluding interviews from selection for social work courses" by Gillian Bridge (in *Social Work Education*, vol. 15, 1996) and "Discrimination in social work–an historical note" by Bill Forsythe (in *British Journal of Social Work*, vol. 25, 1995) are examples of professional journal discussions of these issues.

Political Correctness and Social Work, edited by Terry Philpot (IEA Health and Welfare Unit, 1999) provides a strong account of this conflicted area, placing into perspective the views of Robert Pinker in his article "Playing the devil's advocate" (Community Care 1994).

Social Work and Community Work in a Multi-racial Society, edited by Juliet Cheetham, Walter James, Martin Loney, Barbara Mayor, and William Prescott (Harper & Rowe 1981), marks the phase when social work adopted a multicultural approach. This is also evident in *Teaching Social Work in a Multiracial Society, Curriculum Study Paper 21*, published by CCETSW (1983), and in Vivienne Coombe and Alan Little's training guide, *Race and Social Work*, (Tavistock 1986).

West Indian Children in London by Kathleen Fitzherbert (Bell, 1967) provides an unusual early reference to race as a factor in child care, while *The Nature of Social Work* by Zofia Butrym (Macmillan, 1976) demonstrates the more usual assimilation approach.

The web site of the International Federation of Social Workers (IFSW) is a valuable source of material about current debates within the profession: available at *http://www.ifsw.org/publications*

GILLIAN BRIDGE

SOCIOBIOLOGY

Since the popularization of the term by Edward O. Wilson in 1975, sociobiology has referred to the study of animal behavior from the perspective of Darwinian evolutionary theory. The approach goes back to the work of William D. Hamilton and John Maynard Smith in the mid 1960s however. An older label is ethology, while others prefer behavioral biology or population ecology. Applied to other animals, the subject is relatively uncontroversial, but human sociobiology has been energetically attacked as racist, sexist, hereditarian, social Darwinist, and so on. The core proposition of sociobiology, namely that behavior, like anatomy, has evolved by natural selection, and therefore has a genetic basis, should hardly be controversial.

The sociobiological model is *not* hereditarian; on the contrary, it is premised on the theorem that any phenotype is the product of the interaction of a genotype and an environment. Furthermore, it takes no a priori position on the relative importance of each, which is highly variable from species to species, and behavior to behavior within a species. Nor does sociobiology deny or minimize the importance of symbolic language and culture in humans. Human sociobiologists merely insist that human language and culture themselves evolved biologically, and hence are under some genetic influence, however remote, indirect, and flexible that influence might be. They only reject the extreme environmentalism, holding that humans are equally likely to learn anything with equal facility, and that cultural evolution is entirely unrelated to biological evolution.

A central tenet of sociobiology (as distinguished from the earlier ethology) is the emphasis on individual-level selection as against group selection. Organisms act to maximize their individual fitness (measured in terms of reproductive success), not to benefit the group or species, except insofar as group fitness coincides with individual fitness. Ultimately, the unit of natural selection is the gene rather than the organism, which is, evolutionarily speaking, a gene's way of making copies of itself, an idea popularized by Richard Dawkins.

What seems like altruistic behavior is explained in sociobiology as ultimate genetic selfishness. Beneficent behavior can increase an individual's fitness in two principal ways: through *nepotism* or kin selection, and through *reciprocity*. By helping kin reproduce (nepotism), an organism can maximize its own inclusive fitness, because kin share a certain percentage of their genes by common descent with ego (one-half between siblings and offspring; one-fourth between grandparents and grandchildren, uncles, and nephews; one-eighth between first cousins, etc.). Helping kin reproduce is thus an indirect way of reproducing one's own genes. Between kin, nepotism can be fitness-maximizing even if the behavior is not reciprocated, and indeed many forms of nepotism are highly asymmetrical (for example, between parents and offspring). Nepotism has been found to be a powerful explanatory principle of animal sociality, and is obviously also universal in human societies.

Between unrelated individuals, beneficent behavior can only increase fitness if it is reciprocated, though systems of reciprocity are always vulnerable to cheaters and freeloaders (who seek to avoid reciprocation). In nature, sexual reproduction is a widespread form of reciprocity between males and females; each sex benefits by being "nice" to the other, but nature will not select for unrequited love! Many of the most successful applications of sociobiology have been in the field of male and female strategies of reproduction and "parental investment," and in the resulting mating systems of different species. In humans, systems of reciprocity can be extremely complex and sophisticated, because human intelligence allows for extensive deceit, and hence there is a need to develop complex counterstrategies for foiling cheaters. The conditions for the evolution of reciprocal altruism in humans and other animals have been specified by Robert Trivers.

A neglected aspect of human sociality in sociobiology has been the role of coercion to promote intraspecific and intrasocietal parasitism. Clearly, with the rise of states in the last seven to eight thousand years of human evolution, many relationships are asymmetrical, in that some individuals use coercive means for appropriating resources to maximize their own fitness at the expense of others. Indeed, human societies have become increasingly coercive as they have grown in size and complexity.

Sociobiology should not be seen as a threat to the humanities and social sciences, but as an invitation to incorporate the study of human behavior in the theoretical mainstream of the neo-Darwinism synthesis, the dominant theory of biology for over a century. Its insights complement, specify, and enrich what we have long known about ourselves: that we are a product of both heredity and environment, and that nature and nurture are but the two sides of the same evolving coin.

SEE ALSO: anthropology; Darwinism; environmentalism; genotype; hereditarianism; phenotype; science; social Darwinism

Reading

On Human Nature by Edward O. Wilson (Harvard University Press, 1978) is a statement written for a lay audience, about the relationship between genes and culture, by the man who gave sociobiology its name. The book is scrutinized in *Human Nature and Biocultural Evolution* by J. Lopreato (Allen & Unwin, 1984).

Sociobiology and Behaviour by David Barash (Elsevier, 1981) is a lucid, nontechnical summary of the ideas of the main theoreticians of sociobiology.

Sociobiology, Sense and Nonsense by Michael Ruse (Reidel, 1979) is a thorough review of the scientific, ethical, and ideological arguments pro and con sociobiology, and of their human implications.

CHECK: internet resources section

PIERRE L. VAN DEN BERGHE

SOUTH AFRICA

During the 1970s and 1980s, South Africa's apartheid policy had become one of the great global moral issues, comparable to the debate about slavery or fascism. Apartheid, the Afrikaans word for separateness, denotes a system of imposed racial classification, residential segregation, and denationalization of the majority black population who are excluded from equal rights as citizens.

Among a population of forty-two million, whites, at 12 percent, occupied the top of the racial hierarchy; they were followed by 9 percent so-called Coloreds, as people of mixed origin but mostly Afrikaans cultural background are called; 3 percent Indians, who were mostly imported as indentured laborers to Natal's sugar plantations in 1860; and, at the bottom, 76 percent blacks, who were classified into nine different language groups with tribal homelands. The whites are divided between 60 percent Afrikaners, who controlled political power in the form of the state bureaucracy, and 40 percent English-speakers, who historically dominate a First World economy of sophisticated mining and manufacturing in a Third World country of racial poverty and exploitation.

The grossly unequal life chances based on a system of ethnic patronage under minority domination engendered an early tradition of resistance and dreams of liberation from colonial conquest, beginning with the formation of the African National Congress (ANC) in 1912. The opposition, however, has always been split and weakened by strategic differences about the use of violence, boycotts, and sanctions. Since the 1970s, emerging trade unions politicized labor relations in the absence of legal working-class parties that preceded unionization in Europe and North America. Faced with stronger adversaries and business imperatives, the Afrikaner government attempted to modernize traditional apartheid and buy off dissent through selected co-option in a tricameral parliament. However, the rising costs of minority rule, pressure from both inside and outside, together with the end of the Cold War competition in Africa, finally, in 1990, provided the breakthrough for abolishing formal apartheid and legalizing the banned liberation movements. The nonracial social-democratic ANC and the tainted but still powerful National Party moved toward a system of power sharing. Both major antagonists were too strong to be defeated by the opponent and too weak to rule alone. Both were heading towards an unwilling alliance.

After a four-year period of negotiations – frequently interrupted by breakdowns and violence by both black and white extremists – a transitional constitution was finally agreed upon, and the first democratic elections were held in 1994. Nelson Mandela as President instituted a Truth and Reconciliation Commission chaired by the like-minded Desmond Tutu. Conditional amnesty for politically motivated crimes upon full disclosure proved controversial, but the widely publicized testimony of perpetrators affirmed victims and contributed to political education.

The ruling group retained its two-thirds ma-jority under Mandela's successor, Thabo Mbeki. His centralized style of governing, his turn to neo-liberal economic policies, reluctance to dissociate Pretoria from Robert Mugabe's despotism in Zimbabwe, but above all his inexplicable procrastination in the AIDS crisis brought the ANC government into conflict with many of its former supporters. Corruption scandals in the wake of a massive arms procurement deal added to unease inside and outside. The brain drain continued unabated and the hoped for foreign investment did not materialize. The noble vision of an African renaissance or a much-touted New African Development Plan (NEPAD) remained elusive under conditions of uncertainty about the future.

Nonetheless, the still popular ANC majority government did achieve a considerable improvement in the living conditions of parts of the population. While inequality within each group increased, the income gap between white and black narrowed. A so-called "patriotic bourgeoisie" benefited most from the new order. Affirmative action policies and empowerment in the form of preferential treatment of the historically disadvantaged majority was considered necessary to deal with the legacy of apartheid. However, such policies of differential entitlement inevitably also re-racialized South African society and paradoxically undermined the very colorblind nonracialism in whose name apartheid was defeated.

However, all adversaries are part of an interdependent economy, which holds a potentially buoyant future, given its developed infrastructure, human capital, and remarkable goodwill among the people of all South African segments. Unlike other plural societies with endemic communal conflicts, most South Africans share a common religion and consumer culture in which skin color was merely an artificial marker for exclusion. With the differential privileges now removed and a common society with a federal constitution, proportional voting and a bill of rights, South Africa could develop into the exception to the rule in an increasingly bleak and marginalized continent.

SEE ALSO: Africa; apartheid; colonialism; conquest; culturecide; Doomed Races Doctrine; exploitation; Gandhi, Mohandas Karamchand; human rights; indigenous peoples; Mandela, Nelson; paternalism; race: as synonym;

segregation; systemic racism; *Volk*; white backlash culture

Reading

The Awkward Embrace: One party domination and democracy by Hermann Giliomee and Charles Simkins (Hardwood Academic Publishers, 1999) looks at the troubled post-apartheid transition in South Africa.

Comrades in Business: Post-liberation politics in South Africa by Heribert Adam, F. van Zyl Slabbert and Kogila Moodley, (International Publishers, 1998) provides a liberal-democratic perspective.

The Quakers in South Africa: A social witness by Betty K. Tonsing (Edward Mellen, 2002) is a case study of the Society of Friends' engagement with the issue of racial inequality in South Africa.

South Africa: Limits to change by Hein Marais (Zed Books, 2001) analyzes from an explicitly left, socialist perspective; this may profitably be read in conjunction with Patrick Bond's *Elite Transition: From apartheid to neo-liberalism in South Africa* (Pluto Press, 2000).

South Africa's Racial Past: The history and historiography of racism, segregation and apartheid by Paul Maylam (Ashgate, 2001) reflects on the epic struggle.

KOGILA MOODLEY

SPORTS *see* Ali, Muhammad; Jordan, Michael; Tyson, Mike

STEREOTYPE

Derived from the printers' term for a plate cast from a mold (originally from the Greek *stereos* for solid), a stereotype refers to a fixed mental impression. It is defined by Gordon Allport as: "an exaggerated belief associated with a category. Its function is to justify (rationalize) our conduct in relation to that category." This definition implies a discrepancy between an objectively ascertainable reality and a subjective perception of that reality.

In the field of race and ethnic relations, a stereotype is often defined as an overgeneralization about the behavior or other characteristics of members of particular groups. Ethnic and racial stereotypes can be positive or negative, although they are more frequently negative. Even ostensibly positive stereotypes can often imply a negative evaluation. Thus, to say that blacks are musical and have a good sense of rhythm comes close to the more openly negative stereotype that they are childish and happy-go-lucky. Similarly, there is not much difference between saying that

Jews show group solidarity and accusing them of being clannish. The process of *stereotyping* occurs when the representation of particular groups becomes active.

It is, of course, a difficult empirical question to determine where a generalization about a group ceases to be an objective description of reality and becomes a stereotype. At the limit, almost any statement of group differences can be termed stereotypic, unless it is precisely stated in statistical terms and leaves the issue of causality open. Let us take the example of differential rates of violent crimes between racial groups. African Americans in the USA have conviction rates for crimes of violence that are five to ten times those of whites; they are greatly overrepresented in the prison population; and they also fall disproportionately victim to crimes of violence, frequently committed by other blacks. An unqualified statement such as "blacks are criminals" or "blacks are prone to violence" would generally be labeled a stereotype. "Blacks are more violent than whites," although somewhat qualified, could still be called stereotypic, as the statement implies an intrinsic racial difference in proneness to violence.

The more careful formulations above would probably escape the label of stereotype however, because, even though they state the existence of statistical differences between racial groups, they leave open the question of causality. For example, the higher conviction rate of blacks could be due to hidden class differences rather than to racial differences, or to racial bias in the predominantly white police and courts in arresting and convicting blacks. Indeed, probably all of these factors are at work in producing the statistical outcome.

The relationship between stereotypes and prejudice is also of interest to social scientists. Racial or ethnic stereotypes are generally expressions of prejudice against the groups in question, but insofar as they often have a grain of truth, they may also have a measure of statistical validity, and, therefore, be moderately useful guides for predicting behavior. Since we benefit by trying to predict the behavior of others, and since we all have to rely, for simplicity's sake, on rough and ready categories such as age, sex, class, ethnic group, religion, and the like, implicit stereotypes form the basis of much social life. Such stereotypes do not necessarily reflect deeply ingrained prejudices.

Thus, for example, we know that crimes of violence in the USA are statistically correlated not only with race, but also with age, class, sex, time of day, and urban residence. The old lady who walks past a group of young, black, working-class men, late at night, in a street in Harlem is not necessarily a racial bigot if she feels a twitch of apprehension. She merely applies pragmatic formulas for survival. She probably *is* more at risk in such a situation than, say, at a church picnic. That she is aware of the difference is a testimony to her common sense, not to her racism, though she *may* be a racist.

As a result of the difficulty ascertaining the gap between the objective reality and the subjective perception thereof, the concept of stereotype is not a useful scientific tool in the analysis of behavior, nor has it been used much since the 1980s.

SEE ALSO: bigotry; Irish; prejudice; racial discrimination; racist discourse; representations; scapegoat; xenophobia

Reading

The Nature of Prejudice by Gordon W. Allport (Perseus, 1979) is the "25th anniversary edition" of the 1954 text, which was, in its day, a major statement on the psychology of race relations; the stereotyping process is central.

Race and Ethnic Conflict: Contending views on prejudice, discrimination and ethnoviolence, 2nd edn., edited by Fred L. Pinchus and Howard J. Ehrlich (Westview Press, 1998) reviews the psychological research on prejudice and tries to align this with perspectives derived from sociology, political science and other social sciences.

Stereotype Accuracy, edited by Yueh-Ting Lee (American Psychological Association, 1995), has an opening chapter which traces the history of stereotypes and includes definitions; similar ground is covered in Perry Hinton's *Stereotypes, Cognition and Culture* (Routledge, 2000).

Stereotyping: The politics of representation by Michael Pickering (Palgrave, 2001) considers the contemporary relevance of the term that has a genuinely multidisciplinary heritage, moving between sociology, psychoanalysis, postcolonialism and other disciplines; this might gainfully be read in combination with *Stereotypes and Prejudice: Essential readings* (Routledge, 2000), a collection of old and new essays edited by Charles Stangor.

PIERRE L. VAN DEN BERGHE

STOP AND SEARCH *see* racial profiling

SUBALTERN

Originally a sixteenth-century military term meaning of junior rank (from the Latin *sub*, below and *alternus*, alternate), the term has gained currency principally through the work of Gayatri Spivak. It revolves around the questions of whether the experience of oppression confers special jurisdiction over the right to speak about oppression and whether a representation of this is ever possible in a discourse in which subaltern groups are already "spoken for." Her "Can the subaltern speak?" questioned the credibility of the subaltern woman as a subject already represented as mute or ignored; her speech is, by definition, nonspeech. Speech, in this conception, is not so much about the abilities of subaltern groups to articulate as the reception they are afforded.

Spivak uses the Hindu practice of *sati* in which widows immolated themselves on their husband's funeral pyres as a metaphorical illustration of the plight of colonial women. They have been rendered voiceless by a combination of the patriarchy of their indigenous culture and the "masculinist-imperialist ideology" introduced and imposed by the British Raj.

A journal, *Subaltern Studies* (published by Oxford University Press), has been devoted to trying "to understand the consciousness that informed and still informs political actions taken by subaltern classes on their own, independently of any elite initiatives," as Dipesh Chakrabarty puts it in the discussion to vol. 4 (1985) of the journal. "Subalternaity" refers to the "composite culture of resistance to and acceptance of domination and hierarchy."

Part of this overall project, according to Spivak, is to disclose whiteness as a culturally constructed ethnic identity – constructed, that is, in contradistinction to subaltern minorities who have been subjugated, or silenced. The privileged position of the white male in relation to subaltern groups has been "naturalized" to the point of invisibility. Yet the position of centrality is made possible by the denial of a voice to Others.

SEE ALSO: colonial discourse; diaspora; essentialism; Fanon, Frantz; hybridity; Other; postcolonial; racist discourse

Reading

"Can the subaltern speak?" by Gayatri C. Spivak, in her own collection of essays *A Critique of*

Postcolonial Reason (Harvard University Press, 2001), is a book that encourages us to be self-reflexive and to foreground the privileges that inform our pronouncements on the colonial world.

"Gayatri Spivak on the politics of the subaltern" features Spivak in an interview with Howard Winant (in *Socialist Review*, vol. 20, no. 3, July–September, 1990).

The Postcolonial Critic: Interviews, strategies, dialogues by Gayatri Spivak (Routledge, 1990), edited by Sarah Harasyan, is a guide to Spivak's thoughts.

SYSTEMIC RACISM

Systemic racism is a characteristic of societies in which most major aspects of life are shaped to some degree by core racist realities. It includes five major dimensions: (1) patterns of unjust impoverishment for people of color and unjust enrichment for whites, including the transmission over time of racial inequalities by means of continuing discrimination; (2) the resulting vested-group interests; (3) the alienating racist relation of whites versus people of color; (4) the rationalization of inequalities in prejudices, stereotypes, and ideologies; and (5) patterns of resistance. These dimensions work together dialectically to sustain the reality of systemic racism in societies such as the USA, Great Britain, France, and South Africa.

Unjust impoverishment, unjust enrichment

Current views of systemic racism are influenced by the African diaspora intellectual tradition, a rich source for developing a more accurate picture of the ongoing societal "houses of racism." We will accent here the case of the USA. Drawing on analyses by Frederick Douglass, W. E. B. Du Bois, Oliver Cox, Anna Julia Cooper, Kwame Ture, and Frantz Fanon, among others, recent analysts accent a conceptual framework understanding US racism as centuries-long, institutionalized, and systemic. The first extended analysis of a system of racism was that of Oliver C. Cox, who provided in the 1940s a honed argument showing how labor exploitation of black Americans had created a centuries-old structure of racial classes. Cox writes that the white elite decided "to proletarianize a whole people – that is to say, the whole people is looked upon as a class – whereas white proletarianization involves only a section of the white people" (in *Caste, Class, and Race*, Doubleday, 1948). By

the 1960s a number of black activist analysts were developing a broad institutional racism perspective and an *internal colonialism* overview (for example, Robert Blauner, see below). Critical analysts saw racism as more than demons in white minds, as a complex array of racialized relationships developed over generations and imbedded in all institutions.

Historically, social science study of oppression often accents ambiguous and euphemistic phrases such as "race relations," phrases used by those who view all racial-ethnic groups as more or less responsible for a society's racial realities. White analysts have often written about "race relations" in Western societies, but *racist* relations are not "in," but rather "of," these societies.

Analyzing Europe's colonization of Africa, Du Bois demonstrated that extreme degradation in African colonies was "a main cause of wealth and luxury in Europe. The results of this poverty were disease, ignorance, and crime. Yet these had to be represented as natural characteristics of backward peoples" (in *The World and Africa*, International Publishers, 1946). Unjust and brutal exploitation of African labor and land in colonialism has been omitted from many historical accounts of European prosperity. A similar connection can be made between the immiseration of African Americans and prosperity for European Americans.

The idea of *unjust enrichment* may be used to examine the reality of racial oppression. Unjust enrichment is an old Anglo-American legal term encompassing the receiving of benefits justly belonging to another and the obligation to make restitution for that injustice. Joe Feagin has suggested the parallel idea of *unjust impoverishment* to describe the conditions of those who suffer oppression.

Understanding how undeserved impoverishment and enrichment get reproduced, and institutionalized over generations, is key to understanding systemic racism. In many Western countries, whites are stakeholders in centuries-old hierarchical structures of unequal opportunity, wealth, and privileges stemming from histories of exploitation of people of color. The interests of the white racial class include a concrete interest in labor and other exploitation in the colonial period, as well as a specific interest later in maintaining privileges inherited from ancestors, including what Du Bois called the "psychological wage" of whiteness.

Systemic racism involves recurring, unequal relationships between groups and individuals. At the macro level, large-scale institutions – with their white-controlled normative structures – routinely perpetuate racial subordination and inequalities. Inegalitarian institutions are reproduced by routine actions at the micro level by individuals, as the research of Philomena Essed demonstrates (*Understanding Everyday Racism*, Sage, 1991). Individuals' discriminatory practices express collective interests and regularly sustain the underlying racial hierarchy.

Individuals, whether perpetrators or recipients of discrimination, are caught in a web of racist relations, which distort and alienate what could be egalitarian relationships. Systemic racism categorizes and divides people from each other, thereby severely impeding the development of a common consciousness.

In much recent theorizing about contemporary racial inequalities and conflicts, racial matters have been more or less reduced to issues of class, such as in some Marxist works (such as Melvin M. Leiman's *The Political Economy of Racism: A history*, Pluto Press, 1993), or to issues of socioeconomic status, as in the work of William Julius Wilson (*When Work Disappears: The world of the new urban poor*, Knopf, 1996).

Yet, in their *Racial Formations in the United States* (Routledge, 1994), Michael Omi and Howard Winant have shown that "race" cannot be reduced to ethnicity or class, but rather is an "autonomous field of social conflict, political organization and cultural/ideological meaning." In a systemic racism framework, racial oppression is grounded in concrete advantages whites have gained unjustly, over centuries of colonialism, slavery, segregation, and contemporary discrimination. Systemic racism is more than images, attitudes, and identities, for it is centrally about the creation, development, and maintenance of white privilege, wealth, and power. "Categories are constructed. Scars and bruises are felt with human bodies, some of which end up in coffins. Death is not a construct," write Jorge Klor de Alva, Earl Shorris, and Cornel West, in their essay "Our next race question: the uneasiness between blacks and Latinos," (in *Critical White Studies: Looking behind the mirror*, edited by Richard Delgado and Jean Stefancic, Temple University Press, 1997).

Systemic racism also involves huge psychological, physical, and family costs for the targets of discrimination. These include anger, frustration, anguish, fear and rage – experienced in the immediate moment and accumulated over time.

Systemic racism has a distinctive spatial dimension – for example, it varies in impact at home, work, and in the streets – and a critical temporal dimension, such as the differential collective memories of perpetrators and targets of discrimination.

Reproduction and rationalization

Systemic racism persists across generations by reproducing all necessary socioeconomic conditions. These include a near-monopoly by whites of economic resources and political, police, and ideological power. Systemic racism is perpetuated by social processes that reproduce not only inequality but also the racist relation – on the one hand, the oppressed, and on the other, the oppressors. This alienated relationship is reproduced across all areas of societal life – from one neighborhood to the next, from one city to the next, from one generation to the next.

Reproduced over time are racially structured institutions, such as the economic institutions that imbed the exploitation of black labor and the legal and political institutions that protect the exploitation and extend oppression into other societal arenas. Each new generation inherits organizational structures protecting unjust enrichment and impoverishment. Important too is the reproduction from one generation to the next of the ideological apparatus that legitimates racist oppression. Whites usually develop a strong ideology defending their own conditions as meritorious and accenting the alleged inferiority of those oppressed.

In the US case, by the early 1700s, a system of African American enslavement was entrenched and profitable for white slaveholders and those trading with slave plantations. Slavery was maintained by passing numerous laws and developing courts to sustain them. Slave insurrections had to be protected against, so militias were created to police those enslaved. Slave breeding was expanded so slaveholders did not have to rely on the international slave trade. The political system, including the US Constitution, was shaped to protect slavery. For generations, this imbedded system of systemic racism has been perpetuated and reproduced. Not only do most whites now living benefit from inheritance of economic and cultural wealth from ancestors who profited from slavery or legal segregation, but most also benefit today from job, housing, political, educational and other discrimination, giving them and their children advantages over black Americans.

Important too is the impact of systemic racism on the social, economic, political, and educational resources and opportunities available to oppressed peoples. If the members of a group suffer serious bars to securing the resources necessary for mobility, this restricts their own achievements and shapes the opportunities of generations to come.

Historical analysis indicates that oppression regularly breeds resistance. Racist structures determine lives, but when human agents gain solid knowledge about structures of oppression, they use that knowledge to rebel. Systemic racism theory accents resistance strategies and their impact. Out of their experience with everyday racism comes individual and collective consciousness that periodically leads to protests, demonstrations, and large-scale revolts. The process that reproduces systemic racism has major contradictions. One is that subordinated racial groups have been allowed access to limited resources so that they can survive and be useful in Western economies. When they have secured some resources beyond subsistence, they often have increased resistance to oppression. Human beings have the ability to reflect on circumstances and create, in association with others, a consciousness leading to revolt and change. In recent years we have seen strong antiracist movements in South Africa, France, and Brazil. For example, in the late 1990s France began to transform how it dealt with discrimination, including passing new laws in civil courts, and creating agencies that countered discrimination.

In regard to matters of white-generated racism, the world is slowly changing. Becoming more obvious are contradictions in the global racist order created by the colonial adventures of European nations. People of African descent remain the globe's largest racially oppressed group. Since the 1980s we have seen the systemically racist society of South Africa move from white to black political control and begin to change its socioeconomic system of racism. Few predicted such a sea change. The possibility of a global democratic order rid of racism remains only a dream, but the South African revolution shows that it is a powerful dream. More changes in the world's racist system will likely come as the human spirit conquers the continuing realities of oppression.

SEE ALSO: Africa; antiracism; apartheid; Cox, Oliver C.; cultural racism; diaspora; double consciousness; education; environmental racism; Fanon, Frantz; Hall, Stuart; housing; inferential racism; institutional racism; internal colonialism; Marxism; racial coding; racism; representations; slavery; South Africa; welfare; white race; whiteness

Reading

The Agony of Education: Black students at white colleges and universities by Joe Feagin, HernÃn Vera, and Nikitah Imani (Routledge, 1996) examines systemic racism in the educational system.

Caste, Class, and Race by Oliver C. Cox (Doubleday, 1948) is the classic Marxist exposition cited in the main text above and may profitably be read in conjunction with other historical works referred to, including Robert Blauner's *Racial Oppression in America* (Harper & Row, 1972) and W. E. B. Du Bois's *The World and Africa* (International Publishers, 1965; first published 1946).

Racist America by Joe Feagin (Routledge, 2000) provides an extensive and contemporary analysis of systemic racism.

CHECK: internet resources section under racism

JOE R. FEAGIN AND LESLIE A. HOUTS

T

THIRD WORLD

The origin of this term is generally attributed to Alfred Sauvy who, writing in *L'Observateur* in 1952, used the phrase *le tiers monde* to describe nations ridding themselves of colonialism in a manner similar to the struggle of commoners (the Third Estate) to overcome the domination of the nobility and clergy during the French Revolution. Most Third World countries have a past history of colonial domination and have sought a collective identity which disassociates them politically from either of the two power blocs, Soviet and Western-capitalist. The term also has an economic ambience, implying collectively those countries which through the colonial legacy are exploitatively located in the international economy and which generally lag behind in industrial development. Although the definitional criteria are somewhat different, other terms such as "the South" (as opposed to "the North") and "the developing world" are frequently used with the same connotations and often used interchangeably with "the Third World" in the same texts.

As postcolonial states, most Third World countries have economies historically rooted in a system that tapped their natural wealth and expropriated it for the benefits of colonial powers, their function being to provide raw materials, cheap labor, and markets for developing industrialization elsewhere. Political independence in the aftermath of World War II has done little to change the fundamental characteristics of this system, in which the mechanisms of multinational trade and investment have maintained a neo-colonial economic dependency within a framework of ostensible political independence. In spite of certain successes by Third World countries in producing dynamic economies (largely in East Asia) or in controlling primary production (e.g. OPEC), Third World countries have generally found themselves in a descending spiral of disadvantaged location in the international economic system, thus creating an "international debt crisis" which currently concerns not only themselves but the entire international monetary system. This situation provides regrettable confirmation of President Nyerere of Tanzania's acerbic definition of the Third World as the "Trade Union of the Poor."

Analysis of the Third World's location in a global system of economic exploitation has been largely informed by the works of political economy theorists working within "dependency" and "world systems" paradigms, and by neo-classical economics. While these approaches have undoubtedly been seminal and productive, they have also had the tendency to marginalize the importance of Third World state structures by implying that they have little room for autonomous action. This implication is now being challenged by a Third World scholarship which sees the creation of endogenously derived integrative socioeconomic structures as being a necessary component in economic development. From this perspective the ethnic factor frequently becomes an important variable since many Third World states are ethnically heterogeneous, based as they are on arbitrary partitions of colonialism. For these multiethnic states the goal of making the state a nation, with structures that encourage integrated political and economic participation, is a critical central issue. The locus for the resolution of this issue lies largely within Third World state structures themselves, and the degree to which this objective is achieved will determine in large part the ability of such states to overcome the dependency dimensions of their current international status.

SEE ALSO: Africa; assimilation; capitalism; colonialism; conquest; cultural identity; culturecide; development; ethnonational; exploitation; globalization; human rights; international organizations; Marxism; minority language rights; power ; social Darwinism; South Africa; UNESCO; United Nations

Reading

The Third World, 2nd edn., by Peter Worsley (Weidenfeld & Nicolson, 1977), is an influential examination of the issues in a sociological perspective.

Third World Cities in Global Perspective by David A. Smith (Westview Press, 1995) focuses on global inequality and dependency as a way of exploring city growth in the Third World.

Third Worlds: The politics of the Middle East and Africa, edited by Heather Deegan (Routledge, 1996), argues that grouping the Middle East and Africa as the "Third World" has concealed contrasts – though there are historical and cultural similarities.

MARSHALL MURPHREE

THOMAS, CLARENCE (1948–)

On November 1, 1991, the commission of Clarence Thomas to sit as an associate justice of the US Supreme Court was received. With that appointment, Clarence Thomas became only the second racial minority member to sit on the highest court in the USA. And with that appointment, one of the most controversial, if not *the* most controversial, nominations to the Supreme Court came to an end.

An African American born in poverty and raised in the segregated South, Thomas was a judge of the US Court of Appeals for the District of Columbia, having taken the seat held by the equally controversial Judge Robert Bork only eighteen months earlier, at the time of his nomination. The nomination was made by a Republican President, who did not support the 1964 Civil Rights Act and who, in vetoing the 1991 Civil Rights Act, became at that time the only president in the history of the United States to veto a civil rights bill. The nominee, a conservative Republican who built his professional reputation on a steady, often acerbic barrage of criticisms of civil rights leaders and civil rights programs (such as affirmative action),

was presented to the nation as "the most qualified" person to replace the legendary civil rights lawyer and liberal justice, Thurgood Marshall. Also ironic and controversial was the fact that Justice Thomas personally benefited from affirmative action programs throughout his scholastic and professional life.

Unprecedentedly, Justice Thomas appeared before the Senate Judiciary Committee twice. The first appearance centered on routine questions of judicial temperament and constitutional interpretation, including the nominee's position on the legality of abortion and the doctrine of "nature rights." During these hearings, the nominee made the famous statement that he never discussed with anyone his personal opinion on the famous abortion case *Roe* v. *Wade*.

About a week after these hearings ended but before the Committee voted on the nomination, the Committee was called back into session to consider formally a charge of sexual harassment levied against Thomas by a well-respected African-American woman law professor, Anita Hill. In his most effective performance during the confirmation hearings, Justice Thomas numbed the Democratic senators, all of whom were white and liberal, by accusing them of participating in a "high-tech lynching."

Here, the racial ironies were unmistakable. An African American who has strongly criticized civil rights leaders for crying racism ignores his own advice when under fire – he plays the race card and it comes up aces. Also, the most ardent supporters of civil rights in the Senate, in front of millions of African Americans watching the proceedings on television, were made to look like hooded nightriders from a bygone era. Finally, the sexual harassment charge brought against Justice Thomas was made by a member of his own race who not only had a strong character but also shared much of his political philosophy, including displeasure over the failed Supreme Court nomination of Judge Robert Bork. For some thirty-three hours, Americans were riveted to their television sets watching the hearings, which in addition to the testimony of Justice Thomas and Professor Hill, included the testimony of twenty character witnesses for both sides. In the end, both the Judiciary Committee and the Senate voted to confirm Justice Thomas by the slimmest margin ever.

Justice Thomas has not disappointed his supporters nor surprised his detractors during his years on the bench. His judicial rulings have been consistently conservative. Justice Thomas tends to uphold state rights over federal regulation (what is called the "federalism" principle) and individual autonomy over government control, except in the case of abortion where he favors government-imposed restrictions on the individual's reproductive freedom.

SEE ALSO: affirmative action; African Americans; assimilation; black bourgeoisie in the USA; black feminism; conservatism; empowerment; race card; Simpson case, the O. J.; tokenism; Tyson, Mike

Reading

Advice and Consent: Clarence Thomas, Robert Bork, and the intriguing history of the Supreme Court's nomination battles by Paul Simon (National Press, 1992) is an historical perspective of controversial Supreme Court nominations by a senior member of the Senate Judiciary Committee.

African American Women Speak Out on Anita Hill–Clarence Thomas, edited by Geneva Smitherman (Wayne State University Press, 1995), collects the perspectives of black women scholars and writers.

Clarence Thomas: A biography by Andrew P. Thomas (Encounter Books, 2001) discusses the early life of Justice Thomas, while *Silent Justice: The Clarence Thomas story* by John Greenya (Barricade Books, 2001) attempts to explain why Justice Thomas never asked any questions during oral arguments.

"Gender, race, and the politics of Supreme Court appointments: the import of the Anita Hill/Clarence Thomas hearings" (in *Southern California Law Review*, vol. 65: 1279–1582, 1992) is the most comprehensive collection of analyses of the nomination and confirmation hearings, including writings by Anita Hill and dozens of other scholars, many of whom were directly involved in the hearings.

"The legacy of doubt: treatment of sex and race in the Hill–Thomas hearings" by Adrienne D. Davis and Stephanie M. Wildman (in *Southern California Law Review*, vol. 65, 1992) is a good overview of the Thomas confirmation and may be usefully read in conjunction with other analyses, such as: *The American Dream in Black & White: The Clarence Thomas hearings* by Jane Flax (Cornell University Press, 1998); *The Real Clarence Thomas: Confirmation veracity meets performance reality* by Joyce Baugh and Christopher Smith (Peter Lang Publishing, 2000), which challenges the veracity of statements made by Thomas during his confirmation; *Original Sin: Clarence Thomas and the failure of the constitutional conservatives* by Samuel Marcosson (New York University Press, 2002), which is a critical look at conservative constitutional decision making through the opinions of Justice Thomas; and *First Principles: The jurisprudence of Clarence Thomas* by Scott D. Gerber (New York University Press, 2002) which attempts to find fundamental jurispru-

dential principles in opinions written by Justice Thomas.

ROY L. BROOKS

TOKENISM

As unofficial racial policy or practice in many arenas, tokenism has been described and analyzed by the media and the academic community. A number of scholarly works have described various facets of tokenism as a political resource of powerful white interests, both in the public and private arena of the USA. But the historical work that gave rise to the popular term "Uncle Tom" is Harriet Beecher Stowe's *Uncle Tom's Cabin*.

Tokenism is usually considered a pejorative term similar to "Uncle Tom," used by many in the black community, but also by others, to describe a social situation where blacks, or other people of color, are utilized only for "display" purposes. Both Martin Luther King, Jr. and Malcolm X used both terms – tokenism and Uncle Tom – to describe a major obstacle to racial progress in the United States. In one of his speeches in 1964, "Ballots or bullets," for instance, Malcolm X stated that:

> Just as the slavemaster of that day used Tom, the house Negro, to keep the field Negroes in check, the same old slavemaster today has Negroes who are nothing but modern Uncle Toms, twentieth century Uncle Toms, to keep you and me in check, to keep us under control, keep us passive and peaceful and non-violent.

In a featured *New York Times Magazine* article in June 1967 titled, "MLK defines black power," a similar statement was made by Martin Luther King, Jr., about a sector of "Negro leadership" that had allowed itself to become the representative of white power structures, rather than of the black masses.

What tokenism suggests is that the presence of individual blacks who may be prominent, or in prominent positions, in white institutional settings does not necessarily indicate that: (1) such individuals perform significant or influential roles beneficial to the advancement of blacks as a group; or (2) that the presence of such individuals reflects social parity between blacks as a group and whites in US society.

The function of tokenism as a social phenomenon is to suggest to observers that the rhetoric of racial equality is being adhered to by powerful interests; but this kind of arrangement is not inconsistent with the existence of racial hierarchy where the agendas of powerful white interests, rather than racial or social parity, continue to dominate. As racial policy or practice, tokenism is a way of neutralizing efforts to integrate fully and institutionalize the presence of blacks and other people of color into social and cultural settings where whites continue to have all the power to make and carry out important decisions.

SEE ALSO: antislavery; black bourgeoisie in the USA; integration; King, Martin Luther; Myrdal, Gunnar; Other; paternalism; Thomas, Clarence

Reading

Black Men, White Cities by Ira Katznelson (Oxford University Press, 1973) analyzes the usefulness of political tokenism to local power structures controlled by whites in New York City and Chicago in the early and mid part of the twentieth century.
The Negro in the Making of America by Benjamin Quarles (Collier, 1987) complements the above text in observing the social functions of tokenism.

JAMES JENNINGS

TRANSRACIAL ADOPTION

The problem of identity

In popular terms transracial adoption is taken to refer to the adoption of children seen as belonging to one "race" by parents belonging to another "race." More formally, it refers to those forms of adoption in which the use of race categories is explicitly discouraged as a criterion for placing children with adoptive parents. It is important to note that the defenders of transracial adoption do not advocate deliberately placing children with adoptive parents from dissimilar cultural backgrounds or other "races"; rather, their argument is that when opportunities for placement are limited, race categories should not play a significant role in determining suitable adoptive parents. Transracial adoption is often contrasted with "same-race" or "in-race" adoption.

The phenomenon of children from one particular social milieu being adopted by, or brought up in, families from a different social milieu is neither new nor uncommon. The interesting question for the sociologist is why, principally in the USA over the last fifty years or so, in adoptions where *color* is perceived as significant, the phenomenon comes to be described as transracial. A central element in this description is the inconsistent notions of race that are employed: either race is a fixed attribute of human beings (one belongs to this race or that race by virtue of birth) in which case the race of one's adoptive parents would be irrelevant for the maintenance of one's race throughout one's life; or race is something which has to be nurtured and sustained (one's race is something that has to be learnt or acquired). In the latter instance, it is difficult to see how a child's race could be ascertained in advance of its upbringing, in order to decide which parents would be appropriate for adopting it.

This ambiguity about the meaning of the term race reflects many of the weaknesses associated with lay discourses about race. In particular, assumptions to do with the empirical verifiability of a person's race have frequently come to rest on indistinct claims about cultural and political identities. Debates concerning who should adopt whom and how this may best be regulated thus become entangled with issues of ethnicity, culture and community. So, for example, a key argument of those opposed to transracial adoption is that the adoption by parents of one race of children belonging to another race is to be deprecated on the basis of a putative psychological need for a strong ethnic identity which can be met only by those who have an awareness of the children's "cultural heritage" within their "own community." Furthermore, it is argued, since "white" parents do not experience racism, they are ill-equipped to parent and support adopted "black" children who do.

The relevance of race categories for adoption policy was first mooted in the USA during the late 1940s and early 1950s. Demographic and social changes – concerning contraception, family size, and abortion – combined to reduce significantly the number of "white" children available for adoption, leaving "nonwhite" children as the majority of those who were offered for adoption. The liberalization of attitudes to color and "race" during the late 1950s led to an increasing number of transracial adoptions, that is, "black" children being adopted by "white" parents. Between 1967 and 1972, approximately 10,000

African American children were transracially adopted.

The challenge to transracial adoption arose in the early 1970s, following the annual conference of the National Association of Black Social Workers (NABSW) in Atlanta in 1971. Unsurprisingly in view of the role played by race ideas in US politics, this challenge sought to link transracial adoption to the broader strategies of "race" politics. In particular, it was argued that transracial adoption would inhibit the development of black identity. This was because, even if "white" parents might want children to grow up "black," they lacked the skills, insight and experience to ensure this would happen. The result, as a former President of the NABSW, Morris Jeff, Jr., put it in 1991, was the "creation of a race of children with African faces and European minds" (see Simon, Altstein and Melli, below). Some, such as William T. Merritt, another former President of the NABSW, viewed transracial adoption as a form of "race and cultural genocide."

Opponents of transracial adoption instead advocated "in-race" adoption (often referred to as "same-race" adoption in the UK), arguing that the placement of black children with black parents was key to preserving the cultural identity and integrity of the African American community. This claim was often accompanied by the charge that adoption policy discriminated against working-class African American parents as potential adopters. Some also alleged institutional racism in the adoption system, pointing out that the majority of social workers were white and that their control over adoptions was primarily responsible for the failure to locate suitable adoptive parents from within the African American community.

The Child Welfare League of America, the major professional child care organization in the USA, also began to advocate "in-race" adoption, following intense lobbying from the NABSW. This was a reversion to the position it had held during the first half of the twentieth century when the Jim Crow laws enforced a rigid color bar and widespread social segregation. In the 1980s several US states passed legislation that prohibited or regulated transracial adoption; by the early 1990s opposition to transracial adoption had become "a virtually unchallenged orthodoxy amongst child care professionals" and one that was "constantly reflected in adoption practice," according to Peter Hayes in his article "The ideological attack on transracial adoption in the USA and Britain" (in *International Journal of Law and the Family*, vol. 9, no. 1, 1–22, 1995). Instead, policy emphasis was placed on "in-race" adoption.

However, a number of concerns eventually led to a reaction. These included anxieties about: possible discrimination; the lack of empirical evidence supporting the claims that "same-race" adoption served the best interests of the adopted child; and the responsibility placed on children of color for reproducing African American cultural identity. The Multi-Ethnic Placement Act of 1995 was passed to increase adoption opportunities for the increasing numbers of African American children in foster care awaiting adoption; it aimed to remove the barrier of same-race placement policies. In 1996, the Small Business Job Protection Act, passed by the Clinton administration, prohibited any state organization receiving federal funding from denying a person the opportunity to become an adoptive parent on the basis of "race, color or national origin." On the same grounds, the provision further prohibited a state from denying or delaying the placement of a child for adoption. Unsurprisingly, this has not proven the end of the matter, and opponents of transracial adoption continue to campaign against it.

The human consequences of child care policy

Outside of the USA, the debates about transracial adoption have carried rather less resonance. In Britain in 1983, and taking its lead from the NABSW in the USA, the Association of Black Social Workers and Allied Professions reported to the House of Commons Social Services committee that:

Transracial placement as an aspect of current child care policy is in essence a microcosm of the oppression of black people in society; the most valuable resources of any ethnic groups are its children ... Transracial placement poses the most dangerous threat to the harmonious society to which we aspire. It is in essence "internal colonisation." (in J. Small, "Ethnic and racial identity in adoption within the UK," *Adoption and Fostering*, vol. 15 , no.4, 1991, pp. 61–8).

In 1989, the British Association for Adoption and Fostering (BAAF) summarized the professional position on transracial adoption. Reviewing recent research and debate they noted that "it seems to have produced a broad consensus: that a child's needs are best met in a family of the same race." The basis for this claim was again the insistence that one of the needs of the adopted child "is unquestionably to develop a positive sense of racial identity" (BAAF "Editorial – placement needs of black children," in *Adoption and Fostering*, vol. 13, 1989).

However, the skepticism in the UK towards notions of race, and the higher incidence of "mixed" relationships, have contributed towards a more muted debate, and opponents of transracial adoption have found it harder to establish a significant influence over social policy. Practitioners and academics in the UK are also often more skeptical than their USA counterparts regarding the term "race."

Perhaps as a consequence of the powerful rhetoric linking color with race and cultural identity, the empirical research into transracial adoption is often overlooked. Such research has provided consistent and compelling evidence that transracially adopted children grow up no less emotionally and socially adjusted than adopted children in general. These findings were reaffirmed by the major study on transracial adoption, the Simon–Altstein longitudinal study carried out between 1971 and 1991.

These issues have also influenced policies affecting other groups, of which two include Native Americans and indigenous Australian children. Between 1958 and 1968, approximately 400 children of Native American Indian parents were placed with white families in a joint venture between the Bureau of Indian Affairs and the Child Welfare League of America. By the early 1970s, Native Americans had joined in the denunciation of transracial adoption and in 1978 Congress passed the Indian Child Welfare Act, which virtually prohibited the adoption of Indian children by non-Indians.

In Australia, government policies during the twentieth century (pursued first by the British colonial government and then by the Australian government itself) resulted in many thousands of indigenous children being removed from their families and communities. "Assimilation" meant that under the "White Australia Policy" indigenous and Torres Strait Islander peoples were forbidden to speak their own languages or to engage in distinctive cultural practices. The authorities frequently did not consider indigenous families capable of parenting their own children. As a result, large numbers of indigenous children were removed from their families to advance the cause of assimilation. They were placed in institutions or foster homes, or adopted into non-indigenous families. This practice declined in the 1970s following the establishment of legal representation for indigenous children and their families in removal applications. However, it was not until the 1980s that the practice of removal and placement was finally reappraised. In 1997, the Australian Government published the report of the public inquiry commissioned to investigate these events. Its chief finding was that the most urgent need of separated families was for assistance in family reunion.

Policy governing the adoption of children is immensely important and carries significant human consequences for those involved. The challenge facing those responsible for such policy is to identify the extent to which political rhetoric and common-sense discourses about race, culture and identity are consistent with the empirical evidence about the best interests of the adopted children themselves.

SEE ALSO: Aboriginal Australians; African Americans; American Indians; double consciousness; children; cultural identity; culturecide; indigenous peoples; institutional racism; Jim Crow; multiracial/biracial; prejudice; racist discourse; social work; welfare

Reading

Adoption Across Borders, also by Rita Simon and Howard Altstein (Rowman & Littlefield, 2000), compares various studies and summarizes thirty years of research on transracial and intercountry adoptions.

Black, White or Mixed Race? by Barbara Tizard and Anne Phoenix (Routledge, 1993) is a British-based study of "racial identities" whose chief conclusion is that having a black identity is not related to the color of the parents young people grow up with, but rather to holding politicized views about racism.

The Case for Transracial Adoption by Rita Simon, Howard Altstein, and Marygold Melli (The American University Press, 1994) presents the case for transracial adoption by reviewing the major empirical studies and placing the policy debates within the context of US civil rights legislation.

"Symbolic interactionism, African American families,

and the transracial adoption controversy" by Leslie Doty Hollingsworth (in *Social Work*, vol. 44, no. 5, September 1999), presents a historical review of the debates about transracial adoption. The author uses a symbolic interactionist perspective to argue that African Americans constitute a unique and distinct cultural group and that public policy should preserve cultural realities and favor same-race adoption.

BOB CARTER

TYSON, MIKE (1966–)

American anathema

The youngest heavyweight champion of the world, who was later imprisoned for rape then resumed his professional boxing career under the guidance of Don King, Tyson is one of the most perpetually controversial African Americans of the late twentieth and early twenty-first centuries. Praised in the 1980s and hailed as a member of a boxing pantheon of elite heavyweight champions, Tyson, by the end of the same decade, prompted the magazine *Sports Illustrated* to ask: "Is Mike Tyson the most unpopular heavyweight in history?" Tyson's own behavior over subsequent years could have been designed to answer this. In 1992 he was convicted of rape and spent three years in prison. The conviction coincided with several lawsuits, most filed by women who alleged some form of sexual misconduct. In 1997, in a world title fight with Evander Holyfield, he bit a chunk out of his opponent's ear, an offense for which he was disqualified and suspended from boxing. In the lead-up to his fight in 2002 with Lennox Lewis, Tyson threatened to eat his opponent's babies (even though Lewis did not have children) and attacked him at a press conference.

Describing Tyson as "unpopular" is insufficient: for many he was abominable; a repulsive presence fit for only savagery. And yet, for fifteen years, he was the biggest box office draw in sports, drawing sell-out crowds wherever he fought and even when he did not (he once refereed a wrestling contest). The source of the fascination with Tyson may lie in the conflict that tormented the West in the decades following civil rights. Unburdened of *de jure* segregation and enabled by antidiscrimination legislation, the USA in particular sought to shed its racist past and stride toward an inclusive culture of equal opportunity. Yet, study after study presented a different picture of reality, one in which minority groups, especially African Americans, continued to struggle. Tyson, in his own unwitting way, provided tangible evidence of why this was so.

"I feel like Norman Bates, surrounded by all these doctors," Tyson said when undergoing tests to determine his suitability to fight. The Nevada State Athletic Commission administered the tests. Tyson may actually have been viewed as like the fictional motel owner of *Psycho*: disturbed, dangerous and incapable of the kind of self-reflection that might incline more rational persons to modify their behavior. Punishment seemed to have little effect on Tyson, who, at times, sounded penitent, but acted as if he wished to be anathematized.

Rise and fall

Born in Brooklyn, Michael George Tyson was the product of a dysfunctional family, his father deserting his mother, leaving her to struggle in the Brownsville district – one of the poorest areas of the United States. By the time he was incarcerated at the Tryon School, a correctional facility in upstate New York, Tyson had accumulated an extensive rap sheet; he was thirteen and had been arrested some forty times. In 1980 he was introduced to veteran trainer Cus D'Amato, who had guided Floyd Patterson to the world heavyweight title. Impressed by the untutored power of Tyson, D'Amato offered to train the boy at his Catskill Boxing Club, a sort of live-in training camp. D'Amato was later to become Tyson's surrogate father.

Tyson's ascent to world heavyweight champion was sudden. In November 1986, in his 28th professional fight, Tyson, aged twenty, became the youngest ever heavyweight champion, beating Trevor Berbick in two rounds. D'Amato had died a year before, removing what many believed to be a stabilizing influence in Tyson's life. Jimmy Jacobs, a former handball champion and boxing enthusiast, and Bill Cayton, an entrepreneur, now handled his management; both were white. Of the two, Tyson enjoyed a closer relationship with Jacobs and his death in 1988 left Tyson's business affairs in the hands of Cayton.

As the first undisputed heavyweight champion since Muhammad Ali – and, in many people's eyes, the best – he was able to command higher purses than any boxer in history. In 1987, Cayton negotiated a $26.5m (È15m), multi-fight deal with HBO, the subscription television channel. Discord marked Tyson's reign as champion. Don King was able to persuade him that his interests would be better served if he dispensed with Cayton and acrimonious legal disputes ensued. His marriage to actor Robin Givens overflowed with domestic and commercial conflicts, Givens, at one stage, appearing on national television to announce – in Tyson's presence – that life with Tyson had "been torture … pure hell," and that "he [Tyson] gets out of control, throwing, screaming." Givens continued to make allegations of physical abuse, though without producing proof.

Under the guidance of King, Tyson, having fired Cayton, turned against his long-time trainer Kevin Rooney, with whom he had lived and worked at D'Amato's camp. The decision to release Rooney seemed poorly judged: his style changed as a result and his boxing was never as effective. This became manifestly clear in February 1990 when he lost his world title to James "Buster" Douglas, one of the rankest underdogs in heavyweight title history.

Invited to judge a Miss Black America Pageant in Indianapolis in 1991, Tyson took a special interest in Desiree Washington, one of the contestants. She alleged that he took her to his hotel room where he raped her. Tyson was found guilty and sentenced to ten years imprisonment, four years to be suspended. At the time, he was preparing for a fight against Evander Holyfield that would have earned him $15m. Even while in prison, Tyson continued to spark controversy. Various African American organizations campaigned on his behalf, while women's groups damned him. Like Malcolm X, Tyson underwent a conversion to Islam during his incarceration and promised to emerge a reformed character.

Resuming his boxing career after his release in 1995, Tyson failed to discover his peak form and foundered in a fight against Holyfield. The 1997 rematch revealed Tyson at his vilest: trailing on points and subject to Holyfield's unpenalized headbutts, he spit out his mouthguard and bit a chunk from his opponent's ear. Serving his suspension, Tyson took part in a well-rehearsed wrestling match, in which he served ostensibly as referee. He also had a public argument with King in which he was said to have struck the promoter.

In 1999, shortly after a win over Francois Botha (for which he received $10m), Tyson was sentenced to a year in prison for assaulting two drivers in a Maryland traffic accident in August 1998. Described in court as a "ticking timebomb," Tyson was given the opportunity to appeal, but only on the understanding that he could face a twenty-year sentence if found guilty. He served three-and-a-half months.

Attraction and repulsion

Tyson's first professional fight was on March 6, 1985. Within twenty-one months he was the world heavyweight champion. By the time of his 1997 suspension, he had become one of highest earning athletes in history, challenged only by Michael Jordan. No athlete is able to command purses in the order of $15m per appearance unless there is a public prepared to pay to see him or her. Tyson may have been a repulsive character; but he was also a potent attraction. His big fights were screened pay per view; ringside seats at his fights were rarely available, even at $1,500 each.

The simple explanation of the enduring fascination with Tyson is that he was a good boxer amid a dearth of decent heavyweights. Yet, following the Douglas defeat in 1990, Tyson never mustered another performance to match his early form and his two fights with Holyfield confirmed that he was in terminal decline. Yet, still the interest in him would not abate, not even after his emphatic defeat by Lewis in 2002.

In his book *Tyson* (Pan Books, 1990), Peter Heller quotes Robin Givens: "There's something about Michael that's dangerous. As we all know, that's part of the attraction. It's like enjoying scary movies or roller coaster rides." Tyson assuredly did scare people: all the evidence pointed to the fact that he could not be contained, less still controlled. In the ring and out, he seemed in constant struggle. This has some relevance to understanding Tyson's extraordinary cultural power. Witnessing a Tyson fight, or even just following his exploits, may have had the effect of insinuating fans into a world which was at once strange but entertaining, perilous but beckoning.

Daniel Lieberfeld uses a resonant phrase when explaining why blues music became popular, particularly with white fans, in the 1990s: they were made to feel "party to something primal and uninhibited," he writes in his article "Million dollar juke joint" (*African American Review*, vol. 29, no. 2, 1995). "The allure of the exotic is fundamental to the appeal black culture holds for the mainstream."

Throughout Tyson's career, his feral side was emphasized. He was described as a caged animal, someone that fought on instinct, a fighter who traded on raw aggression. Such descriptions occluded the carefully perfected technique that was born of D'Amato and Rooney's coaching. But they served to project a convenient marketing image: the inhumanly aggressive and invulnerable "Iron" Mike Tyson.

Tyson himself was a willing, if occasionally unwitting, accomplice in this projection. For example, in 1986, following a win over Jesse Ferguson, Tyson told gathered journalists: "I tried to punch him and drive the bone of his nose back into his brain." The quote circulated for long after, a terrifying reminder of Tyson's principal objective when he was in the ring. The writer Joyce Carol Oates famously referred to Tyson's "impassive death-head's face" when trying to fathom out his seemingly self-destructive urges.

It is at least possible that depictions of Tyson as driven by primitive drives on all levels, not just boxing, helped foster an image that was both frightening and marketable. "That was a stereotype, of course," writes Illingworth, one quite common to blacks. And not a new one. In their book *Unthinking Eurocentrism* (Routledge, 1994), Ellas Shohat and Robert Stam write of a process they call "animalization" that was used in racist discourses of imperial days, but which continues to inform present-day debates. It involves "the reduction of the cultural to the biological, the tendency to associate the colonized with the vegetative and the instinctual rather than with the learned and the cultural."

Tyson was attributed the quality of Otherness: a presence somehow in but not *of* mainstream culture; a reminder of what lay outside civilized society, on the fringes of barbarity. Here was a man with boundless wealth, who bought luxuries on an impulse and discarded them without a thought (he once gave away a Bentley to two police officers that were investigating a collision with a parked car). Yet, for all his fame and fortune, Tyson was, in the eyes of the world,

resistant to the most basic civilizing influences. Illingworth suggests that the popular depiction was: "Tyson as some kind of savage on whom the culture bestows all that is noble, only for him to reject the gifts, and the givers, and revert to life on the instinctual level." The adage that "you can take the man from the gutter, but never the gutter from the man" never seemed truer than when applied to Tyson.

In other words, Tyson was a living fulfillment of age-old racist images of black people, images that had sources in the "brute nigger" stereotypes of yore. Blessed with an abundance of brawn, Tyson was a fearful figure; his apparent lack of intellect made him more frightening. Yet, as Givens acknowledged, that was "part of the attraction." Following the misadventures of Tyson made the follower "party to something primal and uninhibited."

It also provided evidence of sorts that, given the opportunity, even the most spectacularly successful blacks are prone to self-destruct. As such, Tyson was the perfect cipher for a culture eager to rid itself of the legacy of pre-civil rights segregation, yet uncomfortable with the prospect of accepting African Americans as fully-fledged equals.

SEE ALSO: African Americans; Ali, Muhammad; Barry case, the Marion; Central Park jogger; consumption; Jordan, Michael; King case, the Rodney; masculinity; Million Man March; race card; racist discourse; scapegoat; Simpson case, the O. J.; Thomas, Clarence

Reading

Blood Season: Mike Tyson and the world of boxing by Phil Berger (Morrow, 1996) is one of several books on Tyson published in the 1990s; others include: Pete Heller's *Tyson: In and out of boxing* (Robson, 1995) and *Bad Intentions: The Mike Tyson story* (Da Capo, 1995), Montieth Illingworth's *Mike Tyson: Money, myth and betrayal* (Grafton, 1992), and Richard Hoffer's *A Savage Business: The comeback and comedown of Mike Tyson* (Simon & Schuster, 1998).

Heavy Justice: The trial of Mike Tyson by Randy Roberts and J. Gregory Garrison (University of Arkansas Press, 2000) is a detailed account of Tyson's rape trial and its context.

U

UNCLE TOM *see* tokenism

UNDERACHIEVEMENT

This refers to a persistent pattern in which one group does less well than might be reasonably expected scholastically. It is premised on the ideological notion of schooling as a good thing and as highly serviceable in modern-day society. It derives from the liberal-democratic assumption that education is the main instrument of occupational and social mobility. Underpinning this is the conviction that the possession of formal educational credentials plays a determining role in the distribution of future life chances. Without these credentials, it is commonly assumed that a person completing secondary education is unlikely to find the sort of job to which she or he aspires, or indeed any job.

Britain's 1944 Education Act was aimed at ensuring that working-class girls and boys had as equal an opportunity of obtaining secondary education as their middle-class counterparts. Nonetheless, research soon revealed that despite obtaining equality of access working-class boys continued to perform less well than their middle-class peers. This concern prompted a new policy in the mid 1960s, with the dissolution of the tripartite system of secondary education and the establishment of comprehensive secondary schools. The imperative for this action was clear: to repair the meritocratic credibility of schools by ensuring that all pupils, irrespective of background, be given an equal opportunity to develop their intellectual potential to the full through unimpaired access to educational institutions and the credentials they offer. In Britain, as in other Western capitalist societies, equality of opportunity is the organizing principle of state education.

Despite the introduction of comprehensive schooling and related initiatives, there remained a significant difference in the academic achievement levels of pupils from working-class and middle-class backgrounds. Now, insofar as this pattern is rarely explained in terms of innate intellectual differences between these two social groups, working-class pupils are considered to be formally "underachieving," that is to say, unlike their middle-class peers they are not realizing their full intellectual potential. A group cannot underachieve if its intellectual and attainment levels have been genetically determined to be lower than the group to which it is being compared. On this view, then, the causes of this relatively lower academic performance lay elsewhere. One of the most popular explanations for this trend is that working-class pupils come from culturally deprived backgrounds and that schools must provide a compensating environment in order to increase their academic performance: hence, compensatory education initiatives. Marxists reject this pathological interpretation, preferring instead to locate the causes of underachievement in the institutional structures of society and their relationship to the education system. Different again is the view that microprocesses of school play the most significant part in this scenario. Here it is argued that teachers perpetuate differential patterns of achievement through their expectations and treatment of working-class pupils. These pupils are stereotyped as low achievers and are offered educational opportunities in accordance with these assessments.

A similar range of explanations has been adduced to account for the underachievement of pupils of African Caribbean origin in British schools. Ever since the early 1960s, research has reported a strong trend toward the lower academic performance of these pupils compared to their white and South Asian pupils. The early and optimistic prognosis that this was a transient phenomenon which derived largely from the pupils' newness in the British educational system and would therefore diminish with the passage of time was no longer tenable in the late 1970s and the early 1980s. In a range of research investigations, including those conducted under the auspices of the Rampton and Swann committees, pupils of African Caribbean origin along with children from Bangladeshi backgrounds were identified as "underachievers." That is, performing less well in public examinations than pupils from other ethnic groups.

Of course, certain educationalists and psychologists, such as Arthur Jensen and Hans Eysenck, argue for the lower innate intellect of black pupils. But for reasons already spelt out, those who adhere to this "scientific racism" argument cannot legitimately typify these pupils as "underachievers." What is more, these arguments have been thoroughly devalued and discredited by evidence which shows that the difference in IQ (in itself a highly dubious measurement) within populations is greater than the difference in average between populations.

What the specific causes of this trend are is a question that has tantalized educationalists for many years, and the answer remains elusive. At the same time, many researchers have been so overwhelmingly concerned with establishing differences, or otherwise, along ethnic lines that they have tended to overlook the significant influence of social class background and gender on performance levels. Black pupils in Britain come largely from working-class families and it has been clearly established that family background has a profoundly moderating effect on school performance levels. Could it be that "West Indian underachievement" is a misnomer and that if the research data were standardized to take into account class and gender backgrounds the results would show few significant differences between black pupils and their white, working-class counterparts?

Perhaps this obsession with achievement in public examinations is misplaced, anyway. While, traditionally, researchers and policy-makers have concentrated their attention on "who gets what," they have ignored the equally important matter: "who goes where – and why?" Put simply, the debate about "underachievement," especially in relation to ethnicity, has only focused on the tip of the iceberg; namely, observable outcomes from schooling. Those researchers who have taken the trouble to dive beneath the surface and attempt to tease out those decisions and processes that influence the selection and allocation of pupils into examination and non-examination classes have revealed a range of insidious patterns which, at the very least, need to be taken seriously in this debate. Is there a tendency for teachers to distract pupils of African Caribbean origin away from academic subjects in favor of developing what they perceive as innate sporting prowess? Are pupils whose main home language is not English regarded as less intellectually capable than their peers whose main language at home and school is English? Are African Caribbean pupils discouraged from competing in high-status examinations because their teachers believe they have difficulties with concentration and perseverance, an "attitude problem," in other words?

Research, based largely on ethnographic methods, has belatedly looked at these and related matters suggesting that "underrated" may be a more appropriate nomenclature than "underachiever."

SEE ALSO: children; cultural identity; Ebonics; education; equality; Freire, Paulo; intelligence; Marxism; merit; multicultural education; social exclusion; underclass

Reading

African American Education: A reference handbook by Cynthia L. Jackson (ABC-Clio, 2001) examines the impact of, for example, all-black institutions, desegregated facilities, testing and legislation, on the education of black pupils; this may well be read in conjunction with an interesting piece of research published as "Black students' achievement orientation as a function of perceived family achievement orientation and demographic variables" by D. Y. Ford (in *Journal of Negro Education*, vol. 62, 1993).

The Art of Being Black: The creation of black British youth identities by Claire E. Alexander (Clarendon, 1996), while not specifically about underachievement, sheds light on why young black people seem locked in the cycle.

The Bell Curve: Intelligence and class structure in American life (The Free Press, 1994) is the controversial text in which Richard J. Herrnstein and

Charles Murray unabashedly assert that scientific evidence demonstrates the existence of genetically based differences in intelligence among social classes and ethnic groups.

Black Students in an Affluent Suburb: A study of academic disengagement by John Ogbu (Lawrence Erlbaum, 2003) attributes the underachievement of black pupils at least partly to their limited aspirations and their attachment to a culture that emphasizes gangsta values; the argument complemented the findings of a report commissioned by the British Office for Standards in Education (Ofsted) which blamed black peer pressure for underachievement (reported in "Black youth culture blamed as pupils fail" by Gaby Hinsliff and Martin Bright, *Observer*, August 20, 2000).

British Educational Research Journal (vol. 19, no. 2, 1993) includes a debate between Barry Troyna and Roger Gomm about how best to interpret in-school processes governing the selection and allocation of ethnic minority pupils to examination groups.

The Science and Politics of Racial Research (University of Illinois Press, 1994) is William H. Tucker's exposÕ of the political and ideological motivations and intentions of those who consider that the "innate inferiority of a race" is still a "proper scientific question."

"Underachievement: a case of conceptual confusion" by Ian Plewis (in *British Educational Research Journal*, vol. 17, no. 4, 1991), lays bare some of the vagueness and disarray associated with the use of the concept in research and may be read with *"Race," Ethnicity and Education* by David Gillborn (Unwin Hyman, 1990) which provides an original and illuminating insight into the complex relationship between ethnicity, education, and achievement.

BARRY TROYNA

UNDERCLASS

The concept of underclass has been used by sociologists to describe the bottom stratum of complex societies, especially in the urban context. Underclass refers to a heterogeneous group rated below those working class with stable employment; it is regarded as beyond the pale of "respectable" society. It includes such social categories as the chronically unemployed, vagrants or transients, the criminal "underground," some occupational groups considered defiling or immoral (e.g. prostitutes), and sometimes, some despised outcaste groups which may be either ethnically or racially defined (e.g. gypsies in Europe, untouchables in India, the Burakumin of Japan, or "ghetto blacks" in the USA).

Near synonyms for underclass are *Lumpenproletariat*, subproletariat, pariahs, and outcaste groups. Each of these terms has special connotations, and tends to be used by social scientists of different ideological persuasions. Thus, *Lumpenproletariat* is generally used by Marxists, and refers more to the economic dimensions of status, while pariahs refers more to the moral devaluation of the status group and is used more by liberal scholars. Underclass is probably the most neutral term.

A key feature of the underclass in modern postindustrial societies is its marginality to the system of production, and its relative redundancy to it. In previous periods of industrialization the bulk of the urban working class consisted of lowly trained and, therefore, interchangeable factory operatives, and the unemployed were a reserve army of the proletariat used to break strikes, keep wages low, and perpetuate the exploitation of the working class as a whole. With the emergence of the postindustrial, social democratic welfare states of Western Europe, Australia, and North America, an increasingly sharp line has been drawn between a stable, secure, working class protected by trade unionism and increasingly employed in skilled service occupations, and an unstable, underemployed underclass subsisting on a mixture of welfare payments and an extralegal underground economy (drug traffic, gambling, prostitution, illegal sweat-shop labor, and so on).

The low skill level of the modern underclass in relation to the increasingly high demands for skilled labor in the mainstream economy combines with the dependency syndrome created by the welfare system to perpetuate the marginality and the superfluity of the underclass. In societies like Britain and the United States, where a substantial sector of the underclass is also racially stigmatized and discriminated against, the self-perpetuation of the urban underclass is further aggravated by racism.

Illegal immigration, as among Hispanics and Asians in the USA, complicates the problem yet more, by favoring the super-exploitation of workers whose illegality excludes them from normal legal protection in wages, employment, and social benefits. An additional factor is the rising number of urban children raised by single parents (overwhelmingly mothers) who, in addition to handicaps of racism and lack of skills, are further marginalized in the system of production by sexual discrimination and their parental responsibilities. For example, an estimated 50 percent of black children in the United States are raised in single-parent families. Many of them inherit underclass status, and are condemned to forming the hardcore of the unemployed ghetto youth. Currently some 40 percent of young urban blacks are chronically unemployed, four times the national average, and subsist largely on welfare and on illegal or fringe activities. The economic dependency of the single mother is often in part the *creation* of the welfare system. The absence of a resident adult male is often a necessary test of qualification for welfare; this, in turn, encourages male desertion and perpetuates the welfare mother syndrome in the underclass.

SEE ALSO: caste; disadvantage; drugs; empowerment; environmental racism; ethnocide; exploitation; homelessness; institutional racism; social work; subaltern; systemic racism; welfare

Reading

Charles Murray and the Underclass: The developing debate, edited by Ruth Lister (Civitas, 1996), has contributions from scholars, journalists and politicians, all evaluating the concept of the underclass.
The Other America by Michael Harrington (Macmillan, 1962) remains the most influential book in the "discovery" of the American underclass.
Social Inequality, edited by Andrõ Bõteille (Penguin, 1969), is a collection of classic articles, both theoretical and empirical, covering many parts of the world.
The Truly Disadvantaged by William J. Wilson (University of Chicago Press, 1987) is an early work on the analysis of underclass formation.

PIERRE L. VAN DEN BERGHE

UNESCO

The United Nations Educational, Scientific, and Cultural Organization (UNESCO) is a specialized agency of the UN that was established in 1946 and has its headquarters in Paris. The preamble to its constitution declares that "the great and terrible war which has now ended was a war made possible by the denial of the democratic principles of the dignity, equality and mutual respect of men, and by the propagation, in their place, through ignorance and prejudice, of the doctrine of the inequality of men and races." In this spirit, the Organization's General Conference (consisting of the representatives of some fifty member-states) in 1950 instructed the Director-General "to study and collect scientific materials concerning questions of race; to give wide diffu-

sion to the scientific information collected; to prepare an educational campaign based on this information."

Accordingly, UNESCO convened a meeting of specialists from a variety of disciplines to draw up a Statement on Race. This was published in 1950. Some of its contentions, and some of the terms used, were much criticized, especially by physical anthropologists and geneticists. Many maintained that the statement confused race as a biological fact with race as a social phenomenon. So UNESCO convened a second meeting that drew up the Statement of the Nature of Race and Race Differences of 1951. As it was thought important to avoid any suggestion that this was an authoritative manifesto embodying the last word on the race question, this statement was submitted for comment to a large number of anthropologists and geneticists. The resulting opinions were assembled and presented in the booklet *The Race Concept: Results of an inquiry* of 1953. In 1964, a further meeting of specialists was arranged to bring up to date and complete the 1951 declaration. This produced *Proposals on the Biological Aspects of Race* (1964). Later, in 1998 the International Union of Anthropological and Ethnological Societies recommended to UNESCO a revision of these proposals prepared by the American Association of Physical Anthropologists. To complement the proposals of the biologists, UNESCO in 1967 convened a committee of experts "to consider the social, ethical and philosophical aspects of the problem." The committee proposed a Statement on Race and Racial Prejudice that included several propositions on the nature of racism, a concept that had not previously featured in UNESCO statements. There is some variation in the endorsement of the four statements by the participants. Only the 1964 statement was described as a text representing the unanimous agreement of those taking part.

In implementation of its mandate, UNESCO commissioned and published (from 1951 onwards) a set of short studies in the series The Race Question in Modern Science, followed by two other series, The Race Question in Modern Thought (stating the positions of the major religions), and Race and Society. It also commissioned pioneering research on racial distinctions in Latin American societies. In more recent times it has been collaborating with the UN Human Rights Center in the preparation of teaching materials that discuss racial discrimination in a human rights context. This is part of its continuing Major Program XII concerned with the elimination of prejudice, intolerance, and racism.

A particularly important development was the unanimous adoption in 1960 by the General Conference of the Convention Against Discrimination in Education. This defines discrimination and binds states parties to undertake various measures to eliminate and prevent it. The Convention was followed in 1978 by the equally important Declaration on Race and Racial Prejudice adopted and proclaimed by the General Conference in 1978. After recalling the four statements mentioned above, it begins in article 1:

> All human beings belong to a single species and are descended from a common stock. They are born equal in dignity and rights and all form an integral part of humanity.
>
> All individuals and groups have the right to be different, to consider themselves as different and to be regarded as such. However, the diversity of lifestyles and the right to be different may not, in any circumstances, serve as a pretext for racial prejudice.

In the event of a state's being involved in a case before the International Court of Justice, or any other international tribunal, its adoption of the UNESCO Convention or Declaration could be cited as a test of its policies, but UNESCO's measures for enforcing compliance with such instruments are weaker than those of the UN International Convention on the Elimination of All Forms of Racial Discrimination.

SEE ALSO: anthropology; environmentalism; hereditarianism; international convention; prejudice; race: as classification; race: as synonym; science; United Nations

Reading

Four Statements on the Race Question (UNESCO, 1969) are the four documents cited in the main text above.
The International Politics of Race by Michael Banton (Polity, 2002) contains a fuller account of UNESCO's publications
The Retreat of Scientific Racism by Elazar Barkan (Cambridge University Press, 1992) has an especially relevant epilogue at pp. 341–6.
CHECK: internet resources section

MICHAEL BANTON

UNITED NATIONS

The main source and authority for international action against racial discrimination is the UN Charter which declares in article 55 that the UN shall promote "universal respect for, and observance of, human rights and fundamental freedoms for all without discrimination as to race, sex, language, or religion." The UN includes a variety of bodies with separate but sometimes overlapping functions with respect to human rights: the General Assembly, the Security Council, the Economic and Social Council (with its subsidiary, the Commission on Human Rights), the Trusteeship Council, the treaty-monitoring bodies and the specialized agencies, including the International Labor Organization (an autonomous institution founded in 1919), and UNESCO.

The Commission on Human Rights has its own subsidiary, originally called the Sub-Commission on the Protection of Minorities and the Prevention of Discrimination but now renamed Sub-Commission on the Promotion and the Protection of Human Rights. Responding to anti-Semitic incidents in Europe in 1959, and to concerns about racist regimes in southern Africa, the Sub-Commission took steps that resulted in 1963 in the General Assembly's adoption of the UN Declaration on the Elimination of All Forms of Racial Discrimination and the similarly titled International Convention two years later. In 1965 also it proclaimed that March 21 (the anniversary of the Sharpeville massacre in South Africa) should be observed as the International Day for the Elimination of Racial Discrimination. Later it designated 1971 as "International Year for Action to Combat Racism and Racial Discrimination," a step followed by making 1973–83 a "Decade for Action to Combat Racism and Racial Discrimination." It was in this connection that in 1975 the General Assembly adopted, by 72 votes to 35, resolution 3379 that "determines that Zionism is a form of racism and racial discrimination." On December 16, 1991 a draft resolution was adopted by 111 votes to 25 according to which the General Assembly revoked the previous resolution.

The General Assembly proclaimed a Third Decade to Combat Racism and Racial Discrimination starting in 1993, but a shortage of funds meant that relatively little could be done to implement its plan of activities. As a separate measure, in 1993 the UN Commission on Human Rights decided to appoint a special rapporteur "on contemporary forms of racism, racial discrimination and xenophobia and related intolerance." The appointment went to a judge of the constitutional court of Benin. The Commission's resolution emphasized "manifestations occurring particularly in developed countries." In the following year, it requested him to examine "contemporary forms of racism, racial discrimination, and forms of discrimination against Blacks, Arabs, and Muslims, xenophobia, negrophobia, anti-semitism, and related intolerance, as well as governmental measures to overcome them." The list of victim groups is an indication of the political forces behind decisions of this kind. This was also the first occasion on which such a resolution mentioned anti-Semitism. As part of its campaign, the UN convened world conferences against racism in 1978, 1983 and 2001.

The Sub-Commission prepared the Declaration on the Rights of Persons belonging to National, Ethnic, Religious and Linguistic Minorities adopted by the General Assembly in 1992. As part of the International Decade of the World's Indigenous Peoples, which started in December 1994, it is hoped to adopt a Universal Declaration on the Rights of Indigenous Peoples (a draft of which has been under discussion for several years) and to create a permanent forum for indigenous people within the UN. It should also be noted that a Convention on the Rights of All Migrant Workers and Members of their Families was adopted in 1991. By August 2001 it had been ratified by sixteen states; it will come into force when it has been ratified by twenty states.

SEE ALSO: human rights; indigenous peoples; International Convention; international law; international organizations; UNESCO; xenophobia; Zionism

Reading

The Charter of the United Nations: A commentary, 2nd edn., edited by Bruno Simma (Oxford University Press, 2002), is a comprehensive reference work.
International Action Against Racial Discrimination by Michael Banton (Oxford University Press, 1996) has details of the initiatives described, while the same author's *The International Politics of Race* (Polity, 2002) updates the account.
United Nations Action in the Field of Human Rights (New York, United Nations Sales No. E.88.XIV.2, 1994).
CHECK: internet resources section

MICHAEL BANTON

V

VIOLENCE

Violence against black populations in Britain and the USA has a long history. From slave days to the present day, violence against blacks has persisted; in the 1990s, high-profile cases such as the beating of Rodney King and the killing of Amadou Diallo remind us that violence is habitual. Britain has a similarly violent history: from the clashes in the dockland areas of London, Cardiff, Liverpool and South Shields between 1919 and 1948 involving attacks on colonial seamen; through the "Nigger-hunting" campaigns of the Teddy Boys in the 1950s and the "Paki-bashing" episodes in the 1960s; to the murders of Gurdip Singh Chaggar in Southall in 1976 and Altab Ali in Whitechapel two years later. The murder of Stephen Lawrence and the subsequent *cause célèbre* it created was a sobering reminder that violence motivated by sheer racism is something of a "way of life" for black people.

Associated with this "tradition of intolerance" have been two significant and insidious trends. First, in contrast to the attacks on black people in Britain and the USA in the earlier part of the twentieth century (and before), it has been possible to discern a move from collective to individualized violence. Second, assailants have tended to depersonalize their victims. "Doing a Paki" has, for instance, endured as a resonant theme since the emergence of British skinhead cultures in the late 1960s; the emergence of US skinheads presaged similar attacks on blacks and Asians.

In Britain, by the early 1980s, it had become clear that these acts of violence were not "just a hiccup" in British race relations, as they had been characterized by the Minister of State at the Home Office on the occasion of Chaggar's death in 1976. No: they constituted a pervasive and corrosive influence on the quality of life experienced by black citizens in modern-day Britain. As a 1989 Home Affairs Committee report put it, harassment constitutes one of the "frightening realities" for black citizens and their children.

The 1980s and early 1990s witnessed a flurry of activity in this area. Initiatives crystallized around a (belated) attempt to document the incidence of harassment, tease out its discernible patterns, if any, and to develop strategies to preempt its occurrence, deal with its perpetrators, and support its victims. Despite the increasing concern shown by national and local politicians, the police, educationalists, community relations activists and antiracist campaigners, the emergent material remains strong on description, weak on definition.

A definition of what exactly constitutes racial, or racially motivated, violence (and cognate terms such as racial incidents, racial bullying, racial attacks, inter-racial conflict) remains elusive. But definitions are important. Why? Because they help in constructing the parameters of empirical research and in clarifying some of the myths, assumptions and stereotypes which prevail in this area.

The operational definitions of a racial incident that currently prevail in statutory agencies, the police force, central and local government, and monitoring groups lead to broad interpretations. That is, whether the perpetration of violence is expressly motivated, or is perceived by the victim as motivated, by "racial" considerations. This is unsatisfactory for three reasons.

To begin with, a racial incident tends to be equated with an overt attack on an individual or group and their property. That is, an easily observable incident that is amenable to monitoring and recording. But this behavioristic definition fails to take into account more subtle, but no less intimidatory expressions of harassment which also define and confine the experience of blacks in Britain: racist graffiti or other written insults; verbal abuse; disrespect toward differences in music, food, dress, or customs; deliberate mispronunciation of names; mimicry of accent; exclusionism and so on.

The other major shortcoming of these definitions is their tendency to conflate "racial" with racism. As a result, they fail to provide the analytical tools for clarifying and interpreting the incidence and direction of conflict between black and white adults and their children. At the level of empirical analysis the broad characterization of conflict between blacks and whites as "racial" constrains us from accounting for the two dominant patterns which have emerged from research in this field. Namely, that black people are more likely to experience "racially" motivated harassment than their white counterparts; and that black children are more frequently subjected to abuse aimed at their perceived "racial" origins than white youngsters.

There is, however, another and more serious weakness with the interchangeable use of "racial" and racist conflicts. Racist attacks (by whites on blacks) are part of a coherent ideology of oppression which is not true when blacks attack whites, or indeed, when there is conflict between members of different ethnic minority groups.

What is omitted from the most popular operational definitions of these incidents is a recognition of the asymmetrical relations between black and white citizens (and their children), and sensitivity to the extent to which the harassment and abuse of blacks by whites is expressive of the ideology which underpins that relationship: racism.

SEE ALSO: Diallo case, the Amadou; ethnic conflict; King case, the Rodney; Lawrence case, the Stephen; policing; racism; sexual abuse; skinheads; social work; white backlash culture; White Power

Reading

Hate Crimes: The rising tide of bigotry and bloodshed by Jack Levin and Jack McDevitt (Westview Press, 2000) focuses on the USA; this may be read in conjunction with *Violence: Diverse populations and communities* by D. De Anda and R. M. Becaerra (Haworth, 2000).

The Hate Debate: Should hate be punished as a crime? by Paul Iganski (Profile, 2002) triggers an interesting debate.

Racial Violence on Trial: A handbook with cases, laws and documents by Christopher Waldrep (ABC-Clio, 2001) is a sourcebook on the myriad cases on violence perpetrated on African Americans in the USA, whereas the focus is on violence against Asians in *Anti-Asian Violence in North America: Asian American and Asian Canadian reflections on hate, healing and resistance* edited by Patricia Wong Hall and Victor M. Hwang (AltaMira, 2001).

Racism in Children's Lives (Routledge, 1992) by Barry Troyna and Richard Hatcher explores the salience of racist name-calling in the lives of young children growing up in predominantly white neighborhoods.

"A typology of racist violence: implications for comparative research and intervention" by Claudio Bolzman, Anne-Catherine Salbert Mendoza, Monique Eckmann and Karl Grünberg in *Comparative Perspectives on Racism*, edited by Jesska ter Wal and Maykel Verkuyten (Ashgate, 2000), collects data from several European nations.

BARRY TROYNA

VOLK

The word corresponding to "people," which in German and related languages is applied to cultural groups and would-be nations. In German, it implies much more than "people" does in English. Since the growth of the Romantic movement from the late eighteenth century, it has signified the union of a group of people with a transcendent "essence." The essence was given different names, for example, "nature," "cosmos," "mythos," but in each instance it represented the source of the individual's creativity and his/her unity with other members of the *Volk*. From there it stemmed a strain in German thought which diverged from traditional Western nationalism and religion. The *Volk* mediated between the isolated individual, alienated by the forces of modern society, and the universe. In *Mein Kampf*, Adolf Hitler criticized the naiveté of the Volkists but made use of their ideas to describe his vision of a racially powerful and united Germany.

A derived word, *Herrenvolk*, means a "masterpeople" and has been used by Pierre van den Berghe to characterize "*herrenvolk* egalitarianism" and "*herrenvolk* democracy." In white supremacist societies such as those of southern

Africa after European conquest, a white minority have been the masters of a larger black population. To preserve their privileged position the whites needed to maintain a front of solidarity, and this required the cultivation of trust and sentiments of equality within their own group. These attitudes contrasted with the assumption of inequality in their dealings with blacks.

SEE ALSO: Aryan; caucasian; Chamberlain, Houston Stewart; fascism; Gobineau, Joseph Arthur de; Haeckel, Ernst; language; nationalism; race: as classification; race: as synonym; Wagner, Richard; White Power; whiteness

Reading

Race: The history of an idea in the West by Ivan Hannaford (Johns Hopkins Press, 1996) identifies Johann Gottfried von Herder (1744–1803) as a key figure in promoting the concept of *Volk*, principally through his 33-volume *Ideen zur Philosphie der Geschichte der Menschhiet* (*Reflections on the Philosophy and History of Mankind*) (1784–91), which focused on culture as a determining factor in history.

The Scientific Origins of National Socialism by Daniel Gasman (Macdonald, London and Elsevier, New York, 1971).

South Africa: A study in conflict by Pierre van den Berghe (Wesleyan University Press, 1965) is the study quoted in the main text above.

MICHAEL BANTON

W

WAGNER, RICHARD (1813–83)

Composer of *Der Ring des Nibelungen* and other classical works, Wagner has been variously portrayed as an anti-Semite who inspired both Adolf Hitler and Houston Stewart Chamberlain with his apocalyptic vision of a third Reich, and an apolitical man of the theater whose oeuvre was perverted by Nazis to propagandize their *Weltanschauung*, or worldview.

Joachim Köhler, author of *Wagner's Hitler*, tends toward the former, presenting an analysis of Wagner that clarifies the role he and his work played in the genocide of World War II. Born in Leipzig, Wagner, the son of a baker's daughter, was brought up with his stepfather, an actor and painter, in Dresden. While his family was poor, Wagner was later to claim aristocratic descent. He moved to Paris where he presented his opera, *Rienzi*, based on the fourteenth-century Roman scholar and politician Cola di Rienzi, whose millennial vision turned on a Reich that would restore the days of empire. The first Reich, or German commonwealth, was the Holy Roman Empire, beginning 962.

Wagner attributed the failure of his opera to the jealousy and personal enmity of his peers, many of whom were Jews, and this seems to have motivated his political activities: he joined Johann Schiller, of the German Freedom Movement, in protests, demonstrations and rebellions, though the execution of the movement's founder, Robert Blum, during the 1848 uprising, convinced Wagner that his politics should be cast in a more literary form. His work from this point contrived to manifest a dualistic conception of a world in which the forces of evil penetrate, sabotage and incapacitate the true Order. Working in exile in Zurich, Wagner worked on a theory of the relationship between art, revolution and the future. As Ivan Hannaford writes: "His magnificent operas, drawn from romantic poems in Middle High German of the twelfth century, celebrated the *Volk* now realized as a new type of man and a new moral order flowing from the artistry of race, language, and nation."

The first Bayreuth Festival was staged in 1876 and was, ostensibly, a literary and arts celebration, though the circle of people who attended were virulently anti-Semitic and committed to the promotion of the third Germanic Reich. Many of the motifs and much of the ideology of Nazism were derived from Bayreuth. Chamberlain, a fellow member of the Bayreuth circle, revered Wagner as a visionary and a "saviour in the mould of Jesus Christ." His hagiography *Richard Wagner* was published in 1895 by Bruckmann, a publishing house that was become one of Hitler's most enthusiastic supporters.

The sobriquet "the Nazi prophet" was often applied to Chamberlain who became an intellectual mentor of Hitler. Chamberlain's suspicion that the malfeasance of Jews was to blame for practically every known adversity came from Wagner. Chamberlain's treatise *Die Grundlagen des Neunzehenten Jahrhunderts* (*The Foundations of the Nineteenth Century*, first published in 1899) implicitly acknowledged Wagner's inspiration: implicitly because it was a Bayreuth tradition to communicate in allusions that only associates would detect. The two-volume work gave historical and philosophical context to anti-Semitism. Wagner's sentiments were evident allegorically: his virtuous characters, such as the *Ring*'s Siegfried are Aryans fighting against the forces of evil, as personified in the likes of

Alberich and Mime, repulsive dwarfs, motivated only by gold. Wagner and his disciples predicated all their endeavors on the principle that money is material power and that Jews were pursuing domination through its acquisition.

Joseph Arthur de Gobineau was another writer who owed an intellectual debt to Wagner. The author of *Essai sur l'inégalité des races humaines* (*Essay on the Inequality of the Human Races*, published in four volumes between 1853 and 1855) warned of the threat to the pure Aryan blood line posed by mixing with inferior races. "Degeneration" would follow, according to Gobineau. The leitmotif is expressed musically in Wagner's *Parsifal*, in which the mystical brotherhood of the Knights of the Holy Grail strive for redemption – a concept that has resonance with the German *Volk*.

Hitler was committed to *realpolitik*, that is, politics based on material, practical needs rather than on ideals or morals such as those depicted in Wagner's operas, on which he doted. This does not diminish Wagner's influence: Hitler acknowledged his inspiration, framing his plans for world domination in Wagnerian terms. As Köhler writes: "His [Hitler's] attempt to translate Wagner's sacred festival drama into the reality of the twentieth century, and to transform the world into a theatre for the demonstration of Wagner's doctrines of regeneration, failed."

Köhler goes so far as to argue that Hitler was "an instrument" who had been "programmed" by Chamberlain, himself in awe of Wagner and convinced of the prophetic properties of his theater. Alternative interpretations suggest that such an association is spurious and that, anti-Semite though he may have been, Wagner had no direct influence on the doctrines that were to plunge the world into war many years after his death. His work may have been appropriated by Nazis, but for political ends that were never entertained by Wagner himself. Opera-lover that he was, Hitler may have found aesthetic and philosophical justification for his anti-Semitism in Wagner's work, but, equally, his hatred may have existed had he never seen or heard of the composer.

"Few are the great artists around whom so much controversy has gathered and who have aroused such extremes of adulation and revulsion," observes Ronald Taylor in his introduction to Köhler's book, which places Wagner firmly on the same historical continuum. "What Wagner urged in words of rabid racial hatred and incitement to political violence," writes Taylor, "Hitler turned into chilling, murderous reality."

SEE ALSO: anti-Semitism; Aryan; caucasian; Chamberlain, Houston Stewart; Doomed Races Doctrine; ethnic cleansing; ethnocide; eugenics; genocide; geometry of race; Gobineau, Joseph Arthur de; Haeckel, Ernst; Holocaust; language; science; *Volk*; White Power

Reading

Race: The history of an idea in the West by Ivan Hannaford (Johns Hopkins University Press, 1996) examines the relationships among the work of a great many theorists of race, including Wagner and, *inter alia*, Nietzsche and Chamberlain.

Wagner's Hitler: The prophet and his disciple by Joachim Köhler (Polity Press, 2001) is the provocative and persuasive thesis that links the concepts articulated operatically by Wagner with the megalomaniac programs of Hitler.

WELFARE

Welfare, or social welfare, refers to the range of social provision provided by state, private and voluntary organizations to respond to the needs of the population. In general terms this covers services such as housing, education, health, social work and the personal social services, and the range of benefit provisions. In the immediate postwar period, the state was the main provider of social provision, but from the mid 1970's, first under Labour and then more generally under the Conservatives, British governments have pursued broadly neo-liberal approaches to welfare. US governments have pursued less liberal policies. These developments have had serious implications for all welfare recipients but particularly those such as ethnic minority groups who experience disproportionate levels of poverty, disadvantage and oppression.

Pathologizing images in welfare

Poverty and class locations have a fundamental impact on people's projected need for welfare provision, their access to services, and their treatment within welfare agencies. For example, in relation to health, the poorest in society suffer from higher mortality and morbidity rates (partly because their poverty results in poorer diets, and they tend to live in inadequate housing in poorer environments). Further, their access to health care is limited in relation to more affluent groups who can afford to pay for and access a wider range of provision outside the state sector. Finally, pathologizing images of the poor often inform the attitudes of welfare professionals. That is, they often perceive that the poor are to blame for their circumstances, rather than seeing their deprivation as arising from economic and social disadvantage.

This relationship is particularly significant amongst Britain's black population, where indicators of poverty demonstrate that black groups are more at risk of high unemployment, low pay and limited social security rights (Labour Force Survey 1997/98, cited in the *Guardian*, February 21, 2000). Yet, despite high levels of deprivation and a greater need for collective welfare provision, the black community suffers unequal treatment from the full range of welfare institutions.

Evidence of how deeply entrenched racism is within welfare organizations has been emphasized and given an increasingly high public and political profile since the inquiry into the murder of Stephen Lawrence in 1993. The findings of the inquiry concluded that racism was institutionalized within British society, and existed within all organizations.

There is widespread evidence of institutional racism across a range of welfare organizations. One of the deepest expressions of institutional racism affecting black people and long documented is the unequal treatment of their children by the education system. For example, in 1999 the Children's Society revealed that black children are six times more likely to be expelled from school than white children (*Guardian*, February 21, 2000). The Ofsted report (2002) entitled "Educational inequality: mapping race, class and gender" suggested that while black children receive high levels of encouragement from home and enter the educational system with high levels of motivation, aspiration and potential, they leave the system with fewer qualifications than their white peers – a clear example of system failure. Over the years there has been a growing concern that diseases such as sickle-cell anemia which predominantly affects Afro-Caribbean males is underresearched and underresourced and not given any priority within the health service. In relation to housing, geographical segregation is often evident.

Although this is often portrayed as "self-segregation," research and evidence have re-vealed that segregation often arises as a result of Local Authority housing allocation policies. For example, the Oldham Independent Review Report (2000) found that local authority housing allocation policies were instrumental in segregating Asian applicants from white households by placing them in lower quality housing on certain estates. Asians who did try to move out geographically were often subject to hostility. In terms of local authority labor representation, the same report found only 2.63 percent of employees working for Oldham Metropolitan Borough Council were Asian, despite the fact that they made up 11 percent of the local population. Black groups have also been discriminated against in terms of legislation that has restricted or denied their right to welfare benefits. For example, the 1981 British Nationality Act excluded British overseas citizens (mainly black citizens) from the right to make any claim on the state, and the 1988 Immigration Act extended this provision. More recently, the 1996 Asylum and Immigration Act has been criticized as impoverishing asylum seekers and refugees, by, for example, withdrawing asylum seekers' rights to income support, child benefits and public housing.

Care and control

Institutional racism also places emphasis on the extent to which notions of inferiority and superiority pervade the welfare system and influence attitudes, policies and practices in organizations. This is particularly significant when discussing the "caring" and "controlling" elements of welfare provision. The black population are over-represented in the controlling aspects of the welfare state such as probation, child protection and mental health services, whilst being under-represented in its more caring aspects, such as domiciliary provision. In such instances stereotypes of, for example, Afro-Caribbean males as being inherently criminal, or the Asian family always being available to care for its dependents, impacts negatively on the relationship that black groups have with welfare organizations. Such stereotypes also help us understand why, for example, Afro-Caribbeans are much more likely than their white counterparts to be diagnosed as schizophrenic under the existing mental health system, whereas there is an under-utilization of mental health services by young South Asian women who have high rates of suicide. Within the educational system there are stereotypes of black children which give rise to negative expectations regarding their behavior and educational potential, and "underachievement" is often depicted as a cultural problem, despite the fact that nearly all pupils in the school system were born in Britain.

Despite evidence that revealed the institutional nature of racism within welfare organizations, up until the 1980s analyses of racism were based on personal and cultural prejudice. In the aftermath of high levels of immigration in the postwar period, when black workers were recruited in increasing numbers to work in sectors of the economy where there were shortages of labor, assimilationist/integrationist perspectives were promoted by politicians and enshrined in legislative developments. The underlying principles were that black groups needed to adopt the "British way of life" and not undermine the dominant white culture. This led to initiatives in the field of welfare such as the employment of bilingual assistants and translators, and the dispersal of black pupils to avoid an undue concentration of "immigrants" in schools. Resources were made available to local councils to fund such provision under Section 11 of the 1966 Local Government Act. This Act legislated for major sources of funding to be made available to offer extra assistance to local councils with high proportions (above 10 percent) of inhabitants of New Commonwealth origin. The dominant ideology of the USA was captured in the metaphor of the melting pot, in which all different cultures would mix and eventually assimilate. As in the "British way of life," ethnic minorities were expected to adapt rather than enrich.

In the 1970s multiculturalism was dominant in terms of "race-relations" developments within welfare organizations. This was informed by the view that contact with other cultural lifestyles would reduce ignorance and prejudice within institutions. Multicultural initiatives were particularly predominant in the field of education, where children were taught about other cultures (sometimes referred to as the sari, samosa and steelband syndrome) in the hope that this would enhance understanding and reduce levels of racism. The focus on individuals and cultures also had implications for welfare professionals. Developments such as Racial Awareness Training (RAT) were introduced to challenge racism, whose aim was to enable professionals to "discover" their personal prejudice. Such developments, although not seeking to pathologize black people, did tend to intensify the defensiveness and guilt that white professionals experienced regarding issues of "race."

Antiracist perspectives

It was in the late 1970s and early 1980s that antiracist perspectives began to emerge, with their focus on structural and institutional racism. Assimilationist/integrationist and multicultural initiatives were criticized as being at best limited in dealing with racism within welfare institutions. Antiracist perspectives instead were concerned with analyses based on why black groups are discriminated against in society, and the way in which practices and procedures within organizations are informed by negative racial stereotypes. As such, antiracism was a much more radical interpretation of racism and social welfare provision, incorporating a belief that the state is not neutral or independent, but is an expression of an economic, social and political system that benefits from racism by oppressing black people.

It was during this period, that the first challenge to institutional racism was made by a state welfare organization, when the Central Council for Education and Training in Social Work (CCETSW) began to take seriously claims of institutional racism in the field of social work education and training. This was a result of increasing concern during the 1980s amongst both black and white sections of the social work academy and profession that the black population were underrepresented, both as workers and as clients in social work agencies, and that when they were represented, they were often pathologized using negative and damaging assumptions, endorsing the white superiority of white culture over other cultures. As a result, developments took place, which constituted a fundamental attempt by CCETSW to make antiracism a central requirement of social work training, and a central component of good social work practice. In future, students were to develop the appropriate knowledge and skills to implement antiracist practice, and organizations providing social work education and training had to have clear antiracist policies.

However, it was after the murder of Stephen Lawrence in 1993 that institutional racism developed a high political and public profile. In early 1997, a coroner's jury, after just 30 minutes of deliberation, returned a verdict of unlawful killing "in a completely unprovoked racist attack by five white youths" (*Guardian*, February 14, 1997). Jack Straw, the Home Secretary at the time, set up a judicial public inquiry into the circumstances surrounding Stephen's death, which was chaired by Sir William Macpherson, and was published as the Macpherson Report. The Report concluded that institutional racism was not only evident in policing practices and procedures, but across a range of institutions.

Both CCETSW and the Macpherson Report, in offering radical interpretations of racism within state organizations, faced a backlash from politicians, the media and professional bodies. CCETSW was accused, for example, of being taken over by zealots, of being obsessed with political correctness and of brainwashing students. Commentaries regarding the Macpherson Report stated that the idea of institutional racism was a wild overreaction, that it made policing unworkable, and that it was an inept and dangerous phrase. This onslaught of criticism has led to antiracist recommendations being undermined and watered down in both instances. For example, in November 1999, the government announced in the Queen's speech that it would not be honoring Macpherson's recommendations to make indirect racial discrimination by the police illegal. Only direct and overt acts of discrimination by the police could be brought to court, leaving the substance of the force's institutional racism untouched

In analyzing the relationship between racism and social welfare provision, there are clear links between the disproportionate levels of poverty faced by the black population, their projected need for welfare services, and the discriminatory nature of provision afforded them. There is also clear evidence of the role of institutional racism within welfare organizations and the negative impact it has on social provision for black groups. However, despite an increasing awareness of the nature of institutional racism and some valiant attempts to counter its impact, it is still met with hostility, defensiveness and denial amongst many welfare organizations and professionals.

SEE ALSO: assimilation; asylum seeker; British Asians; children; disadvantage; education; equality; homelessness; institutional racism; Lawrence case, the Stephen; ; laws: immigration, Britain; multiculturalism; political correctness; prejudice; riots: Britain, 2001; segregation; sexual abuse; social work; underclass

Reading

From Immigration Controls to Welfare Controls, edited by Steve Cohen, Beth Humphries and Ed Mynott (Routledge, 2002), offers an important analysis of a developing "welfare apartheid" informed by racist stereotypes, which has serious implications for asylum seekers and refugees and their access to welfare provision

Tackling Institutional Racism: Anti-racist policies and social work education and training by Laura Penketh (Polity Press, 2000) offers a comprehensive analysis of the development and implementation of anti-racist initiatives in the field of social work education and training.

LAURA PENKETH

WHITE BACKLASH CULTURE

Reaction to apparent threat

The phrase "white backlash culture" (WBC) is generally used to refer to the reaction, from the 1970s onwards, against both an increase in the numbers of minority ethnic populations in the West and those laws, policies, etc. aimed at combating discrimination and redressing inequalities. However, there is much evidence to suggest that WBC has a much longer history, for example the heightened racial violence and lynching, as well as the institutionalization of segregation in the wake of emancipation and reconstruction after the Civil War in the USA. More recently, expressions of WBC have taken a variety of forms including racial violence and abuse; polemical and quasi-academic attacks on affirmative action/antiracist policies and, more latterly, a reaction against those aspects of globalization which appear to threaten white privilege.

WBC, as an overt expression of white consciousness, is more commonly associated with the politics and propaganda of far right-wing organizations which in the US came to prominence in the aftermath of the Vietnam war (Gibson, 1994) and, in the UK, in the 1970s with the influx of immigrants from Uganda and

Malawi. In the USA, the ideologies of such groups were invariably rooted in a mix of Christian fundamentalism, antistatism, survivalism, militarism and overt racism. William Pierce's *The Turner Diaries* spelt out what was for some an apocalyptic yet ultimately utopian vision of a race war between the Organization (or white underground) and ZOG (the Zionist Occupation Government) in which white colluders were to be hung, Jews were to be shot and other minorities exiled.

However, WBC is not restricted to the far right. According to Lemm (1996) Richard Nixon was the first to articulate the values and sentiments associated with WBC when he waged a "culture war" in which he specifically addressed white working-class males. WBC expressed itself increasingly within the political and academic mainstream during the 1980s and 1990s as the press and publishers attacked policies aimed at redressing racial inequalities, in particular those which have been labeled "affirmative action" or "equal opportunities." Accordingly, these critics have argued that white men had become the victims of affirmative action. By way of illustrating this point, *US News* ran a headline in 1989 "No white men need apply" whilst Frederick Lynch, in 1989, wrote a book entitled *Invisible Victims: White males and the crisis of affirmative action* (Greenwood). The idea that white men are the victims of affirmative action implies that such policies have successfully tackled disadvantage and redressed socioeconomic differences between white and minority populations, an assumption, which is not born out in the wealth of official evidence.

Starting with this highly dubious premise, there are three equally suspect substantive criticisms of affirmative/positive action policies. First, it is claimed, they undermine the idea of a meritocracy which is based on the rational allocation of rewards (for example, in education and employment) on the basis of ability (see for example Howard, below). Again there is considerable evidence to suggest that class remains a major determinant of educational success and career destinations, that social networks amongst elite groups continue to play an important role in life chances, and that IQ tests, which are apparently neutral measures of "raw ability," are in fact inherently culturally biased.

Second, it is argued, such policies promote state-induced dependency at the expense of the so-called "can do/will do" culture based primarily on individual effort. This argument is always used very selectively. For example, the agricultural sector in the West, which is highly dependent on state subsidy, is rarely considered alongside others who benefit from state support. On the contrary, according to Prince Charles, farmers would get a better deal if *they* were from a socially disadvantaged group who were benefiting from "politically correct" policies (quoted in *Guardian*, September 23, 2002).

Finally, such policies allegedly curtail freedom, notably those of expression (in the case of the preferred language associated with affirmative/positive action, diversity, etc.), those derived from professional autonomy (e.g. a teacher's control over the curriculum) and those associated with recruitment (i.e. the right to determine selection criteria). The term *political correctness* has been used ironically and pejoratively to attack the allegedly Kafkaesque and doctrinaire framework of such policies and procedures. What is in fact under attack here are those freedoms that have traditionally served the interests of the dominant class (and gender) at the expense of those freedoms that might secure a more equitable distribution of opportunities and rewards.

In the UK the policies of the Conservative governments of the 1980s sought to reverse the initiatives of antiracist local authorities and those promoting multicultural policies. Others who opposed such policies were feted by the Conservative government and tabloid press. Most notable amongst these was a Bradford headteacher, Ray Honeyford, who attacked multiculturalism and blamed it for poor educational standards and the plight of the white working class. Individuals and groups who received support from sections of the tabloid press included the groups of white English parents in Cleveland, Dewsbury and Wakefield, who took their children out of schools committed to multicultural education. These "martyrs" of political correctness were viewed in some quarters as champions of individual rights and freedoms and praised for having escaped the so-called tyranny of a multicultural/antiracist curriculum. The reality is very different. Multicultural initiatives remain marginal to mainstream/core provision, levels of racial harassment remain high, and little progress has been made to change the ethnic profile of senior positions in the public and private sectors.

Fears surrounding immigration and greater diversity coupled with increased opportunities for those beneficiaries of affirmative action or equal opportunity policies have fueled anxiety about national identity, a key aspect of WBC. Hence part of the backlash has been expressed in attempts to redefine what it means to be American, English, etc. in more racially exclusive terms. Politicians, media commentators and academics have all contributed to this debate. A case in point would be Margaret Thatcher's comment in 1978 that Britain was being "swamped" by those of an "alien culture" and that immigration control was necessary to preserve Britain's role in promoting global democracy and freedom. Her party chairperson, Norman Tebbitt, took a different approach to the problem of who was 'in' and 'out', when he invited those of an Indian or Pakistani background, living in the UK, to either support the English cricket team or to simply (re-)patriate, (the famous "cricket test"). The then Conservative prime minister, John Major was somewhat less provocative but no less exclusive when he summed up the quintessential English characteristics in terms of warm beer and cricket. The identity debate has been subsequently taken up by both Labour governments since 1997, particularly in the context of policies on refugees and asylum seekers, and the proposal of the Home Secretary David Blunkett that an English language test be taken by all those wishing to become British citizens. He subsequently backed this up with the comment that English should be the universal language spoken "at home" in the UK. Backlash culture here manifests itself in attempts to define a set of core values associated with Englishness and to obviate the threat as well as define the limits of multiculturalism (see, for instance, Roger Scruton's *The Myth of Multiculturalism* in Palmer's collection)

Thus the apparent differences between backlash culture as expressed in far right and mainstream politics can be overstated. In the USA, David Duke, who began his career as a member of the white student alliance, Ku Klux Klan and Leader of the National Association for the Advancement of White People became a Republican member of the Louisiana Senate and claimed with some justification that the views he advocated from the political fringes had been subsequently taken up by both mainstream parties in the United States.

Likewise, in Britain the agenda of the extreme right-wing British National Party overlaps with the concerns expressed by both Conservative and Labour governments and the Conservative tabloid press. Hence, *The BNP News*, the party's organ, has included stories about immigration and asylum fraud, health risks to whites; cash handouts for black projects, and, of course, narratives of white male victims of reverse racism, all of which, in thematic terms, have been covered in the mainstream tabloid press as well as in some cases taken up by politicians and translated into government policy.

The effort to reassert white privilege

WBC also has an effect on more liberal discourses of multiculturalism, corporate social responsibility, diversity management, etc. Benign attempts to promote and value diversity will always be limited against a backdrop of efforts designed to reassert white privilege. Such reforms are also liable to be appropriated by the dominant group so that what starts out as a positive initiative ultimately is taken over, contained and managed according to white sectional interests. The attempt to market ethnicity corporately through the promotion of local restaurants, festivals and landmarks, is a case in point.

From the 1990s WBC has expressed itself increasingly as an attempt to reassert white privilege in the face of more global concerns. Globalization, which is associated with ideas of interdependence and permeability, has undoubtedly benefited Western governments and their multinational allies. At the same time it is also associated with changes, some of which have been seen as potentially threatening to white privilege and hence cause for countermeasures.

The most obvious feature of globalization in this context is migration. Western governments and the mainstream media have, in concert, precipitated a panic over refugees and asylum seekers focusing on the growing number seeking entry, their cost to the taxpayer, their "moral shortcomings" and their general threat to the health (through the spreading of disease) and well-being of indigenous whites. These views found expression in the UK in a series of laws curtailing the rights of refugees and asylum seekers in terms of residence (through a forced dispersal policy) and access to cash benefits and through a 'streamlining' (i.e. cutting back) of appeals procedures.

The USA and the UK have both cast themselves as "global policeman," a role designed to ensure that their countries' strategic significance and economic interests are maintained as well as to reassert their dominance in the face of global change. So, for example, the alleged economic threat posed by Arab countries since the oil crisis of 1973 has become increasingly seen as one which transcends the market and has in fact to do with a threat to core political and cultural values. Islamophobia has served in part to legitimate the Gulf War in 1991, which, in turn reinforced the notion of the racialized construction of Islamic/Arab terrorism. Events such as the bombing of US embassies in Africa in the mid 1990s and destruction of New York's World Trade Towers on September 11, 2001 in turn provoked an escalation, at a local level, of racist attacks on people assumed to be of Arab/Muslim background.

The expression of WBC varies in intensity and form depending on historic and political factors. What underpins WBC as a whole is the threat posed to white privileges and the anxieties as well as countermeasures such threats provoke. WBC represents an attempt on the part of dominant white groups to reassert themselves in the face of a perceived or potential loss of dominance. The particular forms of backlash culture will depend on the nature of the threat, whether this be based on a heightened perception of numbers of minorities and/or cultural difference (both often media-inspired) or the result of efforts aimed at redressing inequalities through such policies as affirmative action, etc. WBC is as capable of expressing itself through far right-wing politics as it is through more sophisticated philosophical critiques of affirmative action and, as has been suggested, might even be held responsible for the limits and/or the appropriation of more liberal discourses such as multiculturalism by dominant white interests.

SEE ALSO: affirmative action; antiracism; asylum seeker; bigotry; British National Party; culturecide; education; equal opportunity; globalization; Islamophobia; Ku Klux Klan; meritocracy; multiculturalism; neo-nazism; Oklahoma bombing; policing; political correctness; refugee status; reverse racism; September 11, 2001; skinheads; White Power; whiteness

Reading

Backlash by Susan Faludi (Anchor Books, 1992) provides an excellent analysis of backlash culture in relationship to women in the USA.

The Death of Common Sense: How law is suffocating America by P. Howard (Random House, 1994) is an astringent polemic.

Up from Conservatism by M. Lemm (Free Press, 1996) and J. Gibson's *Warrior Dreams* (Hill &Wang, 1994) are two critical discussions of white backlash culture.

Whitewash by John Gabriel (Routledge, 1998) has a chapter on white backlash culture which draws on evidence from the UK and USA.

For two examples written from "within" white backlash culture, see *Invisible Victims: White males and the crisis of affirmative action* by F. Lynch (Greenwood, 1989) and *Anti-Racism: An assault on education and values* edited by F. Palmer (Sherwood, 1986). The latter includes Roger Scruton's essay on cultural relativism, cited in the main text above.

JOHN GABRIEL

WHITE FLIGHT

This term implies disillusionment with, even resentment of, social change. It refers to the movement of whites from neighborhoods and schools that have experienced recent changes in their ethnic composition. The nature of this change is sometimes voluntaristic – the pursuit of employment, perhaps, or cheap housing. It might also be contrived, however, stemming from a general commitment to what is known as the contact hypothesis. This is the belief that direct contact between whites and blacks will lessen the formers' fears about the latters' cultures and lifestyles, attenuate racial prejudice, and enhance the likelihood of integration, racial harmony, and social stability.

Social change along these lines derives from various sources. These include the policies of national governments. For instance, changes in the ethnic population of national states and particular regions within them might derive from alterations in the state's immigration policies. They might also stem from more localized initiatives. The determination, perhaps, of local government to ensure that residential areas and their schools comprise a more heterogeneous ethnic character. Another starting point might be the judiciary. In the USA the desegregation of schools gained momentum after 1954 when, in the *Brown* v. *Board of Education of Topeka, Kansas* case, the Supreme Court ruled that segregated education was unconstitutional.

White flight, then, is a sudden or gradual response to both *de jure* and *de facto* desegregation. Above all, it exemplifies what some white citizens might perceive as their own political inefficacy. Their inability, in other words, to stem the flow of black settlement in their neighborhoods or distract the state from its objective of achieving racial integration. Seen from this perspective, the state's determination to attain the goal of integration is pursued at the expense of the safety of their neighborhoods and schools, the retention of their particular (and traditional) identities, and the sanctity of their cultures and values. In both the USA and Britain, populist alarm at these state-orchestrated maneuvers to contrive a semblance of "racial balance" in neighborhoods and schools has often found a sympathetic ear in respective legislatures. In 1966, Ronald Reagan came to power in California partly on the strength of his committed opposition to the "rioters" in the Watts district of Los Angeles. In Britain, "white flight" was given implicit endorsement and legitimacy by Baroness Hooper, then the Conservative government's spokesperson for education in the House of Lords. In her support of parental choice of schools for their children, a key ideological and policy theme in the 1988 Education Reform Act, Baroness Hooper insisted that the Conservatives "did not wish to circumscribe that choice in any way." Baroness Hooper's pronouncement on the preeminence of parental choice prefigured what some have seen as the state's official benediction for white flight in the education system.

In 1987, Ms. Jenny Carney wrote to the Local Education Authority (LEA) of the British County of Cleveland requesting that it arrange for her daughter, Katrice, to be transferred from her multiracial infants school in Middlesbrough to one "where there will be the majority of white children." Ms. Carney's dissatisfaction with her daughter's school centered on its commitment to a multiracial and multifaith education. "I don't think it's right when she comes homes singing in Pakistani," she informed the LEA; "I know they only learn three Pakistani songs, but I just don't want her to learn this language."

While acceding to Ms. Carney's request, the LEA recognized that it was caught between two pieces of legislation which offered contradictory guidance on this matter. On the one hand, section 18 of the 1976 Race Relations Act states that "it is unlawful for an LEA, in carrying out

its functions under the Education Acts, to do any acts which constitute discrimination." By recognizing that Ms. Carney's request was influenced by the perceived racial characteristics of the school's pupil population, Cleveland was concerned that it had violated this section of the Act and broken the law. On the other hand, section 6 of the 1980 Education Act places upon LEAs a duty to comply with parental preferences as to choice of school, subject to certain exceptions, which were inapplicable here. According to the Commission for Racial Equality (CRE), Cleveland had breached the law; but it had not according to the then Secretary for State for Education, John MacGregor who viewed the 1980 Education Act as sacrosanct on the matter of parental choice. Against this background, the CRE sought a judicial review against Cleveland and the Secretary of State.

In October 1991, Mr. Justice Macpherson resolved in favor of Cleveland. He insisted that section 6 of the 1980 Education Act placed a singular mandatory duty upon LEAs which was not affected by the nature of the parents' requests. Nor did the judge accept the CRE's contention that "segregate" means to *keep* apart. In his view, Katrice's transfer to a school where 98 percent of the children were white suggested that while she was *moving* apart from ethnic minority children (her previous school included 40 percent of pupils of South Asian origin) she was not segregated (that is, kept apart) from them.

The CRE appealed against the decision. But in July 1992 the Court of Appeal upheld the original decision. Whether or not this gives the green light to white flight from multiracial schools remains to be seen. It does demonstrate, however, the weakness of the 1976 Race Relations Act and its inability, in particular, to prevent parents withdrawing their children from schools on explicitly racial grounds.

Can white flight be reversed? An unusual episode in Vicksburg, Missouri, USA, suggests that it can. In 2001, Vicksburg, like most other school districts along the southern Mississippi, was racially segregated in a *de facto* sense. White flight had long since accounted for the large number of white children who were either educated at private or parochial schools, or even educated at home. African American pupils were left to attend overcrowded schools, where there were typically only a handful of whites.

Vicksburg's response was to close down five

schools, renovate several others and build more on the outskirts of town. It also allowed parents to involve themselves in the development of the curriculum. But the most influential reform was known as "controlled school choice": parents were invited to choose from three schools closest to their home. When the selections were in, the school district began deliberations on allocations, and 85 per cent of parents got their first choice. Controversially, race was used as a consideration in making assignments to achieve diversity in each school; the results yielded near-equal counts of black and white pupils. The long-term effects of the Vicksburg experiment are yet to be seen, but the lesson seemed to be that white flight is not as irreversible as many have presumed.

SEE ALSO: bigotry; *Brown v. Board of Education*; busing; education; homelessness; multiculturalism; segregation; white backlash culture

Reading

"Ending white flight" by Jodie Morse at *Time.Com* (2002) is a report of the episode cited in the main text above: available at *http://www.time.com/time/reports/mississippi/vicksburg.html*.

The Logic of Racism by Ellis Cashmore (Allen & Unwin, 1987) provides a testimony to the view that white citizens, especially those in run-down neighborhoods, often invoke cultural differences as a metaphor for their own political impotence and perceived disenfranchisement. The interviews indicate how resentment is evoked once the rights of white individuals are seen to be violated in favor of the rights of groups.

Racial Justice in America: A reference handbook by David B. Mustard (ABC-Clio, 2002) looks at education and housing, among other key areas of division and conflict.

The Struggle for Black Equality 1954–1980 by Harvard Sitkoff, (Hill & Wang, 1981) provides an historical account of campaigners for desegregation in the USA and the white backlash that this movement has engendered.

"Tolerating intolerance" by Carol Vincent (in *Journal of Education Policy*, vol. 7, no. 1, 1992) examines the background to debates within and likely consequences of the Macpherson ruling on the Cleveland LEA case.

BARRY TROYNA

WHITE POWER

White Power is a slogan, battle cry, subcultural marker, and race-nationalist concept integral to the heterogeneous worldwide milieu of "Aryan" activists and ideologues. Coined in 1966 by George Lincoln Rockwell (1918–67), founder of the American Nazi Party and chairman of the now defunct World Union of National Socialists, the concept was formulated in response to the black civil rights movement's fight to end racial segregation in the USA and in the face of more radical demands for Black Power (coined by Congressman Adam Clayton Powell of Harlem and popularized by H. Rap Brown earlier the same year). With the concept of White Power, Rockwell initiated a national socialist shift away from the narrow Aryan/Germanic ultra-nationalist position of Hitler towards the inclusive pan-Aryan race nationalist perspective that informs much of the current white-racist culture. At the time, Rockwell's willingness to include non-Nordic people, such as the Polish, Russians, Greeks, Turks, Spanish, and Italians as "white" provoked ideological resentment from both Hitlerite Nordic purists and believers true to the legacy of Anglo-Saxon supremacy that long had dominated the alchemy of race and nation in American society. Informed by the then culminating process to construct a monolithic "white" race – whereby the previously distinct Nordic, Alpine, Mediterranean etc. "races" metamorphosed into a plethora of different "ethnics" – to secure "white" power over "black" people in American society, Rockwell's thinking was in line with the times and his position would eventually secure the largest following.

Powerlessness and the claim to supremacy

At its heart, invoking the concept of White Power involves a notion of powerlessness, of having been deprived an exalted position conceived of as birthright privileges. Issued at the heights of the conflict over racial segregation, Rockwell's call for White Power came at a time when white racists felt their claims of supremacy were threatened but not yet lost. Although calling himself a revolutionary, Rockwell insisted on loyalty to the constitution and the laws of the United States and believed that the imagined Jewish conspiracy for world dominion could be halted, as it was not yet considered complete. None of Rockwell's organizational efforts achieved any importance before his assassination in 1967. The significance of Rockwell is rather in the legacy he bequeathed the white-racist scene for which the concept of White Power became a unifying tool in the decades to come.

As the 1960s gave way to the 1970s, racial desegregation became more of a reality than a threat and mainstream American society decisively turned towards a multicultural conception of the American "nation." National liberation movements all over Africa and Asia successfully braved the old colonial world order and a series of new states achieved independence. Racism was seriously challenged in science, education, religion, politics, sports, media, and culture. Gradually, racism lost its previous notion of adequacy as a mode of social classification, transforming its believers from good citizens to social villains. Organized white racist opposition to this overall process grew increasingly more radical, desperate and fragmented with each defeat. How could white racism, long thought of as mandated by God and the law of nature, now suddenly be sent off to the garbage heap of obsolete ideas? Cast into confusion, white racist ideologues developed various conspiracy theories alleging that an evil cabal of racial enemies, often but not exclusively known under the acronym ZOG (Zionist Occupational Government), had usurped the power of the US administration and every government throughout the "once white world." The perspective involves an elevation of Jews into an omnipotent body of malicious power; a key component in the conspiracy for world dominion that may also include assorted others such as bankers, plutocrats, aliens, or the illuminati. The cabal is typically thought to be masterminding a plan to eliminate the one force with innate qualities strong enough to thwart their scheme: the freedom-loving white race. Pushing racial equality, multiculturalism, immigration, and re-location of industries from "white" nations to nonwhite countries, the imagined cabal is alleged with blending all the cultures of man into a single soulless, mongrel race of easily manipulated and exchangeable units of production. The white man accordingly is believed to be a rapidly diminishing minority at the brink of extermination. White Power activists see themselves as the "last resort" of a righteous "resistance." The brave heroes that dare to resist ZOG rule risk being assassinated or unjustly thrown into the "federal dungeons." With a logic that might seem bizarre from the perspective of an African, Asian or Latin American, white racists have hereby come to adopt an *underdog* position from which their call for White Power assumes a revolutionary dimension in the mental universe of Aryan activists.

Commenced in the late 1970s and early 1980s, the ZOG theory gained from the dismantling of the Soviet Union whereby communism disappeared as a distracting foe to the radical right, home to many – but far from all – racist activists. The radicalization of the white racist scene in the USA involved a dismissal of the traditional far right as CRAP (Christian Rightwing American Patriots), a phrase coined by White Power ideologue David Lane, imprisoned member of the notorious guerilla group *Brüders Schweigen* (known as the Order after the best-selling race war novel *The Turner Diaries* by William Pierce). Denouncing the traditional far right as blinded by their patriotism to swear allegiance with an administration controlled by racial enemies, CRAP's stance involves two important aspects of the current White Power scene. First, the declaration of war against the federal government facilitated the construction of a global White Power culture by bridging the US scene with European fascism that has been anti-American since the US intervention in World War II. Second, it demonstrates the distinction between, as White Power activists put it, the "right wing" and the "white wing."

Blended ideologies

White Power ideologies typically feature anticapitalist as well as anticommunist sentiments, not infrequently presenting their alternative as the "third position" as seen in the slogan "neither left, nor right, but forward." Politically, White Power ideologues adopt elements from both the right and the left. Hailing god, nation, patriarchy, heterosexuality, social Darwinism, and anti-egalitarianism, White Power activists may also address white working-class issues, environmental concerns, and may want society to provide for elderly poor and single mothers as practical points derived from their ideals of racial solidarity. They may want to curtail corporate power and reorganize production to serve the interest of the people (i.e. the Aryan Folk) rather than the (Jewish) plutocrats. This blend of rightist and leftist themes is part of the logic behind the seemingly paradoxical red–brown alliances, prolific not least in post-Soviet Russia, and a factor behind the electoral inroad of White

Power-oriented populist parties among traditionally leftist constituencies in Western Europe.

The related factors of a generational shift, the rise of the White Power music industry and the revolution of communication technology have accompanied the radicalization of the White Power scene. The past two decades have witnessed the influx of a new generation of racist activists into a scene that had begun to look like a home for retired people. Defined by its lyrics, White Power music covers a wide range of genres, including ska, Oi!, noise, hatecore, nu metal, and folk. Transnational since its inception in the late 1970s and early 1980s, White Power music today is a global industry with several hundred contributing acts from all continents, and has become a prime recruitment tool that has also proved financially profitable. Across the world, white racist concerts organized for April 20 (Hitler's birthday), August 17 (the death of Rudolf Hess), or December 8 (Day of Martyrs) function as revivalist White Power meetings with the musicians acting as high priests inviting born-again Aryans to accept the transformative truth of White Power. White Power music fanzines, such as *Resistance*, *Nordland* or *Blood & Honor* mix reviews of White Power bands with ideological articles and ads by White Power record labels. Pioneering White Power cyber activism was former Ku Klux Klan leader Louis Beam, who in 1984 constructed the Aryan Nations Liberty Net that linked a dozen computerized white-racist information bases. With the first White Power web site *Stormfront* (launched in 1996 by former Imperial Wizard Don Black), White Power cyber activism exploded with several hundred White Power web sites, electronic newsletters, e-zines, dating pages, and chat groups. A main avenue of White Power ideology production and dissemination, the internet allows even the loneliest white racist believer to enter a world in which White Power is at least a virtual reality.

While there are women activists and a few female organizations, the White Power scene is predominantly populated by white males. Through race war novels, White Power music, and the art of White Power, is produced a romanticized warrior ideal which is frequently added to the construction of an Aryan male identity. Knightly values such as courage, strength, honesty, honor, and glory are hailed as primary Aryan virtues. The white woman is presented as an endangered species, a shining jewel of pristine cleanliness surrounded by dribbling perverts at a sinking island in an ocean of filth, setting the stage for the Noble Aryan Warrior to come to her rescue. Frequently illustrated with medieval knights and raging Vikings, White Power tabloids, web pages, and CDs features a bombastic language more suited to heroic legends of the past than contemporary politics. Aryan activism provide its adherents with an opportunity to be part of a Grand Narrative by which he, as warrior, can rise above the trivialities of the everyday commoner and emerge in shining armor at the battleground for the final conflict, lifting his sword for race, nation, blood and honor.

A class analysis of the US scene reveals that the majority of White Power activists come from families where the father had been a military officer, farmer, small businessman, policeman, lower white collar or skilled worker. Activists typically see themselves as descendants of those who "built their country" and thus are entitled to certain "birthright privileges" now being "negated." While surprising to those accustomed to the "white trash" thesis of media produce, this well matches the constituency mobilized by the German NSDAP in the 1930s. Nor does the popular stereotype of the barely literate White Power activist fit a scene in which the level of education is slightly above average. Moreover, the milieu hails the ideals of classic Western learning and most groups expect activists to increase their learning through study.

The myth of racial rebirth

The White Power scene revolves around a mythic notion of racial rebirth, typically specifying rejuvenation through violence as the route of redemption. Transcending national borders, music and electronic communication have facilitated a global flow of ideas, engaging racist radicals across the world in the vision of a future in which race will define nation. Rendered meaning according to context, the notion of White Power has divided the scene into two distinct, albeit not necessarily exclusive, orientations: a narrower ultra-nationalist project to cleanse an already defined nation-state of all considered aliens (e.g. England for the English), and a more ambitious race-nationalist object that transcends the existing national borders, aiming at establishing a transatlantic or even global "white homeland." The mythic core of White Power ideologies may also lend itself to religious interpretations. Comparatively more common to the North American than the European scene, a wide spectrum of white racist religions has become part of the White Power world. Among the more influential are racist recasts of Christianity that identify whites as the chosen people of God and decry Jews as "counterfeit Israel"; euro-tribal constructs that aim at reviving some pre-Christian tradition, such as Celtic, Norse or Greek, typically interpreting the ancient creed as the "racial soul" of the Aryan folk; and occult national socialism that may see Hitler as an avatar of Vishnu or believe that he still is alive as leader of a superhuman Aryan race located inside the hollow earth, as in the esoteric works by Miguel Serrano, the leading occult fascist in the Latin-speaking world.

The mushrooming alternative religions competing for the souls of Aryan activists indicate a final important feature of the current White Power scene: its high level of infighting and fragmentation. Scattered in literally hundreds of mainly dysfunctional and microscopic parties, congregations, secret societies, and armed cells that form and dissolve with astonishing speed, the Aryan "resistance" is anything but united, and spends more time attacking each other than the perceived "racial enemies." This further underscores the importance of White Power as a core concept that enables an otherwise fundamentally factious world to take on a resemblance of unity by offering a symbol vague enough for every believer to project his or her desire upon.

SEE ALSO: anti-Semitism; Aryan; bigotry; Black Power; British National Party; culturecide; Doomed Races Doctrine; ethnocide; geometry of race; fascism; Ku Klux Klan; neo-nazism; Oklahoma bombing; *Protocols of the Learned Elders of Zion*; racism; reverse racism; skinheads; social Darwinism; violence; *Volk*; Wagner, Richard; white backlash culture; white race; whiteness

Reading

Black Sun by Nicholas Goodrick-Clarke (State University of New York Press 2002) analyses neo-nazism as a new alternative religion.
Dreamer of the Day: Francis Parker Yockey and the postwar fascist international by Kevin Coogan (Automedia, 2000) discusses, among other things,

the leftist dimension in postwar transnational fascism.
Gods of the Blood: The pagan revival and white separatism by Mattias Gardell (Duke University Press, 2003) discusses the formation of a White Power culture with a special focus on racist paganism.
The Nature of Fascism by Roger Griffin (Routledge, 1991) is an excellent theoretical analysis of fascism; this may profitably be read in conjunction with *The Emergence of a Euro-American Radical Right* by Jeffrey Kaplan and Leonard Weinberg (Routledge, 1998) which highlights the transatlantic links between the White Power scenes of Europe and the USA.
Religion and the Racist Right by Michael Barkun (University of North Carolina Press, 1997) is a brilliant study of white racist Christianity.
Whiteness of a Different Color by Matthew Frye Jacobson (Harvard University Press 1988) is one of several eminent studies of the construction of whiteness.

MATTIAS GARDELL

WHITE RACE

The invention of white men

The concept of an inclusive category of a white race has its origins in the second half of the seventeenth century and was the result of a social transformation of English, Irish, Scottish, and other European colonizers of America. The transformation entailed homogenizing the statuses of tenants, merchants, planters and so on into a new status – members of a race. As Lerone Bennett writes: "The first white colonists had no concept of themselves as *white* men ... The word *white*, with all its burden of guilt and arrogance, did not come into common usage until the latter part of the [seventeenth] century."

Bennett points out that white servitude was a precursor to the exploitation of blacks: "Before the invention of the Negro or the white man or the words and concepts to describe them, the colonial population consisted largely of a great mass of white and black bondsmen, who occupied roughly the same economic category and were treated with equal contempt by the lords of the plantations and legislatures." Aligning with the plantocracy as "white" meant unburdening themselves of the harshest aspects of bondage.

Theodore Allen favors similar terminology in his *The Invention of the White Race*, which pays particular attention to the experiences of migrant

Irish, once victimized and disparaged as degenerate and not amenable to civilizing influences, yet later transformed into defenders against an exploitative order. The Irish were certainly regarded by English colonizers as an inferior racial group (colonization of Ireland took place through the sixteenth century), but were physically indistinct from the English. There were other groups that would today be recognized as white that were readily associated with savagery. But, it became expedient to co-opt them.

Organized antislavery movements were active in the seventeenth century and their remit included the abolition of both slavery and the slave trade that fed it and the recognition of slaves as sentient human beings, rather than chattels. In repudiation of this, supporters of slavery rationalized the treatment of slaves as livestock by projecting a racist argument. Blacks were slaves, it was contended, because they were so naturally, genotypically, and thus were permanently inferior. As the need for a sharper, clearly defined barrier of delineation became more pressing, so the criterion of color became more useful.

In this context, white skin was imbued with new significance – as a means of control. In late seventeenth-century North America, poor Europeans, some indentured, were endowed with unprecedented civil and social privileges compared to those of Africans. This privilege was an acknowledgment of their loyalty to the colonial land- and property-owning class and established what might be recognized as race privileges. Primary emphasis on race was not, at first, widespread: it occurred only in areas where plantation owners could not form a social control apparatus without the additional support of propertyless groups of European extraction. Virginia and Massachusetts had plenty of white *de facto* slaves and these states promoted the new status. For poor whites, this was a welcome adjustment to a well-established system.

The application of scientific reasoning to the understanding of the white race did not occur until after 1790 with abolitionists by then active and gaining credibility. The concept of a white race became a "rational" defense against the dissolution of slavery and served to enhance the image of black peoples as naturally suited to servitude and labor. Johann Blumenbach's classification, published in 1795, included caucasians, who constituted the light-skinned division of the world's population and were supposed to originate from Caucasus, the mountain range in Eastern Europe. They were, he argued, the most handsome; in contrast to Mongolians and Ethiopians (his other racial categories). Subsequent racial theories strayed only marginally from this conclusion, Aryans (Max Müller) and the Germanic race (Gobineau) being synonyms for whites. The gloss of scientific credibility was lent to the belief in the innate superiority of whites and the European domination of most parts of the world reinforced this.

There was a comparable expediency about the Latin colonial world's invention of a white race. Faced with a confusing range of phenotypical variation in the eighteenth century (Latin colonies did not legislate against the intermarriage or miscegenation of Africans, Indians and Europeans), the Spanish created *los peninsulares*, a category that signified social status and natural advantage. Based on *pureza de sangre* (pure blood), this was a way of separating those born in Spain, including *los criollos*, from all others.

Racial worldview

By the time of publication of John Van Eurie's widely read *White Supremacy and Negro Subordination* in 1861, the concept of a white race was well integrated into what Audrey Smedley calls a "racial world-view" in which social differentiation was understood in terms of natural inequalities. Van Eurie advanced a conception of a white race that bizarrely included, among others, Attila the Hun, Genghis Khan, and Confucius – all leaders of one kind or another, but none of whom would be recognized as white today. This kind of racial worldview could not be sustained without a property that at once excluded inferior races and included (and so integrated) the superior ones; whiteness was that property. Because whiteness signified superiority and privilege, it worked to devalue any skin color that did not qualify and render possessors of that skin Others.

In this sense, the white race developed in contradistinction to blackness, which has a longer genealogy, stretching back to the Christian period when the color acquired negative connotations and became associated with sin and darkness. In his *White on Black: Images of Africa and blacks in Western popular culture* (Yale University Press, 1992), Jan Nederveen Pieterse shows how Islam adopted black to symbolize demons. His study also indicates that blackness appeared in European iconography from the twelfth and fifteenth centuries and was portrayed positively. It seems that only after the seventeenth century and the rise of European colonialism did blackness become denigrated and yoked with savagery and inferiority; though some scholars argue that blackness was linked with inferiority via traditional Christian associations, stemming from the biblical Curse of Ham.

Winthrop Jordan contends in *White Man's Burden* (Oxford University Press, 1974) that, for the colonial English, white was the color of purity and perfection. So the very blackness of Africans' skin was traumatic enough to ensure a European bias against them. The view gains support from Carl Degler's proposal (in *Neither Black Nor White: Slavery and race relations in Brazil and the United States*, University of Wisconsin Press, 1986) that the negative values deriving from the color black served to set Africans apart from other subservient groups.

In contemporary times, whiteness signifies not so much superiority or purity, but privilege and power: it confers advantages and prestige. It also sets normative standards: until recently the term "nonwhite" inscribed deviance and stigmata. Whiteness remains meaningful only in particular kinds of discourses or contexts: specifically, those in which superficial, observable features are supposed to be indices of deeper, perhaps immutable differences. Recognizing color in this way both validates these putative differences, maintains barriers and sustains the myth of a white race.

SEE ALSO: antislavery; Aryan; caucasian; creole; Fanon, Frantz; Garvey, Marcus; genotype; geometry of race; Gobineau, Joseph Arthur de; Irish; miscegenation; *négritude*; Other; race: as classification; race: as signifier; race: as synonym; slavery; white backlash culture; White Power; whiteness

Reading

The Invention of the White Race: Racial oppression and social control by Theodore Allen (Verso, 1994) is a powerful treatise on the construction of the white race as a discrete entity to meet the demands of changing social and ideological conditions; it is complemented by *The Shaping of Black America: The struggles and triumphs of African-Americans, 1619 to the 1990s* by Lerone Bennett (Penguin, 1993) which advances the view that "Black bonds-

men inherited their chains from white bondsmen, who were, in a manner of speaking, America's first slaves."

Race in North America: Origin and evolution of a worldview by Audrey Smedley (Westview Press, 1993) is a study of the establishment of racial conceptions and, as such, shows how the meanings of color terms "insinuated their way, perhaps subliminally" into European – especially English – thought.

White Identities: An historical and international introduction by Alastair Bonnett (Longman, 2000) is an accessible account of the impact of whiteness on a global scale.

"White privileges and black burdens: the continuing impact of oppression" is chapter 6 of Joe R. Feagin's *Racist America: Roots, current realities and future reparations* (Routledge, 2001) and discusses what the author calls "the set of benefits and advantages inherited by each generation of those defined as 'white'."

WHITE SUPREMACY *see* neo-nazism;

WHITENESS

Whiteness is an attribute that is used to describe European heritage people's skin color and, hence, to depict them physically as a race. This identification has tied whiteness to the development of a racial hierarchy, in which it occupies a central position, being used as: (1) evidence of natural, innate, superiority; and (2) the norm and standard of racial identity against which Others (the "nonwhites") are measured. This history has seen older, nonracial, notions of white identity fall into disuse. Before we can explain the role of whiteness in modern racialized societies, it is necessary to understand this transition in a little more detail.

The rise of racial whiteness

People have been calling themselves and others "white" for many centuries and in many parts of the world. The distinction between whites and blacks in the Middle East has been dated to the expansion of Islam into Africa in the eighth century, according to Bernard Lewis, in his *Race and Color in Islam* (Harper & Row, 1971). Sinologists such as Frank Dikötter record that the Chinese "developed a white–black polarity at a very early stage ... and called their complexion white from the most ancient days" (in *The Discourse of Race in Modern China*, Stanford University Press, 1992). The association of whiteness with the upper strata of society is also evident in China. To have a pale complexion was taken to be an indicator of leading a sheltered, civilized life and, hence, as distinguishing one from those such as laborers and peasants, whose skin was exposed to the elements. The link between whiteness and social standing was made in many other places also. In Europe, a sense of this association is retained today in the expression "blue blood," which is used to describe people with an aristocratic lineage. This phrase derives from the notion that the skin of genuine aristocrats is so pale that one can see the blood in their veins. An association between whiteness and purity and, hence, religiosity, may also be discerned in medieval and early modern Europe.

However, none of these forms of white identity indicated a belief in a "white race," or of "white people" as a discrete type or group. A fetishization of whiteness as a key marker of identity developed much later, with the rise of European *racial* thinking and the related belief that *only Europeans could be white*. As this implies, it was once commonplace for Europeans to describe non-Europeans as white: Chinese, Arabs, Indians and many other people who appeared to European travelers to have a pale complexion were called white. It is instructive that the first instance that is recorded by the *Oxford English Dictionary* of white being used as an ethnic term refers, not to Europeans, but to a depiction, from 1604, of indigenous Latin Americans: Grimstone's translation of Acosta's *The Natural and Morall Historie of the East and West Indies* descries "a part of Peru, and of the new kingdom of Grenado, [where] ... the inhabitants are white."

To understand why whiteness became a central marker of European superiority and, therefore, something that non-Europeans were barred from, we must consider its role in the rise of racial thinking. The use of "white" as a term to distinguish a particular race, and as designating the top slot in the racial hierarchy, emerged over a considerable period. In the English-speaking world, it appears to have become a clear, scientifically consolidated phenomenon, in the early nineteenth century. However, even more striking is the colonial context in which whiteness first became a central category in the organization of society. Writing in the early years of the nineteenth century, perhaps the most influential explorer of South America, Alexander von Humbolt, noted that

In Spain it is kind of nobility not to descend from Jews or Moors. In [Spanish] America, the skin, more or less white, is what dictates the class that an individual occupies in society. A white, even if he rides barefoot on horseback, considers himself a member of the nobility of the country. (cited by Magnus Mörner in *Race Mixture in the History of Latin America*, Little, Brown & Company, 1967)

Another illuminating illustration from the Americas of the shift that led towards whiteness being seen as European property may be seen in Nathanial Rogers's editorial intervention on William Wood's 1634 text on natural history, *New England's Prospect*. Following the assumptions of his time, Wood had noted that American natives "are born fair." When Rogers came to edit the text in 1764, this kind of statement was no longer unacceptable but was "one of the popular errors given into by our author" says Rogers. Some years earlier, in 1751, Benjamin Franklin had already indicated how closely access to whiteness should be regulated, a theme that was to dominate discussion of the topic in the USA over the next two centuries. The "number of purely white people in the world is proportionably very small," said Franklin. Moreover, it is "Saxons" (i.e. Anglo-Saxons) who "make the principal body of white people." Other Europeans, Franklin tells us, "are generally of what we call a swarthy complexion" (cited in *Whiteness of a Different Color* by Matthew Jacobson, Harvard University Press, 1998).

The restrictions placed on those who could be classified as white were made inevitable by the developing relationship between whiteness and social, cultural and economic power. This also explains how and why whiteness was "imported" into Europe from settler societies in the mid-to-late nineteenth century and used to narrate and naturalize class distinctions, more specifically to create a metaphorical association between the European underclass and nonwhiteness. An indication of this process may be gained from the depictions of the "savages," "human baboon's" and "toiling slave[s]" found in Booth's 1890 text, *Darkest England and the Way Out*, depictions echoed in numerous other *fin de siècle* tales of what later authors were to call the European "sub-man." These narratives are also illustrative of the removal of whiteness from scientific debate and its absorption into popular culture.

Ironically, racial scientists of the period tended to have a much wider sense of who was white, often including Indians, Arabs and many Africans in what they variously called the white, Caucasian or Aryan race. Yet racial scientists were marginal to the debate: racial whiteness was not about objective facts or natural groups but about the symbolic legitimization and structuring of power relations.

The social and economic role of whiteness (and how it is changing)

Once it had been established as the central symbol of European racial power, whiteness began to take on an important function in the organization of colonial and European societies. Three basic roles may be discerned, the importance and practice of each varying considerably between different countries and regions. The first is *ideological*: whiteness was used as a justification for the power and prestige of European heritage peoples, as well as constituting a site of solidarity and identity for this group. In this way a racial bond was established, a bond which ensured that white people had a cultural and economic stake in aligning themselves with other whites.

Second, whiteness became a mechanism for the *organization of society*. This function is particularly apparent in the logic of imperialism and within colonial societies, where access to different occupations and labor organizations, familial, cultural and social affiliations and economic leverage (i.e., what one's labor was worth) was often determined by one's position vis-à-vis whiteness (either by way of a white/nonwhite binary split or through a gradual loss of socioeconomic power the further away from whiteness one was imagined to be). Third, whiteness developed a *psychological* dimension: the formation of personality through the construction of self and Other became bound up with a racialized set of fears and desires concerning the nature of whiteness (especially in respect to notions of purity and defilement) and its loss or acquisition.

In practice these three aspects of whiteness were mutually supportive. One of the first critical investigators of whiteness as a social and historical phenomenon, W. E. B. Du Bois, writing in the early 1930s about the 1860s and 1870s, noted of "the white group of laborers" in the USA, that

While they received a low wage, were compensated in part by a sort of public and psychological wage. They were given public deference and titles of courtesy because they were white. They were admitted freely with all classes of white people to public functions, public parks, and the best schools … The newspapers specialized on news that flattered the poor whites and almost utterly ignored the Negro except in crime and ridicule. (*Black Reconstruction in America: 1860–1880*, Touchstone, 1995)

DuBois also exemplifies another of the ironies of whiteness: that whiteness is often more visible to people who feel White Power acting against them than to white people themselves. In his essay "The souls of white folk," Du Bois wrote, "Of them I am singularly clairvoyant. I see in and through them" (in Roediger, below).

However, whiteness is not a static phenomenon. Its changing cultural and economic role in the West and across the world shows it to be a persistent but flexible current. Much antiracist discussion of whiteness over the past thirty years has been dominated by a concern to show that whiteness "still matters" and that the hierarchies and inequality associated with it are, if not as bad as ever, at least, "still with us." The problem with this approach is that it makes it hard for critics to respond to, or engage with, some of the most important changes that have influenced the story of whiteness since the start of the last century. These changes have not made whiteness less important but they do suggest that the tradition of fixing it as the unchanging, demonic center of racism is no longer sufficient.

Two of the most significant changes that can be observed are: (1) the demotion of whiteness within public discourse; and (2) the role of whiteness within the symbolic economy of neoliberal capitalism. In respect to the former, it must first be noted that, from the first two decades of the twentieth century, whiteness was beginning to appear a troublesome and increasingly illegitimate form of social affiliation. Within British political and social commentary, a shift can be discerned away from whiteness to less obviously racialized categories. The rise of a "Western" identity appears to be of particular significance in this transition. The development of genetics and the identification of racism with both bad science and bad governments encouraged this development. However, it was also spurred by the egalitarian class logic of white supremacism, which implied that all whites, no matter their class position, were fundamentally of the same kind. This kind of solidarity proved unacceptable to social elitists, who saw in the proletarian "sub-man" and the Bolshevik revolution, dire threats to "Western civilization."

By the end of the twentieth century, only the most marginal of public figures made explicit use of the rhetoric of white superiority. Whiteness was retained in coded and euphemistic forms, but it had suffered a considerable demotion within public discourse. This process has had knock-on effects on the employment and deployment of whiteness in each of the three basic roles of whiteness identified earlier.

The globalization of neo-liberal capitalism and commodity culture also appears to be having a significant impact on the way in which whiteness is employed. Although relatively little research has been undertaken on this relationship, a number of studies on the role of whiteness in advertising and popular culture in contemporary East Asia and South America imply that some new trends in the way whiteness is "used" may be emerging. More specifically, an association of whiteness with an apolitical, consumerist lifestyle is being deployed, so that whiteness can be temporally and symbolically bought into like other lifestyle choices, i.e., owned, mutated, indigenized, mocked, refused. These processes clearly rely on the traditional role of whiteness as an identity and socioeconomic role to aspire to. However, they also suggest that one of the reasons whiteness is proving such a persistent current in the contemporary world is that it is highly adaptable.

SEE ALSO: American Indians; Aryan; bigotry; caste; colonial discourse; cultural identity; Doomed Races Doctrine; double consciousness; essentialism; Fanon, Frantz; Freyre, Gilberto; geometry of race; Hall, Stuart; hybridity; indigenous peoples; *Invisible Man*; Other; Park, Robert Ezra; postcolonial; race: as classification; race: as signifier; race; as synonym; racial coding; racialization; science; sexuality; white backlash culture; White Power; white race

Reading

Black on White: Black writers on what it means to be white, edited by David Roediger (Schocken Books, 1998), is an important collection that gathers analyses from African Americans, from 1830 onwards, on the forms and meaning of whiteness.

Wages of Whiteness: Race and the making of the American working class by David Roediger (Verso, 1992) remains the seminal statement of critical "white studies" in the USA.

White by Richard Dyer (Routledge, 1997) looks at the origins of white identity, its modern cultural expression and relationship with gender.

White Identities: Historical and international perspectives by Alastair Bonnett (Pearson Education, 2000) discusses the development of whiteness around the world as well as the relationship between whiteness and modernity.

"White skin, large breasts: Chinese beauty advertising as cultural discourse" by Perry Johansson (in *China Information*, vol. 12, 2/3: 59–84, 1998) provides a useful illustration of how whiteness is being employed in contemporary cultural politics and commercial life in China.

White Women, Race Matters: The social construction of whiteness by Ruth Frankenberg (University of Minnesota Press, 1993) provides a contemporary, interview-based account of the place of whiteness in white women's lives in the USA.

ALASTAIR BONNETT

WIK DECISION *see* Aboriginal Australians; One Nation

X

XENOPHOBIA

A term that means literally fear of strangers (from the Greek *xenos* for strange and "phobia," a fear or aversion). Once regarded as a psychological condition – used to describe persons who feared or abhorred groups regarded as "outsiders" – its more recent application has been in the context of attacks on immigrants and asylum seekers in Western Europe.

The European Parliament's Committee of Inquiry into the Rise of Racism and Fascism in Europe (1985) identified xenophobia as a new type of specter haunting Europe. The committee's report led to the 1986 declaration against racism and xenophobia signed on behalf of the EU's main institutions and the EU has continued subsequently to use the two expressions as a pair without differentiating between them. The Heads of State and Government of the Council of Europe, in their Vienna declaration of 1993, adopted a plan of action against manifestations of racism, xenophobia, anti-Semitism, and intolerance, which led to the establishment of the European Commission against Racism and Intolerance. In 1993, the UN appointed a Special Rapporteur on Racism and Xenophobia.

In Germany, the word *Rassismus* is uncomfortably associated with the Nazi era. German institutions are more ready to refer to *Fremdenfeindlichkeit* and to translate this into English as xenophobia. This is one factor underlying the increased reference to xenophobia in internationally agreed documents.

In France, sociologists write of a principle of inferiorization and exploitation which allows the victim group a place in society so long as it is at the bottom; and of a principle of differentiation which represents the Other group as so different that it must be segregated, expelled, or destroyed. Opposition to continued immigration, in France as in other European countries, has in the last thirty years lead to more stress upon cultural than supposed biological differences.

If racism and xenophobia are to be distinguished, racism can be seen as relying on ideas of inferiority, whereas xenophobia relies on ideas of fundamental differences between cultures.

SEE ALSO: bigotry; Dollard, John; Other; prejudice; racism; scapegoat; skinheads; white backlash culture

Reading

The Arena of Racism by Michael Wieviorka (Sage, 1995) is a more contemporary treatment of the concept.

"Hostility and fear in social life" by John Dollard (in *Social Forces*, vol. 17, 1938) is an early theoretical statement on fears and prejudices.

Nationalism and Social Theory by Gerard Delanty and Patrick O'Mahoney (Sage, 2002) interprets xenophobia in the twenty-first century as one of the newer variants of radical nationalism.

The Nature of Prejudice by Gordon Allport (Addison-Wesley, 1954) is a classic social psychological text exploring the roots of prejudice.

CHECK: internet resources section under hate groups

MICHAEL BANTON

YOUTH SUBCULTURES

Youth subcultures refer to substrata of young people whose attitudes, identities, tastes, and practices cohere, over time, around a configuration of mutually understood values. While youth subcultures were initially regarded as exclusively white and largely male phenomena, later research focused on their porous mutability and their role in creating new ethnicities that are not bound to traditional, national or local ties and contribute to emerging multicultures.

Though rarely consistent, the stylized practices of subcultures – which are expressed visually through dress and music and aurally through language and argot – may be seen as part of a wider ideological ensemble. Indeed, a feature of youth subcultures is that they are positioned by themselves or others as *sub*terranean, *sub*ordinate and, at least potentially, *sub*versive (*sub* meaning a lower position). "Spectacular" accounts of, for example, skinheads, rastafarians, punks and ravers, sit alongside more prosaic accounts of subcultures in schools, prisons and the workplace. However, having been subject to a series of critiques, the concept of youth subculture has become increasingly contentious and some writers have declared the "death" of the term. We will approach youth subcultures by examining the history of intellectual interest in them, before moving on to an assessment of contemporary developments, particularly in ethnic subcultural fusion.

Beyond deviancy

Producing a rich vein of material from the 1920s, scholars at the University of Chicago's Department of Sociology and Anthropology pioneered subcultural studies. The Chicago School was associated with the exploration of what was thought to be the shadier recesses of society. Its work focused on young gangs, drug-taking and cockfighting groups. In contrast to criminological traditions which held that "deviant behavior" was the product of individual tastes and personality defects, the Chicago School argued persuasively that crime and juvenile delinquency (as it was called) should be understood from *within* the context of the working-class neighborhoods, ghettos and slums from whence they arose. William Foote Whyte's study of Boston gang life, first published in 1943, revealed an organized, hierarchical and rule-bound *Street Corner Society* (University of Chicago Press, 1981). Later studies by, *inter alia* Albert Cohen and Howard Becker, revealed that, judged from the subculture members' perspective, "deviance" was normal rather than pathological conduct.

In Britain, the shift from viewing youth subculture as delinquent gained currency in the research of Jock Young (*The Drugtakers: The social meaning of drug use*, Paladin, 1971) and Stanley Cohen, whose influential work, *Folk Devils and Moral Panics* (Paladin, 1973), demonstrated the important role of the media in amplifying behavior and generating hysterical social reactions. The links between youth subcultures, deviancy and race were later made explicit in *Policing the Crisis* by Stuart Hall, Charles Critcher, Tony Jefferson and John Clarke (Macmillan, 1978). This analysis explored how "mugging" (a term imported from the USA) developed into a *racialized* trope used to draw a fine distinction between black crime and other types of street crime. Dark fantasies of the urban African Caribbean mugger were vividly kept alive in accusatory press reports of the inner-city uprisings that swept through multiethnic parts of Britain in the first half of the 1980s. The racialized portrayal of black youth as wild, rebellious and incompatible with national culture would later be revisited in the popular debate concerning Yardie and hip-hop ("gangsta") culture and, following disturbances in 2001, South Asian youth subcultures.

Hall and his colleagues from the University of Birmingham's Centre for Contemporary Cultural Studies offered several eloquent accounts of youth subcultures, their studies reflecting a commitment to Marxist and neo-Marxist traditions. By adapting Antonio Gramsci's concept of hegemony, the Birmingham School writers elaborated an analysis that interpreted the loaded surfaces of youth style as a cultural arena within which class conflict and struggle symbolically materialized. Here, subcultural practices – as expressed through such diverse groups as Teddy Boys (from the 1950s), mods (from the 1960s), and skinheads and rastas (from the 1970s) – were regarded as a form of *Resistance Through Rituals*, as the title of one of Hall and Tony Jefferson's edited collections expressed it (Hutchinson, 1975). In his essay "The skinheads and the magical recovery of community," John Clarke argued that the youth subculture that aligned itself with neo-nazism and systematically preyed on South Asians, represented "an attempt to re-create through the 'mob' the traditional working class community as a substitution for the real decline ... the underlying social dynamic for style, in this light, is the relative worsening of the situation of the working class" (in the Hall and Jefferson collection, below).

Here, the exhibition of a subcultural identity was a means of expressing and "magically resolving" the crisis of class relations – at least at the symbolic level of the imaginary – using territorial practices and stylistic gestures.

New ethnicities and multiculture

The conventional focus on young white men and class reproduction was to become increasingly difficult to sustain as feminism and race-conscious critiques of subculture came to the fore. A new politics of difference came into being, with its emphasis on hybridity, on postmodernity replacing political economy and class-led analyses. The context in which this change took place was an increasing awareness that young people were living in "New Times," symbolized by globalization, longstanding patterns of diasporic movement and settlement, and a rapid decline in manufacturing industries. Research into what has been called new ethnicities began to explore points of cultural *fusion*, making it increasingly difficult to speak of a distinct "black" or "white" youth subculture outside more hybrid understandings of Britishness. These two-tone dialogs can be found in Dick Hebdige's 1979 analysis of *Subculture: The meaning of style* (Routledge, 1995), in which a multiculture achieved by way of music, language and fashion came to inform and inflect even the "whitest" of youth subcultures, dating from the Teddy Boys of the 1950s. (This argument was extended by David Muggleton in his *Inside Subculture: The postmodern meaning of style*, Berg, 2000). In the postwar resettlement period, during which generations of white and black youth grew up alongside one another, the influence of urban multiculture can be found embodied in the everyday language and stylistic grammar of young people's peer group relations. This is clear from Roger Hewitt's 1986 study *Black Talk, White Talk: Inter-racial friendship and communication among adolescents*, Cambridge University Press).

A focus on merging ethnicities is exemplified in Simon Jones's study *Black Culture, White Youth: The reggae tradition from JA to UK* (Macmillan, 1988) which discloses how a number of white working-class youths could embrace the full blazonary of black style. Les Back's 1996 *New Ethnicities and Urban Culture: Racisms and multiculture in young lives* (UCL Press) emphasizes how porous and mutable the new subcultural forms are and how they recognize no national boundaries.

Terms such as micro-networks, neo-tribes and club-cultures became staples of the subcultural vocabulary in the early twenty-first century. These elastic concepts stretch beyond the local (neighborhood, street, school, etc.) as a bounded space and interconnect with the wider transcultural circuits of globalization. In this respect, the "death of subculture" as a localized class-specific phenomenon is a feature of much contemporary work, culminating in *The Post-subcultures Reader* edited by David Muggleton and Rupert Weinzierl (Berg, 2003).

The intellectual trend in studies of youth subcultures has been away from production to consumption-based accounts. Interest now falls on young people's engagement with, for example, dance, shopping, popular music and cyberspace. In the rush to theorize New Times, the family, local institutions and labor markets have been replaced almost entirely by studies of shopping malls, mobile communications and internet surfing. At the same time, the period of late modernity may be characterized by increased risk and insecurity as the collapse of manufacturing industries and the loosening of national ties continues to shape young lives. The increased choice, flexibility and mobility available to young people in New Times is then curtailed if global change becomes the expression and reinforcement of uneven spatial development. Indeed, despite its emphasis on diversity and cultural intermingling, globalization simultaneously involves the uprooting of local cultures and pastimes and an increased homogeneity.

In the face of such widespread social, economic, political and cultural upheaval, recent studies have drawn attention to the perseverance of local youth subcultures and the continuing significance of place in changing times. Distressingly, the more pluralistic tendencies attributed to globalization – diaspora, hybridity and multiculture – have yet to bridge socioeconomic polarization or to herald a post-racist global society.

SEE ALSO: Central Park jogger; cultural identity; diaspora; globalization; Hall, Stuart; hegemony; hybridity; language; Marxism; media; multiculturalism; neo-nazism; Park, Robert Ezra; post-race; racialization; rap; Rastafari; reggae; representations; riots: Britain, 1981; riots: Britain, 1985; riots: Britain, 2001; skinheads

Reading

Race, Place and Globalization: Youth cultures in a changing world by Anoop Nayak (Berg, 2003) highlights the continuing significance of place in local youth subcultures, using both structural and cultural perspectives; new forms of cultural attachment that invite the replacement of black and white identities are explored.

"Subcultures or neo-tribes? Rethinking the relationship between youth, style and musical taste" by Andy Bennett (in *Sociology*, vol. 33, 1999) exemplifies the theoretical and methodological problems of deploying a subcultural framework in the study of youth.

The Subcultures Reader, edited by Ken Gelder and Sarah Thornton (Routledge, 1997), is the most comprehensive compendium, pulling together key schools of thought in the field; this may be profitably read with *The Post-subcultures Reader* edited by David Muggleton and Rupert Weinzierl (Berg, 2003).

ANOOP NAYAK

Z

ZIONISM

Zionism, in its modern form, developed from a late nineteenth-century belief in the need to establish an autonomous Jewish homeland in Palestine. Theodor Herzl (1860–1904), a Hungarian journalist who lived in Vienna, was eventually persuaded by the events of the Dreyfus case in France and the "pogroms" (i.e. the organized massacre of Jews in Russia) to conclude in his book *Der Judenstaat* that the only way the Jewish people could practice their religion and culture in safety was by having their own nation-state. In 1897, at the First World Zionist Congress in Basle, Chaim Weizmann (1874–1952) insisted that this had to be re-created in Palestine, even though there had been no significant Jewish settlement there after the conquest of Jerusalem in CE 70.

Nevertheless, it was argued that Jews had always considered Palestine their spiritual home, citing that Jews throughout the Diaspora prayed for "next year in Jerusalem." It is, however, equally arguable that Orthodox Jews thought of this sentiment in a philosophical way: a means of affirming old beliefs, not of recommending the formation of a Jewish state with Jerusalem as its capital.

Herzl and Weizmann faced opposition to their ideas from both Orthodox Jews and those Jews who felt themselves to belong to the countries where they and their families had settled. Even after the Balfour declaration of 1917, expressing the British government's sympathy with Zionist aspirations and favoring "the establishment in Palestine of a National Home for the Jewish people," there was not a large migration of Jews to Palestine, which, for hundreds of years, had been predominantly Arab.

Up until World War II, Zionist claims that Jews throughout the world were persistently longing and striving to return to a homeland from which they saw themselves exiled, had very little foundation in fact. Not until after the genocidal anti-Semitism of the Nazi Party had murdered six million Jews between 1939 and 1945 did the classical Zionist theories of Herzl, Achad, and Ha'am, come to mean anything to the Holocaust survivors and Jews throughout the Diaspora.

Just as the pogroms had convinced Herzl, so the Holocaust convinced millions. The majority of Jews now believed that they were a separate people who had suffered unending discrimination and persecution. The only way they could be safe to practice the Jewish way of life was in a Jewish state, controlled and run by Jews and where they constituted the majority. The major theoretical aspiration of Zionism became reality when the Jewish state of Israel was proclaimed in 1948.

While the fundamental demand for the creation of a Jewish state in Palestine had been met, contemporary Zionism means more than pro-Israel support in the Diaspora and more than Israeli patriotism in Israel. Although ideologically it includes both of these, it claims to represent an all-encompassing approach to the problems of the Jewish people. The essential constituents of a Zionist program are contained to a large extent (although not completely) in the resolutions of the 27th Zionist Congress held in Jerusalem in 1978:

- The unity of the Jewish people and the centrality of Israel in Jewish life.

- The ingathering of the Jewish people into their historic homeland, the land of Israel.
- The strengthening of the state of Israel.
- The presentation of the identity of the Jewish people through the fostering of Jewish and Hebrew education and Jewish spiritual and cultural values.
- The protection of Jewish rights everywhere.

The encouragement of *"aliya"* (immigration to Israel) is the primary task of the Zionist movement.

The Soviet publication *Pravda*, in 1971, began an anti-Zionist campaign. Moscow's astonishing charges that Zionist leaders had collaborated with Nazi Germany were taken up by Arab states, then on the crest of an oil boom. Together, the countries were able to cull enough UN votes to push through what is a now infamous resolution. In November 1975, the UN's General Assembly passed resolution 3379, linking Zionism with South African apartheid and condemning it as "a form of racism and racial discrimination." This implicitly denied Israel's right to a legitimate existence.

Zionists emphatically refuted the links, claiming that the resolution conflated nationalism with racism. Some critics and victims of Israel replied that since the time Israel gained a territorial nation (in 1948) it has behaved no better – and sometimes worse – than other nationalist states and movements. The Arab minority of Israel was denied civil rights; many members of that minority were expelled from the lands of their birth; Israel engaged in acts of violence that went beyond a legitimate response to violence committed against it. Defenders and supporters of Israel answered critics by defining their opposition as anti-Semitic.

Changes in political currents in the early 1990s prompted a reconsideration of the resolution. In particular, the Persian Gulf War split the Arab and Islamic worlds and the demise of communism splintered the Soviet bloc. In December 1991, the UN voted 111 to 25 to revoke the 1975 resolution. It was only the second time in its history that the UN had overturned one of its own resolutions.

Martin Luther King famously equated opposition to Zionism to anti-Semitism: "It is discrimination against Jews because they are Jews." In the early twenty-first century, amid conflict in Palestine, the equation was used somewhat promiscuously: those who criticized Israeli policies were frequently denounced as anti-Semitic and, by implication, anti-Zionist. In other words, the term Zionism came to mean something else other than the right to Jewish self-determination. While this is a betrayal of its original meaning, it reflects the manner in which changing historical contexts affect both the content of terms and the uses to which they are put.

SEE ALSO: anti-Semitism; culturecide; diaspora; ethnocide; genocide; Holocaust; migration; nationalism; Other; pogrom; United Nations

Reading

The Idea of the Jewish State by B. Halpern (Harvard University Press, 1969) outlines political developments.

Lost Jews: The struggle for identity today by Emma Klein (Macmillan, 1995) investigates Jews "on the fringes of Jewish life" and how they have sought alternative affiliations to Jewish identity.

The Origins of Zionism by P. Vital (Clarendon, 1975) is a comprehensive guide to Zionism and its roots.

Internet resources

AFFIRMATIVE ACTION

Links to articles on affirmative action provided by *Upstream*.

Affirmative Action

http://www.mugu.com/cgi-bin/Upstream/Issues/affact/index.html

Affirmative Action Review: Report to the President

http://clinton2.nara.gov/WH/EOP/OP/html/aa/aa-index.html
Published in July 1995, the review covers the history and rationale for affirmative action, the results of empirical research on affirmative action and antidiscrimination, justifications for it, and a review of programs in various institutional spheres, including the military and education.

The Affirmative Action and Diversity Project: A Web Page for Research

http://aad.english.ucsb.edu/
Provided from the University of California, Santa Barbara, a large collection of resources relating to affirmative action, including an extensive collection of primary documents, news and announcements relating thereto, definitions of discrimination, economics of affirmative action, articles on individual and group rights, etc.

ANTI-SEMITISM

ADL (Anti-Defamation League)

http://www.adl.org/adl.asp
Reports on contemporary instances of anti-Semitism worldwide, and on extremist groups.

Antisemitism and Xenophobia Today

http://www.axt.org.uk/
The site focuses nearly exclusively on contemporary trends in anti-Semitism, principally in Europe. The *Countries* link provides access to detailed reports on the phenomenon in some particular countries. These provide an overview, historical background to anti-Semitism, the legacy of World War II, some details relating to anti-Semitic and xenophobic incidents, information on Holocaust denial as well as related matters. The *Archive* link includes reports from the Americas, Asia and Australasia, the Middle East and Africa, as well as earlier reports relating to European countries.

The Felix Posen Bibliographic Project on Antisemitism

http://sicsa.huji.ac.il/bib.html
Provided from the Hebrew University of Jerusalem, this is reputed to be the most comprehensive bibliography of anti-Semitism available, including books, monographs and periodical entries. It is divided into two sections, an *Annotated*

Bibliography covering 1984 to the present, and a *Retrospective Bibliography*, at present covering the years 1965–83. The only drawback is that access to the database is via a telnet interface. Most contemporary users will be able to access it by this means simply by selecting the link, but navigation thereon is more complex than selecting links, although after a few minutes experimentation it should be found to work perfectly adequately.

ANTISLAVERY

iAbolish: The Anti-Slavery Portal

http://www.iabolish.com/index.htm
A component of the *American Anti-Slavery Group*, the site provides reports on contemporary slavery worldwide, arranged by region. There are numerous reports available at this site, and links to other campaigning groups associated with slavery in particular places.

APARTHEID

United Nations in the Struggle Against Apartheid

http://www.anc.org.za/un/
Provided by the African National Congress, this site brings together a large collection of UN documents relating to apartheid, including reports, resolutions, seminars, conferences, speeches by the Chairs of the Special Committee Against Apartheid, and UN Conventions. There are also some essays and a chronology of the UN and apartheid.

Other documents relating to countries and regions, boycotts, campaigns and embargoes against apartheid, can be found at *http://www.anc.org.za/ancdocs/history/*

ARYAN

Aryan Invasion Theory Links

http://www.hindunet.org/hindu_history/ancient/aryan/aryan_link.html
The site links to articles/books dealing with the significance of *arya* or *Aryan/s* to aspects of ancient Indian culture and civilization, which explore particularly the notion that light-skinned Aryans invaded and conquered the darker skinned original inhabitants. Such notions were central to Nazi ideology but, as David Frawley explores in one of his contributions, "they did not invent the idea, nor were they the only ones to use it for purposes of exploitation. They took what was a common idea of nineteenth and early twentieth century Europe, which many other Europeans shared" – *http://www.hindubooks.org/david_frawley/myth_aryan_invasion/index.htm*.

Aryan Nations

http://www.gospelcom.net/apologeticsindex/a83.html
Background information, articles and a news database from the Apologetics Index, on this American, anti-Semitic white supremacist hate group. See also entries for Aryan Brotherhood and Aryan National Alliance on the main index at *http://www.gospelcom.net/apologeticsindex/a00.html*

The Aryan Question and Prehistoric Man

http://aleph0.clarku.edu/huxley/CE7/Aryan.html
An essay by L. Huxley, published 1890, in which he discusses the merits of the *Hindoo-Koosh-Pamir* theory, and the confusion caused by the spurious admixing of philological and biological (racial) categories.

Why the Aryan Law?

http://www.calvin.edu/academic/cas/gpa/arier.htm
This is a translation of E. H. Schulz and R. Frercks, *Warum Arierpargraph? Ein Beitrag zur Judenfrage* (Verlag Neues Volk, 1934), a pamphlet that provides background information relating to, and rationalization for, the discriminatory *Aryan* legislation introduced in the early days of the Third Reich in order to reduce the participation of persons of Jewish origin in its social institutions.

ASYLUM AND IMMIGRATION

Asylum Support

http://www.asylumsupport.info/
Site managed by Frank Corrigan. The site in-

cludes links to resources on many issues relating to migration and asylum: *Bill and White Paper* links to resources that include the full text of the Nationality, Immigration and Asylum Bill, background information thereto, the white paper *Secure Borders, Safe Haven*, and a list of advocacy groups. *Publications* links to a lengthy list of document resources, many of which are directly relevant to asylum-migration issues as currently debated in the UK.

asylumlaw.org

http://www.asylumlaw.org/
Information, worldwide, relating to immigration, refugee status, and asylum. In addition to breaking news items, of particular interest is the SUPER Search engine and the HRDE database. Super Search is a meta-search engine that queries fourteen human rights databases simultaneously. They include Amnesty International, the Canadian Immigration and Refugee Board, and the Australian Refugee Tribunal. The latter database includes more than 20,000 decisions. Before use it is worthwhile reading the *About* information.

HRDE is the acronym for Human Rights Documents Exchange, which was a Texas-based organization that compiled reports on various human rights issues, including asylum and refugee status, and collated reports compiled by other organizations, including the US Department of State, the Home Office and the UNHCR. There are some 895 reports in the database, in PDF format. There is no search engine, but those dealing more specifically with asylum related matters are listed from page 18. Earlier pages list reports dealing with persecution in various countries and violations of human rights.

CISNEWS

http://www.cis.org/mail_login.html
This is the URL to subscribe to the mailing list provided by the Center for Immigration Studies, a Washington, DC-based nonprofit research organization. The mailing list, which has some 5,000 subscribers, provides information on immigration news from around the world in the form of two postings a day, one dealing with the US, and the other non-US territories. The Center, at *http://www.cis.org/*, also publishes various reports.

Country Assessments-April 2002

http://www.ind.homeoffice.gov.uk/default.asp?-pageid=88
Produced by the Country Information and Policy Unit of the Home Office Appeals and Policy Directorate, these reports are assessments of those countries that are the source of the largest numbers of asylum applications in the UK. "The purpose of these country assessments is to inform decision-making on asylum applications by Home Office caseworkers and to assist other officials involved in the asylum determination process."

Electronic Immigration Network (EIN)

http://www.ein.org.uk/
The EIN is a voluntary organization with charitable status. The resource is divided into two components. A database of links that is accessible without charge, and a case law database for which there is a subscription charge. The links cover a wide spectrum that goes beyond the confines of immigration and asylum law in the strict sense, but is, nonetheless, very comprehensive, covering immigration law and asylum issues in the UK, Europe, and worldwide.

The Asylum Process in the United States

http://dcc2.bumc.bu.edu/refugees/asylum.htm
Overview of the process with links to relevant reports and sites.

BUSING

Busing: 25 Years

http://www.adversity.net/special/busing.htm#maryland
A series of linked articles examining the impact of busing in Boston following the decision of federal Judge W. A. Garrity to integrate the schools through forced busings. This is one component of the presentation of *Adversity.Net* at *http://www.adversity.net/*, which is a nonprofit educational organization that is opposed to *reverse discrimination*, and which claims that this is a position that is supported by the vast majority of Americans, including minority group members. Their archives include a substantial volume of materials on affirmative action, busing, and similar.

Issues and Views

http://www.issues-views.com/index.php
"The hard copy edition of this newsletter was founded in 1985 by black Americans who advocate self-help and business enterprise and the protection of constitutional rights." Use the Search facility with Busing as the search term to retrieve articles that tend to stress the negative consequences for African Americans of busing.

CASTE

Caste System

http://www.hinduism.co.za/newpage8.htm
Fundamentals of the caste system as described in Hindu sacred texts. See also the link to Untouchables.

CIVIL RIGHTS MOVEMENT

African American Odyssey

http://lcweb2.loc.gov/ammem/aaohtml/exhibit/aointro.html
An online presentation corresponding with an exhibit provided by the Library of Congress that details the stages in the struggles of African Americans to achieve equality in America. Useful as a chronology of major events and a listing of some key figures in the movement.

An Interactive Civil Rights Chronology

http://www.yale.edu/lawweb/jbalkin/brown/index.html
A detailed chronology dating from 1502, when the first Africans arrived in the Americas, to the present.

Civil Rights History Guide: The Struggle for African-American Civil Rights and the Civil Rights Movement

http://history.searchbeat.com/civilrights.htm
A substantial collection of links from *The History Beat*

We Shall Overcome: Historic Places of the Civil Rights Movement

http://www.cr.nps.gov/nr/travel/civilrights/index.htm
A history of the US civil rights movement mapped onto sites of historic interest. From the *Introduction* page select *List of Sites*, which provides biographical sketches of main players, as well as information on various phases of the struggle. See also the links relating to *Strategy* and *The Prize*.

DARWINISM (DARWIN, CHARLES)

Evolutionary Theories in the Social Sciences

http://www7.kellogg.nwu.edu/evolution/
Includes bibliographies arranged by discipline, working papers, book reviews, conferences information, and links to associations and research centers. Somewhat biased toward economic theories, presented by the Kellogg School of Management, Northwestern University.

Evolutionary Theory and Memetics, Links on

http://pcp.lanl.gov/EVOMEMLI.html
From the Principia Cybernetica Web, includes a section on biological evolution and history of evolution, and evolutionary psychology and sociology.

The Descent of Man by Charles Darwin (complete text)

http://www.literature.org/authors/darwin-charles/the-descent-of-man/

The Origins of the Species by Charles Darwin (complete text)

http://www.literature.org/authors/darwin-charles/the-origin-of-species/

ETHNIC CONFLICT

Contemporary Conflicts in Africa

http://www.synapse.net/~acdi20/
The site provides detailed information on major conflicts on the African continent, but also general reports and articles on ethnopolitical conflict that are not regionally specific, for which see the section on *Major Reports*. The image map provides access to links to information relating to

specific countries/conflicts, including historical background, general information, refugees, news and urgent actions. The *Organizations* section provides links to various agencies involved in conflict resolution and management, and peace keeping initiatives, UN and other. The section on *Conflict Issues*, provides links to information on a wide range of matters, including criminal justice and human rights. This is a well-organized site that provides a wide range of useful and interesting information.

INCORE (Initiative on Conflict Resolution and Ethnicity)

http://www.incore.ulst.ac.uk/
The organization was established in 1993 between the University of Ulster and the United Nations University to advance research and policy on the resolution of political and religious conflicts. The site provides a sizable volume of resources relating to these issues. The *Country Guides* provide extensive links to internet resources relating to conflict and ethnicity that are relevant to specific countries and regions. The *Ethnic Conflict Research Digest* includes peer reviewed articles "of recently published books, journal articles and research papers on the dynamics and management of ethnic conflict." The *Information Bank* includes various guides, including bibliographies, training resources, academic programs, etc.

Project on Ethnic Relations

http://www.per-usa.org/
The focus of PER is on the prevention of ethnic conflicts in Central and Eastern Europe, the Balkans, and the former Soviet Union. There are a reasonable number of useful reports here dealing with various facets of ethnic conflicts in these areas, and attempts to resolve them.

Russians in the Newly Independent States: A Bibliography

http://www.riga.lv/minelres/biblio/Bib.htm#Top
An extensive bibliography, dated 1998, published by Hanne-Margret Birckenbach and Boris Tsilevich.

Specialist Group Ethnic Politics

http://www.bath.ac.uk/~mlssaw/ethnic_politics/home.html

A division of the Political Studies Association of the United Kingdom. The site offers book reviews of recent publications and review essays, links arranged by region, information on conferences, a link to the *Global Review of Ethnopolitics*, and promises research papers on the subject.

EUGENICS

American Bioethics Advisory Commission: Introduction to Eugenics

http://www.all.org/abac/eugen02.htm
A brief historical overview from 1883 to the present, with a bibliography.

Eugenics-Genome Project Bibliography

http://clem.mscd.edu/~princer/biblio.htm
This is a reasonably extensive bibliography produced by Rob Prince, The Metropolitan State College of Denver, for a course dealing with American culture and eugenics in the twentieth century, counterpoising thereby, eugenics theory and practice during the early part of the century with the genome project, and the reactions thereto, at the latter end. There is also a bibliography relating to the sterilization of Native Americans during the 1970s at *http://clem.mscd.edu/~princer/STERIL.htm*, and one on the Bell Curve, primarily consisting of magazine articles, but including some books as well, at *http://clem.mscd.edu/~princer/MURRAY.htm*

Future Generations

http://www.eugenics.net/
Links to a collection of articles that support the eugenicist position on intelligence, cloning, etc.

Image Archive on the American Eugenics Movement

http://www.eugenicsarchive.org/eugenics/
This excellent presentation provides a brief history tour with commentary and original graphic images under a range of topics, including social origins, scientific origins, research methods, traits studied, eugenics popularization and sterilization laws. It is also worth looking at the complete archive page, at *http://www.eugenicsarchive.org/eugenics/list_topics.pl*, where the original images are classified under a larger number of topics,

including criminality, immigration, leading eugenicists, and race mixing and marriage laws. For clarity, open the pop-up windows fully.

Institute for the Study of Academic Racism

http://161.57.216.70/ISAR/homepage.htm
Includes links to articles and biographies (e.g. Cattell, Irving, Miller).

SEE ALSO: Intelligence links.

GENOCIDE

Armenian National Institute

http://www.armenian-genocide.org/
The site provides a variety of materials relating to the genocide of the Armenians during World War I. These include copies of some documents, bibliographical materials, a detailed chronology, photo collections, and selected press coverage reports at that time.

Cambodian Genocide Program

http://www.yale.edu/cgp/index.html
This project, headed by Professor Ben Kiernan, is part of the Yale University Studies Program. The resource includes a number of databases, including an extensive annotated bibliography of works relating to Cambodian history and the genocide, photographs, essays, and documents.

International Criminal Tribunal for Rwanda

http://www.ictr.org/
The case materials provide one of the best online sources of information on the 1994 Rwanda genocide.

International Criminal Tribunal for the Former Yugoslavia

http://www.un.org/icty/
The case materials provide one of the best online sources of information on the conflict in Bosnia-Herzegovina 1991–95 and its background. See also the Final Report of the Commission of Experts at *http://www.ess.uwe.ac.uk/comexpert/REPORT_TOC.HTM*

Web Genocide Documentation Centre

http://www.ess.uwe.ac.uk/genocide.htm
This site collates online primary and secondary materials relating to twentieth-century genocides and mass killings, and includes sections on the Holocaust, Kosovo, the former Yugoslavia, East Timor, the Armenian genocide, and Sierra Leone. There is also a book review section subdivided by topic area, timelines, a glossary and biographical materials.

HATE GROUPS

Intelligence Project

http://www.splcenter.org/intelligenceproject/ip-index.html
Publishes a quarterly *Intelligence Report* which "offers in-depth analysis of political extremism and bias crimes in the United States. The Intelligence Report profiles Far Right leaders, monitors domestic terrorism and reports on the activities of extremist groups. Its annual listing of hate groups and Patriot groups is the most comprehensive in the United States." The online archive dates from Spring 1997, all of the articles published from the Winter 1997 edition onward being available online. The *Hate Incident* search facility lists these by state. The *Legal Action* page links to legal news, anti-hate litigation, and to some *landmark* cases.

Links to the Dark Side

http://www.student.uit.no/~paalde/nazismexposed/Scripts/nlinks.html
Links to sites of hate groups.

The Public Eye

http://www.publiceye.org/
Provided by Political Research Associates, "an independent, nonprofit research center that studies antidemocratic, authoritarian, and other oppressive movements, institutions, and trends. PRA provides accurate, reliable research and analysis to activists, journalists, educators, policy makers, and the public at large." The site includes a large number of articles on the subject of extreme groups, including a guide to researching right-wing policy making and funding, and a useful glossary.

The Hate Directory

http://www.bcpl.net/~rfrankli/hatedir.htm
Compiled by Raymond A. Franklin, it is available only in PDF format. The directory includes "Internet sites of individuals and groups that, in the opinion of the author, advocate violence against, separation from, defamation of, deception about, or hostility toward others based upon race, religion, ethnicity, gender or sexual orientation." The October 2001 release ran to 95 pages and lists web sites, mailing lists, newsgroups, Internet Relay Chat[s], Yahoo Clubs and Groups, MSN Groups, and Racist Games available on the Internet. Some of those listed are no longer accessible, but this is usually noted, and they are kept on the listing, for "historical" purposes.

HOLOCAUST

The Nuremberg War Crimes Trials

http://www.yale.edu/lawweb/avalon/imt/ imt.htm#sup
This site is provided by the Avalon Project at Yale University, and provides access to the text of the Trial of the Major War Criminals Before the International Military Tribunal, Nuremberg. In addition, there are various supporting documents, including documents included in Nazi Conspiracy and Aggression.

The Holocaust History Project

http://www.holocaust-history.org/
An extensive collection of essays and documents relating to varied aspects of the destruction of European Jewry.

The Holocaust Project: Multimedia Timebase

http://www.humanitas-international.org/holo-caust/timebase.htm
A very extensive and detailed chronology covering the years 1889–1999.

Web Genocide Documentation Centre

http://www.ess.uwe.ac.uk/genocide.htm
Includes a substantial section on the Holocaust that provides access to primary and other materials relating to the destruction of the European

Jews, including timelines, book reviews, and biographical information on perpetrators.

HUMAN RIGHTS

Office of the United Nations High Commissioner for Human Rights website:

http://www.unhchr.ch/html/intlinst.htm
All UN human rights documents are available for download from this web site. The site also includes links to a wide variety of UN and related web sites providing information on human rights issues, human rights bodies, human rights education, news, conferences and so forth.

UDHR 50 History of the Declaration website:

http//www.udhr.org/history/default.htm.
Honouring the 50th anniversary of the UDHR, this web site provides a comprehensive background to the formulation of the Declaration.

Amnesty International

http://www.amnesty.org/
Current news, campaigns, commentary, reports.

Human Rights Reports

http://www.state.gov/g/drl/rls/hrrpt/
These are produced annually by the US Department of State under the provisions of the Foreign Assistance Act of 1961, and amendments thereto. Arranged by country, they provide useful information, not only on the human rights situation, but also on the general political situation and structure in each. Those for 1999 and 2000 are available online at this site. Reports for 1993–98 are available at *http://www.state.gov/www/glo-bal/human_rights/hrp_reports_mainhp.html*

Minorities Rights Group

http://www.minorityrights.org/
An advocacy organization with consultative status with the UN Economics and Social Council that produces reports on the status of minorities worldwide. A small number of these reports are available online, as well as a training manual, workshop reports and news items.

HUMOR *see* Jim Crow

INDIGENOUS PEOPLES

Aboriginal Studies WWW Virtual Library

*http://www.ciolek.com/WWWVL-Aboriginal.
html*
Annotated links to a wide range of resources on
aboriginal peoples.

Australian Institute of Aboriginal and Torres Strait Islander Studies (AIATSIS)

http://www.aiatsis.gov.au/index.htm
"AIATSIS is an independent Commonwealth
Government statutory authority devoted to
Aboriginal and Torres Strait Islander studies.
It is Australia's premier institution for information about the cultures and lifestyles of Aboriginal and Torres Strait Islander peoples." There
is a useful page of annotated links and access
to the AIATSIS library catalogue, which details
one of the most comprehensive collections
of print materials on Australian indigenous
studies.

Chief George Manuel Memorial Library

http://www.cwis.org/fwdp.html
"This archive was originally authorized by a
resolution of the Conference of Tribal Governments. [It] has grown into the Chief George
Manuel Memorial Library with more than
100,000 documents, reports, and publications
from American Indian nations and indigenous
nations from around the world." More than
1000 documents have been digitized. They include documents classified by region, tribal and
inter-tribal resolutions and papers, internationally focused documents, UN documents, and
treaties, agreements and other "constructive arrangements."

United Nations High Commissioner for Human Rights: Indigenous People

http://www.unhchr.ch/html/menu2/ind_main.htm
UN documents appertaining to indigenous peoples and their human rights.

INTELLIGENCE

Ask Eric

http://ericir.syr.edu/Eric/
This is the largest database of educationally
related information and includes more than one
million abstracts of documents and journal articles. It is updated monthly with the latest available citations. Use the Advanced Search facility
to locate documents relating to intelligence and
race.

History of the Influences in the Development Intelligence Theory and Testing

http://www.indiana.edu/~intell/index2.html
From Indiana University, the presentation examines the subject through brief essays on principal
figures in the development of the field. This can
be explored either through a names index of the
principal contributors, or a timeline, in which the
contributors are subdivided by eras. The articles
provide career information, brief outlines of
central ideas, and references to main works
published by the author. Although the reports
are somewhat schematic, they are useful for a
broad-view based introduction, and for looking
up basic information relating to figures that are
mentioned by writers in passing.

The Bell Curve

*http://www.mugu.com/cgi-bin/Upstream/Issues/
bell-curve/index.html*
Interviews, statements, and book reviews from a
variety of perspectives collated by *Upstream*,
including Charles Murray.

JIM CROW

Jim Crow Museum of Racist Memorabilia

*http://www.ferris.edu/htmls/news/jimcrow/me-
nu.htm*
The museum is located on the campus of Ferris
State University, Big Rapids, Michigan. The
virtual site provides essays on who/what was
Jim Crow, on various stereotypes/caricatures of
Black Americans (brute, jezebel, mammy, picca-
ninny, coon), racist cartoons, and links to other

sites and scholarly essays. The materials are well presented and include graphic and photographic images, and have been written by Dr. David Pilgrim, Professor of Sociology.

The History of Jim Crow

http://www.jimcrowhistory.org/history/creating2.htm
A series of five linked essays, authored by Dr. R. L. F. Davis, the most useful of which is the first, with links to relevant legislation and biographical details of dramatis personae.

KING, MARTIN LUTHER *see* Civil rights movement link

KU KLUX KLAN

Church of the American Knights of the Ku Klux Klan

http://www.americanknights.com/

FBI: Ku Klux Klan

http://foia.fbi.gov/kkk.htm
The 1964/65 investigations of the FBI into the activities of the Ku Klux Klan in relation to violations of civil rights. This is a lengthy document, which is broken down into five parts in PDF format. Substantial portions of some investigative reports/letters have been inked out.

Ku Klux Klan

http://www.spartacus.schoolnet.co.uk/USAkkk.htm
Although this appears to be directed at school children in the UK, a product of Spartacus Educational, it does include a large number of links to movements, historical events, organizations and individuals, all of which form the wider context of the Klan. In the absence of a more in-depth overview, it is useful as a starting point. One of the drawbacks is a lack of adequate referencing of the materials referred to.

Ku Klux Klan Directory

http://www.expage.com/klansmen/

LAW: IMMIGRATION

Electronic Immigration Network (EIN)

http://www.ein.org.uk/
The EIN is a voluntary organization with charitable status. The resource is divided into two components. A database of links that is accessible without charge, and a case law database for which there is a subscription charge. The links cover a wide spectrum that goes beyond the confines of immigration and asylum law in the strict sense, but is, nonetheless, very comprehensive, covering immigration law and asylum issues in the UK, Europe, and worldwide.

UK

Immigration and Nationality Website

http://www.ind.homeoffice.gov.uk/
Official site providing information on the UK immigration process.

USA

U.S.A. Immigration Services

http://www.usais.org/
Official site providing information on US immigration issues.

LAWRENCE CASE, THE STEPHEN

Black Information Link: Stephen Lawrence

http://www.blink.org.uk/default2.asp
Access to the inquiry transcripts, articles on the case, articles following up related issues, and progress reports. Select the *Stephen Lawrence* link from the page index menu.

Home Office Submission to Stephen Lawrence Inquiry

http://www.homeoffice.gov.uk/slinq981.htm
Includes information on Home Office approaches to tackling racist crimes, its views on good practice, and summaries of various reports considered to be relevant, such as British Crime

Survey findings, and a summary of the report on the Perpetrators of Racial Harassment and Racial Violence.

Reclaiming the Struggle: The Lawrence Inquiry One Year On

http://www.irr.org.uk/lawrence/index.htm
Links to articles at other sites, real audio tapes of speeches at a meeting organized by the Institute of Race Relations Monitoring Group and the National Civil Rights Movement, the Institute of Race Relations submission to the Macpherson committee of inquiry, and a *full* list of racially motivated murders since 1991.

Special Report: The Stephen Lawrence Case

http://www.guardian.co.uk/lawrence/0,2759, 179674,00.html
Archived materials from *Guardian Unlimited*, The Guardian newspaper, UK.

The Stephen Lawrence Inquiry: Report of an Inquiry by Sir William Macpherson of Cluny

http://www.archive.official-documents.co.uk/ document/cm42/4262/4262.htm
Complete text.

MIGRATION

Refugees International

http://www.refugeesinternational.org/cgi-bin/ri/ index
Resources available include reports on refugees arranged by region and country, and by issue.

Southern African Migration Project

http://www.queensu.ca/samp/
"The Southern African Migration Project is a multi-faceted research, policy and training pro-gramme designed to facilitate the formulation and implementation of new initiatives on cross-border population migration in the region." Resources include news items arranged by coun-try, a bibliography, speeches, documents, com-mentaries, interviews, and a section on xenophobia in South Africa.

World Wide Web Virtual Library on Migration and Ethnic Relations

http://www.ercomer.org/wwwvl/
Annotated links arranged under organizations, publications, research programs, conferences, and mailing lists.

NEO-NAZISM *see* Hate groups links

PROTOCOLS OF THE LEARNED ELDERS OF ZION

The Protocols of the Learned Elders of Zion.

ftp://ftp.std.com/obi/Rants/Protocols/The_ Protocols_of_The_Learned_Elders_of_Zion
Translated from the Russian of Sergyei A. Nilus by Victor E. Marsden.

The Protocols of the Learned Elders of Zion: A Hoax of Hate

http://www.adl.org/special_reports/protocols/ protocols_intro.asp
A brief historical overview of the role of the protocols in fanning anti-Semitism from the Anti Defamation League.

RACISM

Crosspoint Anti Racism

http://www.magenta.nl/crosspoint/
Links to antiracist (interpreted somewhat broadly) groups arranged by country, listing some 2,000 organizations in 113 countries (No-vember 2002).

European Commission Against Racism and Intolerance (ECRI)

http://www.coe.int/T/E/human_rights/Ecri/ 1-ECRI/
"The European Commission against Racism and Intolerance (ECRI) was set up following a decision of the 1st Summit of Heads of State and Government of the member States of the Council of Europe, held in Vienna in October 1993, and strengthened by a decision of the 2nd Summit held in Strasbourg in October 1997. ECRI's task is to combat racism, xenophobia, antisemitism and intolerance at the level of

greater Europe and from the perspective of the protection of human rights." The two sections most worthy of mention are *Country-by-country Approach*, which provides detailed information on relevant international instruments for the country relating to these matters, constitutional and criminal, and civil and administrative law provisions, administration of justice, specialized institutions, an overview of the situation, etc., and the *Examples of Good Practices*, for which select the *Work on General Themes* link.

European Monitoring Centre on Racism and Xenophobia (EUMC)

http://www.eumc.at/about/index.htm
"The European Monitoring Centre on Racism and Xenophobia (EUMC) was established in 1997 by the European Union as an independent body to contribute to combat racism, xenophobia and anti-semitism throughout Europe. The EUMC works with the Council of Europe, the United Nations and other international organizations. It has the task of reviewing the extent and development of the racist, xenophobic and anti-semitic phenomena in the European Union and promoting 'best practice' among the Member States." The *Publications* link provides access to numerous reports on racism and xenophobia in the member states of the EU sponsored by the center.

ICARE (Internet Centre Anti Racism Europe)

http://www.icare.to/
This site includes a database of antiracism organizations in Europe. The search engine allows filtering by the name of the organization or its abbreviation, city, country, and address. There is a News section that provides reports on racist and intolerance related issues and incidents from across Europe on a weekly basis, and holds archives dating from 1999.

Institute of Race Relations

http://www.irr.org.uk/index.htm
A UK-based organization that was established in 1958, it is an educational charity focused on race relations that promotes their study in the UK and campaigns for their improvement. Its online resources today also include information on

racism and anti-immigration policies in other European countries.

World Conference Against Racism, Racial Discrimination, Xenophobia and Related Intolerance.

http://www.un.org/WCAR/
The conference was held between August 31 and September 7, 2001. The site provides access to the Durban Declaration and Programme of Action, the agenda, and documents of the Preparatory Committee, the most interesting of which are probably the documents of the four regional meetings and the five expert seminars. The latter focuses on these issues in particular regions and the attempts undertaken to combat them.

In Europe

Statewatch

http://www.statewatch.org/
Launched in 1991, *Statewatch*, monitors civil liberties and the state in the EU. It provides reports on these issues, which often are quite detailed. Its database includes some 25,000 items, and lists numerous entries under the categories *asylum, racism, apartheid*, and *racial harassment*, among others. Due to the size of the database, it is worth scrutinizing the list of *Search Terms*, and reading the help file.

REFUGEE STATUS

European Council on Refugees and Exiles

http://www.ecre.org/
"ECRE is an umbrella organization of 73 refugee-assisting agencies in 30 countries working towards fair and humane policies for the treatment of asylum seekers and refugees." Includes current news, documents relating to European policies, responses to proposals and reports.

Guide to International Refugee Law Resources on the Web

http://www.llrx.com/features/refugee.htm
Compiled by Elisa Mason, who worked for six years with the UNHCR, published July 2000.

Refugee Case Law Site

http://www.refugeecaselaw.org/Refugee/Default.asp

Provided by the University of Michigan Law School. "The site currently collects, indexes, and publishes selected recent court decisions that interpret the legal definition of a "refugee." It presently contains cases from the highest national courts of Australia, Austria, Canada, Germany, New Zealand, Switzerland, the United Kingdom, and the United States." Also available are the Home Office Country Assessments.

United Nations High Commissioner for Refugees (UNHCR)

http://www.unhcr.ch/cgi-bin/texis/vtx/home

The site provides information on the activities of the UNHCR, numerous reports on global, regional and country-specific refugee issues, basic texts and statistics.

ROMA

Dom Research Center

http://www.domresearchcenter.com/

The focus of this organization is on research on Gypsy communities in the Middle East and North Africa. Online information consists of news clips arranged by country, regional reports, population charts, and issues of its journal, *Kuri*, published online since January 2000.

European Roma Rights Center

http://errc.org/

This organization monitors the status of Roma in European countries and also provides legal assistance in cases of human rights abuses. The site provides access to a very large volume of information relating to the contemporary situation of Roma in various European countries, information concerning the implementation of Roma rights, a database of European Court of Human Rights cases that have focused on Roma issues, and a mailing list to which interested parties can subscribe and which provides ongoing information on developments. There are also links to other Roma Internet resources.

Roma and Forced Migration: An Annotated Bibliography, Second Edition, 1998

http://www.soros.org/fmp2/html/roma2.htm

An extensive bibliography provided by the Forced Migration Projects. Sections include general bibliographies about the Roma, periodicals that regularly provide information about Roma, the Roma and the Holocaust, and regional and country-specific sections.

SLAVERY

Anti-Slavery International

http://www.antislavery.org/

Tracing its history to the British and Foreign Anti-Slavery Society formed in 1839, the organization now tackles problems of contemporary slavery, particularly in relation to child labor. The site provides a good list of links to other sites involved in antislavery and human rights activities, and also some publications relating to its ongoing campaigns.

Born in Slavery: Slave Narratives from the Federal Writers Project, 1936–38

http://memory.loc.gov/ammem/snhtml/snhome.html

Part of the Library of Congress' *American Memory* project, this presentation "contains more than 2,300 first-person accounts of slavery and 500 black-and-white photographs of former slaves. These narratives were collected in the 1930s as part of the Federal Writers' Project of the Works Progress Administration (WPA) and assembled and microfilmed in 1941 as the seventeen-volume *Slave Narratives: A Folk History of Slavery in the United States from Interviews with Former Slaves*. This online collection is a joint presentation of the Manuscript and Prints and Photographs Divisions of the Library of Congress and includes more than 200 photographs from the Prints and Photographs Division that are now made available to the public for the first time."

Chronology on the History of Slavery and Racism

http://innercity.org/holt/slavechron.html

An extensive chronology/history that is divided

into three periods: 1619–1789, 1790–1829, and 1830–1990s. Compiled by Eddie Becker, it includes graphs, maps and graphics, and links to other resources that are mentioned in the text. The focus is primarily on American slavery and racism, and the information relating to the period 1870–1990 is sparse in comparison to the detailed and extensive information provided for the earlier periods.

SEE ALSO: Civil rights movement links.

SOCIAL DARWINISM

Darwin's Metaphor: Nature's Place in Victorian Culture by Robert M Young

http://human-nature.com/dm/dar.html
Full text, originally published in 1985.

SOCIOBIOLOGY

Sociobiology

http://www.pscw.uva.nl/sociosite/TOPICS/Theory.html#SOCIOBIO
Links to various resources provided by *Sociosite*, a social science subject directory provided by the University of Amsterdam.

UNESCO

http://www.unesco.org/

UNITED NATIONS

http://www.un.org

WHITE SUPREMACISTS *see* Hate groups links

XENOPHOBIA *see* Hate groups links

INDEX

Note: **bold** page numbers denote reference to main encyclopedic entry.

Aaron, Hank 225
AAVE *see* African American Vernacular English
Abiola, Bashorun Mashood 368
abolitionists 35–39, 123–24, 404–5; *see also* anti-slavery
Aboriginal Australians **1–3**, 178, 201–2; Blumenbach's racial taxonomy 166; ethnic identification 142; extinction of 109, 111; genocide 165; Hanson attacks on 177, 282; hereditarian theory 180; internet resources 468; land rights 193; paternalism 310–11; reparations 111; transracial adoption 424; *see also* indigenous peoples
Aboriginal Studies WWW Virtual Library 468
abortion 150–51
Abrams v. *United States* (1919) 128
Abu Hamza xv
Ackerman, Bruce 132
Adarand Constructors Inc. v. *Peña* (1995) 5
ADL *see* Anti-Defamation League
adoption 410, **422–25**
Adorno, Theodor 90, 181, 329, 339
Adversity.Net 463
advertising: beauty ideals 52; conspicuous consumption 91; Jordan 225, 226; racial imagery 299; representations 368; whiteness 454
aesthetics: beauty 50–53; dress 117; negrophilia 299; *see also* body; sexuality
AFDC *see* Aid to Families with Dependent Children
affinity 232
affirmative action **3–6**, 207; color line 87; disadvantage concept 107; equality 130; ethnic monitoring 141–42; internet resources 461; merit 273–74; race card 337; Republican Party 20; resistance to 89; South Africa 413; Thomas opposition to 420; US

colleges 11; white backlash culture 441, 442, 443, 444
Affirmative Action and Diversity Project 461
Affirmative Action Review: Report to the President 461
Afghanistan xviii, 86, 97, 393
Africa **6–9**; blackness 451; Blumenbach's racial taxonomy 166; colonialism 86; conquest societies 89; decolonization 392; Doomed Races Doctrine 108; environmentalism 127; Ethiopianism 135–36, 162, 298; ethnic conflicts 464–65; ethnic identities 170; exploitation 322; Garvey 161–62; indigenous peoples 203; Islam expansion into 451; liberation movements 297, 447; nÕgritude 95, 298; paternalism 310, 311; pluralism 316; refugees 364; serfdom 124; sexuality 397; slavery 403, 404; *see also* Africans; postcolonialism
African American Odyssey 464
African American Vernacular English (AAVE) 236–37; *see also* Ebonics
African Americans xiii, xvii, xx, **9–13**, 310; affirmative action 273–74; AIDS 400; Barry case 49; beauty 51; black bourgeoisie 57–58; black feminism 59; Black Panther Party 60–62; blues music 63; California 240; Central Park Jogger case 76; conservatism 90; criminal justice 12; Doomed Races Doctrine 109; double consciousness 112, 113; drug use and dealing 119–20; Ebonics 121; education 10–11; employment discrimination 4; environmental organizations 205; epithets 128; ethnogenesis 360; families and health 10; Ford 169; humor 195, 196–97; identity 113–15; inferential racism 203, 204; inner-city concentrations 189; intelligence testing 208; *Invisible Man* 211–12; Jim Crow laws 223–

24; linguistic practices 29; Los Angeles 232; lynchings 398; masculinity 263, 264; matrifocality 312–13; media representations 265, 266–67, 370; Million Man March 224, 255, 264, 277–78; minstrelsy 283–85, 399; Myrdal's study 293; naming practices 353; Nation of Islam 294–95; Pentecostalism 314, 315; police brutality 318; politics 12–13; population forecasts 249, 266; poverty 11, 90, 389; race relations 9–10; racial profiling 346; rap music 355–57; reparations 367; repressive environment 38; reverse racism 373; revitalization movement 233; riots 377–78; segregation 389; September 11th aftermath 393–94; sexuality 399; Simpson case 402; slavery 417; transracial adoption 422–23; unemployment 11–12; welfare system 439; *see also* African Caribbeans; black people; Black Power; civil rights movement

African Caribbeans xx, **13–16**, 67; black bourgeoisie 57; class profile 14–15; educational underachievement 429; footballers 255; housing 188; mental illness 270, 271, 272; mugging 456–57; National Front 296; Pentecostalism 314, 315; racial coding 343; reverse racism 373; Rock Against Racism 380; youth 15; *see also* black people; West Indians

African Charter of Human and Peoples' Rights 211, 252

African National Congress (ANC) 258, 259, 413, 462

African Orthodox Church 162

African Union 211

Africans: diaspora 106; whiteness concept 453

Afrikaners 40, 276, 412, 413; *see also* Boers

Afro-Brazilians 65

Afrocentricity **16–17**; black feminism 58–59; essentialism 134; multicultural education 288

agency (human) 68, 116, 264, 361

aggression 108, 329

agriculture: *encomienda* 125; Ireland 213; mercantilism 276; Mexican-Americans 77; Third World 104

Aho, James 300

AIATSIS *see* Australian Institute of Aboriginal and Torres Strait Islander Studies

Aid to Families with Dependent Children (AFDC) 313

AIDS 295, 399–400, 413

AIM *see* American Indian Movement

Aiyetoro, Adjoa 367

Al-Jazeera 394

Al-kalimat, Abdul 58

al-Qaeda xv, xviii, 393

Alagiah, George xiii–xiv

Albania: asylum seekers 46, 97; Kosovar Albanians 137, 139

Alexander, Charles 234

Algeria 7, 8; colonial psychiatry 154; French settlers 276; veil wearing 118

Ali, Ayaan Hris xiv

Ali, Muhammad **17–20**, 224, 294, 401

alienation 90, 91; black people and law enforcement 395–96; mental illness 271, 272; social exclusion 408

Allen, Theodore 449–50

Allport, Gordon 414

alterity: anti-Semitism 31; cultural racism 98; deviant 54–55; Levinas 306; racism 350; *see also* Other/Otherness

Althusser, Louis 175, 179, 200

altruism 412

Alva, Klor de 47

amalgamation **20–21**

Amazon region 22, 23, 64

American Anti-Slavery Society 38

American Civil War 39

American Convention on Human Rights 252

"American dream" 169

American Indian Movement (AIM) 22, 193

American Indians **21–24**, 201, 202, 310; Blumenbach's racial taxonomy 167; Brazil 64–65; English language teaching 121; ethnic identification 142; genocide 165, 306; internal colonialism 209; internet resources 468; Ku Klux Klan view of 233; Las Casas on 238, 239; literacy test requirements for voting 244; media representations 267; reparations 111, 365, 366; sexuality 397; sterilization 465; transracial adoption 424; *see also* indigenous peoples

American Nazi Party 446

Americanization 44, 45, 248

Amin, Idi 8

Ammon, Otto 406

Amnesty International 381, 463, 467

Amritsar massacre 161

ANC *see* African National Congress

ancestral descent 232–33

Anderson, Benedict 95

Andrews, David L. 226

Angelou, Maya 278

Anglo-conformity 44

Anglo-Indians **24–27**

Anglo-Saxons 233, 452

Angola 8, 276, 404

"animalization" 427

anomie 309; *see also* alienation

Anthias, Floya 134, 143

anthropology **27–30**; Boas 64; culture 98; language 235; physical 336, 386, 431; racial classification 334; structuralist 307

anti-Americanism 343–44

Anti-Defamation League (ADL) 278, 461, 470

anti-Muslimism 219; *see also* Islamophobia

Anti-Nazi League 296

anti-Semitism **30–32**, 144; Aryan Republican Army 302; bigotry 53; British National Party 69; British Union of Fascists 327; conceptual problems with term 31; critics of Israel 31–32, 460; Farrakhan 278, 373; Holocaust 182; humor 194; internet resources 461–62; Otherness 306; Pan-German League 174; prejudice 329; *Protocols of the Learned Elders of Zion* 31, 330–31, 373, 470; UN instruments 432, 433; Vienna declaration 455; Wagner 437–38; *see also* Jews

Anti-Slavery International 472

Anti-Slavery Society 406

antiracism **32–35**; beauty images 51; discourse 354; ethnic identities 324; Finot 157; multiracial organizations 292; political correctness 321; press attacks on 370; Rainbow Coalition 220; resistance to systemic racism 418; roots of 32–33; social work 409, 410, 411; spread of 34–35; welfare 440–41; whiteness 453

antiracist education 122, 123, 349, 442

Antisemitism and Xenophobia Today 461

antislavery **35–39**, 404–5, 450; GrÕgoire 172; internet resources 462; Las Casas 238; *see also* emancipation

apartheid **39–41**, 359, 389, 412–13; denial of power 328; housing 189; internet resources 462; Mandela's struggle against 258; racial classification 87; *see also* racial discrimination; segregation

Apte, M. L. 194, 197

ARA *see* Aryan Republican Army

Arabs xvii, 360; Africa 6; anti-Semitism 31; cultural borrowings 146; epithets 128; Israel 107; Israeli 460; religious conflict 139; whiteness concept 453

Arafat, Yasser 259

Archer-Straw, Petrine 299

Arendt, Hannah 31, 155

Arens, R. 100

Aristotle 130, 239

Armenian National Institute 466

Armenians 106, 138, 140, 165, 306, 466

Armstrong, Louis 284

Arnold, Eve 118

art 299; *see also* aesthetics

Aryan Invasion Theory 462

Aryan Nations 300, 330, 448, 462

Aryan Republican Army (ARA) 300, 302

Aryanism **41–42**, 300, 450; beauty 50; Chamberlain 174; Gobineau 172; Haeckel 174; internet resources 462; language 235; Wagner 437, 438; White Power 446, 447, 448, 449; *see also* Nazism; neo-nazism; white supremacism

Asante, Molefi Kete 16, 121

Ashcroft, Bill 84, 85

Asia: Blumenbach's racial taxonomy 166, 167; conquest societies 89; eugenicist fears 398–99; liberation movements 447; refugees 364; serfdom 124; sexuality 397–98; slavery 403; whiteness 454; *see also* Asian Americans; Asians; British Asians; South Asians; Southeast Asia

Asian Americans **42–44**, 310; California 240; English language teaching 121; epithets 128; intelligence testing 181; Los Angeles 232; media representations 267; migration 42–43; population forecasts 249, 266; sexuality 398; television news industry 266; underclass 430

Asians: Africa 8; beauty shops 52; exoticization of Asian women 50, 51; scapegoating 383; *see also* Asian Americans; British Asians; South Asians

Ask Eric 468

assimilation xiii, **44–46**; Aboriginal Australians 2, 3; amalgamation contrast 21; American Indians 23; Australia 424; Brazil 65; Britain 218, 440; Cleaver 84; equal opportunity 123; eugenicist fears 398–99; indigenous peoples 100; integration contrast with 206; Irish Americans 214; monocultural education 122; Motown 287; race relations cycle 309; social inclusion 54; social work 409; United States xvii; *see also* integration

Asylum and Immigration Act (UK, 1996) 435

Asylum and Immigration (Appeals) Act (UK, 1993) 246

asylum seekers **46–47**, 277, 364; British Asians 66; cultural racism 97; globalization 170; homelessness 185; impoverishment of 439; internet resources 462–63; racially motivated attacks 254; racism in sport 256; skinhead hostility towards 403; stress 271; UK immigration law 246; white backlash culture 443; xenophobia 455; *see also* immigrants; refugees

Asylum Support 462–63

asylumlaw.org 463

Atlanta 58, 124, 125

atrocities: Africa 8; Amritsar massacre 161; Beslan school massacre xv; Congo 308; India 139, 161; Ku Klux Klan 234; Nazi 77, 190; Oklahoma bombing 300, 302–3; Sharpeville massacre 40, 432; Soweto massacre 40, 41; Spanish colonialism 238; World War II 190; *see also* genocide

Austin, Regina 92

Australia: assimilation xiii; asylum seekers 46; British settlers 109, 276; colonialism 86; conquest 88; Doomed Races Doctrine 108, 110, 111; ethnic groups 144; Hanson 177–78, 282; Melanesian forced labor 110; One Nation 177, 178, 282, 303–5; racial discrimination 252; racial labelling 336; Salvadorean migrants 143; transracial adoption 424; *see also* Aboriginal Australians

Australian Institute of Aboriginal and Torres Strait Islander Studies (AIATSIS) 468

authoritarian personality 53–54, 329

autonomy: collective right to 193; ethnonationalism 149

avant-garde 299

Ayatollah Khomeini xvii–xviii

Azerbaijan 138, 140

Aztecs 21, 47, 171, 275

Aztlān **47–48**

B-Boys/B-Girls 92

BAAF *see* British Association for Adoption and Fostering

Baartmann, Saartjie (Sarah) 50, 185–86, 399

Babangida, Ibrahim 367

Babington, Thomas 35

Babington, William Dalton 157

Back, Les 256, 324, 457

Bagehot, Walter 406–7

Baker, Houston 356

Baker, Josephine 299, 300

Bakhtin, Mikhail 198

Bakke, Paul Allen 5

Baldwin, James 113, 115–17

Bales, Kevin 405, 406

Balfour, Lawrie 115

Bali bombing (2002) 393

Balkan Wars (1912–13) 137

Ballard, Catherine 187

Ballard, Roger 187

Bangladeshis xvi, 66, 67, 390; census statistics 216; doctors in Britain 268; educational underachievement xx, 217, 429; housing 188; kidnapping and sale of women 405; UK immigration law 246; *see also* British Asians; South Asians

banking 206

Banner, Lois 50

Banton, Michael 143, 176, 338

"Bantustan" policy 389

Baptists 315

Barbados 14, 271

bargaining 361

Barker, Martin 96

Barlow, William 63

Barry, Marion 49, 295, 401

Barthes, Roland 321

Barzun, Jacques 31, 133

basic needs theory 103

Basques 141, 148, 149, 193

Bayreuth Festival (1876) 437

Beam, Louis 448

Beardsley, M. C. 147–48

beauty **50–53**; *see also* aesthetics; body; sexuality

Becker, Eddie 473

Becker, Howard 456

Bedau, H. A. 163

Begun, Yosif 144

Belgium: colonialism 7, 86; ethnic tensions 141; integration 207

Bell, Bernard 113

The Bell Curve (Herrnstein & Murray) 121, 465, 468

Bell-Fialkoff, A. 136, 137

Benedict, Ruth 28, 349, 350

Bengalis 331

Bennett, Lerone 449

Berg, Alan 302–3

Berlin Wall 140

Bernal, Martin 16, 146–47

Bernier, FranÓois 133, 172

Beslan school massacre xv

Betrayed (film) 303

Bhaba, Homi 84, 198

Bible 127, 333, 366, 383, 387

Biddiss, Michael 172

Bierce, Ambrose 54

bigotry xix, **53–57**; humor 196; as pathology 53–54; racial profiling distinction 346; US colleges 11; *see also* prejudice; racism

Biko, Steven 41

bilingualism 279, 282, 290

Billig, Michael 197
Bin Laden, Osama xviii, 393
bio-politics 399
biogenetic law 174
biological differences 28, 29, 59, 165–66; *see also* genetics; genotype; phenotype; scientific racism
biracialism **291–93**, 309
Birmingham: ghettos 167; riots (1985) 375
Birmingham Centre for Contemporary Cultural Studies (CCCS) 175–76, 179, 457
birth control 398
Bischoping, Katherine 164
Black, Don 448
Black and Minority Ethnic (BME) groups 268
black bourgeoisie: Britain 57; consumption 91; United States 57–58
Black Codes 223
Black English 236–37
black feminism **58–60**, 396
Black Information Link 469
"black is beautiful" aesthetic 51, 144
black liberation movement 59
Black Muslims *see* Nation of Islam
Black Panther Party (BPP) **60–62**, 78, 83, 115
black people: Baldwin's theories 116–17; beauty 51–52; children's views 362; consumption 91–92; educational underachievement 339, 440; empowerment 124; female sexuality 397, 399; Garvey 161–62; imagination of tradition 144; intelligence testing 181, 207–8; Ku Klux Klan attacks on 233, 234; literacy test requirements for voting 244; male body 50, 265, 399; masculinity 263, 264–65; media representations 370, 371; multiracialism 291, 292; poverty 439, 441; public sector employment 274; racial coding 343; as scapegoats 383; self-fulfilling prophecies 390–91; sexual abuse 394–96; social work 410; Spike Lee's films 254–55; stereotypes 414; tokenism 421; use of term 9; violence against 434–35; *see also* African Americans; African Caribbeans; Africans; Black Power
Black People's Movement 41
Black Power 19, 20, 41, **62–63**, 229; black bourgeoisie 58; Black Panther Party 60, 83; as replacement to civil rights 82; riots 230; White Power as response to 446
blackness 198, 299, 450–51
Blair, Tony 394
Bland, James 284
Blauner, Robert 168, 209

blues **63**, 426
Blum, Robert 437
Blumenbach, Johann Friedrich 38, 75, 166–67, 386, 450
Blunkett, David 443
BME groups *see* Black and Minority Ethnic groups
BNP *see* British National Party
Boas, Franz 27–28, **64**, 157–58
body: as aesthetic form 117; black male 50, 265, 399; eroticized 50, 397, 399; female 118, 134
Boer War (1899–1902) 40, 160
Boers 7, 40; *see also* Afrikaners
Bogan, Lucille 196
Bogle, Donald 283
Bolivia 276
Bonacich, Edna 274–75
Bonilla, Frank 11
Bork, Robert 13, 420
Boskin, Joseph 197, 283, 284
Bosnia-Herzegovina: ethnic cleansing 136; ethnic conflict 139; "ethnic Muslims" 145; refugees from 185; Roma 382; segregation 390; *see also* Yugoslavia, former
boundaries 369
bourgeoisie: black **57–58**, 91; hegemony 178–79; South Africa 413; *see also* middle class
Boyle's Law (US, 1965) 71
BPP *see* Black Panther Party
Bradford riots (2001) 69, 376
Bradley, Trevor 408
Braham, Peter 326
Braun, Carol Moseley 13
Brazil **64–66**, 276; antiracist movements 418; emancipation 123–24; Freire 158; Freyre 159; indigenous peoples 21, 22, 193, 202, 281; lack of racial boundaries 88; multiracialism 291; racial ancestry 336; slavery 39, 404, 405, 406
Brinton, Daniel 27
Britain: African Caribbeans **13–16**, 248; anti-Irish hostility 213–14; antislavery 35–36, 37, 123; assimilation 44, 45; asylum seekers 46; black bourgeoisie 57; Black English 237; busing 71; colonialism in Africa 7, 86; colonialism in India 24–25, 26, 27, 66, 85–86, 161, 415; colonialism in North America 85; criminal justice policy 319; cultural racism 96; doctors in 268–69; dress 117; education 122, 428, 429; emancipation 123; emigration from 109; English language 280; equal opportunity 129–30; eugenics 150; exploitation of migrants 152; fascism 157;

ghettos 168; "global policeman" role 444; halal butchers 126; homelessness 183, 184; housing 187, 188; immigration law **244–47**, 250, 251, 469; imperialism 117; integration xiii, 206, 207; Islamophobia 215–18; Ku Klux Klan branches 234; labor migration 340; language 236; Lawrence case 252–54, 318–19; Let's Kick Racism Out of Football 255–56; media representations 370; medical schools 268; mental illness 270–72; as multinational state 149; multiculturalism 290; multiracialism 291, 292; National Front 296; nationalism 297; neo-nazism 300; Parekh Report 176, 290, 344; patriarchy 312; Pentecostalism 315; policing 318, 320, 347; politics of difference 176; Powell 326–27; prejudice against Asians 329; race relations law **249–51**; racial discrimination 252, 334; racialization 349; Rastas 358; refugees in 185; riots: (1958) 68, 245; (1981) 15, 318, **373–75**, 384–85; (1985) 15, 318, **375–76**; (2001) 69, **376–77**, 390; Scarman Report 229; "second generation" Asians 143; segregation 331, 390; ska music 365; skinheads 402; slavery 403, 404, 405; social work 409–11; South Africa 40; television humor 195–96; transracial adoption 423–24; underclass 430; violence against blacks 434, 435; welfare 438, 439–40; white backlash culture 441–42; white flight 445; working-class racism 261; youth subcultures 456–57; *see also* British Asians

British Asians xvi, **66–69**; assimilation 45; educational underachievement xx; housing 188, 439; mental illness 270–71, 272; migration and settlement 66–67, 68; prejudice against 329; representations 68–69; riots 376–77; skinhead hostility towards 402; *see also* Bangladeshis; Indians; Pakistanis; South Asians

British Association for Adoption and Fostering (BAAF) 424

British Movement (BM) 69, 70, 296, 402

British National Party (BNP) **69–70**, 296, 300, 326; C18 group 256; riots 376, 377; white backlash culture 443

British Nationality Act (1981) 246, 439

British Union of Fascists 327

Brixton riots (1981) 373–75, 384–85

Brodkin, Karen 29

Bronowski, Jacob 101

Brookes, Rod 335

Brown Berets 78

Brown, H. Rap 446

Brown Man movement 175

Brown v. Board of Education of Topeka, Kansas (1954) 28, **70**, 81, 224, 230, 243, 444

Buber, Martin 306

Buffon, Georges-Louis de 127, 173

Bulgaria 137, 381, 382

Bunyan, John 333

"buppies" 91

Burger King 104–5

Burgess, Ernest W. 309, 310

Burke, Edmund 89

Burma 43, 316

Burma, J. H. 195

Burnley riots (2001) 376

Burns, Robert 333

Burundi 7, 8, 259

Bush, George Sr. 12, 13, 20, 124, 244, 337

Bush, George W. 6, 240, 394

busing **70–72**, 463–64

Butler, Judith 264, 324

Butler, Julius 61

C18 256

California 240, 248, 249, 367

Callaghan, James 250

Callender, Charles 283

Calley, Malcolm 315

Camarillo, Albert M. 11

Cambodia 43, 466

Cambridge, Godfrey 195

Canada: assimilation 100; British settlers 276; conquest 88; ethnic groups 144; ethnic mosaic concept 206; indigenous peoples 21, 22, 23, 24, 100, 202; integration 207; Irish emigration to 213; minority languages 236; multiculturalism xiii, 290; Quebec 141, 149, 193

cannibalism 109, 111

Cannon, Jimmy 18

capitalism **73–74**; black 62; Black Panther Party 61; Cox on 93, 94; exploitation 145, 151, 350; fascism 155, 156; global accumulation 23; hegemony 178, 179; humor 195; ideology of racism 201; inequalities 408; Marxism 293; Motown 287; nationalism 297; race relations 339; rap music as reaction against 357; social ordering principles 28; whiteness 453, 454

Carby, Hazel 264–65

Caribbean: creoles 94; diaspora identities 95; indentured labor 275; Pentecostalism 315; pluralism 316; refugees 364; reggae 365; schizophrenia 271; slavery 404; *see also* African Caribbeans; Jamaica; West Indies

Carlos, John 19, 61–62
Carlyle, Thomas 36, 213–14
Carmichael, Stokely 61, 62, 204, 349, 351
Carter, Bunchy 61
cases: *Abrams v. United States* (1919) 128; *Adarand Constructors Inc. v. Peþa* (1995) 5; Barry, Marion 49; *Brown v. Board of Education of Topeka* (1954) 28, **70**, 81, 224, 230, 243, 444; Central Park Jogger 76; Diageo **104–5**; Diallo, Amadou **105–6**, 318, 346–47; *Dred Scott v. Sanford* (1857) 39; environmental organizations 205; *Fullilove v. Klutznick* (1980) 5; *Gratz v. Bollinger* (2003) 6; *Griggs v. Duke Power Company* (1971) 4; *Grutter* case (2003) 6; *Hopwood, et al. v. State of Texas* (1996) 6; *Johnson v. Board of Regents* (2001) 6; *Johnson v. Transportation Agency, Santa Clara County* (1987) 4; King, Rodney **231–32**, 318, 346, 400; Lawrence, Stephen **252–54**, 318–19, 320, 346, 372, 439, 441, 469–70; *Loving v. Virginia* (1967) 291; *Mabo v. Queensland* (1992) 2, 202; *Martin v. Wilks* (1989) 4–5, 12; Mayagna Community 202–3, 211; *Missouri ex. rel. v. Canada* (1938) 243; *Plessy v. Ferguson* (1896) 70, 223, 243; *Price Waterhouse v. Hopkins* (1989) 244; *Regent of the University of California v. Bakke* (1978) 5; *Richmond v. J. A. Croson* (1989) 5, 12; *Roe v. Wade* 420; *Shaw v. Reno* 12; *Sheet Metal Workers Local 28 v. EEOC* (1986) 4; *Shelly v. Kraemer* (1948) 243; Simpson, O. J. 49, **400–402**; *Smith v. Washington State University* (1996) 6; Tyson, Mike 49; *United States v. Paradise* (1987) 4; *United Steelworkers of America v. Weber* (1979) 3–4; *Wards Cove Packing Company v. Atonio* (1989) 4, 12, 244; *Whren v. US* (1996) 346, 347; *Wik* decision (1996) 3, 304
caste 26, 69, **74–75**; internet resources 464; Jim Crow era 223–24; Myrdal's study 293; positive discrimination policies 107; race relations cycle 309
Castles, Stephen 170, 261
Castro, Fidel 259
Catalonia 149
Catholics: American colonies 247; Irish 213, 214; Ku Klux Klan 233–34; Puerto Ricans 332; as scapegoats 383
Caucasians **75**, 166, 167, 180, 450
Cayton, Bill 425–26
Cayton, Horace 28

CCETSW *see* Central Council for Education and Training in Social Work
celebrities 222, 225
censorship 56
Center for Immigration Studies, Washington 463
Central America: American Indians 21, 22, 23; colonialism 85; Latinos 239; slavery 404
Central Asia 86
Central Council for Education and Training in Social Work (CCETSW) 409, 410, 440–41
Central Park Jogger **76**
Centre for Contemporary Cultural Studies (CCCS) 175–76, 179, 457
cephalic index 64
CÕsaire, AimÕ 153, 298, 392
chain migration 68
Chakrabarty, Dipesh 415
Chamberlain, Houston Stewart **76–77**, 157, 174, 207, 437, 438
Chambers, Robert 174
Chaney, David 56
Chantler, C. 267
Chappelle, Dave 129
Charny, Israel 147, 164
chattel slavery 124, 404–5, 406
ChÃvez, CÕsar 47, **77–78**, 143
Chavis, Benjamin 278, 295
Chechnya xv, 140–41
Cheetham, Juliet 409–10
Chiapas 22, 23
Chicago 168, 367
Chicago School 187, 456
Chicanismo 47
Chicanos 47, 77–78, 143–44; *see also* Mexican-Americans
Chief George Manuel Memorial Library 468
child care: social work 410; transracial adoption 422–24
Child, Lydia Maria 38
Child Welfare League of America 423
children **78–81**; African Americans 11; child labor 171; cognitive/developmental theories 79–80; interpretive reproduction 80; learning racism 78–79; migration schemes 275–76; reading race 362, 363; self-fulfilling prophecies 391; sexual abuse 394–97; transracial adoption 422–24
Children Act (UK, 1989) 409
China: American attitudes towards 44; bigotry against Chinese people 56; colonialism 86; Doomed Races Doctrine 108, 110; film representations 305–6; indentured labor 275; migrants to the United States 42, 43,

209, 247–48, 398; Orientalism 305; patriarchy 313, 314; slavery 403, 405; traditional practices 33; whiteness 451–52

Chinese Exclusion Act (US, 1882) 248

Chinweisu 368

Chirac, Jacques xv

Chow, Elaine 43

Christian Socialism 411

Christianity: Africa 6, 135; American colonies 247; Anglo-Indians 25; anti-Semitism 30; antislavery 35, 36; bigotry 53; blackness 451; Cleaver 83; colonial missionaries 86; crusades xvii; equality 131; fundamentalism 442; Garvey 162; Latin America, 125; Malcolm X's rejection of 257; *nÕgritude* critique of 298; neo-nazism 300; patriarchy 313; Pentecostalism 315; White Power 449

Christy, Edwin P. 283

Churchill, Ward 100

CISNEWS 463

cities: black bourgeoisie 58; British Asians 66; ghettos 167–68; housing 188, 189; Irish Americans 214; Kerner Report 229; Pruitt-Igoe 331; race relations cycle 309; rural-urban migration 276; urban decay 126; urban Indians 21–22

citizenship: Britain 218, 246; globalization 170; Greek conception of 131; language tests 443; Latinos 241; Mexican-Americans 47; multicultural education 288, 289; social exclusion 408; United States 247, 248

civics movement 407

civil disobedience 77, 81, 82; Gandhi 160, 161; King 230

civil rights: Aboriginal Australians 2; African Americans 12; Arabs in Israel 460; feminism 387; legislation 89; Malcolm X on 258; Motown 286; slavery 403; US law **243–44**; *see also* civil rights movement

Civil Rights Act (US, 1964) 3, 4, 82, 224, 230, 244, 286, 420

Civil Rights Act (US, 1991) 4, 5, 13, 244, 420

Civil Rights Commission 6, 82, 244

civil rights movement xvii, 9, **81–83**, 230, 349, 351, 379; Ali 19; Black Power 62; Cleaver on 83; consumption 92; criticism of leaders by Clarence Thomas 420; equal opportunity 129; internet resources 464; *see also* civil rights; King, Martin Luther

civilization: attainment of 127; colonial discourse 84; Gobineau 171–72; Park 309; Western 34, 454

Clarke, John 456, 457

clash of civilizations xiv, 215

class: African Caribbeans in Britain 14–15; Anglo-Indians 26–27; anthropology 28; *AztlÃn* movement 47; bigotry 55; black bourgeoisie 57–58; Brazil 66, 159; Cox 94; educational underachievement 428, 429; ethnic cleansing 138; exploitation 29, 73, 151; fascism 156; health relationship 438–39; life chances 442; Marxism 73, 259, 260, 261; minority status 279; Myrdal's study 293; Otherness 307; proletarianization 416; reduction of racial issues to class issues 417; sexual division of labor 314; social conflict 145; underclass 204, 288, 356, 408, **430–31**; violent crime 414, 415; white supremacism 454; *see also* middle class; socioeconomic status; working class

class struggle 141, 309, 457

classification, racial 333–34, 336, 398; apartheid 412; Blumenbach 166–67, 450; color line 87–88; *see also* hierarchies

Clay, Cassius *see* Ali, Muhammad

Cleaver, Eldridge 61, **83–84**

Clinton, Bill 6, 124, 220, 249

codes **341–45**

COE *see* Council of Europe

cognitive behavior therapy 273

cognitive development 79–80

Cohen, Albert 456

Cohen, Lizabeth 92

Cohen, Robin 301

Cohen, Stanley 456

cohesion 176

Cohn, Norman 31

Cold War 34, 140

Coleman, James 71

collective action 140, 360, 361

collective identity 92–93

collectivism 361

Collins, Patricia Hill 59, 60

Colombia 23, 239

colonial discourse **84–85**, 399

"colonial mentality" 87

colonialism xiv–xv, 28, **85–87**, 322, 388, 416; Africa 6, 7–8, 170; African Caribbeans 13–14; Algeria 154; Anglo-Indians 25, 26, 27; Australia 1; bigotry 55; blackness 451; Brazil 64, 65; capitalism relationship 74; cheap labor 244–45; cultural identity 95; culturecide 100; dominant/hegemonic phases of 84; dress 117, 118; extermination of native races 110, 111; Fanon 154, 155; forced migration 275–76; Gandhi 160; hybridization 198; impact on understanding of race and culture 262; inferential racism 203; internal 23, 168, 192, **209–10**, 416; Ireland 213, 214; languages spoken in 236; *nÕgritude* critique of 298; Orientalism 305; Otherness 307; paternalism 310, 311; Roma 382; sexual domination 397, 398; slavery 404; South Africa 40; Spanish 74–75, 238; systemic racism 417; Third World 419; underdevelopment theory 103; US immigration law 247; white race concept 450; whiteness 452; *see also* decolonization; imperialism; plantations; postcolonialism

color line **87–88**, 114, 250

Combat 18: neo-fascist group 234

comedians 129, 195, 196, 321

Commission for Racial Equality (CRE) 71, 142, 250–51, 255, 377, 445

Commission on Human Rights (UN) 432, 433

commodification: American Indians 23; black culture 370

commodity fetishism 91

commodity production 74

common descent 101

common-sense thinking 179, 201, 260

Commonwealth: British Empire 86; ethnic groups 144; migration to Britain 340, 349; UK immigration law 245, 246

Commonwealth Immigrants Act (UK, 1962) 245

communication: mass 169; nonverbal 354; racial coding 341, 342; racist discourse 351, 354

communications technology 169, 170

Communist Party 61, 212

computer technology 169–70

concentration camps 181, 182

conformity 330

Congo 111, 308–9

Congo-Brazzaville 8

Connolly, Paul 362

Connor, Walker 149

conquest **88–89**

Conrad, Joseph 325

consciousness: false 91, 200; hegemony 178, 179; ideology 200; of race 338–39

consent decrees 4–5

conservatism 28, **89–90**; bigotry 55–56; equal opportunity 129; Thomas 420, 421; transnational communities 106

Conservative Party 90, 96, 245, 326, 438, 442

conspiracy theories 300, 302, 330–31, 373, 446, 447

constraint-choice perspective 189

consumption **90–93**, 408; alienation 91; discrimination 92; mass 169; resistance 91–92;

social identity 92–93; youth subcultures 457–58

contact hypothesis 71, 444

contract workers 151–52, 261

Convention Against Discrimination in Education (1960) 432

Convention on the Prevention of the Crime of Genocide (1948) 99, 147, 148, 163, 164, 181, 190

Convention on the Rights of All Migrant Workers and Members of their Families (1991) 433

Convention relating to the Status of Refugees (1951) 46, 363, 364

Conversi, Daniele 149

Cook, James 1, 86

cool pose 263

Coombe, Vivienne 410

Coon, Carleton 28

Corsaro, William 80

Cosby, Bill 10, 196, 224

Coulthard, G. R. 298

Council of Europe (COE) 210

counseling 273

country assessments 463

Cox, Oliver C. **93–94**, 239, 260, 261, 262, 293, 340, 416

Crane, D. 196

CRAP (Christian Rightwing American Patriots) 447

CRE *see* Commission for Racial Equality

creole **94–95**; Anglo-Indians 26, 27; speech 237

crime: black victims 395; Chicago School 456; hate crimes 10, 233, 319; mugging 456–57; racially motivated 15, 216; racism link 410; racist discourse 353; stereotypes 414, 415; underclass 430; *see also* police; violence

criminal justice 318, 319–20; African Americans 12; Black Panther Party 60; black victims of crime 395; multicultural policy 290; racial profiling 347; *see also* police; prisoners

Critcher, Charles 456

critical gender theory 263

critical race theory 120

critical reflection 158

Croatia 140

Croats 138, 139

Cronon, E. David 161

Crosspoint Anti Racism 470

Cuba: emancipation 123–24; Latinos 239, 240; Mandela's support for 259; Soviet imperial influence 86

Cuffee, Paul 135

cuisine: Asian Americans 43; Indian 66–67, 68, 147

cultural diversity xiv, xvii, xviii, xix; Australia 178; Britain 68; education 99, 122, 123, 253, 288–89; essentialization of differences 97; human rights 192; integration 45, 206; tolerance of 54; *see also* multiculturalism; pluralism

cultural identity **95–96**; bigotry 56; development 103; diasporic 106; dress 117; language 282; mental illness 272; religious faith xix; transnational communities 106; *see also* identity

cultural producers 92–93

cultural racism 54, **96–98**, 216

cultural relativism 32, 371

cultural reproduction 23

cultural rights 192, 193

cultural studies 175, 323, 371

culturalism xiv, 175, 176, 371

culture **98–99**, 287; Anglo-Indians 26–27; black 92, 226, 298–300; colonial discourse 84; dress 117; ethnic change 45; ethnic cleansing 136; ethnic identification 142–43; Gaelic 213; homogenization of 169; hybridity 198; masculinity 263; Orientalism 305, 306; pluralism xix, 316; sociobiology 411; South Asian 68, 69; *see also* cultural diversity; cultural rights; popular culture

culture conflict 272

culture shock 110

culturecide **99–100**, 147, 148, 164

Cuvier, Georges 108, 173, 180, 185, 186, 333, 386

Cyprus 138, 350

Czech Republic 170, 382, 402–3

Dalmage, Heather M. 292

Damas, Lõon 298

D'Amato, Cus 425, 427

Dances With Wolves (film) 24

Darwin, Charles 76, 101, 108–9, 110, 150; Blumenbach's anticipation of 167; internet resources 464; natural selection 127–28, 180; racial classification 333; social Darwinism 407

Darwinism 31, **101–2**; internet resources 464; monism 174; sociobiology 411; *see also* neo-Darwinism; social Darwinism

Davies, Carole Boyce 325

Davies, Christie 195

Davis, Allison 28, 108

Davis, R. L. F. 469

Davis, Sammy Jr. 221

Dawkins, Richard 411–12

Dawkins, Trevor 358

De Gaulle, Charles 392

de-industrialization 171

De Klerk, F. W. 41

debt bondage 405, 406

debt crisis 419

decenteredness 17

Declaration of Linguistic Rights (1996) 281

Declaration on Race and Racial Prejudice (1978) 432

Declaration on the Elimination of All Forms of Racial Discrimination (1963) 192, 432

Declaration on the Rights of Indigenous Peoples (1993) 192–93, 202, 237, 281, 433

Declaration on the Rights of Persons belonging to National, Ethnic, Religious and Linguistic Minorities (1992) 192, 433

decolonization 69, 307, 322; Ireland 214; nationalism 297; Senegal 391; underdevelopment theory 103

deconstruction 321, 323, 324

deculturation 99, 100

degeneration 167, 171, 198, 438

Degler, Carl 451

democide 164

democracy 287–88; equality 131; fascism 157

Democratic Party 12, 285

Denmark 85, 150, 280, 405

Dennis, Norman 253

Denzin, Norman 371

dependency syndrome 430

dependency theory 419

depopulation 109, 110

deportation 137, 138, 240, 393

depression 270–71, 272, 273

Derrida, Jacques 96, 175, 176, 307, 321

Descartes, Renõ 133

descent 232–33

desegregation 70–71, 81, 82, 90, 244, 444, 445, 447

despotism 310, 311

determinism 387, 389

Detroit 29, 169, 228, 285, 378, 379

Deutsche Alternativ 402

developing countries: AIDS 399; asylum seekers 46; development 102; ethnic conflict 104; official languages 236; *see also* Third World

development **102–4**; uneven 74, 297, 458

development racism 203

developmental psychology 79–80

deviance 54–55, 335, 352, 399, 451, 456

Dewey, John 308

di Renzi, Cola 437

Diageo case **104–5**
dialect 45, 121; creoles 94, 95; language distinction 280
Diallo, Amadou **105–6**, 318, 346–47, 434
diaspora **106–7**; black 365; cultural identity 95–96; essentialism 134; globalization 170–71, 458; Hall's conception of 176, 198; Jewish 30–31, 459; Mexican-Americans 47; new ethnicities 369; postcolonialism 325; Roma 381–82; *see also* migration
diffÕrance 96
difference 287, 307; politics of 176, 370–71, 457; race as signifier 335; race relations 340; racist discourse 352; science 386; *see also* cultural diversity; Other/Otherness
differentialism 45
dignity 190, 191, 193
Dik—tter, Frank 451
Dillingham Report (1910) 248
Dinkins, David 13
disadvantage xvii, **107**; affirmative action 3; African Caribbeans in Britain 15; British Asians 66; equality of opportunity 132; mental illness link 270, 272; religious 218; welfare recipients 438
discourse: colonial **84–85**, 399; racist **351–55**, 427
discourse analysis 84, 175, 334–35, 342
discrimination xvi, 349; African Caribbeans in Britain 13; Brazil 65; children's learning 81; Civil Rights Act (1964) 82; constraint-choice perspective 187; consumption as site for 90, 92; Convention Against Discrimination in Education 432; direct/indirect 351, 441; disadvantage concept 107; doctors 269; ethnic monitoring 142; exploitation 152; housing 168, 185, 188, 189, 250; human rights 193; institutional racism 205; Ireland 214; Islamophobia 216–17; Jim Crow era 223; mental illness link 270, 271–72; mixed motive 244; racial profiling 348; racist discourse 351–52; religious 216, 217, 218; reverse 4, 11, **373**, 463; sexual 430; systemic racism 416, 417; transracial adoption 423; US civil rights law 243, 244; welfare 441; *see also* affirmative action; racial discrimination
dislocation 17
disparate impact doctrine 4, 244
diversity *see* cultural diversity
division of labor 74
DJs 355, 365
DNA 389
doctors 268–69

Dollard, John 94, **108**, 340
Dom Research Center 472
dominant ideology 342
domination 179, 198, 200; colonialism 7; racist discourse 352; sexuality 397; *see also* oppression; power
Dominican Republic 211, 239
Doomed Races Doctrine **108–12**
Dortchy, Thomas 104
double consciousness 29–30, 33, 106, **112–17**
Douglas, James "Buster" 426
Drake, St Clair 28
Dred Scott v. *Sanford* (1857) 39
dress **117–19**; French riots xv; Muslim women xiv; veil 118, 154, 313, 314
Drew Ali, Noble 294
"driving while black" (DWB) 346, 347
Drost, Pieter N. 164
drugs **119–20**, 295, 346, 353
Du Bois, W. E. B.: black religions 298; colonialism 416; condemnation of Garvey 162; double consciousness 29, 33, 106, 112–15; epithets 128; Garvey comparison 161; race as signifier 335; whiteness 453
duality 112, 113
duCille, Ann 51–52, 59
Duke, David 443
Dummett, Ann 246
Duncan, Hugh Dalziel 195
Dundee, Angelo 18
Dunkley, H. Archibald 358
DWB *see* "driving while black"
Dworkin, Ronald 131, 132

Eastern Europe: development 102; ethnic conflict 140; expulsion of Germans 137–38; migrants to the United States 29, 44, 248; Roma 381; skinheads 402–3; Soviet imperial influence 86
Ebonics **121–22**, 197, 237
economic factors: Asian migrants to the United States 42; development 102, 103, 104; Latino policy preferences 241, 242; slavery 36, 37; Third World 419; UK immigration law 245
economic justice 83–84
economic migration 46, 363
economics: free market 34, 89, 407; neo-classical 103; rational choice theory 359; social Darwinism 407
ECRI *see* European Commission against Racism and Intolerance

education **122–23**; affirmative action 5–6; African Americans 10–11; American Indians 23; apartheid 41; Asian Americans 43; basic needs theory 103; British Asians xvi, 217; *Brown* v. *Board of Education of Topeka* 28, 70, 81, 224, 230, 243, 444; busing 70–71; Convention Against Discrimination in Education 432; culture concept 99; curricula 253; Ebonics 121; Freire 158; institutional racism 439; Latino policy preferences 241, 242; Mexican-Americans 77, 78; multicultural 99, 122–23, **287–89**, 290, 440; political correctness 321; racial discrimination 119; refugees 185; self-fulfilling prophecies 391; underachievement 217, 339, 428–30, 440; US civil rights law 244; white flight 445; *see also* schools

Education Act (UK, 1944) 428

Education Act (UK, 1980) 445

Education Reform Act (UK, 1988) 445

EEOC *see* Equal Employment Opportunity Commission

egalitarianism: antislavery 38; conservative 129, 130; Finot 157; *Herrenvolk* 435–36; *see also* equality

egocentricity 79, 272

Egypt: ancient 16, 147, 366; colonialism 86; war with Israel xvii

EIN *see* Electronic Immigration Network

elections: empowerment 124, 125; Latino electorate 240, 242; One Nation 303, 304; South Africa 413; *see also* politics; voting rights

Electronic Immigration Network (EIN) 463, 469

Elkins, Stanley 404

Elliott, Jean Leonard 290

Ellison, Ralph 197, 211–12

emancipation 39, **123–24**, 162, 223, 283, 405

emigration: Britain 109; forced 136; Ireland 213, 214

Eminem 299, 357

employment: affirmative action 3–4; African Caribbeans in Britain 14; Anglo-Indians 25; apartheid 40; black bourgeoisie 57; Black Codes 223; British Muslims 217; discrimination 119, 250; environmental racism 126; equal opportunity 129; human rights claims 193; integration 207; labor migration 277; Latino policy preferences 241; Mexican-Americans 77; multicultural policy 290; overseas doctors 268–69; part-time work 206; Puerto Ricans in the United States 332; rational choice theory 359–60; refugees 185; seniority rules 206; training 288; US civil rights law 244; *see also* labor; unemployment

empowerment **124–25**; black feminism 60; consumption 92

encoding/decoding 342

encomienda **125–26**

endogamy 74, 75

Engels, Friedrich 200, 259, 260

English language 121, 236, 280–81; English Only movement 282; Latinos 240; test for British citizenship 443

Enlightenment 288, 306, 307, 388; antislavery 36; Blumenbach's racial taxonomy 166; egalitarianism 38; essentialism 133; Finot 157

entertainment: minstrelsy 283–85; television 267; *see also* media

Entman, Robert M. 266, 267

entrepreneurship 57

enunciation 96

environmental issues 23

environmental organizations 205

environmental racism **126–27**, 203

environmentalism **127–28**, 173; hereditarian theory 180; intelligence 208; sociobiology rejection of 411

epistemic shifts 158

epistemology 59

epithets (racial/slang) **128–29**, 153

Equal Employment Opportunity Act (UK, 1972) 3

Equal Employment Opportunity Commission (EEOC) 3, 6, 82, 244

equal opportunity xiv, xvii, **129–30**, 273; busing 71; ethnic monitoring 142; formal versus fair 132; human rights 191; integration 45, 206, 207; multicultural education 123; UK race relations law 249, 250; white backlash culture 442, 443

equality **130–33**, 387; antiracism 32; antislavery 36, 38; conservative opposition to 89; human rights 190, 191, 193; Jewish conspiracy theories 447; medical profession 269; multiculturalism xix, 290; Parekh Report 176; Reconstruction America 223; UK race relations law 249–50; universalism 34; *see also* egalitarianism

equity: basic needs theory 103; multicultural education 289

Eriksen, H. 149

eroticized bodies 50, 397, 399

Esmail, Aneez 268

Essed, Philomena 29–30, 417

essentialism xiv, **133–35**; amalgamation 21; bigotry 54; collectivism 361; cultural racism

97; dress 118; Ebonics 121; hybridity 198; language 282

Ethiopia 7, 8, 86; Christianity 6; Ethiopianism 135–36, 162, 298; Garvey 162; Rastafari 357, 358

Ethiopian Opera 283

Ethiopianism 135–36, 162, 298

Ethiopians 166, 167, 174, 180, 450

ethnic awareness 170

ethnic cleansing 34, 136–38, 140, 185, 390; see also genocide

ethnic conflict 138–41, 145, 350; developing countries 104; globalization 169; homeless refugees 185; internet resources 464–65

ethnic density 272

ethnic groups 143, 148, 334, 336; see also minorities

ethnic monitoring 141–42

ethnicity 142–46; anthropology 28, 29; British Asians 67; children's learning 80–81; collective rights 193; corporate marketing of 443; development 103–4; dress 117; essentialism 134; globalization impact on 170; Hall 176, 324; homelessness link 185; housing 187, 188–89; identification 142–44; imagination of tradition 144; individual preferences 361; kinship relationships 233; language relationship 235, 236; new ethnicities 324, 369, 457; Puerto Ricans in the United States 332; racial profiling 345, 346; reactions to constraint 145; reading race 362; situational 197; Third World 419; see also race

ethnocentrism 16, 146–47; human rights law 281; interpretive reproduction 80; prejudice 329

ethnocide 23, 147–48, 164; Brazil 65; culturecide comparison 99, 100

ethnodevelopment 103–4

ethnogenesis 360

ethnonationalism 148–50

eugenics 150–51, 386; anthropological views 27–28; internet resources 465–66; reemergence of discourse 400; sexuality and birth control 398–99; social Darwinism 407; see also scientific racism

Eugenics Society 407

EUMC see European Monitoring Centre on Racism and Xenophobia

Eurocentrism 16, 134, 146, 175; dress 117; education 288; Marxism 260, 261–62; political correctness 321; racial coding 343

Europe: anti-Semitism 30–31; asylum seekers 46, 47; Blumenbach's racial taxonomy 166–67; capitalism 73; Chamberlain's theory 76; colonialism xiv–xv; conquest societies 89; ethnic cleansing 137; ethnic conflict 141; Fanon's critique of European humanism 155; far right extremism 318; fascism 155, 156; ghettos 167; Islamophobia 216; languages of 235; migrants to the United States 29, 44, 276; nationalism 297; nÕgritude 135–36; politics of race 322–23; racialization 67, 348; refugees 364; relativism 33; Roma 381–82; skinheads 402–3; slavery 403, 404; White Power-oriented parties 447–48; whiteness 452, 453; xenophobia 455; see also Eastern Europe; European Union

European Charter for Regional and Minority Languages 237

European Commission against Racism and Intolerance (ECRI) 210, 455, 470–71

European Convention on Human Rights and Fundamental Freedoms 210, 246, 252

European Council on Refugees and Exiles 471

European Monitoring Centre on Racism and Xenophobia (EUMC) 216, 217, 218, 471

European Roma Rights Center 472

European Union (EU) 141, 210–11; asylum seekers 46; doctors in Britain 268; xenophobia 455

Europeanization 86

Everington, Sam 268

evolution 101, 102, 109, 387; internet resources 464; social Darwinism 407; sociobiology 411; see also Darwinism

evolutionary psychology 386, 387, 388

Ewe 8

exclusion 339, 408–9; beauty ideals 52; British Muslims 69; cultural racism 54; institutional racism 204; media representations 369; multicultural education 288; socially invented barrier of 112; see also social exclusion

exoticization 50–51, 307

exploitation 151–52, 322; African labor 350; black sexuality 397; colonies of 7; conquest societies 89; globalization 169, 171; ideology of racism 201; Marxism 260; paternalism 310; systemic racism 416, 417; Third World 419; working class 145, 179, 200

extinction 108–9, 110, 174

Eysenck, Hans 429

Falk, David 225

false consciousness 91, 200

family: African Americans 10, 11, 312–13; American Indians 23; black feminism 60;

female subordination 312; Puerto Ricans in the United States 332; sexual abuse 395, 396; single parents 206, 430–31; symbolic role 398; transracial adoption 422–24; *see also* children; marriage

Fanon, Frantz 61, 84, 118, **153–55**, 305, 325

far right: Aryan Nations 300, 330, 448, 462; Aryan Republican Army 300, 302; British Movement 69, 70, 296, 402; British National Party 69–70, 256, 296, 300, 326, 376, 377, 443; British Union of Fascists 327; hate groups 466; National Front 234, 296, 300, 376, 377, 380–81, 402; Oklahoma bombing 302; the Order 300, 302, 303, 447; upsurge in European extremism 318; White Aryan Resistance 402; white backlash culture 441, 443, 444; White Power 446–49; *see also* fascism; Ku Klux Klan; Nazism; neo-nazism; skinheads

Fard, Wallace D. 294

Farrakhan, Louis 19, 277–78, 295, 373

fascism **155–57**, 297; *see also* far right; Nazism; neo-fascism

Faundez, Julio 130

FBI *see* Federal Bureau of Investigation

Feagin, Joe R. 92, 347, 373, 416

Federal Bureau of Investigation (FBI) 61, 115, 258, 469

Federal Writers' Project 472

Feldman, Larry 222

Felix Posen Bibliographic Project on Antisemitism 461–62

female circumcision xix, 97

feminism: black **58–60**, 396; black male responses to 264; Chicano 78; dress 118; Marxist 314; power 263; science 387, 388; subculture 457; *see also* gender; patriarchy; sexism; women

Fenton, Steve 339

Ferdinand, Rio 335

fertility 397, 400

fetishism: commodity 91; South Asian culture 68

feudalism 74, 93, 151, 276

The Fiendish Plot of Dr Fu Manchu (film) 305

Fiji 86, 104

Filipinos 42, 209

film: African Americans: *25th Hour* 255, *A Huey P. Newton Story* 255, *Bamboozled* 255, *Clockers* 255, *Do the Right Thing* 254, *Get on the Bus* 255, 278, *Girl 6* 255, *He Got Game* 255, *Jim Brown, All American* 255, *Joe's Bed-Study Barbershop: We Cut Heads* 254, *Jungle Fever* 255, *Malcolm X* 255, *Matewan* 391, *Mo' Better Blues* 254, *Panther* 61, *School Daze* 254, *She's Gotta Have It* 254, *Summer of Sam* 255, *The Color Purple* 255, *When We Were Kings* 19; American Indians: *Dances with Wolves* 24; Australian Aboriginals: *Rabbit-Proof Fence* 2; neo-nazism: *Betrayed* 303, *Talk Radio* 302–3; Orientalism: *The Fiendish Plot of Dr Fu Manchu* 305–6; Spike Lee films **254–5**, 278

Fingerhut, Natalie 164

Finot, Jean **157–58**

First Nations 21, 24, 193, 202

Firth, Raymond 98, 232

Fisher, Rudolph 196

Fiske, John 372

Fitzherbert, Kathleen 409

Fleras, Augie 290

FLN *see* Front de Libōration Nationale

Florida 16–17, 367

Foner, Nancy 15

football: Let's Kick Racism Out of Football 255–56; violence 98, 256

Ford, Henry 31, 169, 330

Foreman, George 19

Fortier, Anne-Marie 324

Foucault, Michel 176, 264, 307, 321, 342, 343, 388

Fox, George 35

Foxman, Abraham 278

Foxx, Red 195

France: Algeria 7; antiracism 34, 418; assimilation xiii; asylum seekers 47, 277; colonialism 85, 86; differentialism 45; egalitarianism 38; emancipation 123; Fanon 153; French Revolution 89, 108, 131, 296, 306; Grōgoire 172; migration from 276; negrophilia 299; "race relations" term 334; riots xv, 318; Senegalese decolonization 392; slavery 404, 405; xenophobia 455

Frankfurt School 90, 91, 321

Franklin, Benjamin 452

Franklin, Raymond A. 467

Franks, Gary 90

fraternity 233

Frawley, David 462

Frazier, E. Franklin 57–58, 91

Frazier, Joe 19

Fredrickson, George M. 110

free market economics 34, 89, 407

free-rider problem 360, 361

freedom 190, 191, 193

Freeman, Edward A. 214

Freire, Paulo **158–59**

French Revolution 89, 108, 131, 296, 306

Frercks, R. 462

Freudian theory 108; *see also* psychoanalytic theories

Freyre, Gilberto **159**

Front de LibŌration Nationale (FLN) 154, 155

Fullilove v. Klutznick (1980) 5

fundamentalism xvii; Christian 442; multicultural education 288

Furnivall, J. S. 316

Furrow, Burford Oneal 303

Gadhaffi, Muammar 259

Gaelic language 213

Galton, Francis 150, 386, 398

Gandhi, Mohandas Karamchand 77, **160–61**, 328; influence on King 81, 230; Mandela comparison 259

"gangsta" culture 457; *see also* rap music

Gardner, B. B. 108

Gardner, M. 108

Garrison, William Lloyd 38

Garrity, W. A. 463

Garvey, Marcus 51, 61, 135, **161–63**, 257, 298, 357–58

Gaskell, Elizabeth 213–14

Gasman, Daniel 174

Gast, Leon 19

Gates, Bill 169

Gates, Henry L. 335

Gaye, Marvin 286

gender: American Indians 24; anthropology 28; bigotry 55; black feminism 59; Black Panther Party 61; discrimination 29; ethnic cleansing 138; ethnicity 143; masculinity 262–65, 356, 396; minority groups 47; natural rights 190; Otherness 307; sexual abuse 396; as social construct 387; *see also* patriarchy; women

gender order 263

gender studies 263, 264

gendercide 164

General Medical Council (GMC) 268

genes 333–34

genetics 34, 128, 165–66, 334, 386, 387–88, 453; Boas 64; eugenics 150; hereditarianism 180; heritability 180–81; intelligence 121, 208; population 101; reproductive technologies 151; sociobiology 411; *see also* genotype; phenotype

genocide **163–65**, 390; Aboriginal Australians 1; American Indians 21, 22; Brazil 65; conquest 88; cultural 99, 100; definitions of 163, 164–65; Doomed Races Doctrine 111; ethnocide distinction 147–48; internet resources 466; Ireland 213; Otherness 306–7; Rwanda 138, 139; *see also* atrocities; ethnic cleansing; Holocaust

Genocide Convention (1948) 99, 147, 148, 163, 164, 181, 190

genome project 465

genotype 165–66, 411; *see also* genetics

geometry of race **166–67**

George, Nelson 91

Gerland, Georg 109–10

German Freedom Movement 437

Germany: asylum seekers 46, 277; Berlin Wall 140; Chamberlain 76; colonialism 86; emigration of Jews 136; ethnic inequalities xiii; eugenics 150; fascism 156; Gobineau 172; guestworkers 301; Haeckel 174; race concept 322; relocation of Poles 137; skinheads 402; *Volk* 174, 435–36, 437, 438; Wagner 437; war reparations 366; xenophobia 455; *see also* Nazism

Get on the Bus (film) 278

Ghana 8

ghettoization 168

ghettos **167–68**, 189, 266, 318, 331, 389; Chicago School 456; Kerner Report 229; Puerto Ricans in the United States 332

Giddings, Franklin H. 406

Gill, Andy 357

Gilroy, Paul 92, 106, 365, 399

Gimlin, Debra 50

Giuliani, Rudolph 105

Givens, Robin 426, 427

Glasgow, Douglas 98, 204, 379

Gliddon, George Robbins 180

globalization xiv, **169–71**; American Indians 23; Anglo-Indians 27; labor migration 277; language rights 237; neo-liberal capitalism 454; "New Times" thesis 176, 457; race relations 338, 339; transnational communities 106; white backlash culture 441, 443

GMC *see* General Medical Council

Gobineau, Joseph Arthur de 41, 76, 157, **171–72**, 180, 207, 438, 450

Goldberg, David 29–30

Goodrick-Clark, Nicholas 300

Gordon, Milton M. 44

Gordy, Berry 221, 284, 285–87

Gore, Tipper 357

Gorman, Siobhan 347

gospel music 63

Gossett, Thomas F. 64, 157, 239

Gould, Stephen Jay 38, 166, 167
government contracts 5, 12
Gramsci, Antonio 175, 176, 178, 179, 201, 457
Grandmaster Flash and the Furious Five 355–56
Grant, Bernie 375–76
Gratz v. *Bollinger* (2003) 6
Great Britain *see* Britain
Great Depression 248, 399
Greece: conflict with Turkey 137, 141; cultural borrowings 146, 147
Greeks, ancient 131; Afrocentric perspective 16; humor 194; patriarchy 312, 314; slavery 403
Greenwood 377–78
GrÕgoire, Henri 36, **172–73**
Gregory, Dick 195, 278
Gresson, Aaron David 373
Griffin, Nick 376
Griggs v. *Duke Power Company* (1971) 4
group definition 282
group identity 360–61
Grutter case (2003) 6
guestworkers 301, 318
Guevara, Che 61
Guiberneau, Montserrat 149
Guinea 8
Gulf War (1991) 220, 343, 444, 460
Gumplowicz, Ludwig 406–7
Guthrie, Richard 302, 303
GutiÕrrez, JosÕ Anger 77–78
gypsies 45, 184–85, 381; skinhead hostility towards 403; as targets of bigotry 56; underclass 430; *see also* Roma; travelers

Hacker, Andrew 10
Haddon, A. C. 334
Haddon, R. F. 189
Haeckel, Ernst **174–75**
Haile Selassie I 357–58
hair 51, 144
Haiti 37, 86
Haitians 9, 211, 405–6
halal butchers 126
Halbwachs, Maurice 80
Hall, Stuart **175–77**, 324; cultural identity 95, 96; diaspora 106, 198; encoding/decoding 342; "floating signifiers" 335; inferential racism 203–4, 326; media representations 371; new ethnicities 369; race/class relationship 261; youth subcultures 456, 457
Halliday, Fred 218–19
Halliday, R. J. 407
Hamilton, Charles V. 62, 204, 349, 351

Hamilton, William D. 411
Hamm, Mark 302, 303
hands-off policy 318–19
Hanks, Lawrence J. 124
Hannaford, Ivan 166, 437
Hanson, Pauline **177–78**, 282, 303–4
harassment 434, 435; British riots 374; housing clustering as response to 188; overseas doctors 269; police 319; racist discourse 352; United States 10
Harff, Barbara 163
Harlem 168, 212, 257, 332, 415
Harmand, Jules 111
Harris, David A. 346, 347
Harris, Fred 10
Hart-Celler Act (US, 1965) 248
Hartigan, John 29
Hatcher, Richard 80
hate crimes 10, 233, 319
hate groups 10, 466–67
hatred: bigotry 53; Hate Directory 467; religious 218; Wager 438; *see also* anti-Semitism; hate crimes; Islamophobia; racism
hats 118–19
Hattersley, Roy 246
Hausa 170
Hawkins, La-Van 104–5
Hayes, Peter 423
health: African Americans 10; basic needs theory 103; black feminism 60; class relationship 438–39; housing relationship 127; Latino policy preferences 241, 242; mental illness 270–73, 396, 439–40; multicultural policy 290; *see also* medicine
Heath, Anthony xvi
Hebdige, Dick 457
Hecht, Jennifer Michael 157
Hegel, Georg W. F. 306
hegemonic masculinity 263
hegemony **178–80**; education 123; racializing 29; youth subcultures 457
Heidegger, Martin 306
Held, David 170
Heller, Peter 426
hereditarianism 127–28, **180**, 208, 407, 411
Herero people 111
heritability 150, 166, **180–81**, 208
Herrenvolk 435–36
Herrnstein, Richard 121
Herzl, Theodor 459
Hewitt, Roger 457
Hezbollah xvi
Hibbert, Joseph 358

Hicks, Charles 284
hierarchies: Blumenbach's racial taxonomy 38, 166–67; Cuvier 180; Finot's critique of 157; Gobineau 171; language 280–81; multiracialism 292; tokenism 422; whiteness 451; *see also* classification, racial
Hill, Anita 420
Hill, Clifford 315
Hill, George Chatteron 110
Hill, Jane 29
Hinduism: caste 74, 75, 293; patriarchy 313, 314; *sati* 415
Hindus 139, 185, 350
hip-hop culture 92, 457
Hiro, Dilip 315
Hispanics: environmental organizations 205; language 236; literacy test requirements for voting 244; media representations 267; television news industry 266; underclass 430; *see also* Latinos
Hitler, Adolf 50, 172, 381, 435; Haeckel influence 174; Holocaust 182; Wagner as inspiration for 437, 438; White Power 446, 449
Hobbes, Thomas 131
Hoberman, John 204, 226
Hogg, Quintin 327
Hoggart, Richard 175, 176
Holmes, Larry 20
Holocaust 31, 163, 165, **181–83**, 459, 467
Holocaust History Project 467
Holocaust Project: Multimedia Timebase 467
Holyfield, Evander 425, 426
homelessness **183–85**, 408
homoeroticism 399
homogenization 198; cultural 169; globalization 458
homophobia 278, 356
homosexuality xix
Honduras 22
Honeyford, Raymond 216, 442
Hong Kong: English language 236; migrants to the United States 43; UK immigration law 246
honor crimes xiv
Hooker, John Lee 63
hooks, bell 265, 370
Hooper, Baroness 445
Hoover, J. Edgar 61
Hopwood, et al. v. State of Texas (1996) 6
Horowitz, Irving L. 111
Horsman, Reginald 110
Horton, Willie 337
hostels 184
Hottentot Venus 50, **185–86**

House, Callie 366
housing **186–90**; British Muslims 217; constraint-choice perspective 187, 189; discrimination 250; environmental racism 126–27; ghettos 168; homelessness 183–85, 408; mental illness link 272; Pruitt-Igoe 331; racial discrimination 119; refugees 185; restrictive covenants 243; segregation 389, 390, 439
Howard, John 3, 177
Howell, Leonard 358
Howlin' Wolf 63
HRDE *see* Human Rights Documents Exchange
Huggins, John 61
Hughes, Langston 196–97
Hull, Gloria 59
human rights xiv, **190–94**; antislavery 37; claims 193; country reports 467; human unity 191–92; international covenants 190–91, 192–93; international organizations 211; internet resources 467, 468; Islamic codes xix; justifiable restrictions on 191; as legal rights 193; minority languages 281; police abuse 320; racial discrimination definition 252; Roma 472; UNESCO teaching materials 431–32; United Nations 432; *see also* civil rights; political rights; rights
Human Rights Act (UK, 1998) 246, 251
Human Rights Documents Exchange (HRDE) 463
humanism 155, 389
Humbolt, Alexander von 452
humor 129, **194–97**
Hungary 175, 402–3
Hurston, Zora Neale 196
Hutchinson, Earl Ofari 346
Hutton, Christopher 237
Hutus 7, 138, 139, 165, 185, 350
Huxley, Julian 334
Huxley, L. 462
hybridity xix, **198–99**; Anglo-Indians 26; diasporic identities 106; globalization 458; *mestizaje* 32–33; politics of difference 457

iAbolish 462
IBHR *see* International Bill of Human Rights
Ibo 8, 170, 313
ICARE (Internet Centre Anti Racism Europe) 471
ICCPR *see* International Covenant on Civil and Political Rights
Ice Cube 264, 356
Ice-T 356

ICERD *see* International Convention on the Elimination of All Forms of Racial Discrimination

ICESCR *see* International Covenant on Economic, Social and Cultural Rights

identity: African American 113–15; American 113; American Indians 24; Anglo-Indians 26; Baldwin 115, 116, 117; British Asians 67, 68; consumption 92–93; diasporic 106; double consciousness 112; ethnic 29, 67, 143, 148, 233, 360; European 67; Fanon 153; group 360–61; hybridity 198; Irish 214–15; Jewish 460; masculinities 263–64, 265; multiple 307; multiracial 291–92; Muslim 67; new ethnicities 369; New Negro concept 162; Other 306; plurality of xiv; politics of difference 176; psychological interpretations 96; racial 29, 324; racial pride 33; scientific understandings of 388–89; social exclusion 408; subcultural 457; transnational 169; transracial adoption 410, 422–23, 424; Western 215, 453; white 448, 451, 452, 453; *see also* cultural identity; national identity

identity politics 24, 324

ideological state apparatus (ISA) 179

ideology xvii, 179, **200–201**; exploitation 151; fascism 155–56; Marxism 260, 261–62; media representations 371; nationalism 296, 297; racial coding 342–44; racialization 349; racism 349, 350; slavery 405; White Power 448

Illingworth, Montieth 427

ILO *see* International Labor Organization

imagined communities 95

immigrants: Boas' studies 64; Britain 290; colonized minorities comparison 209; education 288; ethnic identities 233; housing 187, 188, 189; humor 194, 195; illegal 246, 248–49, 405–6, 430; integration 45; Ku Klux Klan 234; Latinos 240, 241; media representations 370; racialization of politics 323; social work 409; white 29; xenophobia 455; *see also* asylum seekers; immigration; migration; refugees

immigration: African Caribbeans in Britain 14; Asian Americans 42–43; British National Party 70; British use of term 122; conquest 88; ethnic identification 142; eugenicist fears 398–99; Hanson attacks on 177; internet resources 462–63, 469; Jewish conspiracy theories 447; Latino policy preferences 241, 242; One Nation 303, 304; Powell on 326, 327; race card 337; racist discourse 352, 353, 354; UK law 68, **244–47**, 250, 251, 469; US law **247–49**, 393, 407, 469; white backlash culture 443; *see also* asylum seekers; immigrants; migration; refugees

Immigration Act (UK, 1971) 246

Immigration Act (UK, 1988) 246, 439

Immigration Act (US, 1917) 248

Immigration and Asylum Act (UK, 1999) 185

Immigration and Naturalization Service (INS) 393

Immigration Reform and Control Act (US, 1986) 248–49

imperialism: antislavery movement campaign against 35; bigotry 55; British 117; colonialism distinction 85; hereditarian theory 180; Orientalism 343; Otherness 307; racial 174; racial extinction 109, 111; racism as product of 350; white power 98; whiteness 453; *see also* colonialism

impoverishment 416

INC *see* Indian Nation Congress

Incas 21, 171, 275

incitement to violence 128

inclusion 339, 408; Canada 290; media representations 369; social contract 131

incomes 58, 132

INCORE (Initiative on Conflict Resolution and Ethnicity) 465

indentured labor 275

India: abolition of slavery 405; Anglo-Indians 24–27; Aryanism 462; British Asians 66–67; caste 74–75; colonialism 86, 415; cultural borrowings 146; culture 99; debt bondage 405; English language 236; ethnic conflict 139, 185, 350; Gandhi 160–61; indentured labor 275; languages of 235; mass migrations from 136–37, 138, 277; migrants to Britain 14; migrants to the United States 42, 43; positive discrimination 107; Roma 381; schizophrenia 271, 272; sexually transmitted diseases 399; underclass 430; *see also* Indians

Indian Child Welfare Act (US, 1978) 424

Indian Nation Congress (INC) 160, 161

Indianization 26

Indians xvi, 66, 67, 147; doctors in Britain 268; educational achievement 217; South Africa 412–13; whiteness concept 453; *see also* British Asians; South Asians

indigenous peoples **201–3**; Africa 8; Brazil 64–65; conquest over 88; culturecide 100, 164; Doomed Races Doctrine 108, 109–10, 111; *encomienda* 125; ethnocide 147; genocide 165; human rights 192–93; internet resources

468; land rights 193, 202–3, 211; language rights 281; slavery 404; *see also* Aboriginal Australians; American Indians

individualism: Baldwin 116; human rights law 281; methodological 361

Indonesia: Chinese minority 139; language 236; matrifocality 313; pluralism 316

industrialization 297, 430

inequalities xiii, 179; African Americans 9; American society 226; apartheid 40, 413; colonialism 85, 87; conquest societies 88; educational 439; free market economics 89; incomes 132; media representations 370; paternalism 310; Rousseau 131; scientific racism 38; segregation 390; social exclusion 408; systemic racism 416, 417

inferential racism 98, **203–4**, 326

INS *see* Immigration and Naturalization Service

Institute for the Study of Academic Racism 466

Institute of Race Relations 471

institutional racism xvi, 98, **204–6**, 263, 345; adoption system 423; black activist analysts 416; Black Panther Party 60; British riots 375; homelessness 183; Kerner Report 229; Lawrence case 204, 252, 253, 320, 439, 441; police 319, 320, 377, 385, 441; sexual abuse 396; social work 409, 440, 441; welfare organizations 439, 440, 441

integration xiii, xvii, xix, 45, **206–7**; Aboriginal Australians 2; black conservatism 90; Brazil 159; British context 122, 440; Canada 290; consumption 91; Garvey's opposition to 161; Kerner Report 229; Malcolm X's rejection of 257; UK immigration law 246; white flight 445; *see also* assimilation

intelligence 121, **207–9**; educational underachievement 429; eugenics 398; hereditarianism 180; internet resources 468; *see also* intelligence testing; IQ

Intelligence Project 466

intelligence testing 28, 128, **207–8**; heritability 181; institutional racism 206; *see also* intelligence; IQ

intelligent conclusion 16–17

Inter-American Court of Human Rights 202–3, 211

intergroup relations 350

intermarriage 450; Asian Americans 44; Brazil 65–66; South Africa 87; United States 87; *see also* miscegenation

internal colonialism 23, 168, 192, **209–10**, 416

International Bill of Human Rights (IBHR) 190, 192

International Convention on the Elimination of All Forms of Racial Discrimination (ICERD) 192, **210**, 251–52, 432

International Covenant on Civil and Political Rights (ICCPR) 192, 252

International Covenant on Economic, Social and Cultural Rights (ICESCR) 192

International Labor Organization (ILO) 202, 252, 432

international law: Convention Against Discrimination in Education 432; Convention on the Prevention of the Crime of Genocide 99, 147, 148, 163, 164, 181, 190; Convention on the Rights of All Migrant Workers and Members of their Families 433; Convention relating to the Status of Refugees 46, 363, 364; human rights 190–91, 192–93; humanitarian 136; International Bill of Human Rights 190, 192; International Convention on the Elimination of All Forms of Racial Discrimination 192, **210**, 251–52, 432; International Covenant on Civil and Political Rights 192, 252; International Covenant on Economic, Social and Cultural Rights 192; minority language rights 281; racial discrimination **251–52**; refugee status 363; self-determination 202; UNESCO instruments 432

international organizations **210–11**; African Union 211; Council of Europe 210; European Union 46, 141, 210–11, 268, 455; International Labor Organization 202, 252, 432; Organization for Security and Co-operation in Europe 210; Organization of African Unity 211, 367; Organization of American States 141, 211; UNESCO 28, **431–32**, 473; *see also* United Nations

international relations 74

internet: racist humor 197; White Power web sites 448

internment camps 346, 348, 366–67, 392

intolerance: bigotry 53, 54; tradition of 434; UN instruments 433; Vienna declaration 455; *see also* prejudice; tolerance

Invisible Man (Ellison) 197, **211–13**

IQ 121, 207–8, 388; cultural bias 442; educational underachievement 429; heritability 181; *see also* intelligence testing

Iran xvii–xviii, 46, 215, 314

Iraq xviii

Irish nationalism 260

Irish people **213–15**; ethnic organization in the United States 145; homelessness 184; mental

illness 270; migrant workers 260; racialization 349; as targets of bigotry 56; white race concept 449–50; *see also* Northern Ireland
ISA *see* ideological state apparatus
Islam xvi, xvii; Africa 6, 451; Ali's conversion to 18; bigotry 53; blackness 450–51; Cleaver 83; colonialism impact on 86; Malcolm X 257; marriage xix; patriarchy xiv, 313; political 215; Qutb xvii–xviii; racial coding 343; resistance to racism 33; slavery 403; terrorism xviii; Tyson's conversion to 426; *see also* Islamophobia; Muslims; Nation of Islam
Islamophobia xv, 67, **215–19**, 444; conceptual problems with term 31; cultural racism 97; discrimination 216–17; history and context 215–16; media representation 217–18; rise in 393; *see also* Muslims
Israel xvii, 360, 459–60; anti-Semitism smear against critics of 31–32, 460; deportation of Palestinians 138, 277; patriarchy 313; positive discrimination 107; *see also* Zionism
Issues and Views 464
Italian Americans 144
Italy xiv, 156, 382
Ivory Coast 8

Jackson, Donovan 232
Jackson, Jesse 12, 90, 104, **220–21**, 224, 225, 278, 295
Jackson, Mahalia 63
Jackson, Michael **221–23**, 286
Jacobson, L. 391
Jamaah Islamiya 393
Jamaica: cultural identity 95; dress 117–18; Garvey in 162; Hall 175; migrants to Britain 14, 45; race/class relationship 261; Rastafari 357, 358; reggae 365; schizophrenia 271
James, Walter 409–10
James, William 308
JanMohamed, Abdul R. 84
Japan: American values 391; caste 75; colonial era 86; indentured labor 275; migrants to the United States 42, 43; patriarchy 314; popular representations of the Japanese 306; racism 350; underclass 430
Japanese Americans 279, 346, 348, 366–67, 392
jati 75
Java 313
jazz 299
Jeff, Morris, Jr. 423
Jefferson, Thomas 36–37, 50
Jefferson, Tony 263, 456, 457

Jenkins, Roy 45, 135, 206
Jensen, Arthur R. 181, 208, 429
Jewkes, R. 264
Jews: American values 391; Boas' studies 64; Chamberlain's theory 76; comedians 129; conspiracy theories 330–31, 373, 446, 447; diaspora 106; displacement 137; emancipation 123; emigration from Germany 136; ethnic organization in the United States 145; ethnicity 144; exoticization of Jewish women 50, 51; expulsion from Spain 125; genocide 163, 165; German language use 235; ghettos 167; Holocaust 181–82; humor 194, 195; identity politics 324; Jackson antagonism of Jewish community 220, 295; Ku Klux Klan attacks on 233; as middleman minority 274; migration 275; minority status 279; Nazism 156–57; neo-nazism 300; Otherness 306; Ottoman Empire 360; pogroms 317; positive discrimination policies in Israel 107; prejudice against 329; *Protocols of the Learned Elders of Zion* 31, 330–31, 373, 470; racial coding 342, 343; religious conflict 139; as scapegoats 383; skinhead hostility towards 403; stereotypes 414; as targets of bigotry 56; violent attacks on 303; Zionism 459–60; *see also* anti-Semitism
Jhally, Sut 370
Jim Crow 63, 70, **223–24**, 230, 389; dress 118, 119; drugs 119, 120; humor 195; internet resources 468–69; minstrelsy 283; transracial adoption 423; Tulsa 377; *see also* segregation
Johnson, Lew 284
Johnson, Lyndon B. 4, 5, 82, 228, 230, 266
Johnson v. Board of Regents (2001) 6
Johnson v. Transportation Agency, Santa Clara County (1987) 4
Jolson, Al 284
Jones, LeRoi 284
Jones, Mack H. 124, 125
Jones, Simon 457
Jordan, Colin 69, 327
Jordan, Michael 10, **224–27**, 401, 426
Jordan, Winthrop 37, 451
Jordan-Zachery, Julia 393
journalism 266, 308, 354; *see also* news media
Judeo-Christian tradition 313
justice 130, 132, 290
Justinian 366

Kang, Jerry 346
Kanneh, Kadiatu 118

Kant, Immanuel 131, 386–87
Kashmiris 67, 68
Keith, Arthur 407
Kemp, Jack 124
Kennedy, John F. 4, 82, 214, 230, 248, 257
Kennedy, Randall 128
Kennedy, Robert 230
Kenya 7, 8, 236, 398
Kerner Report (1968) 10, 60, **228–29**, 266, 267, 384
Kersands, Billy 284
Kidd, Benjamin 406
Kikuyu 8
kin selection 412
King, Don 19, 49, 223, 425, 426
King, Martin Luther 9, 77, 81–82, 220, **229–31**, 278; assassination of 83, 115, 231; Gandhi influence on 161; Malcolm X comparison 257; nonviolent civil disobedience 160; tokenism 421; voting rights 243–44; Zionism 460; see also civil rights movement
King, Rodney 105, 224, **231–32**, 266, 318, 346, 400, 434
King, Wallace 284
Kingsley, Charles 213–14
kinship 69, **232–33**, 310, 313
Kipling, Rudyard 86
Kirp, David 71
KKK see Ku Klux Klan
Klein, Naomi 90, 225
Klor de Alva, Jorge 417
Kloss, Heinz 237
knowledge 307, 321, 338, 388
Knox, Robert 39, 180
K—hler, Joachim 437, 438
Korea: migrants to the United States 42, 43; slavery 403
Kosack, – 261
Kosovo 97, 136; see also Albania
Kristeva, Julia 306
Krzywicki, Ludwik 110
Ku Klux Klan (KKK) 224, **233–34**, 300, 377, 443; Aryan Republican Army 302; Garvey's negotiations with 162; internet resources 469; racist humor 197; skinheads 402
Kung Fu (TV series) 305
Kuper, Leo 148, 164, 298
Kurami, Amina Lawal xix
Kurds 148, 193, 281

labor: black feminism 59, 60; capitalism 74; exploitation 151–52; globalization of 171; migrant 151–52, 261, 277, 433; New International Division of **301**; sexual division of 311, 312, 314; see also employment
Labour Party 245, 250, 376, 438, 443
Labov, William 236
Lacan, Jacques 176
Laclau, Ernesto 175, 176
LaFeber, Walter 226
Lakota "Sioux Nation" 22
Lamont, MichÒle 92–93
land rights: Aboriginal Australians 2–3; American Indians 22, 23; as collective rights 193; indigenous peoples 193, 202–3, 211; Ireland 213; South Africa 40
Landry, Bart 58
Lane, David 447
Langan, Pete 302, 303
Langer, Beryl 143
language **235–38**; Africa 8; American Indians 23; Aryanism 41, 42; coding 341–42; cultural rights 193; culturecide 164; decline of 279–80, 281; Ebonics 121–22, 197, 237; educational underachievement 429; epithets 128–29; ethnic cleansing 138; ethnocide 147; Gaelic 213; homeless South Asians 184; hybridity 198; linguistic practices 29; minority language rights **279–83**; multilingualism 122; political correctness 321; race as signifier 334–35; racist discourse 353, 354; sociobiology 411; structuralism 371; youth subcultures 457; see also discourse analysis; English language
Laos 43
LAPD see Los Angeles Police Department
Lapland 111, 193
Laqueur, Thomas 134
Las Casas, BartolomÕ de 126, **238–39**
Latin America: antiracism 32–33; *encomienda* 125–26; indigenous peoples 202; paternalism 310; refugees 364; serfdom 124; white race concept 450; whiteness 452; see also South America
Latinos **239–43**; Central Park Jogger case 76; composition and growth 239–41; education 11; English language teaching 121; environmental organizations 205; exoticization of Latina women 50; family size 10; linguistic practices 29; Los Angeles 232; masculinity 264; political behavior and empowerment 241–43; population forecasts 249, 266; poverty 11, 90; public opinion and policy preferences 241; see also Hispanics
law: African Americans 12; American Indians 24; asylum seekers 46; civil rights **243–44**;

humanitarian 136; indigenous land rights 202; inter-racial sexual contact 398; legal rights 193; race relations **249–51**; racial discrimination **251–52**, 350–51, 358; refugees 471, 472; slavery 404; UK immigration 68, **244–47**, 250, 251, 469; US immigration **247–49**, 393, 407, 469; *see also* cases; international law; Jim Crow; legislation

law enforcement 395–96

Lawrence, Errol 179

Lawrence, Stephen xiii, **252–54**, 362, 434; Diallo case comparison 105; institutional racism 204, 252, 253, 320, 439, 441; internet resources 469–70; media role 372; policing practices 318–19, 320, 346; Race Relations (Amendment) Act 251; youth/police conflict 15

Le Page, Robert 236

Le Pen, Jean-Marie 296

leaders, political: Blair 394; Bush, George Sr. 12, 13, 20, 124, 244, 337; Bush, George W. 6, 240, 394; Chirac xv; Clinton 6, 124, 220, 249; De Gaulle 392; De Klerk 41; Haile Selassie I 357–58; Hitler 50, 172, 174, 182, 381, 435, 437, 438, 446, 449; Howard 3, 177; Jefferson 36–37, 50; Johnson 4, 5, 82, 228, 230, 266; Kennedy 4, 82, 214, 230, 248, 257; Lincoln 39; Mandela 41, **258–59**, 413; Mbeki 186, 259, 413; Nasser xvii; Nixon 4, 62, 442; Reagan 4, 6, 12, 13, 20, 129–30, 445; Smuts 40; Thatcher 57, 96, 129–30, 381, 443; Verwoerd 40

League of St. George 234

learning 158

LEAs *see* Local Education Authorities

Lee, Robert G. 398

Lee, Spike **254–55**, 258, 278

legal rights 193, 281–82, 404

legislation: anti-terrorism 218; antidiscriminatory 409, 418, 425; apartheid 40, 41, 389; Aryan law 462; Asylum and Immigration Act (UK, 1996) 435; Asylum and Immigration (Appeals) Act (UK, 1993) 246; Australia 2, 3; Boyle's Law (US, 1965) 71; British Nationality Act (1981) 246, 439; Children Act (UK, 1989) 409; Chinese Exclusion Act (US, 1882) 248; civil rights 89, 243–44; Civil Rights Act (US, 1964) 3, 4, 82, 224, 230, 244, 286, 420; Civil Rights Act (US, 1991) 4, 5, 13, 244, 420; Commonwealth Immigrants Act (UK, 1962) 245; Education Act (UK, 1944) 428; Education Act (UK, 1980) 445; Education Reform Act (UK, 1988) 445; Equal Employment Opportunity

Act (UK, 1972) 3; eugenics 150; Hart-Celler Act (US, 1965) 248; hate crimes 319; Human Rights Act (UK, 1998) 246, 251; Immigration Act (UK, 1971) 246; Immigration Act (UK, 1988) 246, 439; Immigration Act (US, 1917) 248; Immigration and Asylum Act (UK, 1999) 185; Immigration Reform and Control Act (US, 1986) 248–49; Indian Child Welfare Act (US, 1978) 424; Jim Crow era 223; Local Government Act (UK, 1966) 440; McCarran-Walter Act (US, 1952) 248; Multi-Ethnic Placement Act (US, 1995) 423; multiculturalism 290; National Health and Community Care Act (UK, 1990) 409; Nationality, Immigration and Asylum Act (UK, 2002) 46; Page Act (US, 1870) 398; Public Works Employment Act (US, 1977) 5; Race Relations Act (UK, 1968) 250; Race Relations Act (UK, 1976) 185, 216, 250, 445; Race Relations (Amendment) Act (UK, 2000) 251, 253; racist 323; reparations 365, 366–67; Small Business Job Protection Act (US, 1996) 423; social care 409; transracial adoption 423, 424; travelers 185; UK immigration law 68, 185, 245–46, 439; US immigration law 43, 248–49; Voting Rights Act (US, 1965) 244; *see also* international law; Jim Crow; law; policy

legitimacy 328

Lemkin, Raphðel 99, 147, 163

Lemm, M. 442

Let's Kick Racism Out of Football **255–56**

LÔvi-Strauss, Claude 1

Levinas, Emmanuel 306

Levine, Lawrence 63, 284

Levinson, David 146

Lewis, Bernard 451

Lewis, C. S. 150

Lewis, Justin 370

Lewis, Lennox 425, 426

Lewis, Oscar 332

liberalism 28, 408

liberation 158

liberation movements 8, 297, 447

Liberia 86, 135, 162

Liberty City 380

Liberty Lobby 402

Lieberfeld, Daniel 426–27

Lincoln, Abraham 39

Linnaeus, Carolus 133, 166, 167, 386

literacy 158, 244

literature 84

Little, Alan 410

Little, Earl 257
Livingstone, Frank 28
Local Education Authorities (LEAs) 445
Local Government Act (UK, 1966) 440
location 16, 17
Locke, Gary 43
Locke, John 131
London: ghettos 167; homelessness 183; languages spoken in 236; Macpherson Report 204; riots 373–75, 384–85; segregation 331, 390
Loney, Martin 409–10
Lopez, Jennifer 129
Los Angeles: black middle class 58; ghettos 167, 168; Motown 286; riots (1992) 105, 231–32, 266, 318; Watts riots (1965) 228–29, 250, 378–79, 445
Los Angeles Police Department (LAPD) 318, 400, 401
Louima, Abner 105, 318
Louis, Joe 18, 225
Louisiana Purchase 94
Loving v. Virginia (1967) 291
Lumpenproletariat 430
Lyell, Charles 108
Lyman, Stanford M. 308–9
Lynch, Frederick 442
lynching 114, 212, 224, 383; Ku Klux Klan 233, 234; race card 337; as sexual violence 398; white backlash culture 441

Mabley, Jackie "Moms" 196
Mabo v. Queensland (1992) 2, 202
Mac an Ghaill, M. 263
McCarran-Walter Act (US, 1952) 248
MacDonald, Heather 347–48
McDonalds 171
MacGregor, John 445
McGregor, Russell 110
McGuire, George Alexander 162
McLintock, Anne 368
McManus, Chris 268
Macpherson Report (1999) 204–5, 252–54, 296, 318–19, 320, 377, 441, 470
McVeigh, Timothy 302, 303
madrasahs xv
Magubane, Zine 394
Major, John 443
Majors, Richard 263
Malays 166, 167, 400
Malaysia 140, 236
Malcolm X 9, 18, 230, 257–58, 294–95; assassi-

nation of 115, 258; Cleaver comparison 83; double consciousness 112; dress 118–19; influence on Black Panther Party 61; PG-RNA 367; Spike Lee's film 255; tokenism 421
male chauvinism 61
Mali Federation 392
Mandela, Nelson 41, 258–59, 413
Mao Tse-Tung 61
Maoris 202
Marable, Manning 230
Marcantonio, Vito 144
Marger, Martin 206, 207
marginal man 309–10
marginalization: Aboriginal Australians 2; sexual abuse 395; social exclusion 408
market relations 73, 408
marketing 225
Marley, Bob 358, 364
marriage: Aboriginal Australians 2; African Americans 10; arranged 97; Asian Americans 44; cultural racism 97; endogamy 74; intermarriage 44, 65–66, 87, 450; Puerto Ricans in the United States 332
Marriott, D. 264
Marshall, George 402
Marshall, Thurgood 12, 420
Martin v. Wilks (1989) 4–5, 12
Martinique 95, 153
Marx, Karl 259, 260; capitalism 73; class struggle 174; consciousness 179; ideology 200; influence on Cox 94; migration 276
Marxism 259–62; American racism 293; capitalism 73; class and nationalism 260; Cleaver 83; Cox 94; development 102; Du Bois 115; educational underachievement 428; exploitation 151, 152; Fanon 154; feminists 314; Hall 175–76; hegemony 178; ideology 200, 201, 261–62; Lumpenproletariat 430; migration 68; nationalism 297; race relations 341; reductionism 260–61, 417; youth subcultures 457
masculinity 262–65; rap music 356; sexual abuse 396; see also gender; men
Mason, Elisa 471
Mason, William 234
mass production 169
Matewan (film) 391
Mathews, Robert 303
matriarchy 312, 313, 314
matrifocality 312–13
Mau Mau movement 8
Mauritania 406
Maxi Indians 193

Mayagna 202–3, 211

Mayans 21, 22

Mayor, Barbara 409–10

Mayr, Ernst 101

Mbeki, Thabo 186, 259, 413

Mead, George Herbert 80

media xvi, **265–67**; American Indians 24; asylum seekers 46; British riots 374; eroticized black body 399; humor 195–96; Islamophobia 217–18; Powell 326; race as signifier 335; racial coding 343, 344; racist discourse 352, 354; representations 368–72; September 11th 2001 terrorist attacks 394; stereotypes 347; white backlash culture 442, 443; youth subcultures 456; *see also* film; news media; television

medication 272–73

medicine **267–70**; *see also* health

Melanesia 110

melting pot xiii, xvii, 44, 45, 159, 206, 440

men: black male body 50, 399; black sexuality 399; masculinity 262–65, 356, 396

Mendel, Gregor 102, 166

Menson, Michael 253–54

mental deficiency 150

mental illness **270–73**, 439–40; conditions 270–71; medication and psychotherapies 272–73; reasons for 271–72; sexual abuse victims 396

mercantilism 275–76, 301

Mercer, Kobena 371

merit **273–74**; African Caribbeans 15; conservatism 90; equal opportunity 129, 207; medical profession 269

meritocracy: affirmative action 442; British education system 15, 428; medical profession 269

Merrison Report (1975) 268

Merritt, William T. 423

Merry, Sally Engle 29

Merton, Robert 390–91

Mesopotamia 312

messianic movements 135

Messner, Michael 263, 264

mestizaje 32, 75

methodological individualism 361

Metzger, Tom 402

Mexican-Americans 239, 240, 405–6; *Aztlán* 47; Chávez 77–78; ethnicity 143–44; illegal immigration from 248; internal colonialism 209; *see also* Chicanos

Mexico: American Indians 21, 22, 24; *Aztlán* 47; Doomed Races Doctrine 110; slavery 405

Miami riots 380

middle class: alienation of 91; black bourgeoisie 57–58, 91; consumer discrimination 92; educational achievement 428; hegemony 178–79; King's mobilization of middle-class blacks 230; *see also* bourgeoisie; class

Middle East 397–98, 403, 451

middleman minority **274–75**

migrant labor 151–52, 261, 277, 433

migration xvii, **275–78**; Asian Americans 42–43; Brazil 159; British Asians 66–67, 68; Caribbean 14; Commonwealth 340; difference 307; economic 46, 363; ethnocentric responses from host society 146; globalization 169, 170–71; Indian partition 136–37; internet resources 470; Puerto Ricans 332; racialization of politics 323; rural-urban 276; social ordering principles 28; white backlash culture 443; *see also* diaspora; immigration; refugees

Miles, Robert 261, 262, 350, 373

Mill, John Stuart 157

Miller, W. R. 230

Million Man March 224, 255, 264, **277–78**

Mineta, Norman 43

minorities **278–79**; assimilation 44–45; conquest societies 88; disadvantage concept 107; environmental organizations 205; housing 187; humor 194–95; internal colonialism 209; language rights 237; media representations 265–66, 368–69; mental illness 270; racist discourse 353; social exclusion 408; *see also* ethnic groups

minority language rights **279–83**

Minority Rights Group 467

minstrelsy **283–85**, 399

Mirande, A. 264

miscegenation **285**, 336; Anglo-Indians 25; Asian Americans 44; Australia 2; Chamberlain's theory 76; creoles 94; eugenicist fears 398–99; Latin America 450; slavery 311; *see also* intermarriage; multiracialism

misdiagnosis 271, 272

Miskito 22, 23, 24

misorientation 17

Miss America pageant 51

missionaries: African nationalism 135; Australia 2; colonialism 86; Mexico 47

Missouri ex. rel. v. Canada (1938) 243

mixed race *see* multiracialism

mobilization 140, 149, 230

modernity: bigotry 55, 56; English language 281; "Gothic sociology" 309; Holocaust as man-

ifestation of 182; negrophilia 299; risk and insecurity 458; science 388; Western 34
modernization theory 103
mods 457
Mohawk 24
MolnÃr, VirÃg 92–93
Mongolians 75, 166, 174, 180, 450
Monism 174
monogenesis 167, 186, 386
Montagu, Ashley 28
Montaigne, Michel de 33
Montesquieu, Charles Louis, Baron de Secondat 33
Montgomery bus boycott 230
Moore, Robert 126
Moors 125, 294
"moral alchemy" 391
moral entrepreneurs 56
moral panic 264, 370, 371
morality 36
Mormons 233
Morris, Henry C. 110
Morton, Samuel 109
mosaic metaphor xiii, 206, 316
Moseley, Oswald 327
Moss Side riots (1981) 373, 374
Mossadegh, Mohammed xvii
motherhood: black feminism 60; sexual abuse 396; slavery 397
Motown 221, 284, **285–87**
Mouffe, Chantal 175, 176
Mozambique 8, 276
MTV 221–22
Mugabe, Robert 258, 413
mugging 456–57
Muhammad, Elijah 18, 19, 257, 294–95
Muhammad, Wallace Deen 19, 295
Muharrar, Mikal 347
mulatto 75, 159, 291
Mller, Max 41–42, 450
Multi-Ethnic Placement Act (US, 1995) 423
"multicultural drift" 176
multicultural education 99, 122–23, **287–89**, 290, 440
multiculturalism xiii–xiv, xviii, 45, **289–91**, 370; Britain 68, 69, 218, 440; critiques of 442; equality xix; ethnic identities 324; globalization 458; Hanson attacks on 177, 303; Jewish conspiracy theories 447; media representations 369; "New Times" thesis 176; political correctness 321; as a problem xx; social work 410; white backlash culture 443,

444; youth subcultures 457; *see also* cultural diversity
multiethnic education *see* multicultural education
multilingualism 122, 236, 279
multiracial education *see* multicultural education
multiracialism **291–93**; *see also* miscegenation
Murdoch, Rupert 226
Murji, Karim 384
Murphy, Eddie 195
Murray, Charles 90, 121, 468
Murray, Charles Shaar 286
music: blues 63, 426; commodification of black 370; gospel 63; Jackson 221–22; jazz 299; minstrelsy 283–85; Motown 221, 284, 285–87; popular 56; reggae 237, 358, **364–65**; Rock Against Racism 380–81; skinhead 402; Wagner **437–38**; *see also* rap music
Muslim Brotherhood xvii
Muslim Council of Britain 218
Muslims: asylum seekers 47; black 116; Bosnia 145, 185; British xvi, 67, 69; ethnic cleansing in the Balkans 138; French riots xv; identity politics 324; India 139, 185, 350; racial coding 343; radicalization of xv; Roma 381; September 11th aftermath 392, 393; women xiv, xviii–xix; *see also* Islam; Islamophobia; Nation of Islam
Myrdal, Gunnar 9, 28, 74, 176, **293**, 327, 340
myths 149

NAACP *see* National Association for the Advancement of Colored People
Nabokov, Vladimir 321
NABSW *see* National Association of Black Social Workers
Namibia 8, 111, 165
narrowcasting 267
Nasser, Gamal Abdul xvii
nation: ethnonationalism 148–49; fascism 156; Marxism 260; multicultural education 288; nationalism 296
nation-building xiii; Nigeria 144; South Africa 41
Nation of Islam 61, 135, **294–95**; Ali 18–19, 401; Malcolm X 118, 257, 258; Million Man March 277–78; reverse racism 373
nation-states: citizenship 289; globalization impact on 170; languages 280, 282
National Academy of Science 9
National Association for the Advancement of Colored People (NAACP): *Brown v. Board of Education of Topeka* 70, 81; criminal

justice 12; Du Bois 114, 115; epithets 128; integration 161; Million Man March 278; race card 337; school segregation 243

National Association of Black Social Workers (NABSW) 423

National Basketball Association (NBA) 225

National Coalition of Blacks for Reparations in America (N'COBRA) 365, 367

national consciousness 155

National Front (NF) 234, **296**, 300, 376, 377, 380–81, 402

National Health and Community Care Act (UK, 1990) 409

National Health Service (NHS) 268, 269

national identity: American colonies 247; basic needs theory 103; Ireland 214; Marxism 260; white backlash culture 443; *see also* cultural identity

national security 393

nationalism **296–98**; Africa 8, 135; bigotry 54; birth control 398; black 90, 212, 257, 297; Black Panther Party 61; double consciousness 112–13; economic 90; ethnic cleansing 136, 137; ethnonationalism relationship 149; fascism 156; German 156, 174; Hanson 177; ideology 200; Indian 26, 160, 161; Irish 260; language hierarchies 280; Marxism 260; Mexican-American 47; multicultural education 288; Scottish 149; separatist 335; Third World 102

Nationalist Front (Germany) 402

nationality: children's reading of race 363; ethnic cleansing 136, 138; natural rights 190

nationhood 193, 306

Native Americans **21–24**, 201, 202, 310; Blumenbach's racial taxonomy 167; Brazil 64–65; English language teaching 121; ethnic identification 142; genocide 165, 306; internal colonialism 209; internet resources 468; Ku Klux Klan view of 233; Las Casas on 238, 239; literacy test requirements for voting 244; media representations 267; reparations 111, 365, 366; sexuality 397; sterilization 465; transracial adoption 424; *see also* indigenous peoples

Native Baptism 135

"Native Title" 202

natural resources 23

natural rights 37, 110, 190; *see also* human rights

natural selection 101, 127–28, 334; hereditarian theory 180; social Darwinism 407; sociobiology 411

naturalism 150

naturalization: American colonies 247; Latinos 240–41

nature 386–87

Nazism 136, 322, 387, 388; Aryan Republican Army 302; beauty discourses 50; Chamberlain's influence 77; concentration camps 124; defeat of 34; fascism relationship 156; genocide 163; Gobineau's work 172; Haeckel influence 174; language 235, 237; sterilization 150; Verwoerd's sympathies for 40; Wagner 437; *see also* far right; Hitler; Holocaust; neo-nazism

NBA *see* National Basketball Association

N'COBRA *see* National Coalition of Blacks for Reparations in America

nÕgritude 95, 134, **298**; Europe 135–36; Fanon 153, 154; Senghor 391, 392

negrophilia **298–300**

neighborhoods 187, 188, 189, 318, 444, 445

neo-classical economics 103

neo-colonialism 8, 23, 419

neo-conservatism 371

neo-Darwinism 102, 235; *see also* social Darwinism

neo-fascism 69, 234, 297, 402; *see also* far right; neo-nazism

neo-liberalism 34, 304, 438, 453, 454

neo-Marxism 175, 457

neo-nazism **300–301**, 303; anti-Semitism 31; Britain 327; football violence 256; Islamophobia 216, 218; Ku Klux Klan 233; National Front 296; Roma 382; youth subcultures 457; *see also* far right; neo-fascism; skinheads; White Power

NEPAD *see* New African Development Plan

Nepal 86

nepotism 146, 412

Netherlands: asylum seekers 47; colonialism 85, 86; migration from 276; slavery 404, 405

network migration theory 68

New African Development Plan (NEPAD) 413

New Age travelers 185

new ethnicities 324, 369, 457

New International Division of Labor (NIDL) **301**

New Labour 176

New Negro concept 162

New Orleans 94

"new racism" 322–23, 370

"New Times" thesis 176, 457, 458

New York 168, 378

New York Police Department (NYPD) 318

New Zealand: British settlers 276; colonialism 86; ethnic groups 144; indigenous peoples 202
Newark 228
news media: newspapers 196, 266; racial coding 343; racist discourse 353, 354
NF *see* National Front
NHS *see* National Health Service
Nicaragua 22, 23, 202–3, 211
NIDL *see* New International Division of Labor
Nigeria xviii–xix, 7, 8; English language 236; ethnicity 144; slavery 404; tribal groups 170
"nigga" term 129; *see also* epithets (racial/slang); rap music
Nightingale, Carl H. 91
Nike 171, 220, 224–25
Nixon, Richard 4, 62, 442
Noble Savage 23, 306
nonverbal communication 354
nonviolence 77, 78, 81; Gandhi 160; King 230
normality 55, 56
North America: colonialism 85; Doomed Races Doctrine 108; pluralism 316; refugees 364; slavery 404; *see also* Canada; Mexico; United States of America
Northern Ireland 139, 141, 214, 361; *see also* Irish people
Norway 150, 280, 281–82
Nott, Josiah Clark 180
Notting Hill riots (1958) 68, 245
Noyce, Phillip 2
Nuremberg War Crimes Tribunal 467
NWA 356, 357
Nyerere, Julius 419
NYPD *see* New York Police Department

OAAU *see* Organization of Afro-American Unity
OAS *see* Organization of American States
Oates, Joyce Carol 427
OAU *see* Organization of African Unity
Office of Federal Contract Compliance (OFCC) 5
Oklahoma bombing (1995) 300, **302–3**
Oldham riots (2001) 376–77
Oliart, Patricia 34
Olson, Mancur 360
Olusegun, Kalonji 367
Oman 403
Omi, Michael 28, 261, 417
One Nation 177, 178, 282, **303–5**
oppression: black feminism 59; Freire 158–59; social science study of 416; subaltern 415; systemic racism 417; welfare recipients 438; *see also* domination

order 55
the Order 300, 302, 303, 447
organic intellectual concept 175, 176
Organization for Security and Co-operation in Europe (OSCE) 210
Organization of African Unity (OAU) 211, 367
Organization of Afro-American Unity (OAAU) 257
Organization of American States (OAS) 141, 211
Oriard, Michael 19
Orientalism **305–6**, 343; Islamophobia 215; Otherness 307; sexuality 397–98
OSCE *see* Organization for Security and Co-operation in Europe
Other/Otherness **306–7**; anti-Semitism 31; bigotry 53, 54, 55; colonial discourse 85, 399; cultural identity 96; cultural racism 98, 216; denial of voice to 415; epithets 153; essentialism 133–34; exoticization 50; globalization 170; humor directed at 194, 195; hybridity 198; literary criticism 17; media representations 369; men of color 265; negrophilia 300; Orientalism 305; race concept 335; racial coding 343; racism 350; racist discourse 351, 352–53, 354; sexuality 399; socially invented barrier of exclusion 112; Tyson 427; voice-consciousness 118; whiteness 453; *see also* alterity
Ottoman (Turkish) Empire 86, 360, 403
Oudshoorn, Nelly 134
overpopulation 400
Oxford idealists 407

Pacific islands: Blumenbach's racial taxonomy 166; colonialism 86; Doomed Races Doctrine 108; media representations 267; population forecasts 266
Paganism 300
Page Act (US, 1870) 398
Page, HelÃn 29
Pakistanis xvi, 66, 67, 147; asylum seekers 46; census statistics 216; doctors in Britain 268; educational underachievement xx, 217; housing 188; mass migrations 136–37, 277; *see also* British Asians; South Asians
Palestine 31, 459
Palestinian Liberation Organization (PLO) 259
Palestinians 138, 193, 277, 360
pan-Africanism 114, 368
Panama canal 276
Panther (film) 61
Parekh, Bhikhu 290

Parekh Report (Runnymede Trust, 2000) 176, 290, 344
pariahs 430
Park, Robert Ezra xx, 187, **308–10**, 340
Parks, Rosa 81, 229, 278
particularism 54, 123
paternalism 7, 266, **310–11**
pathologization 438–39, 440
patois 237
patriarchy 263, **311–14**; Brazil 159; colonial women 415; Islam xiv; multicultural education 288; White Power 447; womanist thought 59; *see also* feminism; gender; women
patriotism 149, 300, 447
Patterson, Floyd 18
Patterson, Orlando 399
PC *see* political correctness
Pearson, Karl 110–11, 150
Pentecostalism 15, **314–15**
People United to Save Humanity (PUSH) 220, 225
PER *see* Project on Ethnic Relations
performativity 324
Perot, Ross 203
personality 273, 329
Peru: antiracism 34; colonial labor 276; indigenous peoples 23; slavery 238, 405; white inhabitants 452
Pettigrew, Thomas 330
PG-RNA *see* Provisional Government of the Republic of New Afrika
phenotype **315–16**, 334, 340; Boas' studies 64; Brazil 65–66; genotype distinction 165; intelligence 208; racialization 349; racism definition 350; social races 336–37; sociobiology 411; *see also* genetics
Philippines: English language 236; migrants to the United States 42, 43
Phizacklea, Annie 261
Piaget, Jean 79
Pierce, William 442, 447
Pieterse, Jan Nederveen 38, 39, 299, 300, 368, 450–51
Pinker, R. A. 409
Pitt-Rivers, George H. L.-F. 111
plantations 275, 276, 404, 405, 417, 449; *Invisible Man* 212; minstrelsy 283, 284; paternalism 311; patriarchal relations 159; Puerto Rico 332; race privileges 450; South Africa 412–13
Plato 16
Plessy v. Ferguson (1896) 70, 223, 243

PLO *see* Palestinian Liberation Organization
pluralism xix, 44, **316–17**; Afrocentricity 16; Britain 68; conquest societies 88; denial of 56; education 123; ethnic 143; integration synonymity with 206; *see also* cultural diversity
Pocahontas 397
pogroms 306, **317**, 459
Poland 382, 402–3
police/policing **317–20**; African Caribbeans in Britain 15; British riots 374, 375, 377, 384–85; complaints against 254; Diallo case 105; institutional racism 204; King case 231–32; Lawrence case 252–53; liability for discrimination 251, 253; multicultural policy 290; race card 337; racial profiling 346–48; racist discourse 354; South Africa 40–41
policy: affirmative action 442; behavioral traits 388; criminal justice 319–20; disadvantage 107; housing 189; Kerner Report 229; Latino policy preferences 241; multicultural 288, 289; Parekh Report 176; race relations 249–51; Scarman Report 385; social change 444; social exclusion 408; Thatcherite 57; tokenism 421, 422; transracial adoption 423, 424; urban 126–27; welfare 90, 438–41; *see also* legislation
Policy Studies Institute 268, 269
political capital 242
political correctness (PC) xix, 203, **320–22**; affirmative action 442; Ebonics 121; humor 197; media representations 267; racial profiling 347; social work 410, 441
political entrepreneurs 140
political rights 40, 387; *see also* voting rights
politicide 164
politics **322–23**; African Americans 12–13; antiracism 34; Asian Americans 43; asylum seekers 47; Black Panther Party 60–62; Black Power 62; British National Party 69–70; empowerment 124–25; ethnicity 143; fascism 155–57; Hall 175; Hanson 177–78; Jackson 220; Ku Klux Klan 234; Latinos 240, 241–43; media representations 371; minorities 278; nationalism 296–97; One Nation 303–5; pluralism 316; racial coding 342–44; racialized 67; riots 373–74; South Africa 413; state reproduction of racism 261; voting rights 81–82, 230, 243–44; White Power 447–48
politics of difference 176, 370–71, 457
politics of race 264–65, 322–23, 324
pollution 126

polygenesis 167, 186, 208, 386
polysemy 334
Popat, Andrew 90
popular culture 267, 357, 362, 371; Asian 68; minstrelsy 285; negrophilia 298–99; whiteness 454; *see also* media; music; television
population exchanges 137
population growth 249
populism 445
Portugal: asylum seekers 46; colonialism 7, 85; migration from 276; slavery 404
positive discrimination *see* affirmative action
post-modernism 262, 263, 323
post-race **323–25**
post-structuralism 175, 262, 323, 325; Foucault 342, 343; masculinities 263
postcolonial states 262, 419
postcolonial studies 117, 153, 307, 323
postcolonialism **325–26**; antiracism relationship 34; British Asians 69; cultural identity 95
postindustrial society 430
Poulantzas, Nicos 200
poverty: African Americans 11, 90, 389; American Indians 22; British Asians 66; conservative critique of welfare policy 90; drug use and dealing 119, 120; feminized 288; ghettos 168; mental illness link 270; Puerto Ricans in the United States 332; refugees 185; riots 377, 379; systemic racism 416; urban decay 126; US cities 58; welfare 438, 441
Powell, Adam Clayton 62, 446
Powell, Colin 10
Powell, Enoch 96, 203, **326–28**
power **328–29**; Black Panther Party 61; colonialism 84, 85; exclusionary 288; knowledge relationship 321; literacy as challenge to dominant social order 158; male 263; media representations 371; Orientalism 305, 306; patriarchy 311; race science 388; racial coding 342; sexuality 397, 398; white 98; whiteness relationship 452, 453; *see also* domination; hegemony
powerlessness 395, 446
Pratt, Elmer 61
praxis 158
pregnancy 10
prejudice 53, 56, **329–30**; Burke on 89; contact hypothesis 444; cultural racism 97; Declaration on Race and Racial Prejudice 432; Du Bois on 114; Freudian theory 108; institutional racism 205; religious 218; social Darwinism 407; stereotypes 414; travelers 184; universalism 33–34; *see also* bigotry; racism

Prescott, William 409–10
pretext stops 346
Price-Mars, Jean 298
Price Waterhouse v. Hopkins (1989) 244
pride 33, 52
Prince, Rob 465
prisoners: Aboriginal Australians 2; African Americans 12, 414; British Asians 66; Muslims 216
Project on Ethnic Relations (PER) 465
proletarianization 416
Promised Lands 47
property rights 23, 37, 40, 312
prostitutes 398, 430
protest movements: anti-Vietnam 17; Gandhi 160; systemic racism 418; *see also* civil rights movement; resistance
Protestants 213, 214, 233
proto-nations 149
Protocols of the Learned Elders of Zion 31, **330–31**, 373, 470
Provisional Government of the Republic of New Afrika (PG-RNA) 367
Pruitt-Igoe **331**
Pryor, Richard 129, 195
psychiatry 154, 270, 272
psychoanalytic theories: Dollard 108; Holocaust explanations 182; mental illness treatment 273; patriarchy 314; *see also* psychology of racism
psychodynamic approaches 409, 410
"psychological wage" 416, 453
psychology of racism 349; authoritarian personality 53–54, 329; bigotry 53–54, 55; child development 78–80; Dollard 108; *see also* psychoanalytic theories
psychotherapy 270, 273
Public Eye 466
public space 29
Public Works Employment Act (US, 1977) 5
Puerto Ricans 30, 209, 239, 240, **331–32**
Puerto Rico 123, 125
PUSH *see* People United to Save Humanity

Quakers 35, 247
Quebec 141, 149, 193
Queen Latifa 356
Qutb, Sayyid xvii–xviii

Rabbit-Proof Fence (film) 2
race: American Indians 22; anthropology 27–29; Baldwin 115, 116; black feminism 59; Brazil

65, 66; children's learning 80–81; as classification **333–34**; ethnicity relationship 143, 145; fascism 156; intergroup relations 341; language relationship 235; masculinity relationship 264, 265; media representations 368–72; natural rights 190; Otherness 307; politics of 264–65, 322–23, 324; pre-Darwinian science 102; reading **362–63**; sexual abuse 394–96; as signifier **334–36**; social construction of 348, 387, 388; as synonym **336–37**; tradition versus 33; transracial adoption 422, 423, 424; UNESCO statements 431; *see also* black people; ethnicity; race relations; racial discrimination; racialization; racism; whiteness

race card **337–38**, 400, 420

race relations xvii, 349, 416; as activity **338–40**; anthropology 28; Brazil 65, 66; colonialism influence on 85, 87; as construction **340–41**; Cox on 94; cycle 309, 310; emancipation 123; Freudian theory 108; humor 196; *Invisible Man* 212; legislation 89; media representations 369, 370; Park xx; Powell 326; power relationships 328; sociology of 73; UK immigration law 245–46; UK race relations law **249–51**; United States 9–10; use of the term 334

Race Relations Act (UK, 1968) 250

Race Relations Act (UK, 1976) 185, 216, 250, 445

Race Relations (Amendment) Act (UK, 2000) 251, 253

Race Relations Board 250

race science 385–86, 387, 388, 453

"race suicide" 398

Racial Awareness Training (RAT) 440

racial coding **341–45**

racial discrimination xvii, 334, **345**; African Americans 12; *Brown* v. *Board of Education of Topeka* 70; definition of 251–52; drug use and dealing 119; European Convention on Human Rights 210; international law 192, 210, **251–52**; King case 232; medicine 268; police 251, 253, 317, 318, 319; post-race 323; Rastas 358; rational choice theory 359; UK law 245, 250; UN instruments 432–33; unacceptability of 34; *see also* apartheid; racism; segregation

racial harassment 434, 435; British riots 374; housing clustering as response to 188; overseas doctors 269; police 319; racist discourse 352; United States 10

racial pride 33, 52

racial profiling xv, 105, 251, 317, 318, 319, **345–48**, 393, 394

racial purity: Ku Klux Klan 233; selectionism 407; sexuality 398; whiteness 452, 453

racial rebirth 448–49

racial typology 351

racial ventriloquy 197

racialism *see* racial discrimination

racialization 33, **348–49**, 362; black youth 457; Europeanness 67; Islamic/Arab terrorism 444; media representations 369, 371; politics 323; South Africa 413

racism xx, xxi, 339, **349–51**; Aboriginal Australians 1, 2; African Caribbeans in Britain 13; American Indians 24; anthropology 28, 29; Aryan Republican Army 302; as barrier to integration 207; beauty 50; bigotry 54, 55; biological 34; black feminism 60; Blumenbach's racial taxonomy 166; British National Party 69–70; busing 71; challenges to 447; children 78–80, 81; colonialism 7, 85; colonized minorities 209; color line 87; commonsense thinking 179; critical race theory 120; cultural 54, **96–98**, 216; Diageo case 104; Diallo case 105; double consciousness 29; drug use and dealing 119; educational underachievement 339; environmental **126–27**; epithets 128; ethnic monitoring 142; ethnicization of diverse cultures 134, 143; exploitation 152; Fanon 153, 155; fascism relationship 156, 157; globalization 170; Hanson 178; homelessness 183; humor 197; as ideology 200, 201, 262; inferential 98, **203–4**, 326; internet resources 470–71; Irishophobia 214; Islamophobia distinction 216–17; Kerner Report 229; Ku Klux Klan 233–34; Let's Kick Racism Out of Football 255–56; Marxism 260, 261, 262, 293; media representations 370; medicine 267, 268–69; mental illness 272; multicultural education 288; National Front 296; "new" 322–23, 370; One Nation 305; Parekh Report 344; police 319, 320, 384–85; political correctness 320–21; Powell 326, 327; by proxy 57; racialization distinction 349; reading race 362; representations 368, 369; reverse **373**, 443; Rock Against Racism 380–81; self-contradictions 391; sexual abuse 395, 396; sexual conflict 83; Simpson case 401; skinhead 402; slavery 404, 405; social exclusion 408; social races 336–37; social work 409, 410, 411; sociobiology 411; sociology of race relations 340; sport 263; state responsibility for 129; systemic **416–18**; transracial adoption 422; UN instruments 432–33; underclass 430; UNESCO statements 431; US surveys 80; Vienna declaration 455; violent attacks 434, 435; white feminism 59; xenophobia distinction 455; *see also* anti-Semitism; institutional racism; Islamophobia; racial discrimination; racial harassment; scientific racism

racist discourse **351–55**, 427

Rainbow Coalition 220

Rainwater, Lee 331

Ramsamy, Sam 19

Randall, Dudley 367

Randel, William 234

rap music 92, 129, 147, **355–57**; black male responses to feminism 264–65; mainstreaming of 226; Malcolm X 258; negrophilia 299

rape: Central Park Jogger case 76; Cleaver 83; ethnic cleansing 136; hat wearing by black men 118; masculinity studies 264; myth of black rapist 398; Tyson 426

Rastafari **357–59**; creole speech 237; Ethiopianism 135, 162; imagination of tradition 144; reggae 364, 365; youth subcultures 457

RAT *see* Racial Awareness Training

rational choice theory **359–62**

rationality 166, 388, 407

Rattansi, Ali 306

Ratzenhofer, Gustav 406

Rawls, John 132

reading 158

reading race **362–63**

Reagan, Ronald 4, 6, 12, 13, 20, 129–30, 445

Reaganomics 371

reason 131, 133, 166

reasonable plausibility 16

reciprocity 130, 412

Reconstruction 223, 243, 398

Redfield, Robert 309

redistribution 132–33

reductionism 260–61, 417

Reed, Adolph 112, 113

Reel, Lakhvinder "Ricky" 254

Reeves, Frank 142

reflection 158

refugees 46–47, 277; Britain 290; British Asians 66; ethnicity 143; globalization 170; homelessness 185; internet resources 471–72; multicultural education 288; status **363–64**; stress 271; white backlash culture 443; *see also* asylum seekers; immigrants

Refugees International 470

Regent of the University of California v. *Bakke* (1978) 5

reggae 237, 358, **364–65**

relativism 32, 33, 131, 371

religion: African Orthodox Church 162; American Indians 23; bigotry 53; British Asians 67; cultural rights 193; culturecide 164; ethnic cleansing 136, 137, 138; ethnocide 147; freedom of 363; Ireland 213; messianic movements 135; Otherness 306; patriarchy 313–14; Pentecostalism 314–15; racial classification 333; religious conflict 139; White Power 449; *see also* Christianity; Hinduism; Islam; Jews; Rastafari

religious discrimination 216, 217, 218

Renaissance 33, 288, 306

Renan, Ernest 30

reparations 111, **365–68**, 378

reports: Dillingham Report 248; Kerner Report 10, 60, **228–29**, 266, 267, 384; Macpherson Report 204–5, 252–54, 296, 318–19, 320, 377, 441, 470; Merrison Report 268; Ouseley Report 390; Parekh Report 176, 290, 344; Runnymede Trust Report on Islamophobia 215, 216, 217, 218; Scarman Report 229, 374, **384–85**, 410

representations 265–67, **368–72**; British Asians 68–69; racist discourse 352, 353–54

reproduction of systemic racism 417, 418

reproductive technologies 151, 386, 400

Republican Party 20, 90, 285, 420

resistance 90, 91–92; American Indians 23; cultural identity 95; hybridity 198; systemic racism 418; *see also* protest movements

respect 263

responsibility 205

reverse racism/discrimination 4, 11, **373**, 443, 463

revolution: antislavery struggles 37; Black Panther Party 61; Fanon 155

Rex, John 85, 126, 176

Reyes, Matias 76

Rhodesia *see* Zimbabwe

Rice, Thomas Dartmouth "Daddy" 223–24, 283

Richmond v. *J. A. Croson* (1989) 5, 12

rights: collective 192, 193, 202; cultural 192, 193; equal treatment 132, 191; group-differentiated 282; individual 192; kinship as basis for claims 233; language 237; legal 193, 281–82, 404; minority language rights **279–83**; natural 37, 110, 190; refugees 363; restrictions after September 11th attacks 392–93; UK immigration law 246; voting 81–82, 230, 243–44; *see also* civil rights; human rights; land rights

riots: Britain: (1958) 68, 245; (1981) 15, 318, **373–75**, 384–85; (1985) 15, 318, **375–76**; (2001) 69, **376–77**, 390; France xv, 318;

Kerner Report 228–29; Los Angeles (1992) 105, 231–32, 266, 318; Russia xv; Scarman Report 384–85; United States: (1919) 114; (1921) 377–78; (1965–67) 60, 228–29, 230, 250, 266, 378–80, 445; (1980) 380; (1992) 105, 231–32, 266, 318; (2001) 319; Watts riots (1965) 228–29, 250, 378–79, 445

Ripley, William Z. 157

Rivers, W. H. R. 110

Roberts, Dorothy 398, 400

Robertson, Roland 169

Robeson, Paul 224

Robinson, Cedric 262

Robinson, William "Smokey" 285

Rock Against Racism **380–81**

Rock, Chris 129

Rockwell, George Lincoln 446–47

Roe v. *Wade* 420

Rogers, Nathaniel 452

Rojecki, Andrew 266, 267

Roma 184–85, 288, **381–82**, 472; *see also* gypsies; travelers

Romania 381, 382

Romans: ethnic cleansing 137; humor 194; patriarchy 312, 313, 314; slavery 403

romanticism 31, 306

Rooney, Kevin 426, 427

Rose, Tricia 356

Rosenthal, R. 391

Ross, Diana 221, 222, 286

Rough Sleepers' Initiative (RSI) 183–84

Rousseau, Jean-Jacques 131, 328

Rowe, William 198

Rowland, Dick (Diamond) 378

Roy, Arundathi 344

RSI *see* Rough Sleepers' Initiative

Rummel, R. J. 164

Runnymede Trust: Islamophobia 215, 216, 217, 218; Parekh Report 176, 290, 344

rural–urban migration 276

Rushdie, Salman 216, 343

Russia: anti-Semitism 31, 144, 330; anti-Zionism 460; Caucasians 350; Chechnya conflict xv, 140–41; colonialism 86–87; emancipation of serfs 123; internet resources 465; pogroms 459; *see also* Soviet Union, former

Rwanda 7, 8, 139; ethnic cleansing 138; genocide 165; homeless refugees 185; International Criminal Tribunal 466; racism 350

Said, Edward: cultural permeability xiv, 146; discourse analysis 84; imperialism/colonialism

distinction 85; Orientalism 215, 305, 306, 307, 343; postcolonial literary theory 325

Saleem, Hina xiv, xix

Salvadoreans 143, 405–6

Sambo figure 195, 283, 311

Sami (formerly Lapps) 193, 202, 281–82

Sammons, Jeffrey 17

Sampath, – 264

Sartre, Jean-Paul 306, 325

Sarwar, Mohammed 217

sati 415

Saudi Arabia 314, 403

Saussure, Ferdinand de 341–42

Sauvy, Alfred 419

scapegoating 274, 306, 327, **383–84**; bigotry 56; Freudian theory 108; Islamophobia 218; prejudice 330

Scarman Report (1981) 229, 374, **384–85**, 410

Schelling, Vivian 198

Schiller, Johann 437

schizophrenia 270, 271–72, 439

schools: curricula 99; desegregation 70–71, 81, 82, 243; masculinity 263; Muslim 217; self-fulfilling prophecies 391; underachievement 428–29; *see also* education

Schopenhauer, Arthur 306

Schulz, E. H. 462

Schuyler, George 196

science **385–89**; cultural borrowings 146; Darwinism 101–2; as universalist discourse 34

scientific racism 180, 333, 385–86; American Indians 24; Anglo-Indians 25; antislavery impact on 38–39; Blumenbach's racial taxonomy 166; educational underachievement 429; Finot's critique of 157; language 235, 323; nationalism 297; racialization 349; resistance to 33; types of 351; *see also* eugenics; social Darwinism

SCLC *see* Southern Christian Leadership Conference

Scotland 149

Seagal, Ronald 403

segregation xiii, 90, **389–90**; beauty contests 51; beauty shops 52; Brazil 66; British riots 377; *Brown* v. *Board of Education of Topeka* 28, 70, 81, 224, 230, 243, 444; Du Bois 115; environmental racism 126; eugenics 150; ghettos 168; housing 186, 189, 439; internal colonialism 209; Jim Crow 223–24; Kerner Report 229; Pruitt-Igoe 331; rational choice theory 359, 360; school 71; social exclusion 408; systemic racism 417; United States xvii, 9–10, 80, 243, 423, 445; white backlash culture 441; White Power 446; *see also* apartheid

selectionism 351, 407

self: double consciousness 112; dress 117, 118; Other relationship 306, 307; schizophrenic splitting of 272; Vygotskian theory 80; whiteness 453

self-defense 60

self-deprecation 194

self-determination: Aboriginal Australians 2; Africa 8; Ali 20; Black Panther Party 60; Du Bois 115; ethnonationalism 149; right to 192, 193, 202; Soviet policy 140

self-employment 57

self-esteem 272, 395

self-fulfilling prophecy **390–91**

self-harm 271, 272

semiology 341, 354

Senegal 7, 8, 391–92

Senghor, Léopold Sédar 136, 153, 298, **391–92**

September 11th 2001 terrorist attacks xv, xviii, 128, **392–94**, 444; Islamophobia 97, 216, 217–18, 393; racial coding 343; racial profiling 347, 348; *see also* terrorism

Sep°lveda, Gines de 238, 239

Serbia 136

Serbs 138, 139

serfdom 124

Serrano, Miguel 449

sexism: bigotry 55; Marxism 260; Million Man March 278; political correctness 320–21; rap music 356; social exclusion 408; sociobiology 411; *see also* patriarchy

sexual abuse **394–97**

sexual differences 134

sexual orientation 47; cultural values xix; homophobia 278, 356

sexual politics 60

sexual relations 159, 311, 398

sexual selection 101

sexuality 300, **397–400**; anthropology 28; bigotry 55; black male body 50; Black Panther Party 61; exoticization 50; female subordination 312

sexually transmitted diseases 399, 400; *see also* AIDS

Shah, Samir 344

Shakur, Tupac 224

Shante, Roxanne 356

sharia xvii, xviii

Sharpe, Samuel 135

Sharpeville massacre (1960) 40, 432

Sharpton, Al 104, 105, 224

Shaw v. *Reno* 12

Sheet Metal Workers Local 28 v. *EEOC* (1986) 4

Shelly v. *Kraemer* (1948) 243

Shohat, Ella 371, 427

Shorris, Earl 417

signifier, race as **334–36**

signs 341–42

Sikhs 45, 217, 358

Simmel, Georg 308, 309

Simpson, O. J. 49, 222, 225, 337, 372, 393, **400–402**

Sin, Sin Yi Cheung xvi

Singapore 189, 236, 400

Singh, Gurchand 205, 253

single mothers 206, 430–31

Sinhalese 139

Sinocentrism 288

Sisulu, Walter 258

sitcoms 195–96

Sivanandan, A. 14

ska 365, 448

skin color 51, 52, 78, 324; color line 87; "color tax" 359; environment relationship 127; race concept 335; racial worldview 450; UK immigration law 245

skinheads 327, 374, 380, 382, **402–3**, 434, 457

slang 128–29

slavery 275, **403–6**; abolitionists 35–39, 123–24, 404–5; Africa 7; Biblical justification for 387; bigotry 55; Brazil 65; colonialism 85, 86; emancipation 39, 123–24, 223, 283, 405; *encomienda* 125, 126; exploitation 151, 152; French theorists 173; Freyre 159; Hottentot Venus 186; humor 195; internet resources 472–73; Las Casas 238; Marxism 260; paternalism 310, 311; Pentecostalism 315; power 328; race privileges 450; rebellions 37, 135; reparations 295, 365, 366, 367; Roma 382; sexuality 397; social ordering principles 28; South Africa 39–40; systemic racism 417; United States 113; *see also* antislavery

Slavs 403

Slovakia 170, 382, 402–3

slum clearances 126–27

Small Business Job Protection Act (US, 1996) 423

Small, Stephen xv, xvi

Smedley, Audrey 29, 38, 39, 405, 450

Smith, Adam 89

Smith, Benjamin 303

Smith, Charles Hamilton 180

Smith, Clare 196

Smith, Captain John 397

Smith, John Maynard 411
Smith, Samuel Stanhope 36, 127
Smith, Suzanne E. 286
Smith, Tommie 19, 61–62
Smith v. Washington State University (1996) 6
Smuts, Jan 40
Snell, Richard Wayne 302
Snoop Doggy Dogg 356
social capital 104
social change 56, 444
social class *see* class
social constructionism 324, 340–41, 348, 387
social contract 131
social Darwinism 351, **406–8**; Aboriginal Australians 1; development 102; internet resources 473; linguistic 281; sociobiology 411; White Power 447; *see also* Darwinism; eugenics; neo-Darwinism; scientific racism
social evolution 407
social exclusion xvi, **408–9**; British Muslims 217; homelessness 183
social identity 92–93
social interaction 80
"social mind" 80
social norms 212
social races 336–37
social relations 338, 340
social services 240, 242; *see also* welfare
social work **409–11**; adoption 423; institutional racism 409, 440, 441
socialism 387
sociobiology 310, 387, 407, **411–12**, 473
sociocentric societies 272
socioeconomic status: Latinos 242; reduction of racial issues to class issues 417; whiteness 451–52; *see also* class
sociolinguistics 235, 237
sociology: conflict definition 141; "Gothic" 309; Holocaust explanations 182; masculinity 263; post-race 323; of race relations 340; racism 350
solidarity: African Caribbeans in Britain 15; Black Panther Party 60; Cold War 140; creole speech 237; eroded by consumption 91; "ethnic Chinese" 145; ethnicity 142; group identity 360; national sentiment 296; Puerto Ricans in the United States 332; racial 33; white supremacism 454; womanist thought 59
Solomos, John xv, xvi
Somalia 8
South Africa 7, 322, **412–14**; antiracist movements 19, 418; apartheid 39–41, 359, 389;

British settlers 276; caste 74, 75; colonialism 86; Doomed Races Doctrine 108; Gandhi in 160; Hottentot Venus 185–86; indigenous peoples 109; inter-racial sexual contact 398; Mandela 258–59; racial classification 87; racial labelling 336; rape and sexual coercion 264; Sharpeville massacre 40, 432
South America: American Indians 21, 22, 23; colonialism 85; Doomed Races Doctrine 108; *encomienda* 125–26; Latinos 239; slavery 311, 404; whiteness 454; *see also* Latin America
South Asians 66–69; constraint-choice perspective 187; cuisine 147; doctors 268, 269; entrepreneurship 57; homelessness 184; Islamophobia 216, 218; mental illness 271, 439–40; "second generation" 143; skinhead hostility towards 402; youth subcultures 457; *see also* Bangladeshis; British Asians; Indians; Pakistanis
Southall riots (1981) 373, 374
Southeast Asia: "ethnic Chinese" 145; liberation movements 297; migrants to the United States 43; slavery 403
Southern African Migration Project 470
Southern Christian Leadership Conference (SCLC) 230, 257
Southern states 223
Soviet Union, former: Cold War 34; concentration camps 124; dissolution of 140, 149, 280–81; ethnic tensions 140–41; invasion of Hungary 175; population relocations 138; slavery 405; *see also* Russia
Sowell, Thomas 90
Soweto massacre (1976) 40, 41
Spain: colonialism 74–75, 85, 86, 238, 276, 331, 450; emancipation 123; *encomienda* 125–26; fascism 156; language 280; as multinational state 149; proto-nationalism 149; slavery 404; whiteness 452
speech: mock forms of 29; subaltern 415
Spencer, Herbert 109, 406, 407
Spielberg, Steven 255
Spivak, Gayatri Chakravorty 118, 325, 415
sports: Ali 17–20; black male body 399; inferential racism 204; Jordan 224–26; masculinity 263; race as signifier 335; Simpson 401; Tyson 425–27
Springsteen, Bruce 105
Sri Lanka: abolition of slavery 405; doctors in Britain 268; ethnic conflict 104, 139
St. Louis 331
Stam, Robert 371, 427

state: fascism 155; formation 276–77; Marxism 261; social exclusion 408; Third World state structures 419–20; *see also* nation
Statewatch 471
Stecopoulos, H. 264
Steele, Shelby 57
stereotypes 329, **414–15**; advertising imagery 299; African Caribbeans in Britain 14, 15; American Indians 24; Anglo-Indians 25; bigotry 53, 54, 55, 56; black athletes 335; black males 396; consumption 92; critical race theory 120; educational underachievement 428, 440; humor based on 195; institutional racism 205; linguistic practices 29; Marxism 260; media representations 347, 369, 370, 371; minstrelsy 283, 284; race card 337; racial coding 343; racial profiling distinction 346; racist discourse 352; scapegoating 383; Tyson 427; welfare system 439
sterilization 150, 399, 400, 465
stigma 271, 395
Stoddard, Lothrop 398
Stoicism 131
Stoler, Ann 29
Stowe, Harriet Beecher 37
Straw, Jack 252, 254, 372, 441
stress 270, 271, 272
structuralism 307, 341, 371
Sub-Commission on the Promotion and Protection of Human Rights (UN) 432, 433
subaltern 134, **415–16**
subcultures **456–58**
subjectivity 112, 264
Sudan 7, 8
Suez Canal 175
Sugar Hill Gang 355
suicide 271
suicide bombing 139
Sumner, Walter Graham 406, 407
Supreme Court of the United States 39, 420
Swaziland 8
Sweden 150, 202, 280, 405
Switzerland 150, 207
Sylvester, Roger 254
symbolic communities 93
symbolism 299
syphilis 399, 400
systemic racism **416–18**

Taiwan 43
Taliban 393
Talk Radio (film) 302–3

Tambo, Oliver 258
Tamils 139
Tanzania 8, 419
Taylor, Ronald 438
Tebbitt, Norman 443
technology: globalization 169–70; reproductive technologies 151, 386, 400
Teddy Boys 434, 457
television 195–96, 266; Al-Jazeera 394; media representations 370; MTV 221–22; racial coding 343; satellite technology 226; *see also* media
tenBroek, Jacobus 131
Terrell, Ernie 18
territoriality 193
terrorism xv–xvi, xviii; asylum seekers 47; Beslan school massacre xv; British National Party 70; Islamophobia 218; Oklahoma bombing 300, 302–3; Otherness 307; racial profiling 347, 348; racialized construction of 444; suicide bombing 139; transnational communities 106; "war on terrorism" 45, 348; *see also* September 11th 2001 terrorist attacks
texts: culturalist analysis 371; racial coding 342; racist discourse 351, 352
Thackara, John 326
Thailand 43, 86
Thatcher, Margaret 57, 96, 129–30, 381, 443
Thatcherism 175, 371, 387
theories of race: anthropological 27–29; Aryanism 41–42; Boas 64; chain of being 36; Chamberlain 76–77; Cox 94; Cuvier 186; Doomed Races Doctrine 108–12; environmentalism 127–28, 173, 180, 208, 411; essentialist 133; eugenics 27–28, 150–51, 398–99, 400, 407, 465–66; Finot's critique of 157; geometry of race 166–67; Gobineau 171–72; GrÕgoire 172–73; Haeckel 174; hereditarianism 127–28, 180, 208, 407, 411; linguistics 235; post-race 323–24; race as classification 333–34; race as signifier 334–36; race as synonym 336–37; race relations cycle 309, 310; scientific 385–89; *see also* classification, racial; hierarchies; race; scientific racism; social Darwinism
Third Reich *see* Nazism
Third World **419–20**; development 102, 103, 104; languages 237; modernization theory 103; underdevelopment theory 103, 179; *see also* developing countries
Thirteenth Amendment to the US Constitution 223, 367

Thomas, Brooke 29
Thomas, Clarence 12, **420–21**
Thomas, Elaine 327
Thomas, L. V. 298
Thomas, William I. 309, 390
Thompson, Edward 175, 176
Thompson, Neil 409
Tiedeman, Friedrich 38
Tijerina, Reies Lopez 78
Tishkov, Valery 140
Todorov, Tzvetan 307
Togo 8
tokenism **421–22**
tolerance: Brazil 65; contact hypothesis 71; integration 45; *see also* intolerance
Toll, Robert 283, 284, 285
Torres Strait Islanders 424, 468
Tosh, Peter 358
Tottenham riots (1985) 375
Tower Hamlets 331
Toxteth riots (1981) 373, 374
trade 6–7, 274, 275
trade unions 156, 390–91, 413
Trail of Broken Treaties 22
training: multicultural education 288; overseas doctors 269; Racial Awareness Training (RAT) 440; social work 410
transracial adoption 410, **422–25**
trauma 395
travel 170
travelers 45, 184–85, 288; *see also* gypsies; Roma
tribal sovereignty 22
tribalism 8
Trinidad 99, 264, 271
Trivers, Robert 412
Troyna, Barry 80
Tulsa riots (1921) 377–78
Turkey: Armenian massacres 165; Bulgarian citizens 145; conflict with Greece 137, 141; Kurds 281; Ottoman Empire 86, 360, 403
The Turner Diaries (Pierce) 303, 442, 447
Turner, Henry M. 135
Turner, Nat 37
Turner, Ted 226
Tuskegee experiment 400
Tutsis 7, 138, 139, 165, 185, 350
Tutu, Desmond 259, 413
Tylor, Edward 98
Tyndall, Colin 327
Tyson, Mike 49, 263, 335, 372, 401, **425–27**

UDHR *see* Universal Declaration of Human Rights
Uebel, M. 264
Uganda 7, 8, 137, 399
ugliness 50
UN *see* United Nations
uncertainty 408
Uncle Tom's Cabin (Stowe) 37–38, 421
underachievement 217, 339, **428–30**, 440
underclass 204, 288, 356, 408, **430–31**
underdevelopment theory 103, 179
underprivilege 107
unemployment: Aboriginal Australians 2; African Americans 10, 11–12, 389; African Caribbeans in Britain 15, 272, 380, 439; British Asians 66; British riots 374, 375, 377, 384; Los Angeles 232; National Front 296; social exclusion 408; underclass 430, 431
UNESCO *see* United Nations Educational, Scientific and Cultural Organization
UNHCHR *see* United Nations High Commissioner for Human Rights
UNHCR *see* United Nations High Commissioner for Refugees
UNIA *see* Universal Negro Improvement Association
United Kingdom *see* Britain
United Nations (UN) **432–33**; antiracism 34; Charter of 190; Convention relating to the Status of Refugees 363, 364; establishment of 170; genocide 163, 164; human rights 211; indigenous peoples 22, 202; minority language rights 281; Slavery Convention 403; Special Rapporteur on Racism and Xenophobia 433, 455; web site 473; Zionism 432, 460
United Nations Educational, Scientific and Cultural Organization (UNESCO) 28, **431–32**, 473
United Nations High Commissioner for Human Rights (UNHCHR) 467, 468
United Nations High Commissioner for Refugees (UNHCR) 46, 363–64, 472
United Nations in the Struggle Against Apartheid 462
United States of America (USA): affirmative action 3–6, 87; anthropology 28, 98; anti-Americanism 343–44; anti-Irish hostility 214; anti-Semitism 31; antislavery 36–38, 39, 123; assimilation 44, 100; Baldwin 115, 116–17; beauty ideals 52; black bourgeoisie 57–58, 91; Black English 236–37; black feminism 59; black nationalism 297; Black

Panther Party 60–62; Black Power 62; black war veterans 114; British settlers 276; busing 70–72; caste 74; Central Park Jogger case 76; civil rights law **243–44**; civil rights movement xvii, 81–82; Civil War 39; Cold War 34; conquest 88; Constitution of 128, 131, 223, 247, 252, 367, 417; creoles 94; criminal justice policy 319; Diageo case 104–5; Diallo case 105; disadvantage concept 107; double consciousness 112, 113; drug use and dealing 119; emancipation 123; empowerment 124; English language 236, 280; English Only movement 282; epithets 128; equal opportunity 129–30; ethnic group concept 148; ethnocentrism 147; eugenics 150, 398; family symbolism 398; Garvey 161–62; ghettos 168; "global policeman" role 444; hate crimes 319; housing 187, 189; illegal immigrants 405–6; immigrants to 29, 187, 189, 247–49, 276; immigration law **247–49**, 393, 407, 469; indigenous peoples 21, 22, 23, 24, 100, 201–2; integration 206, 207; intelligence testing 181, 207–8; internal colonialism 209; internment camps 346, 348, 366–67, 392; *Invisible Man* 211–12; Irish emigration to 213; Kerner Report 228–29; Ku Klux Klan 233–34; Latinos 239–43; media representations 265–67, 372; melting pot xiii, xvii, 440; military attacks on terrorist targets xviii; minorities 278, 279; multiracialism 291, 292; Myrdal's study 293; neonazism 300; Park 309, 310; patriarchy 312; Pentecostalism 315; policing 317, 320, 346, 347; politics of race 322; power relationships 328; Puerto Ricans 331–32; race as social construct 334; race card 337; race relations 340; racial ancestry 336; racial discrimination 252; racism 351; racist statutes 27; reparations 365, 366–67; riots: (1919) 114; (1921) **377–78**; (1965–67) 60, 228–29, 230, 250, 266, **378–80**, 445; (1980) **380**; (1992) 105, 231–32, 266, 318; (2001) 319; Roma 382; segregation 80, 389, 444; September 11th 2001 terrorist attacks 392–94; sexuality 397, 398; Simpson case 400–402; single-parent families 430–31; skinheads 402; Supreme Court 420; systemic racism 416, 417; tokenism 421; transracial adoption 422–23; underclass 430; urban decay 126; violence against blacks 434; welfare 438; white backlash culture 441, 442, 443; white flight 445–46; White Power 446, 447; white supremacy 172; whiteness 452; working-class racism 261; *see also* African Americans; Asian Americans; Jim Crow; Mexican-Americans

United States v. *Paradise* (1987) 4
United Steelworkers of America v. *Weber* (1979) 3–4
Universal Declaration of Human Rights (UDHR) (1948) 34, 131, 190–91, 192, 467
Universal Declaration on Indigenous Rights (1988) 192–93; *see also* Declaration on the Rights of Indigenous Peoples
Universal Negro Improvement Association (UNIA) 135, 161, 357
universalism: antiracism 33–34; multicultural education 123; Stoicism 131
unjust enrichment 416
urban areas *see* cities
urban Indians 21–22
utilitarianism 360

Vacher de Lapouge, Georges 406
Vallance, Russ 406
values: American 391; basic needs theory 103; cultural racism 97; dress 117; multicultural education 288; social work 411
Van den Berghe, Pierre 403, 407, 435–36
Van Eurie, John 450
Van Peebles, Mario 61
varnas 75
Vasconcelos, Josõ 32–33
vaudeville 284
veil 118, 154, 313, 314
Venezuela 23
verbal interaction 352
Verity, Robert 109
Verwoerd, Hendrik 40
victim blaming 56, 126
Vietnam 43
Vietnam War 18, 43, 231
Villareal, Roberto 124–25
violence xvi, **434–35**; Britain 14, 327; British Asians xvi; cultural 110; ethnic cleansing 136; Fanon 155; football hooliganism 98, 256; Gandhi 161; Israel 460; Ku Klux Klan 233, 234; Malcolm X 257; pogroms 317; racial rebirth 448; racially motivated 15, 252, 254, 434–35; rap music 356; sexual 398; skinheads 402, 434; stereotypes 414, 415; street 331, 332, 370; United States 10, 11; white backlash culture 441; *see also* atrocities; genocide; lynching; riots

Vogt, Karl 180
voice-consciousness 118
Volk 435–36, 437, 438
Volkish movement 174
Voltaire 127
voting rights 81–82, 230, 243–44; *see also* elections; political rights
Voting Rights Act (US, 1965) 244
Vygotsky, Lev 80

Waddington, C. H. 101
Wagner, Richard 437–38
Waitangi, Treaty of (1840) 202
Waitz, Theodor 157
Walker, Alice 59
Walker, Madam C. J. 52
WAR *see* White Aryan Resistance
war: Africa 8; black soldiers 114; genocide definitions 164; *see also* World War I; World War II
war crimes 139
"war on terrorism" 45, 348
Wards Cove Packing Company v. *Atonio* (1989) 4, 12, 244
Warner, W. Lloyd 74, 94, 108, 293, 340
Washburn, Sherwood 28
Washington, Booker T. 90, 309
Washington, Desiree 426
Washington, Harold 13
WASPs *see* White Anglo-Saxon Protestants
Waters, Muddy 63
Watts riots (1965) 228–29, 378–79, 445
WBC *see* white backlash culture
Web Genocide Documentation Centre 466, 467
Weber, Max 73, 328
Weizmann, Chaim 459
Weld, Dwight 38
welfare 438–41; Aboriginal Australians 2; African Americans 10; Aid to Families with Dependent Children 313; antiracist perspectives 440–41; basic needs theory 103; care and control 439–40; conservative critique of 90; multicultural policy 290; pathologizing images 438–39; social exclusion 408; underclass 430, 431
West, Cornel 91, 112, 231, 356, 417
West Indians: constraint-choice perspective 187; housing 188; reggae 365; *see also* African Caribbeans
West Indies: abolition of slavery 36; US immigration law 248; *see also* Caribbean; Jamaica
Westernization 27

Weston, Horace 284
When We Were Kings (film) 19
White Anglo-Saxon Protestants (WASPs) 195, 214, 233, 279
White Aryan Resistance (WAR) 402
white backlash culture (WBC) 441–44
White Defence League 69, 326
white flight 29, 71, 444–46
White Power 446–49
white privilege 443, 444, 451
white race 449–51
white supremacism: beauty discourses 50; egalitarian class logic 454; Gobineau 172; *Herrenvolk* 435–36; internet resources 462; race concept 335; skinheads 402–3; South Africa 39, 40; White Power 446–49; *see also* Aryanism; Ku Klux Klan; neo-nazism; racism
whiteness 29, 451–54; beauty ideals 52; Caucasians 75; cultural assumptions 113; as culturally constructed identity 415; hegemonic ethnicity 369; Michael Jackson 223; multiracial individuals 291, 292; "Othering" of black subjects 299; post-race thinking 324; "psychological wage" 416, 453; racial worldview 450; reverse racism 373; rise of 451–52; social and economic role of 453–54
Whren v. *US* (1996) 346, 347
Whyte, William Foote 456
Wiggins, David 19, 20
Wik decision (1996) 3, 304
Wilberforce, William 35–36
Wilder, Douglas 90
Wilkins, Roger Jr. 10
Wilkinson, Bill 234
Williams, Patricia 92
Williams, Raymond 175, 176
Williams, Sherley Anne 59
Williams, Vanessa 51
Willis, Paul 91
Wilson, A. N. 30
Wilson, Edward O. 411
Wilson, William J. 58
Winant, Howard 28, 261, 417
Winfrey, Oprah 10, 222
Wirth, Louis 168, 309
Wolf, Naomi 50
Woltmann, Ludwig 174
womanist thought 59
women: Anglo-Indians 25; beauty 50, 51–52; black feminism 58–60; black male responses to feminism 264–65; Black Panther Party 61; class position of 260; emancipation 123;

eroticized bodies 397, 399; exoticization 50–51; fascism 156; homeless South Asians 184; humor 196; kidnapping and sale of 405; Malcolm X on 258; mental illness of Asian women 270–71, 439–40; Muslim xviii–xix; Orientalism 305; patriarchy 311–14; rap music 356; sexuality 397–98; single mothers 206, 430–31; subaltern 415; wearing of the veil 118, 154; White Power 448; *see also* feminism; gender; sexism
women's movement 134
Wonder, Stevie 286
Wood, William 452
Woods, K. 264
Woods, Tiger 225, 335
working class: black 58; Chicago School 456; educational underachievement 428; ethnicity relationship 145; exploitation of 179, 200; fascism 156; industrialization 430; Marxism 260, 261; National Front 296; White Power 447; youth subcultures 457; *see also* class
World Community of Islam 295
World Conference Against Racism, Racial Discrimination, Xenophobia and Related Intolerance (2001) 368, 471
world systems theory 23, 419
World War I: colonialism 7; Du Bois 114; Indian support for Britain 161; intelligence testing 207–8; mobilization 140; reparations 366
World War II: colonialism 7, 8; imperial decline 86; Japanese migrants in the United States 42; Nazi atrocities 190; reparations 366; Senghor 392; US immigration law 248; Zionism after 459; *see also* Holocaust; Nazism
worthlessness 395, 396
Wright, Charles 197

xenophobia 370, **455**; asylum seekers 277; ethnocentrism 146; Hanson 177; Islamophobia 218; multicultural education 288; UN instruments 433

Yanomami 22, 24
Yaqui 24
Yardies 457
"Yellow Peril" 128, 398
Yoruba 170
Young, Arthur 213
Young, Jock 456
Young, Robert xiv, 198
youth: African Caribbeans in Britain 15; British National Party 70; diasporic 106; homelessness 183; subcultures **456–58**
Yugoslavia, former: asylum seekers 46; dissolution into national units 149; ethnic cleansing 136, 138, 140; ethnic conflict 139; International Criminal Tribunal 466; language 237, 280; racism 350; refugees 185, 277; *see also* Bosnia-Herzegovina; Croats; Kosovo; Serbs

zambos 75
Zapatistas 22
zero tolerance 317–18
Zijderveld, Anton 194
Zimbabwe (Rhodesia) 7, 8; British settlers 276; inter-racial sexual contact 398; Mandela's admonishment of 259; South African support for 413
Zionism 350, 360, **459–60**; conspiracy theories 302, 330, 373; UN Resolution against 432, 460; US support for xvii
Zionist Occupation Government (ZOG) 442, 447